BRITISH BATTLESHIPS

Dedicated

to

Sir Stanley Goodall, K.C.B., D.N.C.

Sir Charles Lillicrap, K.C.B., D.N.C.

Sir Victor Shepheard, K.C.B., D.N.C.

and the Officers of

The Royal Corps of Naval Constructors

who made possible

the writing of this Book

BRITISH BATTLESHIPS

"WARRIOR" to "VANGUARD"
1860 1950

A History of Design, Construction and Armament

NEW & REVISED EDITION

OSCAR PARKES
O.B.E., Ass.I.N.A.

With a Foreword by

The Late Admiral of The Fleet The Earl Mountbatten of Burma
K.G., P.C., G.C.B., O.M., G.C.S.I., G.C.I.E., G.C.V.O., D.S.O.

With Four-Hundred-and-Fifty Plans and Photographs

LEO COOPER
LONDON

First published by Seeley Service & Co. Ltd., 1957
Second edition, 1966
Reprinted 1990 by Leo Cooper

Leo Cooper is an imprint of the
Octopus Publishing Group, Michelin House,
81 Fulham Road, London SW3 6RB

ISBN 0–85052–6043

A CIP catalogue record for this book is available
from the British Library

Printed and bound in Great Britain by
Butler & Tanner Ltd, Frome and London

FOREWORD

by

The Late Admiral of The Fleet The Earl Mountbatten of Burma

K.G., P.C., G.C.B., O.M., G.C.S.I., G.C.I.E., G.C.V.O., D.S.O.

Doctor Oscar Parkes' valuable history of British battleships, from the iron-clads of a hundred years ago up to the present day, appears at a historical moment in naval developments; and forms, one might say, a prelude to the warships of the future.

We are now in an interim age in which the aircraft carrier has already replaced the capital ship and the task force the line of battle. With the advent of the atomic age the guided missile launcher will replace the gun turret and the nuclear reactor the boiler furnace. Ships of the future will thus be different in shape as well as different in function; and the revolution thus represented will be just as fundamental as the change from sail driven wooden walls to steam driven iron-clads.

This book therefore marks the end of an epoch—a great epoch—in British naval design and is the dawn of a new era. It is up to us to make the new era as great.

I can earnestly recommend BRITISH BATTLESHIPS not only to those who have served or had members of their family serving in the Royal Navy, but also to those who take an interest in it; and that, surely, includes every British man, woman and child.

Mountbatten of Burma

AUTHOR'S FOREWORD AND ACKNOWLEDGEMENTS

THE Capital Ship of yesterday has been the most wonderful of man's creations. In the years to come her history and development will be a source of interest and research, and it is hoped that this book may go some little way towards meeting a present and future demand by providing an outline of the development of H.M. armoured ships from 1860 to 1950.

For the ships' data I have turned to the official lists, Ships' Covers dealing with their inception and construction, and Ships' Books which cover their subsequent lives, observing the magic words "as fitted" on the Admiralty plans in the case of discrepancies. Occasionally when the evolution of a design is of special interest some of the alternative sketch plans considered by the Board have been included. Already some of the material from official records herein used has been destroyed and cannot be replaced. In compiling the short histories, Admiral G. A. Ballard's splendid series of articles in the *Mariner's Mirror* dealing with the early ironclads added much information not otherwise obtainable.

When the book was commenced it was to have been fully documented, but the space and cost of footnotes ruled this out and these have been severely limited, references being noted in the text.

May I record my most grateful thanks to the Directors of Naval Construction who helped me in consulting their archives, and to their officers who hunted up so much material and information during the War when I was unable to get to London and Bath. I am also indebted to the Director of the Imperial War Museum for permission to reproduce photographs from the Long and Symonds collections now included in that great array of warship albums.

The chapters on the genesis of the "All-Big-Gun" designs were compiled from the correspondence between Admiral Fisher and Chief Constructor W. H. Gard, kindly lent me by Mr. G. G. Evans.

As regards the plans, there is too much difference in ships' lengths for these to be reduced to scale, and the blocks have therefore been made to fit the pages. The elevations show the ships as originally completed, subsequent alterations being shown in detail or in the text sketches. Half deck plans allow for a simple display of side armour, deck protection and bulkheads for the first time.

*　　*　　*　　*　　*　　*　　*

No such history has ever before been attempted, and as no more such ships will be built it forms a unique record of the prime units of naval force upon which the safety, might and majesty of Britain depended for nearly a century.

Commenced in London, 1925
Completed in Ringwood, June 1956.

Oscar Parkes.

AUTHORITIES CONSULTED

Proceedings. Instit. Nav. Archts.
Journal. United Service Instit.
Brasseys Naval Annual.
Report of the Committee on Design 1872.
Report of the Committee on *Inflexible*, 1878.
Report on the Coles turret ship, 1865.
Report on the design of the *Ajax*, *Colossus* and *Imperieuse*, 1875-78.
Court Martial returns on the *Captain* and *Victoria*.
Our Ironclad Warships. Sir E. J. Reed.
Memories of Sir Cooper Key. Vice-Admiral Colomb.
Life of Sir William White. Fredk. Manning.
Modern History of Warships. Prof. Wm. Hovgaard.
Introduction of the Ironclad Warship. James F. Baxter.
Battleships in Action. H. W. Wilson.
Naval Operations. Sir Julian Corbett.
New Light on Jutland. Revd. J. L. Pastfield.
The World Crisis. Sir Winston Churchill.
The Second World War. Sir Winston Churchill.
The Navy and Defence. Lord Chatfield.
It Might Happen Again. Lord Chatfield.
The Navy from Within. Vice-Admiral K. G. B. Dewar.
The "Bismarck" Episode. Capt. Russell Grenfell, R.N.
Life of Sir David Beatty. Rear-Admiral Chalmers.
A Sailor's Odyssey. Viscount Cunningham.
The War at Sea. Capt. S. W. Roskill, R.N.
Operation Neptune. Commdr. Kenneth Edwards, R.N.
The Jutland Despatches.
The Fighting at Jutland. Lts. Fawcett and Hooper, R.N.
The Grand Fleet. Viscount Jellicoe.

CONTENTS

Chapter 1

THE LAST OF THE OLD "LINE-OF-BATTLE" SHIPS

In 1850 the line-of-battle ship was in all essentials the same as she had been for centuries—a little larger and more heavily armed, but built upon the same lines, sailing under the same rig, and carrying her tiers of smooth-bore guns on the same type of carriage. In the days now drawing to a close the British ship-of-the-line floated, if well found, the unquestioned equal or superior to any foreign vessel. Her speed at the most differed by perhaps a knot from that of any possible opponent. On the high seas she feared nothing. There was no sense of insecurity from the possible approach of destroyers, submarines or aircraft; she dreaded no mines or aerial torpedoes; in fact, barring a heavy gale or a lee shore, or an overwhelming assault from several of her compeers, there was nothing to disturb the proud confidence she so rightly assumed.

In comparing our fleet with those of our possible adversaries there was little distinction to be drawn between ship and ship. No grounds existed for comparing the size of their guns, the tactical value of a difference in speed, or the resistance of hulls against cannon fire. The means of waging war afloat was still an art and not a science, and if naval architects were not of one mind, it might only be as to some slight variance in the form of a hull or the amount of beam to be given.

But from the day that steam engines started to oust sail—and with steam came shell fire—all this was changed. In a few years the complete transformation from wood to armour plate was complete, and year by year came startling innovations in the instruments of naval warfare, so that the pride of the fleet one year became out of date by the time she had completed three commissions. The worship of material was to grow apace—the biggest ship . . . the biggest gun . . . the fastest ship—always bigger and better; the men who fought the ships became merely numbers, instead of the deciding factors in most cases.

And when the size of a ship was no longer limited by the length of the bole of a tree, and developments in machinery gave a greater measure of speed than did increase in sail area, ships trebled their tonnage and still cut the water as fast or even faster.

Naturally as size increased numbers diminished, and when the calibre of guns started to grow inch by inch, year after year, until the centre line turret with two huge guns successfully challenged the broadside battery of smaller pieces, then the whole nature of ships underwent a remarkable change. In 1855 it needed the keen eye of a seaman to distinguish between a British and foreign ship; in 1865 their differences were obvious; by 1875 they could not possibly be confused. Individual ships became of more importance and their special features of greater significance; one-, two- and three-deckers gave way to an infinite variety of armoured and unarmoured types in which gun power, armour, speed or endurance were specially favoured. Occasionally certain vessels like the *Minotaur* and *Alexandra* were given pride of place and became aristocrats of the Service, wearing their hauteur in the face of later and finer creations which lacked the kudos of tradition as bestowed by a long line of flag officers; others, unfortunate in their conception, came into the Service under a stigma which time never lifted.

But big or small, acclaimed or derided, they all hold an interest one way or another if only as steps in the evolution of the giants which came to fight in the Great Wars of the twentieth century. And now those giants have passed, and in a few more years the last of the big-gun-carrying battleships will be viewed in much the same way as the seaman in the old *Minotaur* might regard the wooden ships laid up in ordinary—merely as picturesque relics.

But when the wars were over and we came to size up the eternal value of things, it was not the ships but the men who had won.

Chapter 2

THE FIRST SEA-GOING IRONCLAD

THE FRENCH "GLOIRE"

AFTER the conversion of the old two deckers into steam "block ships" for use in the Crimean War, the fitting of steam engines to ships-of-the-line proceeded apace. The French built the *Napoleon* as a steamer, and a very successful steamer, in 1850; we converted the *Sans Pareil* in 1851 and built the *Agamemnon* as a steam two-decker the following year; by 1858 we had built or converted 32 ships-of-the-line, and exactly the same number had hoisted the tricolour on the other side of the Channel. Realizing that the coming of the steamship would effectually wipe out the British accumulated superiority in sailing ships-of-the-line, the French made every effort to keep abreast with our conversions, and succeeded. In August 1855 the *Commission Supérior Centrale* had proposed a programme of new construction comprising 40 screw ships-of-the-line of 70 to 90 guns; 20 frigates; 30 corvettes; 60 despatch vessels and transports—sufficient for the conveyance of an expeditionary force of 32,000 men. But by February 1857 the results obtained by their new *rifled* guns had convinced them that the use of armour had become imperative if ships were to live through an action, and as a result the *Conseil des Travaux* stopped the construction of further wooden ships-of-the-line and concentrated their attention upon the creation of an iron clad fleet.

With the introduction of an entirely new type of fighting ship and the possibilities of the ironclad with a rational conception of its future, the French saw the culmination of their efforts to secure command of the seas. If they could achieve a superiority in ironclads allowing them to tide over the critical period of equality with the British fleet in ships-of-the-line, which we had allowed to come to pass, then Trafalgar and Waterloo might be avenged!

Already several projects for armoured ships had been submitted. Rear Admiral Pellion, Captain Dupré and Lieutenant Duseutre had advocated armoured rams, and Constructors Guesnet, Marielle and Ferranty and Lieutenant Béléguic proposed fast ironclad frigates of 20 to 34 guns with displacements ranging from 1,800 to 4,000 tons. But the Conseil considered that these would all be too small to fulfil the necessary requirements for fast sea-going ships, which included:

(1) A speed of 13 knots for the choice of range and position.
(2) Armour of at least 4 in. thickness over the topsides and extending for 4 or 5 ft. below water.
(3) A command of 7 ft. for the guns.
(4) A stern shaped to give protection to the screw.
(5) Full ship rig for cruising.

Further firing tests commenced at Vincennes in 1856 against various types of armour plate, and the question of adequate backing was thoroughly investigated; then, in order to determine the best methods of construction, targets representing iron and wooden hulls were pounded with solid shot of iron and steel from 30-pdr. and 50-pdr. guns. From these tests sufficient data had been acquired—especially as to the possibilities of iron hulls—to justify a definite launch-out on the new policy when Dupuy de Lôme was appointed *Directeur du Material* on 1 January 1857.

DUPUY DE LOME

No happier selection could possibly have been made. Twelve years before, the new Directeur had submitted his first plan for a sea-going ironclad; his screw line-of-battle ship *Napoleon* had been a triumphant success, and now at the age of forty he was to initiate the greatest revolution in the history of naval construction, as one who "in boldness of conception and in executive skill takes the first place among the naval constructors of our time" (Barnaby).

His ability was backed by the personal interest of Napoleon III, and to this combination of skill and support from the Throne must be accorded the credit of bringing the ironclad battleship into being. And having once decided that the armoured ship was to become mistress of the seas, the French effort to attain maritime superiority was limited only by their national resources for the production of armour and iron plating.

"GLOIRE," 1858

Dupuy de Lôme based the design for his ironclad frigate upon that of his masterpiece, the *Napoleon*, allowing some 500 tons more displacement and increasing the waterline length 19½ ft., but retaining almost the same beam and draught so as to secure finer lines to permit of equal speed with the same engine power. Displacement ran to 5,617 tons, the dimensions being 252½ × 55 × 25 ft., and the wooden hull was plated to the upper deck with

4·3 in. plates in the upper strakes and 4·7 in. in the lower, backed by 26 in. of wood. Along a full-length battery ranged thirty-four 5-ton guns—but at a height of only 6¼ ft. above water, with two more on deck, which limited warlike operations to European waters.

In appearance the *Gloire* made no concessions to conventional profile, being squat and ugly with a straight bow and curved cut-away stern. Originally a barquentine, she was later remasted as a full ship. subsequently rigged as a barque, and finally carried fore and aft sail only.

Actually there was very little invention shown in the *Gloire*. Certain problems regarding stability of a

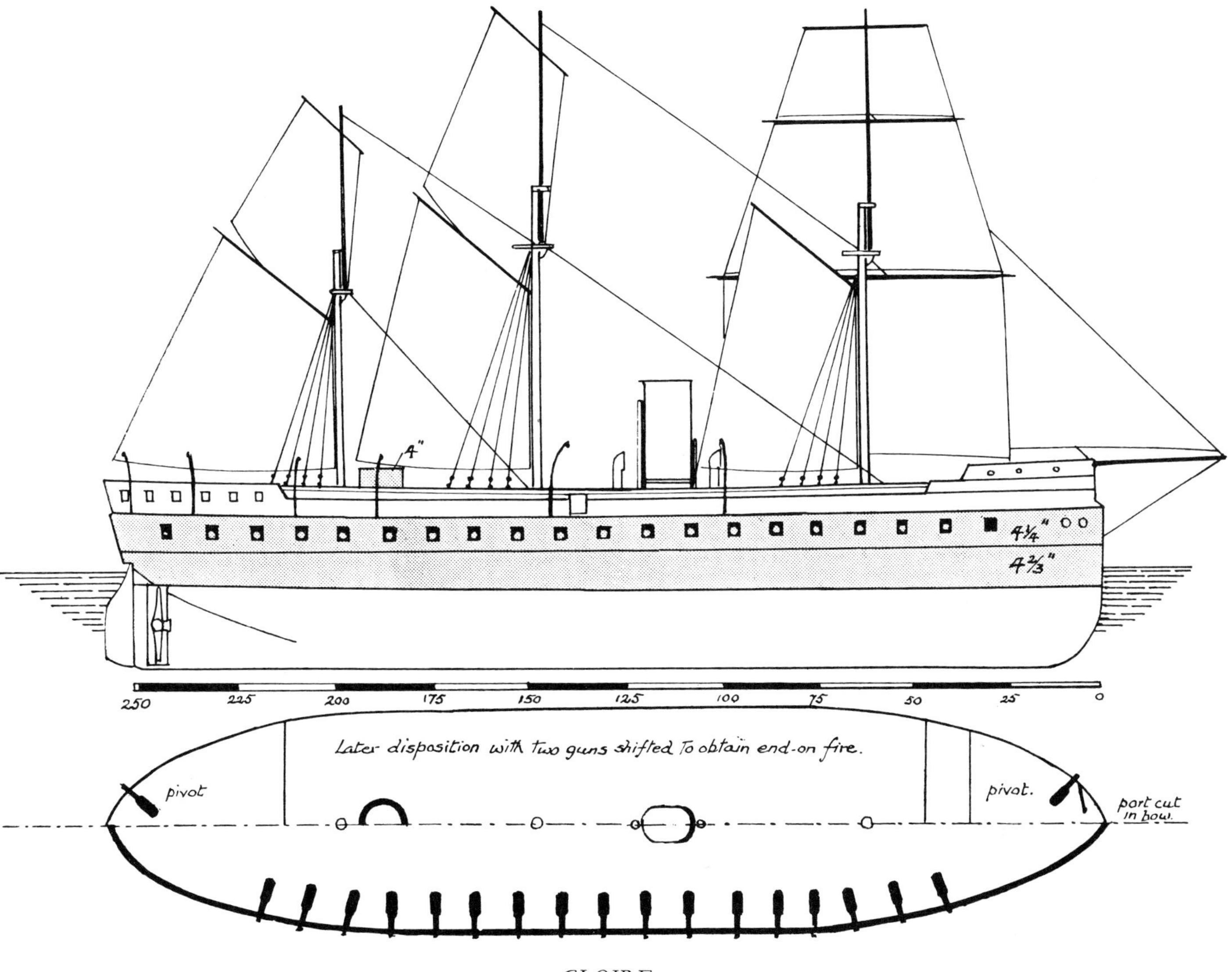

GLOIRE

novel nature due to the armoured hull had to be disposed of, but otherwise she was a straightforward solution to the problem of producing an armoured frigate, whose qualities were a good deal exaggerated in the French press.

FIRST FRENCH IRONCLADS LAID DOWN, 1858

The great revolution in naval architecture was inaugurated in March 1858, when the first four ironclads were ordered—the wooden-hulled *Gloire* and *Invincible* at Toulon, the *Normandie* at Cherbourg, and the iron-hulled *Couronne* at Lorient. This last, designed by Audenet, was built at Dupuy de Lôme's suggestion as an alternative to his own plans. She displaced 6,428 tons and had a sandwich hull made up of 4-in. armour with a 4-in. teak backing, then an iron lattice-work of 1⅓ in. backed by 11-in. teak resting on a ¾-in. iron skin. The *Couronne* proved by far the soundest investment of all the early French ironclads, and when her active career was over became a training ship with chequer sides and a false frigate bow, completing this service in 1909. Subsequently attached to Toulon dockyard, she was still afloat in 1930.

Seeing that Dupuy de Lôme had advocated iron shipbuilding so ardently, the wooden hulls of the *Gloire* and her sisters may seem to belie his reputation for originality and enterprise. That timber was resorted to may be explained by French industrial limitations. A large group of ships had been planned, and as these were to be constructed quickly it was simply a question of making the most of available resources. Had French foundries been in a position to provide all the plating required, as well as the armour, then the *Gloire* class would not have had wooden hulls. By recommending the acceptance of the *Couronne* design by Audenet, the Directeur showed fairness and foresight. As a single ship she could provide experience in the new methods of construction and afford opportunity for putting into practice such features as ram bows and watertight compartments, which were not practicable in timber hulls.

The last two ships of the programme, *Magenta* and *Solferino*, were very different from the *Gloire* group and described as *cuirasses avec spardeck*. Designed by Dupuy de Lôme, they had the distinction of being the only two-decked broadside ironclads ever built, and when first passed into service carried an armament of twenty-four 16-cm. (5 tons) in the upper battery, and sixteen 19-cm. (7·8 tons) and ten 16 cm. in the lower one. Amidships the whole side was covered by 4½-in. armour, but forard and abaft the batteries necessary weight-saving reduced protection to a shallow waterline belt only, leaving the wooden sides exposed. A long ram bow and cut-away stern set them off well, and the *Solferino* created a very good impression when she visited Plymouth in 1856.

With 3,283 h.p. speed was 12·8 knots and full ship rig was spread.

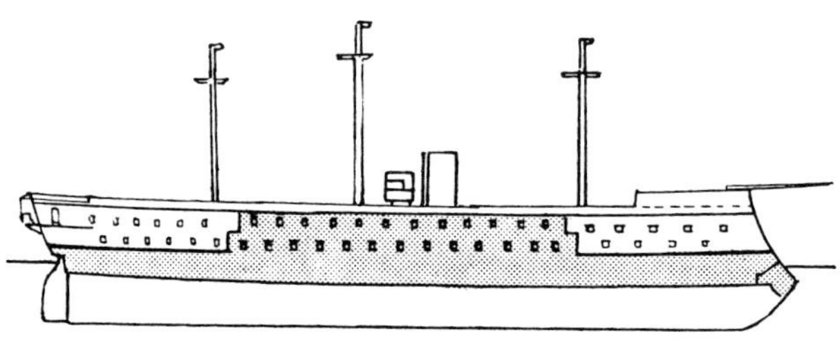

MAGENTA and *SOLFERINO*

At sea they proved good sea boats and much steadier than the *Gloire* frigates, owing to the extra topweight and high centre of gravity.

Chapter 3

EARLY BRITISH IRONCLAD PROJECTS

In this country, however, with a time-honoured policy of preserving the established order of values afloat, the French "New Order" had but little reaction. There was no question of discarding the wooden walls or furthering the use of armour in fighting ships in 1858.

Although we had been persuaded into building the floating batteries, the First Lord, Sir Charles Wood (March 1855 to March 1858) considered that as armoured ships they had not been subjected to any real test under the Russian fire; until more was known about the resistance of armour to heavy guns, he had little interest in sea-going ironclads.

EARLY BRITISH IRONCLAD PROJECTS

Six projects for ironclads had been submitted to the Government in 1856-7. One, from Vice-Admiral Sir Charles Napier, proposed that a three-decker should be cut down to one deck and the weight thus saved expended on side armour to protect a broadside of 10-in. guns. A second, from Captain W. Moorsom, R.N., was along similar lines, advocating a one-decker carrying fifteen to eighteen 68-pdrs. a side with 4 in. iron armour for a depth of 25 ft.

The Surveyor reported that Napier's conversion project would be costly and short-lived, while with adequate stability the battery would be too low. As regards Moorsom's plan, the Board wished to have further information as to the real value of hull armour, and asked the War Department to test both hammered and rolled iron plates and the relative value of both iron and steel.

WOOLWICH ARMOUR TESTS 1857

Experiments carried out at Woolwich in December 1856 and April, May and June 1857 showed that there was little to choose between hammered and rolled plates of 4-in. iron, as both resisted cast-iron 68-pdr. shots at 600 yds., but were broken up by repeated hits—unlikely in action—when the range had been reduced to 400 yds. Wrought-iron shot were far more effective than cast-iron. As an alternative to iron armour nothing thicker than 2-in. *steel* plate was available for testing, and this offered no effective resistance.

Whatever doubts as to the value of 4-in. armour against the heaviest shot may have been entertained by the First Lord, these tests should have dispelled them. If 4-in. iron could keep out 68-pdrs. at 600 yds. there would be no great difficulty in applying it to sea-going ships. The Board, however, took no immediate action and it was left to the initiative of the Controller to submit rough sketches of a proposed sea-going ironclad to the First Lord in February 1858.

FIRST IRONCLAD PROJECT 1858

This was for a 26-gun ship described as a "corvette" (which at that time meant a vessel carrying a scale of armament next to that of a small frigate, whether her guns were carried above or below decks), with dimensions of 280 × 58 × 23¼ ft. and tonnage of 5,600, the ports 10 ft. above water and speed 10 knots with 800 h.p. Armour plates 4 in. thick extended from the upper deck to 5 ft. below the load waterline. The estimated cost was £200,000—which would be about £80,000 more than a standard corvette with the same armament and machinery.

So much for the first proposal of a sea-going ironclad which can be said to have emanated from Whitehall. In strict observance of traditional policy the Board was not prepared to consider the construction of any such vessel liable to initiate a new type of warship—this was three months before anything was known about the *Gloire*—although a sufficient sum had been included in the Estimates under Vote 10 "which," as was pointed out by Sir Charles Wood, "might have been applied to that object [an experimental ironclad] in 1858 if we had gone on with it." There was some doubt as to how the hull was to be kept clean—especially on foreign stations unprovided with adequate docks; also—as an alternative to iron—the Board wanted to know what thickness of the new "homogeneous metal" (a variety of cast steel containing a small amount of carbon, intermediate between malleable iron and cast steel) would be required to resist solid shot—and more especially the new Whitworth *elongated* projectiles. These were a special feature of a new form of artillery developed during the past few years by Joseph Whitworth of Manchester and William Armstrong of Elswick which were to sound the knell of the traditional smooth-bore gun. Armstrong's breech-loaders were destined for a short, unsatisfactory and expensive life afloat, but their method of manufacture and the advantages of rifling were to be the bases for later developments; Whitworth guns were also to have their influence upon future production although not to the same extent.

Chapter 4

THE 1858 "NAVAL SCARE"

In England the naval position was now far from satisfactory.

The news of the commencement of the French ironclad fleet in March did not become known in London until the following May, when it was received with a rising apprehension, which in Parliament and press was fanned into what has become euphemistically termed a "panic" as rumours of a big shipbuilding programme reached Westminster. The *Gloire* and her sisters were described as "huge polished steel frigates" and credited with powers which, although they "plunged some persons into deep distress . . . were manifestly put forward to excite our foolish fears." To allay the well-grounded sense of insecurity caused by these new weapons of war, a Parliamentary Committee was formed in 1858 to enquire into the relative naval strength of the two countries, but the report published the following year did nothing towards providing any reassurance. It made disquieting reading. Omitting all sailing ships—now recognized as having no war value against steamships—it was found that both England and France had 29 ships-of-the-line built or completing, while France had 34 large frigates (not including the ironclads) against our 26.

> "So convinced are naval men in France," note the Committee, "of the irresistible qualities of these ships [the ironclads] that they are of the opinion that no more ships-of-the-line will be laid down, and that in ten years that class of vessel will have become obsolete."

But to meet this alarming situation the Committee could recommend nothing but half-measures. Although the problem of countering the French designs required a drastic change in our appreciation of the elements of sea power, the only course bewildered experts could visualize was an accelerated conversion of the remaining ships to steam!

Behind this very unsatisfactory recommendation was the reactionary influence of Sir Howard Douglas, the veteran artillerist now in his eighty-third year. Implacably opposed both to iron hulls and armour, his advice was still accepted by Palmerston—as he stated it had been by Sir Robert Peel when the decision was taken to convert the *Simooms* into troopers—although the great protagonist of iron ships, John Scott Russell, was very soon to confound his arguments and bring Ministerial opinion into line with scientific achievement.

The Admiralty was therefore in a quandary. There were divided opinions as to whether we should follow the French lead and outbuild them in ironclads; or push ahead with both ironclads and wooden ships, modifying the building programmes as circumstances dictated; or build up our superiority again along traditional lines with the requisite number of wooden ships—which was the course adopted for a short time.

So for the moment wooden walls were given pride of place in Britain's defences, and a further programme of ships-of-the-line was put in hand—of which only those ultimately completed as ironclads were ever set afloat.

Chapter 5

WANING PRESTIGE OF THE THREE-DECKER

WITH the *Howe*, *Victoria*, *Prince of Wales* and *Windsor Castle* the wooden walls reached their acme of development. Apart from great size—and they were twice the tonnage of the *Victory*—their armament consisted of shell guns of the largest calibre with a 68-pdr. mounted up in the bows to provide chase fire which was difficult to secure from the guns at the turn of the bows. All these guns had sights which enabled hits to be made at ranges beyond point-

Three-decker *Victoria* of 6,930 tons displacement launched in 1859 and armed with 62 8-in. and 58 32-pdrs., with 1 68-pdr. chase gun. Fitted with engines of 4,293 I.H.P.—13·14 knots. A second funnel between the main and mizen is here lowered. She was the last three-decker to leave harbour as a sea-going ship, and was flagship C.-in-C. Mediterranean until 1867.

blank, when shells could be driven through the sides of any ship at 1,200 yards or more and then burst inside her. Moreover, with these increased ranges had come a much wider dispersion of fire. A broadside could now be directed at two ships, which was impossible under the "close-alongside" tactics, and thus the need for a three-deck concentration no longer obtained. Under these changed conditions the 130-gun ship was becoming an anachronism. The huge armament meant a great vulnerable target, with a draught of water limiting employment to the high seas and debarring her from operating in shallow waters or off-shore on blockade—which were the conditions chiefly found during the Crimean War. Indeed, the one virtue of the three-decker in 1858 seems to have been the excellent accommodation provided for the Commander-in-Chief and his staff—and the Surveyor was being roundly criticized for constructing such ships! It was claimed that her place in the line could be better filled by the big two-deckers armed with guns of the same calibre and carrying smaller crews.

WALKER'S BIG FRIGATES, 1857

But the relative merits of (1) large and small guns and of (2) concentration of armament versus dispersion were brought to a head when Walker produced the big frigates in 1857. Being nearly equal in size to the *Duke of Wellington* three-decker—or some 440 tons larger than the *Conqueror* two-decker—and armed with heavier guns than either, they bid fair to qualify for capital rank.

The frigates were built in pairs, differing somewhat in dimensions, armament and horse-power, so that *Diadem* and *Doris* could be distinguished in having fewer gun ports and only one funnel.

Diadem	Pembroke 1856	240′×48′×20·6′=2,480 tons. (3,800 displ.)
Doris	Woolwich 1857	I.H.P. 2,685/3,000=11·8-12·1 knots.
		Guns: 20 10-in.; 10 32-pdrs.; 2 68 pdrs.
Ariadne	Deptford 1859	280′×50′×21⅓′=3,204 tons. (4,426 displ.)
Galatea	Woolwich 1859	I.H.P. 3,350-3,517=13 knots.
		Guns: 24 10-in. main deck; 2 68 pdrs. pivot.
Mersey	Chatham 1858	336′×52′×21½′=3,706 tons.
Orlando	Pembroke 1858	I.H.P.=13·2 knots.
		Guns: 20 10-in.; 12 68-pdrs.

As a change from ships built with an eye to construction on the other side of the Channel, the *Mersey* group were replies to a class of American frigates which had created a good deal of interest in this country.

THE AMERICAN FRIGATES

By the Act of 6 April 1854 authorizing the construction of six steam frigates, the Americans had produced a series of remarkable vessels armed with *heavy shell guns*, five of which were frigates and one a corvette with open batteries. Such ordnance promised a superiority in the case of single ship actions much as their predecessors had enjoyed in the War of Independence, when our frigates often had the worst of an encounter because of inferior armament. The *Merrimack*, *Wabash*, *Minnesota*, *Roanoke* and *Colorado* differed slightly in dimensions but were otherwise sister ships; the design of the *Niagara* corvette was entrusted to George Steers of New York, who specialized in fast clippers and yachts and was responsible for the *America*, which had won the Queen's Cup at Cowes in 1851. And whereas certain restrictions governed the design of the frigates, Steers was given a free hand in the corvette for the purpose of ensuring her speed.

U.S.S. Niagara	328 (W.L.)×55×24½ ft.=4,580 tons.
	Guns: 14 11-in.
	Speed: 8·5 knots.
U.S.S. Merrimack	275 (W.L.)×38½×23½ ft.=3,200 tons.
	Guns: 24 9-in.; 14 8-in.; 2 10-in.
	Speed: 9 knots.

Note: The frigate was "Merrima*ck*" officially; she was captured by the Confederates and turned into an ironclad. The U.S.S. *Merrimac* was an iron side-wheel steamer.
The "U.S. Statistical Data of U.S. Ships" credits *Niagara* with 14·5 knots max., 7·4 knots average, and *Merrimack* with 12 knots, average 9 knots.

Steers' efforts as a naval constructor were not particularly successful, as the *Niagara* could only manage 10·9 knots in smooth water under steam and had an average sea speed under steam and sail of 8·5 knots (*The Steam Navy of the United States*, p. 151). But she served a good purpose in helping H.M.S. *Agamemnon* to lay the first Atlantic cable, and her 11-in. Dahlgrens created a considerable impression when she visited this country.

When the designs for the five frigates came to be approved the full significance of steam had not yet been fully appreciated in the U.S. Navy and a traditional pride and reliance in sail could not be surrendered by the old school. It was considered a sufficient concession if steam were admitted as an auxiliary only, and for that reason their keels made them deep in the water and severely limited employment—especially when sent to the China Station. None were flyers and the *Merrimack* was as good as the best. She could chase a quarry at 8·8 knots (1,294 h.p.) in smooth water, and under all conditions of wind and weather at 5·5 knots; under steam and sail she averaged 7·6 knots.

We possibly expected rather a better showing than this, as in his replies Baldwin Walker aimed at 13 knots, which meant providing fine lines and considerable horse-power. It was as much by virtue of the 336 ft. between perpendiculars as by the 4,000 I.H.P. developed on trials that the *Mersey* logged her 13·2 knots, and this extreme length was never exceeded by any other wooden warship. During their construction critics did not hesitate to prophesy that this dimension had been drawn out beyond the recognized limits of timber construction and that the ships would be failures. But happily they did not suffer unduly from longitudinal weakness and were not sold out of the Navy until the middle 'seventies, the *Ariadne* being requisitioned for the *Vernon* torpedo school establishment, being later transferred to Sheerness as a part of the *Actæon*, where she served until the 1920s.

But although not to be included among the capital ships, special interest is attached to these first-class heavy frigates, as besides forming a definite link between the ships-of-the-line and the *Warrior*, they implemented a conception of battle which had grown up since the Crimean War—that of destroying the enemy with impunity either by means of (1) long-range gun-fire or (2) at short range by virtue of armour protection. The big frigates aimed

The 26-gun frigate *Ariadne* launched at Deptford in 1859. One of our largest steam frigates and capable of 13 knots. After her active life she was hulked and lined up with the *Donegal* to form the *Vernon* torpedo establishment at Portsmouth, and later moved to Sheerness and renamed *Actæon* as torpedo school ship there.

at the former method, as their speed was sufficient to enable them to keep beyond range of practically anything afloat, while theoretically their heavy shell guns could deliver broadsides of sufficient weight and intensity to overwhelm any probable opponent. Incidentally our 10-in. shell gun of 86 cwt. was considered too light for its duty and the American model of 107 cwt. regarded as the superior piece.

Nevertheless contemporary critics resented the rationale of the *Mersey* class. They claimed (1) that long-range firing was never satisfactory and had to be followed up by a battering at decisive ranges in order to beat a ship of smaller size, and (2) that speed should only be utilized to bring an enemy of equal size into action, and employed to avoid close quarters only in the case of great superiority on the part of the enemy. By opening the range these frigates might annoy a ship-of-the-line, but could never hope to bring the fight to a successful conclusion. Many preferred the second-class smaller frigates like the *Emerald* with a lighter and more numerous armament, and so voiced an opposition to extreme speed and very heavy guns which persisted right down to the Great War of 1914-18, when Fisher's *Courageous* class were built.

Whether or no the heavy frigates carried enough guns to beat a two-decker, they were certainly of sufficient power to justify some place in the line—possibly as a fast division. They have indeed been described as capital ships because they possessed such fighting ability that their absence from the battle line would have been felt, although never intended to rank with the prime units of the fleet. But as yet it was premature for a one-decker to aspire to line status, although in a few years' time armoured frigates were to replace the two-deckers in our premier squadrons.

Chapter 6

THE FIRST BRITISH SEA-GOING IRONCLADS

On the fall of Palmerston's Ministry in March 1858, Lord Derby headed a Conservative government for a short period of office, the First Lord being Sir John Packington.

Discord between the late Allies had become intensified by the Orsini conspiracy to assassinate Napoleon III, which had been organized in England. An invasion of this country was the common talk of the boulevards; French naval officers were "confident and eager to try their hands," although in former years they had dreaded a naval war; and the Marshals of France, with an army five times larger than the British, regarded us with contempt. Regiments petitioned the Emperor for the honour of being in the van on the march towards London, and the *Moniteur* went to the length of printing the names and addresses of colonels "who demanded to be led to London to hunt down the assassins in their dens."

In order to try to improve our international relations the Queen and Prince Consort visited Cherbourg in August, but the sight of the new fortifications to the roadstead from which the invasion was expected to be launched, together with the great fleet of new ships swinging in that historic anchorage, increased their suspicions as to the ultimate object behind this pageantry. "The war preparations of the French are immense," wrote the Prince, "ours despicable. Our Ministers use fine phrases, but they do nothing. My blood boils within me!"

Since the end of the Crimean War there had been a growing rapprochement between France and Russia which now led to rumours of an Alliance—although actually this was not to be concluded for another thirty-four years. But the possibility of such a combine was a matter for very serious consideration at Whitehall, and one of the first special minutes of the new Board of Admiralty contained the significant remark, "When determining upon the number of ships, and upon the Naval Force generally, which England should have, it should be borne in mind that the navies of France and of Russia may very probably be combined against her." The Surveyor also impressed upon the First Lord the urgent need for increasing the Fleet, declaring:

> "Although a few years ago we were far ahead of them [the French] in respect of screw line-of-battle ships, they are now for the first time equal to us, and unless some extraordinary steps are at once taken to expedite the building of screw ships-of-the-line, the French at the close of next year will be actually superior to us as regards the most powerful class of ships of war."

The Board certainly realized their serious responsibilities and pressed the Government to provide the necessary ships, with such good effect that by the midsummer of 1859 we had 40 two- and three-deckers completed as against only 29 in the spring of the previous year. At the same time there was the problem of the French ironclads, which had assumed grave proportions as their significance became properly realized.

On 28 June 1858 the Surveyor's submission declared that the construction of sea-going ironclads was of the highest importance to ensure the continued supremacy of the British Navy and the safety of the country. In this passage he again voiced the basic policy of the Admiralty:

> "Although I have frequently stated that it is not to the interest of Great Britain—possessing as she does so large a navy—to adopt any important change in the construction of ships of war which might have the effect of rendering necessary the introduction of a new class of very costly vessels, until such a course is forced upon her by the adoption by Foreign Powers of formidable ships of a novel character requiring similar ships to cope with them, yet it then becomes a matter not only of expediency, but of absolute necessity . . .This time has arrived. France has now commenced to build frigates of great speed with their sides protected by thick metal plates, and this renders it imperative for this country to do the same without a moment's delay."

His forceful submission was that two wooden-hulled ironclads should be put in hand at Chatham and Pembroke, and contracts for four more with iron hulls placed with private builders—waiving any objections on the score of fouling, as the ships would be required for home service. The design he prepared for these was for a vessel of 6,096 tons carrying 26 guns, armoured with 4-in. plates from the upper deck to 6 ft. below water, and steaming at 12¾ knots with 1,000 nominal h.p. He estimated the cost of wooden ships to this design as £197,560 and of iron ones £193,340.

But the First Lord, although "very anxious . . . mortified and vexed" by the progress of the French ironclads, with a Board than which "no body of men could have been unanimous on any subject than the Board of Admiralty was upon the necessity of using every effort to recover the ground which had been lost," postponed any construction until the following year, when it was decided that a vote should be made for "at least two wooden frigates being coated with iron."

"ALFRED" TESTS, 1858

Meanwhile Captain R. S. Hewlett of the gunnery school *Excellent*—who had lost no opportunity of pressing for the construction of ironclads—carried through a series of tests against iron plates mounted on the side of the *Alfred* in August and showed the superiority of wrought iron over homogeneous metal or steel—as then made—with the heaviest shot-gun in service, the 68-pdr. In October the first tests of *rifled* guns were made against the *Alfred's* 4-in. plates. A Whitworth 68-pdr. firing *cast-iron* shot at 350 to 400 yds. cracked the plates but only made dents up to 1¼ in. Nevertheless the only *wrought-iron* shot fired before the gun burst pierced both the plate and ship's side of 7-in. oak—a feat not to be equalled for some years, and fine tribute to Whitworth's system although the gun was wrecked. It was also shown that one 68-pdr. shot was more destructive than five 32-pdrs. striking close together.

"EREBUS" AND "METEOR" TESTS, 1858

In the same month experimental firing against the batteries *Erebus* and *Meteor* demonstrated the importance of heavy oak backing to armour, the *Meteor* with the 20-in. of wood putting up a far better resistance than the iron-hulled *Erebus*, in which the frames were displaced by concussion.

RUBBER AND COTTON BACKING

Alternative backing of thick india-rubber and compressed cotton were shown to be quite useless—although again tried out several years later in some of the Federal ironclads during the Civil War.

That the wooden ships were still to be regarded as an integral part of the fleet was made plain by the Surveyor's submission of 27 July in his sensational report on the strength of the French battle fleet. He argued that, though ironclads would increase their superiority in the most formidable class of warships if not countered by similar units in our own fleet, "they must be regarded as an addition to our force as a balance to those of France, and not as calculated to supersede any existing class of ship. Indeed, no prudent man would at present consider it safe to risk, upon the performance of ships of this novel character, the naval superiority of Great Britain."

The Board were inclined to regard the ironclad problem as one suitable for future discussion, but the Secretary Thomas Lowry Corry argued that it demanded immediate attention and was ripe for decision. He carried his point, and on 27 November the Surveyor was directed to submit a project for " *wooden* steam man-of-war to be cased with wrought iron 4½ in. thick"—and the Estimates prepared for 1859 included £252,000 to be expended on two armoured frigates. The British ironclad era had dawned—although Sir Howard Douglas still had the ear of Authority!

The First Lord, however, was more alive to the necessity of unusual efforts than most of his critics in the House, and wrote expressing his personal doubts to Douglas as to the advantages of wood. Scott Russell headed expert opinion, both naval officers' and architects', in advocating iron construction for the new ships, and in view of the gigantic achievements of the mercantile shipyards the Admiralty found themselves no longer able to agree with the aged advocate for timber. A momentous decision was taken, and the old allegiance to wooden walls crumbled. Sir Howard Douglas had to accept defeat in his long-continued struggle against radical change when the Board gave preference to an alternative proposal made by the Surveyor—this time for an iron-hulled ship. The old general who had done so much for the efficiency of the nineteenth-century Navy lost the last round in his eighty-third year, although his convictions never changed. Just before his death, in 1861, he insisted: "All that I have said about armoured ships will prove correct . . . how little do they know of the undeveloped power of artillery"—a prophecy which showed a remarkable prescience of the conditions some twenty years later.

Walker expressed his preference for iron construction while allowing a thickness of wood backing to the armour equal to the side of a timber ship—a very necessary provision, as shown by the *Erebus* and *Meteor* tests. He proposed a frigate in which 4-in. protection was to extend from the upper deck to 5 ft. below the load water-line over a length of 200 ft. amidships with bulkheads at each end, leaving the bows and stern sections unarmoured but subdivided into watertight compartments. The hull would be pierced for 34 guns on the main deck with the 'midships ports at least 9 ft. above water, and two guns on the upper deck as bow and stern chasers. The high speed of 13½ knots would require some 4,000 h.p., fine lines, and great length; for sailing there was to be the rig of an 80-gun ship.

In order to include Chief Constructor Isaac Watts' design in as wide a selection of alternatives as possible, the Surveyor proposed that the Royal Dockyards and private shipbuilding firms should be invited to submit designs embodying the features required by the Board. For the benefit of the Master Shipwrights of the Dockyards—who had as yet had no experience with anything but timber construction—designs for wooden hulls could be submitted for consideration provided that the armour extended from stem to stern.

Although all these designs were rejected in favour of the office one, their details are worth recording:

Designer	*Length ft.*	*Beam ft.*	*Displ. tons*	*Speed knots*	*Wt. of armour* / *displ.*	*Wt. of hull* / *displ.*	I.H.P.
Laird	400	60	9,779	13½	·11	·51	3,250
Thames Co.	430	60	11,180	..	·10	·58	4,000
Mare	380	57	7,341	..	·13	·46	3,000
Scott Russell	385	58	7,256	..	·18	·38	3,000
Napier	365	56	8,000	13½	..	..	4,120
Westwood and Baillie	360	55	7,600	13½	·16	·36	4,000
Samuda	382	55	8,084	13½	·16	·15	2,500
Palmer	340	58	7,690	13½	..	..	4,500
Aberthell (Portsmouth)	336	57	7,668	..	..	..	2,500
Henwood (Sheerness)	372	52	6,507	..	·18	·4	2,500
† Peake	355	56	7,000	..	·14	·46	3,000
† Chatfield	343·6	59·6	7,791	..	·14	..	..
Lang (Chatham) ..	400	55	8,511	15	·14	·53	2,500
† Craddock	360	57·6	7,724	..	·2	·42	2,500
Admiralty (Office) ..	380	58	8,625	14	·18	·52	5,000

† To be built of wood.

Tenders were called for, and that of Ditchburn and Mare of Blackwall—forerunners of the Thames Ironworks—was accepted at £31 10s. per ton B.O.M. on 11 May 1859. The ship was to be launched in eleven months and completed for sea three months later—that is, by July 1860.

FIRST B.L. GUNS. "TRUSTY" TESTS

In January 1859 a test of far-reaching importance was carried out against the 4-in. side of the *Trusty* floating battery, when the first Armstrong breech-loader had its armour-piercing powers tried. Great things were expected of this new type of gun, and Captain Hewlett wrote to the Minister of War "that Mr. Armstrong be desired to consider what description of *shell* he would propose for penetrating the iron plates, for in the event of the shot going through, the shell will be the next consideration of importance." There were full expectations that the shot would pierce the plates and sink the ship, so that plugs and the means of stopping a fracture were all ready.

The result was, to say the least of it, disappointing. Fourteen rounds were fired with wrought-iron, cast-iron and steel shot with 6-lb. charges, at ranges from 450 to less than 50 yds.—but far from piercing the plates, they all had "no serious effect." This, however, was discounted by the Special Ordnance Committee, and having increased the shot to 40 lb. and diminished the charge to 5 lb., it was forthwith accepted for the Service, put into production without any further trials, and became the Armstrong 40-pdr.—a gun less effective than before!

ESTIMATES 1859

On 18 January the Cabinet agreed to what was described as "a great addition to the effective force of the Navy," and Packington announced that the Estimates would involve a "reconstruction" of the Navy—which provoked some alarm abroad and great expectations from the Big-Navy party at home. In his speech on the Estimates, 25 February 1859, he assured the House that the progress of the new French ships and results of our armour tests had convinced the Admiralty that "whatever be the cost . . . it is our duty to lose no time in building at least two." After which fanfaronade an increase in the shipbuilding vote of only £1,000,000, of which £252,000 was to be expended on two ironclads, hardly fulfilled the high expectations aroused. But having passed the vote for commencing the construction of two frigates, no sooner had the tender for the first been accepted on 29 April than the Board began to question the soundness of its decision in view of the great cost of the ship. The advisability of reducing the armour to 2½ in. was actually considered, but the weight of the Surveyor's and Captain Hewlett's opinions carried the day in favour of the thicker plating and heavier displacement. However, before the contract for the second ship could be placed, there was a change in Government in June 1859 and the question of her construction was again in abeyance.

RETURN OF LIBERAL GOVERNMENT, JUNE 1859

When Palmerston—pre-eminently a Big-Navy man—was again returned to power, with the Duke of Somerset as First Lord, it was months before the new Board were able to agree on any sort of forward policy as regards ironclad construction. The Prime Minister was one of Sir Howard Douglas's disciples, and in consequence work on the wooden line-of-battle ships was speeded up so that our old superiority in these could be regained, and a Two-Power standard in them assured by 1861. And this in face of the knowledge that the French had not laid down a wooden ship-of-the-line since 1855!

When Packington enquired about the progress of the further armour tests ordered by his Board, and also when the second ironclad would be commenced, Rear-Admiral Lord Clarence Paget, the new Secretary, replied that there had been delay in the manufacture of the plates for testing and that the second ship would not be proceeded with "until the result of the experiment in the first case had been brought to a conclusion." Then, against his wishes, Paget had to propose the addition of extra wooden capital ships. (In August he had pressed that three ironclads should be substituted for these, and when this course was not approved by the Board, had offered his resignation, although persuaded to withdraw it by Palmerston.) Gladstone favoured the ironclad substitution, but the Prime Minister heartily supported the Board's efforts to regain our predominance in wooden ships.

So hammer and adze continued to echo through the dockyards as useless timber hulls took shape on the building slips. As Sir William White put it (*Quarterly Review*, January 1873): "The conduct of our naval affairs from 1858 to 1860 appears almost inexplicable; and the Admiralty Boards holding office during that period cannot be freed from censure for their sins both of omission and commission. They simply yielded to a *vis inertia* which carried them on smoothly in a well-worn track long after it should have been left; and instead of initiating a policy, or relying, as the French did, upon the skill of their naval architects, they waited for the pressure of public opinion before venturing on anything like extensive changes. . . ."

ALTERNATIVE FOR THE SECOND FRIGATE

In September the question of the second armoured frigate came up for settlement, and the new Board—true to Whig principles—being intent upon a cheaper type, decided that plans for a smaller ship should be considered. The Surveyor therefore submitted a design for one of 5,223 tons whose hull and engines would cost some £52,000 less than those of the frigate already ordered.

While having the same beam, draught and height of battery (which was reduced from 36 to 22 guns), the length was to be only 335 ft.—necessitating a reduction in speed to 12 knots. This, the Surveyor pointed out, would not be sufficient to enable her to avoid action with wooden ships-of-the-line *whose concentrated broadsides might overwhelm her;* nor would it provide that margin of speed which would be required in a ship with an anticipated life of over ten years, if she were to keep abreast of future construction so far as steaming capabilities were concerned.

"BLACK PRINCE" ORDERED OCTOBER 1859

In the face of these arguments it was decided that the second ship should be built to the design already in hand, and in October a contract was placed with Napiers of Glasgow for her delivery in twelve months at a cost of £37 5s. per ton. The first frigate was named *Warrior* on 5 October 1859 and the second at first *Invincible* and later *Black Prince.*

"UNDAUNTED" TESTS, 1859

In August, tests of various types of armour plate as mentioned by Paget had commenced at Portsmouth, with the *Undaunted* as target ship. In these rolled iron proved superior to steel as then made; plates of less than 4 in. were found to be inadequate; and those of laminated armour inferior to the solid plate.

THE 100-PDR. B.L. IN "TRUSTY" TESTS. SEPTEMBER 1859

During the last week in September the keenly anticipated trials of the second type of Armstrong B.L.—the "special gun of large calibre" specifically built as an armour-piercing weapon—were carried out against the iron sides of the *Trusty.* This time there was an expectation of victory of gun over armour, so much so that the order of attack was reversed—the range was to be increased, beginning at 400 yds. and lengthening to 1,000 yds.!

The new piece weighed 65 cwt., was of 6 in. calibre, and fired a charge of 12 lb. of powder. Altogether 22 rounds of cast iron and steel shot were fired, of weights varying from 78 lb. to 100 lb. and specially made for armour piercing with coned or flat heads. Commencing at 400 yds., however, the shot had no effective result. The range was reduced to 200 yds. and finally to 50 yds.—but the gun was still ineffective against the armour! So the shells provided were not required.

B.L. GUNS ISSUED FOR SERVICE

If the tests disappointed the Ordnance Committee, they certainly confirmed the value of the armour selected for the new ironclad. But sixteen days later the War Office ordered a 7-in. model of 82 cwt. firing a shot of 110 lb. with a 13 lb. charge, and this was intended to make good as an armour-piercing gun.

Strangely enough, in July 1864 the Under Secretary for War, referring to the 110-pdr., said: "The House must recollect that when this gun was ordered it was *not intended to be used against iron plates*"—which excuse for the impotence of a gun once so loudly acclaimed meant that the Navy had been deliberately furnished with inadequate weapons.

The Armstrong breech-loading guns introduced into the Service were the

110-pdr. (4 tons and 10 ft. long)
40-pdr. (1½ tons and 10 ft. long)
20-pdr. (½ ton and 5½ ft. long)
12-pdrs. and 6-pdrs.

and something like two and a half millions was spent in equipping the fleet with them between 1858 and 1862.

A fortnight before the *Warrior* took the water a wave of mistrust in the strength and capabilities of the two ships seems to have thoroughly damped the Board's confidence. In the *Illustrated London News* for 8 December 1860 we read:

> "After £250,000 had been spent on her, the Lords of the Admiralty discovered that she is not the description of vessel that will combine stability with invulnerability, but after stopping the work on the *Warrior* for two whole days while deliberations were pending at Whitehall—decided 'that she is not the vessel we could wish for, but after laying out so much money upon her, it will be as well to see what we can make of her.' Thus, while we are wasting our energies on doubtful experiments the Emperor of the French has tested his *La Gloire*, the performances of which have again been reported as having given great satisfaction."

Ten months later the *Warrior* proved that these fears were groundless, and when she was joined in the Channel Squadron by her sister in 1862 the two "black snakes amongst the rabbits" exercised a salutary influence on the other side of the Manche. The Emperor—in spite of many blunders in his switchback career—had "a broader vision of amphibious strategy than the army chiefs of France—or of England either for that matter—who talked of island invasion as if it had no naval aspect. He saw clearly enough that, with such obstructions to be negotiated as the *Warrior* and *Black Prince*, the prospect of the Imperial drum majors ever swinging their batons in the Old Kent Road, was not bright enough to justify a rupture of the correct relations towards Great Britain, which he was careful to preserve to the end of his reign in spite of all pressure to the contrary" (Ballard).

Chapter 7

"BLACK PRINCE" AND "WARRIOR"

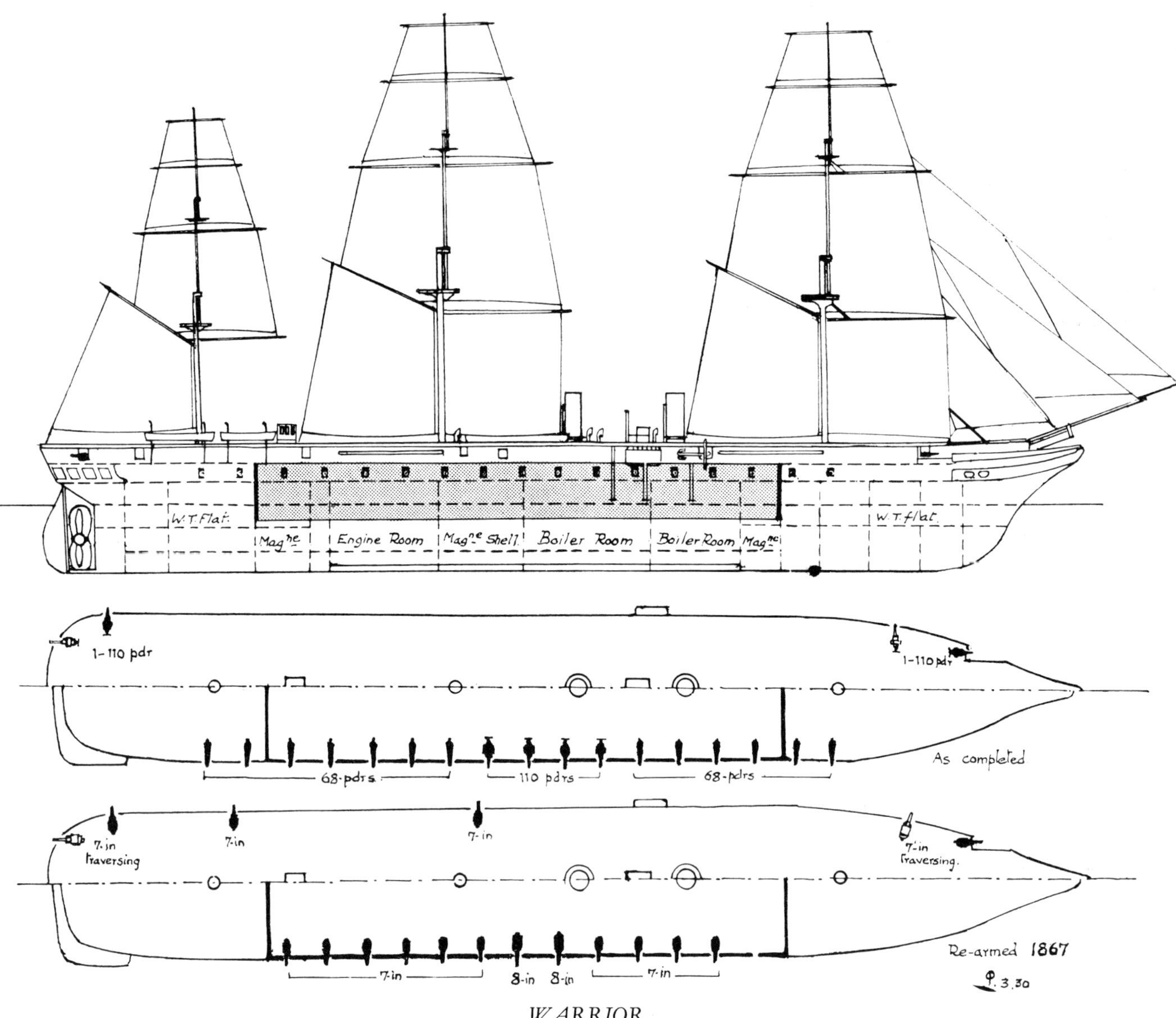

WARRIOR

	Builders	*Laid down*	*Launched*	*Completed*	*Cost*
"*Warrior*"	Mare	25 May '59	29 Dec. '60	24 Oct. '61	£377,292
"*Black Prince*"	Napier	12 Oct. '59	27 Feb. '61	12 Sept. '62	£377,954

Dimensions 380′ (pp) $\times$ 58¼′ $\times$ 26′ = 9,210 tons. Hull 6,150. Equipment 3,060.

Guns	*On completion*	*Re-armed* 1867
	26 68-pdrs.	28 7-in. 6½-ton M.L.R. (24 in "*Black Prince*").
	10 110-pdrs. B.L.	4 8-in. 9-ton M.L.R.
	4 70-pdrs. B.L.	4 20-pdr. B.L.

Armour 4½″ iron. 18″ teak backing. Bulkheads 4½″.
Total weight: 1,305 tons (950 tons plus 355 tons teak).

Machinery Horizontal trunk single expansion. (Penn) N.H.P. 1,250. cyl. 112″, stroke 4′ 4″. Revs. 56-54.
10 Rectangular boilers. 20 lb. pressure.

Trials: "*Warrior*" 5,270 I.H.P. = 14·08 knots.
"*Black Prince*" 5,770 I.H.P. = 13·6 knots.

Coal 850 tons.

Complement 707.

Constructors J. Large and W. H. Walker.

THE basic conception in the design of the *Warrior* provided that she should be able to overtake and overwhelm any other warship in existence. The process by which she was evolved was thus described by Scott Russell:

> "It having been decided that the *Warrior* should carry an armament of forty guns upon one deck, and that a space of 15 feet was required between the guns; this gave, as the necessary dimensions of the battery, a length of 300 feet and a breadth of 50 feet. On this calculation the midship body was formed. Next, in order to attain the desired speed of 15 [*sic*] knots some reduction was necessary in the midship body, while a bow was added 135 feet long, and fine lines were secured for the after body of the ship by giving to the run a length of 90 feet."

FEATURES OF THE DESIGN

In order to attain this unprecedented speed a V-shaped transverse section was adopted for a considerable length forward, which at the suggestion of Scott Russell was not armoured, otherwise there would have been complete lack of buoyancy. As it was, the weight of the first 50 ft. from the bows just equalled the displacement (E. J. Reed, evidence, Turret Ship Committee, 1865, p. 66).

With the *Warrior*, frigates achieved line-of-battle status, not as inferiors to the two-deckers but with an incalculable superiority to the *Howe* and *Victoria*—a state of things which presented the Board with a curious problem. Hitherto the Fleet had been graded in "rates" based on the simple system of truck gun armament, but how the ironclads with their less numerous but far more powerful broadsides were to be shown in this classification perplexed the Board more than a little. There could be no question of abolishing or modifying the time-honoured system of rating, but to include the most powerful warships afloat with the Fourth Raters of 50 guns would have been ludicrous. A solution was found by ignoring the guns and taking the complement of men as a standard, and as that of the *Warrior* was 707 while the Third Rate ship-of-the-line carried 705, the new ships were classed as Third Raters although more than a match for all the First-Rates in the Fleet. Compared with the *Mersey*, the *Warrior's* dimensions showed an increase of 44 ft. in length, 6¼ ft. in beam and 4½ ft. in draught; and whereas the timber ship had overgrown the limits set by the bole of the trees available and showed a tendency to sag under the weight of her engines in consequence, with an iron keel and frames only docking facilities limited dimensions. But in 1861 we possessed only one dock at Portsmouth capable of taking the *Warrior*, and then at high water, and she would have had to be lightened to enter the Canada Dock at Liverpool or No. 1 dock at Southampton. Having a length of 6½ beams, she ran a little finer than the *Mersey*, but in general resembled the big frigates, excepting that her long black hull never received the white chequered strakes of her consorts. The heavy knee bow certainly added to her appearance and appealed to worshippers of tradition when such revolutionary changes were toward. But, like the broad frigate stern, it was an expensive hostage to convention, imposing 40 tons of useless weight, without the excuse of any military qualities, where she could least afford to carry it. Although officially described as possessing a "bow strengthened for ramming," this decoration effectually disposed of the possibility of its being used with any effect, and even proved a measure of safety to her squadron mates—as the ram in peace-time was always more dangerous than in war. On one occasion it certainly saved the *Royal Oak* from the risk of being holed when the *Warrior* crashed along her lee side and carried away the boats and starboard main and mizen chains.

BULWARKS

High bulwarks had been an established feature of the wooden ships for so long that they were fitted in the *Warrior* and subsequent broadside ironclads through sheer force of convention; thus 7 ft. of timber surrounded their upper decks, in spite of its weight and cost and having outlived its usefulness.

In the original draft neither of the two ships was provided with a poop, but some twelve years after completion a light open after shelter deck was fitted to the *Warrior* and a full poop to the *Black Prince*. This to some extent tended to correct their being trimmed by the head owing to faulty disposition of weights. As the French *Couronne*, although laid down in February 1859, did not take the water until March 1861, the *Warrior* had the distinction of being the first sea-going iron-hulled ironclad to be put afloat. But delays were caused by additions to the original design; to reduction in the size of her gun ports; and to the fitting of tongues and grooves at the edges and butts of her plates. This latter very costly procedure was suggested by the curving of the plates tested at Shoeburyness after being struck by heavy shot, but was never repeated in view of the great difficulty in replacing damaged plates. It was therefore a full year after her contract completion date when she entered service.

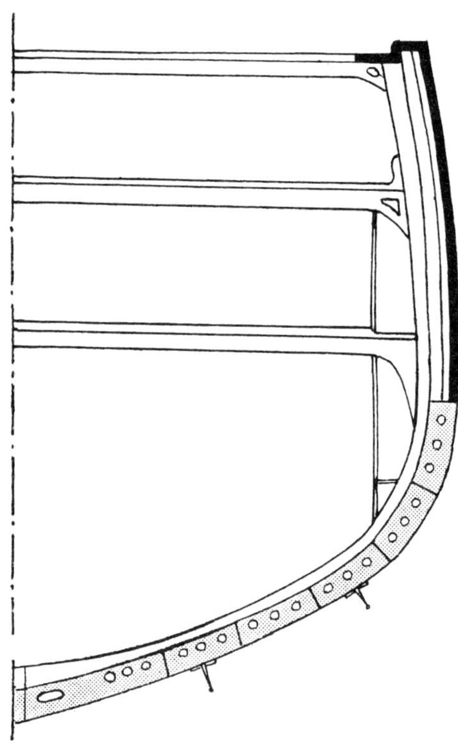
WARRIOR. Section.

STEERING

A weak point in the design was the lack of protection to the rudder head and steering gear, both fitted in conformity with sailing-ship practice, when spare tillers and tiller ropes could be rigged and only injury to the rudder head itself was serious.

SUBDIVISION

In order to offset the risks of flooding from hits in the unarmoured ends, a system of internal water-tight subdivision was applied, running to 92 compartments. This major feature of the design had never been possible in wooden ships, although their hulls were divided off by light partitions. Also for the first time the engines, boilers, coal, ammunition and stores generally were bulkheaded off in a series of self-buoyant chambers, arranged on a plan which became more or less standard for all the later broadside battleships.

DOUBLE BOTTOM

Amidships a double bottom of 57 sections extended under the engine and boiler rooms, but along the rest of the hull the compartments would have been flooded if the bottom plating had been pierced.

HULL WEIGHT

One of the measures of success in a well-designed ship is the excess of weight found in her carrying capacity over the actual weight of a hull of adequate strength. But because of its entirely novel character, lack of experience led to the hull of the *Warrior* having a weight of 4,969 tons against a carrying capacity of only 4,281 tons—whereas a few years later the hull could have been built on an allowance of 3,300 tons.

GUN PORTS

Under the original armament warrant providing 20 truck guns on each broadside, the ports would have been about as large as those in the *Gloire*. But after these had been cut, a system of pivoting the gun carriages under the trunnions of the guns was found practicable and applied for the first time, allowing them to be trained over an arc of 25 to 30 degrees through ports only 2 ft. wide. The ports as cut were therefore plated in to this width, with 7-in. iron reinforcement outside the internal bevel which permitted training, so that the *Warrior's* side exhibited only narrow ports compared with the embrasures through which the *Gloire* fired her guns.

ARMAMENT

According to the first completed draft, only nineteen gunports were altered along each side of the main deck to display thirty-eight 68-pdr. S.B., the other two guns being at the bow and stern on the upper deck. But as the first Armstrong 110-pdr. B.L. were ready for issue during the completion of the *Warrior*, two of these were allotted to her in lieu of the upper deck 68-pdrs. with four 70-pdrs. B.L. as saluting guns, while below a reduction

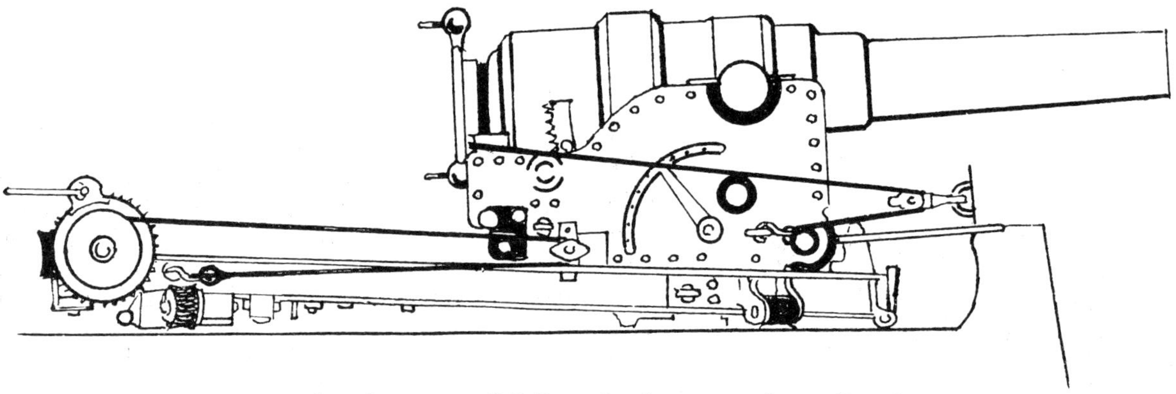
110-pdr. 7-in. 82-cwt. B.L.R., 1860. Armstrong Screw Breech.

was made in the broadside to save weight at the ends of the ship and get rid of some of the unprotected guns. On commissioning then, the main deck showed four 110-pdrs. amidships and thirteen 68-pdrs. on each side, the intention being that she should have a uniform armament of 110-pdrs. when the guns became available. However, firing tests carried out in September 1861 by 68-pdrs. and 110-pdrs. against a cupola aboard the *Trusty* fitted to try out Captain Cowper Coles' proposals demonstrated that the much-vaunted new breech-loading gun was inferior to the 68-pdr. as an armour-piercing weapon—a disconcerting discovery which came as a distinct shock to the Select Ordnance Committee, and effectively prevented the B.L. armament of the *Warrior* from being increased.

In 1867, when the breech-loaders had been discarded and a reversion made to muzzle-loaders, the *Warrior* was completely rearmed with four 8-in. M.L.R. and twenty-eight 7-in. M.L.R., retaining four 20-pdr. B.L. for saluting—the greatest number of rifled weapons heavier than the 6-in. ever carried by a British warship. With these guns the upper deck battery was increased to eight 7-in.—a pair in the bows, a pair in the after part of the waist, a pair on the quarter deck, and a pair at the stern. Four 8-in. 9-tonners replaced the 110-pdrs. in the middle ports on the main deck with 20 7-in. 6½-tonners, all carried behind armour and 8½ ft. above water.

After being rearmed the *Black Prince* carried four 8-in. and only twenty-four 7-in. M.L.R.

In the Ship's Cover is a plan of the *Warrior* showing a high tower aft, unaccompanied by any explanation or descriptive text, but which must have reference to the evidence given by her captain, the Hon. Arthur A. Cochrane, before the Coles Sea-going Turret Ship Committee in 1865, when he said:

> "I should like to show you a drawing of a turret, which if mounted on the deck of some of our ships would be of advantage. It is a drawing of a fixed turret 25 feet high with a revolving gun mounted en barbette. The tower being of this great height enables a plunging fire to be delivered when the enemy ship is in proximity; the shot would take effect over the top of the armour plating and through the decks or bottom of the enemy, whereby all the ships as at present armour plated would be rendered useless."

The somewhat important matter of stability with such a structure did not come in for consideration.

ARMOUR

Unlike the *Gloire*, which was armoured from stem to stern, the *Warrior* carried 4½-in. wrought-iron plating with a backing of 18-in. teak over 213 ft. amidships only, to a height of 16 ft. above water and 6ft. below. These walls were closed at the ends by 4½-in. bulkheads, forming a citadel which was pierced for twenty-six guns, leaving the bow and stern sections of the hull unprotected. At each end therefore was a space of some 85 ft. of thin iron plating without any wood backing, which was just as dangerous from all accounts as the condemned plating in the "Simoom" frigates. Even allowing that the "Simoom" target was made up from inferior metal and that better-quality iron was used in the *Warrior*, the acceptance of conditions rejected twelve years previously is worth noting.

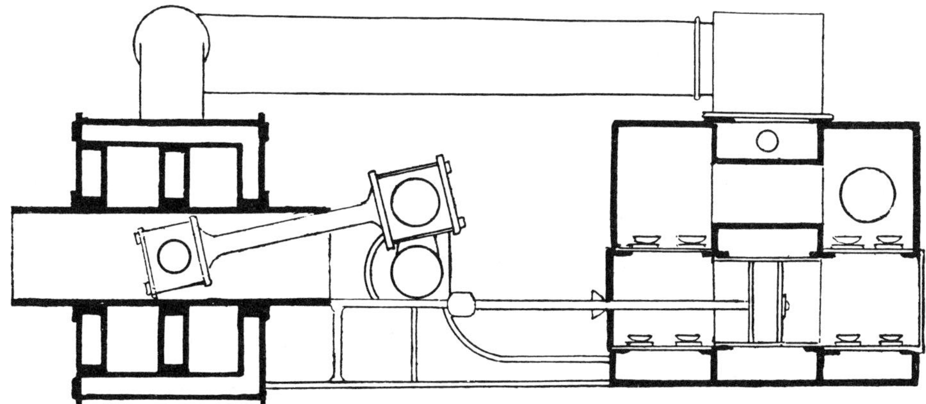

Penn's trunk engine, with jet condenser.

MACHINERY

Penn's trunk engines were by far the best marine type of that period, and those in the *Warrior*, indicating over 5,000 h.p., by a long way the most powerful ever designed for a warship. Trunk engines being without piston rods, needed little floor space without loss of stroke, and their horizontal lie provided large surfaces for the sliding parts with consequent reduction in wear and tear; the propeller drive was left-handed, so that the push and pull of the connecting rods should react upwards on the trunks and so save downward wear on the bearing surfaces. It was only when compounding was adopted by the Service that trunk engines were superseded as unsuitable for dual expansion.

A boiler pressure of only 20 lb. may appear ridiculous but was then considered high. On the measured mile the

Warrior steamed at 14·3 knots, which was unsurpassed by any battleship for some years; the *Black Prince* proved about half a knot the slower in service, her best being 13·6 to 13·9 knots. In the *Warrior* the screw was a two-bladed, 10-ton Griffiths—the largest hoisting propeller ever made—needing 600 men on the falls to the old-fashioned sheers over the stern by which it was raised. *Black Prince* had a fixed propeller.

For the first twelve years there was no auxiliary machinery whatsoever on board except a steam pump, but during their big refits this was geared to work the main deck capstan. Hitherto their ground tackle was the heaviest ever recorded to be dependent upon manual working, and when this gearing was arranged the *Black Prince* became the first ship in the Navy to have a steam capstan, although steam steering was not installed until 1880. The steering gear did not give satisfaction, as the extreme angle of helm did not exceed 18 to 25 degrees; and to secure this there was such a multiplication of tackles between the steering wheels as made the loss of power in friction very considerable and the time of putting the helm over very long. On one occasion the *Black Prince* was turned in a circle with her rudder 30 degrees from the keel line; to put the helm over occupied 1½ minutes, to complete the circle 8½ minutes, and forty men were engaged at the steering wheels and relieving tackles (White, *Naval Architecture*, p. 612).

Steering was by a fourfold handwheel abaft the mizen-mast and conned from a light bridge resting on the quarter-deck bulwarks. In 1861 an elliptical block-house of 4-in. plating was placed under this bridge for the protection of the captain—but as he could neither con the ship from this position nor was any transmission gear installed, it was rather a useless appendage.

COAL

Bunkerage was for 800/850 tons, greater than that of any warship afloat for the next ten years, and sufficient for 1,420 miles at 12½ knots or 2,100 miles at 11 knots. As the engines and boilers weighed 920 tons, the total weight absorbed by steam power was 1,720 tons—or about 19 per cent. of the load displacement. For comparative purposes it may be noted that in the battle-cruiser *Tiger* (1913) machinery and fuel worked out at 23·9 per cent.

RIG

In the early ironclads a full rig was essential as sufficient coal could not be carried to feed the uneconomical boilers and engines during the prolonged passages which every ship might expect in a foreign service career.

From the first it was realised that they could never be regarded as sailing ships in the same degree as were the wooden line-ships, although the steam frigates were capable of as good figures under canvas as any of those without engines.

In combining sail with steam in armoured ships two entirely opposite conditions had to be reconciled—*i.e.*, (1) stiffness to carry sufficient canvas in order to sail well, and (2) steadiness under steam as a gun platform. The heeling due to wind pressure was quite a different thing from heeling due to waves or rolling in a swell, moreover a spread of sail diminished rolling. To stand up to a gale under canvas demanded a high degree of stability—a ship had to be "stiff" with a low centre of gravity; but without the steadying effect of her canvas a "stiff" ship could roll abominably and made a poor gun platform. As the ironclads were intended to fight their guns under steam, it meant that they would have to be made "steady"—*i.e.*, be given a moderate centre of gravity which would diminish rolling under bare poles, but at the same time be sufficiently "stiff" to carry an adequate spread of canvas.

In the case of the *Warrior* it was decided to provide a rig equal to that of an 80-gun ship, as a happy medium which could be carried with safety and at the same time furnish the means for good progress under sail, although the estimated displacement of the ironclad at that time was 8,625 tons and that of the 80-gun ship about 6,000 tons; there was also the advantage of 150 ft. in length with fine lines in favour of speed although disadvantageous to handling and manœuvre.

But a three-masted rig looked very inadequate for such a long hull, and Baldwin Walker was anxious to give the *Warrior* four or five iron masts. But difficulties arose on account of the position of the engines and boilers, although Watts admitted that there would be no insuperable obstacle to erecting an iron mast over the machinery as regards structure; however, "he saw reasons of another nature which appeared to him to make it undesirable to do so," so the three-masted rig was adopted.

When launched it was anticipated that the *Warrior* would be barque rigged, but on completion both were ship rigged on what was to be the maximum spar plan for armoured ships with a total sail area of 48,400 sq. ft. including stunsails. They were the only ironclads ever fitted with wooden lower masts and caps, and on completion the bowsprit was 49 ft. long and 40 in. in diameter with jib boom and flying jib boom in proportion. But as they suffered from excess weight forward this head gear was cut down in March 1862 to a bowsprit 25 ft. long of 24 in. diameter which was stepped on the upper deck—they never had topgallant forecastles—and it was not until the addition of a poop improved the trim that a reversion was made to the original head gear.

Although spreading less canvas than the largest three-deckers with a plain-sail area of only twenty-three times their immersed midships section, the *Warrior* had the advantage of being stiffer and so able to hold on to it longer, while her masts and yards were stouter and heavier in proportion to their length, which allowed for the greater strain.

SAILING

Under canvas she recorded 13 knots under all plain sail and stunsails, which was only to be surpassed by the *Royal Oak* and equalled by the *Royal Alfred* and *Monarch*; the *Black Prince* logged 11 knots only as her best, under whole courses, double-reefed topsails, and topgallants with a 7 to 8 wind on the quarter. The *Ocean's* iron masts replaced her wooden ones in 1875.

Using sail in conjunction with steam, the *Warrior* put up some excellent figures, and it is recorded that on 15 November 1861 during a competitive sea trial she logged 16·3 knots against the 11 knots of the *Revenge* screw two-decker. Again, in November of the same year she ran from Portsmouth to Plymouth in 10 hours at full speed, her maximum being 17·5 knots against the tide, when spreading all plain sail to royals, with the sea smooth and wind on the port quarter (*The Times*, 15 November 1861).

The two funnels were telescopic and lowered when making a passage under sail only. In October 1861 they

This photo of the *Warrior* was taken in Plymouth Sound by Long during her first commission about 1862. She is shown with the short bowsprit and without a poop, and is flying the Red Ensign prior to the White Ensign having been adopted by the Navy. Her famous figurehead is clearly shown, also the wooden davits aft.

were raised 6 ft. to secure a better draught, with the result that the *Warrior's* speed improved by 0·3 knot (5,469 h.p. = 14·3 knots) on a subsequent trial (*The Times*, 17 October 1861).

On account of their great length and slow turning powers they were unreliable when wearing and staying, or rounding-to and scudding. In a seaway they would scoop up green water when their consorts were riding dry—the price paid for too much weight forward in conjunction with the V-section and the pictorial effect of an unsuitable bow.

BILGE KEELS

Two bilge keels were fitted to counteract rolling, and proved more efficacious than had been expected—these being the first ships to have them. As regards behaviour in a seaway, in the Black Battle Fleet they may be placed between the *Achilles* and *Minotaur* which were the steadiest, and the *Lord Warden* and *Lord Clyde* considerably the worst. From the height of their guns above water there would have been no difficulty in working the 68-pdrs. during a 10 to 15 degrees roll.

RAM

It was intended that the strong iron stem should be used for ramming, but, as already mentioned, the heavy iron knee neutralised any possibility of its being effective, while the chances of their being able to strike an opponent at the right angle were problematical, as they were so sluggish in manœuvre that any ship with way on her could avoid a direct blow.

FIGUREHEADS

Both ships were remarkable for their magnificent figureheads—the last ever to be fitted to British capital ships, with the exception of the *Rodney* (1884). Future bow decoration was confined to shield and scroll work, and it was only fitting that the last of this, the oldest form of ornamentation, should have survived to grace the bows of our first ironclads on a scale both of size and craftsmanship commensurate with their importance. That of the *Warrior* is preserved at Portsmouth, and now restored to its original aspect after the shield and sword arm had been allowed to fall away from decay.[1] The carving of the *Black Prince* was 15 ft. high with black armour under a white and gold mantle.

WARRIOR

BLACK PRINCE

CONTRACT LOSSES

Both ships resulted in a loss for their contractors, but in view of the difficulties arising during the initial construction of iron warships a grant of £50,000 was made to the Thames Ironworks to prevent the firm going into liquidation, and £35,000 to Napiers.

EQUIPMENT

In general equipment the two ships were on a par with the other steam line-of-battle ships, having hand steering, man power at the capstan for raising the anchors, hoisting tackle for the heavy boom boats, and sheer legs for raising the propeller. Hoisting screws were only fitted in a limited number of ironclads as the gain in sailing speed was more than offset by the structural weakness caused by the screw well; so for this and other reasons of expediency the hoisting screw was abandoned in the course of a few years. But the traditional methods of steering, weighing anchor, and hoisting out boats persisted in the battle fleet until the gradual introduction of auxiliary steam engines superseded man power. As examples of applied methods of seamanship still in vogue during an era which saw the passing of so many time-honoured naval contrivances, they deserve recording in

[1] When she was in collision with the *Royal Oak* (1868) this huge figurehead was deposited in the gun-room of her next ahead as she overran her, crashed along her side as far as the waist, and sheered off her boats and starboard main and mizen chains.

some detail, and may be taken as applying to subsequent ironclads until mention is made of the steam substitute being fitted.

STEERING

Steering in these ships and in all the earlier ironclads was extravagant in man power, very slow in action, and limited to an extreme angle of helm not exceeding 18 to 25 degrees. As in most matters pertaining to technical equipment afloat, the Controller's department observed an unreasoning adherence to ancient convention by insisting that a full degree of helm should require only three turns of the steering wheel, as this had sufficed for slow-moving sailing ships with narrow rudders; it was this inadequate "reduction gearing" which placed such a strain upon the wheel and demanded so much man power and time to get the rudder over.

In steam ships the screw well precluded the use of the old-type tiller and it was necessary to substitute a cross-piece or "yoke" on the rudder head, where the available space was so narrowed by the run of the ship aft that this yoke had to be very short. Hence there was a loss of power which could only be made good by (1) increasing the purchase in the wheel ropes, or (2) giving more turns to the wheel for any given angle of helm. In (1) friction discounted half the advantage gained, while tradition opposed any alteration in (2). Moreover the belief that everything in a ship ought to be loose and yielding like the sea itself had led to the use of hide instead of hempen ropes, and hide was capable of almost indefinite stretching. Hence muscle was employed stretching wheel ropes and not in putting the helm over beyond a certain small angle.

Anyone who sought to improve steering was called upon to do the impossible—to assist the men at the wheel without either increasing its diameter or exceeding three turns. For years the ingenuity of naval officers and naval architects had been directed towards giving greater power to a lever of given length without shifting its fulcrum—*i.e.*, attempting by means of yokes and purchases to increase power between the wheel of fixed diameter revolving a given number of times and the rudder at a given angle.

It was Captain Cooper Key, when Captain of the Steam Ordinary at Plymouth, who recommended in September 1861 that all ships over 400 h.p. should be allowed four turns of the wheel to put the helm hard over. Next year he asked for a comparative test to be made between hemp and hide wheel ropes, as he believed that hide had only half the *strength* of hemp—a subtle way of side-tracking tradition which favoured hide because of its elasticity.

WEIGHING ANCHOR

The present-day practice of carrying the lead of the hawse-pipes up to the forecastle in battleships was not introduced until the coming of the low-freeboard turret ships in the 'seventies. In all the early ironclads the cables were worked on the main deck, being hove in by means of a "messenger" as the only method by which the massive chain cables could be brought to the main capstan, which stood right aft under the quarter deck. This

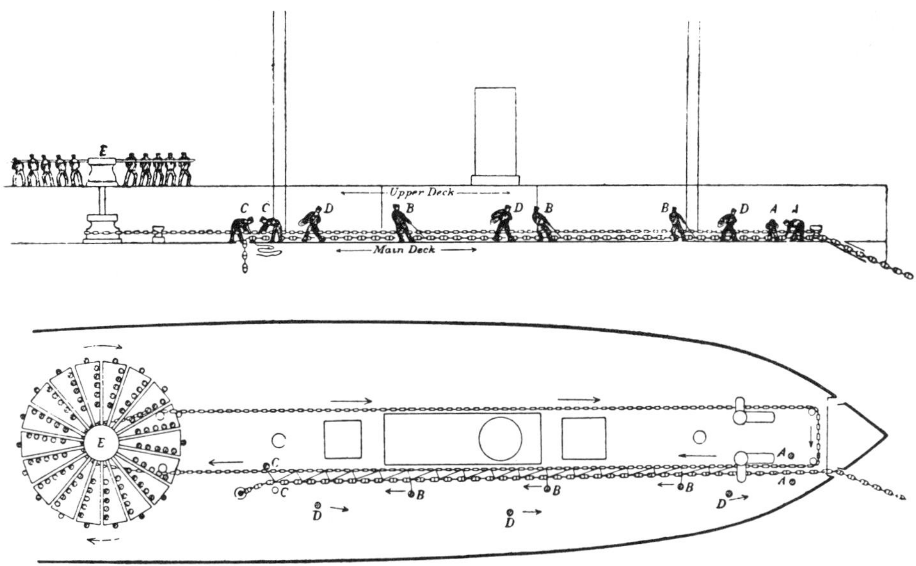

SKETCH OF GENERAL STATIONING FOR WEIGHING WITH A CHAIN MESSENGER
(Not drawn to scale)

Cable deck party: *A*, hands passing the nippers; *B*, hands holding the nipper ends and walking aft with them as the cable comes in; *C*, hands removing the nippers to allow cable to pay down navel pipe; *D*, hands carrying removed nippers forward again for re-passing as required. *E*, quarterdeck capstan with 90 hands on the bars and 10 to 20 on the swifter

(*reproduced from a drawing by Admiral G. A. Ballard in "Mariner's Mirror"*)

system was a survival of the days when the huge hemp cables were too large to wind round the barrel of a capstan for heaving in, and had to be attached by some method to a smaller one that the capstan would receive. This was the "messenger," which was wound three times round the capstan and thence both ends were led forward, one on each side of the deck, to the manger in the bows where each was passed round a roller and lashed together, forming an endless traveller between the capstan and the manger, constantly rotating—forward on one side and aft on the other—as the capstan revolved. As it came up through the hawse pipe the main cable was attached to this messenger by lengths of small rope called "nippers" which were unwound as they reached aft to let the cable pay down the navel pipe into the cable lockers below.

Two specially smart hands, who faced each other just abaft the manger, kept passing the nippers with the cable and messenger between them, while two others removed the nippers at the other end—a risky job requiring great dexterity and strength in the exhausting labour of keeping pace with the messenger and transferring its movement to a bower cable under heavy strain.

In the *Warrior* the hemp messenger was replaced by a chain one with studless links, which caught on teeth forming a sprocket wheel on the lower part of the capstan barrel. Her chain lockers lay abreast the mainmast and the capstan had the usual two barrels on the one spindle, one on the quarter deck and one below, although only the former was usually manned. With five men on each of its eighteen bars and twenty more on the "swifter"—a rope connecting the outer ends of the bars—such a capstan accommodated more than a hundred hands, and when in use presented the appearance of a human whirlpool, all stamping in time to the music of the full band. When the Black Battle Fleet was getting under weigh the operation was accompanied by as much sound as an Aldershot review. The instant the flagship hauled down the signal "Shorten in," every commander ordered "Heave round" and every band struck up one of the recognized capstan tunes, to the music of which the anchors were also catted and fished. But if weighing homeward bound after a three or four years commission abroad, the time was usually taken at the double, and even then the band was apt to get behind the feet (Ballard).

Amidships of "Black Prince" showing sheet anchor

ANCHORS

The ground tackle of the *Warrior* consisted of four Admiralty pattern wooden-stocked anchors (two bowers and two sheets) all of 95 cwt., one 28-cwt. iron-stocked stream anchor, and two iron-stocked 19-cwt. kedges. The bowers were stowed between the cathead and the billboard in the immemorial style; and catted and fished by large hand purchases similar to those in the eighteenth-century models, except that the fish davits were fixtures. The sheet anchors were stowed outboard each side in the fore part of the waist, on hinged crutches to throw them clear on letting go. For stowing again they had to be catted and then transported aft by purchases on the fore and main yards. The stream anchor was kept unstocked and lashed against the mainmast, and the kedges slung on each quarter (Ballard).

"WARRIOR"

Launched by Sir John Pakington at Mare's yard, Blackwall, in mid-winter, when six tugs hauled for an hour to get her down the frozen ways. Commissioned at Portsmouth in August '61; Channel Fleet '61-'64. Escorted the Royal yacht bringing Princess Alexandra from Denmark. Rearmed '64-'67. Channel Fleet '67-'72. (Collision with *Royal Oak* '68; in tandem with *Black Prince* towed the floating dock from Madeira to Bermuda in '69.) 1872-'75 refitted and fitted with poop and steam capstan. 1875-'81 Coastguard ship at Portland. (Particular Service Squadron June-August '78 during Russian war scare.) 1881-'84 R.N.R. training ship on the Clyde. Paid off, but retained on effective list as an armoured cruiser although practically dismantled. Torpedo depôt ship Portsmouth 1904. In 1904 was fitted for service with the *Vernon* torpedo school until the shore establishment was opened, when she was cut down, transformed into an oil pipe-line pier and taken to Pembroke, where she now lies (1953), the precursor of the British armoured fleets.

"BLACK PRINCE"

Was the largest ship to be built on the Clyde when launched. Capsized in dock at Greenock and damaged her masts; arrived at Spithead 10 November '61 with fore and mizen jury masts only. Commissioned at Plymouth May '62. Served in Channel Fleet '62-'66. During '66-'67 flagship at Queenstown. '67-'68 rearmed; '68-'74 guardship on Clyde; '74-'75 refitted and fitted with a poop and steam steering, and wooden masts replaced by iron; '75-'78 Channel Fleet and was flagship of H.R.H. Duke of Edinburgh for Canadian visit. From '78-'96 in Reserve at Devonport as "1st class armoured cruiser." In '96 became training ship at Queenstown and renamed *Emerald* in 1904. In 1910 joined the *Impregnable* at Plymouth. Sold 1923 after sixty-one years' service.

Chapter 8

"RESISTANCE" AND "DEFENCE"

ALTHOUGH the Controller had persuaded the Board not to invest in the slower type of smaller ironclad when the contract for the *Black Prince* was under consideration, their Lordships were still unconvinced that the scale of costs for the first two ships would have to be accepted as a general standard. The fact that only two docks were capable of taking the *Warrior* told against great length, while the former arguments in favour of high speed no longer held good. The Controller had stressed the necessity for speed in ironclads so that they should be able to avoid the concentrated fire from wooden ships, but now it was shown that 4½-in. plates as tested on the *Undaunted* and *Trusty* were capable of withstanding the fire of our latest and heaviest guns. Both these considerations added strength to the argument that it would be advisable to try to construct a smaller and slower type of sea-going ironclad before committing the country to a programme composed only of the largest, fastest and most expensive type of armoured ship.

The Board therefore called for plans for a smaller and slower edition of the *Warrior*, carrying the same armour and mounting the heaviest guns then available. These Walker submitted on 24 November 1859, pointing out that as engine power for 10¾ knots was as much as could be incorporated into the design, the proposed ship would have to be about 2 knots slower than the *Gloire* and unable to bring her into action if she adopted avoiding tactics. Compared with the *Warrior* they would be unsatisfactory ships, but in his anxiety to get the construction of more ironclads under way, the Controller proposed that *six* such ships for "Home Service" be built *faute de mieux*, as by this time it had become absolutely necessary to get ahead with sufficient armoured ships at least to equal the French programme.

But instead of six the Board only asked for the authorization of two. Gladstone urged that work on some of the wooden line-ships be discontinued in favour of a larger number of ironclads, but Palmerston was still unpersuaded that the day of the wooden capital ship had passed and preferred to push ahead with his Two-Power programme of two- and three-deckers. As a result, the Navy was saddled with a couple of ships which would reduce the speed of the *Warrior* in squadron to 10¾ knots, and as fighting units rank inferior to their French opposite numbers both in protection to their batteries and steering gear as well as in armament, speed and sea-keeping qualities. In fact, Sir Nathaniel Barnaby thought so little of them that he estimated their total efficiency compared with the *Warrior* as 1 to 4.

As in the case of the *Warrior* and *Black Prince*, both the new ships were to be entrusted to private shipbuilders, while the resources of the Royal Dockyards were exclusively devoted to the production of wooden ships. The lessons of Sinope and Sebastopol seemed forgotten and no less than fifty unarmoured screw line-of-battle ships and frigates were either laid down, launched, or converted between 1859 and 1860. Of these, many were never to perform any service outside the harbours where they rotted away; some were never put afloat; and a few were to be converted into ironclads as an emergency measure.

"DEFENCE" AND "RESISTANCE"
(1859 PROGRAMME)

	Builders	*Laid down*	*Launched*	*Commissioned*	*Cost*
"*Defence*"	Palmers	Dec. '59	24 April '61	4 Dec. '61	£252,422
"*Resistance*"	Westwood & Baillie	Dec. '59	11 April '61	2 July '62	£258,120

Dimensions 280′ (pp)×54′×25′=6,070/6,150 tons.
Hull and armour 4,500 tons; equipment 1,800 tons.

Guns

On completion "*Defence*"	*On completion* "*Resistance*"	*rearmed* 1867 *Both*
8 7-in. B.L.	6 7-in. B.L.	2 8-in. M.L.R.
10 68-pdrs.	10 68-pdrs.	14 7-in. M.L.R.
4 5-in. B.L.	2 32-pdrs.	

Armour 4½″ wrought iron amidships. 18″ backing.
4½″ bulkheads at ends of battery. Total 950 tons.

Machinery Trunk engines (Penn) I.H.P. 2,540=10¾ knots.
4 rectangular boilers. 20 lb. pressure.
2-bladed screw. 18′ diam.
Coal: 460 tons. Radius 1,200 miles.

Complement 460.

Sail area 24,500 sq. ft.

The special features of these ships were: (1) Ram bows. (2) Double topsails. (3) Iron davits.

In general design these two ships were reduced *Warriors* with one funnel and a ram bow in place of the conventional frigate stem which earned them the name of "steam rams," the *Resistance* being known as "Old Rammo" to the end of her days. The adoption of this form of bow followed the lead of the French, who in their *Solferino* and *Magenta* had incorporated the long projecting stem which was to be such a feature of their ships for the next thirty years—although later it became not so much a ram as a means for providing buoyancy without an excess of

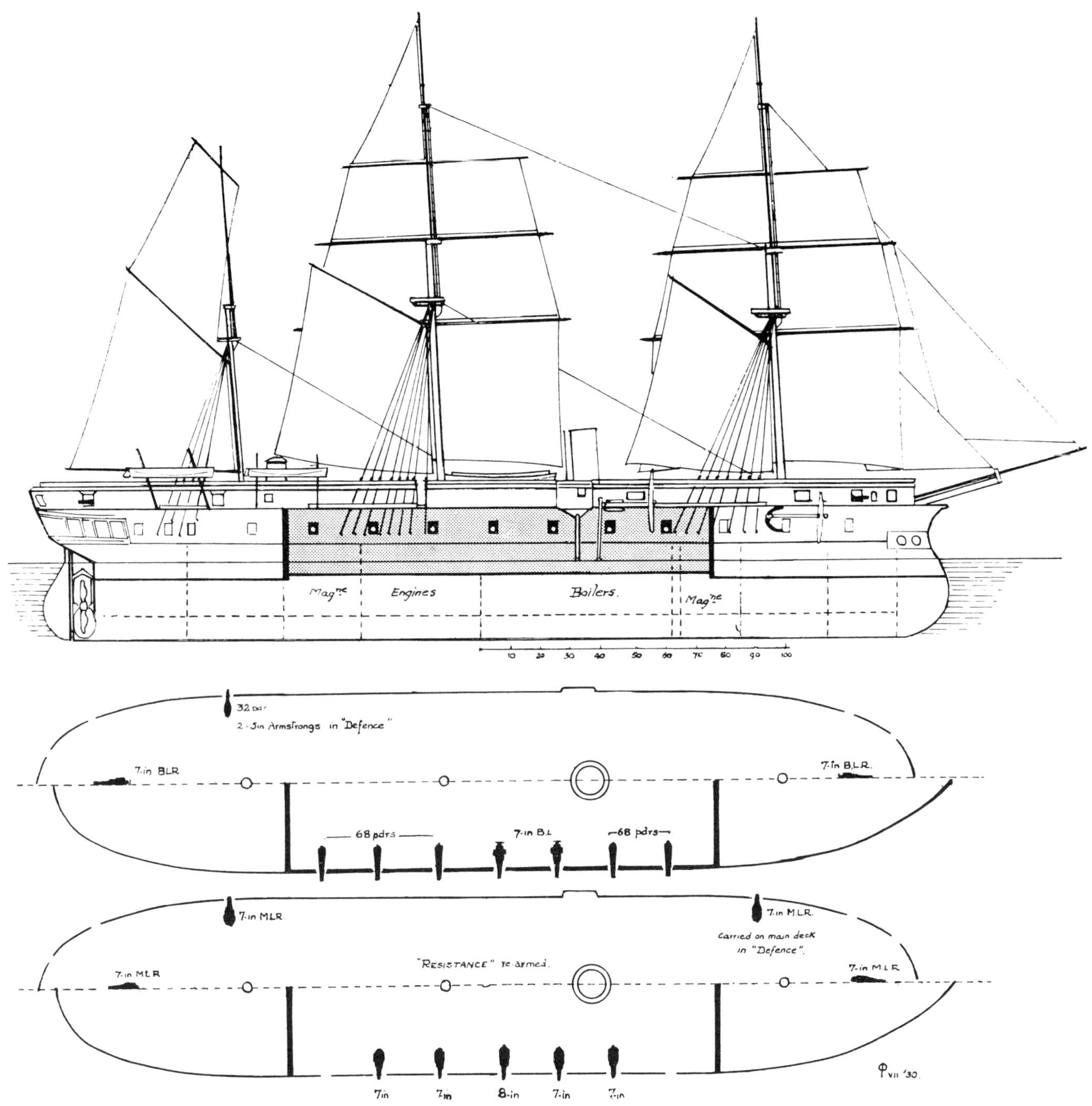

DEFENCE and *RESISTANCE*

(*The Gunter topsails shown were only hoisted in Resistance*)

weight at the bows. With the *Defence* ramming became a recognized if hotly debated method of attack throughout the Victorian era, although it was to prove far more of a potential danger in squadron manœuvres during peace-time than a possible weapon in war.

As completed they were without topgallant forecastles, the bowsprit being stepped on to the upper deck and projecting well below the level of the high bulwarks. At a later date topgallant forecastles were added, but they never had poops and consequently saw all their service as private ships. Internally there were three decks in common with all our broadside ironclads, and the same system of subdivision and partial double bottom as obtained in the *Warrior*. The men were berthed on the gun deck, but most of the officer accommodation, including the wardroom, was below, with miserable ventilation and light.

They were the only ironclads to be painted like the frigates with a white strake along the gun deck, which

The *Resistance* is here shown with her Gunter topgallants replaced by yards, and a fixed bowsprit stepped on to the upper deck below bulwark level. Windsails have been rigged as ventilators, and the tiny charthouse can be seen just before the mizen. Note the ram bow and projecting galleries at the stern.

old-time embellishment, however, was effaced during their first commission. Convention ran to a full frigate stern and exposed rudder head as in the *Warrior*.

So far as hull construction was concerned, these two ships were the most uneconomical ever built for the British Navy, as their hulls weighed 3,500 tons and the total weights carried only 2,492 tons.

ARMAMENT

During this period of gunnery transition when a ship's armament was likely to be obsolete by the time she was ready for sea, few ironclads ever carried their original armament warrant. It was intended that the *Defence* should mount sixteen 68-pdrs. on the main deck and two 68-pdr. pivot guns as chasers, with four 40-pdr. Armstrongs on the upper deck for saluting. But the Armstrong 7-in. 110-pdr. B.L. had commenced its short service

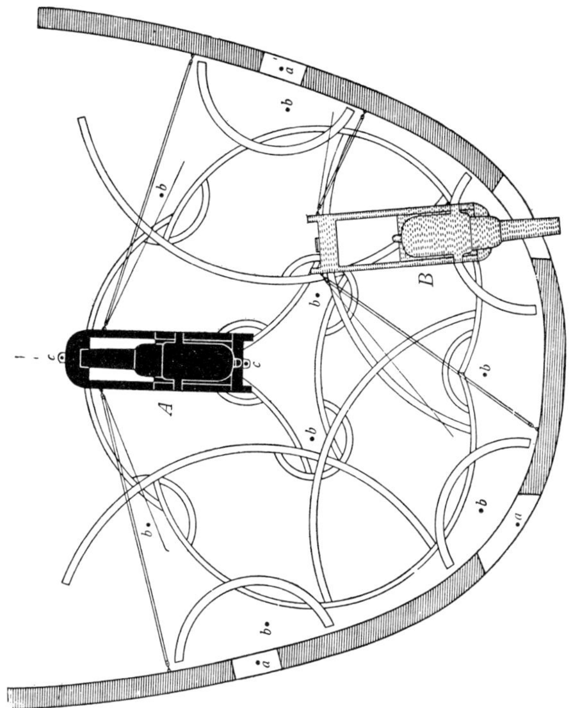

After gun in *Defence* and *Resistance*.

life at the time they were launched and a number were allotted to them. As supplies were limited the *Resistance* received six 7-in. B.L. and the *Defence* eight, each carrying one fore and aft as chase guns, and the rest lined up with the 68-pdrs. in the main deck battery.

On the quarter deck *Resistance* had a pair of 32-pdrs. S.B.—the only examples of this historic piece of ordnance ever to be mounted in a British armoured ship. In their place *Defence* had four 5-in. Armstrong B.L. All these guns were mounted on wooden trucks.

On conclusion of their first commission the entire armament was changed to muzzle-loading rifles on slide mounts, each ship receiving two 8-in. and fourteen 7-in. Of these latter the *Resistance* carried six on her upper deck where they were unprotected but had the advantage of a good command, whereas *Defence* had only four on the upper deck, with a larger number on the main deck behind armour, well protected, but too near the water line for use in a seaway. The port sills of these battery guns had a height of $6\frac{1}{2}$ feet and an arc of fire limited to 25 or 30 degrees before and abaft a transverse line—so that apart from the upper deck bow and stern guns there was no end-on fire. In distinction to the *Warrior* the after guns were mounted on a system of complicated training racers which provided a bearing from two ports in the stern and one on each quarter.

ARMOUR

Like the *Warrior* they were soft-ended, the iron armour covering their sides for only 140 ft. amidships from deck level to 6 ft. below the surface at load draught. This battery was pierced for 7 guns aside and closed by $4\frac{1}{2}$-in. bulkheads, the remainder of the armament being unprotected. The ends were subdivided to localize injury, with water-tight compartments so fitted that they could be flooded to increase immersion if required—a contingency for which provision was made in several subsequent ships, although the circumstances under which it might have arisen are not altogether apparent.

MACHINERY

Penn supplied the machinery for both ships, the trunk engines being of 600 nominal h.p. indicating 2,540 h.p. on trials, during which their designed speed was exceeded by a full knot. *Defence* made 11·3 knots on first trials and 11·6 knots later; *Resistance* at deep draught made 11·8 knots.

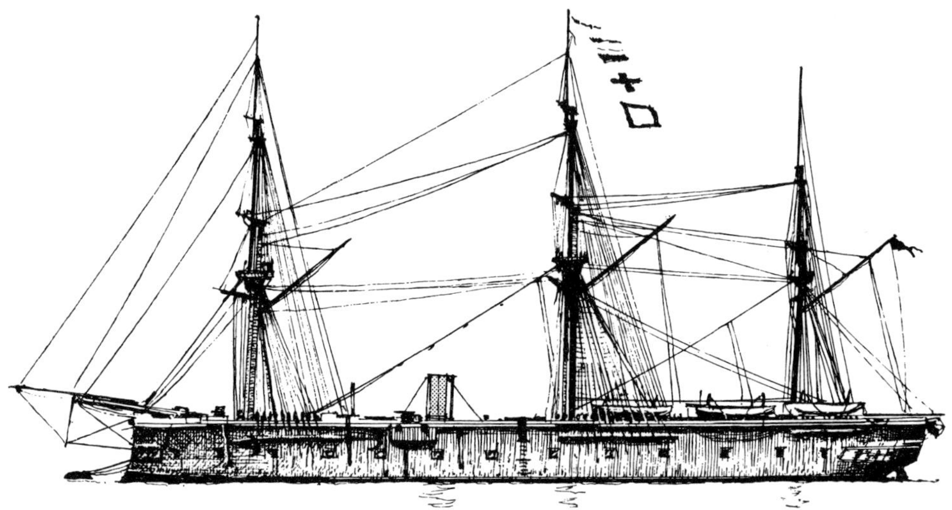

Defence in 1868 when she had been fitted with a topgallant forecastle and a running-in bowsprit, and reduced to barque rig.

In order to diminish drag when under sail, the propeller was made to hoist—which answered better than disconnecting or feathering, the alternatives sometimes employed. Its boss was supported on brackets at the lower end of the stirrup-shaped "banjo frame" with which it could be raised bodily into the circular screw well above water by means of sheers on the quarter deck straddling the opening of the well. The screw fitted on to the shaft by means of a cheese-coupling which was a tight fit and had to be kept clear of barnacles to prevent jamming.

RIG

For safety when ramming the lower masts and bowsprits were of iron. Both ships were selected for experimental rig, being the first in the Navy to be fitted with double topsails—*i.e.*, the sail divided into two with upper and lower yards in order to facilitate handling, a practice which found favour in the Merchant Service with the minimum number of men in a watch to work the sails. The upper topsails were self-reefing on the Cunningham system—a scheme which would have been satisfactory except that wet sails would not roll up properly and caused endless trouble. After tests lasting a year ordinary topsails replaced them. The *Defence* had no topgallants, but in the *Resistance* topgallant sails were rigged on the Gunter plan—a strange-looking top dressing like very elongated jibs hoisted on spars lying close up and down the topmasts which gave the maximum of extra weight with the minimum of canvas. These also were soon discarded.

The disadvantages, from a naval point of view, attendant upon double topsails—6 tons of extra weight aloft, increased resistance when steaming against a head wind, and additional lumber on deck when they had to be lowered plus a much reduced upper sail area—led to their being abolished in 1864 throughout the Service.

When this order came into force both ships were converted to single topsail rig with fidded topgallant masts by their own ship's companies. The *Defence* became a barque from September 1864 to April 1866 and then received full ship rig and a running-in bowsprit: but as the *Resistance* was reported to carry an excess of weather helm she received barque rig only, and did not shed her fixed bowsprit for another ten years.

SEA-GOING QUALITIES

Under sail they were good for about 10½ knots at the best, and handy except in a beam wind, when their slowness in answering the helm constituted a grave defect—and nearly led to the loss of the *Defence* when caught anchored off a lee shore at Pantellaria by a nor'westerly gale while retrieving the gear expended in salving the *Lord Clyde*. With a head wind or following sea they behaved rather better than did the *Hector* and *Valiant* which followed them—which is as much as can be said in their favour; but when it came abeam they ranked with the worst rollers in the fleet.

APPEARANCE

Except for the matter of rig the only standing difference between the two ships lay in the quarter deck davits. *Resistance* had straight wooden ones like the frigates, while in *Defence* the curved iron pattern was fitted for the first time.

"DEFENCE"

Was to have been delivered on 14 March '61 but was not launched until April and delivered in September. Commissioned 4 December and finished 12 February '62. Channel '62-'66. Paid off Plymouth for refit and rearmament. Channel '68-'69; relieved *Royal Alfred* on N. America '69-'70 and then went to the Med. relieving *Prince Consort* '71-'72 (nearly wrecked off Pantellaria). Refit Plymouth '72-'74. Shannon guardship '74-'76; Channel '76-'79 including a year in Med. when the squadron did duty for the Med. Fleet then up the Dardanelles. Paid off '79 and then replaced *Resistance* as Mersey guardship until '85 (collision with *Valiant* 20 July '84 Lough Swilly: sustained an 11-ft. breach in her ram; bows twisted and fore compartments flooded). Plymouth Reserve until '90 when she became our first floating workshop and renamed *Indus* in '98. Was still in existence at Devonport (1940).

"RESISTANCE"

Delivered at Portsmouth 5 December '61, a year later than contract, commissioned in July and completed 21 August '62. Channel '62-'64; Med. '64-'67 where she was the first British ironclad. Paid off Portsmouth for refit and rearmament '67-'69; guardship in Mersey '69-'73. Paid off and recommissioned for Channel '73-'77. Collided with *Devastation* Portland July '74 (slight displacement of armour only). "Particular Service Squadron" June-August '78 during Russian War scare, afterwards reverting to Mersey guardship until '80; paid off Devonport and dismantled. In '85 was selected as target ship and for testing various forms of protection against gunfire and torpedoes—and well justified her name! Sold 1898. Foundered at Holyhead 1899.

Chapter 9

"HECTOR" AND "VALIANT"

As the *Warrior* was still on the stocks, no sea-going ironclad had as yet been tested afloat, and there were still doubts whether iron hulls with their liability to rapid fouling were either suitable for service abroad or could be expected to replace every type of wooden warship. But when the successful trials of the *Gloire* in August-September 1860 established the ironclad as the future ship-of-the-line, the French confirmed their position by bringing in the momentous programme of 1860 which included:

20 sea-going ironclads for the Active fleet.
10 sea-going ironclads for the Reserve.
11 floating batteries,

of which 10 ironclads and the 11 batteries were to be laid down and completed within eighteen months.

In face of this historic effort to regain sea supremacy, conceived on the heroic scale if only on paper, any uncertainty at Whitehall as to the place to be allotted to the ironclad in the immediate constitution of the Fleet was now at an end. The Board were forced to follow suit, but on a scale commensurate with a cautious estimate of the French ability to implement such an ambitious programme, so that between October 1860 and August 1861 the original proposal for 4 armoured ships was increased to 15, and all work on wooden warships was stopped forthwith, excepting those selected for conversion to armour-clads under the Mandate of 1861.

Thus, in the two years from June 1859 to June 1861 the wooden two- and three-decker evolved and perfected during the centuries was eclipsed and supplanted by the ironclad precursors of the present-day battleships.

This reply to the French threat developed in a series of steps as its true significance was confirmed. The first reaction was on 28 September 1860, when Sir Baldwin Walker—now invested with the title of "Controller of the Navy"—proposed that a "Warrior" (the *Achilles*) should be built at Chatham, and two similar ships awarded by contract. Of this the Board approved, although they showed an almost pusillanimous uncertainty in the success of their first ironclads by directing the Controller to report as to their "fitness for use as transports or other duties in case it should be deemed advisable at any time to strip off their armour plates."

In view of which it is hardly surprising that economic expediency subsequently triumphed over confidence in the efficiency of the Constructor's department, and that a couple of modified repeats of the *Defence* were substituted for two larger ships. Out of which the *Hector* and *Valiant* were born.

	Builders	*Laid down*	*Launched*	*Completed*	*Cost*
"*Hector*"	Napiers	Mar. 1861	26 Sept. '62	22 Feb. '64	£294,000
"*Valiant*"	Westwood & Baillie and Thames I.W.	Feb. '61	14 Oct. '63	15 Sept. '68	£325,000

Dimensions 280′ × 56¼′ × 24¾′ (25′ actual) = 6,710 tons (7,000 actual).
Hull and armour 4,500 tons. Equipment 2,130 tons.

Guns

"*Hector*"	"*Valiant*"
4 7-in. B.L.	
20 68-pdrs.	
rearmed 1867	
2 8-in. M.L.R.	2 8-in. M.L.R.
16 7-in. M.L.R.	16 7-in. M.L.R.

Armour Main deck battery 4½″ iron tapering to 2½″ fore and aft. Bulkheads 4½″
Belt 4½″ amidships. Total = 912 tons.

Machinery Return connecting-rod engines. 800 N.H.P. = 11·5 kts.
Trials: "*Hector*" 3,260 I.H.P. = 12·6 knots (Napier).
"*Valiant*" 3,560 I.H.P. = 12·0 knots (Maudslay).
6 boilers. 20 lb. pressure.
2-bladed 20′ screw.

Coal 450 tons. 800 miles radius at full speed.

Complement 530.

Sail area 24,500 sq. ft. as a barque.

Constructors J. Large and W. H. Walker.

Special Features were:

(1) End-to-end battery armour, with incomplete belt.
(2) New form of curved stern affording more protection to the rudder.
(3) Very low centre of gravity.

Together with the "Defences" these ships formed a group of home-defence battleships of the second class which carried no sort of recommendation for the policy of economy responsible for them. In general dimensions they had the same length as the *Defence* but were given 2 ft. additional beam in order to carry 300 tons more armour and heavier engines on the same estimated draught of $24\frac{3}{4}$ ft. But as the science of naval architecture had not then acquired the exact standards of precision of later years, their first trials unfortunately showed them to be deeper than the designed draught by nearly a foot. To prevent further overloading the coal supply was reduced to 450 tons, which precluded employment abroad. So, alone of all the broadside ironclads, they could be fitted with neither poops nor topgallant forecastles because of the extra weights involved.

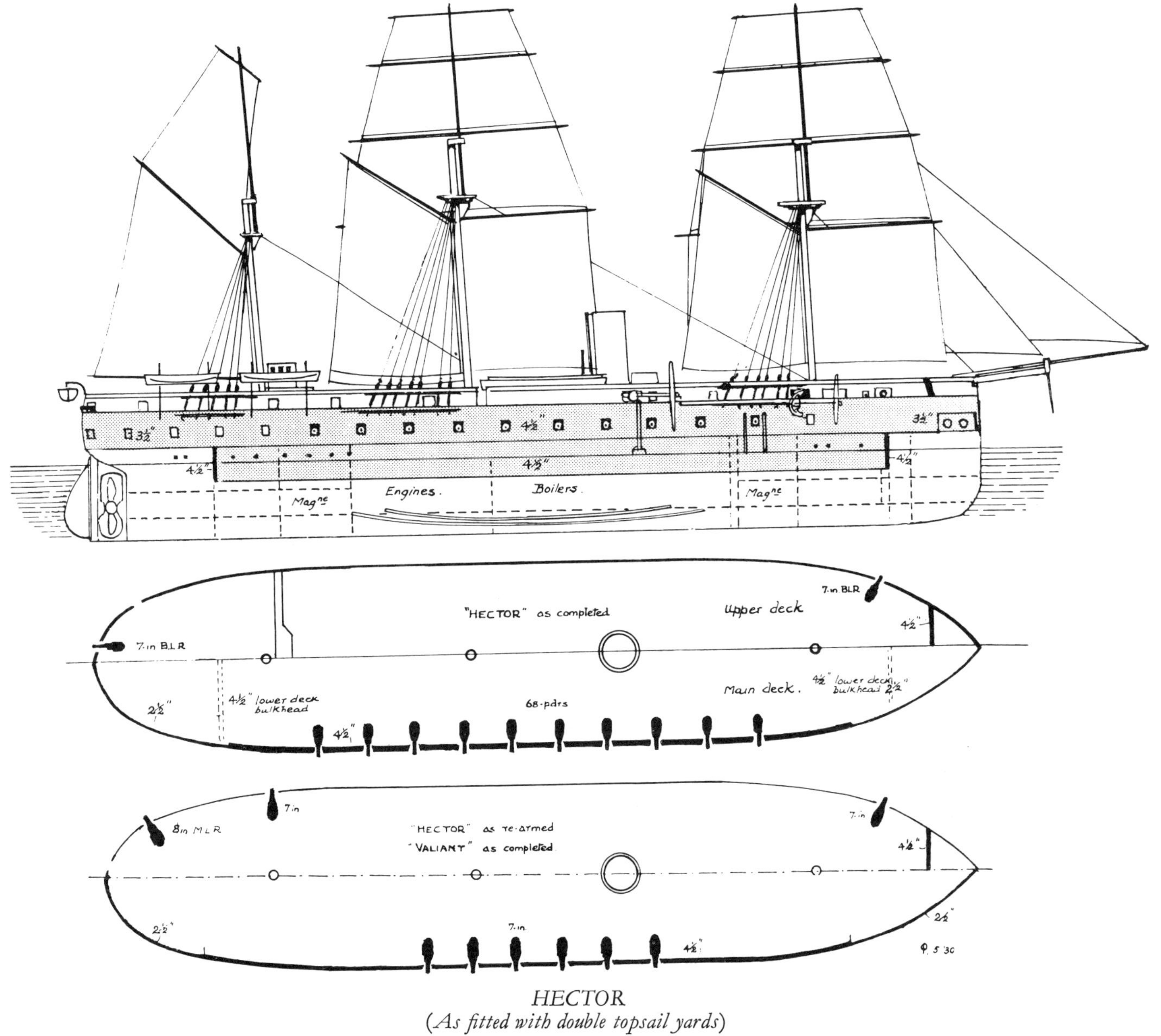

HECTOR
(*As fitted with double topsail yards*)

In appearance they differed from the *Defence* in having a straight stem in place of the ram bow, and—as some protection to the rudder head—were given a French type of stern which rose straight from the counter with a full rounded section, a shape better adapted to a following sea than the time-honoured frigate sterns of the previous ironclads.

Internally their plan was the same as in *Defence* with main-deck berthing for the men, and wardroom and officers' cabins on the lower deck aft. Steering was by hand wheels on each of the three decks, with a messenger capstan for working the anchors. Neither steam steering nor steam capstan was ever fitted.

GUNS

The armament in the first drafts submitted by the Controller was thirty 68-pdrs. behind armour on the main deck and two on the upper deck at the bow and stern. When the Armstrong breech-loaders were issued the warrant was altered to eight 110-pdr. B.L. on the upper deck and twenty-four 68-pdr. S.B. below, but in consequence of their over-draught the full armament was never put aboard, and *Hector* mounted only four 110-pdr. B.L. as upper-deck chase guns and twenty 68-pdr. S.B. in the battery during her first commission.

Valiant suffered such delay during construction, owing to the financial failure of Westwood, Baillie and Co., that by the time she had been completed at the Thames Ironworks the Armstrong breech-loaders had been withdrawn from service, and she was able to ship the rifled muzzle-loaders which had been introduced to replace both them and the smooth-bores. Of the new ordnance two 8-in. M.L.R. were carried on the quarter deck—an unusual position for the heaviest guns—but so placed that they could have been fought in a seaway which would have put

This photo of the *Hector* was taken in 1864 during her first commission when she had double topsail yards and no topgallants. Note the curved iron davits for the quarter-deck boats and plain rounded stern.

them out of action had they been carried behind armour in the battery. On the upper deck she also mounted four 7-in. M.L.R. for the chase, with twelve 7-in. M.L.R. in the battery. No saluting pieces were provided, so that her ceremonial firing was always impressive.

Hector paid off for rearmament in 1867 and entered into her second commission at the same time that the *Valiant* first hoisted her ensign. Both ships now carried the same armament similarly disposed.

ARMOUR

In these ships the French system of end-to-end armour for the battery was adopted, on the insistence of the Secretary, Lord Clarence Paget, the iron being 4½ in. amidships for 216 ft., tapering to 2½ in. at the bow and stern. Below this to 5¾ ft. under water ran a 4½-in. belt, except for 30 ft. at the bow and 35 ft. aft, where the lines were too fine to carry armour without reducing buoyancy to the vanishing point, and the ends were closed by 4½-in. bulkheads. Such a distribution had remained quite unique in our own or any other navy, the invariable custom being to apportion the longest strake of armour to the waterline belt at the expense of the lower-deck side.

Being plated from bow to stern, the battery bulkheads were superfluous and therefore omitted.

MACHINERY

Their return connecting-rod engines were practically identical, although by different makers, having 82-in. cylinders and a 4-ft. stroke. Although fitted with hoisting propellers, the sheers and purchases were never shipped, as both vessels were kept on home service on account of their limited bunker capacity.

Hector was the first British ironclad to be built and engined by the same firm.

RIG

Both ships were to have been double-topsail barques with pole topmasts and no royals, but only the *Hector* was so dressed and then but for a few months. In 1864, when double-topsails were abolished, her ship's company converted her to a full barque with single topsails and royals, and the *Valiant* was similarly rigged on completion four years later. Neither ship ever carried stunsails and in this respect were unique among the battleships.

SEA-GOING QUALITIES

Having neither length to cut through the waves nor a full section forward to allow them to ride well, they suffered in a seaway and were described as "rolling as badly as the 'Prince Consort,' although generally handy in manœuvring and when wearing and in stays." Under her double topsails the *Hector* stood up well under canvas in strong winds and could do something under sail, but both became poor performers when given single topsails. The *Hector* and *Valiant* were designed with a very low centre of gravity, giving a GM of 4½ ft. which afforded too much stability when under steam—with consequent rolling—and was never justified by the restricted sail area afforded them as Home Service ships.

COST

Under the Admiralty system of contract distribution the ships were allotted to northern and southern rivers, the *Hector* being commenced a month after the *Black Prince* was launched at Govan. The *Valiant* was allotted to the Thames, but before she could be put afloat her builders went into liquidation, their work being taken over by the Thames Ironworks Company. In the case of both ships the estimated price for construction was greatly exceeded, and in view of the difficulties attendant upon such contracts a sum of £50,000 was paid to Westwood and Baillie—who had never previously built a warship—and £35,000 to Napiers to cover their loss.

"HECTOR"

Commissioned at Portsmouth January '64. Channel '64-'67; rearmed '67-'68; Southern Reserve '68-'86 during which period she was Queen's Guard at Cowes nearly every summer; Particular Service Squadron June-August '78 during Russian War scare; paid off '86 and lay dismantled in Portsmouth for 14 years when she became part of the *Vernon* torpedo school and the first ship to be fitted with w.t.

Sold in 1905.

"VALIANT"

When Westwood and Baillie closed down in November '61 she was taken over by the Thames Ironworks. After her launch there was a long delay owing to non-delivery of the new M.L.R. guns from the Ordnance Dept.

Commissioned in 1868 as g.s. First Reserve in S. Ireland which duty she maintained for 17 years with one interval for re-boilering. "Particular Service Squadron" June-August '78 (collision with *Defence* 20 July '84, Lough Swilly: lost davits, boats and side fittings, hull damaged and armour plates started). In '85 paid off and for 13 years lay dismantled at Devonport; '98 converted to *Indus* establishment and in '15 to storeship Kite Balloon section as *Valiant III*. In 1926 turned into floating oil tank in Hamoaze, where she was still employed in 1955.

Chapter 10

THE RETURN TO MUZZLE-LOADERS

SINCE its introduction into the Fleet in 1860 the Armstrong breech-loaders had been a source of difficulty, doubt and danger—especially the 110-pdrs. Woolwich Arsenal had become less of a pride than a national humiliation. Instead of a store of modern artillery for future use it was a reliquary of the rifled wrecks and derelicts of the past few years, with hundreds of guns awaiting repair. It had even become the practice to include a list of bore flaws when a gun was issued, and reports from naval officers were like the following:

> "None of the Armstrongs that I have seen have been without flaws. It will be a long time before it bursts, but a gunner does not like to stand alongside a gun with a few cracks in it. I have always felt that I would rather the manufacturers of the gun should fire it than I should." (Gunnery Captain of the *Cambridge*.)

The behaviour of the breech-loaders during the action of Kagosima 14 August 1863 practically settled their fate. Vice-Admiral A. L. Kuper commanding the East Indies and China Station had been ordered to take measures of reprisal against the forts commanding the harbour because of an attack upon British subjects near Kanagawa at the orders of Shimadzu Sabura. Of the ships engaged which carried Armstrongs, the

Euryalus	(35)	mounting	13 B.L.	had	14	accidents	in	144	rounds
Perseus	(17)	,,	5 B.L.	,,	5	,,	,,	111	,,
Argus	(6)	,,	1 B.L.	,,	4	,,	,,	22	,,
Racehorse	(4)	,,	1 B.L.	,,	4	,,	,,	51	,,
Coquette	(4)	,,	1 B.L.	,,	1	,,	,,	37	,,

an aggregate of 28 accidents to 21 guns in 365 rounds from five ships, or a mean of one accident in 13 rounds. In addition the breech-loader's shooting was erratic and often much delayed, shells going "anywhere but straight forward and as much as 600 yards to the left" and a lot failed to explode. Shortly after the action the order came for the withdrawal of the 110-pdrs. from service, and thus the first breech-loading phase came to an end in 1864. Apart from *the method of building the guns* Armstrong's system had been an expensive failure, and the Service was now faced with the problem of finding an armour-piercing gun for the ships awaiting completion.

When considering the selection of such a gun, two questions presented themselves for decision:

(1) Were we to have a new system of *rifled* ordnance or simply revert to smooth-bores and spherical projectiles? Or
(2) Should we develop a new system of *breech-loading* or revert to muzzle-loaders?

Now, although the 68-pdr. had failed to penetrate the *Warrior* target with cast-iron shot, nevertheless its 4½-in. plate and 7-in. timber was pierced when a *steel* shot was used: which raised the question as to whether this well-liked gun could not be retained if supplied with steel shot and shell, with the new gun-cotton in place of gunpowder as a propellent. So served, the gun might very well obviate any revolutionary changes in armament and protection which the Navy neither needed nor wanted; moreover the Board had no wish to embark upon the construction of ships which embodied such changes when two simple and acceptable steps could bring about just as good results. Actually there was no pressing reason why the 68-pdr. should be displaced by a larger gun, or armour increased beyond 5½ in. in thickness. The French *Flandre* class, passed into service between 1863 and 1868, had wooden hulls with 6-in. belts and 4·4-in. over the battery; but owing to inferior methods of manufacture the *Flandre* target required only 16 ft. tons of energy per inch of shot's circumference to penetrate it, while the *Warrior* target called for 33 ft. tons. Thus the French belt and flanks were well within the mastery of the 68-pdr. when the British plating was able to resist the rifled 55-pdrs. and two 110-pdrs. carried by the French ships.

On the other hand, the Americans in developing their own system of big guns preferred a heavy projectile of large size with comparatively low velocity delivering a battering instead of a punching effect. Thus the 15-in. Dahlgrens in the monitors were cast-iron smooth-bores throwing a 453-lb. cast-iron spherical shot with a charge of 60 lb. (equal to about 50 lb. of British powder). In his report "On the Penetration of Armour Plates by Steel Shot" Captain Noble showed that this gun would not penetrate the *Warrior* target beyond a distance of 500 yds. with steel shot, let alone with cast-iron shot, as the low velocity fell off so quickly.

American armour was also inferior to ours, being made up of *laminated* plates up to 6-in. thickness which could be pierced by projectiles effectively stopped by a *solid* 4-in. plate.

Therefore so far as armour and armament were concerned the Navy was content with 4½-5½-in. plating and 68-pdrs. as quite adequate in face of possible opposition from French or American ships.

But arrayed against any conservative policy as regards armament and protection were the combined forces of "progress" mustered by a host of gun designers, manufacturers and iron-masters who produced armour, all busy with new methods of gun construction, fresh forms of rifling, or the rolling of thicker slabs of plating; they applied their inventive or constructive powers to the production of new weapons without considering how the Navy was going to be affected. Behind them was a great weight of public opinion clamouring for the adoption of each nominal advance in offensive or defensive power, and those who clamoured loudest were least able to appreciate the problems involved in the mounting of bigger and bigger guns and the plating of ships with thicker and thicker armour.

In dealing with the complicated gun and armour problem the Navy was at a disadvantage. At the time there was no department of ordnance and no gunnery staff at the Admiralty. Decisions on naval ordnance rested with the Board and practically upon one Lord without any staff whatsoever—and he might or might not consult with the Controller. Pressing for the adoption of new models of bigger guns were the Royal Gun Factory at Woolwich and Sir William Armstrong, with Whitworth in open competition and achieving notable successes in range and

100-pdr "Somerset".

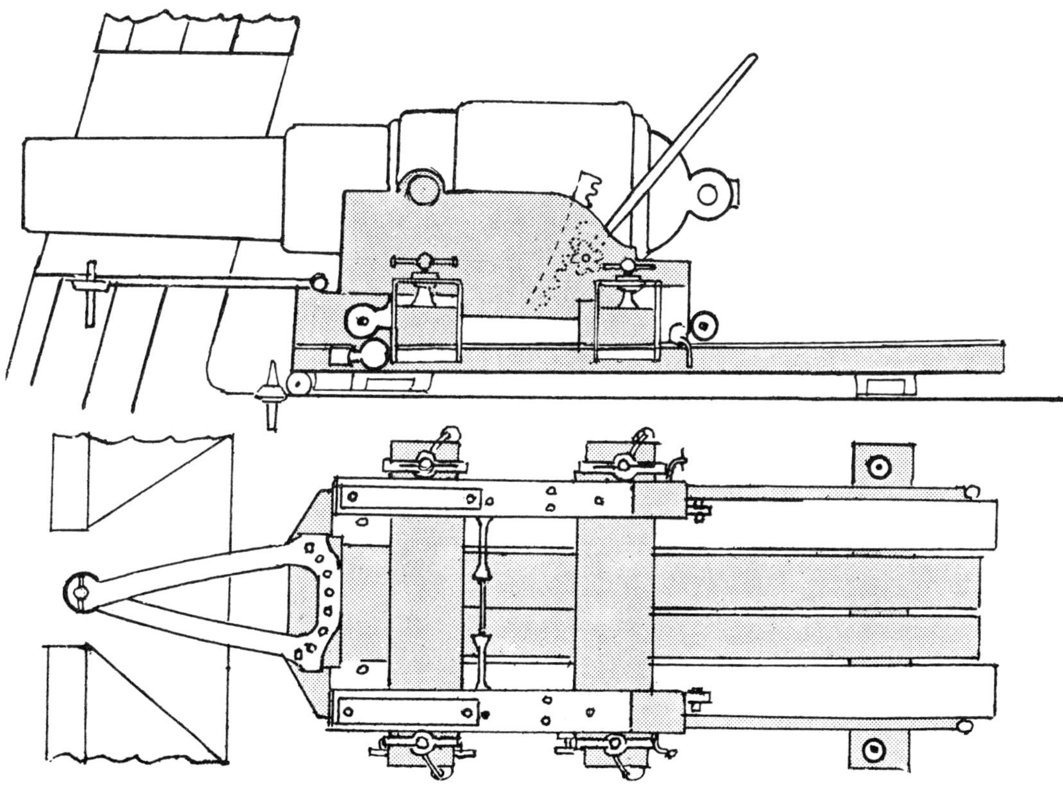

The 100-pdr. "Somerset" on its wooden slide carriage as mounted in the *Achilles*. Flat wooden blocks faced with iron under the slide replaced the trucks, the gun being traversed on metal racers secured to the deck and pivoted on the double bar attached to the front of the carriage and fastened to the sill of the port. Compressors on each bracket of the carriage when screwed up checked the recoil of the carriage on the slide. The gun was raised or lowered by a pinion fitting into a toothed arc attached to the inside of the bracket and worked by the long lever. Excess of recoil was taken up by the preventer rope rove through the cascobel at the breech of the gun and secured to the ship's side. Training was by tackles and handspikes.

penetration with his latest weapons. Advocating novel forms of rifling and construction were Blakeney, Lancaster, Haddan, Scott, Britten, Jeffrey and Horsfall.

Gun mountings were controlled by the Royal Carriage Department at Woolwich, although the Royal Dockyards encroached upon its field of activity. Here again a number of private inventors were busy, of whom Scott, Cunningham and Armstrong were the best known. They sought to fill a demand created by the gun designers and armour manufacturers, involving entirely new conceptions in working big guns on shipboard which directly opposed the age-old prejudices of the seamen.

The task of co-ordinating all these activities fell to the lot of the Captain of the *Excellent*, who alone had a staff competent to consider every problem in naval ordnance and deliver a sound judgment thereon. But as his decision could be accepted or ignored by the War Office (as the controlling authority in all matters relating to the supply of artillery), the Board might be placed in an exceedingly difficult position at times.

Not unnaturally the first proposals for a change in armament came from Sir William Armstrong, who was anxious to redeem the failure of his breech-loaders with another sort of rifled gun. In 1863 the *Excellent* was asked to consider the merits of (1) his wedge system of breech-loading akin to that used by Krupp; and (2) what became known as the "shunt" method of rifling, in which projectiles fitted with copper studs were rammed in from the muzzle base first, with the studs fitting loosely in one set of grooves, to be discharged point first with the studs gripping tightly in another set of grooves and being rotated in the process.

Soon afterwards another type of gun known as the "Somerset" was sent along for trial, a 6½-ton 9·2-in. S.B. muzzle-loader firing a 100-lb. shot with a 25-lb charge of powder. This was an Admiralty design made by Armstrong, and proved the master of 5½-in. plating at 200 yds. with steel shot. With a charge of 33 lb.—which the gun would bear—it was considered that 5½-in. armour could be pierced at 800 yds.

But when it came to employing guns of this size on shipboard the great difficulty lay in providing an efficient mounting. Such appliances as could make them effective did not exist, and when Captain Key of the *Excellent* was called upon to report upon the question of suitable mounting in September 1863, he was forced to say that there were no data—and he could not say what course should be taken. Apart from pivot guns the guns afloat were all mounted on truck carriages of a pattern well over a century old—essentially simple in design, although making great demands upon man power and at sea often dangerous to handle. It was part of the drill in most ships to transport guns working in one port to work them in another; for experience had often shown that the wind and the enemy between them could fix the position of a ship and altogether deprive her of fighting power unless guns could be moved to ports where none were usually carried.

A great improvement upon this traditional mounting had been introduced by Sir Thomas Hardy—Nelson's Hardy[1]—where the gun carriage, with flat wooden blocks faced with iron instead of trucks, worked upon a wooden slide fastened to the ship's side by a "pivot"[2] to allow for its being trained in its port. When fired the gun recoiled on the blocks, its way being checked by a "compressor" attached to the carriage. This, dropping through a slot in the centre of the slide, could be set to grip carriage and slide together, reducing the sudden strain on the breeching, and so the length of the recoil. Heavy 10-in. and 8-in. shell guns at bow and stern of the paddle-frigates were mounted on this carriage-slide principle, which proved satisfactory. But these were "upper deck guns," and it was by no means acceptable to the then naval conception that 'tween-deck guns should have mountings which could not be transported from one port to another. That under steam it would probably take less time to move the ship than shift the gun, was an argument which did not altogether meet the conditions of traditional warfare.

By October 1863 Captain Key had recommended the adoption of this "Somerset" 100-pdr. and fifty-one were put in hand for mounting on a wooden slide carriage on the modified Hardy model. Thirty-five were issued to the *Achilles*, *Enterprise*, *Favorite* and *Research*, but their performance was so poor that production ceased and the remainder were put into store. The trouble was largely due to difficulties in controlling the gun, which was heavier and fired a larger charge than the 112-pdr. B.L., in which the charge had been reduced because of its too boisterous recoil. Armstrong wanted them converted to a 7-in. "shunt" rifle; on the other hand, Key hoped it would be possible to retain the 9-in. bore and steel spherical shot for armour piercing, while giving a light rifling which would allow for an elongated shell of 145 lb. for bombarding and use against wooden ships.

SMOOTH-BORES V. RIFLES

Key set out the pros and cons of the two types at this time, pointing out that no rifled gun had yet been tested by the *Excellent* which was efficient as a broadside gun. The advantages of rifling were: (1) great range; (2) great accuracy; (3) use of powerful shell; (4) retention of velocity to a considerable range and therefore capacity to penetrate armour. Of these (1) and (2) were of value only under special circumstances. The Navy did not ask for fighting at long ranges, nor did it expect accuracy of fire from a rolling ship beyond what could be achieved at short range. The advantages of the smooth bore were: (1) simplicity; (2) rapidity of fire; (3) reduced strain on the gun and therefore greater durability; (4) greater initial velocity. Of these (2) and (4) were not inherent in a smooth-bore system as against a rifled system, although they may have applied to the systems then under consideration. Under ordinary circumstances the accuracy of a smooth-bore could be considered equal to that of a rifled gun at any distance under 1,500 yards, everything depending upon the skill of the captain of the gun. At close quarters the smooth-bore was the superior; great accuracy and long range would be of less value than rapidity of fire, security against derangement of the gun, and penetrating power at short ranges.

Captain Key thought that *smooth-bores* should continue to form the broadside armament, with *rifled* guns on the upper deck and the bow and stern ports of gun decks—always presuming that the as yet untested "shunt" rifling proved satisfactory. By May 1864 the 7-in. "shunt" gun had been tried in the *Excellent* and considerably shaken the position of the "Somerset," being reported as more than equal to naval requirements.

---

[1] Date not known.

[2] Not to be confused with the "central pivot" introduced twenty years later in the Vavasseur mounting. In the case of upper deck guns, "pivoting" meant "traversing" from the centre-line to side ports, by means of roller tracks.

12-TON S.B.

While the 6½-tonner was under test, Woolwich contributed a number of bastard pieces of 10·5-in. calibre and weighing 12 tons. When and if rifled they were intended to throw a 300-lb. elongated shot. Actually only two were so completed; one became unserviceable and the other was retained for flash experiments at Shoeburyness. Thirteen were left as smooth-bores firing a cast-iron round shot of 156 lb. with a 50 lb. charge. However, as the first of the rifled guns to be tested blew out its breech, the charge was reduced to 35 lb., with which it was quite ineffective against the *Warrior* target at 200 yards. Five of the smooth-bore guns were assigned to the *Royal Sovereign* and four to the *Scorpion*, but the latter never received them.

22½ TON S.B.

While the 100-pdr. "Somersets" were being mounted, further development of the smooth-bore continued, and in 1865 four "exceptional monsters" of 13-in. calibre were built by Armstrongs which were to throw a 600-lb. shot. It was intended that these should be rifled, but no decision could be made as to how this was to be done, and the guns remained as smooth-bores. Coles proposed to arm his one-turret project with them, and during the proceedings of the committee which examined his design the 600-pdr. was referred to as "Big Will." Extraordinary claims for penetration at long range were made for it by the Secretary, but enquiry elicited the fact that these performances were based on calculation only from results at short range and with reduced charges.

Its shooting was far too erratic for any such target to have been hit at long range.

These guns were the last smooth-bores to be made. Together with the 12 tonners (as mounted in the *Royal Sovereign*) they were condemned by the Under-Secretary of State and not included in the national store of artillery for appropriation afloat.

An alternative weapon was the Armstrong 64-pdr. with wedge breech-loading, of which eighty-three were in being. But although Captain Key had thought this model fit for service, he was informed that it was not intended to issue it afloat. Breech-loaders by other designers were also under trial from time to time, but none was as satisfactory as the Armstrong wedge. Early in 1866 the B.L. province became limited to field and boat guns only; there was never any real question of substituting them for muzzle-loaders, and Key thought that as no sufficient reason could be shown for preserving a breech-loading system for the smaller guns they might as well be withdrawn from service. These small guns, however, were retained for saluting, boat work, and later as anti-torpedo defence, and proved satisfactory,

In February 1865 Mr. Fraser, the superintendent of the Royal Gun Factories, introduced a muzzle loader built up on a modified Armstrong system with a simpler form of rifling to take studded projectiles, and this 64 pdr. of 64 cwt. was adopted in lieu of the wedge guns. Fraser substituted cheap soft scrap iron of great tenacity for expensive hard iron less suited to dynamic forces, and reduced the number of parts from fifteen or twenty-three to four or six. A steel lining, or "A" tube, toughened in an oil bath, received the rifling. These guns worked out at about £65 a ton instead of £100 a ton for Armstrongs, and apart from the system of rifling were satisfactory. This rifling, at first called the "French," was renamed the "Woolwich" when the grooves were reduced in depth. It consisted of deep broad grooves cut with an increasing twist, each of which received two soft-metal circular studs attached to the projectile. The twist did not attempt to impart rotation until the projectile had proceeded some distance along the bore and attained high velocity.

The "French" rifling was chosen by the Select Ordnance Committee after the 7-in. gun competition of 1865 against the Lancaster oval bore, Whitworth polygonal bore and Scott's iron flanges. The reasons given for deciding in its favour were: (1) the simplicity of its studding on the projectiles; (2) simplicity of grooving; (3) advantage of an increasing over a uniform spiral which can best be realized with a *short bearing* on two points.

In practice the "Woolwich" rifling with studded projectiles was not a success. The studs tended to sheer and the bearing between them was too short; the increasing spiral led to gun damage and sometimes jamming of the shot; there was "wobbling and hammering in the bore" and "puffing" during flight which indicated that a projectile was misbehaving. Sometimes the guns were to blame, sometimes the projectiles; but the result was that the Navy was again landed with a faulty system of artillery which was to endure through the next fifteen years.

HEAVY GUNS 1863-1878

Smooth Bores

	Gun tons	*Proj. lb.*	*Charge lb.*	
9-in.	6¼	100	25	Woolwich "Somerset"
10·5-in.	12	156	35	Woolwich
13-in.	22½	600		Armstrong (not adopted)

MUZZLE-LOADING RIFLES

		Gun *tons*	*Proj.* *lb.*	*Charge* *lb.*	*Velocity* *ft.-secs.*	*Energy* *ft.-tons*	*Pen.** *in.*	*Rifling*
1864	6·3-in.	64 cwt.	64	6 RLG	1,125	570		"Shunt" uniform
1864	6·6-in.	71 ,,	97	25 P	1,416	1,358		Plain groove
1865	7-in.	6½ ton	112	30 P	1,525	1,854	7·7	Woolwich uniform
1866	8-in.	9 ,,	174	35 P	1,384	2,323	9·6	Woolwich increasing
1865	9-in.	12 ,,	253	50 P	1,440	3,643	11·3	
1868	10-in.	18 ,,	406	70 P	1,379	5,356	12·9	
1867	11-in.	25 ,,	543	85 P	1,360	7,015	14·3	
1870	12-in.	25 ,,	608	85 P²	1,292	7,046	13·5	
1871	12-in.	35 ,,	706	140 P²	1,390	9,469	15·9	
1875	12·5 in.	38 ,,	809	210 P²	1,575	13,930	18·4	
1878	16-in.	80 ,,	1,684	450 PB	1,590	29,530	24·7	

RLG=Rifle large grain powder. P²=Modified Pebble.
P=Pebble powder. PB=Prismatic brown.

* Of wrought iron at muzzle
(from List of Service Rifled Ordnance 1886).

Chapter 11

"ACHILLES"

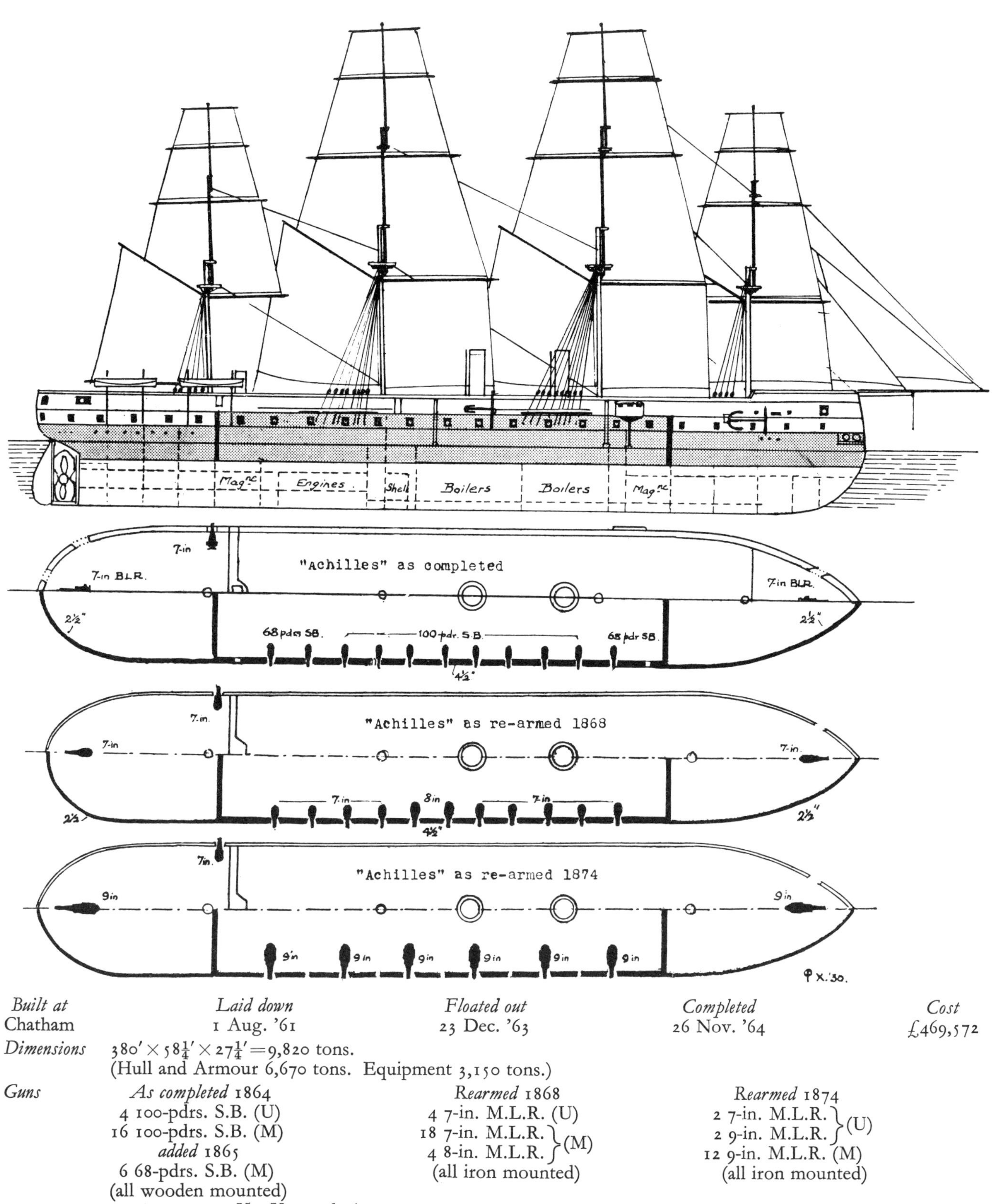

Built at	*Laid down*	*Floated out*	*Completed*	*Cost*
Chatham	1 Aug. '61	23 Dec. '63	26 Nov. '64	£469,572

Dimensions $380' \times 58\frac{1}{4}' \times 27\frac{1}{4}' = 9{,}820$ tons.
(Hull and Armour 6,670 tons. Equipment 3,150 tons.)

Guns

As completed 1864	*Rearmed* 1868	*Rearmed* 1874
4 100-pdrs. S.B. (U)	4 7-in. M.L.R. (U)	2 7-in. M.L.R. } (U)
16 100-pdrs. S.B. (M)	18 7-in. M.L.R. } (M)	2 9-in. M.L.R. } (U)
added 1865	4 8-in. M.L.R. } (M)	12 9-in. M.L.R. (M)
6 68-pdrs. S.B. (M)	(all iron mounted)	(all iron mounted)
(all wooden mounted)		

U=Upper deck. M=Main deck.

Armour	Battery 4½″; belt 4½″-2½″ ends; bulkheads 4½″. Backing: 18″-10″ teak; Plating ⅝″. *Total:* 1,259 tons.
Machinery	Trunk engines (Penn) cyl.: 112″; stroke 4′ 4″; revs. 55. 10 rectangular boilers. 25 lb. pressure. I.H.P. 5,720=14·3 knots. Radius 1,800 miles at 6½ knots.
Complement	709.
Coal	740/1,000 tons.
Sail area	30,133 sq. ft.

Her special features were:

(1) Complete waterline belt with central battery.
(2) A stern shaped to protect the steering gear and rudder-head.
(3) A higher centre of gravity, making her the steadiest battleship in the fleet.
(4) Underwent more changes of rig and armament than any other warship.
(5) The only British warship to have four masts.
(6) Carried the greatest area of canvas ever set in a warship.
(7) The first ship to be designed for a four-bladed non-hoisting screw.
(8) The first iron warship to be built in a Government dockyard.

THIS third ironclad of the programme—of which the *Hector* and *Valiant* were the first to be laid down—was to have been similar to the *Warrior*, and the first drafts of her plans show the frigate bow and stern of that ship. But the question of the unprotected steering gear and rudder-head was raised by Mr. E. J. Reed (then secretary of the Institute of Naval Architects) with the Constructor's Department, and mainly owing to his influence the design was ordered to be recast in January 1861 to allow for a complete belt of armour from stem to stern along the waterline while retaining the same length of battery as the *Warrior*. The useless iron knee-head was done away with and replaced by a slightly outward curved stem, while a stern on the lines of that in the *Hector* was substituted for the wide overhanging counter and "shaped so as to protect the rudder-head, deflect raking shot, and rendering it more fit to receive easily the blows of a following sea." The *Achilles* was therefore a *Warrior* with a complete water-line belt and her ends shaped to the requirements of the new order in fighting ships instead of being reminiscent of the past. She was also somewhat flatter in the floor and carried her engines higher in order to raise the centre of gravity. As the complete armour belt also had this effect—which was increased by other weights above water—the combined effect of these changes was to make the *Achilles* much the steadier ship. Indeed, compared with the other two ships of the Programme it would seem as if Isaac Watts had aimed at testing the extremes of both practicable steadiness and stiffness, as *Hector* with a very low centre of gravity became notorious for her rolling propensities, while *Achilles* won the reputation of being the steadiest ship under steam in the fleet.

CONSTRUCTION

No iron ships had as yet been built in H.M. Dockyards, and in placing the order for the *Achilles* at Chatham the first step was taken towards bringing the service establishments up to the standard of the big private yards in the matter of iron ship-building. There was considerable delay after the instructions to commence work on her hull were received, as the necessary plant for preparing her plates had not been erected, and labour difficulties arose. A number of boilermakers had been specially entered as being skilled in the handling of iron plates, and for a time they were responsible for the construction of the hull. Then came a strike for higher wages; the Admiralty ordered them to be discharged forthwith and in their place ordinary shipwrights volunteered to carry on the work. These men were quickly trained to handle the new equipment and the experiment was successful. As a result, arrangements were made to train these splendid craftsmen in the ways of iron shipbuilding, and from that time constructional work on the hull of iron and steel ships has been entrusted to them. After the keel plate had been laid in the dry dock it was found that much of the material supplied was not up to standard, so that further delay was incurred. Nevertheless she was completed in just over three years, which made a vastly better showing than the long-drawn-out periods required for the later *Minotaur* class.

Internally the *Achilles* generally resembled the *Warrior*. She had no poop and the only break on her long flush deck was an open topgallant forecastle. A light narrow bridge rested on the 7 ft. bulwarks just forward of the mizenmast. This bore a small box of a charthouse just capable of seating two persons, equipped with a telegraph and voice pipe to the engine room and another voice-pipe to the battery controls. Steering orders had to be conveyed by hand signals or direct voice to the fourfold wheel 50 ft. further aft. Not until she was seventeen years old were steam steering-gear and bridge wheels fitted. The hydraulic steering apparatus provided in 1868 proved unworkable.

The ship's company messed in the battery, the officers' quarters being abaft the after bulkhead with the ward-room and most of the cabins on the orlop deck; the gunroom and engineers' mess was on the half-deck. Having no poop, her captain's quarters were right astern on the main deck.

ARMAMENT

In no other British warship has the armament warrant been changed so many times between the dates of ordering and relinquishment of active service. Thus, in March 1861 the *Achilles* was described in the Navy List as a 36-gun frigate, although in the following May her Ship's Book gives the armament as forty-four 100-pdr. B.L., four 40-pdr. B.L., and two 32-pdr. S.B. By 1862 she had become a "50-gun frigate," and the much-vaunted Armstrong 100-pdr. B.L. (also known as the 110-pdr.) having proved inferior to the 68-pdr. S.B. as an armour-piercing weapon, she was given fourteen 110-pdrs., ten 70-pdrs., and twenty-six 68-pdrs. But the 70-pdr. B.L. turned out to be a useless weapon, and by July 1862 another change had been made and she became a "30-gun frigate." All the guns outside the battery were removed and ten 110-pdr. B.L. placed on the upper deck with twenty 68-pdrs. at the ports, the B.L. being retained as chase guns because of their longer range. In December 1863 the *Achilles* received her fourth warrant for a uniform armament of twenty 100-pdr. "Somerset" S.B., of which four were to be on the upper deck and sixteen in the battery—the largest smooth-bores to be mounted on wooden trucks, and with the port sills 9½ ft. above the load line. However, on commissioning, four of the 110-pdr. B.L. were retained for the upper

The *Achilles* only carried this four-masted rig for 7 months when the bowsprit and foremast were removed, the second mast now serving as foremast with the head sails carried to the stem. This photo was taken at Plymouth in 1864, when the battery ports amidships showed the muzzles of 100 pdrs. and 68 pdrs. M.L. The small sponson and waste pipe near the second mast contained the seamen's heads.

deck with sixteen "Somersets" in the battery with six 68-pdrs. In 1868 she underwent complete rearmament with the new muzzle-loading rifles on *iron carriages* which replaced the Armstrongs and smooth-bores throughout the battle fleet. Under the new warrant four 7-in. 6½-ton M.L.R. went to the upper deck, and eighteen with four 8-in. 9-ton at the amidships ports made up the battery, which guns sufficed for six years, when the rapid growth in ordnance necessitated a heavier offensive equipment being substituted. In 1875 the new guns were nearly twice the size and only twelve of these 9-in. 12-ton M.L.R. could be spaced in the battery, the alternate ports having to be enlarged by hammer and cold chisel to accommodate them. Two more 9-in. M.L.R. on turntables giving a 90 degree training replaced the 7-in. at the bow and stern, and of her previous armament only two 7-in. M.L.R. at the quarters were retained.

During her refit in 1889 two 6-in. B.L. were substituted for the 7-in. M.L., and in addition eight 3-pdrs. and sixteen machine guns were added along the topsides.

Being listed as a Third Rate at the time when the Board were uncertain how the ironclads should be classed, her complement of 705 on commissioning was about 50 too few—being made up by supernumeraries until 1874 after which date she carried nearly 100 too many for her reduced armament.

ARMOUR

By accepting some increase in draught and displacement with a reduction of 100 tons in coal supply, the soft-ends of the *Warrior* were replaced in *Achilles* by a continuous belt from stem to stern extending from the battery deck to 5½ ft. below water, affording proper protection to both rudder and steering gear. The battery extended for 212 ft. amidships with 4½ in. faces and end bulkheads.

All armour was in position when the ship was floated out.

RIG

Altogether the *Achilles* underwent three changes in rig, being first completed as a four-master—the only ship

The *Achilles* as rearmed with 9-in. M.L.R. of which six can be seen pointing through the enlarged ports along the main deck. The "bow" mast of the four-master has been removed, and the foremast shifted 25 ft. forward and the bowsprit replaced (1866) and she was rigged as a ship until 1877 when she became a barque.

in the Navy to be so fitted—the masts being called bow, fore, main and mizen. So dressed she carried 44,000 sq. ft. exclusive of stunsails—the largest area ever spread in a warship. Although the earliest reports state that she sailed well, her performance was unsatisfactory with the wind before the beam, and after trials on 14 December 1864 when she had been a month at sea, it was submitted that her bow mast be removed. This was done the following June, but as a three-master without any bowsprit she carried too much weather helm. To correct this, in July 1866 the foremast was shifted 25 ft. further forward and the bowsprit replaced—after which her sailing qualities were regarded as satisfactory for a ship of her length. Her full ship rig was the largest ever carried under the White or Red Ensign and this served until 1877, when there came a reduction to barque. Thus she achieved the distinction of being the only British warship to be canvased under four different plans.

DIMENSIONS OF MASTING

	Victory	*Achilles*
Main truck to deck	183 ft.	179 ft.
Mainmast	119 "	121½ "
Diameter of mainmast	39 in.	40 in.
Main topmast	70 ft.	65 ft.
Main topgallant mast	58½ "	53 "
Main yard	102¼ "	105 "
Main topsail yard	73 "	74 "
Main topgallant yard	48½ "	46 "
Bowsprit	72 "	41 "
Jibboom	53 "	52 "

SEA-GOING QUALITIES

As already mentioned, the *Achilles* was designed to be stiffer than the *Warrior*, and the Constructors Department certainly worked out an almost ideal distribution of weights providing extraordinary steadiness under both sail and steam. But she proved very stiff under canvas, so much so that when caught in a squall which took the main and mizen topgallant masts out of her and split her topsails, a heel of only 10 degrees was logged. Reports of her behaviour under steam show that she rolled less than any other ship of the Channel Squadron of her day. In Admiral Yelverton's report of 1866 she is credited with only 6·6 degrees, with the *Hector* showing 11·3, the *Ocean* 14·3, *Lord Clyde* 16·1 and *Pallas* 17·3 degrees, as the sum of angles to port and starboard.

Steering showed a tendency to be erratic at times owing to reduction in the rudder area—which was only half the size of that in the later *Bellerophon*—and her length made her somewhat difficult to handle, although she was far handier than the *Warrior*. In addition she carried a considerable amount of starboard helm, and her collision with the *Alexandria* in October 1879 was attributed largely to difficulties in controlling her with the hand steering gear when the rest of the squadron manœuvred more quickly under steam steering.

Foreign observers referred to her construction in the highest terms, inasmuch as "during her first ten months afloat not a wine-glass of water had leaked into her hull—a thing unprecedented in the history of shipbuilding." (King.)

APPEARANCE

As a four-master she must have been an imposing sight, but very unpleasing when deprived of her foremast and bowsprit. Under three-masted ship rig Ballard states "she was a very taking vessel to the eye. She sat the water on a remarkably even keel, and it was said of her that the placing and proportions of her spars and funnels were symmetrically perfect in their relation to the general outline and shape of her hull." For the voyage out to Malta in 1902 there were lowermasts and gaffs only, without a bowsprit, and showing double-banked wooden davits amidships—the last warship to carry them. Steaming from Portsmouth the *Achilles* looked still a sizeable ship; when dismasted as the *Egmont* it was remarkable how she appeared to have shrunk and become an insignificant hulk—full rig certainly conferred a sense of size out of all proportion to a ship's dimensions.

"ACHILLES"

Commissioned at Chatham in 1864 for the Channel and served until '68; rearmed and refitted; became guard ship at Portland from '69-'74. Again rearmed, and then went to Liverpool district as guardship '75-'77. Exchanged stations and ship's companies with the *Resistance* of the Channel Fleet in '77 and from there was sent to the Mediterranean in '78 when she was one of the six ships Admiral Hornby took through the Dardanelles. (Collision with *Alexandra* in October '79 when she sustained an underwater leak and the flagship had her boats damaged.) Returned to the Channel in '80 where she completed her sea-going career in '85, twenty-one years after hoisting the pennant. Paid-off she lay dismantled in the Hamoaze until '02 when her name was changed to *Hibernia* for service as depot ship at Malta where she remained for 13 years, being renamed *Egmont* in '04. Returning home in '14 and employed as depot ship at Chatham under the names *Egremont* and *Pembroke* until sold in '25.

The *Achilles* had a great Service reputation and even as late as the mid-seventies was regarded as one of our finest fighting ships. She certainly ranks as Watts' most successful creation.

Chapter 12

THE GENESIS OF THE TURRET SHIP

AT the time when the plans of the *Warrior* were still under consideration a far more novel and epoch-making type of fighting was being evolved in the brain of Captain Cowper Coles, R.N., who was destined to become the most outstanding influence in the history of battleship development. Gifted by imagination and ability to make practical application of his theories, with a dogged persistence which won recognition after long years of official opposition to his inventions, during which he was a sick man, Coles' name will ever be associated with turret ships and the loss of the *Captain*.

There has been much controversy as to who invented the turret ship—John Ericsson, the Swedish engineer, or Cowper Coles. Actually the idea of the revolving gun tower dates back long before either of them started working out their own ideas on the subject—Ericsson himself stated that "this obvious device of installing guns on a revolving platform, open or covered, dates back to the first introduction of artillery." There is also some uncertainty as to Ericsson's claim to have had his first "Impregnable Battery and Revolving Cupola" acknowledged by Napoleon III in 1854, as "a prolonged search has failed to reveal any reference to this proposal of Ericsson's in the archives of the French Ministry of Marine" (Baxter), and although his *Monitor* was ordered for the U.S. Navy in September 1861 subject to very drastic guarantees, the Board had already proposed to construct a fleet of 20 double-turreted ironclads, "the turrets to be of the pattern *advocated by Captain Cowper Coles*, R.N."

"LADY NANCY"

Coles' first conception of what was afterwards to develop into the turret ship was born of the experience derived from the armed raft *Lady Nancy* he designed and built for coastal operations in the Sea of Azoff in 1855. This historic little craft was constructed aboard the *Stromboli* and consisted of twenty nine casks placed in six rows of cradles in a framework of spars 45 ft. long by 15 ft. broad, planked over and carrying a long 32-pdr. of 42 cwt.

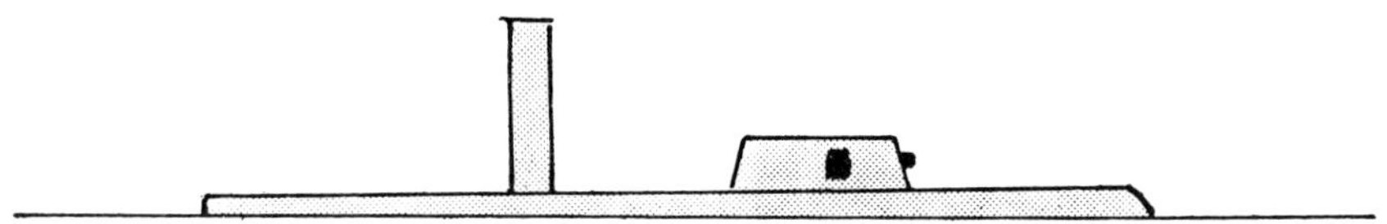

Capt. Coles' proposed armoured raft.

with 100 rounds of ammunition, a 7-in. hawser, and a crew of 18 men. Drawing only 20 in. of water, she was able to approach inshore where shallowness prevented the big ships from venturing, and fired more than eighty rounds at Taganrog with the greatest precision. Although towed more than 200 miles in boisterous weather, not a nail or lashing was started. Perceiving the advantages of a low freeboard and central armament, Coles developed the idea into an armoured raft, for attacking the forts of Sevastopol and Cronstadt, which was to be 150 ft. long, only 20 in. out of water, and carrying one 68-pdr. protected by a fixed hemispherical shield of iron with ports on the face and both sides. A double bottom was provided and the vessel made capable of being immersed from 4 ft. 6 in. to 5 ft. 3 in.; both ends were sharp with a projection of iron to protect the rudder and screw. This raft met with no encouragement from the Admiralty, but from it Coles conceived the idea of the revolving turret for which he filed his first patent on 30 March 1859.

The raft developed into the proposed Cupola Ship of 1859, which was to be of 9,200 tons with ten cupolas carrying twenty of the heaviest breechloaders of the day, two cupolas being raised and placed athwartships to give ahead fire of four guns. The Controller raised a number of objections to the project, pointing out that as the shrouds would considerably restrict the training of several of the guns, the number of these must be reduced or the length of the ship considerably increased. (No rigging was shown in Coles' sketch plan.)

But as a first step towards testing Coles' projects the Board agreed to finance the construction of an experimental turret which was to be commenced at Scott Russell's yard in 1859—but made little headway for the next two years.

In June 1860 Coles took out a further patent for a turret sunk into the crown of an armoured glacis under a light iron deck, over which the guns fired when the hinged bulwarks were dropped, and this was the subject of his lecture to the Royal United Service Institute on 29 June 1860. In the following September and October he submitted two turret ship projects to the Admiralty which were adversely commented upon by three constructors, Watts, Large (Chatham) and Abethell (Portsmouth), who summing up read—

> "In conclusion . . . while ships with the ordinary arrangements for fighting them can, we conceive, be made practically invulnerable, and to a large extent secure from casualty by means of small ports, we do not think it advisable to recommend the adoption of Captain Coles' form of ship which, independently of her peculiar description of armament and mode of protection, labors under every disadvantage in point of efficiency as a sea-going man-of-war."

But Coles enlisted the support of press and public and later of Prince Albert himself, whose advocacy took the practical form of urging Somerset to adopt the turret ship at once, although agreeing that "it would not be prudent to restrict ourselves to vessels of this novel construction, but we should give the country the benefit of possessing some such. Should Captain Coles' plan succeed, his ships will be vastly superior to those we are now building." Coles tells us that the Prince gave him "advice of the greatest benefit . . ., for he had previously turned his attention to the same subject, and was thoroughly conversant with all the mechanical details involved in the execution of my plan." According to Scott Russell, the Prince Consort "had matured an analogous system long before the adoption of the turrets of Coles and of Ericsson . . . and of which he was magnanimous enough to cede the whole public credit to Captain Cowper Coles who also had done the same thing in a somewhat different way" (*The Modern System of Naval Architecture*).

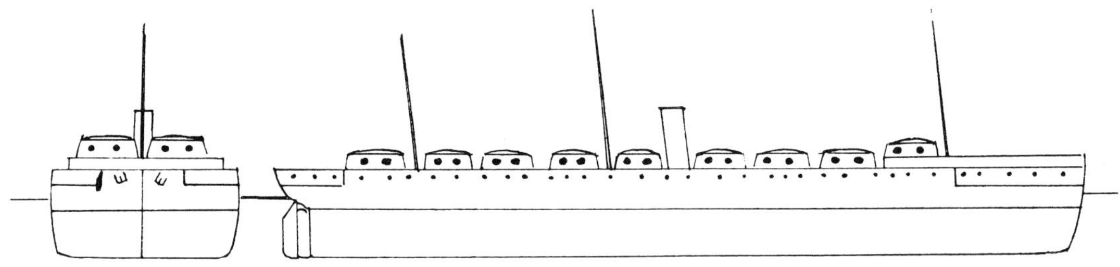

Coles' cupola ship of 1859 with eight cupolas on the centre-line and two abreast up forward to provide axial fire each side of the mast.

EXPERIMENTAL TURRET, 1861

The experimental turret, therefore, was ordered to be completed at Woolwich, erected on board the floating battery *Trusty*, and exposed to severe trials at Shoeburyness. The result of these was so successful that Captain Ashmore Powell described it as "one of the most formidable inventions adapted to naval warfare, as well as coast defences, that has ever come to my notice." After being struck thirty-three times with 68-pdr., 40-pdr. and 100-pdr. projectiles it was in perfect working order and undamaged.

In order to find out whether two guns could be worked in the turret a wooden model was made to house a pair of 100-pdrs. and installed in the hulk *Hazard*—also with satisfactory results.

In October 1861 Coles wrote to the Admiralty:

> "I will undertake to prove that on my principle a vessel shall be built nearly 100 feet shorter than the *Warrior* and in all respects equal to her with one exception—that I will guarantee to disable and capture her in an hour; she shall draw four feet less water, require only half the crew, and cost the country for building at least £10,000 less. I am ready to fall or stand on these assertions."

The Controller discussed the question of the type of ship Coles proposed to build, and although he thought 5,600 tons with sixteen 100-pdrs. under cupolas as too large and expensive, he was prepared to agree to two types with double turrets, one of 2,600 tons and the other of 3,893 tons. But Watts pointed out that both types would be too small and poorly protected to prove successful, and that to afford security against the heavy ordnance then coming into use it would be necessary to have a large ship carrying eight or ten shields with adequate protection and speed. His arguments were accepted by the Board and on 13 January 1862 the momentous decision was made to build a turret ship on Coles' system, the estimates for 1862–63 including a first instalment of £120,000 for the construction of a mastless ironclad to carry twelve breech-loading rifles in six cupolas. In introducing her the Controller stated that—

> "Her dimensions are small (2,239 tons burden—4,032 tons displacement) but it is difficult to see how she could be much damaged in action, and looking at her only as a fighting machine in smooth water, what class of ship yet built could hope to come victoriously out of a contest with her."

Later the plans were modified to allow for larger guns in only four gun houses, and when these were altered in shape from truncated cones to cylinders their descriptive name became "turrets." Known as the *Prince Albert*, this ship marks an epoch in British naval construction as important as was the appearance of the *Warrior*, and if the year 1861 is memorable for the passing of the wooden ship-of-the-line, 1862 is even more so for the advent of the turret ship.

A few days after the Controller gave his description of the ship, news of the actions in Hampton Roads was received in London, telling of the destruction of the wooden frigates *Congress* and *Cumberland* by the Confederate armoured battery *Virginia* (ex *Merrimac*) on 8 March 1862, and her duel with the Union turretship *Monitor* the day following.

This, the first engagement between ironclads, was a drawn battle, as neither ship succeeded in putting the other out of action, and the fight had to be called off when it became apparent that both ships were more or less immune to the opposing gun-fire. Had the *Virginia* used solid shot instead of shells, or the *Monitor* full 30-50 lb. charges instead of only 15 lb. behind her 170-lb. shot, the result might have been different. As it was, there was long-drawn-out and resultless cannonade with the *Monitor* firing once in 7 minutes and the *Virginia* discharging a broadside about once in 15 minutes. Attempts to ram by both ships were frustrated by use of the helm.

These two dramatic actions symbolized the passing of the Old Order and the coming of the New. Beyond providing striking confirmation for the Admiralty policy of changing over from wooden to armoured hulls and adopting the turret, they brought little fresh knowledge which could be applied to British naval construction. But public opinion was profoundly affected and disturbed. There was no real appreciation of the naval revolution which had taken place and the man in the street still accepted wooden walls as the measure of naval power; the fact that we had fifteen sea-going ironclads under construction or completed passed unheeded, and it was believed that the British Navy had been reduced to two ships, *Warrior* and *Black Prince*.

To the boast of American newspapers that our naval supremacy was finished with, *The Times* retorted that it was "safe enough at present," and that our ironclad force was certainly superior to that of the United States, which were not sea-going vessels. If the *Trent* affair had led to war—

> "we should never have left our smart frigates to be encountered by Monitors. We should have sent the *Warrior* and her consorts across the Atlantic, and our supremacy would have been expressed as decidedly, though more compendiously, than ever. We could have done the work of the *Monitor* and *Merrimac* together" (1 April 1862).

The principal features of the *Monitor* may be summarized briefly. She had a submerged, flat-bottomed hull safe from gunfire and protected from ramming by the wide overhang of the armoured raft laid above it. This afforded 2 ft. of freeboard only, so as to minimize target; but ensured steadiness by allowing the sea to wash over instead of breaking against it. The turret revolved upon a central spindle and had to be keyed up from the deck before the steam training gear could be used. In a number of cases Monitor turrets became jammed by hits and debris when in action. Ventilation was through blower trunks aft which were stowed down during battle; or through the turret —which resulted in vitiated air, great heat, and loss of efficiency in the personnel. Owing to the distribution of weights, shallow draught, and great beam, the metacentric height in the Monitors reached the extraordinary figure of 14-15 ft., giving a roll so quick relatively to wave motion that the deck was kept approximately parallel to the surface of the sea.

U.S.S. *MONITOR*

Actions could be fought in smooth water only, as in a seaway with hatches closed and waves breaking over the turret the Monitors were in no state of fighting efficiency. The *Monitor* herself foundered through the pumps being unable to deal with water entering beneath the turret during passage northward from Hampton Roads; the *Weehawken* was lost off Charleston through a wave breaking over her when the fore hatch (which had no combing) was open for ventilation, so that she was swamped and went down in 3 minutes; and the loss of the *Tecumseh* and *Patapsco* after hitting mines was due as much to the water they shipped through deck openings as that entering the breach caused by the explosion.

Following the spectacular success of the *Monitor*, the Federal Government built a large number of single- and double-turreted low-freeboard vessels which were known by the generic term of "monitors." They were mainly designed for coastwise service, but a few were intended to be ocean-going although possessing neither the free-board which would enable them to fight their guns in a seaway, nor the above-deck structure necessary for exercise and the amenities inseparable from a long voyage. Of these the *Miantonomoh* and *Monadnock* of 3,400 tons displace-

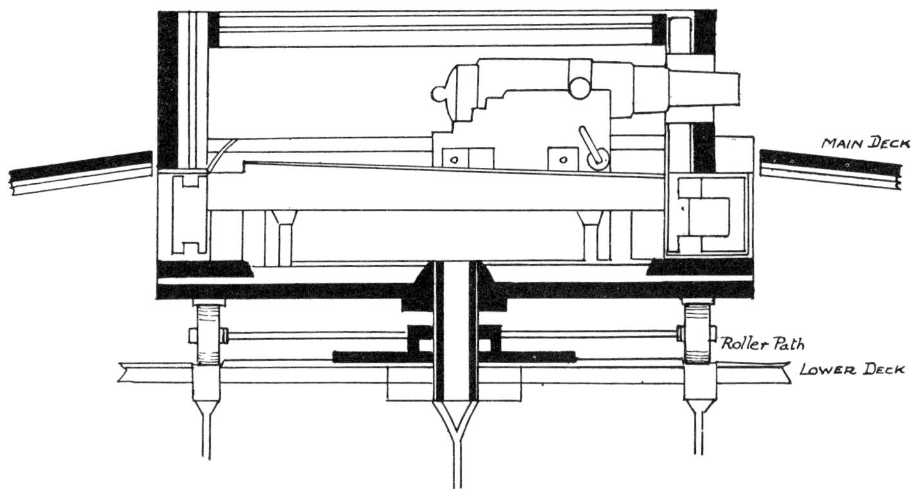

COLES' TURRET

The armoured portion of the turret rose $4\frac{1}{2}$ ft. above the main or weather deck which sloped upwards towards the centre line and served as a glacis. The lower portion revolved upon a central cylinder large enough for men to enter from below, its weight being distributed on bevelled wheels running upon a metal ring like a turntable on the lower deck. Training was by hand power only, both inside and outside the turret by rack and pinion and by a system of hand spikes on the main deck.

The gun carriage ran upon a slide in place of trucks, and both elevation and depression were obtained by raising or lowering carriage, gun and slide by screws at each end of the slide.

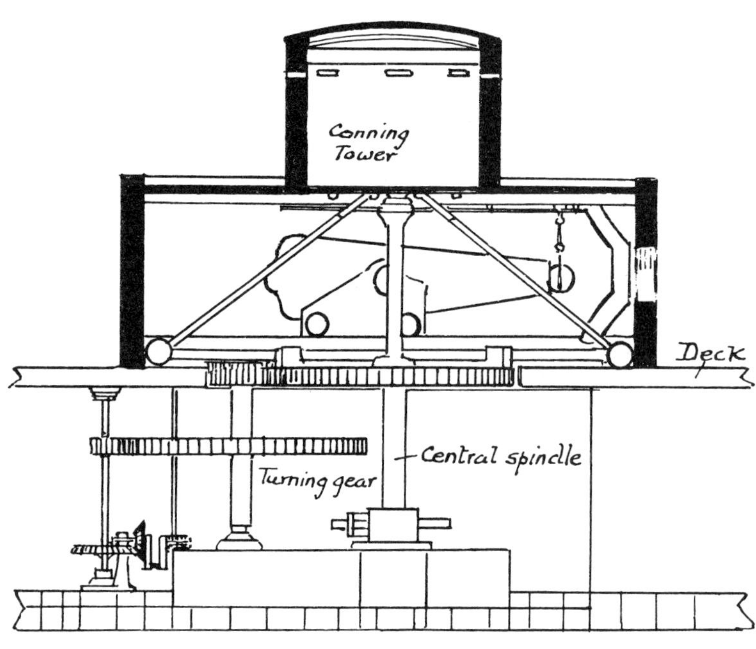

ERICSSON'S TURRET

The turret was supported and revolved upon a central spindle turned by steam training gear. Normally it rested upon the deck, and before training was possible it had to be keyed up by rack and pinion. A conning tower was mounted on the turret roof and turned with it.

Solid iron port-stoppers, hanging from the roof, pendulum fashion, closed the ports when the guns were run in.

ment armed with four 15-in. S.B. in two turrets were actually sent for long sea passages in 1865-6, the former to Europe and the latter from Boston to the Pacific via the Straits of Magellan. They certainly made their destinations, but voyaged under conditions which would have precluded their going into action, as well as being productive of extreme discomfort and unhealthiness to their personnel.

Two big single-turret ocean-going monitors the *Dictator* and *Puritan*, of which great things were expected, were commenced in 1862. *Dictator* displaced 4,438 tons and carried a couple of 15-in. S.B. in a turret 15 in. thick. With 5,000 h.p. her designed speed was 9·5 knots but she averaged about 6; in service she is said to have been an excellent seaboat with a turning circle of 700 feet.

DICTATOR

The *Puritan* was to have displaced 4,912 tons and carried two 20-in. S.B., but after years of delay she was completely redesigned and ultimately completed in 1896 as a two-turreted vessel with a central superstructure.

Mention must be made of these ships as they had a certain bearing upon subsequent British designs, to the extent that the *Miantonomoh* idea was behind the *Cerberus* and through her the *Devastation*, while the Board must have had the *Puritan* in mind when specifying the design of the *Glatton*.

Abroad, the Hampton Roads duel acted as a fillip to ironclad construction, Russia, Spain, Turkey and several of the smaller navies ordered turret ships, although it seems probable that the Danish *Rolf Krake* (Napier) and Italian *Affondatore* (Millwall), both launched in 1863, were ordered before the action. Monitors could make cheap and efficient coast-defence ships, and as such appealed to nations without overseas possessions. And while these powerful little vessels did nothing to influence British construction, they certainly led to changes in our foreign squadrons, which had to be strengthened by armoured units, especially on the South American station, where in later years the Peruvian turret ship *Huascar* caused some unpleasantness when she turned pirate.

Chapter 13

THE TIMBER-HULLED IRONCLADS

The British reaction to France's naval programme of 1860 was both material and psychological, and perhaps greater in terms of national suspicion than in shipbuilding. Napoleon III professed to regard such suspicions as quite unfounded. He considered each nation was entitled to build whatever ships were considered necessary and maintained that neither the French army nor fleet was as yet proportional to the population or resources of the country. But the aged Prime Minister Palmerston had formed very definite opinions as to the ultimate object of the French naval effort and demanded that adequate measures should be taken to meet it. When in January 1861 Lord Clarence Paget, then Secretary to the Admiralty, submitted a plan for limiting both navies while leaving us with an assured superiority, Palmerston would have none of it. He considered it inadvisable either to make such a proposal to France or accept it if made by France to us, since we had to regulate our forces with reference to other Powers besides France.

> "In the next place, such an agreement with any foreign Power would shackle the free action and discretion of England in a manner which we would never submit to; and if such an agreement were made, there must be a perpetual inquisitorial watch kept up by each Power over the Navy and Dockyards of the other in order to see that the agreement was not broken through. This would lead to frequent bickerings, besides being intolerable to National self-respect."

Our requirements might be for double the French force, and if so

> "the Emperor would laugh at us and say 'By all means! I must have 20 or 24 Iron-cased ships—you are quite welcome to have 40 or 48, and I hope you will find money to build them; but do not expect that I am to sit with my hands crossed till you have done so!'"

Such an agreement was proposed in the House in July 1861, and Packington declared that no surer course could be found to lay the foundation of future misunderstandings and quarrels with France than to define in a treaty the number of ships or the relative armaments which the two Powers should maintain.

Meanwhile on 7 February 1861 Rear-Admiral Spencer Robinson succeeded Sir Baldwin Walker as Controller, and his appointment—although not as yet accorded Board status—coincided with a marked increase in ironclad building activities. Following upon a report from our naval attaché in Paris regarding the progress of the French 1860 Programme, the Naval Members of the Board asked for immediate counter-measures. These included the provision of ten seagoing ironclads, and the adaptation of ten or more steam ships-of-the-line for armour protection with a total outlay of £3,000,000.

Gladstone, while protesting against an immediate increase of expenditure before the *Warrior* had run her trials, was willing to accept a bigger appropriation for armoured ships if it could be offset by reduction in expenditure on wooden line-ships. His suggestion was that the vote for the construction of wooden ships should be expended on wooden-hulled ironclads on the French model. But owing to Palmerston's unshaken confidence in wooden line-ships and the heavy demands for material which his Two Power programme was creating, the stocks of seasoned timber—some required up to twenty years' immersion in the ponds set aside in the dockyards for this purpose—were running low. There was a matter of £949,371 included in the 1861–62 Estimates for timber which led to heated controversy in the House. It was suggested that "any Ministry who should send wooden ships of the line to sea to oppose invulnerable iron ships would deserve impeachment," and an amendment deferring any further expenditure on wooden line-ships was only withdrawn when the Secretary stated that the Admiralty merely wished to finish off the conversion to steam of four wooden line-ships and get them out of the docks; and that wood was required for the decks and fittings of iron ships and for the construction of the numerous small warships required on foreign stations.

The Board, however, were far from sharing Palmerston's opinions and pressed for the adoption of its programme of twenty additional ironclads. But despite his opposition to the Prime Minister's wooden ship policy, Gladstone was far too much the economist to accede to such an increase in expenditure, and succeeded in whittling down the number of new ships to nine, pending a definite materialization of the French programme of new construction.

On 8 May 1861 the Controller submitted that the frames of some of the wooden line-ships whose construction had been suspended should be prepared for armouring with 4½-in. plates. He proposed to start with the *Royal Oak* at Chatham for conversion into an armoured frigate of 50 guns with 1,000 h.p. giving a speed of 12½ knots. The approval that this should be done may be regarded as an epoch-making decision, inasmuch as it definitely terminated the "Wooden Walls" era. Henceforth no capital ship was to be constructed without adequate armour protection.

Soon after work on the *Royal Oak*, our seventh ironclad, had been approved, news was received that eight of the ten new French ships had been laid down and that the ninth would be proceeded with as soon as a slip was vacant. This meant that France would have fifteen ironclads built or building and a sixteenth authorized against only seven British armoured ships under construction, a state of things which bid fair to relegate the British Navy to the position occupied by the French a few years previously.

On May 23 the Board, "convinced that none but the most vigorous and energetic measures will prevent the command of the Channel at an early date falling into the hands of the French Emperor," pressed the Cabinet for the immediate construction of more ironclads of the first class, but the Controller—probably sensing Treasury opposition to this—proposed instead that four more of the wooden line-of-battle ships then set up in frame should be completed as ironclads, even though he realized that they would be in every way inferior to iron-hulled ships. Admiral Dundas, the First Sea Lord, capped the Controller's proposal by estimating our requirements to be at least ten ironclads which could be met by the construction of six additional iron-hulled ships plus the conversion of two more framed-up ships-of-the-line and the cutting-down and plating of two teak three-deckers.

But Somerset objected to pressing forward with additional ironclad construction until more definite information as to both design and methods of protection were available, and would have nothing to do with the cheap expedient of cutting down and casing existing two- or three-deckers, believing that they would turn out unseaworthy and inferior fighting ships. But by lengthening the partially completed wooden ships and plating them we could obtain ironclads at least equal to those of the French, although with the same defects; but—and this was a weighty consideration—they could be built without exceeding the current Estimates! On 27 May 1861, therefore, orders were given to proceed with the completion of the two-deckers *Prince Consort*, *Caledonia*, *Ocean* and *Royal Alfred* as ironclads, and three days later Somerset directed that six *iron-hulled* ships should be set up in frame only, pending the results of fresh experiments with regard both to thickness of plating and the advisability of thinner backing or even no backing at all. The Board were left free "either to make a greater progress with a smaller number (three), or to proceed very slowly with the whole six," and they chose the latter alternative pending the results of the *Warrior's* trials and the armour tests at Shoeburyness. The Armstrong B.L. gun lately adopted by the War Office Ordnance Department was being heralded as a long-range armour-piercing weapon which would replace the 68-pdr. smooth-bore; and although the piece afterwards to be known as the 110-pdr. B.L. had not been tested against armour, it was already in production for issue to the Navy with every confidence.

But after calling for tenders for six iron hulls the Board reversed its decision, preferring to push ahead with the three only as quickly as possible. And so on 31 August 1861 the contracts for *Agincourt*, *Minotaur* and *Northumberland* were placed.

A twelfth iron ship was ordered in January 1862 and of an entirely different type—the cupola turret ship to which reference has already been made. She was to be of reduced freeboard, armed with twelve breech-loading guns in six cupolas on the system advocated by Captain Coles, and when completed—but with fewer turrets and heavier guns—she was known as the *Prince Albert*.

Altogether eight timber hulls were taken in hand under the conversion mandate of 1861—the *Royal Oak*, *Prince Consort*, *Ocean*, *Caledonia*, *Royal Alfred*, *Repulse* and *Zealous*—which having been commenced as two-deckers were selected for completion as broadside ironclads—and the *Royal Sovereign* (a three-decker recently passed into service), which was to be cut down and transformed into an experimental turret ship to ascertain the suitability of wooden hulls to carry the new gun houses.

Of the two-deckers, the last three had been laid down in 1859 and work on them advanced to a considerable extent; the other four commenced in 1860 were in frame only and could be adapted for conversion expeditiously and cheaply. The Board therefore decided to suspend labour on the more advanced hulls until the alternative standards of armour, armament and engine power had been tested by experience in the *Royal Oak*, *Prince Consort*, *Caledonia* and *Ocean*. As a result the last three were very much delayed, although put in hand as stopgaps to fill an immediate necessity. Each was completed on a different model as regards armament and armour when the rapid increase in gun calibres and need for better protection to the water-line and batteries led to adoption of a central battery in place of the more widely spaced broadside disposition. As the last of them to enter service, the *Royal Alfred*, did not hoist the pennant until 1867, their descriptions are best withheld until they can be dealt with in chronological sequence.

"ROYAL OAK"

Builder	*Laid down*	*Launched*	*Completed*	*Cost*
Chatham	1860	10 Sept. 1862	April 1863	£254,537

Dimensions $273' \times 58\frac{1}{4}' \times 24/25' = 6{,}360$ tons.
Hull and armour, 3,997 tons; equipment, 2,369 tons.

Guns	*As completed*	*Rearmed* 1867
	11 7-in. B.L.R.	4 8-in. M.L.R.
	24 68-pdrs.	20 7-in. M.L.R.

Armour Battery, $4\frac{1}{2}''$-$3''$; lower deck side and belt, $4''$-$3''$.
Total 935 tons.

Machinery Maudslay, Horizontal reciprocating.
N.H.P. 800 = 12½ knots.
Cyl. 82″; stroke 48″; revs.: 60 p.m.
Boilers—6 rectangular. 20 lb. pressure.
19′ hoisting propeller.

Coal 550 tons = 2,200 miles at 5 knots.

Complement 585.

Sail area With double topsails 25,000 sq. ft.

Special features:

(1) She was the first British wooden ironclad.
(2) Her ratio of weight of armament to displacement was greater than in any British battleship of her date.
(3) She was the first British ironclad to have end-to-end protection along battery, lower deck side and waterline.

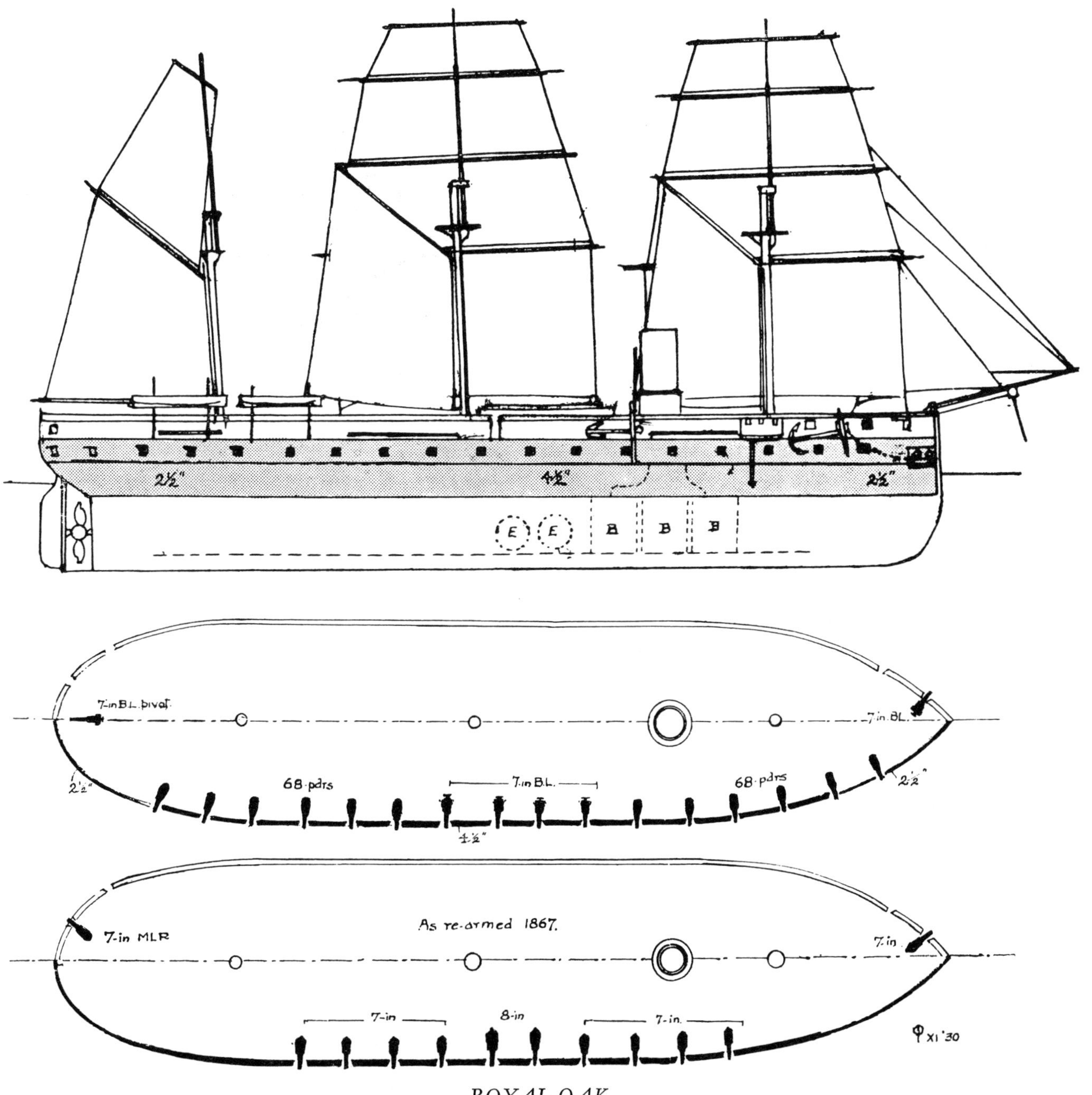

ROYAL OAK

Of the seven two-deckers selected for conversion the *Royal Oak* and *Prince Consort* had been the most recently laid down and therefore at a stage when their construction as ironclads could be most expeditiously carried out. Both were to be finished on the same general plan as regards guns and armour, but it was decided that *Prince Consort* should have more powerful machinery and a higher speed, which required additional boilers necessitating two funnels and a different lay-out below decks. As the *Ocean* and *Caledonia* were also completed to her model they may be described later as a separate group.

Because the process of conversion included lengthening by 21 ft. in order to accommodate the new armament of thirty-six 68-pdrs. on one deck, the *Royal Oak* was divided amidships and separated by hauling the lower half 20 ft. down the slipway. Five frames were then built into the gap and the new section made as rigid as possible by specially stout construction. The original framework at the bow and stern was taken down and rebuilt to give a straight stem and an upright elliptical stern, in conjunction with finer lines at each end—the general effect being to make the bow and stern so similar in profile that she and the *Prince Consort* were known as the "double-enders."

The *Royal Oak* as rearmed in 1867 with her former barque rig altered to that of a ship. Note the flat running-in bowsprit and return to wooden davits which lifted boats higher above water when they were less likely to be washed away.

As the original upper deck was removed she was given a new flush deck plated with ½-in. iron covered by 4-in. oak, and supported by iron beams and stanchions.

Steering was by a threefold wheel on the quarter deck, a double wheel on the main deck below, and another in the wardroom down on the lower deck. There was a light bridge resting on the quarter-deck bulwarks, but no conning tower. A tendency to trim by the bows was accentuated by the addition of a topgallant forecastle after her first commission, making her dip badly in a seaway, so that the contents of the forward shell-room had to be transferred aft to bring her to a more even keel. A poop was never fitted.

ARMAMENT

After the usual changes in armament on paper due to the constant development in ordnance during the 'sixties the *Royal Oak* received the customary combination of Armstrong B.L.R. and smooth-bores—in her case eight 7-in. B.L.R. and twenty-four 68-pdrs. along the battery deck, with three 7-in. B.L.R. on the upper deck as chase guns—two forward and one aft. These she carried until the end of her first commission in 1867, when they were replaced by rifled muzzle-loaders—four 8-in. and sixteen 7-in. along the battery and four 7-in. on the upper deck as chase guns.

ARMOUR

Because of the vulnerability of wooden hulls to shell fire a complete carapace of armour was considered necessary, and for the first time a British ship was as completely protected as the *Gloire*. The 4½-in. iron extended from the upper deck to 6 ft. below water, tapering to 3 in. at 40 ft. from the bow and stern, the battery ports being 7 ft. above water. Beneath this the hull was of 28-in. oak, while below armour level it increased to 32 in. so as to flush with the plating. Being a wooden ship, there could be no water-tight subdivision, nor were there any bulkheads between the engine and boiler rooms.

MACHINERY

The engines were exactly amidships—return connecting-rod drive of 800 nominal h.p. as designed for her when a two-decker, but with a longer screw shaft. On trial she developed 3,000 I.H.P., giving 12·5 knots on the Maplin mile. The six boilers were in two fore and aft groups with the furnaces facing inboard as was the custom at that time.

Although fitted with a hoisting propeller she usually sailed with it merely disconnected, as there were no encircling bulkheads around the well between decks, and the hoisting holes in the lower and main decks (through which the screw and banjo-frame would have to be lifted) were closed by circular covers—which if opened in even a moderate seaway would have led to wholesale flooding.

RIG

As a two-decker a sail area of 33,000 sq. ft. (excluding stunsails) would have been fitted; when converted it was decided to substitute a double-topsail barque rig in which the canvas was reduced to 25,000 sq. ft. with narrow topgallant sails of less than 700 sq. ft. each. This reduced dressing was good enough for home waters, but when there arose the probability of her being sent out to distant stations necessitating long passages when all possible sail would be required, a more generous allowance of canvas was indicated. So when double-topsails and pole topmasts were abolished in 1864 the *Royal Oak* was transformed by her own company into a single-topsail barque with upper sails of full hoist, and in June 1866 square rig was added to the mizen and she became a full ship.

But it was as a double-topsail barque that the *Royal Oak* achieved the highest speed under sail ever recorded by a British armoured ship, when running between Gibraltar and Malta on 9 February 1864 with a clean bottom and under single-reefed topsails, the wind blowing with a force of 7 to 9. Rolling 18 to 20 degrees each way, she logged 13·5 knots—a speed equal to that of the best line-of-battle ships, and the only occasion on which a British ironclad put up better figures under sail than her best under steam.

SEA-GOING QUALITIES

Having a low centre of gravity, the *Royal Oak* was a deep roller and an uneasy gun platform, although by virtue of her lighter machinery she was a little steadier than the three *Prince Consorts*. Handy under steam or sail in all weathers, holding her course in a following sea and riding well in a hard blow, she could have stood up well under a much larger sail area than she ever spread even as a ship.

"ROYAL OAK"

Commissioned at Chatham April '63 for the Channel, and after a few months followed the *Resistance* to the Mediterranean —the first British ironclads to pass the Straits. Paid off for rearming in '67 after which she returned to the Channel for 6 months (was run down by *Warrior* in thick weather when boats, chains, shrouds and back stays were sheered off) and was then sent again to the Mediterranean in '69. At the opening of the Suez Canal she grounded outside Port Said with two others of the squadron on an uncharted bank and was towed off by *Lord Warden* without damage. Returned home at the end of '71 and paid off at Portsmouth for refit, but instead was laid-up as a measure of economy and after 14 years in the fourth class Reserve was sold 30 September 1885.

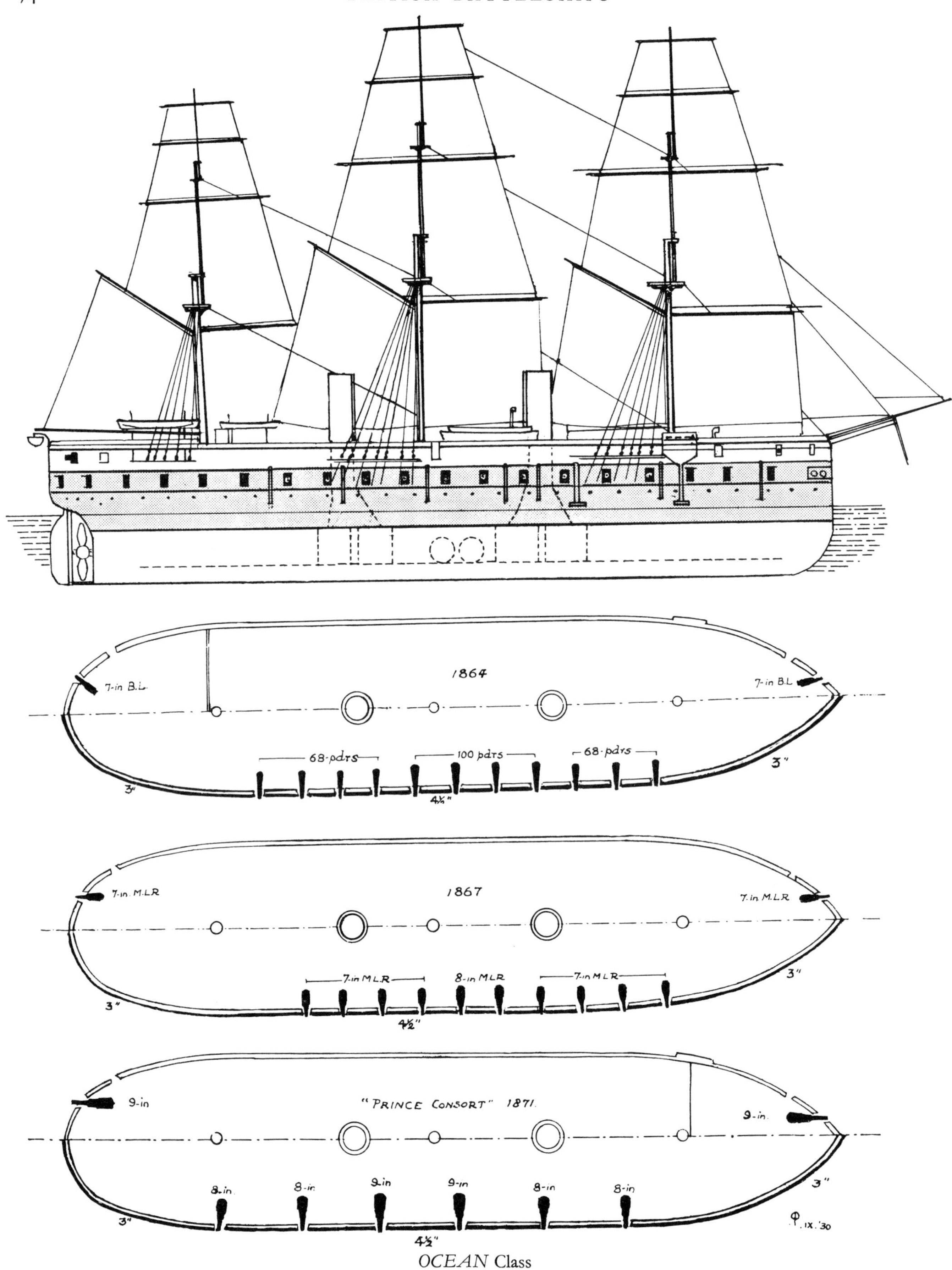
1864
7-in B.L.
7-in B.L.
68-pdrs
100 pdrs
68-pdrs
3"
3"
4½"
1867
7-in M.L.R
7-in M.L.R
7-in M.L.R
8-in M.L.R
7-in M.L.R
3"
3"
4½"
"PRINCE CONSORT" 1871.
9-in
9-in
8-in
8-in
9-in
9-in
8-in
8-in
3"
3"
4½"
Φ. IX. '30

OCEAN Class

"PRINCE CONSORT" (ex-*Triumph*), "CALEDONIA," "OCEAN"

	Builders	*Laid down*	*Launched*	*Completed*	*Cost*
"Prince Consort"	Pembroke	1860	1862	April '64	£266,173
"Caledonia"	Woolwich	1860	1862	July '65	£312,034
"Ocean"	Devonport	1860	1862	July '66	£298,451

Dimensions Original 252′ × 57′ × 25/26½′ = 3,715 tons burden.
Converted 273′ × 58½′ × 24/26¾′ = 4,045 tons burden.
6,830 tons displacement.
(Hull and armour 4,393 tons; equipment 2,534 tons.)

Guns

On completion			*Rearmed 1867*
"Prince Consort"	*"Caledonia"*	*"Ocean"*	*All three*
7 7-in. B.L.R.	10 7-in. B.L.R.	24 7-in. M.L.R.	4 8-in. M.L.R.
8 100-pdr. S.B.	8 100-pdr. S.B.		20 7-in. M.L.R.
16 68-pdr. S.B.	12 68-pdr. S.B.		*"Prince Consort"* rearmed 1871.
			7 9-in. M.L.R.
			8 8-in. M.L.R.

Armour Battery, lower-deck side and belt 4½″-3″.
Total 935 tons.

Machinery Maudslay, horizontal reciprocating.
N.H.P. 1,000 = 12½ knots.
Cyl. 92″, stroke 48″, revs. 56 p.m.
Boilers: 8 rectangular. 20 lb. pressure.
4-bladed 21′ propeller.

Coal 550 tons. Radius 2,000 miles at 5 knots.

Complement 605.

Sail area With double topsails 25,000 sq. ft.

Although built as a temporary measure to maintain our strength in capital ships during a period of emergency, the rate of shipbuilding progress in France proved to be such that no special effort to complete the converted ships expeditiously became necessary. They were, therefore, commissioned at intervals of about twelve months, with a variety of armaments in keeping with the changes and development in gun calibres during the next six years.

The three *Caledonias* were more than half-sisters to the *Royal Oak*, being similar in dimensions but drawing nearly 2 ft. more water aft with corresponding increase in displacement, and with the same protection. But the provision of greater engine power proved to be a mistake. If it could have been achieved without increase in weights the higher speed anticipated might have been realized; as it was, the heavier engines and extra boilers merely gave greater immersion to the hull, increased coal consumption, and diminished steaming radius without any benefit to their rate of progress. In fact, they just about pulled their own extra weight, but with the added disability of hull distortion and sagging which was a cause of constant trouble.

In the Service their construction was regarded as a retrograde movement, their very heavy wooden hulls having only 80 per cent. of the carrying capacity of iron ones. Added to which deterioration in a wooden ship was not far from twice as great during the same period—the usual allowance being that in twelve to fifteen years the casual repairs would about equal the first cost. Nevertheless, they proved to be excellent investments for their expected life of ten or twelve years, and for a considerable period four were serving as flagships on foreign stations. In fact the *Caledonias* formed the backbone of the Mediterranean fleet during their first few years in commission.

ARMAMENT

In offensive power the ratio of weight of armament to tonnage ranked highest among the battleships of their date, and although of considerably less tonnage than the *Warrior* or *Achilles* their broadsides were but little inferior. *Prince Consort* on entering service carried a very mixed armament of seven 7-in. B.L.—three being upper-deck chase guns—with eight 100-pdrs. (amidships) and sixteen 68-pdrs. along the broadsides; *Caledonia* differed in having three more 7-in. B.L. but four less 68-pdrs., four being chase guns. All these were on wooden mountings—the first improvement on the time-honoured truck mounts. *Ocean*, on the other hand, not having been completed until the B.L. and smooth-bores had been withdrawn from service, entered her career carrying twenty-four 7-in. M.L.R. In 1867 the *Prince Consort* and *Caledonia* were rearmed with four 8-in. M.L.R. and twenty 7-in. M.L.R. and the *Ocean* also exchanged her midships guns for 8-in. M.L.R., so that all three were for a time equal in attack. In November 1871 the *Prince Consort* was rearmed for a second time with three 9-in. 12-ton guns on the upper deck, and four 9-in. in line with eight 8-in. 9-tonners along the battery. All these were mounted on Captain Scott's metal carriages which enabled them to be fought in a seaway, and although at that time laid up in Reserve, she was regarded as being one of the best-armed ships we had.

Having no saluting guns, it was necessary to use their main armament on official occasions, which was apt to be a little too impressive in enclosed harbours.

ARMOUR

The hull received a complete casing of $4\frac{1}{2}$-in.–3-in. iron from the upper-deck level to 6 ft. below water as in the *Royal Oak*. For the first time in H.M. ships conning positions were installed, and on each side of the upper-deck amidships was a round pilot tower 7 ft. high and 5 ft. in diameter made of 12-in. timber covered with 4-in. iron,

The *Ocean* in 1868 with full ship rig and original armament. The fixed iron bowsprit is well steeved, compared with the flat running-in one in *Royal Oak*. The pilot towers amidships had not then been fitted. The only known photo of the class showing both funnels raised.

provided with voice pipes to the wheels and engine room. Unfortunately these erections proved quite untenable when the battery was in action, but served a useful purpose as "wash deck lockers."

MACHINERY

In accommodating the 1,000 n.h.p. engines with the additional boilers required, the usual distribution of weights could not be employed. Hitherto the ironclads had provided a full beam abaft of amidships allowing the engines to be placed about one-third of the ship's length from the stern to avoid a long propeller shaft, with the boilers and bunkers grouped further forward to maintain an even keel. But in the *Prince Consort* the only available position for the larger engines was the added central body amidships with the boilers in two groups forward and abaft of them, each group having its coal bunkers abreast of it—hence the unusual spacing of the funnels.

The machinery proved too heavy and caused hull sagging which reached 3 in. in the *Caledonia* before she had been two years afloat—a state of things necessitating frequent adjustments of the shafting. This ran through the foot of the main mast (which straddled it like an inverted V) and down the middle of the after stokehold with furnaces on each side of it—an arrangement which greatly fatigued and hampered the stokers.

On trials the *Caledonia* proved the fastest with 12·9 knots, the *Ocean* logging 12·7 and *Prince Consort* 12·5.

RIG

Only the *Prince Consort* was rigged like *Royal Oak* with double topsails, as by the time the others were completed this rig had been abolished in the Navy. As single-topsail barques they received fidded topgallant masts, and in 1866 yards were added to the mizen which raised them to the dignity of full ship rig; but they could easily have stood up to a much larger sail area than that actually carried.

Having been fitted with iron lower masts intended for double topsails which brought their "tops" 5 ft. lower than normal, the resulting very long mast-heads reduced the height of all the gear above and both the drop and area of the courses and gaff sails. The remainder of their masting and yards was of wood. This reduction in canvas, plus drag from a 21-ft. disconnecting screw, made them indifferent performers under sail despite the *Royal Oak's* record—the *Caledonia* and *Ocean* having 11½ knots to their credit and the *Prince Consort* only 10 knots.

But for all that, to the *Ocean* belongs the distinction of sailing the greatest distance in a day's run ever recorded by a British armoured ship, when on 26 August 1867 she covered 243 knots in the "roaring forties" on her voyage from Gibraltar to Hong Kong.

SEA-GOING QUALITIES

Although handy under both steam and sail, an unusually low centre of gravity giving a G.M. of 6·01 ft. made them very deep rollers and bad gun platforms. In which respect the *Prince Consort*—as being the only one of the trio which served a full commission in the Channel and so came under general observation over an extended period—became the penultimate standard of comparison in the estimation of such excessive stability. As the *Lord Clyde* could record angles during competitive trials far in excess of the other ships, she was beyond comparison as a basis for measurement, so that it was usual to employ the phrase "rolling as badly as the *Prince Consort*" when estimating unusual behaviour in a seaway. In 1872 the *Ocean* rolled 45 degrees to leeward in a "Cape snorter" off Port Elizabeth.

APPEARANCE

In profile they were rather sullen looking and the second funnel between main and mizen served to make them distinctive, if somewhat more ungraceful. Designed with internal scuppers discharging 6 ft. below the load line, their sides later became disfigured by a plethora of scupper-shoots added as the result of the *Prince Consort's* inability to discharge the water she took aboard during an Irish Sea gale on her maiden voyage to Liverpool, during which she was in danger of foundering (*vide Scorpion* and *Wivern*).

All three were launched with flush upper decks, but poops were added to the *Caledonia* and *Ocean*, and topgallant forecastles to *Caledonia* and *Prince Consort*—which increased the maximum draught of the *Caledonia* by 6 in. and of the *Ocean* by 9 in., although by bringing the *Prince Consort* to a more even keel her trim aft was reduced by 3 in. With the addition of forecastles the original fixed iron bowsprits with a marked steeve were replaced by wooden running-in ones—which may be distinguished in photographs by being nearly horizontal.

Although built for temporary service they proved successful ships, and during their short active careers were most important fleet units, being only paid off when iron hulls became available to replace them.

"PRINCE CONSORT"

Laid down at Pembroke in 1860 as the 90-gun *Triumph*, her name was changed in February '62 in memory of Prince Albert. On completion in '64 was ordered to Liverpool to watch Lairds Confederate rams, and was nearly lost on passage. Channel '64-'67 (rearmed); Med. '67-'71. Laid up at Plymouth '71—and again rearmed. By '82 had fallen into disrepair and was sold March '82 for "61/- a ton."

"CALEDONIA"

Not completed at Woolwich until July '65 through delay in delivery of guns. Commissioned as second in command Med.—our first armoured flagship. Poop added '66; temp. flagship Channel for experimental squadron cruises (rearmed

'67) and later relieved *Victoria* (last of the three-deckers) as Flag C.-in-C. Med. until '69, returning home in '72. Guardship in Forth '72-'75; paid off at Plymouth and laid up until she was sold on 30 September '86.

"OCEAN"

Commissioned at Devonport for Channel in '66 but transferred to Med. On 18 June '67 left Gib. for passage to Hong Kong, arriving Batavia after 133 days mainly under sail—the only armoured ship ever to double the Cape under canvas. China '67-'72 without docking, returning home under steam at 4½ knots and arriving at Plymouth 164 days from Singapore. In dockyard reserve until '82 and then sold. From the day she hoisted her pennant until the end of her sea career she never anchored in British waters.

Chapter 14

"MINOTAUR," "AGINCOURT" AND "NORTHUMBERLAND"

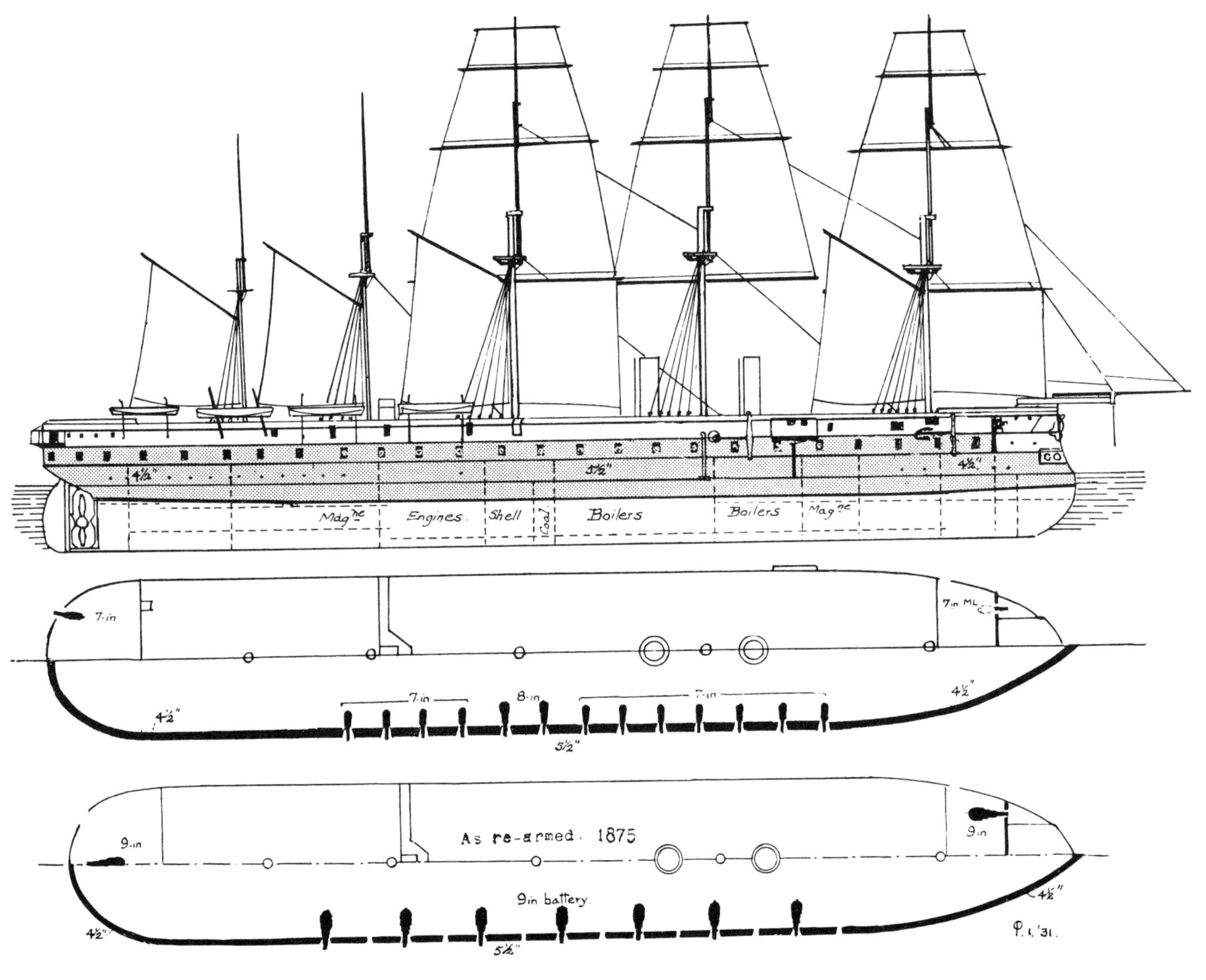

AGINCOURT

	Builders	*Laid down*	*Launched*	*Completed*	*Cost*
"*Minotaur*"	Thames I.W.	12 Sept. '61	12 Dec. '63	19 Dec. '68	£478,855
"*Agincourt*"	Lairds	30 Oct. '61	27 Mar. '65	1 June '67	£483,003

Dimensions $400' \times 59\frac{1}{2}' \times 27\frac{3}{4}' = 10{,}690$ tons.
Hull and armour: 7,560 tons; equipment: 3,340 tons ("*Agincourt*").
" " 7,170 tons; " 3,130 tons ("*Minotaur*").

Guns

On completion	*Rearmed* 1875
4 9-in. M.L.R.	17 9-in. M.L.R. } 2,344 lb.
24 7-in. M.L.R.	2 20-pdrs. }
8 24-pdrs.	

Armour $5\frac{1}{2}''$ iron from upper deck to $5\frac{3}{4}$ ft. below water tapering to $4\frac{1}{2}''$ at the bow and stern. Bulkhead $5\frac{1}{2}''$. Skin $\frac{5}{8}''$; backing 10″ teak. Total 1,776 tons.

Machinery "*Minotaur*" Penn horizontal trunk.
2 cyl. 112″. Stroke 51″. Revs. 58.
I.H.P. (trials) 6,700 = 14·32 knots.
4-bladed screw 24′ diam.
Boilers: 10 rectangular. 25 lb. pressure.
"*Agincourt*" Maudslay. Return conn. rod.
2 cyl. 101″; stroke 54″; revs. 61.
I.H.P. (trials) 6,870 = 14·8 knots.
4-bladed screw 24½′ diam.
Boilers: 10 rectangular. 25 lb. pressure.

Coal 750/1,400 tons. Radius 1,500 miles at 7½ knots (6 boilers), or about 1,000 miles with 10 boilers.

Complement 705 nominal, 800 actual.

Sail area 32,377 sq. ft. (in 1871).

Constructors A. Abethall and J. Large.

Special features:

(1) Designed to carry the heaviest armament afloat behind the thickest armour and at the highest sea speed.
(2) The biggest fighting ships afloat for ten years.
(3) The longest single-screw warships ever built.
(4) Among the best manœuvrers under steam and the slowest and most unhandy of all the ironclads under sail.

It will be remembered that originally the *Achilles* was to have been a 50-gun frigate, but that her armament was reduced to 20 guns by the removal of all the broadside unprotected pieces. For the three vessels of the *Minotaur* class the Board stipulated for a 50-gun frigate design in which a full broadside of what the First Lord called "fighting guns" (*i.e.*, protected by armour) could be mounted, while maintaining the same standard of speed, *without recourse to heavier engines*. Complete end-to-end armour was to be provided—which meant additional length to obtain finer lines with as little alteration to beam and draught as was consistent with the extra load to be carried.

The result was a long, fine hull in which high speed was obtained relative to engine power, and according to Barnaby—

"These ships marked the high water of design of Mr. Watts, and he was blamed by the Controller of the Navy *for the supposed extravagance* of her dimensions as compared with contemporary French design."

This opinion was based on the principle accepted some thirty years later that British designs of given speed, armament and armour must be larger than contemporary foreign ships, as more extended service is required of them with greater demands upon coal and stores. But such argument hardly applied to the *Minotaur*, seeing that she only bunkered 750 tons (with a maximum of 1,400 tons) compared with 850 tons of the *Warrior* and 675 tons of the much smaller *Gloire*, so that the Controller's strictures appear to be justified—although applying to the Board, whose directions tied Watts's hands. Certainly when finally completed the trio turned out to be handy ships, whose guns and armour had so depreciated in relative value during the long period in which they were preparing for sea, that they hardly justified their first cost or the outlay incurred for subsequent alterations. Although achieving much kudos as fighting ships, it was more by virtue of an imposing appearance which afforded a reputation—at least on Southsea Beach and Plymouth Hoe if not in Paris and Rome—long after their battle value had become seriously discounted by the rapid increase in ordnance and need for heavier protection.

Originally all three ships were to have been sisters, but changes in armour and armament were made in the *Northumberland* early in 1865 which placed her in a class by herself, and as such she will be described separately. Together they stood as the longest and largest single-screw fighting ships ever built, and the heaviest in the Navy for the next ten years, uniquely favoured in a rig which comprised the spectacular array of five masts, and in the case of *Minotaur* and *Agincourt* honoured by employment as flagships throughout their active careers.

CONSTRUCTION

The hull was 20 ft. longer than that of the *Achilles* and the sides showed a slight tumble home, with a rounded ram bow and semi-circular, nearly vertical, stern above a low counter.

An open topgallant forecastle and poop gave the suggestion of a slight sheer fore and aft. They were conned from a light bridge fitted with a tiny charthouse which rested on the bulwarks just forward of the break of the poop. Internally were three decks, the height from the floor to the lower deck being 21 ft., from the lower to the main deck 9¼ ft. and from main to upper deck 7¼ ft. From the floor to the main deck the hull was fitted with wing passages 3½ ft. wide which were divided into water-tight compartments, with 15 transverse bulkheads forming the main compartments as in the *Warrior*; the double bottom was confined to the engine and boiler-room sections and contained seven compartments.

On the battery deck there was but a single bulkhead twenty-five feet from the bows, and from that point it was possible to look aft for the whole length of the ship. The men were berthed on this deck, but the officers had their quarters below in the gloom and fœtor of the lower deck, "although aft there was a spacious and void half-deck lighted by four large ports which every commanding officer of the ships and every inspecting Admiral recommended with monotonous emphasis should be made the wardroom, and every such recommendation was turned down by the Board without comment, for no reason set forth in any Admiralty record, or even to guess at, unless as the invincible prejudice of Whitehall against innovations which are not absolutely unavoidable" (Ballard).

They are noteworthy in having been the first of our iron-hulled ships whose carrying capacity (5,232 tons) exceeded the weight of the hull (5,043 tons).

ARMAMENT

As 50-gun frigates it was the original intention to mount forty 100-pdr. Armstrongs in the main deck battery with ten on pivots on the upper deck. But by the time they had been launched the breech-loaders had been withdrawn from service, and when nominally completed in 1865 the *Minotaur* spent a further eighteen months testing out new

Minotaur on completion in 1867 showing four masts with square rig and double topsail yards—a temporary and unsatisfactory dressing soon changed.

guns before being commissioned. By this time very great changes had been made in ordnance design and the 9-in. 300-pdr. 12-ton M.L.R. was in production. Mr. E. J. Reed, who had succeeded Watts as Chief Constructor, wished to demonstrate that a broadside ship could not only mount guns hitherto considered far too big for handling in a battery, but work them just as comfortably as did the experimental *Royal Sovereign* in her turrets. Four 9-in. M.L.R. were therefore included in the main deck armament along with twenty-two 7-in. M.L.R., the chase guns being a 7-in. under the forecastle firing through small embrasures on each side of the bows with another under the poop traversing between square ports on the quarters. Eight 24-pdr. saluting howitzers were carried on the poop.

The 9-in. guns were mounted on Scott's metal carriages and could be loaded by a rammer projecting through a scuttle in the port lid, which remained closed until the gun was ready for firing. These ports were only 2 ft. 9 in. deep and 2 ft. 4 in. wide with internal bevels to give a width of 6 ft. 4 in. and 30 degrees training fore and aft, the sills being 10 ft. above water.

But the 7-in. 6½-ton guns were all mounted on slow-firing rope-worked carriages which were so unsafe that in a moderate swell ships carrying them were virtually disarmed. Hence the *Minotaurs*, although the largest ships in the Navy, were also two of the worse armed. Had the Ordnance Department experts who provided the guns for the Navy ever enjoyed a week's experience at sea in bad weather with their own contrivances, they would doubtless have speedily devised a remedy; but they were dependent for information at second hand from seamen who, though handling heavy ordnance every day of their lives, were technically supposed to be ignorant of artillery, their carriages and stores.

When rearmed in 1875 with a uniform armament of seventeen 9-in. M.L.R. it became necessary to enlarge the alternate ports—which meant cutting through armour, teak backing and the iron skin with hand drill, chisel and hammer, at a cost of £250 per port. The magazines and shell rooms were enlarged and at the ends of the bridge rifle-proof shelters were added containing Elliott's directors, by which the broadside could be fired simultaneously by electrical contract.[1] The *Minotaur* was also fitted with the first searchlight in the Fleet.

At the time the justification of all this expense merely to substitute 9-in. for 7-in. guns was questioned, and

Agincourt as a training ship at Portland in 1898 with barque rig and spare yards crossed on mizen for "ship" effect. The upper deck machine guns have been removed and a boxlike latrine built over the bow 9-in. gun port.

Captain Scott claimed that four 38-tonners—then the largest gun afloat—could have been mounted on the upper deck for the same cost.

About 1883 both ships exchanged two 9-in. for two 6-in. B.L. and in 1891 four 4·7-in. B.L. and some 3-pdrs. and machine guns were added; otherwise the ships retained a M.L. armament throughout their remaining period of service as fighting ships.

For the first time an increase was made over the thickness hitherto employed since the *Warrior*, and 5½ in.

[1] As an alternative to the traversing system a compromise was tried for the 12-ton chase guns, consisting of a turntable flush with the deck combined with racer extensions to three different ports in the bow and four at the stern. Although not altogether a success, the turntable was more satisfactory than the pivotings and swingings of the traversing system.

iron tapering to 4½ in. at the bow and stern covered the sides from the upper-deck level to 5¾ ft. below load water-line. In compensation the backing was reduced from 18 in. to 9 in.—a change which for some time was thought judging by the proving-ground results—to have made the protection inferior to that of the *Warrior*, until it was shown that the powder charge in the 300-pdr. testing gun had been altered from 35 to 50 lb. to increase the penetration of the 150-lb. shot used. The forward bulkhead protecting the bow chaser was also of 5½ in. plate.

MACHINERY

The *Minotaur* was given trunk engines with two 112-in. cylinders on the port side of the shaft balanced by condensers on the other. Driving a 24-ft. screw at 58 revs, she made 14¼ knots at load draught. *Agincourt's* machinery was of the return connecting-rod type by Maudslay, the cylinders being only 101 in. with a slightly longer stroke. Driving a 24½-ft. propeller at 61 revs. she made about 14¾ knots at load draught, although credited with 15·43 knots in some reference books. This latter was logged on preliminary trials when running light and under lower masts only.

Ten boilers were arranged in two rows fore and aft with a central stokehold, badly ventilated and generating a temperature of 130° at full speed. After being re-boilered in 1893 the *Minotaur* made 14 knots with 6,288 I.H.P.

Apart from the main engines there was no machinery on board until 1875, when steam steering was installed; until then handling had been by fourfold wheels on the quarter and orlop decks. As in the *Warrior*, steering was unsatisfactory, and the *Minotaur* with eighteen men at the upper and lower wheels and sixty at the relieving tackles turned a circle in about 7¾ minutes, 1½ minutes being taken in putting the helm over to the very moderate angle of 23 degrees.

RIG

In order to provide their great hulls with sufficient sailing power, five masts were fitted and officially named fore, second, main, fourth and mizen. These were to have had pole topmasts, the first four carrying a course, double topsails and topgallants with gaff try-sails except to the second mast, the mizen hoisting a spanker only. No royals were fitted. But only the *Minotaur* was so dressed. The rig gave an unsatisfactory drive, the yards were removed from the fourth mast, and single topsails with fidded topgallant masts and royals substituted for double topsails on the first three, after which the masts were named fore, second, main, mizen and jigger. To improve appearance in a seaman's eye they often crossed spare topsail and topgallant yards on the mizen, and spare topgallant and royal yards on the jigger, but these naturally carried no sail. The course on the mast between the funnels got badly smoke burnt and was abolished. It was originally intended that the iron bowsprit should be hinged for turning upwards and backwards during action.

After being withdrawn from active service in 1887, they were re-rigged as three-masted barques in 1893-4, and thereby lost their individuality!

Being fitted with screws which only disconnected, a further handicap was added to their difficulties in proceeding under canvas, with the result that they refused to answer the helm properly except under a soldier's breeze, and the best speed ever logged was about 9½ knots under full sail with a 5 to 6 wind on the quarter. Truly no ships ever carried such a display of canvas to so little purpose, and they were regarded as the most sluggish performers under sail of all the ironclads.

SEA-GOING QUALITIES

The *Minotaurs* were regarded as good sea boats, and having a G.M. of 3·87 ft. only, ranked among the steadiest ships in the fleet. Under hand steering they were slow in handling, but after steam steering was fitted were regarded as good in manœuvre. As Admiral Colomb pointed out at the R.U.S.I. in a discussion on the Naval Manœuvres, February 1890:

> "Length did not interfere so much with manœuvring power as people believed, and some of our largest ships are the best manœuvrers; the *Minotaur* and *Northumberland*, two of our longest ships, are also two of the very best manœuvrers we have in the Navy. There is no shadow of question that the *Edinburgh*, which is 75 ft. shorter than the *Minotaur*, takes a full ship's length more space in manœuvring than the *Minotaur* does."

"MINOTAUR"

Ordered under the name of *Elephant*—which was soon afterwards changed—she made a spectacular launch at Blackwall in Dec. '63 after which she took 2 years to complete owing to changes in design, and was 18 months under experimental trials of armament and rig. Commissioned at Portsmouth in April '67 as flag Channel, which proud position she filled for 18 years. (Collision with *Bellerophon*—lost bowsprit and fore topgallant mast.) Refitted and rearmed '73-'75; Channel (flag) '75-'87. Reserve Portsmouth '87-'93; training ship Portland (*Boscawen II*) '93-'05 and Harwich '05-'22 (*Ganges*).

Sold in 1922, 61 years after the laying of her keel.

Throughout her active life the *Minotaur* served as senior flagship with a unique record of pomp and ceremony which she carried with impressive presence. Arrived a day too late for the bombardment of Alexandria. She retained her masts and funnels through a well-preserved dotage, wearing the old-time black, white and buff livery to the end.

"AGINCOURT"

Laid down in dry dock as the *Captain* at Birkenhead and floated out in March '65. Completed '68 and commissioned in June '68 to tow the Bermuda floating dock to Madeira in tandem with *Northumberland*. Channel (2nd flag) '69-'73. (Grounded at Pearl Rock, Gibraltar, and was nearly lost '71.) Channel (flag) '73-'75 during her sister's refit. Rearmed and refitted '75-'77. Med. (2nd flag) '77-'78 (Dardanelles passage with Hornby) and then returned to the Channel as 2nd flag until '89. Paid off in Reserve at Portsmouth '89-'93. Training ship (*Boscawen III*) at Portland '93-'05; at Harwich (*Ganges II*) '05-'09 when she was stripped and converted into a coal hulk at Sheerness (C.109) from '09 to date—a grimy, dilapidated and incredibly shrunken relic of the proud ship which had carried the flags of fifteen Admirals.

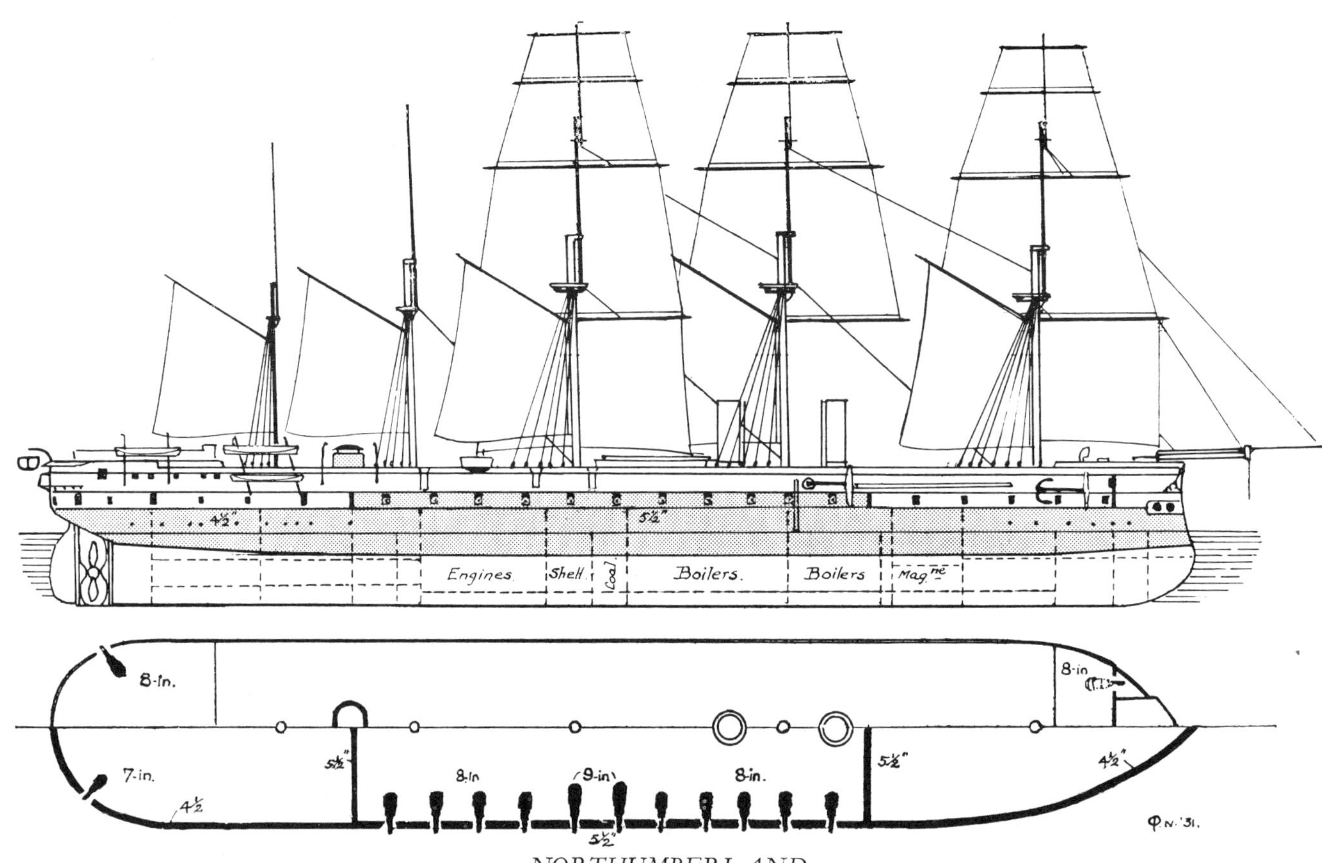

NORTHUMBERLAND

Builders	*Laid down*	*Launched*	*Commissioned*	*Cost*
Mare and Co.	10 Oct. '61	17 Apl. '66	8 Oct. '68	£444,256

Dimensions 400' × 59½' × 27¾' = 10,780 tons.
Hull and armour: 7,340 tons. Equipment: 3,340 tons.

Guns

Designed	*On completion*	*Rearmed* '75
48 68-pdr.	4 9-in. M.L.R.	7 9-in. M.L.R. } 2864 lb.
2 7-in. B.L.R.	22 8-in. M.L.R.	20 8-in. M.L.R. }
8 40-pdr. B.L.R.	2 7-in. M.L.R.	2 20-pdrs. }

Armour 5½" iron from upper deck to 5¾' below water for 184½' amidships with 5½" main deck bulkheads.
Lower deck continuations to bow and stern 5½"-4½".
Backing 10" teak. Conning tower 4½". Total 1,549 tons.

Complement Nominal 705, actual 800.

Machinery Penn. Horizontal trunk engines.
2 cyl. 112". Stroke 4¼'. Revs. 58.
4-bladed Mangin screw.
10 rectangular boilers at 25 lb. pressure.
I.H.P. 6,560 = 14·13 knots.

Coal 750/1,400 tons.

Constructors A. Abethall and J. Large.

Although laid down as a sister to the *Minotaur* and *Agincourt*, the *Northumberland* was altered while on the stocks, after E. J. Reed had succeeded Isaac Watts as Chief Constructor, so that she acquired an individuality of her own. By the time she was laid down what was known as the "68-pdr. period" had merged into the confusion of the ill-starred venture with breech-loaders, and when this in due course had been abruptly terminated in favour of a return to muzzle-loaders, the subsequent growth in ordnance threatened to make these huge ships obsolete before they were ready for sea! The Board therefore decided to give the *Northumberland* the benefit of the new 8-in. gun in place of the 7-in. in the *Minotaur* and *Agincourt* and make allowance for the extra 120 tons of displacement required by curtailing the armoured area. She thus became a reversion to the *Achilles* belt-and-battery type with only 184½ feet of her sides protected instead of 213 feet, and although the superior fighting ship, was always subordinate to her half-sisters in squadron.

ARMAMENT

The battery was much shorter than in the *Minotaurs* and separated by noticeable gaps from the ventilating ports fore and aft, which helped to differentiate her from the other two ships, in which a uniform and unbroken line of square ports ran from stem to stern, although one early photo of *Northumberland* shows her with painted ports filling these gaps. As bow chasers two 8-in. guns behind armoured bulkheads fired through small embrasures

A unique view of the *Northumberland* taken when she was second flagship in the Channel 1873. Note the painted ports (6th from bow and stern) to simulate the *Minotaur* then refitting, the conning tower between the after masts, the gaff on the main, and the full poop. She carried this rig until her 1875 refit when she was reduced to a barque.

beneath the forecastle; abeam, the central battery held two 9-in. and nine 8-in.; astern the muzzles of a pair of 8-in. showed above the sternwalk and a brace of 7-in. below it, all four being without protection.

Actually the *Northumberland* carried 68 tons more of artillery than the *Minotaur*, and by the use of quick-pointing fittings to the guns could work twenty-six heavy weapons under all conditions of weather, and had only two unsafe rope-worked carriages.

When rearmed in 1875, 9-in. guns were substituted for the 8-in. forward; aft, a single 9-in. replaced the pair of 8-in. under the poop, and the aftermost 8-in. guns in the battery were moved to the stern *vice* the 7-in.

To utilize the newly acquired Whitehead torpedo, four discharge carriages were fitted, firing through ports on the main deck; the weapon itself had a speed of 7 knots, a nominal range of 1,000 yards, and an exceedingly unreliable course.

In 1886 two 6-in. B.L. replaced two 8-in. and some light guns were added.

ARMOUR

The 5½-in. battery extended for 184½ ft. amidships with end bulkheads of the same thickness. The whole lower deck side and waterline to 5¾ ft. below load draught was also 5½ in., with 4½ in. at the bow and stern. It was also possible to introduce a $4\frac{1}{2}$-in. plated conning tower between the two after masts—which served to differentiate her from the *Minotaur* and *Agincourt*.

MACHINERY

In machinery and boilers she was a duplicate of the *Minotaur* but was supplied with steam steering gear—a simple apparatus of rotating engine drum with hide ropes to the tiller. Service reports record about $\frac{1}{4}$ knot difference between her and the other two five-masters, and she suffered from a slightly higher coal consumption.

RIG

Originally designed as a three-master and later altered to 5 masts, the *Northumberland's* sail plan was similar to that of the *Minotaur* with the addition of a gaff to the second mast and lower stunsails—which were unique in the Victorian navy. It was her first commander, Captain Roderick Dew, who painted her yards black in order that she might not be submitted to the indignity of ever being mistaken for the other white-yarded five-masters, though

Northumberland as a barque when serving as second flagship in the Channel 1890. Here the spacing between the battery ports and ventilating ports fore and aft is clearly shown.

both happened to be flagships. The same officer was credited with the different naming of the masts—fore, main, mizen, jigger and after-jigger—and was in the habit of setting a lower stunsail triced up on the "main yard" as a flying kite when his "mainsail"—or second course as it was called in the others—had been abolished by Admiralty order.

During her long refit in 1875 the second and fourth masts were removed, and she became a barque. Higher topmasts and topgallant masts with longer yards to the *Achilles* scale were fitted, but produced no resulting benefit to speed under sail, her best under the most favourable conditions being 7 knots.

SEA-GOING QUALITIES

Reed had calculated that while the weight of the first 50 ft. of the *Warrior* equalled the displacement, the same length in the *Minotaur* exceeded displacement by several hundred tons. But by the removal of some 90 ft. of armour from her bows, the *Northumberland* gained in buoyancy and was reported as riding better than the others in a head sea and yawing less when running. But although deprived of a rather large area of armour aft, she still trimmed by the stern—due in part to the additional guns above the counter—which accounted for a loss of 1½ knots under canvas, with the stigma of being the slowest warship when sailing in the whole fleet. In other respects she was like the *Minotaur*—a steady gun platform, able to maintain her speed in a seaway, and satisfactory in manœuvre.

APPEARANCE

As a five-master she could be distinguished from the others by (1) conning tower, (2) gaff on second mast, (3) spacing of main deck ports. She became a three-master nineteen years before her two half-sisters; but when all three were barques the conning tower and steam pipes between the funnels served for recognition—in *Minotaur* these latter were before the funnels, in *Agincourt* abaft them.

"NORTHUMBERLAND"

Laid down at Millwall in 1861, she was five years on the stocks and her construction—although delayed by changes in design—was far advanced when the launching date arrived. But her weight was too great for the cradle and ways—she stuck for an hour while the tide ebbed, then slid down halfway with her after part not water-borne. For a month she was held up by pontoons and shores, but hydraulic jacks and tugs failed to move her at the spring tides. At next high springs the pontoons gave her a lift and she came down with a rush. By now the builders had gone into liquidation and the hull remained as a company asset for eight months until the final instalment was paid by the Admiralty, when she was handed over and completed for sea without delay. Commissioned in '68 for service in the Channel, she helped the *Agincourt* tow the Bermuda dock as far as Madeira. Channel '68-'73. Through faulty cables she collided with the *Hercules* ram in Funchal Roads on 25 December '72 and ripped open her bottom. Rear flag Channel '73-'75; rearmed and refitted '75-'79; Channel '79-'85; refitted '85-'87; relieved *Minotaur* in Channel '87-'90; Reserve at Portland '90-'91 and Devonport '91-'98; training ship for stokers at Nore '98-'09 (*Acheron*). Converted to coal hulk CD.68 (later C.8) in '09.

Sold 1928 and transferred to Dakar.

Chapter 15

THE GENESIS OF THE COAST DEFENCE SHIP—"PRINCE ALBERT," "ROYAL SOVEREIGN," "SCORPION" AND "WIVERN"

NOTWITHSTANDING the success of the *Royal Sovereign* and *Prince Albert*, the employment of the turret for mounting big guns in sea-going ships was dismissed by the Board as an impracticable principle. Both the Controller and Chief Constructor were opposed to its adoption in anything but unrigged ships of low freeboard and then only for *coast defence purposes*—in which it offered a solution to the problem of producing a small but effective ironclad.

Now, naval warfare embraces the possibility of coastal as distinct from high seas operations, the one requiring different types of ships from those designed for contact with the enemy battle fleet. Units intended for coastal service can be of shallower draught, smaller and cheaper than sea-going capital ships; and the provision of some such vessels had been in the mind of the Board when the submission of designs for the *Warrior* was invited in 1859. But *offensive* operations off the enemy coast were not to be confused with a defensive role in home waters, and it was unfortunately this latter service for which the turret ship appeared to be especially suitable. Naval history has shown that the best method of coast defence is to find and destroy the enemy fleet, hence the provision of special ships designed for harbour service only would be the negation of strategy. Both the *Royal Sovereign* and *Prince Albert* were capable of being employed in the narrow seas and off an enemy coast, but at the same time as they were ordered the Controller submitted plans for two iron-hulled turret ships which were only suitable for harbour defence, with the turret offering a solution to the difficulty of providing an acceptable design.

So long as the battle fleets were in being and efficient there could be no question of invasion. But when naval strength had been allowed to decline through false economy, then misdirected attention turned to such substitutes as fortifications and coast defence ironclads. When, in 1804, Pitt had condemned the Government's naval policy, his indictment included the inadequate provision of shallow-draught gun vessels for defence against invasion. Lord Exmouth then clearly formulated the true policy which should always guide the strategy of our naval defence. He said:

> "I do not really see in the arrangement of our naval defence anything to excite the apprehension of even the most timid among us. I see a triple naval bulwark, composed of one fleet acting on the enemy's coast; of another, consisting of heavier ships, stationed off the Downs, and ready to act at a moment's notice; and a third, close to the beach, capable of destroying any part of the enemy's flotilla that should escape the vigilance of the other two branches of our defence. As to these gunboats which have been so strongly recommended, this mosquito fleet, they are the most contemptible force that can be employed. I have lately seen half-a-dozen of them lying on the rocks, wrecked.
>
> As to the probability of the enemy being able, in a narrow sea, to pass through our blockading squadrons with all that secrecy and dexterity, and by those hidden means that some worthy people expect, I really, from anything I have seen in my professional career, am not disposed to concur in it."

Lord St. Vincent was equally emphatic that preparation should rather be directed to keeping the enemy as far as possible from our coasts, and attacking them the moment they left port, than to awaiting them at home. But there were those who claimed that now that sail had given way to steam our former strategy no longer held good. Lord Palmerston in 1860 said: "The adoption of steam as a motive power has totally altered the character of naval warfare, and deprived us of much of the advantages of our insular position." He quoted the opinion of Sir Robert Peel "that steam has bridged the Channel, and, for the purpose of aggression, had almost made this country cease to be an island."

But, as Colomb put it:

> "No change in weapons or method of propulsion can alter the general principles of naval warfare. But this may be fairly advanced, that increased rapidity of movement, improved communications with distant stations, and augmented resources in war material, all tell in the favour of the stronger navy, whether for attack or defence. Squadrons thousands of miles away can now be concentrated at any point, reinforced if threatened, or recalled home, in so many days, while formerly as many months were required. If steam has bridged the Channel, in one sense, it has equally removed the space which intervened between one part of the United Kingdom and another, and has rendered a collection of vessels at any point threatened a matter of a few hours, whereas in former times a contrary wind might delay succour until it was too late. On the whole, therefore, it appears to me that steam would only tell against us in the event of our being completely over-mastered at sea, a contingency it seems unnecessary to dwell upon."

Granted that isolated vessels might evade the blockade and attack seaports, there was still no reason to build coast defence ships when the best coast defence ship is a first-class battleship able to proceed to any point in any weather—and coast defence ships were not the most seaworthy sort of craft.

That France and Russia favoured coast defence ironclads was no excuse for us to follow their example. While they might thus acknowledge inferiority afloat, it was the duty of the paramount Naval Power to maintain an adequately superior force of sea-going ironclads.

Unfortunately for a decade or so this basic principle of defence was ignored, the Fleet was starved, and a Royal Commission in 1859 recommended an expenditure of £10,000,000 on the fortification of our naval arsenals. Remarkably enough, the naval voice was silent, and Captain Cooper Key formed one of the Commission. When Sir Charles Napier protested that "the only sure way to prevent invasion is to have always on hand a superior fleet to the French or any other nation," Lord Palmerston said: "I am not surprised that the gallant admiral should undervalue the strength of fortifications, but, nevertheless, I think the history of war shows that they do enable an inferior force to hold out for a certain time against a superior force."

Another reason for building coastwise warships was put forward as the result of the Russian war. Both in the Baltic and Black Sea it has been the shallow-draught vessels which did all the work, as the enemy battle fleet preferred being sunk at its moorings to coming out into the open. Also during the next few years naval operations in the American Civil War were mainly coastal. With the exception of the blockade runners the Confederates offered no targets upon the high seas calling for the employment of capital ships, while the reduction of coastal defences and maintenance of an inshore blockade had required the services of light-draught ships to stand up to both heavy fortress guns and blockade breakers like the floating batteries of the *Merrimac* type.

Because of such arguments our naval policy for some years to come was largely influenced by provision for coastal operations, in an entire misreading of the lessons of these campaigns as applied to the employment of sea power against the naval forces and trade of a maritime nation.

"PRINCE ALBERT"

Builder	*Laid down*	*Launched*	*Completed*	*Cost*
Samuda Bros.	29 April '62	23 May '64	23 Feb. '66	£208,345

Dimensions $240' \times 48' \times 18\frac{3}{4}'/20\frac{1}{2}' = 3{,}880$ tons displacement.
Hull and armour 2,980 tons. Equipment 900 tons.

Guns 4 9-in. 250-pdrs. 12-ton M.L.R. 6 machine guns added later.

Armour Sides $4\frac{1}{2}''$-$3\frac{3}{8}''$ ends; turrets 10″-5″; deck $1\frac{1}{8}''$-$\frac{3}{4}''$.
Backing: 18″ teak. Total 879 tons.

Complement 201.

Machinery Humphreys Tennant. Horizontal direct-acting.
2 cyl. 72″. Stroke 3′.
N.H.P. 500. I.H.P. 2,130=11·26 knots.
Boilers: 4 rectangular, 23 lb. pressure.
4-bladed 17′ screw. 61 revs.

Coal 229 tons. Full steam $3\frac{1}{2}$ days=930 miles. Economical steaming 7 days.

Constructors C. Paget and W. Gray.

Points of interest:

(1) The first British iron turret ship.
(2) The first to have a definite bridge.
(3) Was retained on the Navy List for thirty-three years—the second longest life of any British capital ship.

In preparing the design for our first turret ship the Board had to decide in what type of hull the new system could best be employed. John Ericsson was building his *Monitor* with a raft freeboard and limiting the armament to a single two-gun turret with all-round bearing—as he put it "two turrets are as unnecessary as two suns in the sky." Coles' 1859 project had provided a full broadside from multiple cupolas, with almost end-to-end armour along her low freeboard sides, and pole masts only. In 1862 his proposed sea-going design retained the low freeboard but concentrated four much heavier guns amidships with a full-length belt and side armour to cover the turret bases, while a novel rig on tripod masts provided the necessary sail power for high seas service.

The Board, however, quite rightly refused to accept this latter as a sea-going ship. Without a forecastle and poop she would not have been seaworthy or properly habitable, and the mast legs—although a clever substitute for standing rigging—obstructed wide arcs of fire fore and aft. Moreover the four heavy guns were of a type not yet accepted into the Service and their mounting presented then unsolved problems.

The armament, therefore, would have to consist of the heaviest available guns—which at the time were the 110-pdr. Armstrongs—and mounted in several cupolas to provide an adequate broadside. This meant that the entire above-water hull would need to be armoured in order to protect their bases, necessitating as much armour as a broadside ironclad plus the weight of the cupolas and deck armour—the latter having a considerable bearing upon stability.

Faced with these conflicting claims of gun-power, armour, stability and rig, the Board decided to model the *Prince Albert* along the lines of the 1859 project, and the Constructor's Department accordingly drew up a less ambitious design in which Coles' assistance was confined to the cupolas only. Freeboard was fixed at 7 ft. to ensure stability while affording a command for the guns equal to that of the average main deck battery in the ironclads. A length of 240 ft. matched that of the largest second-class three-deckers, while a beam of 1 : 5 in conjunction with a shallower draught gave better speed lines.

Since contact with the enemy during bad weather was not regarded as a likely contingency, the turrets could be given end-on fire without being masked by forecastle or poop, while 5 ft. light iron bulwarks hinged to drop outboard during action made for dryness and comfort in a seaway.

Thus the turret produced a new set of values in which a small target and reduced freeboard consonant with

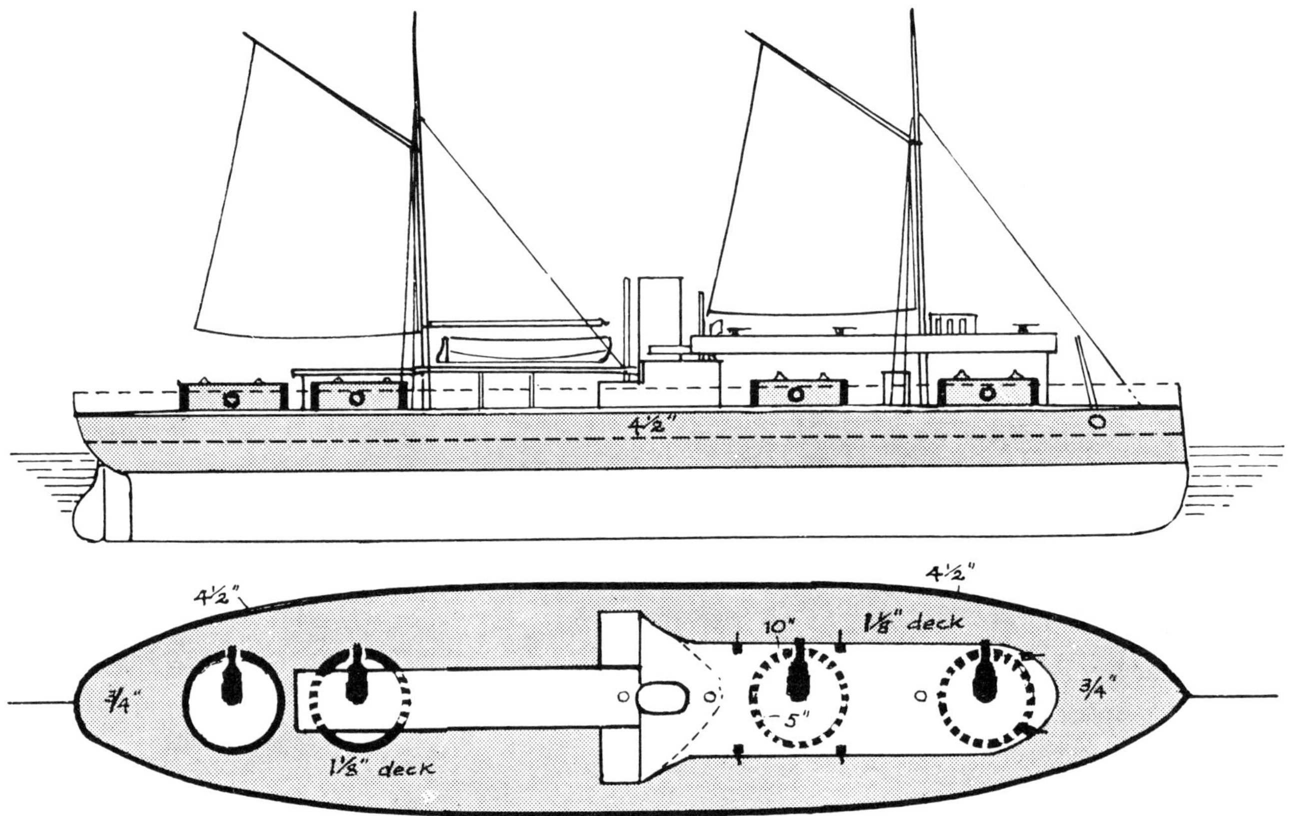

Prince Albert when fitted with flying bridge, charthouse, and machine guns. The gaff sails are for steadying purposes only. The broken line indicates the bulwarks, which hinged out and downwards when the ship cleared for action.

sea-going qualities within certain limits, ranked as assets; a few years before "the bigger the better" had been the axiom behind the line-of-battle ship whose towering walls had now become a liability.

Had the little "P.A." been completed to the original design she would have been an extraordinarily interesting ship. But during her four years construction, guns doubled in size and power and new ships had to be adapted to carry them. Delays in the delivery of material kept the hull two years on the stocks, and then uncertainty about armament postponed completion for nearly as long. Even before the Armstrong breech-loaders were withdrawn from service, Coles was agitating to have her armed with more powerful weapons, and for preference the 12-ton 10·5-in. 300-pdr. then in process of manufacture, which he maintained could easily be worked in his cupolas although impracticable in a broadside battery. Now, in March 1864 Captain Cooper Key of the *Excellent* had given it as his considered opinion that the 6½-ton gun (9·2-in. 100-pdr.) was *the heaviest that could be properly manhandled aboard ship* because of difficulties in providing a satisfactory mounting; hence the Board was reluctant to countenance any change to the 12-ton S.B. then undergoing tests in the *Excellent* which Coles wanted in his turrets. For although the new piece made a good show on paper the Board was not in ignorance of its performances on trial, and appeared quite justified in withholding a decision until after various vicissitudes it appeared likely that the gun would soon be ready for issue. To accommodate the bigger calibre it was decided to reduce the number of turrets to four, and mount a single gun in each of the first three, leaving the fourth with two 110-pdr. B.L. However, by February 1865 the "Woolwich" system of rifled M.L. had been more or less proved and a 12½-ton gun and mounting accepted for service. Four of these were, therefore, assigned to the *Prince Albert*, and when she entered into service early in 1866 her broadside of 250-pdrs. was only one less than that of the contemporary *Bellerophon* of twice her tonnage.

The lay-out on deck was essentially simple—just two turrets before and abaft the funnel with a light superstructure carrying the boats, and an oval conning tower abaft the foremast. The fore-and-aft hurricane deck was not fitted until 1866-7 with the addition of a charthouse the following year.

Prince Albert as she appeared at the 1887 Review at Spithead. Note the threefold steering wheel on the flying bridge abaft the foremast and her Nordenfelt machine guns. The turrets are hidden by the hinged iron bulwarks raised to provide additional freeboard.

ARMAMENT

The original six cupolas were to have been made up of 4-in. plates backed by 16-in. teak to the weight of 80 tons in all. But experiments having shown that thicker armour was preferable to the heavy backing they were replaced by four 111-ton turrets of 5½-in. iron with 10-in. faces and a 14-in. teak backing. The turrets revolved upon a central cylinder large enough for men to enter from below, their weight being distributed on bevelled wheels running upon a metal ring on the main deck like a turn-table. The armoured portion rose 4½ ft. above the weather deck which sloped upwards towards the centre-line with a camber of 2½ ft. and served as a glacis. The roofs had double rails for stowing hammocks and could be used as rifle pits.

Unlike the American turrets which had steam training gear, those in the *Prince Albert* were worked by manual power only—both inside and outside the turret by rack and pinion and by a system of handspikes on the main deck. A full revolution could be made in about a minute by eighteen men, but according to Commander William Dawson:

"The men who control the revolutions are out of sight of the director of the turret, and cannot observe what they are doing nor see the motions of their director; they can only act in blind obedience to his voice, by the inflections of which alone they can guess the urgency or the amount of motion required."

The 12-tonners, then the heaviest guns in the Service, were worked by what was called "machinery" with the carriage running on a slide in place of trucks. To minimize the vertical size of the gun port (through which the gun numbers were exposed to rifle fire) while obtaining adequate elevation and depression, gun plus carriage and slide were bodily raised and lowered by screws acting separately or in pairs at each end of the slide. The change from highest elevation to extreme depression took only 2½ minutes—a great improvement upon the system used in the *Royal Sovereign*.

A few machine guns were afterwards spaced along the flying deck.

ARMOUR

The hull was given 4½-in. plating with 3¼-in. at the ends and 18-in. teak backing; below the ¾-in. glacis deck the turrets were not plated. Although the total weight of armour and backing is given as 879 tons (22·4 per cent. of the displacement), a considerable proportion of this was due to the heavy teak.

MACHINERY

The *Prince Albert* was the first capital ship to be engined by Humphreys and Tennant. On trial she worked up to 2,130 I.H.P. with the boilers showing 23 lb. pressure and the 17 ft. 4-bladed screw making 61 revs. New boilers were installed in 1878, but she never received any auxiliary machinery.

RIG

Coles pressed for a full rig as he wanted her to be a sea-going ship in terms of canvas, but the Board required fore-and-aft steadying sail only.

GENERAL

There were complaints about poor habitability and bad sanitary arrangements, which the Board excused on the grounds that her duties would be confined to harbour service where shortcomings in such respects could be obviated.

In accordance with the Queen's express wishes the little ship was allowed to remain on the Navy List for thirty-three years, and so achieved one of the longest lives on the effective list of any British armoured ship, although during her later years she was of value only as a sentimental relic to the Sovereign.

"PRINCE ALBERT"

Commissioned at Portsmouth 30 June 1866; trials and alterations '66-'67. Passed into 1st Div. Devonport Reserve in July '73. Specially commissioned for the Particular Service Squadron which assembled at Portland under Ad. Cooper Key, August '78 during the Russian war scare; after which she was kept in Reserve, only commissioning for the Jubilee Review in '87 and manœuvres in '89 with the Devonport reserve. Relegated to Dockyard Reserve May '98.

Sold December '99 for £7,025 after 33 years' service.

Looking back along the forty years of slow and often rather confused development which separated the *Prince Albert* from the first all-centre-line *Michigan* of 1905, we can see that in this experimental turret ship Watts produced the perfect battleship in miniature although the Board was far from appreciating it. Unhampered by full rig, the basic design could have been enlarged and given the necessary freeboard for a sea-going type, with paired guns and more localized protection over the turret bases so that something resembling the *Orion* could have been evolved. Such a type might very well have served without much in the way of alterations until the advent of secondary guns.

But because of the overriding demands for sail power the possibilities of the *Prince Albert* as precursor of a sea-going type remained unrealized. Being forty years before her time, she was merely relegated to the backwaters, from where she watched first the passing of a diverse procession of broadside samples born of hemp and canvas, and later the freaks of the "transitional period" which in turn gave way to White's creations. The cycle was completed eleven years after the first turret ship to be built on the Thames had made her final voyage, when in 1910 the keel of the all-centre-line-gunned *Thunderer*, the last Thames-built battleship, was laid down at the Thames Ironworks.

"ROYAL SOVEREIGN"

Built	*Laid down*	*Launched*	*Completed*	*Cost*
Portsmouth	17 Dec. '49	25 April '57	20 Aug. '64	£180,572

Dimensions $240\frac{1}{2}' \times 62' \times 21\frac{1}{2}'/25' = 5{,}080$ tons displacement.
Hull and armour 3,800 tons. Equipment 1,280 tons.

Guns 5 10·5-in. 300-pdr. (150 lb. round shot) $12\frac{1}{2}$-ton M.L.

Armour Sides $5\frac{1}{2}''$; turrets $10''$-$5\frac{1}{2}''$; deck $1''$; conning tower $5\frac{1}{2}''$.
Ship's side 36" oak. Total weight 960 tons. Hull 560 tons.

Complement 300.

Machinery Maudslay. Return connecting rod.
2-cyl. 82", stroke 4', revs. 54.
N.H.P. 800. I.H.P. 2,460 = 11 knots.

Constructors A. Abethall and W. Craddock.

Points of interest:

(1) The first British turret-ship to be completed, and the only one to have a timber hull.
(2) The first British capital ship to carry her main armament outside the hull.

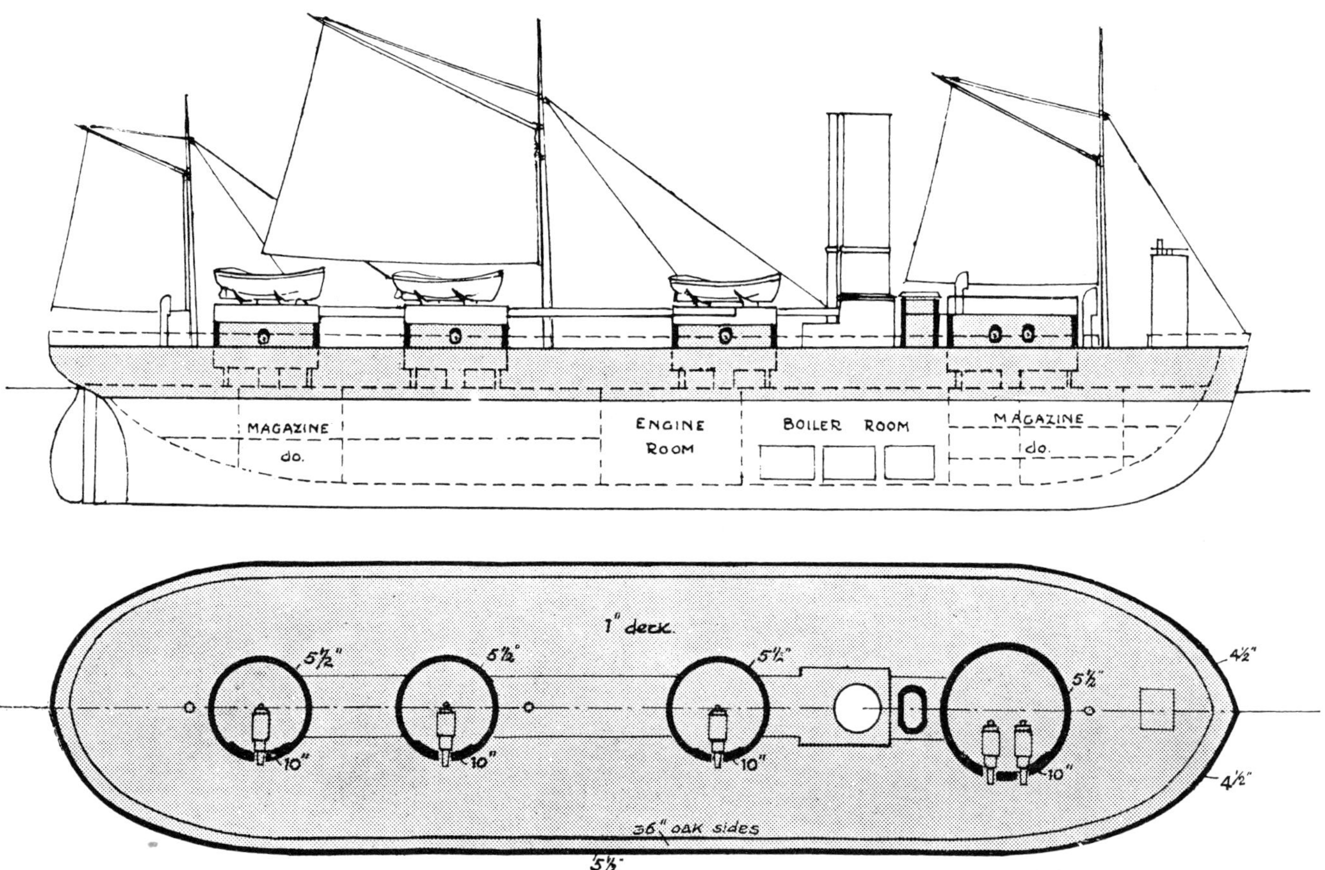

ROYAL SOVEREIGN, 1862.

As the year 1861 is memorable for the passing of the wooden ships-of-the-line, so 1862 is even more so for the advent of the turret ship in the British Navy. At the same time as the *Prince Albert* was ordered Somerset decided to try the experiment advocated by Coles of cutting down a line-of-battle ship, armouring her and equipping her with turrets. Coles declared his belief that in these mastless turret ships we should have the best type of coast-defence vessel, and as something like £20,000,000 was said to be locked up in two- and three-deckers whose fighting value was rapidly reaching a vanishing point, he felt that a full-scale effort to give this moribund fleet another span of usefulness should be made without delay. But the Constructors did not view the project very favourably. Heavy wooden hulls intended for sail power were not shaped for kindliness to turrets, but they conceded that a trial conversion would demonstrate whether the scheme was really worth while when compared with the results obtained with a specially designed iron hull.

The 131-gun *Royal Sovereign* recently completed at Portsmouth was selected, and the order to proceed with her conversion received on 4 April 1862. The process of demolition started three weeks before the keel of the *Prince Albert* was laid at Poplar, and as the wooden hull was cut down the iron one slowly took shape. Both were afloat early in 1864, but the *Royal Sovereign* carried out her gun trials nearly eighteen months before the *Prince Albert* left the Thames.

The work of dismantling all the structure above the lower deck and fitting out as an ironclad took just under two years. For an experiment which might justify considerable expectations Coles urged that she deserved more expeditious labour than was accorded to her; in addition there were delays through the freeboard being cut down too much amidships and having to be built up again. Two years and four months may have seemed a leisurely rate of progress to the inventor intolerant of delay and observing the speed-up being applied to the *Bellerophon* on the stocks.

The *Royal Sovereign* in Plymouth Sound during her first cruises and gun tests. Her four turrets can be seen above the raised bulwarks, with the lion figurehead stowed inboard just forward of the "heads" ventilator. Later the funnel extension was cut down by half.

The hull above water when cut down and armoured resembled a barge, with a length-to-beam ratio of less than 4 : 1—the smallest ever employed in a British armoured ship. The stern was finished off in rounded section to protect the rudder, and the bow only differentiated by the bare indication of a stem piece, while the sides between the foremost and after turrets were parallel to the section of maximum beam, providing great buoyancy. The freeboard ran from 7 ft. amidships to 8 ft. at the bows. Hull and decks were specially strengthened to enable them to withstand such strains as could result from turret weight and firing stresses, the 36-in. timber sides being reinforced by diagonal iron riders while the upper deck beams were double the usual number and attached to iron knees. The turrets were supported upon the main deck and projected through the cambered upper deck as in the *Prince Albert*.

Because the boilers in the three-decker had been placed forward of amidships and there was no question of alterations below decks, the turrets were disposed one forward of the funnel and three abaft it. A light fore-and-aft bridgeway connected these latter, and upon it the davit boats were stowed when at sea. Around the topsides ran thin iron bulwarks 3½ ft. high, hinged to drop outwards when the guns were in action.

Certainly the most imposing feature was the huge funnel, required to provide the necessary draught, but actually only 10 ft. higher above water than those in the *Warrior* with her 17 ft. extra freeboard. An oval conning tower stood between this and the foremost turret, the roofs being connected to form a bridge. Forward of the foremast a tall ventilating trunk screened the galley funnel, and up in the bows a gilded lion striding a pedestal served as a figurehead. For safety at sea this was mounted on rails and could be stowed well inboard.

ARMAMENT

Five 80-ton shields shaped like truncated cones each housing a pair of 68-pdrs. or 110-pdrs. were included in the original design, and Coles records that it took eight months' correspondence to achieve the adoption of the 300-pdr. piece—for which delay he blamed official ineptitude to realize the possibilities of installing the heaviest guns when they could be carried with safety and advantage.

Although nominally a rifled 10·5-in. M.L. firing a 300-lb. elongated projectile, only two of the fifteen guns made were actually rifled (*see* p. 37). The remaining guns being issued as smooth-bores firing either a 168-lb. steel or a 150-lb. spherical shot with a 50-lb. charge, and five of these were allotted to the *Royal Sovereign.* Two were mounted in the foremost and one in each of the other turrets. In 1867 they were replaced by 9-in. 12½-ton M.L.R.

The turrets were similar to those in the *Prince Albert* except that that forward contained two guns, and rose 5 ft. above deck. In all the ½-in. iron skin was covered with 14-in. teak and 5½-in. plating with an additional layer of 4½-in. plating over the face for 6 ft. each side of the ports. The roof of the foremost turret was surrounded by a handrail and served as a bridge; the single turret roofs had hammock rails forming rifle pits. Beneath the main deck below each turret was a 30-ton foundation of timber and iron supports all included in the weights of the turrets—163 tons for the double and 151 tons for the singles.

The 12-ton smooth-bore M.L. had metal carriages and slides of an earlier type than in the *Prince Albert* and were the first of such "heavy" guns in the Service. Being worked by "machinery" in place of ropes, they marked a new era in gunnery; henceforth, Scott's mountings allowed for increasingly heavy guns to be taken afloat and trained with safety and ease in heavy weather. With this mounting and slide the change from highest elevation to extreme depression could be accomplished in half an hour under smooth water conditions. According to the Senior Lieutenant, during her first commission practice from the double turret was as fast as from the singles when an aimed rate of three rounds in five minutes could be maintained. Although 30 men made up the crew for each gun the Gunner stated that he had "superintended casting the gun loose with all the sea-fastenings, running in and running out and loading with 12 gun numbers." It was necessary to discharge the twin guns together as the marines taking numbers three and four declined to go to their station as loaders while alternative guns were being fired on account of the danger of fire being blown back through the port while they were handling 80 lb. of powder. The control officer had to stand with his head partially exposed through the turret roof where "he could be picked off by rifle fire," but despite several applications for a sighting hood or slot in the turret face no such provision was ever made.

To see whether a Coles turret would stand up to heavy gunfire better than Ericsson's, a trial was made on 15 January 1866, when three rounds were fired from a 9-in. gun in the *Bellerophon* with a 43-lb. charge at 200 yds. range against the after turret of the *Royal Sovereign*, in order to test the resistance of the turrets and their liability to jam. Neither the two direct hits on the face and back, nor the glancing hit aimed at the glacis, caused any interference with the turning of the turret, although the plates were dislocated and pierced by the second hit aimed at the back.

The only condition under which concussion was felt inside a turret was in the second one, when the foremost, trained to extreme bearing aft, fired both guns simultaneously. The concussion was "inconvenient" but in no way prevented the men from working the gun. As Captain Cooper Key stated, "I felt it myself, but I am accustomed to it a good deal."

ARMOUR

Because of her greater beam and draught, thicker armour could be carried than in the *Prince Albert* and 5½-in. plating with 4½-in. ends covered the entire hull to a depth of 3 ft. below water. As the 36-in. timber sides formed the backing, the 560 tons listed as armour comprised plating only.

MACHINERY

Engined by Maudslay, the machinery was of the return connecting-rod type with two 82-in. cylinders having a 4-ft. stroke. With 2,460 I.H.P. she recorded just 11 knots instead of 12·25 knots realized as a three-decker—the difference being due to the increased draught as an ironclad.

Coles designed a novel method of working the cables from the lower deck by steam capstans, the men being well protected from fire so that a bow or stern anchor could be let go or picked up while the guns were in action.

RIG

The *Royal Sovereign* had the distinction of being the first British capital ship without square rig, her three pole masts carrying steadying sail only.

SEA-GOING QUALITIES

Having very reduced freeboard with a low centre of gravity, great beam, and a sharp rise in floor, it was only to be expected that the *Royal Sovereign* would roll quickly, although she proved a good if somewhat uncomfortable sea boat. When put into the Portland Race during a heavy gale the roll was 11 degrees each way ten times a minute; but even during her maximum roll of 15 degrees she fired ten rounds from the fore turret without any water entering, the ports being closed by pendulum stoppers during loading.

The maximum draught of 25 ft. militated against general inshore service, and her one and only trip abroad was a run over to Cherbourg in September 1865 made at 6 to 7 knots with a head sea and a wind of 4 to 6. Her Captain reported:

> "As she now stands she is the most formidable vessel of war I have ever been aboard of; she would easily destroy—if her guns were rifled—any of our present ironclads."

GENERAL

As the first demonstration of the practical value of turrets the *Royal Sovereign* proved a complete vindication for Coles' system; but from the "conversion" point of view she showed that the experiment was hardly worth while so long as we had slips available for building iron hulls. Comparing cost and results the specially designed ship would put the razee out of court, especially when experience with the building of iron hulls led to greater economy in weight. In comparing the two turret ships on a percentage basis the advantages of iron construction became more obvious, although the *Royal Sovereign* had thicker armour and an extra gun.

	"*Royal Sovereign*"	"*Prince Albert*"
Dimensions	240′ × 62′ × 23¼′ (mean).	240′ × 48′ × 19½′ (mean).
Displacement	5,080 tons	3,880 tons
Hull	3,240 „ (63%)	2,101 „ (54%)
Equipment	1,280 „ (25%)	900 „ (23%)
Armour	560 „ (11%)	879 „ (22·6%)
Cost	£180,572 (conversion)	£208,345.

As already noted, the "armour" in *Prince Albert* includes the 18-in. teak backing, and the "equipment" of *Royal Sovereign* the 120 tons of timber foundations below the turrets.

General accommodation both for officers and men was regarded as "very fair" by her First Lieutenant, who considered that "no iron ship is very healthy; there is a dampness in them, and in hot weather we feel the want of side ventilation"—which applied specially to the *Royal Sovereign* with no scuttles in her hull. Captain Cooper Key considered that the low freeboard made her living accommodation bad.

"ROYAL SOVEREIGN"

Commissioned at Portsmouth 7 July '64 for Channel cruises and gun tests; became tender to the *Excellent* and paid off in October '66. Again commissioned in July '67 for the Naval Review and later was again attached to the *Excellent* as gunnery ship until replaced by the *Glatton* in July '73, when she was relegated to the 4th Reserve and sold in 1885 for £7,936.

Captain Cooper Key as Captain of the *Excellent* took a keen interest in this epoch-making ship and spent a lot of time aboard her while her turrets and guns were under test. When reporting on her he gave his opinion of the turret system as follows:

Advantages:

(1) Great command of horizontal training which would be especially useful if engines or steering gear were disabled in action; and it might enable a ship in a swell to be placed so as to secure a steady platform.
(2) The power of training while loading, and to turn away the port for safety, to keep the sea out of the port, or to keep the gun bearing.
(3) More complete security for the gun's crew.
(4) The removal of a large portion of the weight in armour from the side to amidships.

Disadvantages:

(1) There were fewer guns, and the offensive and defensive power would be reduced if the turret ship were attacked by more than one ship or fort at the same time.
(2) If one gun or turret were disabled, a larger proportion of the armament would be thrown out.
(3) The turret machinery was liable to be damaged or disabled.
(4) Heavy guns could not be worked with the same rapidity in a turret as on the broadside, as the men have not so much space to work in, and do not stand on a level with the gun carriage.

In the violent controversy then being raged between the advocates of broadside and turret guns the real virtue of the *Royal Sovereign* type was not perceived. If battleships were going to carry eight or ten heavy guns in place of a numerous battery of smaller ones, then it would hardly be possible to design a more powerful ship than one with four or five turrets. Unlike all broadside ships, the *Royal Sovereign* was completely armoured; yet she was essentially a broadside ship capable of fighting any other broadside ship, not only because of the weight of her guns, but because of their number. To equal her, a broadside ship would have to carry double her armament—with the compensating adjustments in other military qualities, and this at a time when it was not considered possible to work anything larger than a 6½-ton gun on the broadside in a seaway (1864).

A year later when 12-ton guns had been experimentally mounted in the *Minotaur* there was no reason why a heavy gun should not be worked as well on the broadside as in a turret. But the advantages of the turret in commanding such an extent of horizontal training was of far more importance than any one of the advantages of the broadside. The question for consideration was whether it counterbalanced the disadvantages.

In the Service the chief objection to the turret ship lay in the difficulty of providing a full rig which would not seriously mask gun-fire. Full rig was regarded as essential for any sea-going ship; hence, although for harbour defence, short voyages, or attacking a fortified position the turret ship would prove of great value, Captain Key did not consider that we could retain that superiority at sea which was necessary to our existence as a first-rate Power, if we armed our fleet for ocean service in all parts of the world entirely on the turret system. In any case, he recommended that turrets should always be designed to carry two guns instead of one, as the increase of weight would be small in proportion to the increase in power. Although the *Prince Albert* and *Royal Sovereign* were the first turret ships to be designed for the British Navy, they were actually antedated on the stocks by two ships laid down at Lairds in 1862 and purchased in 1864, which entered service the next year, some fourteen months after the *Royal Sovereign* had hoisted the pennant. The circumstances under which the *Scorpion* and *Wivern* came to hoist the White Ensign are of interest as providing the first occasion on which warships built to the order of another Government were acquired for H.M. service. In March 1862 Captain James D. Bulloch, naval agent for the Confederate States in Europe during the Civil War, contracted with Lairds for two ironclad double-turret rams to cost £93,750 each, exclusive of guns and ammunition—as part of a considerable programme of armoured ships and frigates which were intended to break the Federal blockade on the Southern ports and lay some of the Northern cities under ransom. Bulloch had ordered them under his own name as a blind, but in January 1863, when they were nearly half finished Lord John Russell, Foreign Secretary, intimated that he was aware of their destination and told Bulloch that they would not be allowed to put to sea unless as the property of a nation not at war.

In order to comply with this, Bulloch arranged with some French bankers to purchase the ships on behalf of the Egyptian Government, with the object of transferring them at sea to the Confederate agents, and to this end they were named *El Toussan* and *El Mounassir*. As the Khedive was known to be in the market for the purchase of ironclads the arrangement seemed plausible enough, but Russell was well informed by the American Minister as to the real state of things, and in October 1863 the ships were seized by the Government and suit instituted for their forfeiture.

At the best this can only be regarded as a very arbitrary step, as Bulloch had been assured by counsel that he was acting within the law if his ships were not sent out armed and equipped—which opinion had been sustained by the Court of Exchequer in the *Alexandra* case, when it was ruled that the subjects of a neutral Power had as much right to sell ships to a belligerent as they had to sell munitions. The Government observed a very shifting policy in holding the two "rams," but already the *Alabama*, built by Lairds, had achieved a great reputation as a Confederate corsair, having managed to slip away from the Mersey what time her exact legal status was being debated. Rather than risk additional complications—and the *Alabama's* depredations were to have dire results upon our exchequer—the Government ordered the Mersey Customs to detain the ships, and in view of the fact that they were well gunned it was thought advisable that the *Prince Consort* should be there in attendance in case of emergency. But although—as already related—the new ironclad failed to make Liverpool owing to stress of weather, there was no mistaking the Government's intention to uphold our newly declared status by armed force, and in order to compromise the dispute as to the exact legality of their seizure, the two rams were purchased for the Navy in 1864 at £30,000 in excess of the contract price, and renamed *Scorpion* and *Wivern*.

"SCORPION" AND "WIVERN"

	Builder	*Laid down*	*Launched*	*Completed*	*Cost*
"*Scorpion*"	Lairds	April '62	4 July '63	10 Oct. '65	£111,614
"*Wivern*"	,,	,,	29 Aug. '63	10 Oct. '65	£118,769

Dimensions $224\frac{1}{2}' \times 42\frac{1}{2}' \times 15\frac{1}{2}/17' = 2{,}750$ tons displacement.
Hull and armour 1,870 tons. Equipment 860 tons.

Guns 4 9-in. M.L.R. (later 6 m.g.).

Armour Sides $4\frac{1}{2}''$-3" (bows)—2" (stern). Backing 10"-8".
Turrets 5" with 10" faces; skin $\frac{3}{4}''$. Total 415 tons.

Machinery Lairds. Horizontal direct-acting engines.
I.H.P. 1,450=10 to 10·5 knots. Max. 11·5 knots.
2 cyl. 56"; stroke 33". Revs. 70.
3-bladed screw, 14' diam.; pitch 20'.
4 boilers. Pressure 20 lb.

Coal 336 tons. Radius 1,210 miles at 10 knots.

Complement 153.

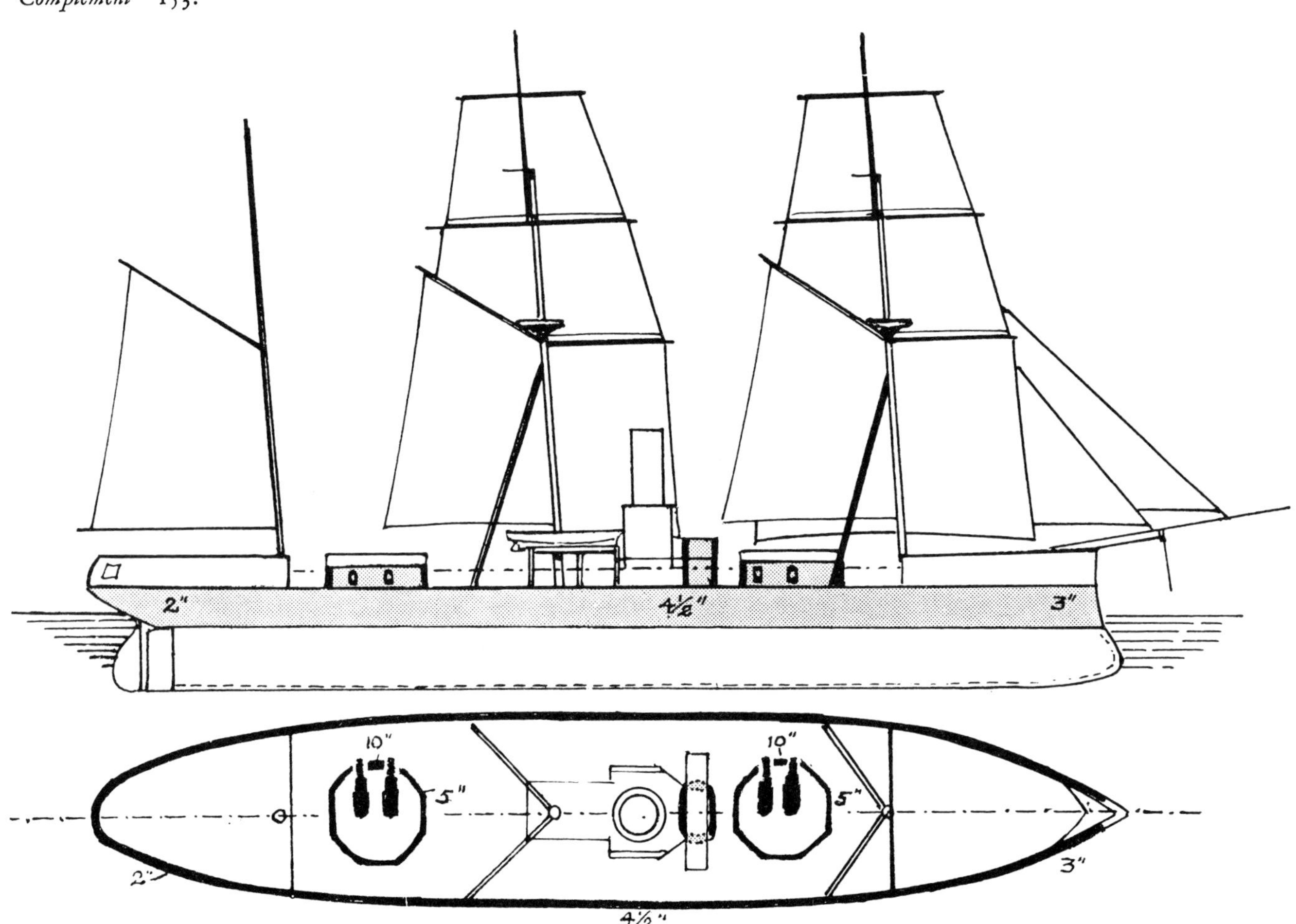

SCORPION and *WIVERN.*

These two were the first of thirteen armoured ships built for foreign navies which have at one time or another been transferred to the White Ensign as an emergency measure. Not having been intended to fill British requirements, all were deficient in some respects and the *Scorpion* and *Wivern* were among the worst of the bad bargains. As units of the Confederate Navy having sea-going qualities possessed by none of the U.S. ironclads, they would probably have been exceedingly troublesome to the Federals; in our own organization they were best employed on local defence duties abroad, where their relative value was highest. Their definite claim to distinction was in being the first turret ships to be built with a forecastle and poop and therefore able to take part in high sea operations, as distinct from the low freeboard monitor types which could not fight their guns in a seaway.

For their size they were good enough little ships, very well armed and sufficiently protected to stand up to anything flying the Federal colours on the high seas, with a radius of action far in excess of that of the *Prince Albert.* Internally the hulls were divided into six main compartments amidships, with smaller ones at the bow and stern, wing passages, and a double bottom from turret to turret.

Amidships the freeboard was 6 ft. only, but hinged bulwarks raised this another 5 ft.; the topgallant forecastle provided "tolerably commodious" accommodation for the men and incidentally was fitted to mount one or two heavy guns if necessary, while in the poop the captain's cabin had ports for two 32-pdrs. Without this additional armament the ships had no chase guns, and omission to fit them was probably due to a desire to test their sea-going qualities before imposing extra weights which would burden their extremities.

ARMAMENT

Early in 1865 the *Scorpion* was allotted four of the 12-ton "300-pdr." smooth-bores firing a 168-lb. shot, but on completion they both carried 9-in. M.L.R.—then the heaviest weapon in the Service and the first to have

The *Wivern* in the Hamoaze 1865, during her first commission. Movable portions of the bulwarks are lowered to expose the turret guns, the hammocks being stowed around the turret crowns to form rifle pits. The funnel extension is lowered. Note the topgallants fidded abaft the topmasts and the steps and hand rails up the struts which do not obstruct the firing arcs unduly.

Captain R. A. E. Scott's iron mounting and slides. This was of a more primitive nature than the model used in the *Royal Sovereign,* and the change from full elevation to full depression took *one hour* in smooth water with an even keel.

A submission was made that 64-pdrs. should be mounted in the forecastle of the *Wivern,* but apart from a few quick-firers no additions were made to the original armament throughout their service.

ARMOUR

The turrets were polygonal with an internal diameter of 23 ft. and of composite construction having 22-in. teak between the ribs at the back of the 5-in. plating, and an inner skin and wooden sheathing to lessen the risk of nuts and screw ends flying off when hit. A patch of 10-in. plating covered the turret faces. The hull sides were completely covered from bow to stern from the upper deck to $3\frac{1}{4}$ ft. below water by armour $4\frac{1}{2}$ in. amidships, tapering to 3 in. forward and $2\frac{1}{2}$ in. aft.

MACHINERY

These were the first armoured ships in the Service to be engined by Lairds, and in them three-bladed screws made their appearance. With a complement of 336 tons, the coal carried equalled one-eighth of the displacement—an unusually high capacity, and provided to allow for extended high-seas operations under the Confederate flag.

RIG

As cruising ships they were heavily rigged for their size with different types of masting. Both were dressed as barques with lower and top masts in one piece, but while *Scorpion* carried double topsails *Wivern* was given struts to her fore and main masts instead of shrouds and hoisted single topsails, topgallants and royals. She was thus the first ship to carry tripod masts—Coles' expedient to avoid masking gunfire by standing rigging. Aloft was another peculiarity, the topgallant masts being fidded on the *after* side of the topmast crosstrees and struck

This photo of the *Scorpion* was taken at Bermuda in 1897. The hinged iron bulwarks have been removed and a light bridge connects the forecastle and poop, with pole masts as a harbour defence ship.

abaft all, thus allowing them to be sent down without lowering the topsails. The mizen carried a spanker and crossed a spare topsail yard.

SEA-GOING QUALITIES

About 1868 their rig was altered to fore and aft sail only. To test behaviour in a seaway both ships were taken into the Portland race with a 10 to 11 wind. The *Scorpion* was laid broadside on with the sea on her quarter and proved buoyant and steady. Her Captain reported: "I found her at all times buoyant and seaworthy and should have no hesitation in taking her anywhere for passage; but as a cruising man-o'-war the discomfort from constantly wet decks would have materially interfered with her efficiency." The *Wivern* with weights in her turrets in place of guns was unquestionably inferior, but this was attributed to the tripod masting.

Later reports show that they behaved well at sea although rolling deeply. *Scorpion* registered over 30 degrees off Dover—how much more is not known as the pendulum on board could not show inclination beyond this. The forecastle kept them fairly dry with wind ahead, but off the bow they became uncomfortable and at times dangerous from the amount of water taken aboard. Before the wind, steering was wild owing to a flat floor and small rudder area; under sail the three-bladed screw made them erratic to the helm.

GENERAL

In front of the funnel—which was telescopic—stood the pilot house, with a light athwartships bridge on the top of it. But as the bridge ladders and stanchions interfered with observation from below, it was regarded as useless and was afterwards replaced by a conning tower. Early in 1867 a flying bridge connecting the forecastle to the poop was added at Coles' suggestion, and greatly improved communication and comfort at sea.

In June 1873 it was decided that *Scorpion* should be deprived of her forecastle and poop, masts and upper deck fittings and converted into a harbour defence monitor with all-round fire. But the work was held up on account of expense and the project abandoned in 1878.

"SCORPION"

Commissioned July '65; Channel '65-'66; refit; Channel '68-'69. Fitted for service at Bermuda where she arrived November '69 and paid off next month. Remained there as harbour ship for 30 years, being fitted with searchlights and q.f. guns in '90. Used as a target and sunk in 1901; raised '02 and sold February '03 for £736. Foundered on her way to Boston U.S.A.

"WIVERN"

Commissioned 28 September '65; served in the Channel '65-'66 (burst a 9-in. gun in '67, the breech weighing aton being blown off owing to flaws in material. With thirteen people in the turret there were no casualties). Paid off in Reserve at Devonport August '68 for refit. Coastguard ship at Hull January '70-October '70 and then Reserve again from '70-'80. Sent to Hong Kong as harbour defence ship '80 being paid off into Reserve there, eventually becoming a distilling ship.

Sold in June 1922.

As an alternative to the cost of building small coast-defence turret ships, Somerset proposed to make further conversions into ironclads from line-of-battle ships, frigates, corvettes and sloops as soon as the *Prince Consort* group were finished and their merits as armoured ships determined. The wisdom of wholesale conversions when applied to all types of fighting ships was questioned, especially as there was still considerable doubt as to the durability of wooden-hulled ironclads; but most of the new French ships being timber built, it was considered justifiable in the light of their experience.

The period was one when the application of armour to a ship was considered almost essential in order to secure her survival under gunfire—which armouring was to include small as well as large vessels, hence the mention of corvettes and sloops. This phase of thought did not last long, but was productive of several interesting armoured ships of small tonnage which now come under review; however, after the three sloops *Research*, *Enterprise* and *Favorite* had been selected for conversion and two corvettes, the *Pallas* and *Penelope*, ordered to be built, the idea of an "all-armoured" navy was discarded. Apart from the three armoured gunboats *Viper*, *Vixen* and *Waterwitch* ordered some years later, armour protection was not applied to ships below capital rank until the introduction of coast-defence turret ships.

The task of redesigning the *Research*, *Enterprise* and *Favorite* as ironclads was entrusted to a newcomer in the Constructor's department, Mr. E. J. Reed—a young and untried naval architect who had attracted the attention of the First Lord and was to have a meteoric rise to fame.

Chapter 16

SIR E. J. REED, K.C.B.

Chief Constructor 1863–70

ON THE retirement of Mr. Isaac Watts in 1863 Mr. Edward James Reed was offered and accepted the post of Chief Constructor by the Duke of Somerset, First Lord from 1859 to 1866. Reed had been apprenticed to a shipwright in Sheerness Dockyard and in 1849 was chosen to enter the School of Mathematics and Naval Construction at Portsmouth then under the direction of Dr. Woolley. His appointment as a supernumerary draughtsman at Sheerness was made in 1852, but finding the routine work without responsibility too irksome, he left the Service the same year. In 1853 he became editor of the *Mechanics Magazine*—which conducted such a crusade against the Armstrong breech-loaders—and also undertook private work as a marine architect, being elected secretary to the Institute of Naval Architects in 1860.

During 1854 Reed had submitted designs for a fast armoured frigate to the Admiralty, but the need for such a type of ship was not admitted and the designs were rejected. In 1861 his second project was placed before the Board—this time for a rigged armoured screw corvette of what was to become known as the "central battery" type, of 2,250 tons B.O.M. and 600 nominal h.p. The design presented an iron ship with a 6-in. armour belt around the waterline from 2 ft. above to 3 or 4 ft. below water with a deck of ¾-in. iron at its upper edge. Above this was an armoured central battery on the upper deck containing six 68-pdr. pivot guns with an armoured ammunition trunk from below the armour deck. Reed claimed that the vulnerability of part of the upper works was compensated by the advantage of weight saving which permitted of high speed and handiness without extravagant dimensions. He acknowledged the assistance of his brother-in-law, Nathaniel Barnaby, of the Controller's Department, in drawing up the design and stated that a shipbuilder of Deptford named Lungley had a patent for the plan in its general form "as it sprang up originally in connection with a patent of his for unsinkable iron ships," the specification of which Reed had drawn.

The following year (1862) a further project was submitted—this time for the conversion of wooden ships into ironclads on a "belt-and-battery" system. This was accorded encouragement, his services being retained by the Constructor's Department. Three small ships recently commenced were selected for such conversion, the work to be carried out under his supervision. He also offered to the Admiralty drawings for two ships which were accepted as welcome alternatives to the larger and more costly projects designed at Whitehall, and these materialized as *Pallas* and *Bellerophon.*

It was the First Lord who was responsible for this unusual procedure in employing extra-departmental assistance. He saw in the young naval architect that promise of originality which he found lacking in the Admiralty establishment; and having committed one such solecism it is not very surprising that he looked beyond the claims of his professional advisers and appointed the newcomer to the position of Chief Constructor on 9 July 1863.

It was hardly likely that the appointment would be regarded with professional or public approval, and in the debate on the Estimates the member for Chatham (Sir F. Smith) criticized it on the grounds that Reed was not properly qualified and "had never built a ship." This the Chief Constructor resented in a letter which led to his being called to the Bar of the Commons as having committed a breach of privilege.

Reed was thirty-three at the time of his appointment, and for the next seven years the Board were to be greatly influenced by a man of forceful personality who was singularly gifted both in exposition and argument, and had very definite and original ideas on ship design. He was responsible for the introduction of double bottoms and subdivision of the hull against the effects of submarine mines (then called "torpedoes"), and believed in short, handy ships with speed secured by increased power rather than through long hulls and fine lines. He realized that there was a limit to the length beyond which the increase in frictional resistance outweighed the decrease in head resistance, and laid down as a principle that "as the extent and thickness of armour are increased, the proportion of length to breadth should be diminished, and the water-line increased in fulness." Reed maintained that the great reduction in the prime cost of short ships more than compensated for the additional steam power. That such short-hulled models could not maintain speed against a seaway was not realized until they had been tested under service conditions, but as at that time the power of manœuvre was rated more highly than fast steaming under adverse weather conditions this failing was not of much moment.

During his régime the rapid increase in gun calibre led to concentration of the armament amidships in central batteries with bow and stern chasers to afford the end-on fire then regarded as of primary importance. Later, when he came to develop his own ideas as regards turret ships, the breastwork type of quasi-monitor was evolved in which armament became limited to a few guns of the largest calibre with massive protection affording the utmost measure of armoured stability.

The ram he regarded as a primary weapon of offence to the use of which the hull lines should be dedicated.

In attempting to combine heavy guns and armour in small hulls he was not altogether successful in his earlier productions which were described by his press critics as "not fulfilling any condition of their specifications, and whose reconstruction begins on the day they are launched." Later he was to be responsible for outstanding successes like the *Hercules*, *Monarch* and—with certain reservations—the *Devastation*. But his tenure of office was associated with opposition to the turret method of mounting guns as opposed to his box-battery disposition until the pressure of public opinion brought about the construction of the *Monarch*. Actually he was not antagonistic to the turret, and afforded Captain Coles considerable assistance with his earlier conceptions, but—and here he stood alone amongst its protagonists—his appreciation of its possibilities ruled out employment on masted hulls where arcs of fire would be limited to the broadside. For this reason he opposed Coles' projects, and when ordered to design the *Monarch* preferred that she should be regarded more as an Office production than his own conception.

Reed's short, tubby models heeled immoderately until he went to the opposite extreme and then had to correct a too high centre of gravity by excessive ballasting. Although not enjoying the same freedom in design as did his predecessor, he was given far more latitude in interpreting the Board's requirements than were his successors; and thanks to the co-operation and confidence accorded to him by the Controller, Sir Spencer Robinson, his own views certainly dominated his designs.

It was held against him that by progressive experiments in individual ships which sometimes diminished efficiency, he built up a fleet of "samples" deficient in the power of combined manœuvre and constructed at unnecessary expense. But such criticism made no allowances for the primary responsibility of the Board for every ship constructed in accordance with definite requirements and restrictions covering displacement, ordnance, protection, speed, bunkerage, and dimensions. The period was one of rapid growth in gun calibres, so that each ship carried progressively larger weapons and thicker armour to withstand the development of artillery abroad; merely to have repeated the *Bellerophon* from year to year would have been to offer foreign gun-layers increasingly easier targets instead of more and more powerful antagonists.

Reed reached the highest position in the Constructor's Department at one bound. For seven years he enjoyed all the advantages of a confidential position with its opportunities for the accumulation of special experience and knowledge. Then, when his services should have been most valuable to the Navy, he chose to accept the higher remuneration of a commercial appointment—although, as he put it, the strained relationships between the First Lord, Mr. Childers, and himself "were not without their effect" in influencing his decision to leave the Service. He did not remain long with Whitworth at Manchester, becoming chairman of Earle's of Hull in 1871 and started practice as a naval architect in London. He secured a seat for the Liberals in Pembroke in 1874 and represented Cardiff from 1880 to 1895; was appointed a Lord of the Treasury in the short Gladstone Government of 1886, and again had a seat for Cardiff 1900–1905. In the House for many years Reed was the bully of the Admiralty. A power of truculent invective combined with scientific training and ability gave him every advantage in debate, although he was more likely to empty the House than fill it. Sir Nathaniel Barnaby, who succeeded him as D.N.C., became his special target. Every design produced at Whitehall was subjected to merciless criticism becoming more pungent and prejudiced as successive types departed more and more from his own constructional theories. Barnaby was debarred from defending the work of his Department, but when Mr. William H. White—who had been intimately associated with most of Barnaby's designs—became D.N.C. the First Lord (Hamilton) allowed him to read a paper at the I.N.A. on the Naval Defence Act battleships in order to meet Reed in open debate. In this encounter Reed was completely ousted and subsequently became a supporter of Admiralty designs.

He was a prolific writer, a keen advocate of technical education and founder of the Royal School of Naval Architecture in 1864, and from 1865–1905 was Vice-President of the I.N.A. Honours included the C.B. (1868), F.R.S. (1876) and K.C.B. (1880). Sir Edward Reed died in London on 30 November 1906 aged 76.

Chapter 17

"RESEARCH", "ENTERPRISE," "FAVORITE" "LORD WARDEN" AND "LORD CLYDE"

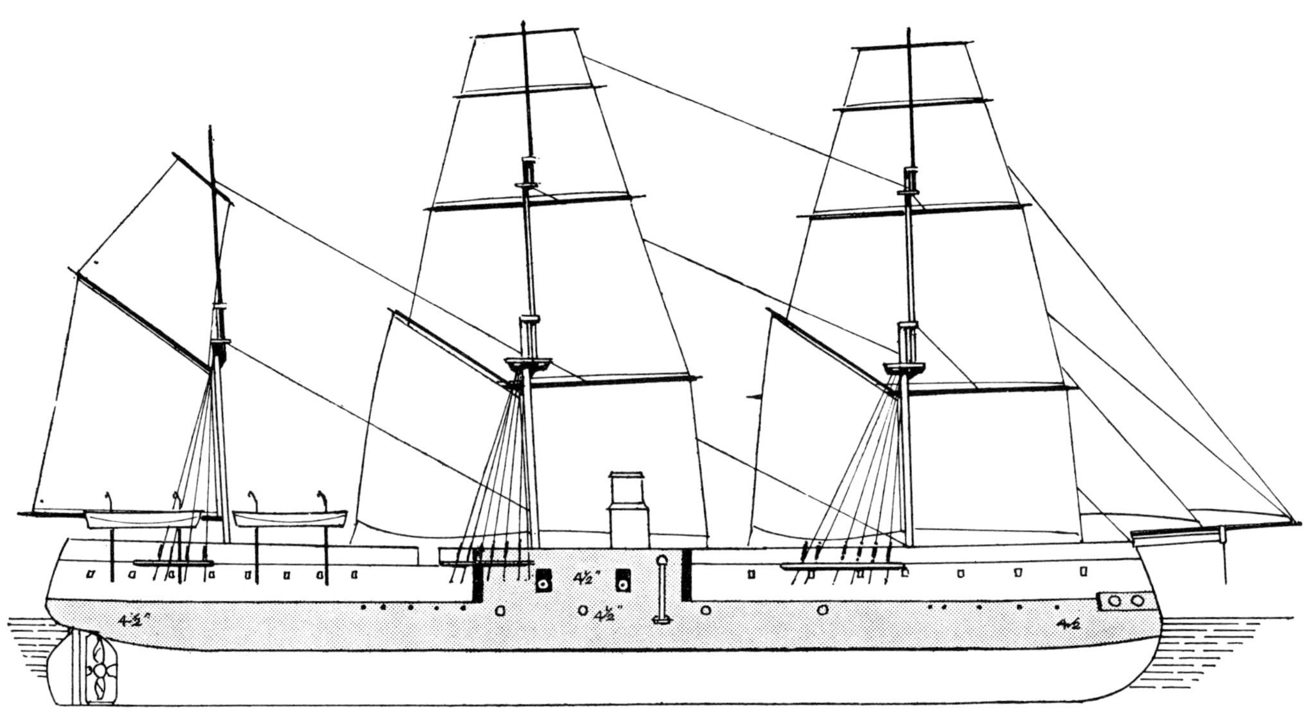

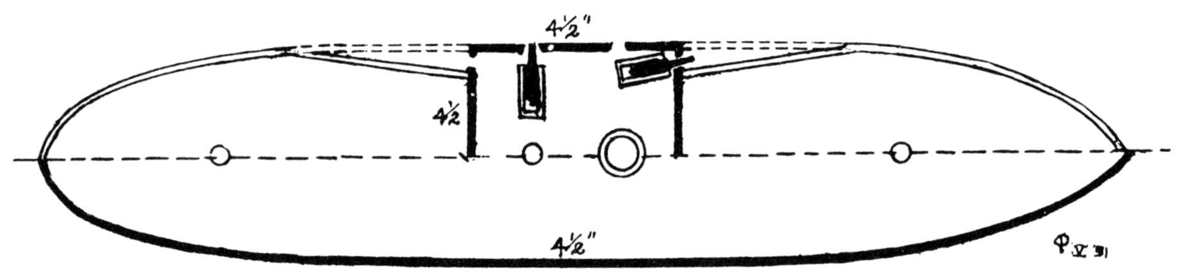

RESEARCH

Builder	*Laid down*	*Launched*	*Completed*	*Cost*
Pembroke	3 Sept. '61	15 Aug. '63	6 April '64	£71,287

Dimensions Original—185′ × 33·2′ × 13/15′ = 1,200 tons.
Converted—195′ × 38·6′ × 13/16·4′ = 1,743 tons.
(Hull and armour 1,280; equipment 620 tons.)

Guns 1864 — 4 100-pdr. Somerset S.B.
Rearmed 1870 — 4 7-in. M.L.R.

Armour Belt and battery 4½″ backing 19½″, bulkheads 4½″.
Total 352 tons.

Complement 139/150.

Sail area 18,250 sq. ft.

Machinery Watt. Horizontal direct. I.H.P. 1,040 = 10·3 knots. Lifting Griffith screw, 12′ diam. 16′ pitch.
2 cyl. 50″. Stroke 24″. Revs. 77/85.
2 tubular boilers. Pressure 28 lb.

Coal 130 tons.

Constructor Chas. Eden.

Special features:

(1) The first light-weight armoured ship to be built.
(2) The first in which provision was made for securing some degree of axial fire from the broadside guns.
(3) The first box-battery ship.

WHEN Reed's proposals to convert the smaller types of wooden-hulled ships into armour-clads were accepted by Somerset as fulfilling Board requirements—and meeting a demand with which the Constructor's Department had been unable to comply—the first vessel to be selected for his prentice hand was the 17-gun sloop *Trent* ordered in November 1860 as one of the *Perseus* class of 950 tons B.O.M. Her name was changed to *Research* when the task of redesigning her as an armoured ship was entrusted to his direction in September 1862. In undertaking her design Reed was faced with greater risks of failure than hopes of success. The Constructor's Department deemed it impracticable to produce a *sea-going* armoured ship of smaller dimensions than 4,000 tons,

Research after her 1869-70 refit when a spar deck was added, and the funnel moved forward of the battery. The two battery ports are open and the recessed hull sides allowing them to obtain some axial fire can be seen clearly.

the only ironclad light-weights at that time being low-freeboard turret ships. To justify her existence, protection would have to be at least 4½ in. and the guns 68-pdrs. or larger, with adequate speed and coal supply.

As sloops carried a heavier armament in proportion to displacement than other types, and were usually slow steamers, the two hulls selected allowed a certain amount of latitude in allotting the various weights to be carried.

Although already a year on the stocks, the *Trent* was only set up in frame so that the necessary modifications could easily be made in her dimensions and form to produce the hull on the lines he had been advocating. Having lengthened her by 10 ft., the beam was increased to a ratio of 1 : 5 and the draught altered to give a trim of 3½ ft. by the stern. Conventional sloop ends were replaced by a ram bow and full oval stern, but the run of the hull profile with topgallant forecastle, poop, and an open waist were retained.

Being a two-decked ship with the main deck just above the water-line, the armament was carried on the upper deck at a height of about 6½ ft. in a 34-ft. box battery amidships. As originally completed the funnel was brought up through this and rose just forward of the main mast; but such an arrangement for protecting the uptakes, although customary in the bigger ironclads with their long batteries, proved quite impracticable when applied to the *Research* with only a very cramped box of armour already overcrowded with four guns, eighty men, the steering wheel, and an ammunition hatch. It was not surprising that inspection reports on her first commissioning complain that the guns could not be properly trained and fired.

ARMAMENT

In place of the former armament of seventeen guns, Reed condensed the offensive power into four 100-pdr. "Somersets," then the most formidable weapon available. As five 32-pdrs. were regarded as equivalent to one 68-pdr. in smashing power, a broadside of two 100-pdrs. would be far more effective than eight of the smaller pieces *against armour*. But was it intended to employ the *Research* against armoured ships? With a two-gun broadside she would have stood a poor chance against opponents of the battle line, whereas when opposing unarmoured vessels the former concentration of smaller calibres would probably have proved the more effective.

For the first time an attempt was made to provide axial fire from broadside guns, and for this reason the *Research* becomes of some historical interest. Reed's scheme was duly approved of by the Controller and Captain of the *Excellent* as an experiment, although its shortcomings were pretty obvious. To allow for fire fore and aft the hull sides before and abaft the battery were recessed and gun ports cut in the bulkheads through which the traversed guns could be pointed towards the bow and stern.

Traversing the guns from the broadside to these end ports meant an extremely risky piece of work in anything of a seaway, and if ever resorted to would have led to difficult and hazardous shooting. However, the *Research* arrangement was followed up in subsequent box-battery ships until embrasures with fixed guns replaced it.

Trial firing before and abaft the beam naturally shook the little ship up considerably, and her critics made the most of it. Minor breakages were grossly exaggerated into major structural damage, and the press worked up quite a scare over "a broken lantern or two and a few cups shaken off their hooks" by the simultaneous firing of all four guns fore and aft.

Describing the arcs of fire from these guns, Captain G. T. Phipps Hornby reported:

> "Judging from what I have seen of the *Enterprise* and the *Research* I should say the bow guns will only train through an angle of 10 or 12 degrees; but then there is a large dead angle before she can bring a broadside gun to bear. To show how large this angle is, I would state an experiment that I saw Admiral Dacres try. He went to inspect both ships at different times; they were lying within two cables of the *Frederick William* 90-gun ship. He said to the Captain, 'Point at the *Frederick William*' the guns being in the broadside ports; he could not bring a gun to bear. The Admiral said, 'Shift the guns'; he could not even then bring a gun to bear. I believe the dead angle was nearly 34 degrees."

A change-over to 7-in. M.L.R. was ordered in June 1866 but postponed, and she did not receive her new guns until the 1869-70 refit.

ARMOUR

This absorbed almost one-fifth of the displacement and so was on a more generous scale than usual and of the same thickness as in the big ships. The belt ran a uniform 4½ in. from 5 ft. below water to 5 ft. above with the same thickness over the battery and bulkheads. Beneath the iron the sides were 19½ in. thick; but for five-sixths of her 195 ft. length the topsides were unprotected wood. As might be expected, there was no weight margin for iron on the decks.

ALTERATIONS

The disadvantages of the open deck amidships soon became manifest and although alterations were decided upon in 1866 it was not until the 1869-70 refit, when she was rearmed, that a spar deck was fitted amidships giving a flush run from stem to stern.

MACHINERY

Horizontal direct-action engines were supplied by Boulton and Watt—the only set made by the famous Soho firm ever to be installed in an armoured ship. The two 50-in. cylinders with a 24-in. stroke worked up to 1,040 I.H.P. for 10·3 knots, steam being supplied by two tubular boilers with a pressure of 28 lb. The bunkers carried 130 tons of coal. No auxiliary steam gear was provided.

RIG

The *Research* was always barque rigged and at her best only 6 knots is recorded. But she was "able to carry sail longer than usual owing to her small spread which the long mast heads enable the ship to carry easily."

Under steam and sail she once made 11·6 knots (31 December 1865), but 9-10 knots was her usual under steam and a meagre coal supply curtailed squadron work.

SEA-GOING QUALITIES

Always reported as a poor seaboat, she rolled abominably and usually remained in harbour during the winter months, justifying the reproach that she was never to be sent over 100 miles away from land. Against a head sea and moderate wind she showed up badly; her captain was once nearly washed overboard and she could hardly make headway on occasion. He reported:

> "I don't consider her, in the old acceptance of the term, a wholesome sea-going ship as compared with wooden ships. At the same time I don't consider she would be in danger of going down in a gale provided proper means were taken to batten her down securely, the means for which, I think, may be improved."

Poor little *Research*! Reed expected great things of her as a light-weight armoured ship, but that she was "probably the very worst vessel, both as a fighting machine and a sea-boat that ever yet went out of a dockyard of any nation pretending to a maritime reputation" (*Standard*, 27 October, 1865) was perhaps a verdict more typical of prejudice against Reed than quite just to an experimental type of ship which could hardly have been more of a success than she proved.

"RESEARCH"

Taken round to Devonport and commissioned in March '64. Channel July '64-May '66. Refit '69-'70; Med. June '71-August '78 when she came home and was placed in Reserve.
Sold in '87.

The second of the three ships selected for conversion by Reed was the 17-gun sloop *Circassian* ordered at Deptford in 1861, her name being somewhat aptly changed to "Enterprise" in July 1862. Although launched and completed after the *Research*, Reed refers to her as "our first small ironclad," so that her design may have been the first to be undertaken.

Although some 400 tons smaller than the *Research*, the same armament was provided, but with less weight of armour; her claim to distinction was in being the first of a "composite" type to be constructed in which a timber hull was combined with iron upper works. This system, while retaining the advantages of wood below water with its slow-fouling properties, rendered the unprotected upper works incombustible. It was intended that the *Enterprise* should be subjected to a long series of tests before this novel form of hull became accepted for other ships. But by the time she commissioned, the decree had gone forth that no further wooden-hulled capital ships were to be built, and the construction of the timber hulls selected for conversion had been advanced too far for such wholesale alterations to be undertaken economically. It was, however, possible to employ composite construction in a number of cruising ships, sloops and gunboats; the French with their limited resources for iron shipbuilding adopted the idea of Reed's and employed it extensively in their armoured ships during the next ten years or so.

Very little was known about the general design during her construction, and Admiral Halstead wrote a discursive letter to the *Daily News* describing her as a new type of cupola ship having a square box in place of a turret—a mistake which arose from her misleading profile when on the slips. Owing to delivery of bad iron from the contractors, construction of the upper ends of the ship was held up while the lower hull and centre section—being of wood—made good progress. Hence the battery could be seen standing up like a tower and suggesting a square cupola (I.N.A. 1863, p. 43).

Having been only a couple of months on the stocks before her new form was decided upon, she can hardly be called a conversion and was practically built anew, the hull being remodelled with a marked ram bow and semicircular stern rising over a low counter. Being a two-decked ship with the main deck just above the waterline, the armament was carried on the upper deck at a height of about 6½ ft. in a 34-ft. box battery amidships. As in the *Research*, the funnel was originally brought up through this to protect the uptakes, but as the same conditions obtained in her battery it had to be moved and led up clear of the forward bulkhead. This change was effected in November 1864 soon after first commissioning.

ARMAMENT

For reasons which do not appear to be on record a mixed armament of two 100-pdr. "Somersets" and two 110-pdr. Armstrong B.L. was allotted for her completion. As the issue of 110-pdrs. ceased the same year it would seem that a shortage of "Somersets" was responsible for thus making things difficult in the magazines. All four guns were replaced by 7-in. M.L.R. during the 1868 refit at Malta.

In order to obtain some sort of axial fire from the battery guns an alternative to the *Research* arrangement was tried in which the topsides before and abaft the battery were slightly laid in and a 12-ft. length of bulwark

"ENTERPRISE"

Builder	*Laid down*	*Launched*	*Completed*	*Cost*
Deptford	5 May '62	9 Feb. '64	3 June '64	£62,474

Dimensions 180′ × 36′ × 12·4/15·10′ = 1,350 tons.
Hull and armour 910 tons. Equipment 440 tons.

Guns	*As completed*	*Rearmed* 1868
	2 100-pdr. Somerset S.B.	4 7-in. M.L.R.
	2 110-pdr. B.L.	

Armour Belt and battery $4\frac{1}{2}''$; bulkheads $4\frac{1}{2}''$; backing $19\frac{1}{2}''$.
Total 195 tons.

Machinery Ravenhill. Horizontal direct-acting.
I.H.P. 690 = 9·9 knots.
2 cyl. 45″; stroke 18″; revs. 90.
Boilers: 2 tubular.

Coal 95 tons.

Complement 130.

Sail area 18,250 sq. ft.

Special feature:
The first ship of composite construction.

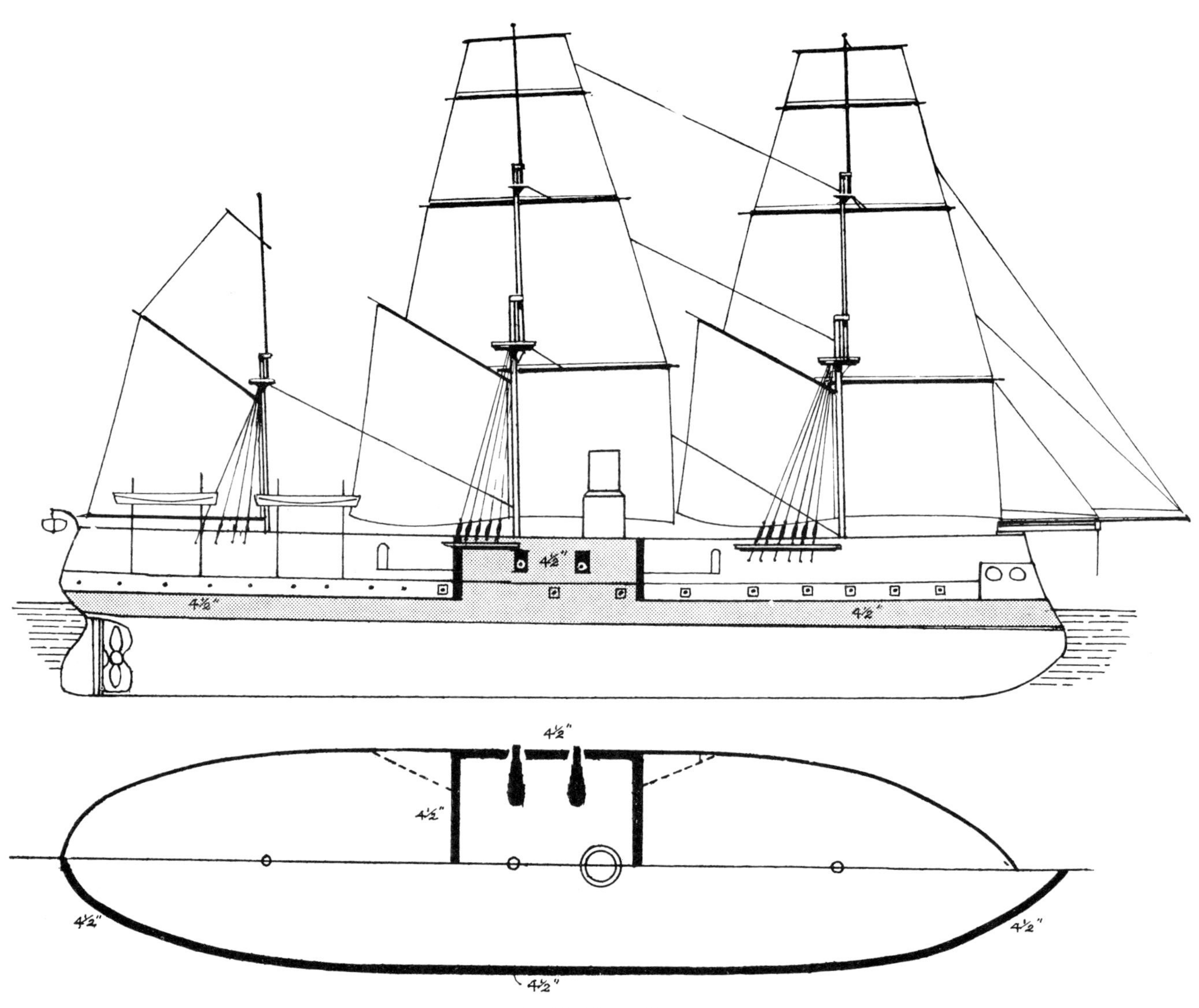

ENTERPRISE

swung inboard like a gate exposing an entry port in the bulkhead to which a gun could be traversed. Only a limited arc of bearing was thus available, and the whole proceeding in practice impressed Reed with the necessity of having as little shifting or removable gear as possible in future ships. Both the 110-pdrs. and 100-pdrs. were mounted on wooden carriages with slides which were troublesome to traverse even on an even keel; in a seaway few captains would have run the risk of casting them loose.

ARMOUR

Owing to the main deck being only just above the water-line, the 4½-in. belt was very shallow and extended below water for 3½ feet only. The box battery was 34 ft. long and 30 ft. across internally faced with 4½-in. iron and closed by 4½-in. bulkheads and a wooden deck above, the guns being carried about 2 ft. higher than in *Research*.

As originally completed the *Enterprise* had her funnel brought up through the battery and close to the main mast as here shown. Later it was moved forward of the bulkhead as in the photo of *Research*. The different arrangement for securing fore-and-aft fire from the battery can be seen, and the narrow belt just showing above the waterline.

As the total weight of armour was only 195 tons—about one-seventh of the displacement—she carried the lowest proportion of any British armoured ship.

MACHINERY

As the first of the few armoured ships to be engined by Ravenhill, she made her 9·9 knots with 690 I.H.P., thus being also the slowest and lowest powered of the protected ships. However, at this period the need for speed in cruising vessels had not been recognized by the Board and our sloops were notoriously slow movers. The *Circassian* was to have been a 11-12 knotter, but "conversion" added 40 tons to the displacement and entailed a reduction in nominal h.p. from 200 to 160, so it is not surprising that a loss in speed resulted.

With a coal supply restricted to 95 tons her bunkerage was below normal, being only one-fourteenth of the displacement instead of the more usual one-ninth.

RIG

Dressed as a barque she carried less aloft than her unarmoured sisters, and although handy and weatherly under canvas was described as undermasted and good for very little in a light breeze. The best recorded in service was 9·8 knots under steam and sail.

SEA-GOING QUALITIES

At sea she was dry, rolling deeply and easily, but always a sluggish mover, losing way quickly in a head sea and barely able to make progress in bad weather.

GENERAL

Accommodation for both officers and men was regarded as "very good" and the ventilation "excellent," so in habitability she seems to have been better off than most of her armoured contemporaries.

Owing to lack of chase guns and limited arcs of bearing by the broadside pieces she was regarded as being incapable of offence through an arc of 120° forward and aft; remarks in this respect under *Research* also apply to the *Enterprise*.

As the response to a passing phase of thought the *Enterprise* and her group were only successful in demonstrating the futility of applying armour to vessels of small tonnage, with resulting loss of speed and cruising ability. The composite construction, however, was cleverly conceived and carried out.

"ENTERPRISE"

Was ordered at Deptford in '61 as the 17-gun sloop *Circassian* but her name was changed—and aptly—in July '62. Commissioned 5 May '64. Channel '64; Med. '64-'71 (rearmed at Malta '68). Returned home and paid off August '71 into 4th Div. Reserve at Sheerness.

Sold in '85 for £2,072.

The third of the ships for whose conversion Reed was responsible was the *Favorite*—named after a French prize—which was one of the 22-gun corvettes of the *Jason* class, commenced in 1860 as part of our programme drawn up in response to the French ships ordered that year. When instructions were issued for her to be completed as an armoured ship the keel had already been two years upon the stocks, and the hull changes were therefore confined to the substitution of a straight stem for the customary knee bow and an oval and upright stern for one of the flat overhanging frigate type. (She carried a topgallant forecastle but no poop, and all ranks and ratings messed and berthed on her one internal deck.) In point of size she was nearly twice the displacement of the *Research* and about half that of the contemporary ironclad frigates, with an armament and weight of protection in proportion, so represented a mean between the armoured sloop and the second-class battleships like *Defence* and *Ocean*. It will be noticed that the guns were the heaviest of the day and the armour of the same thickness as in the bigger ships, thus giving her equality in range and resistance at the expense of speed and sea-going qualities; so that she was the true "pocket battleship," deficient in weight of broadside only in proportion to her displacement, and a better solution to the problem of providing an armoured ship on small dimensions than was thought possible.

ARMAMENT

The box battery extended for 66 ft. amidships and housed four guns aside—originally 100-pdr. Somersets and afterwards 7-in. M.L.R. At the bow and stern were 64-pdrs. as chase guns, and both these and the larger pieces had wooden mountings. The same method of securing a certain amount of axial fire was adopted as in the *Enterprise*, through an ingenious if somewhat precarious arrangement by which 20 ft. of bulwark at the corners of the battery could be hinged inboard to form an embrasure allowing the fore and aft doors of the battery to be used as ports for the traversed guns. But considering the *Favorite's* rolling propensities, any such undertaking could only have been carried out under the most favourable circumstances.

ARMOUR

The complete water-line belt extended from 3 ft. below the load line to the level of the upper deck with a uniform thickness of 4½ in. Above this was the battery with sides and end bulkheads of similar armour, the gun ports having a command of 9 ft. Owing to the height of the upper deck above water it was necessary to curtail the depth of the belt below it, so that a slight roll exposed an unarmoured hull.

"FAVORITE"

Builder	*Laid down*	*Launched*	*Completed*	*Cost*
Deptford	23 Aug. '60	5 July '64	17 March '66	£152,374

Dimensions 225′ × 46·9′ × 20/22·9′ = 3,230 tons.
Hull and armour 2,090 tons. Equipment 1,140 tons.

Guns

As completed	*Rearmed* 1869
8 100-pdr. Somerset	8 7-in. M.L.R. 2 68-pdrs.

Armour 4½″ battery with 19″ backing; bulkheads 4½″.
Belt 4½″, backing 26″; scantling 20″.
Total: armour and backing 560 tons.

Machinery Humphreys and Tennant direct-acting engines.
I.H.P. 1,770 = 11·8 knots.
2 cyl. 64″; stroke 32″; revs. 68.
4 boilers; 20 lb. pressure.
Mangin propeller, 16 ft.

Coal 350 tons.

Complement 250.

Sail area 18,250 sq. ft.

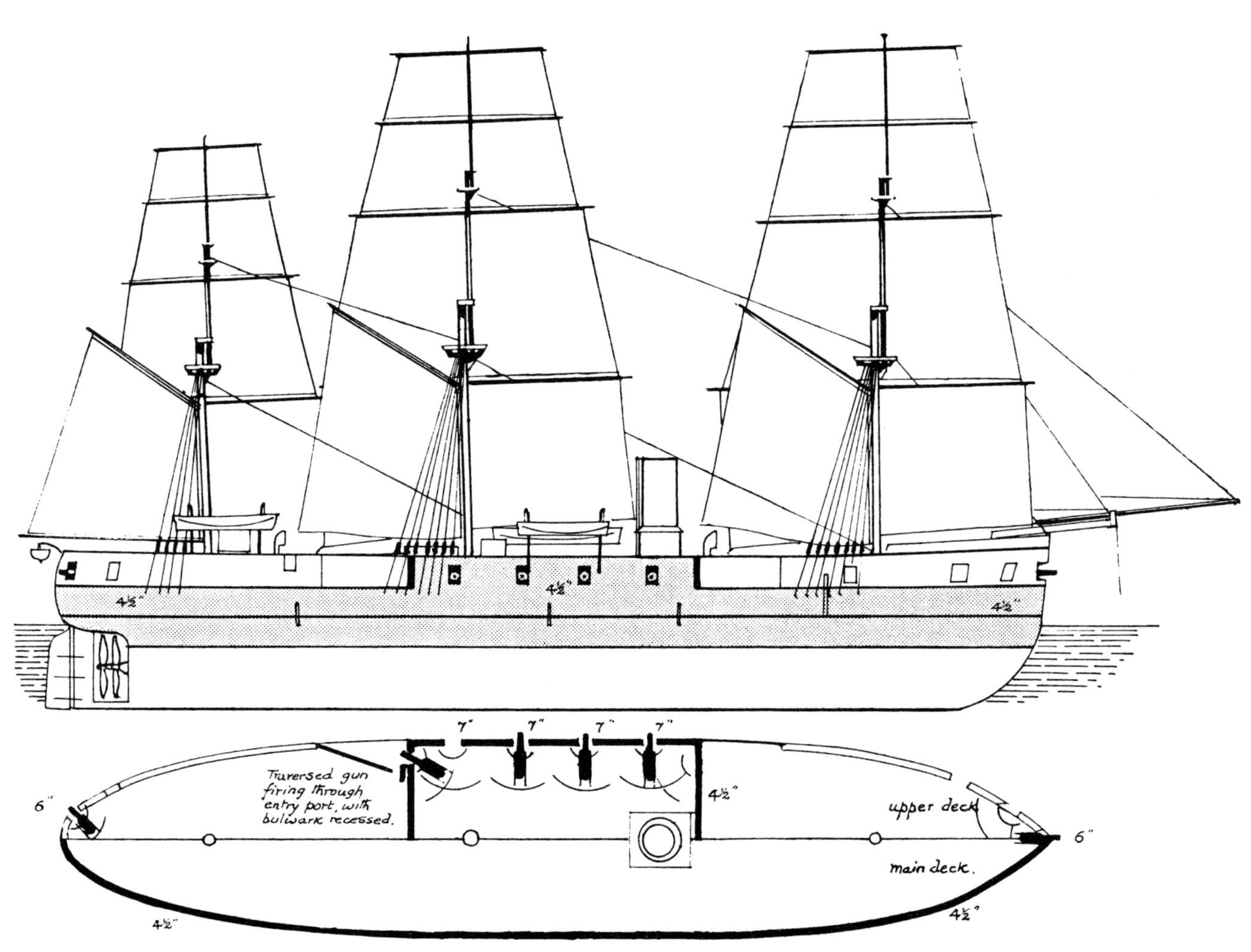

FAVORITE

MACHINERY

In the lay-out of her engines the *Favorite* shared with the later *Lord Warden* as single-screw ships the peculiarity of having her cylinders on the starboard side of the shaft with the condensers to port. The screw was a Mangin with tandem blades, which was unique in the battle fleet as it could be neither raised nor disconnected. This type of propeller was designed to reduce drag under sail without reducing blade surface for gripping the water under steam. There were four blades, but instead of being set as four points on a spherical boss, they were placed in two pairs with the same radial alignment on a long cylindrical boss. They served their purpose with but qualified success and subsequently only appeared in the *Audacious* and *Alexandra*, to be changed when these ships were deprived of their rig. Her best on trials was 11·8 knots under steam.

RIG

The *Favorite* was always ship rigged and well sparred for her size. It will be noticed that there were no channels for the shrouds, the deadeyes being taken down to the bulwarks.

The only known photograph of *Enterprise* taken when she was lying in Plymouth Sound after her first commission in 1869. The recessing bulwarks before and abaft the battery are here laid flush with the side, and the gun port in the bows is closed. Note the height of the masts and absence of channels for the shrouds which are secured to the bulwarks.

Under canvas she was handicapped by the fixed propeller, and otherwise would have cut the water well. As it was, about 10½ knots was her best recorded progress.

SEA-GOING QUALITIES

Although regarded as a good sea boat, she rolled excessively, and on the way out to America it is recorded that she reached 25 degrees one way and 30 degrees the other when there was not a heavy swell, so that her guns could really only be fought in smooth water.

Although provided with more spacious bunkers than normal, she made many long passages under sail, and while on the American station raced with and beat one of our latest and best wooden corvettes. Her return to England was made under canvas until she cast anchor at Spithead.

"FAVORITE"

Commissioned at Sheerness in February '66 for the North American and West Indies station, returning home in August '69 for refit. Relieved *Repulse* as First Reserve guardship on east coast of Scotland '72-'76. Paid off at Portsmouth '76 and laid up in reserve.

Sold 30 March '86 for £3,500.

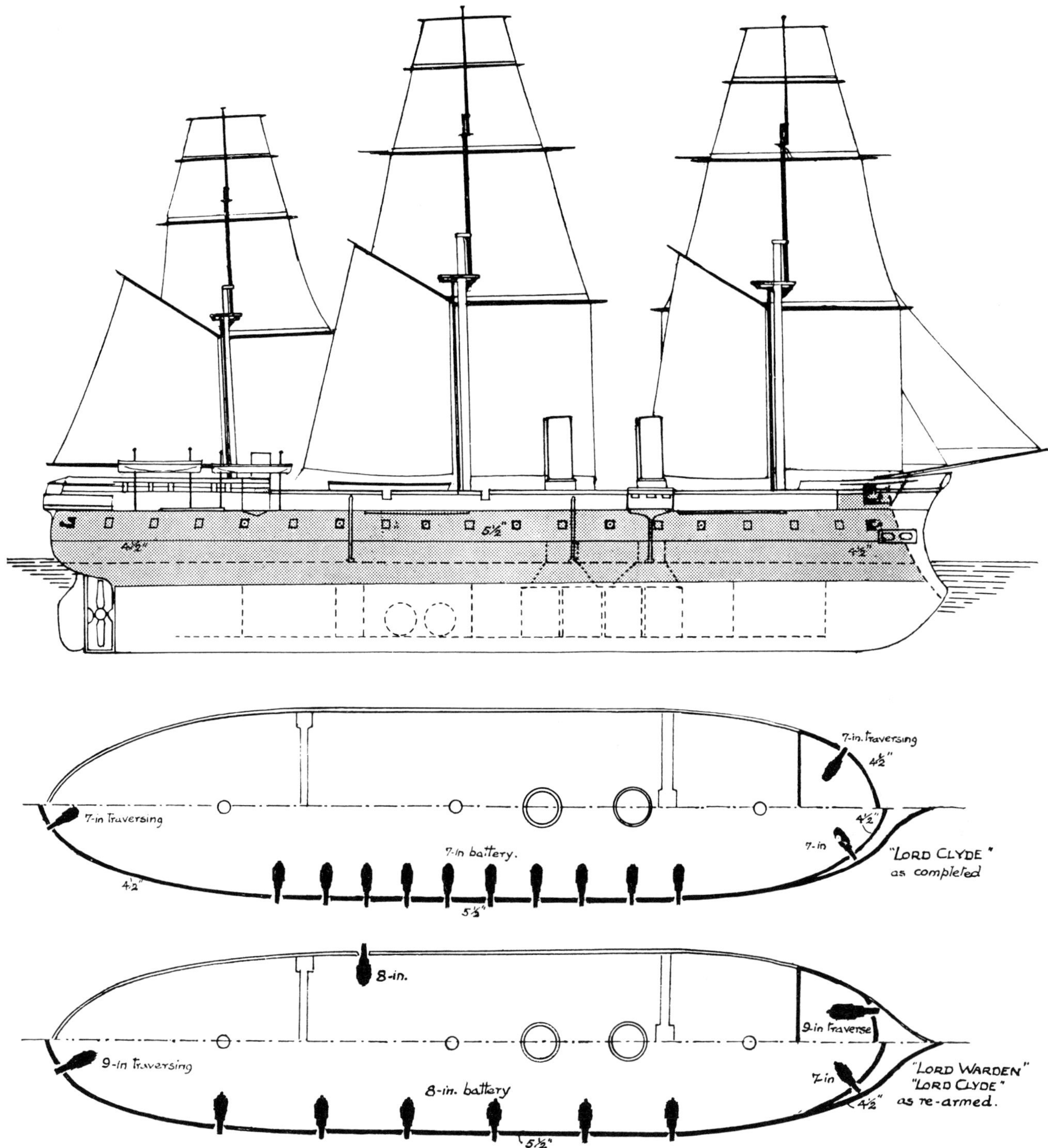

The upper plan shows *Lord Clyde* as completed in 1866; the lower one *Lord Warden* as completed in 1867 and *Lord Clyde* as rearmed in 1870.

LORD CLYDE AND LORD WARDEN

	Builder	*Laid down*	*Launched*	*Completed*	*Cost*
"Lord Clyde"	Pembroke	29 Sept. '63	13 Oct. '64	2 June '66	£285,750
"Lord Warden"	Chatham	24 Dec. '63	27 March '65	30 Aug. '67	£328,998

Dimensions *"Lord Clyde"*: $280' \times 59' \times 23\frac{3}{4}'/27' = 7{,}750$ tons.
Hull and armour = 5,030 tons. Equipment = 2,720 tons.

"Lord Warden": $280' \times 59' \times 24/28' = 7{,}940$ tons.
Hull and armour = 5,180 tons. Equipment = 2,760 tons.

Guns	"Lord Clyde"		"Lord Warden"	
	1866	1870	*As designed*	1867
	24 7-in. M.L.R.	2 9-in. M.L.R.	16 8-in. M.L.R.	2 9-in. M.L.R.
		14 8-in. ,,	4 7-in. B.L.R.	14 8-in. ,,
		2 7-in. ,,		2 7-in. ,,
		2 20-pdr. B.L.		2 20-pdr. B.L.

Armour Belt and sides 5½″-4½″; 1½″ skin; hull 31½″ oak; conning tower 4½″.

Complement 605.

Sail area 31,000 sq. ft.

Machinery "*Lord Clyde*": Ravenhill. Trunk engines. I.H.P. 6,700=13·5 knots.
2 cyl. 116″; stroke 4′.
9 rectangular boilers. 28 lb. pressure.

"*Lord Warden*": Maudslay. Return connecting rod.
I.H.P. 6,700=13·4 knots.
3 cyl. 91″; stroke 4½′. Boilers as above.
4-bladed screw; 23′ diam.; revs. 64.

Special features:

(1) The last true broadside ironclads.
(2) The heaviest wooden ships ever built.
(3) The fastest steaming wooden ships ever built.
(4) The worst rollers in the Battle Fleet.

From the squadron lists of the Black Battle Fleet of the mid-Victorian era the names of two sister ships stand out which have almost human interest—the staunch and impeccable *Lord Warden* and the diseased and unfortunate *Lord Clyde*: the one to reach a ripe old age honoured by unfailing service in the principal commands at home and abroad; the other erratic and always in trouble, doomed to be known as the Queen's bad bargain—the ship which had to be sold out of the Navy ten years after hoisting the pennant without ever having completed one full commission.

Of the five armoured wooden frigates whose construction was sanctioned in 1863, these were the only two to be put in hand, thanks to Reed's influence with the Board; in this respect he rendered a service of the first magnitude. Both in and out of the Service the reversion to wooden hulls for ironclads was regarded as a retrograde step, and the announcement that the keels of two or more were to be laid down was not at all favourably received by the country generally. But in the interests of economy it was decided that the accumulated stores of timber should be used up as likely to be in excess of requirements, although the smaller cruising ships were still to have wooden hulls.

The Chief Constructor was therefore asked to prepare designs for two ships, based upon that of the *Bellerophon*. So while the hull of that ship was being riveted together at Chatham, the adze and augur, mallet and saw were busily employed on the *Lord Warden* being erected on the next slip to her, and on the *Lord Clyde* at Pembroke. As it was anticipated that the timber for these two would not exhaust the supplies available, a third ship, the *Pallas*, was ordered at the same time to utilize the residue—but in view of what afterwards happened to the hull of the *Lord Clyde* it can only be surmised that the resources of Pembroke in the matter of seasoned wood had been vastly over-estimated. Had five such ships been put in hand the results might well have been catastrophic!

In adapting the *Bellerophon's* design and weights to the limitations imposed by a wooden hull, Reed had only the data afforded by the sea experience of the 273-ft. *Royal Oak* upon which to base his drawings—and the sagging propensities of her class had not then become manifest. But experience dictated at least a 20-ft. reduction in length with breadth equal to that of the *Royal Oak*, and the hull was therefore modelled upon these lines in conjunction with an exceptionally strong system of construction. Of the two, the *Lord Warden* was the heavier by 360 tons, drawing a foot more aft—a difference partially accounted for by weightier engines and a poop, and also by the quality of the wood employed, as some of that incorporated into the *Lord Clyde* was not fully seasoned.

Their hulls were a sandwich of wood and iron, being made up of:

(1) A close framework of 24-in. oak ribs, filled in with oak.
(2) A 1½-in. iron skin as a binding.
(3) A layer of 6-in. oak backing for the armour.
(4) Armour of 4½-in. to 5½-in. iron.
(5) A layer of 4-in. oak sheathing 8 ft. deep at the water-line
(6) A thin sheathing of anti-fouling Muntz metal.

forming a compact mass which the much-vaunted American 15-in. gun as mounted in the big Federal monitors, charged with 50 lb. of powder and throwing a 484 lb. shot would fail to penetrate at any range.

A certain amount of iron work in the way of stanchions and beams was used as hull stiffening, the hold being divided into five main compartments by thin iron bulkheads, although these were not regarded as watertight subdivisions. With the exception of the principal officers the entire ship's company was berthed on the lower deck, with a thin partition dividing the officers' quarters from the steerage. The wardroom was ranged round with cabins, the only natural illumination being that which came through the two skylights, one above the other, in the decks above—and this at one end only! The scuttles for the entire deck were 6-in. holes cut through the 3-ft.-thick sides and opening a few feet above water—so that except in harbour they had to be plugged. Rats and cockroaches were "a perfect plague" and the sick list always higher than in the iron ships with their main deck accommodation; the only compensation was that the wooden walls did not sweat, while in cold or heat the temperature was always equable. The *Warden* differed from the *Clyde* in having the seamen's heads in the bows, which gave them the same plough shape as *Bellerophon's*; in the *Clyde* these offices were sponsoned amidships.

The *Lord Clyde* as first completed with all gun ports armed. Note the ram bow and full bowsprit compared with her sister.

The bridge was a light structure placed between main and mizen without any charthouse, beneath which in the *Warden* were bullet-proof pilot-towers sponsoned from the bulwarks.

ARMAMENT

Neither in method of protection nor concentration of armament did the design conform to Reed's conceptions as exemplified in the *Bellerophon*. Twenty 7-in. guns having been decided upon for the battery of the five frigates, and any concentration of heavier guns amidships regarded as a weight imposition unsuitable for wooden hulls, Reed had to content himself with this warrant. On hoisting the pennant the *Lord Clyde* carried twenty-four of these guns—twenty in the battery, two under the topgallant forecastle, and two on the quarter deck. But the *Lord Warden*—which joined her in squadron a year later—reaped the benefit of a rising appreciation as to the ordnance burden which could be imposed upon a timber hull and was able to take with her a much heavier mixed armament of 9-in., 8-in. and 7-in. guns.

As in the *Bellerophon*, there was no attempt to obtain axial fire from recessed ports in the battery and a radical departure was made from former practice by mounting the heaviest pieces at the bow and stern as chase guns. Forward was a 9-in. firing through embrasures on either side of the forecastle and another at the stern with main deck ports on each quarter. To augment the bow fire a couple of 7-in. were placed on the main deck at the turn of the bows—in which position they were useless in a head sea and were generally more of a burden than additions to offence. On the broadside were twelve 8-in. on the main deck and two on the quarter deck just abaft the main rigging, the main deck guns being spaced in alternative ports. This dispersion was adopted to avoid too much burden amidships, and they were the last capital ships to have a "broadside" instead of a "central battery." A pair of 20-pdr. Armstrong served for saluting purposes.

It was not until 1870 that the *Lord Clyde* was similarly armed, and by then the termination of her service career was in sight.

Lord Warden in 1867 with guns in alternative ports only. The knee head prolonging the bows obviated a jib-boom, and the dolphin striker was removed soon after her completion, as well as the spanker boom.

ARMOUR

Except for the upper deck there was end-to-end plating, and here again they were the last broadside ships to be "iron clad" in the full sense of the term. From 6 ft. below water to the level of the lower deck the armour was 5½ in. amidships and 4½ in. towards the bow and stern, an extra 1½ in. of iron being added to the original design between the frames and outer planking; above this along the battery it was 4½ in., so that for the first time flotation was better protected than armament. For 25½ ft. along the forecastle a 4½-in. screen shielded the 9-in. gun. In conjunction with the 1½-in. skin the total protection was the equivalent of 6-in. iron generally, so that the ships ranked with the best protected in the fleet.

MACHINERY

The chief difference between the *Warden* and *Clyde* lay in their machinery, and it was of sufficient importance to have reduced the latter ship to harbour service. The *Warden* had the benefit of Maudslay's 3-cyl. return connecting-rod engines with their cranks set at 120° to each other so that strain and reactions were balanced.

These rendered eighteen years' service in perfect harmony with her hull. But the trunk engines in the *Clyde*—the largest yet made—having only two cylinders set at right angles, caused such reactions that the wooden hull could not stand the strain. Very soon oscillation developed and the engines became worn out inside of two years when a new set had to be fitted.

RIG

Both ships were ship rigged on the second scale like *Bellerophon*, and undersparred for their size. The *Warden* never had a jib-boom because of the projecting knee bow, and only at the beginning of her career did she sport a dolphin striker and spanker boom.

With their full lines it was not surprising that the *Warden's* best was 10 knots and the *Clyde's* 10½ knots, although both were very handy in tacking and wearing. To the *Clyde* belongs the double record of being "the largest ship of any class or kind ever to enter either Spithead or Plymouth Sound under sail alone; performances the more noteworthy from being accomplished under unfavourable circumstances at both anchorages. Never before or since did any ship of the *Lord Clyde's* dimensions enter the Sound without steam" (Ballard). It was as if she realized that her hull belonged to the old order which was quickly passing away—eager to respond to the elemental forces from which the motive power of her long line of ancestors had been derived, but antagonistic to the boiling and straining of the upstart energies which she resented and refused to tolerate.

SEA-GOING QUALITIES

In a class by themselves as the worst rollers in the battle fleet, the *Clyde* usually succeeded in making heavier weather of it than her sister. During 1867 the Channel fleet carried out various rolling tests between August and October, and on occasions when the *Bellerophon* could have fought her guns with safety the seas were washing entirely over the *Clyde's* main deck ports, while she was working through 23° to starboard and 24½° to port. That the *Warden* was somewhat the steadier was due to her midship weights being carried rather higher. After fifteen months' service in the Channel the *Clyde* was transferred to the Mediterranean, where weather conditions would be kindlier to her engines and hull.

Tactical diameter: 600/631 yds. at full power.
378 yds. at 12 knots.

GENERAL

In construction they will for ever represent the finest achievement of the shipwright's craft—the largest[1] and fastest-steaming wooden ships for naval or mercantile purposes ever built in this country or abroad. The success of Reed's conception of a fighting ship—allowing for sea-going qualities—may be gathered from a short comparison with the *Warrior*.

	Lord Clyde	*Warrior*
Length	280 ft.	380 ft.
Armament	376 tons	340 tons
Armour	1,379 "	975 "
Speed	13·4 knots	14·6 knots
I.H.P.	6,064	5,772
Cost	£285,750	£377,292

"LORD CLYDE"

Commissioned at Plymouth June '66. Channel '66-'68. As her engines were showing signs of wear she was sent to the Mediterranean, but after one cruise, when she sprung her steel mainyard, Malta sent her home for new engines. Rearmed and re-engined, and a two-bladed screw fitted. Reserve at Devonport '69-'71. Again sent to the Mediterranean and six months later went ashore off Pantellaria. Pulled off by the *Lord Warden* in a badly strained and damaged condition and towed to Malta. After temporary repairs, was sent home escorted by *Defence*. At Plymouth she was stripped for complete overhaul, when her hull was found to be rotten with timber fungus. For three years every expedient was tried to save her from decay, but to no purpose, and she had to be sold before being too diseased to warrant purchase.

Sold 1875 for £3,730.

"LORD WARDEN"

Commissioned at Chatham July '67. Channel '67 and after a few months transferred to Mediterranean, relieving *Caledonia* as flagship in '69. Flag '69-'75. Took part in the demonstration against the Spanish Communists at Cartagena who were using naval vessels for piratical purposes. Relieved by *Hercules* and paid off for refit. First Reserve in the Forth '75-'78 ("Particular Service Squadron" '78 during Russian war scare); fitted with torpedoes and net defence '84; finally paid off in '85 as her upper works were in such a rotten condition, and her crew transferred to *Devastation*. Although practically excluded from the active list, her sale was postponed for four years and she was not condemned until '89.

[1] The longest ocean-going wooden screw-ship was the warship *Dunderberg* built by W. H. Webb at New York in 1865—too late for the Civil War, and purchased by the French, who renamed her *Rochambeau;* she is listed as 358′ 8″ pp. (377′ 4″ o.a.) × 59′ 7″ × 20′ = 6,949 tons displacement.

Chapter 18

"PALLAS" AND "BELLEROPHON"

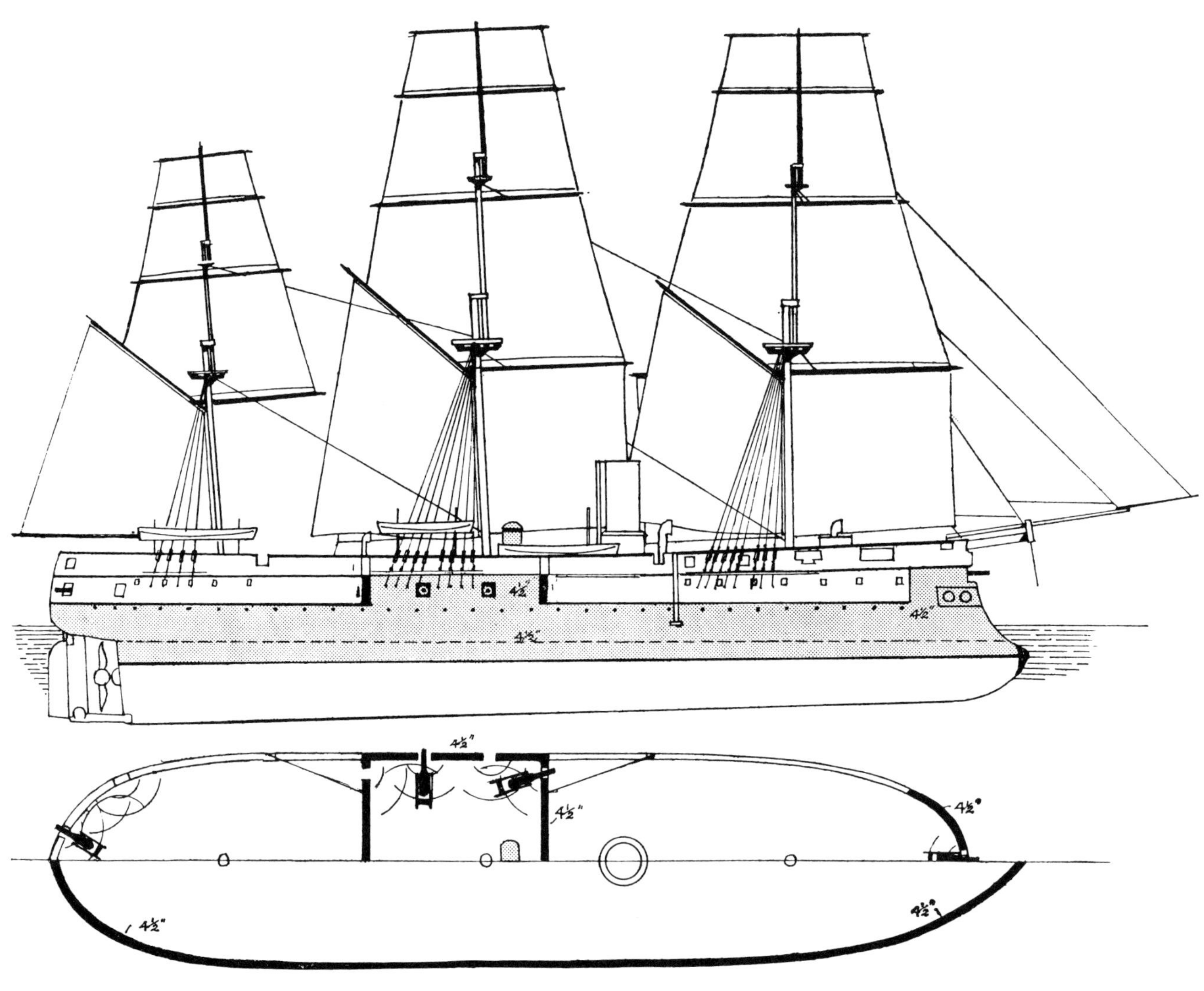

"PALLAS"

Builder	*Laid down*	*Launched*	*Completed*	*Cost*
Woolwich	19 Oct. '63	14 March '65	6 March '66	£190,403

Dimensions 225′ × 50′ × 19′/24·3′ = 3,794 tons.
Hull and armour 2,440 tons. Equipment 1,350 tons.

Guns	*As completed*	*Rearmed* 1866	*Rearmed* 1871
	2 7-in. Armstrong B.L.	2 7-in. Armstrong B.L.	4 6-in. M.L.R.
	4 7-in. M.L.R.	4 8-in. M.L.R.	4 8-in. ,,
		2 5-in. Armstrong B.L.	

Armour 4½″ belt, battery and bulkheads. Backing 22″.
Total 560 tons.

Machinery Humphreys and Tennant; compound horizontal.
I.H.P. 3,580 = 13 knots.
2 high-pressure cyl. 51″; 2 low-pressure 104½″.
4-bladed Griffiths screw 17¾′ diam.; pitch 19⅛′; revs. 68.
4 rectangular boilers. 30 lb. pressure.

Complement 253.
Coal 260 tons.
Sail area 16,716 sq. ft.
Special features:

(1) The first British warship designed primarily as a ram.
(2) A ratio of length to beam of $4\frac{1}{2}$: 1.
(3) A draught 5 to 6 ft. greater aft than forward.
(4) The first warship to have compound engines.

THE *Pallas* was remarkable in being one of the first two armoured ships ever to be built in H.M. Dockyards from plans other than those which originated in the Admiralty, having been designed by Reed as a private

The *Pallas* in Plymouth Sound during her first commission in 1867. Forward of the two-gun battery the forward embrasure shows up black beneath the bulwarks while that aft catches the light. The gun port in the stem is open; the conning tower before the main mast is still to be fitted.

individual and the drawings presented to the Board when his services were first retained for the Constructor's Department.

In the light of her real value in service, it is difficult to imagine this somewhat pathetic little ship as having once been credited with outstanding military qualities—to see her as the embodiment of certain tactical requirements, filling the gap between what the Board demanded and what the Controller could supply! If ever a ship suffered from an overdose of pre-natal praise and post-natal scorn, and passed a life in apologetic humility and premature decay, it was Reed's corvette-ram. But considering the *Pallas* as she would have been presented to Somerset, it is no wonder that she appeared a commendable little ship. Short, and yet promising the then high speed of 14 knots; well protected, and carrying a few guns which had a wide bearing achieved by a hitherto unexploited method for obtaining it; and furnished with a long projecting snout which could be used for ramming in conjunction with rapid powers of turning—she was indeed the *multum in parvo* for which the Board had been seeking in vain!

When designed, there was nothing in the Service analogous to her proportions. It was in the face of established prejudice in favour of great length and much opposition, that the proposal to build a ship only 225 ft. long and to steam anything like 14 knots was accepted by the Constructors. Rig and gun power were to be subsidiary to speed under steam, and an altogether novel form of hull was intended to equip her for the special function of ramming in place of general service, for which she was specifically not intended (Reed, Evidence before Turret-ship Committee, 1863).

Being of a very similar displacement to the corvette *Favorite*, the *Pallas* was given the same rating without regard as to whether her guns were carried above or between decks; and as such, together with the *Favorite* and *Penelope*, she had the distinction of being one of the three armoured corvettes built for H.M. Service.

Although of the same length as the *Favorite*, *Pallas* was a three-decked ship having a freeboard forward of 19½ ft. to the top of the hammock nettings with low 4-ft. fixed bulwarks, her designer now being opposed to these being hinged or movable. Originally there was an open waist with no spar deck, the bows being of extremely bluff mould before being prolonged into the ram. Reed's first draft was for an *iron* ship, but when the building plans were allotted to Woolwich—which was without facilities for fashioning iron hulls—she had to be given the additional draught necessitated by a wooden hull and keel. Her construction was also a measure of economy in utilizing the considerable stores of timber then accumulating in the Dockyards, although as a ram she was essentially of a type for which an iron hull was indicated.

GUNS

The original warrant provided six guns in all, two 7-in. M.L.R. aside in the central battery and either 7-in. M.L.R. or B.L. as chase guns—an equipment which placed her at the bottom of the offensive scale on a tonnage basis. Reed excused this on the grounds that speed was a primary consideration both in her employment as a ram and as a corsair hunter. The four 7-in. M.L.R. were mounted in a central battery with four ports aside, those at the ends being in *deeply recessed embrasures* to afford some axial fire, the arcs of bearing being 30° each way at the broadside ports and 15° and 45° on either side of the line of keel at the bulkhead ports. The bow gun displayed its muzzle under the forecastle, firing through a port in the stem with 10° training from the line of keel, and from 45° to right abeam when traversed to a broadside port; that astern was on the main deck and ranged to 60° from the keel line at the stern port and from 10° before to 50° abaft the beam at the broadside port.

Actually the *Pallas* was sufficiently strong to have mounted 300-pdrs., and her calculations allowed for a surplus buoyancy which would have carried them at her intended load line; but as the ports were only 16 ft. apart instead of 20 ft., Reed was averse to such guns being placed aboard until proper means for working them had been devised—and complained that it was apparently nobody's business to develop methods of training and working such heavy ordnance!

As the bow gun was only 9 ft. above water it was all but swamped by the 7-ft. wave the ram piled up when running light; when down to her marks it could never have been used in a pursuit action.

Soon after entering service 8-in. M.L.R. were substituted for the 7-in. M.L.R. in the battery and a couple of Armstrong 5-in. B.L. added as chase guns to the upper deck; later on, when the early breech-loaders went out of favour, the Armstrongs were replaced by 6-in. M.L.R. (64-pdrs.). A saluting battery was carried on the quarter deck.

ARMOUR

The end-to-end belt was of a uniform 4½ in. from the main deck down to 4½ ft. below water; above this rose the 4½-in. battery amidships with a patch of armour up in the bows forming a screen for the 7-in. chase gun. When refitted in 1872 a conning tower was placed just forward of the main mast—a position selected for the control of broadside fire and affording a limited field of vision forward when the funnel was lowered.

MACHINERY

Her machinery was noteworthy, the *Pallas* being the first[1] armoured ship in the Navy to have compound expansion—in this case arranged on Woolf's tandem system in which the high- and low-pressure pistons worked on the same rod. Although fitted with a four-bladed screw, it was found that she steamed just as well and sailed far better when two of the blades were missing—so these were permanently unshipped. The boilers were fitted with superheaters, a series of tubes at the base of the funnel through which the steam passed with the object of drying it and surcharging it with heat—a contrivance looked on with distrust by her engineers.

Great things had been anticipated in the matter of speed and 14 knots was confidently expected in view of Reed's optimism and the exceptional power provided on the displacement. But at light draught without either

[1] The frigate *Constance* had six-cylinder engines, each triplet consisting of a high-pressure between two low-pressure ones. This machinery was a constant source of extreme worry and anxiety.

guns or sea stores aboard, and under most favourable circumstances, she made only 12½ knots on trial, piling up such a huge bow wave that one Thames pilot called out "Breakers ahead!"—a performance which excited the most scathing comments from Reed's detractors in the press. After her bows had been altered to give a finer run, the bulkheads shifted, and a spar deck added to improve her trim, she managed to reach 13 knots—but was never good for this in service.

RIG

Reed records that the canvas of the *Pallas* was made subordinate to her steam power, in order that her efficiency in pursuit of privateers should not be interfered with by resistance in the air. From first to last she was ship rigged and except for a flying jib had the same sail plan as the *Favorite*; the different mast spacing was due to the main being stepped forward of the engines instead of abaft them. Because of her short tubby hull and non-hoisting screw a matter of 9½ knots was the best recorded under sail—when her performance seemed to depend to an unusual extent upon the circumstances of her handling. Thus in 1866 it was reported:

> "On all occasions of trial, sailing whether on a wind or going free, the *Pallas* proved herself far superior to the rest of the (Channel) squadron. Her power of going to windward is extraordinary."

But the following year we read·

> "The *Pallas* was nowhere from inability to do more";

and again in 1868:

> "The *Pallas* again took a high place."

SEA-GOING QUALITIES

Described as being very stiff, very handy, and very weatherly when close-hauled and equal to a fast frigate when beating to windward, like all the wooden ironclads she rolled deeply in a seaway when under steam, the comparative figures with her squadron mates in the Channel being: *Minotaur* 3·1°, *Bellerophon* 3·6°, *Pallas* 12°.

GENERAL

Both officers and men berthed on the lower deck, the Captain's quarters being aft on the main deck. Accommodation was good for a ship of her size, and for the first time washhouse and bathrooms were provided for the crew.

The rudder was controlled by triple steering wheels on the quarter deck and below it; steam steering gear was never fitted.

"PALLAS"

Commissioned at Portsmouth March '66 for the Channel squadron in which she served until October '69; First Reserve guardship Kingstown until September '70 after which she was paid off and underwent a long refit '70-'72. For the next seven years she served in the Mediterranean, being employed in the demonstration against the Communist pirates at Cartagena in '73. Finally paid off in '79 after a survey in '75 had showed that her hull was generally decayed and that her boilers could only be patched up. Retained in the Fourth Class Reserve at Devonport until sold 20 April '86.[1]

Together with the *Pallas*, the building of the *Bellerophon* came about in so unusual a fashion that Reed's own description of the circumstances is worth recording:

> "In the case of the *Bellerophon* I put the design in a finished form before their Lordships when Parliament had sanctioned the building of 5 armour plated wooden frigates and I requested their Lordships to build this iron frigate from the design as presented to them instead of one of the wooden frigates. As a matter of fact only two of the wooden frigates were built, the *Lord Warden* and the *Lord Clyde*, and the *Bellerophon* was ordered as I had desired. Of course in designing the *Bellerophon* (although I had acted under no orders as I had contemplated putting it forward myself to the Board) I may have been influenced by the known wishes of the Admiralty, but I think I may properly say that the *Bellerophon* represented at that time the kind of ship which I proposed. In all other cases I have acted under the restrictions of superior instructions." (Evidence before Committee on Defence, 5 April 1871.)

---

[1] "The *Pallas* was a rotten old craft and it is extraordinary that such a vessel should have been in commission so late as 1879. In order to keep her plates from falling off, a chain cable was passed under her bottom to frap them in place" (Bacon, *Lord Fisher*, vol. 1, p. 61).

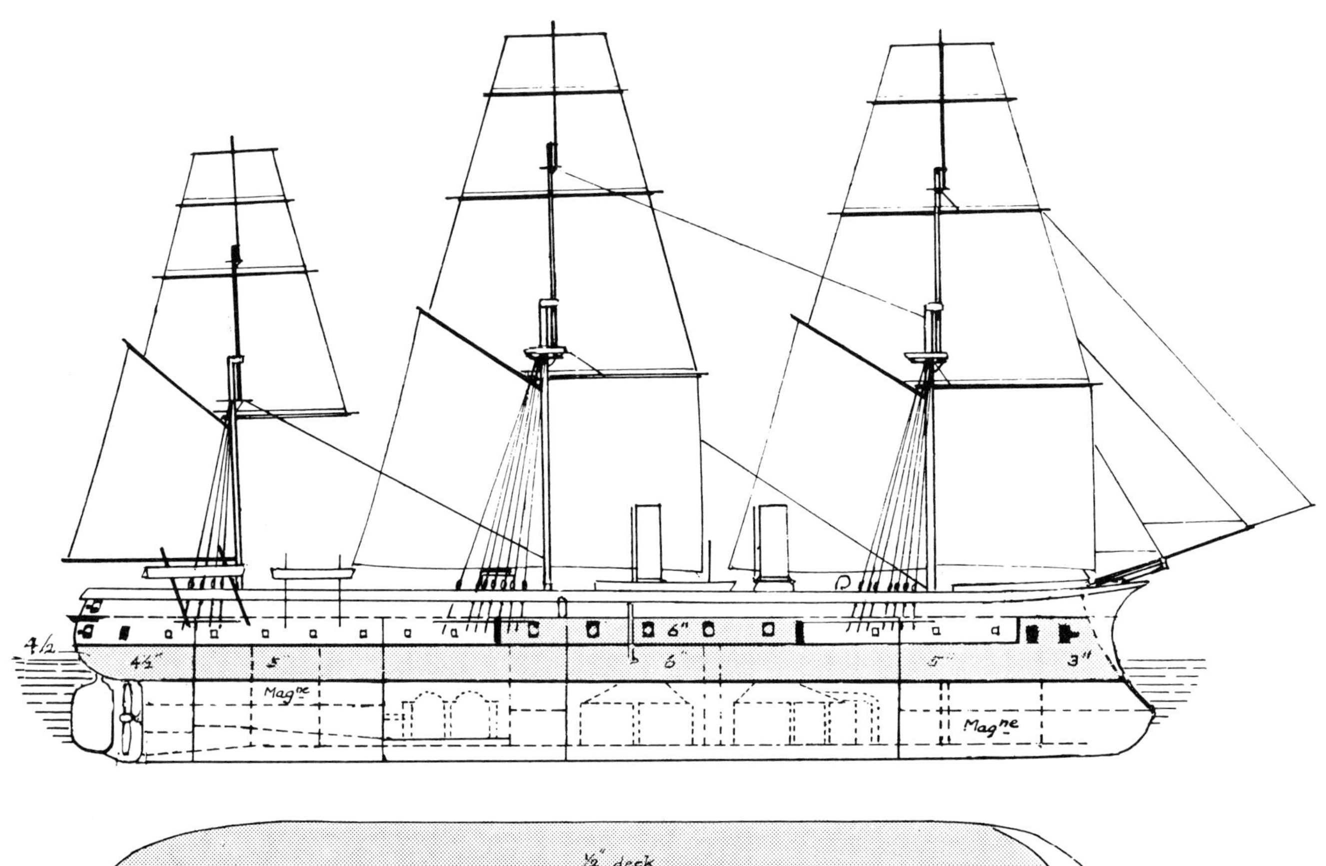

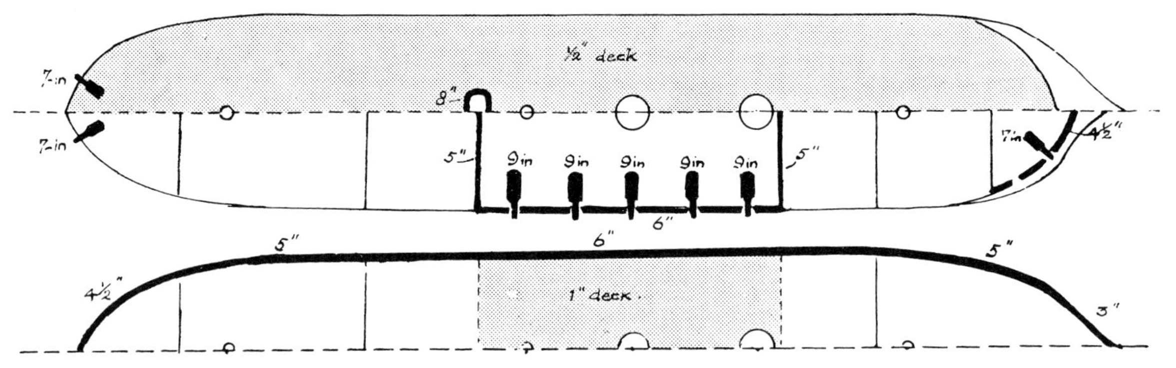

"BELLEROPHON"

Builder	*Laid down*	*Launched*	*Completed*	*Cost*
Chatham	28 Dec. '63	26 April '65	11 April '66	£356,493

Dimensions 300′ × 56′ × $22\frac{3}{4}/26\frac{1}{2}$′ = 7,550 tons.
Hull and armour 4,950 tons. Equipment 2,600 tons.

Guns

1866	1885
10 9-in. M.L.R.	10 8-in. B.L.
5 7-in. „	4 6-in. „
4 Saluting	6 4-in. „
	2 torpedo carriages.

Armour Belt 6′ × 5″ with 10″-8″ backing. $1\frac{1}{2}$″ skin. Battery 6″. Upper deck $\frac{1}{2}$″; main deck under battery 1″. Bulkheads 5″; conning tower 8″-6″. Total 1,093 tons.

Machinery Penn. trunk engine. I.H.P. 6,520 = 14·17 knots.
2 cyl. 112″. Stroke 4′. Revs. = 74.
8 rectangular boilers 27 lb. pressure.
2-bladed screw, diam. 23′, 20′ pitch.

Coal 640 tons. Radius 1,500 at 8 knots.

Complement 650.

Sail area 23,800 (ship).

Constructors F. W. Gray and C. Paget.

Special features:

(1) The first vessel to be built upon the "bracket-frame" system, and to be of steel and iron construction.
(2) The first to mount the 9-in. M.L.R.
(3) The first large ironclad to incorporate Reed's ideas as regards dimensions and hull form, power, and speed.
(4) The only broadside ironclad to have the whole main armament replaced by breech-loaders.
(5) The first battleship to have a balanced rudder.

In the *Bellerophon* Reed had planned a ship of character which stood out boldly from her contemporaries. Where the *Minotaur* had relied upon great length and fine lines for her speed the new model trusted to an increased ratio of horse-power to tonnage; a short central battery with a few large-calibre muzzles replaced long broadsides; 4½-in. armour was discarded for 6-in./5-in., giving a greater resistance but over a more restricted area; a sharp beak ram replaced the cleaver forefoot of the Watts ships, with a noble plough bow conferring an air of aggressive distinction in high relief to the straight sullen stems of her squadron mates.

The *Bellerophon* may be said to have been born of the 9-in. gun out of "ramming tactics." The new Chief Constructor—by persuading a somewhat cautious Board into adopting a larger gun than had as yet been mounted on shipboard—secured the advantages of midship concentration which made for steadier gun sights in a pitching hull. As the main battery was to have the same volume of fire as the twenty 7-in. decided upon for the wooden ships she replaced, the number of guns and the space required to mount them was halved. This in turn reduced the fighting area to be protected, which allowed for a corresponding increase in armour thickness.

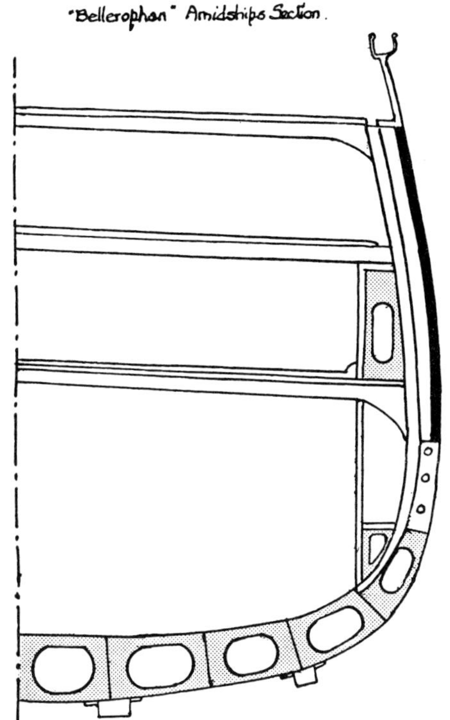

A space of 91 ft. amidships was required for the battery, and fore and aft of this the hull was drawn with full lines so that the beam extended for three-quarters of the length, and given a U-shaped instead of the V section of Watts's ships. Having a bluff bow and semi-oval stern, the ends were buoyant instead of being a burden on the centre section. Deep immersion for the screw was obtained by allowing a trim of 4 ft. by the stern, which made for increased handiness and better steaming when head to wind—although owing to lack of length there was an inevitable falling-off of speed against a head sea despite the full power of her engines.

In *Bellerophon* the longitudinal girder construction used since the *Warrior* was abandoned in favour of Nathaniel Barnaby's "bracket-frame" system with complete double bottoms and cellular division. The difference between the two methods of construction was that in the former the principal members were the strong fore-and-aft girders below the armour belt connected with transverse frames made of plates and angle irons; in the latter the longitudinal girders were deepened and the transverse frames replaced by bracket frames plated along their upper and under sides to form the double bottom. The saving in weight under the "bracket-frame" system was such that 100 ft. of the *Bellerophon's* hull weighed 1,123 tons against 1,303 tons in the *Black Prince*, and by adopting steel wherever possible a reduction in constructional weight of nearly 300 tons was made.

In order to make the ship steady her centre of gravity was raised by means of deep double bottoms and other contrivances for carrying the engines and boilers as high as possible. The forepart of the ship was notably different from that in Watts's models. In both there was the bluff above-water body by which bow fire was obtained, but below in place of a fine V section the *Bellerophon's* U-shaped body was carried with full beam for three-quarters of her length, giving an almost barge-shaped hull with a full rounded bow. As first completed she had a straight sloping stem as in the *Lord Clyde*, but during trials in September 1865 this made her so wet that the profile was changed in November by the addition of a light overhanging knee in which the seamen's heads were placed experimentally. In previous ironclads the heads had been placed forward on the main deck, where difficulties in ventilation had made them objectionable; in the *Bellerophon* they were in the highest part of the ship, decked over and provided with scuttles, with an entry under the topgallant forecastle. Here they proved satisfactory except in a following wind. The new bow certainly helped to make the ship drier, but she piled up a bow wave which was proverbial in the Service and "*Bellerophon's* bow wave in sight" became a standing joke.

Beneath her bluff elliptical counter she carried the first Stanhope balanced rudder in the Service, which did away with the heavy stern post and made steering less laboursome—a welcome innovation as steam steering gear was not fitted until twenty years later. This rudder with an area 25 per cent. greater than that of the *Minotaur*, could be put over to 35 or 40 degrees in about 27 seconds by eight men when steaming as fast as the *Minotaur*, and was as much responsible for her handiness as her short hull.

The shortness of the battery—which incidentally should have carried only four guns aside instead of five, according to reports on facilities for working them—resulted in much improved living quarters for the men; but the presence of the chase guns in the stern made it necessary to move the Captain's quarters to the side, which displaced officers' cabins together with the ward-room, gun-room and engineers' mess and caused them to be taken down to the lower deck, where there was bad ventilation and worse light. When she was selected for Flag duty it was necessary to add a poop for the Admiral's quarters.

GUNS

For the first nineteen years of her long career the battery contained ten 9-in. M.L.R. with two 7-in. M.L.R. in the bows behind armour on the main deck—where it was impossible to work them in a head sea—and three more

The *Bellerophon* on passage between Bermuda and Nassau in 1891 towards the end of her last commission as flagship on the N.A. and W.I. station. She is now armed with B.L. guns, and the conning tower can be seen abaft the main mast.

aft, of which two were on the main and one on the upper deck. This arrangement to obtain axial fire forward from main deck guns was one of those errors in design usually found when a roseate estimation of drawing-board qualities is associated with a lack of sea-going experience—unfortunately rather a feature of Reed's earlier conceptions. The ability for working such large guns as 9-in., weighing 12 tons, from broadside ports had been made possible by the adoption of Captain R. A. E. Scott's iron carriages with mechanical working, but unfortunately with modifications introduced by the Ordnance Department which weakened both carriages and slides. Scott's carriages brought about a revolution in naval armament, so that in course of time 25-ton guns (which with their carriages weighed over 35 tons) were being worked in a seaway on the broadside with far more ease and security than 25-cwt. guns were in 1865. Captain Scott was later appointed Superintendent of Gun Carriages, but until he was in a position to see that his designs went through unchanged it was usual for some "improving" department, committee, or official to introduce modifications which invariably detracted from its efficiency. Until the "improvement" had failed the original design was not admitted, and at one time the departmental contention ran so high that it became necessary for the Board to interpose its authority and order pattern carriages to be made in a Royal dockyard under Admiralty supervision.

Scott's carriages showed great constructional strength; powerful moving machinery unaffected by the concussion of firing; self-acting controlling gear almost independent of human carelessness; a gradual absorption of, rather than a rigid resistance to, shocks; the dispersions of concussions over large surfaces; independence of distortion or other injuries to the ship's side; smoothness and ease of motion in every direction; and safety under all sea conditions.

In 1885, when because of Admiralty insistence the breech-loader had been accepted tardily by the Ordnance Department of the War Office—then responsible for the supply of naval guns—the edict went forth that the *Bellerophon* should be rearmed with them. She was the only one of the old ironclads to have her main armament changed in this way, and it was perhaps just as well that the experiment was not a success, as a demand for naval economy had arisen at that time and it was hoped that money could be saved on new construction by renovating old ships. The new guns were selected as being about the same weight as the 9-in. M.L.R., but extra length made a difficult problem of their accommodation, especially at sea with the ports closed. Ten of the new 8-in. B.L.R. on Vavasseur mountings replaced the battery guns, with four 6-in. B.L.R. in specially constructed embrasures under the poop and top-gallant forecastle in place of the 7-in. chase guns; the saluting Armstrongs gave way to

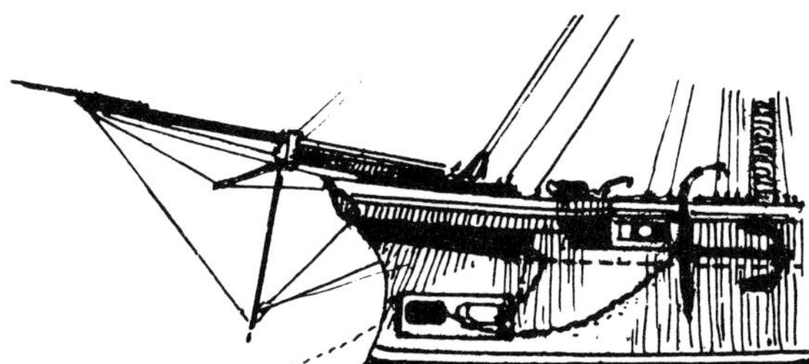

"Bellerophon" after re-armament showing 6-in embrasure.

4-in. B.L.R. which were the earliest form of a special anti-torpedo craft defence, with four 6-pdr. Hotchkiss and twelve machine guns along the upper works.

At the same time the old ship was provided with two carriages for 16-in. Whiteheads discharging through ports on the main deck outside the battery.

The rearmament was the most complete ever extended to an armoured ship; and although furnishing the old vessel with a fictitious fighting value, also served to demonstrate that short M.L. battery guns cannot be replaced efficiently by longer B.L. weapons of approximately the same weight, without undue crowding. Thereafter when elderly ships were subjected to "modernization" their main deck batteries remained unchanged, and B.L. were restricted to upper deck positions.

VAVASSEUR MOUNTINGS

This, the first successful mounting for high-powered B.L. guns, was developed by Mr. J. Vavasseur of Armstrongs in the early eighties. Its distinctive feature was that the recoil consisted of two hydraulic cylinders forming part of the carriage with pistons and piston rods attached to the slide in place of the former compressor brakes. The piston head was designed to give a uniform length of recoil, with the slide inclined upwards at an angle of $7\frac{1}{2}°$ so that gravity ensured the running out.

The system of elevating in the old mounting was a constant source of delay and trouble, as the gear was attached to the recoiling carriage and could not be used for making a correction when the gun was "ready" for firing until the primer had been removed from the vent. Then the gun had to be made "ready" again—by which time another adjustment might be necessary according to the ship's movement. In the Vavasseur mount, elevation and training were effected by hand-worked worm gearing which allowed the gun to be worked up to the moment of firing; and the rope tackles used through so many centuries for working and controlling were at last superseded.

The first Vavasseur mounting designed for use in broadside gun ports worked on the usual rollers and deck racers, with a pivot bar connected to a pivot plate on the deck close to the gun port. The 6-in. gun mount was designed to "house" the gun so that the muzzle should be within the ship's side, and accordingly allowed a recoil of 42 in. Later it was found that "housing" was unnecessary and guns could be made fast with the chase outside the gun port. A later "centre-pivot" mounting superseded this "broadside" pattern which was often considerably affected by alteration in the form of the deck.

The *Bellerophon's* guns all had the "broadside" mounting, and when she departed for her last voyage to the West Indies—in a considerably overloaded condition—her Captain did not consider them to be safe if the ship rolled, there being no proper way of securing them except by the recoil cylinders and the pivot bar tripping toggle, which might work loose. So although the Gunnery Department at the Admiralty was of the opinion that the

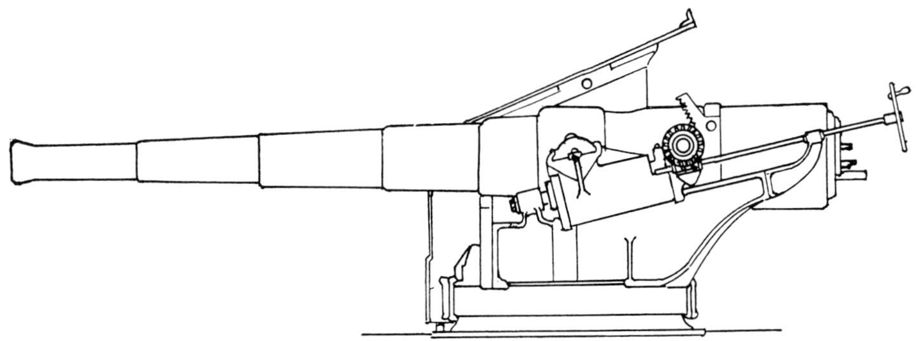

Vavasseur central-pivot 6-in gun. 1881.

vis inertia of the guns would keep them steady and prevent them from taking charge, the Dockyard was persuaded into shoring them up with timber for the trip out.

Incidentally the *Bellerophon* and the small turret ships *Magdala* and *Abyssinia* were the only armoured ships to carry the 8-in. B.L.

ARMOUR

The disposition of protection was similar to that seen in the *Pallas*—a complete waterline belt with a patch amidships along the main deck battery and another up in the bows over the forecastle gun. Compared with Watts's ships, the shorter and more powerful battery was permitted a corresponding increase in armour thickness, leaving the remainder of the main deck—where there was nothing of military importance—unprotected.

From 6 ft. below water to the height of the main deck the belt was 6 in. for its greater length with 5 in. at the bow and stern,[1] backed by 10-in./8-in. teak over a 1½-in. skin. Up in the bows a length of 29 ft. had 4½-in. armour to protect the forecastle gun, and amidships on the main deck was the battery 91 ft. long with 6-in. sides and closed by 5-in. transverse bulkheads. Below the battery the deck was of 1-in. iron, above it ½-in.

An 8-in./6-in. pilot tower was installed abaft the main mast, but it must have been a useless appendage until a wheel was fitted when she received her steam steering gear.

MACHINERY

As already noted, Reed intended to secure speed for his tubby hull by means of increased engine power, hence the *Bellerophon* needed 6,520 I.H.P. to make her 14·17 knots, or 1,000 h.p. more than the *Warrior* for about the same speed. Although less machinery space was available, improved boiler construction allowed for 27 lb. pressure instead of only 20 lb., and because of her exceptionally bluff lines the pitch of her 23½ ft. two-bladed screw was reduced to 20 ft. This, allowing for a maximum of 74 revolutions a minute compared with the 54 of the *Warrior*, gave her the same speed of 14½ knots, although by calculation the older ship should have been the faster. But the *Bellerophon* is described as having the rare and accidental virtue of no propeller slip, and thanks to this she proved very economical at low speeds, being good for 1,500 miles at 8 knots with 640 tons of coal.

In order that her novel lines should be tested at sea as soon as possible, her construction was pressed forward so rapidly that she was ready in twenty-eight months, and sent out on trials with the expectation that no less than 15 knots would be realized—according to the somewhat pompous announcement in *The Times*. But although having the advantages of fine weather and picked coal, only 13·69 knots could be recorded as a four-run average for the first day, and 13·64 knots for the second day's seven tests, owing to the h.p. developed being considerably short of 6,000. Later on, when her boilers and engines were better understood, she did 14·17 knots with 6,520 I.H.P.

RIG

Full ship rig on the second-class scale was carried for the first nineteen years. Not being one of the ships intended for double topsails, her tops were 5 ft. higher than those on the *Minotaur's* lower masts, with the lower yards proportionately raised and the drop of the courses increased; from main truck to deck was 157 ft. to the five-master's 152 ft. During modernization in 1885 she was made a barque. But she was always dull under canvas, and with a disconnected propeller the best ever logged was 10 knots under treble-reefed fore and main topsails and reefed foresail before a moderate gale; in 24 hours her longest run was 182 miles.

Although easily handled as a steamer the dead water she hauled astern made her very sluggish to the tiller under sail, so that she frequently missed stays and refused to wear when the engines had been shut down.

---

[1] The only reference to the 5-in. armour is in the I.N.A. XXX/185, when Sir William White corrected Reed's having credited the *Bellerophon* with a complete 6-in. belt, stating that the plans showed it as being 5 in. before and abaft the battery.

SEA-GOING QUALITIES

Although full lines and buoyancy at the extremities made for dryness in a seaway, her speed fell off quickly against wind and sea—as could only be expected. Lacking the weight of armour in the *Achilles* and *Minotaur* as a steadying influence, she was not so good a gun platform despite the arrangements made to raise her centre of gravity. Her G.M. was 3¼ ft. Hence the rolling tests undertaken with the Channel fleet show that under steam with a long and heavy sea on the quarter the figures would be: *Minotaur* 6·2°, *Achilles* 6·3°, *Bellerophon* 9·4°, *Warrior* 12·6°, *Lord Warden* 14·5°, *Lord Clyde* 21°; and in a heavy Irish Channel sea: *Minotaur* 19°, *Bellerophon* 29° (16° to starboard, 13° to port), *Lord Clyde* 47½°; while under sail with a somewhat heavy sea on the bow and beam the total mean rolls measured by pendulum were: *Minotaur* 4·8°, *Achilles* 5·8°, *Bellerophon* 6·8°, *Lord Clyde* 12·3°.

During all these tests it was claimed that the *Bellerophon* "could have fought her guns with safety, although when rolling through 29° the ports could not have been kept permanently open."

The "Old Billy"—as she was affectionately called throughout the Navy and by her innumerable friends in Halifax, Bermuda and the West Indies—was one of the most popular ships of her day. She still holds the record for the longest spell of service (fourteen years) as a flagship on one station, and despite very poor officers' accommodation remained a sought-after billet until the end of her active career.

"BELLEROPHON"

Commissioned at Chatham in March '66 for service in the Channel, '66-'71 (collided with *Minotaur* in Belfast Lough '68; armour frames driven in 4″-5″ but leakage confined to wing compartments); Mediterranean '71-'72. Refit at Chatham. Flagship on North American station '73—relieving *Royal Alfred*—(run into by s.s. *Flamsteed* when passing mails on the way out, the steamer sinking). Served two commissions until '81, then returned home for refit (with new boilers, B.L. guns and barque rig). Returned as flagship to N.A. and W.I. '85-'92. Paid off at Plymouth and then re-commissioned as port guardship at Pembroke until made non-effective in '03. Converted by Palmers into stokers' training ship *Indus III* Devonport '04 and sold in 1922 after fifty-six years' service.

Chapter 19

"ZEALOUS," "ROYAL ALFRED" AND "PENELOPE"

Of the seven 90-gun two-deckers selected for conversion into ironclads as an emergency measure in 1861, four—the *Royal Oak*, *Prince Consort*, *Caledonia* and *Ocean*—were launched in 1862 and passed into service between 1863 and 1866 in the order named.

Delay in their completion may be excused on the grounds that the French battleship programme was badly in arrears, the completion dates of their ironclads being:

Gloire	1860	*Flandre*	1865
Invincible	1862	*Magnanime*	1865
Normandie	1862	*Savoie*	1865
Magenta	1862	*Surveillante*	1867
Solferino	1862	*Valeureuse*	1867
Couronne	1862	*Gauloise*	1867
Provence	1865	*Guyenne*	1866
Heroïne	1865	*Revanche*	1867
		Belliqueuse	1866

Construction on the three remaining hulls—which were in a more advanced state, having been laid down a year previously—was held up until the results obtained with the *Royal Oak* and *Prince Consort* could be used as a guide to their conversion, and as a result the *Royal Alfred*, *Zealous* and *Repulse* were completed along very different and dissimilar lines. In this respect they form a noteworthy example of the way in which the whole evolutionary process of naval architecture in the mid-Victorian period was profoundly affected and in many ways dominated by the very rapid changes in naval ordnance. When the War Office—upon which the Navy was entirely dependent for its guns—adopted the Armstrong wrought-iron coil system of construction at Woolwich it became possible to produce big guns with a facility hitherto impossible. As a result, calibres increased an inch a year and the successive designs far outstripped the rate of production; a range of new models would be inspected by the Board and the largest and most suitable weapons selected for such new construction as the Admiralty had made provision, but on completion such ships would be markedly outclassed by those on the stocks both by gun power and the protection required to withstand it. And as Armstrong's products were available to foreign Powers and usually ahead of Woolwich, the Navy were at a distinct disadvantage and could only retain some equality by rapidity in construction.

But here again the Service was handicapped by deficient output of ordnance, so that having begun to build a ship to carry the latest type of model there was the prospect of the ship being ready much too soon for her guns unless she was slowed down on the stocks. Such was the case with the *Royal Alfred* and in too many instances during the next twenty years.

It will be remembered that the first four converted ships had been lengthened by 21 ft., but in service the longitudinal hull weakness which soon became manifest in them brought about a Board decision to omit this modification in the *Zealous* and *Repulse*, both of which were subjected to above-water alterations only. As a result the *Zealous* called for less expenditure than any of the wooden ironclads, although against this must be set a reduced fighting equipment of four 8-in. guns compared with the *Ocean* group plus incomplete armour protection and about ¾ knot less speed. But as her service was seen in waters where she reigned supreme, these comparative shortcomings were of little consequence.

The difference in the carrying power between wood and iron hulls is well illustrated in the case of this ship. Her hull weighed 3,067 tons and only carried its own weight (actually 3,055 tons) of armour, armament, engines, coal, etc., whereas had she been built of iron her increased carrying capacity would have allowed for 6-in. armour.

Having had both poop and topgallant forecastle added during completion, she provided a flagship's accommodation. The general construction and lay-out was similar to that of the *Ocean* group although differing in armament, and in profile the *Zealous* would have been difficult to distinguish from the *Royal Oak* except for her foremast being nearer the bow.

ARMAMENT

At the time of her completion the 7-in. M.L.R. had been adopted in place of the Armstrong B.L. and as already noted, formed the equipment of the *Lord Clyde*; a certain number of 8-in. had been issued, but appropriated for the *Lord Warden*, while the *Bellerophon* had first call on the few 9-in. which were ready in 1866. As the *Zealous* was not to be included in the first ranks of our battle fleet, a 7-in. armament was regarded as adequate for

"ZEALOUS"

Builder	*Laid down*	*Launched*	*Completed*	*Cost*
Pembroke	24 Oct. '59	7 March '64	4 Oct. '66	£239,258

Dimensions	$252' \times 58\frac{1}{2}' \times 25'/25\frac{3}{4}' = 6{,}100$ tons. Hull and armour 3,800 tons. Equipment 2,300 tons.
Guns	20 7-in. M.L.R.
Armour	Belt $4\frac{1}{2}''$-$2\frac{1}{2}''$. Battery $4\frac{1}{2}''$. Bulkheads 3″. Pilot tower 3″. Total 790 tons. Backing 30″ teak.
Complement	510.
Machinery	Maudslay. Return connecting-rod engines. Cyl. 82″, stroke 4′, revs. 60. N.H.P. 800, I.H.P. 3,450=11·7 knots. 4-bladed screw. 6 rectangular boilers. 20 lb. pressure.
Coal	660 tons.
Sail area	29,200 sq. ft.
Constructors	J. Large and A. Abethell.

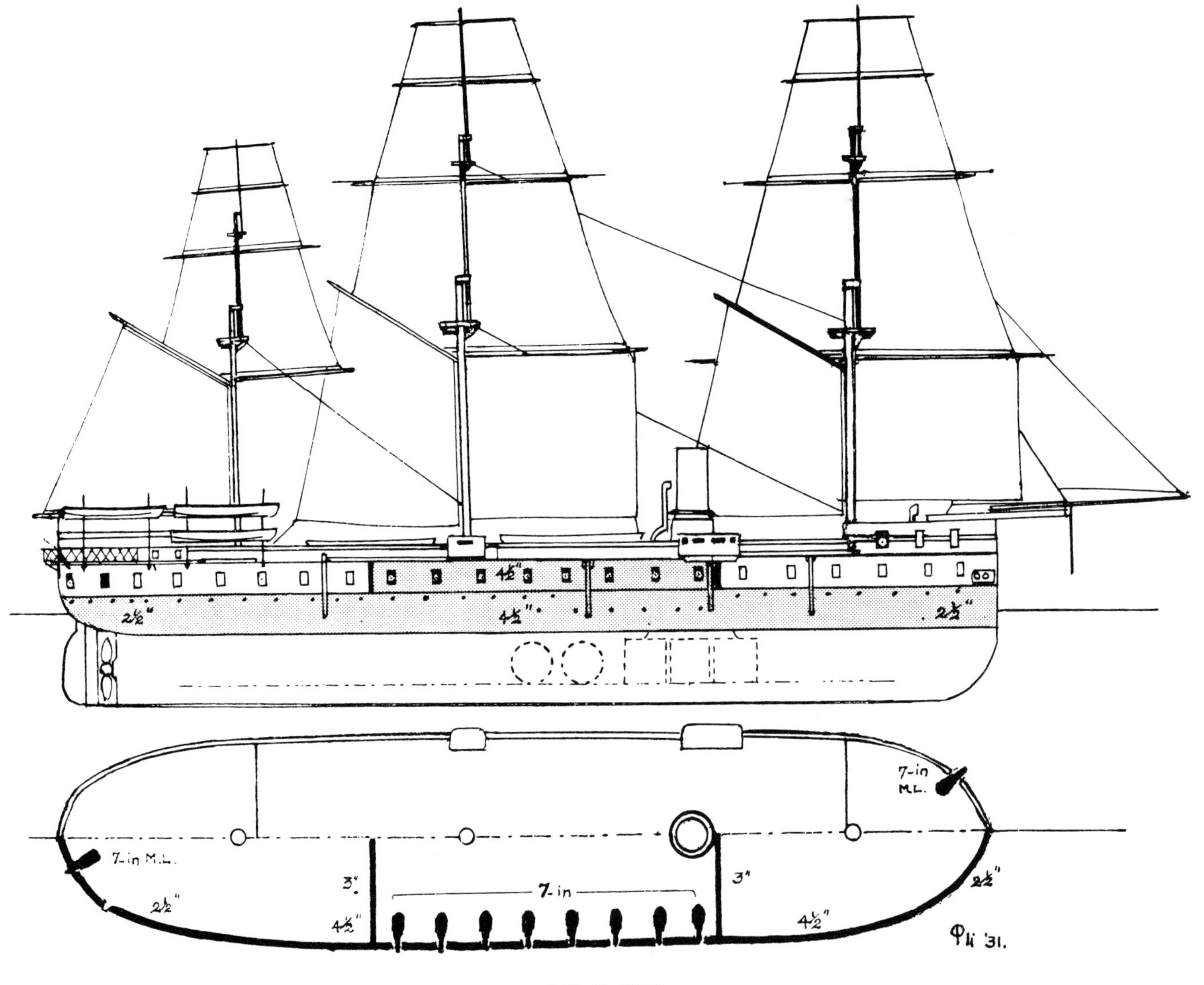

ZEALOUS

her duties and twenty were accommodated—sixteen in the amidships battery and four as chase guns. In which respect she was unique in being the only battleship with a uniform armament of this calibre, and except the *Repulse* the only one to retain her original equipment unchanged throughout her career.

All these guns were mounted on wooden carriages and slides, the ship being sent to the Pacific before the value of mechanical training compared with rope-worked mountings had been appreciated. Hence she became regarded as "the most helpless of the sea-going ironclads" which would be overmatched by the unarmoured cruiser *Inconstant* in moderate weather, and a helpless target in a gale.

ARMOUR

Besides being the most lightly armed of the wooden ironclads, the *Zealous* had also the least weight devoted to protection—790 tons against the 935 tons of the *Ocean*, or 12·9 per cent. of displacement against 13·7 per cent.

The *Zealous* on commissioning at Plymouth as flagship on the Pacific Station in 1866. Both poop and topgallant forecastle can be seen above the line of the bulwarks. She was not to drop anchor in her Home port until '73.

Reed's system of confining protection to the vital parts reduced the full-length plating of the *Ocean* to a 103-ft. battery amidships in the *Zealous* and of 4½-in. iron only, with athwartships screening bulkheads of the same thickness. Elsewhere above the main deck she showed her timbers without even patches of plating around the chase guns. At the waterline and for 6 ft. below, the belt was 4½ in. amidships tapering to 2½ in. fore and aft, so that her shortened model was not responsible for much of the weight saved.

MACHINERY

The lengthened *Royal Oak* with 800 h.p. nominal had made 12·4 knots and stowed 550 tons of coal; the lengthened *Ocean* with 1,000 h.p. nominal reached 12·5 to 12·9 knots and had the same stowage with greater consumption, which reduced their radius. The *Zealous*, unlengthened, shared with the *Repulse* the questionable distinction of being the shortest battleship to carry armour ever built for the Navy, and having a length to beam ratio of 4·3 : 1 was also one of the tubbiest models. Hence her engines working up to 3,623 h.p. only gave her 11·7 knots. But an additional coal supply of 110 tons was some compensation for her deficiencies elsewhere.

The engines were exactly amidships in a single compartment with the boilers.

SAIL

A full ship rig was her dressing from first commissioning to final paying-off, with masts and spars on the second-class scale as in the *Ocean*. Although very handy, stiff, and weatherly under canvas, the four-bladed screw was a big drag and 10½ knots was the best she ever logged. But with six years' service in the Pacific—which station made the least demands upon bunkerage—she covered a greater mileage under sail than any of her contemporaries in the battle fleet, and during her last commission voyaged 30,000 miles with only 1,600 tons of coal expended.

GENERAL

Unlike the other wooden ironclads, she was reported as being a good sea boat and a steadier gun platform than any of them except the *Repulse*, in such weather as would permit of her armament being fought.

As an item of almost antiquarian interest it may be noted that the *Zealous* was embellished with hancing pieces in the shape of life-size female busts at the break of the poop. With the raising of bulwarks in 1800, hancing pieces of every kind had been discontinued and the square breaks entirely undisguised, so this throw-back in the *Zealous* may rank in a minor way with the frigate stern in the *Warspite* and *Impérieuse* (1884) and bow scroll in the *Royal Sovereign* (1889) as the last appearance in H.M. battleships of those features which added to the grace and countenance of the sailing ships.

"ZEALOUS"

Commissioned in September '66 at Plymouth as flagship in the Pacific, reaching Esquimalt ten months later, where she was kept at the end of the telegraph cable from July '67 to April '69. During these twenty-one months she went out for two days a quarter on gun practice—a record stay in port without a break for any British battleship in full sea-going commission in the Victorian Navy. After a nine months station cruise she picked up a fresh crew at Panama which had travelled overland from Colon in January '70. Returned home after 6 years without docking, at 7 knots (best speed) during a five months voyage; struck an uncharted rock in the Magellan Straits but without sustaining serious damage. Paid off at Plymouth April '73; refitted; guardship at Southampton '73-'75; finally paid off and laid up at Portsmouth in '75 and sold Sept. '86 for £6,000.

And so passed the lonely *Zealous*—the ship which never once steamed in company with another battleship, and covered the greatest mileage with cold boilers.

"ROYAL ALFRED"

Having been ordered for conversion in June 1861, work on the *Royal Alfred* was allowed to proceed and her frame had been lengthened before the Board decided to let the final design wait upon the completion and trials of the *Ocean* and *Royal Oak*. During the period at which work was at a standstill Reed became Chief Constructor and responsible for her armament and protection; and as he was able to work on her almost *ab initio* so far as the distribution of her weights was concerned, with 600 tons of additional displacement to expend he decided to equip her with the 9-in. M.L.R. and 6-in. plates introduced in the *Bellerophon*.

Profiting by the experience with the *Royal Oak*, the original 800 h.p./nominal engines were retained as in the *Zealous*. Internally there was the same lay-out as in the *Royal Oak* excepting that the main deck was bulkheaded off fore and aft of the battery, through which the funnel was taken so that the uptakes were behind armour. Intended for flagship duties, she was completed with a poop and also carried a topgallant forecastle, but had no bridge or pilot towers as in the *Lord Warden* and consequently was always handled from the poop. The "heads" were sponsoned off abreast of the foremast and the hull side adorned with scupper pipes as in the *Prince Consort*.

Both officers and men berthed along the lower deck with the discomfort of bad lighting and ventilation inseparable from this arrangement, common to all the wooden ships of her type.

ARMAMENT

The saving in machinery weight—amounting to some 200 tons—allowed for a much heavier armament amidships without straining the hull, and to this extent she was regarded as one of Reed's "box ships." Full advantage was taken of the recent advances in gun power and armour thickness to fit a battery which not only made her the most powerful of the wooden ironclads but also the most heavily armed in proportion to displacement of any British battleship built or building.

Ten 9-in. were spaced five aside in the battery, with eight 7-in. as chase guns, of which four were mounted

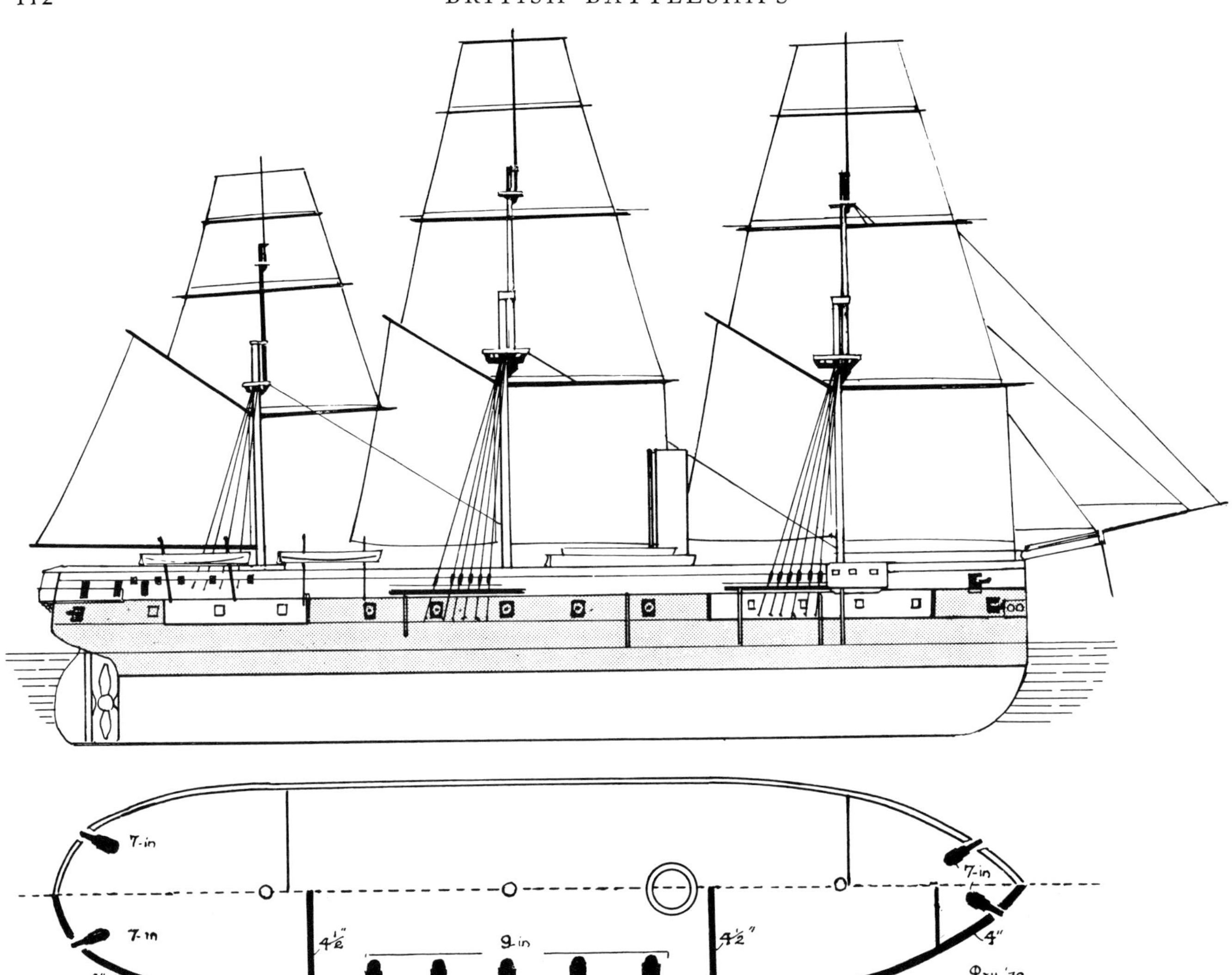

"ROYAL ALFRED"

Builders	*Laid down*	*Launched*	*Completed*	*Cost*
Portsmouth	1 Dec. '59	15 Oct. '64	23 March '67	£282,803

Dimensions 273′ × 58½′ × 23¾′/27′ = 6,700 tons.
Hull and armour = 4,380 tons. Equipment = 2,320 tons.

Guns 10 9-in. M.L.R.
8 7-in. M.L.R.
6 Saluting.

Armour Main deck to 5½′ below water 6″, with 4″ at bow and stern. Amidships battery 6″. Screens and bulkheads 4½″.

Complement 605, exclusive of Admiral's staff.

Machinery Maudslay. Horizontal reciprocating.
Cyl. 82″; stroke 4′; revs. 60.
N.H.P. 800 = 3,230 I.H.P. = 12·36 knots.
6 rectangular boilers. 20 lb. pressure.

Coal 550 tons. Radius 2,200 miles at 5 knots.

Sail area 29,200 sq. ft.

Constructors J. Large and A. Abethell.

Special features:

(1) The best armed in proportion to displacement of any ship in the Battle Fleet.
(2) Was as fast under sail as under steam.
(3) The last timber-hulled capital ship to be built at Portsmouth.

in pairs on the main deck fore and aft, two under the topgallant forecastle and two on the quarter deck—an armament more powerful than that of the heavier *Bellerophon* by three 7-in. For saluting there were six brass smooth-bore howitzers on the poop. The 9-in. 12½ tonners were mechanically worked and could be fought efficiently in a seaway, but the 7-in. 6½-ton guns had the rope-worked slides which militated against their employment in bad weather.

Like the *Zealous*, she completed her service with the same ordnance aboard as on the day she hoisted the pennant.

ARMOUR

By increasing the armour from 4½ in. to 6 in. the area protected had to be curtailed, so that the main deck fore and aft of the battery was bare except for a patch of 4½ in. up in the bows forming a screen for the chase guns, with another length of 26 ft. aft protecting the stern pieces. The battery was 6 in. with 4½-in. bulkheads and

The *Royal Alfred* at Plymouth on passage to the North American Station in 1867. The battery has now shrunk to five guns aside and the ports for her 9-in. M.L. extend from just abaft the funnel to the foot of the mizen.

spread over a length of 115 ft.; it housed the same number of guns as had been crowded into 98 ft. in the *Bellerophon*—a vessel longer by 27 ft. She was therefore more efficiently protected than the earlier *Zealous* or later *Repulse*; but whether the risks from shell-fire against the denuded areas in wooden ships were balanced by increased local concentration of armour over a heavier battery was always a debatable point. However, as it had long since been the practice in French wooden ironclads it was adopted by the Board. From the beginning heavy local protection had been a feature in Reed's designs, and was to be carried to extremes in some ships evolved during the next ten years.

MACHINERY

Engines and boilers were the same as in the *Royal Oak*, but the funnel was about 15 ft. further aft so as to have the uptakes and casings behind armour. Her best trial speed was 12·5 knots.

SAIL

While awaiting her guns the *Royal Alfred* carried barque rig, but in August 1866 yards were crossed on the mizen and full ship rig was retained throughout her career. Although not able to equal the *Royal Oak's* record, she was as fast under sail as under steam with 12·5 knots to her credit under both conditions, and during six years' service as flagship on the North American and West Indies station cut through many thousand miles of grey and blue water without leaving a propeller wake.

SEA-GOING QUALITIES

Being fitted with a poop—which the *Royal Oak* did not carry—and the armour having a centre of gravity about 20 ft. abaft amidships, the *Royal Alfred* trimmed by the stern with a load draught of 23½ ft. forward and 27 ft. aft. This disposition of weights evidently suited her, as although heavier than the *Royal Oak* there was no loss in speed with a similar propeller driving at the same number of revolutions. She was easy to handle under steam or sail, and being light by the head behaved well in a seaway but rolled as badly as any of her half-sisters.

"ROYAL ALFRED"

Was the last timber keeled capital ship to be laid down at Portsmouth. Work was stopped for a time and slowed down for two years, so that she was not put afloat until October '64; and as she then had to wait for the new guns, completion was delayed until '66. Commissioned in January '67 as flagship for the North American station, she arrived at Halifax after a 25 days' passage through the worst of North Atlantic weather with enough coal for one more day's steaming at 5 knots. She remained on duty between Nova Scotia and the West Indies for 2 years, being relieved by the *Defence* while she returned home for docking. A second commission on the same station for 4 years followed. (Grounded on the Bahama Bank and lost her false keel and some sheathing in 1872.) Relieved by *Bellerophon* and returned home to pay off in January '74. Portland Reserve until March '75 after survey of her boilers—which were so eroded that pressure was down to 10 lb. and her speed to 7·5 knots—she was laid up pending an expensive refit until she became obsolete.

Sold in '85 for £5,562.

"PENELOPE"

Builder	*Laid down*	*Launched*	*Completed*	*Cost*
Pembroke	4 Sept. '65	18 June '67	27 June '68	£396,789

Dimensions 265′ × 50′ × 16′/17¼′ = 4,470 tons.
Hull and armour = 2,820 tons. Equipment = 1,650 tons.

Guns 8 8-in. M.L.R.
3 5-in. 40-pdr. B.L.R. (broadside 820 lb.).
2 20-pdr. B.L.R. (saluting).

Armour Belt 6″-5½″-5″; bulkheads 4½″; skin ¾″.
Backing 11″-10″.
Total 688 tons.

Complement 350.

Machinery Maudslay, horizontal reciprocating. I.H.P. 4,700 = 12·7 knots.
6 cyl. 55½″; stroke 30″.
2 Griffiths 2-bladed screws 14′ diam. 15½′ pitch.
4 boilers. 30 lb. pressure.

Coal 500 tons.

Sail area 18,250 sq. ft.

Constructors W. S. Romaine and F. W. Gray.

Special features:

(1) Abnormally shallow draught for her displacement.
(2) Hoisting twin screws.
(3) Twin rudders.
(4) Embrasures for the end battery guns.
(5) Marked steadiness as a sea boat.

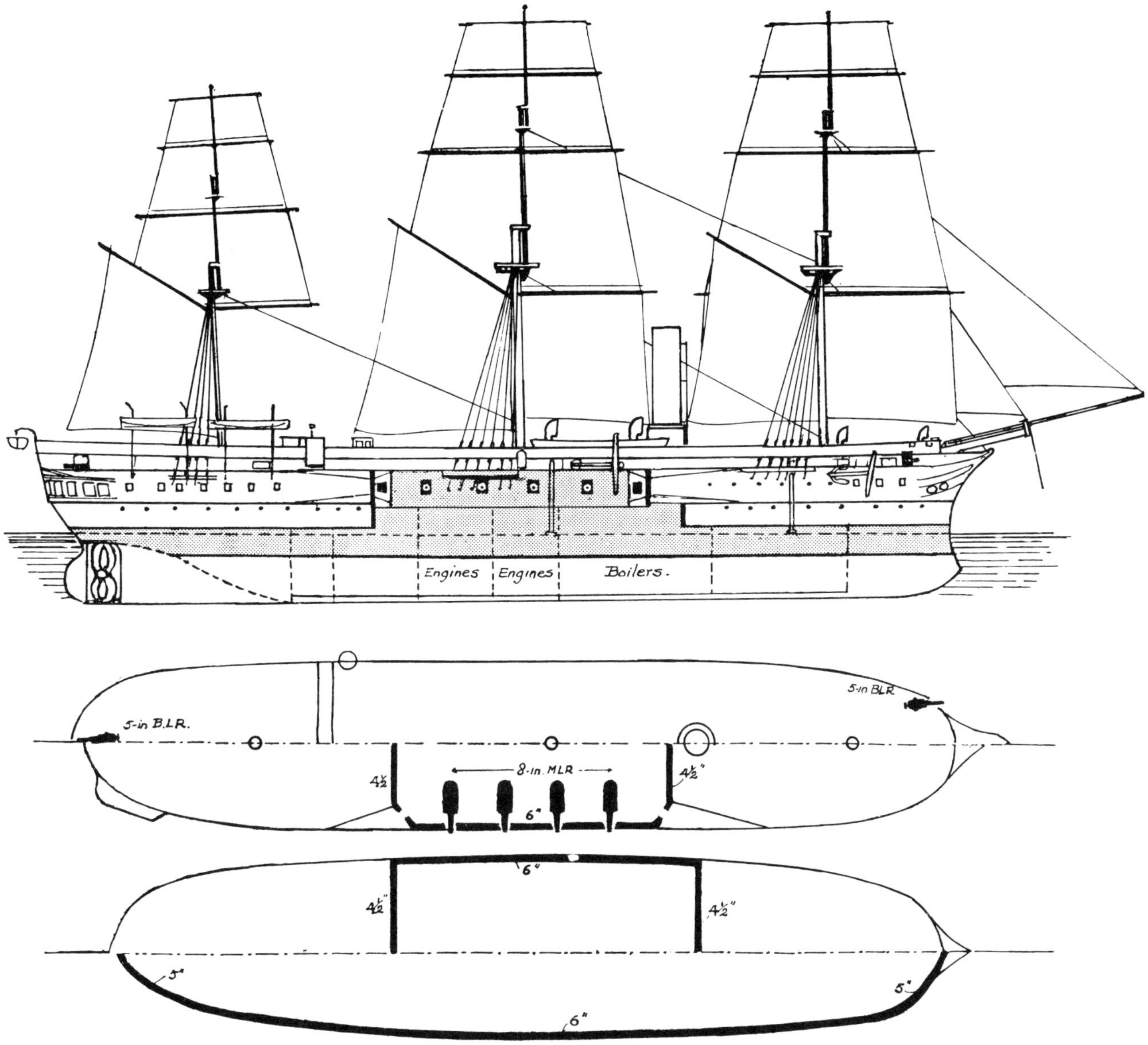

PENELOPE

In the absence from office through illness of the Chief Constructor, responsibility for the *Penelope* was entrusted to his brother-in-law, Mr. Nathaniel Barnaby. She was the last to be laid down of the group of small armoured ships commencing with the *Enterprise*, and being larger than these sloops was officially termed an "armoured corvette"—a corvette being the French rating for what was a large sloop, and at one time only applied to vessels with an open gun deck. Later the description was given to vessels carrying a scale of armament coming between the sixth-rate frigate and medium-sized sloop, whether the guns were decked over or not.

Stern of the "Penelope"

In some respects the *Penelope* was a remarkable specimen of naval architecture, having an abnormally shallow draught necessitating certain limitations in equipment which, in their turn, imposed a variety of constructional expedients destined to remain unique. Exactly for what employment the Board intended her has never been discovered, but presumably for inshore service in the Baltic where the need for light draught armoured units had been appreciated during the Russian war. But in limiting her to 16 ft. forward and $17\frac{1}{2}$ ft. aft her draught was 7 ft. less than that of the 4,140 ton *Boadicea* (1,875)—a corvette most nearly approaching her in displacement—and demanded a very square cross-section to obtain buoyancy; and as the hull immersion was not sufficient for one large propeller she had to be given twin screws, necessitating an experimental and expensive type of stern which has never been duplicated in the annals of naval architecture, although the armoured gunboats *Viper* and *Vixen* had a type of double stern and twin screws.

Because two *fixed* screws in conjunction with a flat bottom, shallow draught, and high freeboard would preclude any possibility of navigable progress under sail, it was decided that they should be fitted for hoisting—a benefit which had been withheld from the *Pallas*, then building. To enable this to be done it was necessary to take the tail shafts *inside* instead of outside the hull, each screw being in a separate hoisting well with a rudder on the after post of the banjo frames, thus creating a stern under-water section which ruined the run of her lines

The *Penelope* at Spithead after her 1887-'88 refit, prior to leaving for Simonstown. Machine guns can be seen on small sponsons up forward and over the after embrasure. Note the projection of the quarter gallery—an unusual feature.

and would have produced a mass of dead water between the rudders. To obviate this the hull was scooped out between them to allow for free water to flow up from the keel—which ingenious solution, however, failed to counteract the other disabilities under which the *Penelope* drifted rather than sailed, as a result of the reduction in her draught.

On the other hand, she naturally had a higher centre of gravity than was customary in the ironclads, and consequently earned a reputation for steadiness and fighting ability in a seaway which was the envy of her consorts rolling their gun ports under, and was to have a marked influence on future ship design.

There were the usual three decks and a topgallant forecastle, but no poop; the officers' accommodation was on the lower deck, with the men berthed forward of the battery.

ARMAMENT

The gun-power provided was generous for her tonnage, with eight 8-in. M.L.R. in a central battery and a 5-in. B.L.R. on each side under the forecastle with a third on the upper deck aft. To secure some axial fire from the battery the end ports were embrasured, an alternative to the recessed sides introduced in the *Enterprise–Pallas* group which were not favoured on account of the shell trap they offered. By employing the embrasure, Barnaby added considerably to the effective fire from the battery, and to the value of the broadside ship as opposed to the turret principle. The 5-in. guns were on truck mountings, and very ineffective weapons; a few quickfirers and machine guns were added during the 1887-8 refit.

ARMOUR

The *Penelope* carried less armour in proportion to displacement than any iron ship in the Battle Fleet (15·4%) and was the only one without belt protection extending up to the main deck. The waterline strake, rising from only 4 ft. below water to 1 ft. 6 in. above at lower deck level, measured 6 in. amidships tapering to 5 in. at the bow and stern, thus leaving an unduly large proportion of her sides exposed. The upper deck central battery was 68 ft. long, flanked by 6-in. iron with 4½-in. bulkheads; below this over the lower deck side was a similar strake, but extending 28 ft. further forward so as to cover the crowns of the forward boilers. Incidentally, the exposed condition of her engine rooms due to the absence of shell gratings nearly led to serious damage at Alexandria, when it was only by good fortune that a shell which entered abaft the armour did not go down into her machinery.

MACHINERY

In designing the machinery Maudslays were faced with the problem of laying two sets of large reciprocating engines on a deck width of 50 ft. Each set was therefore given three small cylinders instead of two large ones, the stroke being reduced to 30 in.—a layout which afforded even running but made for voracious coal consumption, so that although provided with a generous bunkerage the *Penelope* had a very restricted steaming radius.

SAIL

Had this been offset by a good performance under canvas she might have been advantageously employed on distant stations—although not specifically designed for overseas work. But with the exception of the five-masters she sailed worse than any other ship in the fleet, having no grip on the water and drifting to leeward like a tea-tray. A bare 8½ knots was the best ever recorded in her log.

From first to last she was ship rigged, the spacing of the masts being unusual with the mainmast nearer the fore than the mizen. But having only the same sail area as the *Favorite* while exceeding her displacement by 1,455 tons, the *Penelope* was greatly under-canvassed; actually with her twin screws she would have been more serviceable with pole masts and extra fuel. Seemingly the twin screws were of little use when it came to jockeying, and Captain Willes reported on the alleged ability to "point" the ship with them:

> "This is an entire fallacy, as in the *Penelope* which is only 260 ft. long we have found that the screws will not turn the ship at all (pivoting) except in a light wind, and then very unsteadily."

SEA-GOING QUALITIES

As already noted, she was a remarkably steady gun platform. At a draught of 17·4 ft. her metacentric height was 3 ft.; at 18 ft. it was 2·7 ft. Her angle of maximum stability was 40°, but the righting moment did not vanish until 82° inclination had been reached—an extraordinary figure.

GENERAL

After her refit in 1888 she was denied the usual long spell in Reserve and was sent to South Africa as a receiving ship, thus being unique among the ironclads in passing straight from active service to purely subsidiary duties.

In 1896 when the question of her modernization was raised, engines and boilers would have needed renewal as well as armament and it was considered that she was not worth the expense.

"PENELOPE"

Completed and commissioned at Devonport 4 June '68 and served in the Channel until June '69. Then proceeded to Harwich as guard ship where she served 13 years from '69 to '82, with periodic trips with the Reserve Fleet. "Particular Service Squadron" June-August '78 during Russian War Scare. In the summer of '82 her squadron called at Gibraltar, and on account of light draught the *Penelope* was detached for the Suez Canal operations and was present at Alexandria. There she formed the inshore attacking group with *Monarch* and *Invincible* and was placed closest to the western batteries. Firing 231 rounds, she sustained minor injuries and needed a new mainyard and an 8-in. gun damaged by a shell which exploded in the embrasure. Was flagship in Suez Canal until cessation of hostilities and then returned to Harwich for another five years, being paid off in '87. Refit '87-'88 and then sent to Simonstown as harbour receiving ship and in January '97 became a prison hulk until sold for breaking-up at Cape Town in 1912 for £1,650.

Chapter 20

THE DEVELOPMENT OF END-ON FIRE

In 1863 Captain Cooper Key became Captain of the gunnery establishment *Excellent* and responsible for all the tests, trials and reports on new guns, mountings, projectiles, armour, fuses, etc., which were conducted at Portsmouth. In June 1866 he drew up a memorandum on gun disposition in capital ships in which he stressed the necessity for all-round fire with powerful arming of the bow and stern to obviate points of impunity.

This memorandum was to have far-reaching results as it focused attention upon a feature of design which was to be developed out of all proportion to its tactical necessity during the next fifteen years or so, and so deserves recording as the principal influence responsible for what were regarded as the most successful ships in the Reed and Barnaby eras.

Captain Key considered that in single ship actions it was very desirable not to allow the enemy to rake the ship with impunity, as many circumstances might arise to prevent the broadside guns being brought to bear on him; but in a general action it was a point of vital importance. It might be assumed as certain that in a general action a ship would be almost constantly engaged with two adversaries at once; she would, therefore, while engaging one opponent on the broadside find another taking up a position on her quarter, bow, or stern, or whatever point of impunity could be found. This point of impunity should not exist; a ship could not be considered as effectively armed unless she could bring at least two guns to bear on every point of the horizon, either by training them in the ports in which they were carried, or by readily traversing them to other ports. He cited the *Royal Alfred* and *Hector* as quite incapable of coping with a second ship in a general action which might have selected any point for attack more than 30° before or abaft the beam, as they had no bow or stern guns. Attention was necessary to these points, to enable a ship armed on the broadside system to compete with one carrying her guns in turrets. The principal advantage of the latter consisted in enabling each gun to be brought to bear on nearly every point of the horizon. The advantages of the former system should be that guns were at all times pointing in every direction: if this were lost sight of, he considered that ships armed on the broadside must gradually give place to turrets.

These were the arguments which carried the Navy with them. They, of course, strengthened the position of the advocates of turrets; but they also induced Reed to carry out the principle of specific end-on fire in the *Iron Duke* class and *Sultan*, and no doubt contributed towards that absolutely complete adoption of it in such ships as Barnaby's *Alexandra* and the French *Devastation*, and in our purchased ships *Belleisle* and *Orion*. It was a very small step from these arguments to minimize the value of broadside guns altogether, and to exalt the value of "end-on" fire, as was done later in the *Inflexible*.

On the other hand, Colomb pointed out that:

> "although the arguments carried all this weight, it must not be forgotten that those on the other side were not stated. In the first place, all experience was against them. It was obvious that if they apply at all, they must apply with greater force to sailing than to steam ships. It was a question of mobility. If the one ship or the two ships had powers of placing themselves as described, was the ship attacked compelled to maintain for an instant her disadvantageous position? Were not her powers as a sailing ship to move out of such a position immeasurably less than they were when she was a steamer? Yet the wars of a couple of centuries had never raised the question in regard to sailing ships, and the bows and sterns had always remained more or less unarmed.
>
> Was it logical to raise so important an issue without experiment? Was the obvious fact that an ordinary broadside ship could not engage a ship ahead or astern of her if she were deprived of motion, or was without springs on her cables if at anchor, a good argument? Was it not at least necessary to show on paper that positions of ships, or fleets, could be taken up as suggested, and could not be counteracted by movements on the other side? Doubtless there was breadth in such an argument, but it might be said that it wanted depth."

Before terminating his appointment in August 1866 Captain Key put on record his ideas of warship design, which when he went to the Admiralty as First Sea Lord in 1879 served to a large extent as the basis of the plan upon which the *Collingwood* was built.

He was of the opinion that too much importance had of late years been attached to the following points:

(1) *The protection of men's lives in action from the effect of enemy fire.* He would prefer to afford *perfect* protection to the vital parts of the ship such as the water-line, rudder and steering gear, engines, screw and magazines, and utilize all other available weight and space by adding to the offensive power of the armament on every point.

(2) *The attainment of great speed in ships forming a fleet intended to take part in a general action.* He said that the actual speed of a fleet depended upon the speed of any ship which might have her tubes foul, or the machinery in any way partially disabled or defective. The line-of-battle could never move at high speeds or about 11 or 12 knots. Great speed could only be ensured by sacrificing handiness, or stowage, or armament; each of these was of more importance in a fleet than an extra one or two knots.

(3) *The power of shells in setting a ship on fire to a dangerous extent.* He had witnessed the explosion of two hundred and ninety-five shells varying from 150-pdrs. to 20-pdrs. in the wooden target ships *America* and *Alfred*; and although he generally fired twenty shells without visiting the ship, only in one instance was she set on fire to any extent. This was caused by a shell bursting in the side where a previous shell had splintered the planking. Although it had been burning for nearly half an hour, it was put out with a few buckets of water. An efficient fire brigade would obviate all danger of a ship being set on fire by enemy shell.

(4) *The use of the pilot house for the protection of the Captain and other officers.* It was not possible to handle a ship efficiently, or to direct a fleet, from such a position; while the risk incurred by the Captain was less than formerly. Ships now carried only ten guns aside instead of fifty, while a small shot will injure quite as much as a large one and there was nothing in the vicinity of the bridge to burst shells. Exposure to rifle fire could be avoided by $\frac{3}{8}$-in. iron screens in various positions, from any of which the ship could be handled. He submitted that the weight of the pilot tower in the *Bellerophon*—nearly 100 tons—would be better absorbed by eight 7-in. M.L.R. which with all their ammunition would weigh about the same; while it was doubtful whether the tower would resist heavy gun-fire.

He suggested the following points for consideration in the construction of future line-of-battle ships:

(1) They should not exceed 300 ft. in length in order to be capable of rapid manœuvring.
(2) Engines and boiler power should be limited to ensure 12½ knots on the measured mile when fully equipped.
(3) The water-line should be protected by an 8-in. iron belt from 5 ft. below to 2 ft. above the load-line—and a deck of 1-in. plating and 6 in. of planking placed on a level with, or a little below, its upper edge.
(4) The rudder should enter below the water-line; the tiller, rudder, and steering gear (except the wheel) being protected by the belt.
(5) The armament on the gun deck should be 12-ton guns in the midships ports and lighter guns towards the extremities; each gun should train through an arc of at least 72°.
(6) On the upper deck, two guns on a turn-table before the foremast, two other similarly mounted abaft the mizen. No armour was to be on these turn-tables, but rifle-proof protection afforded to the men. The rollers and training-gear to be protected as much as possible by the upper-deck beams and deck. These tables might either revolve inside a bulwark with ports, or the bulwark might be attached to the turntable.
(7) No armoured pilot house, but various rifle-proof positions affording a clear view ahead and astern with speaking tubes to the wheel and engine-rooms.

Captain Key did not see clearly how sails were to be retained. He did not even then think them of propulsive advantage to the ship; but pleaded that the training of seamen by means of "a full rig" should not be forgotten.

The value of this summary of views on armament and design will be seen later on. Of special importance is Key's opinion that it would be better to leave guns' crews unprotected except from rifle-fire than to shield them with armour which could be penetrated. This conclusion was afterwards accepted, and only the advent of small quick-firing and machine guns brought about a return to light protection. Although Key's proposals were not favoured at the time, they certainly formed a very sound general basis for development twenty years later.

Chapter 21

"HERCULES"

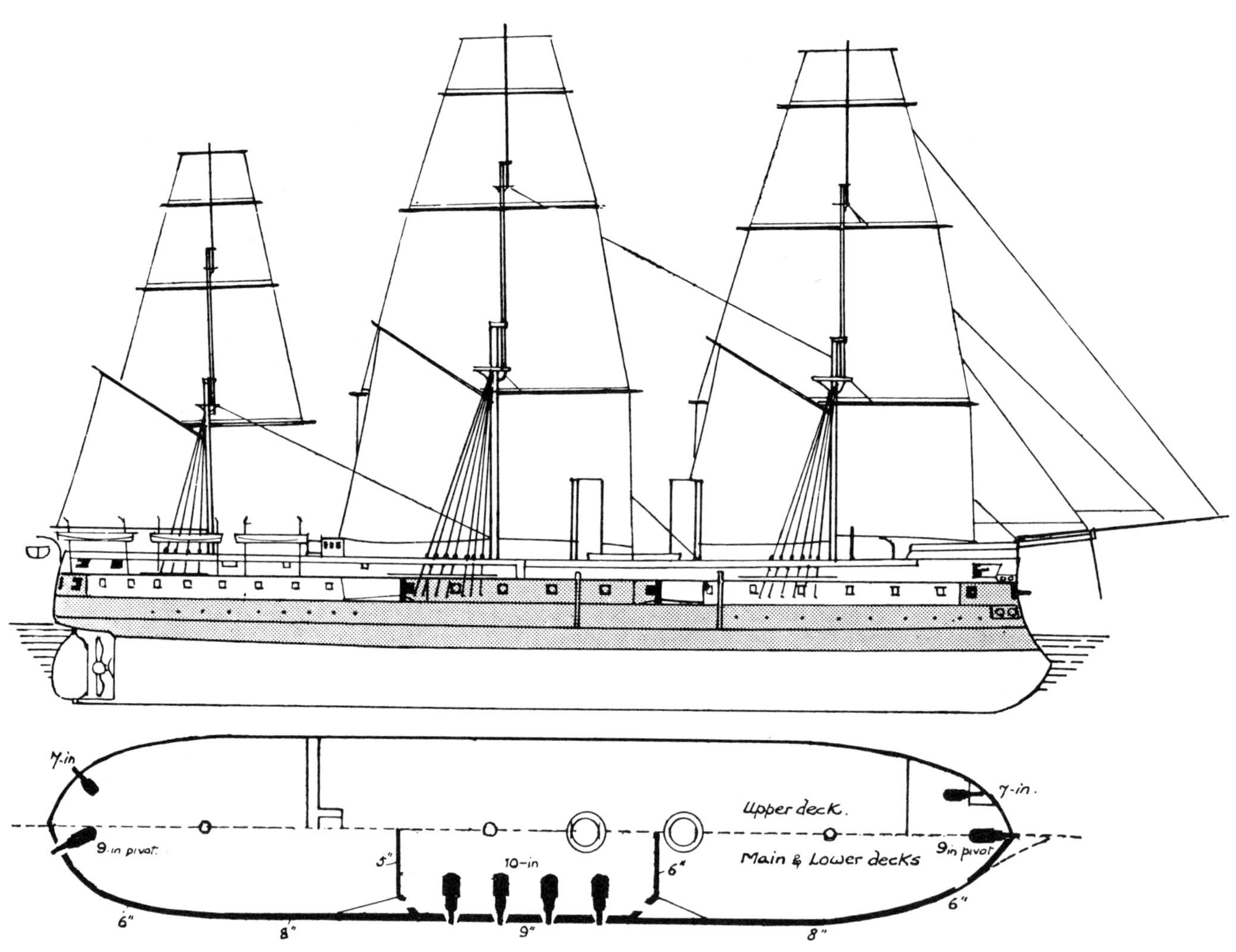

HERCULES

Builder	*Laid down*	*Launched*	*Completed*	*Cost*
Chatham	1 Feb. '66	10 Feb. '68	21 Nov. '68	£377,008

Dimensions 325′ × 59′ × 24′/26½′ = 8,680 tons.
Hull and armour = 5,700 tons. Equipment = 3,130 tons.

Guns 8 10-in. M.L.R. — In 1892 6 4·7-in. Q.F. were added.
2 9-in. ,,
4 7-in. ,, — Later 2 7-in. M.L.R. replaced by 6-in. Q.F.
8 Saluting.

Armour Belt 9″-8″-6″. Bulkheads 6″-5″. Skin 1½″, deck backing 12″-10″.
Total 1,332 tons.

Complement 630.

Sail area 28,882 sq. ft.

Machinery Penn. trunk engines I.H.P. 6,750 = 14·7 knots. 2 cyl. 118″; stroke 4½′; revs. 64.
Boilers, 9 rectangular, pressure 30 lb. 2-bladed screw, 23½′ diam., 24′ pitch.

Coal 610 tons. Radius 1,600 miles at 8 knots.

1892 Inverted triple expansion. I.H.P. 8,500. Speed 14·6 knots.
8 cylindrical steel boilers, pressure 140 lb.
Revs. increased to 88, pitch reduced to 17½′.

WHEN the armament of the *Bellerophon* was under discussion, the Board had accepted the new 9-in. gun only after long debate. While she was still on the stocks the Ordnance Department intimated that a 10-in. piece would soon be available, what time the iron-masters were offering 9-in. plates capable of resisting the 9-in. gun at the then accepted battle range of 1,000 yards. As steel-made 300- to 600-pdrs. of superior quality to the French were now available at Krupps (the Russians actually had some 900-pdrs. under test), the Admiralty could not afford to stand still, and both the new gun and thicker armour were adopted for the *Hercules*, whose keel was laid in the dry dock at Chatham soon after the *Bellerophon* was floated out.

When completed she took her place as the most powerful warship afloat—a proud though shortlived honour, as each successive addition to the fleet of samples now being added to the battle squadrons rose superior to her predecessors in powers of attack and defence.

The general design was that of an enlarged *Bellerophon* with somewhat better lines, and a weight distribution conducive to steadier behaviour at sea. She had a pointed instead of the curved ram, a stern similar to the *Bellerophon*, and a topgallant forecastle, but no poop until prepared as a flagship after her second commission. The rudder was balanced, the steering being worked by a threefold wheel under the break of the poop and another below on the main deck. Improved methods in construction enabled her to be built for only £20,000 more than the *Bellerophon*, although of 1,100 tons greater displacement, while her machinery actually cost less.

She was the first battleship to have the anchor cables led in on to the upper instead of the main deck, as a large gun port in the stem made the provision of a manger impossible, and without it the main deck would have

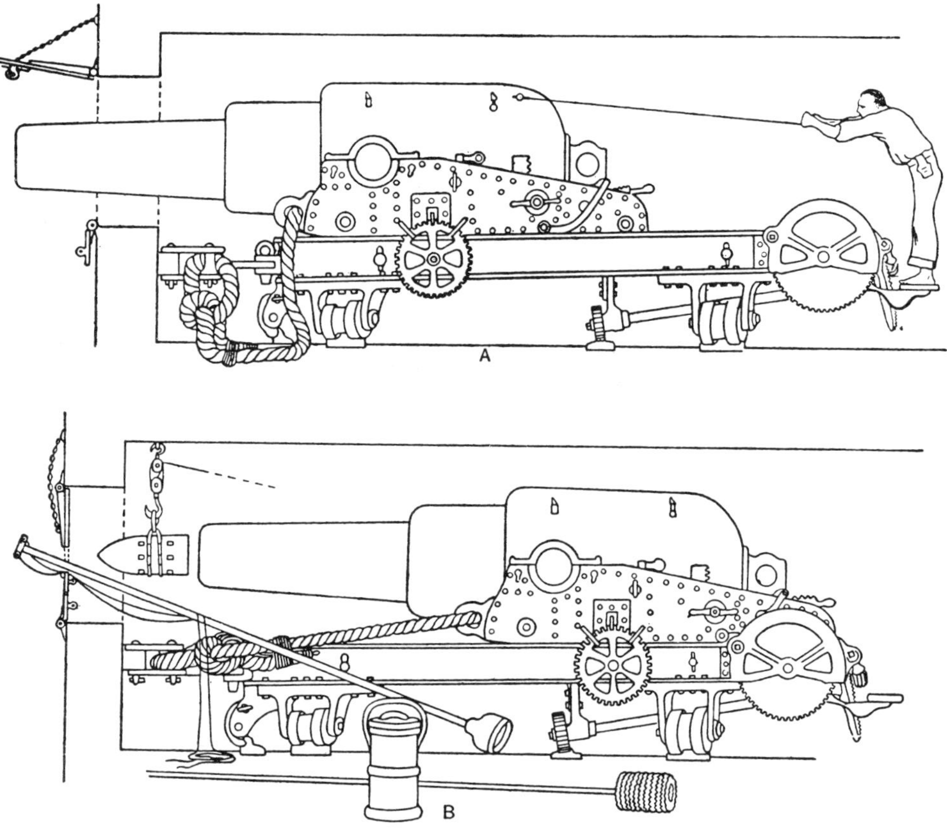

BRITISH 10-INCH RIFLED MUZZLE-LOADER OF 1870 ON NAVAL BROADSIDE MOUNTING WITH GUN'S CREW OF 17 NUMBERS AND TWO POWDERMEN

A. Firing position.
B. Sponging and loading position, with port closed and rammer staff through loading scuttle (disc of scuttle not shown). *(from Ballard).*

been flooded when working anchors in a seaway. No manger was necessary on the upper deck, where flooding would be both unlikely and of little consequence.

ARMAMENT

The *Hercules* shared with the *Lord Warden* the distinction of mounting a three-calibre main armament—to which, in those days, the drawback was not confusion in range determination but multiplicity in projectiles and charges in the shell rooms and magazines. Of the new 10-in. M.L.R., she carried four aside in the central battery—which was 20 ft. shorter than that in the *Bellerophon*—and the end guns could be traversed to fire within a few degrees of the line of keel through indented ports similar to those in the *Penelope*. These 18-tonners charged with 70 lb. of pebble powder threw a 400-lb. projectile with a muzzle velocity of 1,380 ft./sec., the highest rate of aimed fire for a smart crew being one round in 70 secs.

The forward chase guns were two 7-in. M.L.R. under the topgallant forecastle firing through embrasures, and a single 9-in. M.L.R. having a port cut in the stem on the main deck with broadside ports on each side. Stem ports had been used for forecastle guns with a high command in several French ships and were a feature in the

The *Hercules* at Plymouth during her first commission in the Channel 1868-'74, when she was ship rigged and had no poop. Beyond her are the bows of the *Penelope*, with the masts of the *Northumberland* over her stern.

as yet untried *Favorite* and *Pallas*, but at main deck level; the gun may have been less exposed to flooding-out in a head sea than when placed at the turn of the bows as in *Bellerophon*, but was for ever discarded in our Navy after the *Hercules*.

For the after chase there was a 9-in. at the stern and a pair of 7-in. on the upper deck.

Two 14-in. torpedo carriages were placed on each side of the main deck in 1878, and in 1886 net defence was added. In 1883 it was proposed that the *Hercules* should receive a complete B.L. rearmament like the *Bellerophon*, and the Official Return for July shows her with eight 9·2-in. in the main battery and six 6-in. as chase guns with six 4-in. torpedo guns. Experience with the *Bellerophon*, however, put an end to any further B.L. rearmaments in Reed's ships apart from the addition of a few medium Q.F. when they were "modernized" in the 'nineties.

ARMOUR

Distribution was similar to that in the *Bellerophon*, with 9-in. plating over the battery and along the sides, tapering to 6 in. at the bow and stern. The battery was closed by 6-in. transverse bulkheads and the chase guns screened by 6-in. armour to the height of the upper deck. The actual composition of the ship's side was far stronger than the tabulated figures suggest, the components being (1) the 9-in. armour, (2) 10-in. teak backing with longitudinal girders at 2-ft. intervals; (3) 1½-in. skin on 10-in. vertical frames 2 ft. apart filled in with teak; (4) 20-in. teak; (5) ¾-in. plating on 7-in. frames—making a total thickness of iron (without girders or frames) of 11½ in. with 40 in. of teak. On trial at Shoeburyness the mock-up target of the *Hercules*' side resisted a 600-pdr. gun—and the *Warrior's* side was only proof to the 68-pdr.!

Although a conning tower is shown in many published plans of the *Hercules*, actually she did not have one, as they had temporarily gone out of fashion. "The truth was that armoured 'pilot towers' tried in a few earlier ships were no use whatever, having neither steering wheels nor engine-room telegraphs inside. Everybody condemned them, and the argument that they would protect the Captain from being shot by a sniper, like Nelson, was met by the sufficiently obvious reply that if he resorted to a position from which he could not possibly handle the ship, he might as well be shot before going into action at all" (Ballard).

MACHINERY

Better hull lines, increased boiler pressure, and jacketed cylinders in more efficient trunk engines driving a two-bladed screw which had the same diameter but 4 ft. greater pitch than the *Bellerophon's*, secured half a knot more speed with the same horsepower and coal consumption. With 64 revolutions at load draught the *Hercules* made 14·7 knots against the 14·17 of the *Bellerophon*, which was 1,100 tons the lighter, and although both bunkered the same amount of coal the more economical *Hercules* had the advantage of about 100 miles more steaming radius, being able to cover some 1,600 miles at 8 knots. But both ships suffered from deficient fuel supply, and when the *Hercules* was flagship in the Mediterranean she came to rely upon the *Devastation*—which had thrice her bunkerage—for the wherewithal to complete a cruise when the call upon her own resources had been too heavy.

Excepting a combined steam pump and capstan (which was becoming a standard fitting during the later 'sixties), there were no engines apart from the main machinery until steam steering gear was added in 1874; when re-rigged in 1892 she received a steam hoist for the boat derrick.

SAIL

It had been intended that her masting should be on the second scale, but when it became known that Coles' *Captain* was to carry sail on the maximum scale, Reed gave both *Monarch* and *Hercules* squarer yards and extra canvas "in order to prevent facetious representations concerning the relative sailing qualities of the various vessels."

Her sail plan was therefore on a par with that of the *Achilles* with 17-ft. instead of 20-ft. mastheads, and an 81-ft. lower foremast in place of 86 ft.; and being the only one of the six specially heavily rigged battleships to have the shortened mastheads, the mainsail was the largest to be set by any vessel in the Fleet. Inclusive of stunsails her total sail area was 49,400 sq. ft., of which 24,400 were square sails, 9,700 fore-and-aft sails, and 15,300 stunsails.

But in spite of this spread of canvas she was an indifferent performer, with 11 knots as her best recorded effort under sail—a knot better than the *Bellerophon*.

Her lower masts with identity plates were later used as derrick stumps on the building slip at Chatham.

SEA-GOING QUALITIES

With a metacentric height of 2·69 ft. she rolled about seven times a minute and as a gun platform proved steady, being a good sea boat generally, although with a tendency to yaw when running. The Earl of Clanwilliam reported in 1870:

> "The *Hercules* displayed very good qualities during a gale off Cape Finisterre; she was very steady; the heaviest lurch was from 12° to 13° with a fierce gale and a very heavy sea, both on the beam. But I regret to say she is a most difficult ship to steer under all circumstances from the large weather helm she carries, without a speed of 4 to 5 knots, more especially when running before the wind. When the gale commenced she steered so wildly and broached-to so often, that I gave up the idea of running out the gale and hove-to with fore and main trysails and fore staysails, using steam with about 20 revolutions. I believe the battery guns could have been worked and the ship taken into action at any time during the gale, using steam with full power."

Having finer lines and a freer flow of water to the rudder she manœuvred better under sail than the *Bellerophon*, and would both tack and wear under favourable conditions.

MODERNIZATION

Like so many of the old ironclads, the *Hercules* was subjected to a certain degree of extensive refit in the early 'nineties, when her value as a fighting ship was somewhat over-estimated. In this expensive but futile "modernization" two 6-in. Q.F. replaced the forward 7-in. M.L.R., and six 4·7-in. Q.F. were spaced three aside along the upper deck above the battery, with nine 6-pdrs. and thirteen 3-pdrs. scattered over the topsides—which additions to her offence enabled the old ship to eke out a further twelve years with the Reserve ships at Portsmouth as a "third-class battleship." Experience with the *Bellerophon* precluded any rearmament in the battery—although by this time there was not a single muzzle-loading gun mounted in the French battle fleet.

All sail power was removed and a couple of military masts together with rather imposing funnels helped to give her an up-to-date appearance above, which tended to accentuate the pathetic ineffectiveness of the grand old hull below. Inverted triple-expansion engines by the Greenock Foundry Co. replaced her obsolete machinery,

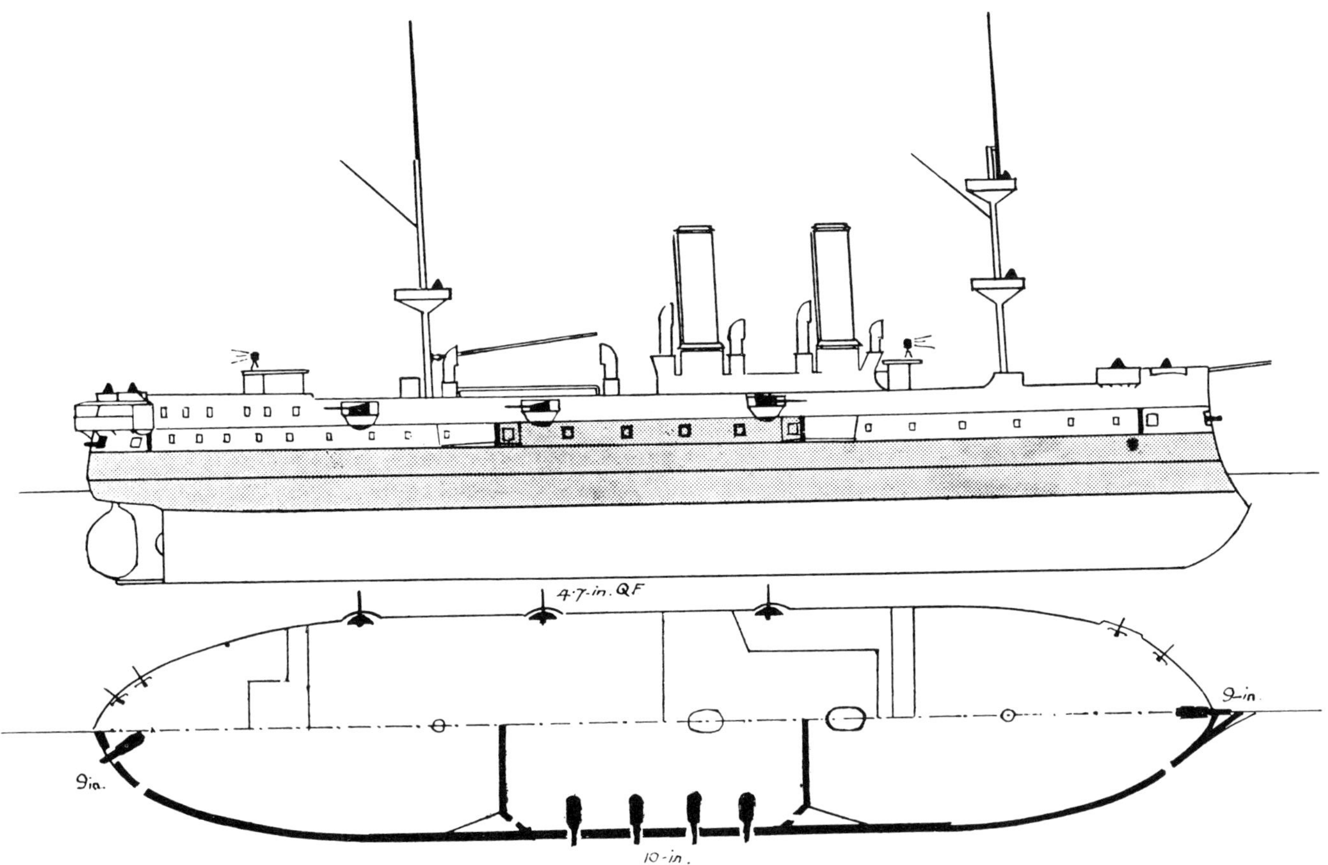

HERCULES. Modernized, 1892

and eight cylindrical boilers with steam pressure raised from 30 to 140 lb. increased revolutions from 64 to 88; but reduction in propeller pitch from 24 ft. to 17½ ft. allowed for only 1 knot more speed—and then with excessive vibration. Fuel consumption was certainly lowered, but as sea-time during the rest of her life only amounted to seven days, the new machinery was practically unused when she was relegated to harbour service in 1905.

That this policy of partial modernization—fitting new machinery while retaining the old armament—found favour in certain circles may be gathered from the following extract from "Brassey," 1892 (Engineering section):

> "One of the most judicious and sensible steps ever taken by any Board of Admiralty has been the fitting of some of our older ironclads with new machinery. Such ships as the *Minotaur*, *Hercules*, *Monarch*, and others, built with a scrupulous and conscientious attention to strength that it is much to be feared no longer survives as a first principle in our dockyards, may some day form an invaluable second line of battle. When the first race and battle are over, and the swift and the strong are all *hors de combat*, the victory will remain with the Power that can bring into action the most efficient unwounded reinforcements."

"HERCULES"

Commissioned at Chatham '68 and served in Channel from '68-'74. (In July '71 was selected to tow the *Agincourt* off the Pearl Rock, Gibraltar, then in danger of complete loss under difficult conditions, which duty she performed successfully, thanks to consummate seamanship. Collided with and rammed *Northumberland* 25 December '72 which drifted on to her bows during a gale at Funchal. Outer bottom torn open and wing compartments filled.) Refit '74-'75. Flag Mediterranean '75-'77. Paid off Portsmouth; commissioned in '78 as flagship of Admiral Cooper Key's Particular Service Squadron during the Russian Crisis of '78; guardship in Clyde '79-'81; flagship Reserve Fleet '81-'90 (Admiral Hornby's Particular Service Squadron 1885, and cruise to Baltic under Duke of Edinburgh). Modernized '92-'93; and in Reserve at Portsmouth '93-'04. Temporary harbour flagship of C.-in-C. '04; depot ship at Gibraltar as *Calcutta* '05-'14, then towed home and "Fishguard 11" as part of the artificers training establishment at Portsmouth—a roofed-in hulk unrecognizable as the ship which was regarded as the well-nigh perfect example of naval architecture of her day and "Reed's Masterpiece."

Chapter 22

TURRET VERSUS BROADSIDE SHIPS "MONARCH" AND "CAPTAIN"

If the story of how Ericsson introduced the turret into the U.S. Navy is the most dramatic in the history of warship construction, that of Coles' fight to get his turret accepted by the Admiralty is the most tragic. Under the stimulus of Civil War, events moved fast in favour of the little *Monitor*, and her historical debut placed her inventor in an unassailable position as ship designer and constructor. Over here, Coles fought year after year

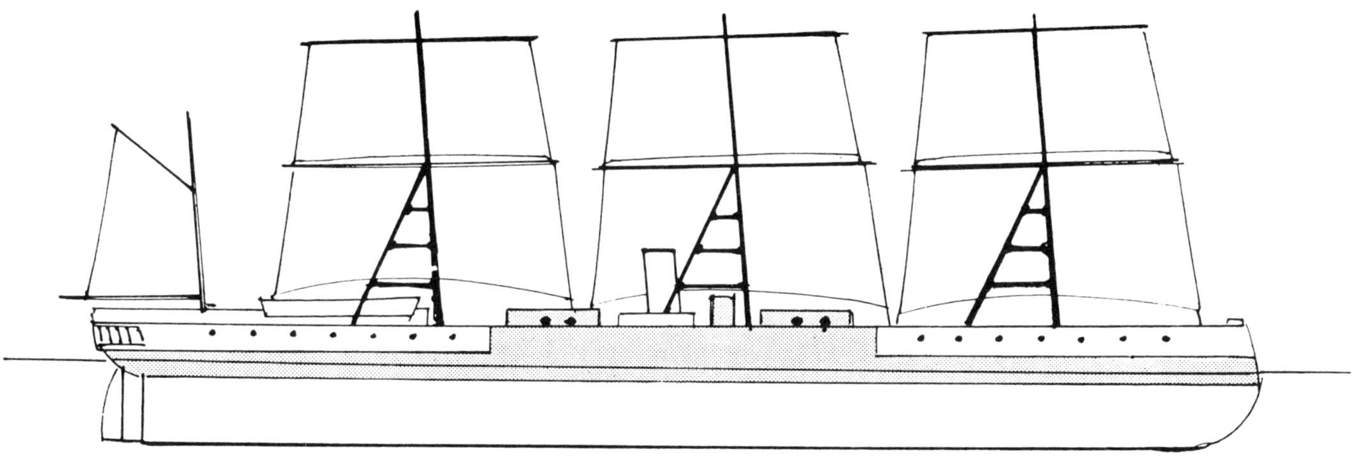

Coles' proposed Turret ship, 1862.

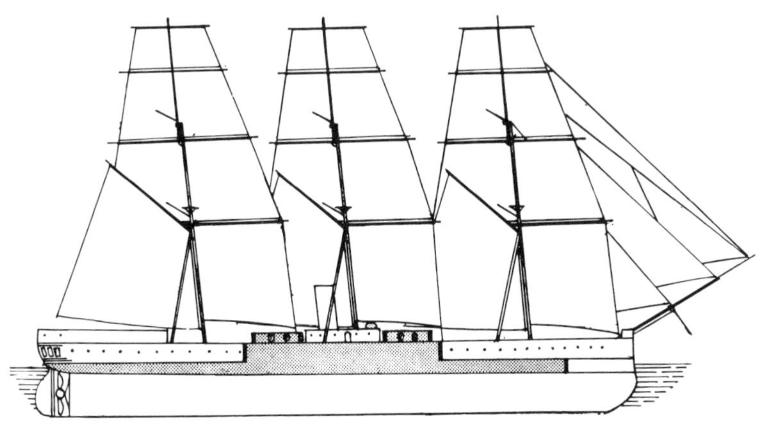

Coles' proposed Turret ship of 1863.
(Coles-Barnaby design.)

to get a sea-going turret ship built—only to be subjected to departmental obstruction and frustration while suffering the handicap of constant illness, which prevented him from putting his views before the Committees called to consider them, and finally fated to have the ship of his dreams built over-weight, so that under stress of weather she was to shatter the hope of success her achievements seemed to justify before taking him down in the vortex of her foundering.

From the day that the *Royal Sovereign* and *Prince Albert* were ordered Coles never ceased from advocating the advantages of the turret as against broadside armament in sea-going battleships. By lectures, articles, and letters to the press he built up such a substantial case in favour of his system that by 1864 the leading newspapers were almost solidly on his side.

The fantastic ten cupola design of 1859, which had been turned down by the Admiralty constructors as an impracticable application of his principles, was followed in 1862 by a more acceptable type which he introduced during a lecture at the R.U.S.I. This was for a two-turret type rigged with four masts, three of which were tripods designed to avoid masking the guns by shrouds and rigging. But Coles made no pretence of being a naval architect when it came to working out the design of such a ship as a practicable proposition. Skilled assistance was needed before drawings could be submitted to the Board, and he therefore applied to the Admiralty for the loan of an experienced constructor, and the following year Mr. Nathaniel Barnaby was directed to assist him in drawing up calculated designs for his proposed ship, the first plan being dated March 1863.

In general the Coles-Barnaby design was based upon the 1862 model but given three tripods with full and equal rig. The B.O.M. tonnage was 3,700, dimensions being $280 \times 54 \times 24\frac{1}{2}$ ft. with 12 knots speed, and four 300-pdrs. were to be mounted in two turrets. The sail area was considerable, amounting to 33,000 sq. ft. Incidentally it should be noted that all Coles' sea-going projects were intended to be canvassed on the maximum scale and he relied upon the tripod system of masting to carry this.

The Board, however, decided that it would not be expedient to embark upon the construction of any further turret ships until the two coast-defence ships had been tested. But after the success of the *Royal Sovereign*, Coles pressed the Board to extend their experiments to a sea-going type. He had hoped for a favourable reaction to the design drawn up by Barnaby—but the Board ignored it and Coles was never able to discover what had become of his drawings.

Towards the end of 1864 he attacked official inertia from a fresh angle. Reed's *Bellerophon* and *Pallas* having been accepted as official standards in medium and lightweight armoured ships, Coles determined to put forward competitive designs to their displacement, from which hard-and-fast comparisons could be made. Starting with

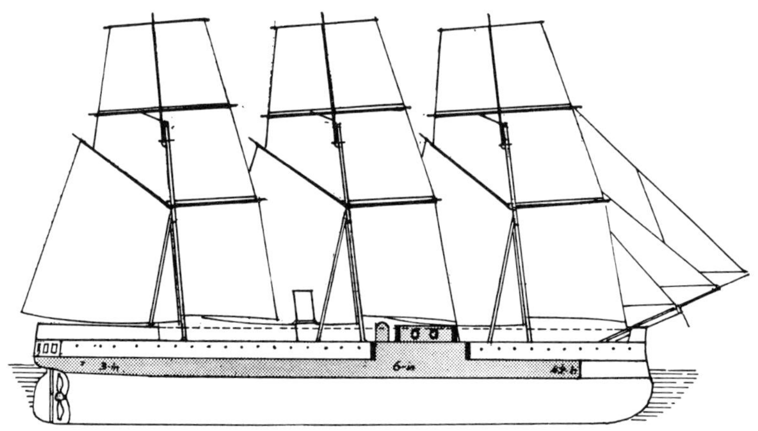

Coles-Scullard design.

the *Pallas*, he asked that he should be allowed the use of her drawings for tracing dimensions and planning the structure, with the services of a competent draughtsman and naval architect for drawing up a turret ship design which should compete with Reed's armoured corvette. He wrote the Board:

> "She shall be equal if not superior to any of them in the essentials of a man-of-war in speed, defence, sea-going qualities, and decidedly superior in offensive powers. The designs shall be submitted to be reported on by a committee of naval officers and eminent ship-builders *half of whom I shall nominate*."

The Chief Constructor was quite agreeable for the plans of the *Pallas* to be loaned, and urged Coles to take the *Bellerophon* as his model as likely to lead to the evolution of a more satisfactory turret ship, the *Pallas* being of wood. Actually Coles made use of both sets of drawings, taking the smaller ship as his model for dimensions and the larger one for general constructional details. The services of Mr. Joseph Scullard, Constructor at Portsmouth Dockyard, were placed at Coles' disposal, and in due course the designs for a ship smaller than the 1863 project and carrying her armament in one turret only were submitted to the Board.

This ship compared with the *Pallas* as follows:

	Turret Ship	*"Pallas"*
Dimensions	225′ × 49′ × 22½′.	225′ × 50′ × 21½′ (mean).
Displacement	3,996 tons.	3,794 tons.
Designed h.p. and speed	3,600 = 13·8 knots.	3,580 = 13·8 knots.
Guns	2 600-pdrs.	4 100-pdrs. 2 110-pdrs.
Armour	Belt 6″-3″. Citadel 6″. Turret 6″.	4½″. 4½″.
Weight of broadside	1,200 lb.	310 lb.
Weight of armour, etc.	664 tons.	560 tons.
Sail area	18,218 sq. ft.	16,716 sq. ft.

In every way the turret ship would have been far superior to the corvette, which could not have fought her guns in a seaway and commanded only restricted arcs of fire concentration.

In April a committee was appointed to consider the proposed turret ship, but none of its members were nominated by Coles. They were Vice-Admiral Lauderdale (chairman), Rear-Admiral H. R. Yelverton, Captain H. Caldwell, Captain John J. Kennedy and Captain Henry B. Phillimore; and all the witnesses examined were more or less in favour of the turret excepting Reed and the Controller. Rear-Admiral Elliot stated:

> "For a vessel of the same displacement I prefer the plan proposed to any other I have seen or heard of for a sea-going armour-plated man-of-war full-rigged ship."

Through illness Coles was unable to attend any of the meetings and in due course a Report was made. But it was not until the following August that he was able to reply to the many objections which were marshalled up against the design. Coles disposed of them in summary fashion. Their general tenor may be judged by the following:

> A.1: "The possibility of a shot entering the top of the turret when the vessel was rolling or exposed to plunging fire."
>
> Answer: . . . when the turret top was 16 ft. above water and the *Pallas* guns only 9 ft.
>
> B.1: The possibility of the ship being boarded and the turret jammed by wedges.
>
> Answer: . . . when any boarding party could be swept off the ship—and if a wedge were driven from above to jam the 4-5 inches between base and deck it could be easily driven out again by men from below.

However, the Committee, although not in favour of the one-turret armament, wished the system to be given a trial in a sea-going ship; in accordance with their recommendations the *Monarch* was then designed by the Constructor's Department and the drawings sent to Coles in March 1866. Coles proposed alterations which included:

(1) The lowering of the height of the turrets.
(2) Removal of the forecastle and poop.
(3) Placing the guns 15 ft. above water instead of 17 ft.

In his letter he said:

> "Allow me here to observe that in designing the ship one of the chief merits of the turret system, that of firing right ahead with her heaviest ordnance, appears to have been discarded and the broadside plan substituted by weighting the ends with guns and armour so antagonistic and fatal to sea-going qualities and high speed. I must therefore most respectfully but earnestly record my opinion that a sea-going turret ship should not be loaded with the bow and stern weight as proposed in the *Monarch*, that her turrets should not be deprived of fore and aft fire, and that it is disadvantageous and unnecessary to add to her tonnage by giving her guns the unprecedented height of 17 ft. out of water, tending to make her top-heavy and to labour heavily in a seaway. A good sea boat does not altogether depend upon height out of water, but upon form, and the extremities of the ship being kept light in proportion to their displacement."

The Board, however, could not accept Coles' recommendations, and the *Monarch* was put in hand as a ship which he considered "did not represent his views of a sea-going turret ship or one which could give his principles a satisfactory and conclusive trial."

Soon after the *Monarch* was ordered it became obvious that Coles' supporters in Parliament and the press and public were not going to be satisfied with the Admiralty design for a turret ship. Ever since the introduction of ironclads the official policy towards the maintenance of naval supremacy had been subject to constant criticism, and a large number of politicians and journalists were far from being inclined to "trust the Admiralty." Controversy grew more acrimonious and partisanship ran higher, until things reached a state when the Admiralty were being censured from both sides of the House. And unfortunately there was schism in the Board itself. The naval members were at one with the Controller and Chief Constructor in regarding Coles' conception adversely, while the First Lord (Somerset) held the opposite view and championed Coles. Between the two sides the Naval Lords were in a quandary.

They might have asserted their professional authority and resigned; or acquiesced to the public demand and given Coles a free hand at Whitehall; or pursued a middle course—which they did. As a compromise the Board agreed to finance the construction of a turret ship to Coles' design which should be built by one of the firms officially nominated.

Of these Coles chose Laird Bros., who held a position second to none in the shipbuilding world and had already built several turret ships for foreign navies; and Lairds accepted the responsibility of designing and building the ship, to which the name *Captain* was given as the First Lord's own choice. Thus shortly afterwards the Birkenhead firm had under construction two ships bearing the name of Nelson's commands, *Captain* and *Vanguard*, both of which were destined for short careers terminating in tragedy.

By now there were three very definite schools of thought as to the type of sea-going ship in which turrets should be mounted:

(1) Coles put forward the claims for a freeboard of 8 to 11 ft. with turrets carrying the heaviest guns, provided with an all-round fire and heavily rigged with tripod masts.

(2) Reed objected to the rigged turret ship, but if masting was required, then he would place his turrets towards the ends of the ship where the guns would have a training on either side of the fore and mizen masts. He preferred to mount turrets fore and aft on a breastwork through which all ventilators could be led and deck openings properly protected, with a flying deck and *light signal masts only*. He favoured a medium freeboard of about 12 ft. amidships and regarded the monitor hull as inadmissible except in a harbour defence ship.

(3) The Board wished to combine turrets with masts and yards on a high freeboard hull, fitted with forecastle and poop. Adequate rig was regarded as essential, since there was little faith in the reliability of steam propulsion, and the then low boiler pressures and uneconomical types of machinery meant heavy coal consumption and restricted radius. With the limited bunkerage of the period it was felt that speed could be increased and fuel saved by the provision of sail rather than that masts and yards should be discarded in favour of an equivalent weight in coal.

But the essential virtue of the turret was its all-round bearing. Circumscribe this by shrouds, rigging and the superstructure necessary for the proper working of sails, and half its value would be thrown away. A rigged turret ship Reed regarded as an anachronism—a low-freeboard one as a danger; he impressed the Board with his belief in the central battery as the best method of mounting guns in rigged capital ships and pointed out that *on a given displacement twice as many guns could be so carried with equally good protection as in a turret ship.*

The Controller, Sir Spencer Robinson, was definitely opposed to the sea-going turret ship and it was owing to his influence with the Board that Coles had such a long and difficult fight. In 1867, soon after the contract price for the *Captain* had been fixed at £335,000, he stated:

> "While I say, and say with a certain knowledge and clear conviction of the fact that a turret ship for coast defence and for the purpose I have named is the very best weapon you can use, I use my own judgment, and I have within myself as clear a conviction, founded upon argument, reflection, and logic, that this may not be the best vessel for sea-going and cruising purposes" . . . "and the greatest opponent to the turret system as applied to a sea-going ship is Captain Coles—and for this reason—that in my judgment he has advocated impossibilities." (R.U.S.I., 1 May 1867.)

In his detailed Report to the Board dated 26 April 1865 the Controller had been more favourably disposed towards the turret ship than his evidence before the Committee seemed to imply, and on the question of sail power some of his observations were extremely pertinent and anticipated a reaction against masts and yards which was not to become general in the Service for some years to come.

> "So many officers, whose judgment is of great weight, consider the large sail power so essential to a sea-going man-of-war, that it is with diffidence that I state my deliberate conviction that all the essential qualities of a steam-ship of war, especially of an iron-clad, are jeopardized by a large system of sail power, and that my objections to it are not diminished by carrying the sail on tripod masts—an extremely ingenious arrangement.
>
> If there are practical reasons which render it almost impossible to raise the screw of a well-designed iron-clad—and in this design it is not proposed to do so—then the large sail power, in my opinion, fails to effect its intended purpose, and is only mischievous in action, in a gale of wind, or in steaming with foul winds.

> If, however, a large sail power is required in a sea-going turret-ship, it can only be obtained by the ingenious invention of Captain Coles."

Meanwhile Coles' conceptions were materializing.

In July 1866 Lairds' plans were sent to Whitehall for inspection and on July 20 the Chief Constructor reported that:

> "The *Captain* had been well designed and proportioned and would not materially differ from a ship that would have been prepared in this department had Their Lordships seen fit to sanction in our designs an upper deck 8 ft. above the water."

And that:

> "It was embarrassing to find Coles has accepted from Messrs. Lairds and forwarded to Their Lordships as a perfectly satisfactory proposal a design embodying so many features against the adoption of which he has energetically remonstrated when proposed by the Department at various times during the last 2 years."

this last paragraph having been occasioned by the inclusion of the forecastle and poop which Coles had all along declared to be unnecessary and serious encumbrances, depriving the turrets of all axial fire. But experience in their foreign-ordered turret ships had shown Lairds that a low or medium freeboard vessel could not fight her turret guns in a seaway when awash, and that only the bow and stern superstructures as fitted to the *Scorpion* and *Wivern* could keep her moderately dry. To which decision Coles had to bow—and sacrifice his long-cherished tenets.

In June 1866 the *Monarch* had been commenced as an office design conforming to the requirements of the Committee of naval officers and members of the Constructor's staff. Six months later the keel of the *Captain* was laid in the dry dock at Birkenhead as a Lairds' design embodying all the features of Coles' conception, with the addition of forecastle and poop.

"MONARCH"

Builder	*Laid down*	*Launched*	*Completed*	*Cost*
Chatham	1 June '66	25 May '68	12 June '69	£354,575

Dimensions $330' \times 57\frac{1}{2}' \times 22\frac{1}{2}'/26' = 8{,}300$ tons.
Hull and armour 3,486 tons. Equipment 4,814 tons.

Guns	1869	1871	*Added on "modernization"*
	4 12-in. M.L.R.	4 12-in. M.L.R.	4 12-pdrs.
	3 7-in. "	2 9-in. "	10 3-pdrs.
		1 7-in. "	

Armour Sides 7″-6″-4½″; bulkheads 4½″-4″; bow screen 5″.
Turrets 10″-8″; conning tower 8″; backing 12″-10″; skin 1½″-1¼″.
Total 1,364 tons.

Complement 530-575.

Sail area 27,700 sq. ft.

Machinery Humphreys and Tennant, Return conn. rod.
I.H.P. 7,840 = 14·9 knots.
2 cyl. 120″, stroke 4½′.
2-bladed screw, 23½′ diam., 27′ pitch, 63 revs.
9 boilers. 30 lb. pressure.

Coal 600 tons. Radius 2,000 miles.

1892 Re-engined and re-boilered.
Maudslay inverted triple expansion. I.H.P. 8,216 = 15·75 knots.
8 cylindrical boilers. 150 lb. pressure.
Radius 6,000 miles.

Special features:

(1) The first sea-going turret ship.
(2) The first British warship to mount 12-in. guns.
(3) The fastest battleship of her day.
(4) Had the longest life on the effective list of any British armoured ship.

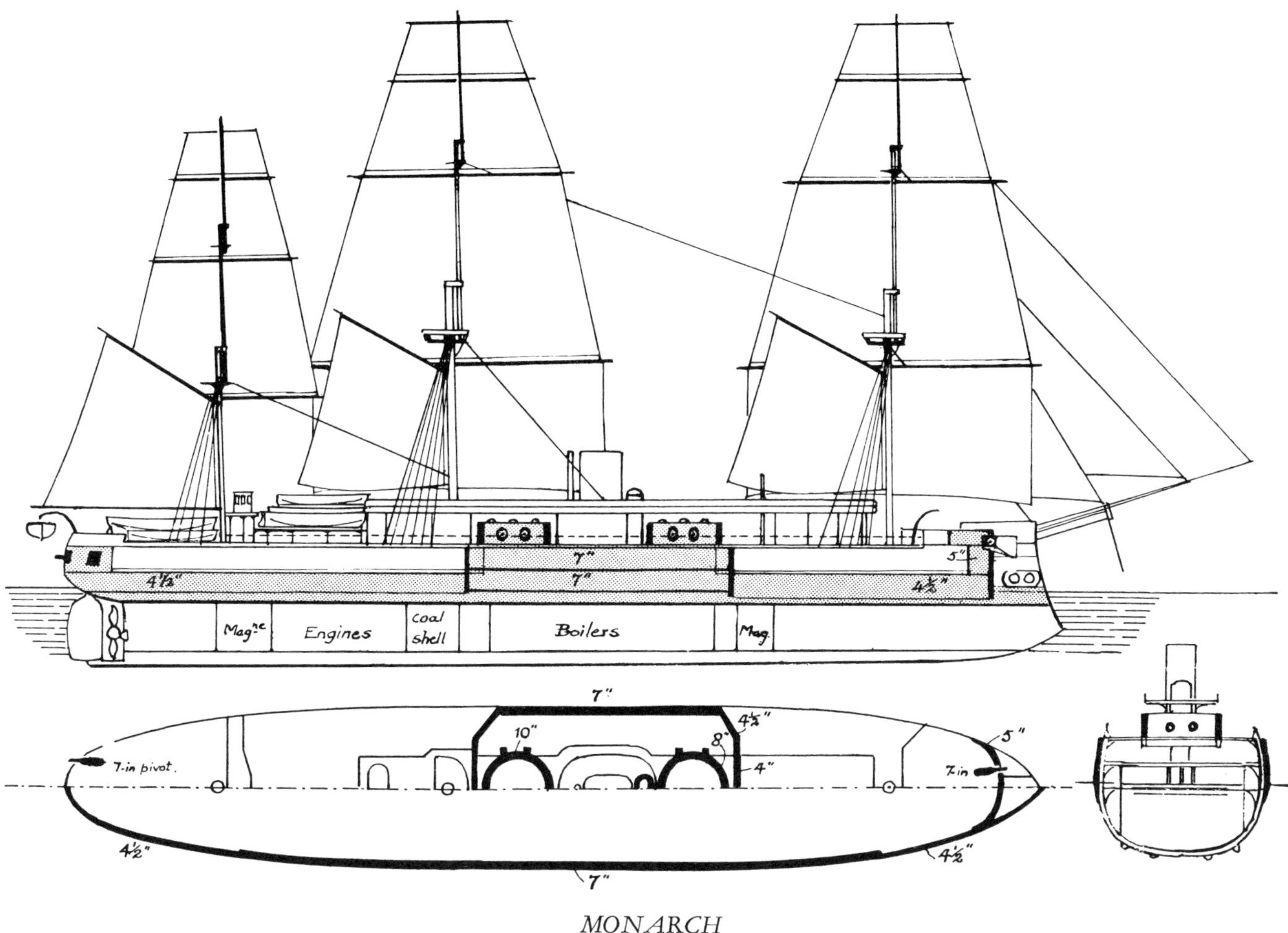

MONARCH

The design of the *Monarch* as a sea-going turret-ship was dictated by the Board's decision that she was to have a forecastle and carry full sail—dominating features to which everything else had to be subordinated. It meant depriving the turrets of any axial fire and placing them amidships; devising methods of keeping the gunfire clear of shrouds and rigging; and generally reducing what should have been an all-round fire to the level of a revolving central battery.

Reed took little pride in her, although it would be hard to say that a more successful ship had hitherto been put afloat, in so far as she fulfilled in every respect the intentions of her designers. But whatever her virtues were as a ship she fell far short of his conception of a fighting machine, and upon this standard he judged her, writing in March 1869, that it was "his clear and strong conviction that no satisfactorily designed turret ship with rigging has yet been built, or even laid down," and that "the middle of the upper deck of a full-rigged ship is not a very eligible position for fighting large guns." His statements before the Committee on Designs in 1871 partly indicate the changes he would have preferred in the *Monarch* or in subsequent ships of her type, viz.: A freeboard of 12 ft.; no forecastle or poop; turrets wider apart, with masts before the fore and abaft the after one carrying light rig only, and allowing the guns to fire past them axially.

That the Board viewed the conception of their first sea-going turret ship in a somewhat parsimonious spirit may be gathered from the preliminary drafts which showed that the tonnage proposed was on the low side and allowed for an armament of 15-ton guns and only 6-in. armour. Reed pressed for a greater latitude in displacement so that he could provide 25-ton guns and 7-in. protection, and this was finally conceded.

The hull was simply that of a central battery ship, with three decks, a topgallant forecastle, but no poop. There was the pointed ram and curved stem of Reed's previous ships but with finer lines, the proportion of length to beam being 5·7 : 1 instead of 5·5 : 1 (*Hercules*) to as low as 4·5 : 1 (*Pallas*). As a matter of fact, the ratio in the *Monarch's* proportions was not exceeded by any British battleship until the *Dreadnought* (1905), which was practically 6 : 1. The freeboard amidships was 14 ft., the guns firing 3 ft. above deck at a height of 17 ft.—or 7 ft. more than that of any battery in the Fleet; and a considerable amount of ingenuity was shown in the rearrangment of the upper deck structures to allow for as wide and unencumbered an angle of fire as possible from the turrets.

In the absence of the usual fixed bulwarks—which were replaced by light iron plates dropped outboard on hinges when the ship was cleared for firing—the 500 hammocks were stowed on a flying bridge deck extending from fore mast to quarter deck. This structure was supported on trunks protecting the mess-deck ladders, funnel base, and casing around the main mast; and being a vulnerable structure it was not loaded with anything likely to foul the turrets beneath in case of damage, although at a later date some machine guns were spaced along it. The boats were nested before and abaft the mizen, and hoisted by the spanker boom.

In front of the funnel was a small conning tower with vision limited to beam arcs and fitted with a steam steering wheel, the chart-house being a diminutive pen placed on the quarter deck bridge, from which the ship was usually handled despite the disadvantages of an unusual amount of obstruction from rigging and super-

The *Monarch* at Portsmouth during her second commission 1874-'76 when she had been reduced to a barque, and a wooden bowsprit fitted—here seen with the jibboom run in. Machine guns were not mounted on the flying deck until her refit in '85.

structure. Hand steering was provided by a triple wheel aft and a second one below it, with tillers on the main and lower decks.

ARMAMENT

Two turrets rose amidships on the centre line and from their oval ports peeped the muzzles of the first 12-in. guns in the Navy—25-ton M.L.R. throwing a 600-lb. shell sighted to 7,000 yards, and firing a double round in two minutes. Training was by steam with accessory hand gear. These 600-pdr. guns—which Coles proposed as the armament for his single turret design—were a tremendous increase over the preceding 10-in., and the trial model earned the sobriquet of "Big Will" in the Service. But for some time after commissioning neither the guns nor mountings were altogether successful.

The short forecastle was divided by a cross bulkhead into the "heads" forward and a battery aft containing two 7-in. M.L.R. chase guns firing through embrasures on each bow at a height of $16\frac{3}{4}$ ft. above water. Aft there was a third 7-in. ranging through three ports on the main deck 8 ft. above water. These guns were replaced by 9-in. pieces after the first commission.

In 1878 two torpedo carriages firing through ports on the main deck were added to her equipment.

ARMOUR

Protection along recognized lines for the hull provided a complete 7-in. to $4\frac{1}{2}$-in. belt rising from 5 ft. below water to main deck level. Amidships came the citadel with 7-in. sides and $4\frac{1}{2}$-in. to 4-in. ends with angled corners, containing the turret bases and part of the magazines; the bow guns fired through a 5-in. screen winged back along the forecastle for their side protection and dropping down to the belt as a defence against raking fire. The 5-in. to $4\frac{1}{2}$-in. armour to these was not thick enough to offer protection against medium-size guns and only added weight to the bows, detracting from her steaming against head seas, which she was unable to do when cleared for action without endangering her masts. The stern chaser was similarly protected.

The two turrets were of the same diameter as those in the *Prince Albert* (26 ft.) but only 7 ft. high and made of 8-in. plates with 10-in. faces around the ports.

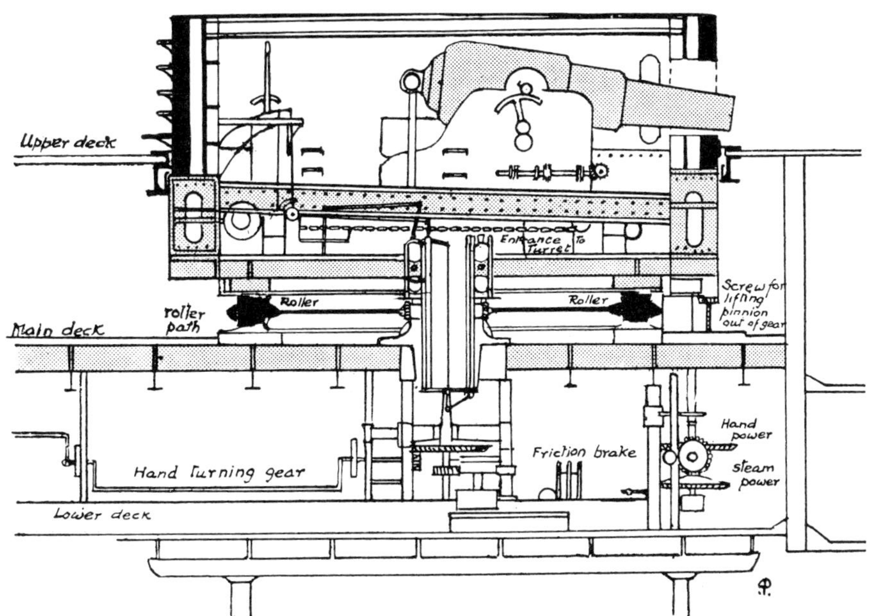

Turret of *MONARCH*.

MACHINERY

Equipped with the most powerful set of engines as yet seated on the bed-plates of a British man-of-war, the *Monarch* made 14·9 knots with 7,840 i.h.p., and so captured the *Warrior's* long-standing record over the measured mile with $\frac{1}{4}$ knot superiority over her squadron mates. That she only had a single screw was practically her one point of inferiority to the *Captain*.

Steam blast was fitted for the first time and proved efficacious but extremely wasteful of steam and fuel; fan engines were fitted in the stokeholds in 1870, but the closed stokehold and forced draught was not to be introduced for another ten years.

In her, auxiliary machinery became a necessary and integral part of the equipment, and with turret engines, steam capstan and steam steering the *Monarch* may be regarded as the forerunner of the present-day system of wholesale auxiliary machinery for every purpose.

SAIL

When Coles decided to dress the *Captain* with the maximum standard spar plan of the British Navy, Reed obtained the Board's permission to increase the canvas to be carried in the *Monarch* from the second-class scale to the heaviest, so that there should be no possibility of the Admiralty model being outsailed. In consequence of having to place the masts in relation to the turrets their spacing was unusual, with a span of 155 ft. between the fore and main. Except that the lower masts were 79, 81 and 63 ft. from deck to cap compared with 86, 86 and $67\frac{1}{2}$ ft. in the *Achilles*, the *Monarch* carried full ship rig with spars equal to those of the six battleships canvassed to the maximum scale. With this wind-trap she once logged 13 knots under plain sail and weather stunsails—a record among the battleships only exceeded by the *Royal Oak* with 13·5 knots. In 1872 her mizen was altered to barque rig and all the steel yards were replaced by wooden ones on a smaller scale; also the fixed iron bowsprit was changed for a runner-in of wood which lay on the topgallant forecastle.

Reed complained of the difficulty in arranging the rigging so as to obviate interference with gun fire at extreme arcs of training—*i.e.*, 20° with the line of keel. In the *Captain* the ropes were worked from the flying deck; in the *Monarch* this carried a few boats aft and was mainly for the passage of officers above the turrets. Reed says:

> "The ropes will be worked upon the upper deck over which the turrets have to fire, consequently a thousand contrivances have had to be made for keeping both the standing and running rigging tolerably clear of the guns."

Actually the main "contrivance" was the reduction in number of the shrouds of the fore and main lower rigging, which were made thicker in compensation. In comparison with other rigged turret ships this problem of shrouds and gun fire was very happily arranged in her case.

SEA-GOING QUALITIES

The *Monarch* sailed well but could neither stay nor wear with certainty without using her engines; until the fore part of the balanced rudder was cut down her steering was bad, and when running before the wind it was almost impossible to keep her from broaching-to.

In bad weather she is reported as being "everything that could be desired as a sea boat, buoyant and at the

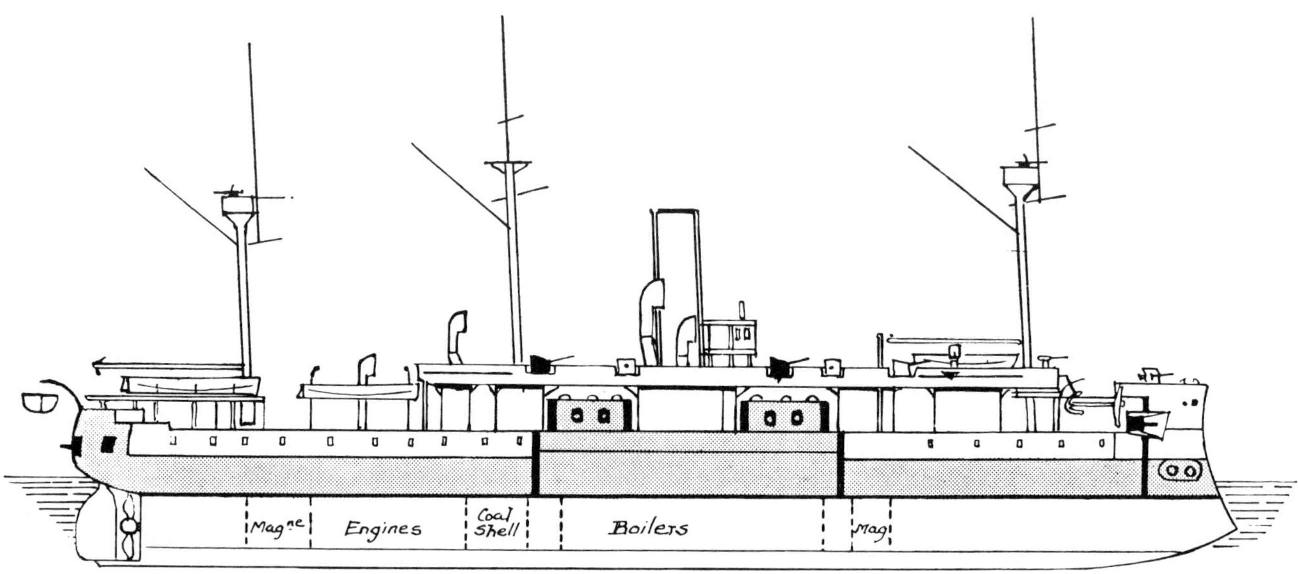

MONARCH modernized.

same time remarkably steady. On no occasion did she roll more than 15° and that quite the exception. She shipped no water whatever, and did not strain a rope-yarn. Her guns were capable of being fought either to windward or leeward with the same ease as at Spithead during bad weather."

Also "she can carry a press of sail, beat to windward by tacking, and in a fresh breeze outsail *Inconstant* and *Volage*."

Her G.M. was only 2·37 ft. and according to Admiral Henry Boys she would appear to have been rather tender, as he stated in the R.U.S.I. (20 April 1887): "When at anchor the *Monarch* was seldom on an even keel, generally laying over as much as 3 or 4 degrees by the pendulum—and then would suddenly change over from one side to the other without apparent cause." Empty bunkers would give her a 5° list, and a change from loading to firing positions in the guns caused a marked inclination.

MODERNIZATION

In 1890 she was taken in hand for "modernization," but for reasons which have not been recorded no effort was made to bring the obsolete M.L. armament up-to-date, although B.L. guns could have been substituted without any great difficulty. But £136,000 was wasted in providing new triple-expansion engines and cylindrical boilers, and thereafter she was able to make 15·75 knots—about ·75 knot better than was logged on first trials—

which sufficed to take her out to Capetown as guardship and a final spell of stationary dotage. At the same time she was deprived of her rig, given military tops to the fore and mizen, a tall imposing funnel, a chart house, ventilating cowls and the usual topside garnishing of small quick-firing and machine guns to excuse retention on the effective list for another six years, when work on her was brought to a belated conclusion in 1897—the longest period for refitting yet recorded.

That the saving in weight due to abolition of rig was not of such consequence as had been made out was explained by Reed (*Naval Science*, July 1873) using the *Monarch* as an example. He showed that the total weight of masts, sails and rigging was below 210 tons, and including stores added on account of her sailing equipment, 250 tons would be the outside limit of what had been termed "the endless stores and weights connected with the sail equipment." Reducing her crew by half would mean another 125 tons and say 100 tons by removal of fittings more or less closely connected with the sail power and larger crew. This total of 475 tons he did not regard as very much to distribute over additional coal and armour, and after alterations the weight of the hull would be 3,386 tons and of equipment 4,829 tons—or about 41 per cent. of displacement would go into hull and 59 per cent. into disposable carrying power, as against 42 per cent. hull and 58 per cent. carrying power as

The *Monarch* at Chatham on completion of her seven years refit in 1897, with military rig, a tall funnel, big cowls, a bridge before the funnel, and some machine guns along the flying deck. Over her bows are the funnels of the *Illustrious* completing for sea.

a rigged ship. On the other hand, had the *Monarch* been *designed* as a "mastless" ship, not much less than 1,100 tons could have been added to her carrying power.

Apropos of reconstruction, one of the major difficulties attendant upon any scheme involving additional weights to a ship is the maintenance of adequate stability. It is the common experience that the constant additions and alterations to every ship of war leads to a steady sinkage and consequent loss of stability, which in these earlier battleships averaged about $\frac{3}{4}$ in. every year. This increase in draught corresponded roughly to an amount of 1 ton for every £150 spent on alterations, additions, and painting, and on this basis it was fairly easy to estimate the additional draught with loss of freeboard which was always accompanied by what at times was a serious loss of stability.

That the *Monarch* was thus retained as an effective fighting unit in the Navy List for thirty-three years may be regarded as high tribute paid to a satisfactory ship, but for the fact that her obsolescence coincided with a period when neglect to replace worn-out tonnage had resulted in an accumulation of thirty-eight ironclads armed with muzzle-loaders being still classed as effective.

That wartime duties in Table Bay would not expose the old ship to serious danger may be accepted as an excuse for this last spell of service which allowed her to exceed the effective life of the *Prince Albert* by one year.

"MONARCH"

Commissioned at Chatham May '69, and served in Channel until '72. (Crossed to U.S.A. in company with U.S. Corvette *Plymouth* which she outsailed, voyaging to America and back without any fuel shortage, using sails as auxiliary. During home run did 242 miles in one day, thus missing the *Ocean's* record by one mile only.) Engaged in competitive trials with *Captain* in which she proved superior on every count, during summer of '70; followed by 15 months in the Channel and then paid off for refit (given barque rig).

Served in the Channel '74-'76 when she was sent to the Mediterranean, returning home for refit in '77. Again up the Straits '78-'85 and was present at the bombardment of Alexandria when she fired 125 12-in., 54 9-in. and 21 7-in. shells.

Became stationary at Alexandria, where she swung round her moorings year after year owing to fuel restrictions. During the Russian war scare of '85 she was ordered to Malta flying the flag of C.-in-C. Lord John Hay, but owing to the collection of marine growths in her stern tube linings she broke down at sea and for some days her whereabouts was unknown. Eventually, after much searching and anxiety, she was picked up, towed to Malta, repaired, and sent home under escort. Refit '85. Again served in the Channel from '85-'90 and then paid off for a long refit. Modernized '90-'97; sent as half-complement guardship to Simons Bay '97-'02; reduced to depôt-ship and renamed *Simoom* in '04. Brought home in '05.

Sold 1906.

Her heavy armament excited a lot of interest in America, and the idea was spread that she was powerful enough to bombard the Atlantic seaboard towns with impunity. At that time the great American philanthropist, Samuel Peabody, who had spent 3 million dollars in housing the poor of London, was lying dead in London; and when John Bright received an anonymous telegram from America "*First and best service possible for "Monarch" bring home Peabody*," he acted upon it at once. The *Monarch* sailed with the body, and thus became a messenger for harmony and peace. Many years later Bright met Andrew Carnegie, and learned that he had despatched the cable—aged 34.

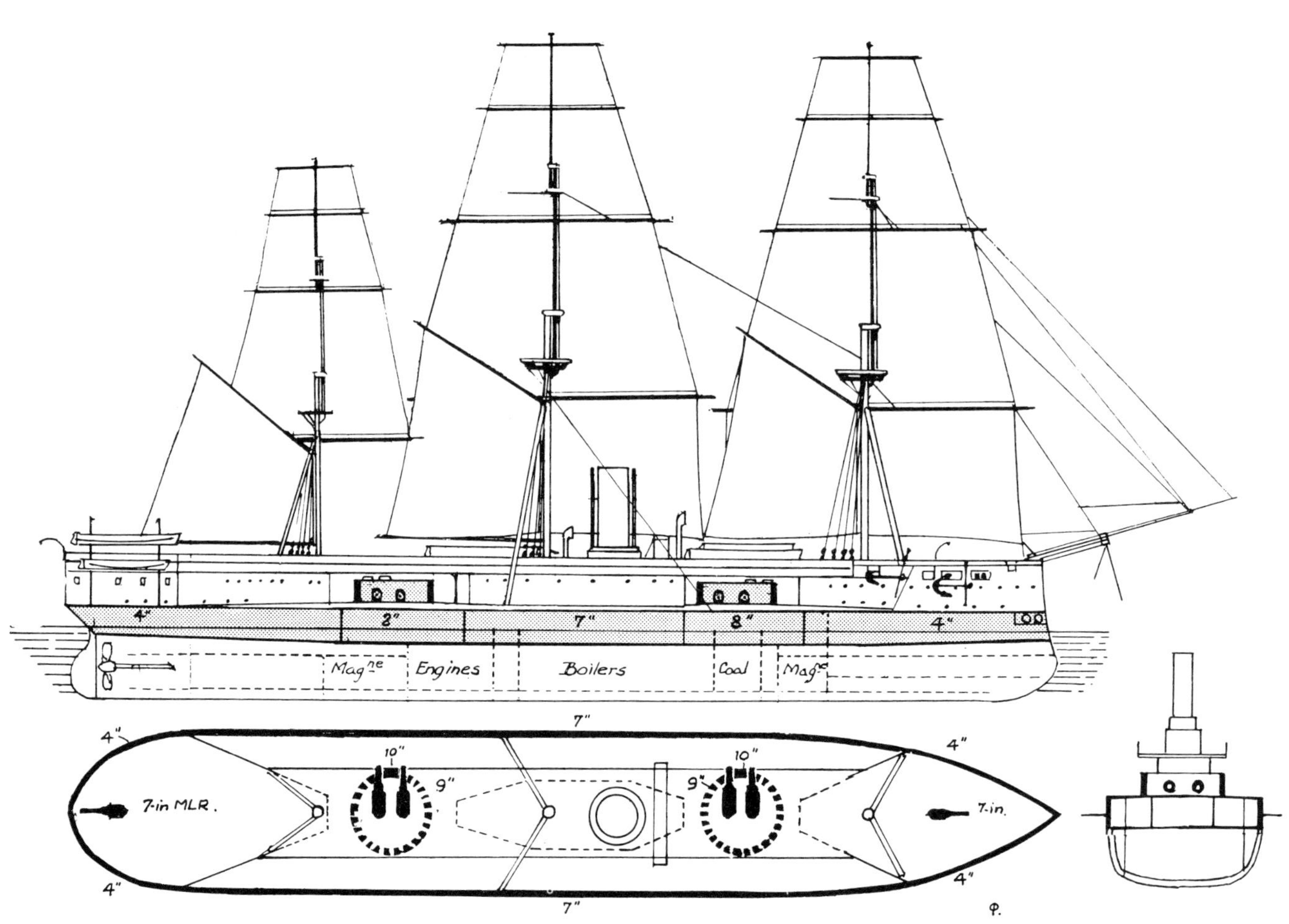

CAPTAIN

"CAPTAIN"

Builders	*Laid down*	*Floated out*	*Completed*	*Cost*
Lairds	30 Jan. '67	27 March '69	Jan. '70	£335,518

Dimensions 320′ × 53¼′ × 22½′/23½′ = 6,963 tons (designed).
× 24¼/25½′ = 7,767 tons (as built).

Guns 4 12-in. M.L.R.
2 7-in. M.L.R.

Armour Belt 7″-4″; turret bases 8″; turrets 9″, face 10″; conning tower 7″; backing 200 tons.
Total 1,190 tons.

Complement 500.

Sail area 26,322/37,990 (full) sq. ft.

Machinery Two sets trunk engines. I.H.P. 5,400 = 14·25 knots.
4-cyl. 90″; stroke 3¼′; revs. 74.
2 2-bladed screws, diam. 17′, pitch 21½′.
8 rectangular boilers. 30 lb. pressure.

Coal 600 tons (full).

Special features:

(1) Our only two-decked sea-going battleship.
(2) Had the greatest proportionate length to beam of any capital ship for the next thirty-five years.
(3) Had the lowest freeboard of any British sea-going armoured ship.

Although Coles is usually held responsible for the design of the *Captain*, his share in her did not go beyond the general conception of a special type of fighting ship from a seaman's point of view, with guns mounted in turrets of his own devising. Lairds accepted the onus of producing a ship to fill Coles' requirements, but did not hesitate to introduce such modifications as they considered necessary, such as forecastle and poop, which were entirely foreign to the seaman's conception. They were the architects, and the success or failure of the ship lay in their calculations and drawings. Coles was concerned in getting his projects materialized by the most capable naval shipbuilders in the country, who had already constructed several turret ships which had made their way safely across to South America; and owing to illness he had far less of a hand in the production of the *Captain* than he had anticipated.

The striking difference between the *Captain* and the *Monarch* was in the former having only two complete decks instead of three, so that her upper deck corresponded to the main deck in the rest of the contemporary battleships. This was designed to be 8½ ft. above water only, whereas the *Monarch* had a freeboard of 14 ft.—although the actual difference in sea-going trim was to be tragically increased. A sort of vestigial upper deck was made up of the forecastle and poop, which at the break were continued inboard towards the turrets and then joined by a flying deck which spanned them and rested upon the notorious "coffin-shaped" superstructure amidships through which passed the funnel uptakes, main mast, engine-room skylights and stokehold ventilators. This narrow flying deck carried the hammocks in a sort of parapet on each side, as well as three boomboats, a conning tower, and bitts and fife-rails for the running rigging of the fore and main masts; it was the muster deck for all divisions and drills when at sea, and for working the sails—although affording precious little space for running sheets and halliards. Before the funnel it was crossed by a light bridge fitted with the engine-room telegraphs and voice pipes to the triple wheels on the poop and lower deck.

There was a slight ram bow, a vertical semi-circular stern, a single unbalanced rudder, and twin screws; in dimensions she was 10 ft. shorter and 4 ft. narrower than the *Monarch*, the ratio of length to beam being 6 : 1—proportions not equalled until the *Dreadnought* (1905)—but as the amidships section was full, and the maximum breadth carried well fore and aft, there was a certain amount of compensation for what was a deficiency in beam.

GUNS

The two turrets were widely separated, slightly higher than those in the *Monarch* but less in diameter, and the two 25-tonners in each swung round only 2¼ ft. over deck and barely 9 ft. above water. Although the deck was awash in moderate weather, the guns were never inconvenienced from water inside the turrets and made efficient shooting in heavy seas when trained on the weather beam. When going through the motions of firing the guns were trained out of action to lee or windward for loading.

Being masked by superstructure, the turret guns had no axial fire and this was provided by a single 7-in. M.L.R. on the forecastle 20¾ ft. above water and another on the poop at a height of 18 ft., both being unprotected. Coles preferred this arrangement to that adopted in the *Monarch* as allowing a higher command and saving the ends from being weighed with armour which could not resist medium gunfire.

ARMOUR

But the entire hull to deck level had 7-in. to 4-in. plating increased to 8-in. for 80 ft. along the turret bases, the turrets themselves being 10 in. on the faces and 9 in. elsewhere with a backing of 11-in. teak. Armour totalled 1,190 tons against the 1,364 in the *Monarch*, but was generally thicker through having less area to cover.

MACHINERY

The *Captain* was the second British capital ship to have twin screws; and only three more were to be built with the single propeller permitting the attendant risks of breakdown. In the case of the *Penelope* two propellers had been provided as a matter of expediency; in the *Captain* duplication of machinery halved the risks of complete loss of tactical movement, improved manoeuvring powers, and incidentally permitted its manufacture at Birken-

The *Captain* at Plymouth, taken on the eve of departure for her last cruise. Compare her low freeboard with that of the *Monarch* which had lowering bulwarks in addition, and abnormally high masting. Note the topgallants are fidded abaft the topmast, and that there is a boom to the main trysail—a unique fitting.

head, where workshops were not equipped to handle the heavy castings and forgings necessary in single engines of the same horse-power.

Two sets of trunk engines were coupled to outward turning two-bladed screws which at 74 revolutions under full power across Stokes Bay gave 14½ knots.

To minimize overloading, the full complement of 600 tons of coal was only once shipped. Under steam she was not as economical as the *Monarch*, although some 500 tons smaller.

SAIL

Both ships carried the same coal supply, but the *Captain* was unable to stow any outside her bunkers (a customary practice in her contemporaries) and the provision of sail power was regarded as essential if she were to aspire to blue water status. But instead of being content to mast his creation for the lowest scale of canvas—which would have been quite satisfactory—Coles chose to equip her with the heaviest masts and maximum spar plan then employed—almost as a gesture of superlative confidence in her ability to carry anything up aloft and also as some insurance against the handicap of twin-screw drag and dull sailing. If the Admiralty was surprised,

Lairds accepted the added weight without demur, and fitted the *Captain* with the tallest and heaviest masts in the Fleet—the main lower mast being 96 ft. from cap to gunwale level against the highest of 86 ft. in any other ship. Owing to the position of the turrets her masts were better placed for sailing than in the *Monarch*, but from its proximity to the funnel the main rigging would soon have become smoke rotted. To obviate any interference of gun-fire by the shrouds Coles employed the tripod system which had solved the problem in the little *Wivern*, iron legs serving both as shrouds and stays. The standing rigging secured to the flying deck consisted of rope ladders for the men to reach the tops. Rigged in this way the *Captain* was always ready for action. The *Monarch*, on the other hand, took at least 1½ hours to prepare before being able to close an engagement after a chase under sail. Aloft there were several peculiarities in gear. The topgallant masts were fidded abaft the topmasts as in the *Wivern* and for the same reason; in place of the usual topmast and upper back stays the topmasts and topgallants were stayed to iron out-riggers spread from under the tops and topmast caps; and the main trysail had a boom like the spanker and could remain spread on any point of sailing as there was no mizen stay to interfere with its swing. The original plan was for the lower masts and topmasts to be made in one piece as in the case of all previous tripod masts, but in 1868 it was found desirable to fid the topmasts, and slightly modify the proportions of the spars while retaining approximately the same area of 26,322 sq. ft. This worked out at 22 sq. ft. to areas of midship section compared with 35 to 36 sq. ft. in high freeboard ships.

Actually the hurricane deck was increased in length and breadth during construction, adding topweight but providing necessary space for working the sails. Although at first the new conditions were found difficult, Captain Burgoyne wrote in July: "Now that the men are beginning to get used to the narrow deck the work goes like a glove." On her first cruise she confirmed Laird's opinion that she would be as stiff as other ironclads of recent construction. In a wind of 6-7 and a heavy sea she lurched to 13-14 degrees when wearing, the heel being what was expected from the calculations made as to her sail-carrying power. Captain Commerell considered her rather a stiff vessel under sail with an easy and slow roll. To Captain Burgoyne she appeared to stand up well under canvas—he considered the *Captain* a "most complete success—a most comfortable and easy ship and in my opinion one of the most efficient men-of-war in the world."

EQUIPMENT

Officers and men, excepting the Captain, Commander and Navigator, berthed on the lower deck at water-line level, where there were scuttles and plenty of free ventilation—which virtue curiously enough was overlooked by the Controller when he reported upon the accommodation on his first visit to the ship. Illumination was through large dead-lights in the deck, and in this respect was better than usual. Generally the equipment was primitive, but a patent capstan and steam drive were provided.

RESPONSIBILITY OF CONSTRUCTION

For a considerable period the ship was held up owing to difficulties in getting the question of responsibility for her design and construction satisfactorily settled, as Coles was a sick man and could not live at Birkenhead during the long period when his services were required to supervise every phase of the ship's growth. In the end the Controller agreed to shoulder his work "by inserting in every clause of the Contract where Captain Coles had been named the words 'Controller of the Navy' and by their Lordships directing me to assume towards the contractors with reference to the 'Captain' the same duties and position I occupied with respect to the *Agincourt* built by the same firm." Lairds agreed to this and also to the building of the ship in accordance with the original design subject to any modifications in detail which were mutually agreed upon and approved of by Coles.

STABILITY

The tragedy of the *Captain*, owing to lack of stability, was attributed at the Court Martial to:

> "A miscalculation on the part of Lairds through which the ship floated deeper than was intended—a discrepancy which the Controller described as a 'serious and unexampled error' in constructural calculations."

This stricture upon the Laird brothers' skill as naval architects was not altogether warranted—the error in constructural calculations must be blamed to the yard staff rather than office. The ship did not float too deeply because of mistakes in calculating her displacement from accepted data, but because of the use of overweight material—a very different thing when the matter of professional reputation is concerned.

When Reed came to scrutinize closely the details of the design he noted that:

> "In my preliminary report I expressed no doubt as to the stability of the ship, but on investigating the matter I find that the centre of gravity of ships armed and plated in the proposed manner is situated higher than would appear probably at first sight, and I would advise that Messrs. Laird be requested to satisfy themselves on this point, especially as it is proposed to spread a large surface of canvas upon the *Captain*."

To which Lairds replied on 15 August:

> "We have carefully considered the position of the centre of gravity and the disposal of weights and have no reason to fear that the vessel will be deficient in the stability necessary. We may observe that in the event of the vessel being light with all coals burnt out, it is provided that the space under the double bottom may be filled with water as ballast."

And as demonstrating the difference between high and medium freeboard it is worth noting that the *Monarch* had her metacentre $1\frac{1}{2}$ ft. above the water-line, while that of the *Captain* was $7\frac{1}{2}$ ft. below it (*Naval Science*, April 1872).

So much for the alleged error in calculation which would have affected the first principles of the ship's stability; the actual cause of the tragedy lay in the omission to observe adequate checking and supervision of weights.

RESPONSIBILITY FOR WEIGHTS

Coles wished to have Admiralty supervision at Birkenhead during the period of construction as was customary in the case of contract-built ships, but to this the Board declined to agree on the ground that the responsibility for producing the *Captain* lay with Lairds and himself; the most they would accede was the appointment of an overseer to approve the *quality* of the material used, but without exercising any supervision in checking its weight. To this deviation from standard practice it is possible to attribute the chief factor in the loss of the *Captain*. Lairds kept the Resident Inspector supplied with a full list of all the material used in her construction and this was forwarded to the Controller's Department; but in many cases weights were introduced which had not been originally provided for owing to the difficulty in estimating figures for some portions of so novel a design, and frequently additions had to be made consequent upon experiments and information obtained after the design had been decided upon.

Reed would not allow the word "approved" to be used, implying Board sanction for even minor details in connection with the ship—always "no objection would be offered"; he was determined that full responsibility should rest with Lairds. And it is recorded that some of the arrangements which were "not objected to" by the Controller did contribute both to the extra weight and to the reduction of stability in the ship—such as the increased height of the poop and forecastle and additional length and breadth of the hurricane deck.

EXCESS WEIGHT

Now, it was a common experience on the part of the Admiralty surveyors that every private shipbuilder tended to underestimate the weights which his ships had to carry, or were being put into them—with the consequence that until the advent of the *Monarch* no ironclad had floated at her designed draught. In two specific cases quoted by Barnaby at the Court Martial as much as 2 ft. $3\frac{3}{4}$ in. (*Tamar*) and 2 ft. $10\frac{1}{2}$ in. (*Orontes*) excess draught had already resulted, although in the case of these ships forecastles and poops had been added to the original design. The *Warrior*, *Agincourt* and *Bellerophon* had considerably exceeded their draughts and Lairds had learned a lot from the *Agincourt*. Realizing something of what was going to come about with the *Captain*, they asked to be allowed to dispense with the iron plating behind the armour, which they considered could be omitted with safety—but it was not allowed, although dispensed with in several armoured ships built after the *Captain*.

As already noted, in the case of the *Captain* the Admiralty officer who usually received instructions to see that the weights were not in excess did not receive the customary orders, and as a result Barnaby stated that during his visit to Birkenhead in September 1867 he saw:

> "That there was no evidence of the care and vigilance which are to be found necessary in armoured ships in order to procure precise draught of water. Messrs. Laird weighed I believe very carefully the materials which they put into the ship, but I saw in the distribution of the materials many instances of too large an amount of material expended in order to produce the desired results in strength of structure . . . and we know that there were some things which were omitted from the calculations (the turret engines) as to the weights which were to be carried."

That such a state of things was not passed without comment was to be expected despite the reading of the contract, and again Barnaby stated:

> "My officers are uniformally instructed to mention to Messrs. Laird as occasion might offer, what they more than once mentioned to me, and what I saw myself upon my visits to the ship, and mentioned to the firm viz. that throughout the building of the ship iron was being put into her in larger quantities than would have been deemed necessary in the building of such a ship in Her Majesty's Dockyards, or under my direction."

The recorded calculations show that the total displacement required was 6,866 tons, and the drawings allowed for 6,950—a surplus of 84 tons to the good. If the essential benefit of an official check on the weights had been available the *Captain* might have been a successful ship. But week by week tragedy permeated more and more into her hull as lack of official supervision allowed a hundredweight here and a ton there in girders, scantlings, plates, decks, turrets, engine-room equipment, and a hundred and one separate parts which go to every foot of a ship's length to be worked in aboard, so that when she was taken out on trial her draught was 24 ft. 1½ in. forward and 25 ft. 6¼ in. aft instead of 22 ft. 6 in. and 23 ft. 6 in.; when fully laden for sea the mean draught was 25 ft. 3 in., giving her a freeboard of 6 ft. 6 in. instead of 8 ft. 6 in., with a displacement of 7,837 tons.

The additional weight[1] was mainly absorbed by the following items:

	tons		*tons*
Stores and fittings	81	Rifle tower	2
Turrets	25	Iron hull	77
Guns and carriages	20	Deck	26
Appendages to turrets	45	Poop }	
Engines	72	Forecastle }	133
Turret engines	55	Hurricane deck }	
Armour	51	Woodwork, etc.	152
Backing	41	Cement and sand	52
		Glacis plates	25

Total 857 tons—in the total of 860 tons calculated by Lairds.

STABILITY

On 27 March 1869 when she was floated out of dock, Mr. F. K. Barnes of the Constructors Department noted that the ship was going to be very much overweight—by at least 427 tons—and her immersion increased by at least 13 in. if the complement remained at 400 men. If, however, the authorized complement of 500 men were to be accommodated there would be a further increase of 1½ in. in the draught.

During completion Lairds had gone into the question of stability and calculated that she would be unsafe beyond an angle of 21° inclination—or less than one-third of the *Monarch's* angle of safety. So when the ship left for Portsmouth on 24 February 1870 to receive her coal and ammunition a letter was sent asking that she should be subjected to the practical test of inclination in the dockyard basin for these figures to be checked. There was no mention of her stability being in doubt—low freeboard ships were not intended to roll like those higher out of water—and the inclination test was regarded as more or less of academic interest in recording the qualities of a novel and experimental type of ship. Although approved of on 26 February the test was not carried out until 29 July; the data secured were only worked out by 23 August when it became known that her danger angle was 21°—as Lairds had calculated. Both Coles and Captain Burgoyne in command were aware of this, but owing to press of work at the Admiralty and the fact that the papers were not marked "urgent" the result was not communicated to Admiral Milne in charge of the squadron to which the *Captain* was attached.

As it was, no doubts were entertained about the *Captain's* stability, although visiting officers accustomed to high freeboard regarded the low hull with misgivings. Captain Burgoyne was quite confident in his command, and although the Admiralty had demurred against paying the last instalment on her purchase from Lairds on account of the increased immersion, it was agreed that this should be settled if her sea-going tests were carried through successfully. Had the purport of Lairds calculation been promulgated and the inclination tests worked out at once, there would have been no question of such a proviso—the ship would never have gone to sea with the risk that such tests might not be terminated successfully.

After carrying out a series of thoroughly comprehensive trials with the *Monarch*, the *Captain* joined the rest of the squadron at sea. Having weathered a full gale successfully and proved herself under steam and sail as well as at target practice, she appeared to have confounded her critics.

Reed alone was consistently apprehensive about her, but unable to impress his misgivings upon Mr. Hugh Childers, who had succeeded Somerset as First Lord. The apparent triumph of the *Captain* over her detractors made Reed's position very difficult, especially as Childers had appointed his own son to the ship as a measure of appreciation of her novel fighting qualities in opposition to the Chief Constructor's views.

As a culmination to the antagonism which the *Captain* had engendered between the civilian members of the Board and their professional advisers, Reed resigned office on 8 July 1870—nominally to take up a position with Whitworths, although, as he put it, "this cause had its weight in all that happened."

---

[1] Reed in his evidence before the Committee of Building and Repairs 1885 stated that the material was not weighed (p. 112), which is hardly borne out by this list.

INCLINATION TEST

On returning to Portsmouth in July, the *Captain* was subjected to an inclination test, and her angle of extreme heel with safety judged to be from 15° to 16° in smooth water.

Minor repairs were carried out before the ship went off on a three-weeks shake-down gunnery cruise—during which she was deemed to have realized the standards laid down and the contract with Lairds completed accordingly. Having joined the rest of the Fleet, she left for Gibraltar on 4 August with Coles on board as a privileged observer.

LOSS OF THE "CAPTAIN"

At sea on 6 September the Admiral made a visiting inspection and towards evening it came on to blow. When the ship was heeling 13½° and taking water over the deck he questioned her condition with Coles and Burgoyne, but with their assurance in her safety returned to his flagship.

Conditions became worse and by midnight a full gale was roaring with a heavy and confused sea. The *Captain*, under double-reefed topsails and fore topmast staysail, had both watches crowded on the superstructure trying to lower the topsail yards. But the ship was heeling too much for them to come down and at 12.15, when a blast of exceptional violence carried away twenty-three sails in the squadron, the *Captain* was thrown over beyond her safety limit, lay on her beam ends, and foundered bottom upwards. She carried with her Captain Coles and 472 officers and men—her entire complement with the exception of 17 men and the gunner who managed to get ashore in the pinnace.

THE "CAPTAIN" COURT MARTIAL

From the evidence given at the Court Martial it is clear that the builders did not regard the extra draught as endangering her stability, and the Admiralty were satisfied with Lairds assurance and the results of the first trials, to the extent of taking no steps to make the inclination test an urgent matter, or to communicate the results obtained to Admiral Milne while the fleet was at Vigo from August 25 to September 1. Both officers and men regarded her as a fine ship and had no doubts about her safety, describing her as "the most perfect sea boat they were ever in."

Two extracts from the Court Martial are worth quoting as having a bearing on the omission to acquaint the Admiral with the results of the stability tests:

Captain Commerell, V.C.:

> "Do you think that a diagram together with an official intimation that 21° was the point which would assuredly capsize the *Captain* would have had a great influence upon the officers entrusted with the experiment, and that in dealing with the *Captain* the same as other ships entailed a grave responsibility? I ask this, as an officer who has had the *Captain* under his orders and who, with that diagram before him, would not have dared to keep the ship under sail one single night."

Mr. Reed:

> "The *Captain* was built to be under the same conditions as other ships and I believe—although I regret to have to state it—that if any such information emanated from the Admiralty it would have resulted in the strongest efforts to prove the Admiralty wrong, and to carry all possible sail . . . My belief was that the unseaworthiness of the *Captain* was a cause of anxiety to many who professed to believe in her, and what I thought would happen with the *Captain* was this—that she would have the highest possible reports to begin with; that she would be very carefully nursed through her early career until admissions of her deficiencies became slowly admitted, and that before she got through a commission she would be condemned as utterly unfit for the Naval Service. That in 1869 I did what I thought was right in the matter in resisting to the utmost degree in my power a desire on the part of the First Lord to increase the number of *Captains*. That resistance I repeated, and again and again repeated basing my objections upon the danger which was involved in the *Captain* herself; and when I found my resistance was useless I retired from duty and undertook to submit my resignation from my office. The proposal to repeat the *Captain* was withdrawn—but I am out of office and the son of the First Lord is amongst the unhappy victims of the loss. I wish the Court to believe that my actual departure from office at length did not arise from this cause—but it had its weight in all that has happened . . . and that I had the strongest reasons for not keeping up a systematic assertion of the dangers incurred in the *Captain*."

To Captain Burgoyne, Reed had expressed himself very definitely:

> "I don't want to say any more against her, but I am glad that it is your fate and not mine to go to sea in her."

Burgoyne's confidence defied criticism, which sought to impress upon him the particular danger of her capsizing under canvas.

In the words of Mr. Barnaby: "In building the *Captain* it was known that a great experiment was being made, that that experiment was made with reasonable prospects of success, and that, like many other experiments, unforeseen accidents caused it to fail." And the failure was a crowning tragedy in the life of Cowper Coles, who lived only long enough to experience what must have seemed a catastrophic end to his great work. But a few years later the fleets of the world proclaimed that his turret was everything he had claimed for it.

The Court found that:

> "H.M. Ship *Captain* was capsized by pressure of sail assisted by the heave of the sea; and the sail at the time of her loss (regard being had to the force of the wind and the state of the sea) was insufficient to have endangered a ship endued with a proper amount of stability."

Chapter 23

CONVERSION OF WOODEN SHIPS INTO IRONCLADS

AFTER the successful conversion of the *Ocean* group of two-deckers into ironclad frigates and the *Royal Sovereign* into a turret ship, it was only natural that, having been shown this seemingly cheap and economical way of utilizing obsolete tonnage, the public were persuaded that its scope could be vastly extended with every advantage both financially and materially.

A number of professional naval architects and amateur publicists hastened to air their views in the press and

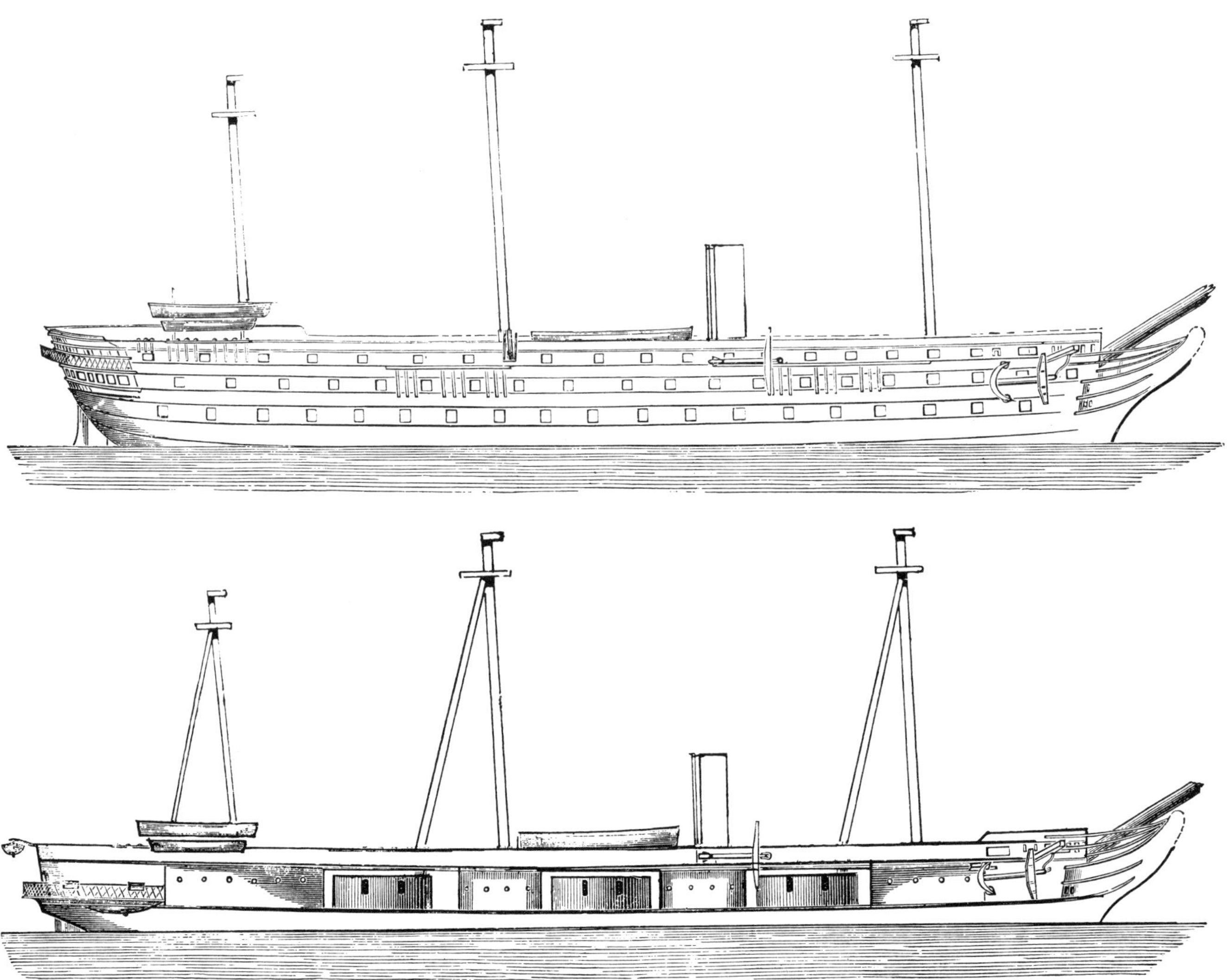

Henwood's proposed conversion of a three-decker into a three-turret monitor, 1869. The figures he submitted applied to a 90-gun two-decker, although the resulting turret ship would have been similar to that above.

many remarkable "conversions" were advocated—some seemingly practical and worth while. Amongst these latter the proposal fathered by Mr. C. Henwood—a naval architect of repute—created the most interest as having been delivered at the Royal United Service Institution in a paper read on 5 April 1869 with Admiral Sir Henry Codrington, K.C.B., in the chair.

Mr. Henwood proposed to cut down the *Duncan* class of 90-gun two-deckers to the lower deck, armour the remaining 4 ft. of freeboard end to end, and mount three two-gun turrets along the centre-line, retaining a high forecastle and poop connected by a fore-and-aft bridge. There would be full ship rig with tripod masts, and the result was to be a sort of six-gun *Captain*, the converted ship displacing 6,265 tons against the *Duncan's* 5,920 tons, with a draught of 25 ft. and a monitor deck 4¼ ft. above water.

Public opinion approved of the *Captain*, and the "Henwood monitor" scheme which combined the then attractive features of the *Monitor* with all the accepted advantages of a fully rigged sea-going ship, received considerable support—except from official quarters.

Reed took occasion to explain why in his book *Our Ironclad Ships* (1869), and showed that the Constructive staff at the Admiralty fully realized the capabilities of the old wooden ships for rapid conversion into broadside ironclads or monitors, to the extent that detailed designs had been prepared for the work to be carried out *if and when* the necessity arose. But without that necessity no more wooden ship conversions would be undertaken. Compared with iron-hulled ships the timber hulls were more or less decayed and weak; were of deeper draught than required for coast defence; were slow and had comparatively wasteful engines needing a larger coal supply; and could not carry so great a weight or thickness of armour as new iron ships, the mere hulls of which could be very cheaply and quickly built by the great private firms of the country.

Also a wooden ship with a heavy hull and great weights of engines, boilers, etc., low down was likely to roll much more heavily than an iron ship with different structural arrangements; and the only satisfactory means of reducing rolling to any extent would be by carrying out the *breastwork monitor system in combination with low freeboard*—as had been provided for in the designs prepared at the Admiralty. For while a tendency to roll would be somewhat checked by water working over low freeboard decks, in any but a breastwork monitor this would prevent the guns being fought. But, so far as the Henwood monitor was concerned, the Secretary of the Admiralty stated in the House that, instead of having a freeboard of 4 ft. as was estimated, the upper deck would only have been a few inches above water when all the weights intended to be carried were on board. Apart from her, discussing the projects in general, calculations showed that none of our screw line-of-battle ships could be converted into efficient sea-going monitors having the necessary sail power and crews required to work them under sail, together with the weights of stores and equipment required in a full-rigged ship. They could be made into (1) partially armoured broadside ships, or by giving up masts, spars, sea stores, and a large weight of equipment be turned into (2) coast-defence monitors; but even such conversions would not be justifiable except as a war emergency.

The conversion of the *Royal Sovereign* with 560 tons of armour cost £150,000, whereas the more durable and efficient *Cerberus* hull with 670 tons of armour was contracted for £99,000, and the hull of the *Glatton* with 1,065 tons of armour only cost £163,000 (with 12½ per cent. establishment charges).

One useful outcome of the conversion agitation was that it led to the interesting information about the plans for utilizing the old wooden hulls should war emergency make such steps necessary; and especially the fact that Reed was prepared to alter them into breastwork monitors. It was with great regret that the search for these plans had to be relinquished without result, as the metamorphosis of a *Duncan* into a *Devastation* would have been well worth recording.

As during the ten years which had elapsed since the completion of the *Warrior* carrying 68-pdrs. and 4½-in. armour, development of the capital ship had produced the *Monarch* with 25-ton 12-in. guns in turrets and vastly superior protection, it was indeed strange that a wooden-hulled battleship with her guns on the broadside should have passed into service in 1870. And yet the last of the converted two-deckers whose construction was undertaken as a quick and economical method of creating an armoured fleet in the emergency of 1861 was not completed until her services had become almost superfluous.

For various reasons the Board thought fit to suspend work on the *Repulse* for a full five years before her conversion was taken in hand, instead of merely slowing down construction as in the case of the *Royal Alfred* and *Zealous*. She was therefore completed long after the other six had been commissioned, and hence assumes an historical interest in having been the last capital ship to be built of wood as well as the last of a long line which included the *Henri Grace a Dieu*, *Sovereign of the Seas* and the earlier *Britannia's* to rise into shape at Woolwich Dockyard during the 400 years it had been established. Soon after she glided into the muddy waters of the Thames, the yard was closed as a Gladstonian measure of economy and the *Repulse* had to be towed down the river to Sheerness for completion.

DESIGN

By 1864 Mr. E. J. Reed had been for some eighteen months in charge of the Construction Department at Whitehall, and his ideas on armament and protection were carried out in the plans sent to Woolwich when resumption of work on the *Repulse* was authorized. Two years before she was launched the *Bellerophon* had taken her 9-in. guns afloat, and by the time the *Repulse* arrived at Sheerness the 10-in. guns of the *Hercules* had set up a higher standard of armament values which determined that 4½-in. iron could no longer be regarded as adequate protection, while a complete carapace as in the *Ocean* was impossible to provide. Instead, thicker armour had now to be concentrated over much smaller vital areas, leaving the rest of the hull open to attack; hence in the *Repulse* the 103-ft. battery of the *Zealous* was further contracted to 70 ft. allowing armour to be increased to

"REPULSE"

Builders	*Laid down*	*Launched*	*Completed*	*Cost*
Woolwich Sheerness	29 April '59	25 April '68	31 Jan. '70	£183,640

Dimensions 252' × 59' × 22'/26'. Displacement 6,190 tons. Hull and armour 4,310 tons. Equipment 1,900 tons.

Armament 12 8-in. M.L.R. 2 Saluting. 4 16-in. torpedo carriages. Broadside = 1,140 lb.

Armour Belt 6"-4½". Battery 6" with 4½" bulkheads. Skin ¾". Total 1,040 tons. Ship's side 31" oak.

Complement 515.

Machinery Penn. trunk engines; N.H.P. 800. I.H.P. 3,350 = 12½ knots; cyl. 89", stroke 4 ft.; revs. 59; 6 rectangular boilers at 30 lb. pressure; 2-bladed screw 19' diam.

Coal 460 tons.

Sail area 29,200 sq. ft.

Special features:

(1) Our last wooden capital ship.
(2) The only wooden ironclad with a knee bow and rounded stern.
(3) Bridge placed forward of funnel for the first time.

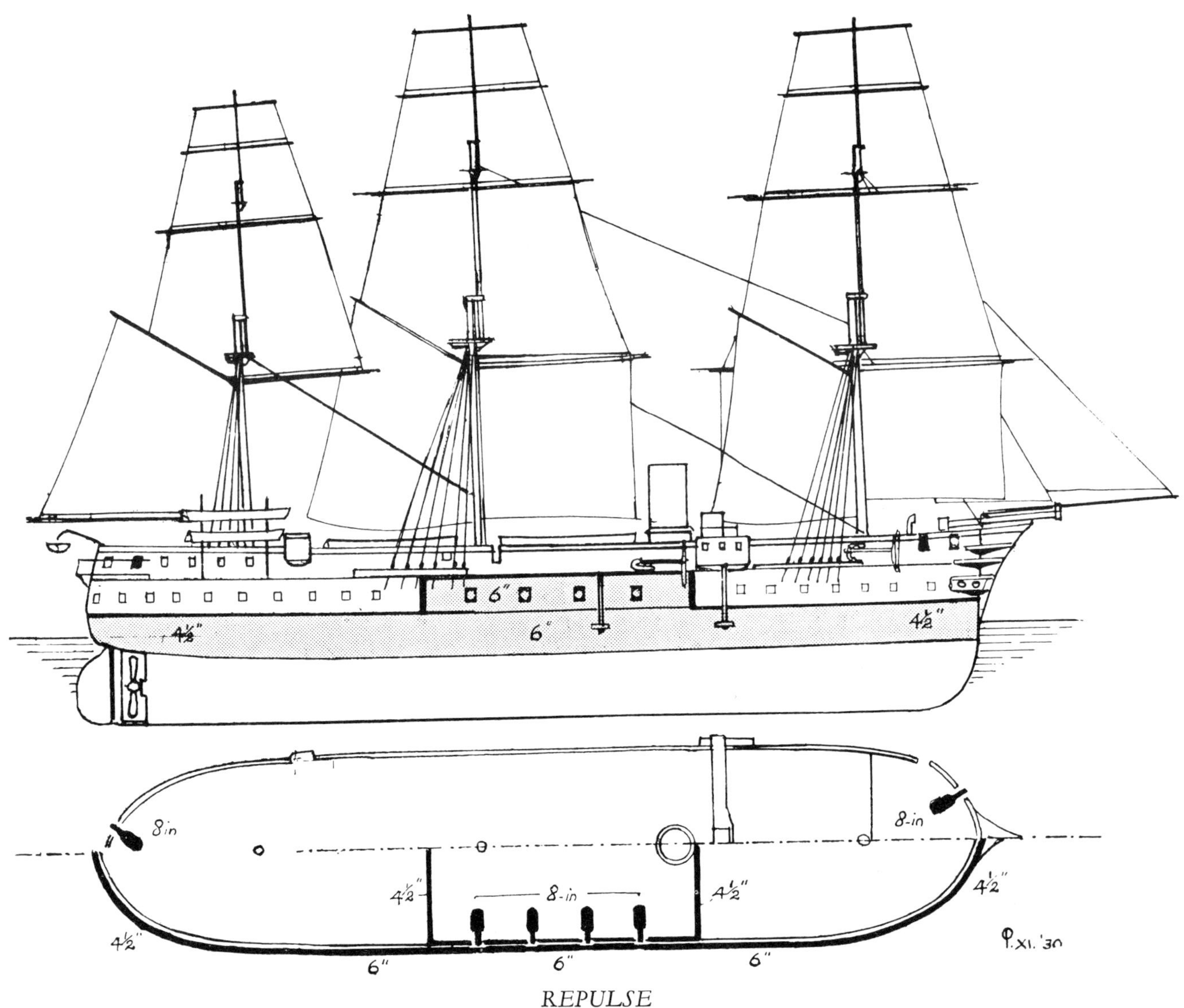

REPULSE

6 in. and gun calibre from 7 in. to 8 in. Hence, as this entailed 33 ft. more of main deck timber being exposed on each side, the *Repulse* became more vitally committed to destruction by gun fire than had ever been anticipated when thinner armour ensured immunity from shell fire. That she should not be exposed to ordeal by battle through conflict with her peers was more or less assured by despatching her to the Pacific station, on the completion of which service she took her place in the Reserve as a second-line unit.

Although but little altered below the water-line, the *Repulse* underwent greater changes above it than did any of the previous ships, with an immersion line changed by disposition of weights so that she drew 22½ ft. forward and 26 ft. aft—a feature shared in common with most of Reed's earlier designs. Owing to restrictions in the length of the building slip at Woolwich there was no question of her being lengthened, and in this respect *Repulse* and *Zealous* differed from the earlier five ships. But such short, tubby models had shown a marked tendency to dip in a head sea, and the *Prince Consort's* experience on her first passage north pointed the necessity for modifications up topsides to obviate flooding of the decks. For this reason very high bulwarks were provided with

The *Repulse* leaving Portsmouth after her 1877-80 refit, for guardship duties at Hull. Note the knee bow and figurehead, and chart house before the funnel. After the *Lord Warden* she was the best-looking of the wooden ironclads, and our last wooden battleship.

a rise in sheer fore and aft which made her hull unique in the battle fleet of the period, and kept her decks high and dry so that the conspicuous scupper shoots of the *Ocean's* were not required. A marked peculiarity was the light knee bow fitted as a sentimental embellishment to the last of the timber hulls. Although to the ship-lovers of the period this may have seemed an anachronism when associated with a full rounded stern, in modern eyes accustomed to clipper bows and cruiser sterns it was certainly an improvement on the sullen stems of her half-sisters. Its æsthetic effect was sadly marred by the running-in bowsprit breaking the continuity of rising line which the earlier fixed type with a well-marked sheer would have carried out handsomely.

Intended for service as an overseas flagship, the *Repulse* was completed with a topgallant forecastle and full poop; but because of the space required by the two guns astern the Captain's quarters had to be placed under the poop and the Admiral's on the main deck. But whatever she lacked in military qualities the *Repulse* had the reputation of furnishing the best accommodation of any ship of her time, and with a poop open to the quarter deck having cabins ranged fore and aft on each side, and most of the officers enabled to bunk under an open port in the tropics, she presented very greatly improved living conditions. The short central battery also permitted of main-deck berthing for a large portion of her ship's company without the usual mess tables between the guns, while the open lower deck was unencumbered by bulkheads and wing passages provided in iron hulls.

For the first time the bridge and chart house were placed forward of the funnel, instead of being right aft at the break of the poop where there were only small pilot towers on each beam.

ARMAMENT

Four of the twelve 8-in. guns were mounted on each side of the amidships battery without any provision for axial fire by means of embrasures. Two more were under the forecastle and two aft, with a saluting battery of 20-pdrs.

During the long refit after paying-off in 1877 she received a torpedo armament of four discharging carriages and twelve Whiteheads, together with a couple of Thornycroft second-class torpedo boats for which crutches were fitted on the bulwarks amidships just abaft the sheet anchor. But as she did not serve again overseas, and the boats were not required for home service, they made the passage abroad on their own bottoms under escort.

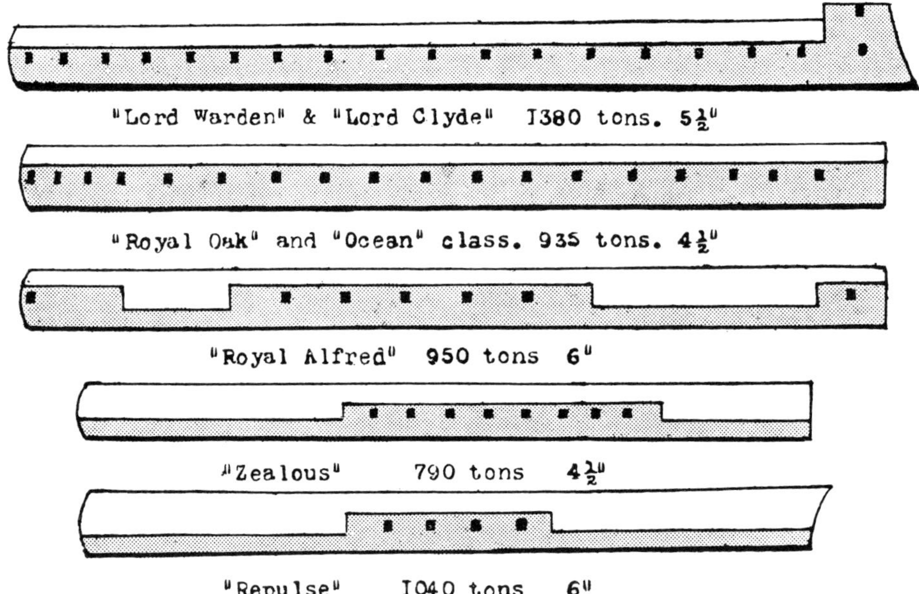

Scale diagram showing arrangement of side armour, its weight and maximum thickness in nine wooden battleships.

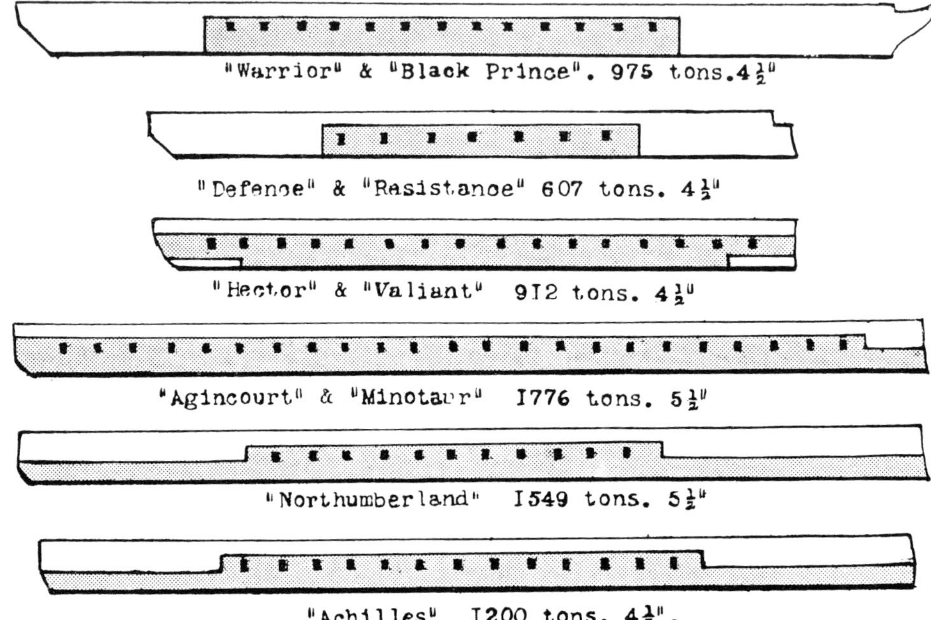

Scale diagram showing arrangement of side armour, its weight and maximum thickness in ten broadside ironclads.

ARMOUR

Protection was on the same scale of resistance as that in the *Royal Alfred*, although lacking bow and stern armour to the chase guns, with 6-in. plating tapering to 4½-in. fore and aft along the waterline and 6-in. over the central battery which was closed by 4½-in. bulkheads against raking fire. Nevertheless it totalled 1,040 tons against 950 tons of the earlier ship owing to a larger proportion of thicker metal, and greater depth below water.

When the torpedo tubes were fitted, net defence was also added which—except the *Lord Warden*—no other wooden ship carried.

MACHINERY

Alone among the converted ships the *Repulse* was driven by trunk engines. These had originally been made for the three-decker *Prince of Wales*—which was never completed—and being on a lighter scale than those in the *Lord Clyde* the troubles developed in that ship did not arise. The propeller was also smaller, with two instead of four blades, and fitted for hoisting. On the Stokes Bay mile 12½ knots was recorded with 58 revolutions—which was no improvement on her seven-year-old half-sisters. So far as fuel was concerned, she stowed least of all with 450 tons, which curtailed steaming radius by a third—being good for about 1,800 miles at 5 knots—and made her very much dependent upon sail. When refitted in 1880 the propeller pitch was altered from 28 to 26 ft. and boiler pressure reduced from 30 to 20 lb., after which she logged 11 knots with 2,734 i.h.p. at 56 revs., under less favourable circumstances than had obtained on her first trials, with 3,350 i.h.p.

SAIL

Masted on the second scale, the *Repulse* carried ship rig throughout her career, and differed from the other conversions by having fore and main lower masts 3 ft. shorter but with the tops raised 3 ft. to give the same drop in the courses. Under canvas her best was 10½ knots.

SEA-GOING QUALITIES

Excellent as a sea boat alike under both steam and sail, she steered well, and in contrast to the other wooden ironclads was a moderately steady gun platform, although stiff and heavy for the canvas carried—in which respect she resembled the *Achilles*. Thus, on one occasion she lost mainyard and jibboom, with a close-reefed fore topsail, top staysail, and three davit boats.

With the sole exception of the *Zealous* no other armoured ship covered more mileage with cold boilers.

"REPULSE"

Conversion commenced 25 October '66; completed for trials 21 August '69 and on commissioning in March '70 was sent as guardship to Queensferry, where she remained for two years. Selected as flagship to take over from the *Zealous* for the Pacific command and spent five years sailing the western coast of America from British Columbia to Patagonia. When relieved by the *Shah* in '77 her captain chose to round Cape Horn under sail rather than cut through Magellan Straits under steam, and it was seven weeks before she made Rio and forty-five days later ere she steamed past the Spithead forts—the only British armoured ship ever to round the Horn under canvas. Refitted '77-'80; guardship at Hull '81-'85; joined Admiral Hornby's "Particular Service Squadron" June-July '85; paid off into 4th class Reserve '85-'89 when she was sold, although still as sound as ever—the last British timber-hulled capital ship.

At the time the *Monarch* was launched twenty-nine British and twenty-six French armoured ships of various types had been put afloat, namely:

British		French	
Warrior	*Ocean*	*Gloire*	*Surveillante*
Black Prince	*Prince Consort*	*Invincible*	*Valeureuse*
Defence	*Caledonia*	*Normandie*	*Belliqueuse*
Resistance	*Royal Oak*	*Solferino*	*Ocean*
Hector	*Royal Alfred*	*Magenta*	*Alma*
Valiant	*Lord Warden*	*Couronne*	*Atalante*
Achilles	*Lord Clyde*	*Gaulois*	*Armide*
Minotaur	*Zealous*	*Flandre*	*Reine Blanche*
Agincourt	*Repulse*	*Heroïne*	*Montcalm*
Northumberland	*Pallas*	*Guyenne*	*Jeanne D'Arc*
Bellerophon	*Enterprise*	*Magnanime*	
Hercules	*Favorite*	*Provence*	Harbour defence
Penelope	*Research*	*Revanche*	*Taureau*
Monarch	*Royal Sovereign*	*Savoie*	*Cerbère*
Prince Albert			

of which the British list comprised some twenty-one different classes exhibiting a wide variety of experimental construction as against only eight French types, in which homogeniety was more favoured than a wide individuality embodying various improvements in construction or equipment.

Chapter 24

"AUDACIOUS" CLASS AND "SWIFTSURE" AND "TRIUMPH"

AFTER laying down the *Monarch* and authorizing Coles to proceed with the *Captain* to his own designs, the Board had to consider the question of providing a number of smaller second-class armoured units suitable for service on distant stations to which the French were already sending their "cruising ironclads" like the *Belliqueuse* as armoured nuclei to their squadrons. And although the press was vociferous in its demand for turret ships and blamed the Admiralty for not having accepted Coles' projects at his own valuation, it was decided to hasten slowly and await the trials of the *Monarch* and *Captain* before embarking on any smaller editions of them. For service in China and the East Indies sail was still regarded as essential, and Reed never altered his belief that the central battery was the best method of gun disposal in a rigged ship. The five-year-old *Defence* was therefore selected as a basis upon which a new type should be modelled, and Reed used her dimensions in drawing up a design in accordance with the 3,000 tons *Bom* prescribed by the Board. This however only allowed for 6-in. armour and an armament of eight 9-in. and two 6½-in. guns; to be carried at 12 knots with stowage for 330 tons of coal and crew of 400. By special directions she was to hoist a larger spread of canvas than had ever been given to an ironclad on a mean draught of 22 feet.

Neither the Controller nor Reed were satisfied that ships so poorly protected and armed would be suitable, and asked for a moderate increase in tonnage and cost to allow for 8-in. armour and 12-ton guns. When this was proposed to the Board as allowing the ships their proper equipment as second-class ironclads, there was great difficulty in obtaining the necessary sanction, which was yielded with reluctance. Again and again instances of Robinson and Reed having to press for a greater latitude in dimensions and fighting power over and above the limits laid down by the Board occur during their close association, and that they were almost invariably successful in getting what they wanted speaks well for the weighty influence Reed's councils exercised through the Controller.

In March 1867, when the Estimates were drawn up, the provision for new construction was not regarded as adequate, so Lord John Hay and Admiral G. H. Seymour handed in their resignations—and obtained the necessary ships!

At least four ironclads were required, but when it came to placing the contracts, only two were laid down to Reed's plan in the first instance. Before making a definite decision about the others the Board—in accordance with an undertaking given to the House—repeated the procedure observed in the case of the *Warrior*, and asked a number of leading shipbuilders to submit their own designs—with the promise that the third and fourth ships should be placed with the firm which submitted drawings for a ship within the limits of size and cost, if considered to be appreciably better than the Chief Constructor's project.

The results of this competition were decidedly instructive. The London Engineering Company proposed a broadside ship of 3,800 tons; Mare and Company a combined broadside and turret ship; Palmers a broadside ship with a movable upper deck battery of 9-in. guns; the Thames Ironworks a broadside ship much like the *Invincible*; and Napiers, Samudas and Lairds each designed a turret ship—a sufficiently diverse selection, which were placed before the Chief Constructor for adjudication. It is hardly surprising that none were found to be without some feature or other to which exception could be taken, and the outcome was the same as on the previous occasion—the two remaining ships were built to Admiralty design. Lairds' plans for a turret ship, however, were considered to have such high merit that the firm was awarded a contract for the *Vanguard* as a placebo, without any competitive price being sought. The fourth ship, *Iron Duke* was assigned to Pembroke Dockyard.

And so for the first time since the *Ocean* class were converted, a group of homogeneous ships were built to one design—an economic and efficient procedure not to be repeated until the *Admirals* were ordered sixteen years later.

In drawing up the *Audacious* design Reed set out to secure two features of outstanding military importance which had never as yet been incorporated into a British capital ship:

(1) A steady gun platform under steam in a seaway while still retaining adequate performance under sail.
(2) Axial fire from the main armament in all weathers.

In the *Penelope*—not then complete—shallow draught and plenty of beam was to provide steadiness for the gun sights but a poor performance under canvas; in these ships the Chief Constructor decided to reduce the *Defence's* draught by 3 ft. and fix the necessary higher centre of gravity by additional weights up topsides, at the same time slightly increasing the displacement by adopting a squarer section and fuller lines. Both requisites (1) and (2)

"AUDACIOUS" Class

	Builder	*Laid down*	*Launched*	*Completed*	*Cost*
"*Audacious*"	Napier	26 June '67	27 Feb. '69	10 Sept. '70	£256,291
"*Invincible*"	Napier	28 June '67	29 May '69	1 Oct. '70	£249,203
"*Iron Duke*"	Pembroke	23 Aug. '68	1 March '70	21 Jan. '71	£208,763
"*Vanguard*"	Laird	21 Oct. '67	Floated out	28 Sept. '70	£262,664

Dimensions 280′ × 54′ × 22′/23·2′ = 6,010 tons. Hull and armour = 3,880 tons. Equipment = 2,100 tons.

Guns 10 9-in. M.L.R.; 4 6-in. M.L.R.; 6 20-pdr. saluting.

Armour Belt 8″-6″; bulkheads 5″-4″; skin 1¼″; battery 6″-5″-4″; backing 10″-8″ teak. Total 924 tons.

Complement 450.

Sail area 25,054 sq. ft. (ship).
23,700 sq. ft. (barque).
"*Vanguard*" 21,520 sq. ft.

Machinery "*Audacious*" and "*Iron Duke*"—Ravenhill; "*Invincible*"—Napier; "*Vanguard*"—Lairds.
Two sets of 2-cyl. horizontal return connecting-rod engines; cyl. 72″; stroke 3′. I.H.P. 4,830 = 13 knots.
2 Mangin screws (afterwards replaced by Griffiths). Revs. 74. 6 rectangular boilers, 30 lb. pressure.

Coal 460 tons.

Constructor Alexander Milne.

Special features:

(1) They were the steadiest gun platforms in the Fleet.
(2) Could command axial fire from the main armament in all weathers.
(3) Were without wing bulkheads.
(4) Their sail area was greater in proportion to displacement than in any other capital ship.

AUDACIOUS Class.

were secured by moving four of the 9-in. guns from the main to the upper deck and accommodating them in a separate battery 16 ft. above water, which by projecting out well beyond the hull sides provided the corner ports with end-on fire—the first application of a system proposed by Captain Symonds, R.N. The form above water was determined by the fact that the then First Lord (Packington) made references in public hardly complimentary to the proposed appearance of the ships, which led to modifications excused by Reed when he stated, "I put a knee to the head, and an old-fashioned stern on to gratify public taste." But as the necessary ram could not be combined with a frigate stem this latter had to go, although the square stern was retained and provided Admiral's quarters until a poop was added when the ships were nearly at the end of their active careers.

Owing to the tumble-home of the hull sides and bulwarks the upper deck was narrow and cut up into fore-and-aft sections by the transverse walls of the battery, through which were communicating passages closed by armoured doors—all of which interfered with the working of sails and boats and restricted the use of the deck

The *Invincible* off Plymouth on commissioning in 1870. The photo shows her cut-away stern and quarter gallery windows (mostly painted) with the original short steam pipe abaft the funnel.

generally. Internally it was the opposite, as the short main-deck battery allowed for the officers' quarters being brought up from below, so that for the first time the wardroom enjoyed a quarter-deck hatchway, and cabins were properly lighted and ventilated by big square ports. The men had better berthing forward, with room to sling over 400 hammocks without using the flats.

But below was the serious defect in the design destined to result in the *Vanguard* disaster—*i.e.*, the absence of wing passages.

This failure to provide necessary longitudinal bulkheading exposed any of the big compartments to flooding in the event of the ship's side being pierced between water level and the double bottom—a defect aggravated by the main deck being only 3 ft. above water so that a loss of trim would result in the flooded compartment overflowing on to the deck above through the hatches—this being long before the days of high hatch-coamings.

Having already added to the burden up topsides by providing an upper deck battery, Reed may have sought still further to affect his weight distribution by this cutting-out of longitudinal bulkheads in addition to effecting economies in the hull framing. But from the plans of the engine-room it would appear that the space occupied by the machinery would not allow for wing bulkheads. In any case the net result of these measures to raise the centre of gravity were only too successful.

The Controller has recorded how Reed knew perfectly well that the efforts to economize weight—not strength—in the lower hull might require the addition of ballast to bring the ships to their proper draught of water, and the requisite amount would have to be ascertained when all their weights were aboard. Incidentally he made it clear that such an expedient had to be employed because deficiencies in his staff were such that all the necessary calculations for such distribution of weights as would obviate ballasting could not be worked out without considerable delay, and as well as the assistance of additional data not then available.[1]

It was never Reed's intention to allow the ships to go to sea before inclining tests had been made and the exact position of the centre of gravity determined; but unfortunately his resignation was handed in three months before their completion and the *Invincible* was sent out on trials in an incomplete state without being tested or ballasted, owing to a misunderstanding of orders sent during the Controller's absence through illness.

Before being ballasted the G.M. was 2 ft. only, and in consequence the *Invincible* showed herself steady as a fort under steam, but with a wind on the beam, although without sail and gallant masts on deck, she listed 17°. This condition was corrected by 360 tons of cement and iron being worked into her double bottom—thus adding non-productive weight and increasing risks of injury and hull strain if holed or grounded. After which she rode

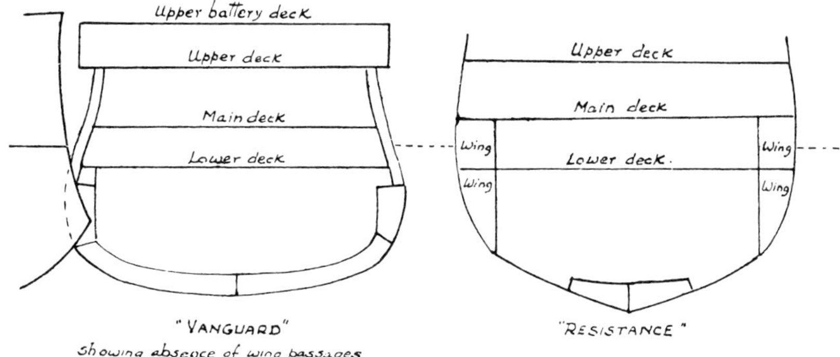

"VANGUARD"
Showing absence of wing passages

"RESISTANCE"

a foot deeper with a loss of 0·4 knot under steam. The G.M. was increased to 3 ft. and thereafter the class were still magnificent gun platforms, able to make steady shooting when their consorts would be rolling their gun ports under; and for this reason ranked higher in the Battle Fleet than mere size would warrant.

ARMAMENT

The ten 9-in. were grouped amidships on two decks—three aside in the main deck battery and four in an upper deck box battery with corner ports to give axial fire. For the displacement this was a very powerful equipment which had the advantage of being situated amidships where it suffered least from pitching, and having four guns which could be worked under weather conditions which would have placed all the guns in the Battle Fleet out of action excepting those in the *Monarch* and the bow chasers in *Lord Warden* and *Lord Clyde*.

This upper deck battery was good in its way, but led to the guns being bunched up amidships immediately over the boilers and inconveniently remote from the ammunition and shell rooms.[2]

Outside the armour were four truck-mounted 6-in. 64-pdrs., two forward and two aft, which required personnel out of all proportion to their fighting value. There were also six 20-pdr. Armstrongs for saluting purposes. In December 1879 the *Invincible* took out the first six Nordenfelt guns supplied to the Mediterranean. In the middle 'eighties these and the 64-pdrs. were replaced by six or eight 4-in. B.L. as anti-torpedo guns.

In 1878 four main deck 14-in. torpedo carriages disposed fore and abaft the battery were added, and towards the end of their sea-going careers torpedo net defence was fitted.

For their displacement, therefore, they were well armed, and although referred to as "second class ships" were far superior in every way to the *Alma* group of 3,788 tons which the French were completing at that time for service on distant stations.

ARMOUR

In accordance with the generally accepted principle in naval architecture of the period that a ship's protection should be on a scale roughly comparable to her armament, the belt was increased to 8 in. amidships—the thickness her 9-in. guns could pierce at the then maximum fighting range of 1,500 yards. This covered the engine and boiler room compartments and extended from 5 ft. below water to only 3 ft. above at full load, owing to the

[1] The Constructor's Department had grown but little in the last ten years and comprised three Assistant Constructors, a Surveyor of Contracts, a Secretary to the Chief Constructor, and ten draughtsmen.

[2] It also raised the centre of gravity considerably more than Reed really required and was largely responsible for the ballasting.

lowness of the main deck, tapering fore and aft to 6 in. where the compartments were smaller and of less vital importance. Above this, the sides were unprotected, excepting for the 59 ft. of the battery which was covered by 6-in. plating with a 5-in. bulkhead forward and a 4-in. one aft. Because of these soft sides it was predicted that a shot striking above the belt could go right through the ship and smash away the armour on the opposite waterline, as the protective deck was only 4 ft. above water and made of $3\frac{1}{2}$-in. wood covered by $\frac{1}{4}$-in. steel.

A "pilot tower" stood above the upper battery, a light structure of 3-in. plate which could accommodate one man, and furnished with a single voice pipe to the fighting wheel in the battery below.

In her refit at Chatham in 1889-90 the *Audacious* discarded her barque rig and was given a couple of fighting tops for 3-pdrs., some 4-in. B.L. and a number of machine guns which can be seen on the forecastle and over the battery amidships. This photo was taken at Portsmouth before she took over duty as guardship at Hull.

MACHINERY

At a time when twin screws were not regarded with any favour either in naval or mercantile circles at home or abroad—and the French were not to adopt them in big ships until 1879—the Board showed commendable enterprise in ordering twin sets of engines for the *Audacious* class, although—as in the case of the *Penelope*—it was more on account of necessity than any recognition of the tactical benefits provided. Only by virtue of smaller screw diameter employed in the dual drive could the required reduction in draught be attained. Now in masted ships the great drawback of twin screws was that they could not be hoisted without some such constructional makeshift as was employed in the *Penelope*—so in the *Audacious* class none was attempted. Having two sets of engines, there was not the single-screw ship's dependence upon sail power in case of a breakdown, and the value of their canvas was assessed accordingly. At the best it meant considerable help in coal saving when running before the wind, and even if the quartette were somewhat slow and leewardly when the funnel was down, their tremendous spread of canvas provided an adequate alternative to depleted bunkers.

The *Invincible's* machinery wore out so soon that, as a penalty, Napiers were not awarded another machinery contract for ten years.

SAIL

When completed with ship rig they spread a greater sail area in proportion to displacement than any other capital ship; the hoist from trucks to deck being equal to that of the *Agincourt* and *Hercules*, with fore and main lower masts of 79 and 84 ft., topmasts of 65, and topgallants of 50 ft. The lower yards, however, were only 96 ft. instead of 105 ft. and the topsail yards 71 ft. instead of 74 ft. But after the loss of the *Captain* during their first year in commission there was a reaction towards lighter masting which led to the yards being removed from the mizen in all four ships, and topmasts being cut down in the *Vanguard* by 10 ft. and in the others by 6 ft.

On passing into Reserve the *Audacious* had her yards removed and was given fighting tops on the fore and mizen in acknowledgment of the passing of her sailing days, but was the only one of the class to be so altered.

SEA-GOING QUALITIES

Reporting on the *Audacious* during her passage out to China, Admiral Ryder wrote to the Controller:

> "Whatever objections may have been raised to ships of the *Audacious* class, the longer experience I have of them the more I am struck with their wonderful steadiness. I have just lately made a passage, running before a heavy sea and strong wind, all my stern ports barred in, and to my great surprise the ship did not roll more than 2° to 1° each way. I half made up my mind to broach her to, to see what she would do in such a sea, but the helmsman did it for me. In giving the ship a yaw he brought her to the wind, and positively to our surprise, she declined to take any notice of the sea at all. An ironclad flagship the French *Atalante* accompanied me. We were both proceeding before the same sea, my flagship rolling 2° to 1°, the other rolling 20°."

Because of the drag of their screws they were slow under sail, and with comparatively shallow draught and flat bottoms failed to hold the water when close hauled.

Deficient fuel was sometimes a cause for anxiety, and *Iron Duke* with bunkers and battery filled with coal could only make the passage from Aden to Ceylon at 4 knots, arriving with less than sufficient for one day's steaming.

In the *Iron Duke* the rudder was hinged, in the rest it was balanced—which made steering easier under steam but detracted from their sailing powers so as to make them almost unmanageable under canvas only.

In order to test an alternative to the heavy and expensive copper sheathing used to militate against fouling by barnacles and weed, experimental zinc sheathing under water was tried in the *Audacious*.

"AUDACIOUS"

Damaged when launched in a gale, and was the first iron-hulled British warship to float lighter than designed. Taken from Govan to Plymouth for completion and commissioned October '70 as guardship at Kingstown. Transferred to Hull '71-'74 and paid off at Chatham for recommissioning as flagship of China command '74-'78 (collision during typhoon at Yokohama). Relieved by *Iron Duke* and paid off at Chatham; guardship at Hull '78-'80; refit '80-'83 (new boilers, poop, etc.) and then relieved *Iron Duke* as flagship for two commissions, returning in '89; refit at Chatham '89-'90 (4-in. B.L.; military rig, etc.) and then served a third spell at Hull from '90-'94. Laid up in 4th Reserve '94-'01 and then converted into training hulk *Fisgard* at Portsmouth '02-'14. Towed to Scapa '14 and became receiving hulk *Imperieuse* until '19, then removed to Rosyth as receiving hulk *Victorious* until 1927.

Sold 15 March 1929.

"INVINCIBLE"

Completed at Plymouth and commissioned October '70 as guardship at Hull '70-'71; Mediterranean '72-'76; paid off at Plymouth for renewal of boilers and engines prematurely worn out; Mediterranean '78; joined *Swiftsure* to guard Bulair lines when Fleet was up Dardanelles; landed troops on acquisition of Cyprus; joined Admiral Hornby's squadron in Marmora and then transferred temporarily to the Channel. Returned to Mediterranean and then recommissioned in March '82 (Bombardment of Alexandria 11 July '82 expended 140 9-in., 131 6-in., 5,000 m.g. against Fort Mex). Paid off at Portsmouth '86; conveyed relief crews to China; guardship at Southampton '86-'93; removed from effective list and in '01 converted into t.b. depot *Erebus* at Sheerness '01-'06; transferred to Portsmouth as *Fisgard II* '06-'14; foundered in Portland Race 17 September '14 with loss of 21 hands when being towed to Scapa Flow.

"IRON DUKE"

Commissioned at Plymouth January '71 as First Reserve guardship until September, when she went to China as flagship and was the first capital ship to use the Suez Canal. Relieved by *Audacious*, she paid off at Plymouth May '75 and in July became guardship at Hull. Sunk the *Vanguard* in collision 1 September '75 and afterwards took that ship's place at Kingstown until July '77. Refit '77-'78. Flagship of China command '78-'83 (towed off P. and O. *Bengal* ashore in Red Sea '78); aground on Woosung Reef for 5 days and towed off by U.S.S. *Monocacy* in '79; went ashore off Hokkaido '80 and had to be repaired at Hong Kong (the last occasion on which a British capital ship hoisted her big guns in and out with her own gear). Refitted and reboilered '83-'85 and then joined Admiral Hornby's Particular Service Squadron April-August '85 and afterwards the Channel squadron until '90, when she reverted to First Reserve guardship until 1900. Cut down to coal hulk and finished her days in Kyles of Bute until sold in '06.

"VANGUARD"

Completed and commissioned at Plymouth October '70 (proved the fastest of the four, making 14·5 knots on trials). Guardship at Kingstown '70-'75; sunk by *Iron Duke* in collision off Dublin Bay in a fog 1 September '75—no lives lost. She was struck between the boiler and engine rooms, flooding both compartments and sank 70 mins. after in 19 fathoms. The first capital ship in the annals of the Navy to be sunk by collision.

"SWIFTSURE" and "TRIUMPH"

	Builders	*Laid down*	*Launched*	*Completed*	*Cost*
"*Swiftsure*"	Palmers	31 Aug. '68	15 June '70	27 June '72	£257,081
"*Triumph*"	Palmers	31 Aug. '68	27 Sept. '70	8 April '73	£258,322

Dimensions 280′ × 55′ × 24·5′/26·1′ = 6,910 tons.
Hull and armour = 4,570 tons. Equipment = 2,140 tons.
280′ × 55′ × 24·8′/26·7′ = 6,640 tons.
Hull and armour = 4,680 tons. Equipment = 2,150 tons.

Guns 10 9-in. M.L.R.; 4 6-in. M.L.R.; 6 20-pdr. saluting.

Armour Belt 8″-6″; battery 6″-5″-4″; skin 1¼″; bulkheads 5″-4″. Backing 10″-8″ teak. Total 975 tons.

Complement 450.

Sail area Plain 32,900 sq. ft./41,900 full.

Machinery Maudslay.

Constructors Alexander Milne and G. H. Seymour.

Special features:

(1) The last British capital ships of less than 8,000 tons, and
(2) The last to have no guns above 9-in. calibre.
(3) The first British battleships to be sheathed and coppered.
(4) The last to have hoisting propellers.
(5) *Swiftsure* was the last British flagship to fly an Admiral's flag at the topgallant masthead in a rigged ship, and
(6) The last rigged battleship to hoist sail during fleet manœuvres.

Although apparently only single-screw sisters to the *Audacious*, the *Swiftsure* and *Triumph* had such different hulls from the original quartette that they must be regarded as qualified to rank as a class by themselves. For whereas the *Audacious* had been designed to secure a steady gun platform in conjunction with shallow draft without much consideration for sailing qualities, for the two later ships the Board stipulated that good performance under canvas was to rank with ability to steam well—which may be taken to represent the difference in requirements between foreign stations such as the Mediterranean or China and the Pacific.

Of our eight areas of separate naval responsibility the Pacific ranked as by far the largest. Vast distances had to be covered and consequently good performance under sail was of paramount importance on a station where supplies of coal were limited and very expensive. And as the station included the South American western coastline where very unsettled republics maintained armoured ships liable to rebellious demonstrations of a piratical nature, the need for armoured ships able to fight under steam in order to maintain British prestige and interests was now an essential. The *Shah* and *Huascar* duel had demonstrated that.

In designing the *Audacious* Reed had been given the *Defence* as a model for length and beam, and employed twin screws to get propulsion upon a much reduced draught when displacement was maintained by such expedients as a flat bottom, square bilges, and no rise in floor. To make her a good gun platform the weights had been kept high and the metacentre low, so that while she was steady in a seaway she lacked stiffness to carry the canvas necessary to compensate for her limited bunkerage.

But when it came to drawing up the requirements for the future flagships on the Pacific station, there was no need for reduced draught or twin screws, and instead a single hoisting screw in conjunction with ample draught for good sailing was very much indicated. Hence the Chief Constructor was directed to reverse the former procedure and submit a draft plan of an *Audacious* with the under-water hull of the *Defence*. Thus above the waterline and in her bows the *Swiftsure* presented all the features of the *Audacious* except at the stern, while below her marks there was a return to the hull lines of six years before. The obvious difference between the two classes lay in the shape of the stern, where the wide transom, high counter and projecting taffrail had given way to an elliptical stern narrowing from the quarter to a circular end with a low counter and receding taffrail.

This alteration meant a reduction in weight at some height, with the addition of structural weight below due to increased draught, all of which combined to afford better stability in carrying sail.

It may here be mentioned that one of the recommendations of the Committee on Designs was that the

The *Swiftsure* and *Triumph* differed from their earlier half-sisters in having full ship rig and an elliptical stern with a row of real and painted windows. Here the *Triumph* is off Plymouth on her first commission for the Channel in 1873.

Swiftsures should be completed as two-gun turret ships with some lighter guns in unprotected positions. The weight of armour was to be the same, with the battery plating concentrated as an armoured base to the turret.

SHEATHING

As British docking facilities in the Pacific were non-existent until the dockyard at Esquimalt was completed in 1886, a reversion was made to the former practice of sheathing the underwater hull with copper—which had been abandoned because of the process of electrical erosion set up by copper in contact with iron under water affecting the lower strakes in the armoured wooden ships. Both zinc and Muntz metal reduced fouling but were inferior in this respect to copper, so the former practice was modified by introducing a double layer of 3-in.

planking extending to 3 ft. above water, which was covered by tarred felt before being coppered. This system reduced galvanic action and prevented fouling to an extent sufficient to justify its adoption for foreign service.

As finally approved the completed design had the same length (280 ft.) and beam (54 ft. exclusive of sheathing) as *Audacious* and *Defence*, but with the maximum draught of 26 ft. and a single screw. Calculated displacement was 6,700 tons, exceeding that of the *Audacious* mainly from the greater depth of hull, and of the *Defence* partly from the somewhat fuller lines and partly from the extra beam due to sheathing.

The deck arrangement followed that of *Audacious* with a short open topgallant forecastle and no poop, and the usual 6-ft. bulwarks carrying hammock troughs enclosed the whole deck outside the upper battery. Across the quarter deck ran a light bridge carrying a chart house, with the triple hand wheel underneath and fitted with voice pipes to the two fighting wheels below and behind armour. At sea boom boats were stowed on top of the upper battery. Bower cables were worked on the upper deck, but sheet cables on the main.

All ranks and ratings were berthed on the main deck, the men forward of the battery and the officers abaft—a change from the usual berthing on the lower deck which marked the beginning of its abandonment. The men

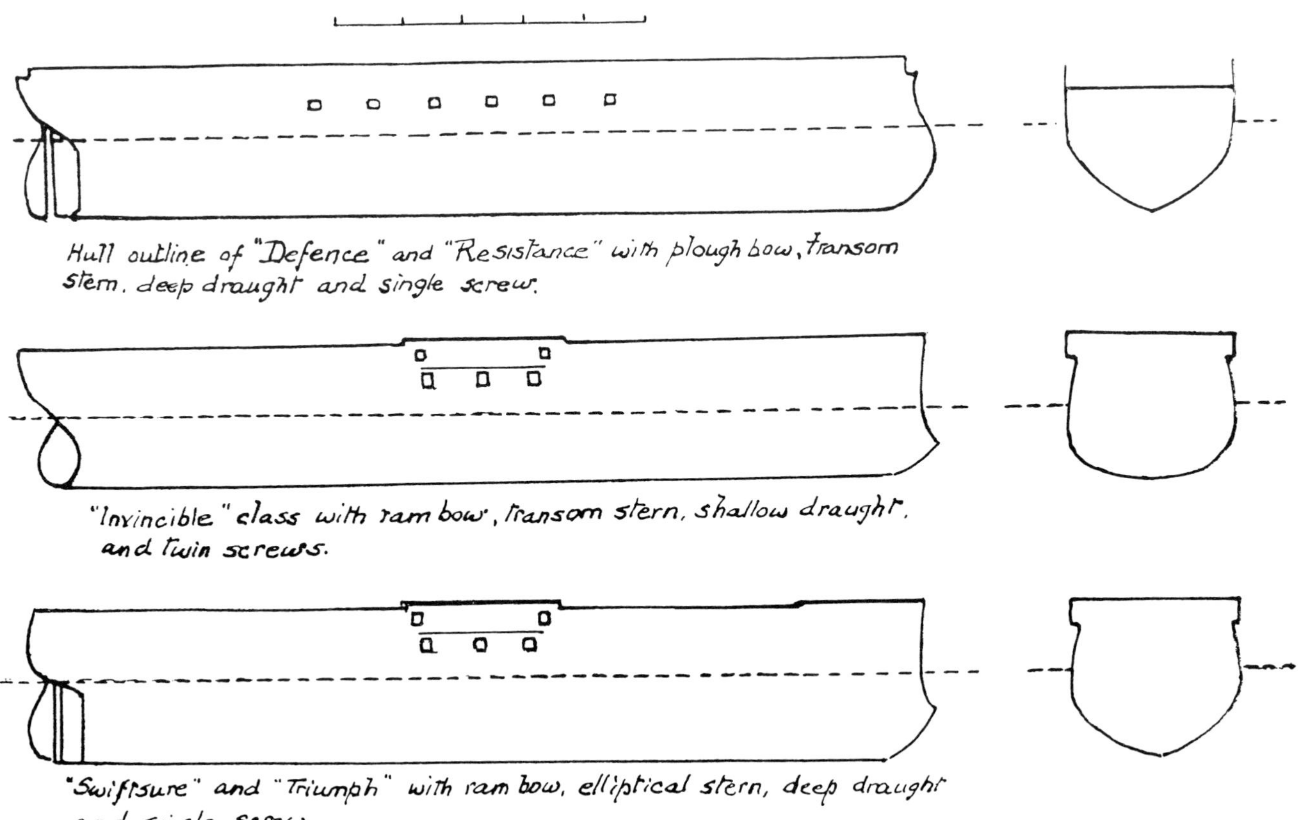

disliked having to sling hammocks in a battery, and as the officers' accommodation was excellent and well lighted the ships were popular and healthy.

ARMAMENT

As in the *Swiftsure*, the four 9-in. M.L. in the upper box battery trained from abeam to the axial line, with six 9-in. below as the main deck broadside. Four rifled 64-pdrs. (6-in.) converted from smooth bores and truck mounted did duty for upper deck chase guns, two forward and two aft, each having a broadside and a chase port. In 1882 these practically useless pieces were replaced by four 5-in. firing a 50-lb. shell in the *Triumph* and eight 4-in. with a 25-lb. shell in the *Swiftsure*. Some 6-pdr. and 3-pdr. pedestal mounted guns were installed at the same time as additional anti-t.b. defence.

In 1880-82 when the "fish" torpedo had reached a stage of development sufficient to justify its being carried by capital ships, both vessels received four launching carriages—a light steel open frame-work carriage standing on rollers with an air impulse rod in a swinging breech-end cover—placed at special ports fore and abaft the main deck battery.

PROTECTION

This followed *Audacious* lines with the same absence of longitudinal wing bulkheads.

MACHINERY

Both were driven by Maudslay's horizontal twin-cylinder return connecting-rod engines turning a two-bladed hoisting screw of 23½ ft. diameter. They were the last of the few capital ships fitted with this device which had otherwise been abandoned as the space, inconvenience and hull weakness resulting from the banjo hoist and well did not compensate for hoisting advantages under sail in home waters. Both ships touched 13¾ knots on trial, with *Triumph* indicating the higher horse-power. Their bunkerage of 550 tons was sufficient to give 1,600 miles at 6 knots.

They were provided with steam steering gear and a steam capstan for working cables.

SAIL

As first completed they were ship rigged with 32,900 sq. ft. of canvas (to which stunsails could add another 9,000 sq. ft.) with their main trucks 170 ft. above deck, fore and main yards 96 ft., and fore and main topsail yards 71 ft. long. In common with other ships having a length of about five times their beam they were apt to carry too much weather helm when sailing full and by—a tendency increased by the hoisting propeller, which left a void between stern post and rudder post, thus reducing the resistance to leeway aft.

After their first commissions in European waters, where movements were mainly carried out under steam, they were converted to a large-scale barque rig under which they sailed as well as ever (22,750 sq. ft.). Given favourable trade wind conditions they could have covered any distance above 1,200 miles more quickly under sail than at the economical speed imposed by their coal supply. Moreover, they proved handy and reliable in tacking and wearing, due to ability to stand up with only a little ballast to a larger canvas area in proportion to tonnage than any other British armoured ship. As fighting ships their value was enhanced by remarkable steadiness in heavy weather.

Built side by side at Palmers Yard, they spent their active careers doing turnabout as flagships on the Pacific Station.

"SWIFTSURE"

Commissioned at Devonport September '71 for experimental service with the Channel squadron. Had no equal in sailing and was only left astern by the wooden frigate *Aurora* reported as among the fastest sailers in the Fleet of all time. Steam steering fitted and she relieved the *Defence* up the Straits in August '72, remaining on the station until October '78. (Took part in the Cartagena incident, a demonstration against mutinous Spanish ships; Hornby's passage of the Dardanelles 1878.) Paid off at Devonport for refit and given barque rig, torpedo equipment, a 25-pdr. B.L. battery, and Admiral's quarters as relief flagship to *Triumph* in Pacific from March '82 to December '85 and then refitted at Devonport (new boilers). In Reserve until second spell in the Pacific April '88 to October '90, when she was relieved by *Warspite* and became flagship Devonport Reserve until August '91. Guardship for 2 years, then reduced to Fleet Reserve until '01 when as *Orontes* she served as hulk for stores.

Sold July '08 for £17,550.

During the Manœuvres of 1893 the *Swiftsure* asked permission to spread sail to enable her to keep station, as her steaming power was not equal to the speed ordered for her squadron. This was the last occasion on which sail was used by one of H.M. battleships with the fleet at sea.

"TRIUMPH"

Commissioned at Devonport March '73 for the Channel and later transferred to the Mediterranean (Cartagena incident). Paid off '77 and hastily prepared as flagship in Pacific to relieve the *Shah* after her indecisive action with the piratical Peruvian turret ship *Huascar* May '78 to October '82, when relieved by *Swiftsure*. Paid off at Portsmouth and reboilered, Whiteheads, 25-pdrs., etc. Returned to Pacific as flagship from January '85 to December '88 (Admiral Baird) (during this commission the dry dock at Esquimalt was completed). Her relief by *Swiftsure* terminated her foreign service career and after Devonport Reserve in '89 she was flagship at Queenstown from February '90-September '92. Paid off into Fleet Reserve at Devonport until July '00 and then surrendered her armament to become depôt at Plymouth. Hulked and machinery removed '03; renamed *Tenedos* t.s. for boy artificers at Chatham. Tender to *Warrior* '05 at Portsmouth; became *Indus IV* at Devonport '10; towed to Invergordon in '14 as floating store *Algiers*.

Sold November '21 for £10,775, after having remained afloat 13 years longer than her sister.

Chapter 25

EROSION AND FOULING

A MAJOR problem in the maintenance of iron ships was the control of erosion and fouling, especially on foreign stations. With timber hulls the teredo worm was the menace, and both this and marine growths could be countered by copper sheathing, in which the anti-fouling properties are due to the action of sea-water forming oxychlorides and other soluble salts which do not adhere to the uncorroded copper, and are continually being washed away, leaving a smooth surface upon which plants and animals cannot become attached. The sort of copper used largely determined the rate of wastage, and much attention was directed to securing the minimum of wear consistent with retention of anti-fouling properties. The attachment of the copper sheets presented no difficulties as they could be nailed directly on to the wooden skin; but with an iron hull any such intimate connection leads to galvanic action between the copper and the iron, and even a very indirect connection is sufficient to produce galvanism, with consequent pitting and erosion.

To overcome this galvanic action two thicknesses of wood were laid between the iron and the copper, the inner thickness being bolted to the iron with galvanised iron and the outer thickness bolted to the inner with "naval brass," these not coming into contact with the hull or the bolts of the inner thickness. This system was found to be satisfactory after twelve years' experience with ships on foreign stations. Of the battleships the *Swiftsure*, *Triumph* and *Neptune* were so treated.

The expense of copper led to experiments with other metals, the *Royal Oak* being sheathed with Muntz metal, which like copper is electro-negative to iron and also requires wood sheathing. But when docked after six months in the Mediterranean her bottom "was found to be foul beyond all conception"—which seems to have been sufficient evidence to warrant no further tests.

Zinc, on the other hand, being electro-positive to iron, does not need wood sheathing, and when used as a sheathing to wooden ships was not very successful in preventing fouling, as there was not sufficient metal contact to produce galvanic action. Various methods of affixing zinc sheathing to an iron hull were proposed, and that adopted in the Navy entailed laying a single thickness of 3-in. to 4-in. planking against the hull and bolting it to the plating; to this the zinc sheets were nailed. The strakes of the planking were not caulked and water finding its way under the sheathing could pass freely through the seams to the iron skin. A certain amount of metallic connection between the zinc and the iron came through the iron stem and stern post, but not enough to ensure much galvanic action.

Only the *Audacious* and *Temeraire* of the capital ships were so sheathed, and the results chronicled in the case of the *Audacious* are worth mentioning.

While acting as guardship at Hull near the sea where the water is brackish, no fouling or oxidation took place whatever and it was thought that the whole question had been settled satisfactorily. Her 1880-83 refit included fresh sheathing for service as flagship on the China Station, and here it was a very different story. As Rear-Admiral Philip Colomb put it:

> "In the *Audacious*, where I served for more than three years, I thought some of the strongest language I have ever thought in my life . . . on the question of the enormous quantity of fouling that went on with zinc sheathing. I never saw anything like it. I never knew any kind of bottom foul so rapidly or to such an extent as on that zinc sheathing of Her Majesty's ship *Audacious*."

The fault lay in the wood sheathing. Had it been possible to fix the zinc directly on to the outer skin the galvanic action would have been unimpaired. This slowly erodes the zinc, producing a thin greasy lamina to which barnacles and grass cannot adhere as it is being continually washed away by passage through the sea water. But with the wood almost eliminating galvanism the zinc was just as much an attachable surface to zoophytes and grass as iron.

Chapter 26

"SULTAN"

PENDING the results of the experimental turret ships *Monarch* and *Captain*, the broadside system of mounting the main armament was to hold pride of place as the best method of disposition of heavy guns in a rigged ironclad, and in 1869 the *Sultan*—named after Sultan Azizieh of Turkey, who was visiting England—was ordered as a still further addition to the ever-growing array of individual types which now composed the Battle Fleet.

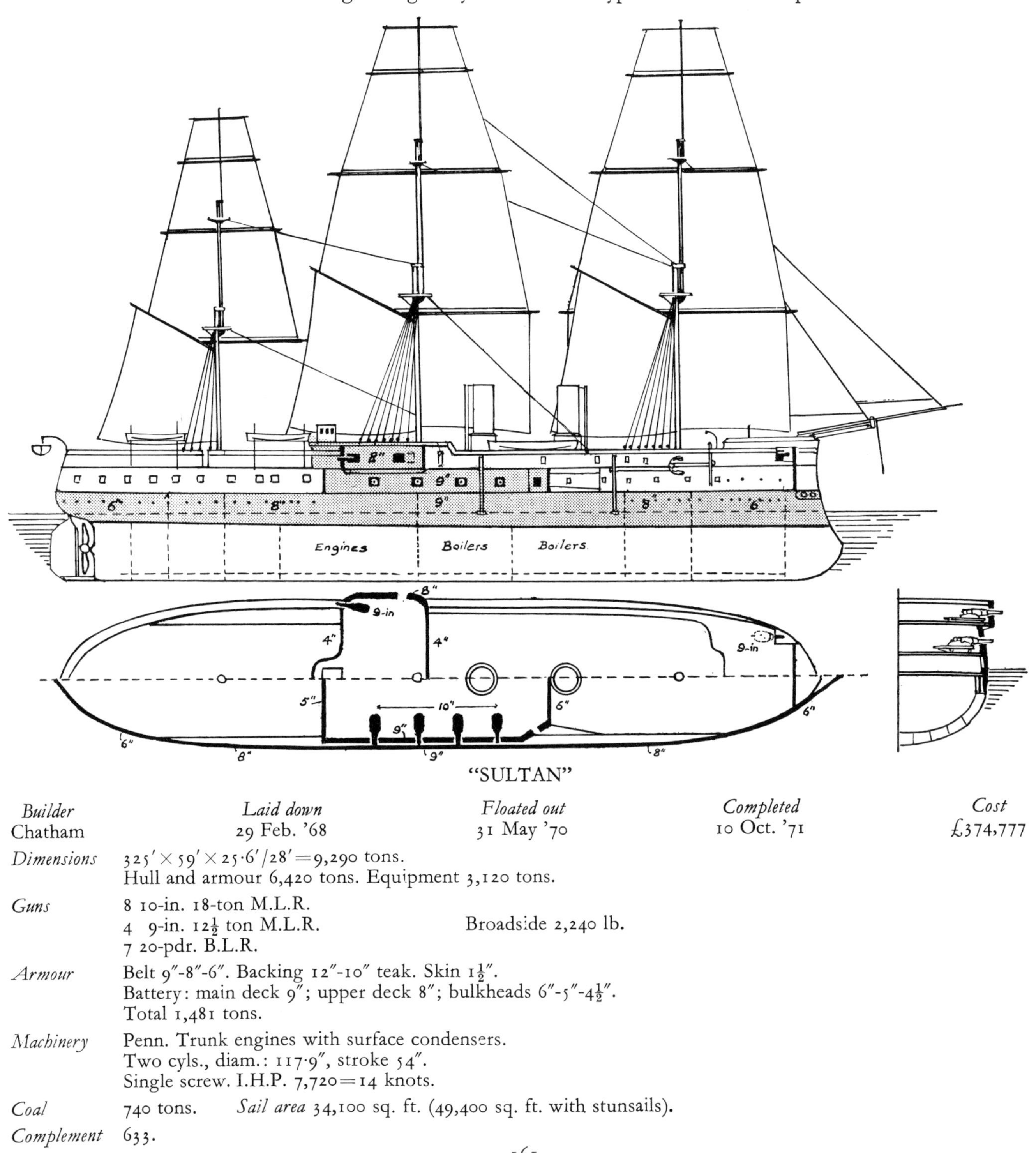

"SULTAN"

Builder	*Laid down*	*Floated out*	*Completed*	*Cost*
Chatham	29 Feb. '68	31 May '70	10 Oct. '71	£374,777

Dimensions 325′ × 59′ × 25·6′/28′ = 9,290 tons.
Hull and armour 6,420 tons. Equipment 3,120 tons.

Guns 8 10-in. 18-ton M.L.R.
4 9-in. 12½ ton M.L.R. Broadside 2,240 lb.
7 20-pdr. B.L.R.

Armour Belt 9″-8″-6″. Backing 12″-10″ teak. Skin 1½″.
Battery: main deck 9″; upper deck 8″; bulkheads 6″-5″-4½″.
Total 1,481 tons.

Machinery Penn. Trunk engines with surface condensers.
Two cyls., diam.: 117·9″, stroke 54″.
Single screw. I.H.P. 7,720 = 14 knots.

Coal 740 tons. *Sail area* 34,100 sq. ft. (49,400 sq. ft. with stunsails).

Complement 633.

The design of the *Sultan* was based upon that of the *Hercules* with an upper deck armoured battery in place of the main deck bow and stern guns. As in the *Audacious* class—which had been laid down a few months previously—stability was diminished in order to secure greater steadiness at sea by raising her centre of gravity. As the upper battery meant a topweight of some 300 tons this excessive weight was but partially offset by various expedients, one of which was the lowering of the main and lower decks and restricting the height of the watertight bulkheads to main deck level. As hatchways at that period did not have high combings, this meant that in case of flooding with increased immersion the water in one compartment might rise to the top of the bulkheads

Shown as a ship in the plan, the *Sultan* was reduced to barque rig during her refit in 1876, when her stability was in question. She is here seen under plain sail and easy steam in the Mediterranean when H.R.H. the Duke of Edinburgh was in command. The fighting top to her mizen was not fitted until 1879.

and then spread fore and aft along the main deck and down the hatchways of other compartments. In fact, it was this very cause which led to the sinking of the *Sultan* eight days after she had struck a reef in 1889.

The hull was modelled to give one of the roundest forms of midship section ever adopted up to that time or for the next twenty years, and this together with a metacentric height of less than 3 ft. was successful in earning her the reputation of being one of the steadiest ships afloat. But although her dimensions were the same as in the *Hercules* with a foot more draught, the alteration in disposition of weights introduced problems of stability which needed practical experience to confirm their solution, and when tests came to be carried out it was soon evident that Reed had been too lavish with his top weights and that the *Sultan* was tender.

In order to restore her stability excessive ballasting had to be resorted to as in the *Audacious* quartette, some 600 tons of cement and iron being placed in the double bottom. The addition of this deadweight, which added to her risks if grounded and might well have been better utilized, caused a lot of adverse comment at the time and remained a black mark against the design.

ARMAMENT

The main deck battery carried the same number of 10-in. 18-ton guns as the *Hercules*, but was lengthened by 12 ft. with the after embrasure suppressed. In order to reduce the size of the gun ports without limiting the field of vision they were designed with their lower portions exactly corresponding to the space filled by the lower half of the gun in extreme training, while the upper portions were enlarged laterally to give full arcs of view. They allowed for 70° of training, 10° of elevation, and 5° of depression, the port sils being 11 ft. above water.

In order to secure axial fire from the main deck battery, the foremost gun on each side was mounted on a turntable so that it could be trained from the broadside to fire through an embrasure dead ahead. Lacking embrasures, there was no axial fire from the after battery guns, this being provided by a single 9-in. gun on each side bearing 45° ahead of the beam through a broadside port and dead astern through an after one, the bulwarks being recessed to allow for this. As the two ports were too far apart for the employment of a turntable, the gun had to be traversed from one to the other by a complicated system of deck racers over which it was pivoted and swung. In order further to reduce top weights the ready-rack ammunition for these upper deck guns had to be moved to the main deck—a drastic departure from British gunnery tradition. But here the question of its accommodation raised a problem. For while solid shot could be stowed with safety in an exposed position, it was deemed advisable that shell should be kept below the waterline unless they could be stowed behind battery armour—and there was no room for the upper battery shell in the main deck battery, where all available space was taken up by the ready-racks therein required. So in the case of the *Sultan* the risk of stowage outside the battery walls had to be accepted; but as these shell would be the first to be expended in action the innovation was not regarded as risky.

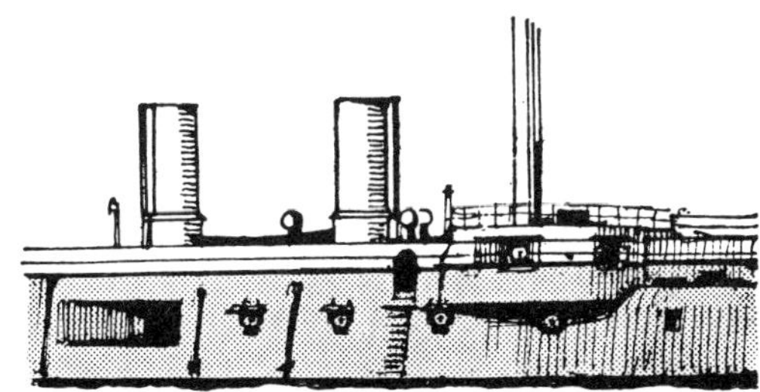

SULTAN, port side, amidships.

By suppressing the bow and stern main-deck guns which were such an objectionable feature in the *Hercules*, fire ahead was provided by a pair of 9-in. high and dry under the topgallant forecastle, where they were protected by a cross-deck bulkhead without side armour. All her guns had Scott's mountings which made for safe and rapid handling in bad weather, and in this respect *Sultan* was the best equipped of her contemporaries.

Nine years after her completion she was fitted with four carriages on the main deck for Whitehead 14-in. torpedoes, two forward of the battery and two aft. Seven 4-in. 25-pdr. B.L. on Vavasseur mountings were placed on the upper deck as an anti-torpedo craft defence, with nineteen light and machine guns, a couple of Gatlings being housed in a military top on the mizen mast. This was the first plated-in masthead position to be fitted in a British warship. Hitherto it had been the practice as part of the exercise "General Quarters" to hoist light guns to the "tops" on the lower masts, which were just screened with canvas as weather protection.

A couple of torpedo boats were also added to her equipment stowed abreast the mizen on crutches above the spar deck; and as both were retained while she was up the Straits they evidently proved more satisfactory there than in Home waters. She also received two searchlights.

In the Official Return for July 1883 the *Sultan* is listed a complete B.L. armament of eight 9·2-in. on the main deck, four 8-in. on the upper deck as chase guns, and a torpedo battery of seven 4-in. guns. This was during the period when *Bellerophon* was undergoing her rearmament, and with the experience of long guns in her battery no more of Reed's ships had their main armaments changed.

ARMOUR

Protection was along *Hercules'* lines, the waterline belt being 9 in. amidships tapering through 8 in. to 6 in. at the ends with a backing of 12-in.–10-in. teak on a $1\frac{1}{2}$-in. skin. The main deck 10-in. guns fired from behind 9-in. plating with a 6-in. angled bulkhead forward and a flat one of 5 in. aft. Amidships the upper battery sponsoned out and formed the distinguishing feature of the ship. This was of 8 in. with $4\frac{1}{2}$-in. bulkheads.

The total weight of armour and backing was 1,481 tons as against 1,332 tons in the *Hercules*—or 16 per cent. of the displacement.

MACHINERY

Penn's engines were of the simple pressure type with twin-trunk cylinders, surface condensers, and tank boilers working at a 30 lb. load. There was a single two-bladed screw and a level 14 knots was recorded on trial with 7,720 i.h.p. Outside her engine room steam was only supplied to her cable capstan and steering gear.

Ventilation was defective and remained so until the 1879 refit, when additional cowls and fans were fitted. She was also given new boilers and on a 6-hour trial developed 7,736 i.h.p. with only 28 lb. pressure.

SAIL

After cruising under full ship rig for four years she was reduced to a barque in 1876 and had her fore and main shortened by 20 ft., as her stability seems to have still been in question. In 1879 she received her mizen fighting top.

Although originally canvassed on the first scale with her main truck 178 ft. above deck, she was as sluggish under sail as the *Hercules*, being handicapped by the screw not revolving when disconnected even at 6 knots. She stayed well, but took a long time to wear, and early reports state that the obstruction caused by the upper battery and restricted beam due to the recessed topsides was against quick working of the sails.

SEA-GOING QUALITIES

With her small metacentric height and full body she was a remarkably steady ship, taking about 8½ seconds to roll from starboard to port, compared with 8 seconds in the *Hercules* and 7 seconds in *Bellerophon*. But despite the reduced bow and stern armament she was described as "an uncomfortable pitcher."

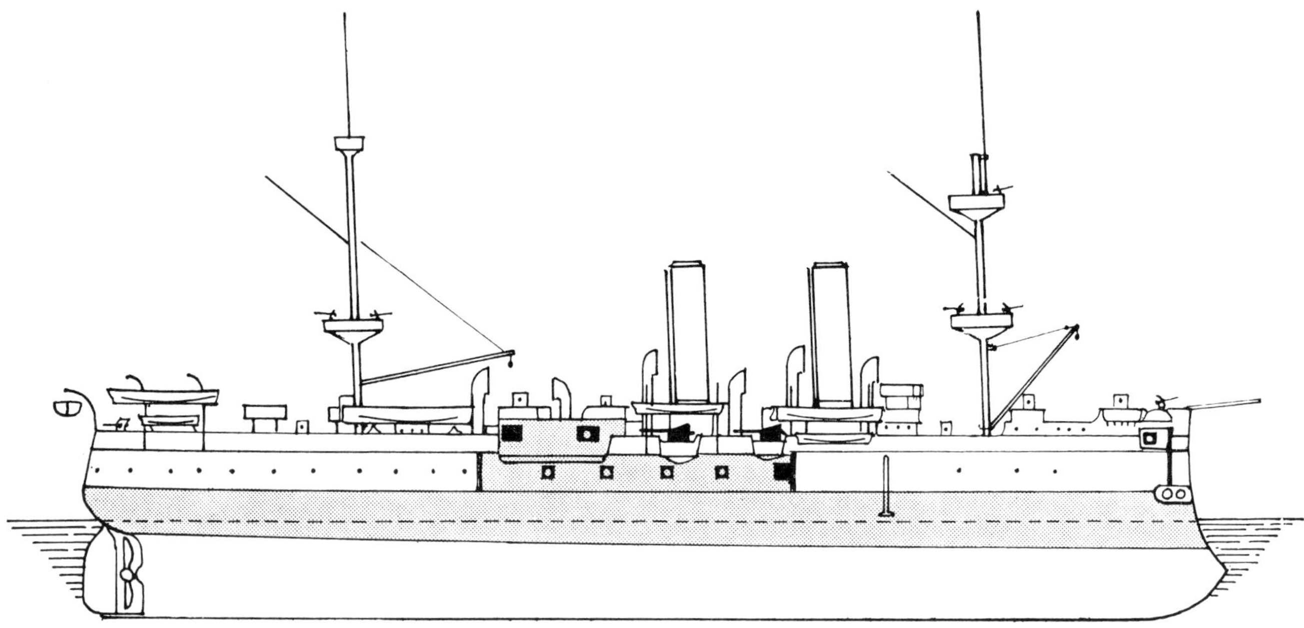

SULTAN modernized.

GROUNDING AND SINKING

On 6 March '89 she grounded on an unknown rock in the South Comino Channel, Malta, and ripped her bilges open. Efforts to pull her off by the *Temeraire* were unsuccessful and she slowly flooded. In a heavy gale on the 14th she slipped off and sank. It was feared that her recovery was impossible, but at length the Italian firm of Baghino and Co. undertook to raise her for £50,000, and on 27 August she was taken into Malta Dockyard, where preliminary repairs were undertaken. In December she left for Portsmouth under escort, making the passage under her own steam at about 7 knots, and anchored in Spithead on 22 December.

MODERNIZATION

Between 1893 and 1896 over £200,000 were spent in bringing her back to a fighting condition, although the old ship was never worth it. Nothing could be done to strengthen the original M.L. battery, but four 4·7-in. Q.F. mounted on the upper deck amidships, together with thirty-one Q.F. and machine guns distributed over the topsides, provided some anti-torpedo defence. A new set of engines by Thompsons of Clydebank enabled her to attain 14·6 knots with 6,531 i.h.p. but with intense vibration. As the new vertical machinery altered her weight distribution a waterline girdling of 9-in. teak was added to provide additional beam and raise her metacentre.

To set off the old hull in modern style she was given a couple of military masts, two tall funnels, a number of cowls, and a double bridge forward. After which she still retained a likeness to the *Hercules* but could be distinguished by her upper battery and a small upper top on the main mast.

During this period, when naval economy had become a political catchword, obsolete ships were retained in the Navy List to swell the roll of "Third-class Battleships," whose M.L. guns were supposed to have a "second-line" value if and when the later ships were knocked out. But in her new guise the *Sultan* was only once seen at sea—in the manœuvres of 1896. Thereafter she lay in the Portsmouth steam basin until 1902 when her scandalous if pathetic retention on the fighting list was terminated in a general scrapping of the M.L. gunned old warriors.

After sinking in the Comino Channel in 1889 the *Sultan* was raised, temporarily repaired at Malta, and sent to Portsmouth, where later she underwent "modernization" with new engines, the addition of some 4·7 in. Q.F. amidships and numerous machine guns, a military rig, double bridge, and tall funnels, cowls, etc. Here she is seen on leaving the Dockyard in 1896.

"SULTAN"

Commissioned September '71 at Chatham for the Channel.

1876 Refit; light guns added and rig reduced to barque.

1876 Mediterranean under Capt. H.R.H. the Duke of Edinburgh. One of Admiral Hornby's squadron up the Dardanelles.

1879 Refit and reduced to Reserve.

1882 Nominally in Channel but detached to reinforce Admiral Seymour in the Mediterranean. Present at bombardment of Alexandria and had 2 killed and 8 wounded from a hit in the forecastle battery.

1884 Sunk a French transport by collision after parting her cable in the Tagus (December).

1885 June-July. In Admiral Hornby's Special Service Squadron during Russian war scare.

1886 Channel, but detached to Mediterranean.

1889 Grounded in Comino Channel 6 March and later sank. Raised and temporarily repaired at Malta; arrived Portsmouth nine months later. Placed in Reserve.

1893-1896 Modernized. Additional guns; new machinery. Went on manoeuvres '96. Remained in Reserve until '06.

1906 Dismantled and hulked as *Fisgard IV* artificers training ship until 1931 and then became mechanical repair ship.

1940-1945 Depôt ship, Portsmouth minesweepers.

1947 Sold.

Chapter 27

THE BREASTWORK MONITORS

DURING 1867-68, when the question of Colonial Defence was under consideration, the Colony of Victoria wished to build a monitor for the defence of Melbourne. There were financial restrictions which limited size, and as the vessel was to be used for harbour defence only it was suggested by the Victorian authorities that a monitor fitted with a Coles turret passing through the deck would be adequate. This both the First Lord and Reed declined to consider on account of the difficulties in making the deck water-tight. After much discussion Reed agreed to a new type of monitor designed specially with careful regard to the harbour at Melbourne—and he found the requirements as regards ordnance and armour very difficult to meet under the restrictions imposed.

The *Cerberus* was built to this design and was noteworthy as being the first of a series of "breastwork" monitors incorporating Reed's ideas as to the principles upon which low-freeboard turret ships should be based.

In the following year, when the Indian Government required armoured ships to strengthen the forces at Bombay, the construction of similar vessels was decided upon. One of these was the *Magdala*, a sister to the *Cerberus*; but for the *Abyssinia* the plans of a rather smaller ship were accepted from Messrs. Dudgeon of Poplar.

Although built for Colonial Governments these three little ships were always included in the listed strengths of the Navy, and may be described here with advantage as forming a connecting link between the first phase of ironclad design which ended with the *Sultan* and *Monarch* and—after the intervention of a series of small coast-defence monitors—the second phase commencing with the *Devastation*. The central-battery *Alexandra* and hybrid *Temeraire* may be regarded as developmental survivals of individual interest, but of no importance so far as their influence upon subsequent design was concerned except so far as the *Temeraire* carried the first form of primitive barbette in our Navy. Of the Brazilian and Turkish ships purchased in 1879 it need only be said that they were in, but not of, the Navy.

The difference between Ericsson's and Reed's conceptions of a turret ship will be readily understood.

Ericsson was satisfied to lead his hatchways, ventilators and turret machinery through the deck without the provision of combings or proper means of keeping the hull watertight, and in consequence his creations were fit for river or harbour operations only, when the hatchways could be kept open without undue risk of swamping. Raft freeboard and no encumbrances on deck to mask the all-round firing arcs of his turret guns was what he aimed for, although experience was to show that both the little conning position and engine room suffered from concussion.

Reed accepted the low freeboard principle because of the steadiness it provided, besides allowing armour saved on hull sides to be applied to deck protection. But as the funnel uptakes, turret bases and air shafts would all need separate protection, he adopted an armoured breast-work to enclose them all as an equivalent in weight which at the same time gave the turrets a much-needed freeboard and allowed shafts and hatchways to be taken up to a comparatively safe height.

Between the harbour defence ship and the sea-going battleship the difference was merely a matter of degree—the *Devastation* was to develop out of the *Cerberus* in due course. But what made them both possible was the lack of necessity for masting in the case of the *Cerberus*, and the adoption of twin screws in the *Devastation* as a provision against engine breakdown—rendering sail unnecessary as a means of continuing a passage.

So long as a sea-going rig was deemed essential Reed insisted on high freeboard; but when masts and yards had no longer to be reckoned with as an influence on design, then he was willing to adopt drastic reductions in hull height in conjunction with the breastwork for turret ships.

It has been claimed for the *Royal Sovereign* and *Prince Albert* that they anticipated the gun distribution of the *Dreadnought* (1905) in carrying several turrets along the centre-line. By the same token in the *Cerberus* we have the germ idea of the principle upon which all battleships from 1885 to 1905 were based—the placing of the main battery in armoured positions fore and aft with uninterrupted bow and stern fire and wide arcs of bearing upon either beam. But between her and the *Trafalgar* of 1887 there was to be a strange medley of large and small armoured ships indicative of the confused and almost chaotic condition of policy governing design, which was not to become more or less settled until the *Royal Sovereign* (1889) emerged.

No armoured ships of our naval forces received such meagre recognition on entering service as Reed's first breastwork monitors. Having been built for Colonial navies the fierce light of criticism was withheld, the technical press according them but one picture and a passing reference, as their lives were to be spent in the quiet dignity of self-satisfied oblivion in overseas harbours. And yet as examples of naval architecture they were deserving of a full measure of publicity, being the first examples of an entirely novel type of fighting ship which was to be the embryo of future development. Graduating by the process of trial and error, the conception of the *Cerberus* was to mature through the *Devastation*, *Dreadnought*, *Trafalgar* and *Royal Sovereign* to the classical success of the *Majestic*. Certainly it was a far cry from the little harbour monitors to White's most successful creations, but

"CERBERUS" and "MAGDALA"

	Builder	*Laid down*	*Launched*	*Completed*	*Cost*
"*Cerberus*"	Palmers	1 Sept. '67	2 Dec. '68	Sept. '70	£117,556
"*Magdala*"	Blackwall	6 Oct. '68	2 March '70	Nov. '70	£132,400

Dimensions $225' \times 45' \times 15{\cdot}3' = 3{,}340$ tons.
Hull and armour=2,640 tons. Equipment=700 tons.

Guns 4 10-in. M.L.R. ("*Magdala*" 1892 4 8-in. B.L.).

Armour Sides 8″-6″; breastwork 9″-8″; turrets 10″-9″.
Deck $1\frac{1}{2}$″; breastwork deck 1″; backing 11″-9″.

Complement 120/155.

Coal 120/210 tons maximum.

Machinery "*Cerberus*" by Maudslay; "*Magdala*" by Ravenhill.
Twin screws.
"*Cerberus*" I.H.P. 1,370=9·75 knots.
"*Magdala*" I.H.P. 1,436=10·6 knots.

Constructors R. W. Pasley and Alexander Milne.

Special features:

(1) The first British ships to have low freeboard.
(2) The first to have breastwork protection.
(3) The first to have a central superstructure with fore and aft turrets.
(4) The first in which sail power was dispensed with.

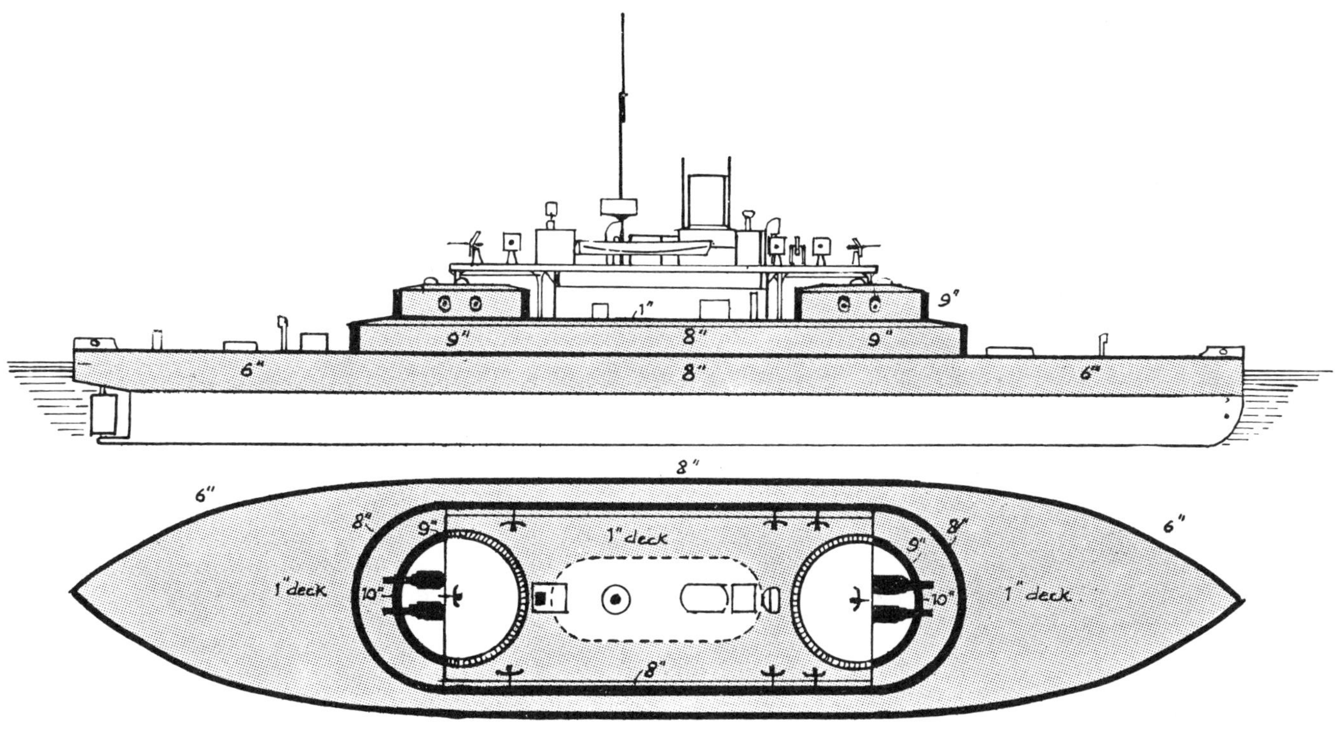

CERBERUS

the ancestry is there as represented by end turrets with a central superstructure, and a mere pole in place of the towering timber of antiquity.

In every way the *Cerberus* was a complete break from established tradition with an appearance different from anything as yet seen afloat. The hull gave a freeboard of $3\frac{1}{2}$ ft. only, with a central breastwork for $112\frac{1}{2}$ ft. amidships rising 7 ft. above the deck. This did not extend to the full beam by the width of a gangway on either side. Between the turrets and extending well over them was the raised shelter deck for the navigating positions and boats. By such structural expedients Reed retained the characteristic low freeboard of the monitor but raised his turrets to allow for their being fought clear of wave wash, with the provision of quite a spacious hurricane deck.

ARMAMENT

The original four 18-ton 10-in. guns were retained in the *Cerberus* throughout her career, but in 1892 *Magdala* was given 8-in. B.L. Machine guns were placed at the ends of the hurricane deck some years after they entered service.

ARMOUR

The turrets were 26¼ ft. in diameter with 9-in. armour on 11-in. backing, except over the faces, where it was 10-in. with 9-in. teak behind. They were always hand worked.

The hull sides received 8-in.–6-in. armour with 11-in.–9-in. backing, the deck being of 10-in. teak with 1½-in.

The *Cerberus* off Melbourne on one of the occasions when she put to sea for gunnery practice.

plating. Heavier protection was given to the breastwork which had 9-in.–8-in. sides and ends, with a 1-in. iron deck on 10-in. teak.

MACHINERY

In these ships twin screws and a balanced rudder ensured good manœuvring and replaced sail power, as once at their destination they would never be required to make long sea passages. *Magdala* was the faster by nearly a knot.

"CERBERUS"

When first completed the *Cerberus* had a flying deck extending beyond the turrets for the stowage of extra boats, and pole masts at each end of the breastwork. But the voyage out to Melbourne promised a hazardous experience and it was decided to ensure her safety by building up temporary sides from the curve-in of the breastwork to the bow and stern, leaving a low freeboard well amidships. As this temporary freeboard was taken up to such a height that the crowns of the turrets only just showed above it, and a full three-masted rig was provided, she looked rather like a miniature edition of the *Monarch*.

Loaded with 210 tons of coal, the draught was 15 ft., giving a metacentric height of 3½ ft. and an angle of maximum stability of 25° vanishing at 39°. During the passage, which was made largely under sail and in the face of considerable difficulties, she rolled only 15° in heavy weather.

At Melbourne part of the projecting ends of the shelter deck were removed with the build-up, and the rig altered to a single pole abaft the funnel. She was always based at that port and apart from short trips for gunnery practice did no sea time. When struck from the active list she became a depot ship at Williamstown until July 1936, then as a final term of service she was scuttled and used as a breakwater.

"MAGDALA"

Made the passage out to Bombay in the depth of winter without convoy, as the builders and officers employed by them considered her to be sufficiently seaworthy to run the risk—nor did the insurance offices hesitate about covering them. She was rigged, but not built up like *Cerberus*, and went out under canvas with the reluctant permission of the Admiralty given on the understanding that the navigating party would observe and strictly abide by certain rules as to heel, etc.

Luckily the wind did not exceed a force of 5 with 7 ft. waves, and water came on deck in small quantities only. She was very stiff under canvas with all sails set except topgallants, and never rolled more than 12°.

At Bombay the rig was removed, the hurricane deck was shortened so that it did not overlap the turrets, and a single pole mast stepped forward of the funnel.

Her life was spent in Reserve at Bombay with occasional trips for firing practice.

Sold 1903.

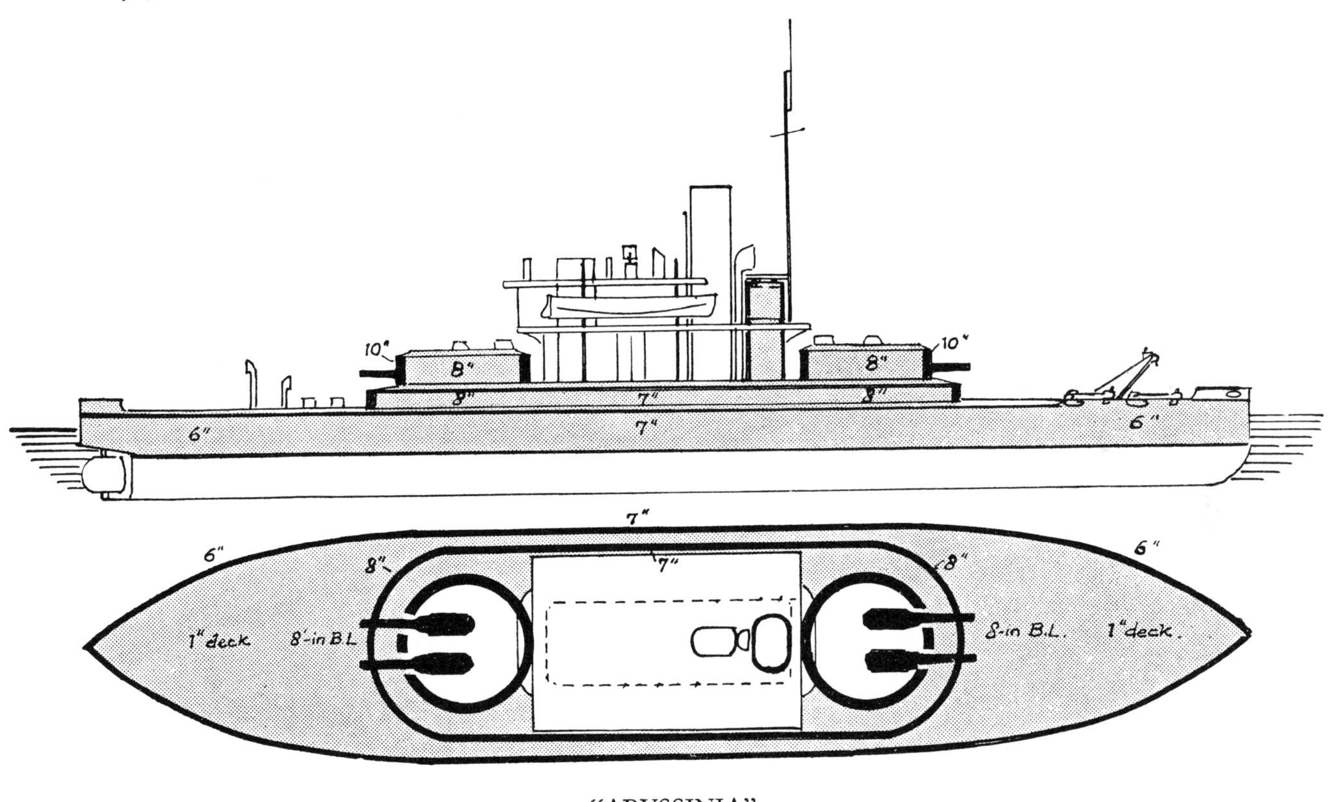

"ABYSSINIA"

Builder	*Laid down*	*Launched*	*Completed*	*Cost*
Poplar	23 July '68	19 Feb. '70	Oct. '70	(Unknown)

Dimensions	225′×42′×14·6′=2,900 tons. Hull and armour=2,200 tons. Equipment=700 tons.
Guns	4 18-ton 10-in. M.L.R. (Rearmed 1892 with 4 8-in. B.L.)
Armour	Sides 7″-6″; breastwork 8″-7″; turrets 10″-8″. Deck $1\frac{1}{2}$″-1″; skin $1\frac{1}{4}$″-1″; backing 11″-9″ teak. Total (excluding turrets)=556 tons.
Complement	92/100.
Coal	92 tons.
Machinery	Dudgeon. Twin screw. I.H.P. 1,200=9·59 knots.

When the India Office asked the Board of Admiralty for advice as the best type of ship for the defence of Bombay, the Controller recommended the construction of large monitors carrying the heaviest guns and protected by 12-in. plating on the sides and 15-in. on the turrets, at a cost of about £220,000 each. Such ships, however, would considerably exceed the intended expenditure, and after a year's correspondence smaller and more lightly armed monitors were decided upon for which specifications were drawn up and tenders obtained.

In the opinion of the Controller and Chief Constructor none of the designs submitted were as suitable as that of the *Cerberus*, which the India Office were pressed to accept, but on the score of economy it was decided that, of the two ships to be built, one, the *Magdala*, should be of the *Cerberus* design while the second, the *Abyssinia*, costing some £20,000 less, was placed with Dudgeons of Poplar.

Although the *Abyssinia* was very similar to the *Cerberus* there was slightly less freeboard; a breastwork shorter by 12½ ft. and a little lower; and turrets 2 ft. larger in diameter; also in places the armour was 1 in. thicker, but she carried less coal and had a lower designed speed. As fighting ships there was little to choose between them, but the *Abyssinia* was probably considerably better value for the money.

The design having been made subject to conditions laid down by the Chief Constructor, she was commenced in July 1868 and completed in October 1870—a month before the *Magdala*. It was found that the angle of maximum

As more or less of a stationaire at Bombay the *Abyssinia* had cabins fitted aft, and it will be seen that she lacked the flying-deck extensions over the turrets. The photo was taken after she had been rearmed with 8-in. guns in 1892.

stability was 21° and that all stability vanished at 41·5°, compared with 25° and 39° of the *Magdala*. When it came to arranging for the overseas passage there was such complete confidence in her sea-going abilities that it was decided to let her go out as she was without the hull being built up or any steadying sail fitted. Escorted by hired steamers, she made the trip under her own steam and in better time than the other two.

"ABYSSINIA"

At Bombay she was kept in Reserve, and when there was some question as to whether she was intended for general coast defence or merely harbour defence duty her book records: "A doubt exists as to the seaworthiness of *Abyssinia* in all weathers; but with due precaution and moderate weather she can proceed over considerable distances." In 1892 she was rearmed with four 8-in. B.L. Apart from periodic excursions for firing practice she led an idle and uneventful life in harbour, and when the Indian Harbour Defence service ceased in '03 she was sold locally and broken up.

"GLATTON"

Although the *Glatton* was not passed into service until three months after the *Hotspur* had hoisted the pennant, she had been laid down two months earlier and so may be regarded as preceding her in chronological order.

In general design she will always rank as one of the curiosities of the Navy—a Board model designed for duties which were never specified. In February 1863 the Board had asked for a "low monitor of moderate speed and the smallest possible dimensions capable of carrying 12-in. armour and guns of 25 tons in one or two turrets," and these were submitted by the Controller on 7 April. The single turret design was selected, as the provision

"GLATTON"

Builder	Laid down	Launched	Completed	Cost
Chatham	10 Aug. '68	8 March '71	24 Feb. '72	£223,101

Dimensions 245′ × 54′ × 18·5′/19·5′ = 4,910 tons.
Hull and armour = 3,680 tons. Equipment = 1,210 tons.

Guns 2 12 in. 25-ton M.L.R. (later 9 smaller guns).

Armour Sides 12″-10″; breastwork 12″; turret 14″-12″; conning tower 9″-8″-6″; deck 3″; skin 1½″-2″; backing 21″-15″ teak.
Total = 1,743 tons.

Complement 185.

Coal 240/540 tons.

Machinery Lairds. I.H.P. 2,870 = 12·11 knots.

Constructor Alexander Milne.

Special features:

(1) The first British single-turret ship.
(2) Carried the highest percentage of armour of any British armoured ship.
(3) Had the lowest freeboard of any ship in the Navy.

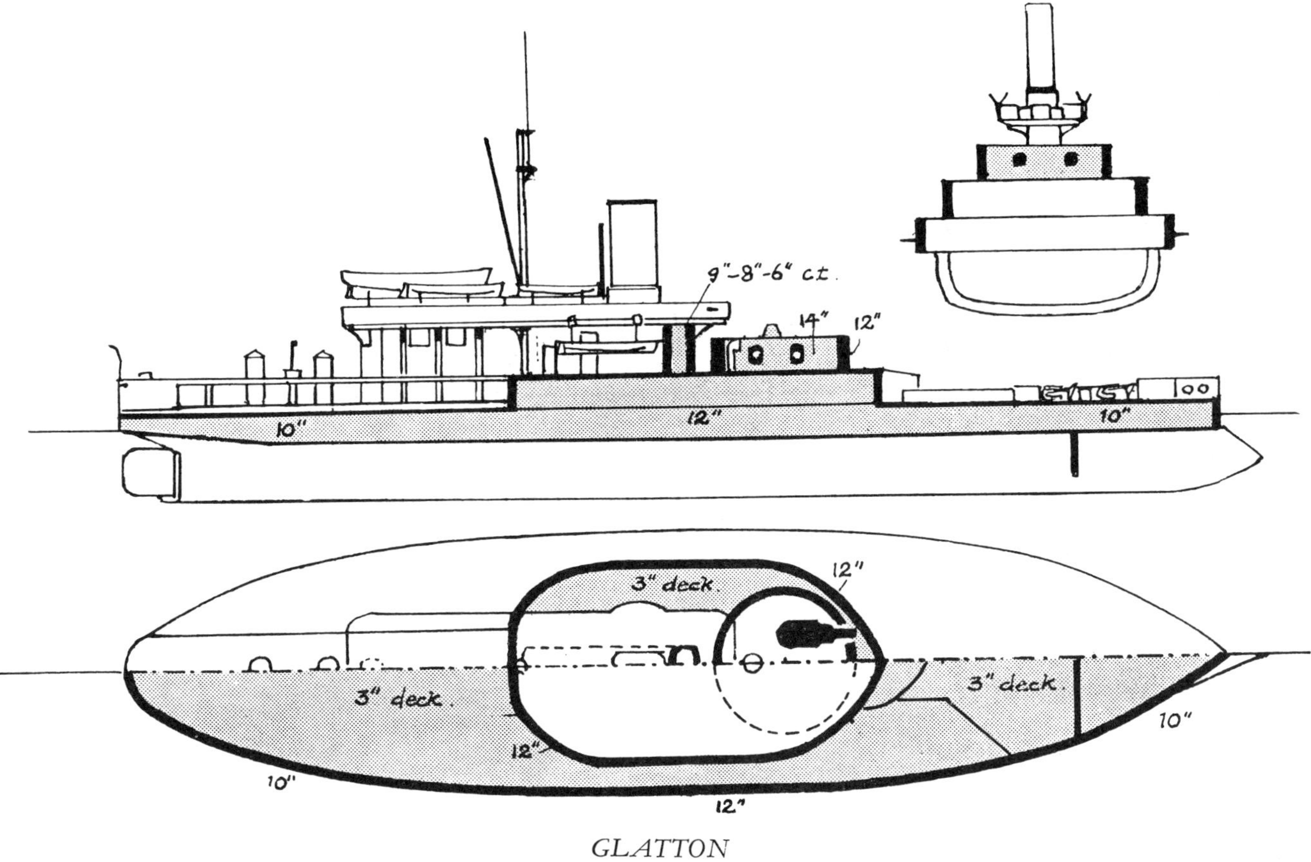

GLATTON

of two turrets upon the dimensions given would have meant a general reduction of 3 in. in the armour—a sacrifice "inconsistent with proper safety."

No specific information as to the proposed duties of the ship was afforded, but the Controller inferred that she was to be for "the defence of our own harbours and roadsteads, and for attacking those of the enemy." Reed himself described her as "a very exceptional vessel designed under a very peculiar stress of circumstances," and evidently viewed her alleged duties with a certain amount of suspicion, as "there is no vessel with the objects of which I am less acquainted than the *Glatton*. She was designed strictly upon orders which I received and upon the object of which I was never informed." Before the Committee on Designs his scathing comments upon her lack of sea-going qualities suggest that he considered she was intended for a wider sphere of activities than the harbour defence duties to which she was perforce relegated by a freeboard which apparently precluded any idea of operations at sea excepting in calm weather. In their Report the Committee stated that she did not answer to the conditions of a first-class coast-defence ship through not being "fully equal to the most formidable sea-going ships with an ability to proceed in all weathers to any part of our own coasts."

This appreciation of the proper qualities for ships intended for coast defence was also an apt criticism of the weak and unseaworthy vessels which were being added in considerable numbers to foreign navies for employment in estuaries and rivers. In our own Service the difference between coast defence and sea-going ships lay *only* in the smaller coal supply which might be carried by the former—at least in theory. But owing to the dictates of economy and an entirely wrong conception of what was implied by "coast defence," the Navy was to be burdened by a number of feeble ironclads whose value was confined to the swelling of Navy Lists and whatever service they could render as local training ships.

So far as the *Glatton* was concerned, she stands out as the acme of uselessness. Having the freeboard of a harbour defence ship combined with the draught of a sea-going one, and carrying the heaviest guns of her day

This excellent view of the *Glatton* proceeding to Spithead for gunnery practice gives a good idea of her low freeboard, curious superstructure housing the boats, and the flying deck aft pierced by ventilators. Except for the addition of the small guns on the superstructure, her appearance was unaltered throughout her life.

in an impregnable hull whose radius of action was severely circumscribed by very restricted bunkerage, she was beset with limitations which relegated her employment to zones where she was never likely to be employed.

From the indication of the features required in the *Glatton* the Board appear to have taken the big U.S. monitor *Dictator* as a model with the addition of a breastwork to give hatchway freeboard. The Chief Constructor was fully aware that this vastly over-rated American floating fort with a huge 15-in.-gunned turret upon a raft hull was quite unsuitable for British service—but my Lords did not discuss their project with him. Reed may, therefore, be relieved of the stigma of the *Glatton's* creation, although the ugly little ship had a personality which gained for her a curious and almost affectionate interest quite distinct from that afforded by any other warship.

Together with the *Cyclops* class which were to be laid down a couple of years later, the *Glatton* possessed the distinction of being the lowest freeboard ship in the Navy. Nominally she was to have been 3 ft. amidships and $4\frac{1}{2}$ ft. at the bows with a draught of 19 ft., but when going into action it was intended that 320 tons of water should be admitted into special tanks—which were otherwise to be used as additional coal bunkers—so as to increase her immersion to 20 ft. Here we get a classical example of the low-freeboard fallacy and the ridiculous expedient resorted to in order to obtain it—proceeding to sea with 240 tons of coal only so that the reserve bunkers could be flooded! In their criticism of the design the Committee on Designs rightly considered that the *Glatton* would be unmanageable in such a condition, and dangerous in heavy seas.

ARMAMENT

The two 25-ton 12-in. guns with their muzzles $11\frac{3}{4}$ ft. above water, fired from a 12-in. turret, thickened to 14 in. on the face, and were intended to have an all-round bearing, as the superstructure had been made narrow enough for the guns to be trained aft on each side of it. The Controller claimed that:

> "No point on the horizon upon which at least one of the turret guns cannot be brought to bear. This important object has never before been obtained in a single-turret ship, and has only been gained in this case by means of very great consideration and devising effect."

No records are available as to the blast effects when this astern fire was carried out, but the French thought fit to make the same arrangement in their *Tempête* class a few years later—probably with the idea that such provision would only be used during retreat when concussion damage would be of little consequence.[1]

A tube was provided inside the turret with a platform for the control officer whose head was protected by an armoured hood with sighting slots.

ARMOUR

The *Glatton* stands out as the best protected ship of her day with 35 per cent. of her displacement devoted to armour. The side plating was $6\frac{1}{2}$ ft. deep with an upper half of 12 in. backed by 18-in. teak, and a lower half

of 10 in. with 21-in. backing, all built upon a skin of doubled 1-in. plating. Some 35 ft. from the bows there was a transverse bulkhead below the belt for magazine protection—a novel feature which was to appear in several ships during the next few years.

Amidships came the breastwork enclosing the turret base, funnel uptakes, hatchways and ventilating shafts, $6\frac{1}{2}$ ft. high and 12 in. thick covered by a $1\frac{1}{2}$-in. deck. As low freeboard demanded special deck protection against plunging fire the weather deck was made of 3-in. plating with 6-in. wood—the total weight for her 11,348 sq. ft. of deck being 608 tons. In order to preserve the monitor principle of a low hull steadied by waves washing over it, the breastwork was not brought out to the hull sides, but the Committee on Designs considered that if light extensions from the breastwork were fitted as superstructure they would add considerably both to her accommodation and safety. But although shown in some published plans of the ship, these were never fitted.

Owing to the restricted freeboard there would have been no object in fitting the customary longitudinal wing bulkheads, and in consequence a full-length double bottom with the skins 4 ft. apart had to do duty for these; in addition the combined overhang of armour and backing which formed a $2\frac{1}{2}$-ft. projection below water was regarded as "affording great protection to the inner bottom against the attack of rams." This again was another of the original *Monitor* features which also contributed to steadiness in a seaway, although in the case of the U.S. monitors the prominent knuckle of plating caused considerable hull strain when impacting rising water.

---

[1] Admiral G. A. Ballard informed the writer that when he was in the ship, stops had been fitted which precluded the guns being trained much abaft of amidships, but this was several years after her completion.

SPEED

Designed for $9\frac{3}{4}$ knots only, the *Glatton* exceeded all expectations by making 12 knots on trials. In manœuvring she was handy and turned quickly, but proved difficult to steer on a given course. Her books contain no records of any tests to determine behaviour in bad weather, but she had a calculated stability up to $47\frac{3}{4}°$, while a list of $6\frac{1}{2}°$ immersed the deck and 23° put the edge of the breastwork below water.

SEA-GOING QUALITIES

Comparing the behaviour of high and low freeboard ships, Admiral Boys speaking at the R.U.S.I. in February 1889 said:

> "In the first place, we are not to suppose that we shall fight all our actions in a gale of wind or steaming against a sea. I do not think our ships should be exactly built for that purpose, but built for the occasion of fighting actions, which is more frequently the case in moderate than in heavy weather. I can give you a practical experience of what I thought was a great triumph for the low bow. I had to take the *Glatton* from Portsmouth to Portland for some experiments to be made in firing at her turret by the *Hotspur* at Weymouth. In those days these low freeboard turret ships were not supposed to be very safe to move about alone, and the *Bellerophon* was ordered to accompany as a convoy. We steamed against a summer south-westerly gale. The *Bellerophon* having to steam further out never came near us; we got to Portland an hour before her, and while she was pitching her bows into a head sea we were going through it extremely comfortably. Of course a good deal of sea came over the decks, but it all ran off again. In that case I certainly considered the behaviour of the *Glatton*—it was not a very heavy sea—was better than that of the *Bellerophon* and she was a steadier gun-platform."

TURRET TESTS

On 5 July 1872 her turret was subjected to test firing from the *Hotspur*. The first shot missed—and by missing was to have a considerable influence on future naval designs; the second displaced a plate at a line of junction and remained embedded in the backing; the third shot struck the glacis, penetrated the turret plating above for 15 in., and then rebounded broken up. No damage was done to the interior of the turret, nor was its working affected—as demonstrated by the guns being fired with full charges afterwards.

GENERAL

The fore part of the superstructure carrying the flying deck was armoured to serve as a conning tower—a dangerous position if the guns were ever fired aft! This flying deck housed the boom boats and davit boats at sea, and was fitted with a few machine guns in later years. The breastwork deck was carried aft as a narrow viaduct forming the quarter deck and this, together with the curious superstructure, gave her a unique and interesting profile which was far more French than British.

Although fitted with a ram, it was only a prolongation of the hull plating without any armour reinforcement and, if employed, likely to be as much a menace to her own safety as a weapon of offence.

"GLATTON"

Commissioned in May '72 for Dockyard Reserve as tender to the gunnery school *Excellent* and throughout her career was based on Portsmouth and could be seen swinging around moorings in the upper reaches of the harbour or pushing her way out past Spit Fort for firing practice. Particular Service Squadron June-August '78. In '81 she was fitted to discharge 14-in. torpedoes. Was specially commissioned for the 1887 manœuvres and together with the *Prince Albert* entrusted with the defence of the Thames estuary—her only recorded sea time. In September '89 came reduction to 2nd class Reserve and in November '96 to Fleet Reserve, but degradation to Dockyard Reserve did not come until November '01. The following year she was listed for sale, passing into the shipbreakers' hands in 1903.

Chapter 28

THE ADVENT OF THE IRONCLAD RAM "HOTSPUR" AND "RUPERT"

With the coming of steam the possibilities of ramming were renewed, and naval authorities generally visualized a steam-driven ram which they credited with almost supreme power of attack. In both France and England the armoured ram was advocated as a dire opponent of the ironclad in fleet actions, either during first-line attack or as a "chooser of the slain" coming up from the rear after the vanguards had clashed. As the battle formation then in favour was "line abreast" and fleets were expected to charge one another bows on and engage in a general mêlée under a pall of the dense white smoke generated by pebble powder, opportunities for employing the ram would be quite favourable in theory. But officers with a more practical grasp of realities pointed out that so long as a ship had any way on she could avoid the ram by a turn of the helm, and that results could only be expected when the enemy lay disabled and a sitting target. Admiral Sartorius actually wanted to cut down the *Great Eastern*, cover her with shot-proof iron plate, fit screws at each end, install a heavy gun armament, and use her as a ram. For protection from boarding she was to have towers from which scalding water could be pumped on to the deck. It is difficult to believe that such a fantastic proposal was ever made, but it was, and received the reception it deserved.

During the American Civil War ironclads used or attempted to use their rams time and again, but without any great success, except under very favourable circumstances. Although the *Merrimac* holed the wooden frigate *Cumberland* with the first blow of the ram to be chronicled in modern history, neither she nor the *Monitor* were able to injure each other by bow attack in the subsequent duel. During the fighting on the Mississippi various small ships with strengthened bows were used as rams, but as often as not injured their own consorts. The *Albemarle* sunk the *Southfield* when the latter was lashed alongside another gunboat (*Miami*) with spars and chains, the intention being that the two ships should catch the ram of the Confederate ironclad between them and then board her. Later the gunboat *Sassacus* rammed the *Albemarle*, but only succeeded in smashing up her own bows and getting put out of action by gunfire. At Mobile Bay the Confederate ironclad *Tennessee* missed the *Hartford*, then the *Brooklyn*, then the *Lackawanna*, and when offered as a target to the *Monongahela* received only a glancing blow which did her no harm.

By far the most interesting of the rams was the little *Manassus*—a tug boat converted into an ironclad at the expense of the citizens of New Orleans. She had the appearance of a floating cigar surmounted by two funnels abreast with a single 32-pdr. carronade firing through a shuttered port up forward, the ram being a solid beak of 20 ft. of wood. The whole hull was covered by a carapace of 12-in. oak enclosed in 1½-in. iron armour.

Although this sinister looking little craft was destined for a short life only—the 1½-in. armour being too thin to stand up to the heavy fire against which she was exposed during the fight for the passage of the New Orleans forts in October 1861—Federal reports speak of her as "the most troublesome vessel of them all." Her chief claim to historical importance is that her exploits were to start a new vogue in warships having far-reaching consequences.

It was four years before her first repercussion can be recorded when Dupuy de Lôme designed the *Taureau*, laid down at Toulon in 1865. This was a 2,718-ton turtle-decked spur-bowed wooden-built and armour-plated craft carrying a single 9·5-in. gun forward on a revolving platform in a fixed turret, able to make 12·5 knots, and possessing a remarkably small turning circle. To all intents and purposes she was an enlarged *Manassus* with a turret gun in place of the carronade, being designed primarily as a ram and armed only as a secondary means of offence. As anything else but a harbour defence unit the *Taureau* was "pour rire," and she and her four sisters of the similar but slightly larger *Belier* class spent their entire lives in dockyard basins. However, by the time she was ready for sea in 1866 the battle of Lissa had been fought and forthwith the ram leaped into favour as a primary weapon of offence. In this engagement—which was more a series of evasions and accidents punctuated by catastrophes than a classical naval battle—Tegetthof's orders to the Austrian ships were clear and definite—"Ram everything grey." His own fleet had black hulls with different coloured funnels to aid identification, and the battle may be described as a mêlée in which the Austrians steamed backwards and forwards trying to ram the disorganized Italian fleet and failing to do so.

But there was one signal success—the sinking of the *Re d'Italia* by the *Ferdinand Max*. The Italian ironclad had already been struck aft and with her rudder carried away lay helpless in the grain of Tegetthof's flagship as she loomed out of the smoke and charged her at 11½ knots. Driving her projecting bow through the iron and wood, but without experiencing any damage from the concussion, the *Ferdinand Max* reversed engines as the *Re d'Italia* swung over from starboard to port, and drew clear of the doomed ship as she went under. Having already aimed oblique blows at the *Palestro* and *Re d'Italia* without effect, this second attack with such dramatic results proved an epoch-making encounter—for over thirty years afterwards the ram was to be accepted as a weapon of offence!

The Italian Admiral Persano, charging about in the turret-ram *Affondatore*, could twice have beaked the wooden two-decker *Kaiser*, but each time his nerve failed him at the critical moment. Other unsuccessful attempts during the battle are chronicled, the targets having way on in every case. So that although the ram based its reputation upon Lissa, the one successful encounter was magnified out of all proportion in comparison with the many abortive attempts at ship charging, which were put down to the confusion caused by the smoke from Austrian gun fire. In fact Sir George Sartorius—whose advocacy of ramming was to result in the construction of the *Polyphemus* some years later—wanted unarmed rams so that there should be no possible cause or temptation to distract the attention of the commander from ram power.

Reed was a convert to the new weapon and recorded his convictions in *Our Ironclad Ships* (1869) at a time when the rapid increase in gun calibres threatened the value of iron armour:

> "While gun-makers and others therefore indulge in the complacent belief that armour is in vain and that the gun is all in all, I am obliged to maintain a wholly opposite position, and I assert with confidence that just as the *Hercules* is at this moment impregnable in the region of the water-line to the attack of any and every gun afloat in any part of the world, so the ships of the future may in like manner be endowed with a like impregnability against the guns of the future; and my conviction is that before armour ceases to be superseded as a defence against guns, guns will themselves be superseded as a means of attack and the ship itself—viewed as a steam projectile—possessing all the force of the most powerful shot, combined with the power of striking in various directions—*will be deemed the most formidable weapon of attack that man's ingenuity has devised.*"

Admiral Colomb, one of the most profound students of naval affairs of his day, writing as a Captain in 1867 (R.U.S.I.) upon "Lessons from Lissa," stated that:

> "The power of the new weapon was conclusively proved, and it is henceforth impossible to doubt its practical value. The rise of the ram in foreign estimation is one of the most remarkable features of the age. Dating from the first utterances of our gallant Admiral of the Fleet, Sir George Sartorius, the ram has carried all navies by storm, and, so far as I can gather, except in Russia, without enquiry. When I read my paper on Modern Naval Tactics, here, in the year 1865, and acknowledged myself a complete convert to Sir George Sartorius' views, English naval opinion was incredulous. Admiral Boutakov had written ably on naval tactics, but had nowhere expressed a conviction that the ram governed the tactics of the future, although an enquirer so acute and unprejudiced could not avoid allusion to its growing importance. In France, a system of tactics based wholly on the supposed unrivalled empire of the gun existed, and there was only a faint glimmer of an idea that the old line of battle was about to fall from its high estate.
>
> Now look at the change. Admiral Boutakov (see Appendix) has worked at the ram question to an extent unattempted by us; and Russia has drawn up her scheme of naval evolutions on the avowed principle that the ram is the only weapon of value against a fleet. France has pushed her old system of evolutions into the background, in the firm belief that *the ram, and the ram only, need be feared at sea.*"

When dealing with the trials of the Channel Fleet in 1868 (Parl. P. No. 500), Admiral Warden expressed a far more conservative opinion based rather upon the misses than the hits at Lissa:

> "The subject of ramming I approach with great diffidence. It is one which exists principally in the region of speculation. I am not one of those who think that in the next naval war ramming will rank before artillery as a mode of attack; but I believe firmly that it will play a very important and formidable part in all future engagements.
>
> Possibly some naval actions will be decided by the independent and energetic action of some individual captain seizing the fortunate moment and the right opportunity for running down his enemy at a high speed.
>
> It is as clear as anything can be that so long as a ship has good way on her, and a good command of steam to increase her speed at pleasure, that ship cannot be what is called "rammed"; she cannot even be struck to any purpose so long as she has room and is properly handled.
>
> The use of rams, it appears to me, will only be called into play after an action has commenced, when ships, of necessity, are reduced to a low rate of speed, probably their lowest. I therefore apprehend that it would be consistent with prudence and good tactics always, when going into action, to hold in reserve a portion of the squadron or fleet to act as rams; and that when action had commenced, and noise and smoke and fire were doing their work, the reserve to be brought into play, to act independently as circumstances might require.
>
> I believe also on this subject as well as on very many others connected with naval warfare, that the first great action which takes place at sea between ironclad squadrons will dissipate and cast to the winds many of our preconceived opinions and theories, disturb many of our prejudices, and throw an entirely new light on the whole subject."

Such opinions, however, were very much in the minority. The ram had become to be regarded as almost a weapon of precision when compared with the gun plus the low standard of accuracy in shooting which then obtained. Given speed and rapid powers of manœuvre, everything was to be expected from ships specially designed for ramming whether armed or without guns. Actually only a few "rams" were to be built in the succeeding years, and all turned out to be of no military value.

In this country the demand for a specialized use of the new arm found expression in the *Hotspur* and *Rupert*. For a time these little ships were assigned a battle value as rams which was entirely fictitious; as this waned, their reputations came to rely upon whatever value could be credited to their turret armament—which relegated them to the lowest category of armoured ships.

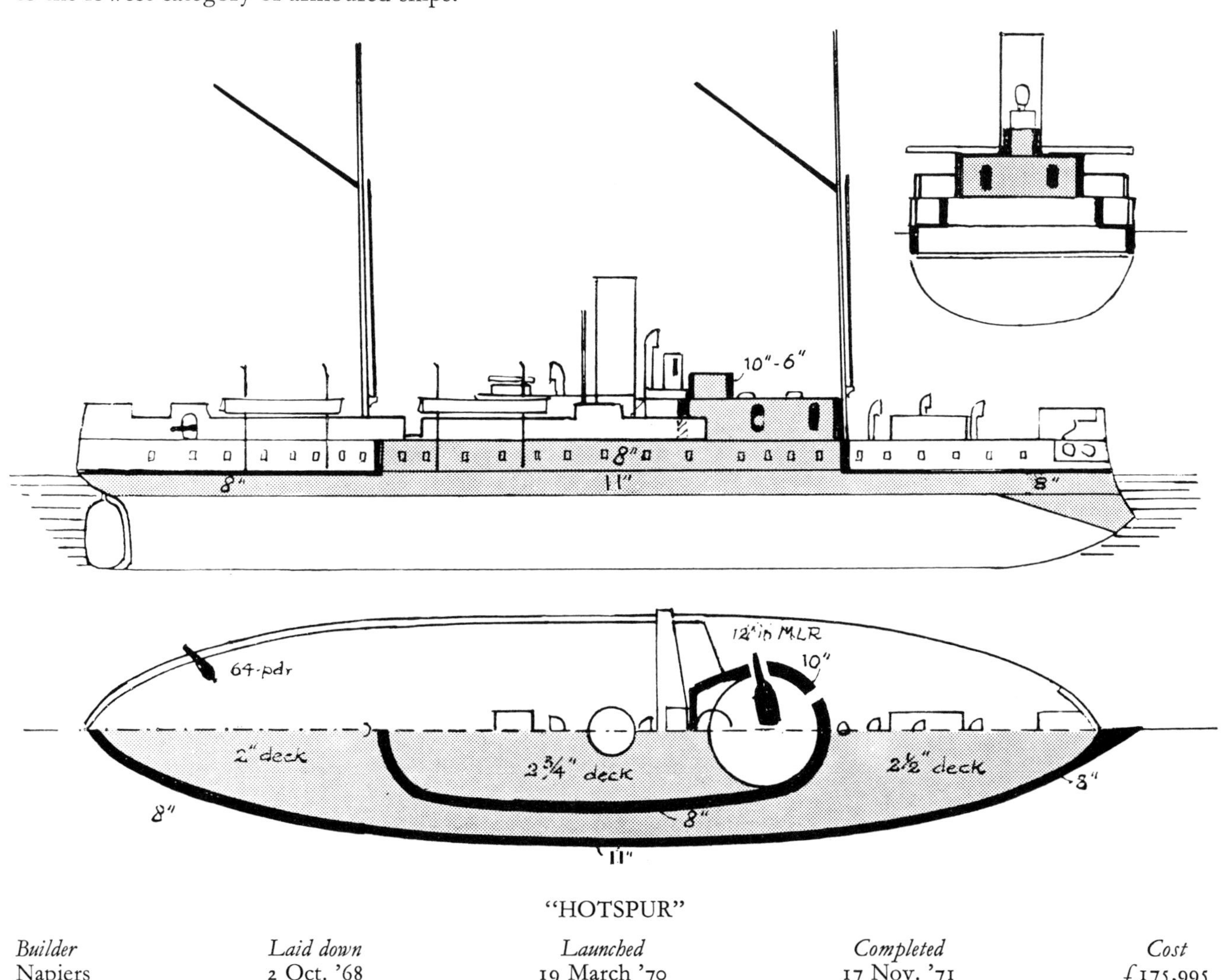

"HOTSPUR"

Builder	*Laid down*	*Launched*	*Completed*	*Cost*
Napiers	2 Oct. '68	19 March '70	17 Nov. '71	£175,995

Dimensions 235′×50′×19′/20·8′=4,010 tons. Hull and armour 2,800 tons. Equipment=1,210 tons.

Armament

1871	1883
1 12-in. 25-ton M.L.R. 2 64-pdrs. M.L.R. } =672 lb. broadside.	2 12-in. M.L.R. 2 6-in. B.L. 8 3-in. 8 M.G. } =1,364 lb. broadside.

Armour Belt 11″-8″; breastwork 8″; turret 10″-8½″; conning tower 10″-7″-6″; decks 2¾″-2″: 1½″-1″ (upper). Total 1,260 tons.

Complement 209.

Coal 300 tons.

Machinery Napier. I.H.P. 3,500=12·65 knots.

Special features: (1) The first British warship to be built as a fleet ram.
(2) The only British warship to have a fixed turret.
(3) The first to have an armoured breastwork inside the hull in place of side armour above the belt.

N

If the *Glatton* represented the Board's reaction to the big U.S. monitors, then the *Hotspur* can be taken as a reply to the French *Belier* class of ram. But whereas the *Belier* was fit for nothing but harbour defence work, the *Hotspur* was designed to work with the fleet despite her low power, poor speed and wretched coal supply. As the accepted conception of a ram was a low-lying hull with a long snout, the *Hotspur's* freeboard was restricted to 8 ft. forward for roughly a third of her length, and from that point to the stern high bulwarks were added.

The ram projected 10 ft. from the bow perpendicular, and for the first time was reinforced by a prolongation of the belt. This was to be her principal weapon. The gun could prepare the way for its use, although the design did not permit of gun fire being brought to bear upon an enemy ahead. Indeed, for the first ten years of her life the only battle value which can be assigned to the *Hotspur* lay in her spur—and although this was highly rated at the time, as first completed she was the most useless unit ever built for the battle line.

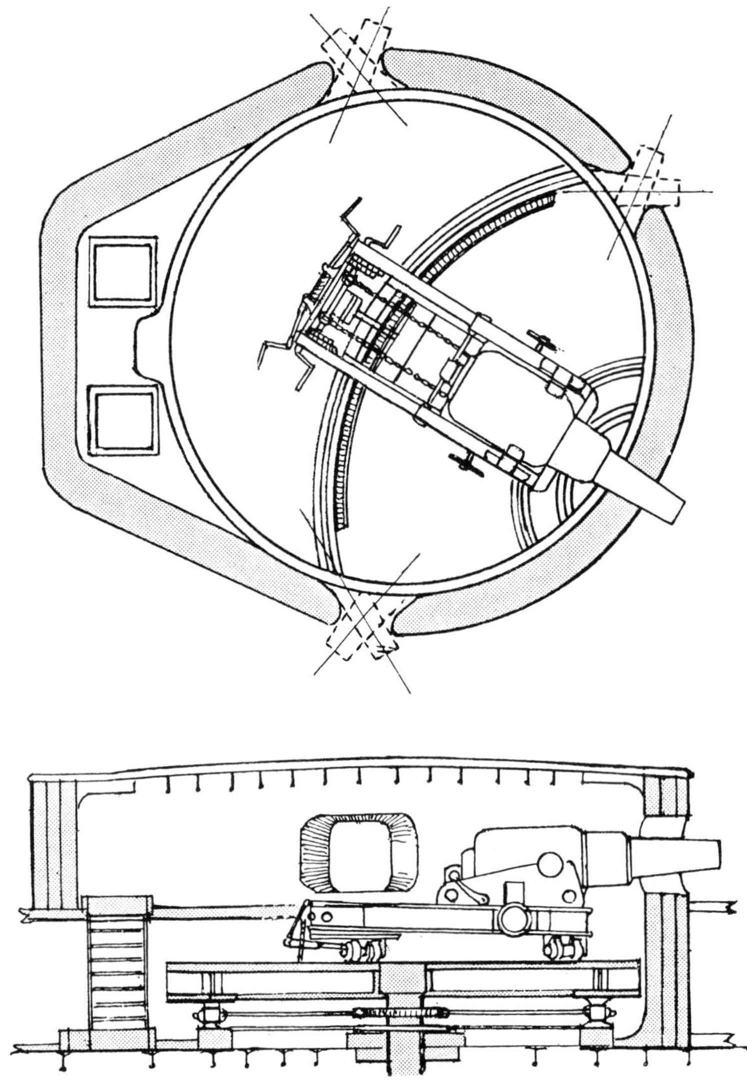

HOTSPUR. Section through fixed turret and moving turntable.

Against the lofty broadside ships of her day the *Hotspur* must have looked quite a formidable curiosity, possessing the menace of a new weapon credited with exaggerated powers, driven forward by a well-protected hull presenting a very small target although at not more than average speed. She was actually a three-decked ship, but as the main deck was only a few inches above water there was a freeboard formed by the upper deck which was flush from bow to stern with a spar deck running aft from abaft the turret.

ARMAMENT

As it was considered unlikely that a revolving turret would stand up to the shock of ramming, the Board decided that the single 25-ton gun mounted on a Scotts carriage which constituted her main armament should be placed in a fixed turret pierced by four large ports to give bow and abeam fire—a poor sort of substitute for the turret proper and more of a shell trap than a protection. In practice it was found that the deck was not strong enough to stand being fired over, so the gun was restricted to a bearing on either side only. Fire astern was from two 64-pdrs. on wooden trucks, one on each quarter training through embrasures; these guns required seven times the number of men between them as did the 12-in. gun under the same conditions at sea.

With which limitations to the use of her armament, the *Hotspur* more or less conformed to the Sartorius requirements, as her Captain would not have been able to employ the gun against any ship he proposed to ram by direct bows-on approach, although it could have been used in the tactics outlined by Captain Colomb in 1871.

ARMOUR

A complete 11-in.–8-in. belt was provided covering the lower deck side to 5 ft. below water, and this was carried down to reinforce the ram—the first instance of this very necessary provision to strengthen what was

HOTSPUR

to prove a structural weakness in ships whose spur was merely a prolongation of the hull plating. In Admiral Warden's opinion the bow best adapted to ramming was that of the *Achilles*, which could be used to deliver a straight smashing blow down a ship's side above and below water, opening up all the decks to an inrush of water. Her heavy, slightly curved stem piece was well able to withstand the impact and could be withdrawn without being twisted and wrenched. The *Ferdinand Max* had a bow somewhat on these lines, and that her wooden hull came off scot-free after sinking the *Re d'Italia* led to an entirely erroneous estimate being formed as to the damage the attacking ship was likely to sustain with another shape of bow.

With an under-water spur projecting 10 ft. or so, collision would result in its being driven deeply into the opposing hull, to become impacted as the two ships continued their way—and unless specially strengthened would probably be wrenched off or opened out. The *Glatton's* ram could have suffered in this way, but in the *Hotspur* the beak was less pronounced and being well reinforced by armour was less liable to damage. It was a pity that so much virtue was placed in the exaggerated ram bow. Although it gave a speedy and formidable aspect to a ship and vested her with powers of ramming which were never more than academic, it was actually a source of weakness and danger, as peace-time collisions between consorts were to demonstrate time and again.

Over the belt the main deck was 2½ in. thick forward, 2¾ in. amidships and 2 in. aft. Above this the hull side was unarmoured, but internally came the 8-in. curved breastwork enclosing the turret base, funnel uptakes and hatchways—an uneconomical albeit weight-saving device upon which Reed set great store, although it found little favour outside the Constructor's Department. Above this was the upper deck, 1½ in.–1 in. thick, so the ship was particularly well protected against plunging fire.

On top of the turret was a small conning tower, and between this and the telescopic funnel a narrow bridge and chart house were worked in. It is strange that this eminently satisfactory layout, which after many years was to become a standard practice, was not adhered to in subsequent ships, but as will be seen, conning towers were to be placed here, there and everywhere before the *Hotspur* arrangement was finally accepted.

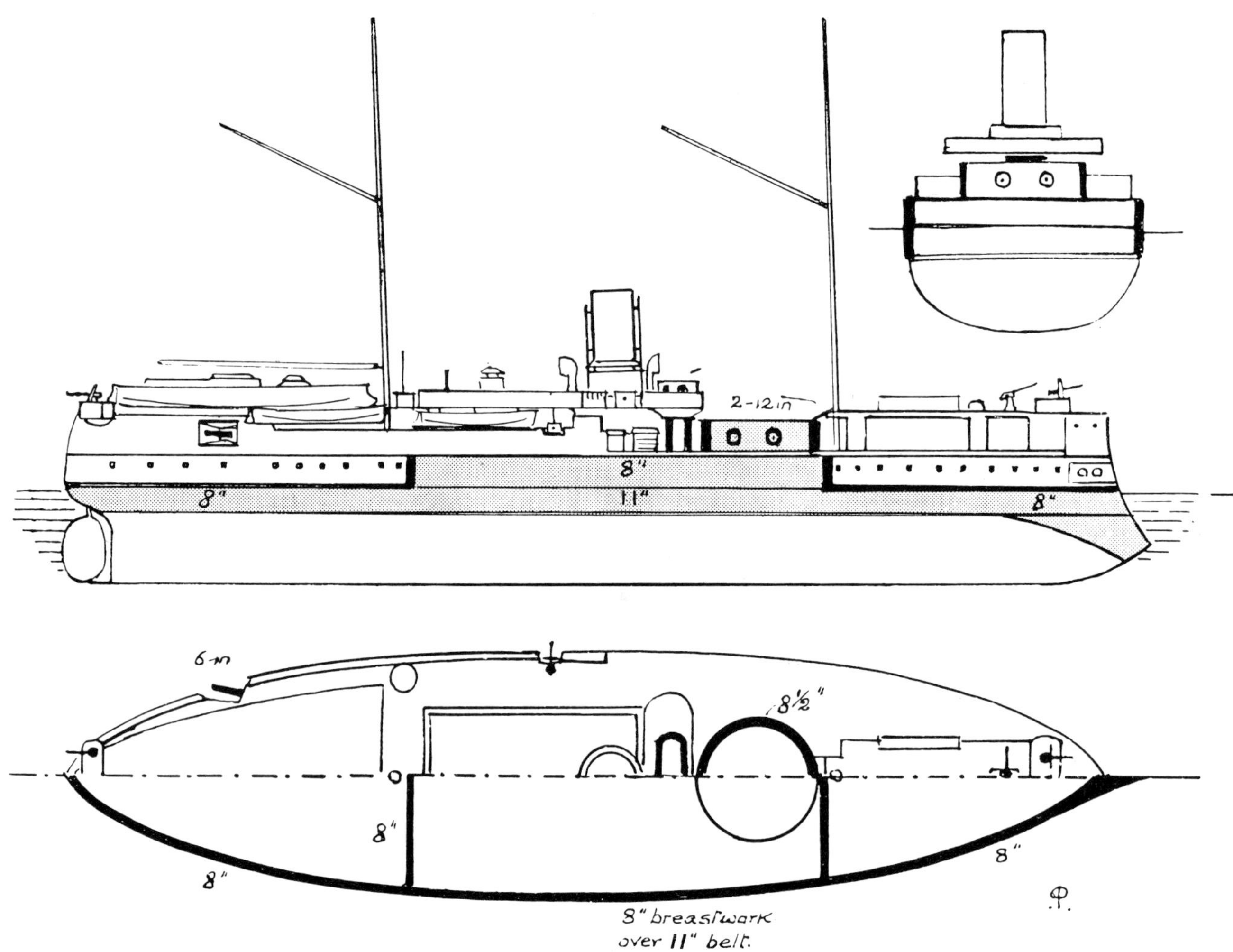

HOTSPUR. Reconstructed.

SPEED

Although a good turn of speed was regarded as essential in a ship intended for ramming, the *Hotspur's* best was 12·6 knots on trials—which, considering that her proportion of length to beam was 4·5 : 1, was good even for the power provided. At sea she behaved well under all conditions, being a good gun platform and very handy, with a turning circle of about 400 yards. But she suffered from the inevitable disability attendant upon low power and a tubby hull—inability to make progress against a heavy sea. Her reports show that she was easily stopped when bad weather was against her, and in 1888 after the manœuvres it was decided that for this reason and because of her small coal supply she was unfit for Fleet work and should henceforth be employed on harbour defence duties only.

RECONSTRUCTION

It was decided in 1877—six years after her completion—that nothing short of complete reconstruction would suffice to make an efficient fighting ship of the *Hotspur*, but not until 1881 was she sent up to Lairds for her long list of shortcomings to be made good at a cost of £116,600.

As in the *Rupert* (commenced in 1870) a twin-gunned revolving turret had been fitted without any apprehension as to its being jammed when the ram was employed, the alterations to the *Hotspur* included the substitution of a similar gun house made up of the compound armour recently introduced by Cammells (2¾-in. steel on 5¾-in. iron) with two 12-in. M.L.R. in place of the single gun. A couple of 6-in. B.L. replaced the smooth bores, with some small quick-firing guns along the topsides.

Drastic alterations were effected in her protection, the internal breastwork being removed and replaced by side armour, with transverse bulkheads to form a central citadel. But this entailed so much additional weight and cost that no other breastwork ships were so treated. Some steel superstructure was added to make her more habitable, and by the addition of a flying deck forward connecting the bow structure—which was enlarged to form a false forecastle—with the roof of the turret, accommodation was provided for some small guns besides making for better conditions at sea. She was also given a larger conning tower and chart house, some new boilers,

HOTSPUR

steam steering gear, a turret engine, torpedo fittings, and a second-class torpedo boat which was stowed on the spar deck aft under the steam derrick.

But when large-calibre B.L. guns came to be introduced into the Service she was not considered to be worth a subsequent rearming, and so the M.L.'s had to serve her for another twenty years with a rapid decrease in her battle efficiency. Towards the end of her career she became one of the notorious "coffin ships" whose retention in the Navy List was a political scandal.

"HOTSPUR"

Commissioned at Devonport in November '71 and suffered from collision with a tramp steamer in '72. Retained in 4th Reserve until June '76 and then went to the Mediterranean until May '78, when both she and the *Rupert* served in the Sea of Marmora during the Russo-Turkish war. Devonport Reserve '78-'81. Reconstructed at Lairds '81-February '83 and attached to *Cambridge* as gunnery tender until April '85. Joined the Particular Service Squadron between April and August '85; afterwards served as guardship at Holyhead with periodic spells at sea for manœuvres until May '93. In Reserve at Chatham between '93 and '97 and then went out to Bermuda where she remained as guardship until '03. Struck off the effective list and sold in August '04 for £4,328.

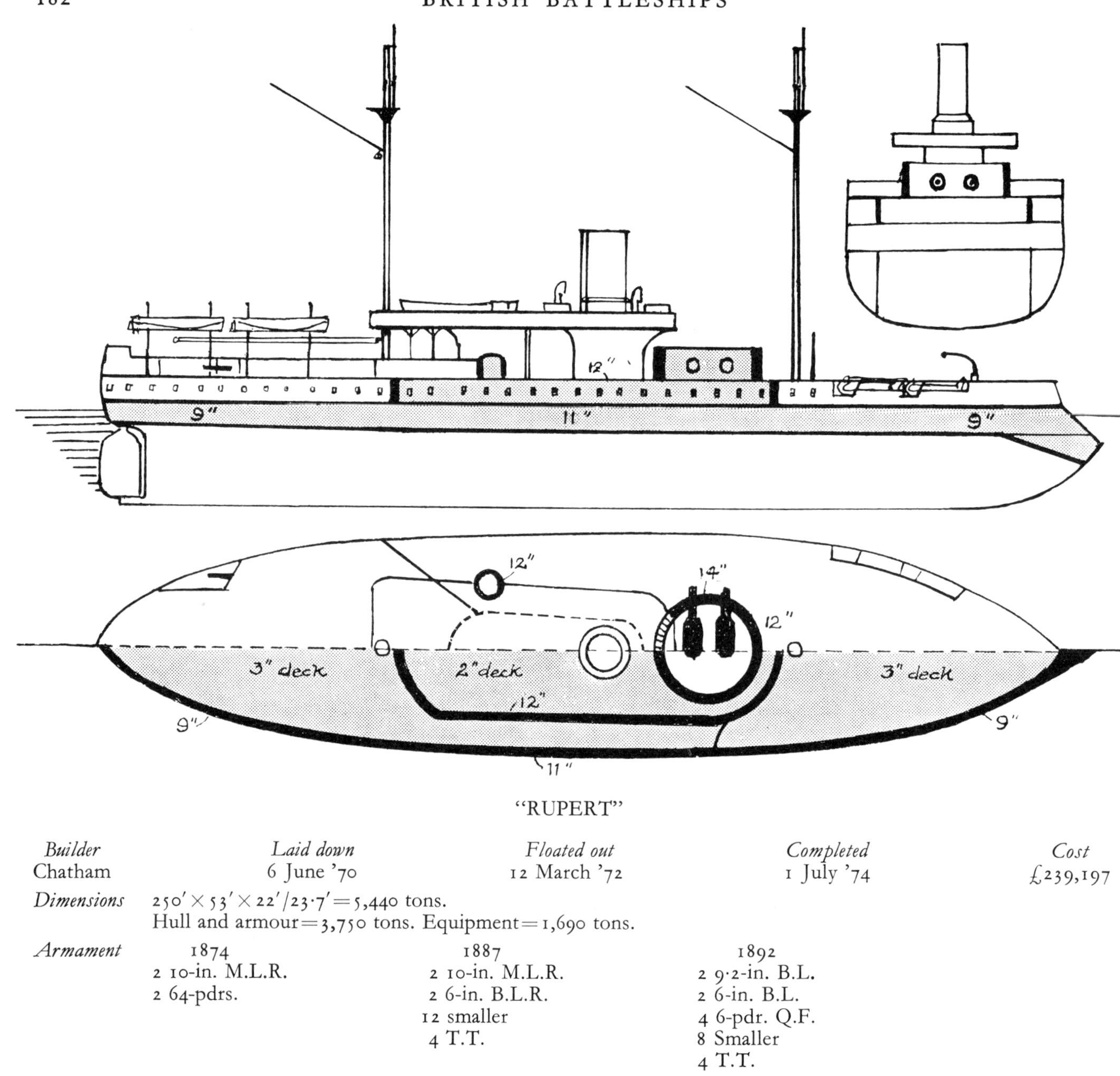

"RUPERT"

Builder	Laid down	Floated out	Completed	Cost
Chatham	6 June '70	12 March '72	1 July '74	£239,197

Dimensions 250'×53'×22'/23·7'=5,440 tons.
Hull and armour=3,750 tons. Equipment=1,690 tons.

Armament

1874	1887	1892
2 10-in. M.L.R.	2 10-in. M.L.R.	2 9·2-in. B.L.
2 64-pdrs.	2 6-in. B.L.R.	2 6-in. B.L.
	12 smaller	4 6-pdr. Q.F.
	4 T.T.	8 Smaller
		4 T.T.

Armour Sides 11"-9"; breastwork 12"; turret 14"-12"; conning tower 12"; deck 3"-2"; skin 1¼"; backing 14"-10". Total=1,505 tons.

Complement 217.

Coal 550/390 tons.

Machinery Napier. I.H.P. 4,200=12 knots (trials 4,630=13·5 knots).

Constructor Alexander Milne.

Special features:

(1) The last armoured ship to carry 64-pdrs.
(2) The first to undergo reconstruction which included B.L. guns and new machinery.

A second ram of the *Hotspur* type was projected in 1868, but not actually commenced until nearly two years later, as a *Hotspur* armed with a *Glatton* turret and crowned with something of her superstructure.

As a coast-defence ship compared with the *Glatton*, gun power was sacrificed in order to secure greater handiness for the purpose of ramming, and the Board recorded that great things could be expected of her in defence of our harbours and when working in conjunction with the Fleet—although she was not supposed to be a sea-going vessel.

Compared with the *Hotspur* she was given an increase in displacement of 1,400 tons with a considerable addition to the draught—which verged on that of a sea-going vessel—two 10-in. in place of the single 12-in. gun, and thicker armour. What arguments were advanced in favour of the revolving turret cannot now be ascertained, but the Board decided that it could be expected to withstand the shock of the ram and had the *Rupert* designed accordingly. It will be seen that there was no question of trying to provide a theoretical all-round fire from even one gun as in the *Glatton*; instead the arc was limited from ahead to just abaft of amidships on either side, where a small "fighting tower" was placed which allowed for a good view of what was going on abeam, but somewhat limited vision ahead and only on a straight course. Her Captain regarded them as almost useless."

Although the forecastle was kept clear of the latrine and some of the fittings which so encumbered the *Hotspur*, gunfire was obstructed by a foremast and shrouds which her first Captain described as "an unmitigated evil." The fore-and-aft rig was supposed to provide for progress in case of an engine breakdown, but the foresail

RUPERT

merely made the ship plunge and was almost impossible to work under weather conditions, and the sail effort was of so little avail that the masts were dismissed in the same report as "not worth the inconvenience and expense of keeping them up."

The extent to which the ram as a primary weapon was accepted by a considerable proportion of naval officers may be gauged from the following report by Captain W. E. Gordon (February 1878) which was fully endorsed by Admiral Commerell and was largely responsible for the subsequent *Hero* and *Conqueror*. Referring to the *Rupert* as a ram, he says:

> "She is a comparatively simple weapon within the capacity of an ordinary man to make the best use of, whereas the Captain of the *Alexandra* or *Temeraire* in action would be like a man armed with sword, rapier, rifle and pistol, trying to use them all at the same time. No man's faculties are equal to making the *best use* of such complicated machines."

The annotations against the Admiral's report are mainly in agreement, especially as regards the masts and fighting towers, but when it comes to eulogizing the *Rupert's* capabilities as a ram we find "Good in theory but not prac-

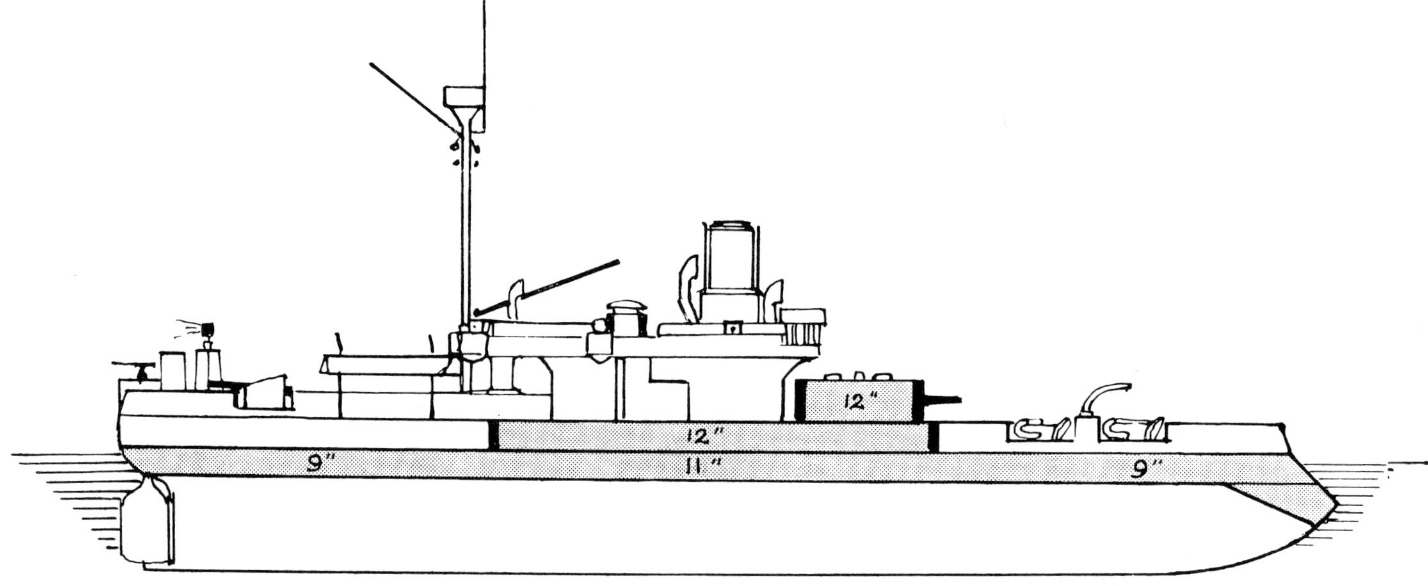

RUPERT, Altered.

ticable supposing enemy has 14-15 knots and *Rupert* 11-12." Captain Gordon's proposals for modifications to his ship were kept in mind when she was modernized in 1891-93 and carried into effect when the *Conqueror* was designed in 1878.

ARMAMENT

The ram was shaped and armoured as in the *Hotspur*, but with somewhat more projection and support from the belt at the lower edge. It was certainly a formidable beak, capable of stoving-in an enemy's side without much risk of being wrenched about in the process.

Although carrying two 18-ton in place of 25-ton guns, the turret was 2 ft. more in diameter than the *Glatton's*, and slightly higher. It was made up of 12-in. plating with 14-in. on the face. As rams were only supposed to concern themselves with an enemy on or just off the bow, or when avoiding action brought her abeam in passing, the turret guns could be trained to about 45° abaft the beam. But as there was room for small guns in the after

breastwork a couple of 64-pdr. M.L.R. were placed there for whatever good they might be. And she was the last armoured ship to carry this direct descendant from the 68-pdr. S.B. of our first ironclads.

ARMOUR

As completed, protection was along *Hotspur* lines with a complete water-line belt of 11 in.-9 in. and an internal breastwork amidships. This, however, was 12 in. instead of only 8 in. and accounted for most of the 245 tons of additional armour carried. Above the belt ran a 3-in. deck, with an upper 2-in. one covering the breastwork, so that excepting for an inch difference on the belt the armour was equal to that in the *Glatton* and absorbed 27·6 per cent. of the displacement. There was a small 12-in. pilot tower on each side amidships—a unique feature which appeared in no other warship, British or foreign.

RUPERT, Reconstructed.

SPEED

Unlike the *Glatton*, the *Rupert* failed to make her designed speed, and instead of the 14 knots which had been anticipated, about 12 knots was her best in service during the first twenty years of her career.

There are few records as to behaviour at sea in her books, but she is described as "rolling heavily but not uneasily" and reaching 30° in a moderate swell—when she would have been no match for the *Hotspur*! This was prior to her reconstruction, after which her vertical engines, new armament and additional weight up topsides would tend to raise the centre of gravity so that possibly she became a steadier gun platform.

RECONSTRUCTION

By 1891 the *Rupert* had reached a stage when nothing short of reconstruction would justify her retention on the active list. Like the *Hotspur* she had never been satisfactory, although her troubles arose from equipment rather than shortcomings in design. Underpowered with chronically troublesome boilers, she needed careful nursing to make 10 knots; 18-ton M.L. guns were too feeble to justify their retention when even the 25-tonner was obsolete, especially when served by a very defective ammunition supply with difficult stowage; and her general equipment needed drastic overhaul and renewal. She was therefore put in hand for what may be described as a properly balanced reconstruction, such as no capital ship had as yet received. The *Bellerophon* had been rearmed but left with her old boilers and machinery; *Hercules*, *Monarch* and *Sultan* were re-engined, re-boilered and generally furbished up, but retained their original M.L. guns so that the work done on them was wasted; *Hotspur* had been transformed before B.L. guns were available for the turret, so that she rapidly became obsolete; but *Rupert's* defects were generously rectified and she was given a fresh lease of life afloat.

The M.L. guns were replaced by 9·2-in. B.L. as the nearest equivalent in weight, and later model 6-in. placed aft with four 6-pdr. and six 3-pdr. Q.F. and four light guns spaced along the topsides. Changes in protection such as had been carried out in the *Hotspur* entailed too much additional weight, but two sets of triple-expansion engines and new boilers were installed, and with 6,000 h.p. (f.d.) in front of her screws she at last made the 14 knots for which her armament had been compromised—although at a 25-ft. draught. Additional weight having brought her marks down by 2½ ft., the after torpedo tubes just abaft the mast were now awash and her freeboard reduced to 6 ft. To correct this condition of things only 390 tons of coal were allowed instead of 550, and the after bunkers kept empty so as to preserve the use of the tubes, which in 1894 were altered to take 14-in. torpedoes. But even this limited supply was 40 tons more than the fuel complement stated on the original data sheets, so that at normal draught she still had more than the then allotted bunkerage.

And last but not least, she became a seemly looking little ship, with a handsome funnel; a military mast in place of the mixed rig carried for several years; and some fine upstanding cowls indicating a healthier condition of things below decks.

"RUPERT"

Commissioned May '76 at Devonport. Mediterranean '76-October '86. Reserve Portsmouth '80-'85. Particular Service Squadron April-August '85. Hull portguard ship August '86-March '90 (q.f. guns mounted on flying deck '87). Reserve at Portsmouth March '90. Reconstructed and rearmed '91-'93. Portguard ship Pembroke July '93-May '95. Fleet Reserve Devonport. Portguard ship Gibraltar December '95-May '02 during which she spent quite half her time in Egypt. Fleet Reserve, Devonport, '02-'04; portguard ship, Bermuda May '04-'07.

Sold July '07 for £11,355.

Chapter 29

REVERSION TO BREECH LOADERS NOT RECOMMENDED

During 1868 the Ordnance Select Committee pressed the War Office to again adopt the breech-loading system and start another gun revolution. Their report was forwarded to the Admiralty and referred to the Director of Naval Ordnance for consideration. Rear-Admiral Cooper Key submitted the following memorandum to the Board on 15 September 1868, and the Board in forwarding it to Sir John Packington, the War Minister, declared that they "fully concurred" with it.

> "This report of the Select Ordnance Committee on the advantages of breech-loading 'in an abstract sense' calls for little comment. That the power of loading at the breech has some advantages is unquestioned; but the practical questions are: (1) Is any one of the known systems of breech-loading as applied to heavy guns so efficient as to be worthy of adoption? (2) Has any proved itself sufficiently satisfactory to authorize the experiments that would be necessary to ascertain its merits with guns of 10-in. calibre and upwards?
>
> Looking at the very good results obtained from our own muzzle-loading guns up to 12 tons weight, both as regards rapidity of fire and perfect safety, as compared with the serious accidents which have happened at different times with the French and Krupps systems of breech-loading, I do not hesitate to answer the first question in the negative.
>
> With reference to the second, we are met at once by the enormous outlay that would be involved in a satisfactory solution. The breech-loading system is certainly not required for guns of 12 tons weight and under. We should therefore undertake the experiments with guns of 18 tons; and what system of breech-loading and construction should be our starting-point? I do not consider that either the Government or the Country would feel satisfied unless the experiments were conducted on the same basis as those for breech-loading small guns—viz., an invitation for universal competition.
>
> The cost of such a measure puts it out of the question. I do not, therefore, consider that the substitution of a breech-loading system for that now adopted for our naval ordnance should be seriously entertained."

Today such an ultra-conservative outlook would suggest something akin to a conspiracy of obstruction, but it must be remembered that the Admiralty was only just out of the wood after the Armstrong fiasco and the subsequent confusion with regard to ordnance. No responsible administration would desire to open the whole matter again after so short an interval.

In justification it may be said that while the one thing which breech-loading was calculated to improve was energy, that was the one quality thought least of in the Navy, where it was held that except against armour, increased energy could only in theory improve shooting. As accurate shooting was discounted by the unsteadiness of the ship as a gun platform, it followed that decisive results could best be obtained by superior shell fire at close range; and it was this combination which found general acceptance afloat. That ability to close the range with an enemy bent on conducting an action at long bowls *postulated superior speed* was apparently neither here nor there—the sea speeds of British squadrons showed little if any advantage over the French. But at this period the French breech-loaders were inferior to our muzzle-loaders both in energy and rapidity of fire. According to a writer in the *Revue Moderne* for December 1868 their breech arrangements were by no means satisfactory, and under the most favourable circumstances the heaviest guns (24 cm. and 27 cm.) could not be fired faster than once in two minutes, while our 12-ton and 18-ton M.L. would have loosed off three or four rounds in the same time. He considered our 9-in. 12-ton as more powerful than the heaviest French gun, and attributed this to their bad powder and faulty construction by which initial velocities did not much exceed three-fourths those obtained with our guns.

Ordnance tables of the period list the following figures for the two types in each fleet:

	British		*French*	
	9-in.	*10-in.*	*24-cm.*	*27-cm.*
Projectile-lbs.	250	400	317	475 lb.
Ft.-tons	3,496	5,160	2,821	3,871
Ft.-secs.	1,420	1,364	1,115	1,188

So that while not accepting the French statements as conclusive, the above figures for similar types of shot show a marked British superiority both in range and hitting power which combined with extra squadron speed would have raised the White Ensign high above the Tricolor.

Hence the wisdom of the Admiralty in preferring to retain the muzzle-loaders was justified, at any rate for the next few years.

Chapter 30

THE STATE OF THE FLEET IN 1868

From December 1868 to February 1874 a Liberal Government under Mr. Gladstone was in power, with Mr. Hugh Childers at the Admiralty until March 1871. His Board included:

Vice-Admiral Sir Sydney Dacres, K.C.B.
Vice-Admiral Sir R. Spencer Robinson, K.C.B. (controller).
Captain Lord John Hay, C.B.
G. O. Trevelyan, Esq., M.P. (succeeded by the Earl of Camperdown in 1870).

This administration will always be a memorable one. Mr. Childers had great administrative ability, was an untiring worker although in poor health (he started at 9 a.m. at the Admiralty and finished his Parliamentary duties about midnight, rarely exceeding three hours' sleep), but was disposed to concede too much to the opinions of others in a desire to temporize and conciliate. Against a wall of opposition his outstanding reform was a scheme for age retirement in the Navy which brought to an end the scandal of delayed promotion, want of employment, and favouritism which for so long had evaded drastic action. He also changed the composition and distribution of the Fleet and ended the routine by which a ship relieved after three years was replaced by another of similar type whether or not such services were necessary. Squadrons were strengthened in some cases, reduced in others, and a number of useless ships brought home. He inaugurated large works at Chatham and Portsmouth, strengthened home defences, and formed an up-to-date training squadron.

But in his reorganization at the Admiralty when outlying departments were brought under one roof, he also changed the business distribution of the Board in a way which impaired the flexible character of the administrative machinery. The Board was reconstructed, and afterward consisted of the First Lord responsible for the business of the Admiralty; the first Naval Lord responsible to him for business relating to personnel and for the movements and condition of the Fleet with the Junior Naval Lord as his assistant; the Controller responsible for the material side of the Navy; and the Parliamentary Secretary assisted by the Civil Lord in charge of finance.

Each Lord was restricted to the business assigned to him and practically rendered the meetings of the Board valueless—so that their number fell from 249 in 1866 to 33 in 1870 and none of these lasted more than half an hour and many of them much less.

The First Lord wished to be accessible at all times and in consequence the Members of the Board were in and out of his room all day long causing grave departmental confusion, delay, and disputes. The First Naval Lord had previously exercised personal supervision over the Controller's department—now in the charge of an officer of his own rank—and the dissensions with frequent threats of resignation were a topic of general conversation in the office. But when as the result of a joint threat of resignation by the Controller and Chief Constructor in July 1870 Reed left the Admiralty, Spencer Robinson preferred to retain his position. It was subsequently found necessary for Mr. Gladstone himself to address a letter to him, to acquaint him that his name would be omitted from the next Admiralty patent, and on 14 February 1871 Captain R. Hall, C.B., was appointed Second Naval Lord and Controller.

In the spring of 1869 when the Channel, Mediterranean and Reserve Squadrons were assembled for a combined cruise Mr. Childers decided to take command with the Admiralty flag hoisted aboard the *Agincourt*. This unprecedented step confusing executive with administrative functions led to quite a variety of troubles. Legally an Admiralty order required the signature of two Lords and a Secretary before its disobedience became a criminal offence, and the idea of a Board having to agree before a signal could be hoisted under the Admiral's flag—had full punctilio been observed—would have made the proceedings ridiculous rather than merely incongruous.

The Reserve Squadron on this occasion comprised:

Agincourt	(ironclad)	*Duncan*	(2-decker)	*Mersey*	(frigate)
Hector	,,	*St. George*	,,	*Cadmus*	(corvette)
Valiant	,,	*Trafalgar*	,,	*Scylla*	,,
		Donegal	,,		
		Royal George	,,		

At this time it was the practice to keep the latest ships in the Steam Reserve, and one of the results of this cruise was a reorganization of the various squadrons which relegated the old ships-of-the-line to dockyard reserves.

Childers' first concern on the material side was the provision of additional armoured ships. In view of the fact that the late Board was not proposing to build any more ironclads in the ensuing session, he called for a survey of the plans of broadside and turret ships considered by his predecessor in order to put himself *au fait* with the most recent developments in design. The turret ship appealed to him strongly, but as the *Captain* had not yet been floated out and the *Monarch* was six months from completion their respective merits had still to be tested. But both were ships of heavy tonnage, and in the meantime Childers was desirous of ascertaining whether a smaller type of turret ship with sea-going qualities was practicable.

In January 1869 Reed was therefore authorized to prepare designs for a turret ship of 3,000 tons B.O.M. mounting two large guns and able to steam at 14 knots with coal for an ocean voyage. Sail was to be provided, but only on a limited scale. Reed went carefully into the suggestion and on 3 February 1869 reported that such a ship would be impracticable. But the question of the provision of such ships having been thus raised, he seized the opportunity of advocating his own conception of a sea-going turret ship and two days later came forward with a proposal for a two-turret ship of 4,400 tons B.O.M. (9,035 tons displacement) which was submitted to the Committee on Designs (of which Coles was a member) and approved on 15 February 1869.

In drawing up his specification, the Chief Constructor considered it desirable that the following features should be embodied:

(1) A hull plated with 12-in. armour over the vital parts.
(2) Decks plated with 2-in. iron.
(3) Two turrets plated with 12-in. armour and 14-in. round the ports.
(4) Each turret to contain either two 25-ton or one 50-ton gun.
(5) A speed of 12 knots or thereabouts.
(6) A most powerful ram bow.
(7) Twin screws, with two sets of engines upon each.
(8) An uninterrupted range of horizontal fire without any drawback or compromise; and therefore no masts or rigging whatever—mere drying poles only.
(9) A small crew.
(10) A side constructed expressly against ramming.
(11) A radius of 4,000 miles at 10 knots continuously.
(12) Monitor form with elevated breastwork.

In the House on Friday, 2 April 1869, by a majority of 79 it was decided that the Navy required three more battleships—although 46 members considered that whether England did or did not want three new ships, it was certain that she did not want three ships of the kind proposed. But for Childers' threat to shut up dockyards and commence wholesale discharges of operatives it is more than probable that the vote would never have been passed at all. As it was, provision was made for the commencement of two such ships in the Estimates for 1869-70 to be called *Devastation* and *Thunderer*, and for a third, the *Fury*, during the following year.

As first proposed the design for these ships called for the most controversial type of warship as yet put forward by the Constructor's Department, and from a sea-going aspect quite the most ill-conceived in certain respects. It was fortunate both for his reputation and the welfare of the men who served in the *Devastation* and *Thunderer* that Reed's original drafts were materially altered after he had resigned office and the most glaring deficiencies made good so far as progress of construction permitted.

Reed's *Devastation* was simply the little *Cerberus* enlarged and developed to sea-going proportions up to the limits in displacement stipulated by the First Lord. Because of this restriction her nature was altered to the extent of making her of low instead of medium freeboard forward, with the loss of water-line armour for 65 ft. from the bows. Instead of 12 ft. of freeboard forward there was only 9 ft. with a sunk forecastle to provide accommodation and extra buoyancy, and the ram had to be left without any reinforcement from the belt.

The outstanding feature of the design was, of course, the "monitor" hull of 4½ ft. height above water from the break of the forecastle to the stern—an aftermath of the visit paid to British and European ports by the U.S. double-turreted monitor *Miantonomoh* in 1866-67 during a voyage from America and back of 17,767 miles. Now the essential virtues of the monitors' invulnerability and extreme steadiness lay in their raft freeboard and shallow draught—in the case of the *Miantonomoh*, 3 ft. and 12½ ft. respectively—which provided a very large initial stability and a *metacentric height of* 16 *ft.* Had the side freeboard been high this excessive stability would have resulted in troublesome and dangerous rolling, but because the seas could wash over her decks she enjoyed almost complete immunity from wave effects. On the other hand, this half-tide rock existence meant constant battening down, with the risk of being swamped if a deck aperture were opened, and a dreadful state of things below decks. So far as fighting was concerned, there could be no question of effective shooting under such conditions.

Childers quoted American reports that these large monitors were healthy and on the whole quite pleasant ships to live in, but the following letter from one of our Captains who visited the *Miantonomoh* on her arrival gave a rather more truthful impression of the state of things aboard:

> "I went on board the *Miantonomoh* shortly after her arrival at Spithead from America. I never saw such a wretched, pale, listless set of officers and men. They seemed to have no 'go' left in them and crawled about

the decks in a state of debility, one and all. I was shocked and immensely struck by their inactive appearance, which remained vividly impressed on my mind's eye. More than one officer declared he would not for any consideration, of his own free will, go through the same experience gained by his voyage across the Atlantic. The vessel was compared to a dungeon under water filled with a stifling atmosphere by a steam engine; the crew had no place to go in bad weather, all the openings being battened down in a very light breeze, and the foremost cowls, which were very high, and through which the engines and fans on the lower deck drew the fresh air, were turned aft to keep the water out, so that for days and nights the crew were kept below living upon and breathing over and over again their own breath. After a resuscitation on English beef-fêtes and dinners, the *Miantonomoh* had her character and capabilities changed in a wonderful way with the returning health and spirits of those on board. She was called a good sea boat, could fight her guns during heavy weather (they never having been cast loose at sea). She was a model of comfort and security, as the turrets afforded fresh air and a promenade. I sincerely trust we shall not waste money on any costly turret vessel until the capabilities of the *Monarch* and the *Captain* have been shown."

Reed looked to the low freeboard as a help towards securing steadiness at sea, with a turret and hatchway freeboard of $11\frac{1}{2}$ ft. provided by the breastwork amidships to give fighting efficiency. The claims of habitability he either overlooked or failed to appreciate, but what the Service and technical press thought about the new ships was expressed by the *Engineer*, 9 April 1869, in the downright fashion then usual in discussing naval affairs.

"It would be absurd to assume that because monitors of the American type are steady, our new turret ships, with a much higher centre of gravity, and a totally different disposition of weights, shall also be perfectly steady in a sea-way. It also remains to be seen whether sea-going ships can be trusted at sea without masts and sails; but on this point we shall not dwell just now. We have said sufficient, we think, to show—First, that the only precedents which can be adduced to justify the construction of the proposed vessels at all must be sought in the American navy; in the second place, that we have learned nothing from America or any other nation as to the powers possessed by monitors of fighting their guns in a sea-way; and, thirdly, that even if we had, the difference between the proposed turret ships and any monitors yet constructed is so great that very little can be predicated about the first from experience with the second; that, therefore, lastly, the proposed ships will be merely experimental. But this much admitted, it follows, we think, as a natural consequence, that the experiment should be carried out on as moderate a scale as may be found sufficient for trying the principles involved fully and fairly; and to this end it would suffice to build one ship instead of three. To build one is good policy; to build two is a mistake; but to build three is a political crime. It is a direct sin against economy.

We now come to consider the proposed ship from a new point of view, even more important than that from which we have already regarded it. We have shown what experience does *not* teach us about these ships of the future. It remains to be seen what experience does teach us. And the lesson admits of being very briefly stated. It is simply that the proposed ships will be practically uninhabitable. Ventilation must be secured when at sea by use of fans. The unfortunate crew will know nothing of the breezy deck so dear to every sailor. The boatswain will never pipe all hands on deck, for all hands could not find standing room on the platform between the turrets. At least sixteen hours out of the twenty-four will be passed below by every man on board—that is to say, in lamplight, or something very little better. On tropical stations the vessels would be absolutely uninhabitable, and yet they are specially designed to remain as much as thirty days at sea without going into harbour once. Heaven help the crew told off in the new craft for blockade duty!"

In Reed's *Devastation* the only structure on the weather deck was the breastwork, which encircled the turrets and left a gangway of 6 ft. along each side. Above this and between the turrets rose an imposing superstructure crowned with a flying deck through which the funnels and trunks were led, and providing stowage for the boom boats and all davit boats when at sea. There was to be no masting, but just a drying pole at each end of the breastwork.

That she proved a greater success than was thought possible by her critics was largely due to the modifications the design underwent between April 1869 and her completion in April 1873. Taking her by and large the *Devastation* must be ranked with the *Warrior*, *Royal Sovereign* and *Monarch* as the fourth milestone in British capital ship development—the first sea-going mastless turret ship, carrying the heaviest guns afloat in combination with the most complete system of protection, engines for twin screws, a good turn of speed, and a wide radius of action.

A year after the keels of the *Devastation* and *Thunderer* had been laid came the loss of the *Captain*—and forthwith the boldness and originality of the new design became suspect. Being low freeboard turret ships it was held that they would behave in the same way as Coles' ship and be overwhelmed by the sea despite the absence of masts and yards. Such was the general opinion in the Service; and it was reflected by universal distrust ashore due to a very natural ignorance of the principles involved in the design, plus a reactionary prejudice against a type of ship which had been officially condemned and suffered tragic loss.

Barnaby wrote:

> "This was the general naval opinion—but the Navy did not distinguish between two very different uses of freeboard. Height of side out of water is required in a sailing ship, where the sails are secured and cannot be immediately loosed in a squall, in order to provide a margin of stability to right the ship from a sudden heel. A high side is even more influential than a broad beam in giving this margin of stability. In an unmasted ship, with great beam, high side freeboard is not only not required for this purpose—it is an evil, because it will set up quick and deep rolling among waves." (*Naval Development*, p. 74.)

Although the most satisfactory course would have been to place before the House a full and sufficient explanation of the fundamental differences which existed in regard to safety between the *Captain* and the vessels designed by the Constructor's Department, such a course would have taxed to the utmost the energy and ability of any statesman who elected to take the bold course and face the storm. Unfortunately Childers had identified himself so closely with the *Captain* and her supporters that such a course was impossible, and before Parliament met he decided to appoint a Committee of Inquiry which could clear the decks and restore public confidence.

As Sir Spencer Robinson pointed out, the appointment of this Committee was "an expression of doubt on the part of the Admiralty of the day whether they, their predecessors, or their servants, were competent to fill the posts entrusted to them," with especial reference to himself and Reed—who had then left office. Whether or not my Lords mistrusted themselves and their advisers it was certainly the easiest way of meeting the difficulty and one which later was to become the favourite method in Government departments—*i.e.*, by the appointment of a Royal Commission. Thus the First Lord by discrediting those acting under him was able to assume the position of an impartial observer, and secure valuable time—which in the vicissitudes of our political life often serves just as well as "clearing your yard-arm." In this case the Minister who constituted My Lords when the inquiry was set on foot had run his course and disappeared from power before the wisdom of his action had been tested.

THE COMMITTEE ON DESIGNS

And so to vindicate the new principles now governing design, and restore public confidence in the *Devastation* class and other recent warships, a Special Committee was appointed by the Admiralty consisting of the highest professional and scientific authorities in England. They were asked to enquire into and examine "the designs upon which ships of war had recently been constructed" with special reference to the stability of armoured ships and the best means of securing a sufficient reserve of buoyancy. The first meeting was in January 1871 and a report upon the *Devastation* appeared the following March. Apart from proposals for certain modifications which in no way affected the basic design the findings were in favour of the type and in every way expressed confidence with regard to the designs examined. The full reports were later published as a bulky tome which gratuitously presented to foreign navies a vast amount of valuable information which otherwise might have been regarded as confidential, and at the cost to the British taxpayer of many thousands of pounds.

It also contained several important suggestions which were to have a most influential effect upon future designs—especially the *Inflexible*. The leading problems in design were fully discussed and a wide range of expert opinion sounded upon the subject of armour and its application in future capital ships.

Although it was evident the gun was now superior to the armour of the day—and the three ships of the *Devastation* type were to be the last "ironclads" in the old meaning of the term and the last to have more than very partial armour protection for the next fifteen years—the Committee as a whole was favourable towards the heavily plated battleships; and as the necessity for impenetrable armour was assumed, there was no call for any investigation into the alternative method of protection—*i.e.*, an overwhelming superiority of fire. Indeed, as the Committee was not asked to include gun power in their deliberations it is not altogether surprising that the gun—except incidentally in its relation to armour—was neglected. In consequence the ship was considered as an end in herself and not as a means—which on the whole is the difference between the points of view of the naval architect and the naval officer.

In this respect the Committee differed from Sir William Armstrong who had been invited by Lord Dufferin to give his views upon the value of armour as a defence against shell-fire. In his reply Sir William Armstrong said:

> "At present it is only the most recent of our armour-clads that have any pretence of being considered invulnerable. All the earlier vessels when built had just as much claim to be so regarded as the strongest ships of the present day; yet they are now left completely behind and are, in my opinion, much inferior to well-constructed unarmoured ships. I venture to ask, what reason have we to suppose that the powers of attack will not continue quickly to overtake the increased powers of resistance, which we are applying at great increase of cost and at a sacrifice of general efficiency. Every addition to the weight carried for defence

must be attended with a diminution of armament and speed, unless the size of the ship be increased in a very rapid proportion. A continual addition, therefore, to the thickness of armour involves either a continual reduction of offensive power, or such an increase in the size of the vessel and its consequent cost, as must limit the production of sea-going ships to a number inadequate for constituting an efficient Navy."

He went so far as to recommend the reduction of armour to a minimum—merely retaining some bow plating as defence in an end-on attack, and advocated the construction of smaller and faster unarmoured ships with hulls closely subdivided to preserve flotation, well armed with guns and torpedoes. His argument was that the loss of such ships would not be calamitous; that they would not become out-of-date; and that numbers were a necessity if commerce were to be protected.

Such a conception, while it might appeal to some naval officers, did not commend itself to those interested in the constructional side of big ships and the maintenance of their stability and buoyancy by armour if necessary. A solution was needed for defence against the rapidly increasing size and power of naval ordnance otherwise than by plating of 20 in. or over. While it was still possible to allow the thickest armour over gun positions and the engine and machinery spaces amidships, an end-to-end Reed belt of adequate thickness appeared out of the question on the grounds of increased displacement and expense—and anything less than armour capable of defeating the greatest projectiles now being manufactured abroad was held to be worse than useless.

SIR WILLIAM THOMSON'S PLAN

Sir William Thomson proposed a central armoured citadel of minimum dimensions and maximum strength of armour, and to form around this and extending out to the ship's sides a belt of cork 9 or 10 ft. deep, resting on an armoured deck 5 or 6 ft. below water. On applying this principle to the *Devastation* type it was found that by substituting some 500 or 600 tons of cork for an equal weight of armour this proposal could be carried out, but that no increase in the thickness of armour on the breastwork was possible.

REED'S PLAN

The late Chief Constructor had an even more extraordinary conception. He proposed that an armoured citadel should be the central portion of the hull *with the ends unarmoured.* Instead of the usual complete belt there was to be a waterline deck with a thick armoured deck some 6 ft. below it, and when going into action the space between them should be filled with water. The citadel was to provide all the buoyancy required, the ends being not required to contribute anything either to buoyancy or stability. If the ends were filled with cork, shells might blow it out, and he preferred flooding with water so that shell-fire could do nothing to jeopardize safety. When not in action the ship could be lightened, and benefit by decreased displacement and additional speed. But he pointed out that his calculations showed that on the grounds of structure and stability this system could only be applied to ships of *over* 6,000 *tons* and with a proportion of length to beam of 4·5 : 1.

ELLIOT AND RYDER PLAN

A third suggestion of a similar nature came from Admiral George Elliot and Rear-Admiral A. P. Ryder, who in a minority report advocated a full-length raft body at and below the waterline, with an armour deck several feet below water and a thwartship bulkhead forward. A double skin open at the top of the raft body would allow it to be used for stowage of water, coal, provisions, cordage, etc., with subdivisions on the cellular system. Hatchways coming up through the raft body would have to be enclosed by cofferdams with movable armour gratings for action.

The Committee, in taking a general survey of these alternatives to complete belt protection, remarked that while it was difficult to increase materially the thickness of armour applied in the usual manner to sea-going ships in the form of a belt around the ship, besides local protection for guns, men, etc.,

> "It is not by any means certain that some method may not be devised of securing the requisite reserve of buoyancy by other means than by armour plating. Were this accomplished, the area of armour might be diminished, and its thickness increased in a corresponding degree. The ship would then comprise a very strongly plated central citadel, surrounded and supported by an unarmoured raft constructed on a cellular system, or containing some buoyant substance such as cork, which without offering any material resistance to the passage of projectiles, would not be deprived of its buoyancy by penetration."

This was the important proposal later to be adopted in the Italian *Duilio*, our own *Inflexible* and types derived from her, and in a modified form in the "Admiral" class.

Other recommendations made included:

(1) The use of bilge keels of greater depth than had hitherto been customary to give greater stiffness with steadiness of gun platform.

(2) The introduction of compound engines for greater economy.

(3) The use of incombustible materials for all cabin fittings, linings, etc., in the vulnerable parts of a ship.
(4) A composite armament of protected and unprotected guns, the latter of smaller calibre for use against unarmoured target where a rapid and well-sustained fire would be of more importance than penetration.
(5) The adoption of "displacement" tonnage in place of the arbitrary "Builders Old Measurement" figures —which conveyed about as good an idea of a ship's size as did the "nominal" h.p. of an engine's output.

The abandonment of sail power was also recommended by a majority of the Committee in respect to all first-class sea-going warships even when designed for foreign service. It was pointed out that it was impossible "to unite in one ship a very high degree of offensive and defensive power with real efficiency under sail." Sail rigging was a danger in action owing to its inflammable nature and risk of falling masts and spars which might obstruct guns and screws. It limited the arcs of fire of guns and prohibited the full use being made of turrets, and absorbed weight which could be expended to better advantage in fuel, especially in twin-screw ships where the risk of break-down requiring the use of sail power was obviated. Added to which there was the increased resistance to progress against the wind, and cumbering-up of deck space when masts and yards were struck.

But a dissentient minority favoured the retention of sails and included the Controller, Rear-Admiral Houstan Stewart, the Director-General of Naval Ordnance, Captain Arthur Hood, and Dr. John Woolley, the naval architect, whose recommendations the Board accepted. They considered that improvements in marine engineering might put a different face upon the question, but until very great improvements were made, there was little hope of steam ships performing cruising service without the aid of sail power.

While the retention of canvas might apply to the smaller craft, there was no question but that the days of sail were over so far as armoured ships were concerned, and what the Board failed to realize was that compound engines and twin screws constituted those "very great improvements" which had already placed us upon the threshold of the "mastless" capital ship. It is of interest to note that Reed favoured sail, Barnaby opposed it, and W. H. White (a future D.N.C.) agreed with the minority.

There was also a Minority Report drawn up by Admiral Elliot and Rear-Admiral Ryder which included alternative designs for all types of warships under construction or planned for that period (October 1871) based upon a system of armament in which two or more heavy guns were carried inside armoured towers on the centre-line at the bow and stern, in conjunction with a number of unprotected lighter pieces. The guns—ranging from 25 to 50 tons—were to be mounted upon a special revolving and inclined carriage designed by Captain Scott which allowed them to be raised hydraulically above the edge of the tower or barbette for firing, and on recoil nested in it for loading. The ships were to be of high freeboard and fitted with sail power. The general idea followed rather upon French lines and later found expression in the *Temeraire*.

But the prime cause for the Committee having been commissioned was the ill-repute of the *Devastation*, and the report upon her was issued within two months. Already her plans had undergone a certain amount of revision. Reed had resigned his office in July 1870 and Mr. Nathanial Barnaby having been placed in charge of the Constructor's Department as President of the Council of Construction, several alterations had been drawn up by his officers with a view to improving her stability, habitability, and protection. These were placed before the Committee and included:

(1) Extension of the breastwork out to the sides and astern as superstructure.
(2) Addition of an armoured bulkhead forward below water affording extra protection to engines and magazines.
(3) Substitution of 35-ton guns for the original 25-tonners.

These changes were estimated to result in an increase of 6½ in. in the mean draught, lowering the forecastle deck to 8 ft. 6 in. while raising the amidships freeboard to 10 ft. 9 in. This increase in height amidships which obviated the steadying effect of waves on the deck was not anticipated to cause any appreciable differences in steadiness during weather in which actions might be fought.[1]

While the Committee agreed that the *Devastation's* stability at 43½° was ample for safety against the rolling action of waves and wind pressure, they recommended that the angle of vanishing stability of future large mastless ships should not be less than 50°—which has steadily increased ever since to upwards of 70°. They found that the additional superstructures incorporated in the design nearly doubled the moment of maximum stability and vastly improved the accommodation for officers and men. In effect these transformed the *Devastation* from what well might have been a floating nightmare under many conditions of service to quite a reputable standard among ships of her type when turret armament came to replace the old broadside distribution in the new additions to the battle fleet.

As a fighting ship the *Devastation* satisfied the Committee as being of a type which should serve as a model for future capital ships, which when based upon different "centres of naval power" abroad to be established where

[1] The recognized proportion then observed was that for a ship of not more than five breadths in her length, the height of freeboard should be one-eighth of her beam.

requisite, could operate in defence of the Colonies and overseas possessions to better effect than ships of such limited fighting power as the *Monarch*. The indefinite nature of the words "where requisite" and difficulties as regards docking and supplies robbed the proposal of any immediate value, so that it could only be regarded as a fragmentary effort towards the establishment of a grand scheme of Imperial Defence, which could never take practical shape until the relations between the mother-country and her dependencies were entirely different from those then existing.

So far as rigged ironclads were concerned, the Report recommended that *no more* "first-rates" of a full-masted type should be built, either on the turret system or with broadside armament. However, both these recommendations were ignored as the Board chose two broadside designs, the *Alexandra* and *Temeraire*, for the ships laid down in 1873, and by the following year the rapid development of heavy guns abroad had made the *Devastation* system of protection seem no longer practicable.

Chapter 31

"DEVASTATION" AND "THUNDERER"

	Builder	Laid down	Launched	Completed	Cost
"*Devastation*"	Portsmouth	12 Nov. '69	12 July '71	19 April '73	£361,438
"*Thunderer*"	Pembroke	26 June '69	25 March '72	26 May '77	£368,428

Dimensions 285' × 62·3' × 26'/27·6' = 9,330 tons. Hull and armament 6,070. Equipment = 3,310 tons.

Armament "*Devastation*" 4 35-ton M.L.R. "*Thunderer*" 2 35-ton M.L.R. 2 38-ton M.L.R. Both 1891 4 10-in. B.L. 6 6-pdrs. 14 smaller.

Armour Sides 12"-10"-8½"; breastwork 12"-10"; turret 14"-10"; conning tower 9"-6"; deck 3"-2"; skin 1½"-1¼"; backing 18"-16". Total = 2,540 tons.

Complement 358.

Coal 1,800 tons ("*Devastation*"). 1,600 tons ("*Thunderer*"). Radius 4,700/10; 2,700/12½ (full sea speed).

Machinery "*Devastation*": Penn, direct-acting trunk. I.H.P. 6,650 = 13·84 knots. 2 cyl. 88"; stroke 3¼'.
"*Thunderer*": Humphreys and Tennant. Horizontal direct-acting. I.H.P. 6,270 = 13·4 knots. Revs. 75; 4 cyls. 77"; stroke 3½'.
In both: 8 Rectangular boilers. 27-30 lb. pressure; two 4-bladed Griffiths screws; 17½' diam.; 17-22' pitch.

Constructor Alex. Milne.

Special features:

(1) The first sea-going "mastless" turret-ships.
(2) The first sea-going ships of the quasi-monitor type.
(3) The first to have hydraulic loading gear ("*Thunderer*").

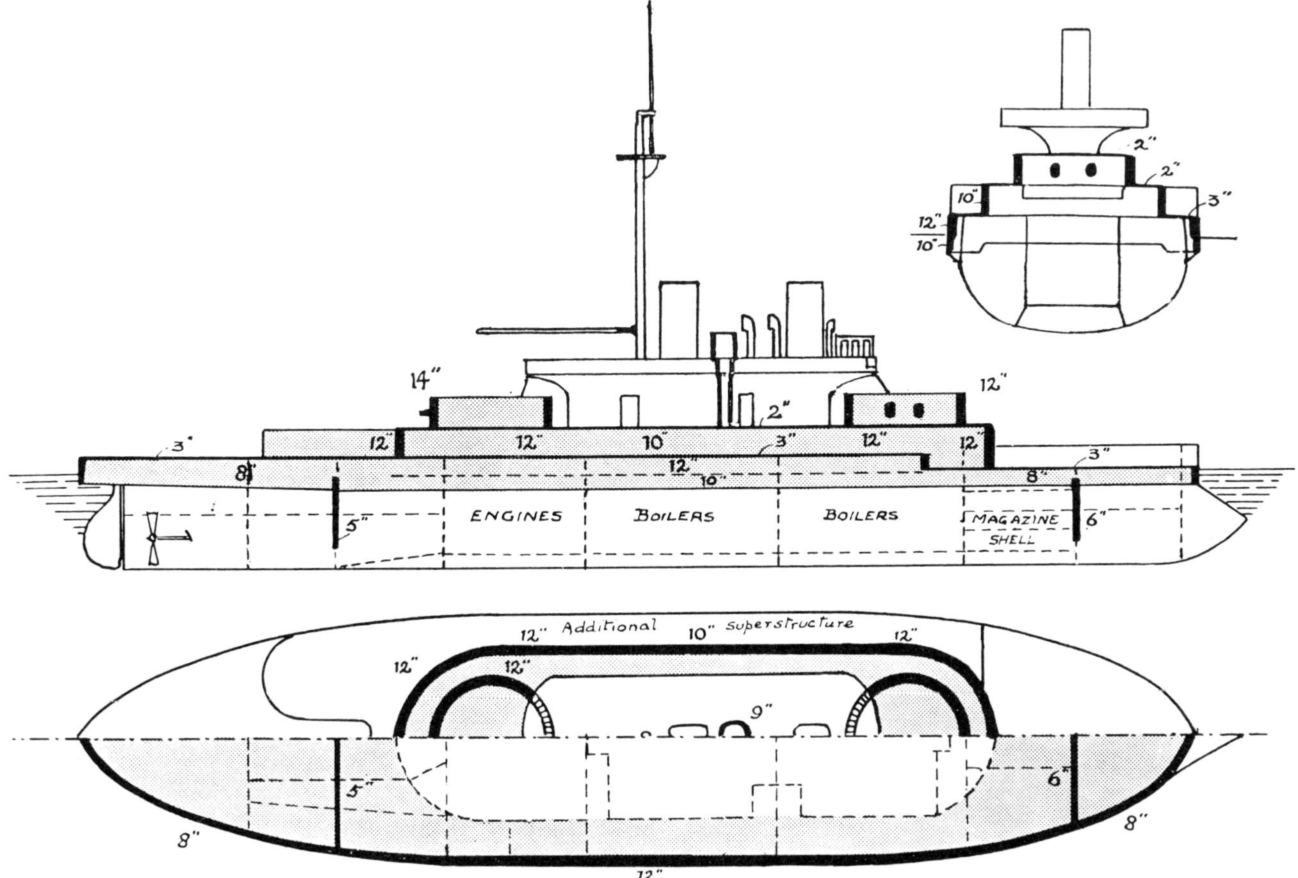

Devastation as modified by Barnaby with superstructure extending from the breastwork to the deck edge and continued aft forming a *cul-de-sac*.

The *Devastation* as conceived by Reed and modified by Barnaby was an epoch-making design unique in the revolutionary features she embodied. By virtue of her quasi-monitor hull, turret armament and its distribution, absence of masting, twin screws and huge coal supply she was even more of a wonder ship than the *Dreadnought* of 1906. But whereas the *Dreadnought* evoked criticism from some quarters on account of her size and one-calibre armament, the *Devastation* when she joined the flag was condemned generally and on all counts.

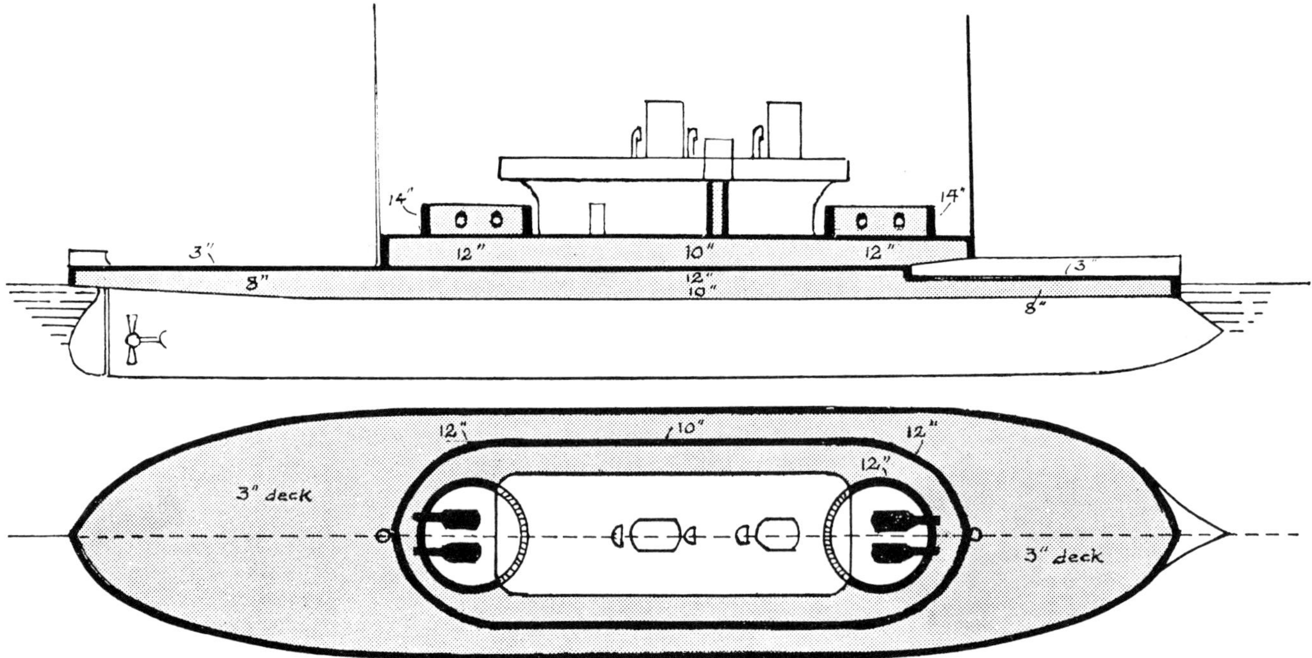

Reed's original design for the *Devastation* with a passage running between the armoured breastwork and the deck edge.

HULL

The outstanding feature of the original design has been the *all-round low freeboard*, adopted for reasons given in an official report when the plans were first submitted:

> "The freeboard of the low armoured deck, 4½ ft., while much more than has been given to American monitors, is low enough to effect a considerable saving of armour, and to greatly favour the steadiness of the ship in waves. It is at the same time high enough to give such a margin of buoyancy as will make the internal division of the ship into watertight compartments to a large degree effectual."

After-part of the *Devastation* showing the *cul-de-sac* formed by the superstructure to allow for the turret guns to be depressed when trained aft.

By leaving a broadway gangway between the armoured breastwork and the ship's side Reed had allowed ample deck space over which waves could act as a steadying factor; as modified by Barnaby this space was covered by a light iron superstructure extending transversely to the sides to give a good freeboard, and about 30 ft. towards the stern where it formed the notorious *cul-de-sac* which provided well-lit accommodation for the officers. These additional superstructures were strongly objected to by Reed on the grounds that a shell-burst inside them with resultant flooding might seriously affect stability. If the extra covered deck space had been insisted upon, he would have preferred to have extended the breastwork out to the sides in the first place.

A novel hull feature was its square section with the maximum beam running for two-thirds of its length, the bottom being almost flat, with the sides rising vertically from a rather tight bilge, full lines at both ends, a big pointed ram, and a submerged counter.

By dispensing with sail power a number of advantages both structural and tactical were secured for the first time in a sea-going ship:

(1) Direct ahead and astern fire was secured for the main armament, with uninterrupted arcs of bearing on the beam.
(2) Decreased range of stability, rendered possible by a general lowering of the height of the ship and absence of bulwarks. This contributed towards a steady gun platform.
(3) Only 28 per cent. of the displacement absorbed by the hull proper with 72 per cent. available for carrying purposes.
(4) Marked reduction in complement.

With the abolition of masts and yards drastic changes could be made both in freeboard and hull proportions not to be employed with safety in former hulls when every allowance had to be made for (1) the impulsive action of wind on sails, and (2) the effect of waves in the causation of rolling. Critics of the *Devastation* sought to show

Devastation as she appeared after her refit in 1879 with a fighting top and some light machine guns along the hurricane deck. Hitherto her armament had consisted of the four turret guns only.

that she relied upon low freeboard for stability, whereas Reed claimed that more trouble had been taken in devising means for making her *steady* than in any previous design, and that low freeboard was not the prime factor in securing easy motion in a seaway. Certainly with her centre of gravity 3 ft. below the legend waterline and a metacentric height of 4 ft. there would be a marked disposition to rolling, which the square section and overhang of the armour belt would largely correct, although this latter feature eventually had to be modified.

Certainly no warship had ever left harbour under such a cloud of pessimism and dismal forebodings as the *Devastation*; and no warship of such novel design more completely justified all the confidence reposed in her by her constructors.

ARMAMENT

The *Devastation* embodied the conception that the gun as the most decisive weapon at sea became most effective when mounted in limited numbers of the largest calibre and with the widest arcs of training.

The turrets were 30½ ft. in diameter with their port sills 13 ft. above water. Both ships were to have carried 25-ton 12-in. M.L. guns mounted on Scott's carriages, but at an early stage the later model 12-in. of 35 tons was substituted firing 706-lb. projectiles with a charge of 110 lb. afterwards increased to 140 lb., giving an m.v. of 1,390 ft. secs. The turrets were steam trained and the guns hand worked, necessitating crews of twenty-two men in each turret. Full elevation was 14° 10″ with 3° 10″ depression, and it took thirteen minutes to pass from one to the other. In order to allow for full depression when firing dead astern the after superstructure was cut away in a bay—which also afforded scuttle space for the cabins it accommodated.

Soon after her completion the *Thunderer's* forward guns were replaced by Armstrong 12·5-in. M.L.R. for which the new hydraulic system of loading was introduced, the old carriages being retained. By this system the crews were reduced from twenty-two to ten for the pair of guns—which greatly lowered the casualty risk in the turret—and for the first time external loading was given a trial. This entailed depressing the guns while the turret was being turned from the firing position until the muzzles were over either of the loading tubes which led up from the lower deck 30° on each side of the middle line.
Hydraulic pressure then forced the rammer, cartridge and projectile up the tube and into the gun; after loading, the turret was unlocked, turned towards the target, and the guns fired by electrical control from the conning tower if required.

This system afforded the M.L.R.s very much the same facilities as did fixed loading positions in the early types

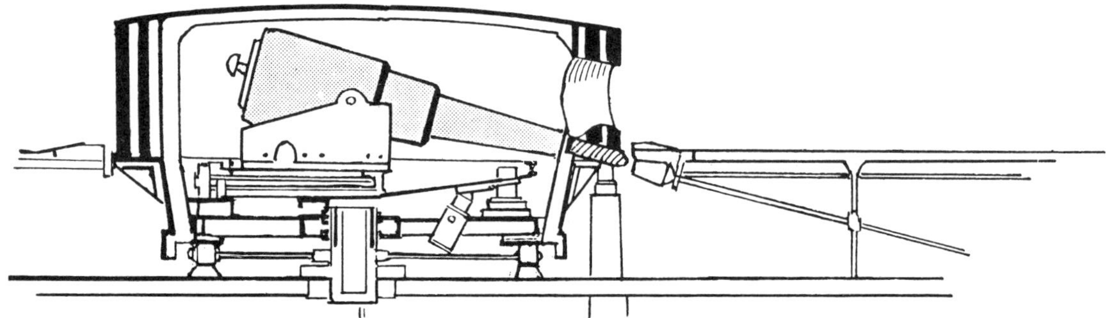

Turret in *Thunderer* showing 38-ton gun depressed for loading.

of B.L. guns, and was so satisfactory that but for the explosion of one of the *Thunderer's* Armstrongs in 1879 during practice firing it is probable that the return to B.L. guns in 1886 would have been postponed for a few more years.

This accident occurred off Ismed on 2 January 1879 and the circumstances are described by Admiral of the Fleet the Rt. Hon. Sir E. H. Seymour in his book *My Naval Career and Travels*.

> "Both turret guns were being fired simultaneously, and evidently one did not go off. It may seem hard to believe such a thing could happen and not be noticed, but from my own experience I understand it. The men in the turret often stopped their ears, and perhaps shut their eyes, at the moment of firing, and then instantly worked the run-in levers, and did not notice how much the guns had recoiled. This no doubt occurred. Both guns were at once reloaded, and the rammer's indicator, working by machinery, set fast and failed to show how far home the new charge had gone. This too may seem unlikely, but no doubt it happened; and the gun on being fired burst, killing two officers and several men, and wrecking the turret. Experiments made with a similar double-loaded gun, burst it in exactly the same way."

The loading numbers on the deck below would have been unaware of any misfire, as the concussion was "so tremendous that it was impossible to hear whether one gun or two had been fired" (Beresford). For some years the turret guns constituted their sole armament and it was not until the late 'eighties that quick-firers were mounted on the hurricane deck. When "modernized" they were given 10-in. B.L.—the heaviest hand-worked gun in the Service—and several 6- and 3-pdrs.

ARMOUR

A contemporary writer most aptly described the ship as "an impregnable piece of Vauban fortification with bastions mounted upon a fighting coal mine."

After the sequence of central battery ships with their rapidly diminishing armoured areas the *Devastation* class came as a welcome return to the true "ironclads"—and were destined to be the last of them! When designed they were impervious to any gun afloat except the largest at close quarters—although the new pebble slow-burning powder was to make this immunity a matter of a few years only. Reed wanted to armour every foot of above-water surface, but restrictions in displacement forced him to leave the forecastle unplated and the ram without any reinforcement from the belt. His original plan would have resulted in an unhealthy and uncomfortable ship, which Barnaby's superstructures certainly obviated, although offering a large area of thin ironwork as a hostage to enemy shell-fire.

Compared with previous Reed designs, the proportion of displacement allotted to armour was a striking testimony to the advantages accruing from the use of a low freeboard hull in combination with turret armament and twin screws in place of sail power, as the following percentages demonstrate:

	Displacement	*Armour weight*	
Hercules	8,680 tons	1,332 tons	15·3 per cent.
Audacious	6,010 ,,	924 ,,	15·3 ,, ,,
Monarch	8,300 ,,	1,364 ,,	16·4 ,, ,,
Devastation	9,330 ,,	2,540 ,,	27·2 ,, ,,

To this extent the *Devastation* fulfilled Reed's conception of the first essential in the military qualities of a capital

Thunderer during the Manœuvres of 1900 with the *Vindictive* of Zeebrugge fame and cruiser *Blenheim* above her stern. In her big refit of 1889-91 she was rearmed with 10-in. B.L. guns and more light pieces, additional bridgework, signalling pole forward of the modified funnels, and a different mast. Although her forecastle would be awash in a seaway she was remarkably steady.

ship—to remain afloat in action. But with only four guns delivering a poor volume of fire even by the gunnery standards of the day, she was what her critics called a "You can't hurt me and I can't hurt you" ship.

Both turrets were of 12-in. plates on 17-in. backing with 14-in. faces on 15-in. backing, the armour being in two layers separated by teak.

The end-to-end belt, shallowing to waterline level forward, was 12 in. amidships and 9 in. at the ends backed by 18-in. teak from upper deck to 5¾ ft. below water, where it thinned to 10 in. amidships and 8½ in. towards bow and stern. This belt projected 2 ft. on each side and as the lower edge was not faired off it acted as a side-keel of great efficiency in adding resistance to rolling. There was, however, the drawback that when rolling in a seaway the emersion and immersion produced considerable shocks on the under side of the projecting armour so that after several trials it was decided to "fill-in" the projection. This done, the vessel proved to be steady and well-behaved. Special protection to the magazines was afforded by 12-in. submerged transverse bulkheads fore and aft—a development of the "Glatton" system.

Arising above the hull was the internal breastwork 10 in. thick amidships and 12 in. around the turret bases, surrounded by Barnaby's light superstructure which flushed it up to the sides and provided the notorious *cul-de-sac* double bay aft.

Low freeboard laid the decks more open to attack than in the higher broadside ships, and consequently horizontal armour absorbed a considerable proportion of the weight allotted to protection. Over the breastwork the deck was 2 in., with 3 in. on the upper deck amidships and 2 in. aft; on the belt deck the plating was 3 in., the total weight of deck protection including glacis plates and armoured skylights being 556 tons—an increase of 153 tons over Reed's original estimate. Throughout the hull and turrets the skin was 1¼ in.

Although there was a bridge at the forward end of the hurricane deck, the armoured pilot tower of 9-in. to 6-in. plating weighing 110 tons was placed between the funnels with a communication tube leading down to the breastwork deck.

The system of subdivision was greatly extended in these ships, with sixty-eight compartments in the hold space and thirty-six in double bottom and wings. Of the latter the largest held 50 tons of water—equal to 1½ in. immersion—and the whole double bottom flooded by 1,000 tons of water ballast gave additional immersion of 28 in. only.

MACHINERY

The machinery for both ships was contracted for prior to the adoption of compound engines in the Service. The *Devastation* had Penn's famous trunk type and was the last capital ship to receive them. On trials in September 1872 at a mean draught of 26 ft. 5 in. she made 13·8 knots with 6,637 h.p. at 76·7 revolutions and a boiler pressure of 27 lb.

The *Thunderer* was given horizontal direct-acting engines by Humphreys and Tennant, the first capital ship contract to be executed by this famous firm. After recording 13·4 knots with 6,270 h.p. the trials were held up by a boiler burst in July 1876 due to sheer carelessness through a stop valve being closed in a boiler in which both safety valve and pressure gauge were defective. In January 1877 during a six hours full-speed run in the Solent with the wind between 7 and 9 and a rough sea she worked up to 5,749 h.p.—or just 149 h.p. beyond the contract figures.

Extraordinary interest in the ships had been aroused by the time the *Devastation* was ready for her trials in the summer of 1873, as both ashore and afloat she was regarded as unsafe to go to sea. In addition her novel design and grotesque appearance, the heavy gun power and massive protection, built up a ship personality such as had never before existed. But the public was still loyal to masts and yards, and this top-heavy looking Goliath, low-decked and high-superstructured, trusting to machinery alone for long ocean passages, and flaunting a grim nakedness aloft, was regarded as fit for harbour service only. Comparing her with the *Monarch*, the bias of public opinion can hardly be wondered at, and no British warship before or since has evoked so much apprehension. The notice found affixed to her gangway when commissioning at Portsmouth, "Letters for the 'Captain' may be posted aboard," well summed up the general feeling as to her chances for survival at sea.

A preliminary cruise did nothing to allay anxiety. She developed condenser trouble which caused a heave-to for a time, and this breakdown brought forth jeremiads anent the shortcomings of machinery and dangers of relying upon mastless ships. Her habitability was also censored and hope expressed that she would be laid up as a drill ship. Altogether the *Devastation* had a thoroughly bad press and the public expected tragedy when she was sent out to face the Atlantic.

But the Board thought otherwise. They knew she would meet all expectation, and to give her a thorough testing in company she left port with the *Agincourt* representing the old type of long-hulled ships and *Sultan* as the best of the later Reed models.

SEA-GOING QUALITIES

They were ordered to proceed to Berehaven and from there to make cruises into the Atlantic when suitable rough weather presented itself. To gauge the comparative pitching, a broad white stripe was painted on the *Sultan's* side representing the *Devastation's* upper deck. On September 9 she went out with the *Sultan* into lumpy and irregular seas to face a 45 m.p.h. gale, raising waves 16 ft. high and up to 400 ft. long. Going head to sea at 7 knots the turret ship had the better of it. Although her forecastle was swept by green Atlantic she rose readily, and it invariably happened that the seas broke upon her during the upward thrust of the bows, thus acting as a retarding force which limited the succeeding pitch, so that the angle between extreme elevation and depression of the bows was only 7½°. Both ships behaved well when placed broadside on to the sea, and rolled very little. A week later she took the *Agincourt* out to face a nor'westerly gale with 450 to 600 ft. waves running 20 to 26 ft. high, and here the older ship had somewhat the better of it, although her greater length gave her the appearance of pitching through a greater angle. The *Devastation* averaged from 5° to 8° with 11¾° as a maximum.

> "A wall of water would appear to rise up in front of the vessel, and dashing on board in the most threatening style as though it would carry all before it, rushed aft against the fore turret with great violence, and after throwing a cloud of heavy spray off the turret into the air, dividing into two, to pass overboard on either side. All the hatchways leading below from the upper deck were closed; it was not, however, thought necessary to close the doors in the sides of the trunks leading up from the main hatchways to the flying deck, most of the men on deck preferring to remain here under the overhang of the flying deck."

The greatest angle rolled through was when proceeding at 7½ knots with wind and sea on the quarter; then she registered 13° to windward and 14½° to leeward when pitching through 5° to 6°. On the whole she was considered to have behaved better than the *Agincourt*, rolling more slowly and less deeply—in fact, just as her constructors had anticipated.

But if the low forecastle had certain virtues, it also produced unforeseen limitations in the matter of sea-going qualities, which the bow wave and forecastle flooding very soon demonstrated would have to be on a less ambitious scale than intended. When designed, sufficient fuel for a passage to America was allowed them, but after a taste of full Atlantic weather their sphere of activities was limited to Home waters and the Mediterranean.

Curiously enough it was always the *Thunderer* which was held up as a model for steadiness. Admiral Colomb used to refer to her as "that steady old rock which nothing disturbs," and "as steady as the old *Thunderer*" meant full marks as a gun platform.

REFITS

Although at the conclusion of the first Mediterranean commission the Captain of the *Devastation* spoke of her as being "wholesome and comfortable for the officers and men and everything he could wish for"—at least so Admiral Inglefield assured a public meeting—nevertheless her big refit in 1879 included "improvements in the sanitary and ventilating arrangements, the former having been particularly defective during the late commission." Her machinery was given a complete overhaul, and six Nordenfelt guns were mounted on the hurricane deck with a Gatling in the top added to the mast as defence against torpedo attack—which by this time had become a definite although somewhat exaggerated menace. A torpedo port was also cut on each side of the breastwork for 14-in. carriages and an additional steam cutter fitted with torpedo dropping gear accommodated—the stowage being 12 Whitehead torpedoes. The *Thunderer* was similarly refitted in 1881; in 1877 she had been fitted with experimental torpedo nets.

Between 1891 and 1892 both ships were rearmed with 10-in. B.L. 29-ton guns firing a 500 lb. projectile (*Thunderer* by Armstrong and *Devastation* by Whitworth) and given six 6-pdrs. and eight 3-pdrs. in place of the Nordenfelts.

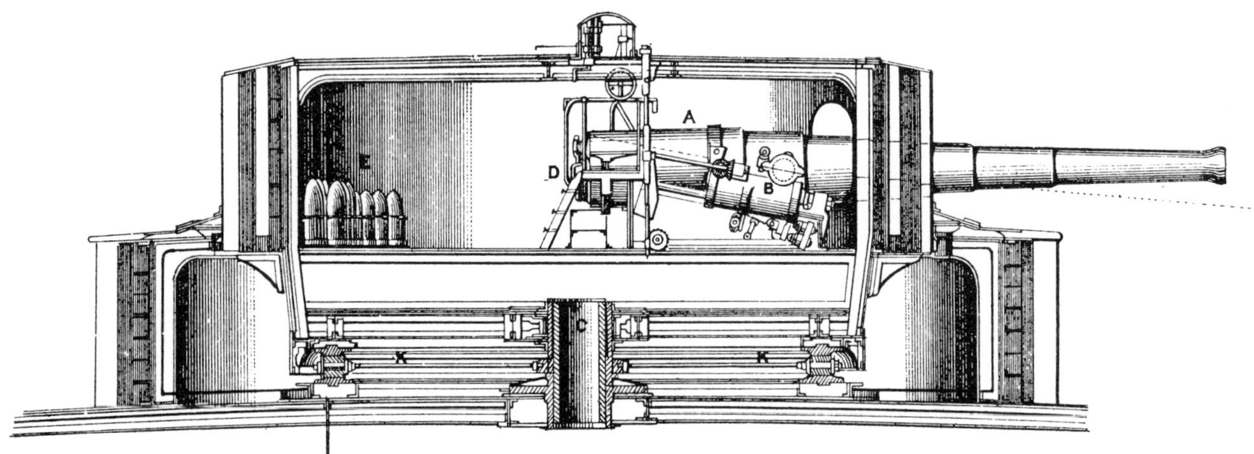

The old machinery was replaced by inverted triple expansion engines and cylindrical tubular boilers generating 7,000 h.p. (f.d.) driving three-bladed screws of 16 ft. diameter which raised their extreme speed to 14·2 knots. The coal supply—which previously stood at 1,800 tons in the *Devastation* and 1,600 tons in *Thunderer* or three times that carried by the masted ships—was reduced to 1,200 tons. Both ships were re-masted, *Thunderer* receiving a heavy signalling pole forward which served to distinguish her from her sister; a flying bridge was added and new funnels rounded off a general effect of modernization.

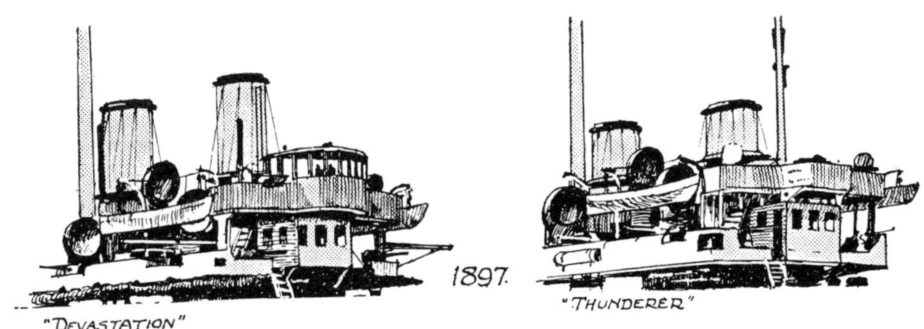

By this time public opinion had veered round to an opposite extreme and had adopted the two ships as symbolic of British sea power, more by virtue of their names and appearance than anything else. But for some years following her gun and boiler accidents the *Thunderer* was regarded as a hoodoo ship, being kept in Reserve at Malta and listed as undergoing repairs.

In the Service their popularity steadily increased as the years went on. Ten years after they had hoisted the pennant during which time the *Alexandra*, *Temeraire*, *Inflexible*, *Colossus* and *Collingwood* had paraded the latest ideas in gun distribution and armour protection before critical and prejudiced naval officers, these once derided "mastless" turret ships held an unshaken pride of place despite various shortcomings. In 1884 Admiral J. C. Wilson voiced what was a widely held service opinion at an R.U.S.I. meeting when the most acceptable type of battleship was under discussion:

> "I also agree with my friend Captain Colomb that we have no type of ship to my fancy equal to the *Dreadnought* or to the good old *Thunderer*. Give me the *Thunderer*, the hull of the *Thunderer*; she had bad engines, she was not arranged as I would like inside, she was badly gunned as we know, and she had not enough light guns or sufficient armaments; but she carried 1,750 tons of coal, could steam at 10 knots from here to the Cape, and could fight any ship of her class on the salt water."

"DEVASTATION"

The first iron ship to be built at Portsmouth. Commissioned January '73 for Particular Service. From May '74 to April '75 she was in the Channel (was rammed by *Resistance* at Portland July '74; armour displaced but no leakage) and then transferred to the Mediterranean untii 7 November '78 when paid off at Portsmouth for refit. (Whiteheads; Nordenfelts; s.l.), and afterwards kept in Reserve until April '85 when she was commissioned for Particular Service with Admiral Hornby's "Evolutionary Squadron." From August '85 to May '90 was portguard ship at Queensferry (collided with *Ajax* before 1887 Jubilee review). Paid off at Portsmouth for long refit '91-'92 and rearmed, etc. From '93 to January '98 was portguard ship at Devonport and in Reserve there until April, when she went to Bantry as coastguard until June, and then returned to the Devonport Reserve. From November '98 until April '02 was portguard ship at Gibraltar but actually spent most of her time with the fleet, Paid off in Reserve at Portsmouth in April '02, was refitted in '04, and made non-effective in '07.

Sold in May 1908 for £21,700.

"THUNDERER"

Boiler explosion during trials July '76. Commissioned May '77 for Reserve Fleet Particular Service Squadron June-August '78 and Channel (was fitted with 16-in. experimental torpedoes). Went to the Mediterranean in '78 (gun explosion 2 January '79 with 11 killed and 30 injured). Paid off in Malta Reserve in '81 (was given 14-in. torpedoes, enlarged chart house, etc.), but served with the fleet between '85 and '86. Paid off at Chatham for refit and in January '88 joined the Portsmouth Reserve. Big refit '89-'91 (rearmed, new machinery, etc.). Again served in Mediterranean from March '91 to September '92 by which time constant trouble with boiler tubes caused her to be sent home, and paid off into Chatham Reserve. In May '95 went to Pembroke as portguard ship until December 1900 when she joined the Fleet Reserve at Chatham. Refit '03. Was made non-effective in '07, and transferred to Portsmouth.

Sold in July 1909 for £19,500.

Chapter 32

THE BARNABY ERA

As already mentioned, Mr. E. J. Reed relinquished his position as Chief Constructor on 9 July 1870. During his seven years at Whitehall naval construction both in design and development had passed through a somewhat critical period, the adoption of the turret system being marked by the controversy and uncertainty which time and again has accompanied the introduction of novel conceptions into the Service.

Although complaining that his projects were considerably circumscribed by Board requirements which in many cases he regarded as ill-formed and not conducive to the efficiency of the ships concerned, Reed was certainly allowed far more latitude in his work than any subsequent officer in his position. If Isaac Watts had been given practically a free hand in designing the early ironclads, it was because the Board relied almost solely upon the Surveyor for professional advice, and he in turn depended upon the ability of the Chief Constructor to fulfil requirements without himself being in a position to exercise any critical control of the designs produced. During Reed's régime the Board had the advantage of greater experience in ironclad ships, although their exercise of authority was more frequently than not directed towards undue restrictions in tonnage and cost. But the close collaboration which he always observed with Sir Spencer Robinson was of immense benefit to the Service. The Controller had a tremendous opinion of Reed's abilities and gave him wholehearted support throughout the period of their association. When Reed resigned Robinson viewed his departure as a national calamity. He urged the First Lord to appoint Mr. Nathaniel Barnaby to the vacancy as being imbued with the Reed tradition, but Childers was at that time vastly impressed by the design of the *Captain* (which had apparently vindicated his confidence in her and was still two months from catastrophe), and elected to offer the post to Mr. William Laird, but was unable to persuade him to accept it. After which rebuff Barnaby was given the title of "President of the Council of Construction" until 17 August 1875, when he was appointed Chief Constructor.

Nathaniel Barnaby was born at Chatham 25 February 1829 and entered the Service as a naval apprentice at Sheerness, aged 14. Having won a scholarship at Portsmouth naval school in 1848, he became a draughtsman at Woolwich dockyard in 1852, and in 1854 was appointed to the Department of Naval Construction to assist in the design of the *Warrior*. When Reed, who had married Barnaby's sister—became Chief Constructor in 1863, Barnaby was made head of his staff, in which capacity he worked on most of the designs for new ships, including the *Monarch*. On Reed's resignation he became President of the Council of Construction and Chief Naval Architect in 1872 at the age of 43; three years later this post was changed to Director of Naval Construction. Barnaby was awarded the C.B. in 1876 and the K.C.B. in 1885, when he resigned his post for reasons of ill-health. He died 15 June 1915 at the age of 86.

Sir Nathaniel Barnaby was in charge of the Constructor's Department for thirteen years, and his tenure of office was marked by exceptional difficulties both from the material and financial aspects of design. In arming his ships he had to contend with a rapid increase in calibre from 12-in. 35-ton M.L.R. to 16·25-in. 110-ton B.L.R. at a time when there was a marked diversity of opinion as to the value of huge ordnance and considerable fluctuation in the size of the guns selected for primary armament. In addition the secondary armament was introduced and added further problems to the question of a properly balanced design.

Armour, on the other hand, did not keep pace with gun power. Enormous thickness of wrought iron, and later of compound iron and steel, was required to keep out the heaviest projectiles, thus limiting the areas it was possible to protect and complicating the difficulties of defence along the waterline.

Torpedo warfare also developed rapidly and led to further problems. Indeed the potentialities of the torpedo-boat were exaggerated to such an extent that by the 'eighties it was seriously regarded as having ousted the battleship from her pride of place, and that the construction of heavily armed and armoured units would cease. Comparisons between the cost of torpedo craft and battleships and the vulnerability of the big and very expensive ship to the attack of small boats which could be built in swarms for the same expenditure reacted strongly on battleship construction. Displacement was deliberately cut down for the sole purpose of reducing the financial loss consequent upon the sinking of a battleship. The proper reaction to torpedo attack should have been increased dimensions with constructional provisions for meeting it; but as the period was one of naval apathy and extreme economy, the policy of limiting financial loss made a more practical appeal to the Board than did the alternative of granting increased dimensions and constructional measures to try and obviate it.

The Barnaby era may be divided roughly into four periods during which the design of capital ships underwent markedly characteristic changes:

1. (*a*) Complete hull protection with fore and aft turrets (*Dreadnought*, *Cyclops*).
   (*b*) Complete belt and broadside batteries (*Alexandra*, *Temeraire*).
2. Central citadel with en echelon turrets (*Inflexible*, *Ajax*, *Colossus*).
3. Short belt with barbettes (*Collingwood*, *Imperieuse*).
4. Bow turrets only (*Hero*, *Sans Pareil*).

Thus the ships for which he was responsible ranged from the last of the rigged broadside ironclads to turret ships carrying the largest calibre guns ever mounted in a British battleship, and included such controversial designs as the *Inflexible* and the *Admirals*—an extraordinary assortment of types without precedent in a period of only thirteen years. Most of his productions evoked more hostile than favourable criticism, and while their shortcomings were usually attributed to their designer, actually Barnaby was allowed considerably less latitude than his predecessors, and it will be seen that the Board's responsibility was almost as much actual as it was virtual; in some cases his alternative suggestions would have resulted in far more satisfactory ships.

BARNABY'S CREED

In Reed's ships *offence* was secondary to *defence*, with flotation dependent upon belt and side armour; Barnaby, on the other hand, placed attack before defence, his creed being:

> "There should be the greatest possible offensive power and the defensive arrangements should be such as to ensure the ship, as far as possible, and in equal degrees, against all the various modes in which she may be disabled or destroyed. From this it will follow that it should not be in the power of the enemy to disable the ship by one single blow delivered by any means at his command."
>
> "In a well-designed ship there should be defence for the propelling power, for the steering-power, and for the floating power against the gun, the ram, and the torpedo. To a large extent defence against the ram and torpedo must rest with the officer in command, but to resist them he requires that speed and steering gear as well as floating power should be equally defended against the gun which he cannot avoid. The avoidable weapons are provided against, by material defences, far less than is the gun which cannot be avoided; and equality of defensive power is obtained by reckoning the skill of the seaman as part of the defence against ram and torpedo."

From 1871 the growth in the power of naval guns, due to improved gunpowder as well as increase in calibre, was out of all proportion to the resistance of the armour opposed to them. A year or so after being laid down the erstwhile impregnable *Devastation* could have been smashed by the guns of the *Monarch* with their improved charges, while her 35-ton guns were being surpassed by European models. At home Sir Wm. Armstrong was prepared to accept orders for 14-in. guns throwing half-ton projectiles with a charge of 2 cwt. of powder which could not be resisted by less than 20 in. of armour; and Sir Joseph Whitworth undertook to make 11-in. pieces capable of penetrating 16-in. iron at 1,000 yards, and a 13-in. gun effective against armour up to 24 in.

Against the menace of such weapons the Reed standards of protection appeared useless, and some alternative system of ensuring defence and flotation had to be considered in which the weight allotted to armour could be concentrated over vital areas. Even the advent of compound armour did little to relieve the Constructor's difficulties in providing adequate protection, as breech-loading guns of ever-increasing calibre were being introduced abroad. Hence Barnaby was forced to adopt amidships turrets with the heaviest protection possible over a central citadel in conjunction with unarmoured ends and elaborate subdivision. He was also restricted to revolving turrets, as the French *barbettes* were impracticable with the muzzle-loading guns which the Ordnance Dept. refused to discard. But the turret system made great demands upon displacement as their turning machinery had to be heavily armoured and placed below decks—which meant low freeboard to save weight. On the other hand, barbettes containing the gun training engines carried their weapons at a greater height, the French being satisfied with an unprotected base and an armoured ammunition tube to the magazines. But even when breech-loading guns had become available and the barbette system introduced in the *Admiral* class, the Board thought fit to return to turrets with the restrictions these imposed upon design.

In January 1871 Admiral Sir Spencer Robinson was relieved from the post of Controller which he had held for ten years and Captain Robt. Hall took his place, who in turn was followed by Rear-Admiral Wm. Houstan Stewart[1] in April 1872—an appointment associated with a temporary setback in battleship design through the building of the *Alexandra* and *Temeraire*. Stewart was one of the three members of the Committee on Designs who had favoured the retention of sail power and also opposed the recommendation that the *Swiftsure* should be built as a one-turret ship, and as the other two members, Captain Arthur Hood and Dr. Woolley, retained influential posts at Whitehall, it is not difficult to account for this brief but interesting reversion to the masted broadside capital ship.

It will be remembered that two of the recommendations of the Committee backed by Barnaby were that:

(1) No more lightly armoured and masted ships like the *Monarch* or *Sultan* should be built.
(2) Additional ships of the *Devastation* class should be ordered.

and Reed's description of the Board's response to these is worth noting:

> "Did the Admiralty adopt their advice? Not in the least. They neither built the latter nor ceased to build

[1] From January 1869 until March 1872 and again from April 1882 onwards the Controller was a Lord of the Admiralty.

> the former; but on the contrary, and as we think most wisely, ordered two new broadside ships of the *Sultan* class with some modifications, which do Mr. Barnaby the more credit as they have been made in ships of which he, curiously enough, disapproves."

Both these ships were laid down before the *Devastation* was ready for sea—the Board required more battleships and evidently preferred to proceed with accepted and satisfactory types rather than run any risks with additional low-freeboard turret ships. Barnaby was thus given the opportunity of producing the last of their line and incidentally two of the best-known ships of the mid-Victorian Navy—the *Alexandra*, as nearly perfect a specimen of the broadside ironclad as could be imagined, and the *Temeraire*, a broadside ship with two guns on the centre line *en barbette*.

But neither of these ships can be regarded as really belonging to the Barnaby era, the *Alexandra* being a greatly improved Reed model and *Temeraire* a hybrid owing something to Reed and something to Admirals Elliot and Ryder. The *Dreadnought* and *Cyclops* group also come into the same category—the former was merely a modified *Devastation*, and the latter adapted from a design Reed had drawn up for the Victorian Government. It was not until 1874, when the *Inflexible* was laid down, that the first typical Barnaby battleship came into being.

It is a shipbuilding aphorism that if a ship looks bad she generally is bad. The extent to which this applies to Barnaby's productions is perhaps a matter for individual opinion, but whatever their shortcomings from a military aspect they were mostly unattractive and cumbersome looking. Apart from the *Alexandra* and *Admirals* they had confused and irritating profiles without symmetry, and an ugliness in the matter of masts and funnels which carried no excuse from a utilitarian standpoint. Following in Reed's footsteps Barnaby favoured beamy models, and this characteristic became accentuated when he came to adopt Froude's formula in drafting dimensions. Thus, in the citadel ships carrying amidships turrets at low freeboard, in conjunction with big barracks of fore and aft superstructure tailed with uncompromising sterns, there was certainly little scope for the higher æstheticism in the modelling of profiles. The worst of the lot were the *Ajax* and *Agamemnon*, but in all subsequent ships the influence of his chief assistant, Mr. W. H. White, becomes apparent, the later *Colossus* and *Edinburgh* being topped and tailed into something like seemliness.

* * * * * * *

MR. GOSCHEN SUCCEEDS MR. CHILDERS 1871

When illness compelled Mr. Childers to retire from the Admiralty in March 1871, Mr. G. J. Goschen was appointed to succeed him—a statesman of acknowledged ability and a leading Cabinet minister. No change was made in the Board, but in May 1872 Rear-Admiral J. W. Tarleton, C.B., was appointed Second Naval Lord and Captain Robt. Hall left the Controller's office to become "Naval Secretary"—a fresh post.

Goschen carried out his predecessor's policy, and the formation of the Naval Volunteers was his best remembered contribution to the Service during the three years he was at the Admiralty.

Chapter 33

"FURY"

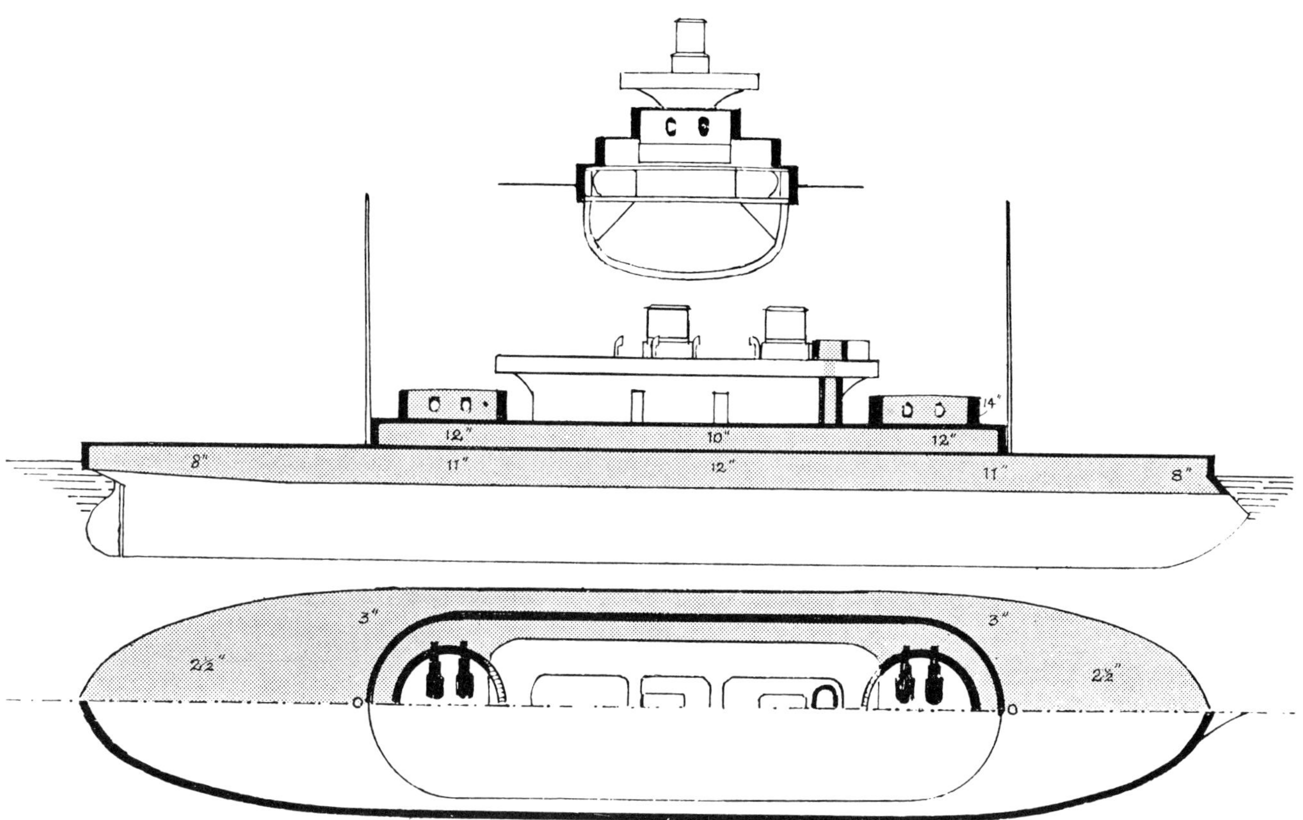

Reed's design for the *Fury* showing the low bow, passage between the citadel and deck edge, and drying poles only.

"FURY"

Builder	*Laid down*
Pembroke	10 Sept. '70 (construction ceased in 1871 and design cancelled).
Dimensions	320′ × 62¼′ × 26′ = 10,460 tons.
Guns	4 12-in. 25-ton M.L.R.
Armour	Sides 12″-11″-8″; turrets 14″; breastwork 12″-10″; decks 3″-2½″; skin 1½″. Total = 3,330 tons.
Machinery	Horizontal low pressure engines. 7,000 h.p. = 13·5 knots.
Coal	1,600 tons. Radius at 10 knots 4,000 miles.

For the third ship of the *Devastation* class which had been included in the Estimates for 1870 the First Lord, Mr. Hugh Childers, waived restrictions on tonnage, and allowed Reed to design the *Fury* with a free hand as a bigger and faster edition of her prototype.

The general differences in design were slight. She was some 35 ft. longer, with a nominal h.p. of 7,000 against the 5,600 of the earlier ship to give a knot more speed; the belt was continued to the bows, and although the general thicknesses of armour were the same, protection showed an increase of 790 tons due to the additional length.

Construction had proceeded to a stage when the hull had been built up to the armour deck, and then all work was suspended during the sittings of the Committee on Designs in 1871, as the findings of the Committee had included several proposals for increasing the stability of the *Devastation* type which could be applied to the *Fury*. These included radical alterations in the matter of the citadel, and the better to incorporate them together with improvements in armament and protection it was decided that she should be redesigned and rebuilt as a new ship. Every drawing which had been made by Reed was cancelled and an entirely new set made by Mr. W. H. White, who had been appointed to supervise work at Pembroke Dockyard. White was instructed to produce plans in accordance with his own ideas, and the new ship was renamed *Dreadnought* in 1874.

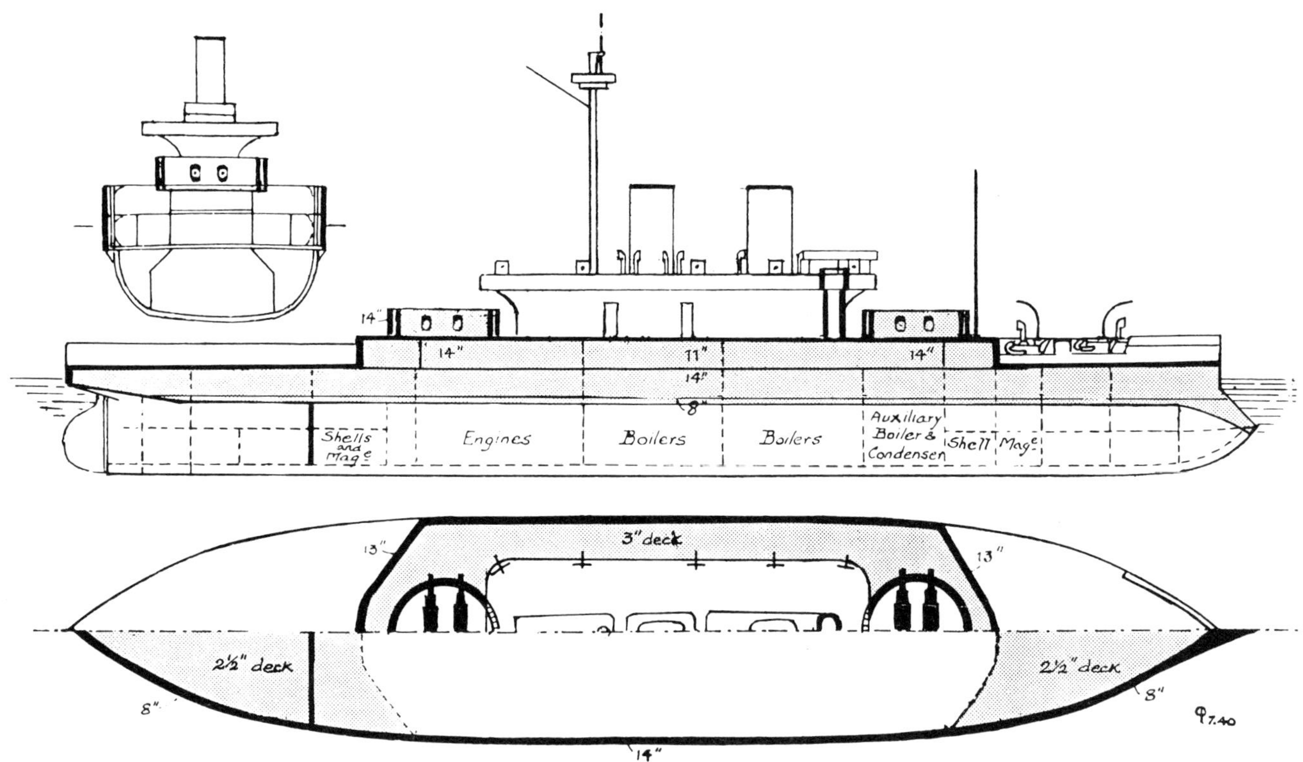

The *Fury* as altered by Barnaby to become *Dreadnought*. Note the built-up hull fore and aft, breastwork extended to the hull sides, and thicker armour.

"DREADNOUGHT"

Builder	*Laid down*	*Launched*	*Completed*	*Cost*
Pembroke	1872	8 March '75	15 Feb. '79	£619,739

Dimensions 320′ × 63¾′ × 26¼′/26¾′ = 10,886 tons.
Hull and armour 7,286 tons. Equipment 3,600 tons.

Guns 4 12·5-in. 38-ton M.L.R.
(6 6-pdr., 12 3-pdr., 9 smaller added later.)
Weight of guns and ammunition 400 tons.

Armour Sides 14″-12″-11″-8″; turrets 14″; bulkheads 13″; conning tower 14″-8″-6″; decks 3″-2½″; skin 1½″.
Total 3,690 tons (33·8 per cent.).

Complement 369.

Coal 1,200/1,800 tons. Radius at 10 knots 5,700 miles.

Machinery Compound vert. triple exp. by Humphreys and Tennant.
I.H.P. 8,210 = 14 knots.
H.P. cyl. 66″; two L.P. 90″; stroke 4′ 6″.
2 Griffiths screws 4-bladed. 20′ diam. pitch 21′-26′.
12 boilers. Total weight of machinery 1,430 ton .

Constructor Alex. Milne. W. H. White.

Special features:

(1) The first ship to have a longitudinal bulkhead amidships.
(2) The first—other than the *Pallas*—to have compound engines.
(3) The last British battleship to have overall armour as a true "ironclad."
(4) Carried the thickest *complete* belt of any British battleship.
(5) The first ship to have artificial ventilation.

When work on the *Fury* was suspended, Barnaby made certain proposals for alterations in her design which were placed before the Committee on Designs, although never formally submitted to the Board. These changes he anticipated would cause an additional 6 in. immersion, with reduction of the freeboard fore and aft to 4 ft. They included:

(1) Carrying out the breastwork flush with the hull-sides to provide a freeboard of 11½ ft. amidships with 12 in. plating. This would provide a larger reserve of buoyancy and stability and could accommodate the entire crew. It would be lighted and ventilated from above.
(2) Completion of the armour belt forward and taking it down to the ram, thus rendering the forward bulkhead introduced into the *Devastation* unnecessary.
(3) Subdivision forward as in *Devastation*.
(4) Placing the turrets 10 or 12 ft. *each side of the centre line* so as to allow fire from three guns ahead and astern. Thus placed they would tend to diminish rolling.
(5) An open flying deck made of iron bars 9 ft. above water for working the anchors. He did not consider lifting power was required forward in such a ship, and pitching would be reduced by not having a forecastle. The fore part was to be regarded as a mere prolonged snout under water acting like a bilge-keel, *with the breastwork as the true bow*.

Of these Nos. 1, 2 and 3 had already been worked into a proposed plan for a modified *Devastation* which was included in a Committee on Designs Minority Report signed by Admirals Elliot and Ryder. They had also advocated that the breastwork should be extended right to the bow and stern by light plating, thus providing a flush deck—a modification which removed the ship from the category of monitor. In her final form the *Dreadnought* incorporated these four proposals, although the adoption of the flush deck was delayed. After being redesigned the name *Fury* was retained for over a year, and during this period the superstructure extension of the citadel was rounded off short of the extreme bow and stern which were kept low to act as steadying influences against pitching. It was not until the trials of the *Devastation* in 1873-4 had demonstrated the attendant shortcomings of a low bow in setting a practical limit upon the power of driving a ship against a head sea, that the plans were altered to allow for a flush deck from bow to stern.

REED'S CLAIM TO THE "DREADNOUGHT"

For nearly twenty years Reed chose to regard the *Dreadnought* as one of his own creations, and in a pamphlet on *The Proposed Further Outlay on the Navy* he had written:

> "Now the last and most powerful ship which I designed at the Admiralty was the ironclad *Dreadnought*. It is a literal fact (and not a boast on my part, for the ship had the benefit of some improvements which were not mine) that this ship—now stationed in the Mediterranean—is still regarded by many naval officers as by far the best and most powerful ironclad yet completed in our Navy."

He stressed the point that the *Fury* was framed and nearly plated and that the changes involved no undoing of the work already done—from which he submitted that all the reconstruction she underwent must have been reconstruction at or above the water line.

In correcting this impression in 1889, White dealt bluntly with his old chief. Years of acrid criticism had culminated in Reed's taunt:

> "The day for getting the best possible ships out of our Whitehall Office is past and gone."

And White took occasion at the I.N.A. meeting in 1889 to put the facts on record:

> "If the dimensions of the *Fury* and *Dreadnought* are looked at, it will be seen that the extreme breadth of the ship was altered, and various changes made. When we come to the question of what the new design involved, perhaps it will be as well to make a statement once and for all which can be revived. I personally was intimately concerned with the reconstruction of the *Dreadnought*. I was at Pembroke detached from the Admiralty for many months in connection with that matter, and what I have to say is this—that the *Dreadnought* differs from the *Fury* in every feature of great importance except the disposition of the armament. The armour 13-14 in. thick instead of 12 in.; it is brought out at the sides in the form of a citadel instead of being on a narrow breastwork; the guns are worked on the hydraulic system of mounting and are of another type of gun; and as regards machinery, she has inverted vertical compound engines instead of horizontal low-pressure engines. There was also an entire rearrangement of the coal supply. The ship was redesigned throughout. It was a thing which would have had to be done in any case, owing to the adoption of the compound engines, and the improved performance of deep draught twin screw ships."

Despite which, the *Dreadnought* will always be regarded as a Reed ship. The basic conception of the type belonged to Reed and subsequent alterations improved but did not change her into anything which could be included in the category of Barnaby productions. She was the last of the true ironclads having a hull almost completely covered with what soon became known as "pie-crust"—iron armour adequate enough for her date of conception, but vulnerable to moderate-sized guns by the time she was completed. Altogether it accounted for nearly 34 per cent. of her displacement, while her four guns absorbed 4·8 per cent. and discharged only one round every half-minute, so that the discrepancy between offence and defence was even greater than in the *Devastation*.

GUNS

The *Fury* had been designed for 25-ton guns, but these were changed to the 38-ton model bored out to 12·5 in. so as to fire an 800-lb. shell with 160-lb. charges. As in the *Thunderer* the operating gear was hydraulic with steam training for the turrets.

On account of the risk of interference no secondary guns were mounted, although in his modified *Fury* designs submitted when the *Inflexible* was under consideration Barnaby showed how these could have been accommodated

Dreadnought cleared for action in Malta harbour with bulwarks in the bows lowered, railings laid on deck, topmast struck, and boats trailed astern. Beyond her is the Indian troopship *Serapis*.

(p. 247). During 1885 ten Nordenfelts were mounted on the hurricane deck, which were replaced by 6- and 3-pdrs. in 1894—then considered heavy enough to repel torpedo attack.

Considering how well she stood in Service esteem, it is strange that she was never rearmed like the *Devastation* and *Thunderer* during her refit in 1894. Writing in 1897, Captain Garbett states "the *Dreadnought* is to have her muzzle-loaders replaced by breech-loaders" (*Naval Gunnery*, p. 77), so the change was under consideration as part of her big refit in 1897-98. But by that time the old ship was not worth heavy expenditure in her turrets, magazines and engine rooms, and in consequence she stands out as one of the few ships built in the 'seventies which retained her original guns and engines throughout her career.

ARMOUR

In the *Devastation* there was a central breastwork enclosing the turrets with a passage 10 ft. wide between it and the side of the ship; this was repeated in Reed's *Fury*, but in the *Dreadnought* the armour was extended out to the hull sides, forming a citadel 144½ ft. long with oval ends making it 184 ft. in the middle line. This citadel was roofed by a 3-in. weather deck, the main and lower decks being unarmoured. The turrets revolved upon the main deck, below which was the hydraulic training and steam turning gear, and it will be appreciated that this machinery was not separately enclosed but relied upon the citadel for protection. A shell entering the citadel might therefore put both turrets out of action, and Reed's narrower breastwork reduced this risk in proportion to its deck space and width at the ends. In broadening it to form a citadel considerably more armour was required, but as a set-off to these disadvantages the additional space enclosed afforded increased stability and buoyancy, and gave an unobstructed upper deck with better quarters for officers and men.

Amidships the side plating was 11 in. with 14 in. for about 20 ft. at the turret bases; with oval bulkheads across the ends to deflect a raking hit.

Below the citadel ran a 14-in. belt rising about 3 ft. above water and tapering to 8 in. at its lower edge $5\frac{1}{4}$ ft. below; before and abaft the bulkheads this tapered to 8 in., and rose 4 ft. above water, dipping to reinforce the ram and rising slightly over the rudder. No British warship ever carried a thicker complete belt than this. Behind it ran deep coal bunkers covering the engine and boiler rooms amidships with a 22-ft. athwartships bunker forward and an 8-ft. one aft.

Before and abaft the citadel the main deck was $2\frac{1}{2}$ in. thick to bows and stern, lying flat above the belt. In the *Devastation* there were thwartships ammunition-room bulkheads fore and aft below the belt; in the *Dreadnought* that forward was replaced by a transverse cable locker, the after one being retained.

MACHINERY

When referring to the origin of the *Dreadnought* White stated that she would have had to be redesigned in order to carry compound engines—which covered an innovation of extreme importance. Since the end of the 'sixties the Board had been experimenting with compound machinery in the corvettes of the *Amethyst* and *Thetis* classes with both low-pressure rectangular and high-pressure cylindrical boilers, and the success of the latter in service led to their adoption in the *Dreadnought* and *Alexandra* launched a month later. Compound engines required double the pressure sufficient for the simple type and the frequent failure of the early installations in the Navy and Merchant Service through insufficient *steam power* delayed their general acceptance for a long time; it was therefore a big step forward when the two 4,000-h.p. sets of machinery were ordered. The provision of vertical instead of horizontal cylinders brought about the abandonment of one of the fixed principles in design—that screw machinery should lie below waterline protection; and in making the change it was decided that compounds should only be installed in armoured ships where the plating abreast the engines was high enough to shield the tops of the cylinders—which ruling for a long time precluded unarmoured ships from the benefits of economical speed.

The *Dreadnought* was the first battleship to be designed for compound engines since Wolff tandem cylinders were placed in the engine room of the little *Pallas*, and each of her twin screws was driven by a set of vertical inverted three-cylinder engines with the 66-in. high-pressure exhausting into two 90-in. low-pressure cylinders. Auxiliary machinery was by this time being more widely employed and there were engines for ventilating, fire pumps, steering, turret turning, capstans, etc., to a total of twenty-nine.

She was noteworthy in being the first ship to have a longitudinal bulkhead dividing the engine and boiler rooms which extended from 40 ft. short of the stem to about the same distance from the stern. This allowed for the boilers being placed back to back along the bulkhead instead of face to face as formerly, when the firemen had furnaces in front and behind them! There were also athwartships bulkheads to the boiler rooms making two 42-ft. rooms forward and two 40-ft. rooms aft.

Artificial ventilation was introduced in the *Dreadnought* after the reports from the *Devastation* in the Mediterranean, and that she was the first ship to have it may rank as a notable distinction.

SEA-GOING QUALITIES

Forward the freeboard was $10\frac{3}{4}$ ft., aft 10 ft.; and owing to the breastwork deck having been carried forward to the bows, the anchor cables worked under this forecastle, as in the old *Royal Sovereign*, instead of upon it.

At sea she proved very steady, rolling less than her two half-sisters—but inclined to pitch. In heavy weather, ahead or following seas could sweep her from end to end, and if she made her speed more easily than did the *Devastation* she was certainly wetter, although spared the effects of a following sea breaking into what was referred to as "the objectionable *cul-de-sac*" aft in that ship.

GENERAL

Often referred to as "the naval officer's beau-ideal of a battleship" she certainly looked the part and somehow managed to sustain her reputation as the best protected ship in the Navy long after her once impenetrable armour had become "pie-crust." Broad flat funnels gave her a dignity which was not enhanced when they were heightened in 1898, but she lacked the long chases of 10-in. B.L. given to her half-sisters which would have helped to save her face during the years of her third decade.

In every way the *Dreadnought* was a singularly successful ship, and when the *Trafalgar* design was proposed some ten years later the first drawings show almost her replica. She stands out as the only battleship built during the Barnaby era which was never a target for adverse criticism, and was considered fit for effective service twenty-five years after first leaving Pembroke Dockyard.

Dreadnought after her refit in 1899 when the funnels were raised and additional machine guns mounted. She is wearing the grey livery which replaced the black, white, and buff in 1903, and is lying in the Hamoaze as part of the Dockyard Reserve.

"DREADNOUGHT"

Commissioned in 1879 for trials after being nearly seven years under construction at Pembroke. Fitted with torpedo gear and placed in reserve at Portsmouth until 1884. Went out to the Mediterranean on 14 October '84 where she remained for ten years, paying off at Chatham for refit in September '94. From March '95 to March '97 was coastguard ship at Bantry. Big refit at Chatham when she received new boilers, raised funnels, additional q.f. guns, etc. Manœuvres 1900 and 1901 when she was rated as a second-class battleship. In July 1902 joined *Defiance* at Devonport as tender and served as a depot ship for T.B.'s at manœuvres. In 1905 took her place in the Dockyard Reserve and was moved from the Hamoaze to the Kyles of Bute.

Sold in July 1908 for £23,000.

Chapter 34

COAST-DEFENCE SHIPS, 1870

At the same time as the *Fury* was laid down four "coast-defence" ironclads were also commenced for completion as quickly as possible. As they stand out as the most unsatisfactory group of ironclads ever to fly the White Ensign, the reasons for their construction may best be given in Sir Spencer Robinson's own words:

> "During the war scare of 1870, when there was a possibility of this country becoming involved and our ports subjected to enemy attack, the Board had to consider the question of local coast defence against the kind of vessels (and how they would be armed) which would attempt the destruction of the large commercial and manufacturing towns situated on our coast. No large heavily armoured, deep draughted ships of war can approach the most defenceless of these harbours. A serious attack would have to be made by light vessels—probably a mixture of armoured and unarmoured ships . . . and you will easily see that the superiority on all points rests with the class the Admiralty adopted as part of a system of coast defence."

In order to implement this futile defensive policy the Board decided that the safety of our ports would best be assured by the provision of "harbour defence" monitors, four in number, and both in the interests of economy and expediency the *Cerberus* design was selected and slightly modified as being most suitable for an Emergency Programme.

The ships were very quickly put afloat—*Cyclops* slid into the Thames ten months after her keel was laid—but when the immediate necessity for their services had become less definite, construction was slowed down and several years elapsed before they presented themselves for employment, although delivered from the builders and nominally completed in 1872.

As ships of war they were held in ridicule throughout the Navy, and one of the Board who ordered them afterwards wrote to *The Times*:

> "The Constructive Dept. was ordered to build ships that could easily be run over in mid-ocean; which could not possibly float in shallow water; that could not go from one port to another except after careful study of the barometer; that could go to the bottom readily in a very heavy seaway and in a variety of other ways; and that possessed the smallest amount of offensive power and the maximum amount of defensive power. That problem the Constructive Dept. has solved very faithfully and exceedingly cleverly in giving us 'coast-defence' ships which cannot defend our coasts . . . and what on earth do 'coast-defence' ships mean?"

Although built to a design which was specifically drawn up for a harbour defence ship, they came to be regarded as "coast defence" ships able to proceed to any point off our shores if and when their presence was required—and as such were expected to be able to put to sea with safety. Before their completion the Committee on Designs of 1871—when investigating the diversities and discrepancies of the ships of this period—made a unanimous report that "if a certain superstructure extending along a good portion of their sides was not put on, they would be safe to go from port to port *only* in fine weather," and recommended that the breastwork be extended out to the ships' sides and plated in, both to afford better accommodation and as a measure to improve stability.

The Constructor's Dept. had already proposed such breastwork extensions as a precautionary measure because the available data for calculating the stability of low freeboard ships in a seaway lacked the proof of practical experience. However, for reasons which could only be given by the Board which thought fit to order them, they were completed as designed and the prescribed alterations were not made until 1886-9. When added, this superstructure provided space for a Captain's cabin and better accommodation, a reading room, sick-bay, etc., and made the ships safer and considerably more habitable.

GUNS

If the *Rupert's* armament bore the lowest ratio to tonnage of any of the coast-defence ships, the *Cyclops* class had the advantage of the opposite extreme, as each ton of armament only required 48 tons of displacement. Their four 10-in. 18-tonners were mounted on Scott's compound pivoting carriages with hydraulic jacks instead of levers, and were far more efficient guns as regards training and handling than any previously sent afloat.

When they came up for alteration an anti-torpedo battery of four 3-pdrs. and five machine guns was placed on the hurricane deck, with a couple of searchlights.

ARMOUR

The above-water hull was completely covered with armour, which exhibited the same high ratio to displacement as did the armament, equalling the ratio in the *Glatton*, in being one-third of their tonnage. But having two turrets

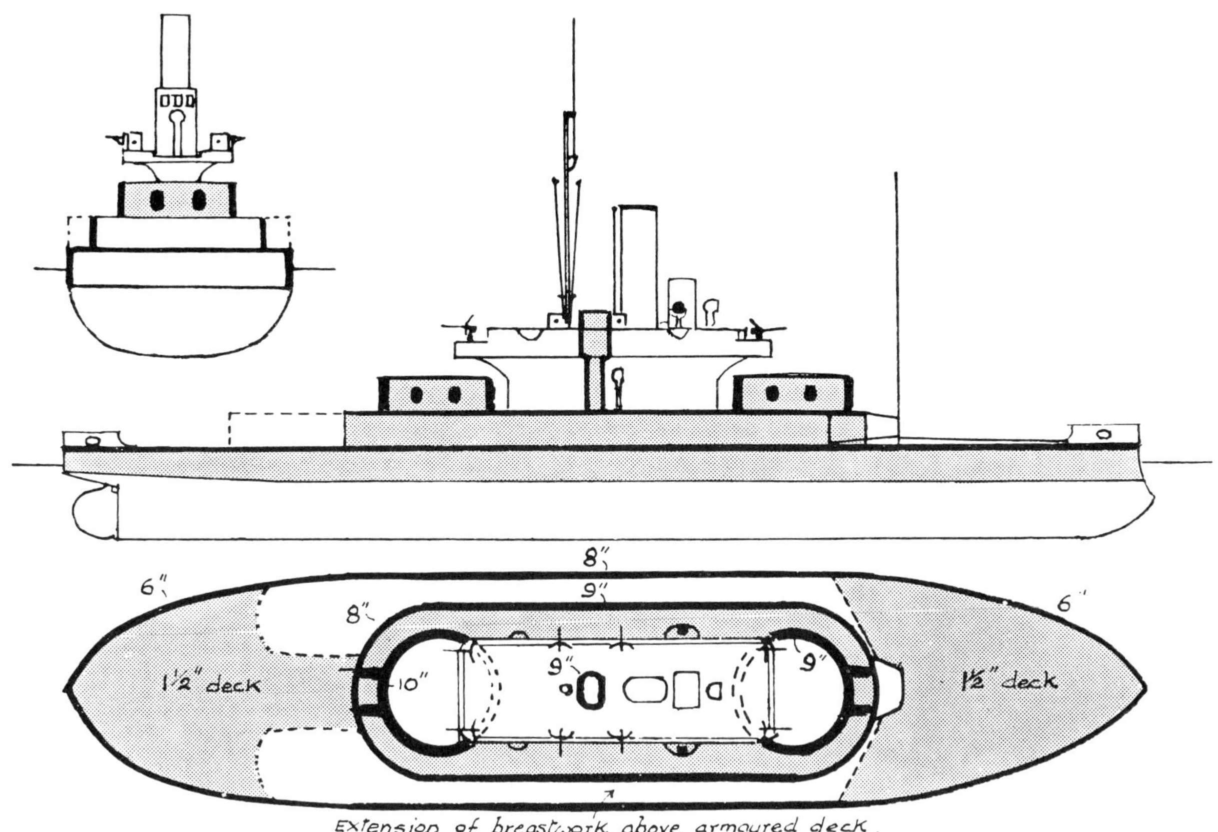

CYCLOPS

THE "CYCLOPS" CLASS

	Builders	*Laid down*	*Launched*	*Completed*	*Cost*
"Cyclops"	Thames I.W.	10 Sept. '70	18 July '71	4 May '77	£156,782
"Gorgon"	Palmers	5 Sept. '70	14 Oct. '71	19 March '74	£141,254
"Hecate"	Dudgeon	5 Sept. '70	30 Sept. '71	24 May '77	£143,310
"Hydra"	Napiers	5 Sept. '70	28 Dec. '71	31 May '76	£194,334

Dimensions 225′×45′×16·2′=3,480 tons (when altered 3,560 tons).
Hull and armour 2,730. Equipment 750 tons.

Guns 4 10-in. 18-ton M.L.R. Broadside 1,640 lb.

Armour Sides 8″-6″; breastwork 9″-8″; turret 10″-9″; conning tower 9″-8″; deck 1½″; skin 1¼″-1″; backing 11″-9″ teak. Total 1,130 tons.

Complement 156/191.

Coal 270 tons.

Machinery *"Cyclops"* *"Hydra"* John Elder. 2 sets compound tilt-hammer;
2 high pres. cyls. 31″; 2 low pres. 57″; stroke 27″.
"Cyclops" 1,660 h.p.=11 knots.
"Hydra" 1,472 h.p.=11·2 knots.

"Hecate" *"Gorgon"* } Ravenhill. 2 sets 4 cyl. simple horizontal direct action; cyls. 45″ diam.; stroke 24″.
"Gorgon" 1,670 h.p.=11 knots.
"Hecate" 1,755 h.p.=10·9 knots.

and a larger breastwork there was considerably more area to be covered, so that the 10-in. plates on the turret faces were the thickest aboard. However, as they were not intended to meet anything more formidable than light craft in shallow waters it was amply sufficient.

The sides were 8-in. amidships with 6-in. ends, the ram being bare. Amidships the breastwork rose 9¾ ft. above water, with 9-in. plating on the sides and 8-in. across the curved ends; at each end of this were the turrets, 9 in. with 10-in. faces. Both the main and breastwork decks were $1\frac{1}{2}$ in., and the skin $1\frac{1}{4}$ in. to 1 in.

RIG

As a relic of the original *Cerberus* rig the *Cyclops* and *Hecate* always carried a forecastle pole stepped to the port side of the turret which was used for the boat boom guys and as a drying mast; *Gorgon* and *Hydra* had a main mast only.

SEA-GOING QUALITIES

As might be expected, they took no part in the general activities of the fleet, and remained year in year out swinging around their moorings in the dockyard harbours. In April 1878 they were not distributed between the ports, but all four were attached to Sir Cooper Key's "Particular Service Squadron" which assembled at Portland Roads and remained in being for four months during the Russian-Turkish war scare. Being considered unsafe for the passage to Berehaven, they stayed behind under the shadow of the Bill until the formation was dispersed.

Hecate when in the Particular Service Squadron 1878. The breastwork enclosing the turrets and superstructure comes up short of the ship's side before the passageway was plated in, and she is without any anti-torpedo armament. Note the triple steering wheel forward of the little chart house.

But in 1887 all four were commissioned for the manœuvres and made sea passages. The *Gorgon* struck heavy weather outside Queenstown and in Admiral Ballard's opinion "was not so bad as a torpedo-gunboat, although she yawed a lot." But if very uncomfortable they were considered safe by those aboard. After the breastwork extensions were fitted things improved considerably, although—like the *Devastation*—they suffered in a seaway from the *cul-de-sac* aft. The angle of maximum stability was 25° vanishing at 39·25°.

ALTERATIONS

The four were taken in hand between 1885 (*Hecate*) and 1889 for additional superstructure around the breastwork, and both the breastwork and upper decks were strengthened. A watertight bulkhead and an additional flat were worked in at the bows and a false keel added. With the addition of quick-firing guns the shape of the hurricane deck was modified.

The *Cyclops* at Spithead during the Manœuvres of 1890. Her sides had been plated in amidships and machine guns—seen on the flying deck—added during her refit of 1887-89.

"CYCLOPS"

Delivered at Devonport for completion from builders January '72 and placed in Reserve until finally ready for sea in April '77; 1st. Div. Reserve; Particular Service Squadron April '78-August '78; paid off into Reserve, Chatham. Altered '87-'89 (superstructure, net defence, q.f. guns) Portsmouth; Manœuvres '87, '89, '90, '92; Fleet Reserve; '01 non-effective list.

Sold August '03 £8,400.

"GORGON"

Delivered from the builders April '72 and placed in Reserve at Devonport. Served as tender to the *Cambridge* 74-'77 and then commissioned for the Particular Service Squadron from April-August '78. Tender to *Cambridge* from '78 onwards. Altered '88-'89. Manœuvres '87, '89, '90, '92. Fleet Reserve at Devonport until placed on the non-effective list in 1901.

Sold '03 £8,400.

"HECATE"

Arrived at Devonport from builders April '72 and was not completed until '77. Commissioned in April '78 for the Particular Service Squadron and paid off in August into Reserve at Devonport. Altered '85-'86. Manœuvres '87, '89, '90, '92. Fleet Reserve at Devonport until made non-effective in 1901.

Sold '03 £8,400.

"HYDRA"

Arrived at Devonport from builders August '72 and underwent a leisurely completion until '77. Commissioned April '78 for the Particular Service Squadron, paying-off in August at Sheerness. Served as tender to the *Duncan* going into the basin during winter. Altered '88-'89.

Manœuvres '87, '89, '90, '92. In Fleet Reserve at Chatham until made non-effective in 1901.

Sold '03 £8,400.

Chapter 35

"ALEXANDRA" (ex "SUPERB")

Builder	*Laid down*	*Launched*	*Completed*	*Cost*
Chatham	5 March '73	7 April '75	31 Jan. '77	£538,293

Dimensions 325′ × 63·8′ × 26′/26½′ = 9,490 tons. Hull and armour 6,160 tons. Equipment 3,330 tons.

Armament

1877	1891	1897
2 11-in. M.L.R.	4 9·2-in. B.L.	4 9·2-in. B.L.
10 10-in. M.L.R.	8 10-in. M.L.R.	8 10-in. M.L.R.
6 13-cwt. B.L. (2,658 lb.)	6 4-in. B.L.	6 4·7-in. Q.F.

Four torpedo carriages.

Armour Sides 12″-10″-8″-6″; bulkheads 8″-7″-6″-5″; decks 1½″-1″; skin 1½″; backing 12″-10″ teak. Total 2,060 tons.

Complement 674.

Sail area 27,000 sq. ft.

Machinery Humphreys: vertical inverted compound.
I.H.P. 8,610 = 15·1 knots.
Twin screws; Mangin type. 21′ diam.
H.P. cyl. 70″; two L.P. cyl. 90″ (two sets).
12 boilers. 60 lb. pressure.

Coal 500/680 tons.

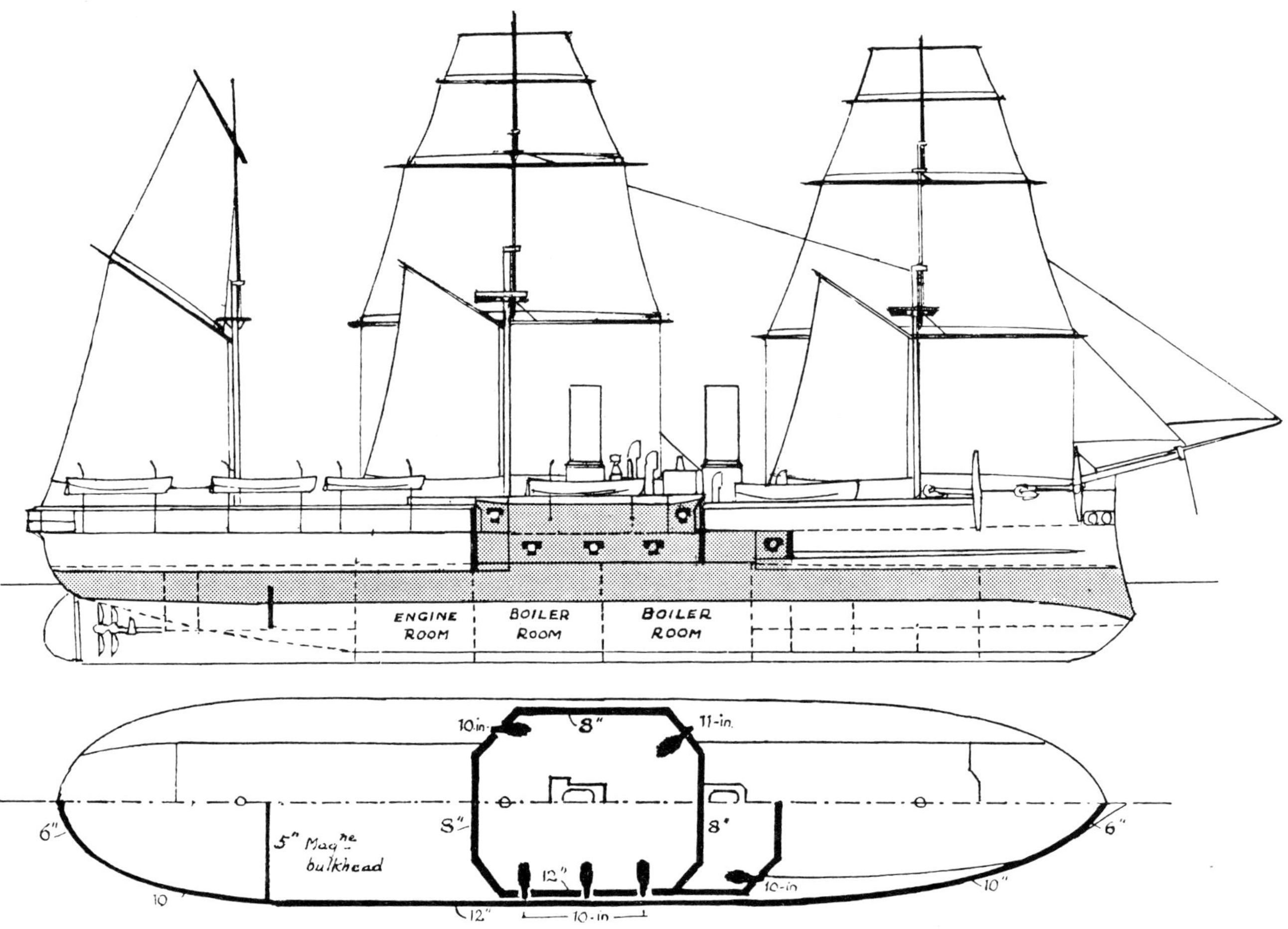

The *Alexandra* as completed with barque rig and a four-bladed Mangin propeller. Note the comparatively short masts and broad yards, and the height of the 10½ ft. upper battery and main deck aft. The transverse bulkhead just forward of the mizen was to protect the magazine from raking shots under water.

Points of Interest:

(1) One of the last two broadside ironclads to be designed at Whitehall, and the last to carry her main armament below decks.
(2) The most successful central battery ship ever built, and the fastest battleship of her day.
(3) The first ship in which the broadside was deliberately sacrificed to obtain bow fire.
(4) The only British battleship with axial fire broadside ports on both upper and main decks.
(5) Served as a flagship throughout her active career.
(6) One of the only two ships to carry 11-in. guns.

The *Alexandra* in Malta harbour in 1887 as flagship of the Duke of Edinburgh with Prince George of Wales serving as a lieutenant. The Duke had her painted white for coolness and she is here shown dressed ship on Queen Victoria's birthday. Note the 4-in. B.L. above the battery amidships and machine guns on and below the bridge.

In their report the Committee on Designs had recorded the following opinion:

"It is with much reluctance that a majority of our number have arrived at an opinion *adverse to the full rig for ironclad ships*. We all view with regret what presents itself to the minds of most of us as the inevitable failure of the attempt to unite in one ship a very high degree of offensive and defensive power with real efficiency under sail and find ourselves compelled to regard the attainment of this very desirable object as an insoluble problem."

Nevertheless when the Board came to determine the nature of the battleships to be commenced in 1873 the minority opposed to this sound advice had sufficient influence with My Lords for a reversion to be made to the rigged broadside type and as such the *Superb*—afterwards known as the *Alexandra*—was laid down one month before the *Devastation* commenced her trials.

Her name was changed to *Alexandra* when she was released into the Medway at high water on 7 April 1875 by H.R.H. The Princess of Wales (afterwards Queen Alexandra) in the presence of the Prince of Wales, the Duke and Duchess of Edinburgh, the Duke of Cambridge, the Duke and Duchess of Teck, the entire Board of Admiralty with the majority of the Cabinet and over one hundred members of Parliament. She was the first British Ironclad to be launched by a member of the Royal Family and the first since the Reformation whose birth was attended by a religious ceremony—in this case conducted by the Archbishop of Canterbury.

The *Alexandra* marked the end of the long series of progressive steps in the development of the broadside ironclad, and as is usually the case when something akin to perfection is attained afloat—as measured by the tactical standards of the day—she was virtually obsolete before hoisting the pennant. But she stands out as a queen among ships, flagship in the Mediterranean for a full term of active service, and flagship of the Reserves up to her final commission when she headed the line of the "B" fleet in the 1900 Manœuvres, and fired her guns for the last time at the Coronation Review in 1902.

It was indeed a strange irony which gave Barnaby—whose influence favoured the turret ship—occasion to produce a disposition of artillery allowing for an end-on concentration which was to find so much favour with contemporary and later critics. Reed stopped short with recessed ports and sponsons and was vastly satisfied with the *Audacious* and *Sultan*. But in 1869 the Austrian Chief Constructor, Chev. J. von Romako, had prepared designs for the *Custozza* class in which most of the broadside guns had direct ahead or astern fire. These were

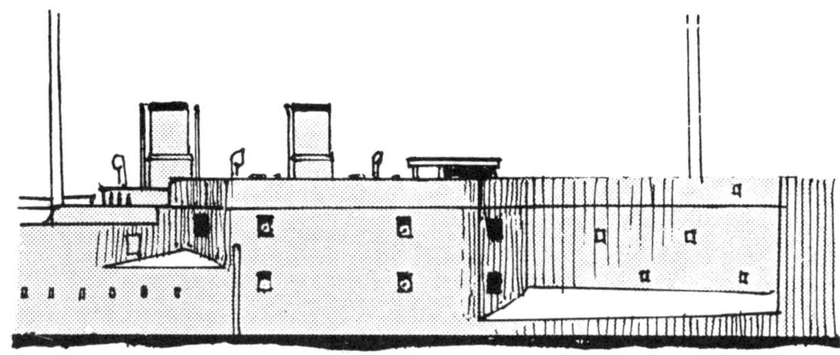

Central battery of the Austrian battleship *Custozza*, which influenced Barnaby in designing the *Alexandra*

mounted in a two-decked "bow battery," the sides being inclined inboard forward and the upper deck aft recessed at an angle to allow four guns to fire forward, and two at 56° from the keel-line aft.

Barnaby adopted this two-deck battery, and as our gunnery people objected to one gun firing immediately over another, the lower battery was extended forward about 25 ft. to form a pair of steps up the ship's side—as square, harsh, and uncompromising a set of obstacles as had ever been placed in the run of a wave along the hull of a warship.

Had French constructors tackled the same plan it is not difficult to visualize their treatment of the battery ends—a fairing of the sides so that the sea met kindlier curves which might shoulder water aside rather than oppose it with a flat buffeting. But how the *Alexandra* was going to face up to a head sea and fight her guns does not seem to have been a matter of much moment.

Needless to say axial fire was not carried out during the usual gunnery exercises as the resultant damage could not be accepted during peace time. Although only superficial it cost money to repair, so firing practice was restricted to bearings on which it did not occur.

That the design of the *Alexandra* was fundamentally faulty was not admitted for many years—the tactics of the day favoured a disposition in line abreast, and it was asserted that a ship must be prepared to fight end-on or else expose herself to be rammed. But line abreast could only be employed against an enemy in similar formation—and there was no way of making an opposing fleet fight an end-on action if it did not choose to do so. In any case an end-on battle would become a broadside one after a very short time.

Although of the same length as the *Sultan* (325 ft.) the beam was 4 ft. more and she floated on an even keel, whereas Reed's ship trimmed nearly 3 ft. by the stern. The *Alexandra* had slightly the higher freeboard.

In contriving his end-on fire Barnaby subjected the ship to certain rather serious inconveniences, as the sides forward and abaft the central battery had to be set back so far that the width of the upper deck between bulwarks was no more than 38 ft. anywhere—or about equal to that of a corvette. Forward of the battery the lower gun was also embrasured, so that the hull contraction had to be carried down to within 6 ft. of the waterline—which greatly reduced berthing space for the ship's company. But only the upper corner ports of the after end of the battery were set back—to have given the lower guns end-on fire would have meant constructional difficulties and too great a restriction of accommodation. So the officers' half of the ship was very spacious.

Besides being constricted the open deck area was also very limited in length, as the *Alexandra* had both topgallant forecastle and closed poop together with a battery which filled the entire waist and divided the deck into two wells surrounded by bulwarks 7 ft. high. Of these wells, that forward from forecastle to battery bulkhead was only 85 ft., while the after one from battery to poop (50 ft.) served as the quarter deck.

The ship was conned from a charthouse and bridge spanning the quarter deck, but there was also a smaller bridge between the funnels which was afterwards enlarged for this purpose. A fore-and-aft bridge connected the upper battery and topgallant forecastle.

Below she had exceptional head room, with 10½ ft. between decks in the upper battery, 8½ ft. in the lower one, and 9 ft. along the main deck forward and 10½ ft. abaft it—considerably more than in the greatest ships of today. The messes forward were 11½ ft. high, well ventilated and well lit, but only measuring 65 ft. by 40 ft. owing to the set-in of the hull sides—which did not provide liberal room for 350 ratings. The lower deck was 7 ft. throughout.

Wardroom, gunroom and engineers' mess with most of the cabins were on the half deck, the Admiral's quarters and cabins of the principal officers being under the poop.

GUNS

The armament as originally planned was to have been twelve 10-in. 18-ton guns, but in 1876 it was decided that two 11-in. 25-tonners should be mounted forward in the upper battery with the port sills 17 ft. above water. These guns were made especially for the *Alexandra* and *Temeraire* and never appeared in any other capital ship. Thanks to Captain Scott's mountings these last broadside ships were therefore armed with weapons which a few years previously had been regarded as impossible to work except in a turret.

For the first time end-on fire became of primary importance in a central battery ship, the 11-in. guns being placed in the forward ports with training from dead ahead to only slightly abaft the beam. They fired 543-lb. shells with a charge of 85 lb. of pebble powder at a muzzle velocity of 1,320 ft. sec.—and were actually sighted for 10,000 yards! With a first-rate crew a maximum rate of two rounds in three minutes was recorded. The after guns were 10-in. trained from end-on to 5° before the beam, and fired a 406-lb. projectile with a charge of 70 lb. and m.v. of 1,380 ft. sec. A very smart crew could get off eleven rounds in twelve minutes with this gun, but an average rate of fire was one aimed round in a minute and a quarter.

The lower battery was separated by an armoured bulkhead into two compartments, the after one being a replica of that above it but with three ports a side for 10-in. guns; the forward one presented the corner ports with a 10-in. firing from dead ahead to 7° abaft the beam. In practice, training right ahead and astern caused too much damage to the ship's structure.

Six 20-pdr. Armstrongs were carried on top of the battery for saluting, which in 1884 were replaced by 4-in. B.L. with 25 lb. shells and Vavasseur mountings. At the same time ten 1-in. Nordenfelts firing a 1-lb. shot were placed along the upper works for torpedo defence.

MODERNIZATION

In 1889 after twelve years' unbroken service up the Straits the ship was taken in hand for partial conversion and four 9·2-in. B.L. replaced the guns in the upper battery. These fired a 380-lb. projectile only, but had double the rate of fire and twice the range of the M.L. guns. The Nordenfelts were also replaced by six 6-pdrs. and twelve 3-pdrs., the 4-in. being retained until 1897, when they were changed for 4·7-in. Q.F. Both Whitehead torpedoes and searchlights were recent inventions, and the *Alexandra* was the first battleship to carry them into the Mediterranean. Her twelve torpedoes were 16-in. diameter with a 60-lb. charge, a speed of 8 knots and a range of about 700 yards. They were fired by air impulse from open iron framework carriages on rollers through ordinary ports, two being on the main deck up forward and abaft the battery. After her first commission these very unreliable weapons were replaced by the 14-in. Mark II with only a 34-lb. charge but ranging 600 yards at 19 knots from a tube discharge.

Finally there were twelve 500-lb. mines—as carried by most of the battleships of that day—which could be fired by electrical contact.

ARMOUR

So far as defence was concerned, the *Alexandra* suffered less from the inherent demands of her type than might have been expected, and could claim to be the best protected ship in the Service after the three big turret-ships. The end-to-end belt 10½ ft. deep was 12 in. amidships thinning down through 10 in. to 6 in. at the ends. The lower battery had 12-in. sides with 8-in. bulkheads, but only 8 in. could be allowed above this for the heaviest guns in the ship. There was no conning tower until the reconstruction in 1890, and the upper battery served in lieu of this.

Some 65 ft. from the sternpost a 5-in. transverse bulkhead protected the magazine from raking shots below the waterline aft.

In common with all the central battery ships she suffered from having the guns immediately over the boilers so that there was no room for the magazines and shell rooms conveniently below them. Consequently the main magazine was abaft the engine room with the main shell room forward of the boilers, the ammunition from both having to be conveyed along the lower deck each side of the funnel and engine-room enclosures to the battery hoists; this meant keeping the watertight doors open in the intervening bulkheads.

MACHINERY

The trials of the *Devastation* having shown that she had been allowed an excess in machinery weight, the *Alexandra* was only given 8,000 h.p. instead of the 9,000 h.p. intended, which saved a matter of 175 tons. This was expended in thickening the upper battery armour from 6 in. to 8 in. with a general increase over the hull of 1 in.—and all without any detraction from the intended speed.

Although laid down and launched before the *Alexandra*, the *Dreadnought* did not hoist the pennant until two years after the broadside ship had entered service; hence the *Alexandra* can claim to be the first of H.M. battleships to take afloat vertical compound engines served by high-pressure cylindrical boilers acting at 60 lb. in place of

The *Alexandra* in 1900, with military rig, raised funnels, 9·2-in. guns in the upper battery, and 4·7-in. guns in shields amidships. This was her last appearance at sea, when she was to be flagship of the "B" fleet in the Manœuvres—a fitting end to a career marked by twelve years' service as flagship in the Mediterranean.

the 30-lb. rectangular pattern. Twelve of these were set back to back in two rows separated by a longitudinal bulkhead with the furnaces facing outwards opposite the doors of the central bunkers. Each engine drove an outward-turning Mangin screw of 21 ft. diameter. In addition to the main engines there were a pair of 600-h.p. auxiliaries for turning the screws when under sail in order to lessen their drag; and if necessary these engines could also move the ship at 4½ knots.

Special care was paid to ventilating arrangements, and apart from a more numerous array of cowls than usual the three masts were intended to act as air shafts and provided good uptakes, being fitted with stoppers to cut out draught in case of fire.

When completed for sea the *Alexandra* had a speed higher than any battleship afloat (or for ten years afterwards) and only three superiors in steaming endurance—the *Devastations*. At 66 revolutions on the Maplin mile she just exceeded 15 knots and could have done better in deep water. With full bunkers of 680 tons of coal some

3,800 miles could be covered at 7½ knots. As a steamer she once distinguished herself by towing a troop transport which had broken down on the way to Egypt at a good 12 knots—which was more than the transport ever did under her own power!

RIG

Being fitted with twin screws and able to cross the Atlantic under steam, there was no necessity for her to have been given masts and yards, but convention and prejudice decided that she should be heavily square rigged as a barque for the first twelve years of her service. The sail plan differed from the standards then in use in having considerably less hoist in proportion to spread so that she presented rather a squat appearance among her consorts. Masted on the second scale with the main truck 155 ft. above deck, she was sparred more heavily than ships like the *Achilles* on the first scale, the 53-ft. topmasts being only a foot longer than the topgallant yards, compared with the 65-ft. mast and 46-ft. yard in *Achilles*. The jibboom was 64 ft. from knightheads to point—the longest ever carried and unique in measuring more than her topmasts; but after the second commission this was removed as its gear occupied space on the topgallant forecastle required for the 3-pdrs. Excluding stunsails she could hoist 27,000 sq. ft. of canvas requiring 24 miles of rope rigging with a combined weight of spars, sails and rigging and spare gear of 150 tons.

At the best the *Alexandra* was a sluggish performer under canvas. Twin-screw ships suffered from the drag

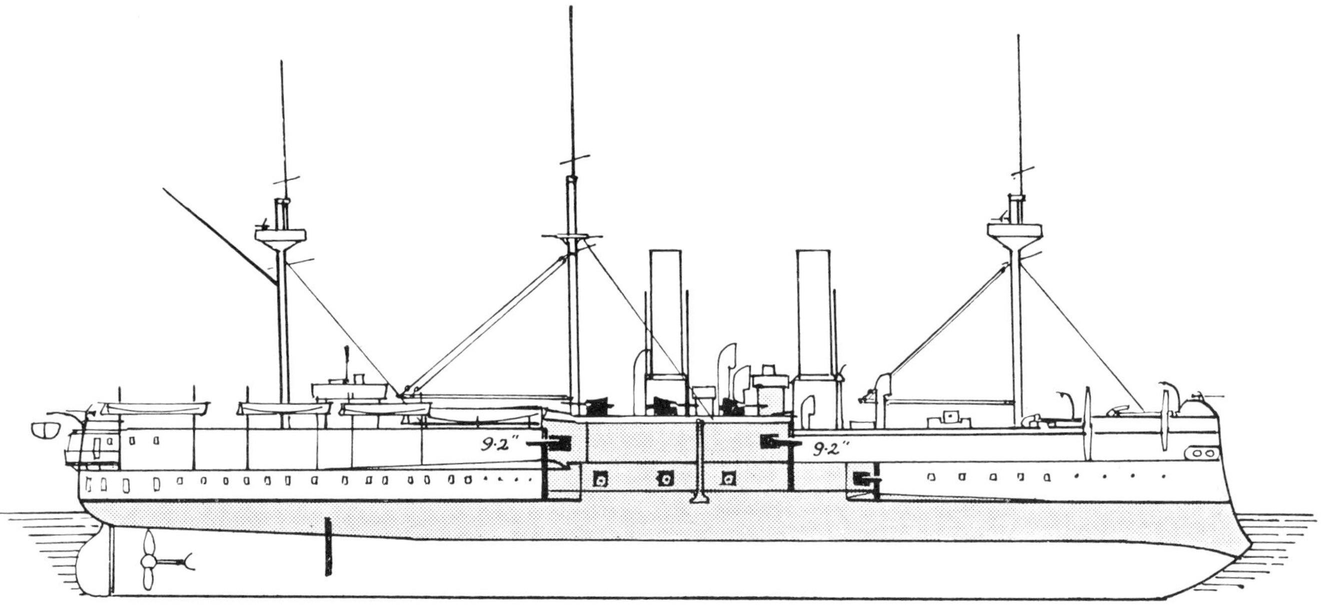

ALEXANDRA. Rearmed.

of propellers and tail shafts, and were too square in section to hold a lee; consequently, although easy to handle under sail, she never managed more than 6 knots.

SEA-GOING QUALITIES

As might be expected the embrasured hull was not kindly to the sea. When steaming into any sort of weather she was as wet forward as a half-tide rock, and it was quite impossible to drive her against a full gale. Her commander thus described her behaviour (R.U.S.I. March 1889):

> "Steaming in the *Alexandra* against a gale in really rough weather was one of the most fearful things I have ever witnessed. The seas would come in clean over the bows; the structure forward was not sufficient to keep them out, and great difficulty was experienced in getting the water off the ship afterwards."

Otherwise she was a good sea boat, and to the end of her service able to make a steady 13 knots and more when required.

ALTERATIONS

During 1889-90 when the 11-in. guns were replaced by 9·2-in. B.L. she was stripped of her canvas and reduced to pole topmasts. The lower masts were cut down to 63, 69 and 59 ft. respectively and fighting tops carrying

3-pdrs. fitted to the fore and mizen. For hoisting in boom boats, etc., a steam-worked derrick was fitted to the fore mast. The bridgework between the funnels was enlarged and a number of cowls proclaimed improved ventilation; new boilers were installed, and a 12-in. conning tower fitted between the funnels.

In May 1897 three 4·7-in. Q.F. a side replaced the 4-in. B.L. over the battery, and the following year the funnels were raised, the extra draught enabling her to keep her speed to the end.

GENERAL

Fitted with experimental wireless telegraphy for 1899 manœuvres—the first warship to carry it—and as senior ship in the Mediterranean a peak of perfection in white enamel, polish and burnished equipment was attained which became a byword in the Service.

With the passing of this the last and finest of our broadside ironclads, a definite fleet link with the *Warrior* was severed.

For twenty-three years she had served as flagship, and when leading the line of her low freeboard squadron in 1900 she had an opportunity of showing her sea-going qualities to every advantage, providing a happy memory for those who loved a noble ship.

"ALEXANDRA"

Commissioned at Chatham 2 January '77 as flagship Mediterranean which exalted duty she performed until '89 without leaving the station. In '78 Vice-Admiral Hornby led his fleet consisting of the *Agincourt*, *Achilles*, *Swiftsure*, *Temeraire* and *Sultan* through the Dardanelles—cleared for action and with the upper spars sent down, entering the straits at daybreak in the teeth of blinding snowstorm and gale from the eastward. Owing to her davits being turned inboard the compass was affected and the *Alexandra* grounded on a shoal just below the narrowest part of the strait. The *Sultan* was detained to assist her while the rest of the squadron proceeded to Gallipoli and she was got afloat in time to anchor off Nagara that night, and to appear at the head of the squadron off Constantinople on the morning of February 15th. Collision with *Achilles* during squadron tactics. In '82 for the bombardment of Alexandria the flag was shifted to *Invincible* as having lighter draught; she fired 48 11-in. and 221 10-in. shells and received 24 holes above her plating but no serious injury. For her fourth commission in 1886 the Duke of Edinburgh hoisted his flag and Prince George of Wales, afterwards King George V, joined as a watch-keeping lieutenant. In June '89 she was paid off at Chatham for modernization and in '91 became flagship of Reserves at Portland. In February '92 appointed coastguard ship at Portland and so served until April '01—her last spell at sea being as flagship of the "B" fleet in the 1900 manœuvres. Thereafter her rating was reduced to third-class battleship and she joined the Fleet Reserve at Chatham, being relegated to Dockyard Reserve in April '03 as mechanical training ship for seamen.

Sold October '08 for £21,750.

"TEMERAIRE"

Builder	*Laid down*	*Launched*	*Completed*	*Cost*
Chatham	18 Aug. '73	9 May '76	31 Aug. '77	£489,822

Dimensions 285′ × 62′ × 26·8′/27·2′ = 8,540 tons.
Hull and armour 5,730 tons. Equipment 2,810 tons.

Armament 4 11-in. 25-ton guns.
4 10-in. 18-ton guns.
6 20-pdrs. (replaced later by 6 4-in. B.L.).
2 Torpedo projectors.

Armour Belt 11″-9″-6″-5½″; barbettes 10″ fore, 8″ after; battery 8″; bulkheads 8″-5″; deck 1½″-1″; backing 12″-10″; skin 1½″.
Total 1,900 tons.

Complement 531/580.

Coal 400/620 tons.

Sail area 25,000 sq. ft.

Machinery Humphreys and Tennant: 2 cyl. comp. vert. inverted.
I.H.P. 7,520 = 14·65 knots.
H.P. cyl. 70″, L.P. cyl. 114″; stroke 46″; revs. 70.
2 Griffiths screws; 20′ diam.
12 boilers in four sets; 60 lb. pressure (tested to 120 lb.).
30 other steam engines.

Points of interest:

(1) The first barbette ship in the Navy.
(2) The tubbiest of the broadside models.
(3) The largest brig ever built. Had the longest lower yards ever carried in a British ship.

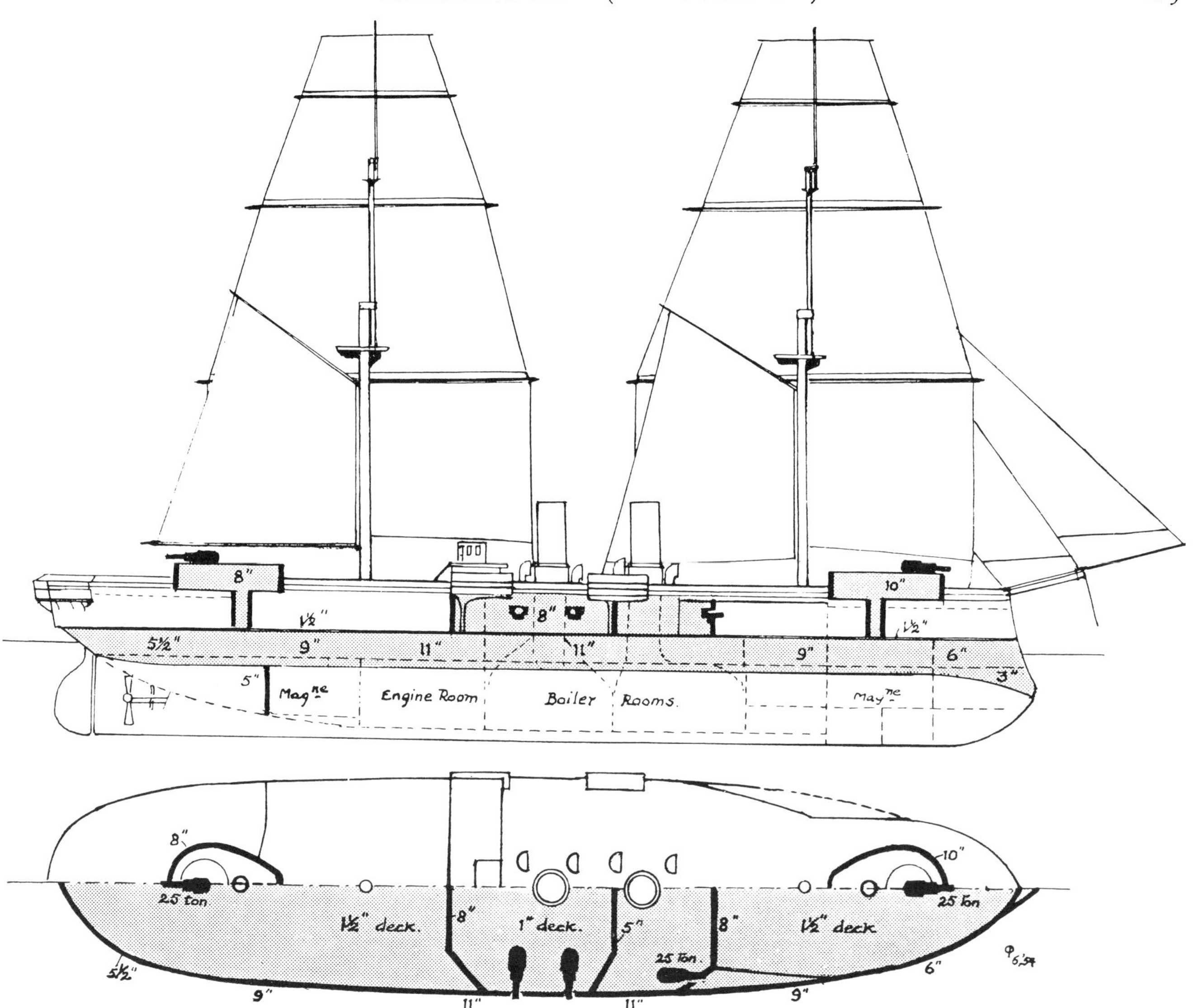

The "Great Brig" *Temeraire.* Compare the height of her masts and width of her spars with those of the *Alexandra.* The foresail was the largest unit of canvas ever stitched in an Admiralty sail loft. Her 11-in. guns are shown peeping over the barbettes in the firing position, but normally were lowered inside them.

Soon after the *Alexandra* was commenced, the keei of a second battleship was laid down on an adjoining slip at Chatham—where the big frigate *Raleigh* was already under way. The Eastern yard was thus greatly favoured at the expense of Portsmouth, where only the *Shah* (frigate) was building, Devonport being still restricted to small ship construction.

The *Temeraire* ranks in a class by herself, having been designed to carry an experimental system of mounting the largest guns which, though satisfactory, proved uneconomical and was never repeated.

She came into being as the direct result of a Minority Report by two members of the Committee on Designs, Admirals Elliot and Ryder, which set out alternative designs for all types of warships under construction or planned for that period (1871), based upon a system of armament in which two or more heavy guns were mounted inside armoured towers on the centre-line in conjunction with a number of smaller unprotected pieces.

The proposed ships were all of high freeboard, and the big guns ranging from 25 to 50 tons were to be mounted upon a special revolving and inclined carriage designed by Captain Scott, R.N., which allowed them to be hydraulically raised above the edge of the tower for firing and nested in it for loading.

Instead of duplicating the *Alexandra* the Board decided to give this system a trial, the *Temeraire* being designed as a broadside ship on the Reed model with two of her heavy guns in towers instead of in an upper deck battery. In the original sketch plan the proposed length was 320 ft. with 60 ft. beam, which closely approximated to the dimensions of the *Hercules* and *Sultan*, then accepted as model hulls. Later a preference to quicker turning then preferred for ramming tactics led to 40 ft. being lopped off forward, so that she became a little shorter than the *Devastation* with a proportion of length to beam of 4·6 to 1—the lowest of any of the broadside ships.

In order to keep down freeboard in view of the barbettes, the arrangement of the forecastle and poop was peculiar. Instead of being at full height for entrance at upper deck level these rose barely 4 ft. and were entered by short steps leading down to the doors. The height of the bulwarks was also curtailed and instead of being 6-7 ft. were only 4 ft., making it easy to see outboard all round but affording less shelter against wind and sea. Having no upper deck battery she was spared the handicap of cramped deck space, and with the barbettes placed well up to the bow and stern, the guns had clear arcs of fire, and to this extent the *Temeraire* conformed to Reed's idea of a rigged turret ship. But such barbettes naturally weighed considerably less than revolving turrets (with their armoured bases) which could not have been carried at anything like the same height above water.

There was no conning tower, the ship being worked from a bridge abaft the funnels.

To prevent fouling the hull was sheathed with wood and copper as an alternative to zinc, which had proved of no value in the *Audacious*.

In the matter of accommodation the *Temeraire* ranked high above the earlier broadside ships with their lower

A photograph taken in 1881 in the Mediterranean with *Temeraire* in the foreground, *Invincible* beyond her, and *Monarch* in the distance. The *Temeraire* shared with the *Alexandra* the distinction of being the only rigged battleships on the station to be painted white. The embrasured port for the broadside 11-in gun can be seen beneath the forward funnel.

deck cabins, as she provided main deck living quarters for all ranks and ratings except the captain, commander and chaplain, whose cabins were under the poop. The wardroom was moved to the stern above the counter as in the wooden ships-of-the-line, with a few cabins opening out of it on one side and a full row of square ports on the other side and aft. The remaining cabins and gun-room, engineers' and warrant-officers' messes stood on the spacious half deck, each with a square port opening outwards and backed by a sliding glass sash. But bathrooms had still to be introduced and smoking was restricted to the half deck, wardroom officers using the starboard side and all others the port.

The forward mess deck lay between the bows and the battery and was better than in the majority of vessels as to light, space, head room and ventilation.

ARMAMENT

With the *Alexandra* she shared the distinction of carrying 11-in. guns, and her outstanding feature lay in two of these being mounted in barbettes with disappearing mountings. This system was originated by Captain Eades of St. Louis, U.S.A., in 1861 for the *Winnebago* class of monitors which he built for the Federal Mississippi service, in which steam power worked the guns. Steam had been replaced by compressed air and water in the Moncrieff mounting for coast-defence guns, which in turn gave way to hydraulic power in the Rendel adaptation for the *Temeraire*.

The system offered complete and continuous protection both for the gun's crew and the gun whilst it was being loaded, and so differed radically from the French type of barbette in which the guns were mounted clear of the rim and were fully exposed together with the crews. This was considered an advantage over closed turrets as the target could be seen more clearly and the "freedom and morale of the gunners better assured." So long as big guns only had to be faced this argument might be advanced; but when the *Nordenfelt* gun came along and crews could be swept down at the close ranges then accepted for battle, then the French had to fit domed shields to rotate with the gun. This barbette-shield combination was the precursor of our present-day barbette-turrets, but it was to be many years before their adoption in our Navy.

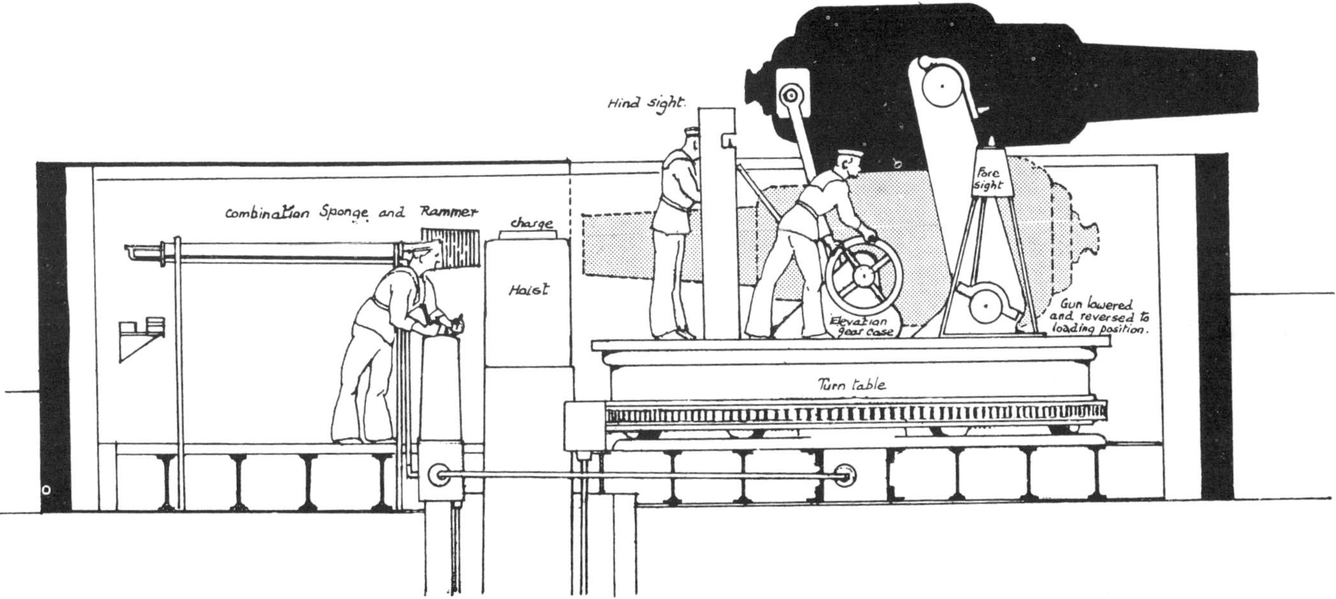

Longitudinal section of the *Temeraire's* barbettes with the gun raised for firing in the fore-and-aft line, or (in lighter shade) lowered for loading.

Since the scale will not allow for full details of the hydraulic mechanism, only the valve-box and main pressure pipes are shown; some other minor details are also omitted.

The ammunition hoist is shown as up for loading with the upper chamber of the carrier holding the powder charge. The dotted line in the covered part of the barbette shows the position of the hand turning gear which could be rigged in case of a breakdown in the engine. Hand loading was also possible but slow.

The figures are shown at the stations in which the gun could be handled by a crew of three. One is at the gunlayer's position, one at the right-hand elevation wheel and one at the control levers whereby the gun was loaded, raised or lowered, and turned, and the ammunition hoist moved up or down; a full crew numbered six, but merely duplicated these duties. As the mounting was unique in the navy, the drill was never included in any book issued to the fleet, but was left to the Gunnery Lieutenant and Commanding Officer.

The barbettes were pear-shaped and 9½ ft. deep, rising about 4 ft. above deck and measuring 33 ft. fore and aft and 21½ ft. across. The shape was necessary to allow both for the gun to rest in the wide end and when loading, with the hydraulic rammer, almost as long as its bore, to lie opposite its muzzle in the narrower part. This narrow end was roofed over with iron sheeting. On the floor of the wider end was a massive hollow turntable rotated by hydraulic presses attached to it and bearing the mounting and gun. This was raised and lowered by elbowed levers of which the heads were attached to the trunnions, the elbows to bearings on the platform, and the lower ends to the hydraulic presses. The raising and lowering of the gun, the ammunition hoist, the rammer, and rotation of the platform were operated from a cased stand of four control levers placed just behind the hoist. When trained on the target the gun was laid for elevation by a bar connection on each side of the breech to elevation arcs, graduated in degrees and enclosed in gear cases on the turntable, with a double gearing operated by a hand wheel. The foresights were on tall tripod stands beside the trunnion arms, with the hind sights in 6-ft. rifle-proof shields to the rear of the breech occupied by the gun-layer and officer of the barbette. When the gun-layer had set his sight for range and alignment it automatically indicated the correct elevation for the gun, which he read off and passed to the two numbers at the elevating wheels. Firing was by a hand battery or ordinary lanyard and friction tube. Six numbers formed the full crew, although three could keep the gun in action. Each barbette could train through 240°.

The gun always sank to the same plane of 3° inclination for loading with its muzzle pointing towards a port in the narrow end to which powder and shot were brought up by a two-part hydraulic lift and forced home in turn by the hydraulic rammer. The hydraulic engines were below the waterline. An aimed round could be fired in 1¾ minutes, and Admiral Ballard thus described the whole operation:

> "The mechanism worked without a hitch and almost without a sound. It was interesting to watch from an outside observer's standpoint. At first nothing was to be seen but the surrounding parapet; then quite silently except for a slight hissing, the gun would suddenly appear coming up from inside and swinging round simultaneously towards the target, in a fashion rather suggestive of an elephant getting on its legs, and turning to make a charge. It checked and steadied, while the gun-layer passed the degrees of elevation, and got the reply 'Elevation correct.' A momentary pause followed and then came the full-toned bellow of an old-fashioned muzzle-loader using pebble powder, as it sent the shell away—easily seen in flight when clear of an immense cloud of white smoke—while the hydraulic buffers in the raising mechanism checked the recoil. And almost immediately the gun was turning back and sinking down all in a combined movement to the loading position. In a few seconds it had totally disappeared."

But although the system was entirely satisfactory so far as shooting was concerned, it was too uneconomical in space and weight to justify further employment. For while the *Dreadnought's* turrets of 32½ ft. diameter could accommodate two 38-ton guns, the 33 ft. of the *Temeraire's* towers housed one 25-tonner only and so quite precluded such barbettes being used for larger weapons. Thus an excellent system for coast-defence guns where space and weight are of no consequence was never again seen afloat, and the *Temeraire's* officers and men had the handling of a method of gun service unique in sea history.

So much for the *Temeraire's* most interesting weapons. The bulk of her armament was carried in an octagonal central battery bulkheaded off into a fore and after part. The first contained another pair of 11-in. 25-tonners mounted on iron broadside carriages and slides and served by hand, with a crew of seventeen and two powdermen. Deeply embrasured ports gave an arc of fire from right ahead to abeam. The after part housed four 10-in. of 18 tons in pairs on the broadside firing of a 400 lb. shell with a 70 lb. charge, the mountings being similar but lighter. As completed an anti-torpedo battery of four 20-pdr. Armstrongs on wooden chock carriages were at ports in the waist and quarter deck, but after her first commission these were replaced by six 4-in. 25-pdrs. B.L. on Vavasseur mountings (1884) with a dozen 6-pdrs., quick-firers and Nordenfelts ranged along the bulwarks added in 1880. Two torpedo carriages ejecting Whiteheads by air impulse fired through ports abaft the battery, the *Temeraire* being the third British battleship to include torpedoes in her armament.

When the entire battery of four 10-in. and four 11-in. went into action 138 men were needed to keep up the ammunition supply, so that each gun required as many men to feed it as to fight it. Watertight doors in two bulkheads had to be opened to supply shell from the shell-room to the 11-in. guns in the fore battery and the doors in one bulkhead to supply powder—or else powder and shell had to be sent via the upper deck.

Incidentally it may be noted that nearly all the ships at the bombardment of Alexandria suffered minor damage caused by their guns, and the *Temeraire* more than most. Her after barbette gun could not be trained on any bearing whatever without damage to the fittings and bulkheads under the poop, so quarterly practice with the gun's crew was carried out in the fore barbette for three out of the annual four firings.

Although over 1,000 tons smaller than the *Alexandra*, the *Temeraire's* gun-fire concentration was considered to be but little inferior while enjoying greater accuracy and freedom of range. Upon broad arcs the armaments were:

	Alexandra		*Temeraire*	
Ahead	2 25-ton 2 18 ,,	1,898 lb.	3 25-ton	1,629 lb.
Abeam	1 25 ,, 5 18 ,,	2,573 ,,	2 25 ,, 2 18 ,,	1,898 ,,
Astern	2 18 ,,	812 ,,	1 25 ,,	543 ,,

ARMOUR

The *Temeraire* was the last ship to be designed and built for the British Navy during the next twenty years to have a complete waterline belt. Curiously enough textbooks and descriptions of the ship all credit her with 11 in. amidships and 10 in. at the ends—a girdling of quite impossible generosity towards the bows and stern. Actually the 11 in. amidships thinned down through 9 in. to 6 in. forward and 5½ in. aft with 3 in. taken down over the ram. This served as a bulkhead to the fore magazine, the after one having a below water 5-in. bulkhead beneath the barbette. The battery surrounded by 8-in. armour and divided by a 5-in. bulkhead formed the only patch of protection along the main deck. Along the top of the battery lay a 1-in. deck with 1½-in. beyond it over the belt to the bows and stern.

The two barbettes were unequal in thickness, that forward being 10 in. with only 8 in. on the after one; the hoists ran up armoured tubes.

MACHINERY

As in the *Alexandra* the machinery was of the vertical compound type, but owing to lack of space there were only two cylinders in each set—a 70-in. h.p. and 114-in. l.p. For the first time wrought iron, brass and steel entered into the construction of machinery in place of cast iron only, and in their day the engine rooms of the *Temeraire* were show places.

A central longitudinal bulkhead with athwartships screens divided the boiler rooms into four sets each containing three boilers with a working pressure of 60 lb. tested to 120 lb.

Running light over the Stokes Bay mile she made 14·65 knots with an I.H.P. of 7,697 and a coal consumption of 2¼ lb. per h.p. per hour—which was low considering that the furnaces had been pressed to the full regardless of economy. A twelve-hour full-speed trial at sea showed her mean speed to be between 13 and 14 knots, but exceeding 14 knots in smooth water.

Unlike the *Alexandra* she had Griffiths two-bladed screws which gave excellent results for the power indicated and, compared with the four-bladed pattern, caused a minimum of drag under sail.

For auxiliary machinery she carried a steam steering engine and steam capstan, plus twenty-eight starting, pumping, ventilating, hoisting and generating engines. With 620 tons of coal in her bunkers compound engines gave her a steaming radius of nearly twice that of the older battleships of her size, so that the provision of sail was superfluous. But so strong was the influence of Service custom that the usual sacrifices in design had been made so that she might carry a full dressing of canvas, and in this lay the *Temeraire's* second claim to distinction—the "Great Brig."

SAIL

To avoid interference with fire from the after barbette the mizen was deleted, and an outsize in brig rig planned to make up for the deficiency. As such she became the largest vessel ever handled under two masts. In her height of 169 ft. from main truck to deck she was exceeded by the *Warrior*, *Black Prince* and *Achilles* (all 175 ft.) and *Hercules* (177 ft.), but in spread she outreached them all. Her fore and main yards measured 115 ft., that being 8 ft. more than the main yard of the *Victory*, 1 ft. more than that of the *Marlborough* and 6 ft. longer than those in the *Warrior* group, being the biggest spars ever crossed in a British ship. Her topsail (78 ft.) and upper yards equalled those on the *Marlborough's* main mast and—except for the *Alexandra's*—were by 4 ft. the longest in the British service (78 ft.). The foresail was the largest unit of canvas ever stitched in an Admiralty sail loft, containing 5,100 ft. and weighing 2 tons; and her main trysail the largest ever on a gaff head (49 ft.), with 3,200 sq. ft. before stretching.

All her spars were wooden except the iron lower masts, and on account of the barbette the bowsprit had to run in on the main deck instead of the topgallant forecastle, so that in a head sea, water used to come aboard through the bowsprit hole.

Despite such a wind-trap up aloft the *Temeraire* was a sluggard under sail, but—because of her dimensions—amongst the handiest in the fleet. On one occasion Captain Gerard Noel sailed her up the five-mile length of Suda Bay in fourteen tacks (May 1891).

> "The wind was steady, but dead foul and too squally for carrying royals. Engines were stopped at the entrance and sail made on the starboard tack shortly before one o'clock to begin the long beat up that lasted till six; during which those enormous yards were boxed fourteen times through the full round of their swing, with all the attendant business on tacks, sheets, bowlines, weather braces, lifts and trusses. The rest of the fleet (all 'mastless' turret ships) had arrived in the morning and everyone who had not already gone ashore was watching the *Temeraire*, including the Admiral. She presented a spectacular finish to the centuries of such movement under the pennants of the British Mediterranean command, which was talked of for many years after on that station" (Ballard).

But the Board's efforts to perpetuate sail were far from being appreciated by her first inspecting Admiral, who wrote, "The masts are too heavy and seriously compromise her fighting efficiency; the foremast would easily be brought down and should be a tripod; the bowsprit should be removed"; and in 1881 criticism was more severe; "She should be dismasted except for a military mast aft fitted with a fighting top and a Gatling gun, and she should have a proper conning tower." In dealing with these reports Barnaby wrote somewhat naïvely to the Controller: "If the rig is now reduced there will be no compensation for the sacrifices in guns and armour which were made to secure it."

SEA-GOING QUALITIES

Reports state that "she steered and stayed well, and wore very well in 8 mins. under sail in a moderate sea." In a seaway she behaved properly and was described as unusually steady so that the barbette guns could always be worked, although the forward battery ports might have to be kept closed. In bad weather there were occasions when in the Channel Fleet only the *Monarch* and *Temeraire* could have fired a gun.

But the curtailment of her length up forward from the original plan shifted the centre of gravity of her armament and armour with a consequent tendency to force her down by the head. Her ship's book recounts that her pitching was slow and very deep with a tendency to hang in an unusual manner at the bottom of her plunge, which at first "was very startling to the officers and men." When full of coal and drawing 28 ft. forward her first Captain considered that she was overweighted at the bows and could not face the conventional Atlantic gale.

The *Temeraire* in the Hamoaze when relegated to Fleet Reserve. Stripped of her yards with a steam hoist to her boat boom, and raised funnels all resemblance to the "Great Brig" had vanished. Lined up in the *Indus* establishment she lay minus main mast and after funnel, and as *Akbar* at Invergordon she was a funnelless and mastless hulk.

Actually her behaviour in one was seen to be not in the least dangerous, and Barnaby explained "that the motion was slower than they had been accustomed to owing to the distribution of weights," and that at normal draught she was designed to trim 6 in. by the stern; while the alterations proposed by her Captain, such as shifting the anchors further aft, would have little effect. Instructions were issued that excess of coal should not be carried in the bow bunkers.

GENERAL

In 1899 she was dismantled aloft and given light signal yards only, being denied the military rig which afforded some sort of "modernized" appearance to the *Sultan*, *Hercules*, *Neptune*, etc.; with tall funnels and a short make-believe bowsprit she became a nondescript-looking craft easily distinguishable for what she was, although bearing little semblance to the "Great Brig," and for years lay up the Hamoaze, her sea time finished.

Although often referred to as the "Happy Brig," the sobriquet was not altogether complimentary, having been earned during the period she was commanded by Captain Gerard Noel, when at one time under various counts, all, or nearly all, her wardroom officers had managed to get themselves put under arrest.

"TEMERAIRE"

Commissioned at Chatham August '77 for the Mediterranean, where she served for the next fourteen years excepting for a short spell during the winter of 1887-88 when she was in the Channel Squadron. Was one of Admiral Hornby's squadron which forced the Dardanelles in a blinding snowstorm in '78. Retained in the vicinity of Constantinople for the next twelve months, then assisted in taking Cyprus from the Turks and ended her first commission in Malta in '81. Took a prominent part in the bombardment of Alexandria on 11 July '82 when she silenced Fort Mex, shared Fort Pharos with the *Inflexible* and assisted with Fort Moncrieff. Fired 136 11-in. and 84 10-in. shells, her shooting being favourably commented upon by observing U.S. officers. Recommissioned at Malta 1884 and some of her crew took part in the desert fighting at Tel-el-Kebir and Abu-Klea. For some months was station flagship of H.R.H. the Duke of Edinburgh. Paid off at Portsmouth '87 and joined the Channel Squadron for a few months; then returned to the Mediterranean for her three last years of her active service (rammed by the *Orion* when ordered to exchange stations in their respective columns during manœuvres. Struck abreast engine room ripping outer skin and flooding a wing compartment).

Paid off at Devonport June '91. Reserve Fleet until May '93 when she went into the Fleet Reserve. Relegated to Dockyard Reserve in November '01 and next year became depot ship for the Fleet Reserve. Converted by Palmers into a machinery workshop 1904-06 and formed part of *Indus* establishment until 1915 when her name was changed to *Akbar* and she was transferred to Liverpool as a reformatory ship. During the war she served as a depot ship at Invergordon.

In May 1921, forty-four years after she first steamed down the Medway, she was sold for £5,725.

With the laying-down of the *Alexandra* and *Temeraire* what may be regarded as the second phase of the first period of the Barnaby era came to an end. So far the dictates of the Board had allowed but little scope for individuality in design, although the ships stand out as the most popular and successful he ever produced. From now onwards the huge weapons Armstrong had prepared to supply in 1871 became available for shipboard and the former balance between guns and armour changed to the great advantage of the gun. A new system of protection had to be evolved to counteract this, and with the employment of that system in a modified degree the first typical Barnaby ship, the *Shannon*, came into being.

Chapter 36

THE "DARK AGES" OF THE VICTORIAN NAVY

THE ten years following the laying-down of the *Alexandra* and *Temeraire* may well be called the "dark ages" of the Victorian Navy. For six years the Conservatives under Disraeli were in power, during which time the Service was openly neglected. For his first year in office the First Lord was Mr. Ward Hunt, who although anxious to do his best for the Service proved quite unable to make any stand against Disraeli's policy of drastic naval economy, and may well be remembered as our most ineffective naval administrator. In the House he was mainly concerned with an Agricultural Bill and discussions on guano, but was a sick man most of his term of office and died in 1877. The naval portfolio then went to Mr. W. H. Smith, who served until May 1880.

Although the cost of individual ships was rising rapidly, the Estimates were kept at round about £11 millions, and our administration was mainly a matter of waste and reckless economy which might well have succeeded in endangering the peaceful security of the Empire. In Admiral Hornby's opinion.

> "We have ships without speed, guns without range, and boilers with only a few months' life in them. This is called economy, but it is really only not spending money, closing the purse strings, and keeping our Fleet in such a state of inefficiency and unpreparedness as to render it comparatively useless should we at any time become involved in war with a Maritime Power."

New construction was reduced to five armoured ships in five years. Of these the *Inflexible* was commenced in 1874 with pæans of laudatory comment which afterwards changed to critical apprehension when her stability in action was questioned. Having produced her, the Board became more concerned about reduction in displacement, thus limiting the liability of battleship tonnage being lost through torpedo attack than in adding to the number of capital ships, and turned to cheaper diminutives, the *Ajax* and *Agamemnon*, as a solution to their difficulties two years later.

These three ships, together with the *Nelson* and *Northampton*, represented the sum total of the additions to our armoured strength until 1878, when the Russian war scare led to the purchase of the *Orion*, *Belleisle*, *Superb* and *Neptune* from Turkey and Brazil.

But apart from the parsimonious attitude of the Treasury some excuse for the lack of stronger action on the part of the Board may be found in the general tendency to question whether the big battleship could still be regarded as the foundation of naval strength. With her very status under question and every element of her being—gun-power, armour, speed and size—subjects for the keenest controversy, it is not surprising that the Admiralty were constrained towards a policy of delay and caution while its mind was being made up. Which may be construed either as a sound conservative outlook or as the opportunism of incompetency.

In assessing this attitude of mind it must be remembered that the essentials of naval policy, strategy, tactics and ship design were not yet regarded as a matter for close study or experiment. Our naval needs had never been properly formulated; there was no department charged with either the study of attack and defence, naval intelligence, or defence of our seaborn trade; naval manœuvres were unknown; and no large-scale experimental tests were ever carried out.

Writing in 1871 in the *Royal United Service Institute Journal* on the "Attack and Defence of Fleets," Captain P. H. Colomb stated:

> "If I were to make the assertion that the designs of our ships arise more out of instinct and tradition than out of any comprehension of how they are liable to attack and how they are capable of defence, I should raise a feeling of incredulous surprise. . . . You would be constrained to rely on the general proposition that the ships were designed to use their guns and perhaps their rams for attack; and their armour for defence against guns. Beyond this you could not go."

But if instinct and tradition served well enough until 1871, the need for a sounder basis of opinion and decision became increasingly evident in the subsequent years. Guns were continually increasing in size and power; iron armour in moderate thickness provided poor protection for the close-quarter fighting still accepted for battle owing to the low standard of shooting and slow rate of fire common to all fleets; the torpedo was developing into a weapon which had to be taken into account, although still relatively feeble and inaccurate in practice; and the ram was coming more and more into favour for fleet work as suitable tactics were being evolved. Nothing approaching any basic conception as to the most efficient form of battleship design for British requirements had as yet been formulated. During the 'seventies armoured additions to the Fleet included:

(1) Breastwork monitors
(2) A masted turret ship (purchased)

(3) A two-storey central battery ship
(4) A central battery ship with barbettes
(5) Casemate ships (purchased)
(6) A one-deck battery broadside ship (purchased)
(7) Citadel turret ships
(8) Small redoubt single turret ships
(9) Partially belted broadside ships

none of which offered any solution for the difficulties to be met as regards gun calibres, protection and disposition of armament. Opinion was sharply divided as to whether a few large guns were preferable to a number of smaller ones; whether medium armour and fewer guns was better than an overwhelming offence with limited waterline protection; whether the French high freeboard was preferable to the medium or low freeboard we affected; or even whether a host of torpedo craft, and gunboats carrying heavy artillery, should be the reply to battleships.

With regard to the use of the ram, Captain Philip Colomb has shown (1) that the best method of attack was not straightforward charging at the enemy, but in manœuvre which brought the ram inside the turning circle of the opponent while keeping him outside its own. (2) That the approach should be at least 4° off the bow so that gun-fire with its resulting cloud of thick smoke did not obscure vision; and (3) that speed was not of so much consequence as ability for quick manœuvre and determination to press home the attack.

And in addition to all the other problems besetting the design, there was the damned, but not yet dead, influence of sail power which might descend like a blight upon any projected warship to the vast detriment of her efficiency. Both the *Alexandra* and *Temeraire* had suffered big sacrifices in guns and armour for the sake of masts and yards, which by the most simple calculations were shown to be a useless economy in motive power.

Even in the case of small ships, careful records showed that the weight of masts and yards, if translated into bunkerage with hulls designed for speed and stability under steam, made for a far more efficient and economical fighting unit than when the conflicting demands of steam and sail—with the retarding influence of rigging in a head wind—had to be allowed for.

But "Tradition" died a lingering death in Whitehall. During 1876 a sail-minded Admiralty spent £113,000 on coal and £123,000 on raw hemp, canvas and the like, and the *Shannon*, *Nelson*, *Northampton* and *Inflexible* were still to cross royal yards before the captain of the *Imperieuse* came to write the death warrant which led to the replacement of spars and cross-trees by signalling yards and fighting tops.

* * * * * * *

Meanwhile the French had pushed ahead with their first and second-class ironclads, coast defence and harbour defence ships until they were equal if not superior to us both in numbers and tabulated gun power. By 1878 the ships completed for England, France and Russia, subsequent to the list for 1865, were:

England		France		Russia
A	B	*A*	B	*A*
Thunderer	*Scorpion*	*Colbert*	*Tonnere*	*Pedr Veliky*
Devastation	*Wivern*	*Trident*		*Minin*
Dreadnought	*Glatton*	*Richelieu*		*Kniaz Pojarski*
Alexandra	*Hotspur*	*Marengo*		*Pervenetz*
Temeraire	*Rupert*	*Ocean*		*Kreml*
Sultan	*Cyclops*	*Suffren*		*Netron Menia*
Audacious	*Hecate*	*La Galissonniere*		*General Admiral*
Invincible	*Hydra*	*Victorieuse*		*Gerzog Edinbourski*
Iron Duke	*Gorgon*	*Triomphante*		
Vanguard		*Redoubtable*	C	B
Swiftsure		*Alma*	*Onandaga*	*Ad. Lazareff*
Triumph		*Armide*	*Belier*	*Ad. Grieg*
Shannon		*Atalante*	*Bouldogue*	*Ad. Chichagoff*
		Jeanne D'Arc	*Tigre*	*Ad. Spiridoff*
		Montcalm		
		Thetis		C
				Tcharodika
				Smertch
				9 small monitors

A=Sea-going. *B*=Coast defence. *C*=Harbour defence.

Although this counting of heads shows us at a considerable numerical disadvantage, the position was actually very different. Individually the French ships were smaller than ours with wooden hulls, inferior protection, and lacking watertight subdivision; their general weight of armament was lighter, and although armed with breech-loaders these did not confer any advantage in offensive power. The Russians made a good show on paper and were rated as battle-worthy in the absence of definite information to the contrary, but really were full of defects and would have been of little consequence as fighting ships. Hence our position was not as dangerous as comparative tables would indicate, although this was hardly appreciated at the time.

Subsequent to the construction of these ships, the following were laid down:

	England		France	
1874	*Nelson*	7,630 tons	*Fulminant* (c)	5,574 tons
	Northampton	7,630 „	*Tempete* (c)	4,523 „
	Inflexible	11,880 „		
1875	Nil		*Vengeur* (c)	4,523 „
1876	*Ajax*	8,660 „	*Turenne*	6,400 „
	Agamemnon	8,660 „	*Bayard*	5,881 „
			Devastation	10,200 „
			Courbet	10,200 „
1877	(Nil)		*Admiral Duperre*	11,100 „
			Tonnant (c)	4,707 „
			Furieux (c)	5,560 „
1878	*Neptune*	9,310 „	*Terrible*	7,200 „
	Superb	9,170 „	*Requin*	7,200 „
	Belleisle (c)	4,870 „	*Indomitable*	7,200 „
	Orion (c)	4,870 „	*Caiman*	7,200 „
1879	*Colossus*	9,420 „	*Duguesclin*	5,869 „
	Edinburgh	9,420 „	*Formidable*	11,441 „
	Conqueror (c)	6,200 „	*Admiral Baudin*	11,380 „
			Vauban	5,900 „
	12 ships	97,620 „	18 ships	132,458 „

(*c*) Coast Defence ships.

During the period 1874-9 the French ships were built of iron and generally had heavier armaments than ours. The above series of reduced British programmes enabled the Tricolour to fly level with the White Ensign, and by 1880 the British Navy could no longer claim even a "One-Power Standard!"

THE "SHAH" AND "HUASCAR" ACTION

29 May 1877

This action between two British unarmoured ships and the most notorious ironclad of her day may be mentioned because it was the first occasion on which a Whitehead torpedo was used in actual war, while the poor shooting and its negligible results give a fair idea of the marksmanship of the period and the failure of our guns to achieve anything like the armour penetration registered on the proving ground.

In May 1877 one Nicholas de Pierola, leader of the defeated party in a Peruvian revolution, seized the little turret ship *Huascar* as she lay in Callao harbour and proceeded to steam up and down the coast bombarding such towns as refused to pay ransom and molested several British ships. As the Peruvian Government disclaimed all responsibility for such piratical behaviour Rear-Admiral de Horsey, in command on the Station, decided to compel her surrender.

The *Huascar*, built by Lairds in 1865, was a 1,130-ton, 10-knot, low freeboard single turret ship carrying two 10-in. Armstrong M.L.R. throwing a 300-lb. projectile, two 40 pdrs., and one 12 pdr. Her turret armour was 5½ in. on 14-in. teak, with 4½ in.-2½ in. along her sides. Freeboard was 4½ ft. only and her bows were specially strengthened for ramming.

Admiral de Horsey's flagship was the *Shah*, one of Reed's three big unarmoured frigates carrying an exceptionally heavy armament, with a trial speed of 16·4 knots. She carried two 9-in. 12-ton M.L.R. (capable of piercing 9½ in. of iron at 1,000 yards) on upper deck pivots, eight 7-in. (7½-in. iron at 1,000 yards) on each side, and eight 64 pdrs. of no account against armour.

The corvette *Amethyst*, of 1,970 tons, was armed with fourteen 64 pdrs.

As the *Huascar* drew only 14 ft. against the *Shah's* 27 ft., she tried to reach shoal water off Ylo, but the *Amethyst* managed to prevent this and fire was opened at 1,000 yards range at 3 p.m. With the *Shah* steaming to and fro the *Huascar's* gunners could not hit her, although such manœuvring prevented good practice by the British, especially as the low freeboard turret ship made a poor target, and fire had to be suspended at intervals to avoid dropping shells into Ylo. *Amethyst* kept up an accurate and steady fire but could only damage her opponent's upper works. After two hours' gunfire the *Shah* launched a torpedo, but the range was too great and its speed too low to reach the target. At 5.45 the action ceased as the rebel had gone in close to the town, and next day she surrendered to the Peruvian fleet.

The *Huascar* was struck by 60-70 shot, mainly on her upper works, with several glancing blows on her side armour. Only one 9-in. common shell had pierced the 3½-in. plating above the waterline, causing casualties, and there was one dent on the turret from a 7-in. shot. During the two and a quarter hours the *Shah* had fired 280 rounds of which 30 are supposed to have scored hits; neither British ship had more than a few ropes cut, and by manœuvre had prevented the use of the ram.

Although the action attracted but little public interest, it focused attention on the need for an armoured flagship on the Station and the poor penetration by supposedly armour-piercing guns such as were carried by many of our battleships.

Chapter 37

THE COMING OF THE PROTECTIVE DECK

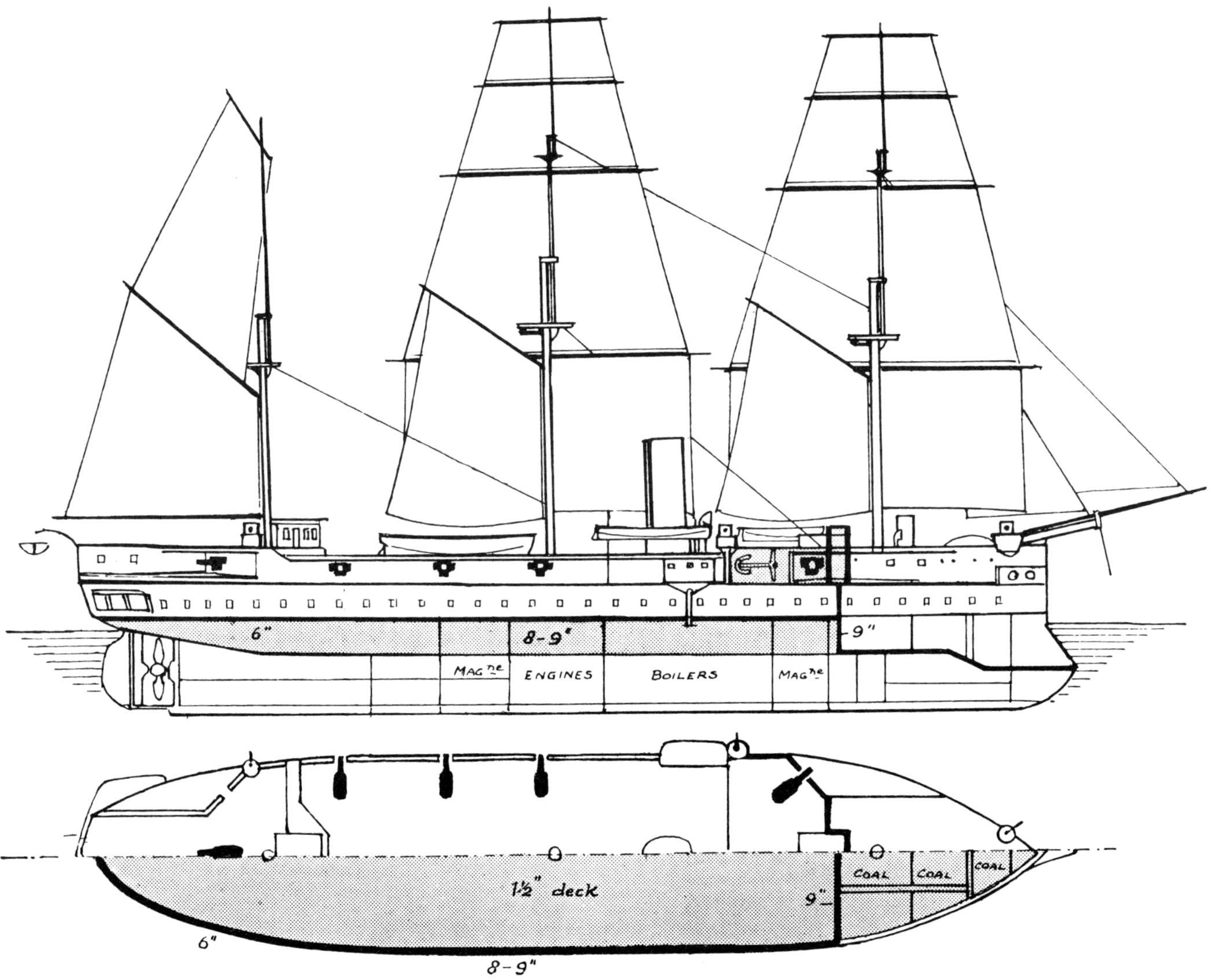

The *Shannon* was the first of Barnaby's designs in which the waterline belt forward was replaced by a submerged armoured deck with coal bunkers above it. Note the large embrasures to obtain axial fire, and the overhang of the quarter galleries.

"SHANNON"

Builder	*Laid down*	*Launched*	*Completed*	*Cost*
Pembroke	29 Sept. '73	11 Nov. '75	17 Sept. '77	£302,707

Dimensions 260′ × 54′ × 21′/23·6′ = 5,390 tons (5,670 tons finally).
Hull and armour 3,500 tons. Equipment 1,940 tons.

Armament 2 10-in. 18-ton M.L.R.
7 9-in. 12-ton M.L.R. 4 Torpedo tubes (1881).
6 20-pdrs.

Armour Belt 9″-8″-6″; bulkheads 9″-8″; conning tower 9″-4″; decks 3″-1½″-1″; skin 1¼″; backing 12″-10″.
Total 1,060 tons.

Complement 452.

Coal 280/560 tons; wood and zinc sheathed.

Machinery Lairds. Comp. horizontal return-conn. rod.
2 H.P. 44″; 2 L.P. 85″; stroke 4′; I.H.P. 3,370=12·25 knots.
Single screw 19½′ diam.; pitch 18′-22′; revs. 70.
8 cylindrical boilers. 70 lb. pressure.

Sail area 24,000 sq. ft. (as ship rigged). 21,500 (barque).

Points of interest:

(1) The first British armoured cruiser.
(2) The first ship to have a protective deck and subdivision in place of a complete belt.
(3) The last British armoured ship to have full ship rig, and a single screw.
(4) The ship for which no useful active employment could ever be found, as being too weak for the battle-line and too slow for a cruiser.

As a fighting ship the *Shannon* possesses little interest; but as an example of naval architecture she stands out as the armoured ship in which (1) a protective deck was first introduced and (2) which assumed the rank of "armoured cruiser" for the first time. As such she has a very definite place in the history of naval construction.

Her first official classification was as a broadside armour-belted cruising ship with the status of a second-class

Showing the after torpedo-net booms, quarter-gallery windows and embrasure for after 12-ton gun.

battleship—and as such comes within the scope of this survey. Intended to carry the flag on distant stations where the routine of service entailed prolonged sea passages, provision was made for sufficient armament and protection to match foreign contemporaries of her rating; but nothing could justify her employment in either of the battle squadrons, for which she was quite unsuited. As a second-class battleship she could have engaged in a duel with such foreign armoured units as were likely to be encountered abroad, but when it became necessary to bring her home, being hopelessly slow for a cruiser, no use beyond that of coastguard ship could be found for her. So of her twenty-one years' service exactly three were spent on foreign stations, ten as a coastguard ship, and nearly four in the Reserve. The remaining four years were passed in repairs and refits.

The genesis of the *Shannon* was probably inspired by the Russian cruiser *General Admiral* laid down in 1870 armed with four 8-in. and two 6-in. guns in an open central battery and protected along the waterline with a complete shallow armour belt—the first "armoured cruiser." She was completed in 1874.

ARMAMENT

The gun distribution was peculiar and interesting. As active service abroad would probably include ship duels; the *Shannon* was designed to fight bows-on or with the enemy well on the bow. Her two 10-in. guns were therefore mounted towards the rear of the long forecastle and fired through deep embrasures which allowed for arcs of training from dead ahead to just abaft the beam. These guns were protected by a 9-in.-8-in. transverse bulkhead angled to form the embrasure port faces, and then taken back as side armour forming a wide screen intended to shield the amidships battery from raking fire.

Amidships were six 9-in. on the open deck, exposed to gun fire and damage from falling spars and rigging. It was intended to withdraw the men from these guns to the armoured forecastle after they had been laid, and fire them by electricity when passing the enemy if an attempt to ram failed. Otherwise they could have been fought as in an ordinary corvette. Aft was the seventh 9-in. mounted on a central pivot for traversing to either side and firing through deep embrasures allowing direct fire astern with a bearing to slightly ahead of the beam.

This gun was covered by the poop deck. Viewed from the quarter these embrasures moulded the stern in a most distinctive way and their effect was accentuated by the sponsoned gallery windows.

Six 20-pdrs. provided a saluting battery.

ARMOUR

The chief feature of the ship lay in the waterline system of protection. Hitherto the belt had been complete except in the case of some of the early ironclads. In the *Shannon*, Barnaby introduced a new system of defence

The *Shannon* in Plymouth Sound after machine guns had been added in 1881. The conning tower forms part of the structure abaft the foremast, with a boat atop. She is home from the Pacific Station where she was not allowed to fire her 10-in. guns because of the cost of sending ammunition out there.

in place of waterline armour, which although regarded with distrust and suspicion in his subsequent designs, was in course of time to be accepted as a normal and adequate method of safeguarding the waterline in lieu of, or as an adjunct to, armour. As thus embodying Barnaby's chief contribution to naval architecture the little *Shannon* received a distinction which ensured her a definite niche in the progress of design.

The belt was 9 ft. deep with 5 ft. below water, measuring 9 in.-8 in. amidships and 6 in. aft, but ending abruptly 60 ft. from the bows with a 9-in. transverse bulkhead. Forward of this and from its lower edge a 3-in. armour deck ran down to the ram 10 ft. below water, leaving a space between it and the lower deck to be filled by coal bunkers flanked by stores, with the cable tier right in the bows. These "coal tanks," as they were called, were another special feature, and when full would limit any flooding through a shot hole, being well separated by cofferdams.

Above the belt the armour deck was 1½ in. only, shielding the magazine, machinery and steering gear from plunging fire. Had there been twin screws she would have had a submerged armour deck aft, but the single screw precluded this. Abreast the engines and boilers, and forward of the bulkhead, the side between the main and lower deck was protected by cofferdams made up of iron boxes 2 ft. wide filled with old rope, canvas, etc.

The armoured forecastle was fitted with communications to engine-room, helm and battery and intended to serve as a conning position. In 1875 a small conning tower was added just abaft the foremast and above the bulkhead, and at the same time deck plating over the boilers was thickened—first examples of the additional weights to be added which eventually brought her a foot overdraught.

RAM

The *Shannon* was distinguished by having a triangular ram projecting 8 ft. from the stem which was detachable and supposed to be stowed on board during peace time so as to obviate the risk of injuring a consort—a liability becoming increasingly frequent. The fitting of this ram could only be performed in dock; and as there was no room for it abroad, Service tradition averred that it was generally chasing her around the world when not in store at Devonport. Arising out of this state of things was the facetious taunt that the ship's officers could not be trusted to handle her if and when it ever were fitted, through lack of practice in avoiding ships in company.

MACHINERY

Lairds were responsible for the engines, which were a small set of their compound, horizontal, return connecting-rod type with the two h.p. cylinders placed behind and bolted on to the two l.p., and the pistons attached with a single piston rod so that they worked simultaneously. The eight boilers were back-to-back against the bulkhead and faced the bunkers, with other bulkheads separating them from the engine room and after holds. The single Griffiths screw was two-bladed and lifting—the last to be so fitted in one of H.M. capital ships.

With a bunker capacity of only 560 tons the *Shannon* was intended more for sailing than steaming, and 12·2 knots was the best recorded speed—a ridiculous figure for an alleged cruiser.

Incidentally, as there were apprehensions in some quarters as to the possible dangers of going into action with high-pressure steam in the boilers, the engines were designed to work the steam expansively to any desired extent, with a special arrangement of valves to allow for low-pressure steam down to 2 lb. being admitted directly into the low-pressure cylinder.

RIG

Great store was set upon sail power in this ship and coal supply suffered accordingly, the original bunkerage being only 280 tons. In 1875 the yards, masts and rigging were increased in weight and a full ship rig was to be set, but after an experimental cruise in 1876 this was reduced to barque with the foremast shortened, the bowsprit and jibboom reduced. As a barque there were no stunsails, which could easily have been carried as her reports made her out to have been a dull sailer despite the hoisting screw.

SEA-GOING QUALITIES

Described as a very steady gun platform and extremely handy, her sea-going qualities were well spoken of and she seems to have been very adequately fitted for the Pacific Station. That she had to be recalled was probably owing to ammunition difficulties. Being the only ship on the Station with 10-in. guns, there was no reserve of ammunition for them: her Captain had orders not to carry out 10-in. target practice, as it was a most expensive undertaking to send out heavy shells all the way round the Horn to the magazines at Esquimalt.

GENERAL

Apart from her shortcomings as a warship, the *Shannon* was not altogether a success as a ship. Too much had been attempted on too small a displacement, and when she should have been completed something else was thought of which might make her more efficient—and forthwith placed on board. In July 1876 she was to all intents and purposes ready for sea when entering Plymouth Sound, but for the next twelve months the Dockyard laboured to make her better and better. Whiteheads and torpedo fittings with six 20-pdr. guns were added; the armour on the conning tower was increased and it became part of a considerable deck structure upon which a boat was stowed; armour glacis plates around the lower deck hatchways were thickened; a variety of heavy fittings were installed, and the coal supply raised from 280 to 470 tons, and crew increased from 350 to 450.

Owing to a miscalculation she was a foot overdraught in 1876, and when again commissioned in September 1877 matters were much worse. Her rig was reduced, but trouble with the engines kept her in Dockyard hands for another eight months. Ultimately the maximum bunkerage was fixed at 560 tons on a displacement of 5,670 tons full load.

No changes were ever made in her main armament as she was not worth it, but a few machine guns were added in 1881.

"SHANNON"

Commissioned 17 July '77 for Particular Service. The next year she underwent considerable alterations at Devonport and the rig was reduced. In March '78 she joined the Channel fleet for a shake-down cruise and then went to China in April but was ordered home in July when further changes were put in hand at Devonport; Commissioned December '78 for the Channel; was employed in the Mediterranean for a time and in July '79 went out to the Pacific for a couple of years returning to Devonport in July '81 and placed in the 4th Div. Reserve for a long refit. In May '83 became tender to the *Warrior* at Portsmouth. In June proceeded to Greenock as coastguard ship until August and then moved to Bantry. (Joined Admiral Hornby's Particular Service Squadron June-July '85 during the Russian War scare.) Reduced to Fleet Reserve in May '93 and Dockyard Reserve January '98.

Sold December '99 for £10,105.

"NELSON" and "NORTHAMPTON"

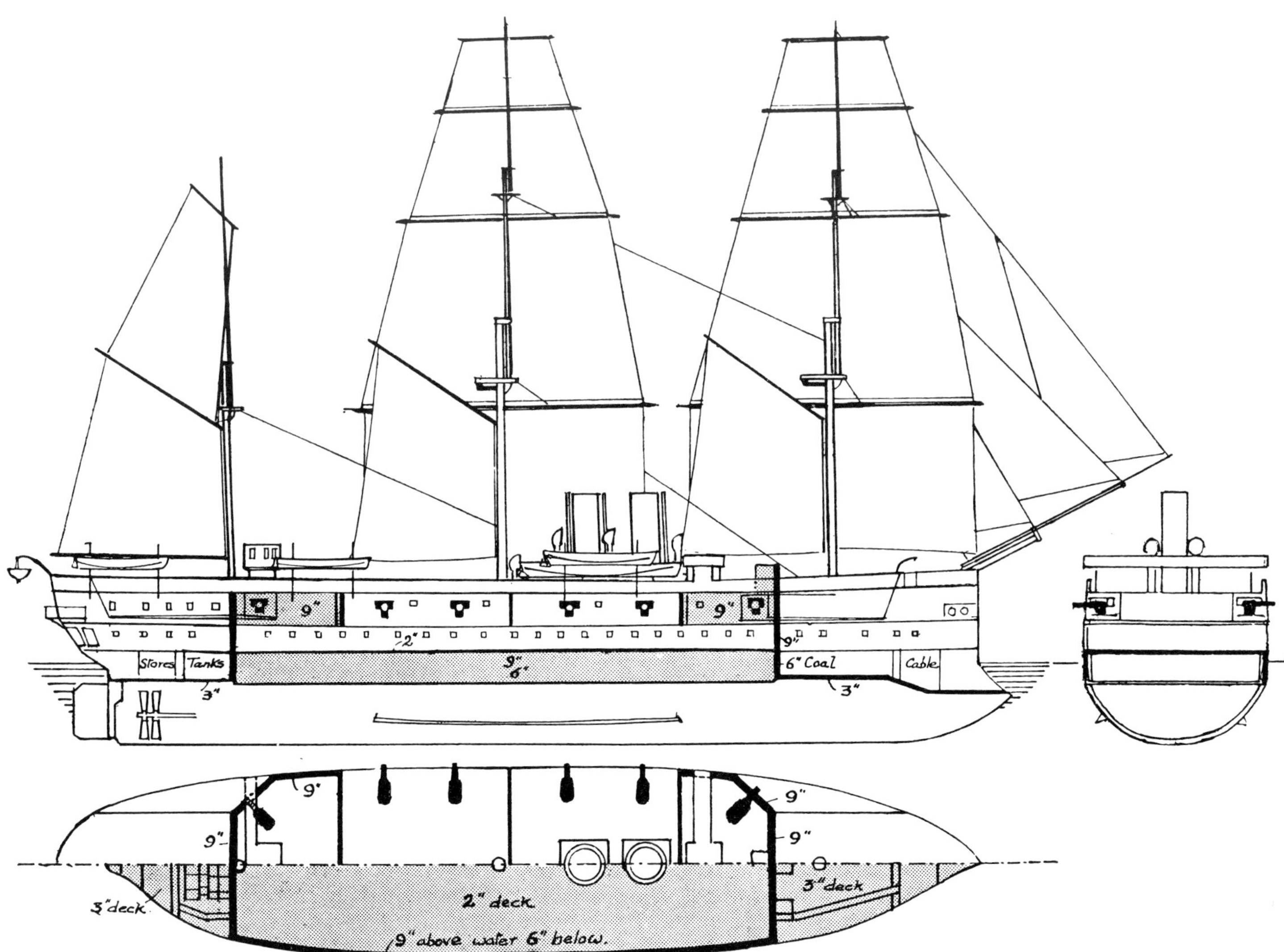

In the *Nelson* and *Northampton* the *Shannon* scheme of waterline protection was extended by confining the belt to the length of the battery, and entrusting the ends of the ship to a strong underwater protective deck with sub-division of the hull above it. Note the armour screens dividing the battery, and a broadside in place of a traversing gun in the after embrasure.

"NELSON" and "NORTHAMPTON"

	Built by	*Laid down*	*Launched*	*Completed*	*Cost*
"*Nelson*"	Elder & Co.	2 Nov. '74	4 Nov. '76	26 July '81	£411,302
"*Northampton*"	Napiers	26 Oct. '74	18 Nov. '76	7 Dec. '78	£414,441

Dimensions 280′ × 60′ × 23·9′/25·9′ = 7,630 tons ("*Nelson*" = 7,473 tons).
Hull and armour 4,680. Equipment 2,920 tons.

Armament 4 10-in. 18-ton M.L.R. Two 60′ torpedo boats.
8 9-in. 12-ton M.L.R.
6 20-pdrs.
16 machine and boat guns.

Armour Belt 9″-6″; bulkheads 9″-8″-6″; conning tower 9″; decks 3″-2″; skin 1¼″; backing 12″ teak.
Total 1,562 tons.

Complement 560.

Coal 540/1,150 tons.

Sail area 24,766 sq. ft.

Machinery "*Nelson*": Elder & Co.; I.H.P. 6,624 = 14 knots.
Two sets 3 cyl. vertical compound, inverted.
H.P. cyls. 60″; L.P. 104″; stroke 3½′; revs. 75.
"*Northampton*": Penn. I.H.P. 6,073 = 13·17 knots.
Two sets vertical inverted compound.
3 cyls. 54″; stroke 3¼′; revs. 82.
2 screws; Mangin 2-bladed, double; diam. 18′.
10 oval boilers; 60 lb. pressure; 30 furnaces.

Radius 3,500/12½ knots; 5,000/10½ knots.

Sail area 24,766 sq. ft.

Points of interest:

(1) The last British capital ships to carry their main armament on the broadside and between decks.
(2) The first armoured ships to have a protective deck at each end.
(3) The first armoured ships in which gun protection was sacrificed to provide thicker belt armour and heavier guns.
(4) Had variable expansion engines.

(Although laid down some months after the *Inflexible*, the *Northampton* was completed three years earlier and so is included here for comparison with the *Shannon*.)

The Service generally regarded the *Shannon* with very lukewarm favour as being a ship "deficient in warlike qualities," and in the *Nelson* class which followed her Barnaby sought to make good her deficiencies by an increase of 40 per cent. in displacement which allowed for 1¾ knots increase and three more guns.

But the *Nelsons* still had the grave defects of the *Shannon* in lacking suitability for any clearly defined tactical use—like the old Fourth Rates, which were not heavy enough to meet ships-of-the-line nor fast enough to catch frigates. They were indeterminate intermediates, of questionable battle value by the standards of the day, and too large for commerce protection generally.

Barnaby, however, had very definite ideas as to their value:

> "What services are these ships designed to perform, and what promise is there of performance? They may be looked upon as armoured ships having to meet armoured ships—or, as protected cruisers; and their very first duty would be to relieve the *Bellerophon* on the North American station."

Apart from their value as armoured units he pronounced them to be his ideal of cruising fighting ships.

On the other hand the Controller held that:

> "They were no part of what was called our battle fleet; their object was not to take part in a close engagement but to roam over the seas and drive away unarmoured fast cruisers from harrying our commerce—a flying squadron not for a moment to be confused with our ironclad ships."

This diversity of opinion can be explained by the purely personal opinions of the two officers as to what constituted the protection necessary for a capital ship. Barnaby was to become a great advocate of the submerged armour deck in place of vertical waterline plating, while Houstan Stewart was still wedded to Reed's belt-and-battery system—and so quite unable to visualize the *Nelsons* as adequate additions to the battle line. Actually, they served as flagships on distant stations, afterwards being relegated to guard ship and reserve service at Home—never faced with possible opponents of armoured status abroad, and hopelessly deficient in speed for any cruiser duties.

We get a good conception of what Barnaby wished to create by accepting his description of the design as being that of the *Bellerophon* with the battery opened out and the side armour removed to obtain heavier guns and better protection along the waterline. Comparing the plans of the ships it is difficult to credit the *Nelson* with carrying so much more armour and on that score being better equipped for the battle line, apart from her superiority in gun fire.

The following figures convey a good idea of both the "battleships" and "cruiser" qualities of the *Nelson*.

		Nelson	*Bellerophon*	*Iron Duke*
	Length	280′	300′	280′
	Beam	60′	56′	64′
	Draught	24·7′	24·8′	22·8′
	Displacement	7,473 tons	7,550 tons	6,010 tons
	I.H.P.	6,624	6,520	4,020
	Speed	14	14·17	12·8
Armour	Total tonnage	1,720	1,273	1,082
	Average thickness	7·28″	5·28″	5·7″
Guns	Weight	533 tons	420 tons	351 tons
	Broadside	1,800 lb.	1,595 lb.	1,378 lb.
	Coal	1,200 tons	645 tons	460 tons
	Canvas sq. ft.	24,770	23,400	22,750

The *Northampton* as a boys' training and recruiting ship when she was visiting the Clyde, about 1896. A fighting top has been fitted to the mizen, and a number of machine guns can be seen along the topside. For her employment she presented an impressive and comfortable appearance.

In place of iron the *Nelson's* side was made up of 1-in. steel plating and it was argued that if shot could not be kept out it should be let in and out again with as little resistance as possible, preventing splinter effect by adequate screening. In effect let the heaviest armour be provided for sheltering engines and boilers, but for the rest buoyancy and stability should be ensured by watertight compartments, armour decks below water, cofferdams and steam pumps. Thus an "All-or-Nothing" system was advocated as in the *Iron Duke*, but at the expense of gun protection.

In general design the *Shannon* was followed with (1) an extra deck so that the amidships guns were covered in; (2) an under-water armour deck aft as well as forward in place of belt armour; (3) twin Mangin screws instead of a hoisting propeller; and (4) an extra 9-in. gun on each side, and two 10-in. aft in place of a 9-in. on a central mount for traversing.

ARMAMENT

It will be seen that there was 181 ft. between the end bulkheads in the *Nelson* to 91 ft. in the *Bellerophon*, while in Reed's cramped batteries there was always the risk of a shell entering through one of the large ports and doing widespread damage as the guns were not screened. Barnaby provided splinter screens of 1-in. steel between the 12-tonners, which were well spaced and in pairs; the 18-ton guns deeply embrasured fore and aft had heavy armour all round them and arcs of fire on the beam and axially. But whereas Reed's central battery was well placed where accurate shooting was possible in a head or following sea, Barnaby's wider disposal exposed the important guns to the full effects of pitching in ships which were lively at sea.

As in the *Shannon* salvo firing was to be the special form of attack, the guns being loaded and laid under cover of the end bulkheads and fired electrically without the crews being exposed in a close engagement. The broadside having been discharged, she was then to turn bows on, reload, and again manœuvre for another

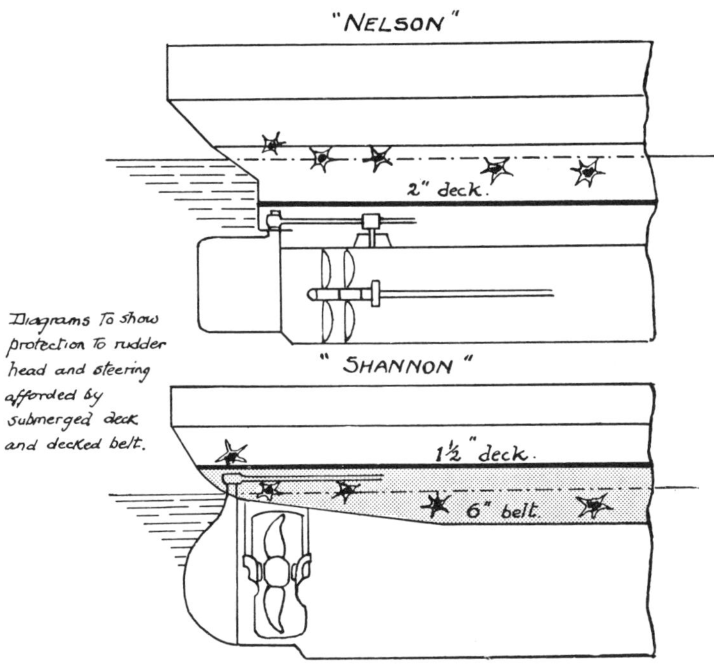

Diagrams to show protection to rudder head and steering afforded by submerged deck and decked belt.

broadside. Such tactics were only suited to a duel and quite out of the question in a line-of-battle action, so that as flagships on distant stations they were well equipped to deal with possible antagonists.

The ram was a triangular plate sharply pointed and set 11 ft. out from the stem, with sides reinforced by 3-in. plates in a continuation of the armour deck. Unlike the *Shannon's* it was a fixture.

ARMOUR

For waterline protection the *Shannon's* partial belt plus armour deck forward was replaced by a central belt with armour decks at each end—very much akin to that devised for the *Inflexible*.

The belt amidships extended for 181 ft.—the longest ever fitted in a Barnaby deck-and-belt ship—altogether 9 ft. deep with 4 ft. above water being made up of two strakes, an upper one of 9-in. iron upon 10-in. teak and a lower of 6-in. iron on 13-in. teak. At each end was a cross-deck bulkhead 9 in. above and 6 in. below water, rising to the upper deck 22 ft. above, where it was angled off to form corner ports for the 18-ton guns and then flanked down the hull side for 27½ ft. as a wide screen for the battery.

R

Above this ran a 2-in. armour deck covering the engines, boilers and magazines; fore and aft of the bulkheads it was continued to bow and stern as 3-in., and on the lower deck covered the stern post and sloped down to meet the ram. Between this deck and the main deck the space was filled by water-excluding stores, coal, and water tanks, to prevent flooding if the unprotected sides were pierced. As a substitute for the *Shannon's* belt, it was considered that 3 in. at 4 ft. below water was a far better provision for keeping the ship afloat—given sufficient stability—than 12 in. of vertical armour. It was a matter of non-vital importance whether a shot struck at the waterline or not. In a belted ship a shell piercing at this point might either blow up the ship or completely flood one end and render the magazine useless, the amount of water admitted being sufficient to make her unmanageable. In the *Nelson* the water admitted would leave the ship with her sea-going and fighting qualities practically unimpaired.

The difference between the protection afforded to the steering gear by an under-water deck and a belt is clearly shown on p. 241. In the *Nelson* the gear was well below water, and supported by the deck beneath the armour deck, which might be driven down without damaging the steering. But the *Shannon's* gear was above

During 1889-91 the *Nelson* was modernized by the addition of some q.f. and m.g., torpedo discharge ports, and a military rig as masts and yards were being discarded in armoured ships. She is here seen at Malta during one of her trooping runs.

her single hoisting screw and might well have been reached by a shell piercing the belt; in a twin-screw ship the steering gear could be placed lower, but even then was more easily reached through thin side armour or an above-water deck than through an under-water deck.

MACHINERY

Penn's engines for the *Northampton* had three equal-sized cylinders capable of being worked as simple expansion high-pressure at full power, or as compound during economical steaming when only the foremost cylinder would be at high pressure; at reduced power they could also be used as simple expansion with low-pressure steam.

On first trials she required 10° of starboard helm, so for the second series the propeller blades were reduced to give more clearance with the ship's run; but with 6,062 h.p. only 13·17 knots was realized. This time the weather helm was only five degrees. Even after further modifications to screws and rudder these figures were not improved upon and she was always about a knot slower than the *Nelson*, even when using the steam blast.

RIG

Both were barque rigged and very taut in proportion to spread, with a sail area of 24,766 sq. ft. In wartime only the lower masts were to remain standing. In 1886 *Northampton* had a fighting top fitted to the mizen and in her 1889 refit *Nelson* was remasted with tops on the fore and mizen. With the drag of twin Mangins and long shafts it is not surprising that they were poor performers under sail—lively, and with an easy motion in a gale of wind, but otherwise very steady.[1]

SEA-GOING QUALITIES

Specially built for prolonged cruising, they were good for 7,000 miles on 1,000 tons of coal, or a continuous speed of 7 knots for forty days; no rigged ship up to this time had carried more than 970 tons—which was bunkered in the *Superb*—so that 1,150 tons was a special allowance with an eye to their overseas employment.

GENERAL

The two names did not pair happily, *Northampton* having no naval significance and was "selected" in order to gratify the constituents of the then First Lord, Mr. Ward Hunt. During her employment as a sea-going training and recruiting ship for boys she did a lot of port-to-port visiting with a brass band and other allurements. With high wall sides, a broad windowed stern, ornate bow scrolls, and a general appearance of comfortable well-being, she was a handsome and impressive ship; and for ten years the *Northampton* proved as great an attraction to the youth of the country as could have been selected from the Navy List.

"NELSON"

Commissioned at Chatham in July '81 for the Australian station as commodore's ship until January '85 when she was fitted with extra cabins as flagship. Returning to Chatham in January '89 she underwent a three years' refit being fitted with four 4·7-in. and q.f. guns, nets, torpedo ports and a military rig. In October '91 became guardship at Portsmouth for three years, being transferred to Fleet Reserve in November '94 where, apart from trooping runs to Malta she remained until April '01 and then degraded to Dockyard Reserve. In December '01 was hulked and became T.S. for stokers until sold in July 1910 for £14,500.

"NORTHAMPTON"

Commissioned September '79 at Chatham as flagship for N.A.W.I. station where she remained until '86. In April was temporary reserve ship at Portsmouth and in November went to Chatham in 3rd Reserve. Commissioned for manœuvres in '88, and in March '89 went to Sheerness as flagship. Took part in manœuvres '90, '91 and '92; in August '93 joined A reserve at Sheerness and in February '94 the Fleet Reserve. Commissioned as sea-going T.S. for boys in June '94 and so employed until November '04 when she was paid off into Fleet Reserve and sold at Chatham in April '05.

---

[1] Appointed to the *Northampton* as Captain in 1888, Admiral Sir Robert Hastings Harris wrote, "She was anything but a comfortable command as a fighting ship. The dockyard authorities, who were quite aware of her defects and who knew that as a fighting ship she was a sham, would not spend any money on her. Among the most disagreeable of her unremedied characteristics was the inability to steam more than ten knots at full speed; a steam capstan that as often as not refused to lift her anchors; and steam steering gear which, if hard put over, rather rapidly in an emergency, at once locked itself permanently at either hard-at-starboard or hard-a-port, as the case might be, and required to be tinkered with for at least ten minutes before it could be moved again."

Chapter 38

THE ADVENT OF THE MONSTER GUN

ALTHOUGH both Armstrong and Whitworth had announced in 1871 that they were prepared to supply guns far bigger than any yet mounted afloat, there was no question of the Board exercising any initiative in adopting these large calibres. British policy was based upon the sound principle of preserving the *status quo* and not hastening the obsolescence of the ships we had by progressively increasing the size of artillery, which inevitably would lead to similar armaments abroad. The Admiralty preferred to leave the initiative to foreign Powers knowing full well that we could always overtake and outbuild them. The Ordnance Department had progressed as far as the 12-in. gun and there the Board was prepared to stop as having secured as large a weapon as sea warfare demanded.

It was left to the Italians to initiate the monster gun era which provided such a difficult problem for the naval constructors in the 'seventies.

Hitherto their battle fleet had consisted of weak broadside ships and one turret ship—the notorious ram *Affondatore* which Admiral Persano had selected for his flagship at the battle of Lissa in 1866, when he had to retire after suffering defeat by an inferior Austrian force under Admiral Tegetthoff. During the next six years only two small central battery ships were launched and Italian pretensions afloat were apparently at a low ebb.

It was, however, a lull before a Naval Renaissance, brought about by the threat of French maritime power in the Mediterranean. Italy saw her long and vulnerable coastline at the mercy of French ships of no great individual fighting power and only moderate speed, and in reconstructing her naval defences decided upon the provision of a limited number of giant ships rather than of a larger number of less powerful units.

The great constructor Benedetto Brin brought this policy into materialization through a series of huge battleships, unique in their originality of conception and portentous fighting qualities, of which the *Duilio* and *Dandolo* were the first to be laid down in 1872. Together with the *Gloire* and *Dreadnought* of thirty years later they proved to be the most provocative capital ships ever built.

"DUILIO"

Brin intended his ships to have the heaviest guns combined with the thickest armour and highest speed, but on a tonnage which *should not greatly exceed* that of our *Dreadnought*. No details of the original design are obtainable, but the hull was 20 ft. longer and nearly a foot broader than that of the British ship, with a complete waterline belt and four 38-ton guns. But in order to ensure that the two ships should not be outmoded during construction, there was to be a latitude in the matter of gun calibre with a corresponding elasticity in design so that compromises could be made to allow for a much heavier armament.

At that time the pernicious results of meddling with design during construction had not been appreciated, and it was the common practice to introduce all sorts of modifications in order to bring a ship suffering from belated building into line with new developments in armament and protection. In the case of the *Duilio* the latitude allowed was unfortunately exercised to the full, with far-reaching repercussions in our own Construction Department, as it brought about the first monster gun phase and all the expediencies in methods of protection which had to be adopted in battleships of limited displacement during the next decade. We were quite content with the 38-tonner, but when Armstrongs announced that they were prepared to supply 15-in. guns of 50 tons, the *Duilio* was promptly authorized to receive them. The sum total of weights thus entailed required considerable changes in hull and equipment weights, but, as will be seen, there came a further rise to 17·7-in., necessitating even more extensive changes in protection, and Reed recorded:

> "I visited Spezia and found they were in great difficulties. They had made miscalculations; they were obliged to contract the armour, and the proposal at the time was to put in some boilers outside the armoured part of the vessel. Then having got the ships in that state they had to defend them and do the best they could with them. Then they took the next step and said 'We will build ships with only patches of armour here and there to protect this and to protect that, but as we know that their floating power is unprotected, we will give them abundant speed to keep them well out of the way of all armoured ships.' " (*R.U.S.I.*, 26 November 1884.)

If he had stuck to 38-tonners Brin could have made the *Duilio* and *Dandolo* thoroughly efficient and well-balanced fighting machines fit to hold their own against any opposition in the Mediterranean. But by vastly over-gunning them their actual fighting value was sadly diminished. Their hulls would never have withstood the stress of continuous firing, while the chances of securing a hit with such slow-firing weapons was out of all proportion to their smashing power, compared with the handier and more accurate guns they replaced.

What were of greater consequence were the problems in protection arising out of the introduction of these great guns. In setting the lead with a 15-in. calibre, Brin realized that he was giving hostages to fortune. Other Powers could follow suit, and the *Duilio* might become exposed to the risk of combat with ships similarly armed despite a high legend speed. Hence protection must needs be adapted to withstand such fire. Anything along *Dreadnought* lines with a wide spread of armour was apparently precluded. Only a very limited area could be made impregnable to 15-in. gunfire, and Reed's facetious comment more or less described the system which had to be adopted, although it was along the lines he himself had proposed before Lord Dufferin's Committee on Designs. Brin seized upon the suggestions made in the Report the previous year, and planned the citadel *cum* raft-body idea in a modified form.

Fore and aft turrets had to go by the board, and to get some sort of all-round fire he mounted the four big guns in two turrets 18 in. thick placed slightly *en echelon* amidships upon a citadel of just less than one-third of the ship's length and plated with 17-in. armour. Below this ran a waterline belt 169 ft. long, 21½ in. thick at the upper edge and 12 in. at the lower, with 16-in. end bulkheads. Above the citadel and belt the deck was 3 in. with

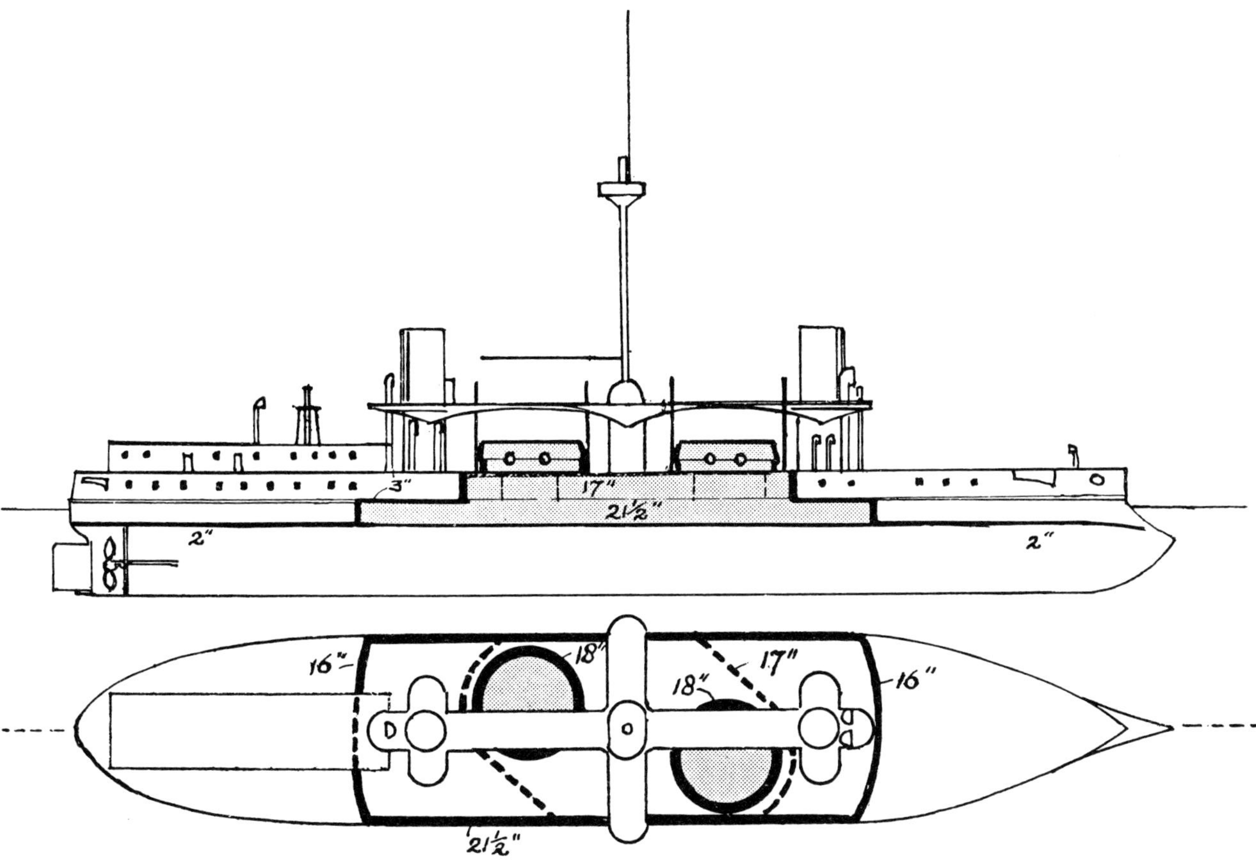

Carrying four 100-ton guns in a heavily armoured citadel at 15 knots the Italian *Dandolo* and *Duilio* introduced the monster gun, and created a big impression. They had a thick belt amidships and relied upon a protective deck and subdivision for integrity fore and aft. The largest and most powerful battleships of their day which served as a model for our *Inflexible*.

2 in. from the lower edge of the belt to the bow and stern. Altogether the armour amounted to 2,559 tons, which worked out at 24·5 per cent. of the designed displacement of 10,400 tons or 22·8 per cent. of her actual 11,140 tons; and for the first time steel armour was employed in place of iron. It is of interest to note that the armour was ordered from Cammell and Co., the guns and mountings from Elswick, and the engines and boilers from Penn. All the iron and steel used in construction came from France, so that the Italian share in the ship was confined to design and assembly.

It will be seen that the underwater deck completely shut off the lower part of the hull, and Brin *relied upon this* to provide stability and buoyancy (Barnaby, Memo. to First Lord 16 April 1877), with close sub-division above the deck to localize flooding in action. There was also the armoured stability afforded by the citadel and belt, but to what extent this entered into Italian calculations is uncertain. When our own citadel ships came to be designed it played a vital part, and reliance upon the raft body for stability would have placed them in a hazardous condition. It must therefore be assumed that much the same conditions would have obtained in the

Duilio in practice if not in theory, although in discussing the citadel-raft type of ship the Committee Report did not contemplate the protection even of the requisite buoyancy by armour, and were prepared to trust the floating power of such vessels to the unarmoured raft constructed in cells and containing buoyant substances.

In this the Committee was diametrically opposed to the views of the late Chief Constructor, Reed, who regarded himself as the "author of the 'citadel system' " (*Modern Ships of War*, p. 69). Reed laid down what he considered to be the basic principles of the type, and while ignoring inherent stability due to the raft body stressed the importance of the armoured citadel:

> "The question of leaving so-called armoured line-of-battle ships without armour at the extremities is first one of principle, and afterwards one of degree. The principle (which should be observed in the design of every armoured vessel which is intended for the line of battle, or for those close and severe contests of ship with ship which will probably supersede in a great degree the system of fighting in line of battle) is this; the proportion which the armoured citadel bears to the unarmoured ends must always be such as to enable the ship to keep afloat all the time the armour itself holds out against the attacks of the enemy; so that injuries to the unarmoured ends, however great or multiplied, shall not alone suffice to destroy the ship. Whatever may occur in the future to interfere with the application of this principle—and I do not deny that such interferences may arise under certain perfectly conceivable circumstances—nothing has yet happened to justify its abandonment, or even to justify the remotest chance of its being violated.
>
> "Where ships are formed with fine water-lines, and the two opposite sides are consequently very near to each other for many feet, it is quite unnecessary to cover them with armour. The buoyancy comprised between the two sides at such parts is very small and consequently penetration can let but little water into the ship, and do but little harm."

In addition to carrying by far the heaviest guns and thickest armour yet considered for service afloat, the *Duilio* was also to have the high mobility essential in the scheme for defence of the Italian coastline and ports, and was accordingly engined for 15 knots—equal to the highest speed ever recorded for any capital ship.

This decision to undertake the construction of the most powerful warships yet conceived must be regarded as an example of confidence as remarkable as it was courageous in view of Italy's financial position and the somewhat limited attainments of her naval personnel. That the *Duilio* and *Dandolo* ever justified their existence is an open question, seeing how soon they were outmoded. But at the time of their inception they were certainly regarded with a good deal of apprehension and awe, and provoked Barnaby into proposing the *Inflexible*.

THE 'NEW "FURY"'

The British 1873 programme provided for the commencement of one battleship only, which was officially referred to as a "New *Fury*." She was to combine heavy guns, thick armour and great handiness with the greatest possible speed. Bunkerage was to be sufficient for operations in the Channel, Mediterranean or the Baltic, with proper sea-going qualities for those waters and as little sail-power as was consistent with peace-time duties. There could be no question of any more broadside ships—the *Duilio* had set a standard which made the recently commenced *Alexandra* and *Temeraire* appear very second-rate—and Barnaby was faced with the problem of going one better than his confrere in Rome while conforming to the Board's requirements.

Thus the *Duilio* radically changed our outlook upon both guns and armour. In one step the completely ironclad ship like the *Dreadnought*, having her thickest plates 14 in. and as nearly invulnerable from bow to stern as could be conceived, had to be discarded. The citadel-raft hull, put forward and discussed by the Committee on Designs as an intriguing solution to future possibilities in the matter of protection *if bigger guns than 12-in. were to be adopted*, became of immediate import—the *Duilio* had turned such possibilities into realities. The Admiralty became faced with a succession of problems in battleship design which was to last for the next ten years—a period to be marked by more controversy over the battle-worthiness of our capital ships than ever before or since.

A preliminary draft plan and an appreciation of the military qualities of the type of ship he proposed, together with several alternative sketch plans, was submitted by Barnaby to the Controller on 3 June 1873. Taking the *Fury* as a model, he showed how improvements in her could be effected by:

Plan A: Cutting out the belt fore and abaft the citadel and substituting transverse armour bulkheads.

Plan B: Adding a third turret amidships containing a single 50-ton gun to No. 2 plan, but reducing speed from 14 to 13 knots.

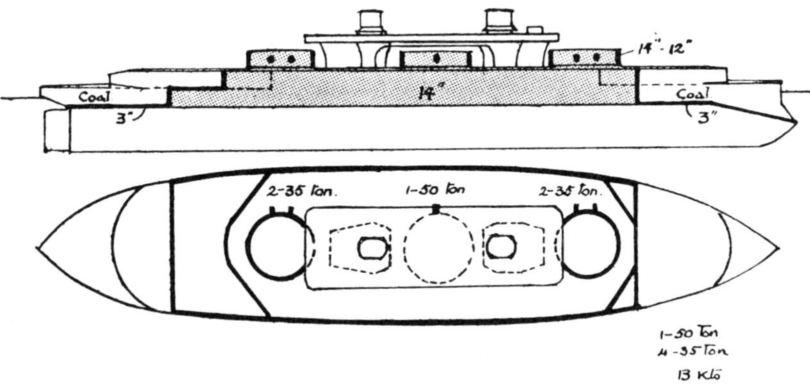

Plan C: Abolishing the flying deck and mounting two 18-ton guns in small centreline barbettes on the citadel. Speed 13 knots. Armour and freeboard reduced.

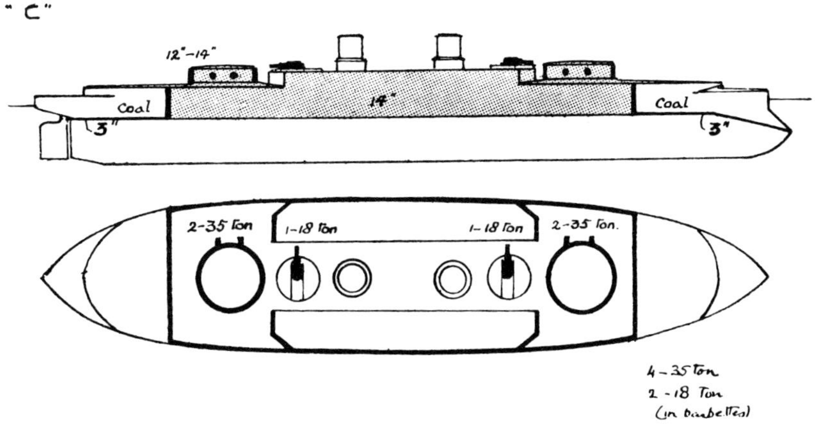

Plan D: Similar to plan A with four unprotected 12-ton guns on the flying deck. Speed 14 knots.

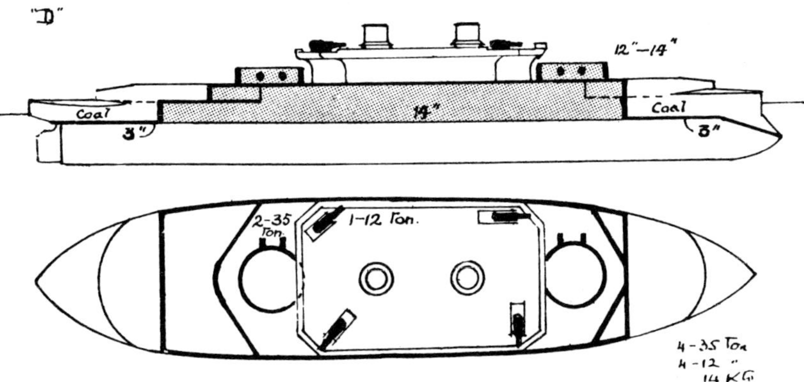

(These sketch plans show the original bow and stern of the *Fury* as modified by Barnaby before the sea trials of the *Devastation* had demonstrated the defects of the low bows. At this date a "false bow" was under consideration for the *Fury* and the flushing of her decks fore and aft had not been definitely decided upon.)

The fourth sketch (E) shows a radical departure from all previous capital ship designs, which had been prepared by Mr. Hounsom of the Constructor's Department for the Emperor Napoleon III and sent to the Controller by the Duke of Edinburgh a few weeks previously. Instead of reporting upon it at once, it had been retained for submission with the other designs for the new ship. A broadside of seven 35-ton guns *en barbette* was certainly worthy of serious consideration, but no figures as to tonnage and cost are available. It was essentially a design in which the volume of gun fire was relied upon to beat down opposition and so save the exposed gun crews—and as such would doubtless have found supporters amongst the critics of Barnaby's designs.

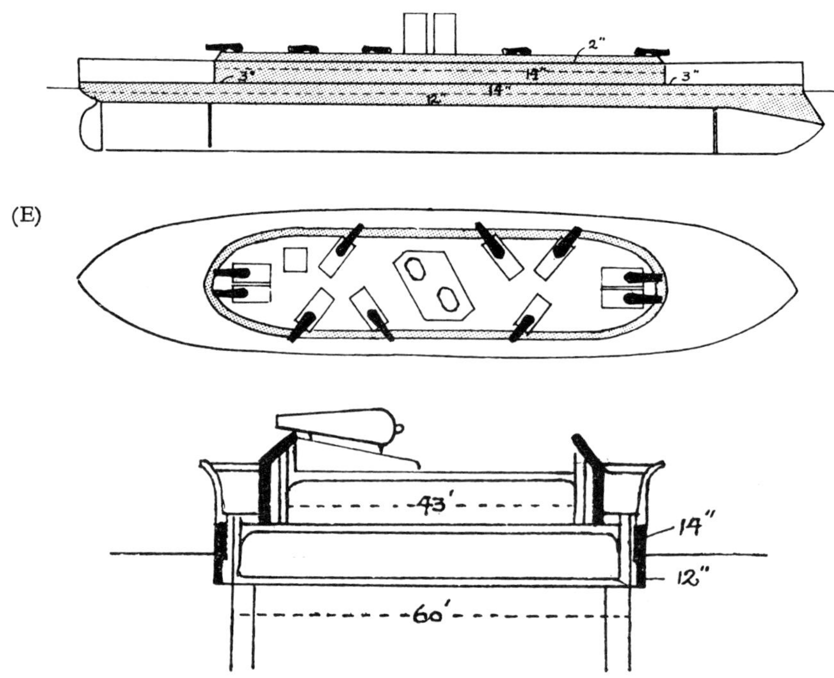

But these modified *Fury* projects held no solution for the *Duilio* problem, and this Barnaby fully realized.

According to a legend in the Constructor's Department he therefore put his appreciation of the position to the Controller in this way. That the time had come for us to build a ship of outstanding power and size with the highest speed, thickest armour, and heaviest guns which should be so large and costly that any foreign competition would be out of the question. He pointed out that it would take four years to build the ship, during which time great advances could well be made in big gun design—and that it required less time to construct a new gun than to complete a hull. Both Woolwich and Elswick were arranging for 60-ton guns and he proposed to step out and use the same calibre as the Italians, preparing the designs with a view to adopting still heavier weapons should they become available. So far as armour was concerned, he did not consider it essential that our ships should always have to be impregnable to the heaviest existing guns, but that it was necessary for British ships to have guns of *the most powerful* description, "even up to *hundreds of tons* if such masses of material could ever be wrought."

If necessary the change-over to such guns was to be effected by "some easy modification in her construction hereafter," but as such a substitution would entail larger turrets, much heavier mountings and ammunition supply, and a general stiffening up of the scantlings and structure to withstand the additional strain of firing, Barnaby's proposal to compensate for the extra weight of the guns by doing no more than simply to remove the armour from the turrets, retaining just a musketry-proof gun house, appears somewhat naïve. This sacrifice of armour he justified on the grounds that machinery had made it possible so to reduce the gun crews as to make the impregnability of the turrets less important so far as the preservation of life was concerned; the increase in the size of the guns themselves was in itself a protection from injury by direct hits. As he was precluded from exceeding the dimensions of the *Fury*, it would not be possible to protect the vital parts against gunfire heavier than 60-tonners; the turrets themselves could not be made proof against the guns they carried, but would be penetrated by them at 600 yards, so that turret armour could be reduced with a certain amount of justification.

On the other hand, Barnaby did not consider that any increase in the penetrating power of guns would make it desirable to dispense with hull armour merely because it could be defeated by some guns at certain ranges. It would always remain impenetrable to all guns beyond certain ranges and to many guns at all ranges, and must therefore be advantageous as a means of security to the vital parts of a ship. But the limits to armour thickness he considered would be found in the size and cost of the proposed ship, where the protection afforded would be proof to the 60-ton gun and the maximum we should ever be expected to provide. Actually the 24 in. of the *Inflexible* was the thickest armour ever to be taken afloat.

The characteristics of the new ship would therefore be:

Speed 14 knots, and coal for 3,000 miles at 10 knots.
Four 60-ton guns with 100/120 rounds of ammunition per gun, in turrets of 16″ armour.
Armour of 24″ to machinery, boilers and magazines.
Cost not to exceed *Fury*.
Passage of Suez Canal when lightened of coal.
Decks fore and aft about 17 ft. out of water, without interference to direct fire in line of keel of at least two guns.
Two masts for signalling, with crows nests but no yards.
Beam and draught not to exceed what will allow entry to docks at Portsmouth, Chatham, Malta and the lift dock at Bombay.

(It was pointed out that to make her capable of entering dock at Devonport or Bermuda it would be necessary to reduce the beam so much as to deprive her of stability when the ends were perforated and injured.)

When all these desiderata came to be translated into elevation and plan, Barnaby could do no better than follow the same principle as the Italians, and in adopting the citadel and cellular raft he produced a ship very much upon the same lines as the *Duilio*. But while Brin had kept to a low forecastle with some superstructure aft for boat stowage and accommodation, Barnaby provided high superstructures at each end, and a shorter citadel with the turrets set further from the centre-line.

This disposition of turrets was supposed to allow for axial fire—three guns in *Duilio* and four in the *Inflexible*, although Barnaby officially claimed that only one gun from each turret would fire fore and aft. Actually in both ships concussion limited axial fire from 20° to 30° of the line of keel, and cross-deck discharge with such short guns shook things up unpleasantly.

Barnaby explains how the *en echelon* position came to be adopted in his *Naval Development* (p. 75) when he says:

> "But long after the success of the *Devastation* in ordinary weather at sea had been proved, it was held in Parliament and the Press that the low hatchway freeboard forward and aft . . . were dangerous features in a sea-going ship. There was no sound foundations for these objections, but they were very influential in determining the form of the upper works of the *Inflexible*; and high hatchway freeboard was given to her from stem to stern. This made it necessary to place the turrets *en echelon*."

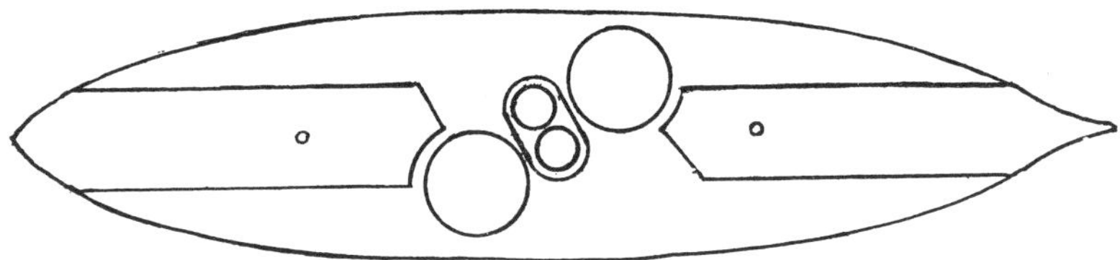

The original lay-out of superstructure and funnels in the *Inflexible* with flying bridge amidships omitted. As the funnels were liable to blast damage, they were shifted to before and abaft the turrets and the after superstructure widened.

The original draft and specifications were considerably altered by Captain Hood who, having changed his opinion since the *Devastation* report, objected to the proposed rig; the thickness of turret and belt armour; shape of superstructures; and position of the funnels. He showed that if the masts and yards were abandoned there would be a saving of about 100 tons which could be best utilized by (1) increasing the turrets from 16 in. to 18 in. (56 tons); (2) increasing the under-water belt from 12 in. to 16 in. with a reduction on the waterline from 24 in. to 22 in. Also that the forward superstructure should be reduced in width by 5 ft. to improve axial fire, with alteration in shape to both superstructures amidships to lessen concussion effect and increase the angle of training of the after turret. The position of the funnels he regarded as unsatisfactory; they should be placed in the centre-line, one before the foremost turret and the other abaft the after one with an air shaft between them.

INCREASE TO 80-TON GUNS

Actually the Woolwich 60-ton gun was never put into production, but in 1875—a year after the keel-plate of the *Inflexible* had been laid—the first 80-tonner was completed, with a calibre of 14·5 in. After a series of experiments this was bored out to 15-in.; and having been well tested was again bored out another inch so that 16-in. became the final calibre.

When the Ordnance Department intimated that this "Woolwich Infant" would be available by the time the ship was ready to receive her armament, the *Inflexible* was adapted for them in accordance with the Biggest-Possible-Big-Gun policy.

But happily this change-over involved no sacrifices in armour, as the additional weight in guns, mountings, ammunition, etc., were accommodated by the simple expedient of increasing draught 1 ft. and displacement by 800 tons. So with her new guns the ship reached 11,880 tons and drew a mean of 25 ft.—one foot more than had been intended for allowing her to dock at Bombay.

"DUILIO" GIVEN 100-TON GUNS

As a response to this attempt to deprive them of the Big Gun kudos to which they had aspired in the *Duilio*, the Italians decided upon a gesture of friendly rivalry and arranged for Armstrongs to deliver 17·7-in. 100-ton M.L.R. in place of the 60-tonners—and to this ace gun the Admiralty had no trump. The Navy being restricted to Woolwich could not turn to Elswick, and the Ordnance Department were not contemplating larger calibres than 16-in. But in 1878 four of these 100-ton M.L.R. were bought from Elswick, two being mounted at Malta and two at Gibraltar.

Chapter 39

"INFLEXIBLE"

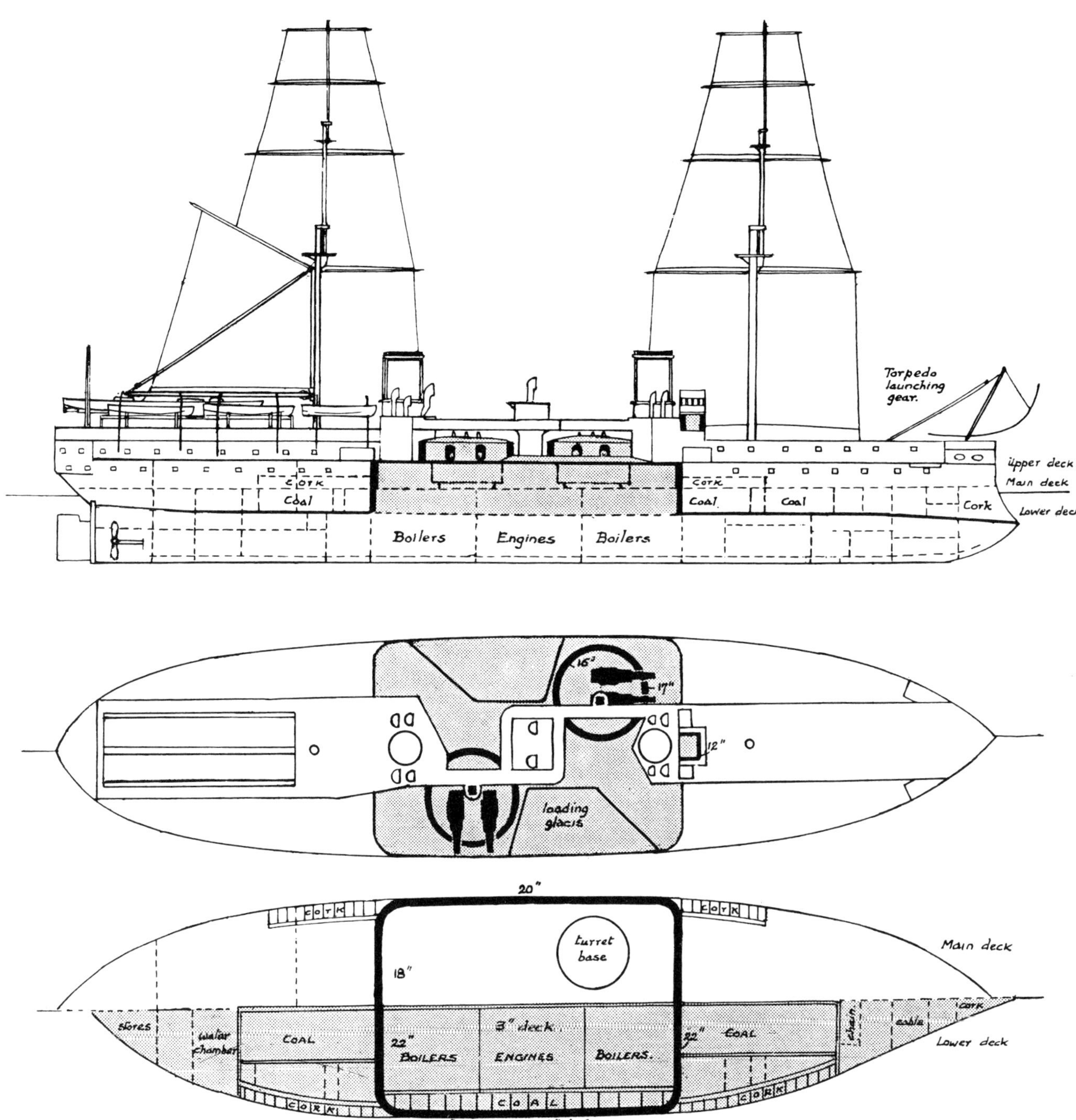

The *Inflexible* was modelled upon the *Duilio* but with waterline armour confined to the citadel, and a thick protective deck fore and aft as in the *Nelson*. Magazines and shell rooms were in the large compartments under the deck and beneath the masts.

"INFLEXIBLE"

Built at	*Laid down*	*Launched*	*Completed*	*Cost*
Portsmouth	24 Feb. '74	27 April '76	18 Oct. '81	£812,485

Dimensions 320′×75′×24·5′/26·5′=11,880 tons.
Hull and armour 7,720 tons. Equipment 4,160 tons.

Guns 4 16-in. 80-ton M.L.R. } 6,955 lb. 2 submerged tubes.
6 20-pdrs. 2 carriages.

Armour Citadel 24″-20″-16″; bulkheads 22″-18″-14″; turrets 17″-16″ (compound); deck 3″; conning tower 12″; skin 1″.
Total 3,275 tons (27·5 per cent.)

Machinery Elder & Co. 2 sets 3-cyl. inverted compound.
One H.P. cyl. 70″; two L.P. cyls. 90″; stroke 4′.
12 boilers; 60 lb. pressure.
Twin 2-bladed screws 20′ diam.; revs. 65.
I.H.P. 8,407=14·75 knots (light draught).

Complement 440.

Coal 1,200/1,300 tons.

Sail area 18,500 sq. ft.

Constructor Alex. Milne.

Features of interest:

(1) *En echelon* turrets amidships carrying the heaviest guns in the Service.
(2) An impregnable citadel carried in a hull having high fore and aft superstructures, with the ends covered by an armoured deck below water above which was extensive sub-division to localize flooding.
(3) Thicker armour than any ship before or since; "compound" used for the first time.
(4) Two 60-ft. torpedo boats and a novel torpedo equipment with the first submerged tubes.
(5) A ratio of length to beam of nearly 4 : 1.
(6) The greatest metacentric height of any British warship to date.
(7) Anti-rolling tanks.
(8) Electric light.

THE *Inflexible* is one of the milestones in the history of British naval architecture, both as the precursor of central citadel ships and as the first capital ship in which the under-water armour deck was used in place of vertical armour along the waterline. Certainly the central box citadel had only a transitory influence in battleship design, but the under-water deck was to develop into a standard feature in all navies.

Apart from these architectural features she was a complete departure from all previous standards of design, and of gun power, armour thickness and disposition of armament. Introduced as the fighting machine *par excellence*, with every pretension of initiating a new scale of military values in general, her sponsors were merely successful in defeating their own ends by subsequent modifications, so that the *Inflexible* became an unfortunate example of what may be called precocious hypertrophy.

For the first year of her conception she enjoyed an enthusiastic press; then came accusation when her stability in battle was questioned; later, her ability to remain right side up in face of the enemy having been more or less vindicated, she enjoyed a brief spell of public confidence and pride. But as lighter and faster-firing guns came into favour her reputation in the Service started to decline, and within five years of hoisting the pennant, breech-loading ordnance was ousting her from the front rank.

But whatever her defects may have been, the *Inflexible* stands out as the greatest of Barnaby's conceptions by virtue of novelty in design rather than on account of her great guns and massive protection. She was certainly an extraordinary ship, and to a large extent embodied the solution of the problem of biggest gun *v.* thickest armour as then presented. But at the best she proved no more than a qualified success. We should have done better by ignoring the *Duilio* as we did the rest of Brin's monster creations; apart from the fact that the Italians have always built better ships than they could fight, the *Duilio* with her slow-firing and slower hitting guns—which had to be discharged one at a time to avoid structural damage—would never have been much of an antagonist even for one of the proposed types of modified *Fury*. But unfortunately the Board was persuaded that "it was necessary for British ships to have guns of the most powerful description," and so the *Inflexible* became the first of our "biggest gun" disappointments, to be later joined by the *Benbow*, *Sans Pareil*, and *Furious*.

Behind them all was the hope that an opponent could be disposed of by a single knock-out blow, the lucky hit which has never yet been registered against an armoured ship in the history of naval warfare. A single knock-out hit might be expected from well-controlled salvo fire, but not from the spasmodic discharge of a single monster gun. It was fortunate that our first biggest-gun phase began and ended with the *Inflexible*.

THE CITADEL RAFT

To visualize the designer's conception of the ship she should be regarded as consisting of three separate parts:

(1) A central citadel 110×75 ft. rising 9½ ft. above water with the turrets at opposite corners and enclosing hydraulic loading gear, magazines, etc., to a depth of 6 ft. below. This was protected by armour in two thicknesses separated and backed by teak totalling 20-in. iron and 21-in. teak above water; 24-in. iron and 17-in. teak at the waterline; 16-in. iron and 25-in. teak below water.
(2) An under-water hull limited above by the 3-in. armour deck extending from ram to rudder-head, with the engines and boilers below the citadel and elsewhere cut up into watertight compartments.
(3) The hull and superstructure above this deck before and abaft the citadel, unprotected and structurally only serving to provide increased stability.

The *Inflexible* in Malta harbour during her first commission with the peacetime brig rig. This view shows how a nominal all-round fire could be obtained from each turret, with the muzzles of the starboard guns projecting beyond the flying bridge; in practice only one gun on each side had axial fire owing to blast effects.

It was laid down specifically by the constructors that *the citadel was inherently stable* and that "with any possible damage to the unarmoured ends by shot or shell she will continue to float with perfect safety before any damages are made good"—and this quite properly was stressed as a most important point.

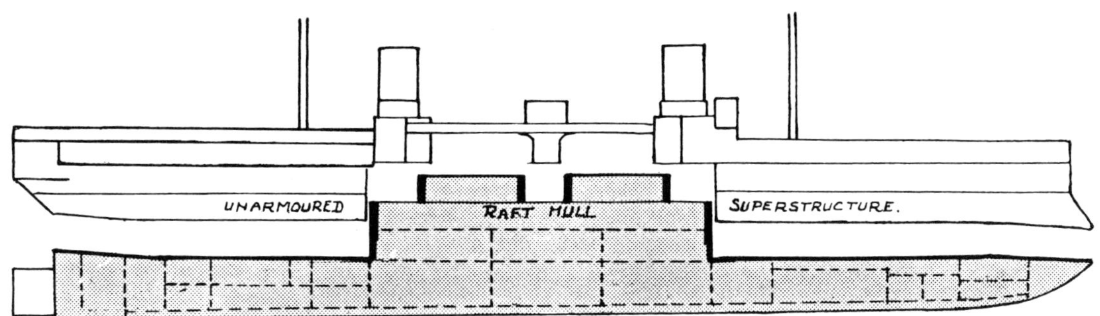

The conception of the *Inflexible* was of an unarmoured but buoyant superstructure carried upon a raft hull limited above by the armoured deck and citadel.

NOVEL DIMENSIONS

Being of the Reed tradition, Barnaby favoured curtailment of length in proportion to beam, and in the *Inflexible* he planned the tubbiest hull of any warship yet constructed. In working out her lines advantage was taken of William Froude's researches into ship proportions by means of models towed in a tank which had demonstrated that a ratio of 4½ (length) to 1 (beam) could be employed without loss of speed or increase in power to displacement. As it was necessary to provide as great a beam as possible in order to secure the widest arcs of fire from the turrets as well as hull security and stability, the benefits of Froude's work can be seen in the *Inflexible's* 14 knots achieved with only 8,000 h.p., although she was 320×75 ft.—actually a ratio of nearly 4 : 1.

But when the *Inflexible* was designed there was little or no sea-going experience with very short and broad ships to demonstrate their loss of speed against a head sea. The "skimming dish" sort of hull was excellent in theory and in the model tank, but showed up badly in service. This was not properly realized for some time to come, and meanwhile Barnaby was satisfied in keeping his hulls short, cutting down displacement, and getting his speed without a great expenditure of power.

Thus, the *Inflexible* was undoubtedly the most graceless ship to date, especially from bow and stern when the great beam was accentuated by narrow superstructure flanked by the huge turrets which showed up like haystacks. Whatever lines she may have had were broken up by every sort of protuberance possible with two ugly funnels to complete a thoroughly ungainly profile.

GUNS

The 16-in. M.L.R. fired a 1,684-lb. projectile with a muzzle velocity of 1,590 ft. secs. able to pierce 23 in. of iron at 1,000 yards. The firing rate was about one round per gun every two minutes.

When first completed she carried six 20-pdrs. for saluting and torpedo defence; in 1885 these were replaced by 4-in. 22-cwt. B.L. and in 1897 by 4·7-in. Q.F. There was a proposal to instal a battery of 6-in. Q.F. in 1900, but this fell through as the old ship was not worth it. The magazines and shell rooms lay below the armoured deck beyond each end of the citadel.

TORPEDO EQUIPMENT

Her torpedo armament comprised two 14-in. carriages above water and two *submerged* tubes at the bows—the latter being fitted experimentally and for the first time in an armoured ship. Over the bows there was also a peculiar scoop down which a torpedo ran when released, and a contraption of sheers aft by which one could be thrown out—neither of which methods of launching was of any value and only gave endless trouble.

Two second-class torpedo boats, stowed on skids on the after superstructure, were supposed to be used for night attack, but proved to be of little service except under very favourable conditions.

TURRETS

As in the case of the citadel armour, the turrets were built up in sandwich form with an outer layer of 9-in. compound and an inner of 7-in. iron, backed and separated by a total of 18 in. of teak, with 1 in. thicker armour and less teak at the faces. They were 33 ft. 10 in. diameter externally and weighed 750 tons each. For working them Rendel's hydraulic system—experimentally tried in the *Thunderer*—was installed in place of steam, and a complete rotation could be made in just over a minute. The guns were mounted on blocks sliding along fixed beams with hydraulic cylinders taking the recoil, and on the reverse running the gun out again.

Owing to their length, loading had to be performed outside the turret, the duplicate fixed stations being under the armour deck which was raised and inclined upwards at the base of the turrets to form a glacis. When the muzzles were depressed they came under the edge of this deck—an arrangement which was certainly an improvement upon the loading ports in the *Thunderer*.

PROTECTION

The central box citadel upon which the stability of the ship depended has already been described. Its length, 110 ft., was fixed as being the utmost which could be protected by the 24-in. plating required to keep out 16-in. projectiles; to have lengthened it in order to gain in stability would have meant thinning the armour and sacrificing the greater for the less. Thus a single shell sent through the armour might disable the ship, but no single hit could possibly destroy the unarmoured structure; and as first designed the citadel had ample stability to maintain the ship afloat and in a fighting condition, independently of any damage to the unarmoured ends.

Beyond the citadel waterline buoyancy was secured by the armour decks in conjunction with subdivision and cofferdams, cork, and canvas. The 6½-ft. space between the main deck just above the waterline and the armour deck below it was divided into compartments filled with coal or stores in water-tight tanks, forming a raft from which any sea-water entering through a shell hole would be limited by the content of the compartment, which

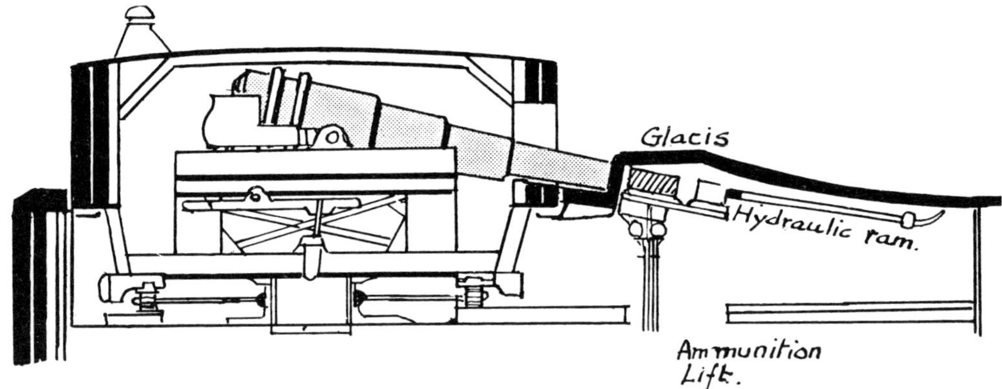

Turret turned inboard with guns depressed below glacis for loading.

for the greater part was coal. Indeed, one of the disadvantages of the design was that two-thirds of the fuel would have to be stowed away outside the citadel surrounded and covered by water when the ship went into battle to prevent it taking fire from shell explosion. Fuel available for action would be only 400 tons, to be stowed in the fighting bunkers and kept ready for use.

For about 70 ft. each end from the citadel the space between these coal bunkers and the ship's side was made up of compartments 4 ft. wide and filled with cork, and internal to this was a cofferdam 2 ft. wide packed with canvas and oakum which also extended across the ship at the end of the coal spaces.

Small-scale experiments with 68-pdr. shell on iron boxes filled with cork soaked in calcium chloride had shown that it did not catch fire easily and could be usefully employed for excluding water, while the canvas and oakum tended to be driven into shot holes and helped to plug them.

Theoretically, with every compartment thrown open to the sea, the cork walls perforated, and the internal cofferdam destroyed, the ship would still have been safe and able to fight. Unfortunately when the guns were increased from 60 to 80 tons the whole foundation of the ship's stability was altered. As Barnaby put it, "the change in armament made us more dependent upon the integrity of the unarmoured parts of the ship than we were when the ship was first designed." The bugbear of radical changes in a completed design brought about the almost inevitable results, and whereas a longer citadel with increased buoyancy had been vetoed because it might expose thinner armour to perforation, heavier guns had been accepted without taking into account the consequent *loss in armoured stability*, which placed the ship at the mercy of the unarmoured structure.

SUPERSTRUCTURE

The fore and aft superstructures raising the upper deck to a height of 17 to 20 ft. gave her a good performance in a seaway and contributed substantially to stability, besides providing accommodation required for the officers. The forward superstructure had a width of 21½ ft., the after one of 30 ft. Between the funnels rose an air trunk supporting the control station which was connected to the superstructures by narrow fore and aft gangways. Although there was supposed to be direct fire along the axial line fore and aft, concussion effects were too severe for this to be employed except as in an improbable emergency in action and cross-deck fire shook things up considerably, making the control station most unpleasant.

This control station is not shown as a protected position, but in the small-scale official plan there is a small armoured tower in front of the forward funnel. As this was surmounted by the charthouse and flanked by cowls which must have blocked vision most effectively, it can be dismissed as any sort of conning tower. As yet the need for a strongly armoured central control position was not apparent. The means for transmitting orders and communications were still very imperfect, so that the conning tower as was developed in later years could not yet be an efficient central control station. It was therefore neither possible nor justifiable to expend weight for such a purpose, which explains why "pilot towers" and the early conning towers were small, inefficient and poorly protected.

SPEED

On first trials the *Inflexible* developed 8,407 h.p. with a mean of 14·75 knots during four runs over the Stokes Bay mile, running light and drawing only 18 ft. 10 in. forward and 23 ft. aft. But the four-bladed screws were regarded as overmuch for her engines, and accordingly replaced by two-bladed before further tests were made. Ventilation proved very defective and the engine-room became unbearable, so that two upcast shafts leading

The *Inflexible* as portguard ship at Portsmouth in 1896. Fighting tops replace the brig rig which was removed ten years previously. The raised deck forming the glacis beneath which the gun muzzles dipped for loading can be seen beneath the starboard turret trained for cross-deck firing.

to the funnel casings and two more to cowls were fitted together with fans and fresh air leads which corrected the temperature both in the citadel and below decks.

Under natural draught she made 12·8 knots with 6,500 h.p., and towards the end of her service was worth about 10·5 knots.

SEA-GOING QUALITIES

In order to ensure stability should her ends be shot away the metacentric height was fixed at 8 ft.—which made her liable to roll quickly. Although somewhat steadier than had been anticipated she had a period of 5½ secs. compared with 7 secs. in the *Bellerophon* and 8 secs. in the *Hercules*—which was regarded as a slow-moving and steady ship. So in order to secure a better gun platform without decreasing stability the innovation of anti-rolling tanks was introduced and fitted fore and aft—although that forward was generally used for stores. These were big ballast tanks, cross-connected by pipes through which the water passed when the ship rolled but with a time lag calculated to counteract this. No results from their employment are recorded in the ship's book, but it is stated that in practice the water did not move quickly enough and the roll was frequently augmented rather than reduced (*Lord Fisher*, vol. 1, p. 75).

In all the *Inflexible* only put in seven years' fleet service, with two spells up the Straits, where her amidships freeboard of only 10 ft. was not a great drawback.

RIG

Although intended to fight under pole masts only, the *Inflexible* was given a brig rig as a peace-time dressing so that the ship's company could participate in evolutions aloft with the rest of the Fleet.

The lower masts were 78/75 ft., topmasts 46 ft. and topgallants 39 ft., with lower yards 79½ ft., topgallants 45 ft. and royals 36½ ft., giving a total sail area of 18,500 ft., she had no head sails.

This rig, as Barnaby was careful to point out, was "not fitted in deference to the views of naval officers, but was part of the design of the ship, and commended by those with whom the final decision rested"—a delightful dig at Whitehall prejudice. But whoever insisted on the absurd wind-trap was guilty of an expensive blunder, although the ship only had to suffer its drawbacks for four years. By 1885 masts and yards had given way to fighting tops, and when refitted in that year she was reduced to pole masts with a circular fighting top and light signal yards. In 1900, when she was to have been "modernized" with a 6-in. Q.F. battery, a *Sultan* rig with two tops in each mast was prepared for her at Portsmouth Dockyard. But, as in the case of the *Dreadnought*, Treasury sanction could not be obtained for the expenditure, so these masts lay for years up by the coal wharf as a reminder of what the old ship might have looked like in her dotage. Internally her layout was complicated compared with the simple systems which obtained in previous ships, and during her first commission the confusion below was only overcome by the ingenuity of her first Captain, John Arbuthnot Fisher.

> "The *Inflexible* was of novel construction, full of complicated machinery, numerous compartments, and tortuous passages; men used to lose their way altogether amidst the mazes of this iron labyrinth, and knew not what deck they were on, what compartment they were in, or whether they were walking forward or aft; so it occurred to the Captain that if he had to take his ship into action there would be pretty general confusion down below, and that there would be very little chance of his orders being transmitted or attended to, so he set to work in earnest, and with the assistance of his Officers, and by adopting various and ingenious devices such as painting bulkheads and passages with different colours and various other novel plans, he succeeded after several months of close personal supervision and attention in evolving order out of chaos, and rendered his ship a valuable fighting machine; but the various and sometimes irksome drills which went on below by candle-light and which were so absolutely essential to the fighting efficiency of the ship, made no show; nobody knew from outside what was going on within, and the probability is that the other ships' companies were under the impression that the crew of this gallant ship spent most of their time in sleeping, which impression would no doubt be strengthened when Officers from other ships came on board and saw men emerging from the gloomy depths below, blinking and winking like owls in the daylight.
>
> "Be that as it may, when the Admiral's inspection took place but scant credit was given to the Captain and his Officers for all the pains and trouble they had taken to get their ship into fighting order, and as they could not cross topgallant and royal yards and shift topsails quite so smartly as other ships in the squadron, they found themselves but lightly thought of, and suffered under the cold shade of official displeasure. Then the gallant Captain bethought himself that this was unpleasant, and would be bad for the *morale* of his men. So having got his ship into fighting efficiency with but scant credit for it, he set to work with equal energy to exercise his men aloft, for he had masts and sails too, and in a very short time his ship succeeded in shifting a topsail a few seconds quicker than any ship in the squadron. Then she immediately rose from the depths of official displeasure to the highest pinnacle of fame—she acquired the proud title of 'the smartest ship in the squadron' and nothing was good enough for her." (Captain Penrose Fitzgerald, R.U.S.I. paper "How can we make the most of our ships?")

"INFLEXIBLE"

Commissioned at Portsmouth 5 July 1881 and completed in October when she proceeded to the Mediterranean. Was present at Alexandria where her firing was very impressive and accurate although not so destructive as had been anticipated. She fired eighty-eight 16-in. shell against Ras-el-Tin, Mex, Ada and Pharos forts and sustained the most damage of any of our ships. One 10-in. shell struck below the waterline outside the armour and glanced upwards, perforating the deck and killing the carpenter and an officer directing a 20-pdr. on the superstructure. The concussion of her guns injured the upperworks and smashed some boats. Returned to Portsmouth full of defects in 1885 for refit. Rig removed, tops fitted, and small guns changed. From February '85 she was in Reserve, commissioning for the '87 Review and manœuvres in '88 and '89. In July '90 again went up the Straits where she remained until November '93, and then returned to Portsmouth as portguard ship for four years. Reduced to Fleet Reserve in October '97 and Dockyard Reserve in November 1901.

Sold in September 1903 for £20,100.

Chapter 40

THE "INFLEXIBLE" COMMITTEE

IN 1875 when the ship had been a year on the stocks the late Chief Constructor, who had recently paid a visit to the Italian yards and inspected the *Duilio* and *Dandolo*, sprang a bombshell by declaring them to be "unsafe for battle, and exposed beyond all doubt or question to speedy destruction"—a statement which reacted on the *Inflexible* as being designed on the same system.

The charge was repudiated by the Italian Government on the grounds that Reed could not possess the confidential particulars for making the necessary calculations relative to their stability. But it was realized that Reed was in a position to obtain quite as much essential material as was necessary to make an accurate estimate upon which to base his statement, and public anxiety in this country was not allayed by the Italian denial. Believing that in the new ship approaching completion they would possess the most formidable and perfect war machine afloat, an opinion to the contrary from such a competent authority could only be regarded as a matter for serious consideration.

Reed's calculations were published in *The Times* of 18 June 1876 and brought before the House. He claimed that having gone fully into the calculations of the *Inflexible* the result of the cork chambers being destroyed could only be complete loss of stability and capsizing. When the ship was ordered the Constructor's Department undertook that the armoured citadel would have ample stability for keeping the ship afloat in an upright position without any assistance from the unarmoured ends; and he contended that every heavily armoured ship had been designed to comply with this condition. Since the design was first prepared considerable modifications had been introduced and the *Inflexible*, instead of having an ample reserve of stability after the unarmoured structures had lost their buoyancy, would not have sufficient for withstanding the heave of the sea or even the action of the rudder. Also, he pointed out that whereas the original design provided ample stability within the citadel, the Admiralty was now trying to prove that such stability was really unnecessary.

The Admiralty defence of the *Inflexible* mainly turned upon Reed's contention that the cork packing would be blown out and the cofferdams destroyed by shell-fire. Barnaby claimed that the possibility of the ship being reduced to this state was infinitely remote. The cork packing was adopted to preserve the solidity of the side walls, water being supposed to flow freely through holes made in them; and the other materials for cofferdams were intended to exclude water from the coal spaces notwithstanding perforation.

But while accepting these aids his department was not prepared to trust to the extreme improbability that all compartments could possibly be riddled in action, for although in fighting a ship of her own class the number of projectiles she could receive in her unarmoured ends under the water and in its immediate neighbourhood would not be numerous, yet in a long engagement with many adversaries she would be exposed to heavy fire from a large number of light guns. It was estimated that 300 hits would be necessary to reduce the ship to a "riddled and gutted condition."

It was therefore provided that when completely riddled under water and every compartment thrown open to the sea, the cork walls perforated and the cofferdams destroyed, she should be safe and able to fight. In such a condition her range of stability would be 30°.

Replying to this, Reed pointed out that although there would be stability when the ends were riddled this had nothing to do with his objections, which were that wherever a shell penetrated, "*riddling*" would not be the result *but complete destruction of the surrounding chambers*. When the ship was thus "gutted" there would be no stability to represent a curve. He did not base his argument on "the preposterous conditions that the fore and after ends of the ship are to be utterly demolished," but that shell-fire would destroy the water-tightness of a structure of half-inch iron even when situated a little below water level in a smooth sea. Also the very principle of the ship provided for bunkering 800 tons of coal in the unarmoured ends, "surrounded and covered by water when the ship goes into action" to bring her well down to her fighting draught. As for their Lordships' reminder "that even if the ends were blown out there remained the remedy of admitting 400 tons of water-ballast into the double-bottom of the citadel" which would at once have the effect of increasing stability," he pointed out that this would add another 20 inches to the damaged draught of 27 ft. leaving a deck freeboard of 5½ ft. only, which would accentuate the difficulties and dangers of her condition.

In order to settle the controversy the Admiralty appointed a committee on 16 July 1877 consisting of Admiral Sir James Hope, Dr. Woolley, Mr. G. W. Rendel and Mr. William Froude to investigate the charges made by Reed—distinguished men well able to weigh evidence from a Service, naval architect's, engineer's and scientist's point of view.

Their report was presented on 4 December 1877 and generally upheld the Admiralty claim that the *Inflexible's* stability was sufficient in view of the highly improbable event of her having all her stores and cork blown out by shell-fire. If ever she were so damaged, the metacentric height would have been only 2 ft., her condition of stability only $17\frac{1}{2}°$ with the ship in a highly critical state, limited in speed and turning power, dangerous to manœuvres against ram and torpedo, and requiring caution in even running out the guns because of heeling.

The Committee expressed the opinion that future progress in armoured ships lay in a combination of effective armour and some system of cellular or equivalent structure, and indirectly admitted the desirability of increasing the safety of vessels of the *Inflexible* type by the following recommendations:

(1) Extension of the cork chambers longitudinally to the extreme ends of the ship and upwards to the main deck.
(2) Reduction in the inclining moment due to the running-out of the guns (as designed 1,600 ft. tons).
(3) Increase in pumping power (in *Inflexible* as designed this was only 4,500 tons an hour).
(4) Systematic experimental enquiry into the best form and distribution of the cells at the ends of ships of this type; and concerning the best material, if any, with which the cells may be wholly or partially filled.
(5) Increase of beam in future vessels of this type in order to increase transverse stability. Experiments with models had shown that even a considerable increase in the extreme breadth of the *Inflexible*, if accompanied by a corresponding fining of the ends so as to keep the displacement unaltered, would if anything diminish the resistance of the intact vessel to propulsion at high speed.

During this enquiry construction on the ship was suspended and her completion delayed for nearly a year in consequence. By the time she passed into service the glamour of her size and gun-power caught the public fancy and she was just as much of a sensation as the *Dreadnought* which followed her a quarter of a century later. How she would have acquitted herself in action may be judged to some extent by the experience of the Chinese turret-ships *Chen Yuen* and *Ting Yuen* at Yalu. These were central citadel ships with soft ends, and modified editions of the *Inflexible*. Exposed to the concentrated fire of the Japanese ships, the latter was hit close on 200 times and the former nearly as often; but in neither case were the unarmoured ends blown to pieces, and the British ship would hardly have become a sitting and almost helpless target as was the case with the Chinese ships.

Chapter 41

THE PASSING OF MASTS AND YARDS

WHEN the big sheer legs at Portsmouth lowered the heavy lower masts of the *Inflexible* into position, the occasion was one of some historical interest in marking the last time that one of H.M. ships-of-the-line would be masted to carry canvas. Although three more armoured units were to be provided with masts and yards, the *Shannon*, *Nelson* and *Northampton*, they were intended for service as flagships on distant stations and belonged to the new category of "armoured cruisers" in which a good spread of canvas was still regarded as necessary. A fourth armoured cruiser the *Imperieuse* did make an attempt to justify her brig rig, but only succeeded in putting *finis* to the use of sail in heavy ships. For a few more years the age-old method of wind propulsion was to serve its term in corvettes and smaller vessels, and then as these were gradually withdrawn from service we watched the passing of the most romantic feature which ever graced a ship-of-war.

When Sir Spencer Robinson expressed his adverse opinion to the use of sail in armoured ships in April 1865, he was almost a voice crying in the wilderness; ten years later the younger generation of naval officers were starting to criticize the use of sail in large ships, and Captain Philip Colomb wrote a paper showing that it was an entire mistake to suppose that there was any economy in fully rigging steam vessels. His figures demonstrated in the case of the flagships of the China Station that the very least cost for the pleasure of carrying about masts and yards was £1,730 a year. He traced the flagships through 23,000 miles, the gunboat *Dart* through 12,000 miles, and the *Egeria* through nearly 11,000 miles. Every hour and mile was accounted for, and the "economy" was a dead loss. It cost more coals to carry around the masts and yards than was gained by them, and this was when the compound engine was just coming in. In the *Minotaur*—used as a training ship—the masts and yards did not suffice for gymnastic purposes and the ship was equipped with regular gymnastic apparatus.

In 1882 Captain Penrose Fitzgerald, a particularly plain-spoken critic, gave it as his opinion that the two years' cruise with the big *Inconstant* and *Bacchante* and a squadron of corvettes, when nine-tenths of the distance were covered under sail, could not be justified as a period of training.

> "The detached squadron has not been a success unless it be considered simply as an escort to the Princes during their visit to Australia and Japan, but as a training school for officers and men it has not been successful—that is to say, it has not trained them nor exercised them in subjects which would be useful to the country in wartime.
>
> Sending steamers which sail badly to make long passages under sail is inconsistent with the spirit of the age, and with the rapid means of progression which is now universal; it is waste of time, and both Officers and men know this, and it disgusts them.
>
> The men read now much more than they used to, and they know perfectly well that a high state of efficiency in 'shifting topsails' will be of no use to them in wartime, nor enable them to fight their ship any better than if they had never seen a topsail yard in their lives. They look upon it as a gymnasium at which so much useless work is done, like carrying shot or any other manual labour." (R.U.S.I., 1887.)

In 1887 we had fifteen rigged ironclads in commission, six with twin and nine with single screws. Captain Fitzgerald put forward the strongest possible case for unrigging these ships, although he considered that sail could be retained in the smaller cruising ships which lacked adequate coal bunkerage, and his contentions found full support at a big representative gathering at the R.U.S.I. in March 1887. The principal arguments for the abolition of sail in ironclads were as follows: Their weight caused increased immersion, they occupied valuable space both on deck and below which might be devoted to warlike stores. They tended to mask the fire of guns, and there was a probability of wreckage from them fouling the screws in action. Finally, and as the most potent argument against them, they diverted so much attention, energy and resources of Officers and men from the real work of their profession and study of modern warfare. Evolutions aloft were so showy and attractive with so much swagger about them, and the smart shifting of topsails and topmasts had for so long earned the Admiral's approval and the First Lieutenant's promotion, that the fact of these time-honoured signs of "efficiency" having nothing to do with the fighting efficiency of the ship had been lost sight of.

The chief arguments for the retention of masts and yards were: The engines might break down, and without sails the ship would be perfectly helpless; that masts and yards helped to steady a ship in a gale and stop rolling; and (greatest argument of all) if they were abolished we should lose with them the fine, dashing, showy and somewhat risky gymnastics which produced such a hardy and courageous type of seaman.

Critically examined, these arguments held no water. If a single-screw ironclad broke down in peace time while in squadron, she could be taken in tow by her consorts; if when alone she would be reported by some passing vessel and very soon picked up, as our ironclads did not do much cruising alone in remote and unfrequented waters. In such a case the sails would be of some use, as in the case of the *Monarch* when she broke down between

Alexandria and Malta (*q.v.*), but even so the chances of loss would be too remote to justify retention. If she broke down in a gale of wind on a lee shore she would drift ashore just as surely and more rapidly with masts and sails than without them; if she were in a position to get soundings before she reached the rocks she would have a better chance of riding it out at her anchors without masts and yards than with them.

Lastly, she might break down in action. If in a single action she would certainly be rammed and sunk, and all the sails in the world would not help her. If in a general action, and she were not rammed by friend or foe, she would be taken in tow by whichever side won—and it could not be suggested that if the enemy gained the day any rigged ship would be allowed to escape under sail.

The second argument that sails steadied a ship in a gale was partially true, but experience with the ironclads had shown that the best way to treat them in heavy weather was to furl the square sails and lay them to under very easy steam with the head two or three points from the wind, and set trysails with the sheets hauled amidships.

Masts and yards had been the means of bringing our guns into action for generations, but that end was now served by steam; high masts would only serve as beacons above the smoke of action to show the enemy where to fire. Sail drill used to be very much overdone, and Captain Fitzgerald quoted the case of a corvette in which he served when the Captain kept the men sending up topgallant masts, crossing topgallant royal yards, hauling out a bowline, etc., striking bowline, repeating it from 7.50 a.m. to 1 p.m., so that two men were invalided out from the effects of over-exertion.

Captain Fitzgerald's paper and the discussion which followed must have played their part in hastening on the gradual abolition of sail from the ironclads. As the big ships came into dockyard hands for large refits, opportunity was taken for substituting fighting masts and fitting signal yards in place of the great wind-trap aloft, so that within a few years only the *Swiftsure* and *Triumph*, which played Box and Cox as flagships on the Pacific Station, and the training ships *Minotaur*, *Agincourt* and *Northumberland*, remained as the last descendants of the traditional battle fleet.

Chapter 42

"AJAX" AND "AGAMEMNON"

	Built at	Laid down	Launched	Completed	Cost
"*Ajax*"	Pembroke	21 March '76	10 March '80	30 March '83	£548,393
"*Agamemnon*"	Chatham	9 May '76	17 Sept. '79	29 March '83	£530,015

Dimensions 280′ × 66′ × 23′/24′ = 8,510 tons.
Hull and armour 5,820. Equipment 2,690 tons.

Armament 4 38-ton 12·5-in. M.L.R.
2 6-in. B.L.
21 smaller guns. } 3,400 lb.

Armour Citadel 18″-15″; turrets 16″-14″; bulkheads 16½″-13½″; conning tower 12″; deck 3″; teak 18″-9″.
Total 2,223 tons (26·1 per cent.).

Complement 345.

Coal 700/960 tons.

Machinery Both by Penn. Inverted compound. I.H.P. 6,000 = 13 knots.
3 cyls. 54″; stroke 3¼′.
Twin screws 18 ft. diam.; revs. 70.
10 return tubular boilers; 60 lb. pressure.

Constructor Alex. Milne.

Points of interest:

(1) The last battleships to be armed with M.L.R.
(2) The first to have a secondary battery as well as anti-torpedo guns.
(3) The most unhandy capital ships ever to fly the White Ensign.

In the *Ajax* and *Agamemnon* Barnaby succeeded in producing two of the most unsatisfactory battleships ever built for the Royal Navy. Such appreciation as they ever earned was officially inspired and voiced in the press during their construction; once they had put to sea defects and deficiencies became only too manifest, and thereafter they ranked as the black sheep of the Battle Fleet.

Having accepted the *Inflexible* as the model upon which future types of battleship were to be based, the Admiralty decided that the next ships should be smaller and cheaper editions, just as the *Warrior* was followed by the *Defence* and *Hector* classes. This policy of reaction to any increase in displacement and the confounding of cheapness with merit was to crop up sporadically during the next twenty years, as instanced by the *Centurion*, *Renown* and to some extent the *Canopus*; in none of these was the saving in expenditure commensurate with the loss in fighting power, and the *Ajax* and *Agamemnon* were the worst examples of this particular form of futile economy.

In drawing up the specifications for the *Inflexible* the Board had directed that the draught should not exceed a mean of 24 ft.—although this was afterwards increased by a foot when the heavier guns were adopted. For the *Ajax* the mean was to be 23½ ft. for service in the shallow waters of the Baltic and Black Sea if necessary, with a reduction in displacement of 3,000 tons representing a saving of some £300,000 on each ship. In having to work to these limitations the Director of Naval Construction was faced with a difficult task, as the length and beam were to be fixed by the Froude ratio of 4½ : 1, or—as recommended by the *Inflexible* Committee—with even a higher proportion of beam and finer ends to obtain the required speed of 13 knots.

The minimum beam was fixed by the diameter of the turrets—28 ft. externally or 4½ ft. less than those in the *Dreadnought* for similar guns. As in the *Inflexible*, the citadel was about 10 ft. wider than their combined diameters. This allowed for a length of 297 ft. with Froude's ratio, or 280 ft. with the 4·2 : 1 of the *Inflexible*—which was what Barnaby used. He pointed out that to have made the ships any wider would have meant fining the ends to obtain the necessary speed, and so cramping accommodation; to have made them shorter would have meant insufficient bilge keel to check rolling and not enough armour depth to prevent the unarmoured hull from exposure on rolling. Also with a shorter citadel the four guns could not have been sufficiently staggered to fire abeam.

Although model experiments showed the apparent suitability of the dimensions decided upon, the ships suffered from excess of beam and were most unhappy at sea.

In fact, these diminutives of the *Inflexible* had all her defects and none of her alleged virtues. The Secretary to the Admiralty acknowledged that:

"In one important particular the *Ajax* and *Agamemnon* are inferior to the *Inflexible*. The central citadel

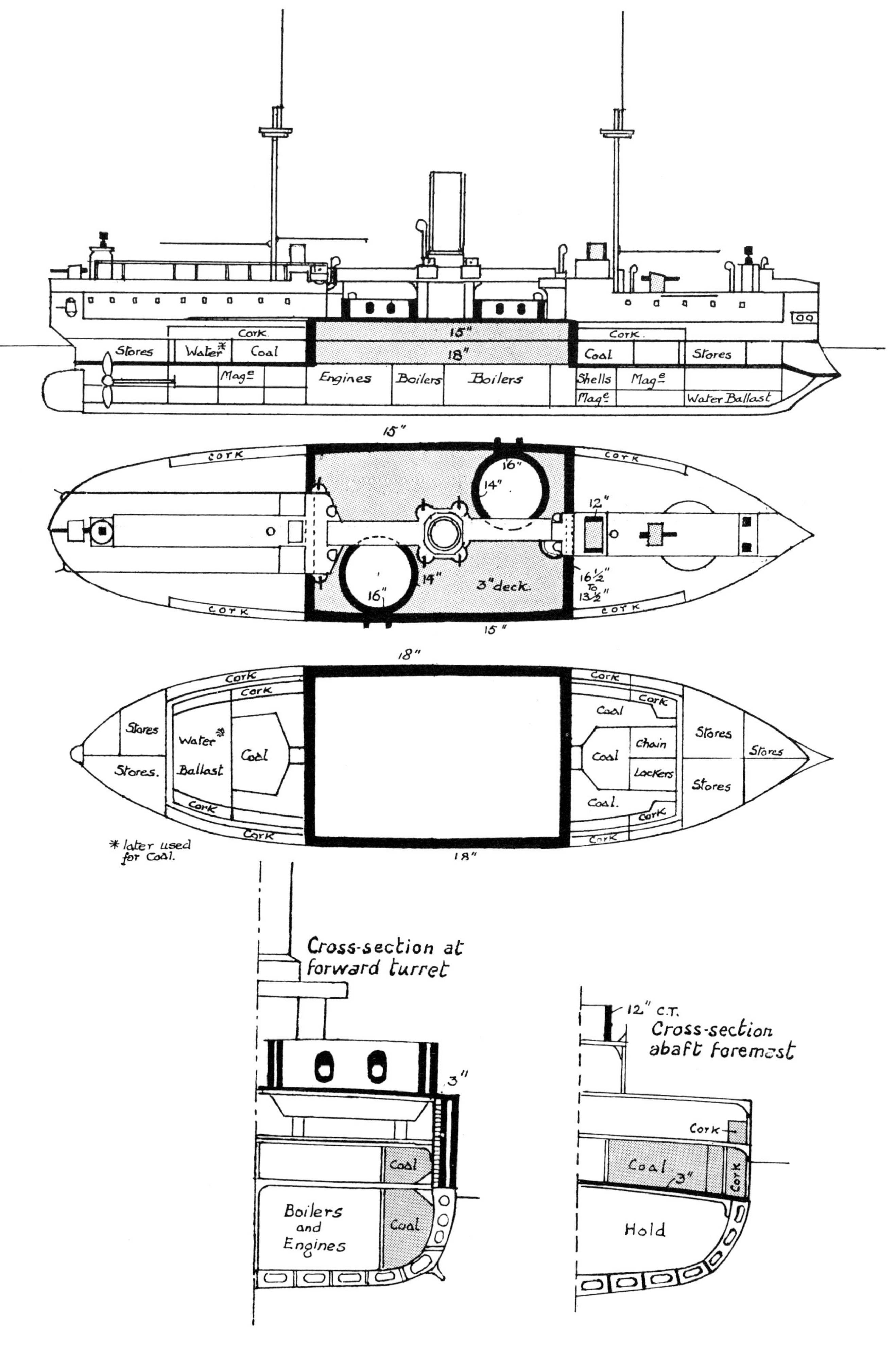

Cork.
Stores
Water*
Coal
15"
18"
Cork.
Coal
Stores
Mag^e
Engines
Boilers
Boilers
Shells
Mag^e
Mag^e
Water Ballast
15"
CORK
16"
14"
12"
14"
16"
3"deck.
16½"
To
13½"
CORK
15"
18"
Cork
Cork
Stores
Water*
Ballast
Coal
Stores.
Cork
Cork
Cork
Coal
Cork
Coal
Chain
Lockers
Stores
Stores
Stores
Coal.
Cork
Cork
18"
* later used for Coal.
Cross-section at forward turret
3"
Coal
Boilers and Engines
Coal
12" C.T.
Cross-section abaft foremast
Cork
Coal
3"
Cork
Hold

is not, as it was in the case of the *Inflexible*, of sufficient displacement to secure the stability of the ship should the unarmoured ends be destroyed."

Actually the reverse was the case, the ships being so constructed that they were dependent upon their unarmoured ends for ability to float right side up and were the worst examples of abuse of the citadel system.

Like the *Inflexible* they took an unconscionable long time to complete, as from 1872 onwards the Government both under Disraeli and Gladstone tried to run the Navy as cheaply as possible. Each Board was faced with the same financial difficulties during the next twelve years until the inevitable crisis arose, and meanwhile diminished votes towards new construction prolonged building periods and piled up costs, overheads, and interest until ships estimated at £500,000 apiece were actually costing £700,000, of which at least £100,000 was dead loss.

Being built under the stigma of the *Inflexible's* alleged shortcomings, it is little wonder that they were born of distrust and controversy. Their prototype had been heralded as the world's biggest warship and had the kudos of carrying the thickest armour and guns twice as heavy as any in the Fleet—but these ships were simply reduced copies with her defects exaggerated! Moreover, as they happened to be the only big-gun armoured ships to be laid down in the years 1876-77-78—during which time the French commenced a dozen such, all completely belted and with armour as thick or thicker—it is little wonder that they came in for every sort of adverse criticism.

The *Agamemnon* in Plymouth Sound in 1884, painted white for her commission out East. The short 6-in. B.L. are beneath the forward boom and right aft, and she has the cutaway stern associated with her erratic steering.

The *Devastation* had been completed three years when the *Ajax* was laid down, and a comparison may help to bring out the chief points of Barnaby's model.

	"*Devastation*"	"*Ajax*"
Dimensions	285′ × 62·3′ × 26·9′.	280′ × 66′ × 23·5′.
Displacement	9,330 tons.	8,510 tons.
Guns	Four 35-tons.	Four 38-tons.
Armour	2,540 tons (Hull 10″-12″).	2,223 tons (short citadel 15″-18″).
Coal	1,800 tons (maximum).	960 tons (maximum).
H.P. and Speed	6,650 = 13·8 knots.	6,000 = 13 knots.
Cost	£361,438	£548,393.

ARMAMENT

The four biggest guns which could be mounted in the *Ajax* were the 12·5-in. 38-tonners, but several alternatives were considered before the main armament was definitely settled.

In August 1878 Elswick had produced a new type of 8-in. M.L.R. of 11½ tons firing a 180 lb. projectile with a muzzle velocity of 2,116 ft. secs. and giving a much greater penetration than the 35-ton gun, though of course without its smashing power. Also there was a 12-in. M.L.R. of 38 tons which was expected to rival the 80-ton gun in penetration, and approaching completion an 8-in. breech-loader which would equal the muzzle-loader in power.

It was realized that the perforating power of these guns with their greater range were more likely to find favour in the Service than smashing power with lower velocity—especially when associated with a slow rate of fire. Indeed there was a likelihood that the size of future ships in relation to the power of their armaments might be considerably reduced, while the value of side armour would be lessened. The whole *Inflexible* conception was vitally affected by such weapons, and especially by the possibility of introducing the Armstrong 38-tonner firing a 640-lb. projectile with a m.v. of 2,000 ft. secs., allowing a gain in penetration of more than 50 per cent. over the short guns already ordered for the ships.

In November 1878 a model was prepared showing how these long M.L. models could be loaded in 28-ft. turrets. It was an engaging proposition, but with the great disadvantage that in action the four loading chambers and the two ports in each turret would have to be kept open and the turret flooded if seas came aboard. However, any change to the longer B.L. guns or to a system of loading M.L. outside the turret would involve "large considerations which could not be disposed of hastily"; and as the long guns were not then made and would have to be tested, it was settled that the ships should be completed for the short 38-ton chambered guns and work on the hydraulic mountings went ahead.

But a few months later came the explosion of the *Thunderer's* 38-tonner, and work was again suspended pending the result of the enquiry.

One of the recommendations of the Committee on Designs was that unarmoured secondary batteries should be carried for employment against unarmoured areas, and these ships were the first in which a definite three-calibre armament was mounted. It was rather a curious mixture of guns and not without a certain historical interest. The 12·5-in. M.L.R. with their turret ports 10 ft. 7 in. above water and loaded from inside the turret were the last muzzle-loaders to be mounted in a British capital ship. The secondary armament—decided upon in November 1884—were short 6-in. B.L., one being placed well back on the forward superstructure and the other right aft. Both were replaced by 6-in. Q.F. in 1897. Against torpedo attack, then entrusted to small launches only, a number of Nordenfelts and light guns were mounted in little sponsons around the funnel and on the superstructures. For torpedo attack a 60-ft. launch was carried on skids under the main derrick.

ARMOUR

Although nominally a citadel ship in which ability to float was vested in the integrity of the citadel, no matter what damage might be suffered by the unarmoured ends, actually armoured stability in these ships was so compromised that the very reverse was the case. With a citadel 6 ft. shorter and 9 ft. narrower than in the *Inflexible* the narrow margin of safety in that ship had been cut too fine and it provided insufficient buoyancy and stability to maintain the hull right side up if the unarmoured ends became waterlogged despite the smaller turrets and lighter guns. Also in the general scale-down armour thickness had to suffer, so that instead of 24 in. the sides could only be composed of 10-in. and 8-in. plates separated and backed by 10-in. teak, reduced below water to a similar sort of sandwich with a total 15 in. of iron. Being specifically designed for end-on action the fore and after transverse bulkheads became of special importance and received almost the thickest armour of all, totalling 16½ in. above and 13½ in. below water—the latter being but little less than in the *Inflexible*. A 3-in. deck covered the entire citadel. Under favourable conditions the citadel walls were reinforced by coal, as armoured wing bulkheads helped to form longitudinal bunkers along their full length.

Before and abaft the citadel protection was confined to a 3-in. under-water deck with the main deck just above the waterline and the intervening space filled with coal, stores, and a water ballast tank aft. Also for 70 ft. before and abaft the citadel there ran a double belt of cork separated by a cofferdam for a height of 6 ft. above and below water—a ceinture of questionable value upon which the life of the ship in action more or less depended.

The turrets received 14-in. compound armour with 16-in. faces which compared well with the 16 in. to 17 in. in the *Inflexible*.

During the Barnaby era various positions were assigned for the conning tower—such as it was—and the *Inflexible* carried her square box on the island between the funnels where vision was largely confined to either beam. In the *Ajax* it was moved to the forward superstructure and placed on top of the charthouse behind the mast, upon which lofty if very insecure foundation it commanded wide arcs of vision. The 12-in. iron rectangular box was still nothing more than an armoured pilot house containing a few voice pipes, with a vision slot of 18 in. between the crown and the sides. It could have afforded little sense of security in action, being liable to come tumbling down with the wreckage of the charthouse or disappear over the ship's side from a direct heavy gun hit. Indeed, it is remarkable that such thick protection should have been allotted to a structure so poorly equipped and sited.

SEA-GOING QUALITIES

In reducing Froude's ratio for the lines of the *Ajax* Barnaby defeated his own ends. Instead of producing an economical ship able to make 13 knots with a minimum of power, he burdened the Navy with a couple of unreliable steamers which ranked with that handful of designs that never evoked a good word even from the men who had the responsibility of handling them.

The most objectionable and perplexing characteristic of their behaviour at sea was the large amount of helm, sometimes to port and sometimes to starboard, required to keep them on a straight course. Remaining at either the one or the other unchanged for hours or even days together, it would occasionally and without the least warning or apparent cause change sides and then again remain for an indefinite period in the new position. Up to 10 knots they were safe enough to manœuvre in company with a squadron, but at higher speeds the angle of helm increased so rapidly that they became positively dangerous in company or in narrow and crowded waters. At full speed (13 knots) the helm angle was never less than 18°, and when the reversal occurred and the ship took charge they would fly off at right angles before the helm could be corrected. On one occasion the *Agamemnon* with her helm amidships turned a complete circle to port in 9 mins. 10 secs.

The explanation of this phenomenon lay in the handling of their dimensions. Being of great proportionate beam and moderate draught, also very flat-bottomed and of full lines, they were apt to behave more like trays than ships, and the Captain of the *Ajax* reported:

> "My belief is that on such occasions a huge body of water changes from one quarter to the other, and affixes itself there like a clam. From that moment the helm is carried the reverse way to what it was before."

This conclusion agreed with the observed results when the tank model of the ship was used for experimental tests by Mr. R. Froude using both hand and mechanical towing and steering. Consequently he was able to indicate the changes necessary to the stern for this sheering tendency to be overcome. A snub fitted to the upper edge of the rudder to increase its area had made no difference, as it was found that the leaving-lines or run of the hull were so blunt as to engender a large mass of dead-water with a one-sided flow. This had been observed to some extent in the *Northampton* and *Inflexible*, but was greatly accentuated in the *Ajax*.

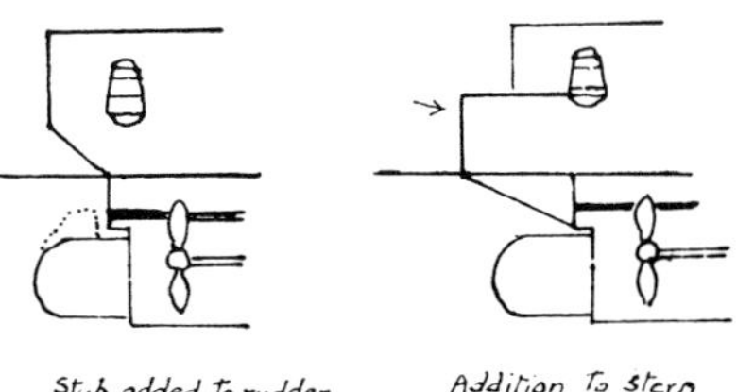

Alterations effected on the sterns of the *Ajax* and *Agamemnon* to correct their steering.

On the strength of the results obtained with the model fitted with extensions to the stern, a long deadwood was added to the *Ajax* and *Agamemnon*, after which they were reported as being fit to work with a squadron, although still requiring an uncertain amount of helm at slow speed which made the steering of a straight course very difficult. In thick weather they came to be regarded as no fit company for a squadron at sea and were directed accordingly. "Take station on the horizon" being the reputed signal.

In anything of a seaway they lurched and plunged in a manner all their own, and when the Fleet left Spithead after the 1889 Review the *Standard* reported:

> "The erratic *Ajax*, for example, would dart out of line at times, making a wide sweep, and as she plunged into the seas would send the spray flying showers hundreds of feet high, while great seas swept her forward decks."

As was the case with the *Belleisle* and *Orion*, one of the ships passed her active career abroad while the other spent her time in the Coastguard or Reserve, standing-by for the possibility of service in the shallow waters for which their draught fitted them, and which no other heavyweights of their day could have performed.

"AGAMEMNON"

On completion at Chatham in April '83 she was ordered to Devonport as drill-ship, and there received considerable additions to her equipment. Commissioned in September '84 for service in China and shadowed the Russian armoured cruiser *Vladimir Monomakh* for the passage out, during the war scare. Ran aground several times in the Suez Canal and held up traffic for some days. Returned to the Mediterranean in March '86 and had her stern altered at Malta. From February to November '89 did temporary duty on East Indies station, and served as one of the blockading fleet at Zanzibar against coast slaving traffic (at one time had 7 officers and 73 men on the sick list out of 400 complement). Rejoined Mediterranean fleet until October '92 and then paid off at Devonport into Reserve. In '96 was reduced to Fleet Reserve and made non-effective in November 1901. Sold 1903.

"AJAX"

Commissioned 30 April '85 at Chatham for Admiral Hornby's Particular Service Squadron until August when she went to Greenock as coastguard ship. Her stern was altered at Chatham in '86 when she returned to Greenock and served there with periodic sea-time at manœuvres for the next five years (collided with *Devastation* off Portland in '87). Paid off in Reserve at Chatham in April '91 and two years later went into Fleet Reserve. Reduced to Dockyard Reserve in November 1901.

Sold March '04.

Chapter 43

THE RUSSIAN WAR SCARE PURCHASES

DURING the Russo-Turkish war of 1878 there was a possibility of our being drawn into conflict with Russia. The Reserve was mobilized and resulted in the formation of a strange conglomeration of ships known as the "Particular Service Squadron" which assembled in Portland Roads under Admiral Sir Cooper Key and remained in being from April until August. This international tension was also responsible for the purchase of four armour-clads, at a first cost of two millions—the *Belleisle*, *Orion* and *Superb* under completion for the Turkish Navy and the *Neptune* in hand for Brazil. Having been built under what Reed described as "very peculiar circumstances in some cases," they required heavy dockyard expenditure to convert them to British standards in armament, construction and equipment. But at the best they were bad bargains and their acquisition was described as "one of the regrettable results of mean economies in the provision of defence which invariably lead to extravagant and aimless expenditure when necessity arises."

There was, however, another aspect of their purchase. The Turkish ships had to be detained in proper observance of our neutrality obligations and we were more or less obliged to take them over in recompense to their builders, as had been the case with the *Scorpion* and *Wivern*. Britain at that time—and for another thirty-odd years to come—kept her private yards busy with naval orders from abroad which could always be regarded as potential reserves for our own Fleet, although the ships might differ broadly from British practice. At a later period the standard of construction and general trend of design of such ships was approximated to Admiralty requirements, but in the 'seventies the private builders allowed themselves considerable latitude in filling foreign specifications, so that a strange diversity of fighting ships steamed from the Thames and Tyne.

"BELLEISLE" AND "ORION"

Designed in Constantinople for service in the Eastern Mediterranean and Black Sea, these ships appear to have been primarily intended for use as rams, with gun power as a secondary weapon. They made no pretence of being sea-going vessels and were quite unfit to accompany a fleet at sea on account of their low speed and limited coal supply which also precluded them from blockading work. But if the red cross of St. George had been opposed to the blue saltire of St. Andrew the two ships had qualities of short range efficiency that could have been applied to purposes of advanced strategy in the Black Sea or Baltic without the necessity of risking more valuable vessels. As in the case of the big monitors during the World Wars, they were shallow-draught fighters never intended for the battle line, but well suited for coastal operations.

When first taken over the *Belleisle* was listed as an "Armour-plated Ram," while the later *Orion* appeared as an "Armoured Corvette"; later both were elevated to the rank of "Second class Battleships" and finally received proper recognition as "Coast Defence Ships."

The hull was short and tubby, 20 ft. longer and 7 ft. broader than that of the *Cyclops* with the full beam extending nearly half the length, well squared at the bilges and full-lined at the extremities, with but little rise of floor. Although having but small reserve buoyancy, the watertight bulkheads were not carried to upper deck level. The design was unique in having an almost *Hotspur* hull with a central battery in place of the fixed turret, and for their tonnage they were sturdy little ships which would doubtless have served Turkish requirements very satisfactorily. But when incorporated in our Navy List they had to be judged from our standpoint, and here gun power ranked considerably higher than ability to ram. Vice-Admiral Colomb summed up their battle value from a gunnery aspect when he wrote:

> "The *Belleisle* was the negation of any approved form of battle; she was equally weak and equally strong in every direction and the expression of despair over the idea of any recognized method of fighting at sea."

Which, of course, was only to be expected of a ship not intended for the line of battle. On the other hand, the guns were well placed for ramming tactics—*i.e.*, training over a wide arc forward for opening an attack, and equally over the quarters for when an attack failed.

ARMAMENT

Reed always maintained that on a given weight eight guns could be mounted on the broadside, four on each side of the ship, about as effectively as four guns could be worked in two turrets, and moreover be pointed at eight different targets if required, instead of only two. The *Orion* demonstrated this so far as the number of weapons was concerned, as she carried four 12-in. against only two in the *Glatton*, one in the *Hotspur* and two 10-in. in the *Rupert*, although with lighter protection. Certainly in the *Glatton* too much weight had been allotted to armour, although the Board had turned down a two-turret alternative design on the grounds that a second gun position would have meant an unacceptable reduction in armour thickness; the *Hotspur's* single gun with its limited arcs of fire would have made no sort of a show in a duel, and the *Rupert*, although a much heavier ship, suffered every sort of disadvantage except somewhat better protection.

"BELLEISLE" (ex *Peik-i-Sheref*) and "ORION" (ex *Bourdjou-Zaffer*)

	Builders	*Laid down*	*Launched*	*Completed*	*Cost*
"*Belleisle*"	Samuda		12 Feb. '76	19 July '78	£267,179
"*Orion*"	Samuda		23 Jan. '79	3 July '82	£295,761

Dimensions 245′×52′×20·9′/21·1′=4,870 tons.
Hull and armour 3,270 tons. Equipment 1,570 tons.

Armament 4 12-in. 25-ton M.L.R. } broadside 1,268 lb.
4 20-pdrs.
2 torpedo carriages.

Armour Belt 12″-7″-6″; battery 10″-8″; bulkheads 9″-6″-5″; conning tower 9″; decks 3″-2″-1″; skin 1¼″; backing 16″-10″. Total (never tabulated).

Complement 235/249.

Coal 450/510 tons.

Machinery Maudslay. 2 sets horizontal direct action.
2 cyl. 65″. Stroke 30″. I.H.P. 3,200=12·2 knots.
4 boilers. 20 furnaces.

Points of interest:

1) Only British ships to have their entire armament in an upper deck central battery.
(2) Only British ships to carry 12-in. guns on the broadside.
(3) Their armament absorbed a higher percentage of the displacement than in any other British ship.
(4) The last British ships to carry their guns in a central battery and the only ones having the magazine beneath it.

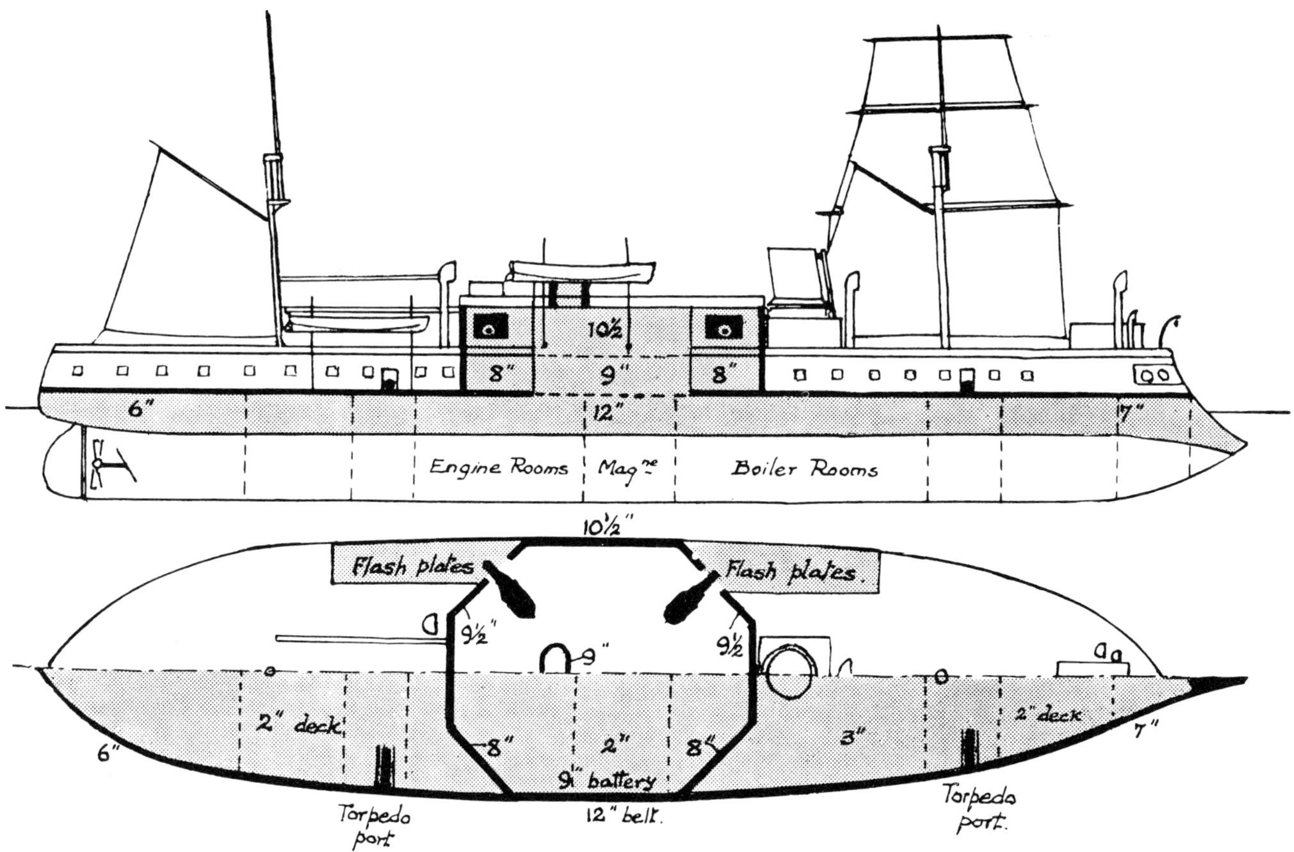

The *Belleisle* is here shown with the rig carried for two years and a short funnel. For the first time magazines were sited beneath the battery separating the boiler and engine rooms.

The original equipment would probably have been four 18-ton guns in common with those in the *Superb*, as when the *Belleisle* was taken over the first item listed under alterations in her progress book is "Enlargement of ports to take 25-ton guns." Other structural alterations to fit her for British service included extra bunkers and cabins, some stiffening of the long ram, and provision of torpedo discharge gear.

The four 25-ton guns were disposed at the corners of an octagonal battery situated on the upper deck amidships, the ports being large enough to allow for a nominal training arc of 120°, permitting a concentration of two guns directly ahead or astern and two over a limited area on the beam; elsewhere only one gun could be brought to bear. This four-gun battle-box was Reed's equivalent to a single turret which could point two guns through about 270°; and although an excellent distribution of gun power when employed as a support to the ram, it offered no advantages for use in line-of-battle. So far as this country was concerned, if any knell had been needed to the central battery these ships provided it; and if the *Orion* could claim any distinction it was in being the last ironclad with her big guns so mounted to be completed for the British Navy. Abroad it survived for a few more years in the Argentine *Almirante Brown* (1880), French *Courbet* (1882) and German *Oldenburg* (1884).

That 12-in. guns were ever mounted on the broadside was a noteworthy refutation of the opinions expressed in 1865 before Captain Scott's mountings had been adopted. In the *Orions* the four big guns absorbed a greater

The *Belleisle* is here shown in the Hamoaze just before her first refit when the funnel was raised. The fore yards were removed in 1880.

percentage of the displacement than had been allotted to offence in any other British battleship; they could bring one to bear on any point of the compass, and if required on four different targets—a questionable advantage in later days when concentration of fire in salvoes marked the peak in efficient shooting, but a very real advantage according to gunnery requirements in the eighties. Our one-turreted ships when operating in coastal waters against a single opponent might very well find themselves in the position of being unable to bring their big guns to bear; in a purely broadside ship, or one of the *Monarch* type, there would have been wide "angles of immunity" which did not exist in the *Orion*.

Six 3-pdrs. and a couple of searchlights were mounted on top of the battery some years later (1886), when the ships were also given torpedo net defence. The two 14-in. torpedo carriages were at main deck level.

PROTECTION

Although not on the ponderous scale of the *Glatton* the *Orion's* protection was very adequate for defence against the type of craft which she would be likely to have encountered in the defence of the Dardanelles, and considerably more substantial than we had put into our *Cyclops* class. The waterline belt 10 ft. deep of which 5 ft. was below water at load draught was 12 in. amidships with 7 in. at the bow—where it was taken down over the ram—and 6 in. aft. Amidships the battery rising from the main deck in two storeys, the upper one containing the guns carried $10\frac{1}{2}$ in. plating on the sides and $9\frac{1}{2}$ in. over the end bulkheads. It was described as being somewhat cramped for working the 25-tonners; the lower storey contained the "ready rack" shell supply and magazine uptakes, and as a redoubt was given 9-in. sides and 8-in. ends. The outstanding virtue of the design was the placing of the magazines directly beneath the battery—an advantage unique at that period.

A 9-in. plated rectangular pilot tower perched on top of the battery, later crossed by a light bridge carrying the searchlights.

Horizontal main deck plating over the engines and boilers was 3 in. and beyond that 2 in. to the bow and stern.

MACHINERY

Handiness rather than speed was the essential in ramming tactics, and as engines and bunkerage had to be restricted in compensation for the armament, the ships were not good for much more than 12 knots and bunkered 450 tons or 510 at a pinch. Twin screws made for handiness and ability to navigate in shallow waters which would have been impossible with one large propeller.

The *Belleisle* at Spithead for the 1889 Review. Her funnel has been raised, and some 3-pdrs. mounted on the battery above which is a searchlight platform.

SEA-GOING QUALITIES

Not being intended as sea-going ships they were never tried out in really bad weather, but the records show that *Belleisle* rolled easily and quickly, burying herself in a force 6 wind. In a head sea she was brought up almost to a standstill, and in ordinary weather rolled to such an extent as to render her guns unworkable. The great ram, projecting 10 ft. beyond the bows under water, represented 8 ft. of solid iron forging, and was responsible for a huge bow wave and green over the forecastle even in calm weather.

But under the favourable conditions in which they were designed to operate they proved very handy, circling at full speed in $3\frac{1}{2}$ minutes over 420 yards. Their radius of action at full speed was about 1,000 miles.

GENERAL

Their equipment generally was poor, *Orion* being taken over in an unfinished condition was given a steam capstan and steam steering, but *Belleisle* had man-handled ground tackle all her life. Periodic requests for the fitting of a steam capstan were made, but as the First Lord (Northbrook) put it quite bluntly in 1884, "These ships are hard bargains and I grudge spending money on them"—a typical example of niggardliness which condemned the ship's company to a vast amount of unnecessary labour. The request was dropped in 1886, and so the *Belleisle* finished up as the only British capital ship without power to her capstans.

When completed *Belleisle* was given a square rig on the foremast with yards of 52, 41 and 27 ft., but in 1880 these were removed; thereafter the remaining gaffs were euphemistically called "schooner rig." *Orion* was never rigged.

As designed the funnel nicely cleared the battery, but in 1879 *Belleisle* had hers raised 16 ft. This extension was made in *Orion* before her completion.

At the time of the launch of the *Orion* the Service press regarded these ships very favourably, and the *Broad Arrow* (8 February 1879) considered that:

> "Having regard to the armament and armour, speed and coal endurance, fighting qualities and cost of building, we consider that the *Belleisle* and *Orion* are not excelled by any type of war vessel afloat. For the sum of £300,000 one of these vessels can be built, so that two can be obtained for the cost of one *Vanguard* and more than three for that of one *Inflexible*. There is ample duty in the Royal Navy for at least six of such vessels . . . and it behoves us to maintain on the Pacific Station vessels of the *Orion* type, than which none in existence are better adapted for the service to be performed . . . and far more likely to be advantageously employed than the Invincible class, to say nothing of such worn-out specimens as the *Hector*, *Valiant*, *Resistance* and *Lord Warden*."

Just how ships with a *Brassey* radius of 1,000 miles could operate over the vast spaces covered by the British command in the Pacific, and face the weather there encountered, evidently did not enter into the editorial calculations. Not surprisingly it remains as about the last favourable press they got. Thereafter their shortcomings at sea damned them as serviceable fighting ships.

As in the case of the *Ajax* and *Agamemnon*, one of the pair served her full term of years in Home waters while the other saw considerable service abroad.

"BELLEISLE"

Taken over from Samudas in a completed condition and commissioned 2 July '78 as coastguard ship at Kingston where she served for the next fourteen years, changing her anchorage only when visiting the other ports in the Irish command, her quarterly firing practice, the annual squadron cruise, and refit at Devonport.

In April '93 she paid off into the "B" Reserve at Devonport passing into the Fleet Reserve in May '94 and was finally paid off in May 1900 at Portsmouth and fitted out as a fleet target—the first armoured ship to be so utilized since the *Resistance*. The *Majestic* fired 15 rounds of 12-in., 100 6-in. lyddite at bow and battery, and 100 6-in. common shell at the stern plus 400 3-in. various and 750 3-pdr. Lyddite was then a novelty and the effects were dramatic against the unarmoured ends. While the 6-in. Common destroyed as a box could be smashed up with an axe, Lyddite pulverized wood completely leaving nothing but dust. Holes in the deck showed edges like dry rot, and there was no sign of any charring. Where 6-in. common shell burst between decks, the deck above showed no sign; but Lyddite left huge holes with the deck bulged up and thick cross beams showed no power of resistance. One shell entered the battery through a gun-port and wrecked all the gun-sights although the guns were uninjured. The conning tower was not hit.

The wrecked ship was towed back to Portsmouth and fitted with 6-in. plates to represent a section of the *Drake* and 4-in. plates for the *County* class, and on 19 February '02 was fired at by the gunboats *Pincher* (9·2-in.) and *Comet* (6-in.) with informative results. On 3 September '03 she was used to test the effect of a torpedo explosion against a "mock-up" filled with cellulose to represent a method of protection advocated in France. The alleged swelling effect of the cellulose in closing up the hole could not be ascertained as the explosion blew the target sky high and filling the ship which slowly settled into thick mud. After five weeks' work what remained of the *Belleisle* was raised on 8 October '03 and sold for £8,600.

"ORION"

Not being in such an advanced stage as her sister when purchased in February '78 she was rather more generously fitted out. Commissioned 24 June '82 for Mediterranean[1] (collision with *Temeraire* when changing station during exercises) and paid off into Reserve at Malta May '83. Commissioned April '85-'88. Shadowed a Russian armoured cruiser out East[2] during the strained relations following the "Penjdeh incident" and stayed as guardship at Singapore (then quite undefended) until '90 when she returned to Malta 2nd class Reserve. Repair and refit. Paid off into Dockyard Reserve at Chatham September '93 and declared non-effective in November 1901. In April '02 became parent ship for T.B.D. Malta and in July '04 depôt for Malta R.N.R. Served a brief commission in December '06. Became *Orontes* store ship at Devonport in '10 until sold June '13 for £13,725.

---

[1] To join the squadron expected to bombard Alexandria, but arrived 14 days too late. Landed parties to occupy Ismailia and formed part of Naval Brigade at Tel-el-Kebir.

[2] *Orion* was enabled to overtake and pass the Russian, as at Aden and Colombo the Admiralty agents bought up the entire stock of coal, and regretted they could only supply enough to allow her to proceed at half speed. At Singapore she found the *Orion* (which had traversed the Bay of Bengal during the favourable season), and beyond that port to Vladivostock she would be looked after by the *Audacious* and *Shannon*.

"SUPERB" (ex *Hamidieh*)

Builders	*Laid down*	*Launched*	*Completed*	*Cost*
Thames I.W.	1873	16 Nov. '75	15 Nov. '80	£531,846

Dimensions 332·3′ × 59′ × 24·4′/26·5′ = 9,710 tons.
Hull and armour 5,830 tons. Equipment 3,340 tons.

Armament			1891
	16 10-in. M.L.R.	3,248 lb. broadside.	12 10-in. M.L.R.
	6 20-pdr. B.L.		10 6/35 B.L.
	10 boat guns.		6 6-pdrs.
	4 Mark II torpedo carriages.		10 3-pdrs.
			4 T.T.

Armour Belt 12″-10″-7″; battery 12″; bulkheads 10″-7″-6″-5″; conning tower 8″; decks 1½″; skin 1½″; backing 12″-8″.

Complement 620/654.

Coal 600/970 tons.

Machinery Maudslay. Direct acting horizontal type.
2 cyls. 116″; diam. stroke 48″.
I.H.P. 6,580 = 13·2 knots. 67 revs.
Single screw 23′ diam.; pitch 19½′.
9 Rectangular boilers; 30 lb. pressure.

Points of interest:

(1) Had the largest battery of one-calibre big guns ever mounted in any British battleship.
(2) The first ship to have two conning towers.
(3) The last and best protected of the broadside ironclads.
(4) Fired heaviest broadside of any British battleship to date.

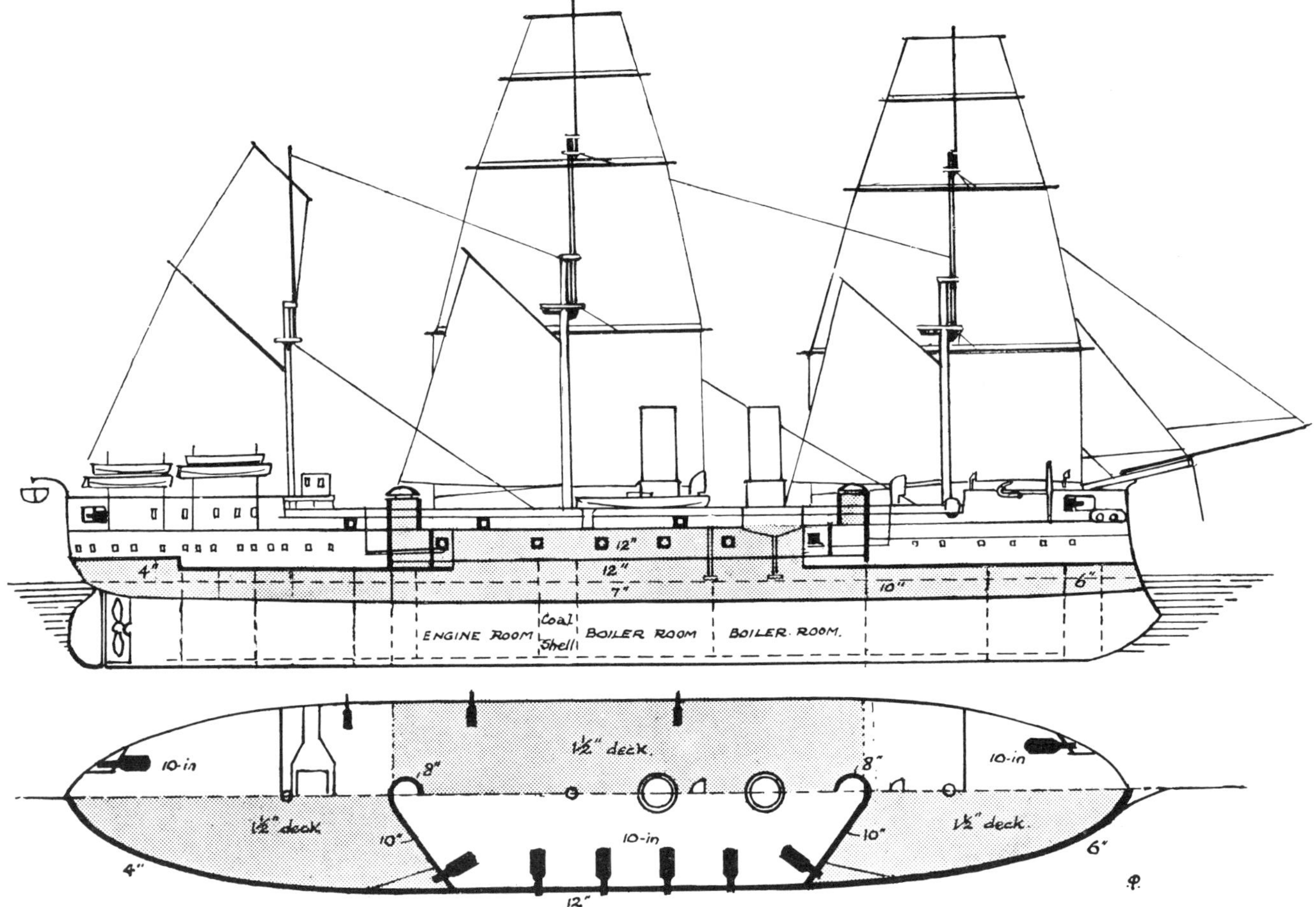

The *Superb* as rearmed for H.M. service showing her sixteen 10-in. M.L.R.—the largest battery of one-calibre big guns ever mounted in a British battleship. Note the two conning towers.

The *Hamidieh* has been designed by Reed for the Turkish Government and completed in 1877, but detained because of neutrality obligations and purchased February 1878, being passed into service during 1880 after extensive alterations.

From her original drawings she was simply an enlarged *Hercules* with twelve 10-in. M.L.R. in the central battery, two 7-in. M.L.R. on the upper deck fore and a single one aft as chase guns. For H.M. service she underwent alterations which kept her in dockyard hands for eighteen months and included raising and lengthening the forecastle and poop to allow for a 10-in. M.L.R. being embrasured on each side forward and aft in place of the pivoted 7-in. M.L.R. on the centre line, thus giving her a single-calibre main armament of sixteen guns—the largest ever mounted in a British ship. Additional lighter pieces were also fitted, with torpedo gear, searchlights, and extra coal bunkers and cabins. The mess deck being very lofty, an additional wooden deck was worked in about 5 ft. below the beams and used for slinging hammocks—being always referred to as the "slave deck." Later, when the battery was also used for messing, this "slave deck" was discarded.

Both topgallant forecastle and poop were long and commodious, the latter being the longest in the Service.

The *Superb* was distinguished by her long battery, long topgallant forecastle, and the longest poop in the Service. She is here seen in the Mediterranean where she served for seven years.

The ship was worked from a light bridge crossing the bulwarks just forward of the mizen, and a novel feature was the provision of a conning tower at each end of the battery.

ARMAMENT

The battery extended 111 ft. between the end gun ports—38 ft. longer than in the *Hercules*—with axial fire obtained from guns mounted in the embrasures instead of their having to be transferred from the broadside ports. Six 20-pdr. saluting guns were placed in the waist.

As a one-decker she was distinctly inferior to the *Alexandra*, but for Mediterranean and Black Sea fighting the long main deck battery did not present the same drawbacks as it did for oceanic service—where in bad weather the ports would have had to be closed—and the Turks preferred the guns on one deck as conducive to easier working.

ARMOUR

For a broadside ship the *Superb* was very well protected with a belt 12 in. amidships thinning at the lower edge and tapering through 10 in. to 6 in. at the bows and 4 in. aft. It did not reinforce the ram. The battery also had 12 in. plating, the 10 in. end bulkheads being lapped around the bases of the conning towers. Her armour was thus generally thicker than in the *Alexandra*, but no protection could be provided for the chase guns either by way of screens or side plating, as the 10-in. pieces were considerably heavier than any previously carried at the bow and stern.

The 8-in. conning towers had light domes allowing for a sighting slot 18 in. deep; in both the equipment included controls for the steam steering gear. A $1\frac{1}{2}$-in. deck covered the belt and roof of the battery.

MACHINERY

Turkish requirements having been satisfied with a nominal 13 knots, the *Superb* fell a little below recent British standards in respect of speed, and also in having the old and less expensive type of horizontal engines and rectangular boilers. But bunkerage exceeded the *Alexandra's* by nearly 100 tons at full capacity.

On passage 10 knots seems to have been about as much as she could manage—the discrepancy compared with trial figures being accounted for in the ship's book by vagaries on the part of the patent log.

SAIL

The *Superb* was barque rigged on a modified second scale. At sea reports state that she was very stiff under canvas and could not be made to wear even after all the ship's company had been sent aft to help get her off

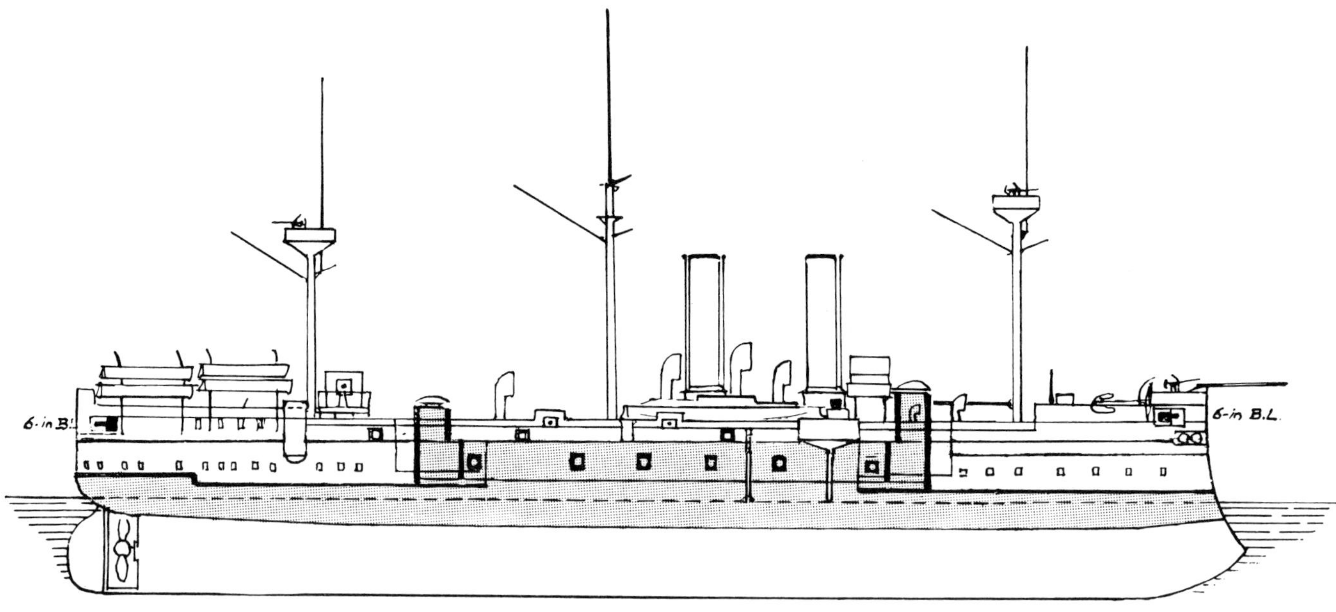

SUPERB modernized.

the wind; consequently although her yards slightly exceeded the scale, she was never able to proceed under sail with banked fires let alone with cold boilers.

SEA-GOING QUALITIES

Her reports describe her as very steady and holding her way well in the head sea; easy to handle under steam, but quite unmanageable under sail. Apparently only once during her seven years in the Mediterranean was there an opportunity of reporting upon her behaviour in bad weather, and on that occasion the clinometer registered 18° to leeward in a 7 wind, her left-handed screw requiring as much as 12° of starboard helm.[1] Why she should need from 8-12° of permanent helm angle to overcome a tendency to swing to port instead of to starboard as was usually the case, has never been explained—possibly the shape of the rudder had something to do with it. But it meant that she needed more room for a turn to starboard than to port, and suffered from rudder drag.

ALTERATIONS

As completed she had vertical funnels, but in 1881 these were given a rake, with additional lower casings and steam pipes. Thereafter her profile was distinctive and unseemly. After taking part at Alexandria—where

[1] New nomenclature=rudder to starboard.

she received minor injuries from 10-in. shell and one large hole 10 × 4 ft. from a burst near the battery embrasure—her refit included a new after bridge.

From 1887 to 1891 the *Superb* underwent the customary "modernization" with a set of triple-expansion engines and four double-ended and one single-end cylindrical boilers. Under forced power she then made 14·5 knots with 8,500 I.H.P. Her yards were removed, the masts lowered, and fighting tops fitted to the fore and mizen with 3-pdrs. in each and a steam derrick to the main mast—which had been taken out of the *Warspite*.

The M.L. guns in the central battery were retained, but those in the bow and stern embrasures and upper deck amidships were replaced by 6-in. Q.F. with six 6-pdrs. and ten 3-pdrs. over the upper works.

A second-class torpedo boat was stowed amidships alongside the new tall funnels; and torpedo net booms and a full set of cowls completed the furbishing-up for a fresh spell of duty at home. The saving in weight on the new machinery amounted to 300 tons, and the distance she could steam with a given quantity of coal doubled.

In August 1898 the 4-in. B.L. were replaced by 4-in. Q.F. guns.

As some indication of the relative value of sister ships under different flags, it may be noted that the Turkish

The *Superb* was under refit from 1887-91 when the 10-in. M.L. in the embrasures and 20-pdrs. amidships were replaced by 6-in. B.L; triple expansion engines and cylindrical boilers installed, and a military tops added to her fore and mizen. For three years she served as guardship in the Clyde where this photo was taken.

Messudiyeh (torpedoed by s/m. B.9 in 1914) was completely reconstructed in Italy in 1902 and given two 9·2-in. in turrets fore and aft; twelve 6-in. Q.F. in the main battery; fourteen 12-pdrs. and ten 6-pdrs. Twin screws, triple-expansion engines and 16 Niclausse water-tube boilers produced 11,000 h.p. and 12·5 knots. The old armour was retained on the belt, with Harvey steel to the battery. And with it all the load displacement was reduced to 8,972 tons!

"SUPERB"

Commissioned at Chatham 4 October '80 for the Mediterranean where she remained for the next seven years. At Alexandria she fired 310 shells from her 10-in. guns. Paid off at Chatham in May '87 for reconstruction and then commissioned in April '91 as coast guardship on the Clyde until May '94 when she was paid off in Fleet Reserve at Chatham and did not go to sea again until the 1900 manœuvres when she was rated as a second-class battleship. Next year she dropped into the third class and in '04 was used as an overflow hospital for infectious cases. Then for a year or so she lay grey and stripped in the Kyles of Bute until sold in March '06 for £19,000.

"NEPTUNE" (ex *Independencia*, Brazil)

Builders	*Laid down*	*Launched*	*Completed*	*Cost*
J. & W. Dudgeon Millwall	1874	Feb. '78	3 Sept. '81	£600,000 plus £89,172 alterations

Dimensions 300'×63'×25'=9,310 tons. Hull and armour 6,080 tons. Equipment 3,090 tons.

Armament 4 12-in. M.L.R. 2 9-in. M.L.R. 6 20-pdrs. B.L.R. Tubes 2 14-in.

Armour Belt 12"-9"; redoubt 10"-8"; bulkheads 8"-6"; turrets 13"-11"; conning tower 8"-6"; decks 3"-2"; 1½"-1" over breastwork; skin 1¼"; backing 15"-10". Total 2,118 tons.

Complement 541/465: smaller when re-rigged.

Coal 670 tons. Radius 1,480/10 knots.

Machinery Penn. Trunk engines. I.H.P. 7,993=14·2 knots.
2 cyls. 127" diam. with 47" trunks; stroke 4½'.
Single Griffiths 4-bladed screw. 26' diam.
23' pitch. 70 revs.
8 boilers. 32 lb. pressure.

Points of interest:

(1) The last British battleship to have a complete waterline belt for the next twenty years.
(2) The most costly warship built to that date.
(3) The last British rigged turret ship.

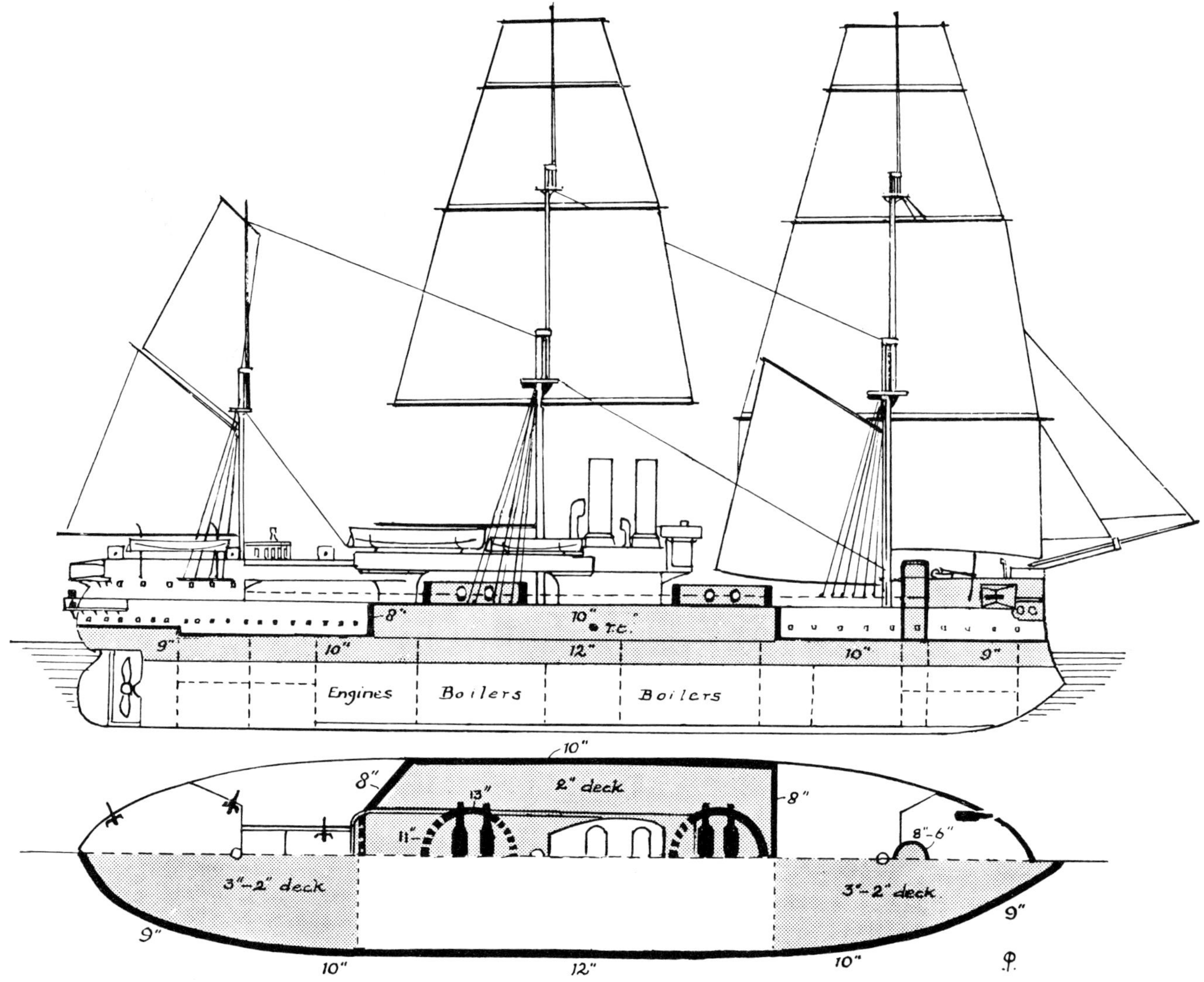

The *Neptune* stripped of her double topsail yards and rigged as a full barque after her purchase from Brazil and conversion to H.M. service. The main course was never hoisted because of its proximity to the funnels.

During the early 'sixties a number of small coast-defence turret ships had been built in this country for the South American republics, and served as armoured nuclei for the scratch collections of vessels which formed their several navies. In 1872 Chile placed an order with Samuda's for a couple of medium-sized central-battery ironclads to the designs of Sir Edward Reed—sea-going vessels capable of overwhelming anything belonging to the maritime States in the southern-western hemisphere—which gesture was followed by the arrival of a Brazilian Naval Commission in this country with instructions to arrange for the construction of a sea-going turret ship of the largest size to be armed with the heaviest guns available and carrying a full head of sail.

The *Devastation* was then the cynosure of foreign naval interest, and the Brazilians wanted a "rigged *Devastation*" designed by Reed to their requirements. In view of the late Chief Constructor's antipathy to rigged turret ships and the incompatibility of the *Devastation* design with sail power, it will be appreciated that he did not approach the project with any great enthusiasm; and the plans were drawn up under what he termed "peculiar circumstances."

Although a rigged *Devastation* was an anachronism, the Brazilian authorities thought fit to sacrifice valuable military qualities and harass the whole design for the sake of a canvas dressing only capable of supplying a limited power of movement under favourable circumstances and, moreover, destroyed any resemblance to their British

The *Neptune* in Plymouth Sound on first commissioning in 1883. Three years later the yards on the main mast were removed because of smoke rot.

ideal by adding a poop, forecastle and upper works for the working of a full barque rig, thus depriving both turrets of the axial fire which was their essential virtue.

One feels that Reed could have had little say in the general lay-out of the ship, and the full specification suggests that he was only making the best of a bad job. The resulting *Independencia* had but little in common with the *Devastation* and resembled a modified *Monarch*. Whatever value she may have possessed for the Brazilians—and strangely enough they ordered two more ships of a similar type in 1883-84—as *Neptune* she became a white elephant in our own organization, being a thoroughly bad ship in most respects—unlucky, full of inherent faults and small vices, and at times a danger to her consorts.

Although the Brazilians were anxious to get possession of her as soon as possible, it was nearly two years before the contract could be placed and four more before she left the ways, by which time her owners valued her potential services so highly that when the British Government came to exercise their right of purchase in the emergency of 1878 the price demanded and paid was £600,000. As the completed *Devastation* and *Dreadnought* cost less than £370,000 apiece for the same tonnage, we paid a hard price for an unsuitable ship, and what is more had to go on paying heavily for repairs after her launching damage; alterations to enable service models to replace Whitworth guns; and a general tinkering-up lasting some three years after the first trials at sea. Altogether the taxpayer had to find £690,000 before this bad bargain joined the colours, and apart from the far bigger *Inflexible* and *Benbow* the *Neptune* proved our most expensive battleship prior to the *Royal Sovereign.*

Although passing a more or less uneventful life, she entered her element and made her last voyage under sufficiently dramatic circumstances.

By stopping on the ways while being launched her bows were left overhanging on the end of the building slip, with the result that the bracket system of construction showed up badly—when got off and towed to Samuda's it was found necessary to take out and rebuild the bottom for the greater part of the amidships section. As the French put it, "Her frames cross one another only the better to cut one another." At the end of her career, when taken in tow for removal from Portsmouth Harbour, she took charge, rammed and nearly sank the *Victory*, collided with the *Hero*, and was only just prevented from wrecking her way upon other ships.

HULL

Of medium freeboard like the *Monarch*, she had the full, beamy underbody of all Reed's ships, which was teak sheathed and coppered, the hull containing three decks with ten transverse w.t. bulkheads rising to main deck height and providing good vertical security. The ram bow had no reinforcement by the belt, and the curved elliptical stern boasted two stern-walks as the canopy carried a breast-rail for many years—a unique feature.

Compared with the *Monarch* the *Neptune* was 30 ft. shorter, 5½ ft. wider, and drew nearly 5 ft. less water; her citadel extended 32 ft. more on the sides and had a shade less freeboard; the armament was somewhat heavier and protection thicker. But whereas the *Monarch* introduced the rigged turret ship and fulfilled all her constructor's requirements, the *Neptune* only emphasized the inherent shortcomings of the type and did nothing to enhance Reed's reputation.

In appearance the main difference lay in the *Neptune* having two funnels, no extension of the flying deck over the fore turret, and with larger and more widely separated turrets the main mast had to be stepped close abaft the funnels. Amidships the superstructure carried a hurricane deck which extended aft in two stages to the poop, being supported by boiler and engine-room hatchways.

ARMAMENT

As *Independencia* the intention was to arm her with Whitworth guns—four 35-ton 12-in. in the turrets and a couple of 8-in. under the forecastle. These were hexagonal-bored B.L. of a type alien to the Service, so to avoid adding to the multiplicity of models already afloat they were replaced by Woolwich 38-ton M.L.R. and 9-in. 12-ton M.L.R. Unfortunately the scantling in the wake of the turrets was not up to Admiralty standards, and the damage sustained under full charges necessitated these being reduced from 200 lb. to 180 lb., so that her fighting punch suffered considerably. The turrets were of 28 ft. diameter and 7 ft. high above deck, with two loading positions and hydraulic rammers opposite the ammunition hoists on each side of the main deck. Bow fire by the 9-in. was through embrasures on each side, with protection by 8-in. plating which extended the length of the topgallant forecastle. Training was limited to 45° from the axial line owing to the presence of a large hatchway between the guns, which cut away the rear racer circuits of the gun slides and so prevented any broadside training. As the expense of structural alterations correcting this defect would have been heavy, the hatch was allowed to remain.

No provision was made for gunfire astern, presumably because the Brazilians never expected the *Independencia* to show her hind-quarters to an enemy, plus the necessity for providing sufficiently luxurious upper deck accommodation for an admiral. Here again the cost of alterations and necessary strengthening precluded the provision of a stern-chaser in the *Neptune.*

The original armament included ten 20-pdr. Armstrong B.L.—discarded in favour of the more efficient type of Nordenfelt anti-t.b. gun, which were subsequently twice changed. The final battery of fourteen 6-pdr. and 3-pdr. quickfirers was distributed along the topgallant forecastle, flying deck and poop.

A single torpedo tube was cut through the main deck armour amidships on each side for taking the 16-in. Whitehead—the first model with a range of 800 yards at 7 knots—and these again were discarded in favour of a 14-in. model of treble the speed and range.

PROTECTION

Although the total weight of armour in the *Neptune* is not entered in official lists, it must have absorbed a considerable proportion of the 1,000 tons difference in displacement compared with the *Monarch,* as her advantage ran to 5 in. over the belt and 3 in. on the citadel. The belt was shallow—only 8½ ft. deep of which 3 ft. was above water—and of 12 in. amidships tapering to 10 in. and 9 in. at the ends. Above this ran a 3 in.-2 in. deck. The former Reed breastwork was replaced by a full-width citadel (112 ft. long at the sides and angled in aft to enclose the after hatchways) made up of 10-in. plating with 8-in. end bulkheads, and crossed by a 2-in. deck. This contained the boiler and engine room hatches, scuttles to shell rooms and magazines, ventilating shafts, and turret bases.

As Barnaby was now committing the Navy to citadel ships with unarmoured ends, the scale of protection in the *Neptune* was very favourably regarded and provided her one redeeming feature.

The turrets were 3 in. thicker than in the *Monarch*, being 11 in. with 13-in. faces and a 13 in.-15 in. teak backing.

The break of the forecastle was selected for installing a conning tower of 8 in.-6 in. plating, from which a clear view forward and abeam could be obtained without the smoke interference which so militated against the amidships position. Unlike the towers so far fitted in H.M. ships, it had a strong armoured foundation, and although not provided with a wheel or compass may be regarded as the first adequately installed conning position to be carried in a British battleship. The drawback to the site selected was the inordinate length of communications to turrets, machinery spaces, and fighting wheel amidships, with the greater liability of these being cut when in action. Normally the fore end of the flying deck formed the conning position, and here the shelter was fitted with a wheel, compass and engine-room communications with flying bridge extensions projecting well beyond the ship's sides.

MACHINERY

At a time when our engineering shops were busily engaged turning out compound engines with their saving in fuel and increased radius of action, the decision to equip the *Independencia* with a single set of old-fashioned trunk engines must have been dictated by reasons of economy and time of delivery. Compound machinery could not have been obtained at short notice, whereas simple pressure engines built on speculation, or from countermanded orders, had become cheap and available at short notice. And so Penns of Greenwich saw the last and largest set of trunk engines they ever provided for a battleship—or probably any other vessel—lowered into the machinery rooms of the *Independencia*. They had the biggest cylinders ever to be installed in a man-of-war—127 in. with 47-in. trunks giving an effective diameter of 118 in.

A contract horse-power of 8,000 was the highest ever obtained from two cylinders, and on trials in February 1878 at 8,950 tons displacement she developed 8,832 h.p. and a mean of 14·65 knots with 71 revs. But ventilation was so faulty that the stokehold temperature reached 163° and the men were unable to keep at work—especially as the furnaces faced amidships, which meant that the stokers had fires back and front. After improved ventilation had been arranged she was credited with 13·4 knots at 6,000 h.p.

The *Neptune* was a notorious glutton for fuel and Sir George Tryon described her as being "a weak ship in her engines and consuming a coal-mine daily." As she only bunkered 670 tons there was hardly sufficient for a 1,500-mile voyage even at 10 knots with a clean bottom.

Steam was raised in equally antiquated boilers, her eight rectangular tanks working at 32 lb. pressure occupying excessive space which could otherwise have been utilized for coal.

Auxiliary machinery was confined to steam pumps, cable holders and steering gear. For some reason or other the big main derrick for hoisting out the boom boats had no winch, and the purchases had either to be manned or else taken through a long series of leading blocks along the waist right forward to the cable capstan at the break of the forecastle.

SAIL

The decision to rig the *Independencia* may have been largely influenced by the performance of the *Monarch* under sail, although her extra 1,000 tons displacement postulated a much greater area of canvas, which could not be provided. As it was, her main mast was uncomfortably near the funnels although they had been put in sideways with the narrowest diameter in the fore and aft line to get them as far forward as possible.

Although the forecastle and poop deprived the turrets of axial fire they were angled to allow for wide arcs on the broadside which were not masked by rigging. The foremast was just abaft the forecastle and could be worked from the hurricane deck; all fittings, bitts and leads were so arranged as to be out of the line of fire when cleared for action. Of the fore- and main-mast shrouds, only two were left on each side when cleared for action, and these took their chance of being shot away. The main mast could also be worked from the hurricane deck when necessary and the mizen rigging from the poop.

In the matter of rig the *Neptune* ranks with the *Achilles* in having undergone three changes. As *Independencia* she was a barque with double topsails, which was changed to a standard topsail rig for British service. But the main mast was so close to the funnels that sail and rigging became smoke-rotted and the mast had to be stripped; after which she sailed under fore and mizen only—a most unsightly combination, "like a half-dressed harlot" in lower-deck parlance. But with such a scanty dressing the ship could never answer her helm without help from the engines, and at best the canvas only added a knot to her steaming speed.

In 1885 (Malta) there is a note in the Ship's Book recording that the tops had been plated-in on all three masts, and in all probability the yards were removed; in any case, the days of sail power in battleships were over and the following year she was re-rigged with a couple of tall masts each carrying a lofty fighting top—too gawky for looks and of a type shared by the *Warspite* and *Imperieuse*.

SEA-GOING QUALITIES

When fully rigged, her stability was reported to be superior to that of the heavy unmasted ships, but was peculiar inasmuch as it vanished at an angle where normally it should have gone on increasing—due to difference in slope of the bilge. Thus, the *Monarch* would have reached her maximum stability at 50°, slightly passed it at 58° and capsized at 69°; the *Neptune* was the more stable at 30°, fell away rapidly to 50° and would have turned turtle at 58°. She rolled heavily, manœuvred badly and was a shocking sea boat.

A feature of her steaming was the bow wave, which rose up 10 to 11 ft. as a solid wall bigger than the *Bellerophon's*, and streaming past left a broad channel of dead water following astern. In a 5 to 6 wind with a heavy beam sea her book records the deck as being continually awash and at times several feet deep in water, as the scuppers were inadequate.

On first commissioning she was attached to the Channel Fleet; but after two years' experience with her behaviour a transfer was made to the Mediterranean as being a more suitable cruising ground. Then, after less than three years' service with the sea-going squadrons, came relegation to coastguard duty, what time the *Monarch* had still to serve a full commission in the Channel.

During her refit in 1886 the *Neptune* was remasted with military tops at a greater height than usual, and fitted with net defence and some m.g. A photo taken in 1887 when ready for the Spithead review.

GENERAL

Under the poop was accommodation for an admiral and his staff, but as the *Neptune* was never a flagship her wardroom officers benefited accordingly. In general she provided better quarters for officers and men than any other of H.M. ships, owing to her freeboard, absence of guns between decks, and comparatively small complement as a turret ship.

She could boast of being the first warship to be fitted with a bathroom[1]—an innovation of Brazilian specification—and became notorious for a 12-ft. skylight through which the wardroom was usually flooded when at sea. According to Thames-side tradition her fittings in the wardroom and some cabins were of solid silver—but these did not survive Dockyard alterations.

"NEPTUNE"

Completed at Portsmouth '78-'82. Commissioned 28 March '83 for the Channel with a transfer to the Mediterranean in '85. Paid off July '86 at Portsmouth for refit (new rig, net defence machine guns, etc.). Became coastguard ship at Holyhead in May '87 until November '93, then paid off into Fleet Reserve at Portsmouth and Dockyard Reserve in November '01. Sold in September '03 and made a spectacular passage down the harbour on October 23 '03 when she rammed the *Victory*, collided with *Hero* and had some close shaves with other ships.

Sold 1903 for £18,000. Broken up at Lenwerder 1904.

[1] Since the *Pallas*.

Chapter 44

NOVEL FOREIGN WARSHIPS

FROM the end of the 'seventies to the middle of the 'eighties the future of the battleship as a big-gunned and heavily armoured unit of sea power appeared to be precarious. Artillery had acquired a mastery over armour which threatened to restrict its use to very thick plating for the defence of gun positions only, leaving flotation to close subdivision and the submerged protective deck. And when weapons of 100 tons had been sent afloat and the production of 200 tonners discussed, it seemed as if the only reply to the smashing power of these slow-shooting monsters was the reduction and distribution of target so that a number of small fast vessels armed with either light guns or a single heavy gun would replace the big but very vulnerable capital ship.

Also, torpedo attack from being a minor hazard looked like becoming a major menace when Whitehead's ingenuity had transformed Captain Luppis's crude invention into a weapon of some precision. Small fast torpedo boats replaced ship's pinnaces, and there seemed to be no way of resisting this devastating under-water attack, launched from a host of tiny cheap craft operating under the cover of smoke or darkness. Faced with the risk of knock-out blows above water from huge shells and below by increasingly heavy charges of high explosives, it is small wonder that ships like the *Inflexible* were no longer regarded as the prime units of naval power, but rather as expensive and exceedingly vulnerable targets whose day of fighting invincibility had passed.

But those who realized the then limits of torpedo warfare—the unseaworthiness of the small boats, difficulties in bringing off a night attack, and vagaries of the torpedoes themselves—were more concerned with alternative battleship conceptions and the relative merits of medium or heavy gun power. Barnaby's citadel designs carrying a few monster guns and a patch of massive armour did not appeal to practical seamen who realized that battles would be won by ships which could hit often and keep on hitting. Reed's *Sultan* and *Hercules*, armed with a good broadside of medium artillery, were still favourites afloat, where even under favourable circumstances naval gunnery remained a matter of a few hits to many misses, and the chances of securing a hit with 80-ton guns in a topsail breeze against a moving target were slight.

In 1871 Captain Colomb had drawn attention to the shooting of the *Monarch*, *Captain* and *Hercules* against a rock off Vigo during a practice run of six minutes at a range of 1,000 yards, when it was calculated that had fire been directed against one of these ships, out of twelve rounds there would have been only one direct and one indirect hit—with an even chance that the former might have penetrated the armour! Had the rock been a moving ship there might well have been no hits upon which to base calculations.

Another incident which made a deep impression upon the memories of many observers was the failure of the *Hotspur* to hit the *Glatton's* turret at short range in Portsmouth Harbour. If a carefully laid gun at point blank missed at 200 yards in a flat calm, the fighting value of a ship armed with only two or four of such weapons, although impressive on paper, might be very different in practice.

Arguing upon these grounds, many distinguished naval officers rated the faster firing and more numerous broadside batteries above the limited discharge from turrets, and the good general protection in Reed's designs as more likely to survive an action than a citadel ship with her waterline protected by what was termed "contrivances." Advocates of the citadel, on the other hand, argued that as the enemy could only pierce such armour by the heaviest guns, our ships might expect to face a slow and inaccurate fire at long range which would not be directed against their unarmoured ends.

In contrast to the British "citadel" type three foreign ships were laid down about 1879 which added further complications to the battleship controversy.

(1) The French *Amiral Duperré* with four barbettes carrying the heaviest guns, and a complete waterline belt of thick armour.
(2) The Italian *Italia* with four monster guns and no side armour at all.
(3) The Chinese gunboat *Lung-Wei* carrying two of the most effective guns afloat.

"AMIRAL DUPERRÉ"

Although Dupuy de Lôme had designed a most efficient type of turret for the small coast-defence ironclads, the French preferred open barbettes for their high freeboard sea-going ships which until 1879 had been armed with a combination of upper deck barbette guns and a main deck central battery. In the *Amiral Duperré* of 11,000 tons launched that year the following features were incorporated:

(1) Four 13·4-in. guns in upper deck 12-in. barbettes 28 ft. above water.
(2) A heavy secondary battery of fourteen 5·5-in. unprotected along the main deck amidships.
(3) A high freeboard hull with a complete but narrow waterline belt of 22-in. iron tapering fore and aft.
(4) A speed of 14 knots.

On paper the *Duperré* made quite a brave show and Reed laid great stress upon her complete belt in most of his tirades against Barnaby's citadel ships. Actually she was a most vulnerable ship carrying a belt which would be generally immersed at sea, and when pierced above the water-line cursed with the short range of stability under such conditions which went with marked tumble-home sides and narrow deck. Her direct influence upon British design could be seen in the later *Warspite* and *Imperieuse*, but generally she demonstrated (1) the high

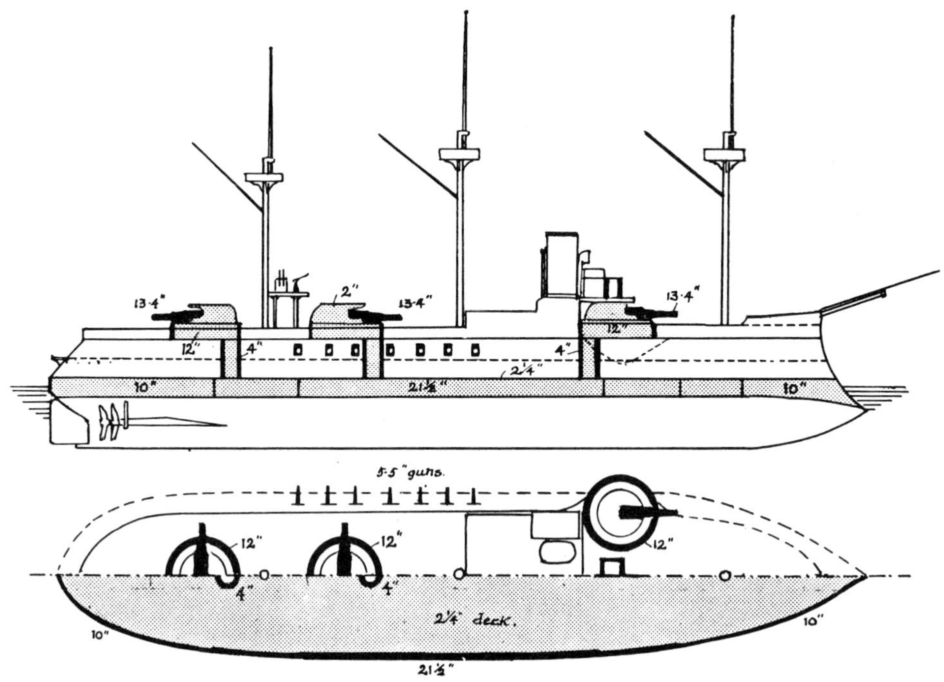

French battleship *AMIRAL DUPERRÉ*

command which could be obtained with barbette mountings, and (2) drew attention to the value of secondary guns in the attack of unarmoured areas—also the fact that provision would have to be made against such fire in future designs.

"ITALIA"

Far from being influenced by Reed's direful prophesies as to the likely fate of the *Duilio* and *Dandolo* in action, the Italian Government laid down two even more extraordinary ships, *Italia* and *Lepanto*, in 1877-78 which embodied principles in attack and defence of such a revolutionary nature that for a time they dominated naval thought and discussion.

Italy had required something faster and more seaworthy than the *Duilio*, with an armament which could tackle anything afloat, speed greater than that of any capital ship, and at the same time be capable of carrying a large number of troops "to ensure that any attempt at invasion or bombardment might be frustrated."

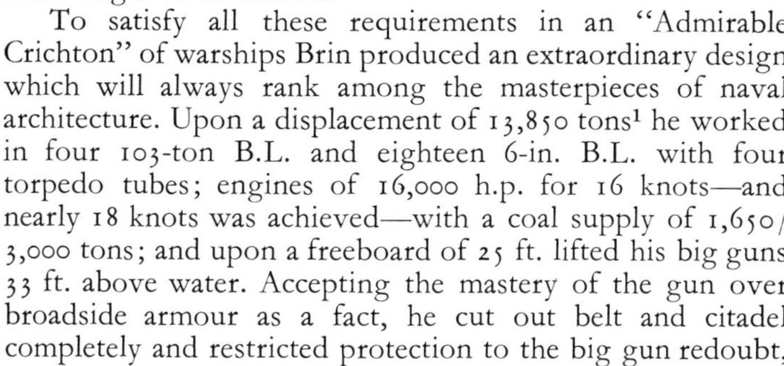

To satisfy all these requirements in an "Admirable Crichton" of warships Brin produced an extraordinary design which will always rank among the masterpieces of naval architecture. Upon a displacement of 13,850 tons[1] he worked in four 103-ton B.L. and eighteen 6-in. B.L. with four torpedo tubes; engines of 16,000 h.p. for 16 knots—and nearly 18 knots was achieved—with a coal supply of 1,650/3,000 tons; and upon a freeboard of 25 ft. lifted his big guns 33 ft. above water. Accepting the mastery of the gun over broadside armour as a fact, he cut out belt and citadel completely and restricted protection to the big gun redoubt,

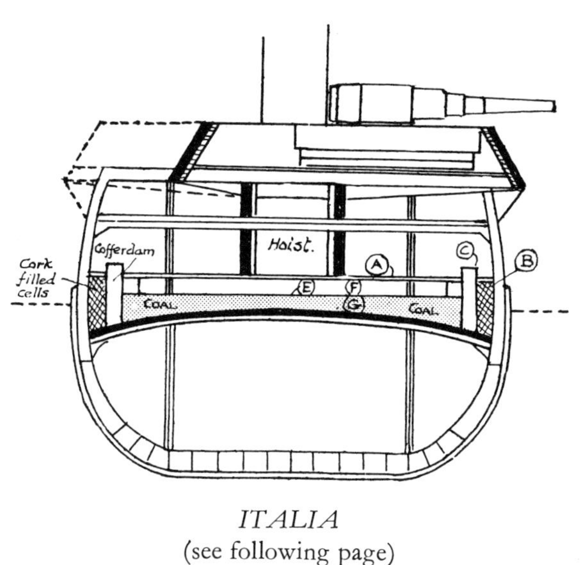

ITALIA
(see following page)

[1] Subsequently increased to 15,000 tons with 1,700 tons of coal and only eight 6-in. guns.

ammunition hoists, funnel bases and submerged deck with an intricate system of bulkheads and subdivision aided by elaborate pumping arrangements to secure flotation. Actually the total armour with backing was 3,012 tons—22·3 per cent. of the normal displacement.

From the plan it will be seen how the *Italia's* buoyancy and stability in action depended exclusively upon a cellular raft running the full length of the ship—an adaptation of the *Inflexible's* unarmoured ends and the proposals contained in the Report of the Committee on Designs. In the transverse section the 3-in. curved protective deck ran 6 ft. below the waterline, and 11 ft. above this was a plain unarmoured deck (*a*) with two longitudinal bulkheads at each side forming an outer cellular layer (*b*) and an inner cofferdam (*c*); between the inner of these bulkheads was fitted an intermediate watertight deck (*e*) dividing the space into (1) an upper part closely subdivided into empty compartments (*f*) and (2) a lower part filled with coal (*g*).

Glacis armour protected the boiler hatches from the protective deck to a height of 3 ft. above the waterline.

Although the cellular layer was never adopted in this country Mons. Emile Bertin when Chief Constructor for the French Navy employed it in conjunction with a thick and narrow waterline belt instead of side armour, as will be seen in descriptions of some of his designs hereafter. To this extent it is worth recording in some detail, as the success or failure of rival systems abroad can well be of more interest and significance than accepted methods of protection employed in our own ships.

The whole design was made practicable by the adoption of a huge central barbette of 19-in. compound armour

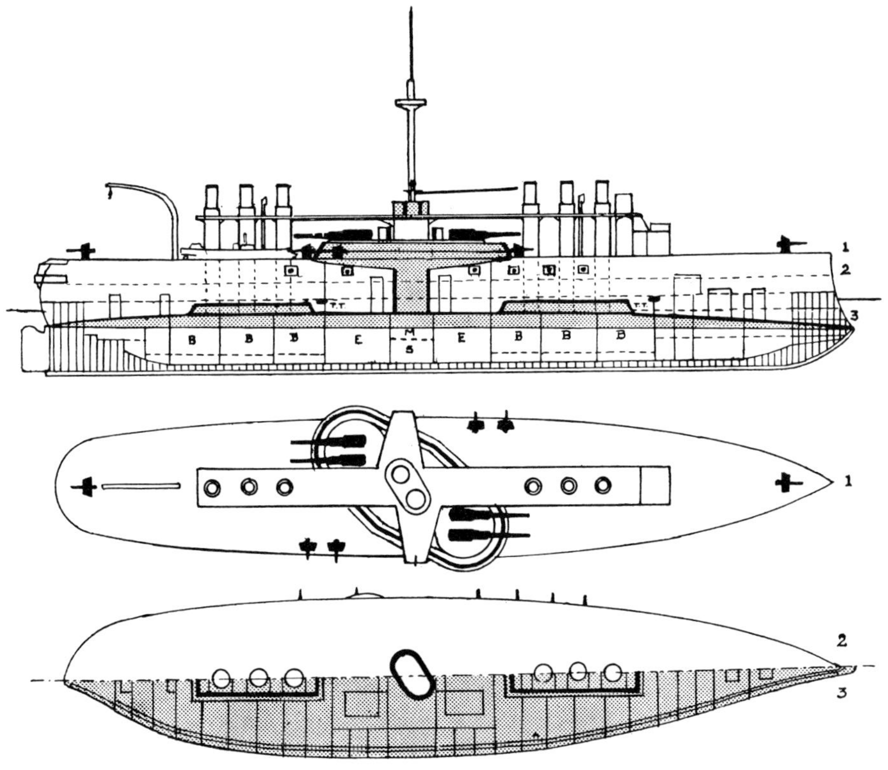

Italian battleship *ITALIA*

placed diagonally across the deck with a pair of guns on turntables at each end. In practice the rate of fire of these huge weapons was one round in four to five minutes, and the 6-in. could not be used while they were in action; in the end the secondary battery was whittled down to eight guns only.

But Brin could not foresee either the coming of the quick-firing gun or the development of high explosive shells, both of which revolutionary factors in determining design coincided with the *Italia's* entry into service and caused her value to slump completely. She could no longer be regarded as a battleship but only as a huge protected cruiser—a prototype to our *Furious* of forty years later. Colonel G. Rosso had to describe her as "a brilliant but unlucky conception of the mind of a great naval architect" (Inst. Nav. Arch. 1911), and although she engaged the attention of our constructors for some years—Barnaby putting forward the design for "a much improved *Italia*" in 1879—she was never thought much of in the Service, and Captain Penrose Fitzgerald—describing her at the R.U.S.I. in 1883—was prepared to pit the *Hercules* against her with odds on the British ship.

But, like the *Duperré*, she presented breech-loaders *en barbette*, a heavy secondary battery, high speed and high freeboard as definite factors in design which were to become essential features in British ships within a few years.

CHINESE GUNBOATS

At the other end of the scale from big guns and heavy armour was Sir William Armstrong advocating fast unarmoured deck-protected ships carrying many light or one or two large guns. His views were epitomized in the *Lung-Wei* type of gunboat Armstrongs built for China in 1881. These carried a single gun in a fixed turret at each end—10-in. 25-ton B.L. which were more powerful than any other gun afloat at the time excepting the huge M.L.R. in the *Inflexible* and *Duilio*, and these they completely surpassed in efficiency. With a strong protective deck and steaming at 16 knots with coal for 4,000 miles at cruising speed, they combined the power to hit hard with ability to escape from any armoured ship afloat—and caused a great impression when they called at Portsmouth to show off.

Presenting a very small target and able to choose their range, it appeared that the ordinary battleship would be in for a very rough time of it if opposed by a number of such gunboats equivalent to her own cost. Presented

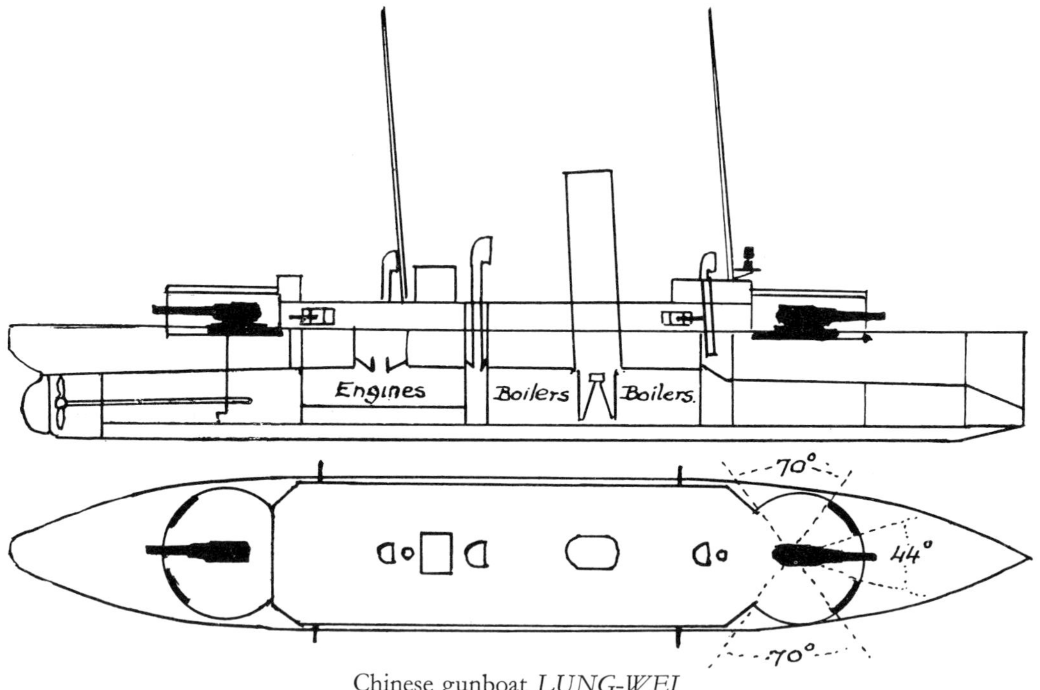

Chinese gunboat *LUNG-WEI*

in this light they made a great appeal to those who thought in terms of numbers and cheapness, coast defence and local operations. Time and again the construction of such ships for our own use was urged upon the Board, but the "home defence" policy was always successfully countered by the "blue-water" school who based our needs on the sound basis of naval history and its lessons. The *Lung-Wei* was not the type which could fight her guns in Channel weather, and for their passage out East both ships had their ends built up flush with the boat deck. But in 1882 Sir William Armstrong gave it as his opinion that "at present not a single ship in the British Navy is competent to engage them, that could overtake them in pursuit or evade their attack when prudence dictated a retreat," and his views were shared by a number of authorities responsible for the moulding of public opinion.

But while adhering to a big-ship policy the Board and its professional advisers were fully alive to the risks to which capital ships were exposed from specialized smaller craft, and Barnaby speaking at the Instit. of Naval Architects in 1876 had stated that:

> "The torpedo could be made, within the proper range of its operation, invincible. The possibility of attack by armoured rams or torpedo-ships, or by numerous unarmoured vessels of that kind, exposed the costly armour-clad ships to a risk which they ought never to encounter alone. The assailants ought to be brought to bay, before they could get within striking distance of the ironclads, by consorts, armed, like the attacking vessels, with the ram and with the torpedo, and which must, like them, run the risk of being sunk. Each costly ironclad ought to be a division, defended against the torpedo and ram by small, numerous, but less important parts of the general force."

Which of course was sound enough in theory, but in practice would limit or even do away with the use of ironclads themselves at sea. Such small craft could not be expected to keep company with big capital ships in wide operations, and their protection would therefore limit the use of ironclads to coastal or confined waters.

With a view to providing protection along these lines an experimental fleet ram, the *Polyphemus*, was laid down in 1878 to the designs of Chief Constructor Philip Watts, which was intended to accompany a squadron of battleships in a protective capacity generally.

"POLYPHEMUS"

In his *Naval Development* (p. 163) Barnaby claims that one of his greatest personal efforts was to get the ram recognized both as a big ship weapon and also as the sole arm of offence in a special vessel of small size with speed superior to the battleships of the day. The *Polyphemus* was originally intended as a ram pure and simple.

But when the Whitehead was adopted, the Board decided to equip her with torpedoes and a light armament against boat attack. As a torpedo-ram Barnaby rather lost interest in her. He considered that the introduction of torpedoes had made the ship too costly for numbers to be built, whereas it was possible that the type would have been continued and improved had the simplicity of the ram been adhered to. From a Service point of view the *Polyphemus* was regarded with considerable respect, and great things were expected of her in wartime—especially by those who had served in her.

But as a sea boat she condemned herself, for even in favourable circumstances she behaved like a half-tide rock and the crew as often as not were confined below. This, her principal defect, was to have been remedied in a second vessel—under consideration in 1886—by allowing a considerable increase in freeboard with adequate superstructure for accommodation, drill and exercise. This project was dropped, however, in favour of an alternative type, the "torpedo-cruiser," such as had been evolved at Elswick for the Austrian Navy in the *Leopard* and *Panther*, provided with higher speed, a good ram bow and better armament. On these lines the *Fearless* and *Scout* (1885) presented greater possibilities for warfare on the open seas, and the impracticable battleship screen of small rams, gunboats and torpedo launches became merely a first step towards what we now know as a "well-balanced fleet" with cruisers, scouts and sea-going torpedo craft supporting and protecting the capital ships. The formation of such composite squadrons commenced with these two ships.

Within the past ten years the following accidents had demonstrated tragically the dangers of the ram in peacetime:

1869. The Russian ironclad *Kreml* rammed the frigate *Oleg*, sinking her with the loss of 16 men.
1871. The Russian ironclad *Ad. Spiridoff* rammed her sister the *Ad. Lazareff* which was only saved from sinking in Kronstadt harbour by the speedy arrival of pumps from the dockyard.
1873. The Spanish ironclad *Numancia* rammed the corvette *Fernando el Catolica* and sank her, all the crew except five being drowned.
1875. The French ironclad *Jeanne d'Arc* rammed the despatch vessel *Forfait* which was sunk but without loss of life.
1875. H.M.S. *Iron Duke* rammed and sank the *Vanguard*, but without loss of life.
1877. The French ironclad *Thetis* rammed the ironclad *Reine Blanche* which was run ashore to save her from sinking.
1878. The German ironclad *Konig Wilhelm* rammed and sank the turret ship *Grosser Kurfurst* with the loss of nearly all the officers and men.

As demonstrating the necessity for having the ram securely built into the bow in order to withstand the twisting and wrench effect of oblique collisions it may be noted that although the *Iron Duke* hit the *Vanguard* at 7½ knots when the latter was making 6 knots athwart her bows so that the armour of the damaged ship was driven in bodily and a huge hole made in her side, the ram and bow of the *Iron Duke* were practically uninjured—striking evidence of their strength and proper construction, although the belt was not taken down to the spur. In contradistinction with this the *Konig Wilhelm* was nearly sunk after striking her consort in consequence of having the ram unsupported and being without a collision bulkhead.

In the short summaries of the ships' careers the note "Particular Service Squadron" for 1878 or 1885 refers to two special mobilizations of the Reserve Fleet which were ordered during periods of strained relations with Russia. In 1878 the assemblage took place at Portland between June and August, and Admiral Sir Cooper Key with his flag in the *Hercules* assumed command over a very mixed squadron consisting of:

Hercules (flag), *Warrior*, *Valiant*, *Resistance*, *Hector*, *Penelope*, *Lord Warden*.
Cyclops, *Hecate*, *Gorgon*, *Hydra*, *Glatton*, *Prince Albert*, *Thunderer*.
Boadicea (unarmoured frigate).
Blazer, *Bustard*, *Tay*, *Tweed* (river gunboats).
Lively (paddle despatch vessel).

With the assumption of more cordial relations with Russia this strange assortment of ships was dispersed and Cooper Key went to the Admiralty as First Sea Lord under Mr. W. H. Smith for the last year of Disraeli's term of office. His selection marked a breakaway from traditional practice whereby the Sea Lords were of the same parliamentary colour as their civilian head, as although Key rarely expressed particular political opinions his sympathies turned towards Liberalism; hence when the Conservatives left office in 1880 he was able to retain his position in the new Gladstone Government.

The seven years during which Cooper Key was at Whitehall proved to be one of the most momentous periods for the Navy and the turning-point in its material progress. It covered the return to breech-loading guns and the rearmament of the Fleet; the revitalization of design and acceptance of new principles in armament and protection; and transition from national apathy towards naval affairs to the crescendo of agitation for a stronger Fleet.

Chapter 45

THE RETURN TO BREECH-LOADING GUNS

During this period the great increase in armour thickness had made the armament manufacturers turn their attention towards improvements in ordnance whereby higher velocities and increased penetration could be obtained without merely enlarging the bore and weight of the gun; and the discovery that slow-burning large-grain powder could be used to develop sustained pressure led to changes in gun design which inevitably resulted in the readoption of the breech-loader.

When this new powder was fired in the short M.L. guns, the projectile left the muzzle before the charge was properly consumed, so that burning powder scored the decks of the turret ships. A longer chase was clearly indicated, and in 1878 Sir Andrew Noble and Professor Abel carried out a series of experiments at Elswick with longer guns loaded with slow powder, and showed that much higher velocities could be obtained than was possible with violent powder in shorter guns of similar weight.

When it was also discovered that a greater amount of large-grained powder could be burned without increase in the maximum pressure if the charge were "air-spaced"—that is, by making the powder chamber larger than the actual charge—the system of thus "chambering" guns was introduced, with additional external strengthening over the breech end. With M.L. guns chambering could not be carried out to any great extent, although it was applied with good results to the 38-ton and 80-ton models. Moreover, the increase in length necessary to obtain the benefit of the "large" powder meant loading arrangements outside the turret or—in the case of the smaller guns—great expense of manual labour in ramming the charge and projectile home. With breech-loaders the additional length was no objection, and there was also the advantage that the men were less exposed when loading and that the smoke was discharged outside the turret instead of the recoil bringing the still smoking muzzle inside the turret on return to the loading position.

The earlier breech-loaders had been dangerous because they could be fired without the breech being properly closed. With the new guns which Elswick offered to the Admiralty for trial this fault had been obviated by automatic safety devices attached to the breech which prevented the gun being discharged until the interrupted-screw action had locked. This device had been adopted from the French in preference to Krupp's wedge system, and was to remain our standard breech mechanism for upwards of fifty years.

On the Continent the use of breech-loaders had been general for many years, and in 1875 the so-called "mantle-ring" gun was produced in which a mantle or jacket shrunk over the breech end of a light rifled steel tube took the place of the massive inner body of Krupp guns. Hoops of short length were shrunk on outside to provide general strength. This gun gave a great increase of power out of all comparison with the performance of corresponding muzzle-loaders which by now had outlived their reputation for strength and simplicity. Moreover, the *Thunderer* explosion had done much to shake public confidence in their reliability.

In April 1879 a committee was appointed to consider whether a return to breech-loaders was indicated. But the Admiralty acted somewhat in advance of extraneous opinion and in the August sent a number of naval officers over to Meppen to witness and report upon the trials of the new Krupp guns. What they saw created a great impression, and the Board's decision was made without more ado. And so in the month when the 100-ton M.L. was undergoing proof at Woolwich and the 80-tonners for the *Inflexible* had almost reached completion, the great change-over was initiated in favour of the long B.L. with Elswick breech-mechanism for the *Colossus*, *Majestic* (later *Edinburgh*), *Conqueror*, and the newly designed *Collingwood.*

The War Office—which was responsible for providing the artillery—thereupon decided to manufacture a 12-in. B.L.R. in accordance with a Woolwich design, and in the meantime an experimental 43-ton 12-in. B.L. was ordered from Armstrongs for delivery in ten months. The Woolwich design was for a 25-cal. piece, and as the limit of length admissible in these ships was 27¾ ft. this measurement was provisionally accepted. But the finished design did not receive approval until February 1882; the weight of the projectile was not decided upon until September; and the weight of the charge only finally determined in March 1884.

But the change-over to breech-loaders was to be marked by both danger and delay—danger because of faulty material and obsolete methods of construction, and delay which held up deliveries so that ships came to be commissioned without all their big guns aboard. That all was not well with the methods of production at the Royal Ordnance Factory was first realized in 1880, when a very remarkable petition was presented to the Commons signed by eminent Fellows of the Royal Society including Sir Henry Bessemer, which contained the following:

> "That your Petitioners have devoted special attention to questions of gunnery and to the construction of ordnance. Certain of them have attained some eminence as metallurgists, engineers and inventors. Their theoretical studies and practical knowledge lead them unhesitatingly to the belief that the system of heavy ordnance now in use and known as the Woolwich system is inefficient and dangerous . . . Your Petitioners

look with dismay upon the defects of the English heavy guns, and they are of the opinion that these defects seriously endanger our naval supremacy and national safety . . . false information and wrong principles have been officially disseminated and taught in both Services."

It was not until 1884 that the Superintendent of the Factory admitted that the Woolwich guns were obsolete and that even in 1875 we were, to the knowledge of Woolwich, "distanced in the artillery race." But in addition to supplying inferior material the War Office chose to ignore the Admiralty demands for ordnance and included in their estimates only such amounts as they considered convenient, generally averaging two-thirds of the sums asked for between 1881 and 1886. The Navy, moreover, were in ignorance as to the various reserves of ammunition available at home, as these had to be pooled with the Army, whose requisitions would be served first in an emergency leaving the Navy with whatever was left over.

It was not until November 1886, when Captain J. A. Fisher was appointed Director of Naval Ordnance, that the chaos in ordnance and stores was taken in hand, and a departmental campaign started which led to the Navy assuming responsibility for its own guns, ammunition and stores a few years later.

Prior to preparation of the designs for these ships in the spring of 1878, Barnaby made submissions for a departure from the Froude ratio of dimensions which had been used in the *Inflexible* and *Ajax* in order to give them a length of 350 ft. with 68 ft. beam. His argument was that the ram and torpedo had made speed of more importance than handiness both in offence and defence, and that as it could not be obtained in short ships without large engine power it would be better to reduce the size and cost of machinery and also fuel consumption at the expense of additional length. He pointed out that when there was plated protection from end to end a long ship was wasteful of armour, but this did not apply to citadel designs. Thus the *Ajax* could be lengthened to 350 ft. with advantage if by so doing speed could be increased from 13 to 14½ knots and coal endurance raised to that of the *Devastation*.

But the Board turned down this recommendation and fixed on 325 ft. for the length of the *Colossus*—the same as in the *Hercules*, *Sultan*, and—within a few feet—*Dreadnought* and *Inflexible*; her dimensions therefore added 5 ft. to the *Inflexible's* length and deducted 7 ft. from her beam, giving proportions of 4·7 : 1.

In the original calculations the draught was fixed at a mean of 25 ft. 9 in. giving 9,150 tons displacement with a full coal supply of 950 tons. But various additions made to equipment totalled up to 510 tons, adding 9 in. to the draught and necessitated a readjustment of weights. Consequently the normal coal complement was reduced to 850 tons, and the full load displacement fixed at 9,520 tons with 26½ ft. draught.

"COLOSSUS" and "EDINBURGH" (ex *Majestic*)

	Built at	*Laid down*	*Launched*	*Completed*	*Cost*
"*Colossus*"	Portsmouth	6 June 79	21 May '82	31 Oct. '86	£661,716
"*Edinburgh*"	Pembroke	20 March '79	18 March '82	8 July '87	£645,138 (£662,773)

Dimensions 325′×68′×25·3′/26·3′=9,150 tons.
Hull and armour 6,150 tons. Equipment 3,000 tons.

Armament 4 12-in. 45-ton B.L. guns.
5 6-in. B.L.
4 6-pdrs. (added later).
20 smaller.
Tubes:
2 14-in. above water.

Armour (compound) Citadel 18″-14″; bulkheads 16″-13″; turrets 16″-14″; conning tower 14″; deck 3″-2½″; skin 1″; teak 22″-10″.
Total 2,414 tons (26·3 per cent.).

Complement 396.

Coal 850/950 tons.

Machinery "*Colossus*" Maudslay. "*Edinburgh*" Humphreys.
2 sets inverted direct compound.
D.H.P. 6,000=14 knots. I.H.P. 6,808=16 knots ("*Edinburgh*") light.
7,488=16·5 knots ("*Colossus*") draught.
H.P. cyl. 58″; 2 L.P. 74″; stroke 39″.
Twin screws; 4-bladed diam. 17′ 8″; pitch 17′-20′; revs. 86.
10 elliptical tubular boilers. 64 lb. pressure.

Points of interest:

(1) The first British battleships to carry breech-loaders.
(2) The first to have compound armour generally in place of iron.
(3) The first in which steel was used for general construction.
(4) The last of the citadel ships proper.
(5) Had a metacentric height of 9 ft.

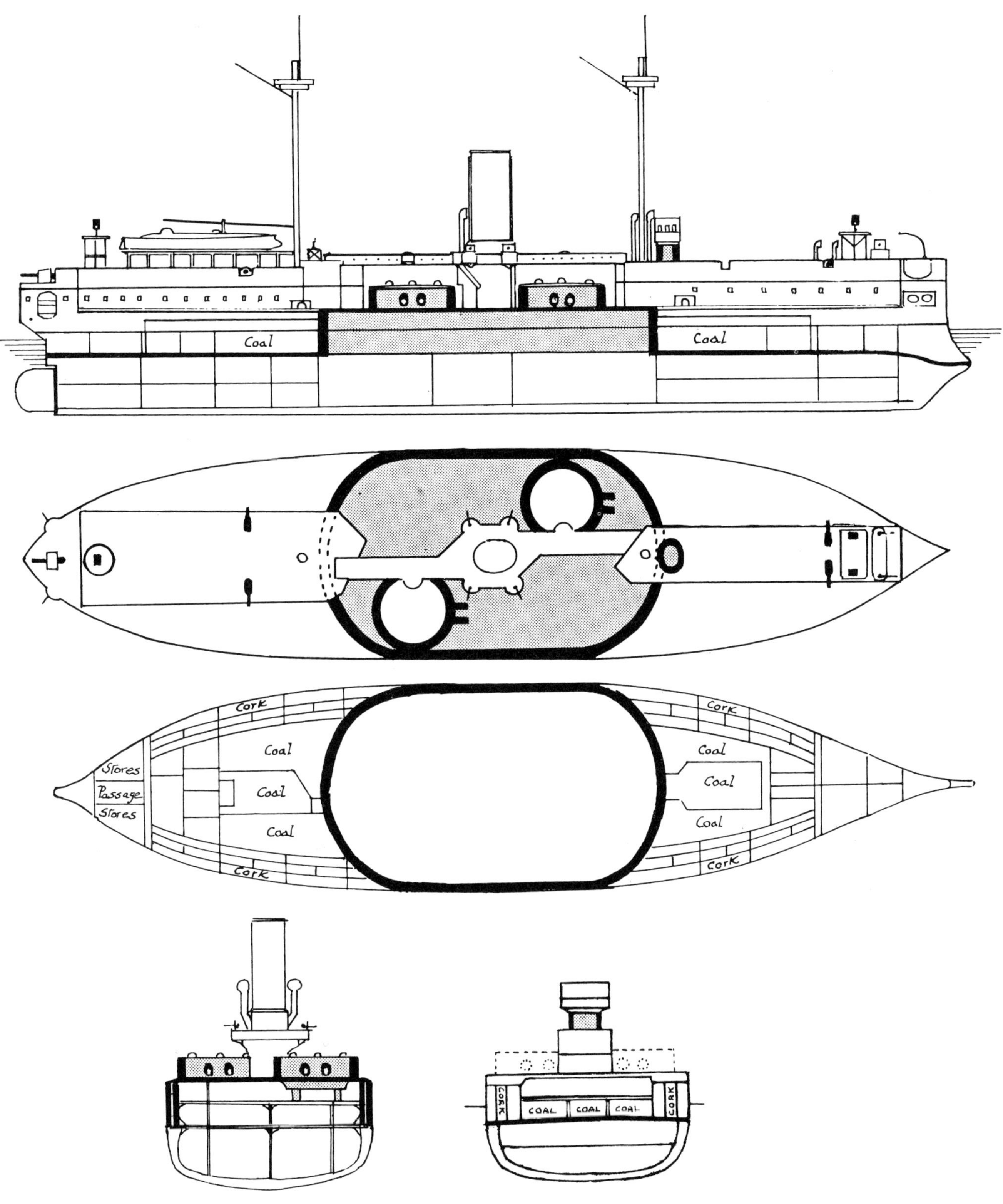

COLOSSUS AND EDINBURGH

ARMAMENT

As originally planned they were to have carried four 38-ton M.L.R. and four 6-in. B.L., being *Agamemnon's* with a knot more speed and better sea-going and sea-keeping qualities. But in 1882 when Woolwich had at last broken away from the M.L. tradition and produced an acceptable design the Board were able to arm the ships with 12-in. 25 cals. B.L. guns—the first to be mounted in British ships. So when the great sheer-legs at Portsmouth slowly lowered the new weapons into her turrets the *Colossus* could boast of being the battleship in which M.L. guns, iron construction and iron armour were all discarded for the first time.

Owing to their method of manufacture the first batch of 12-in. guns were faulty and one burst on trial in the *Collingwood* on 4 May 1886, while the *Colossus* was still completing. The original charge of powder was 400 lb., but this was reduced first to 290 lb. and then to 222 lb.—the charge used when the gun exploded. As a result, the Captain of the *Colossus* was directed not to fire his big guns during the first cruise, and the whole batch had to be withdrawn from service for chasehooping.

An increase in the secondary armament from two to five guns was allowed at the expense of the turret armour, reduced from 16 in. to 14 in. to allow for the additional weight involved. As in the *Italia* the 6-in. guns were

The 12-in. guns of the *Colossus* were loaded in the same way as the M.L.'s in the *Inflexible*, but in reverse—the charge was rammed home from below the deck into the breech, the gun being elevated or depressed by a hydraulic ram under its rear end.

widely distributed as the system of definite battery grouping had not yet been adopted, and the main object was to place them as far from blast effects as possible. These B.L. guns were replaced by 6-in. Q.F. in April 1898.

The torpedo tubes were placed forward in a transverse battery under the armour deck.

Contrary to expectations no trouble arose from smoke or fumes in the turret, as the interval between firing and the return to the loading position before opening the breech gave ample time for combustion products to escape through the muzzle; and not until all-round loading and rapid fire came into practice many years later did air-blast have to be employed to clear breech-loaders of fumes. At target practice in 1887 the *Colossus* made record shooting by getting off four rounds from one gun in six minutes and scoring three hits at 1,500 yards when at full speed.

ARMOUR

The citadel measured 123 ft. along the middle line—compared with 104 ft. in *Ajax* and 110 ft. in *Inflexible*—and shaped a broad oval so that all hits would be more or less converted into glancing blows. With 18-in. sides and 16-in. ends it extended from 6 ft. 6 in. below water—6 in. deeper than in the previous ships—to the main deck height of 9 ft. 6 in. As already noted the turrets had 14-in. plates with 16-in. over the faces and were slightly larger than in *Ajax*.

The position of the conning tower under the charthouse forward of the fore mast calls for a short comment. Hitherto conning towers had been placed in a variety of positions—right aft; between the funnels; at the break of the forecastle, etc.—and in *Ajax* found itself on the roof of the charthouse abaft the fore mast with a commanding if somewhat precarious position. But in their recent ships the French had found that a full field of vision for axial and broadside fire could only be obtained from forward of the fore mast, and placed their conning towers accordingly with bridge and charthouse above and abaft them, where if wrecked, vision would not be obstructed. This position was selected for the *Colossus*, but with the charthouse *placed on its crown*—the first step was taken towards the thoroughly unsound practice, which was to obtain for so many years of hiding the conning tower away under the fore bridge usually amidst a nest of small guns with stanchions and other obstructions to vision.

In these ships steel was first used in general construction, only the heavy forgings like stem and stern posts being made of iron. And whereas in the *Ajax* only the turrets had compound armour, in the *Edinburgh* both turrets and citadel were of steel-faced iron.

The same system of armour deck, cork compartments, cofferdams, and subdivision was followed, but on a more extensive scale. And as some indication of its value it may be noted that when the *Edinburgh* ended her days as a fleet target in 1908 she was towed back to Portsmouth stern first on an even keel without her unarmoured ends being blown away or extensively damaged, after enduring a more devastating fire than she would have experienced in possible action during her active life. In which connection it was rather a caprice of Destiny that although the *Inflexible* Committee had recommended that the citadel system of protection should be put to a

The *Colossus* as gunnery tender at Portsmouth in 1904, showing full net defence and the high mast heads of her later years.

practical target test, this was never done until the *Edinburgh* firing took place a quarter of a century afterwards—and then with quite a different object!

SEA-GOING QUALITIES

Both ships did well on trials, the power developed exceeding contract by record figures. Running light *Colossus* reached 16·5 knots with 7,488 h.p. and *Edinburgh* 16 knots with 6,808 h.p., at which speed in calm water they threw up a remarkable bow wave which rose like a solid wall for 13 ft. and passed unbroken for some distance aft, the "like of which had never previously been observed."

As sea boats they can only be described as passable, with a quick and deep roll, and carrying considerable weather helm with a wind on the beam or quarter. Owing to the gun ports being only 12 ft. above water, at 13° inclination the muzzles dipped into the sea when trained abeam, and when rolling the chases were submerged several feet by moderate waves—a phenomenon which could not happen with the short M.L. guns.

That they would be rather unhappy at sea was inevitable, as their metacentric height was 9 ft.—a foot more than in the *Inflexible*. This was due to the fact that while in the well-protected monitors and *Dreadnought* type it had been possible to assure stability with a metacentric height of from 2½ to 5 ft., in the citadel ships where unprotected ends might be damaged a much greater degree of stability had to be provided, and the metacentre was raised accordingly. But as increase in this direction shortens the rolling period and makes for bad shooting, some return to steadiness had to be provided by long deep bilge keels and anti-rolling tanks. Without the use of the tanks the *Edinburgh's* period for a full swing from side to side was 9 secs.—a great improvement upon the 5½ secs. of *Inflexible*; 40 tons of water reduced the angle of roll from 6° to 4½°, but as the period could not be prolonged to 10 secs. this success was not worth mentioning. Large Atlantic waves have a period of about 10 secs., so that modern battleships with a 16 secs. period are very steady when among them; but such waves would synchronize with the *Edinburgh's* roll when abeam, making changes of course necessary to avoid danger. Further experiments showed that 100 tons of water gave the best results, increasing the rolling resistance at 10° by 43 per cent. Two feet added to the bilge keels added 67 per cent. to resistance at all angles of roll, but the water chamber was more effective at small angles; for violent rolling the bilge keels proved more efficient. As the "ballast water" washing to and fro fetched up "with shocks of great violence," making it difficult to stand on the deck above the tanks, their retention was not recommended, especially as the space was required for other purposes.

They were bad at manœuvre with large turning circles and slow on the helm.

APPEARANCE

To distinguish them it was only necessary to notice that in *Colossus* the steam pipes were level with the funnel top—in *Edinburgh* below it; also in later years *Colossus* had very high mast heads.

"COLOSSUS"

Took over seven years to complete, running speed trials in January '84 and gun trials in July '85. Commissioned at Portsmouth 13 April '86 for Particular Service and in August joined the Channel fleet for tests. Detached for Special Duties in October and then being formally completed was sent to the Mediterranean in April '87 where she remained for six and a half years, returning to take up duty as coastguard ship at Holyhead in November '93. Eight years later in '01 was paid off and passed into the Fleet Reserve at Portsmouth; transferred to Dockyard Reserve in '02 but in January '04 was given a fresh lease of life as tender to the *Excellent* with duty as guardship at Cowes in August '04. Ordered to be sold in September '06 and towed away for breaking up in October '08. £18,500.

"EDINBURGH"

Ran her steam trials in September '83 but completion delayed over armament. Commissioned at Portsmouth for Jubilee Review in July '87 and proceeded to Mediterranean in August where she remained until January '94. In February '94 became coastguard ship at Hull, soon after exchanging to Queensferry with *Galatea*. Joined Fleet Reserve at Chatham in September '97—in May '99 being temporary flagship at the Nore. Became tender to *Wildfire* at Sheerness October '99 and acted as gunnery ship until March '05 when she joined the Special Reserve at Chatham.

Used as target for experimental firing in '08, she was fitted with modern armour plates fully supported, for testing hits at oblique impact with filled A.P. shell as supplied for war use. As a result of these trials the Controller (Jellicoe) instructed the D.N.O. in October '08 to produce designs for A.P. 12-in. shell and above which would pierce thick armour at oblique impact in a fit state for bursting. Jellicoe then hoisted his flag as C.O. Atlantic Fleet, but owing to technical blunders in his absence this instruction was not carried out. Thus at Jutland we lost the advantage of our heavy guns while handicapped by our thinner armour.

Chapter 46

GENESIS OF THE "CONQUEROR"

In describing the *Rupert* mention was made of a report on the ship by her Captain (February 1878) in which he sketched out certain alterations which would correct her faults and increase her efficiency considerably. Although not carried out in full when the *Rupert* was modernized, these suggestions served as the basis for the design of the *Conqueror* and for that reason the sketches which accompanied them are worth inclusion here. In some cases it is not easy to understand how a ship came into being unless there is some knowledge of the why and wherefore, and the *Conqueror* is a case in point.

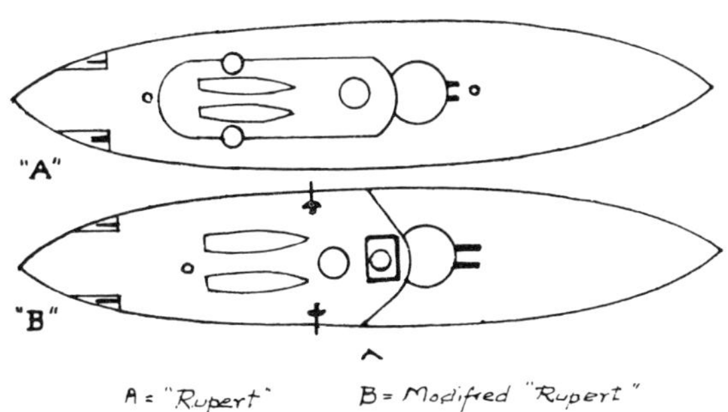

Sketch A shows the *Rupert* as she was in 1878 with a central flying deck and an angled breastwork aft, two "fighting towers" with obstructed vision, and a couple of pole masts.

Sketch B shows the alterations proposed by Captain W. E. Gordon, with high bulwarks as far forward as the breakwater and armour plates around the steering position forward of the funnel, and one mast only.

Captain Gordon described the *Rupert's* fore mast as an "unmitigated evil," and the sail effort as not worth the inconvenience and expense of keeping them up. The vessel was to be regarded primarily as a ram with gun power only auxiliary. As Captain Gordon put it, "The ram is a comparatively simple weapon within the capacity of an ordinary man to make the best use of, whereas the Captain of the *Alexandra* or *Temeraire* in action would be like a man armed with sword, rapier, rifle and pistol, trying to use them all at the same time. No man's faculties are equal to making the *best use* of such complicated machines."

Captain Gordon's remarks and sketches were submitted through Admiral Commerell, who gave them full endorsement, "recommending the type as more nearly approaching what a ship-of-the-line should be than any other I have seen." But his views of the simplicity of ramming were not shared by the Controller, who noted that they were "good in theory but not practicable supposing that enemy has 14-15 knots and *Rupert* 11-12." Neither apparently took relative powers of manœuvre into consideration, which Colomb had shown to rank higher than speed (see Appendix), but in other respects the type of ship found favour with the Board as the *Conqueror*, designed in accordance with sketch B, was laid down in April 1879. The First Lord, in proposing the Estimates for 1878-79, thus introduced the ship:

> "She was intended to be an improved *Rupert*. The *Rupert* would commend herself to the judgment of naval officers as being a handy and convenient vessel. It was proposed to build another of the same class, with more powerful guns in her single turret, namely guns of 38 tons instead of 18 tons with economical engines of modern type and great coal-endurance."

"CONQUEROR" and "HERO"

	Built at	*Laid down*	*Undocked*	*Completed*	*Cost*
"Conqueror"	Chatham	28 April '79	8 Sept. '81	March '86	£401,991
"Hero"	Chatham	11 April '84	27 Oct. '85	May '88	£388,764

Dimensions	*"Conqueror"* 270′ × 58′ × 22′/24·3′ = 6,200 (4,110/2,160 tons). *"Hero"* 270′ × 58′ × 21·7′/25·8′ = 6,440 (4,200/2,240 tons).
Armament	2 12-in. 25 cal. B.L. 6 above water 14″ t.t. 4 6-in. B.L. 1 torpedo launch. 7 6-pdr. q.f. 1,628 lb. 13 smaller.
Armour	Belt 12″-8″; citadel 12″-10½″; turret 12″-14″; conning tower 12″-6″; decks 2½″-1¼″; skin 1″; backing 13½″-9″; bulkheads 11½″-11″-10½″. Total 1,700 tons (27·4 per cent.).
Complement	330.
Coal	*"Hero"* 620/500. *"Conqueror"* 650/500 tons.
Machinery	*"Conqueror"* Humphreys & Tennant. *"Hero"* Rennie. 2 sets 3-cyl. inverted comp. I.H.P. 4,500 = 14 knots. 1 H.P. 54″. 2 L.P. cyl. 70″; stroke 3′. Twin screws 14′ diam.; pitch 16½′-18½′. 8 cylindrical tubular boilers. 24 furnaces. 70 lb. pressure.

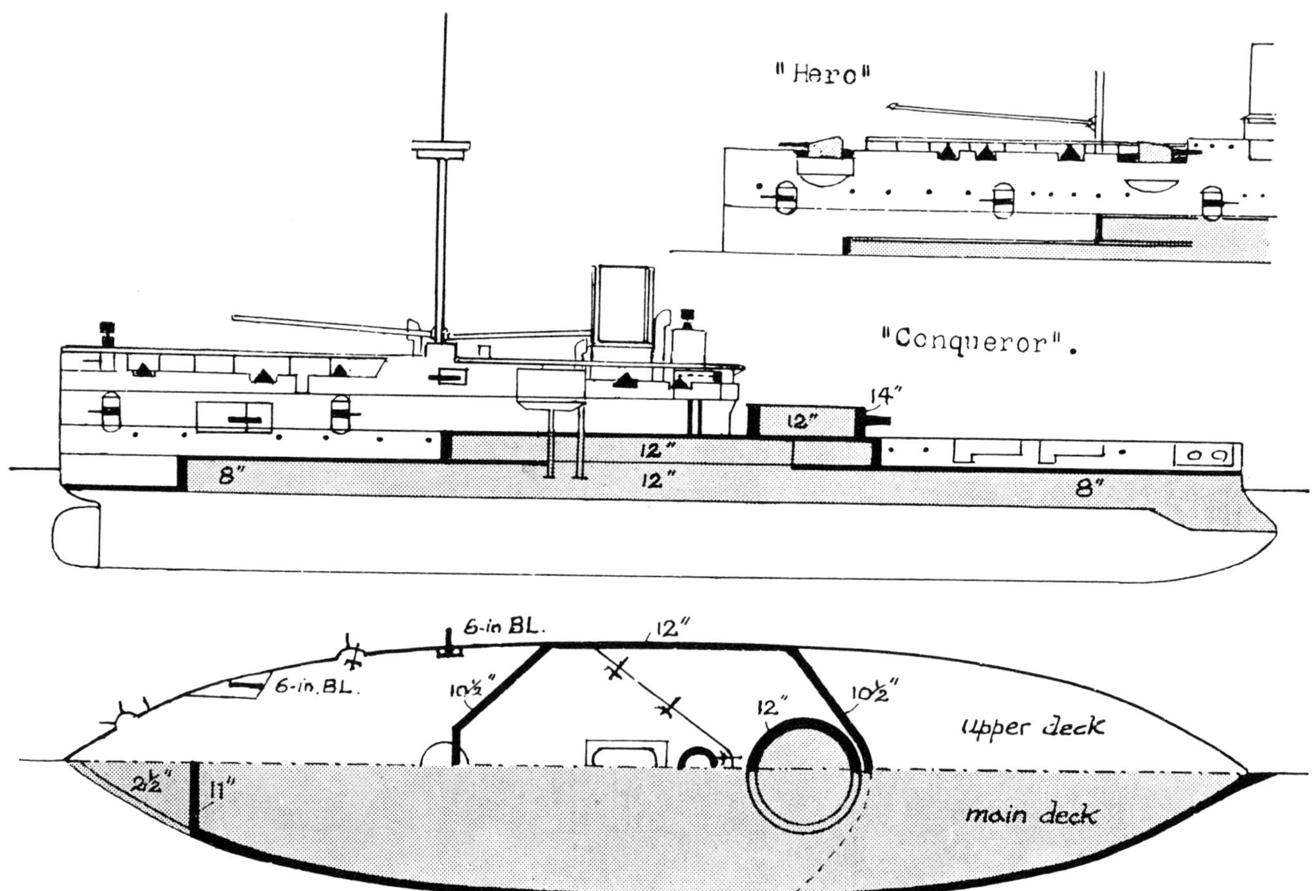

In the *Conqueror* and *Hero* protection was by an almost complete belt with a thick redoubt enclosing the turret base and funnel uptakes. In the *Conqueror* the 6-in. guns fired through embrasures in the superstructure, in the *Hero* they were raised to sponsons on the boat deck.

During the seven years in which the *Colossus* and *Edinburgh* were being built, a smaller single-turret battleship the *Conqueror* was constructed in dry dock at Chatham, the three enjoying a building period about on a par with that observed in the most leisurely of the Continental dockyards. Five years after she was laid down a second ship of the same class, the *Hero*, followed her on the blocks and hoisted the pennant two years after her sister had left the Medway—two of the most useless turret ships ever built for the Navy.

At the time end-on fire and ramming tactics were still in favour and the *Conqueror* is described as representing the views of those who considered fewer heavy guns in a small, well-protected, fast and handy hull designed for ramming preferable to ships like the *Colossus*—and costing much less. Whether the Controller Vice-Admiral Sir William Houstan Stewart had intended her as an economical addition to the sea-going fleet or as an oversize coast defender is uncertain—but that she could ever be anything more than a make-believe sea boat was hardly to be expected. Although sent out on manœuvres for some years, the two ships never earned anything but scathing criticism and were fit for nothing except the harbour service as gunnery tenders in which their lives were spent.

Coming as a break in the line of citadel ships, the *Conqueror* with her orthodox belt-redoubt protection was not an example of atavism, but merely marked the limits in displacement and proportions beyond which Barnaby's system could not be applied. A length to beam of 4·5 to 1 and 6,000 tons had been laid down as necessary for stability, and her 6,200 tons with 4·6 to 1 offered little margin towards safety—hence a reversion to the modified *Rupert* distribution of armour.

ARMAMENT

The short 12-in. guns were always regarded as too near the deck, and if discharged straight ahead likely to damage fittings in their line of fire besides straining the hull. Owing to blast effects on the bridge it was found inadvisable to fire them abaft the beam, so the arcs of bearing were limited to something like 45° on each side.

Conqueror had two of her 6-in. guns mounted in the superstructure and two on the upper deck; in *Hero* all

The *Conqueror* at Spithead in her early days. Note the short chases of the 25 cal. 12-in. guns and the second-class torpedo boat with funnel lowered stowed below the after boom.

four were in sponsons on the upper deck, with wider arcs of training. They also carried a tertiary battery of six 6-pdrs. and five 3-pdrs. with some machine guns, thus introducing the diversity of small gun calibres which further complicated magazine arrangements and the fleet ammunition supply.

The six 14-in. above-water torpedo tubes was the heaviest armament yet mounted; they were supposed to come into play if a ramming attack failed, when the ships would otherwise have been practically helpless owing to lack of gunfire astern.

HERO

ARMOUR

Some 1,700 tons of compound armour equal to 27·4 per cent. of the displacement provided considerably better protection than in the *Rupert*, the belt being 12 in. amidships tapering to 8 in. forward and finishing 27 ft. short of the stern with an 11-in. bulkhead. A 2½-in. deck covered the steering gear. The 58-ft. redoubt enclosing the turret base and funnel uptakes had 12-in. sides and angled 10½-in. bulkheads at each end. This replaced the internal breastwork of the *Rupert*, with all the advantages of side armour in protecting stability.

As in the *Colossus* a conning tower (with an extension down to the redoubt) was placed in what was to become the traditional position—at the forward end of the superstructure. Above this was a charthouse and bridge with wings extending right abaft the funnel—the most efficient and commodious yet afforded to any ship and the forerunner of the great structures developed forty years later.

SEA-GOING QUALITIES

With a forecastle freeboard of 9½ ft.—over a foot less than in the *Dreadnought*—there could be no pretence of their being anything but bad sea boats, and in a moderate swell when the *Benbow* would be rolling 5° the *Conqueror* worked through 18° to 20°. During the 1890 manœuvres she actually rolled 35° one way so that the cutter stowed at bridge level was washed from its davits. Shooting was difficult as the bows were usually buried in a cataract of foam, and the mess deck on the main deck forward became almost uninhabitable in anything of a seaway owing to leaky forecastle fittings. Admiral Mayne reporting on the 1889 manœuvres said: "What they would have become after the big guns had been fired over them a few times is at present left to the imagination." Being short and beamy speed fell off quickly in a head sea, although they could make 14 knots under natural draught in smooth water. Reports show them to have been handy, steering well and answering the helm quickly—so fulfilling requirements for ramming.

Apart from a month at sea on the few occasions when they took part in the manœuvres, both ships spent all their days in harbour—the *Hero* at Portsmouth and *Conqueror* at Devonport. For full fifteen years they were familiar features of the dockyard waterways, and their passing marked the disappearance of home-welcoming and affectionately regarded links with the Victorian navy. When the grey livery was introduced in place of the black, white and buff, it was generally remarked that no ships were changed more—and to their disadvantage—than these two.

"CONQUEROR"

Commissioned at Chatham 5 July '87 for the Jubilee Review. In September joined the Devonport Reserve, becoming tender to the gunnery school *Cambridge* in '89. Apart from going out on manœuvres in '88, '89, '90, '91, '92 and '94 she was never out of sight of land. Paid off in July '02 and was banished to Rothesay in '05 until sold in April '07 for £16,800.

"HERO"

Commissioned at Portsmouth May '88 as tender to the gunnery school *Excellent* where she remained until relegated to the Dockyard Reserve in February '05. Commissioned for manœuvres in '88, '89, '90, '91. In November '07 became a target ship and was sunk off the Kentish Knock on 18 February '08.

Chapter 47

GENESIS OF THE "COLLINGWOOD"

THE problem of providing a suitable design for the next large armoured ship as a reply to the French *Formidables*—which carried three 75-ton B.L. on the centre line and twelve 5·5-in. along the main deck—gave the Constructor's Department every sort of difficulty. During 1879 Barnaby submitted various tentative suggestions to the Board, which although catholic in their range of variety showed a certain lack of originality and very little conception of our real requirements in the matter of sea-going battleships. They included:

(1) A much improved and powerful edition of the *Italia*.
(2) An improved *Inflexible*.
(3) An *Inflexible* along the lines suggested by Reed which could go into action with her ends flooded.
(4) A *Dreadnought* with central citadel and unarmoured ends.

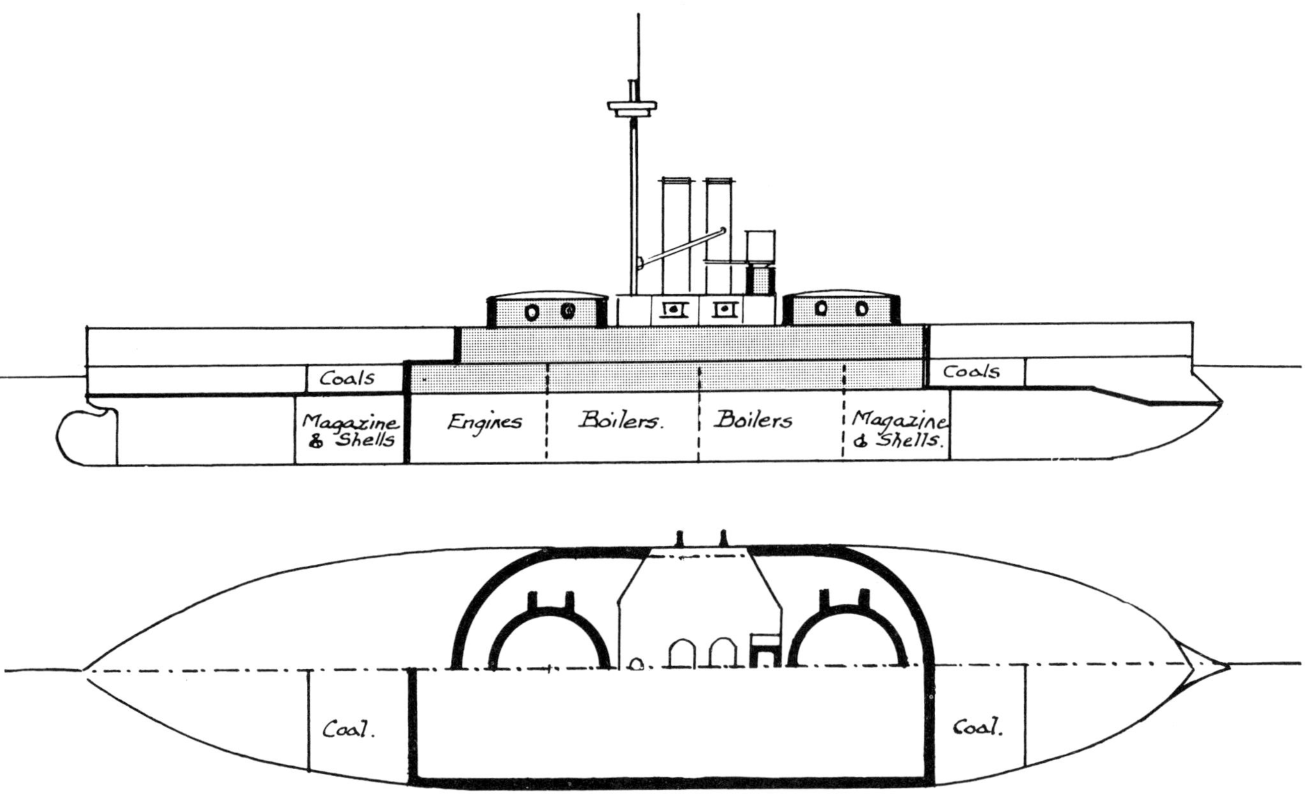

Proposed improved *DREADNOUGHT*, 1879.

These were under consideration for months, but the Board would have none of them. The *Italia* design had been ridiculed in debate and something better than turret ships with guns only 12 or 14 ft. above water was required. Moreover, the First Sea Lord, Admiral Sir George Wellesley, gave directions that displacement was to be under 10,000 tons—a limit which in the opinion of the Construction Department meant second-class ships and precluded the production of a design which could compete with the larger French and Italian models.

As a basis from which a suitable design might be evolved Barnaby turned to the French *Caiman* class laid down the previous year—a low-freeboard type in marked contrast to the high-hulled sea-going battleships of the *Formidable* and *Courbet* classes on the stocks or completing for sea. The *Caiman* belonged to a group of four large-size coast-defence ships of 7,200 tons with 14½ knots designs speed. A huge 16·5-in. was mounted fore and aft on a low 18-in. barbette, with a central superstructure housing four 4-in. guns at the corners and fourteen Q.F. on the upperworks and masts. The complete belt of 19½ in. amidships tapering to 12 in. at the bow and stern was covered by a 3-in. deck and provided unusually solid protection but along a depth of only 7½ ft. Altogether the four ships constituted a very formidable fighting unit.

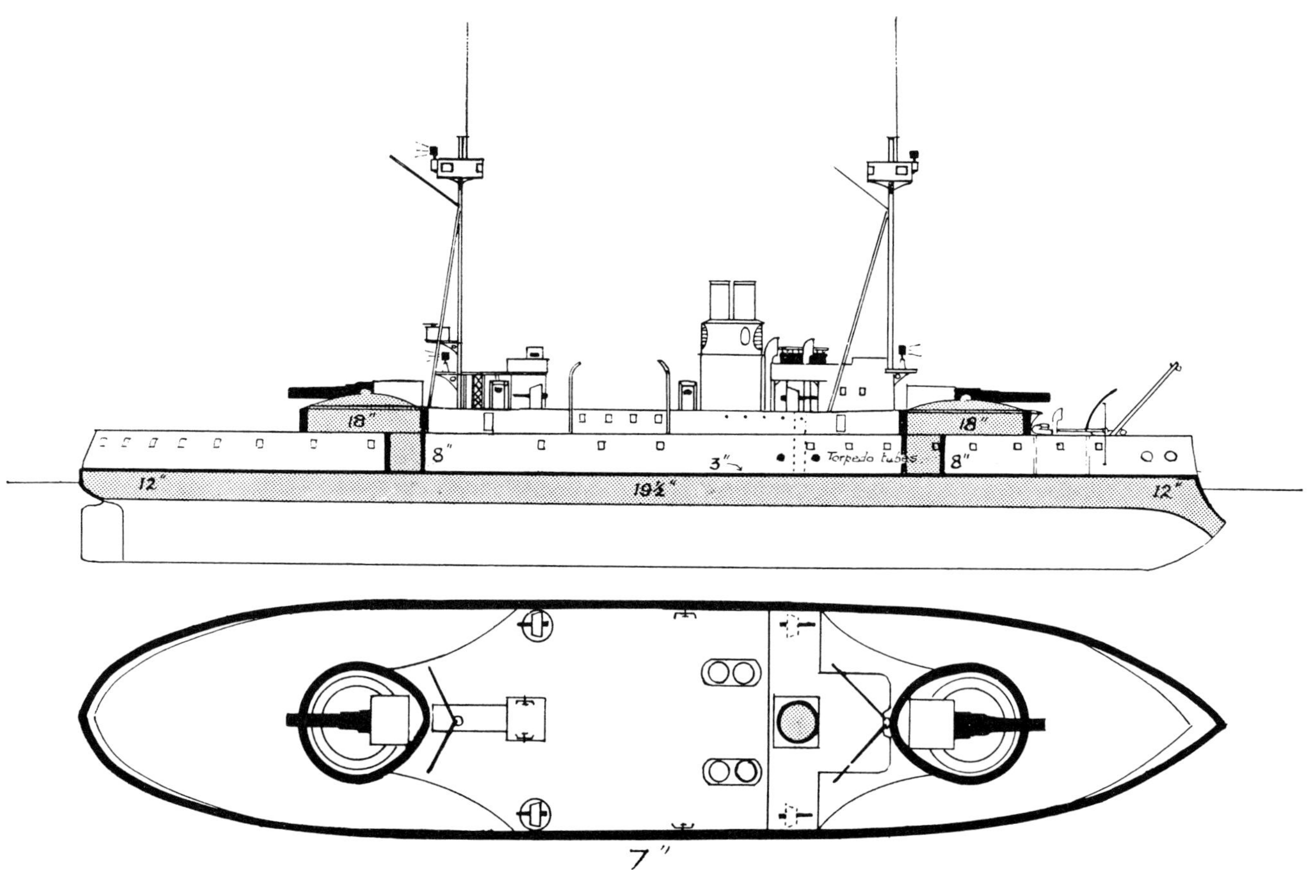

The French coast-defence battleship *Caiman* which served as a model for the *Collingwood* initial design.

According to Vice-Admiral Colomb the initial design was to have had two guns at the bow and stern on turntables with a strong broadside armament between them, the guns being muzzle-loaders ("Memoirs of Sir Cooper Key" p. 426). With the abandonment of the muzzle-loader this design was re-cast, and a rough pen-and-ink sketch preserved in the "Collingwood" Cover (undated) shows what may be accepted as the genesis of the ship, and from which the elevation below has been scaled off.

There is a freeboard of two decks with single large guns on low turntables as in *Caiman*, and the only protection for the loading numbers a low screen at the rear. The armament was to be two 80- or 100-ton breechloaders plus four or more smaller guns capable of piercing 6-in. plates at 1,000 yards—which would be the measure of the 6-in. gun. A 100-ton gun is shown in the elevation.

While the Board aimed at the same displacement as the *Caiman*, the dimensions were very different:

"*Caiman*"	278′×59′×24½′=7,230/6,000. 14·5. Two 42 c.m. Four 10 c.m.
"*Collingwood*"	325′×65′×23=7,200/5,000. 14. Two 80/100-ton. Four smaller.

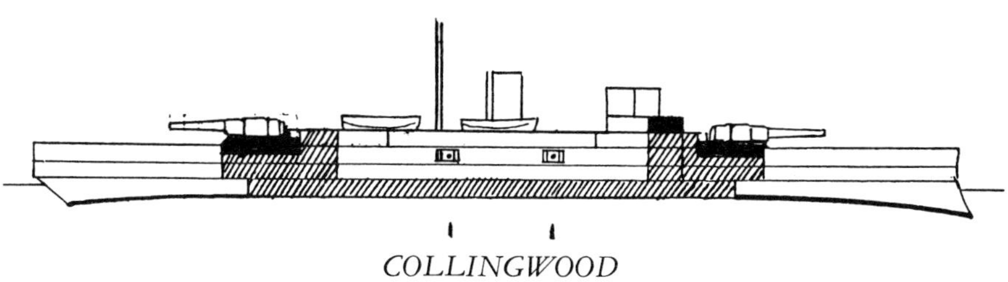

COLLINGWOOD

It will be noticed that the proposed length is 325 ft. figures which seem to have been regarded with some veneration as having contributed towards the success of the *Hercules*, *Sultan*, *Dreadnought* (320 ft.), *Alexandra*, *Inflexible* (320 ft.) and *Colossus*. This addition of 47 ft. in length with 6 ft. on to the beam and 1½ ft. less draught postulated hollow lines fore and aft such as were characteristic of the final design of the *Collingwood*. The metacentric height was to be 6 ft. with a 75° range of stability.

Armour thickness was to be not less than 12 in. compound and arranged from what weight was available, allowing for a waterline belt 6 ft. deep with the upper deck 9 ft. above water.

In discussing the mounting for the big guns Captain Watson absolutely condemned the *Temeraire* system, which he considered could not well be in action five minutes in a well-fought engagement, although practice from these guns was perfect at long range—which is interesting as being the only adverse criticism of this mounting from a fighting point of view which the writer has come across.

Thus when Admiral Sir Cooper Key became First Sea Lord in 1879 these first tentative sketches showing a general approach to his ideal of 1866 came up for consideration. He saw for the first time in our Navy a proposal for the particular disposition of armament he had advocated—guns at the bow and stern on turntables with a broadside battery in between them; no rig; and the broadside guns protected as he had laid down in his sketch—that is, not protected at all.

In order to meet the conditions laid down for an acceptable British edition of the *Caiman*, Barnaby states:

> "We got the design of our first heavily armed barbette ships 2,000-odd tons larger than the French design which was actually before us when their Lordships decided to enter upon the consideration of such a class of ship."

From 7,230 tons the final displacement rose to 9,500 tons with another 3 ft. added to the beam (68 ft.) with a much thicker belt, increase in speed, and the secondary battery a deck higher.

To Mr. W. H. White, Barnaby's most trusted and competent assistant, was given the task of working out the complete design incorporating the required armament and speed, coal storage, etc., in conjunction with the most adequate system of protection possible upon the displacement allowed. In the survey of this, two points of great difference arose—the underwater armoured deck and the conning towers. The former was an integral part of the basic conception, which could not be modified; the latter Key had always protested against, but machine guns counted for more than rifle fire, and the heavy towers provided had become a necessity.

With the change to B.L. guns the Controller, Sir Houstan Stewart, was able to recommend a new and suitable mount. Instead of the towers installed in the *Temeraire* or the low type of barbette favoured by the French he was able to place before the Board a new conception for mounting heavy guns invented by Mr. George Rendel of Elswick. This was a half-size edition of the huge central barbette in the *Italia*, upon which was mounted a pair of guns at a greater height than possible in a turret and without any increase in the weight of protection.

Compared with the turret, the advantages of the barbette as then devised were briefly as follows:

(1) Being a fixed breastwork the only machinery required was for the gun turntable, so that the armoured breastwork or citadel protecting the turntable and turning gear as well as the transport of ammunition for a turret could be dispensed with.
(2) This saving in weight allowed the guns to be carried at about twice turret height—*i.e.*, 28 ft. against 12 ft.—making the guns drier in a seaway, less affected by spray, and giving a better plunging fire, which was then considered of great importance as the armoured deck was regarded as the most vulnerable part of a battleship.
(3) The turning gear was better protected.
(4) Elevation and depression were not limited by the height of a turret or the size of ports.
(5) There was not the same restriction in working and breathing space as in a turret, where the air sometimes became so foul that in the *Duilio* the guns could only continue to be worked when a plate had been lifted from the turret roof.
(6) The small openings of turret ports limited sighting vision, and the laying of guns could not be performed so easily as in an open barbette.

In the *Collingwood* provision was made for the acceptance of new tactical ideas—the discarding of end-on methods of fighting with the recognition that battleships would have to operate in line ahead while concentrating their fire on the beam. In the *Alexandra* and citadel ships broadside fire had been curtailed in order to provide arcs of bearing ahead and astern, but the new ship was to bring her entire main armament to bear on either side and only two guns fore and aft. In addition, the rapid growth of the French torpedo fleet necessitated some provision for a more powerful secondary battery than was carried in the *Caiman*, both as a defence against torpedo craft and for use upon the unprotected parts of armoured ships.

Thus it will be seen that the prospect of having to face a heavy volume of fire from a numerous battery of secondary guns such as had been introduced in the *Italia* opened up entirely new problems in the matter of protection.These 6-in. B.L. could not be used when the big guns were in action, and could only play their part against capital ships when the range had been closed. This meant that instead of concentrating armour to meet a very slow and uncertain fire at long range by big guns only, it had become necessary to devise a method of distribution which placed it to the best advantage for the protection of guns, boilers and machinery, also to preserve stability as far as possible in a protracted action against big, medium and small guns.

White's solution to the problem was considered the best possible under the circumstances. He concentrated his armour along a short and heavy water-line belt amidships, covered it with a strong deck, closed the ends with heavy transverse bulkheads, and flanked both ends and sides with coal bunkers. From the lower edge of the bulkheads the protective deck was extended to the bows and stern as in the citadel ships, with the space between it and the main deck closely subdivided into watertight spaces for patent fuel, water ballast, stores and cables. The barbette with its thick armour floor which served for protection against shells bursting in the hull below was connected to the top of the armoured deck by an armoured ammunition tube. The gun numbers, behind thick armour, had a machine-gun-proof plate covering the top of the barbette between them and fire from the enemy fighting tops.

Barnaby claimed for this system in the *Collingwood* that—

(1) The guns and gunners were exceedingly well protected for the size of the ship.
(2) The ventilating tubes communicating with the boilers and engine rooms, and the tubes for bringing ammunition through, were equally well protected.
(3) The engines and boilers were better protected than if the same weight were carried along as a complete belt.
(4) The magazines, shell-rooms and steering gear were much better protected by the under-water deck than if the sides had armour not projectile proof, and the underwater deck removed from where it was underneath the coal and water to the top of a belt above water.
(5) Over the unarmoured ends for half the ship's length it was a matter of *non-vital* importance whether a big-gun projectile struck at the water-line or not. In a belted ship such a projectile striking at this point might either blow up the ship or completely flood one end and render the magazine useless. The amount of water admitted would, in the belted ship under the above circumstances, be so great as to render her quite unmanageable and an easy prey, even if it did not at once sink her outright. In the *Collingwood* the amount of water under these circumstances would be so moderate in amount as to leave the ship with her sea-going and fighting qualities practically unimpaired.

On the other hand, the ends of the vessel being only of thin plate were readily penetrable by even machine guns, which would probably lead to diminution of speed and stability. But to have carried the belt to the ends while retaining all the existing qualities of the ship would have needed considerably more than 1,000 tons extra displacement; and with such a belt the ship would be less safe against certain risks than she was; *i.e.*, the steering gear would be more exposed, the magazines and shell rooms more easily reached, and big gun fire would more completely flood one or both ends than when the armour deck was well under water. The belted ship was (1) exposed to precisely the same defect of getting water in on her armour deck—although it was nominally above water—if holed at a height reached by waves in a seaway; and (2) the alternation of the belt going under and coming out of the water offered no impediment whatever to the accumulation of a fatal quantity which—unless localized by intact subdivision—would capsize the ship.

Experiments and careful calculations showed that the sinkage of the various citadel ships after (1) riddling or (2) coaling, compared with earlier partially belted types, was:

	With unarmoured ends riddled. Full coal and stores	*With unarmoured ends riddled, but with half coal and stores*	*Due to coaling*
"*Warrior*"	32 inches	—	16 inches
"*Resistance*"	42 "	—	16 "
"*Inflexible*"	23 "	19 inches	27 "
"*Agamemnon*"	22 "	20 "	20 "
"*Colossus*"	18 "	16 "	22 "
"*Collingwood*"	17½ "	15 "	22 "
"*Camperdown*"	14 "	12 "	22 "

"COLLINGWOOD"

Built by	*Laid down*	*Launched*	*Completed*	*Cost*
Pembroke	12 July '80	22 Nov. '82	July '87	£636,996 (£627,375)

Dimensions 325′×68′×25·10′/26·11′=9,500 tons.
Hull and armour 5,980. Equipment 3,520 tons.

Armament 4 12-in. B.L. 45-ton. 6 6-in. B.L. 12 6-pdrs. 14 smaller. Torpedo tubes 4.

Armour (compound) Belt 18″-8″ with end bulkheads 16″-7″; barbettes 11½″-10″; tubes 12″-10″; conning tower 12″-2″; screens to battery 6″; deck 2″-2½″-3″; skin 1″; teak backings 20″-10″. Total 2,575 tons.

Complement 498.

Coal 900/1,200 tons.

Machinery Humphreys, 2 sets compound inverted 3 cyl. One H.P. 52″, two L.P. 74″; stroke 3½′. I.H.P. 7,000=15·5 knots; forced draught 9,600=16·8 knots. Boilers 12 cylindrical (new '97); 90 lb. pressure. 36 furnaces. 2 screws 18½′ diam.; pitch 19′-17½′.

Radius 7,000 miles at 10 knots.

Points of interest:

(1) The first British ship to have breech-loading guns in barbettes.
(2) The first battleship to steam at 16 knots.
(3) The first British battleship to have vertical armour limited to the waterline.
(4) The first to have secondary and tertiary guns grouped as batteries.
(5) Bunkerage giving a wider cruising radius than any other ship.
(6) Big guns carried five feet higher than in any previous ship.

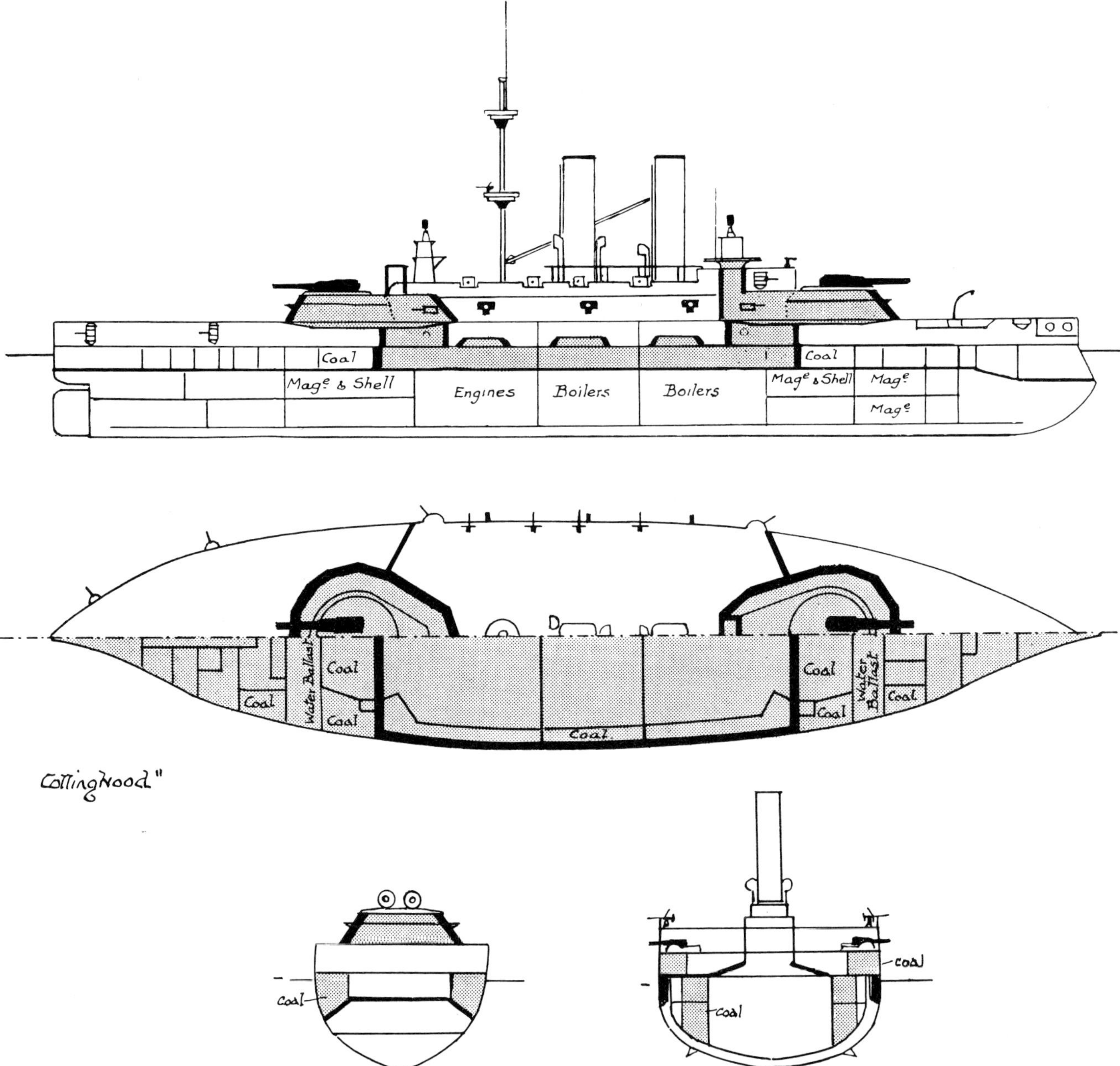

In the *Collingwood* waterline protection was confined to a short narrow belt over the machinery spaces, the magazines under the barbettes being beneath a deep protective deck. Below water the ends were fined with close subdivision to minimize flooding.

In the history of British naval development the *Collingwood* marks the point when design crystallized into a type which could serve as a basis for group construction for the first time since the *Iron Duke* class were built. Hitherto our battle fleet had been built up by ships in ones and twos of every variety in shape and size; henceforth—with but a few regrettable lapses—they were to be added in homogeneous groups in which a steady policy of development by gradual improvement was to be observed. And it was the misunderstood and much maligned *Collingwood* which heralded a transformation of the battle fleet from a collection of samples to a series of sealed pattern squadrons.

Her one outstanding fault was lack of freeboard, and as the attainment of 16 knots meant considerable compromise in design, much of what had been sacrificed for the extra speed was largely sacrificed in vain, owing to her inability to face up to a seaway. Doubtless but for displacement restrictions she would have carried a higher forecastle and justified her engine room when full speed was ordered—as it was she buried her anchor gear in green seas and cascades of foam with a magnificent exhibition of thwarted effort.

A comparison between the *Colossus* and *Collingwood* will show that, although of the same dimensions, the barbette ship had a hull some 170 tons lighter carrying 520 tons more equipment, and costing £21,000 less.

The *Collingwood* at the 1902 Review. The boat deck had been carried aft forming a bridge, and the ship presented a well-balanced and handsome profile although dwarfing her 12-in. guns.

Incidentally cost had now risen from the £38 a ton of the *Devastation*—our cheapest tonnage—to £67 in the *Collingwood*; the *Neptune* was still the most expensive at £74—excluding armament in each case.

In place of the narrow superstructures in the *Colossus* there was a large central superstructure containing the secondary battery—which was to become a standard feature in battleship design for the next two decades. The top of this superstructure formed the hurricane deck along which the quickfirers were spaced, thus allowing full provision for three types of armament in separate batteries.

ARMAMENT

The position of her guns—22 ft. above water instead of only 12 ft.—secured a far better command of fire than in any other ship, and being well separated in self-contained redoubts there was for the first time no possibility of both pairs being put out of action by a single shell.

Originally the 12-in. guns were 43-tonners, but after one had burst on trials the additional strengthening made them 45 tons. With a charge of 295 lb.—reduced from 400 lb.—the 714-lb. projectile had a muzzle velocity of 1,892 ft. secs. and was capable of piercing 20½-in. iron at 1,000 yards.

The pear-shaped barbettes, 60 ft. long and 45 ft. wide, had sloping eleven-faced sides 11½ in. thick with a 10-in. rear, and 13-in. teak backing. The 10-ft. ammunition trunk was of 12 in.-10 in., and could be used for ventilation by upcast draught which cleared the interior of smoke after firing. The guns, mounted on a turntable without protection from above, had centre-line loading positions with the breech over the ammunition trunk, and were depressed 13° to receive the projectile and charge. When fired abaft the beam there was no damage to the superstructure from blast effects.

Instead of the scattered secondary armament of the *Colossus*, the 6-in. guns were grouped amidships three aside with their ports 14 ft. above water. The centre guns had 57° training before and abaft the beam; the end ones bore 57° fore and aft respectively, but for lack of training space only 30° towards amidships. The only hull protection was provided by 1-in. plates around the ports, but raking fire was to be excluded by 6-in. bulkheads angled from the barbettes at each end of the battery, and damage localized by splinter screens between the guns.

Four of the 6-pdrs. were at the corners of the battery, and eight spaced above on the boat deck; the smaller quickfirers fired from little sponsons aft, also from the superstructure and fighting tops.

The torpedo ports opened above water on the main deck below the corners of the superstructure.

PROTECTION

Although referred to officially as a "citadel ship," this description was an absurd misnomer—all that remained of the citadel was a narrow belt extending from 5 ft. below water to 2½ ft. above, which covered 140 ft. amidships. For a depth of 4 ft. it was 18 in. thick, thence tapering to 8 in. with a 15-in. backing at the lower edge, and closed at each end by bulkheads 16 in. at the upper part and 7 in. below. This "citadel" enclosed the barbette trunks and protected the engine and boiler rooms. It was covered by a 3-in. armour deck. From the lower ends of the belt 2½-in. decks ran to bows and stern, dipping to reinforce the ram and covering the magazines, shell rooms, steering gear, etc. As already described, the space between this lower deck and the main deck was cut up into compartments for coal, patent fuel, stores, water spaces and cable lockers as in the citadel ships, but without the cork and cofferdams. Considerable use was also made of coal bunkers in this system of defence, experiments having shown that loose fuel had an extraordinary value in neutralizing the explosive effect of shells. Along the sides below the armour deck the bunkers were 9 ft. deep and across the end bulkheads 21 ft. deep—a very useful thickness when full, although such consumable stores made for a somewhat variable factor in protection. The whole citadel was thus entirely surrounded by deep bunkers, which also formed the only resistance to shell entering below the battery deck.

It will be seen that the underwater form of the *Collingwood* was very different from previous models, her narrower ends considerably reducing the size of any compartments flooded. For this reason continuations of the belt to bow and stern, although costing as much per foot as amidships, would have much less value in protecting buoyancy and stability. Batnaby considered that even in a larger ship with more weight of armour available, he would have preferred to expend it in thickening the decks, the amidships belt, and in increasing the height of the belt, rather than employ it in taking a belt along the whole length of the water-line.

It was not until 1889 that the *Collingwood* was officially vindicated so far as the buoyancy value of her unarmoured ends was concerned. The occasion was the debate at the I.N.A. on White's designs for the Naval Defence Act ships, when Lord Charles Beresford said that he wished someone would have the courage to fill the unarmoured ends of one of the "Admirals" with water. White, apparently to the surprise of his audience, said that this had been done in the *Collingwood*, and that the experiment had justified her designers, since in this condition the ship had manœuvred with a loss in speed of only half a knot.

SPEED

Considerable interest was attached to the *Collingwood's* speed trials as she was the first big ship to be cursed with forced draught. On the final contractors' six-hour trial at full pressure under n.d. she made 16·6 knots with 8,369 h.p. when drawing 23½ ft. and displacing only 8,060 tons; forced draught developed 9,573 h.p. but with an addition of only 0·24 knots (16·84 knots). Her screws were considered to have too great an area, and although the pitch was fined from 19 to 17½ ft., the engines could not use all the steam generated under a draught of 1 in. pressure.

SEA-GOING QUALITIES

Although speed was not much affected in moderate weather it was greatly reduced in a head sea or swell, and whenever the green came over the forecastle the crew's quarters were rendered uninhabitable—a constantly recurring trouble owing to leaking decks. In a beam sea she might roll 20° each way, and the water beating against the fore barbette in a mass of foam and spray made the working of the guns extremely difficult. She was regarded as handy at 6 knots or over.

A lot of her trouble in a seaway was due to the hollowed lines fore and aft in the underwater form, which greatly reduced buoyancy and so caused her to sink into the trough of the sea when the bow, offering but small resistance, was soon buried in the advancing wave slope and driven deeply through it by the well-immersed propellers. Had displacement restrictions allowed for an additional forecastle deck she and her half-sisters would have been far better sea boats and fighters.

GENERAL

The *Collingwood* always looked a good deal lighter than the rest of the "Admirals" because of her tall, thin funnels. As first completed there was only an upper top in the mast and her appearance was considerably improved when the lower top was added and an after bridge and charthouse fitted.

"COLLINGWOOD"

Commissioned at Portsmouth 1 July '87 for the Jubilee Review, paying off in Reserve in August. Joined up for the manœuvres from July-September '88 and then went into Reserve again until the '89 manœuvres after which she was prepared for the Mediterranean where she served from November '89 until March '97 (refit Malta '96). Was coastguard ship at Bantry from March '97 to June '03 and then paid off into B Reserve at Devonport being transferred to East Kyle in January '05 where she remained until sold on 11 March '09 for £19,000.

Chapter 48

CRITICISM OF THE "COLLINGWOOD"

When Barnaby placed his signature along the margin of the *Collingwood's* plan, he must have done so with pride and satisfaction. To have broken away from the central-citadel type of turret ship and assumed full responsibility for a new type of goodly countenance, well charged with both weapons of attack and powers of defence, and able to steam towards the enemy faster and keep the seas at speed longer than any of her consorts, was indeed the culmination of months of application and anxiety on a scale enjoyed by no other creative workers of his race. His constructors had achieved what he considered was the finest fighting machine afloat and on a tonnage well inside the restricting limits set by the Board—a notable turning-point in British naval design and the precursor of those magnificent groups of battleships which her Constructor, W. H. White, was to produce when he later became D.N.C.

But if no warship of the mid-Victorian era could be immune from criticism, certainly Barnaby's battleships received more than their fair share, owing to Reed's implacable opposition towards any addition to the battle fleet which was not more or less of a mobile armoured target. In the case of the *Collingwood* the Board's requirements as laid down had been well and truly fulfilled, and Reed could have done no better—or even as well. Additional displacement was allowed for the five later units of the class which was expended in heavier armament, otherwise they presented the same characteristics.

When details of the *Collingwood* were first announced, Service appreciation of the various types of battleship was very mixed. The Navy, had it been polled in 1879, would have declared for the *Achilles* as the nearest possible approach to the perfect ironclad, with the *Bellerophon* and *Hercules* representing the *Achilles* with her supposed faults corrected. The *Devastation* type was not yet admitted, chiefly because it lacked sail power; and the *Alexandra* challenged the mastless *Dreadnought* to maintain her place. The much vaunted *Inflexible* was as far as possible from reconciling the incongruities of other types, for there was no sort of criticism to which she did not offer herself. (*Memories of Sir Cooper Key*, p. 42.)

The *Collingwood* had the same proportions allotted to guns and armour as the *Inflexible*, but with an increased rate of fire from two to nine rounds a minute, and to this extent she initiated a principle opposed to that of the *Dreadnought*. In her rapidity of fire was to be regarded as a defensive measure, and it was this little-understood and less appreciated principle which evoked the storm of disapproval against the *Collingwood*.

Admiral Custance stressed this when he stated that:

> "It showed the mistake, first, of not assigning the proper reasons for any change in principle initiated, and secondly, of not winning over naval opinion beforehand. The *Collingwood* was condemned by the Navy, not for lack of gun-fire—which was still her real weakness—but for want of armour which still absorbed four times as much weight as her armament, or nearly one-third of the whole weight of the ship. The Navy, as a whole, was quite unaware that defence really depended more on gun-fire than on armour, and during the long discussions which took place, hardly any attention was called to this point." (*The Ship-of-the-Line in Battle*, p. 43.)

But it was not the actual weight of armour but its method of utilization which was criticized. The Navy found it impossible to accept the thick but short and narrow belt as a real measure of protection, and rejected the idea that with her ends riddled the *Collingwood* would remain safe and stable. Whenever the "Admirals" crop up in the naval biography we find the same bitter sarcasm directed at their system of water-line protection, their low freeboard and general wetness, and the vulnerability of the barbettes, guns and gun crews. The results recorded when the ends of the ship were flooded had never been circulated in the Fleet, so that the *Collingwood* only widened the gulf which had been growing rapidly between the executive and the Constructor's branch. Undoubtedly Sir Thomas Symonds and Admiral J. R. Ward voiced the Service when they said:

> "The result of this riddling there can be very little doubt about in the mind of any practical seaman who has ever seen a partially waterlogged ship and has realized the power of loose water. When told that their ship is quite safe and manageable, and in fact in no worse condition with six or seven hundred tons of water in her than she was without it . . . they naturally open their eyes wide and say this sort of thing is quite new to us—it is directly contrary to all our previous experience of the behaviour of ships at sea; so that as practical seamen we venture to doubt your assumption, and all the figures and calculations in the world will not convince us."

In January 1885, after Barnaby had produced a monograph on the recent Admiralty designs, these officers admitted that they thought that an underwater deck and shortened belt necessarily involved the continuous admission of water when there was perforation at the water-line—that there would be no cessation of inflow and that the ship would inevitably founder.

Reed's position as defined in his own words was:

"I, for one, close at once with the doctrine that, in building a first-class battleship for this country, armament considerations ought to take first place. I may be entirely wrong. It may be that the importance I attach to keeping a ship or a series of ships (which cost a million apiece carrying many lives) afloat is excessive; but to my mind . . . when you are dealing with a line-of-battle ship, the first consideration, I think, should be that that ship should be kept afloat by thick armour." (*Trans. I.N.A.*, vol. XXX, p. 181.)

He added that in his opinion the matter of armament and its disposition was a secondary consideration. To which Lord Armstrong made the pertinent reply:

"that if we render a ship absolutely safe from being sunk by modern artillery, we shall simply eliminate its power of sinking anything else."

In *The Times* of 19 February 1885 Reed attacked this latest design for lack of armoured stability, and was prepared to demonstrate to any competent tribunal that there was not one of the citadel ships which could not be either capsized and sunk, or sunk without capsizing, without any shot or shell whatever being directed against their armoured portions.

As Barnaby in his official position was unable to reply to these attacks, White—who had left the Admiralty early in 1883 to enter the employment of Sir William Armstrong, Mitchell and Co. as Warship Designer and Manager of the naval construction branch of the firm—wrote at great length to explain the means employed to secure buoyancy and stability in the *Collingwood*, and the following extracts associate his authority with the design:

"Summing up the foregoing statements, I desire to record my opinion, based upon complete personal knowledge of every detail in the calculations and designs for the 'Admiral' class, that the disposition of the armour belt (in association with the protective decks and cellular sides, water-tight compartments, etc., existing in the unarmoured portions of the vessels situated above the protective decks) is such that the buoyancy, stability, trim, speed and manœuvring capabilities are well guaranteed against extensive damage from shot and shell-fire in action. And, further, that in these particulars the 'Admiral' class are capable of meeting, at least on equal terms, their contemporary ships in the French Navy . . . It is undoubted that great differences of opinion prevail, but it must not be forgotten that the Board of Admiralty, by its recent decision announced in the House of Commons, has reaffirmed the opinion that the artillerists regard the existing disposition of the armour as satisfactory. This has been done after the attention of the Board and the public has been most strongly directed to the supposed dangers incidental to the rapid destruction of the light superstructures lying above the under-water decks of the 'Admiral' class. It would be folly to suppose that in such a matter any personal considerations would prevent the Board from authorizing a change which was proved to be necessary or advantageous." (*The Times*, 4 April 1885.)

Reed's reply in *The Times* four days later was as concentrated a broadside as the "Admirals" ever received, but one paragraph only is sufficient to epitomize his opinion of them:

"Mr. White coolly tells us that the *Collingwood* with five hundred tons of water logging her ends to a depth of seven or eight feet will not be much worse off than a ship whose armour deck stands two and a half or three feet above the water's surface, and his reason is that even above this latter deck the water would flow in when the ship was driving ahead with an injured bow. I will only say that sailors of experience see a very great difference between the two cases, and I can but regard such theorizing as very unfortunate basis for the designs of Her Majesty's ships. . . . It distresses me beyond measure to see our ships constructed so as to impose upon them the most terrible penalties whenever their commanders dare, and dare they ever have and dare they ever will, to close with their foe and try conclusions with him. It has been my painful duty over and over again to hear foreign officers entreat me to use all my influence against the adoption in their Navy of ships with so little armoured surface as ours. On one occasion the *Collingwood* herself was imposed upon them as a model to be imitated, and I was besought to give them a safer and better ship. 'How could I ever steam up to my enemy with any confidence,' said one of the officers concerned, 'with such a ship as that under my feet?'"

Both Spain and Japan had invited specifications for battleships in the early 'eighties from Armstrongs, and White had submitted modified editions of the *Collingwood*. As neither nation placed their orders with the Tyneside firm it is more than likely that Reed's fulminations were instrumental in these contracts going abroad.

But Reed did not intend to provoke a scientific discussion. His object was to upset thoroughly the public sense of security in the Navy and confidence in the Admiralty—which was already being subjected to harsh criticism—so that if changes in naval administration which had for some time been impending, or even imminent, became a matter of immediate concern, he might, being a member of Parliament, realize his political ambition by a return to the Admiralty either on the Constructive or Administrative side.

The result of the controversy in *The Times* was very different from what he had intended. His authority had been challenged and his reputation as a naval architect impaired; and if in the future the choice of a successor to Barnaby lay between him and White, the latter was assured of official support.

Chapter 49

THE "IMPERIEUSE" AND "WARSPITE"

GLADSTONE GOVERNMENT 1880

JUST before the *Collingwood* was laid down the Beaconsfield Ministry with Mr. W. H. Smith as First Lord came to an end, and in May 1880 Mr. Gladstone was again at the head of the Government with Lord Northbrook at the Admiralty. His Board was a particularly strong one of which every member had made his mark in the Service. Upon taking office the Members were:

Admiral Sir Cooper Key, K.C.B.
Vice-Admiral Lord John Hay, C.B.
Rear-Admiral Anthony Hiley Hoskins, C.B.
Thomas Brassey, M.P. (afterwards Lord Brassey), Civil Lord.
Controller: Vice-Admiral Sir William Houstan Stewart, K.C.B.

In view of the parsimonious policy pursued by the previous Government this Board aroused great expectations in and out of the Service, which unfortunately were far from being fulfilled. As the Duke of Somerset had occasion to observe: "The mind of man does not go back to the time when the management of the Navy by the Admiralty was not a subject of dissatisfaction"; but, as Lord Brassey himself admitted, "the Northbrook administration shared in more than ordinary degree the unpopularity to which, after an extended term of service, every Admiralty seems to be doomed."

Northbrook was a politician and a very strong party one at that. Having from early days imbibed the extreme views of economy and retrenchment associated with Liberalism, he was always more solicitous to keep down the Estimates than to incur any expenses which he thought might be embarrassing to the Ministry. In many ways he was aided and abetted by various members of his Board, who at first being unable to decide what types of warships were really required—and so held up construction for years—then favoured designs which aroused bitter antagonism in the Service. But whatever reasons or excuses may be put forward by apologists for the policy which obtained between 1880 and 1885, the Northbrook Administration has become symbolic of Navy starvation; the extent to which the stigma is deserved may to some extent be judged in the chapters which follow. As might be expected the long years of procrastination and excuse resulted in a Naval Panic and were terminated by what then ranked as a large Programme of Construction.

The new Board inherited control of a Navy not even superior to that of France either in battleships or cruisers; although neither in Parliament nor the country was there any general feeling that things were not as they should be. At this period the Navy had no press. There were no writers or publicists in or out of the Service with a mission to educate public opinion on the subject of Sea Power; and as the Reform Bill had made a fetish of Economy and Retrenchment it became just a matter of course that the Navy should be singled out as the first victim of Mr. Gladstone's financial myopia, since great reductions in expenditure could be effected by paying-off ships, discharging workmen from the Dockyards, and ceasing to purchase stores.

Ten years before, Mr. Childers—with full public approval—had set reduction of expenditure above the maintenance of naval force and the Board had acquiesced without much demur. A precedent had thus been established which blinded even the Navy itself to its true position. Sir Cooper Key himself as a Royal Commissioner on Fortifications had looked towards *military* forces as at least a possible alternative to naval power in defence against invasion. Hence the fact that the French Fleet equalled our own did not give rise to any special alarm. Moreover, as no type of battleship had been or could be decided upon, and the Board was by no means convinced that the *Collingwood* was worthy of being repeated and developed any more than were the *Devastation*, *Alexandra* or *Temeraire*, there was ample excuse for a policy of *laisser faire* during the next couple of years before any steps were taken to increase the Battle Fleet.

But while we contented ourselves with the *Collingwood*, the French made 1880 a record year by laying down the *Hoche*, *Neptune*, *Magenta* and *Marceau*, all of about 10,600 tons, bringing their total since 1874 to 22 ships of 164,451 tons against our 13 ships of 107,220 tons. The design of these ships is of some interest as they introduced an armament distribution which was to influence our own Constructors. First drawings show a light, three-pole, fore-and-aft rig for which the heavy fighting masts were substituted when the big blast-screen superstructure came to be added. But before the end of its first year of office the Board was forced to the conclusion that it would be necessary to lay down some second-line ships for service overseas and also to increase our rate of shipbuilding—now being spun out to seven years with the *Ajax* and *Agamemnon*. But there were two important considerations to be settled before discussing new designs—guns and sails. The number and size of guns and their disposition opened up big possibilities, but the provision or not of rig was the great stumbling block.

Although calculations clearly proved that sail power in armoured ships was the reverse of economical, the necessity for saving coal by the use of sails had been so impressed upon the naval mind that it was as yet impossible for the delusion to be shaken off. New ships, therefore, might have to carry long breech-loaders in conjunction with a heavy rig—and how this was going to be contrived seems to have been a matter of much doubt and perplexity.

Ultimately our specified requirements for ships able to overtake cruisers and out-fight second-class battleships on foreign Stations included (1) high freeboard; (2) at least four big guns and several secondary ones; (3) high

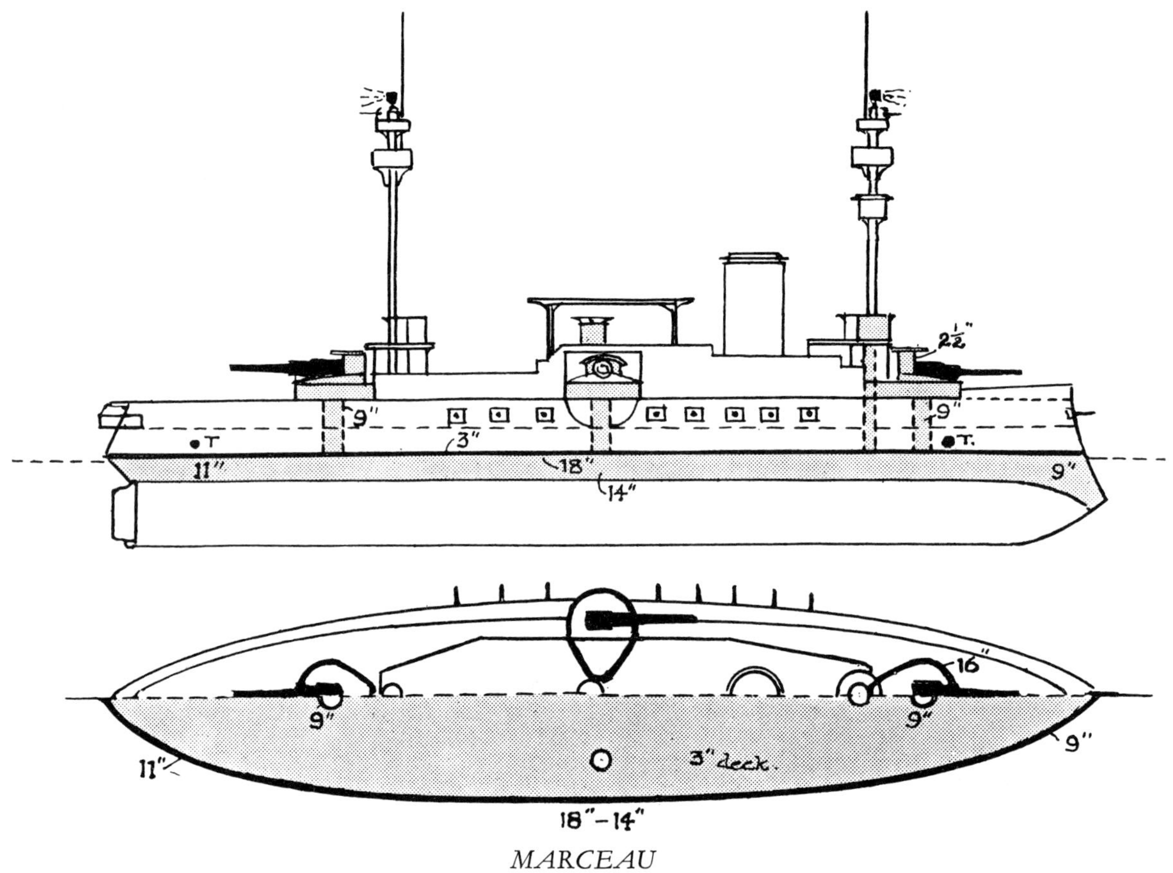

MARCEAU

speed; (4) full square rig in conformity with traditions of service abroad. And in seeking their solution the Board again turned to France.

The *Magenta* as first planned suggested a type basis which might fill the bill. On paper the French gun disposition allowed for a three-gun concentration on all bearings against the *Collingwood's* two or four, and appeared preferable for ships which would more likely be involved in duels than fleet actions. The *Imperieuse* and *Warspite* were planned accordingly, being officially known as "Armour-plated steel barbette ships."

"IMPERIEUSE" and "WARSPITE"

	Built by	*Laid down*	*Floated out*	*Completed*	*Cost*
"Imperieuse"	Portsmouth	10 Aug. '81	18 Dec. '83	Sept. '86	£543,758
"Warspite"	Chatham	25 Oct. '81	29 Jan. '84	June '88	£538,797

Dimensions 315' × 62' × 26' 3"/ 27' 3" = 8,500 tons.
Hull and armour 5,190 tons. Equipment 3,210 tons.

Armament 4 9·2-in. 24-ton B.L. — Torpedo tubes.
10 6-in. B.L. — 6 above water (18-in.).
4 6-pdrs.
16 smaller.

Armour Belt 10"; with 9" end bulkheads; 8" barbettes with 2" shields; 3" hoists; 9" conning tower; 4" deck fore and aft; 2" over belt; teak backing 10".
Total 1,405 tons.

Complement 555.

Coal	900/1,130 tons.
Machinery	"*Imperieuse*"=Maudslay. "*Warspite*"=Penn. 2 sets 3-cyl. inverted compound. I.H.P. 8,000=16·1 knots; forced draught 10,000=16·7 knots. Cylindrical and oval boilers.
Radius	5,500/10 knots.
Sail area	20,575 sq. ft.

Points of interest:

(1) The last armoured ships to be designed with square rig.
(2) The first to carry the new 9·2-in. B.L.
(3) The only British ships to carry their main armament in four separate positions, French fashion.
(4) The only British ships to have marked French tumble-home sides.
(5) Had the thickest armour decks of any ships until the *Majestic* (4″-2½″) and not exceeded until the *Powerful* (6″-3″).
(6) Exceeded designed displacement by 1,000 tons.

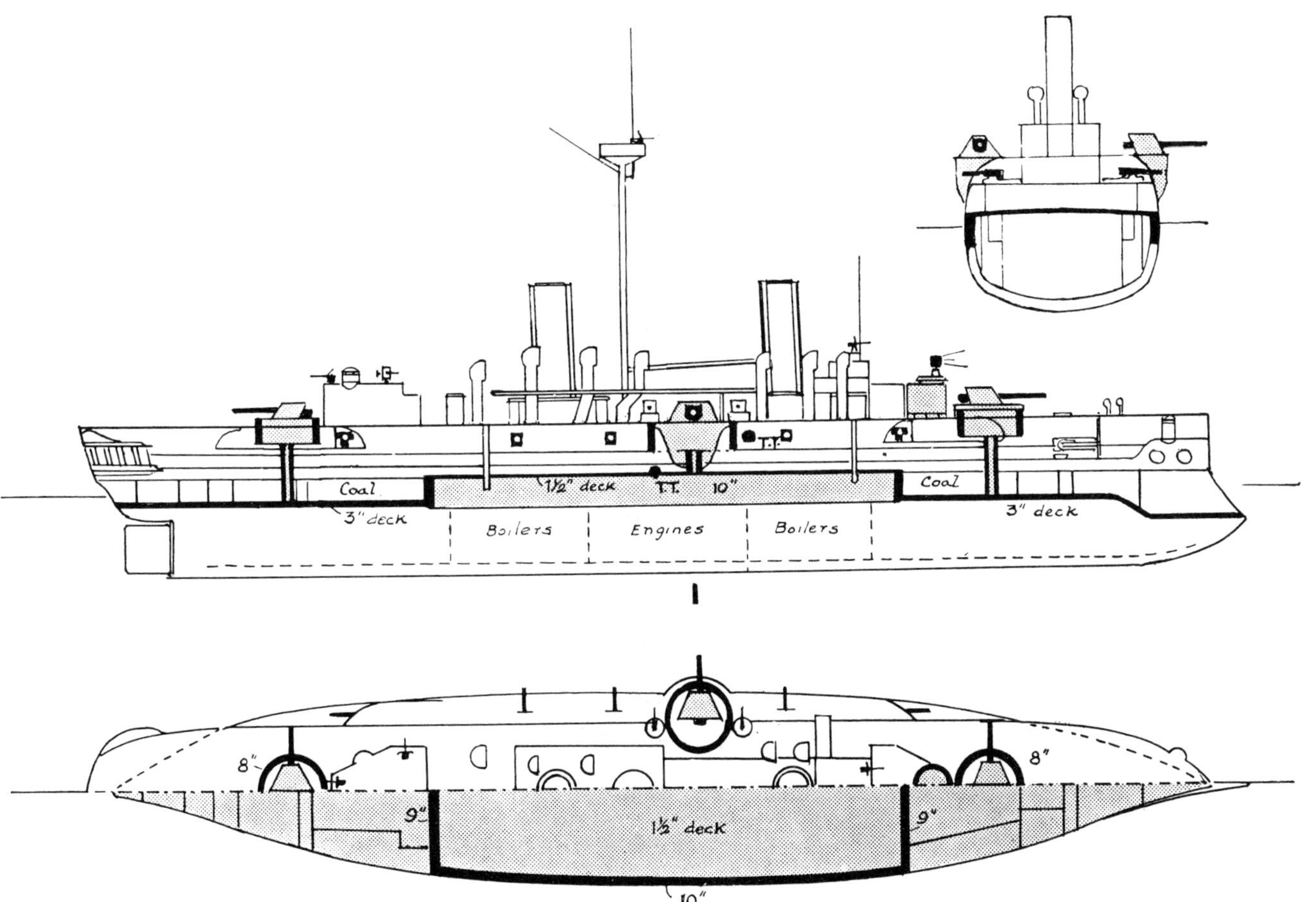

"*Imperieuse*" with altered rig and full secondary battery of ten 6-in. guns.

Of the *Imperieuse* and *Warspite* the best that could be said of them was that they could take a broadside of three 9·2-in. and five 6-in. guns into action at 16 knots. So far as the design was concerned, they rank with the black sheep of the Victorian armoured ships, and in the House Admiral Sir John Commerell referred to them as "amongst the most complete failures of modern ships; badly designed; badly carried out, and absolutely dangerous," although this was rather harsher criticism than they deserved. After alterations and when regarded as "protected" cruisers only, they could be listed as quite useful flagships, and the Russians thought so much of them that they produced a very near copy in the *Admiral Nachimoff*, and what is more kept her on the China Station under a full brig rig for many years.

The tribulations of the *Imperieuse* arose through changes in equipment during construction and centred about her coal supply, belt submergence, and inability to sail. As the finished ship differed considerably from the original plans, it will be as well to dispose of her initial troubles before commencing any detailed description.

As first proposed a bunkerage of 400 tons at 24 ft. 11 in. load draught was considered ample, but in 1884 an increase to 900 tons was ordered and later on the 18-ton 9·2-in. and 4½-ton 6-in. were replaced by 22-ton and 5-ton models respectively, with mountings to match. The complement was also raised from 430 to 514 with corresponding stores, and 10 tons added to the rigging. As a result of all these additional weights to a small ship, the mean draught was increased by 2 ft. and the belt submerged by that amount, so that only 14 in. showed above water.

But this condition of things was to be aggravated in a way not anticipated in the office calculations, as owing to faulty weight-recording during construction the line of flotation was deeper than had been estimated for the tonnage and material nominally to be absorbed.

As originally brig-rigged and due to grave alterations in weights during building *Imperieuse* was highly unsatisfactory. Her sailing qualities were poor and the removal of the heavy masts proved a considerable benefit.

Thus, in discussing the *Imperieuse* a late Chief Constructor informed the writer that:

> "Everything going into the ship had to be weighed on a special weighing machine by a Recorder of Weights (apart of course from the very large items which would be weighed on the railway apparatus). I noticed that the record of weights for the *Imperieuse* was stationary and was told quite frankly by the Recorder that he had orders from the Foreman not to record any weights for her as she was overweight already. The Foreman stood his ground. 'It would never do to show any more weights,' he said, 'because the weight allowed by the Admiralty has already been exceeded.' It was then my duty to invite the Foreman to appear before Mr. Henry Deadman, Chief Constructor of the Dockyard, and I can assure you that Mr. Deadman was too much shocked to be amused."

To provide for any apprehensions about her stability the water-line teak sheathing was made 10 in. instead of 4 in., giving an increase in beam of 12 in. and about 6 in. additional metacentric height.

When first commissioned for trials the displacement had reached 8,500 tons. The Board were anxious for a good report on her sailing as so much had been compromised to secure this, but although the heavier and much tubbier *Temeraire* had put up quite a good show under canvas the very different lines and lighter brig rig of the *Imperieuse* refused to respond. Sail proved more of a hindrance than a help. It took a strong breeze to make her move at all, and she carried so much weather helm that it was difficult to steer her or keep her off the wind.

Her Captain reported:

> "She stayed from port tack in 12 minutes, and then it was 16 minutes before she gathered way on the new tack. She came up well to the wind within one point, where she hung; then gathered 3 knots sternway and I had practically to make a stern board to get her round.
>
> Having carefully noted the saving of coal by the increase of speed given by sail power under various conditions and trials, the weight of her masts and sails, the wind they held when steaming against it, the difficulty in steering without steam, and therefore the danger of collision and necessity for always having steam ready, I am decidedly of the opinion it is most undesirable to retain her masts and sails. I consider they give only a minimum of good to a maximum of evil. I am also of opinion her fighting power would be much endangered by retaining the amount of rigging required for perhaps occasionally using sail to assist steam power; and although when going into action I presume all masts, yards, etc., above the tops would come down, there would still remain a large amount of wire-rigging and gear to not only foul the propellers, but endanger the lives of the barbette guns' crews underneath, and perhaps block the barbettes and prevent them from working, thus increasing the risk of accident and inviting disaster. The weight of the masts, yards and stores connected with them should be taken into consideration; the same weight in coal, not only for use but for protection, would be of so much more value. Should her masts be removed, I venture to suggest her derrick be lengthened and fitted with a military top."

In the face of such a report, prejudice and sentiment had to go by the board, the heavy masts were taken out of her, and a 35-ton military mast was stepped in place of the derrick stump amidships with a saving of 100 tons. Henceforth fighting tops and searchlight platforms were to replace the wind-trap in armoured ships, so that in a few years only the *Minotaur* amd *Agincourt* were able to scrve as remembrances of former days.

The *Imperieuse's* masts were put into the *Northampton*, but failed to improve her sailing qualities; those of the *Warspite* went into the *Superb* after her long refit, but only carried fighting tops.

Deprived of her masts the *Imperieuse* became a very different ship, and at 8,400 tons completed her trials satisfactorily. But she could hardly be ranked as an armoured ship and became the target for much satirical abuse, with Reed in the forefront of her detractors.

HULL

The provision of direct fore and aft fire from the beam barbettes meant constricting the topsides to allow for sponsons, with a pronounced tumble-home to secure full beam at the water-line. Had the tumble-home sides followed a seemly line from bow to stern they could have added a certain distinction and dignity; as it was, the general effect was marred by embrasures, gun ports, sponsons, and a plethora of scupper pipes, with a huge anchor port at the bows.

She was 10 ft. shorter and 6 ft. narrower than the *Collingwood*, with less spindle-like lines, a broad flare forward, wide overhanging counter and frigate stern fitted with a dummy six-window gallery—a most incongruous garnishing on a par with the stem of the old *Repulse*.

ARMAMENT

The four 9·2-in. revolved in small circular barbettes served by armoured tubes leading down to the protective deck. Small superstructures served as screens to protect the conning tower and control position aft from blast, but axial fire from amidships so shook up things on deck that the arcs of bearing were restricted to 140°. To this extent the gun distribution fell into line with *en echelon* turrets, and the only alternative was the *Collingwood* system, except that no twin 9·2-in. mounting was available which did not nearly halve the rate of fire.

As for the 6-in. guns, although ports were cut for ten, weight restrictions limited the early armament to six; later, when given a full complement of ten, two were to be landed in peace-time and the positions used as cabins. In April 1893 the Ship's Book credits *Warspite* with eight, and it is not until March 1900 that she appears to have had all ten aboard.

In March 1887 the torpedo tubes amidships were raised 2 ft. to keep them above water.

PROTECTION

For 140 ft. amidships a 10-in. compound armour belt covered the water-line to a depth of 8 ft., of which 3¼ ft. should have been above water at the original displacement of 7,600 tons. The end bulkheads were of 9-in., and this armour was regarded mainly as protection to the engine and boiler rooms, so that its relation to water level was immaterial. Above this ran a 2-in. deck and—as in the *Collingwood*—flotation beyond the belt relied upon an armoured deck in this case 4 in. thick in place of 3 in. in the battleship. Between this deck and the main deck above elaborate subdivision served instead of armour, with coal bunkers 38 ft. long before the belt and 35 ft. abaft it running the full breadth of the ship. A second tier of bunkers ran along the lower deck side above the belt, and with a full complement of fuel aboard the *Imperieuse* practically submerged the belt and depended upon coal for above-water protection. Actually it was of little consequence whether the belt showed above water when there was so little margin, but the further the ships steamed the more it became a water-line defence. Quite rightly the Board placed a much extended radius of steaming as of more consequence than whether the belt peeped above water or not. In any case a water-line hit was likely to be a very remote contingency in action, as practice shooting had shown it was almost impossible to register one even with careful aim at short range. Far more important were hits along the lower deck which might cause flooding above the armour deck when the tumble-home meant a diminishing water-plane on heeling with increasing loss of righting moment. Here coal provided a very

Without her original brig-rig and with a relatively light military mast *Imperieuse* was a greatly improved vessel. But in spite of many modifications she remained the target for much satirical comment.

real protection and the ships would probably have been a good deal safer on leaving harbour with full bunkers than when a foot or so of armour was above water.

SPEED

Although displacing 1,100 tons less than the *Collingwood* an additional 1,000 h.p. produced about the same speed, so that the *Imperieuse's* lines were not as successful as in the Pembroke ship. But 16 knots being well in excess of her contemporaries abroad, she could depend upon bringing her guns into action. With 10,000 h.p. (f.d.) she made 16·75 knots.

At less than 5 knots steering was liable to be erratic, but above 10 knots was satisfactory.

As gun platforms they were steady, the *Imperieuse* in company with *Colossus* only rolling $3\frac{1}{4}°$ when the turret ship was working through 17° and taking water into her turrets.

APPEARANCE

Both ships presented the same asymmetrical profile with the ragged line of cowls and boat fittings, and a flag pole forward; in *Warspite* this came just abaft the fore barbette, while *Imperieuse* carried hers on the chart house.

"IMPERIEUSE"

Commissioned at Devonport 28 August '86 for passage to Portsmouth where she completed for sea and was passed into Reserve. Extensive trials resulted in her rig being removed. Commissioned July-August '87 for the Jubilee Review and then placed in Reserve until March '89 when she was sent to China as flagship and so served until '94. Paid off at Portsmouth in June '94 into Reserve for long refit and rearmed November '94 with eight 6-in. q.f., increased to ten in February '97.

Went to the Pacific as flagship in March '96 returning home in August '99 for refit at Chatham. Commissioned for '03 Manœuvres and in September paid off into Reserve until February '05 when she became Depôt for T.B.D. at Portland as *Sapphire II*. In April '09 was attached to 2nd Division Home Fleet and in June became an independent command for Capt. in Charge at Portland. On 24 January '10 she flew the flag of R.A. 1st B.C.S.

Her connexion with Portland ended in December '12 and having been condemned she passed to the shipbreakers after twenty-seven years' service.

Sold 24 September '13 for £35,555.

(*Note*.—The *Imperieuse* postal base serving at Scapa until 1919 was not this ship but the old central battery *Audacious* q.v.)

"WARSPITE"

Commissioned at Chatham 20 June '88 for the manœuvres and in September paid off into Reserve, until the following summer when she again joined the fleet for exercises. In February '90 was sent out to the Pacific to replace *Swiftsure* as flagship and there remained until June '93 when she paid off at Devonport into B reserve. In August '93 went to Queenstown as portguard ship until December '96 when she returned to Chatham and paid off into the Fleet Reserve A for a refit. Went out to the Pacific again in March '99 as flagship relieving the *Imperieuse* until July '02 when she joined the Chatham Reserve.

Sold 4 April '05.

Chapter 50

THE BOMBARDMENT OF ALEXANDRIA

During 1882 public interest in the Navy was aroused over the part it played in the Egyptian Crisis and subsequent campaign, and a brief summary of the events which led to the intervention of British naval forces in Near Eastern political affairs may be of interest.

In 1875 Lord Beaconsfield's administration had purchased the Suez Canal shares owned by Ismail Pasha, Khedive of Egypt, in order to relieve the disorder into which the finances of the country had fallen owing to his extravagance. Enormous loans had been floated in London and Paris, but after a dozen years of reckless squandering he reached the end of his financial tether and had to default to his creditors, and in order to protect the bondholders a joint accountancy control by the British and French Governments over Egyptian finances was insisted upon. But Ismail found this check upon his inordinate expenditure too irksome and dispensed with its services in 1879, whereupon—as Egypt was still nominally a vassal State under the suzerainty of Turkey—the Sultan Abdul Hamid was called upon to depose him. When dethroned in June 1879 Ismail retired to Naples with an immense fortune and was succeeded by his son Mohammid Tewfik with an Anglo-French direction over his finances.

Faced with considerable economies, the Egyptian officials and army fostered the growth of an "Egypt for the Egyptians" party, and when anti-European sentiment boiled over, a new leader, Arabi Pasha—a brigadier in the Egyptian Army with great influence over the troops—organized the opposition and took over control as Minister of War. Under his initiative the authority of the Khedive was repudiated in May 1882, but when Great Britain and France threatened to intervene he was obliged to resign. However, on 27 May he was reinstated with the power of a dictator.

At this point France was in favour of military intervention, but the Gladstone government preferred to send a note to the Sultan calling his attention to the crisis which had developed in his vassal State. A joint Note was, however, sent to Arabi and a large international fleet collected at Alexandria to back it up. Then a change of government in France complicated matters by repudiating direct intervention—although willing enough to profit by any action taken to defend her financial interests—and Britain was left either to back out or exercise force. For a time the British Cabinet waited upon the fickleness of French diplomacy while a special conference of Ambassadors discussed the situation at Constantinople; and then, when anti-foreign riots made further delay impossible, the British Admiral was authorized to act and leave further debate to the diplomats.

The Mediterranean Fleet under Admiral Sir Frederick Beauchamp Seymour, which assembled before Alexandria in July 1882, consisted of the battleships

Inflexible	*Sultan*	*Superb*
Monarch	*Temeraire*	*Penelope* (detached from
Alexandra	*Invincible*	the Home Reserve)

and gunboats *Beacon*, *Bittern*, *Condor*, *Cygnet*, *Decoy* and paddle despatch boat *Helicon*. The big ships differed in every particular—design, armament and machinery. Only the *Invincible* had any sisters—the rest were solitary models. Between them they mounted 16-in., 12-in., 11-in., 10-in., 9-in., 8-in., 7-in. and 6-in. guns; below water they carried single or twin screws; simple or compound, horizontal or vertical engines; and high-pressure cylindrical or low-pressure rectangular boilers. One thing they had in common was sail power.

Since the middle of June their decks had been crowded by refugees, the *Monarch* having 700 of all ages and colours aboard. Special watch was kept against surprise attack by mines—of which Arabi had plenty—or spar torpedoes, and at night each ship was surrounded by wire hawsers rigged out on booms. Admiral Seymour demanded that the constant work of strengthening the forts which had gone on for the last month or so must cease, but was assured that none such was in progress. On 10 July he sent an ultimatum to the effect that unless the works were surrendered at once for disarmament he would open fire the following day.

This was a signal for all the foreign ships to depart, and as the warships were played out of harbour by our bands the last of the refugees were packed off in a P. and O. liner detained by the Home Office. At 10 o'clock that night the ships moved into their assigned positions, the Admiral having previously transferred his flag from the *Alexandra* to the *Invincible*, whose lighter draught permitted her to berth with the *Penelope* in the inner harbour.

Alexandria at that time ranked as a first-class sea fortress mounting about 250 guns, but of these only 44 were modern rifles equal to those in the ships, the remainder being smooth-bores of little effect against armour. Afloat the eight British battleships carried ninety-two guns of 6-in. and upwards, but as five of them could only bring one broadside into action the total available for simultaneous bearing upon the enemy was forty-three. And if the ships had the advantage of twelve big-calibre guns they would have to fight with the sun in the gunlayers' eyes under all the handicaps suffered when ships were pitted against shore batteries.

But it cannot be said that the forts were formidable, as none were of modern construction and most of them were ancient and built of poor material. Judging from his operation orders, Seymour did not anticipate much danger to his ships. Captains were allowed to anchor or not at their own discretion when within range, and a number of forts were to be attacked simultaneously instead of fire being concentrated upon the strongest and the others reduced in succession. At the same time the Admiral appears to have been in two minds as to the resistance he might encounter, as he contemplated the possibility of two or three days being required to effect their reduction.

All ships cleared for action on the 10th, topgallant masts being struck and bowsprits run in; the gunboats sent down all their yards, but the ironclads only their upper ones. In the evening the *Monarch*, *Invincible* and *Penelope* were anchored inshore with *Alexandra*, *Sultan*, *Superb*, *Temeraire* and *Inflexible* outside the breakwater with the gunboats. At 7 a.m. on the 11th the first shot was fired by order from the *Alexandra* and a signal for general action hoisted in the *Invincible*, which was employed as flagship. The weather was fine and clear with an onshore breeze which made spotting difficult when powder smoke formed dense clouds a hundred feet high before dispersing.

The Egyptian gunners, although mostly inexperienced, replied quickly and stuck to their guns when exposed to superior fire and with but little protection in the case of the smooth-bores. Our shooting was controlled so far as smoke allowed by officers stationed in the tops, and was as good as might be expected under the circumstances. But over 50 per cent. of shells either failed to burst, burst prematurely, or split on striking. One unexploded shell from the *Penelope* was found in a magazine containing 400 tons of powder, and only ten out of the forty-four rifled guns were silenced when the "cease fire" was sounded at 5.30 p.m., although no reply had been received from the forts for some time.

The best shooting seems to have been made by the *Inflexible* and *Temeraire* with their hydraulically worked guns, but on the whole the damage done was hardly commensurate with the amount of ammunition expended.

To a large extent this may be excused by the fact that only about one-third of the squadron ammunition was suitable for fortress attack, the bulk being armour-piercing Palliser shells with a small bursting charge. Such common shell with a heavy bursting charge as could be served out had the Pettman percussion fuse of War Office design, and this failed to function in a lamentable way. With reliable shells the action would probably have been over in a few hours, instead of dragging on until the common shell was nearly all gone in some ships.

Our casualties were 5 killed and 28 wounded, while the Egyptian losses were about 150 killed and 400 wounded out of the 2,000 engaged. The forts were not abandoned until the 13th, a few shots being fired on the 12th before a flag of truce had been hoisted. Damage done to the ships was small; the *Inflexible* sustaining the most injury, having been hit outside the citadel by a 10-in. shell below water which turned upwards, pierced the deck, and caused casualties in the superstructure; her unarmoured parts were pierced in several places and a good deal of damage done to the upper works and rigging. *Monarch* and *Temeraire* escaped hits, but the *Alexandra* was struck sixty times—twenty-four being outside the armour. *Sultan* came through with a plate started on the water-line, some boats damaged, and holes in funnels and masts; *Invincible's* armour showed several hits and the unarmoured hull was pierced in a number of places; *Superb* received a severe hit just above the water-line with a shell hole 10 ft. long and 4 ft. wide, and two other hull wounds. *Penelope* was hulled in eight places and had a narrow escape from one shell which entered the battery, struck the engine-room hatch-coaming, fell into the engine room and was caught on a grating. In all cases the resistance of armour proved to be better in action than estimated from proving ground results, and none was penetrated at ranges varying from 1,500 yards to 4,000 yards.

The action marked the last occasion on which the British Battle Fleet fought with muzzle-loading guns, and the first in which it was protected by armour.

It secured the safety of the Canal against a threatened *coup d'état* and paved the way for the subsequent military operations which led to the battle of Tel-el-Kebir on 13 September, and the capture of Arabi next day, which ended the first stage of the Admiralty dealings with Egypt and allowed the Board to rest from its labours—which had been exacting and most successfully conducted through a trying period.

Chapter 51

DECISION TO BUILD THE "ADMIRAL" CLASS

FACED with the French quartette of ships for 1880, the Board could not rest content with the sterility of the Constructor's Department for an indefinite period. Although public opinion was quite indifferent to the critical state of affairs which might develop when substantial naval equality between France and England could be regarded as a menace to political peace, it was not the business of the Admiralty to start a naval scare—especially as the French programme of new construction, which had been sustained by loans, ceased in 1881.

Retrenchment had incurred a certain risk, and the proper course now was to seize the opportunity of making good our leeway without unduly disturbing the electorate. But the problem of what type of ship in which to invest still remained.

In considering the design of the *Collingwood* it could be admitted that she had a good measure of the qualities demanded by the unsettled naval opinion of the day, although her system of protection was not favoured afloat. However, no better model for a First Line ship had been put before the Board. A bold policy was indicated and had to be adopted. It was high time that the long series of experimental types should give way to some degree of homogeneity in design.

And so a similar situation to that which had confronted Sir John Hay in 1867-68, when he ordered the four *Iron Dukes* and two *Swiftsures*, was dealt with in a similar way; and although the prototype was still on the stocks, five somewhat more powerful sister ships were laid down in 1882-83.

Thus the materialization of Sir Cooper Key's ideal of 1866 brought about (1) an abandonment of sail power, (2) the rejection of tactical ideas which reached a climax in the *Inflexible*, and, above all, (3) the adoption of breech-loading guns—a distinction shared with the contemporary *Colossus*, *Edinburgh* and *Conqueror*. The Woolwich-Armstrong breech-loading guns introduced by the Naval and Military Ordnance Committee formed in 1881 were as follows:[1]

	Tons	*Mark*	*Cals.*	*Length in ft.*	*Charge lb.*	*Projectile lb.*	*Muzzle velocity*	*Muzzle energy*	*Penetration of iron at 1,000 yds.*
16·25 in.	110	I	30	43·6	960 S.B.C.	1,800	2,087	54,390	32 -in.
13·5 ,,	67	II	30	36·1	630 S.B.C.	1,250	2,016	35,230	28 ,,
12 ,,	45	III	25·25	25·7	259 P.Br.	714	1,914	18,130	20·6 ,,
10 ,,	29	II	32	28·5	252 P.Br.	500	2,040	14,430	20·4 ,,
9·2 ,,	22	I-II	25	20·9	144 P.Br.	380	1,800	8,622	16·1 ,,
9·2 ,,	24	II-V	29	21·7	166 P.Br.	380	2,036	11,230	18·3 ,,
8 ,,	13	III	25·6	18·8	100 P.Bl.	210	1,953	5,554	13·4 ,,
6 ,,	5	VI	26	13·6	45 P.Bl.	100	1,960	2,663	10·5 ,,
5 ,,	2	III	25	10·4	16 S.P.	50	1,800	1,124	6·1 ,,
4 ,,	13 cwt.	I	14·8	4·9	3·5 R.L.G.	25	1,180	241	3·4 ,,
4 ,,	26 ,,	IV	27	9	12 S.P.	25	1,900	625	5·4 ,,
12-pdr.	7 ,,		28	7·6	4 S.P.	11·5	1,720	249	—

SHIP TYPES MOUNTING 16·25-IN. TO 8-IN. GUNS

16·25 in.	.. ..	*Benbow*, *Sans Pareil.*
13·5 ,,	.. ..	*Admirals*, *Nile*, *Royal Sovereign.*
12 ,,	.. ..	*Colossus*, *Conqueror*, *Collingwood.*
10 ,,	.. ..	*Centurion*, *Devastation* (R), *Sans Pareil.*
9·2 ,,	.. ..	*Warspite*, *Alexandra* (R), *Rupert* (R).
8 ,,	.. ..	*Magdala* (R), *Abyssinia* (R), *Bellerophon* (R).

(R) = rearmed.

[1] Compiled from the Official "List of Service Ordnance," 1891.
S.B.C. = Slow burning cocoa. P.Bl. = Prismatic black.
P.Br. = Prismatic brown. S.P. = Small pebble.
R.L.G. = Rifle large grain.

"ANSON," "CAMPERDOWN," "HOWE" and "RODNEY"

	Built at	*Laid down*	*Launched*	*Completed*	*Cost*
"*Anson*"	Pembroke	24 April '83	17 Feb. '86	May '89	£662,582
"*Camperdown*"	Portsmouth	18 Dec. '82	24 Nov. '85	July '89	£677,724
"*Howe*"	Pembroke	7 June '82	28 April '85	July '89	£639,434
"*Rodney*"	Chatham	6 Feb. '82	8 Oct. '84	June '88	£665,963

Dimensions "*Anson*" "*Camperdown*" { 330′ × 68½′ × 27·4′/28·4′ = 10,600 tons. Hull and armour 6,650. Equipment 3,950 tons.
"*Howe*" "*Rodney*" { 325′ × 68′ × 27·4′/28·4′ = 10,300 tons. Hull and armour 6,430. Equipment 3,870 tons.

Armament 4 13·5-in. 67-ton B.L. guns.
6 6-in. 26 cal. B.L.
12 6-pdrs.
17 smaller.
Torpedo Tubes.
5 above water.
("*Rodney*" had no bow tube).

Armour (compound) Belt 18″-8″; bulkheads 16″-7″.
Barbettes: "*Howe*" and "*Rodney*" 11½″-10″.
"*Anson*" and "*Camperdown*" 14″-12″.
Tubes 12″; conning towers 12″-2″.
Screens to battery 6″.
Upper deck amidships 3″; under water deck 2½″; skin 1″.
Total 2,880 tons (28 per cent.).

Complement 525/536.

Coal 900/1,200 tons.

Machinery "*Anson*," "*Howe*," "*Rodney*"—Humphreys. "*Camperdown*"—Maudslay. 2 sets compound inverted 3 cyl. One H.P. 52″; two L.P. 74″; stroke 3½′; revs. 100. I.H.P. 7,500 = 15·7 forced 11,500 = 17·4 knots. Boilers 12 cylindrical. 90 lb. pressure. 36 furnaces. 2 screws 18½′ diam.; pitch 19′-17½′.

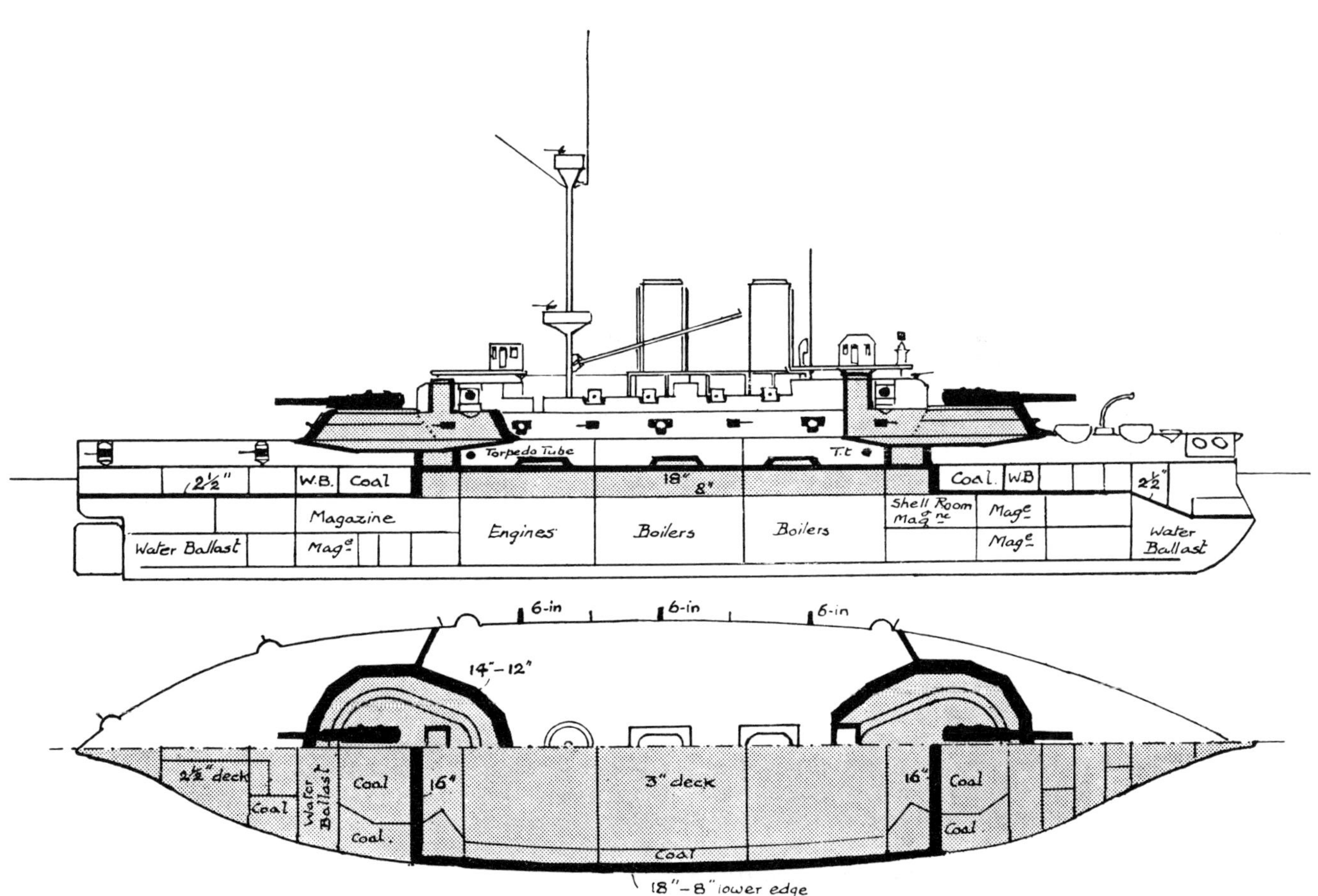

CAMPERDOWN

In selecting the main armament for the Dockyard-built ships the Board favoured the 13·5-in. gun, Woolwich model, as being of nearly the same weight as those the French were mounting in the *Formidable* and *Admiral Baudin*. It was a much more powerful weapon than the 12-in. of the *Collingwood*, being capable of piercing the thickest armour in any warship afloat at 3,000 yards.

In the first two vessels to be laid down, the *Howe* and *Rodney*, the dimensions of the *Collingwood* were repeated, except that in order to accommodate the additional weight of guns, mountings and ammunition the draught had to be increased from 26 ft. 4½ in. to 27 ft. 10 in. with a rise in displacement of 800 tons to 10,300 tons. In view of their low freeboard this extra 18 in. immersion was a handicap at sea, especially as when carrying full bunkers there would be a further increase in draught of 6 in. But seemingly the results of low-freeboard steaming in a seaway did not count for much so long as the big guns had the high barbette command, while the extra immersion of the belt was of little account as it was always likely to be submerged when at sea.

The *Howe* about 1902 with the mast head semaphore used for long distance signalling. The high signal mast detracted from the symmetry of these ships, and an inconspicuous upper fighting top was introduced in place of the large top in *Collingwood* and *Benbow*.

In *Anson* and *Camperdown* the barbettes had 14 in.-12 in. plating instead of 11½ in.-10 in., making an addition of 350 tons to the armour total, while the belt was 150 ft. long instead of 140 ft., taking the displacement to 10,600 tons. But to carry this extra weight without further increase in draught they were lengthened 5 ft. and given 6 in. more beam.

ARMAMENT

The 13·5-in. gun weighed 67 tons, was 36 ft. long, and capable of penetrating more than 27 in. of iron at 1,000 yards with a 1,250 lb. projectile and charge of 630 lb. S.B.C. powder (later 187 lb. of cordite). They were carried at a height of 20 ft. above water and had a command of 270° training across bows and stern.

PROTECTION

This was similar to that in *Collingwood*, with the difference in length of belt and thickness of barbette armour already mentioned, and a considerable narrowing of the ammunition tubes.

MACHINERY

The nominal h.p. was increased by 500 for the same speed.

GENERAL

Owing to delays in manufacturing the 67-ton guns and deciding the weight of their projectile and charge—which held up work on the magazines and hoists—the completion of all four ships was inordinately prolonged, so that despite the good intentions of the Board about accelerated construction, they did not hoist their pennants until six or seven years after being laid down. The delay over the guns was due to the faulty principle of placing liners in the bores which cracked during proof, and it took a long time to repair these and make the guns efficient. Meanwhile the *Admirals* propped up the Dockyard walls, until they could be fully or even partially armed, for as late as spring 1890 the *Howe* had only two of her big guns aboard.

In *Anson* and *Camperdown* the 6-in. B.L. were later replaced by 40 cal. Q.F.; in the other two ships the 26 cal. guns were "converted."

SEA-GOING QUALITIES

The 1889 Manœuvres Report on their sea-going qualities describes them as good sea boats with speed not affected when steaming against a moderate wind and sea. But their low freeboard was considered as rendering

Italian *Sardegna* class showing hood over barbette protecting the gunners compared with the open barbette top in *Camperdown*.

them unsuitable as sea-going armoured ships for general service with the fleet, as "their speed must be rapidly reduced when it is necessary to force them against a head sea or swell" (see *Benbow*).

In addition, the barbettes had merely light canvas covers which were easily washed away, so that there was little to prevent quantities of water from finding its way down below. When steaming against a gale the *Camperdown* is described as having shipped hundreds of tons in a few hours so that the magazine passages were knee-deep in water. The Italian *Sardegna* class with very similar barbettes were later given light steel shields which remedied this defect, and it was a pity that the *Admirals* could not have been similarly treated.

APPEARANCE

Although sister ships, each had distinctive details by which it was interesting to identify them. *Rodney*, the first to be delivered, had a single fighting top like *Colossus*, but later was masted like the others with a large lower and small upper fighting top; and about 1896-97 all except her were given a tall signal mast forward in place of the short pole. Otherwise they could best be distinguished by the arrangement of their tertiary batteries. *Anson* had her first three 6-pdrs. amidships well spaced from the fourth. *Howe* had them in groups of two. *Camperdown*, as *Howe*, but had prominent steam pipes. *Rodney* had a short pole before the bridge (p. 323).

"ANSON"

Arrived at Portsmouth from Pembroke in March '87 and for two years lay waiting for guns while slowly completing for sea. Commissioned 28 May '89 as R.A. Flag Channel fleet. In September '93 went up the Straits where she served until January 1900 (refit Malta '96). Paid off at Devonport into C Reserve and transferred to A Reserve in February '01, commissioning for the new Home Fleet in March '01. In May '04 paid off into B Reserve at Chatham.

Sold 13 July '09 for £21,200.

"CAMPERDOWN"

Commissioned at Portsmouth 18 July '89 for Home Fleet manœuvres, going into reserve in September. In December '89 went to the Mediterranean as flagship until May '90 when she was transferred to the Channel (flag) replacing the old *Northumberland*. Paid off May '92 in Fleet Reserve A commissioning for manœuvres in July '92 after which she again was sent up the Straits. Collided with and sank the *Victoria* on 22 June '93 and was under repair from July to September. During '96-'97 underwent a large refit when the chart-house was altered and the signal mast stepped. Paid off at Portsmouth in September '99 B Reserve and in May 1900 into Dockyard Reserve C. Commissioned July 1900 as coastguard ship at Lough Swilly until May '03 when she paid off into B Reserve at Chatham and was prepared as berthing ship to submarines at Harwich where she lay from October '08 until sold 11 July 1911 for £28,000.

"HOWE"

Delivered at Portsmouth 15 November '85 for guns to be fitted and commissioned 18 July '89 for manœuvres. In May '90 replaced the *Iron Duke* in the Channel and on 2 November '92 during the Mediterranean cruise grounded on Ferrol Rock; was salvaged by a Swedish firm under extraordinary difficulties and floated off 30 March '93; completed temporary repairs at Ferrol in April. Paid off at Chatham for a full overhaul costing £45,000. In October '93 relieved the *Edinburgh* in the Mediterranean coming home in December '96 and was then stationed at Queenstown as portguard ship. Served there, with periodic absence for manœuvres, until October '01; Devonport Reserve until July-September '04 manœuvres, which was her last spell of sea time. Moored in Hamoaze in Fleet Reserve until sold on 11 October 1910 for £25,100.

"RODNEY"

Commissioned at Chatham 20 June '88 for Home Fleet and was flagship at manœuvres; from August '88 until July '89 was in reserve at Portsmouth. Manœuvres July-September '89 and then relieved the *Monarch* in the Channel where she served from May '90 to May '94, and then went to the Mediterranean. Returned home in September '97 and served as coastguard ship at Queensferry from September '97 to February '01 when she was relieved by *Anson* and paid off into Chatham Fleet Reserve B. In July '06 was shown in Special Reserve and sold on 11 May '09 for £21,350.

Damage sustained by the "Camperdown" in collision with "Victoria"

Before the *Camperdown's* way was stopped her stem had penetrated 6 ft. into the *Victoria*, and then the sterns swung together about 20°, which exaggerated the injuries to both ships. *Camperdown* injured her stem piece and damaged the thin plating at the port bow, so that a considerable amount of water was quickly shipped and she was soon down by the head. But for the prompt action of her carpenter, who succeeded in building a wooden barrier across the main deck, she might very well have been lost. As it was, the water rose to the top of the barrier but did not overflow it. Her metacentric height became almost nil, and but for careful handling and smooth water she would have turned over.

In these ships every bulkhead and platform was perforated to permit of "drainage" water being conducted from *any* compartment—including the chain locker and coal bunkers—to the main drain and thence to the engine room. Every perforation was fitted with a valve of some kind, but many were very inaccessible and dust and grit often prevented their being closed properly. The seepage into the *Camperdown* was instrumental in a considerable modification being adopted with drainage in subsequent ships.

"BENBOW"

Built by	*Laid down*	*Launched*	*Completed*	*Cost*
Thames I.W.	1 Nov. '82	15 June '85	June '88	£764,022

Dimensions $330' \times 68\frac{1}{2}' \times 27{\cdot}4'/28{\cdot}4' =$ 10,600 tons.
Hull 6,580. Equipment 4,020 tons.

Armament
2 16·25-in. 110-ton B.L.
10 6-in.
12 6-pdrs.
20 smaller.

Torpedo Tubes.
1 bow.
4 beam.

Armour (*compound*) Belt 18″-8″; bulkheads 16″-7″.
Barbettes 14″-12″; tubes 12″.
conning towers 12″-2″.
Screens to battery 6″.
Decks 3″ upper amidships, 2½″ to ends; skin 1″.
Total 2,880 tons (27·1 per cent.).

Complement 523.

Coal 900/1,200 tons.

Machinery Maudslay, 2 sets compound inverted 3-cyl.
One H.P. 52″, two L.P. 74″; stroke 3½′; revs. 100.
I.H.P. 7,500=15·7; forced 11,500=17·4 knots.
Boilers 12 cylindrical; 90 lb. pressure.
36 furnaces.
2 screws 18½′ diam.; pitch 19′-17½′.

Points of interest:

(1) The first ship to carry the 110-ton B.L. gun.

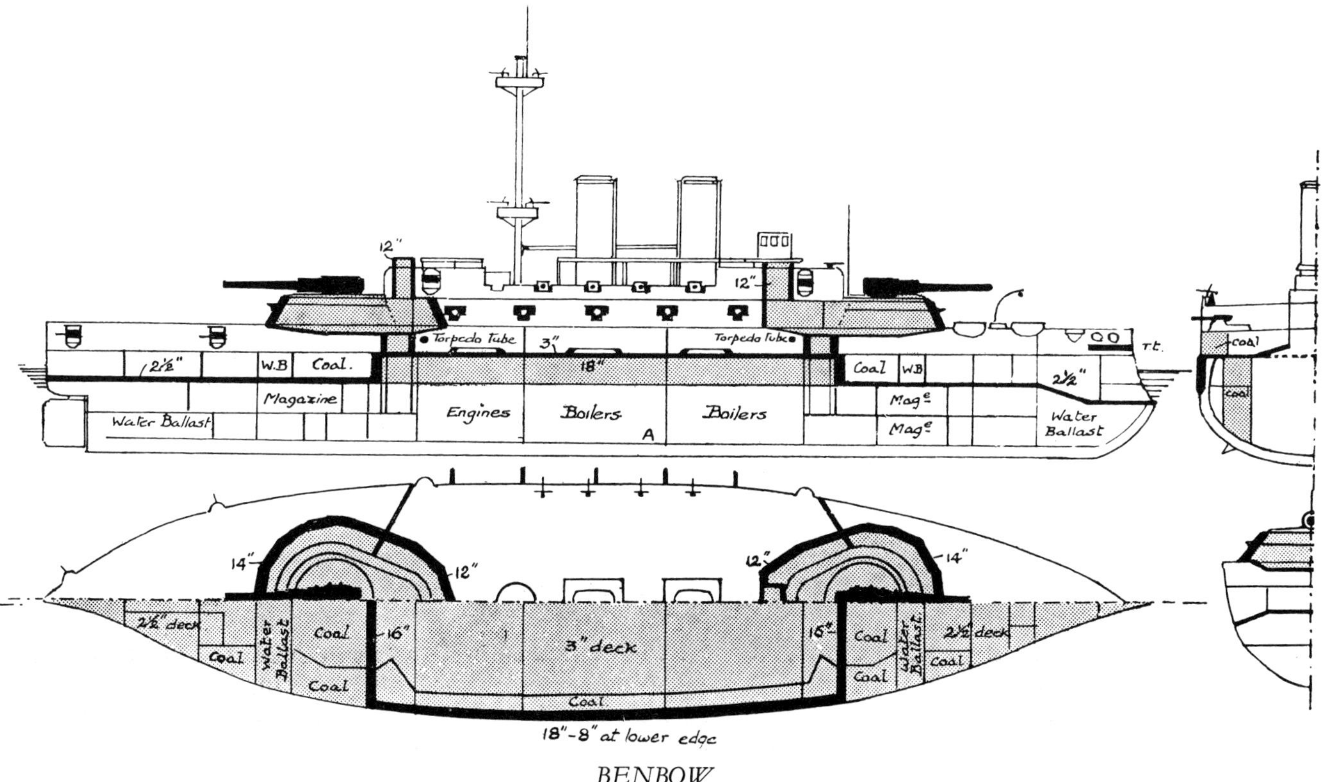

BENBOW

When distributing the orders for the second batch of the *Admiral* class the lack of suitable building slips in the Dockyards made it necessary to place the *Benbow* out to contract, and the Thames Iron Works were able to start work on the first British battleship awarded to Blackwall since the *Cyclops*.

In conformity with the decision to accelerate construction, her contract stipulated delivery in three years—which meant avoiding any delay in the matter of armament supply. As it was very doubtful if Woolwich would be able to deliver any of the new and untried 13·5-in. B.L. for a considerable period, an alternative heavy gun had to be selected which could be supplied in good time and thus avoid the expense incurred by delay with the contractors. The choice lay between a repeat of the *Collingwood's* 12-in. or in turning to Elswick for their 110-ton 16·25-in. B.L.—which was the only other large "known" gun available, and which the Italians were mounting in their three new 11,000-ton battleships of the *Andrea Doria* class. As the French had put three 75-ton B.L. into their *Formidable* class, our little 12-in. 45-tonners seemed an inadequate sort of response—although perfectly capable of smashing up either of these two ships. And so the "One knock-out blow" school of thought got the decision and the design of the *Benbow* was modified to take one 110-tonner in each barbette in place of two 13·5-in. As a set-off to the weight saved, the battery was enlarged from six to ten 6-in. guns.

Although the possession of this giant armament gave the *Benbow* a special kudos, they were by no means an effective substitute for the 13·5-in., being slow in handling and slower in hitting, with a much shorter life, and a tendency to droop at the muzzle as a final disability. The inner tube could not stand up to more than 75 rounds—and then its renewal was a costly and difficult business—while the rate of fire in practice was one round every four to five minutes, although credited with trial firing of three rounds in six minutes starting with the gun loaded.

The *Benbow* was generally considered to be the best steamer of the *Admiral* class, having reached 8,658 h.p. under natural draught and logged 17·5 knots with 10,860 h.p. when running light under 2-in. pressure. As, however, she was the only one to have her speed measured by patent log, a comparison of trials could be mis-

With her two huge 110-ton guns the *Benbow* stood high in the public estimation. She is here seen during the 1904 Manœuvres as a unit of the "B" Fleet in the grey livery introduced the previous year.

leading. But that, when hard put to it, she was capable of making a better show in a seaway than might be thought possible on account of her low freeboard, may be gathered from her performance during the 1903 Manœuvres. On 7 August a gale was experienced which caused the fleet to straggle greatly, and only the *Benbow* kept up with the flagship *Revenge*, leaving the *Royal Oak*, *Sans Pareil* and *Hood* hull down astern and the *Royal Sovereign* out of sight.

Reports state that at sea she was very steady, although even in gentle weather her forecastle would be awash at a moderate speed; in a seaway it dipped and rose in a smother of green seas and foam, so that she and her sisters made a magnificent spectacle as a squadron. Nowadays (1935) to have watched the Mediterranean Fleet at sail drill or a Battle Fleet under full canvas are memories of the privileged few; today we may count ourselves fortunate who can say, "I saw the *Admirals* at sea."

"BENBOW"

Delivered from the builders to Chatham in August '86 and commissioned 14 June '88 for the Mediterranean where she served until October '91, and then paid off at Chatham into Reserve. In June '92 commissioned for manœuvres and from July to September the next year; Fleet Reserve B until March '94 when she went to Greenock as coastguard ship until April '04. Remained in B Reserve Devonport swinging around her buoy in the Hamoaze until sold on 13 July '09 for £21,200.

Rodney as completed with single fighting top.

Chapter 52

PROBLEMS OF THE EARLY EIGHTIES

CARNARVON COMMITTEE 1879

THE political history of the Navy at this period, with its devious tensions and lapses into blind neglect which led up to the Naval Defence Act of 1889, entered upon a fresh cycle in September 1879 when the Carnarvon Committee was formed to consider the question of Colonial Defence. The Russian scare of the previous year had revealed such complete lack of organization for the conduct of a naval war, for the protection of our commerce, and for the defence of our overseas possessions that the Government formed a strong committee of naval, military and civilian experts who were commissioned to make a thorough investigation of the whole problem. The members were all Liberals and all "Big Navy" men. In due course a Report was presented which was sufficiently disconcerting to cause it to be made very secret—so much so that its contents were not divulged until the Colonial Conference of 1887—the gist being that the Navy was not nearly big enough for the duties it would be expected to fulfil and that its strength would have to be increased with as little delay as possible, and to an extent which would mean additional expenditure requiring a rise of threepence on the Income Tax.

Needless to say no Gladstone Cabinet could be expected to countenance such taxation, especially as there had been no mandate to increase the Navy at the 1880 Election, and it was decided that the exigencies of the Prime Minister's financial reputation necessitated the postponement of any action. To the politicians our weakness afloat as demonstrated by the Carnarvon Report was of quite secondary importance to the game of party politics, and the Navy being regarded as non-political ground the two parties came to an agreement that any campaign to obtain an increase in the Naval Estimates should be held over until 1884.

NEW CONSTRUCTION 1880–84

In view of this decision the Board decided that no extreme protest was indicated. It was content to pursue its policy of hastening slowly with fresh construction, while pushing ahead with breech-loading rearmament and the completion of ships already in hand. So between 1880 and 1884 the armoured tonnage laid down and expenditure on Shipbuilding and Ordnance amounted to:

	England			France		
		Tonnage	Shipbuilding and Ordnance		Votes 11, 12, 15-20	and Budget Extraordinaire
1880	*Collingwood*	9,500	£3,425,803	*Neptune*[1]	10,581	£2,898,112
1881	*Imperieuse*	8,400	£3,736,669	*Hoche*	10,650	£3,120,899
	Warspite	8,400		*Magenta*[1]	10,581	
				Marceau	10,581	
1882	*Howe*	10,300	£4,156,644	Nil		£3,254,569
	Rodney	10,300				
	Camperdown	10,600				
	Benbow	10,500				
1883	*Anson*	10,600	£4,245,382	Nil		£3,383,346
1884	*Hero*	6,200	£4,607,237	*Brennus*	10,600	£3,175,359
				C. Martel	10,600	
		84,800	£20,171,735		63,593	£15,832,285

The French programme was afterwards mulcted of the *Brennus* and *Charles Martel*, which were to have been armoured on the British system; their construction was abandoned and two other ships with the same names commenced some years later.

NEW CONTROLLER BECOMES SEA LORD

In 1882 two notable changes were made at the Admiralty which indicated how much the question of *material* was governing the situation, and how ready the Board was to face it. The Controller, Rear-Admiral Thomas Brandreth (appointed December 1881), was made a Lord of the Admiralty, and an additional Civil Lord was created "who should possess special mechanical and engineering knowledge as well as administrative experience to assist the Controller in the business relating to material."

[1] These ships were stated by the First Lord to have been commenced in 1882 and 1883 respectively.

ADDITIONAL CIVIL LORD

Mr. George Rendel of Armstrongs was appointed to the new post, and he came with a great reputation having been responsible for such innovations as the Chilean protected cruiser *Esmeralda*, the Chinese gunboats, and barbettes for the *Italia* and *Collingwood*.

POLITICAL TRUCE ON NAVAL AFFAIRS

The Egyptian War showed the Navy to advantage, and both the bombardment of Alexandria and the Nile operations reacted to our national prestige at the expense of France. Naval power had been exercised to safeguard British interests when another nation equally threatened had preferred to climb down, and the man-in-the-street was in good conceit with the Fleet. But the change in the general naval situation as shown by relative increase in new construction was outside his cognizance, and the years slipped past with little or no light being thrown upon the coming state of things either from the platform or in the press, nor through criticism of the "Wait Awhile" policy with which the Admiralty was content.

Certainly Lord Henry Lennox—who had been Secretary under Packington—Admiral Sir John Hay and Sir William Armstrong all drew attention to our naval weakness between 1882 and 1884, but they were voices crying in the wilderness. *The Times* dismissed this "art of the alarmist" as "putting forward fancy figures and then arguing they were correct," while deprecating a larger expenditure on shipbuilding and even objecting to too close a scrutiny of ships and guns. "Jervis and Nelson," it observed, "never did such things, and as for the doubt that must hang over naval battles—numbers might not count for much!"

But the Board did go to the length of putting up Lord Alcestor (Admiral Sir Beauchamp Seymour) to pen a monitory letter to *The Times*, though the short discussion it evoked was too much concerned with detail and too little with policy for public interest to be aroused, and as an attempt at educational propaganda it fell flat.

TORPEDO VERSUS BATTLESHIP

In July 1884 Lord Sidmouth drew attention to our naval deficiencies in the House of Lords and in his reply Lord Northbrook made use of an expression which—separated from its context—was made to bear a construction such as was never intended, and is to this day preserved as a reproach to the First Lord and to Sir Cooper Key who inspired it.

Lord Northbrook said:

> "When the noble Marquis said that it would be desirable that the Admiralty should have an unlimited amount of money to spend on the present types of ships of war, he felt bound to say that he was not of that opinion. *The great difficulty the Admiralty would have to contend with, if they were granted three or four millions tomorrow for the purpose referred to, would be to decide how they should spend the money.* Anyone who had paid attention to the progress made in the construction of guns must be aware that the guns put on board the newest types of ships would be able to destroy any armour which could be put on a vessel. We were now obliged to leave portions of our vessels undefended, and to protect only certain vital parts. In every new vessel the armour had to be thicker, and, unless ships were built of a larger size, a great portion of them must be penetrable. Therefore the difficulty at the present time was whether it was desirable to increase the number of these enormous ships of war; and that was a difficulty felt not only at our own Admiralty, but, as he knew, by those who had to conduct the affairs of other countries. Then there was another consideration which made it doubtful whether it would be wise to spend a great sum of money now upon such ships. Some of the best naval officers in this country thought that, in the event of another naval war, the torpedo would be the most powerful weapon of offence, and would be able to dispose of the most formidable ships in the service of this or any other country. Therefore it would be most imprudent greatly to increase the number of these enormous machines."

This of course merely reflected the opinion of his chief professional adviser, and Sir Cooper Key was far from happy about the future of heavily armoured battleships, sharing the growing apprehension which had come to regard them as in a defenceless position when attacked by torpedo boats—unless nets were to prove a more efficient defence than seemed likely.

To a large extent opinion had been built up on the *Oberon* experiments at Portsmouth and various tests undertaken abroad when explosive charges were detonated against or at graduated distances from hulks to ascertain the effects of torpedo or mine. Torpedo boats were still small and averaged under 100 ft. in length, but were growing rapidly in size and speed. No full-scale manœuvres had been carried out to test their efficacy under service conditions at sea, but exercises showed that boats attacking by night on fleets at anchor or at slow speed ought generally to be successful. Opinion abroad was to the effect that an attack could only be repulsed by gunfire when not more than one boat attacked one ship, and that night attacks *must always be in favour of the torpedo.* Daylight attacks conducted in the French navy showed that three boats were sufficient to destroy one ship which had had full warning, and that was when allowance was made for gunfire hits scored within torpedo range.

Experiments in both the British and French Navies indicated that while ships were being fitted with large numbers of machine guns there was no evidence that these had the power to stop a torpedo boat—in fact most hits were obtained when the attacking boat was well within torpedo range. In the absence of larger and longer ranged quickfiring guns it looked as if booms and *nets* provided the only available defence for ships at anchor, and that at sea only high speed would ensure safety.

Certainly in the face of this menace from the omnipotent torpedo the future of the big ship appeared decidedly hazardous—just as it had been when shell-fire was first directed against wooden hulls.

Thus Lord Northbrook summed up the situation as it appeared to the Board—that the types of ship we required was so uncertain that any hurried expenditure would most probably be only wasted. But robbed of their context his words were made to imply that we had an ample sufficiency of naval force and no more money was wanted.

TORPEDO NET PROTECTION

The nets referred to were of the early Bullivant type made up of steel wire rings 6½ in. diameter joined by small steel rings, and weighing only 1 lb. per sq. ft. They were slung out on long booms triced up high above water by stays from the derricks or mast heads and trailed to hull depth; extended trials proved them capable of stopping the slow 14-in. torpedo, which it was feared might then explode and destroy the net.

H.M.S "HOTSPUR" with early type of torpedo-net crinoline

The booms were carried along the sides in turret ships, but usually stowed inboard in broadside ships except for a pair triced up at the bows and stern. The cumbersome crinoline took a long time to get fixed into position and longer still to restow, and could only be used with the ship at anchor.

In due course a more satisfactory method of laying out the nets was evolved with the booms nearly flush with the water and the nets hanging down some 25 ft. So fitted, a ship could proceed slowly without the nets being swept to the surface and was safe at sea. But the coming of the net cutter fixed to the nose of the torpedo changed all that, and the crinoline was generally discarded abroad although retained in this country—probably because "Out nets" was good drill and a useful evolution.

ANTI-TORPEDO PROTECTION

The first proposals for armour protection against under-water attack were made by Reed in 1884 in a patent specification for a system which he hoped to get incorporated in the battleships of the Northbrook Programme.

In his specification submitted to the Admiralty, the design for a ship he named the *Enterprise* was modelled upon the *Conqueror* and included an armoured double-bottom 4 in.-3½ in.-2½ in. with the thickest portion over the sides with the 8-ft. space between it and the thin outer bottom subdivided transversely and longitudinally. This armoured screen ran under the machinery, boilers and magazines and, as he described it:

> "The torpedo will be stopped and compelled to explode outside of the inner bottom, and the debris of that bottom will be dashed against the inner armour, which will of course be vastly more difficult of penetration by this debris than the ordinary ⅜-in. steel plating which at present is all that separates the boilers etc. from the outer bottom."

The scheme worked out satisfactorily as regards weight in several designs he had prepared, and he claimed that it possessed the additional advantages of stopping shell hits below the water-line and "localizing the injurious effects of ramming."

The deep double bottom of necessity raised the boilers and engines so that they were partially above the water-line and directly exposed to gunfire which could penetrate the belt.

In their investigation of the question of stability the officers of the Controller's department considered the case in which damage from ram or torpedo was supposed to be confined to one side of the ship.

> "It is supposed that the connection between a water-tight transverse frame and two deep longitudinals are destroyed; these longitudinals are 13½ ft. apart at the outer plating. This would open six compartments to the sea, and if such an accident were to occur while the ship was floating with riddled ends she would capsize, although the inner bottom might remain intact."

Chiefly for this reason the Board was unable to accept Reed's proposals, but it was pointed out that a vessel

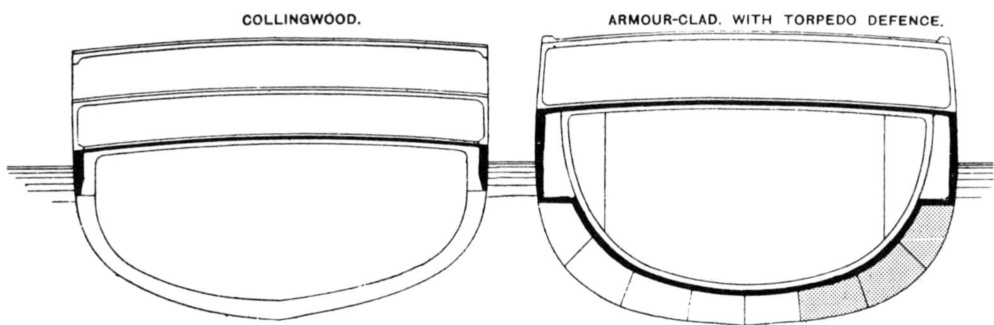

of this type to do the same work as the existing larger vessels in the Navy would have to be at least 1,500 tons heavier; and that her side armour, although very considerably thinned, would be required to protect both engines and boilers as well as the mechanism for working the guns. In the design of the *Enterprise* Barnaby stated:

> "he had shortened the belt, giving exactly the same proportionate area of water-line protected as in the *Admirals*, and he submits to a sinkage on perforation much more than twice theirs, in a ship two-thirds their size."

It will be noted that the Admiralty constructors riddled the ends of the ship before entering upon any calculations as to stability after what could only have been the maximum under-water damage inflicted by a single hit on the most favoured spot for the torpedo. Reed, however, must be given the credit of having put forward what seems to have been the first proposal for armour protection against torpedo attack, and thus anticipated various schemes of a similar nature tried out twenty years afterwards, especially that incorporated into the giant Japanese battleships *Yamato* and *Mutsu* (1941).

Chapter 53

THE NORTHBROOK PROGRAMME

It was not until the autumn of 1884 that public feeling with regard to our maritime position underwent a change, and the first mutterings of the storm which was to bring about the Naval Defence Act five years later began to stir the country.

"TRUTH ABOUT THE NAVY" ARTICLES

Both Parties had agreed that a naval "panic" should be postponed until now, and it was a Liberal paper which initiated it. During the recess before the General Election Mr. H. O. Arnold-Forster proposed a series of articles on the state of the Navy to Mr. W. H. Stead, then editor of the *Pall Mall Gazette*. These were to be based upon information supplied by the Hon. Reginald Brett (later Lord Esher), then private secretary to the Secretary of State for War, and Captain J. A. Fisher of the *Excellent*. On September 15 the first of the famous "Truth about the Navy" series of articles appeared, which very successfully focused attention upon the deficiencies of the Fleet in ships, equipment, organization and personnel. In face of such convincing statements and masterly arguments a swing-over to a demand for naval reform was at once manifest in the press generally. But nothing could be done until the return of Lord Northbrook from Cairo, where he had been putting Egyptian affairs in order, that country now having partially passed under our protection.

"NORTHBROOK PROGRAMME"

On 10 November the First Lord spoke at the Guildhall and admitted that it was desirable steadily to increase our strength in armour-plated ships and cruisers, paying particular attention to the provision of speed in the smaller classes of vessels. This heralded the "Northbrook Programme" of 1884 by which an additional £3,100,000 was to be devoted to new construction during the next five years and resulted in the battleships *Victoria* and *Sans Pareil*, seven belted cruisers of the *Australia* class, six torpedo cruisers of the *Archer* class and fourteen torpedo boats.

The Board excused the delay in asking for more ships on the grounds that had this programme been put forward *before* the public expression of feeling it would in all probability never have been accepted; as it was, the naval sense of the country having been aroused, *the provision for new ships was scouted as inadequate*. In the Service the First Lord was credited with the outlook of a managing director of a bus company, solely concerned with cutting down working expenses and renewals; and Cooper Key's unpopularity became extreme. His contemporaries on the Flag List regarded him as weak and time-serving, an administrator with brains but without backbone and too much concerned with keeping his seat on the Board to enter effective protest against a policy about which the Navy itself had been practically silent and accepted without remonstrance for the past five years.

Key's own view of the position was recorded in a letter to Admiral Sir Geoffrey Phipps Hornby—then C.-in-C. at Portsmouth—dated 2 December 1884:

> "It is rumoured at Portsmouth that I am opposed to the increase in the Fleet—I wish to disabuse *your* mind on the subject. If you had seen what I have written, heard what I said to the Board, you would know I have been disturbed about the absurdly small sum the Government are asking for. I have protested against this as insufficient and have scarcely slept for the last five nights having been so worried about it. . . . I could not very well resign on the point as we have had no more reason for that than we had three months ago. I have always deprecated asking for a very large lump sum for shipbuilding purposes—it will only induce other Nations to make another start. When I found the feeling of Parliament and the Country I advocated a larger expenditure, and was very much disappointed when we did not get it. But now we have got a half-loaf which is about what I originally asked for, I cannot say that I resign because the press has gone beyond that, although I much regret that we did not go beyond it also."
>
> "I believe that if our successors maintain the expenditure we have ensured for the next few years, we shall have no reason to doubt our position in the future—unless the other countries go ahead; then we must go farther ahead also."
>
> "We have now twenty-seven ironclads in commission. The French have eleven. We could commission thirteen more within a month. I cannot find that the French have more than two ready and one of these has her boilers condemned (*Richelieu*). Many of our ships are of obsolete types—so are many of theirs. Moreover, being of wood theirs cannot last long. I should have no fear whatever of war with France and Russia now, so far as our Navy is concerned; but I do fear that a relative strength in five years' time will be much too near equality for safety."

RUSSIAN CRISIS, 1884

During that month the stupid truculence of the Russians brought an increasingly difficult international tension to the very verge of hostilities. Crossing the boundaries of Bulgaria and Afghanistan, their troops occupied frontier towns, and the notorious General Skobeleff declared that it was "a political necessity for Russia to possess herself of India." The Foreign Minister, Lord Granville, had declared his opposition to these new territorial encroachments, but as if determined to force a war on us, the Russians persisted in their advance through Afghanistan.

Our response was immediate. The Reserves were called out and the Admiralty, having obtained the cession of the island of Port Hamilton, south of Korea, as an advanced depôt on the line to Vladivostock, hoisted the British flag there on 2 April 1885 and connected it to Hong Kong by telegraph. Every Russian ship outside her ports was shadowed by a sufficient British force, sometimes leading to delicate situations. On one famous occasion the *Agamemnon* under Captain Long, when covering Admiral Crown in the *Vladimir Monomakh*, entered Yokoska with the full broadside of the Russian ship trained upon his water-line and upper works without knowing whether hostilities had broken out or not.

PARTICULAR SERVICE SQUADRON, 1885

Admiral Hornby was selected to command a Baltic Expeditionary Fleet which was to be made up to 12 iron-clads, the *Polyphemus* and *Hecla*, 6 cruisers, 13 gunboats, 8 armed merchant ships and 16 torpedo boats which assembled in part at Portland during June 1885. This second Particular Service Squadron was "a menagerie of unruly and curiously assorted ships" consisting of the:

Minotaur (Flagship), *Agincourt*, *Hercules*, *Sultan*, *Penelope*, *Iron Duke*, *Lord Warden*, *Repulse*
Devastation, *Ajax*, *Hotspur*, *Rupert*
Shannon
Hecla (torpedo depôt ship), *Oregon* (merchant cruiser)
Conquest, *Mersey*, *Leander* (cruisers)
Polyphemus (torpedo ram)
Cormorant (sloop), *Racer*, *Mariner* (gunboats)
Snap, *Pike*, *Medway*, *Medina* (river gunboats)

However, so conciliatory a note was received from St. Petersburg that the prospects of war became remote and the ships of Hornby's Squadron were employed in exercises to test both their sea-going qualities and machinery, and the value of the new torpedo boats, mines, booms and general anti-torpedo equipment. The outstanding incident was the charging of the boom at Berehaven by the *Polyphemus*, and the value of the larger torpedo boats was well demonstrated. Much was learned about torpedo attack and the best means of breaking down an enemy's defences against it, or—as the lessons were taken to be read—how our ships could best protect themselves from an enemy's torpedo boats.

Chapter 54

THE RETURN TO TURRET SHIPS

When the design for the two new battleships came to be discussed, changes in the Board brought about a marked deflection from the principles of attack and defence upon which the *Admirals* had been based. Rear-Admiral Thomas Brandreth having been appointed Controller with a seat on the Board in December 1881, there was no longer any enthusiastic advocacy for barbettes—in fact, the question of replacing them by turrets in the *Admirals* had been considered, but as the cost of the alternative schemes meant expenditure of £40,000 to £100,000 and considerable delay in getting the ships to sea, the barbettes were retained.

In formulating the plans for the new ships, naval opinion ruled out the *Admirals* with their limited armour protection along the waterline and lack of it beneath the gun positions, and voiced an old allegiance to turrets and complete belts. But economy and a demand for more moderate dimensions stipulated that cost need not exceed *half that of the "Inflexible"*—or £400,000, the cost of the *Conqueror*.

A sister to this little coast defence ship, the *Hero*, had been laid down in April 1884, and the demand was for something in the nature of an improved *Hero* with:

> "a cumbrous superstructure, an effective minor armament and an 18-ton gun protected by a half-turret in the stern. Such a vessel should have been built at a cost which would have given us for the same aggregate expenditure two improved *Conquerors* as against one *Sans Pareil.* When, however, the design for the new ships was seriously considered, the same elements of fighting efficiency were insisted upon as in the case of a battleship of the first class, and the *Conqueror* type as reproduced to meet all the new conditions as to thickness of armour, and calibre of armament was increased from 6,200 to 10,470 tons and the cost was doubled." (*Naval Annual*, 1887, p. 103.)

To the strange mixture of types then under construction—the *Colossus*, *Admirals*, *Imperieuse* and *Conqueror*—the reactionary *Sans Pareil* merely accentuated the confusion of thought which then obtained. The *Conqueror* idea was faulty enough for a coast-defence ship; as applied to a seagoing ship—for which a powerful all-round fire is essential—it was inexcusable.

The four French contemporary ships *Hoche*, *Marceau*, *Magenta* and *Neptune*, against which the new design would be directed, were high freeboard vessels of about 10,600 tons carrying four 13·4-in. guns in a lozenge disposition instead of three along the centre line. While this obviated the *Baudin's* troubles in firing over the deck amidships, it introduced blast complications which limited the arcs of fire so that the end guns could only be used over about 180° and those amidships over 90°. Seventeen 5·5-in. guns were carried along the main deck—eight aside amidships and one in the bows. Side armour was limited to a thick and narrow end-to-end belt topped by a 3-in. deck leaving the rest of the hull exposed to small calibre gunfire. The original plans show three pole masts carrying light fore-and-aft rig and superstructure confined to a flying bridge amidships, but they were completed with two heavy military masts and a considerable amount of superstructure which in the *Hoche*, *Magenta* and *Neptune* was built up to provide accommodation and act as a blast screen.

"SANS PAREIL" and "VICTORIA" (ex *Renown*)

	Built by	*Laid down*	*Launched*	*Completed*	*Cost*
"*Sans Pareil*"	Thames I.W.	21 April '85	9 May '87	8 July '91	£778,650
"*Victoria*"	Elswick	23 April '85	9 April '87	March '90	£777,239 (£844,922 with armament)

Dimensions 340′ × 70′ × 26·6′/29′ = 10,470 tons (11,020 tons normal load). Hull and armour 7,420. Equipment 3,600 tons.

Armament			
	2 16·25-in. 110-ton B.L. guns.	T. Tubes.	1 bow.
	1 10-in. 29-ton B.L.		1 stern.
	12 6-in. B.L. (later Q.F.)		2 sub.
	12 6-pdrs. 20 smaller.		2 carriages.

Armour (compound) Belt 18″; bulkheads 16″; submerged deck fore and aft 3″; turret 17″; redoubt 18″; side to 6″ guns 3″; screen bulkheads to battery 6″; conning tower 14″-2″ top; backing 6″-7″ teak. Total 2,950 tons.

Complement 430; as flagships 550-583; 595 (in '05).

Coal 750/1,000 tons. Radius 7,000 miles at 10 knots.

Machinery Two sets triple exp. Humphreys. Cyls. 42″, 62″, 96″; stroke 4′ 3″. I.H.P. 7,500 = 15·3 knots; f.d. 14,000 = 17·2 knots. 8 4-furnace boilers; 135 lb. pressure. 2 screws.

Points of interest:

(1) The last single-turret battleships in the Service.
(2) The first to have triple expansion engines.
(3) Carried the highest percentage of armour of any sea-going ships since the *Dreadnought.*
(4) *Victoria* was the first battleship to be built by Armstrongs, and the first to be built, and armed by her contractors.

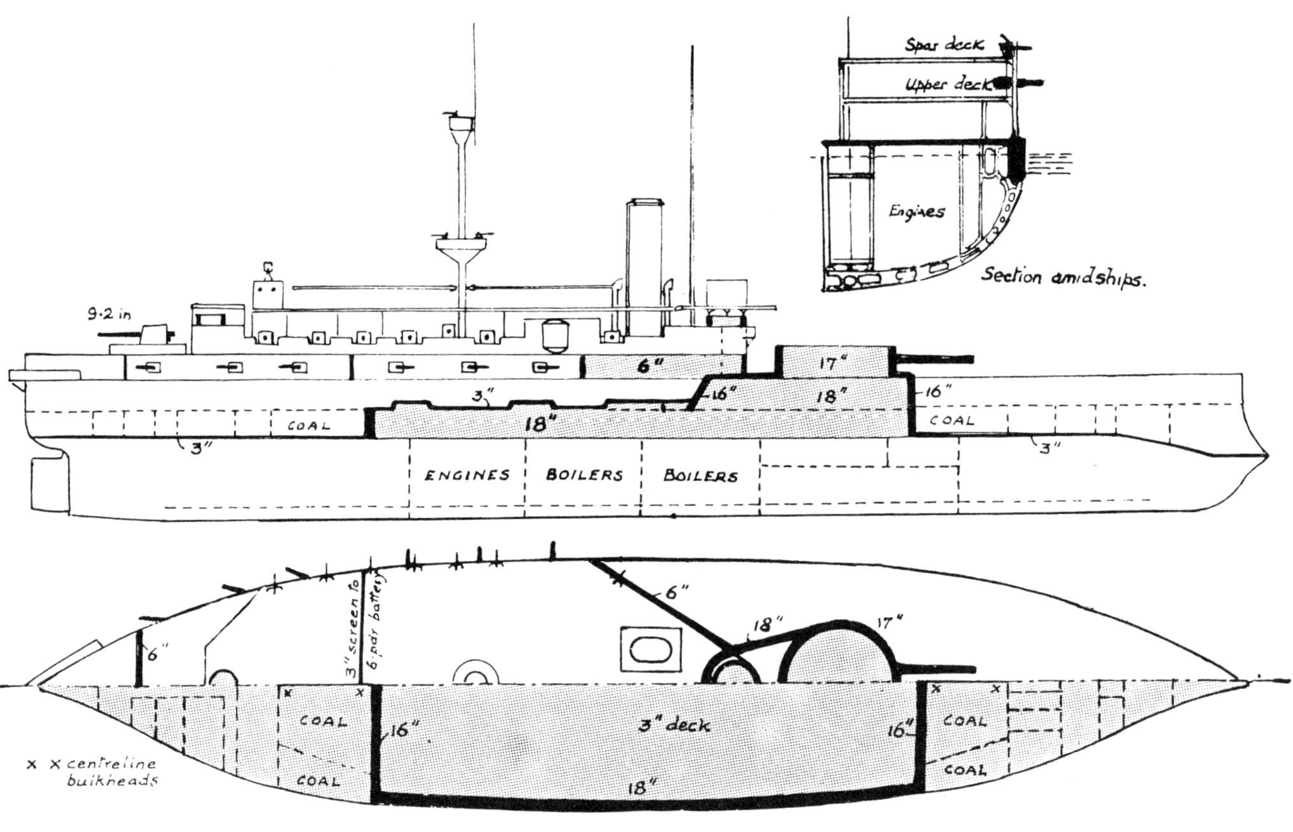

SANS PAREIL

Various reasons have been put forward to account for the design of these ships. It has been stated—

(1) That the Board required the heaviest type of ordnance which could be mounted upon the limited displacement, and as the weight involved by mounting the *Benbow's* guns in separate turrets was out of the question, they had perforce to be paired in one turret forward.
(2) The Board was also supposed to have been influenced by what were known as "Mediterranean considerations"—which at that time included the possibility of having to force the Dardanelles. This operation was regarded as one where bow fire would be preferred to a divided armament necessitating manœuvre to bring the after gun into action. Hence a single turret forward was favoured, except by a Board minority who visualized a wider scope of activity for the ships, and as a concession to whom the after gun was included.

In the absence of any official records showing how such a sound tactical conception as embodied in the general lay-out of thc *Admirals* came to be discarded in favour of a retrograde design like the "improved *Conqueror,*" it is fairly safe to assume that Barnaby had little or no say in the matter—the *Sans Pareil* was a "Board model" and he merely designed her to instructions received. But from the alternative sketch plans preserved in the "Ships Cover" it is possible to follow her evolution pretty clearly.

Six sets of plans lettered "A" to "F" were considered, of which "A" and "D" are missing. It would certainly have been interesting to have seen Barnaby's first interpretation of the improved *Conqueror* as shown in "A". If there was any question of including an 18-ton gun astern—which is unlikely when we have plan "E" before us—it is evident that lack of heavy fire astern ruled "A" out. In plan "B" of 3 September 1884 Barnaby got over this shortcoming by adding a single turret to each beam, giving an ahead fire of four 63-tonners, with three

The *Sans Pareil* during the manœuvres of 1904. Except that low funnel casings had been fitted, she was practically unaltered since her first commission.

abeam and two astern—a very remarkable layout. Torpedo defence was to be secured by the provision of twenty-two 6-in. and thirteen 6-pdrs.—an extraordinary battery for that or any other period. As the boiler rooms were separated by a central ammunition passage the ship would have had four funnels.

A month later we get plan "C", as likely as not put forward by the Chief Constructor as a personal suggestion, as it bears the imprint of being pure Barnaby. It is, of course, a turret edition of the *Admirals* with a two-deck secondary battery and—what should be carefully noted—separate citadels for the turrets.

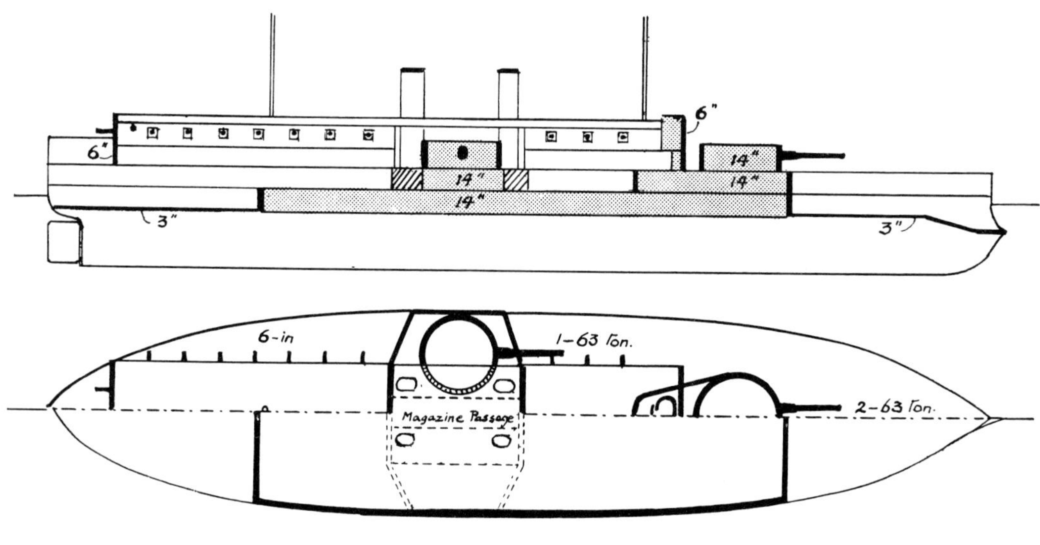

"B" design. 3 September, 1884.
10,000 tons. *Guns:* 4 63-ton; 22 6" B.L.; 13 6-pdrs.

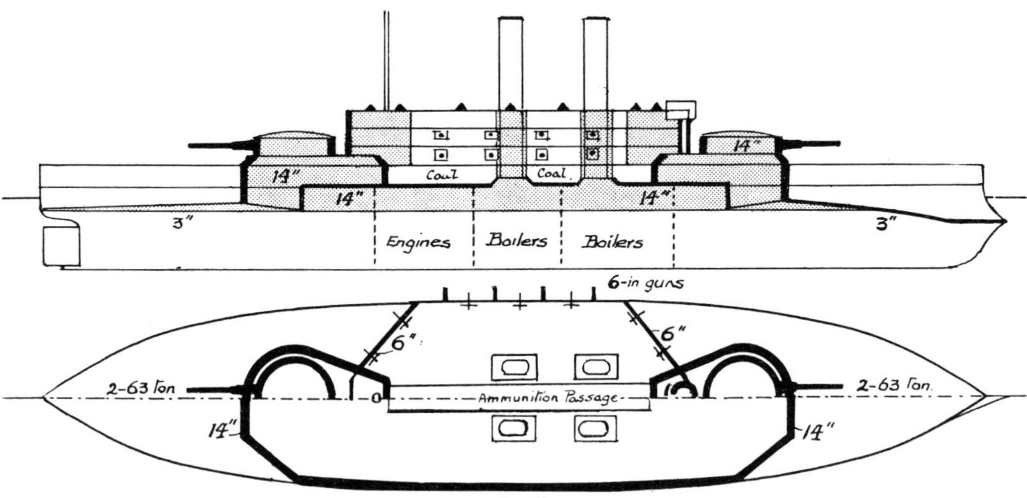

"C" design. 6 October 1884.
Dimensions: 340′×75′×27½′=11,700 tons. *Guns:* 4 63-ton; 16 6″; 14 6-pdrs. *Freeboard:* 10′.
Gun command 16′. *Training:* 135.

Like the *Northampton*, she was intended to come into action on the bow, as the battery was unprotected apart from the armour screens at each end. It is a thousand pities that the Board could not accept the design—possibly 11,700 tons was the deciding factor against it.

Plan "D" has not come to light, and again the possibilities are intriguing. But in November the Board got back to the original idea in plan "E"—which although 5 ft. shorter than the final 10,470 ton *Sans Pareil* with the same beam and draught, was calculated to be of 10,150 tons. Turret, redoubt and belt were all of 20-in. compound armour with two 63-ton guns up forward and a couple of 6-in. firing through a screen to look after affairs astern. This very inadequate provision of offence aft led to a curtailment of the 6-in. battery in the final plan "F" and the addition of a 10-in. gun at the stern as mentioned in "Brassey." But no explanation is forthcoming to account for the jump from perfectly adequate 13·5-in. to 16·25-in. guns which required a 2-in. reduction over the turret, redoubt and belt to keep displacement down to the Board limits.

But judging by the way in which the 13·5-in. gun was accepted in all the preliminary designs, there seems to have been no special demand for anything bigger. The *Benbow's* armament was not arrived at by a process of hypertrophical development, but selected *faute de mieux* when it appeared that construction was going to be held up by delays in the production of the new 63-tonner at Woolwich; also the *Sans Pareil's* final design was decided upon about the time that the *Admirals* were being launched. Hence it was more than likely that the same considerations forced the Board into repeating the *Benbow's* armament. That Elswick also experienced trouble with

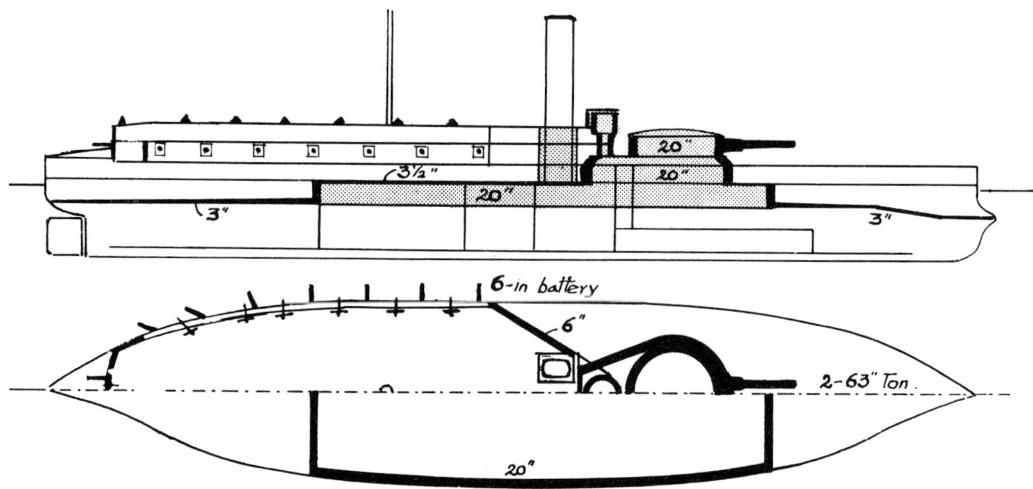

"E" design. 17 November 1884.
Displacement: 10,150 tons. 335′×70′×26′ 6″. *Guns:* 2 63-ton; 16 6″; 13 6-pdrs. I.H.P. 9.800=16 knots.

their monster 16·25-in. pieces and so kept the *Sans Pareil* and *Victoria* in dockyard basins for 3 to 4 years was unfortunate; but even had they been armed by Woolwich it would not have made much difference, as the *Admirals* did not get their full complement of 13·5-in. guns until 1890.

HULL

Compared with the *Benbow* the *Sans Pareil* was 10 ft. longer, 1½ ft. more in beam, and about the same mean draught, giving some 400 tons more displacement. There was the same underwater fineness at the ends and spur ram, but the rudder was narrower. Freeboard at load draught was about 12 ft., but with the turret taken as far aft as possible the longer forecastle gave more buoyancy forward.

Over 6,000 tons dead weight had been worked in the *Sans Pareil* when she went down the slipway—the greatest weight launched in this country since the *Great Eastern.*

ARMAMENT

The turret carried guns only 15 ft. above water as against two barbettes giving a 22 ft. command in the *Benbow*, but it was altogether a far better protected position with the base enclosed in a redoubt. But the great weight of turret and base restricted freeboard, any increase of which would have meant more weight at a greater height with consequent impairment of stability. In theory the guns should have ranged through an arc of 300 by angling the superstructure, but as in practice the deck buckled under ahead fire and the superstructure became shaken up considerably when the turret was trained much abaft the beam, the blast-free arcs were a lot less than usually shown.

During proof at Woolwich one of the *Victoria's* guns was found to have bent, and when again submitted for acceptance was put through a long series of trials which brought out other defects. It was therefore rejected and replaced by one specially strengthened, which served as a model for those in the *Sans Pareil* and held up her commissioning a further sixteen months.

The 110-ton gun was never tested to destruction, and although supposed to have a life of seventy-five rounds, this estimate was often questioned. It was a slow firer, never made good shooting, and proved costly to repair and reline. As Lord George Hamilton said in his statement on the 1890-91 Estimates:

> "While it is held fitting and proper that the Navy should have a few 110-ton guns, it is intimated that their extended use is no longer thought desirable. These monsters are treated with a sort of gingerly consideration, which leaves the impression that they are privately regarded as a highly respectable blunder. Many things are left unsaid which might very well be said about them, but as the Admiralty seem desirous to revert quietly to more manageable and less costly weapons, it is no longer necessary to criticize them severely."

Aft, the 10-in. gun was of 30 cals. weighing 29 tons and firing a 500-lb. projectile with a muzzle velocity of 2,040 ft. secs., able to penetrate 20·4 in. of iron at 1,000 yards. Incidentally, the following rule-of-thumb for armour piercing was accepted at that period subject to certain assumptions. Taking the calibre of the gun as a measure of the armour, it was found that no shot could perforate a plate unless it had over 1,000 ft. velocity for each calibre in thickness. Thus a 10-in. projectile needed over 1,000 ft. velocity to perforate a 10-in. plate; over 1,500 ft. velocity for a 15-in. plate, and over 2,000 ft. velocity for a 20-in. plate. The *Sans Pareil's* gun was therefore effective against the armour of any French ships except the *Baudin*, *Formidable* and *Duperrè*.

Sans Pareil showing after 10-in. gun.

In all the preliminary designs Barnaby had provided a very powerful secondary battery and a number of 6-pdrs.—then the largest Q.F. guns—for torpedo defence. Being relatively slow firing the 6-in. B.L. did not demand the same amount of ammunition as the later quick-firers, and weight in guns could be carried to maintain a volume of fire which in later ships depended upon greater magazine capacity. In the *Sans Pareil* the exceptionally long superstructure allowed for batteries of six 6-in. guns aside, with a 3-in. hull "affording protection against tertiary fire"—these being the days when theory of attack presumed the main armament to be directed against heavy armour, leaving unprotected parts to smaller guns without much regard for the normal hazards of gunnery and such a heresy as big guns "firing into the brown." Against raking fire the batteries had 6-in. angled bulkheads forward which also acted as blast screens to the turret guns, with transverse screens between the third and fourth guns to localize damage. The guns weighed 5 tons, were 26 cals. long, and fired a 100-lb. projectile about four times a minute.

On the deck above, 6-pdrs. fired through open ports with a 3-in. transverse screen aft, and twelve 3-pdrs. and eight machine guns were distributed over the topsides and fighting tops.

Of the eight torpedo tubes, two were above water at the bow and stern, two above water and one submerged on each beam. Altogether the *Sans Pareil* had eight different sizes of ordnance aboard, and commenting upon the manœuvres of 1889 Rear-Admiral Richard Mayne pointed out that it was inevitable that the greatest confusion would prevail during action over her ammunition supply.

> "There are made for the Naval Service something like ninety different descriptions of guns, and it is an old story now that a ship was filled with ammunition at Malta and sent off in great haste to Alexandria, and upon her arrival there it was found that only one ship had any guns which could use the ammunition brought. . . . We have now a 6-pdr. quick-firing gun and a 3-pdr. quick-firing gun. If the 3-pdr. is large enough why have the 6-pdr? If it is not large enough, why have it at all?
>
> The multiplicity of torpedo tubes is also a great mistake, and the bow tube on which so much trust has been placed, and on which so much ingenuity has been shown in cutting away the stem to place it, is worse than useless."

ARMOUR

The system of protection was very different from that in the *Conqueror*, where there was almost complete water-line armour and a central citadel. For the first time a turret base was encased in a separate redoubt which also included the foot of the conning tower, the turret being 17 in. and the redoubt 18 in. Amidships the belt covered 152 ft. and was 18 in. with 16-in. bulkheads at the ends—12 ft. longer than in the *Admirals* and a foot deeper (8½ ft.). An *end-end belt* had been considered, but it would have meant a reduction to 14 in. with 12-in. ends; to have retained the 18 in. amidships and added 12 in. continuations to bow and stern would have brought displacement to over 11,000 tons—a 500-ton increase which the Board was not prepared to countenance. Instead, the submerged 3-in. deck fore and aft with water-line subdivision as in the *Admirals* was again employed, but as the hull before and abaft the citadel was markedly tapered, the longer belt was in fact not necessary as the estimated loss of buoyancy by complete riddling of the unarmoured ends *above* the protective deck could only amount to 41 tons with a sinkage of 2 in. The effect of the admission of a considerable quantity of water below the deck may be judged from the experience in the *Sans Pareil*—whose longitudinal bulkheads forward had been removed after the sinking of the *Victoria*, early in 1901. When exercising her submerged tubes in Sheerness harbour for some unstated reason the submerged room was flooded with several hundred tons of water. The bulkheads held, a mat was got out, and the water pumped out by the ship's own appliances—the effect of the flooding being to sink the bows 3 ft.

As already noted, the sides over the battery were 3 in. with 5-in. screen bulkheads, and the conning tower 14 in. with a 2-in. top.

With a displacement percentage of 28·1 the *Sans Pareil* carried a greater proportion of armour than any other Barnaby battleship except the *Dreadnought*—and, of course, the *Cyclops* group.

MACHINERY

Triple-expansion engines by Humphreys and Tennant were installed for the first time in these ships, and both did very well on trials, developing over 500 h.p. more than the designed power at natural draught and 2,000 h.p. more with closed stokeholds. On trials the 4 hrs. mean was:

"*Sans Pareil*"	14,482 h.p. (f.d.)=17·75 knots.
"*Victoria*"	14,244 h.p. (f.d.)=17·3 knots.

and at natural draught both made 16 knots with just over 8,000 h.p.

Although of the same h.p. as the *Benbow*, there were only eight boilers instead of twelve and working at 135 lb. pressure instead of 90 lb. This allowed for four boilers aside in two compartments with an amidships ammunition passage running between them, the uptakes combining into two widely separated funnels athwartships—here introduced for the first time, although a common feature in French ships.

As completed the *Victoria* had very short funnels which did not provide much natural draught, so in July-August 1890 they were lengthened by 17 ft. The *Sans Pareil* always had high funnels.

SEA-GOING QUALITIES

With the same 12 ft. freeboard as the *Benbow* they were best suited to Mediterranean service, although in a seaway they proved steady and did not appear to suffer as much from their low freeboard as did the *Admirals*, owing to their longer forecastles. But when steaming at 17 knots even in smooth water the bow wave washed the forecastle, so that nothing like full power could be developed when driven head to sea if the turret guns were to be fought efficiently.

GENERAL

Although both ships had run their steam trials in 1888, the delay in supplying the big guns held up completion for 2 to 3 years, the *Sans Pareil* being sixteen months later than her sister. They were the last battleships to be designed by Sir Nathaniel Barnaby, and although regarded as his most successful productions any real approval they evoked seems to have been limited to a select circle of officers.

"SANS PAREIL"

Commissioned at Chatham for the manœuvres on 8 July '91, and went into Reserve at the end of August. In February '92 she was sent to the Mediterranean and there served until April '95 being then paid off into the Fleet Reserve at Sheerness as portguard ship and tender to *Wildfire*. In May '98 became an independent command as guardship and carried out this duty until December '03 excepting for a spell between April '99 and January '00 when she was under refit and relieved by *Edinburgh*. After January '04 her last years passed in the Fleet Reserve until sold on 9 April '07 for £26,000 under the Fisher scrapping policy.

"VICTORIA"

Delivered from Elswick at Chatham on 16 April '88. Completion was delayed through a fault developing in one of the big guns. Commissioned 19 March '90 as flagship Mediterranean in place of the *Camperdown*. Grounded at Snipe Point, Platea, on 29 January '92 and floated off on 4 February, during which period the ship's hammocks were never got down; she was lightened by 1,253 tons, temporary bulkheads and cofferdams built in, and finally *Edinburgh* and *Dreadnought* pulled her off. Refitted at Malta, being the first ship to enter the new Hamilton dock. Reassumed her command in May and was sunk by collision with *Camperdown* 22 June '93 with the loss of Vice-Admiral Sir Geo. Tryon, 22 officers and 336 men.

Barnaby's régime lasted through a thankless period marked by extreme growth in guns and thickness in armour which made the necessary compromises in weight and distribution more and more difficult along the lines he favoured and under the limitations in displacement imposed by the Board. During 1884 he went on sick leave prior to resignation and in his absence from Whitehall the preparation of the next pair of ships was entrusted to the Council of Construction.

BATTLESHIP DISTRIBUTION

1891

Channel	Mediterranean	North America and West Indies	Coast Guard and Reserve
Anson	*Benbow*	*Bellerophon*	*Ajax*
Camperdown	*Collingwood*		*Belleisle*
Howe	*Agamemnon*		*Hotspur*
Rodney	*Colossus*		*Northumberland*
	Edinburgh		*Neptune*
	Dreadnought		*Audacious*
	Trafalgar		*Invincible*
	Victoria		*Iron Duke*
	Inflexible		*Triumph*
	Temeraire		

Chapter 55

THE LOSS OF THE "VICTORIA"

THE Mediterranean Fleet was proceeding from Beirut to Tripoli and the collision occurred during preparatory manœuvres before anchoring off that town. The subsequent court martial did nothing to clear up the uncertainty as to why Admiral Tryon, leading the starboard division, ordered the two columns of his fleet to turn 16 points inwards from a distance of six cables only, when he had decided on eight cables—the minimum distance for safety in view of the tactical helm in force in the squadron which gave a turning diameter of 800 yards.

The ships were in two columns of line ahead steaming E. by N. and should have been at a distance of ten cables (2,000 yards) for the turning movement to have been performed which would bring them W. by S. at two cables distance—the proper interval both between ships in column and between columns for an anchoring station. But the *inward* turn was a manœuvre for which there was no diagram in the signal book, although it contained a signal for columns to wheel sixteen points *outwards*, and Tryon overcame the deficiency by the use of divisional signals:

> "Second division alter course in succession 16 points to starboard preserving the order of the fleet."
> "First division alter course in succession 16 points to port, preserving the order of the fleet."

Now Tryon was a master tactician who delighted in ordering what were regarded as complicated manœuvres which were invariably safe, but which he never explained beforehand although glad to discuss them afterwards. The captains of the fleet realized that at six cables such an inward turn would be dangerous, and Rear-Admiral Hastings Markham—leading the port column in the *Camperdown*—suspecting a mistake ordered his flag-lieutenant to make an enquiry by semaphore. But before this could be made a signal came from the Commander-in-Chief asking what the Rear-Admiral was waiting for; and Markham, thinking that something other than what he had at first imagined must be intended, and having every confidence in Tryon, ordered the signal to be acknowledged.

The *Victoria's* two signals were at once hauled down, the helms of the two flagships were put over—to the full in *Victoria*, but to 28° only instead of 35° in the *Camperdown*—and at 3.31 p.m. the short prelude to tragedy commenced. As the ships neared one another the port engine of the *Victoria* was reversed, and when about 10 points round both engines were put "full speed astern." The *Victoria* turning in a smaller circle than the *Camperdown* was slightly in advance, so that the stem of the *Camperdown* struck her on the starboard bow 10 ft. abaft the anchor at an angle of about 68°, both ships steaming at 5 to 6 knots.

The impact swung the *Victoria* nearly 70 ft. to port and the *Camperdown's* ram penetrated to 9 ft. at a depth of 12 ft. below water; then the sterns started swinging together, enlarging the breach and destroying the watertight connexion to the side plating of two important transverse bulkheads just abaft the site of collision. When the ships drew apart the breach extended some 28 ft. below the forecastle deck and 18 ft. below the water-line with an area of 100 to 110 sq. ft. As the order to close water-tight doors and hatches was not given until a minute before the collision (and normally three minutes was required for this operation), only a few had been secured before many compartments were flooded which had not been breached, and a rapid list to starboard brought the battery door under water. Steaming slowly with both screws in an endeavour to reach shallow water, the *Victoria's* main deck was 13 ft. under water as far as the battery. The forward battery door, two foremost ports and turret ports were still open, and when the ship lurched there was an inrush into the battery and through open hatchways into the hull which destroyed stability, so that the stern was raised showing the port screw above water. Then she fell over slowly to her side and with increasing rapidity turned bottom up and went down by the head at an angle of about 30° to the vertical.

The court martial at Malta did nothing to explain how Tryon could have arrived at the conclusion that six cables apart was a safe distance from which two columns of battleships could be turned inwards. But he did order and countenance such a manœuvre; and it cannot be assumed that any question of risk was entailed—since everything known of Tryon is directly opposed to the possibility of his exposing ships to needless danger—we can only suppose that either—

(*a*) The manœuvre intended was different from that which was carried out, or
(*b*) Tryon made a mistake.

(*a*) The theory that a different manœuvre was intended was put forward by Sir William Laird Clowes in a letter to *The Times* and explained at full length in *The Royal Navy*, Vol. VII, pp. 415-26. It is based on the interpretation of the words "preserving the order of the fleet" in each signal. This, Sir William contended, should be accepted in its literal meaning—*i.e.*, that when the turn had been completed the starboard column would *still be to starboard*. Only by one division turning outside the other could this have been achieved—a combined turn inwards would have *reversed* the order of the fleet. He writes:

> "I am aware that to the ordinary naval mind the direction implies no more than that the body of ships (in this case a division) to which the signal is made is to preserve its own order. What I feel is that such a direction should have been interpreted by the light of the conditions existing at the moment, and that Tryon probably anticipated that the peculiar conditions would lead his subordinates to attach to the direction the importance which, I suspect, he did."

The printed proceedings of the court martial show that the officers examined were not questioned as to what they personally understood by the words "preserving the order of the fleet," although both Rear-Admiral Markham and Captain Brackenbury of the *Edinburgh* both thought that it might be Tryon's intention to circle *outside* the second division. This was explained on the grounds that the signal to the second division had been hoisted superior and lowered first, without taking into account that Tryon would not anticipate his subordinate officer committing the solecism of crossing his bows and so had turned under full helm for Markham to circle around him. If such had really been Tryon's intention, then the collision occurred through Markham taking the inner instead of the outer circle.

The outstanding objection to this theory is that if the "order of the *fleet*" and not merely the "order of the *divisions*"—had been retained, the whole purpose of the turn would have been defeated, as its object was to place the flagship at the head of the port or inshore column when they arrived off Tripoli. The recognized position of the senior flagship would be as near to the town or its principal landing place as possible, and at Tripoli the landing place is in the western part of the bay. By "retaining the order of the *fleet*" the *Camperdown* would have occupied the leading inshore berth which the Admiral intended for the *Victoria*.

(*b*) That Tryon made a mistake is explained by Admiral Mark Kerr in *The Navy in My Time* (p. 31). He says:

> "Half-circle turns are very seldom executed, while quarter-circle turns in manœuvres are constantly made. When manœuvring the Fleet, one gets accustomed to allowing two cables of sea-room for a quarter-circle turn, and I felt sure that this was the cause of the mistake. The two lines were six cables apart. The harbour was astern of them, and they were to enter it at two cables apart. The Admiral evidently forgot for the moment that the half-turn circle required more sea-room for the inward turn of each of the leaders, which was to reverse the course the Fleet was steering, and, at the end of the turns, to leave the two lines two cables apart. If someone had happily suggested to him that he was forgetting that the turns would be half-circle and not quarter-circle, and that consequently three and a quarter cables instead of two cables would be required for each turn, and, to carry out the manœuvre the distance apart of the lines must be increased to eight and a half cables before the turns were made, all would have been well. . . . A little over a year later I met a lieutenant who had been in the *Victoria* with me, and was the officer of the watch on the bridge near the Admiral when the fatal collision occurred. I gave him my opinion of the cause of the accident as above, and he replied 'That was exactly the reason. The Admiral himself told me that that was the mistake he had made. I could not make up my mind what I would do if I was called as a witness, for we had all been told by Captain Maurice Bourke that we were to do everything to preserve Sir George's reputation. I could not make up my mind whether I was to perjure myself or not, but fortunately I was not called to give evidence.' "

Many questions both technical and material were raised by the disaster, and although the court martial could fix the responsibility for the collision, it did not feel called upon to express any opinion upon the causes for the capsizing of the *Victoria*. Not unnaturally public opinion became concerned as to the powers of resistance of our latest battleships. A ship holed amidships might well be exposed to the risk of foundering, but an impact up at the bows—where there was a close system of compartments to localize inflow—should not have resulted in catastrophe. Were the central citadel ships, with inadequate protection for half their length, all exposed to loss in this way?

As might be expected, Sir Edward Reed was only waiting for a suitable opportunity to attack an Admiralty design which had so far escaped his criticism, and in the course of a debate on the Naval Estimates in the Commons he contended that the loss of the *Victoria* was solely due to defects in design—the unarmoured ends and alleged longitudinal bulkheading—and that failure to close the water-tight doors had nothing to do with it. "An unarmoured end of a ship suffered injury and the ship went to the bottom," and he went on to name a dozen others "that were likely to capsize in a similar manner if they received like injury." He argued that if the armour had been complete it would not have been penetrated by the *Camperdown's* ram—or to a much less extent; and that the longitudinal bulkhead confined the water admitted to one side of the ship and caused her to capsize.

Although Reed never lacked the courage of his own opinions, such criticism was pure casuistry, and savoured more of the ignorant opportunist than a man of established ability. He might well have waited for more detailed knowledge of the actual conditions which caused capsizing before lowering his reputation as he did.

A full investigation based on the court martial evidence was carried out, and by calculation and experiments with models the behaviour of the ship was carefully accounted for. It was shown that the water admitted *above* the protective deck caused a loss of buoyancy of only 108½ tons, while that admitted *below* this deck accounted for 1,001½ tons, and assuming that the *Victoria* had an impenetrable belt up to her bows, the *Camperdown's* ram would still have holed the thin bottom plating below the belt, admitting the same quantity of water below the protective deck. Moreover the Report showed that there was *no* central longitudinal bulkhead[1] forward of the stokeholds and engine room—which were not affected by the collision—and that the short compartment bulkheads did not produce any marked one-sided loss of buoyancy. One of the chief causes why she listed to starboard was that open doors allowed water to find its way from bunkers above the protective deck down through the coal-shoot and so fill No. 7 bunker just before the forward starboard stokehold. This flooding and that of the compartments opened out accounted for the 20° angle of heel preceding the sudden lurch which put the battery ports under.

With a metacentric height of 5 ft. there was no lack of stability, which reached its maximum at a heel of 34½° with a full range of 67½°. Had it been possible to get the water-tight doors and ports closed in time, the ship would have remained afloat under control with a heel of 9° and able to make port under her own steam.

When the Report complete with calculations and model experiments was presented to Parliament, Reed publicly denounced the conclusions arrived at and promised to furnish a full reply which would controvert them. This promise was never fulfilled.

---

1 Nevertheless the Ship's Book of the *Sans Pareil* contains an entry relative to the removal of the longitudinal bulkhead (not specified) after the loss of the *Victoria*.

Chapter 56

"NILE" AND "TRAFALGAR"

In the last Estimates introduced by Lord Northbrook the construction of two more battleships was authorized, but no design had been approved by the Board when Mr. Gladstone resigned on 9 June 1885. Lord Salisbury accepted office although he did not command a majority in the House, and Lord George Hamilton received the First Lord's portfolio.

Pending a general election the Conservative naval policy was limited by the prospect of an early dissolution, and there could be no question of any supplementary programme of construction. In any case, the First Lord realized that, before construction on a big scale could be undertaken, vast changes would have to be made in administration both at the Admiralty and in the Royal Dockyards. Years of *laisser faire* and financial stringency had played havoc with personnel and material, the predominating influence of the Treasury having reduced the naval establishments generally so that they functioned more or less like a firm on the verge of bankruptcy.

Under the circumstances Hamilton decided that a clean sweep was a necessary preliminary to the extensive reorganization and reform he had in mind, and the Board was subjected to what could still be regarded as a routine change of the Naval Lords—but for the last time. Henceforth political considerations were to play no part in Admiralty appointments. Sir Cooper Key—who had but seven months to serve before reaching the age of retirement—went as chairman of the new Nordenfelt Company. Although leaving the Service under a cloud, he will always be remembered as a wise and conscientious administrator who had done much for scientific education during his years at Greenwich when first head of the new Naval College.

In addition to these routine changes the Chief Constructor tendered his resignation on the grounds that his health was no longer capable of sustaining his official duties and responsibilities.[1]

The new Naval Lords were Admirals Sir Arthur Hood, Sir Anthony Hoskins and Captain Codrington. Vice-Admiral Brandreth retained his position as Controller for a full term until November, when he was succeeded by Vice-Admiral William Graham.

The First Lord took an early opportunity of consulting Hood as to Barnaby's resignation, and in his own words:

> "Hood knew a great deal of the technical side of design and construction of ships. He was also a high gunnery expert. He was altogether opposed to Barnaby's theories and he strongly advised me to make an effort to bring back to the Admiralty Mr. W. H. White, who had recently left the Service to become head of Armstrong's shipbuilding yard. I made further enquiries, and found that all who knew White had a very high opinion of his capacity. To bring a public servant back into the Service as head of a department over those who had remained was an unusual procedure, and sure to lead to protest. . . . Both White and Armstrong behaved with patriotism and promptitude. White gave up a large income, and Armstrong surrendered a man who he knew to be one of the first naval architects of his time.
>
> In pushing this arrangement through I had relied upon Hood, but had forgotten to consult the Controller in whose department the Chief Constructor was. The Controller was naturally very much annoyed, but was a high-minded gentleman and he ultimately accepted my explanation that it was from inadvertence rather than intention that he had been ignored. It was just as well that I did not consult him, for the officials in his department would have made such objections that I should have had much difficulty in getting the matter through. As it was, the two Senior Constructors resigned, but as they were near the age of retirement their loss was soon made good."

He sent White a letter dated 28 July 1885:

> "Sir Nathaniel Barnaby has resigned his post, though his resignation has taken the shape of two months' leave. I shall be glad if I could secure your services as his successor.
>
> Whoever succeeds him will for years to come occupy a most prominent and responsible position, for the retirement of Mr. Rendel from the Board of Admiralty, and my determination not to fill his post, will give the Chief Constructor an authority for the future even greater than that which he occupied for the past few years.
>
> There are a number of reforms which I believe can be advantageously carried out, both in the dockyards and the Admiralty itself, and I shall personally be glad to do all I can to expedite and support any arrangements

[1] His grandson Mr. K. C. Barnaby writes: "Actually Barnaby's retirement was not really due to his illness nor was it the result of any disagreement with the Board over his designs. The real cause was that he had become extremely tired of the perpetual quarrels with his brother-in-law Reed, which were making things difficult for family relations. He was very fond of his sister and the two families were close neighbours."

which your varied experience, in dockyards and private establishments, would advocate as tending to economy, expedition, and efficiency."

It was agreed that Mr. Philip Watts should fill his place at Elswick, and White became Director of Naval Construction on 1 October 1885, with the title of Assistant Controller from 17 December 1885.

As it was customary for the preliminary designs of new ships to be evolved and discussed many months before the Estimates were presented, it may be presumed that Barnaby would have prepared sketch plans for consideration by the Northbrook Board early in 1885. Unfortunately no record of them can be traced, but we know that the type favoured had a twin turret fore and aft in separate redoubts, and quite possibly would have been very much along the lines of sketch plan "C" of 11,700 tons submitted for the *Sans Pareil*—even if this actual drawing did not again come up for consideration now that additional displacement was available.

However, during Barnaby's absence from office the new First Sea Lord cancelled the decisions of the outgoing Board, and set the Constructors to work out a design to his own specifications. The Chief Constructor was placed in a very difficult position, and wrote White on 22 August 1885 as follows:

"Replying to a note from me concerning a projected visit to the United States, Lord George Hamilton informs me that he expects me *to hand over the duties* to you at the end of two months' sick leave. This will mean that I shall be responsible for all that is done. But Morgan, under Hood's direction, is preparing the new 11,800 ton ship with a single citadel, although on the 28 July the Board had accepted a double citadel. Since I left they have issued a minute cancelling the former. If they had taken you into their confidence I should have offered no objection. I have told the First Lord that I shall, under these circumstances, resume duty until you join me, and that in the interim I shall ask you to confer with me. I have not been to the office since the 6th and had sent for all my papers, but I shall go there on Monday, and stop until you come."

A joint memorandum from Barnaby and White sent to the First Lord was in the following terms:

"Having regard to the facts hereafter stated, we are of opinion that before any new first-class armourclads are ordered it is desirable to appoint a new Committee on Designs, of which the constitution should resemble the Committee of 1871.

(1) That very wide differences of opinion prevail as to the continued use of thick vertical armour, and as to principles which should govern the distribution of protective materials on warships.

(2) That the relative advantages and disadvantages of the turret and barbette systems of mounting heavy guns may now be considered more definitely than has hitherto been possible, good examples of each type being available for inspection and trial.

(3) That new conditions have to be met owing to the rapid development of quick-firing guns, these conditions affecting not merely the structure of ships and disposition of protection, but the arrangement of the main armament.

(4) That at the present time we stand committed to an expenditure on armourclads which are as yet incomplete of £6,500,000 approx. of which say about one-half has still to be met on hull, engines, gun-mountings, etc., extending over the next four or five years. The whole building resources of the Dockyards, so far as they are available for armourclad construction, can be usefully employed in pushing forward with the greatest possible rapidity the completion of these vessels.

(5) The ordering of two such vessels as are now contemplated would amount to a further expenditure of, say, two millions in the same time.

(6) That the commencement of the work on the hulls of these vessels at an early date, while leaving open grave questions affecting armour and armament, could only lead to delay in ultimate completion. This would be especially true of a dockyard-built ship.

(7) Having today seen for the first time the drawings prepared by the Chief Constructor in accordance with the Board minute of 12 August, we are of the opinion that the type with the two citadels approved on 28 July is preferable to that approved on the 12 August with the single citadel, on the assumption that the cost of the two types is to be practically the same.

Should their Lordships decide to order these vessels to be built, we would suggest that the plans be signed by the Chief Constructors who have prepared them; and marked by Order of the Board."

Although this memorandum was described as extra-official, it was necessary to record dissent from the proposed design for future reference, and the First Lord accepted this point. But he would countenance no delay over the commencement of the two ships, and in his reply said that although improvements in them might be suggested, the delay and extra expense which constant alterations entailed more than counterbalanced the advantages they might bring—and the Dockyards needed employment!

Only two of the preliminary sketches have been preserved. That dated 8 July is presumably Hood's first reaction against "Barnaby's theories"—to revert to a type which was still regarded as the naval officer's ideal, and repeat the *Dreadnought* with heavier guns and armour while retaining her defects in having a single citadel and no secondary armament.

Apparently more enlightened opinions prevailed on 28 July and a two-citadel plan was approved by the Board although, as already mentioned, this was not preserved in the *Trafalgar* folio. But if it were the *Sans Pareil* C plan or some modification of it with more side armour to bring the displacement up to 11,800 tons, then the two-decked secondary battery being unprotected on the face must have violated Hood's own conceptions profoundly. While accepting the Board's decision he evidently decided that a compromise might be equally well received and had the *Dreadnought* design recast with the addition of an armoured secondary battery but retaining the single citadel. This was approved of on 12 August and the plans entrusted to Mr. Morgan and Mr. Crossland assisted by Constructor Allington and Assistant Constructor J. H. Cardwell.

Although the *Nile* and *Trafalgar* eclipsed any of Barnaby's productions as fighting ships, they did so only by virtue of a big increase in displacement which was almost entirely devoted to protection, and which would never have been sanctioned by previous Boards. Thus, their equipment tonnage was within 20 tons of that of the *Sans Pareil* with a fractional loss in speed, but the weight of hull and armour rose from 7,420 to 9,010 tons—so that 1,590 tons were added to the displacement to secure improved protection—an allotment which would never have been countenanced by Barnaby.

Hood had reverted to Reed's maximum standard of protection, and Barnaby and White could see to what

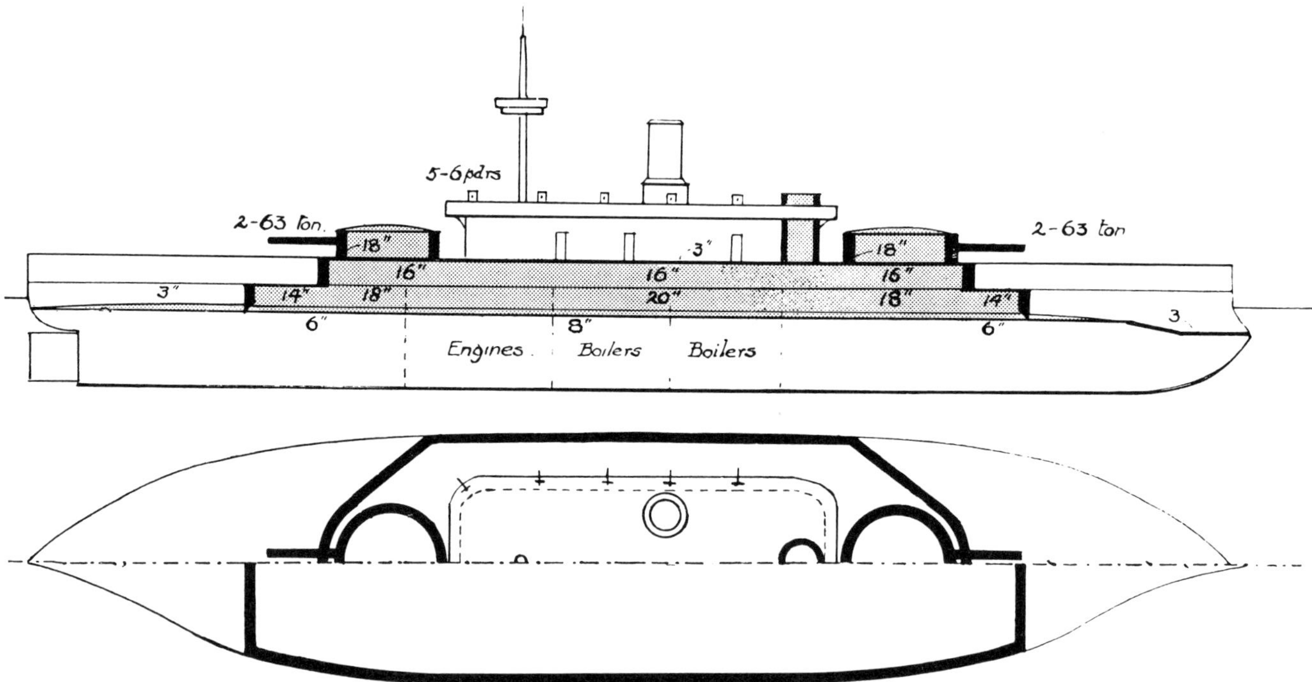

The first design for the *Trafalgar* was based upon the *Dreadnought* with 13·5-in. guns, thicker armour, and ends with a protective deck instead of belt armour.

greater advantage that increase of 2,000 tons over the *Admirals* might have been expended. Both would have employed barbettes, with separate citadels at the expense of side armour; and White would certainly have preferred greater length and more freeboard to secure a higher sea speed. The handicap of low freeboard to speed in a seaway had not as yet been realized by Hood—although White had occasion to appreciate the advantages enjoyed by French high hulled designs, so far as dry decks and clear gun sights were concerned.

However, we can accept Hamilton's insistence upon the necessity for getting more armoured tonnage into commission as justified. Whatever improvements a Committee on Designs might have introduced, the Navy was well satisfied with the ships as they were, and even after twenty years' service they could claim to be good second-line reserves.

During the time they were on the stocks the menace of the torpedo was allowed to dominate the conception of naval warfare to such an extent that battleships apparently stood for little more than helpless targets instead of being capable of destroying anything afloat. Thus, in his description of the *Trafalgar* when moving the Estimates for 1886, Mr. Hibbert (Financial Secretary to the Admiralty) indulged in prophesy to the extent of saying:

> "I may safely say that these two large ironclads will probably be the last ironclads of this type that will ever be built in this or any other country."

"NILE" and "TRAFALGAR"

	Built by	*Laid down*	*Launched*	*Completed*	*Cost*
"*Nile*"	Pembroke	8 April '86	27 March '88	10 July '91	£765,615 £885,718 total
"*Trafalgar*"	Portsmouth	18 Jan. '86	20 Sept. '87	March '90	£739,541 £859,070 total

Dimensions 345′ × 73′ × 28′/29′ = 12,590 tons (11,940 tons designed) with 27′/28′ draught. Hull and armour 9,010 tons. Equipment 3,580 tons.

Armament 4 13·5-in. 67-ton.
6 4·7-in. Q.F. (later 6-in. Q.F.)
8 6-pdrs.
9 3-pdrs.
Torpedo tubes (1890).
1 bow and stern.
2 submerged.
2 above water.

Armour (compound) Belt 20″ amidships tapering to 14″ at the ends and 8″-6″ at lower edge; bulkheads 16″ ford. 14″ aft; main citadel 18″-16″; bulkheads 18″.
Turrets 18″; conning tower 14″; battery bulkheads 5″, side 4″; deck throughout 3″; skin $2\frac{1}{2}$″-$1\frac{3}{4}$″; backing 10″-4″.
Total 4,226 tons (33·5 per cent.).

Complement 577.

Coal 900-1,200 tons.

Machinery "*Nile*" by Maudslay; "*Trafalgar*" by Humphreys.
Two sets of triple exp. H.P. 7,500 = 15·1 knots.
F.D. 12,000 H.P. = 16·75 knots.
6 cylindrical boilers.

Radius 1,050 miles at 16·25 knots.
6,500 miles at 10 knots.

Points of interest:

(1) The last single citadel turret ships to be built.
(2) The first British battleships to carry a quick-firing secondary armament.
(3) The heaviest British battleships to date, and carrying the highest percentage of armour to displacement.

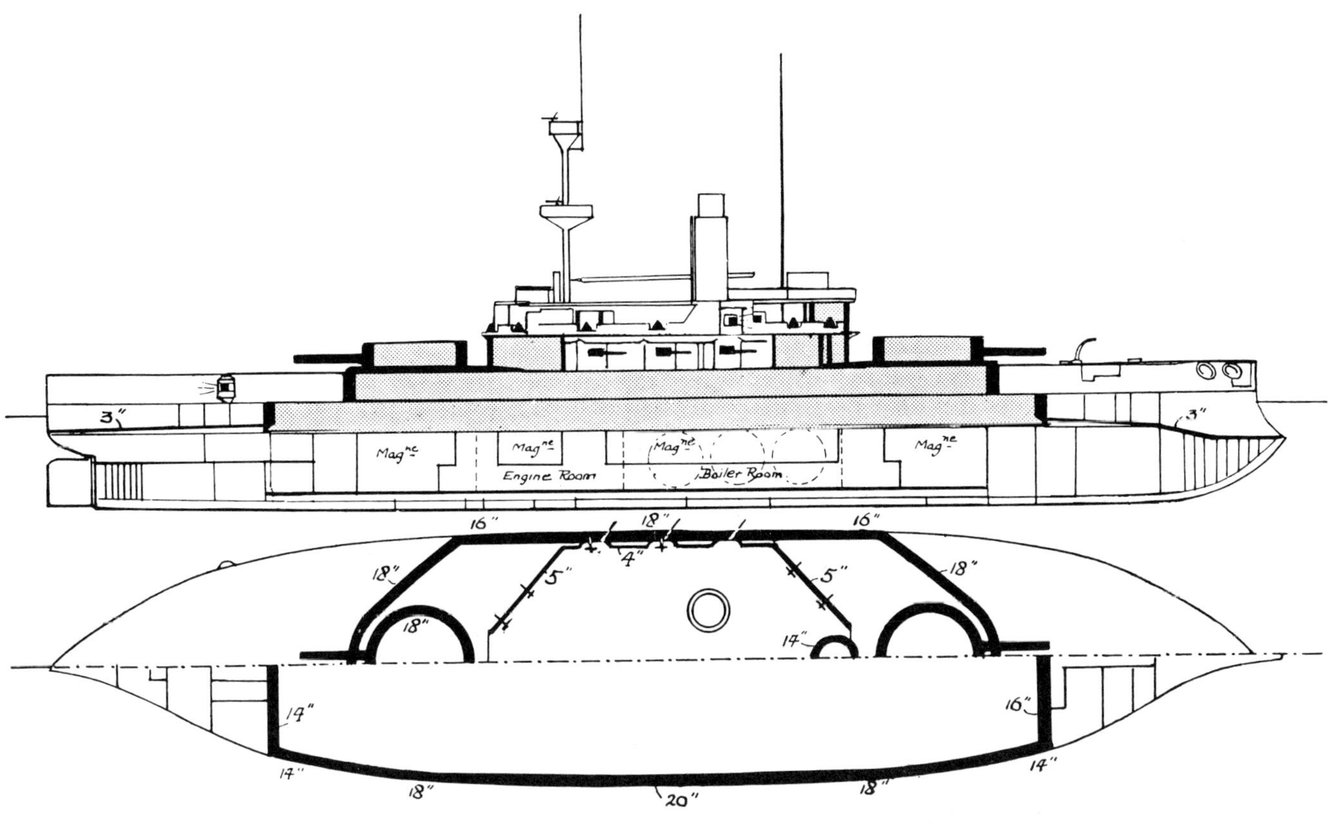

NILE

However, the eclipse of the battleship was not to be achieved for another sixty years, and in March 1889 the First Lord explained that:

> "I had hoped some two years ago that the *Nile* and *Trafalgar* would be the last battleships laid down in this country. It then appeared as if there was to be a general cessation of armourclad building owing to the appearance of the torpedo boats. But the powers of these torpedo boats had been greatly exaggerated by naval officers. France suspended her battleship building and other nations followed her example; but since then, owing in part to the invention of quick-firing guns, there has been a return to the building of battleships."

As originally designed these ships were to have been of 11,940 tons displacement with a secondary battery of ten 5-in. B.L. and the upper edge of the citadel 11 ft. above water, but modifications during construction took the displacement to 12,590 tons and added a foot to the draught. With full bunkers they would have been down another 6 in. Although the change in armament was all to the good, it served to focus attention on the very undesirable practice of introducing extensive alterations or additions during construction to which nearly every ship was subjected to some extent. As these almost invariably resulted in increased displacement the Board

The *Trafalgar* as she first appeared with short funnels and a 4·7-in. gun battery in 1890. The next year her funnels were raised by 17 ft. and the battery changed to 6 in. Q.F. in '96.

directed that in future what was to be known as a "Board margin" of 4 per cent. of the displacement was to be included in the legend tonnage to allow for such contingencies.

HULL FORM

Below water the hull lines were slightly finer than in the *Sans Pareil* with more cutaway under the ram and a larger rudder. Owing to the much shorter forecastle the lack of freeboard caused greater inconvenience in a seaway, but as both ships spent their active service careers in the Mediterranean this was minimized.

ARMAMENT

Although 14 ft. above water the horizontal axis of the turret guns was only 3½ ft. above deck, and as it was considered quite possible that the decks would be severely damaged if they were fired directly fore and aft, White insisted that battle tests should be carried out and the matter settled. Full charge rounds were therefore fired direct ahead with 3° of elevation, and the only injury worth recording was a depression of about 2 in. in the deck near the water ridge, bending a beam below and fracturing one of the stanchions on the forward mess deck.

Improvements in the handling and control of the hydraulic gear and mountings greatly facilitated loading arrangements, and on trials four rounds were fired singly in nine minutes; eight could have been loosed off in the same time had the guns been worked as a pair. With a practised crew it was accepted that the firing time could be regarded as two minutes only.

As designed the secondary armament was to have been eight 5-in. B.L., but the success of the Elswick 4·7-in. Q.F. with its long range, rapidity of fire and accuracy of aim justified its adoption in place of the larger B.L., and six were substituted in January 1890. The eight B.L. weighed 135 tons, while the extra ammunition for the Q.F. brought the weight of the new battery up to 185 tons. Ten rounds were fired from each of the port guns in an average of 1 minute 20 seconds for the ten—and forthwith the torpedo menace began to assume its proper proportions.

In October 1896 the *Trafalgar* was given six 6-in. Q.F. in their place, the *Nile* being similarly rearmed during the following year. Submerged tubes were added to both ships in August 1890.

The *Nile* could be distinguished by her taller funnels which extended beyond the casings. In 1904 she was in the commissioned Reserve and took part in the manœuvres. Over her stern is the cruiser *Blake*.

ARMOUR

The *Trafalgar* had the highest percentage of armour to displacement of any British battleship except the *Glatton*, some comparative figures being:

	Displacement	*Armour*	*Per cent.*
Dreadnought	10,820	3,257	33
Glatton	4,910	1,743	35
Collingwood	9,500	2,575	27
Victoria	10,470	2,950	28
Nile	12,590	4,226	33·5

The belt was 230 ft. long—68 ft. longer than in the *Sans Pareil*—and 20 in. (thinning to 8 in. at the lower edge $5\frac{1}{2}$ ft. below water) amidships tapering through 16 in. to 14 in. (with 6 in. lower edges) beyond the turrets.

The end bulkheads were 16 in. forward and 14 in. aft. There was a submerged deck in place of the *Dreadnought's* belt at the extreme ends, the hull being so fined that but little extra immersion would have resulted from flooding.

Above the belt came the citadel 192 ft. long, with 16-in. side plating amidships, 18-in. across and around the turret bases, and covered by a 3-in. deck—the single citadel to which Barnaby and White had objected. Owing to their low freeboard the possibility of deck hits were regarded as a matter of some moment and 3-in. steel was not much protection although as much as could be afforded.

When rolling 10° from the vertical, the ships would present a deck target having a vertical projected height of 13 to 14 ft. four or five times a minute, perforation of which might involve serious damage to the turret bases and loading apparatus. But the risk of both turrets being put out of action by heavy shell perforation was minimized by internal armoured traverses.

The secondary battery had 4-in. sides and 5-in. angled ends, with the guns in slight sponsons and firing through a curved shield.

MACHINERY

Being fitted with engines of the same power as the *Sans Pareil* although of some 2,120 tons greater displacement, they were not expected to equal her in speed, although *Trafalgar* made 15·1 knots under natural draught and 17·2 knots with closed stokeholds. But she piled up such a bow wave when at full speed, even in calm water, that there was no question of a sea speed of anything like this. Actually the hull lines were admirably moulded for the maximum speed intended (16½ knots) but not for more, especially with a freeboard of only 11¾ ft.

The *Nile* developed a maximum of 10,112 h.p. at natural draught, but the speed was not taken; at forced draught she averaged 12,102 h.p. and 16·8 to 17 knots. But with a wind of only force 3 to 4 and not sufficient sea to lift the ship when steaming down Channel, the forecastle was always awash with clouds of spray breaking over the turret.

The *Trafalgar* was completed with very short funnels like the *Victoria*. These were deficient in natural draught, so 17 ft. was added to them in April 1891, the estimated increase in draught being $\frac{1}{16}$ in. for every 10 ft. in height. The *Nile* had not been put into commission when this change was made, and in her the casings ended considerably short of the caps, giving her a very characteristic difference from her sister.

"TRAFALGAR"

Dockyard re-organization greatly curtailed the building period and the ship was officially stated to have been completed in the unprecedentedly short time of three and a quarter years. Actually she was kept waiting for her guns and was not ready for service until March '90 being commissioned on 2 April as 2nd Flagship Mediterranean where she remained for seven years. Paid off October '97 at Portsmouth and became port guardship until August '02; then derated to Fleet Reserve A, and in September '03 to Dockyard Reserve. In April '05 transferred to Reserve Fleet, Devonport, and in March '07 to Sheerness where she served as turret and submerged tube drill-ship for two years until replaced by *Vengeance* in April '09 when she reverted to 4th Division Home Fleet at the Nore.

Sold 9 March 1911 for £29,500.

"NILE"

Was ready for trials in July '90, but as guns and mountings had not been delivered she had to run them in ballast. Commissioned at Portsmouth 30 June '91 for manœuvres, after which she went to the Mediterranean to replace *Benbow* and remained up the Straits until January '98 when she became portguard ship at Devonport. In February '03 joined the Dockyard Reserve and then commissioned in Reserve March '03. When the Home Fleet was formed she was given a nucleus crew and joined the 4th Division at Devonport; in June '11 was relegated to the E Division and put on the sale list.

Sold 9 July '12 for £34,900.

These ships were best suited to the Mediterranean, where they passed their active service, and suffered less from reduced freeboard than when relegated to Home Service. As fighting ships they commanded the highest esteem, and for use up the Straits the writer has heard them preferred to the *Royal Sovereigns* on account of their small target and massive protection.

Chapter 57

SIR WILLIAM WHITE

Director of Naval Construction 1886–1903

William Henry White was born at Drews Cottage, Devonport, on 2 February 1845, being nominated to the entrance examination at the Dockyard in 1859, when his inability to reach the required standard in height was overcome by the aid of folded blotting paper in his boots. Having satisfied the examiners in March, he commenced work as an apprentice on 1 July aged 14 at a wage of three shillings a week, being first employed on the line-of-battle-ship *St. George*, then undergoing conversion to steam. Gaining an Admiralty scholarship in 1863, he was selected as a candidate to the recently opened Royal School of Naval Architecture at South Kensington, having headed the list of students from all the Yards—which position he held throughout the course.

His first employment took him back to Devonport in 1865, and then to Chatham the following year—first as an additional and later as a third-class draughtsman, working on structural details in the *Bellerophon* and *Hercules*. When his apprenticeship terminated and he passed out of the School, he entered the Admiralty and was employed drawing up specifications of ships with the calculations and estimates of weight and speed as preliminaries to design. Very soon he became personal and confidential secretary to Mr. E. J. Reed until his resignation in 1870, when he continued to act for Mr. Barnaby, who became President of the Council of Construction. In November 1870 he was appointed Instructor on Naval Design at Kensington, and in 1872 became Secretary to the Council of Construction. From that date until 1883 there was no work done by the Admiralty designing staff in which he did not play a large or in many cases a leading part. Between 1872-3 he supervised the work at Pembroke Dockyard, including the redesigning of the *Fury*, and then being transferred to Portsmouth became supervisor to the *Inflexible*. After the loss of the *Captain* in 1870 he and Mr. W. John were placed in charge of the stability calculations required by the Committee on Designs, and found it necessary not only to make a considerable extension of known methods but to devise new ones in explaining the behaviour of ships under steam and canvas in a wind and a seaway.

In March 1875 he became Assistant Constructor, and was married in the same year. His *Manual of Naval Architecture* published at this time became a world-wide classic, and in 1880 he submitted a memorandum recommending the formation of a Royal Corps of Naval Constructors which was established by Order in Council in August 1883.

White left the Admiralty in 1882 to enter the employment of Sir Wm. Armstrong, Mitchell and Co. as Warship Designer and manager of their warship construction branch, and for the next three years became responsible for the early Elswick cruisers. On the resignation of Sir Nathaniel Barnaby he again entered the Admiralty as D.N.C. when 40 years of age. His first duty was to draw up a scheme for reorganization at the Admiralty, the Dockyards, and the various staffs, with the rank of Assistant Controller. In 1888, when the agitation for a Naval Defence Act was reaching its climax, he produced his revolutionary designs for the barbette ships of the *Royal Sovereign* class from which were developed the *Majestics* and all the subsequent types associated with his name, together with their contemporary protected and armoured cruisers. The outstanding features of White ships were barbette mountings, high freeboard, wide distribution of armour with a deeply curved protection deck, and casemate protection for the secondary armament associated with main deck batteries.

On 3 July 1900 catastrophe darkened his wonderful career when the new Royal yacht *Victoria and Albert*, successfully launched the previous year, heeled over in dock during her completion. Although a perfectly designed vessel with every allowance for ample stability, she had been overloaded with absurdly heavy fittings on and above the upper deck without White's knowledge, so that the Report made after her launch was entirely untrustworthy in regard to the estimation of weights to be added before completion. In addition she had been floated in dock with almost empty bunkers and water in only three boilers when in an unstable condition with a small negative metacentric height.

As D.N.C. White accepted full responsibility and all the blame, although the culprit was Mr. W. E. Smith, Chief Constructor at Pembroke, who had immediate supervision of the design and calculations. When the necessary adjustments of weights had been carried out the yacht fulfilled every expectation in speed, behaviour at sea, stability and comfort, serving the Sovereign for forty years without fault.

But shock, the sense of disgrace to a man who had made his reputation by original work and calculations on stability, and rancour shown by Parliament and press, brought on a nervous breakdown. After a Report from a Committee which investigated the accident the Board's decision was that:

> Their Lordships are of opinion that you committed a very serious error in judgment in not sufficiently impressing upon your subordinates the novelty and importance of the task entrusted to them, and in not satisfying yourself that the instructions issued by you for the guidance of your department were being complied with.

In April 1901 White submitted proposals for the *King Edward VII*, his last design for a battleship. But by the time the final drawings were completed he had left the Admiralty, and the plans were formally signed by his successor Mr. Philip Watts. During the past year he had been really unfit for work, and wearied his staff by lack of decision and constant worrying about trivial matters, so that loyalty gave way to a change in feeling which slowly hardened into resentment. On 30 October he sent in his letter asking for retirement and the official announcement that he had retired was made on 6 December.

His last day of office was 31 January 1902, when, after sitting alone for some time, he went into the room of his senior assistants and said, "I am going now. Good-bye to you all!" But no one rose from his seat, and there were no farewell handshakes. He turned and walked down the stairs alone, and it was only his old messenger who came forward and said, "May I shake your hand, Sir William, and say how sorry I am you are so ill as to be obliged to leave us!"

And so he passed from the scene of his labours, his triumphs, and fall, a broken-hearted, disappointed and worn-out man.

During the next few years he travelled extensively in the U.S.A. and Canada. At home his contributions to the lay and technical press were voluminous, and mainly in support of the antagonists to the *Dreadnought* and *Invincible*. He could see the huge fleet he had created threatened with speedy obsolescence by ships which he considered too big and costly, vulnerable to torpedo attack, and lacking the 6-in. batteries which he held were necessary for inter-ship actions. One of his seventy-odd letters to Admiral Sir Reginald Custance will suffice to show his opinion of the new designs:

> ". . . I know all about *Invincible's* armour and think it will be worse than you say when she is deep-laden. 12-in. guns with 7-in. barbette armour do not commend themselves to me.
>
> I agree with you about *Dreadnought* armament. The disposition is viciously bad. About her manœuvring and stopping powers, I have heard conflicting accounts, her great weight and very fine form and features influencing her behaviour."

On 27 February 1913 Sir William had a stroke at his office in Victoria Street and died the same evening.

The White Era was the very antithesis to that of Barnaby. In place of a motley assortment of entirely different types of turret and barbette ships of which not one could be selected as the type of battleship for the future, White produced a barbette ship which fulfilled all requirements and set an entirely new fashion in armament and protection, high freeboard and a noble profile.

Sir William was a Fellow of the Royal Society; Vice-President of the Institution of Naval Architects; Past President of the Institutions of Civil Engineers, Mechanical Engineers, Marine Engineers, and the Institute of Metals, and President-Elect of the British Association; Honorary Member of the American Society of Mechanical Engineers, of Civil Engineers, of Naval Architects and Marine Engineers, and numerous other foreign bodies. The high esteem in which he was held may well be summed up by the judgment of Sir Henry Campbell-Bannerman, a former Secretary of the Admiralty and later Prime Minister, who once said that he knew three "men," and coupled the name of Sir William White with those of two of the noblest public servants of the day.

Chapter 58

THE "RESISTANCE" EXPERIMENTS AND THE NAVAL DEFENCE ACT

WHEN the new Board took office the armoured ships already in hand included eleven battleships and seven belted cruisers, plus the *Nile* and *Trafalgar* of the 1885 Estimates, and the immediate necessity was not so much a nominal increase in the numerical superiority of the battle fleet, as increased efficiency in the Dockyards to bring about accelerated construction. The block in heavy gun production at Woolwich was also made an urgent matter so that no future delays would hold up completion. Drastic reduction of wasted expenditure in maintaining a lot of obsolete ships was also to be effected, as the Navy List was cluttered up by too many slow and poorly armed small craft long overdue for replacement by faster and well-armed gunboats suitable for the manifold duties they were called upon to perform on distant stations.

So far as battleships were concerned our position was strong enough despite the imposing array of French armoured ships. Some twenty-eight of these had wooden hulls without water-tight compartments, and actually only ten sea-going units were acknowledged as being available in the Report on the Estimates for 1886 presented to the Chamber of Deputies. Moreover their new construction was proceeding at an even more leisurely rate than our own, the percentage towards completion being:

	Commenced		*Completed*
Requin	1878	7,200 tons (90 per cent.)	1885
Formidable	1879	11,441 „ (85 „ „)	1889
Neptune	1880	10,581 „ (45 „ „)	1892
Hoche	1881	10,650 „ (56 „ „)	1890
Magenta	1881	10,581 „ (38 „ „)	1892
Marceau	1881	10,581 „ (48 „ „)	1891

Not that not a single ironclad laid down during Lord Northbrook's term of office had as yet been launched.

With the exception of *Lord Warden* and *Repulse* all our wooden ironclads had been discarded, but the early broadside ships were now obsolete and due for replacement. However, before undertaking the extensive programme which was now very definitely indicated, the various problems raised by the introduction of secondary batteries and new explosives as well as the development of torpedo warfare had to be investigated. Even the continued existence of the heavily armoured battleship was being questioned, and although the *Trafalgar* certainly put an end to the "10,000 ton limit" which had so hampered our constructors for years and provided a type which found favour afloat, it looked as if she might be the last of her line. With the triumph of attack over defence, design was in a transitional stage. It was seriously contended that some other type of capital ship would have to be evolved in which speed and gun power on a smaller displacement, relying upon cellular and deck protection rather than masses of armour for flotation, would permit of a larger number of ships being built for the same expenditure.

"RESISTANCE" EXPERIMENTS AUGUST 1886

As a step towards the solution of these problems the old ironclad *Resistance* was selected as a target ship, and White was present at the first series of experiments in which she was subjected to gunfire from various calibres against special armour plates and coal-bunker defence as well as to torpedoes and high explosives. The results were never fully divulged, but they served to clear up many outstanding questions and guided White in formulating the designs for the Naval Defence Act battleships and cruisers which he was called upon to prepare in a year or so.

As the same sort of problems were affecting capital ship construction abroad, our position was not jeopardized by the delay; and these attacks on the *Resistance*—which were continued for some years until the ship was a tattered shell—furnished an insight into battle conditions which resulted in the designs of British ships being raised to levels of incomparable superiority in both attack and defence over their Continental contemporaries.

DOCKYARD REFORM

During 1885 White took in hand the reorganization of the Dockyards which in 1884 had been reported as only suitable for repairing work, but a few years later were to become the cheapest and most expeditious building yards in the world. Until various reforms had been carried out new construction was to be restricted to small cruisers and sloops. He also stressed the unfortunate results of the fundamentally unsound policy of restricting the annual votes for ships being built which led to delay, waste and excessive overhead charges and showed that votes should be increased by at least 50 per cent.

GLADSTONE'S GOVERNMENT. 1886

In the General Election of 1886 Mr. Gladstone was again returned to power. He placed the Marquess of Ripon in charge of the Admiralty and made Sir Edward Reed a Lord of the Treasury, the Board including:

Admiral Lord John Hay, K.C.B.
Vice-Admiral Sir Anthony Hoskins, K.C.B.
Vice-Admiral W. Graham (Controller).
Captain J. E. Erskine.

This Government lasted only six months before being defeated on the Home Rule Bill in June, but as the First Lord gallantly withstood all pressure to reduce the Estimates, the policy of the previous Board could be continued during that short period.

RETURN OF LORD SALISBURY: 1886

The July elections returned Lord Salisbury as premier, and Lord George Hamilton resumed his labours at Whitehall. The Sea Lords were:

Admiral Sir Arthur Hood, K.C.B.
Vice-Admiral Sir Anthony Hoskins, K.C.B.
Vice-Admiral W. Graham (Controller).
Captain Lord Charles Beresford.

The outstanding event in this Administration was the Naval Defence Act of 1889 by which seventy ships were added to the Fleet at a cost of £21,500,000—a far larger programme of construction than the First Lord visualized and beyond anything the Board had imagined to be necessary. Cooper Key had foreseen a period of difficulty ahead, but anticipated that a *regular yearly increment* of new ships would avert this. Instead of which, no battleships were provided between 1885 and 1889 because of the (1) necessity for preparing the Dockyards for the faster construction of larger ships, and (2) problems affecting design of battleships.

Certainly the *Sans Pareil* was *pour rire* as representing any justification for the delays of the Northbrook Board on this second account; the *Trafalgar* exhibited defects which if not apparent to Hood were obvious to White; and the latter realized that it would need experimental proof of the soundness of his convictions before they could be accepted and the new ships modelled accordingly.

On the financial side Lord George Hamilton was exceedingly fortunate in having Mr. W. H. Smith as First Lord of the Treasury and Mr. Goschen as Chancellor of the Exchequer, both having held office as First Lord and quite ready to provide the necessary funds to put the Fleet upon an effective footing. No First Lord had been favoured with such Treasury support since Sir James Graham during the Crimean War.

Shortly after joining the Board Beresford drew up a Memorandum on War Organization calling attention to the immediate necessity for creating a Naval Intelligence Department which should also be charged with War Staff duties. He showed that there was no real organization for war; that personnel was far below requirements and stores were sadly deficient; that there was no arrangements for the control of merchant shipping, transport of coal, ammunition or stores, and a lack of hospital ships. And that whereas in the past the old Navy Board had been responsible for the provision of all matters of supply, leaving the Lords Commissioners free to conduct war, now with the Navy Board abolished the Naval Lords were wholly occupied with routine business arising from the peace organization.

The Memorandum was laid before the Board, who came to the unanimous conclusion that the statements were exaggerated, and that as a Junior the Fourth Lord was meddling with high matters not his business. Beresford, however, obtained permission to show the memorandum to Lord Salisbury, who after making enquiries from three Admirals accepted it *in toto*. The Naval Intelligence Department was formed, but the War Staff proposal was dropped and did not become carried into effect until 1912.

On 13 October 1886 the substance of this confidential memorandum was published in the *Pall Mall Gazette*, having been stolen by an Admiralty messenger, who was afterwards trapped and brought to trial.

In December 1886 the Chancellor of the Exchequer, Lord Randolph Churchill, resigned as a protest against extravagance and waste in the Services, and Mr. Goschen received his portfolio.

The efficiency of the Fleet was now bound up with the efficiency of the new Intelligence Department, and towards the end of 1887 the First Lord thought fit to cut down the salaries of the head officers, Captains W. H. Hall, R. N. Custance and S. M. Eardley-Wilmot, by £950—a breach of faith which reacted against the Department and had far-reaching consequences. As a protest to this and in order to force the hand of the authorities to undertake reorganization and adequate strengthening of the Fleet, Beresford resigned from the Board on 9 January 1888 and embarked upon his crusade both in the House and throughout the country for a larger, better equipped and properly organized Fleet.

STARTING-POINT OF THE NAVAL DEFENCE ACT

The Estimates for 1886-87 authorized the construction of small cruisers and sloops—and one experimental torpedo-gunboat, the *Sharpshooter*. The following year White took the initiative in submitting a Report showing the probable waste of the Navy during the years 1888-92, with a list of the ships he would propose to lay down at once and necessary new construction for the next four years—an outline for the proposed reconstruction programme based upon replacement of obsolete vessels of all types. The total net reduction in numbers was seventy-two ships valued at £7,500,000 (which included the five *Audacious* class), and White assumed that a similar number would replace them with a total outlay on hulls and engines of £9,000,000. If the *Audacious* quintette were retained the outlay would be £7,500,000.

Actually when it came to writing off the old ships and removing such a display of names from the Navy List the Board jibbed, and between April 1889 and April 1894 the only deletions were:

4 battleships (*Defence*, *Hector*, *Valiant*, *Warrior*)
8 wooden cruisers
8 wooden sloops
10 gun vessels

so that the new programme materialized as additions rather than merely replacements. The *Audacious* class actually served to swell the Return until 1900, and most of the early ironclads were re-boilered and "modernized."

This Report of White's may be regarded as the genesis of the Naval Defence Act of 1889. Armed with his figures and tables, the First Lord saw the Controller and First Sea Lord and put this summing-up of the situation before the "Select Committee of the House of Commons on the Naval Estimates for 1888" which sat in June of that year. He told them that although financial considerations were necessarily the basis of all proposals for a shipbuilding programme, the paramount considerations were the requirements of the Navy; that the list was not a grandiose table of additions to the Fleet, but merely of ships which would take the place of those in various categories deemed obsolete by 1892. But when it came to enquiry as to the basis upon which the necessary strength of the Fleet came to be calculated Hood stated that "never in the whole course of his experience had he known of a scheme comprehending the naval requirements of the Empire to be laid before the Board." The method of preparing the Estimates was for the First Lord to state what sum of money the Cabinet felt disposed to grant for the Navy, leaving it to the Naval Lords to get as much value as they could through an administration which was neither economical nor efficient. That the Board was not seriously perturbed about our weakness at sea may be gathered from Admiral Hood having also stated that he "would have preferred by the end of 1890 to have had six more fast cruisers, but did not consider it a point of vital importance." But having admitted that no comprehensive scheme for the Empire's requirements had ever been considered, his estimate was perhaps a little haphazard. The First Lord, however, stated that he was satisfied with the relative superiority of the Navy, and had the support of his naval advisers.

On Beresford's resignation Rear-Admiral Hotham was appointed to his seat, and in July 1888, immediately before the Manœuvres, the Naval Lords were asked *to make a confidential report on the requirements of the Fleet in case of a war with France*, stating what force would be required to protect our coasts against invasion or bombardment, and Malta and Gibraltar if they were attacked; what force would be required to afford reasonable protection to trade routes and relief to coaling stations if attacked; and finally, what force would be necessary in a war with France and Russia should it be necessary to defend Constantinople.

Having dealt with the strategic problems, the Naval Lords proposed a programme of construction to be spread over five years which should include sixty-five ships—eight first-class and two second-class battleships; eight large cruisers of 19½ knots; twenty-five second-class cruisers; four third-class cruisers; and eighteen torpedo-gunboats. The total cost for hull and engines alone was estimated at £14,500,000 with an annual expenditure of £700,000. There was also this very important corollary:

> "That the shipbuilding programme will be further considered not later than 1892-3, with a view to prevent any discontinuity in new construction, and more especially to provide for the laying-down of new ships in the Dockyards early in 1893-4; so that proper employment may be found for the men as the ships of the Special Programme pass out of hand."

So far discussion on the new programme had been confined to the Admiralty. In his *Memoirs* Beresford recalls that during November 1888, when Mr. Goschen had expressed disapproval at his line of action, he told him he was going to ask for seventy ships to cost 20 million sterling. The Chancellor said that this was preposterous and that he wouldn't get even three ships if he asked for them—*as they were not wanted!* Which may be taken as a fair indication of the Cabinet's outlook in that month.

On 13 December Lord Charles challenged the Shipbuilding, Maintenance and Repair vote in the House and forcibly drew attention to the shortcomings of Admiralty policy, expounding his own programme, which was to include four large and ten smaller ironclads, forty cruisers of different classes, and torpedo craft—seventy vessels in all, to be built at a cost of £20,100,000.

Hamilton received these proposals with caution. He was far from saying that the Fleet was strong enough, and told the House that during the next year he hoped to lay before them a larger and more comprehensive programme than was provided by the current Estimates, "desiring that when they moved, their movement should be genuine and prolonged."

During February 1889 the Report on the Manœuvres of 1888, which had been entrusted to Admirals Sir William Dowell, K.C.B., Sir R. Vesey Hamilton, K.C.B., and Vice-Admiral Sir Frederick Richards, K.C.B., was presented to both Houses. It was a masterly document which extended far beyond its terms of reference. Besides criticizing the performance of various classes of ships, it formulated the principles of British sea power and definitely affirmed the absolute necessity for establishing and maintaining a Two-Power Standard. It reported that the Fleet was "altogether inadequate to take the offensive in a war with only one Great Power," and that "supposing a combination of two Powers to be allied as her enemies, the balance of maritime strength would be against England." The gravity of this Report could not be ignored, although the Board attempted to mitigate its effect before publishing it as a White Paper. Sir Arthur Hood preferred to traverse its opinions as regards the utility of certain types of ships at sea; the First Lord attempted to show that our deficiency was more apparent than real, and due to exceptional causes unlikely to recur—altogether an ineffective and injudicious defence.

Of course the position taken up by the Board may have been just a political manœuvre—an apparent reluctance to accept the verdict of the Three Admirals in order to harden the pressure which Parliament and the country were bringing to bear upon the Treasury. The Conservatives had accused the Liberals of neglecting our defences in 1884, and if they could be induced to retort in favour of a large naval programme, then the responsibility for a rise in the Income Tax could be divided. Certainly after three years of silent work the administration reforms had been carried into effect and the new organization was ready. The Admiralty was prepared; the Dockyards were properly equipped for a spectacular showing when the ships were ordered; and all the critics, the Three Admirals, Lord Charles Beresford, Lord Brassey and the indefatigable Sir Edward Reed may just have been flogging a willing horse. But the prime effect was that on 7 March 1889 Lord George Hamilton introduced the Naval Defence Act, and provided for the construction of seventy ships between 1889 and 1894, including:

7 *Royal Sovereign* class battleships		14,150 tons
1 *Hood* ,,		14,150 ,,
2 *Centurion* class ,,		10,500 ,,
9 *Edgar* class large cruisers	(*circa*)	7,700 ,,
8 *Astraea* class ,,		4,360 ,,
21 *Apollo* class ,,		3,400 ,,
4 *Pallas* class ,,		2,575 ,,
18 *Sharpshooter* class torpedo gunboats		735 ,,

The total cost was to be £21,500,000 of which £10,000,000 was special expenditure out of the Consolidated Fund, to be spread over the seven years ending 31 March 1896 to defray the cost of thirty-two ships built by contract; and £11,000,000 to be included in the naval votes for the next five years ending 31 March 1894 in payment for thirty-eight ships allotted to the Dockyards.

The actual relative strengths of the British, French and Russian Fleets in armoured ships of consequence may best be judged from the following lists. A number of ancient and obsolete vessels have been omitted, including the French *Flandre* and *Alma* classes, and a lot of French and Russian harbour-defence monitors and armoured gunboats which merely provided imposing names for nominal returns as their most valuable feature.

BATTLESHIPS—I

England (22)		France (14)	Russia (7)
Nile	*Colossus*	*Marceau*	*D. Apostoloff*
Trafalgar	*Ajax*	*Magenta*	*Sinope*
Victoria	*Agamemnon*	*Neptune*	*Tchesme*
Sans Pareil	*Inflexible*	*Hoche*	*Ekaterina II*
Benbow	*Alexandra*	*Formidable*	*Pedr Veliki*
Anson	*Dreadnought*	*A. Baudin*	*Alexander II*
Rodney	*Devastation*	*Caiman*	*Nicolai I*
Howe	*Thunderer*	*Indomitable*	
Camperdown	*Temeraire*	*Terrible*	
Collingwood	*Superb*	*Requin*	
Edinburgh	*Neptune*	*Devastation*	
		Courbet	
		A. Duperré	
		Redoubtable	

BATTLESHIPS—II

England (15)		France (7)	Russia (1)
Sultan	*Triumph*	*Ocean*[1]	*Gangut*
Penelope	*Hercules*	*Marengo*[1]	
Hero	*Bellerophon*	*Suffren*[1]	
Conqueror	*Northumberland*	*Friedland*	
Audacious	*Minotaur*	*Colbert*[1]	
Invincible	*Agincourt*	*Trident*[1]	
Iron Duke	*Achilles*	*Richelieu*[1]	
Swiftsure			

ARMOURED CRUISERS

England (13)		France (7)	Russia (8)
Warspite	*Immortalite*	*Duguesclin*	*V. Monomakh*
Imperieuse	*Narcissus*	*Vauban*	*D. Donskoi*
Nelson	*Orlando*	*Turenne*[1]	*G. Edinbourski*
Northampton	*Undaunted*	*Bayard*	*G. Admiral*
Shannon	*Warrior*	*Victorieuse*[1]	*Ad. Nachimoff*
Aurora	*Black Prince*	*Triumphant*[1]	*Pamiat Azova*
Galatea		*Galissonniere*[1]	*Kniaz Pojarski*
			Minin

COAST DEFENCE

England (11)		France (6)	Russia (7)
Belleisle	*Hydra*	*Furieux*	*Ad. Chichagoff*
Orion	*Rupert*	*Tonnant*	*Ad. Greig*
Glatton	*Scorpion*	*Tonnerre*	*Ad. Lazareff*
Gorgon	*Wivern*	*Vengeur*	*Ad. Spiridoff*
Cyclops	*Hotspur*	*Fulminant*	*Charodeika*
Hecate		*Tempete*	*Rusalka*
			Smertch

[1] Wooden hulls.

Chapter 59

THE GENESIS OF THE "ROYAL SOVEREIGN"

WHILE on holiday after an accident in August 1888 White was recalled to meet the Board at Devonport and directed to prepare designs for an improved *Trafalgar* with a freeboard of 11½ ft. There was to be the same main armament but with the guns 2 ft. higher and the turrets 2 ft. deeper; a secondary battery of ten 6-in. guns, and as many 3-pdrs. and machine guns as could be placed. Protection was to follow *Trafalgar* in thickness and disposition. Speed, however, was to be raised to 17 knots (n.d.) with a coal supply for 7,000 miles at 10 knots and bunkerage 25 per cent. above normal complement.

This would represent Hood's ideal battleship without consideration of size and cost, and in complying with these directions White submitted alternative designs and a memorandum in which he criticized both *Trafalgar* and this improved edition of her. When completed he estimated that *Trafalgar* would displace 12,500 tons with 900 tons of coal aboard, and an extreme draught of just on 29 ft. with a mean of 28¼ ft.; and the steps by which the size of the new design was forced up to what would have been an unacceptable figure are worth setting out in some detail, as showing how what appear to be very moderate additions to freeboard, speed and armament react in their demands by big additions to displacement.

In submitting the design embodying the new proposals White pointed out that:

> "The modified *Trafalgar* . . . is a vessel of about 16,000 tons displacement, including the Board margin of 600 tons. This great increase compared with the *Trafalgar* is principally due to the following causes:
>
> (1) The "open stokehold" speed of 17 knots being about half a knot faster than the estimated forced-draught speed of the *Trafalgar*, the horse-power has to be increased by nearly 70 per cent. and the weight of machinery about 50 per cent. (560 tons).
>
> (2) The coals have to be increased by 300 tons.
>
> (3) The citadel has to be lengthened from 193 ft. to 240 ft. in order to provide the greater space required for machinery, boilers and communications. This involves an addition of about 240 tons of armour to the citadel.
>
> (4) The belt has to be lengthened from 230 ft. to 280 ft. in order to provide the same proportionate length of armoured water-line. This involves an additional weight of over 200 tons.
>
> (5) Raising the axes of the guns 2 ft. involves an addition of 120 tons to the weight of the turret armour.
>
> (6) The increase in auxiliary armament involves an addition of about 270 tons.
>
> (7) To carry these increased loads at the higher speed necessitates an addition to the dimensions of the ship, and consequently to the weight of hull, amounting to 1,000 tons.
>
> (8) In this larger ship with greater power and more numerous guns the complement would have to be increased from 540 to 700 with additional stores.
>
> It may be anticipated that the new ship would cost about £185,000 more for hull and engines; for hydraulic machinery, gun mountings and torpedo gear a further increase of about £10,000 may be expected. In round figures, including stores for first fitting, the cost would be about £200,000 more than the *Trafalgar* or about £1,000,000 excluding guns."

To the design of this modified *Trafalgar* White added a series of five designs for turret-ships on the same model in which the Board conditions were not fully realized and displacing 16,000 to 11,700 tons (the latter for comparison with the new French *Brennus*). He also pressed the *claims of the barbette* in three designs of 15,000, 13,700 and 11,700 tons and pointed out that in recent French and Italian ships the gun axes were 26 to 29 ft. above water; in the Russian ships 22 ft.; and in the *Admirals* 21 ft. In his proposed designs the armoured walls of the barbettes were to be vertical and carried down to the protective deck, and the freeboard 18 ft. against 11¼ ft. in the turret ships with the gun axes 23 ft. above water instead of 17 ft. In length, depth and thickness the armour belts were to be the same as proposed for the turret ships, with the barbette protection equal to the redoubts of the turrets.

But fundamentally the great difference between the turret and barbette ships lay in the disposal of the armour. In the central citadel ships with a lower freeboard and smaller target a far greater proportion of the sides could be armoured, while the armour if carried up from the belt not only protected the guns but could also be made to protect stability at considerable angles of inclination. On the other hand, White observed "such protection of stability has been abandoned in all navies with a view to securing the lessened risks arising from a wider dispersion of the heavy guns placed in separate armoured positions, as well as the higher efficiency of the auxiliary armament."[1]

---

[1] This conception was faulty and soon to be relinquished in favour of armoured stability.

As Hood and White differed over this armour disposition a meeting was held in the First Lord's room on 16 November 1888 at which were present the members of the Board, Captain Fisher the D.N.O., Admirals Dowell, Vesey Hamilton and Richards, Vice-Admiral Baird, Captain Lord Walter Kerr and the D.N.C., for the purpose of a full discussion—and no body of men could have spoken with greater authority. Their conclusions were printed in a White Paper presented to Parliament in February 1889, the features of the new battleships agreed upon being:

(1) The big guns should be in two separate redoubts separated by the secondary battery—as opposed to the amidships citadel of the *Inflexible* or the redoubt of the *Nile*.

(2) The secondary battery should be mounted on two decks to secure maximum distribution against rapid-fire guns.

(3) A speed of 15 knots with natural and 17 with forced draught should be provided.

(4) It was preferable to dispose the weight of armour

(*a*) available for water-line protection in the form of thick armour on the belt for a large portion of the length, but not carried to the ends.

(*b*) From belt to main deck as 4 in.-5 in. armour associated with coal bunkers and compartments.

(*c*) To allow for proper protection for the crews of the secondary guns.

(5) The ships should have high freeboard.

(6) The big guns should be in barbettes and should be of about 50 tons weight and 12 in. calibre. As no such guns were then available the first three of the eight first-class ships should have 13·5 in. calibre weapons of the well-tried and successful model.

The design was a compromise between the *Anson* and *Trafalgar* made possible by improvements in armour which allowed for a greater proportion of the sides to be covered without increasing its percentage of displacement. Tests in March 1888 of Cammell's steel-faced plates mounted on the *Nettle* gave excellent results, and steel plates made by Vickers—then a new firm—were nearly as good; John Brown's compound plates were also of excellent quality, and these three firms undertook to make experimental 4-in. plates suitable for upper hullside armour. In June 1889 Jessops of Sheffield produced a *nickel-steel plate*, and this alloy was taken up by the other manufacturers.

The decision to mount the guns in barbettes was a victory for White. As a concession to Hood's recommendation that one of the three ships to be laid down in the Dockyards should be on the turret system, that allotted to Chatham was so designed and given the name of *Hood*.

"ROYAL SOVEREIGN" CLASS

	Built by	*Laid down*	*Launched*	*Completed*	*Cost*
"*Empress of India*" (ex "*Renown*")	Pembroke	9 July '89	7 May '91	Aug. '93	£912,162
"*Ramillies*"	Thomsons	11 Aug. '90	1 Mar. '92	Oct. '93	£980,895
"*Repulse*"	Pembroke	1 Jan. '90	27 Feb. '92	Apl. '94	£915,302
"*Resolution*"	Palmers	14 June '90	28 May '92	Nov. '93	£953,817
"*Revenge*"	Palmers	12 Feb. '91	3 Nov. '92[1]	March '94	£954,825
"*Royal Oak*"	Lairds	29 May '90	5 Nov. '92[1]	June '94	£977,996
"*Royal Sovereign*"	Portsmouth	30 Sept. '89	26 Feb. '91[1]	May '92	£913,986

Dimensions 380′×75′×27′/28′=14,150 tons (Deep load 15,585 tons).
Hull and armour 9,640. Equipment 4,500 tons.

Armament 4 13·5-in. guns.
10 6-in. Q.F.
16 6-pdrs. Q.F. (5,500 lb.)
12 3-pdrs. Q.F. broadside.
Tubes: 2 submerged forward.
4 above water abeam.
1 above water stern.

Armour (Compound and steel) Belt 18″-16″-14″ ends, with 16″-14″ bulkheads; decks 3″-2½″.
Barbettes 17″-16″-11″; main deck casemates 6″; side above belt 4″; screen bulkheads 3″; fore conning tower 14″, after one 3″; backing 8″-4″.
Total 4,560 tons (32·2 per cent.).

Complement 712.

Coal 900/1,100 tons (1,490 tons maximum).

Machinery 2 sets 3 cyl. vert. trip. exp. H.P. (nat.) 9,000=15·5 knots.
H.P. (f.d.) 11,000=16·5 knots (maximum H.P. 13,360[2]=18 knots).
8 cylindrical single-ended boilers. 155 lb. pressure.

---

[1] Undocked. [2] "*Royal Sovereign*" only.

Radius 2,780/14; 4,720/10.

"*Empress of India*," "*Repulse*" and "*Royal Sovereign*"=Humphreys and Tennant.
"*Ramillies*"=J. and G. Thomson. "*Resolution*" and "*Revenge*"=Palmer.
"*Royal Oak*"=Laird.

Points of interest:

(1) The first British high-freeboard battleships to carry all their main armament on the weather deck.
(2) Our first to carry their secondary armament in casemates.
(3) Our first to exceed 12,000 tons.
(4) Our first to have steel armour.

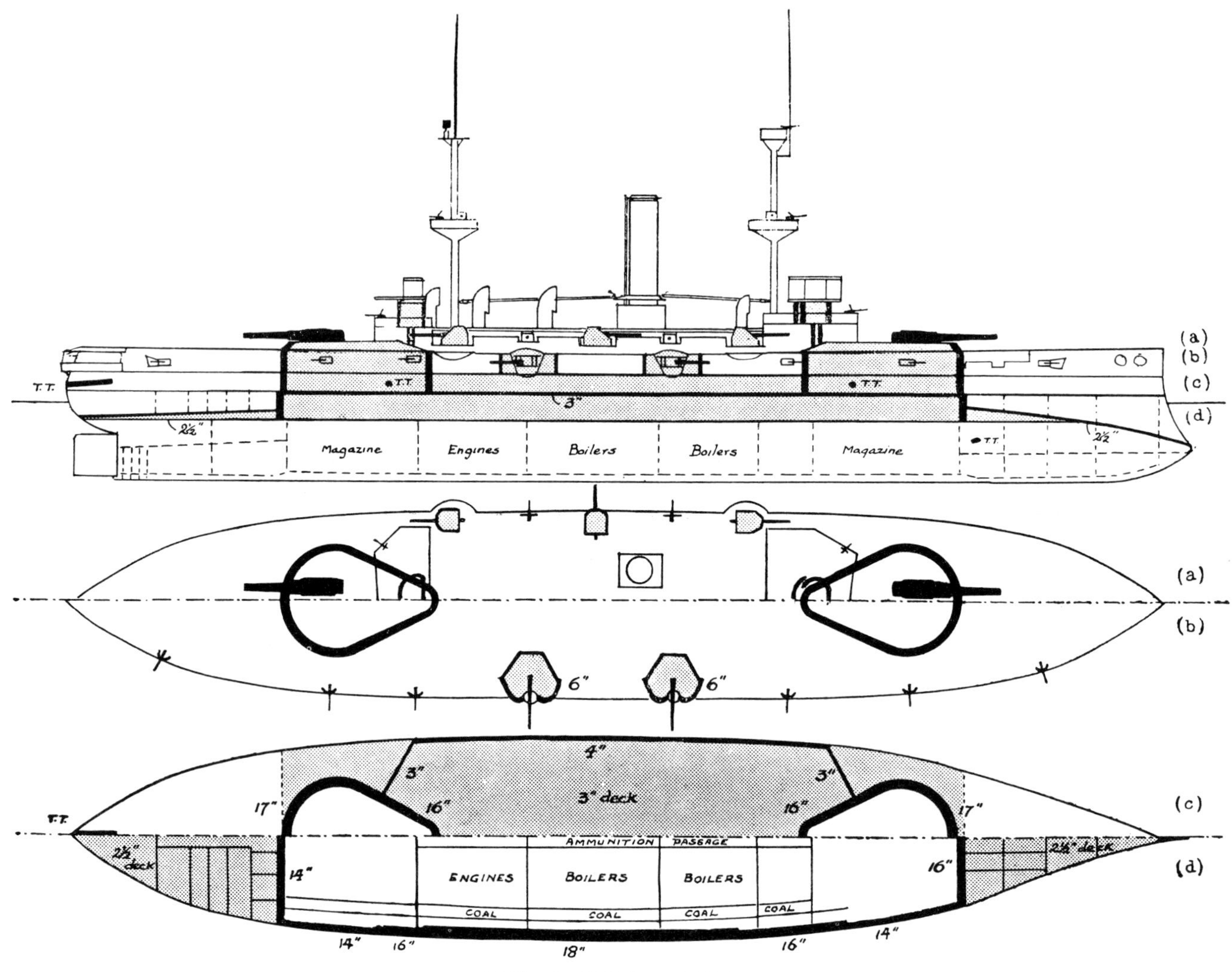

ROYAL SOVEREIGN

When White materialized the requirements of the Board in his design for the *Royal Sovereign*, he provided the Navy with the finest group of fighting ships afloat, which sat the water with majesty and distinction. For the first time since the *Devastation* set a new standard for unsightliness, a British battleship presented a proud, pleasing, and symmetrical profile which was unmatched by any other warship afloat, initiating a new era of Vulcanic beauty, after two decades of sullen and misshapen misfits.

In placing the contracts it was decided that the first group should go to the Dockyards, where matters of detail could be decided without delay, and worked out by an experienced staff in consultation with naval officers. At Portsmouth no building slip was long enough and a dry dock had to be requisitioned; Pembroke had the slips but needed new cranes for heavy equipment and had to send her ships to Chatham for completion; Devonport had not yet been promoted to battleship construction. It was intended that the building period should be three years, but in the case of the *Royal Sovereign* special efforts were made to get completion earlier so that she could be tested in advance of the others, and a record of two years and eight months from keel-laying to commissioning was achieved under the drive of Admiral Superintendent J. A. Fisher.

HULL

The outstanding feature of the *Royal Sovereigns* was their high freeboard. For the past fifteen years or so most of our armoured ships had suffered from low forecastles, since the turret, for reasons of weight and protection, imposed this restriction upon vessels of moderate displacement. But by adopting the barbette principle White was enabled to give his ships both higher freeboard and the greater speed this permitted. It was by now realized that the height of the bow determines the speed at which a ship can be driven against the sea. With a given freeboard, when a certain speed is reached, which depends upon the state of the sea, the form of the bow, and other factors, so much water will come aboard and head resistance increase to such an extent that it becomes both undesirable and impossible to raise speed any further. The *Trafalgar*, *Sans Pareil*, *Hero*, and the rest of the

The *Royal Sovereign* when flagship of the Channel Fleet in 1893. Compare her dry forecastle with that of the *Thunderer* in a similar seaway.

smaller turret ships all suffered in this way, in anything but calm weather, and the *Hood* was to put finish to both low freeboard and the revolving turret in H.M. ships.

Apart from the matter of speed, higher freeboard is also necessary to avoid to a large extent clouds of spray sweeping over the ship when steaming against wind and sea, and markedly interfering with gun sighting and ranging. In heavy weather low freeboard ships had to close gun ports or worked certain guns with difficulty, and conditions between decks greatly detracted from the efficiency and comfort of the crew. The higher the speed the more serious these evils become, and the higher must be the freeboard and gun mountings in order to avoid or diminish them. Having a length of 380 ft., the *Royal Sovereigns* were not likely to meet waves as long as or longer than themselves, whereas ships shorter than 350 ft. suffered accordingly, and would therefore *require a higher freeboard than longer ships*.

Now increase in freeboard can be secured in various ways; (1) by a rising sheer of the deck; (2) by the addition of a forecastle; or (3) by the extension of this into a complete deck. As the turret ships suffered from green seas over the forecastle and were liable to be pooped by a following sea, White overcame both these disabilities in the *Royal Sovereigns* by the addition of a whole deck. But as this additional freeboard raised above-deck weights very considerably and so also the position of the vertical centre of gravity—which has to be kept as low as possible compatible with requirements of steadiness as opposed to stiffness—White revived one of the old sailing ship features to help conteract such a tendency by giving the *Royal Sovereigns* quite a marked "tumble-home."

This inclination inboard of the hull sides above the water-line probably had for its object a saving of weight in the upper part of the structure, and perhaps a reduction in stiffness in order to obtain easier movement in a seaway; but according to one of his constructors this tumble-home was adopted by White for no better reason than "that it looked so well in the French ships." Certainly the D.N.C. had a great respect for Bertin and his designs, but contemporary battleships across the Channel were sadly lacking in initial stiffness. Thus, the *Magenta* heeled about 8° when her rudder was hard a-starboard at a speed of 15·8 knots and with her guns in line with the keel. But when these were trained abeam away from the centre of the turning circle, her heel increased to about 15°, and a major factor in lowering initial stability (the heel up to 15°) is the tumble-home side.

ARMAMENT

Owing to the high freeboard of 18 ft. only the crowns of the barbettes showed above deck and carried the guns at a height of 23 ft. They were pear-shaped with end-on loading positions only, from fixed ammunition trunks at the apex shaft; an upper storey contained the turn-table, the lower the hydraulic turning engines, etc.

In White's barbette the weak underpinning in the *Admirals* was replaced by heavy armour walls down to the

The *Revenge* (later-*Redoubtable*) off the Belgian coast in 1914. Over the bows is Admiral Wilson's minesweeping gear; removable bulges had been fitted, but that on the port side has been removed after a collision. Casemates protect the upper deck 6-in. guns, and she carries the special control tops on the foremast fitted when gunnery tender at Portsmouth. She was listed to secure additional gun elevation.

belt level. These were 17 in. with 16 in. at the apex and 11 in. where covered by the lower deck side armour. They left the guns exposed and openings around and beneath the turn-table were a source of weakness—corrected in the Italian *Sardegna* class having barbettes like the *Admirals* (1888), by the fitting of armoured shields to the barbettes. These served as a model in all subsequent British ships.

For the secondary battery the same arrangement was used as had been introduced in the cruisers *Blake* and *Blenheim* of the 1888 Programme with the upper deck guns behind shields and those on the main deck in 6-in. casemates. This allowed for the guns being well separated, but in placing them on the main deck the Board's instructions to White set the fashion for a faulty distribution which persisted in British and foreign designs for the next decade despite the very obvious disadvantages of a low and wet command, flooded battery decks, and inability to use the guns in a seaway.

White had wished to place the upper guns in casemates as well, but the Board attached a good deal of importance to keeping the boat deck as free and unencumbered as possible and only shields were approved of. But in his calculations White allowed for casemates being fitted when required, and when objections to upper deck obstructions were overcome by experience, opportunity was taken to add this necessary protection some ten years later.

Although appearing to afford protection to the gun's crew, experience in the Sino-Japanese War showed that thin screens or shields were useless or worse. They only served to explode shells which might otherwise have passed the gun, sending a blast of splinters across the deck to the opposite gun; or, if they passed the gun, might be caught and exploded by the shield on the far side instead of passing out of the ship. After the *Royal Sovereigns* we reverted to the time-honoured formula that a gun should be protected by approximately its own calibre in armour thickness or else left exposed.

Compared with Barnaby's proposals for secondary batteries ten guns appeared somewhat meagre for the displacement, but White took occasion to point out that these Q.F. guns with their mountings and ammunition supply were the equivalent of twenty 6-in. B.L. with their normal supply, and exceeded 500 tons—or two and two-thirds times the weight of the *Trafalgar's* six 4·7-in. Q.F. and practically equal to the total weight of armament proposed for the *Fury* of 1870.

A wide distribution was arranged for the 6-pdrs. on the upper and main decks; the 3-pdrs. were on the shelter decks and in the fighting tops.

In place of 14-in. torpedoes a new model 18-in. was carried, and the original seven tubes were reduced to three during reconstruction.

ARMOUR

Allowing for the additional deck height in freeboard it will be seen that the protection was arranged as a combination of the *Anson* and *Trafalgar* systems with the good points of both. The main belt 250 ft. long extended for two-thirds of the length and was 8½ ft. deep with 5 ft. under water, being closed by a 16-in. bulkhead forward and 14-in. aft. When the design was under discussion White recommended that the bows should be lightly armoured before the citadel so as to maintain speed should she be struck up forward during a pursuit action, but the conclusion reached by the Committee and confirmed by the Board was that the ends should be left unarmoured; an under-water deck with ample subdivision was considered the best arrangement. In place of coal in the *Anson* and 18-in. armour in *Trafalgar* the *Royal Sovereign* had 5 in. of Harvey steel (nickel steel in *Ramillies*, *Repulse*, *Revenge* and *Royal Oak*) backed by deep bunkers, which was considered enough to burst medium Q.F. shell, and prevent free perforation of this area by the quick-firing guns coming into service.

It was this thin steel plating—which had been found "satisfactory" for such protection in the *Resistance* experiments—which brought forth a tirade against these ships by Sir Edward Reed. But, as White pointed out, Reed could have no knowledge of experimental data upon which to base his opinions of the damage likely to happen to lightly armoured structures in action. To have added thick plating above the belt would have greatly increased the size of the ship, and White had submitted alternative designs showing possible dispositions of the protective material within the limits of weight available; it was the province of the naval officers to determine from their knowledge of gunnery that disposition of armour which they considered had the balance of advantage.

The main deck was left unprotected except for the 6-in. casemates here introduced for the first time, and then only after the most careful consideration and discussion. The great French constructor M. de Bussy had adopted the small turret for housing 7·6-in. and 6·4-in. guns in the famous cruiser *Dupuy de Lôme* ordered in 1888 and

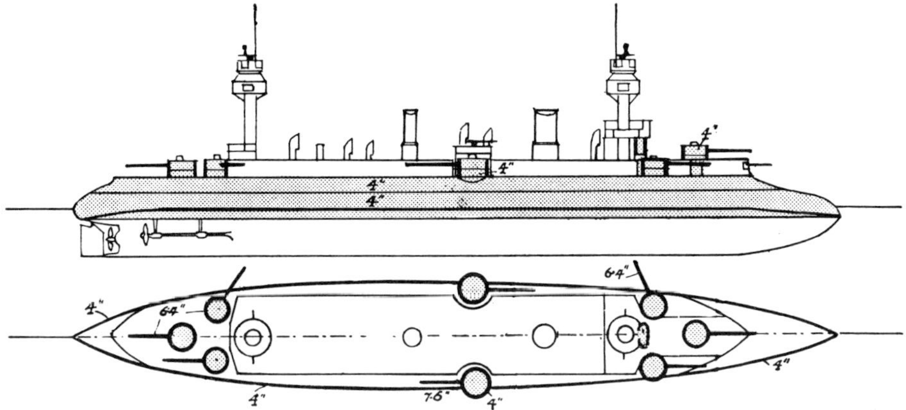

French armoured cruiser *Dupuy de Lôme* which created a sensation with all her guns in turrets having wide arcs of fire, and the hull protected by 4-in. plating. The extraordinary bow was so shaped to secure buoyancy forward without a forecastle exposed to gun blast.

a similar system was proposed for the *Royal Sovereign*. But the Board eventually decided against the turret as involving mechanism for its turning which did not give the same facility as was obtained by manual power when the protecting armour was fixed and the guns mounted on central pivots.

Had the turret been accepted secondary armaments would have been confined to upper deck positions—as is the general practice today—and our battleships for the next ten years would have been spared their most objectionable feature—*i.e.*, main deck casemates.

In the *Dupuy de Lôme*, de Bussy also introduced two other features which deserve recording as having influenced British design: (1) a complete ceinture of 4-in. steel over the hull and (2) the vaulted protective deck

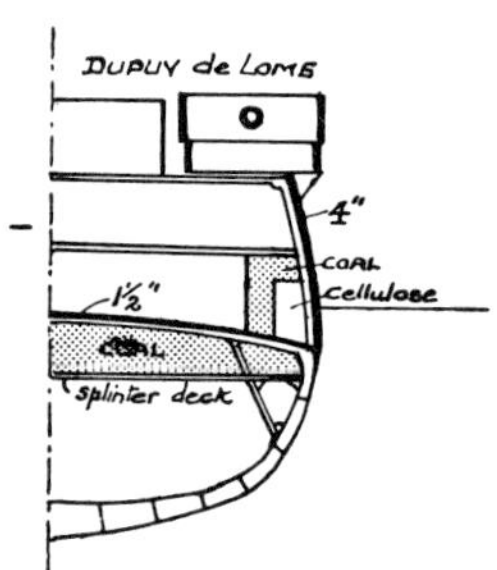

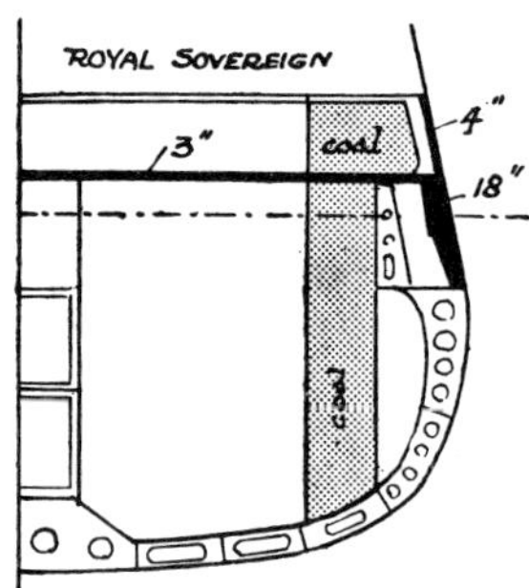

joining the *lower edge* of the belt instead of lying across the top of it. It will be seen from the hull section sketch that below this deck ran a splinter deck, the space between them being filled with coal, while more bunkers and a cofferdam filled with cellulose extended along the waterline. In theory this cellulose was to swell up under the action of sea water and close up shot holes—and apparently answered pretty well in small-scale experiments, although more likely to be blown away *en masse* by medium shell fire. In any case, its use was condemned in our Service, although for a time the water-lines of numerous French ships relied upon it for protection.

The small water-line cofferdam found favour and afterwards was quite extensively employed, appearing in the U.S. *Virginia* and *Connecticut* classes as late as 1904. The value of the protective deck being curved down to the lower edge of the belt—an adaptation of the curved deck in the Elswick cruisers *Esmeralda* and *Piemonte*—appealed to our constructors and in a modified form appeared a year or so later in the *Renown*.

By covering the hull completely with thin armour de Bussy carried into effect the lessons drawn from firing trials against the old ironclad *Belliqueuse* when the widespread damage caused by shell fire against unprotected structures was dramatically demonstrated. On the other hand, 4-in. armour was sufficient to explode shells outside the ship with insignificant damage.

White, however, had another opinion about thin armour, and argued that such meagre protection could be seriously damaged and great havoc wrought inboard by cheap chilled Palliser projectiles instead of high-explosive shells. On which grounds he preferred simple coal defence above the curved protective deck for the big cruisers *Blake* and *Blenheim* (1888), although in the following year he changed his views, preferring to follow the French lead in the *Royal Sovereign* by covering the flanks with 4-in. Harvey steel backed by coal.

The 5-in. casements afterwards fitted to the upper deck 6-in. guns were of Krupp non-cemented steel, and the net weight added about 100 tons.

Over the belt the deck was 3 in., with 2½-in. curved decks running to the bow and stern.

SPEED

Owing to their length and lines—which were calculated for a higher speed than could be given to the low freeboard *Trafalgar*—only 9,000 h.p. was allowed for 16 knots and 13,000 f.d. for 17·5 knots. Actually only the *Royal Sovereign* was driven to develop this power and for the rest of the class the maximum was fixed at 11,000. Loaded to a mean draught of 27½ ft. the name ship reached 18 knots with 13,360 h.p.—the first armoured ship to touch this figure. With a pressure in the stokeholds of 1½ in. all went well for the first three hours; but during the last hour of the trial the tubes of two boilers began to leak, causing a considerable drop in power, so that data for the first three hours were used to calculate results.

Incidentally, at this period a pressure of 2 in. was permissible on the builders' four hours forced draught trial, and even with new boilers the terrific strain due to uneven expansion of the tubes and elements led to endless trouble—either at the time or a later period when former exposure to breaking-down strain developed weaknesses which in time became manifest.

In 1892 forced draught was irrevocably condemned by marine engineers after having been adopted by all navies with quite inexplicable imprudence. At the best it only saddled a ship with a fictitious ability to make a speed which could never be attempted under service conditions without risk of breakdown. In practice it ruined so many boilers and laid up so many ships that less than 1-in. pressure became the recognized limit as against ½-in. which constituted natural draught.

All the class exceeded their nominal power by 200-500 h.p., and running light achieved from 15·25 (*Empress of India*) to 17·8 knots (*Repulse*); at modified forced draught they ranged from 11,571 with 17·25 knots of the *Ramillies* to 11,608 with 18·27 knots developed by the *Royal Oak*, all being at less than legend displacement.

COAL SUPPLY

Being designed to allow for a Board margin of 4 per cent., the legend displacement was calculated to include an unappropriated weight of 500 tons. During construction various additions amounting to 250 tons were deducted from this, but on completion it was found that the actual balance allowed for 1,100 tons of coal to be carried on the designed trim of 1 ft. by the stern and 27½ ft. mean draught. The wing spaces abreast the bunkers (nominally reserve bunkers) could therefore be filled under normal conditions, providing a complement of 1,450 tons.

STABILITY

Unusual problems were presented in arranging for stability, as calculations had to take account of unprecedented loads of armour, height of guns and barbettes, and other factors giving unusually large moments of inertia tending to long periods of oscillation even if good metacentric height was provided—and 3½ ft. G.M. was aimed at. This, it was calculated, would give a period of oscillation as great as, or in excess of, that of the old *Hercules*, *Sultan*, *Monarch* and *Invincible* classes which were all steady gun platforms. Moreover the range between deep and normal load was expected to reach 2,000 tons in displacement change, and suitable arrangements had to be made to allow the ships to pass from one load to the other without alteration in metacentric height. On completion the inclination tests showed that the metacentric height was 3·6 and centre of gravity only 1¾ in. below the calculated position in *Royal Sovereign*, and 4 in. in *Ramillies* with her heavier machinery.

SEA-GOING QUALITIES

As completed they were without bilge keels, as it was considered that the influence these could exert on a hull of such large dimensions and great inertia would be negligible, while their presence would interfere with docking facilities. Moreover, having been designed for a long period of oscillation it was expected that they would make steady gun platforms in heavy weather. But as it happened practice was very far from conforming with precept under certain conditions, when the ships were liable to develop a deep and disconcerting roll. Thus, in December 1893, the *Resolution* during passage from Plymouth to Gibraltar met exceptionally heavy weather with a *short steep* sea which moved her so badly that she had to be brought up head to sea, and was finally forced to put about and return to Queenstown owing to shortage of coal. At the same time the torpedo-gunboat *Gleaner* made far better weather of it than her great consort, and was able to proceed to her destination.

Although the "rolling *Resolution*" sustained no material damage from the water which had found its way below through open communications, the press carried all sorts of alarmist reports that she was in danger of foundering and had sustained severe structural damage.

Bilge keels were then ordered to be fitted—although there was a considerable weight of opinion in the Constructors Department that these would be of no avail—and the *Repulse* then completing was the first to receive

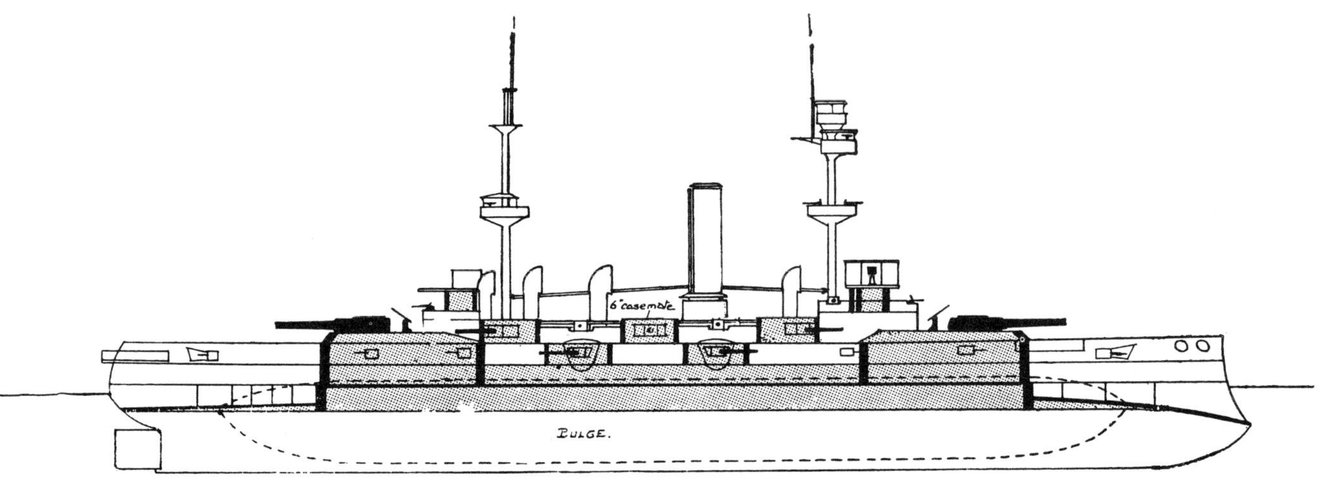

REDOUBTABLE (ex-*Revenge*)

them (200 ft. long × 3 ft. deep). In a comparative test with the *Resolution* she rolled only 11°, when the latter ship registered 23°, and with this corrective the class proved steady gun platforms and comfortable sea boats. The period for the double roll was 16 seconds.

ALTERATIONS

During the long refits between 1902-4 the upper deck 6-in. guns were given casemates which added considerably to their fighting value—the shields had always been a weak point. About 1907 the fighting tops were converted into range-control positions, and when the torpedo nets had been lowered clear of the main deck guns the *Royal Sovereigns* achieved their most utilitarian appearance with a remarkable air of solidity in keeping with a reputation for being the most substantially built ships ever produced.

In August 1914, when the call went out for all available naval tonnage, all excepting the *Revenge* had passed into the shipbreakers' hands. She was rescued from the Motherbank, specially fitted with bulges, and performed yeoman service off the Belgian coast despite the drawbacks of a 28½-ft. draught aft, remaining on the Navy List until the end of hostilities.

"EMPRESS OF INDIA"

Commissioned at Devonport 4 September '93 for Channel (2nd Flag) to December '95 (bilge keels fitted '94). Re-commissioned as private ship in Channel to June '97 then transferred to Mediterranean for four and a half years. (Cretan operations '97-'98.) In October '01 became flag S.N.O. Irish Coast. Long refit '02 (casemates fitted, etc., and net shelf lowered) 2nd Flag. Home Fleet September '02-May '04 and then private ship to February '05. Commissioned in Reserve. Refit Devonport '05 and f.c. fitted (collision with s/m A.10 Plymouth Sound 30 April '06). S.S. ship May '07-April '09 and then joined 4th Division Home Fleet, Devonport until '11. Placed in Mat. Reserve and collided with German barque *Winderhudder* while being towed to Motherbank by *Warrior* and underwent temporary repairs before being laid up. Used as target ship and sunk by gunfire off Portland Bill November '13. Total service in commission eighteen and a half years including two and a quarter years in Reserve.

"RAMILLIES"

Commissioned Portsmouth 17 October '93 for Mediterranean (flag)—October '03 (bilge keels fitted Malta '94). Paid off Chatham for refit '03-'04 (casemates fitted, etc.); Manœuvres July-September '04; Fleet Reserve Chatham to November '06. (In collision with *Resolution* 15 June '06 near Sheerness and afterwards long refit Chatham.) Commissioned for Home Fleet March '07 (f.c. fitted); 4th Division Devonport April '09-August '11; Paid off and towed to Motherbank. Sold at Portsmouth 7 October '13 for £42,300.

Total service in commission sixteen and three quarter years.

"RESOLUTION"

Commissioned Portsmouth 5 December '93 for Channel—October '01 (bilge keels fitted '94; collision with *Repulse* 18 July '96). c.g.s. Holyhead November '01-February '02 then became 2nd Flag. Reserve Squadron. Refit Devonport '02-'03 (casemates fitted etc.). On passage Holyhead to Plymouth 27 February '03 lost rudder and damaged hull and steering gear. Commissioned January '04 as portguard ship Sheerness—June; July-September manœuvres; p.o. into Fleet Reserve. Commissioned January '05 in Reserve Chatham (collision with *Ramillies* 15 July '06); refit Chatham; S.S. Devonport February '07-April '09 then to 4th Division H.F.

P.O. August '11 and towed to Motherbank where she was run into and damaged by S.S. *Seapoint* 5 March '12.

Sold 1914.

Total commissioned service sixteen and a half years.

"REVENGE"

Fleet Reserve Portsmouth 22 March '94; commissioned 14 January '96 Flag. of Particular Service Squadron (formed at the time of European unrest following Jameson Raid)—November '96. Mediterranean 2nd Flag December '96 (Cretan operations '96-'97)—June '00. P.O. Fleet Reserve until April '01 then became c.g.s. Portland, and Flag. Reserves February '02: Flag. Vice-Admiral Home Fleet October '02; long refit Chatham '02 (casemates fitted, etc.) to '05; Commissioned Reserve Portsmouth replacing *Colossus* as gunnery ship September '06 (in collision with S.S. *Bengore Head* 7 January '08, and with H.M.S. *Orion* in Portsmouth Harbour 7 January '12 (severely damaged and flooded); repaired '12. As gunnery ship had large square control top on foremast. During '12 big guns replaced by 10-in. but 13·5-in. remounted October '12; Mat. Res. Motherbank April '13-October '14; returned to general service. Operations off Westende and Belgian Coast being renamed *Redoubtable* 10 August '15; big guns relined and reduced to 12-in. bore with a range of 16,000 yards increased by heeling the ship; below the water-line external "bulges" were added as torpedo exploding screens. Drawing up to 29 ft. was very unsuitable for coastal work in shallow water and minefields, but figured in several operations and was afterwards very useful in carrying out firing trials in the Thames on which the subsequent long-range bombardments were based. Displacement in 1917 at load draught 14,635 tons. Afterwards replaced and subsequently paid off. Tender to *Victory* 1 January '18-February '19 and then placed on sale list.

Sold 6 November '19 for £42,570.

"REPULSE"

Commissioned 21 April '94 Channel and served eight years (collision with *Resolution* 18 July '96) transferred to Mediterranean for temporary service March '02. Refit April '03-December '04 (casemates fitted, etc.) Dockyard Reserve February '04 and passed into Commissioned Reserve Chatham January '05; refit '06-'07; 4th Div. H.F. Devonport April '09 until replaced by *Majestic* as parent ship of battleship group in August '10. Towed to Motherbank 1910.

Sold 11 July '11 for £33,550.

"ROYAL OAK"

Reserve Portsmouth 12 June '94. Commissioned 14 January '96 for Particular Service Squadron until November '96; refit Portsmouth; Mediterranean March '97-June '02; refit Chatham (casemates fitted, etc.); 2nd Flag. H.F. February '03 and later in Channel until March '05; Commissioned Reserve Chatham (small-arms magazine explosion 11 May '05)' f.c. fitted '07; H.F. Devonport April '09 and tender to *Repulse* July '10; Dockyard Res. December '11 and towed to Motherbank August '13.

Sold 1914 for £36,450.

"ROYAL SOVEREIGN"

Commissioned 31 May '92. Flag. Channel and with *Empress of India*, *Repulse* and *Resolution* formed part of Lord Walter Kerr's Squadron at opening of Kiel Canal June '95; private ship Channel from December '95 transferred to Mediterranean June '97-August '02 (6-in. gun explosion November '01. Six killed, 19 injured). Portguard ship Portsmouth '02-May '05; refit '03 (casemates fitted, etc.); Dockyard Reserve Devonport May '05-February '07 and then commissioned as S.S. ship; 4th Division H.F. April '09-'13; passed into Material Reserve '13.

Sold 7 Oct. '13 for £40,000.

(*Note:* S.S. (special service) ships were commissioned with skeleton crews.)

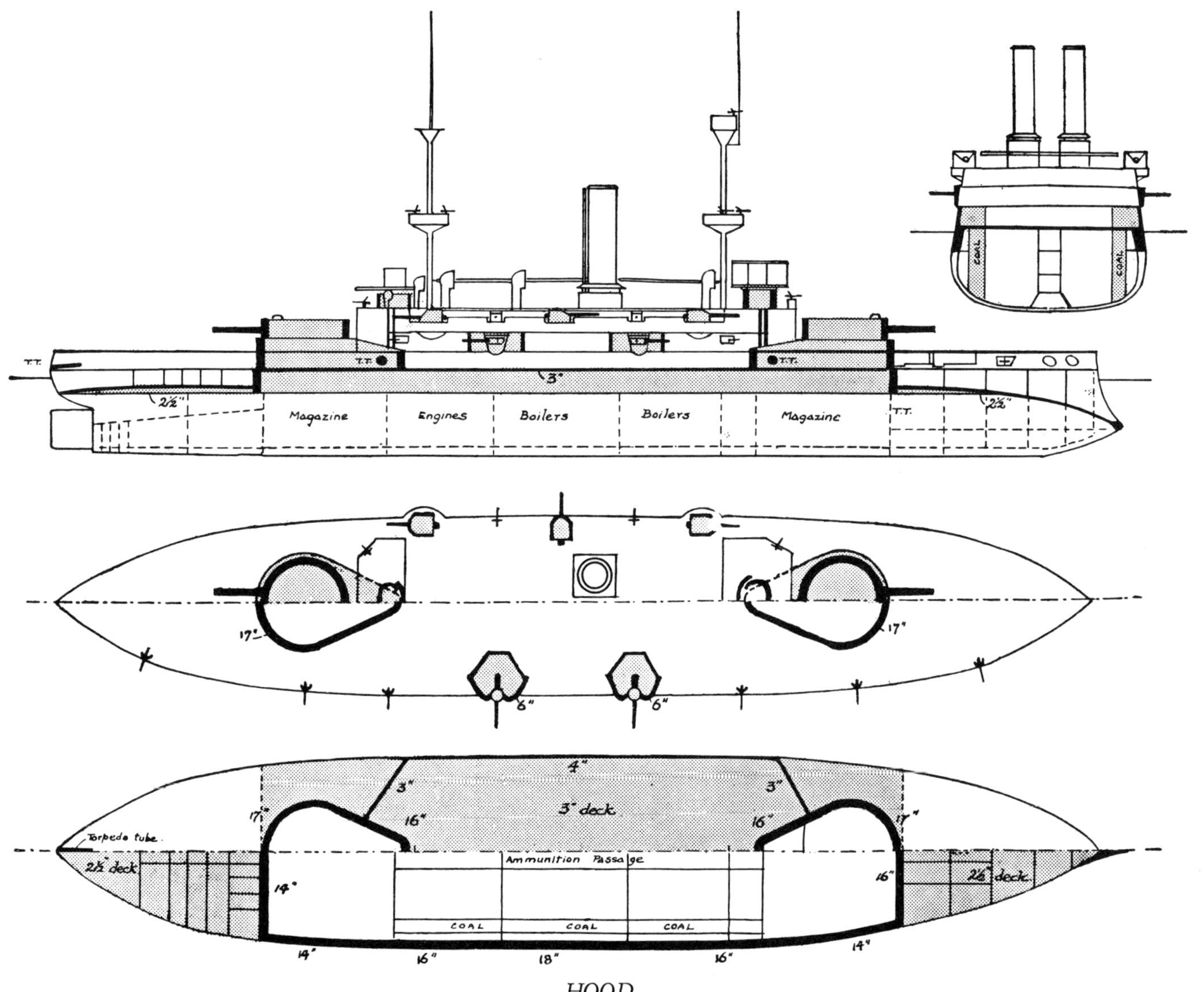

HOOD

"HOOD"

Built at	*Laid down*	*Launched*	*Completed*	*Cost*
Chatham	12 Aug. '89	30 July '91	May '93	£926,396

Dimensions 380'×75'×27'/28'=14,150 tons (deep load 15,588 tons). Hull and armour 9,640. Equipment 4,500 tons.

Armament 4 13·5-in. 30-cal.; 10 6-in. Q.F.; 10 6-pdrs.; 12 3-pdrs.
Tubes (18-in.): 1 above water astern. 2 submerged forward. 4 above water abeam.

Armour (compound and steel) Belt 18"-16"-14"; fore bulkhead 16", after one 14"; turrets 17"-16"-11"; main deck casemates 6"; side above belt 4"; screen bulkheads 3"; fore conning tower 14", after conning tower 3"; backing 8"-4". Total 4,560 tons.

Complement 692.

Coal 900/1,100 tons (1,410 tons maximum).

Machinery Humphreys and Tennant 2 sets 3-cyl. vert. trip. exp. H.P. n.d. 9,000=15·7 knots; 11,000 f.d.=16·7 knots. Boilers 8 cylindrical; 155 lb. pressure.

Radius 2,780/14; 4,720/10.

Points of interest:

(1) The last British battleship to have reduced freeboard.
(2) The last British turret-ship.
(3) The ship upon which bulge protection was first tested experimentally.

In deference to the express wishes of the First Naval Lord, Admiral Hood, the eighth of the first-class battleships was built as a turret ship—and proved a very qualified success compared with the others. In defence of her construction it may be claimed that she definitely settled any doubts as to the superiority of the barbette, the *Royal Sovereigns* outmatching her on all points. She took the water at Chatham as the last British turret ship in direct descent from Coles' *Royal Sovereign.*

With a freeboard of 11¼ ft. only her big guns trained 17 ft. above water as against 23 ft. in the others, and although the turrets were fine massive-looking structures compared with the barbettes and afforded solid protection to guns and personnel, they could not make as good shooting in a seaway. Lack of freeboard also told against her qualities as a sea boat and restricted speed in bad weather.

In most other details she was similar to the barbette ships, but when it came to adding casemates to the upper deck 6-in. guns it was found that her stability would not stand the extra top weight.

During her first period at sea she was very slow in answering the helm and did not turn well, but improved after bilge keels were fitted in 1894.

For some years after barbettes had been given armoured hoods they retained their name, but gradually the word "turret" came into use in describing the hood or gun house, leaving "barbette" for the fixed base. Finally it ousted it altogether and all gun houses, large or small and armoured or not, became known as "turrets," while barbettes were often referred to as "turret bases."

"HOOD"

Commissioned 1 June '93 for Mediterranean and served there until April 1900; refit Chatham; portguard ship Pembroke December 1900 and then transferred to Mediterranean until December '02; long refit Chatham '02-'03 (four above-water tubes removed, etc.); Home Fleet June '03-September '04; passed into Fleet Reserve. Commissioned in Reserve January '05-February '07; Devonport Division Home Fleet February '07-July '10. Became receiving ship Queenstown and landed her 6-in. guns. Removed from fighting list March '11, towed to Portsmouth and placed in Material Reserve. Used as target for torpedo tests and upon outbreak of War was sunk to block the southern entrance to Portlands Road where her hull still remains.

Total commissioned service eighteen years.

HOOD

Although the handsomest and most formidable looking of the *Royal Sovereign* group, the *Hood* lacked sea-going qualities because of low freeboard, and want of sufficient stability precluded upper deck casemates being fitted. She is here shown in 1893 before leaving for the Mediterranean.

1896

CHANNEL	MEDITERRANEAN	CHINA	COAST GUARD AND PORTGUARD
Magnificent	*Ramillies*	*Centurion*	*Benbow*
Majestic	*Revenge*		*Colossus*
Prince George	*Hood*		*Edinburgh*
Empress of India	*Barfleur*		*Dreadnought*
Repulse	*Anson*		*Sans Pareil*
Resolution	*Camperdown*		*Devastation*
Royal Sovereign	*Collingwood*		*Thunderer*
	Howe		*Inflexible*
	Rodney		*Alexandra*
	Nile		*Rupert*
	Trafalgar		
	Devastation		

Chapter 60

"MODERATE DIMENSIONS" BARFLEUR, CENTURION AND RENOWN

When drawing up his proposals for the battleships which would be required under the Naval Defence Act, White assumed that no second-class ships would be built. He held very definite opinions upon the necessity for British ships being equal to or better than the best built abroad, and had no use for the second best whether from the "economical," "moderate dimensions," "size *v.* numbers," or any other point of view. But in March 1889 the Controller and D.N.O. (Captain Fisher) asked for outline drawings for two second-class battleships. These were intended for use on the China and Pacific Stations, with a maximum draught of 26 ft. for navigation of the Chinese rivers; radius of action was to be the same as *Imperieuse* but with only 750 tons of coal instead of 900 by virtue of triple-expansion instead of compound engines; speed was to be 16½ knots with n.d. and 18 knots under f.d.

Prime cost was fixed to show a 30 per cent. saving on that of the bigger ships—and this determined their size, as to effect such a reduction 4,000 tons had to be knocked off the displacement. In a ship so much smaller it meant reducing the armament from 13·5-in. and 6-in. to 10-in. and 4·7-in. guns with only 12-in. armour available for the belt in place of 18-in., and 9-in. on the barbettes instead of 17-in. They were, however, to be given the same freeboard, manœuvring powers, bunkerage, and sea-going capacity; and in general cost and maintenance seven *Centurions* were to equal five *Royal Sovereigns*.

The armament White proposed was four 10-in. and eight 4·7-in., the latter behind shields on the *upper deck* a full 21 ft. apart, where they stood a better chance than between decks when attacked by H.E. shells. In arranging protection he again put forward the proposal made for the *Royal Sovereign*—that thick belt armour be abolished in favour of a uniform medium thickness over the area from lower edge of belt to main deck in combination with a thicker and curved protective deck as in the *Blenheim*. But the Board decided to retain the thick belt and flat deck, although in the later *Renown* and *Majestic* they were to be discarded in favour of a wider covering of thinner armour, and a *Blenheim* deck.

Although time has shown that the construction of second-class ships merely to avoid expenditure is false economy—when the passing of the years provides them automatically—these two ships were intended for duties beneath the dignity of a first-class battleship but beyond the nominal fighting power of our cruisers. Russia had been sending large armoured cruisers carrying 8-in. and 6-in. guns out China way; and as an answer to these, light battleships of high speed able to act in concert with the cruiser force out there were considered necessary. As the Russians could steam round about 15 knots under favourable conditions, the *Centurions* would have been well able to deal with them—and it is on these grounds that their value should be appreciated during their earlier years of service. Otherwise it would seem that the Navy was saddled with a couple of very inferior battleships which quickly reached the limit of their effective employment abroad, and were only fitted for more or less subsidiary duties at home.

"BARFLEUR" and "CENTURION"

	Built at	*Laid down*	*Launched*	*Completed*	*Cost*
"*Barfleur*"	Chatham	12 Oct. '90	10 Aug. '92	June '94	£533,666
"*Centurion*"	Portsmouth	30 March '90	3 Aug. '92	Feb. '94	£540,090

Dimensions 360′ × 70′ × 25′/26′ = 10,500 tons.
Hull and armour 6,800. Equipment 3,700 tons.

Armament
4 10-in. 29 tons/32 cal.
10 4·7-in. Q.F.
8 6-pdrs.
12 3-pdrs.
4 smaller.

Torpedo tubes:
2 submerged forward.
4 above water beam.
1 " " astern.

Armour (compound and steel) Belt 12″ with 8″ bulkheads; side above belt 4″ (Harvey).
Deck 2½″ (nickel steel); barbettes 9″ with 6″ (Harvey) hoods; 3″ lower deck bulkheads; 4″ (Harvey) main deck casemates; forward conning tower 12″; after conning tower 3″; backing 9″-6″.
Total 2,350 tons (22·4 per cent.).

Machinery Both by Greenock Foundry.
Two sets vert. triple exp. H.P. 9,000 = 17 knots. 13,000 (f.d.) = 18·5 knots.
Cylindrical boilers.

Radius About 6,000/10.

Coal 750/1,125 tons. *Constructors* Edwin Beaton. J. H. Narbeth.

Complement 620.
Wood and copper sheathed for foreign service.

Points of interest:

(1) Our last battleships to have the main protective deck across the top of the belt.
(2) The first to have hooded barbettes, and big guns with all-round loading positions.
(3) The first to undergo reconstruction as distinct from "modernization" since the *Hotspur*.

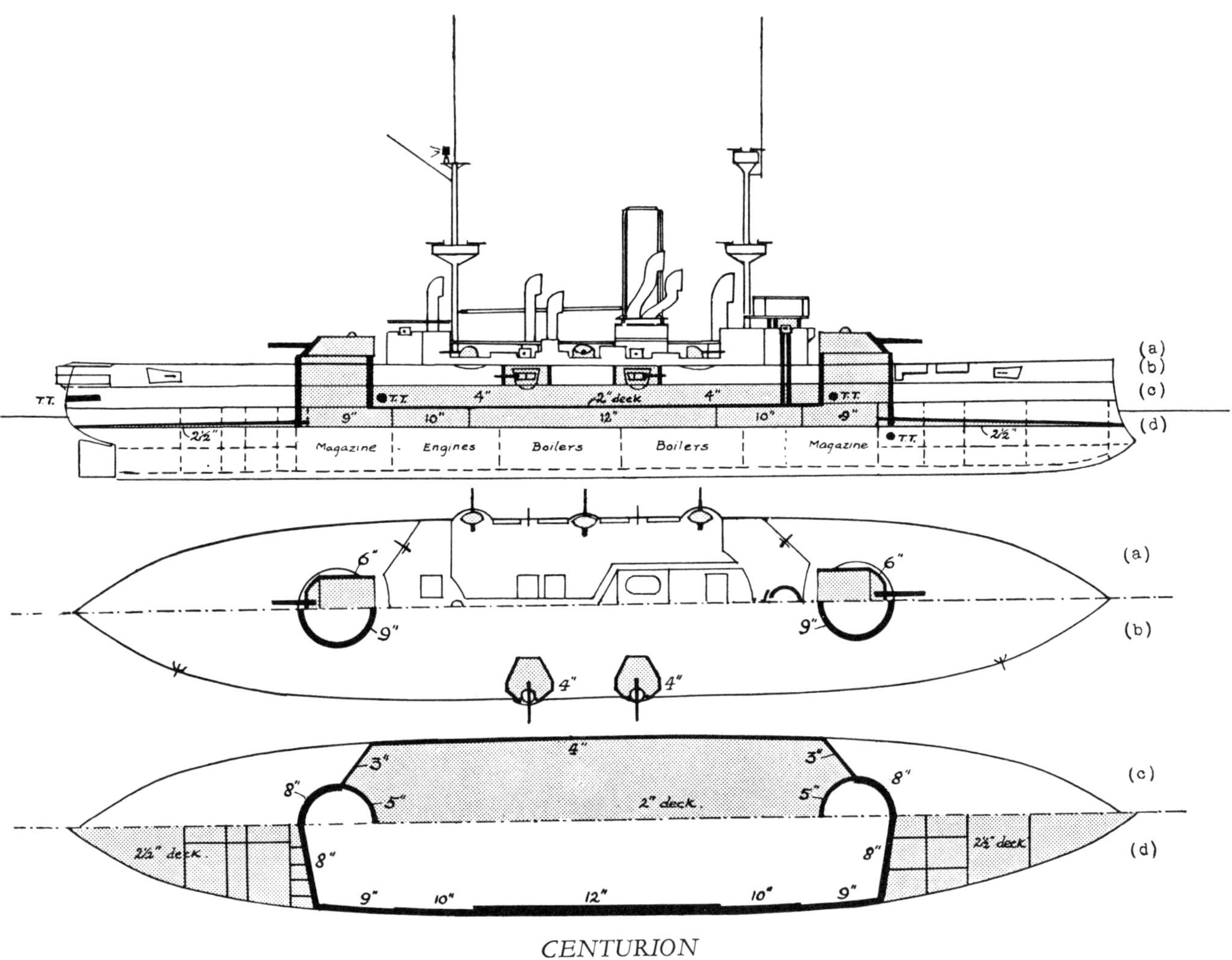

CENTURION

In general appearance there was a close resemblance to the *Royal Sovereign*, but as—owing to magazine arrangements—the central ammunition passage could be omitted, the boilers were brought to the centre line and the funnels closely paired. Their internal arrangements showed a great improvement on previous designs and served as a model for subsequent battleships.

ARMAMENT

The 10-in. guns fired a 500-lb. round capable of piercing 20½-in. iron at 1,000 yards, and noteworthy as being the first high-trajectory pieces of heavy ordnance in the Service. Both steam and hand training gear were fitted, and as the latter necessitated both gun and crew being above the protective top of the turn-table it was necessary to provide an armoured shield with the rear left open to give proper working facilities. These 29-ton guns were the largest in the Service to be hand worked, but their breech mechanism proved difficult to manipulate and the system was recognized as being much inferior to the hydraulic gear as used for the larger calibres. The mountings were designed by Whitworths, who contrived to accommodate them in circular instead of pear-shaped barbettes, with considerable economy in weight. Siemens electric gear was fitted experimentally in *Barfleur* as an alternative, by which they could be brought from 7° depression to 35° elevation in 14 seconds. Loading was made possible in all positions of training by placing the loading chamber under the gun platform and revolving with it, the ammunition passing up a central tube and then up an incline to the breech of each gun.

Inspection reports show that the training arrangements were unsatisfactory, as the steam gear could not arrest the turning motion sufficiently quickly and the hand gear was not adequate. Hydraulic gear was fitted in all subsequent ships.

With a freeboard forward of 22 ft. with 17 ft. amidships and 19 ft. aft the forward guns were 25 ft. above water and the after one 22½ ft.

SECONDARY BATTERY

In the original design submitted in March 1889 the 4·7-in. guns were to be on the upper deck, but at the Board meeting on 30 August it was decided that ten should be disposed as in the *Royal Sovereign*, the displacement being increased by 250 tons so that 4-in. main deck casemates could be worked in without encroaching on the Board margin.

Nowadays it appears a feeble secondary equipment for a battleship, although seemingly adequate on the *Trafalgar* standard, and appeared to be their one feature upon which the Service was critical.

The *Centurion* before leaving for her first commission on the China Station in 1894, with her insignificant battery of 4·7-in. Q.F.

ARMOUR

The belt of compound armour covered 200 ft. with a thickness of 12 in. amidships and 9 in. at the ends, tapering to 8 in. at the lower edge and crossed by 8-in. bulkheads; of its 7½ ft. depth, 5 ft. was below water. Above this the lower deck side was of 4-in. Harvey steel carried on by oblique bulkheads to the barbettes, which had a maximum thickness of 9 in. reduced to 5 in. within the shelter of this plating. The main deck was unprotected except by the 4 in.-2 in. Harvey casemates.

The protective deck was 2-in. nickel steel where the 4-in. armour topped the belt, and 2½-in. over the remainder to the extremities.

As the weight of armour and backing totalled only 2,350 tons—or less than 25 per cent. of the displacement—the *Centurions* fell short of accepted standards in the matter of protection, even when allowing for the extra resistance of steel.

SPEED

Both ships had the reputation of being good steamers although always needing more than the legend 9,000 h.p. for 17 knots. Their trial speeds were:

Barfleur	*Centurion*
9,934 h.p. = 17·1 knots.	9,703 h.p. = 17·5 knots.
13,163 „ = 18·5 „	13,214 „ = 18·5 „

These results were obtained on normal draught, but with a patent log—which was regarded as liable to inaccuracies at such speeds.

RECONSTRUCTION

In June 1901 Captain J. R. Jellicoe of the *Centurion* submitted that her fighting efficiency would be greatly enhanced if the torpedo tubes were removed and 6-in. substituted for 4·7-in. guns. As Naval Assistant to the Controller he had been closely associated with the design of the ships, and when the *Centurion* returned home in September 1901 his appointment as naval secretary enabled him to supervise the office work of their reconstruction, which was left in the hands of Constructor J. N. Narbeth, who had been responsible for the original sketch plans.

A drastic scheme for remodelling the secondary battery was drawn up along the lines of the *Renown* with end casemates superimposed and a clean sweep made in the arrangements amidships. But ten 6-in. Q.F. mounted

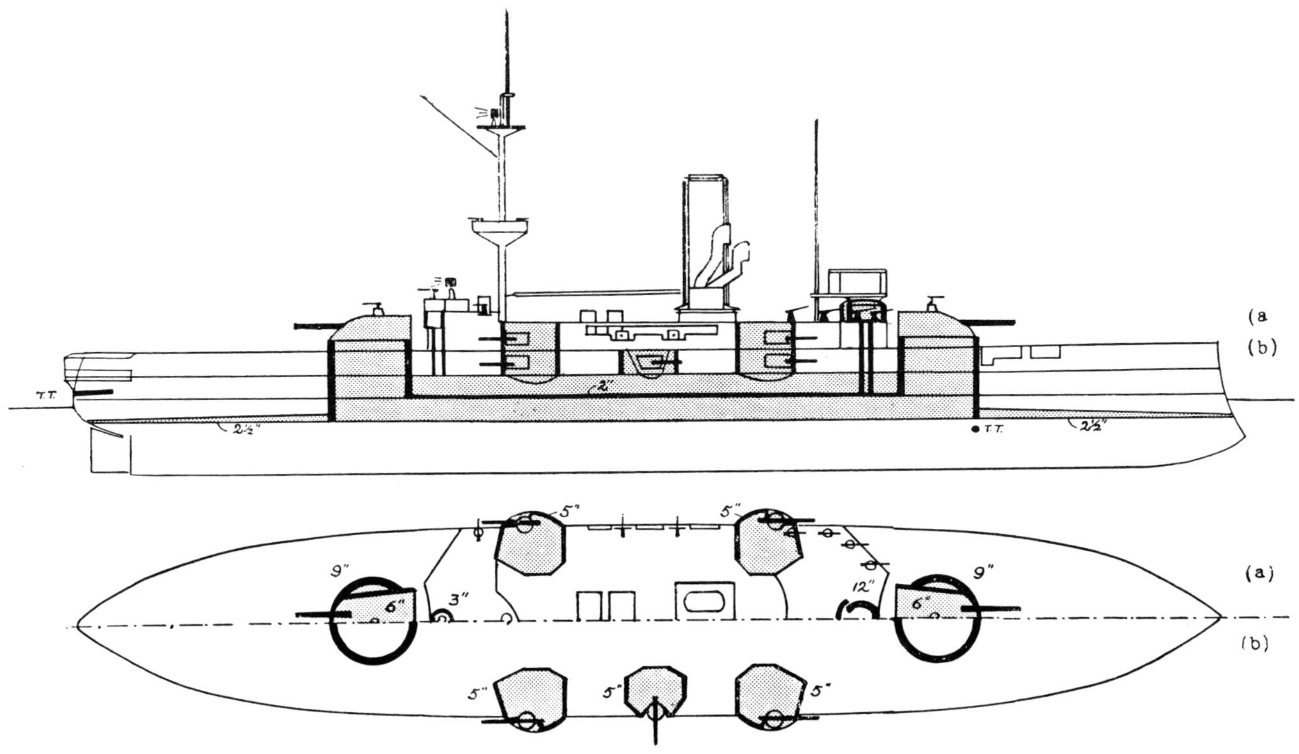

CENTURION reconstructed.

in four double and two single casemates, together with their ammunition, meant a very considerable addition to the ship's weight. In compensation, every scrap of superfluous metal was taken out—superstructures, the after bridge, foremast (saving 20-odd tons), all heavy fittings and lockers, etc.—totalling 352 tons including the former main deck casemates (125 tons). Altogether 430 tons of new material was worked in—of which the 5-in. K.N.C. casemates accounted for 300 tons—making a net addition of 78 tons only. The draught was practically unaffected, and the general distribution of weights when adjusted to retain the same metacentric height left the good sea-going qualities of the original design unimpaired.

Boilers and machinery were thoroughly overhauled and made good, but there was no question of pressing the boilers beyond full power at natural draught, as by this time forced draught could not have been used without the certainty of serious damage and risk to personnel. The speeds obtained were

Barfleur	*Centurion*
9,137 h.p.=16·75 knots.	9,270 h.p.=16·8 knots.

at a mean draught of 26·7 and 25·7 ft. respectively, the *Centurion* being recorded as "foul." Neither in speed nor stability were the ships adversely affected, the improvements to both offence and defence providing striking testimony to the advantages possible under the system of detailed weights supervision recently introduced.

DIFFERENCE

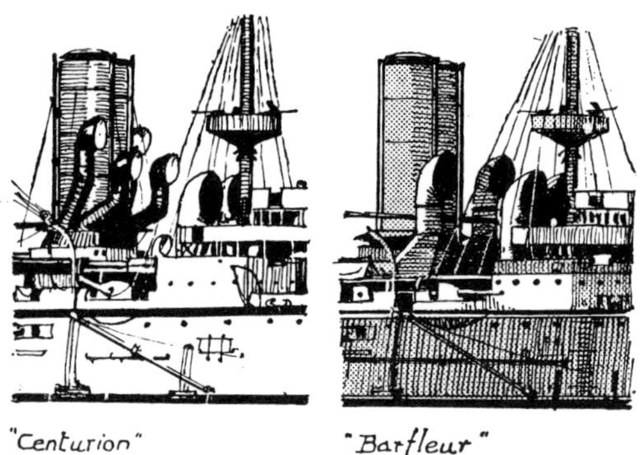

To show difference in ventilating cowls.

Reconstruction cost *ca.* £125,000.

Both before and after reconstruction *Centurion* had *two* ventilators with angled trunks each side of the funnels, while *Barfleur* had a large one with a straight trunk.

"BARFLEUR"

Passed into reserve at Chatham on 21 June '94 and commissioned for manœuvres July-September. Proceeded to Mediterranean February '95 where she relieved the *Sans Pareil* (refits at Malta '96-'97 and '97-'98) and transferred to China September '98 as R/A flagship. Returned to Devonport in January '02 and passed into Fleet Reserve. From August '02 to July '04 underwent a complete reconstruction. Commissioned for manœuvres July-September '04 (collided with *Canopus* in Mounts Bay 5 August '04) and then went into Fleet Reserve A. January '05 commissioned in reserve and in February took out a fresh crew to *Vengeance* (China). Flagship of Portsmouth Reserve from May '05; repair and refit '05-'06; March '07 reduced nucleus crew; April '09 joined 4th Division Home Fleet until June when she went to Motherbank.

Sold 12 July '10 for £26,550.

"CENTURION"

Commissioned at Portsmouth 14 February '94 as Flagship China (bilge keels fitted at Hong Kong '96-'97) and served there until September '01. Paid off at Portsmouth into Fleet Reserve C for reconstruction. Commissioned November '03 for China until August '05 (collision with *Glory* 17 April '04) then paid off into commissioned reserve at Portsmouth from September '05 to May '07 when she became a special service ship with reduced nucleus crew. April '09 4th Division Home Fleet. June '09 went to Motherbank.

Sold 12 July '10 for £26,200.

During 1891 the Board were pressing for a new type of 12-in. gun, and the design of the battleships to carry it came under tentative discussion. Early in the following year, as the dimensions and ballistics of the new piece were still unsettled, a revision of the shipbuilding programme became necessary. The Estimates for 1892 provided for the commencement of three battleships of a new type, but in face of the delay in providing their heavy ordnance, two ships were postponed until the following year and a decision taken to build the third to a modified *Centurion* design.

Upon completion of the *Repulse* work had to be provided for Pembroke Dockyard, to which this vessel—the *Renown*—was assigned as a measure of stop-gap employment *faute de mieux*.

In August 1892 a change in Governmnet again placed Mr. Gladstone in power for the fourth and last time, with John Poyntz, 5th Earl Spencer, K.G., as First Lord—who showed his administrative courage by retaining the naval members of the late Board and forming the strongest administrative unit which had ever sat round the big table in the Board Room at Whitehall. (Admiral Sir Anthony Hoskins, Vice-Admiral Sir Frederick Richards, Rear-Admiral Lord Walter Kerr, and Rear-Admiral John A. Fisher as Controller and Third Lord from February 1892.)

White had as his advisers Captain Cyprian Bridge (Director of Naval Intelligence)—a determined opponent of increasing dimensions—and Fisher, whose ideal armament for a battleship at this time was "the lightest big gun and the biggest secondary gun," so that both favoured a diminutive like the *Renown*. There was, in fact, some question of building the three battleships to her type, and Fisher thought so highly of her that he wanted a class of six,[1] but although she was regarded as comparing very favourably with any other battleships building in Europe in the matter of speed, protection and secondary battery, her main armament was recognized as being too weak—and the Navy was fortunately spared any more like her.

[1] As he personally informed the writer in 1918.

The *Barfleur* at Portsmouth after reconstruction at Devonport 1902-'04. She has lost her foremast and after bridge, and the whole amidships section has been rebuilt with a 6-in. battery in casemates. Wind sails replace all but the forward cowls.

"RENOWN"

Built at	*Laid down*	*Launched*	*Completed*	*Cost*
Pembroke	Feb. '93	8 May '95	Jan. '97	£709,706 £41,500 (armament)

Dimensions 380′ × 72′ × 26¾′ = 12,350 tons.

Armament 4 10-in./40 cal.
10 6-in. Q.F.
12 12-pdrs.
12 3-pdrs.
10 smaller.

Torpedo tubes:
4 18-in. submerged.
1 18-in. stern, above water.

Armour (Harvey). Belt 8″-6″ with 10″-6″ end bulkheads.
Barbettes 10″ with 6″ shields; casemates 6″ (main deck) and 4″ (upper deck); lower deck side 6″; deck 3″ slopes, 2″ crown, 3″ ends; conning tower 9″. Total 2,700 tons.

Complement 674.

Coal 800/1,760 tons.

Machinery Maudslay Son and Field. Two sets vert. trip. exp. H.P. 12,000 = 18 knots. 2 screws; 8 cylindrical boilers at 155 lb. pressure.

Radius 8,500/15.

Points of interest:

(1) The first British battleship to have a curved protective deck.
(2) The first battleship to have upper deck casemates.
(3) First British battleship to have all-steel armour.
(4) The last British second-class battleship.

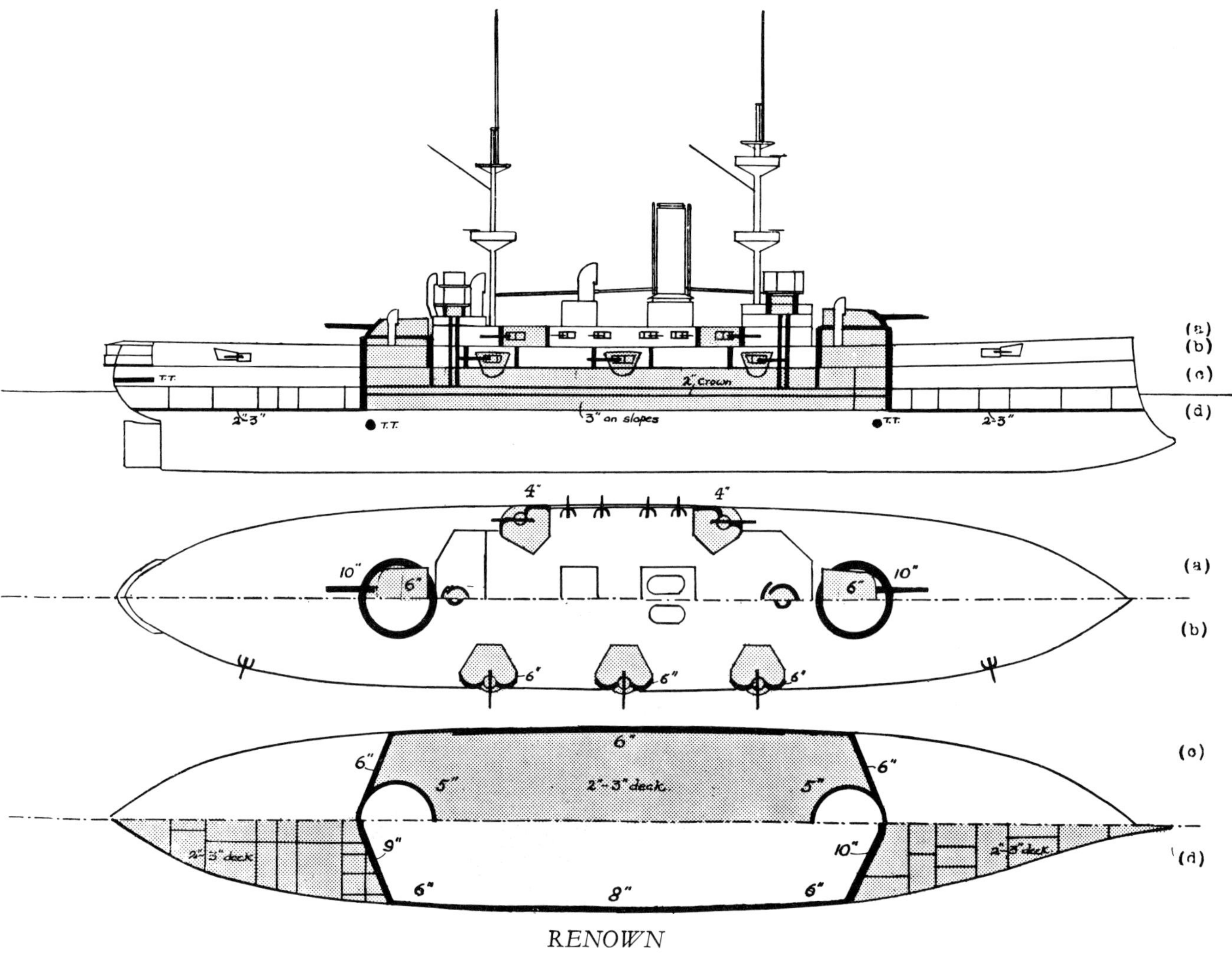

RENOWN

Originally the *Renown* was to have been the first of a new class to carry 12-in. guns, but when it became evident that the new weapon would not be ready for some time her design was prepared for the same main armament as the *Centurion*, but in conjunction with a heavier secondary battery than existed in any European battleship.[1]

The quick-firer had by now acquired an importance out of all proportion to its calibre value, owing to the large areas left open to attack in recently completed foreign ships; consequently adequate protection to the gun crews had to be provided, and objections to upper deck corner casemates on obstruction grounds went by the board.

A better system of protection was also to be introduced based on the distribution of armour White had proposed for the N.D.A. battleships, and in both this respect and her secondary armament she served as a model in our own and foreign navies for many years to come, thus meriting an importance far beyond her value as a fighting ship. But such as it was, her value rapidly deteriorated after five years' service, when an adaptability to the ceremonial side of the Service more or less relegated military qualities to the background, so that she became rated more highly as a yacht than as a ship of war.

With marked sheer both fore and aft and a graceful profile the *Renown* was always regarded as one of the prettiest ships in the Service, while the closed 12-pdr. battery amidships and heavier foremast providing a sense of solidity lacking in the *Centurion*.

ARMAMENT

The 10-in. guns were 40 cal. pieces which could be elevated to 35°, and having hydraulic training gear did

[1] The U.S.S. *Indiana* had eight 8-in. and four 6-in. guns.

not suffer from the creeping defects inherent in the steam gear of the *Centurion*. Except that the shields had closed backs the gun positions were similar, but the loading position was end-on only.

Of the ten 6-in. guns, four were placed on the upper deck in 4-in. casemates at the corners of the 12-pdr. battery and had axial as well as beam training, the casemates serving as battery screens. The other six guns had 6-in. casemate protection along the main deck, thus reversing the disposition in the *Royal Sovereign* with a corresponding drop in fighting efficiency. Wide areas of training (45°) were secured for these main deck guns by means of small sponsons, the ports being closed by hinged screens when in a seaway to prevent flooding. The gun fired through a curved shield which turned with it and largely occluded the port, the arc of fire being 45° before and abaft the beam. Rate of fire was six rounds in 50 seconds or in service sixteen rounds in three minutes.

In this ship the 12-pdr. battery amidships became a definite feature which persisted for over a decade. The guns fired through ports instead of being in the open, but the thin steel plating offered no real protection against

The *Renown* in 1904 commissioned for manœuvres. The main deck 6-in. guns had been removed in 1903 and this was her last spell of operational service in the fleet.

the smallest projectiles. The remaining four guns were at first in fore and aft hull ports and later moved to the shelter decks.

ARMOUR

Two new features of major importance were introduced—viz.:

(1) The protective deck sloped down to meet the lower edge of the belt instead of being laid flat on top of it,
(2) Water-line armour was reduced in thickness to allow for better protection along the lower-deck side.

The combination of the *Blenheim's* protective deck with belt armour introduced a system which was adhered to for 20 years in our own Navy and eventually came into general use abroad. To a projectile piercing the belt it provided a deflecting resistance of 3-in. steel at 45° inclination with coal bunkers above and below—nominally the equivalent of 6-in. vertical armour. And as experience had shown that while water-line hits were unlikely, the chances of hitting became greater as height above water increased, the wisdom of concentrating armour along a narrow belt became more than questionable. When the design of the *Royal Sovereign* was under discussion White had shown that the protection of stability by armour had been abandoned in all navies in favour of the lessened risks arising from a wider dispersion of guns and increased efficiency of the auxiliary armaments and had provided a thick belt with only 4-in. plating over the flanks as defence against above-water holing. In the *Renown* he was prepared to modify this conception to the extent of limiting the belt to 8 in., giving it the benefit of curved deck reinforcement, and increasing the plating over the hull side above to 6-in. As 6-in. Harvey was reckoned as two and a half times as strong in defence as the 4-in. armour in the *Royal Sovereign*, the *Renown* presented a far sturdier target than figures might suggest.

The difference between the new British system and those which obtained abroad may be seen in the following sections of typical battleships:

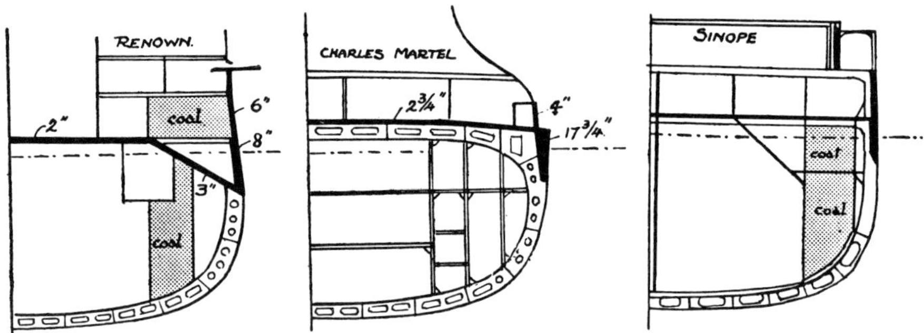

Cross sections of British, French and Russian battleships showing disposition of side armour (sadly lacking the *C. Martel*) and its conjunction with the armoured deck. Note how in the *Renown* the deck is sloped to the lower edge of the belt giving additional side protection to the machinery spaces.

Thus, in the case of the *Massena*, *Carnot* and *Charles Martel* there was a narrow 18-in. belt which rose only 20 in. above the designed load water-line, at the top of which lay a 2¾-in. steel deck. Above this was a strip of 4-in. steel only a metre high, and above that the hull was unprotected. Which meant that from a height of about 5½ ft. over the water-line the sides could be riddled by the lightest Q.F. guns, and water could enter *above* the belt when they rolled only 9°. Compare this with the *Renown* having 6-in. armour carried up 9¼ ft. above water to the main deck—the danger of water accumulating on the protective deck was incomparably diminished.

In the *Charles Martel* it will be noticed that 3 ft. below the protective 2¾-in. deck there is a thin "splinter deck" formed by a continuation of the double bottom. This was intended to stop fragments from hits on the deck above coming through into the hold, and also to keep out water coming in through holes in the armour deck. Actually the two decks were too close for any splinter stopping to be effective.

Bertin wanted to provide a cellular layer with armour decks at top and bottom of a much higher belt, but as this would have meant increasing displacement by some 3,000 tons the full development of his system had to wait for eight years until the much larger ships of the *Republique* class could incorporate it.

Another interesting departure in the *Renown* was the abolition of the usual citadel transverse bulkheads. In their place the two armour strakes were inclined inwards and wrapped around the barbette bases, so offering a greater area of protection from the beam—another feature which persisted for many years.

Because of the additional protection to stability offered by the flank plating it was possible to reduce the belt to 210 ft. as against 250 ft. in the *Royal Sovereign* which had the same length (380 ft.) beyond which the protective deck and subdivision replaced armour. This absence of bow and stern belt has so often been cited as a grave defect in White's earlier ships that its actual significance must be appreciated in the light of calculations made for the *Renown* on the assumption that all the numerous watertight compartments above the water-line had been completely riddled and destroyed.

(1) If the forward end only were injured as assumed, the bow would be depressed 3½ ft. below and the stern raised 1½ ft. above the designed load draught, giving a freeboard forward of 21½ ft. This was the worst that could happen so far as change of trim was concerned, with no serious effect upon her manageability.
(2) If similar injuries were received aft the stern would be depressed 3¾ ft. and the bow lifted 2½ ft.—without any appreciable effect upon her manœuvring qualities.
(3) If both ends were injured, she would sink about 17 inches, leaving her broadside armour 8 ft. above water, and her control but little affected. Under these circumstances her speed would depend upon the nature of the injuries received.

"Soft-ends" were retained until 1897, when the *Formidable* was laid down, but in her the thin belt extensions to bow and stern were more in the nature of a placebo than anything else.

PEED

The *Renown* proved to be the best steaming capital ship yet built for the Navy. Her trial results were:

	Air pressure	*Revolutions*	*Mean h.p.*	*Speed*
8 hours n.d.	·27 in.	97·8	10,708	17·9
4 „ f.d.	1·7 „	104·5	12,901	19·75

with an economical speed of about 15 knots with 6,000 h.p. and coal consumption of 1·88 lb. per I.H.P. per hour. Being a good sea boat, steering well and rolling easily, she was well fitted for the duties of battle-ship-yacht between 1902 and 1905.

GENERAL

During the time she was Admiral Fisher's flagship, 1900-01, the after bridge—an encumbrance of doubtful value—was shifted to abaft the foremast and the flash plates removed from the quarter deck to facilitate dancing—always her Admiral's athletic and social diversion. Twice favoured by Royalty for passage to India, her white and buff became grey in 1905, when she was relegated to dockyard service; and in 1909 the press recorded that "the *Renown* has again moved under her own steam" when her propelling machinery was used for the last time—only twelve years after she had hoisted the flag and performed but eight years of nominal sea service.

"RENOWN"

Left Pembroke 1896 for completion at Devonport and was passed in Reserve January '97. Commissioned June '97 as flagship for the Jubilee Review and then went as flagship N.A. and W.I. Vice-Admiral Sir John Fisher hoisting his flag 24 August '97, and two years later when appointed to the Mediterranean he transferred her there as flagship until February '02. Fitted for conveying T.R.H. The Duke and Duchess of Connaught to India, and main deck 6-in. guns removed October '02. On return p.o. into Fleet Reserve Portsmouth until July '04 and then commissioned for manœuvres. Big refit '04-'05. Commissioned Reserve February '05. Prepared for conveying T.R.H. the Prince and Princess of Wales to India April-October '05 (all 6-in. guns removed). On return went into commissioned Reserve May '06 and joined 4th Division Home Fleet '07. Tender to *Victory* October '09 and became stokers t.s. at Portsmouth (run into by water tanker *Aid* 26 September '11 with slight damage). Turned over to c. and m. January '13 and towed to Motherbank December '13.

Sold 1914.

Chapter 61

FRENCH BATTLESHIPS OF THE PERIOD

FRANCE being our principal naval rival, a few notes on contemporary French battleships may be included here to indicate some of the more striking features of their productions. Incidentally there were considerable differences in general appearance between ships which were nominally of the same class, as although the broad features of design were supplied by the Chief Constructor a good deal of latitude was allowed to the principal constructor at each Dockyard in the matter of detail—superstructure, masts, funnels, etc. Hence a sequence of ships which would have been of a class in our Service bore but little outward resemblance to one another and gave the impression of a fleet of samples.

To those interested in the appearance of ships this latitude had everything to commend it. Since the 'seventies French designs had exhibited a strong leaning towards the bizarre and "fierce-face." Piled-up superstructure, preposterous masts, uncouth funnels, tumble-home sides and long ram bows with no attempt at achieving any symmetry or balance in profile produced an aggressive appearance in marked contrast to the restrained and more harmoniously efficient ensemble of our own ships. They favoured small turrets which made the guns look over long, and grouped their secondary guns near the main armament for reasons of protection and magazine distri-

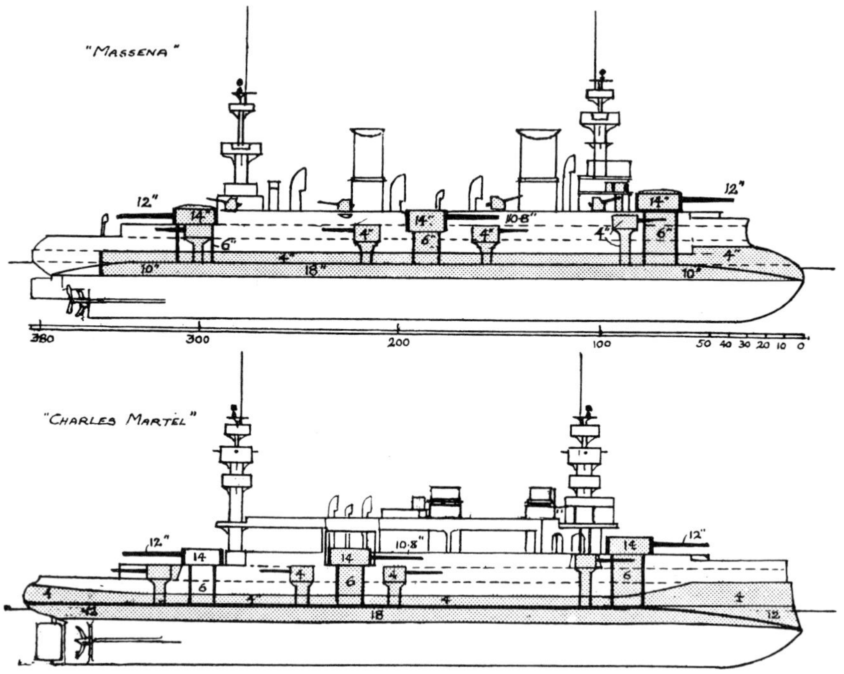

The *Massena* (1893) and *Charles Martel* (1895) are typical examples of the formidable appearance affected by French battleships of the period. Big guns were mounted singly in end and beam turrets with the secondary 5·5-in. also in single turrets sited near their bases. The *Massena* was one of the earliest warships to have triple screws. Note the shallow belts and lack of any armour above.

bution—although providing grounds for the criticism that one well-placed shell could put the whole group out of action.

But although well armed the system of protection left much to be desired, the hulls above the shallow belt being naked to attack. In order to secure end-on fire the topsides were constructed with a sharp tumble-home below the turret bases, which reduced stability at moderate and greater angle of keel. This tendency was theoretically overcome by high freeboard and enormous superstructure, but as these upper works presented a vulnerable target easily demolished by shell-fire and raised the centre of gravity of the ship, any flooding above the belt was likely to prove fatal when the inherent small moment of stability became still further reduced.

The *Carnot* and *Charles Martel* were laid down in 1891 and completed in 1896; the *Massena* was building from 1892 to 1898 and *Bouvet* from 1893 to 1898. *Massena* was the first battleship to have triple screws. All four were good for 17 knots at sea.

The *Bouvet* was the last French battleship to carry her guns in single turrets; thereafter the British system of twin turrets fore and aft was favoured.

Chapter 62

THE COMING OF THE "DESTROYER"

In the spring of 1892 Mr. Yarrow, then building torpedo boats on the Thames for our own and most of the foreign navies, informed the Controller, Rear-Admiral Fisher, that he had visited some of the French shipyards and was in possession of details regarding their new very fast torpedo boats. But if Fisher would like him to produce faster boats far in advance of the French, he would undertake to do so. Fisher at once asked for an official report on the French boats and his proposals to the Admiralty for a design which would surpass them. Yarrow's suggested dimensions were 180 ft. long by 18 ft. beam, and 4,000 h.p.

Fisher asked what he proposed to call them. "That's your job," replied Yarrow. "Well," said Fisher, "we'll call them '*Destroyers*' as they're meant to destroy the French boats." So the new type were at first called "torpedo boat destroyers" and later "destroyers" for short. Two designs were submitted both 180 ft. × 18 ft. 6 in. × 5 ft. 3 in., displacing 240/260 tons (*Havock*) and armed with three 18-in. tubes and one 12-pdr. and three 6-pdr. guns, but *Hornet* was fitted with the new Yarrow water-tube boiler and made 27·3 knots with 4,000 h.p., while the *Havock* with locomotive boilers reached 26·7 knots with 3,500 h.p. at 165 lb. instead of 180 lb. pressure. A noticeable feature in the trials of both vessels was the absence of all vertical vibration. In February 1893 *Hornet* made 28 knots on trials as the fastest vessel in the world.

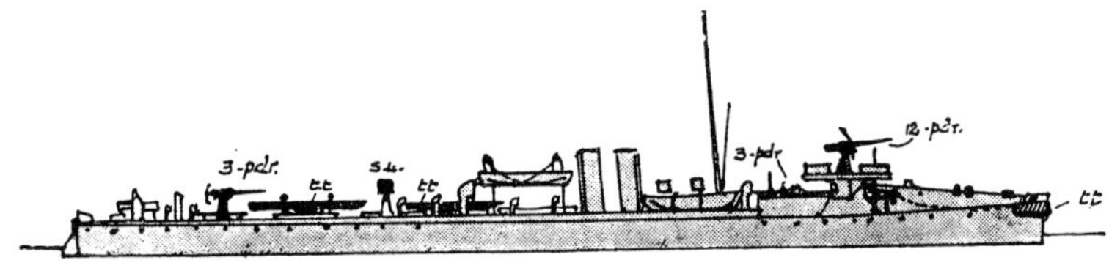

H.M.S. Havock

The Board was so satisfied with these pioneer vessels that a large number of contracts were distributed among numerous firms with complete detailed drawings of their machinery—a step taken without Yarrow's knowledge. At a loss to know how this dissemination of information came about, Yarrow inserted an advertisement in the press offering £200 reward for information leading to the discovery of the person offering the drawings for sale, which soon brought the Admiralty procedure to light. Yarrow felt that in distributing his complete designs to competitive firms without first obtaining his consent the Admiralty were giving away the results of original work and experience which did not belong to them. He refused any monetary compensation as he was fighting for a principle, and it was not until the matter had been taken up in Parliament that the Secretary to the Navy issued a statement acknowledging the value attached to Yarrow machinery designs and the fact that they had been used as a guide to contractors for destroyers since ordered. Such interchange of plans is now common practice, and if the particular firm sacrifices something today it will probably reap the benefit tomorrow. But the principle has formed a bone of contention at different times over gun-mountings, engines and submarines; and the Admiralty have always insisted on their point of view with the dictum, "If you do not care to work with the other firms for the good of the Navy, then you will no longer be asked to tender." And as the prestige of Admiralty work means so much in securing foreign contracts, contractors recognise an advantage which outbalances any loss which community of design may entail.

The early destroyers gave a lot of trouble at first. Engines and boilers caused many breakdowns, hulls showed signs of overstrain, and there was often excessive vibration. They were very wet, vastly uncomfortable, and bad rollers—in fact too small and lightly built for the exacting duties required of them. Gradually these early troubles were overcome when displacements rose and a full raised forecastle replaced the turtle deck forward. Later the adoption of turbine machinery and oil fuel with a more extensive use of high tensile steel in hull construction produced much more habitable and reliable ships with fine sea-going qualities.

Although originally intended for destroying torpedo boats by virtue of higher speed and heavier guns, their torpedo armament permitted subsequent employment as torpedo boats; in due course when the smaller boats became obsolete the destroyer succeeded to the major rôle of torpedo boat, and as such developed into an insidious menace to the battleship demanding ever-increasing measures of offensive and defensive protection.

Chapter 63

AGITATION FOR SMALLER BATTLESHIPS

DURING 1892-93 the characteristics of the *Royal Sovereigns* and a promise of increased displacement in the *Majestic* type brought about an agitation against the size and cost of battleships in both Service and political circles. The Liberals were opposed to any increase in naval expenditure on traditional grounds, and bigger battleships meant bigger Budgets; in naval circles there was a considerable reaction against monster guns which so largely dictated the size of ships designed to carry them; and on the Board itself the question arose as to whether a curtailment of speed and coal supply would not produce a more economical type of ship.

To a large extent the question of size arose out of discussions on the best form of convoy protection, and the defeat of the privateers proposed by French strategists of the "Jeune École." Numbers and not individual power were required to keep the Channel free to commerce, and at a Board meeting on 2 December 1892 a proposal was made to build some battleships of limited speed and coal supply which could be used for restricted service in the Channel or near our coasts.

The qualities of offence and defence necessary to meet the most modern French or Russian ships were to be preserved, so that they would be coast defenders of a type never previously considered and very different from the mistaken conceptions built during the Transition Period.

White prepared a memorandum on this subject for the Board, and taking the *Royal Sovereign* as a basis for calculations showed that the items on which savings would be possible were: (1) hull, including the protective deck, (2) engines, (3) equipment. By allowing 14 knots instead of 16½ knots for the eight-hour n.d. trials there would be a continuous sea speed of 12 knots with an outside saving of £60,000; and this would be effected by halving the bunkerage and allowing about seven days' steaming at 10 knots, or something like 1,600 knots with 80 tons for auxiliary purposes.

These figures, he considered, were sufficient justification of the view always maintained by the Admiralty that the construction of vessels of low speed as compared with contemporaries abroad was not justified by the possible economy so obtained.

In another memorandum of 5 December 1892 "On the Characteristics and Dimensions of Battleships" he dealt with the subject from a general point of view, when reviewing the claims made by advocates of smaller ships of certain types which had been championed as capable of defeating the big battleship.

> "The general idea underlying all these proposals is that even in the largest ships there are considerable areas of the upper works unarmoured, and liable to speedy destruction by shell-fire from guns of moderate calibre, with quick-loading mechanism and high explosives as the bursters. Moreover, the armour extends but a moderate distance below the load-line in still water, and either a moderate angle of roll or change of water-level due to wave motion may expose the weak bottom below the armour to perforation by chance projectiles, which would readily find access to the vitals.
>
> Taking these facts into account, it is urged that there is no need to carry armour-piercing guns of great power, that moderate calibres (9·2-in. or 10-in. at the most) should not be exceeded, and few of these carried. Quick-firing guns of 6-in. calibre and below, it is considered, should form the bulk of the armaments. A moderate number of these should be mounted in one ship, in order to diminish the risk of serious loss involved in the destruction of a unit of an attacking force. Since armour protection has the restricted value above described, it is argued that it may be dispensed with, or made very moderate in thickness and extent. In this manner the size and cost of individual ships can be kept within modest limits.
>
> The capital expenditure on a few large battleships carrying heavy guns in strongly armoured positions, and a great weight of armour on certain portions of their hulls, can be made to produce a considerably greater number of smaller ships, each of which, it is considered, is as efficient against underwater attacks as larger ships. The united action of these smaller ships against the less number of vessels of larger type would, according to the advocates of the former, almost certainly secure their victory. Probably there would be the loss of several of these smaller vessels, but their greater number would give a margin for such losses, and still leave a force available for simultaneous attacks from different directions. Such attacks, it is thought, would be most difficult to deal with on the part of commanders of the fewer but larger ships, and the multiplication of rams and torpedoes associated with increase in numbers would have an overwhelming effect.
>
> For many services besides fleet actions—such as covering a stretch of coastline or sweeping an area of sea—the increase in numbers would be of immense value. With larger numbers in a fleet small squadrons could be detached from the main body without seriously crippling the force. In short, increase in numbers is held to favour both the power of *concentration* and of *distribution*, according as the necessity of the moment may dictate; so that there is an elasticity in the employment of a force not attainable with a few large ships representing the same capital expenditure."

Having thus stated the claims for smaller dimensions with scrupulous fairness, White proceeded to explain his objections. In the maintenance of speed at sea and in steadiness of gun platform the larger vessels were superior; they were less likely to be put out of action by a single blow, either from gun, ram or torpedo; and carrying their armament on a single bottom, and under one direction, gave them a greater power of concentrated attack; the fire of heavy guns in well-protected positions might be reversed until it was possible to deliver it with the maximum effect; and a good action could be fought with the secondary armament alone. Small ships could not carry heavy armour-piercing guns in well-protected positions, and destruction of unarmoured upper works was accomplished more rapidly when big guns were associated with quick-firers.

Turning to the tactical question involved, he remarked that many of the most experienced naval tacticians regarded the hypothetical *concerted attack* by several smaller vessels on a single large one as impossible in practice, while they ran serious risks of ramming or injuring each other during action.

> "In fleet actions the corresponding risks would be even greater. Supposing seven or eight large ships opposed to twenty or thirty smaller ones, the difficulty of concerted attack, even in the earliest stages of an action, would be great, and it would become practically impossible later on. While the comparatively few large ships might act together and concentrate their attack on any selected portion of the flotilla of small ships, the corresponding concentration by a crowd of small ships would be impracticable . . . and the smaller ships would run great risks of being destroyed in detail by the larger."

A 9,500-ton type, of which twelve could be built at the cost of eight *Royal Sovereigns*, was also being advocated by Lord Brassey, Captain Eardley-Wilmot, and others. These, White showed, might equal the larger ships in speed, steadiness and steaming radius, but thinner armour and lighter guns had to be accepted as the price paid for four additional rams and twenty-four torpedo tubes. They would be intentionally inferior to the first-class battleships of France and Russia, although our *Royal Sovereigns* were actually cheaper than their foreign contemporaries.

> "Ramming and torpedo attacks are effective only in the closest action. The attack by, and defence against, artillery are possible under modern conditions at considerable ranges. By general consent the gun armament is still treated as of the highest importance, and it can only receive its fullest development on the larger ships. Adequate protection against heavy guns in the ships now built or building for foreign navies can only be obtained in large ships. Mere statements of *maximum* thickness of armour are misleading . . . the real question to be determined is, in short, what qualities of speed, coal endurance, armament and protection ought to be associated in the battleship which is intended to form one in a fleet designed to meet other ships built or building."

"Moderate dimensions" in 1893 equalled the biggest ships of twenty years before, as in turn the biggest ships in 1893 would have been very moderate dimensions twenty years later. Whether belonging to the Victorian, Edwardian or Georgian eras, the arguments for and against them have remained the same, and what White wrote may be taken as applying to the claims put forward for smaller battleships time and again in the next forty years.

Chapter 64

THE "NAVAL SCARE" OF 1893, AND THE SPENCER PROGRAMME THE "MAJESTIC" CLASS

In his statement upon the Naval Defence Act Lord George Hamilton had specifically stated that the new construction thereby provided was not to be regarded as a temporary spurt which would ensure naval supremacy, but rather as the commencement of a steady accumulation of strength year by year through successive programmes commensurate with our requirements as they presented themselves. Upon relinquishing office he left behind him a memorandum indicating what his Board considered the minimum programme of new construction for which immediate provision was necessary, and this included three battleships for 1892 and two more in 1893.

Only the *Renown* was commenced in 1892, and when it seemed as if 1893 would be passed without fresh keels being laid the opinion of the country quickly became manifest. Again Lord Charles Beresford drew attention to our cruiser weakness, and in an address to the London Chamber of Commerce on "The Protection of the Mercantile Marine in War" made a call for an expenditure of 25 millions spread over three-and-a-half years. Vice-Admiral P. H. Colomb supported this necessity in the *United Service Magazine*, and letters and articles from naval officers appeared in the press. Lord George Hamilton raised the question in the House and pinned the Government down to a statement of our requirements.

Now, in 1889 Lord Salisbury's Government had waited to be convinced of the necessity for a big increase in expenditure and on the strength of that conviction had carried public opinion with them in passing the N.D.A.; but in 1893 Mr. Gladstone's Ministry regarded reduction of expenditure upon defence as a moral virtue, and needed drastic coercion before doing their plain duty.

Early in November 1893 Lord Spencer had asked White to prepare a statement showing the estimated expenditure on new construction for the next five years, with dates of laying down and completion of the ships it was proposed should be built in reply to the French programme introduced by Admiral Gervais—which included the battleships *Bouvet*, *Charlemagne*, *Gaulois* amd *St. Louis* ordered in January 1893.

The situation against which provision had to be made was likely to develop in 1896-7. The years 1894-5 would see nineteen British first-class battleships ready for service against ten French and three Russian, as several included in the lists for 1889 had passed into the second line. But owing to the ships completing afloat or well advanced on the stocks, France and Russia would steadily improve their position unless we laid down more ships in 1894; during 1896 they would certainly complete six battleships, bringing them up to practical equality in numbers with our own if the *Renown* and two ships it was proposed to lay down could be ready by then. In addition to first-class ships France would have four powerful *Bouvines* class in the second line, and Russia would also have added some of a similar type.

White regarded it as imperative that *at least* six first-class ships should be laid down during the years 1894-96 and completed in 1898, this being the *minimum addition* which would keep the Navy abreast of France and Russia in completed ships.

Lord George Hamilton's resolution in the House was "that in view of the critical years ahead immediate and considerable additions to the Navy were necessary"; to which Mr. Gladstone replied with an amendment intended to delay any such action:

> "I may venture to assure the House on the responsibility of the Government that neither the House nor the Country need entertain under the existing circumstances, the smallest apprehension as to the distinct supremacy of Great Britain."

and Sir William Harcourt for the Exchequer pretended to represent the professional advisers of the Admiralty when he declared that the existing condition of the Navy was satisfactory—both omitting any reference to "the critical years ahead."

Lord Spencer at once protested against these statements without waiting for any action from the naval members of the Board, who were prepared to resign in a body if their advice was rejected. (Admiral Sir Frederick Richards (August 1893) Rear-Admiral Lord Walter Kerr; Rear-Admiral Sir John Fisher; Captain Gerard Noel.) Faced with a political crisis, the Liberal, Government had to trim its sails to the rising storm. Sir William Harcourt managed to explain his words away and Sir Frederick Richards disposed of the Prime Minister's statement as "a misunderstanding between bare equality and real equality for the Fleet occupying the inferior strategic position."

The First Lord then presented a draft Programme for the years 1893-98 and the Cabinet received it with bad grace; but in face of the threatened resignation of the Sea Lords had no alternative but to accept the situation. All credit is due to Lord Spencer for carrying through his great Programme in the face of opposition by his colleagues and antagonism from a hostile and influential section of the Liberal party. The resulting increase in the Estimates was mainly responsible for Mr. Gladstone's retirement, and Sir William Harcourt made his reputation on the Exchequer by a readjustment of the Death Duties providing for an increase in armaments to which he remained opposed.

The full Spencer Programme of 8 December 1893 was to have included:

7 Majestics.
2 Powerfuls.
6 Diadems (1st class cruisers).
12 Talbots (2nd „ „).
4 Pelorus (3rd „ „).
6 ram cruisers.
7 torpedo gunboats.
2 sloops.
82 destroyers.
30 torpedo boats.
1 torpedo depôt ship.

at a total cost of £31,000,000 spread over five years.

Later the number of cruisers was reduced, the *Diadems* held over and only nine *Talbots* laid down. Four ram cruisers (*Arrogants*) were commenced in 1895.

"MAJESTIC" Class

	Built at	*Laid down*	*Launched*	*Completed*	*Cost*
"*Majestic*"	Portsmouth	Feb. '94	31 Jan. '95[1]	Dec. '95	£916,382 £70,100 (guns)
"*Magnificent*"	Chatham	18 Dec. '93	19 Dec. '94[1]	Dec. '95	£909,789 £70,100 „
"*Hannibal*"	Pembroke	1 May '94	28 April '96	April '98	£906,799 £57,360 „
"*Prince George*"	Portsmouth	10 Sept. '94	22 Aug. '95	Nov. '96	£895,504 £70,100 „
"*Victorious*"	Chatham	28 May '94	19 Oct. '95	Nov. '96	£885,212 £70,100 „
"*Jupiter*"	Clydebank	26 April '94	18 Nov. '95	May '97	£902,011 £65,640 „
"*Mars*"	Lairds	2 June '94	30 March '96[1]	June '97	£902,402 £61,950 „
"*Cæsar*"	Portsmouth	25 March '95	2 Sept. '96	Jan. '98	£872,474 £64,420 „
"*Illustrious*"	Chatham	11 March '95	17 Sept. '96	April '98	£894,585 £76,291 „

Dimensions 390′×75′×26½′/27½′=14,900 tons.
Load draught=14,560 tons ("*Cæsar*") to 14,890 tons ("*Jupiter*").
Deep load =15,730 tons ("*Cæsar*") to 16,060 tons ("*Jupiter*").

Armament 4 12-in. 35 cal. (80)
12 6-in. 40 cal. (300)
16 12-pdrs. (300)
12 3-pdrs. (500)
Total 1,580 tons (including Turntables and gun shields).
Torpedo tubes:
18-in. { 4 submerged. 1 above water (stern).

Armour (Harvey). Belt 9″ amidships with 14″ bulkhead for'd and 12″ aft.
Barbettes 14″×7″; shields 10″; casemates 6″; decks 4″, 3″ and 2½″; conning towers 14″ and 3″.
Total 4,535 tons=30·4 per cent.

Machinery "*Majestic*," Vickers. "*Victorious*" Hawthorn. "*Magnificent*" and "*Illustrious*" Penn. "*Jupiter*" Clydebank. "*Hannibal*" Harland and Wolff. "*Mars*" Laird. "*Prince George*" Humphreys and Tennant. "*Cæsar*" Maudslay.
Two sets 3 cyl. invert. triple exp. 4-bladed screws 17″ diam.
Boilers 8 cylindrical single ended; 155 lb. pressure.
H.P. 10,000=16·1 knots; f.d. 12,000=17 knots. 106 revs.

Coal 900/1,900 tons; plus a subsequent provision of 400 tons oil in all except "*Jupiter*" and "*Illustrious*."

Complement 672.

[1] Floated out.

Points of interest:

(1) Marked the return to 12-in. guns.
(2) Last battleships to have oval barbettes.
(3) Largest class of battleships ever built.
(4) Introduced a general design which with certain modifications served as a pattern for all the battleships of the White Era.

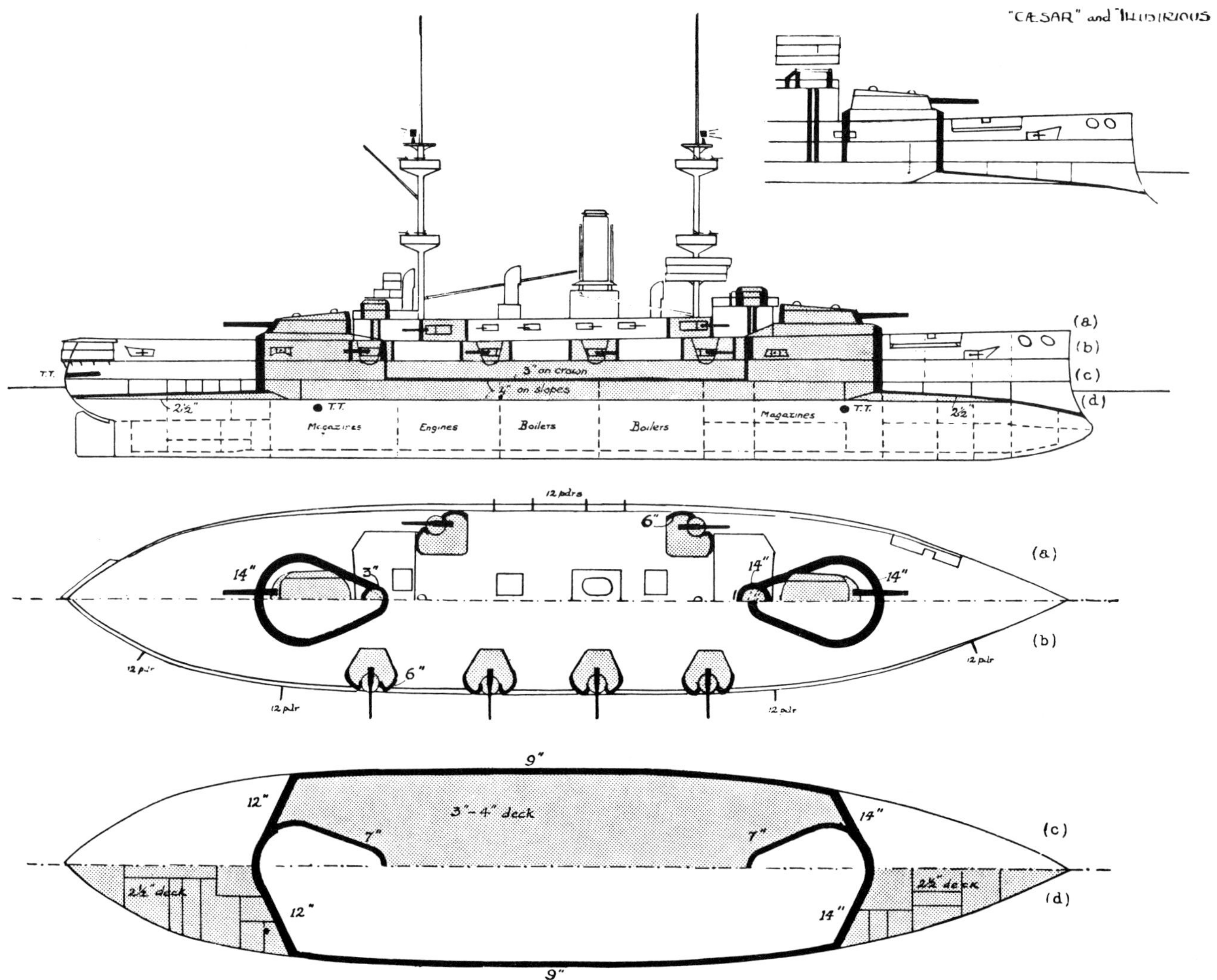

In the *Majestic* class the 18″ lower and 4″ upper belts gave way to a uniform 9″ over the whole citadel. In *Cæsar* and *Illustrious* there was a reduction in the size of the barbette, and the bridge was placed above the conning tower instead of around the base of the foremast.

White's ideas found their full expression in the *Majestics*, which were the finest specimens of naval architecture of their day. He had the advantages of Harvey armour and the new wire wound 12-in. gun, both of which favoured reductions in weight with increased efficiency; also the incubus of a 4 per cent. Board Margin was removed, and instead a reserve of only 200 tons had to be allowed in the legend displacement. Actually the Margin would have amounted to 500 tons, and as this load had to be carried at the same speed and draught it would have meant an increase of 1,000 tons displacement. As White pointed out, the *Majestic* would not have a narrow belt, but a wall of armour rising 9½ ft. above water, and that if in an extreme case 400 tons were added to her weight the extra immersion would only be about 8 inches; consequently the special reason which gave rise to the Margin—the lowering of the top of the belt in narrow-belted ships—did not apply to her.

In the original design the extra reserve tonnage was found by increasing the mean load draught from 27 ft. 6 in. to 27 ft. 10 in. with a displacement of 15,000 tons; actually it was found possible to reduce the legend to 14,900 tons, retaining the original draught.

GENERAL FEATURES

In general lay-out the *Majestic* was a 12-in. gunned *Renown* with additional secondary guns and thicker armour, and although only 10 ft. longer had the mass effect of a much larger ship because of her magnificent masting, which afforded a really noble profile. But the tumble-home of the *Sovereigns* was somewhat accentuated and proved a very questionable feature, as it detracted from buoyancy when the metacentric height was already small, although with a strake of 9-in. armour above the belt the *Majestic* was not so exposed to the loss of initial stability as the thin-sided *Sovereign*.

In all but the last three ships to be laid down the forebridge was built around the base of the mast so that the conning tower should be clear of wreckage; in these three the risk of the mast being involved with bridge damage was considered of more importance, so the chart house was shifted further forward. Also the communication tubes from conning tower to bridge were more easily arranged in this latter position. *Majestic* and *Magnificent*

Mars when in the Channel Fleet 1898. As completed she differed from the rest of the class in having torpedo nets stowed on a shelf below the main deck casemates instead of above them, and was the first battleship to be fitted for oil burning.

had pole instead of striking topmasts for some years, and *Mars* carried her torpedo shelf below the main-deck batter—to which position it was afterwards moved in the others.

HULL WEIGHTS

Both the *Royal Sovereigns* and *Majestics* were always spoken of as being exceedingly strong and well-built ships—the former especially. This was partly due to a growing practice of providing battleships with fittings of extraordinary strength and weight compared with those in cruisers, so that they came to be regarded as useful repositories for every sort of heavy fitting. The *Royal Sovereigns* suffered a lot from this extravagance—so much so that one contract-built hull reached 5,700 tons against 5,340 tons in a Dockyard-built hull when the weight as designed was only 4,850 tons. While special efforts were made to build the *Majestic* and *Magnificent* in record time, care was taken to check the customary freedom in the use of overweight material, with the result that the

Majestic had a 5,717 tons hull as against the 5,650 allowed. With the contract-built ships supervision was not so strict and the heaviest reached 6,030 tons. Incidentally the competition between the first two ships to reach completion became so keen that irregularities in the delivery of material were connived at—or even arranged for. Thus Lord Charles Beresford, then Captain of the Steam Reserve at Chatham, writes: "During 1893-4 the *Magnificent* was being built by Chatham in rivalry of Portsmouth, which was building the *Majestic*. It was becoming a close thing, when the *Magnificent* received from the manufacturers a lot of armour plates which *might* have gone to the *Majestic*, and which enabled us to gain a lead." It was generally held that "should" would give a more truthful picture than "might."

ARMAMENT

The change from 13·5-in. to 12-in. guns meant a saving of about 140 tons and this was used to increase the secondary armament from ten to twelve guns, with eight 12-pdrs. replacing 6-pdrs., making sixteen in all. Also the new Elswick mountings allowed for a further reduction in weight, which was absorbed by fitting hand gear as well as hydraulic power for working the big guns, with the provision of thickly armoured hoods over the barbettes.

The new 12-in. 35 cal. wire-wound guns weighed 46 tons and fired an 860-lb. shell capable of piercing 33-in. iron at 1,000 yards.

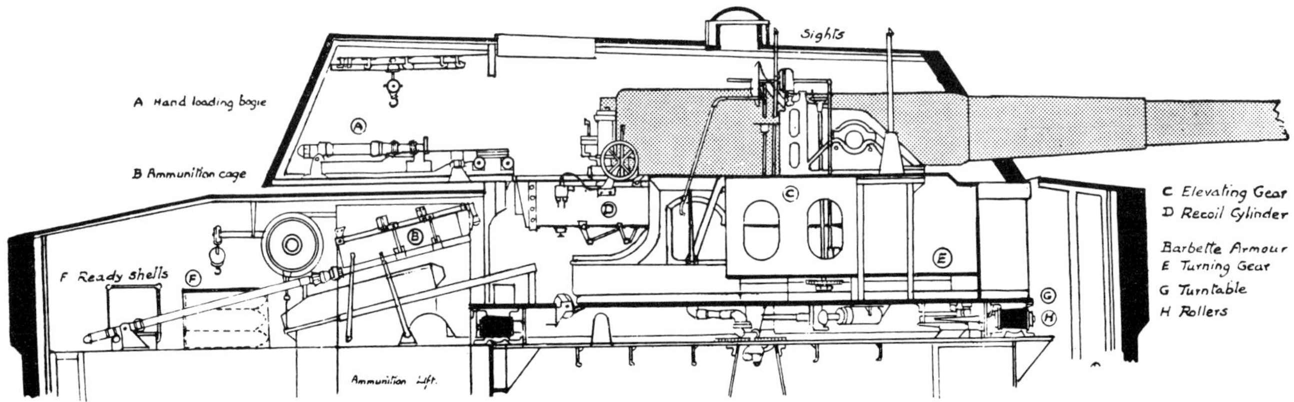

Barbette mounting in "MAJESTIC"

There were some small differences in detail in the mountings of the *Majestic* and *Magnificent*, but the loading arrangements were substantially the same for all nine ships. The fixed loading position was on the middle line at the pointed end of the barbette, with a rectangular hoist from the magazine and shell room. The shell and charge fell out on either side of the trunk and a fixed hydraulic ram in line with either gun rammed them home at an elevation of 13½°. All-round loading was also provided for eight rounds per gun; the projectiles were carried in a small bin at the rear end of the turntable and the cartridges were hoisted through a fixed trunk in line with the axis of rotation of the turntable. Small hydraulic rams fitted in the rear portion of the shield were used for loading these few rounds. The rate of fire was three rounds in four minutes and the ammunition supply eighty rounds per gun.

In *Cæsar* and *Illustrious* a very important change was made in the 12-in. gun mountings somewhat on the lines of that introduced by Armstrongs for the Italian *Re Umberto* (1887). The fixed loading position and rear hoist necessitating the very heavy pear-shaped barbette gave way to an all-round loading position with a cylindrical barbette. An all-round loading station was fitted in the hood, and the turntable carried a shell chamber in which twenty-four shells per gun were stowed; it also carried two hydraulic rams for loading. A fixed central ammunition trunk led from the magazine and shell room to this chamber and loading was at any degree of training but at a fixed elevation of 13½°.

Thus for the first time a break was made in the ammunition hoists and a very necessary safety measure introduced; this arrangement also allowed for a much accelerated rate of fire. The guns were worked by hydraulic power, and the moving weights balanced with the guns in the "run-out" position. This mounting and barbette was a basic model for subsequent installations in British and most foreign navies until twin were superseded by triple and quadruple mountings.

The barbettes were 14 in. thick above the main deck and 7 in. below it behind the side plating, with 10-in. sloping-sided shields. Forward the command was 27 ft. and aft 23 ft.

Eight of the twelve 6-in. guns were carried on the main deck with all the disadvantages entailed by such a restricted command in heavy weather—a disposition which was to persist in all White's battleships and most of their foreign contemporaries despite its obvious drawbacks. Not until the middle of the Great War was this battery suppressed in some of the later classes and half the guns raised to the upper deck.

Four of the 12-pdrs. were placed behind a thin screen between the upper deck 6-in. casemates on each side, and the remainder on the main deck fore and aft; the twelve 3-pdrs. occupied the fighting tops.

Ammunition for all these auxiliary guns passed on the under-side of the armour deck through passages which connected the magazines fore and aft, and communicated with the casemates and decks by vertical hoists. Electric hoists were subsequently fitted for the 6-in. guns.

As a point of interest the 12-in. guns and shields from *Mars*, *Magnificent*, *Illustrious* and *Victorious* were transferred in 1915 to the *Lord Clive* group of monitors and when given extra elevation made good shooting up to 21,000 yards.

Besides the seventeen 18-in. torpedoes carried for the submerged beam and the above-water stern tubes, five 14-in. were included for discharge from the picket boats.

Owing to the substitution of cordite for gunpowder the full 12-in. charge weighed only 167½ lb. against 295 lb. of powder in the earlier marks, which mainly accounted for the total weight of service ammunition inclusive of metal cartridge cases carried in the *Majestic* being only 335 tons as against 300 tons in the *Anson* for the main armament alone. Cordite also admitted of the supply for the secondary guns being raised from 200 to 300 rounds per gun.

ARMOUR

In these ships it would seem as if White was reverting to Reed conceptions, in that armour protecting stability along the lower deck side had the same importance as that defending the engines, boiler rooms and magazines. But in stressing the virtues of the armoured stability in his ships Reed made a virtue of necessity—he was compelled to find heavy plating for the lower deck side because it was part of the single-citadel wall where perforation might have put both turrets out of action. In the *Majestic* White allowed ample water-line security by combining belt armour with a thick inclined deck and wide coal bunkers, so that it was economically possible to provide against the effects of *secondary guns over areas which were not liable to such attack a short time previously*. And his big guns were safe and isolated in their separate barbettes.

In the *Renown* a first step had been taken towards equal protection along the water-line and lower deck sides; in the *Majestic* both strakes of armour were of the same thickness, giving a 16-ft. deep citadel of 9-in. steel for 220 ft. amidships which was joined up to the barbettes by a 14-in. bulkhead forward and 12-in. aft. Inside this citadel and affording mutual reinforcement was the curved protective deck, 4 in. thick on the 40° slopes to the lower edge of the belt with 3 in. on the crown. From the ends of the citadel it ran as 2½ in. to bow and stern, the sides being of ½-in. plating only. As on one occasion a picket boat rammed the *Illustrious* in Malta and holed her through this "soft-end," the class were afterwards sheathed with thick wood to prevent such a humiliation occurring again. But as such sheathing was usually resorted to for increasing beam and affording some additional stability (as in the *Sultan*), this precaution was taken as an indication that the ships were deficient in this respect—which stigma these excellent sea boats never outlived!

The total weight of armour apart from casemates was 4,055 tons compared with 4,050 tons in the *Royal Sovereign*; and the casemates weighed 480 tons against 160 tons in the earlier ship, giving a grand total of 4,535 tons—or 30·4 per cent. of the displacement.

SPEED

Their 3-stage compound engines were always reliable, and *Hannibal*, fitted by Harland and Wolff—the first battleship to be engined by this firm—had the reputation of being the most economical steamer of the class.

	Eight hours N.D. trials				*Four hours F.D. trials*			
	Mean draught	*I.H.P.*	*Revs.*	*Speed*	*Mean draught*	*I.H.P.*	*Revs.*	*Speed*
"*Majestic*"	25′	10,418	100·5	16·9		12,097	106	17·9
"*Magnificent*"	25′	10,301	96	16·5	24′ 8½″	12,157	100·3	17·6
"*Hannibal*"	25′ 3″	10,357	97	16·3	25′	12,253	103	18
"*Prince George*"	25′	10,464	97	16·5	25′	12,253	101·7	18·3
"*Victorious*"	25′ 8″	10,316	98·6	16·9	25′ 2″	12,201	105·3	18·7
"*Jupiter*"	25′ 10″	10,258		15·8	25′ 10″	12,475		18·4
"*Mars*"	25′	10,159	98	15·9	25′	12,434	104·2	17·7
"*Cæsar*"	26′	10,630	96	16·7	26′	12,652	101·8	18·7
"*Illustrious*"	26′ 3″	10,241	96·5	15·9	26′	12,112	99·5	16·5[1]

[1] Run in boisterous weather, affecting speed.

All results were obtained with the ships running light. They proved very handy at sea, with turning circles of 450 yards at 15 knots; the marked sheer at the bows gave a freeboard of 25 ft. forward with 17 ft. 3 in. amidships and 18 ft. 6 in. aft.

With metacentric height of 3·4 they proved steady gun platforms, the period for the double roll being 16 seconds.

But this low measure of stability, in combination with longitudinal bulkheads without adequate means for quickly righting the ship by flooding opposite compartments, was to prove a vicious feature in White's creations—which, like most of their contemporaries were in no shape to resist two torpedoes. Thus, the *Majestic*, *Goliath*, *Formidable*, *Cornwallis* and *Russell* all either capsized quickly or listed heavily before going under, the list precipitating their foundering and resulting in loss of life. In some cases the ship might have been saved if kept upright, but constructional protection against mines and torpedoes was to be of almost secondary importance for years to come until increased dimensions would allow for the necessary subdivision. Meanwhile low stability to secure a steady gun platform was of greater moment than a high metacentre.

FIRE CONTROL

When fitted for fire control the upper fore top and after lower top were enlarged and given head screens, except in the *Magnificent*—whose foremast might have belonged to the *Formidable*.

OIL FUEL

Mars was the first large ship to have oil fuel, and used to advertise her progress from harbour by a pall of smoke worthy of the best Japanese steam coal. All were so fitted subsequently, except *Jupiter* and *Illustrious*. In the earlier mixed-fuel ships the oil was sprayed on to the coal and not burned separately.

TORPEDO NETS

In the *Mars* the torpedo net shelf was experimentally lowered a deck and ran below the casemates, in which position it proved far more satisfactory—especially when the heavy Gromet net of closer mesh and weighing 5 lb. per sq. ft. was adopted. Added to which, if damaged in action portions of net could not foul the guns. The crinoline was only partial, the extreme bow and stern being kept clear so that a ship could proceed slowly and a damaged net would be less liable to foul the propellers—although in later classes, having inward turning screws, this risk was likely to be increased. In 1906 the Channel Fleet with nets down steamed at 6 knots.

Net cutters to deal with the heaviest mesh were of (1) the pistol type evolved by the French, which discharged automatically upon hitting the net, and (2) a scissor type. The former worked well enough experimentally, but did not score much success under realistic conditions. The closer mesh apparently defeated the scissor cutter, and both in our own and the German navies heavy nets were regarded as more or less torpedo proof. But France discarded the net; the Russians fitted it in some ships and not in others; for a short time it was carried in the Italian *Duilio* and *Italia* classes; and the Americans ignored it.

With main deck shelves "Out nets" became an evolution performed in an astonishingly short time, the nets being dropped and swung out into position on their 30 ft. booms in 10 *seconds* and refurled on to the shelves in 1 *minute*. The record times were even less, as recorded in the *Venerable*, 1905. (*The Navy and Defence*, p. 61, Chatfield.)

GENERAL

Caesar, *Hannibal* and *Illustrious* were greatly delayed by labour troubles.

Illustrious' first steam trials were not satisfactory, and she was to experience a lot of engine-room trouble when up the Straits.

FUNNEL MARKINGS

With ships of a uniform grey from 1903 onward identification largely depended upon funnel markings, first introduced in the Channel Fleet. These followed no set sequence until 1911, when a class displayed bands of white, red and black in their alphabetical order. These were all removed at the outbreak of war.

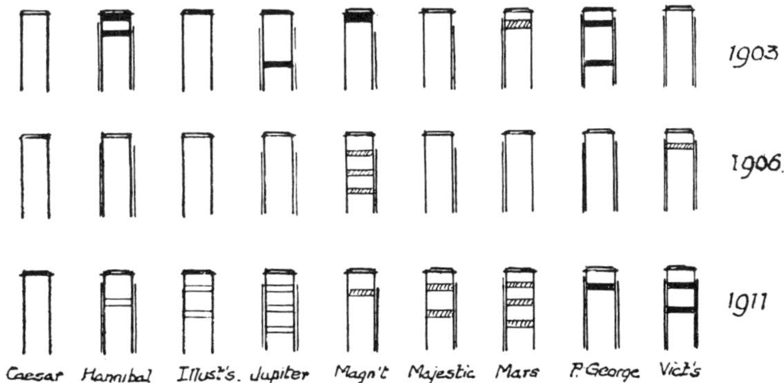

"MAJESTIC"

Commissioned Portsmouth 12 December '95 as Flagship Channel on which duty she was employed for eight years; p.o. Portsmouth February '04. Commissioned July '04 Channel (coal gas explosion 14 December '04; 1 killed, 2 injured) and transferred to Atlantic August '06; commissioned Reserve October '06 Home Fleet Nore, February '07; refit Chatham '07-'08 (f.c. and w.t. fitted) January '08 Home Fleet Devonport; February-June '08 temporary Nore Division Home Fleet; June '08-August '09 Devonport Division Home Fleet (nucleus crew); parent ship for battleships from August '10-May '12. In 3rd Fleet Devonport from May '12 (collision with *Victorious* 14 July '12 with no damage to *Majestic*) then 4th Division Devonport until August '14.

War: Commissioned Devonport for VII B.S. August '14; October part escort to Canadian convoy; Channel and Dover patrols; (bomb. Lombardsyte) 1915. Mediterranean fitted as mine-bumper for first Dardanelles operations and bombardment of 18 March; flagship of Admiral Nicholson 26 May, and sunk by U.21 next day off Gaba Tepe in seven minutes, thus starting and ending her life as a flagship.

Anchored with her nets out as close inshore as possible in the midst of transports discharging stores, with destroyers patrolling outside and trawlers forming a cordon the old ship seemed safe enough. But a periscope broke water 400 yards away and the track of a torpedo was seen coming through one of the few gaps in the screen of transports. It went clean through the nets without a check and hit amidships. Another followed instantly and in seven minutes the famous old ship, pride of the old Channel Fleet in whose design the whole thought and experience of the Victorian era had culminated, capsized. Good discipline resulted in all but forty of the crew being saved, and they were killed in the explosions or were caught in the nets.

She capsized in nine fathoms of water and for months lay resting on the stumps of her masts, her green keel awash like some great fish. Then in a gale at the end of the year her foremast gave way and she disappeared.

"MAGNIFICENT"

Commissioned Chatham 12 December '95 as 2nd Flag. Channel and so employed until February '04; p.o. Devonport for refit; July '04 Channel, transferring in December to Atlantic Fleet (gun explosion 14 June '05 with 18 casualties); November '06 commissioned Reserve Chatham transferring to Nore Home Fleet February '07; flag C.-in-C. (temporary) November '07; refit '07-'08 (oil fuel, f.c. fitted); 2nd Flag. Home Fleet August '08-January '09; February '09 Flag Nore Home Fleet (nucleus crew); February '10 Flag V/A Home Fleet 3rd and 4th Divisions (sternwalk damaged by S.S. *Veratyr* at Sheerness 3 December '10). February '11 tender to *Vivid* as turret drill ship; May '12 sea-going gunnery t.s. Devonport; became independent command September '12 (grounded near Cawsand Pier in fog 16 June '13 with slight damage); July '13 3rd Fleet Devonport.

War: Commissioned for IX B.S. Humber; transferred to Scapa defence; turrets removed for monitors and used as trooper for Mediterranean September '15 (Suvla landing). Afterwards employed upon miscellaneous subsidiary duties and finished as an ammunition store, Rosyth until '19.

Sold 1921.

"PRINCE GEORGE"

Commissioned Portsmouth 26 November '96 for Channel (in collision with *Hannibal* 17 October '03 with damage to plating, framing, and bulkheads. No blame attributable). Repairs '03. June '04 big refit (oil fuel, f.c., etc.) January '05 commissioned in Reserve; transferred to Atlantic Fleet February '05 and to Channel July '05; (damaged by collision with German cruiser *Freidrich Karl* at Gibraltar 31 March '05 attrib. to German ship) March '07 Flagship Portsmouth Division Home Fleet to February '09 (w.t. fitted '09) (5 December '09 broke adrift at Portsmouth and collided with *Shannon*—struck below armour shelf and much damaged) December '09 Portsmouth Division Home Fleet (nucleus crew); refit '10; August '11 Devonport Home Fleet; June '12 VII B.S. 3rd Fleet until '14.

War: Commissioned as Flag VII B.S. August '14; Channel operations; fitted as mine-bumper for Dardanelles passage; bombardments from March '15; hit badly 2nd May, repaired Malta; covering force at Suvla; hit by torpedo which failed to explode during Evacuation of Helles 9 January '16; p.o. Chatham and used as auxiliary sick-bay; miscellaneous dockyard duties, and finished up as T.B.D. depôt ship.

Sold 1921.

"MARS"

Commissioned Portsmouth 8 June '97 for Channel (gun accident 14 April '02) serving until August '05; large refit (first battleship to be fitted to burn oil fuel); March '06 commissioned Reserve, Portsmouth; October '06 Channel; March '07 Devonport Division Home Fleet; 30 March-27 May '07 Channel temporarily during refit of *Commonwealth*; June '07 Devonport Home Fleet (Nore Division temporarily during October '07). In 3rd and 4th Divisions until May '12; refit '08-'09 and November '11-March '12; until '14 in 4th Division Home Fleet Devonport.

War: Intended for IX B.S. but sent to Humber defence; September '15 to Mediterranean as trooper (turrets transferred to monitors); covered Anzac and Helles evacuations January '16; p.o. '16 and became depôt at Invergordon.

Sold 1921.

"JUPITER"

Commissioned 8 June '97 at Chatham for Channel and served until January '05; large refit Chatham; August '05 commissioned Reserve Portsmouth; September '05 Special Service and later Channel; February '08 Portsmouth Division Home Fleet; June '08 temporarily to Nore Home Fleet; October '08 Portsmouth Home Fleet (nucleus crew) Flagship from February '09-June '09 and then 2nd Flagship 3rd Division Home Fleet. Refit '09-'10 (f.c. fitted) June '12 sea-going gunnery t.s. Nore; refit Portsmouth '11-'12; January '13 3rd Fleet Pembroke; December '13 3rd Fleet Devonport.

War: Commissioned for VII B.S. guardship Humber and Tyne; sent to Archangel as ice-breaker and by reaching the port in February '15 established a record; remained until May and then to Channel; '15-'16 service in East Indies and Egyptian waters; '17-'18 Special Service; p.o. '19.

"HANNIBAL"

Completed at Portsmouth April '98 and placed in Fleet Reserve. Commissioned 10 May '98 for Channel where she served until transferred to Atlantic Fl. in December '04 (collision with *Prince George* 17 October '03, no damage); February '05 Channel; August '05 p.o. Devonport; June-November '06 large refit (oil fuel, f.c. fitted) October '06 commissioned in Reserve January-June '07 Channel; July '07 Devonport Division Home Fleet until '14 (struck sunken reef Babbacombe Bay 19 August '09 and severely damaged for 60 ft.; in collision with T.B. 105 29 October '09; no damage to *Hannibal*). Temporary g.s. Devonport June '10; refit November '11-March '12.

War: Intended for IX B.S. but sent to guard Humber and later Scapa; September '15 to Mediterranean as trooper (turrets transferred to monitors); during '15-'16 on Special Service.

'16-'19 East Indies and Egypt.

Sold 1920.

"VICTORIOUS"

Joined Fleet Reserve Chatham 4 November '96 and commissioned 8 June '97 for Channel; January '98 to Mediterranean and thence to China (grounded on and off in Suez Canal February '98), returned to Mediterranean March '00-August '03 (refit Malta '00-'01) p.o. Chatham refit '03-'04 fitted as flagship; February '04 R/A flag Channel and afterwards Atlantic (run into by T.B. 113 in Hamoaze 14 July '04 and side plating damaged; January '07 Chatham Home Fleet; temporary Flagship C.-in-C. Nore '08; reduced to nucleus crew March '09; refit oil, fuel, f.c., etc. April '09 Nore Division Home Fleet. flagship Vice-Admiral temporarily in '09 (explosion in coal bunkers 5 June '10) January '11 Devonport Division Home Fleet; August '11 reduced to nucleus crew (in collision with *Majestic* during manœuvres 5 June '10 in fog; sternwalk damaged and starboard engine disabled, no blame). May '12 3rd Fleet Devonport; refit December '13.

War: Intended for IX B.S. but sent to Humber defence.

Base ship at Scapa for dockyard workers early '16-'19.

Sold 1923.

"CÆSAR"

Commissioned Portsmouth 13 January '98 to Mediterranean but joined Channel temporarily and arrived Malta May '98; refit Malta '00-'01; remained up the Straits until October '03; p.o. Portsmouth refit (nets lowered) February '04 Flagship Vice-Admiral Channel; Atlantic December '04; March '05 Flagship Rear-Admiral Channel; (collided with and sunk barque *Afghanistan* off Dungeness 3 June '05. Bridge, boats, davits, etc., port side carried away and large hole in waterline at bows; repaired Devonport) December '05 Flagship Rear-Admiral Channel; Atlantic as temporary Flagship February '07. May '07 Devonport Home Fleet (primary f.c. fitted '05 and completed '07) refit Devonport '07-'08; May '09 Nore Home Fleet and Flagship Vice-Admiral 3rd and 4th Divisions temporarily May-June '09; April '11 Devonport 3rd Division Home Fleet; March '12 4th Division Home Fleet reduced nucleus crew; from May '12 in 3rd Division and later 4th Division Home Fleet.

War: Commissioned for VII B.S. Channel operations and with Southern Fleet; '15-'18 North America and West Indies and Atlantic cruises; '18-'19 Mediterranean and Black Sea.

Sold 1921.

"ILLUSTRIOUS"

Commissioned at Chatham May '98 for Mediterranean where she served for six years. (Crete insurrection operations, September-December '98.) Channel July '04-'08 (R.A. November '06-September '08). Reserve Portsmouth '08-'12. 3rd Fleet Devonport '12-'14. (Manoeuvres '12 V.A. 2nd B.S.)

War: Was guardship in succession at Loch Ewe, Lough Swilly, River Tyne and Humber in '14. January-March '15 and June '15 detached service. (May '15 was listed in Channel or Southern Fleet.) Ammunition store ship Tyne '16-'17; store ship Portsmouth '17-'19. Paid off March '20 for disposal.

Sold June 1920.

Chapter 65

THE SINO-JAPANESE WAR 1894–95

THE naval actions of this war were fought between the well-equipped and well-led Japanese and the often poorly equipped and badly led Chinese. In tonnage, in number of men, in Q.F. guns, and above all in speed and the more modern type of their ships, the Japanese fleet was superior. The Chinese had one advantage in two second-class battleships of 7,400 tons; the Japanese possessed three protected cruisers each mounting a 12·5-in. Canet gun, but these by no means lived up to their reputation and did little damage.

In the Yalu battle the battleships *Ting Yuen* and *Chen Yuen*, gunned and generally protected like the *Edinburgh*, put up such a good fight against the Japanese Q.F. guns that they were responsible for Admiral Ito's withdrawal at the end of the day. Their unarmoured ends were not a menace to their stability, but finished up more or less intact and their armour was unpierced.

On the material side the battle of the Yalu demonstrated:

(1) The advantage of speed and the offensive rôle.
(2) The advantage of Q.F. guns.
(3) The necessity for special precautions against fire, and of removing all woodwork.
(4) The uselessness (or worse) of thin shields to guns.
(5) The necessity for not having accumulations of heavy gun charges in exposed positions.

As regards (4) the conclusion is drawn rather from the action on 25 July and the attack on Wei-hai-Wei than from the Yalu battle. On 25 July the shield of the *Tsi Yuen's* starboard 8-in. gun was struck by a shot, causing some loss to the gun's crew, and sending a shower of splinters across the deck, which killed or wounded nearly the whole crew of the opposite gun of similar calibre. As the result of this experience the Chinese landed all their gun shields before the Yalu fight, including the 1-in. shields to the 12-in. guns in the *Ting Yuen* and *Chen Yuen* (which looked like heavy turrets), but not the light turrets to the bow and stern 6-in. guns. Another instance was at Wei-hai-Wei, when a shot from the Chinese batteries struck the shield of a machine-gun in the cruiser *Yoshino*, killing two and wounding seven men, none of whom would have been touched but for the protecting (?) shield. As for torpedoes, the Japanese never fired any and never intentionally closed to within fair torpedo range. The Chinese ships fired one or two, but rather to get rid of them in view of the danger of their being struck by a shot than of damaging the enemy. The Chinese went into action with torpedoes in tubes, pistols inserted, and spare torpedoes in trollies at hand, but when shells began to burst about the ships the torpedoes in the tubes were fired off, although there was no enemy within 2,000 yards, while the warheads were taken off spare torpedoes and stowed below. The sudden sinking of the *Chih Yuen* was put down to the explosion of one of her own torpedoes.

While this evidence did not detract in the slightest degree from the value of torpedoes, it indicated the advisability of their discharge from below water and with the satisfactory development of the Elswick submerged tube. Above water discharge in British battleships was limited to bow and stern tubes which could not be properly sited and operated below water.

While the conduct and fighting experiences of this war had no effect upon battleship design, it was the first in which warships made extensive use of quick-firing guns, and torpedo craft were employed in mass attacks against battleships and cruisers. What was of more significance was the fact that Asiatic nations made use of European methods of warfare for the first time, and that Japan was able to defeat her vastly more powerful adversary in a series of overwhelming victories under the leadership and direction of her own naval and military commanders after all European officers had been withdrawn from their tutorial positions. And this only a comparatively short time since she had emerged from a state of feudal isolation.

Henceforth Japan had to be reckoned with as one of the naval Powers in the Far East, and from that day her position became stronger and stronger as her fleet grew and improved. Both China and Japan had looked to Britain and Germany as well as their home yards for their warships, and to Germany for their military organization and training. As military power made a greater appeal to the Japanese people than did the hitherto almost unknown navy which was almost entirely officered by scions of the Samurai, it was to Germany that the nation tended to turn for guidance in the direction of their Services after the close of hostilities.

China had no option but to accept Japan's terms for peace and the territorial demands which represented the reasonable fruits of victory. But the secession of the Liao-tong peninsula together with Port Arthur was wholly unacceptable to Russia, who saw her dreams of expansion in the Far East placed in jeopardy and had her own eyes fixed on Port Arthur. She therefore evoked the French Alliance to secure an evacuation of this very desirable territory and invited this country and Germany to join in bringing direct pressure against Tokio. The British Government refused to be associated with such power politics, but Germany—with ulterior objects of her own—joined the forces against Japan, who was compelled to hand back the surrendered territory to China.

Russia had annexed Vladivostock in 1860; in 1898 she forced China to hand over Port Arthur, which was to become her base for a greatly enlarged Pacific fleet and a necessary move towards the domination of Manchuria. French support for her ally was natural, but Germany's interference was absolutely gratuitous and uncalled for, as she had at that time no possessions in North China which could be affected by the so-called "upset in the balance of power." The two useful missionaries whose murder subsequently served as an excuse for her annexation of Kiao Chao were still at their labours, and she had no diplomatic excuse for assisting to bully Japan out of her hard-won spoils.

The Japanese felt this interference and insult bitterly as a stab in the back from a false friend, and she never forgave it. The result was that instead of turning towards Germany for professional help in equipping her services after the war she came to Britain for tuition, and placed her orders with Armstrongs and Vickers instead of Krupps. Later the friendship was to ripen into a full alliance which otherwise might have been concluded with Germany—and an alliance between Germany and Japan in 1914 would have resulted in a very different course of hostilities in the Far East, and placed Australia and India in jeopardy. Of all the false steps taken by Wilhelm II his severance of friendship with Japan was destined to prove our greatest blessing.

Realizing that their position at Wei-hai-Wei opposite to Port Arthur would be strategically false when the Russians had turned the port into a fully equipped and fortified naval base, the Japanese wisely offered the place to Britain and our flag was hoisted there in May 1898. It was never made into a fortified base, but served as an exercise ground and sanatorium for the Fleet.

Chapter 66

THE "CANOPUS" CLASS

LORD ROSEBERY had succeeded Mr. Gladstone as Prime Minister in 1894, and recommended White for the K.C.B. in the New Years honours. In May 1895 there was a Board conference on the ships to follow the *Majestics* and provisional agreement was reached as to their leading features:

(1) Main armament to be the same as in *Majestic*.
(2) Height of those guns above water the same as in *Centurion*.
(3) Speed, coal supply and secondary armament the same as in *Renown*.
(4) Water-tube boilers proposed in place of cylindrical, but these being lighter, questions of stability arose which needed investigation.

The approximate dimensions, displacement and cost, with a sketch design, were submitted on 23 May.

Before any decision was reached the Conservatives were returned to power, with Lord Salisbury as Premier and Mr. Goschen (who had joined the Liberal-Unionists) at Whitehall, after a lapse of twenty-one years. In Goschen the Navy was fortunate, for of the many good First Lords, few better combined a sleepless vigilance with an absence of any sort of nervous extravagance (John Buchan, *Scottish Review*, 14 February 1907.) The Board was only altered by Sir Frederick Bedford taking the place of Lord Walter Kerr, who had assumed command of the Channel Fleet. It was not until December that the proposals in the original report on the new ships was confirmed.

In outlining the features of the *Canopus* class a fresh influence on British sea power had now to be taken into account, as Japan had ordered two first-class battleships in England and these White foresaw would make a very important alteration in the alignment of power in the East.

> "Should the Japanese succeed, as seems probable, in refitting the captured Chinese ships, including the battleships, their fleet will receive in the next two or three years a very great accession of strength, which obviously must have a direct bearing in the types and numbers of ships of the Royal Navy required for the defence of our interests in Eastern seas."

He had proposed that a special class of battleship should be designed for the China Station, having greater length in order to secure the lighter draught required for passage through the Suez Canal. As neither of the new Japanese ships was to be sheathed and coppered, he put it forward that this considerable addition to hull weight (which could increase draught by over a foot) should be omitted, as we had docking facilities at Hong Kong which obviated any difficulties from fouling.

At a meeting on 1 June the complete design was again considered and it was found possible to allow for twelve 6-in. guns instead of only ten, all having casemate protection as in the *Majestic*. The upper fighting top was removed from each mast so that only six 3-pdrs. were needed, but the 12-pdrs being increased from eight to ten.

WATER-TUBE BOILERS

Although considerable advance had been made in the design of machinery, the boiler lagged behind the engine in British practice, our engineers having devoted their energies too exclusively to the using of steam when made, rather than to the making of it—at least, so far as large ships were concerned. On the other hand, for some years the French had been making great strides with water-tube boilers, the *Brennus* (1891) being the first battleship to receive them. Two main types were being developed (1) with large tubes for bigger vessels and (2) with small tubes for torpedo craft and third-class cruisers. Belleville produced the first type to be successful, other makers of large-tube boilers being Niclausse, Babcock and Wilcox, Yarrow and Durr. Pressures rose to 250 or even 300 lb.

The small-tube boiler was introduced by Du Temple in France and soon afterwards by Thornycroft in this country, who fitted them to the torpedo-boat *Arieta* built for Spain, and got 26 knots out of her in 1887. Later British makes were the Yarrow, Reed, White, Babcock and Mumford, all of which were tried out in destroyers or gun boats. Pressures were at first 220 lb. and later 250 lb.

Although good results were being obtained in small craft, the big boiler makers with huge sums invested in plant for manufacturing cylindrical generators were united in opposing any change in established practice so far as big ships were concerned. Our first ship to have water-tube boilers was the torpedo-gunboat *Speedy* of the *Alarm* class (810 tons). This novel type was intended to steam at 21 knots with 4,500 h.p., but their locomotive boilers proved unequal to the demands of the engine room and we had to be content with 3,500 h.p. f.d. and from 19 to 19·5 knots; but the *Speedy* managed 3,046=18·5 knots at n.d. and 20·2 knots at 4,703 h.p. f.d.

In 1895 our first torpedo gunboat the *Sharpshooter* (735 tons)—which had failed to make her designed speed by a couple of knots during 1890-91—was given Bellevilles and reached 3,238 h.p. (n.d.) with 19 knots by the log, after which other vessels of her class exchanged their fire-tube boilers for various types with water-tubes for experimental tests. Of these the *Sheldrake* (Babcock and Wilcox) obtained the best results.

The advantages claimed for water-tube boilers were: (1) higher working pressures, (2) saving of weight, (3) rapid steam raising, (4) economy in fuel, and (5) facility in repairs. Forced draught and high pressures were very hard on the shell boiler, but high pressures were necessary if full value was to be got out of multiple-compound engines, with the result that breakdowns were becoming a serious problem. Thus, after her long refit in 1891, when she had received new engines and boilers, the *Thunderer* was ordered to the Mediterranean; but on arrival there she started to develop such leaky tubes that Sir George Tryon insisted on her removal from his squadron as being no longer an effective unit. After a limping and inglorious passage home her tubes were doctored with Humphreys' ferrules, after which she managed to run to Madeira and back at 13 knots without further trouble. These ferrules turned out a remarkably lucky temporary expedient which enabled much good work to be got out of bad boilers. But nobody was going to design a new boiler with the idea that its tubes should be ferruled. In fact it looked as if finality had been reached in boiler construction on the old lines, and results with water-tube boilers in France and with the Danish cruiser *Geiser* (Thornycroft boilers made under licence by Burmeister and Wain) indicated an inevitable change-over to the new order.

When it became known that the Russians were likely to equip their big cruisers with Bellevilles, the Board decided to fit them in the *Powerful* and *Terrible* and the *Canopus* class; and as they had not as yet been tried in any large British ships all sorts of trouble were freely prophesied. It is sea-going human nature patiently to suffer accustomed evils, but to be very intolerant of new difficulties; hence what might be only a trifling and remediable defect in a water-tube boiler would be regarded as outweighing all the long-standing troubles experienced with the older type. The new boilers required more skilful attention than the old, and as the Admiralty instructions for tending them were not such as would tend to get the best results if strictly adhered to, a variety of difficulties had to be overcome during the first few years until proper training and practical working knowledge brought about a more satisfactory state of things.

Meanwhile the Battle of the Boilers raged with violent denunciations from the old guard led by Sir William Allen in the House, and a Committee of Enquiry was appointed which in an interim report recommended that no more water-tube boilers should be fitted. As a sop to public opinion—which had been thoroughly prejudiced against the Belleville—a compromise was adopted temporarily, and mixed installation of water-tube and cylindrical boilers were installed in some ships. When tests had shown that the Niclausse was inferior to the Belleville—which ceased to be troublesome by the time the agitation had died down—all new battleships were fitted with the latter until it was finally displaced by the Babcock and Yarrow large-tube types.

"CANOPUS" Class (1896-'97 Estimates)

	Built at	*Laid down*	*Launched*	*Completed*	*Cost*
"*Canopus*"	Portsmouth	4 Jan. '97	12 Oct. '97	Dec. '99	£866,516
"*Glory*"	Lairds	1 Dec. '96	11 March '99 (floated out)	Oct. '00	£841,014
"*Albion*"	Thames I.W.	3 Dec. '96	21 June '98	June '01	£858,745
"*Goliath*	Chatham	4 Jan. '97	23 March '98	March '00	£866,006
"*Ocean*"	Devonport	15 Feb. '97	5 July '98	Feb. '00	£883,778
"*Vengeance*"	Vickers	23 Aug. '98	25 July '99	April '02	£836,417
					(Guns in all £54,800)

Dimensions 390′×74′×25′ 10″/26′ 6″=12,950 tons (about 13,150 tons at load draught; 14,320 tons deep load).

Armament 4 12-in. 35 cals.
12-in. 6.
10 12-pdrs.
6 3-pdrs.
2 Maxims.

Torpedo tubes:
4 18-in. sub.
Torpedoes carried:
18-in. 14.
14-in. 5 (boats).

Armour Belt (K.C.) amidships 6″; bow 2″; bulkheads for'd 10″-8″-6″; aft. 12″-10″-6″.
Barbettes (K.C.) 12″-6″; shields 8″.
Casemates (H) 6″; decks (M) 2″×1″.
Conning towers (H-N) 12″ and 3″.
Total 3,600 tons.

Machinery Two sets 3 cyl. vert. invert. triple exp.
H.P. 13,500=18·3 knots.
Boilers 20 Belleville with economizers.
Engines and boilers by: "*Canopus*" Greenock Foundry. "*Goliath*" Penn. "*Glory*" Laird. "*Ocean*" Hawthorn Leslie. "*Albion*" Maudslay. "*Vengeance*" Vickers.

Coal 800-1,800 tons.

Complement 682.

Points of interest:

They were the first British battleships to have:

(1) Water-tube boilers.
(2) Krupp armour.
(3) Sponsoned casemates to obtain end-on fire from main deck guns.
(4) A natural draught speed of 18 knots.

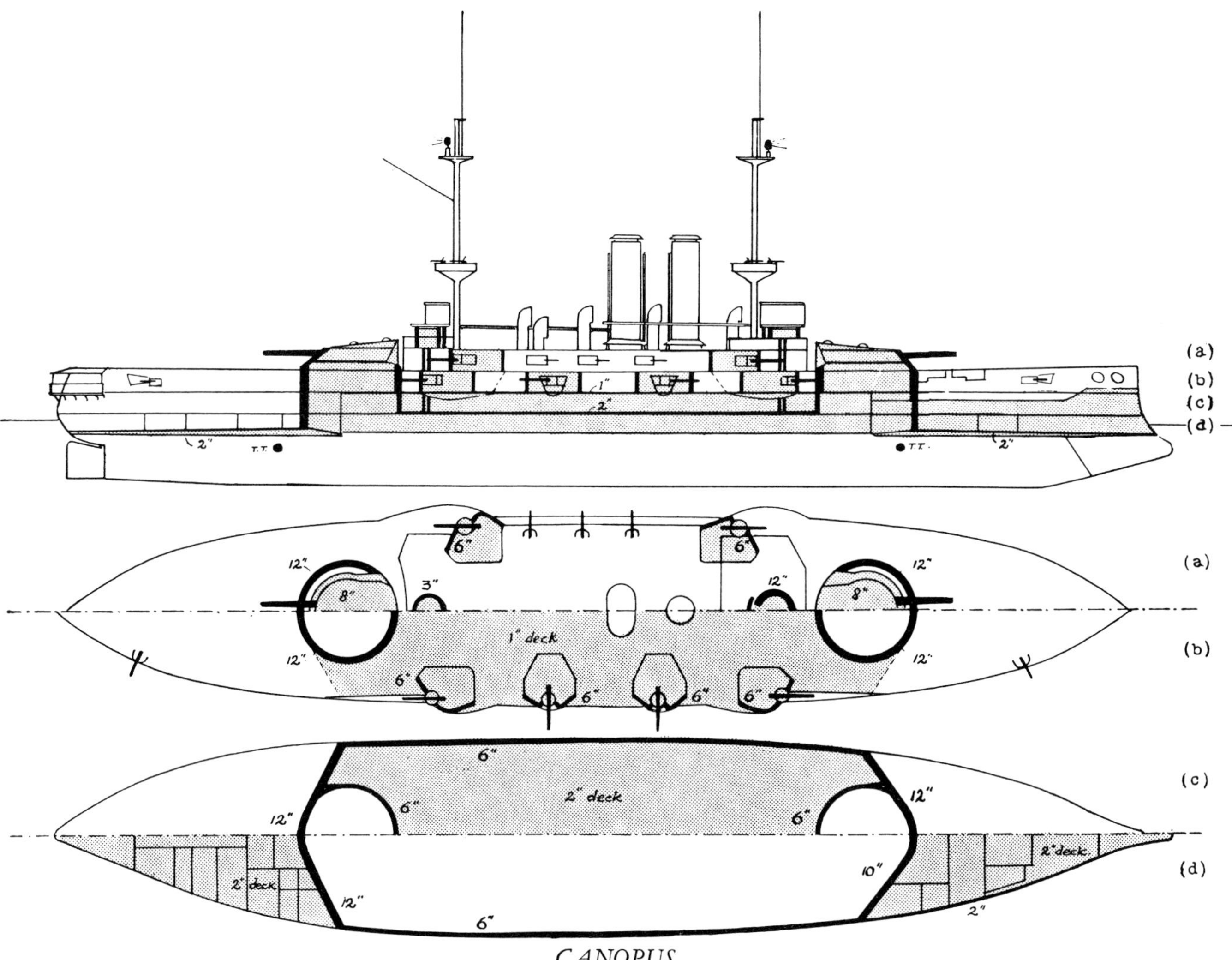

CANOPUS

In the *Canopus* the 3-in. protective deck of the *Majestic* was replaced by an upper 1-in. and lower 2-in. deck for defence against mortar fire.

The first five ships were laid down under the 1896 Estimates and the *Vengeance* under those for the following year. When introduced by the First Lord he referred to them as "improved *Renowns*," and the Constructors Department always regarded them as second-class battleships because of their thinner armour. Having the same length as the *Majestic*, their manœuvring powers were practically the same, as although the shallower draught tended towards a larger turning circle, the deadwood fore and aft being cut away compensated for this. Indeed the bow was quite a feature of the ships, the forefoot being steeply inclined with the most prominent ram of anything in the Fleet bar the *Polyphemus*; aft the cut-away was only slight compared with subsequent designs. All exceeded their designed displacement by some 200 tons.

ARMAMENT

Guns and mountings were similar to those in the *Majestic* with circular barbettes as in the *Cæsar* and *Illustrious* and the same loading arrangements—*i.e.*, at any angle of training, but at a fixed elevation of $13\frac{1}{2}°$. *Vengeance* was

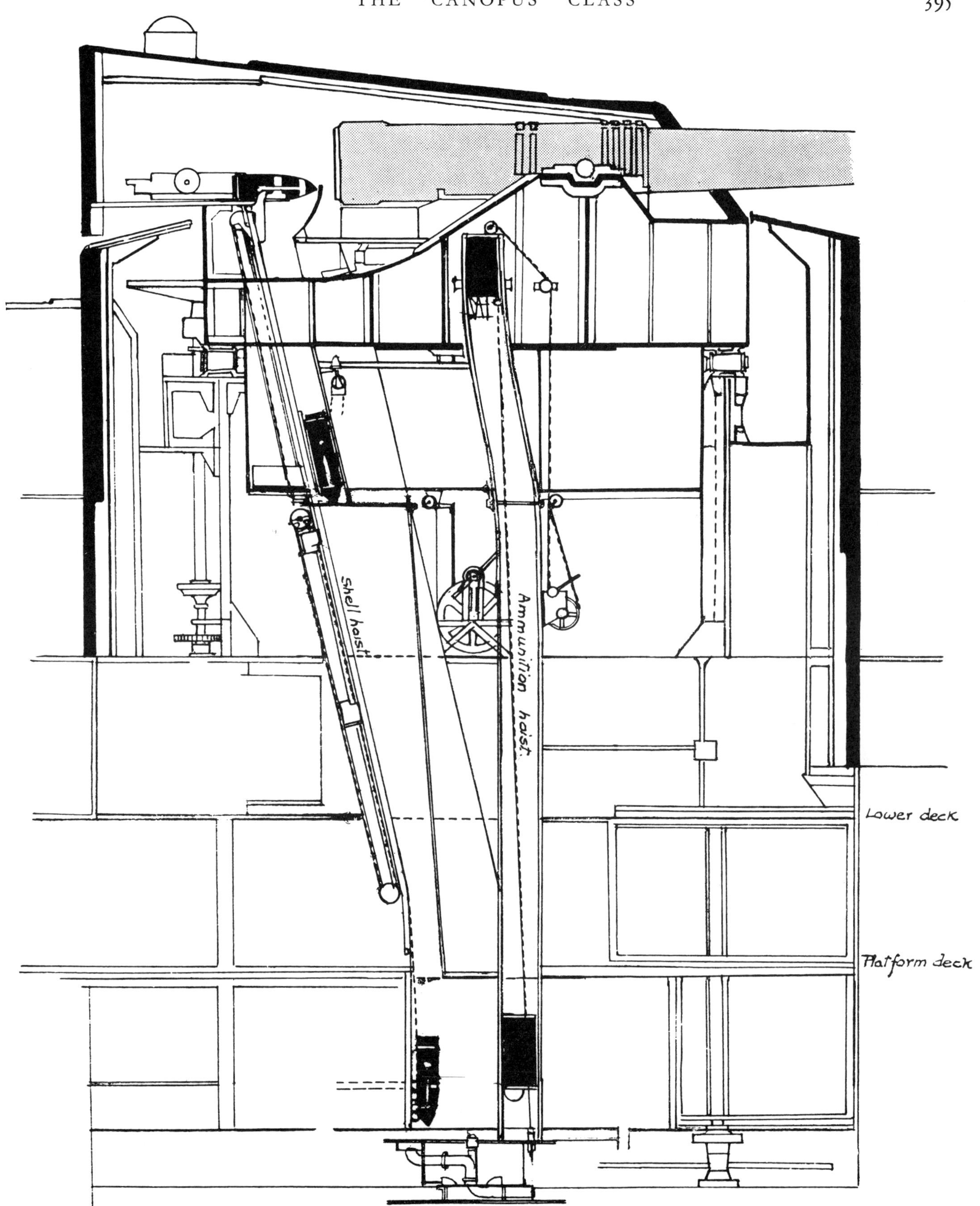

Section barbette in *Albion* and *Glory* to show alternate powder and shell hoists direct from magazine and shell rooms to guns and horizontal loading position.

supplied with Vickers new chain rammer for loading at any elevation, which was successful in reducing the time of firing from 45 secs. to 32 secs. a round. Her turrets had angled plates instead of curved fronts and flat sides, and so set the fashion which was to become universal.

On the main deck the end casemates were splayed out into sponsons to afford end-on fire, the guns being 12½ ft. above water.

Three 12-pdrs. aside formed batteries on the upper deck, with single guns towards the bows and stern on the main deck. The 3-pdrs. occupied the fighting tops.

PROTECTION

The outstanding feature in the protection of these ships was the introduction of armour made by the Krupp process which was used for the belt and barbettes. Its increased resistance is shown by the comparative figures:

5¾-in. Krupp—7½-in. Harvey—12in. Compound—15-in. Iron

or ratios of 1: 1·3: 2·08: 2·6.

Vertical armour was disposed as in the *Majestic*, but generally reduced in thickness, the belt being of 6-in. Krupp instead of 9-in. Harvey—or the equivalent of 15 in. in place of 18 in. of iron. It extended for 195 ft.—25 ft.

Vengeance as flagship African Station. The fighting tops were adapted for gunnery control in 1912, and short topmasts were a wartime feature. The second funnel had its greatest diameter athwartships (see plan), but they appeared to be the same size when viewed abeam.

less than in the *Majestic*—with a width of 14 ft. of which 9 ft. was above and 5 ft. below water; forward it was closed by a bulkhead 10 in.-8 in.-6 in. and aft by one of 12 in.-10 in.-6 in.—the difference being accounted for by the addition of a 2-in. bow belt rising nearly to the level of the hawse holes and taken down to the forefoot and reinforcing the ram.

It will be remembered that when White had proposed something of the sort for the *Royal Sovereign* the Board considered the armour deck and subdivision sufficient to maintain buoyancy forward. But when the *Canopus* design was under consideration the risk of the forecastle being riddled by tertiary fire and swamped by the bow wave led to the addition of this 2-in. plating. It would, of course, have been useless against medium guns except at very long range.

There was no question of any public agitation against "soft-enders" having been responsible for this additional plating in the hope that it might be fobbed off as "a complete belt forward." Like the curved armour deck, the high belt of average thickness, and upper deck casemates, it was one of White's earliest suggestions which was now adopted and developed in subsequent designs.

A notable feature was the additional above-water armour deck decided upon when the Board was informed that the French were contemplating the mounting of howitzers for high-angle firing as a means of attacking decks. White then proposed that the *Canopus* be given an upper 1-in. steel deck 9½ ft. above water as a roof to the citadel, which would be strong enough to explode any shells at main-deck level. Actually the French went no further than to test out a 5·9-in. military howitzer in the little gunboat *Dragonne*, and without any very satisfactory results. But because of this 1-in. upper deck, the main deck had to be reduced to 2 in. for its entire length.

Above the belt the barbettes were 12 in., below it only 6 in., with 8-in. shields. Both upper and main deck casemates were 6 in.—although old reference books credit them with 5 in. only. Similarly the first five ships are shown with Harvey-Nickel armour and only the *Vengeance* with Krupp; but in official lists only the casemates are given as Harvey with Harvey-Nickel conning towers, the side armour and barbettes being Krupp Cemented.

Special attention was given to reinforcing the ram. This was made up of a cast steel stem piece into which was worked the armour deck, with a 2-in. stiffening plate and the 2-in. side armour over the ordinary skin and framing. Thirteen of the forward frames were webbed with steel plating and the spaces filled with cork up to the level of the armour deck, giving a good solid mass, stiff yet elastic. That it could stand impact was shown when the *Ocean* missed the "hole in the wall" on leaving Portland in a thick fog, and displaced several of the heavy blocks of stone forming the breakwater without any damage to her beak (1902).

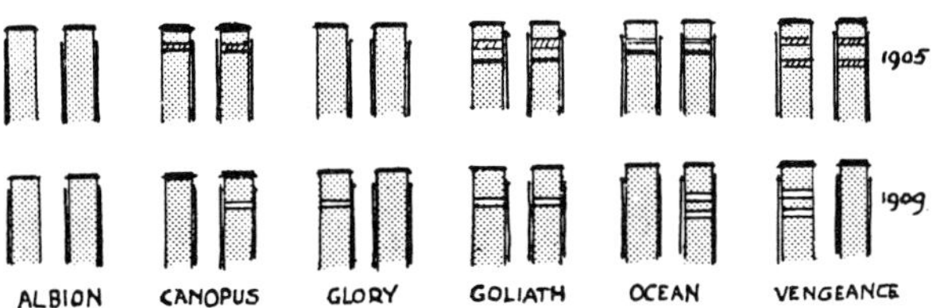

In 1905 the funnel bands were red; in 1909 white.

MACHINERY

As our first battleships to have water-tube boilers the class proved good steamers, their twenty Bellevilles with 33,780 sq. ft. of heating surface generated 13,500 h.p. against the eight cylindricals with 24,400 sq. ft. giving 10,000 h.p. in the *Majestic*, allowing an increase of nearly 2 knots. On the 8 hrs. full power trial they made from 13,728 h.p. and 18·5 knots (*Ocean*) to 13,918 h.p. and 18·4 knots (*Goliath*).

Albion made her runs in a gale and recorded 17·8 knots with 13,885 h.p. *Vengeance* was regarded as the best steamer of the class.

GENERAL

Owing to different distribution of boilers a reversion was made to fore and aft funnels, the second having its greatest diameter athwartships. When fire controls were fitted, the additional top built on the foremast "starfish" was at first square; this was retained in *Vengeance* but later replaced by one both larger and oblong in the rest; the main fighting top was screened but otherwise unaltered, except in *Albion*, where an extension was added.

The class formed the backbone of the China Squadron for some years and proved excellent ships for the station, serving there until the Japanese Alliance allowed them to be brought home and incorporated with the Home Fleet. During the war they were ubiquitous, serving as far afield as Archangel, East Africa and the Falkland Isles,

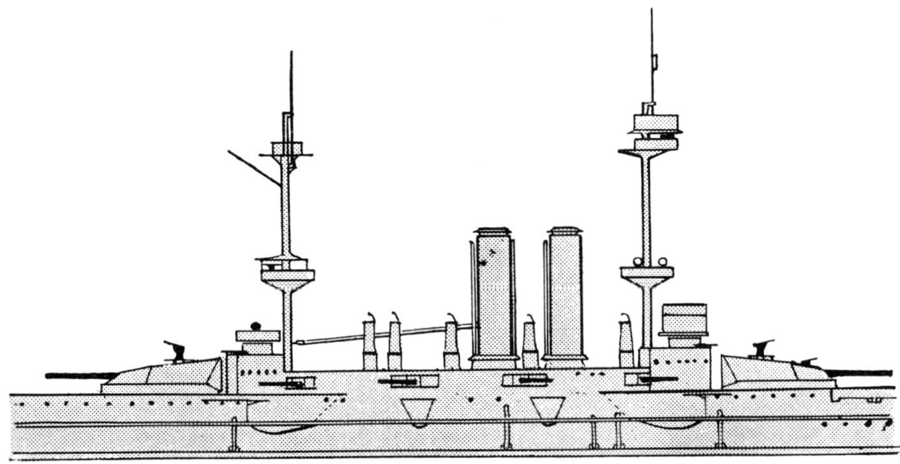

Canopus 1917 with her main deck batteries suppressed and 6-in. guns in place of the 12-pdrs. amidships.

thus showing that armoured ships—even when obsolescent—can be employed on subsidiary operations and emergency duties having no relation to the services for which they were primarily intended.

In 1917 the main deck batteries in *Canopus* and *Glory* were suppressed, two 6-in. on each side replacing the amidships 12-pdrs. And so, twenty-odd years after they were designed, four unprotected guns on the upper deck were considered better value than eight in armoured casemates a deck lower. Several of the *King Edwards*, *Duncans*, *Formidables*, *Drakes* and *Kents* were so treated, towards the end of War I, and so belatedly and unobtrusively one of the major features of White's designs was wiped out and the fashion set for similar changes to be made abroad.

"ALBION"

Her wash when launched wrecked stands along the slipway, 34 spectators being drowned, mostly women and children.

Commissioned June '01 for China where she served until '05, joining the Channel Fleet in August (collision with *Duncan* at Lerwick 26 September '05, no damage). In April '06 commissioned Reserve Chatham for refit (machinery and boilers) until December '06. February '07 temporarily attached to Home Fleet Portsmouth; March '07 Atlantic Fleet (refit Gibraltar '08-'09 when f.c. were fitted). August '09 Parent Ship 4th Division Home Fleet Nore; May '12 3rd Fleet Nore (refit Chatham '12). During '13 at Pembroke.

War: August '14 8th B.S. Channel; '14-'15 Cape and East Africa. February '15 Dardanelles. Took part in the bombardments during February and March; covered landing at Helles 25 April (hit badly on 28 April and 2 May). Aground off Gaba Tepe. Transported troops to Salonika October '15. During '16-'18 East Coast, England. Became accommodation ship at Devonport in '18.

Sold 1919.

"CANOPUS"

Commissioned 5 December '99 for Mediterranean where she served until April '03; big refit at Lairds May '03-June '04; manœuvres '04 (run into by *Barfleur* in Mounts Bay, 5 August '04, slight damage); p.o. into Fleet Reserve: January '05 commissioned Reserve Portsmouth; May '05 commissioned for China, but joined Atlantic Fleet; transferred to Channel January '06; (primary f.c. fitted) May '07 Home Fleet Portsmouth (nucleus crew); refit '07-'08; April '08 Mediterranean until December '09; joined 4th Division Home Fleet; May '12 Nore 3rd Fleet (reduced to 4/5 power '10); refit Chatham July '11-April '12; '13-'14 3rd Fleet at Pembroke.

War: 7 August '14 8th B.S. Channel; 23 August guardship at St. Vincent; October South American station and guardship at Port Stanley and Abrolhos Rocks November-December; January '15 sent to Dardanelles and took part in actions of 2 March and 18 March; covered landings in April blockade of Smyrna; covered landings in May; returned home in '16 and went into Reserve at Chatham as accommodation ship until p.o.

Sold 1920.

"GLORY"

Commissioned Portsmouth November '00 as flagship, China station, where she served until October '05 (collision with *Centurion* 17 April '04) when she went into Commissioned Reserve Portsmouth before joining Channel Fleet until October '06. Commissioned Reserve Portsmouth Home Fleet February '07. Refit March-December '07 (f.c. mag. cooling, engines, boilers); Mediterranean Fleet September '07-April '09; 4th Division Home Fleet (nucleus crew); refit Chatham August-December '10; 3rd Fleet Nore May '12 transferring to Portsmouth April '13.

War: August '14 8th B.S. Channel. Escorted Canadian convoy October '14 and then went as flagship to North America covering New York to Panama. During '14-'15 in Atlantic and N.A.W.I., and then joined Mediterranean fleet June '15, guarding Suez Canal and covering East Indies and Egypt during '16. Between '16-'19 was in North Russia and Murmansk.

Re-named *Crescent* as depôt ship Rosyth.

Sold 1922.

"GOLIATH"

Commissioned at Chatham 27 March '00 for China station where she served until '03 (refit Hong Kong September '01-April '02). After refit at Palmers January-July '04. Manœuvres July '04 and then went into Commissioned Reserve Portsmouth. In May '05 commissioned for China but joined Mediterranean and transferred to Channel December '05-March '07 when she reduced to nucleus crew Home Fleet. Refit August '07-February '08 for engines and boilers. Fractured propeller shaft on passage to Malta where she was in dock October '08-January '09. In April '09 joined 4th Fleet at Nore with red n.c. becoming Flagship Rear-Admiral 3rd and 4th Divisions Home Fleet. Refit Chatham '10-'11.

(Primary f.c. fitted '06. Completed '07-'08.)

During '13-'14 with 3rd Fleet at Pembroke.

War: August '14 8th B.S. Channel, and then for defence of Grand Fleet anchorage at Loch Ewe. Took part in the Ostend operations and in September '14 went to East Indies for escort duties. Took part in Rufigi river operations against *Konigsberg* in November '14 and transferred to Dardanelles in April '15. Covered the Helles landing and was damaged 25 April and 2 May.

Sunk 13 May '15 by 3 torpedoes from a Turkish t.b. manned by Germans. 570 killed.

"OCEAN"

Commissioned Devonport February '00 for the Mediterranean, transferring to China January '01 where she served until August '05 (damaged by typhoon September '02). Refits '01, '02-'03, '05. Returned home August '05 for Commissioned Reserve Chatham. In January '06 joined the Channel Fleet until June '08 (refit '06-'07) when she went to the Mediterranean. Refit '08-'09 when f.c. was fitted. In February '10 joined the 4th Division Home Fleet. Refits '10 (boilers) and '11-'12. May '12 3rd Fleet Nore. During '13-'14 in 3rd Fleet at Pembroke.

War: August '14 8th B.S. Channel and Queenstown; September '14 to East Indies for convoy service and in October took part in Persian Gulf operations. February '15 Suez Canal patrol and Dardanelles. Bombardments during February-March '15.

18 March. Hit by mine and shell fire. Abandoned 7.30 p.m. and sunk in Morto Bay at 10.30 p.m.

"VENGEANCE"

Our first battleship to be built, armoured, gunned, and engined by one firm.

Commissioned April '02 for Mediterranean; June '03 ordered to China where she served until April '05, returning home to Commissioned Reserve Devonport. Refit '05-'06 (engines, boilers, condensers). In the Channel from May '06-May '08 when she joined the Home Fleet Portsmouth with n.c. (collision with S.S. *Benyon Head* 13 June '08 with slight damage repaired by ship's owners). February '09 Home Fleet Nore (grounded at entrance to London River 28 February '09 without damage; collision with *Biter* in fog 29 November '10 with damage to booms and net shelf); parent ship to Special Service vessels. April '09 gunnery drill ship. July '12 3rd Fleet Nore. Refit 1912.

Siemans' system of f.c. fitted.

1912-'13 8th B.S. '13-'14 gunnery t.s. Nore.

War: August '14 8th B.S. Channel and Atlantic; Cameroons operations November '14 Egypt, Cape Verde station, and Gibraltar Flagship of Admiral de Robeck January '15 and ordered to Dardanelles. Took part in bombardments of 18 February and 18 March, covering the landing at Helles 25 April. Went as guardship Egypt November '15 and '15-'17 served in East Indies and Egypt, East Africa and the Cape.

1918-'19 Ordnance depôt, Devonport.

Sold 1921.

Chapter 67

THE SPANISH—AMERICAN WAR

THE naval engagements of this war added nothing to what was already common knowledge. At Manilla Bay a huddle of old gunboats made a sitting target for well-armed American cruisers, and at Santiago four poorly equipped armoured cruisers put up a running fight against four battleships and two large armoured cruisers of vastly superior strength. Wholesale fires did most of the damage, and the Board of Examination concluded that "the use of wood in the construction and equipment of warships should be reduced to the utmost minimum; that loaded torpedoes above the water-line are a serious menace to the vessel carrying them; that the value of rapid-fire batteries cannot be too highly estimated; and, finally, that all water and steam piping should be led between the protection deck, or below the water-line, and fitted with risers at such points as may be considered necessary."

All of which merely confirms the observations drawn from the Sino-Japanese war, while the necessity for eliminating woodwork was stressed by our Committee on Designs in 1870. That ships would suffer from the blast effects of their own guns was more or less accepted, although certain vessels like the *Texas*, *Boston* and *Indiana* class demonstrated the extent to which arcs of fire would have to be curtailed, especially when wing turrets trained towards the axial line.

While the *Oquendo* trio with their thick belts and bald hulls soon succumbed, the *Colon* showed the value of a good coat of medium armour; with an adequate supply of coal aboard she would have outpaced her opponents and got away. As it was, she had to be put ashore when her bunkers gave out, showing little damage after making a fine run for 70 miles.

Chapter 68

EXPERIMENTAL GUN POSITIONS ABROAD

THE turn of the century marked the end of the "four 12-in. and twelve 6-in. gun" era, during which White's designs had served as models the world over. Heavier secondary batteries were now becoming the fashion, and a number of interesting experiments were carried out abroad in order to find positions for the smaller guns which would allow for a wide blast-free arc of bearing.

Not that these directly influenced British practice, but as tentative steps in the general scheme of evolution they call for passing reference.

U.S. TWO-STOREY TURRETS

In the coast-defence battleships of the *Indiana* class authorized in 1890 eight 8-in. guns in four twin turrets were mounted at the sides of the superstructure and suffered a good deal from blast interference. When the *Kearsarge* and *Kentucky* came to be designed in 1897, four 8-in. in twin turrets were placed on top of the 13-in. guns, where it was claimed that:

(1) A gain of 90° on broadside was obtained.
(2) There would be no interference from blast.
(3) A well-protected base and ammunition supply were obtained without extra weight, as well as a high command.
(4) The fire of all four guns could be controlled by one officer.

Against these were the following disadvantages:

(1) The 8-in. guns could not be fired separately.
(2) Both pairs of guns depended upon one control.
(3) Firing one gun disarranged the other three.
(4) Four guns could be disabled by a mishap to the turret.
(5) Undue weight concentration upon the roller-path and turret supports.
(6) Difficulties in dismounting the 13-in. guns.
(7) Additional top weight affecting stability necessitated a low freeboard.
(8) Extra structural strength required below the turrets because of weight and firing stresses.

In the succeeding *Alabama* and *Maine* classes the 8-in. guns were omitted, but reappeared again in the *New Jersey* group (1902) because of the good results obtained from them at Santiago in the Spanish-American war.

By now the old-fashioned turret had been replaced by a gun house more along British lines, and in the *New Jersey* four of the eight 8-in. were carried in pairs on top of the 12-in. guns. But although the technical difficulties experienced in the *Kentucky* were stated to have been overcome, the arrangement was abandoned in the *Connecticut*

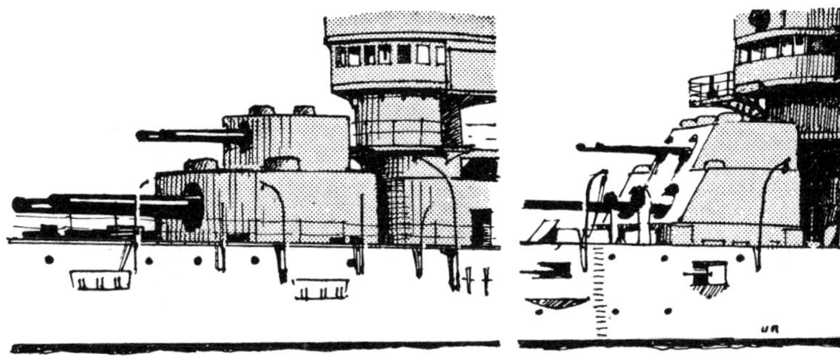

Kearsarge and *Kentucky* with 8-in. guns on top of the 13-in.

New Jersey class with 8-in. above the 12-in. guns.

class which followed them. The risk of the simultaneous disablement of four guns was said to have been the objection, but the writer never heard an officer who had served in the *New Jersey* class say a good word for the superposed turrets.

Thus the two-storey turret was ruled out as a practical expedient in armament distribution, and led to such

American innovations being regarded as of the "lick creation" order—which later on found prejudice against the *South Carolina* arrangement. The four-gun *Normandie* turret of 1913 grew out of the triple introduced in the *Dante Aligheri* and had nothing in common with the *New Jersey* grouping.

SUPER-FIRING

On the other hand, the arrangement employed to give wide arcs of bearing to a single 5·5-in. gun in the *Henri IV* (1897) was of far greater consequence in the long run. In designing this 8,800-ton coast-defence ship Emile Bertin, although greatly hampered by financial restrictions, produced a most interesting and unique sea-going monitor which incorporated novel features in hull design, armament and protection.

Above the low hull rose three tiers of superstructure giving a high bow but allowing the main deck to act as a sort of bilge keel when the ship was rolling, and producing a very steady gun platform. She carried a single 10·8-in. gun fore and aft with nests of three 5·5-in. amidships, and a single 5·5-in. in a small turret aft raised a deck in order to give wide arcs of fire on the beam and astern over the after turret.

To test the effects of firing, sheep were put in the 10·8-in. turret, and although they seemed little the worse for it, one or two suffered from excessive fright. An autopsy on two showed that the heart of one and the brain of the other were affected—but how much to concussion shock and how much to terror it was difficult to say. It was, however, assumed that men would have suffered relatively little.

But the interesting point was noted that the maximum blast occurred at right-angles to the gun muzzle, so that the control officer using the lower turret hood could be affected through a wide arc of fire. The gun, in fact, was so placed that it caused the greatest inconvenience at other gun positions; had its muzzle projected beyond the lower sighting hood a good deal of the blast effect astern might have been avoided, but the short chase did not allow for this.

As the *Henri IV* took five years to build (1897-1902), comment on the value of the after 5·5-in. was reserved until her trials, when the effects on the sheep were generally exaggerated—at any rate, the value of super-firing was heavily discounted. That such a position secured training over both beams was lost sight of in this country—in fact, Sir John Biles was successful in persuading the Japanese not to have a centre-line gunned cruiser built to Bertin's designs. We were still faithful to the broadside battery in 1902 and the advantages of the small turret, for secondary guns—already realized in France, Russia, Sweden and to some extent Italy and Germany—were not to be admitted for another year or so. Hence the influence of the *Henri IV* experiment was largely of a negative nature—although accepted *in toto* years afterwards—a common fate of innovations appearing before their time.

French *Henri IV* showing a 5·5-in. gun firing over the 10·8-in—the first example of superfiring to obtain axial bearing.

Chapter 69

THE "FORMIDABLE" CLASS AND THE "LONDON" CLASS

When the Japanese followed the *Fuji* and *Yashima* with the 15,000-ton *Shikishima* and *Hatsuse* and the French went to increased displacement in the *Jena*, it was felt that more powerful ships than the *Canopus* were indicated for the 1897 Programme.

Improvements in armour, machinery and boilers had allowed for weight saving with increased efficiency in the last design; but a longer and heavier 12-in. gun was now being made of higher velocity and energy with a mounting permitting rapid loading in any position. These guns in turn required larger and heavier turn-tables, bigger barbettes and heavier mountings, so that an increase of 150 tons carried high up had to be provided for. White proposed a modified *Majestic* to embody all the improvements introduced since her design but without increase in displacement, and this became known as the *Formidable*.

He also put forward a proposal for increasing the secondary battery to fourteen guns as in the Japanese ships, while keeping the displacement to 14,900 tons. As an alternative with only twelve guns this figure could be reduced by 200 tons. The Board, however, preferred the smaller number of guns on the grounds that upper deck casemated guns, while increasing offensive power in heavy weather, would cause "a serious obstruction to ordinary traffic along the upper deck and involve a sensible increase in the complement." Instead of accepting any reduction in tonnage, it was thought preferable to increase defence by the use of the new 9-in. Krupp armour on the citadel with greater security to buoyancy and stability, in view of the probable improvement in guns and projectiles abroad. This additional armour raised the displacement to 15,000 tons—or 100 tons more than the *Majestic*.

Comparison between the *Formidable* and *Hatsuse* of the same tonnage always favoured the latter, especially because of the heavier secondary battery with six guns on the upper deck. Hence the reason why the British ship was "under-gunned"—according to her critics—is instructive as showing that the onus of deciding what offensive or defensive equipment a ship should carry primarily rests with the Board. White had to undergo acid criticism for alleged under-gunning in his designs during the following years, through this point not being appreciated by his detractors.

Three "FORMIDABLE" Class (1897 Programme)

	Built at	*Laid down*	*Launched*	*Completed*	*Cost*
"*Formidable*"	Portsmouth	21 March '98	17 Nov. '98	Sept. '01	£1,022,745
"*Irresistible*"	Chatham	11 April '98	15 Dec. '98	Feb. '02	£1,048,136
"*Implacable*"	Devonport	13 July '98	11 March '99	Sept. '01	£989,116
					(Guns in all £74,500)

Dimensions 400′ (431¾′ o.a.)×75′×25′/26·10′=15,000 tons.

	At load draught	*At deep load*
"*Formidable*" "*Irresistible*" "*Implacable*"	14,480	15,805 tons

Armament 4 12-in. 40 cal. (80)
12 6-in. 45 cal. (200)
16 12-pdrs. (300)
2 12-pdr. boat.
6 3-pdr. (500).
2 Maxims. Total (including turntables and gun shields)=1,730 tons.

Torpedo tubes:
4 18-in. submerged.

Armour Belt and lower deck sides (KC) 9″; bulkheads 12″-10″-9″.
Side plating forward 3″; aft. 1½″.
Barbettes 12″-6″; shields 10″-8″.
Casemates 6″; conning towers 14″ and 3″.
Communication tubes 8″ and 3″.
Decks lower 2½″-2″; middle 3″-2″; main 1″.
Total 4,335 tons.

Machinery "*Formidable*" by Earl. "*Irresistible*" by Maudslay. "*Implacable*" by Laird. Two sets 3 cyl. vert. triple exp. H.P. 15,000=18 knots. 109 revs. Boilers 20 Belleville with economizers. 37,000 sq. ft.

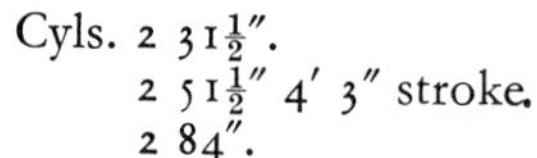
Cyls. 2 31½".
2 51½" 4′ 3″ stroke.
2 84".

Coal 900/2,000 tons=3,000/8,000 miles at 10 knots. 300 lb. pressure.

Complement 780; as flagship 810. ("*Implacable*" in '17=710.)

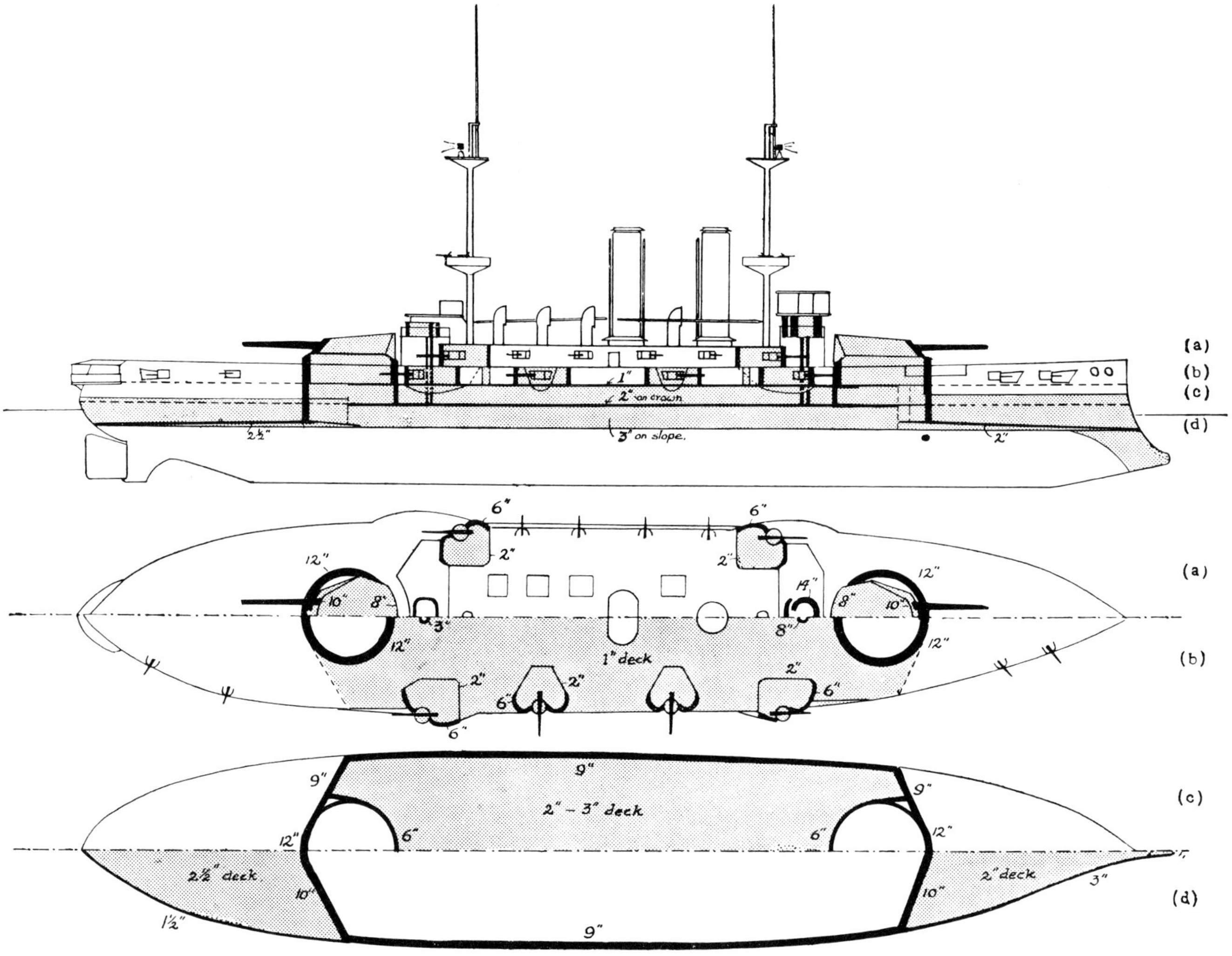

"FORMIDABLE"

Although based on the *Majestic*, the *Formidable* presented an improved *Canopus* design ranking as the most powerful European battleship model of her day. An office estimate of 5,650 tons had been allowed for the hull—the same as in the *Majestic*—but keen inspection of material weights resulted in a saving of 40 tons, so that for the first time the designer's figures were realized—a great improvement upon former practice. The load draught displacement was actually only 14,480 tons, with full load 15,805 tons—or 805 tons above the legend displacement.

A new type of stem was introduced in which the scarf at the water-line was abolished and a 34-ton casting forming the ram was carried far enough aft to run with the supporting plates and doubling of the ship's side right into the rabbets without curvature in the fore and aft line. This system—affording better support to a stronger ram—was copied in Germany and later in France.

ARMAMENT

The 12-in. guns were 40 cals. long, weighed 50 tons, and fired an 850 lb. round with 2,612 m.v. and an energy of 40,086 ft. tons; loading could be carried out at any elevation or direction. In terms of steel penetration, they could pierce a 12-in. plate at 4,800 yards as compared with 3,100 yards for the previous 35 cal. piece. The

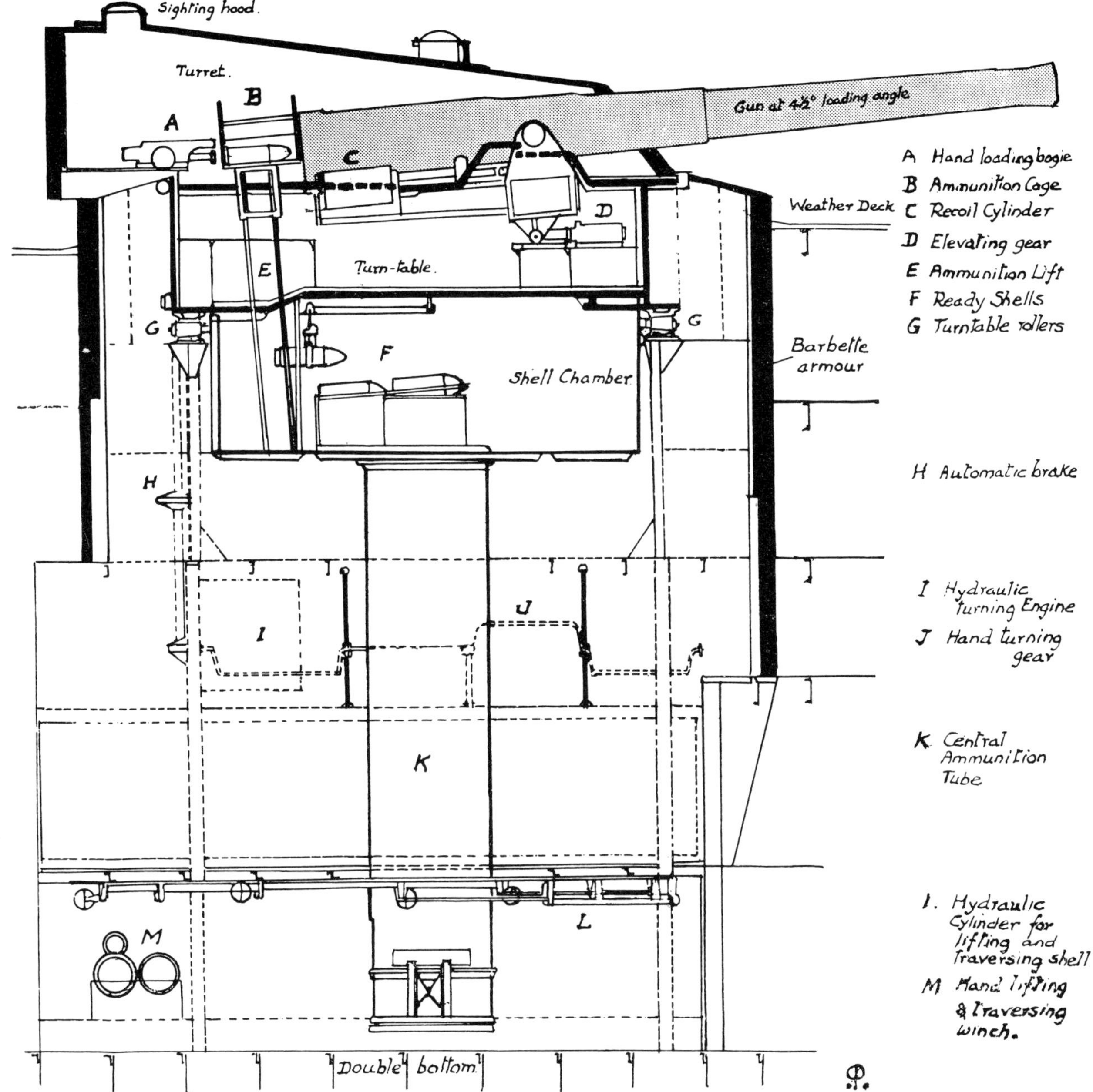

Section of *Formidable's* barbette showing the ammunition hoist interrupted at the shell chamber instead of being continuous from magazine to guns as in previous classes.

12-in. mounting was noteworthy in having an ammunition hoist interrupted at the shell chamber and designed to safeguard against cordite fire in the upper part of the hoist flashing down the central ammunition tube to the magazine. Above the side plating the barbettes were 12 in. and 6 in. behind it, with 10 in.-8 in. gun shields. Both upper and main deck casemates were 6 in., the end ones being broadly sponsoned for axial fire. Of the 12-pdrs., the amidships batteries held four aside with four forward and aft in main deck ports, the six 3-pdrs. being in the fighting tops. The stern torpedo tube was suppressed and two submerged tubes aside placed under the barbettes; three of the steam boats could be armed with 14-in. torpedoes.

PROTECTION

Both the main belt and lower deck side had 9-in. Krupp steel for 218 ft. amidships, making a citadel 15 ft. deep of which 4¾ ft. was below water. This was closed by 9-in. bulkheads above the lower deck and 10-in. below it. Forward a 12-ft. strake of 3-in. plating ran to the bows with 1½ in. aft to the stern for about 8 ft. deep. This last length of plating had a collision protection value only, although superficially it served to make up a complete water-line belt which in later designs was to become proper armour.

Horizontal armour followed the *Canopus* arrangement with a main deck of 1 in. over the citadel and a middle deck 2 in. on the crown and 3 in. on the slopes extending down to the lower edge of the armour. Beyond the citadel ran the under-water protective deck 2 in. forward and 2½ in. aft, with the usual hull subdivision, so that there was no departure from established practice occasioned by the thinly armoured ends, although their provision necessitated reducing the barbettes from 14 in. to 12 in.

MACHINERY AND SPEED

Compared with the *Majestics*, by the adoption of water-tube boilers the h.p. was raised from 12,000 f.d. to 15,000 n.d., giving an increase from 17 to 18 knots—which for practical steaming purposes was regarded as a gain of two knots. On the 30 hours run at four-fifths power all three ships made just over 11,600 h.p. and from 16·8 to 17·5 knots the 8 hours full power gave an average of 15,500 h.p. and 18·2 knots.

Although generally regarded as handy ships they suffered from inward turning screws which, although giving

The *Implacable* at Mudros 1917 with her main deck batteries suppressed and 6-in. guns mounted in place of the 12-pdrs. amidships. Note that she has had stockless anchors fitted.

greater drive, slightly higher speed and decreased fuel consumption, were troublesome when leaving moorings at slow speed as they refused to bring the stern up to the wind when turning from rest, so that they merely lay broadside on.

With a metacentric height of 4·46 at load condition their period of double roll was 14 secs. and a stability range of 65·2°.

The class differed from previous ships in having the steering engines in the engine rooms, with electric motors for the fans and after capstan, which obviated steam pipes running aft. Telemotor gear in five different positions controlled steering engines in place of shafting, and loud-speaking telephones were fitted in place of voice tubes.

Although carrying stocked anchors, the first tests with a stockless pattern were made in the *Formidable* during 1901, when she was able to ride out three days of heavy weather in Spithead using one stockless anchor only. But the change-over was delayed until the last of the *Duncan* class were designed.

GENERAL

In appearance they were heavier-looking editions of the *Canopus*, with funnels wider apart and an extra 12-pdr. gun aside in the battery.

During 1916 the surviving *Implacable* had her main deck 6-in. battery plated in, four of the guns being placed a deck above in the former 12-pdr. battery, where they fired through large ports with light shield protection only—a very necessary change allowing at least eight guns to be worked in all weathers, although weight distribution precluded casemates being fitted as in the *Royal Sovereigns*. The heavy 12-pdrs. were reduced to eight and shifted to the shelter decks, with a couple of 3-pdrs. retained for saluting.

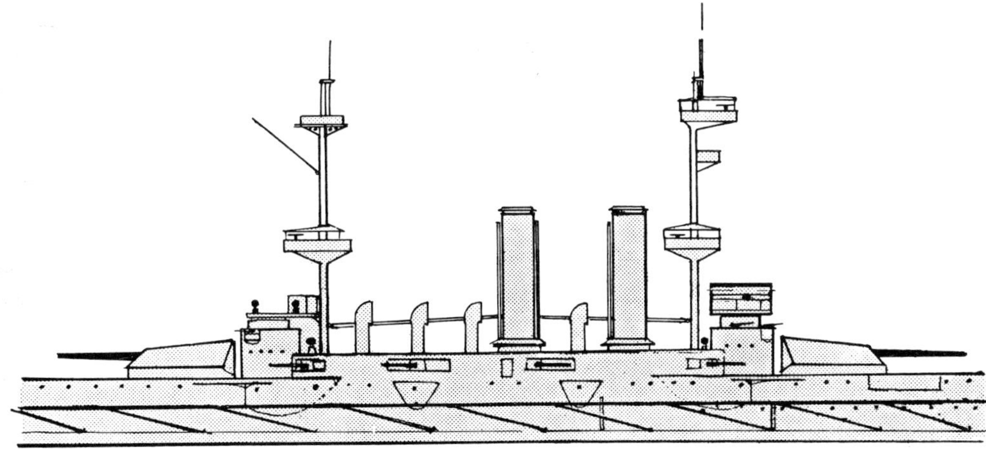

IMPLACABLE, 1917

When fire control was fitted both fighting tops were screened and elongated positions added to the forward searchlight top.

Completion of the *Formidable*, *Irresistible*, *Venerable* and *Albion* was delayed by the liquidation in 1899-1900 of Maudslay Son and Field and Earle's S.B. Co., who had their machinery in hand. Also strikes in the engineering shops, various difficulties incidental to the substitution of Krupp for Harvey armour, and the adoption of Belleville boilers, held up the completion of most ships at this time.

"FORMIDABLE"

Commissioned at Portsmouth for Mediterranean 10 October '01-April '08 (f.c. fitted at Malta during refit December '04-April '05); transferred to Channel. Refit Chatham August '08-April '09; 1st Division Home Fleet April '09-June '09; Atlantic June '09-May '12; refit Gibraltar; reduced to nucleus crew for 2nd Fleet 5th Squadron Nore, and between August and October '12 developed serious defects in boilers owing to hard and continuous steaming when undermanned. 5th B.S. '12-'14.

War: Served in 5th B.S. on Channel patrol and torpedoed by U.24 on 1 January '15 in bad weather with a loss of 35 officers and 512 men out of 780.

"IRRESISTIBLE"

Commissioned at Chatham for Mediterranean 4 February '02-January '08 (collision in fog with Norwegian S.S. *Clive* 3 March '02. Considerable damage sustained. Grounded Malta 9 October '05, temporary repairs) primary f.c. fitted '05-'06; refit Malta October '07-January '08; Channel January '08 (collided with schooner 4 May '08 in fog, no damage or blame) until '09 when she joined 1st Division Home Fleet; reduced to nucleus crew May '10; refit Chatham June '10-February '11 and then went to Nore Division Home Fleet. Joined Portsmouth sub-division Home Fleet in August '11 and in November went to Tyne while her crew carried out trials of *Monarch*. March '12 Devonport Division Home Fleet. 5th B.S. '12-'14.

War: Served in 5th B.S. on Channel patrol; February '15 sailed for Dardanelles; in 2nd Division B.F.; Bombardments of 26 February and up to 18 March when she was mined at 4.15 p.m., abandoned, carried within range of the Narrows forts, and sunk by gunfire about 7.30.

"IMPLACABLE"

Commissioned Devonport for Mediterranean 10 September '01-May '08 (primary f.c. fitted '04-'06) (boiler explosions 12 July '05—2 killed, many injured and 16 August '06). Refit Chatham '08-'09 (f.c. completed). Channel February '09; 1st Division Home Fleet April '09; transferred to Atlantic June '09-May '12; transferred to 3rd B.S. 1st Fleet and in May '12 to 2nd Fleet Nore with nucleus crew; 5th B.S. '12-'14.

War: Served in 5th B.S. Channel patrol; ordered to Dardanelles in March '15, covered landing at Helles 25 April; and subsequent operations. Ordered to Adriatic to reinforce Italian fleet May '15. Between '15-'16 operated from East Indies to Egypt then returned to Mediterranean for '16-'17 (armament altered); Northern patrol '18-'19.

Sold 1921.

The 1898 Programme provided for three battleships, and on 6 June the Board considered proposals for a new design as a reply to recent Russian construction. In dealing with the genesis of the *Duncan* class Mr. J. H. Narbeth, Assistant Director of Naval Construction, stated in a paper read before the I.N.A. in April 1922:

> "About 1896 the newspapers reported that Russia was building a number of cruisers. The building of second-class cruisers instead of battleships also received some amount of credence from the action of the Czar in connection with the Hague Conference. The vessels were next reported as armoured cruisers, but when the available particulars of the vessels were pieced together it was revealed that they were not cruisers but very speedy battleships—the ships known later as the *Peresviet* class."

(As the naval reference books for 1896 listed the *Peresviet* class as 12,674-ton turret ships of 17·5 knots and the second-class cruisers of the *Pallada* type were shown a year later, this special piece of intelligence work responsible for the *Duncan* design in 1898 does not suggest that the Controller's Department was kept *au fait* with progress abroad.)

But in order to expend economically the sum voted for labour and with a view to getting it distributed upon a broad basis for rapid building during the following year, it would have been necessary for the drawings and specifications of the new ships to be at the Dockyards by the early autumn—and in view of the heavy demands upon the Controller's office at that period, this was found to be impracticable. White therefore suggested that the *Formidable* plans should be repeated for three ships, allowing rather longer than normal for the preparation of the new design (*Duncan*), and to this the Board agreed.

Certain modifications which had been accepted for the *Duncans* were incorporated in the *Londons*, making them into transitional ships between the *Formidables* and *Duncans*, and although generally listed with the *Formidable* the major points of difference are noteworthy.

Provision was made for the seventh and eighth ships of the *Formidable* group in the Estimates for 1900 (*Queen* and *Prince of Wales*).

Five *LONDON* Class (1898 and 1900 Estimates)

	Built at	*Laid down*	*Launched*	*Completed*	*Cost*
"*Bulwark*"	Devonport	20 March '99	18 Oct. '99	March '02	£997,846
"*London*"	Portsmouth	8 Dec. '98	21 Sept. '99	June '02	£1,036,393
"*Venerable*"	Chatham	2 Jan. '99	2 Nov. '99	Nov. '02	£1,092,753
"*Queen*"	Devonport	12 March '01	8 March '02	March '04	£1,074,999
"*Prince of Wales*"	Chatham	20 March '01	25 March '02	March '04	£1,193,380

Dimensions 400′ (431¾′ o.a.) × 75′ × 25½′/26½′ = 15,000 tons.

	At load draught	*At deep draught*
"*Bulwark*"	14,490 tons	15,700 tons
"*London*"	14,420 "	15,640 "
"*Venerable*"	14,690 "	15,850 "
"*Queen*"	14,160 "	15,415 "
"*Prince of Wales*"	14,140 "	15,380 "

Armament 4 12-in. 40 cals. (80).
12 6-in. 45 cals. (200)
16 12-pdrs. (300)
2 12-pdrs. (boat).
6 3-pdrs. (500)
2 maxims.

Torpedo tubes:
4 18-in. submerged.
(18 18-in. and 6-14-in. torpedoes carried.)

Protection Belt 9″-3″; after bulkhead 12″-10″-9″; end plating bows 3″ stern 1½″.
Barbettes 12″-8″-6″; shields 10″-8″.
Ammunition tubes 2″; conning towers 14″ and 3″.
Casemates 6″; Decks: lower 2½″, 2″ and 1″; middle 2″ and 1″; main 2″ and 1½″.

Machinery Engines by: "*Bulwark*" Hawthorn Leslie. "*Queen*" Harland and Wolff. "*London*" Earle. "*Prince of Wales*" Greenock Foundry. "*Venerable*" Maudslay.
Two sets vert. triple exp. 15,000 H.P. = 18 knots.
Boilers: 20 Belleville with economisers. Pressure 300 lb.
Babcock and Wilcox in "*Queen*."

Coal 900/2,000 tons. Radius 3,000/8,000 miles at 10 knots.

Complement 714-733.

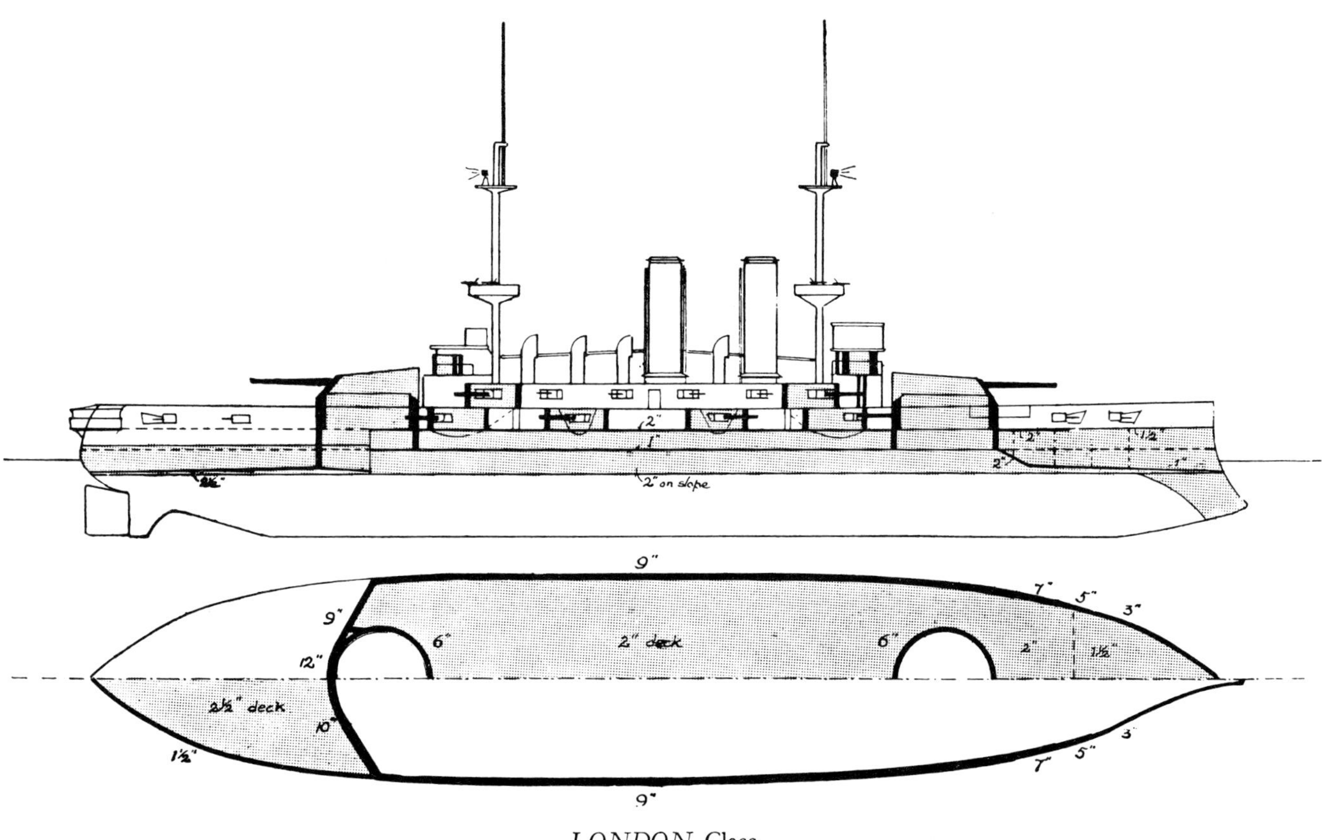

LONDON Class

In appearance they differed from the earlier trio in having (1) no lower-deck scuttles forward, and (2) open 12-pdr. batteries amidships in *Queen* and *Prince of Wales*, as absence of protection was now considered to be somewhat safer than the shell-burster screen walls, marking a step towards the later theory that small guns were safest in the open.

ARMAMENT

Similar to that in the *Formidable*.

PROTECTION

As a better defence against high-angle fire the order of thickness in the armour decks was reversed, plating being placed on the main deck over the citadel with 1½ in. in the forecastle. Below it ran a 1 in.-2 in. middle deck. Forward of the citadel the 1-in. lower deck was given a 2-in. slope to meet the middle deck before the barbette.

The forward citadel bulkhead was dispensed with, and the side armour carried forward in steps of 7 in., 5 in. and 3 in. with 2 in. right in the bows worked on to a double thickness of skin plating—the arrangement fixed on for the *Duncan* and observed in the rest of the pre-*Dreadnoughts*. Thus the Reed complete belt was largely carried into effect now that steel armour afforded a reasonable measure of protection against medium-calibre guns.

The main belt was 250 ft. long and 15 ft. deep, of which 10½ ft. was above and 4½ ft. below water.

GENERAL

London was one of the ships selected for the first experiments in naval aviation, and during 1912 a sloping trestle runway erected from the forward shelter deck to the bow gave a launching run to seaplanes.

In 1916 both *London* and *Venerable* had their secondary guns changed as in *Implacable*, and when converted into a mine-layer in 1917 *London* had her after barbette removed and a 6-in. gun placed on the quarter deck, all the barbette and casemate guns being taken out.

For experimental flights with seaplanes the *London* and *Hibernia* were fitted with a runway over the forecastle in 1912 and successful flights were made.

"BULWARK"

Commissioned at Devonport for Mediterranean (flagship) 18 March-February '07 (primary f.c. fitted '04-'06). February '07 Flagship Home Fleet (grounded near Lemonlight North Sea 26 October '07 when avoiding fishing boats, with slight damage). Refit '07-'08; August '09 Channel (f.c. completed '08); April '09 1st Division Home Fleet; March '10 Home Fleet Nore (nucleus crew) as flagship Vice-Admiral 3rd and 4th Divisions; April '11 became private ship; June '12 5th B.S. 2nd Fleet Temporary Rear-Admiral August-September (grounded twice on Barrow Deep off Nore on repair trials May '12 damage to bottom plates); '12-'14 5th B.S.

War: In 5th B.S. Channel. Blown up off Sheerness 26 November '14 by internal explosion.

"LONDON"

Commissioned Portsmouth 7 June '02 as Flagship Coronation Review; then Mediterranean until April '07. June '07 Home Fleet Nore (suffered a lot from overheating bearings and leaky condensers and during '06-'07 with cracked cylinders). June '08 Flagship Rear-Admiral Channel; big refit Chatham '08. '10 Flagship Rear-Admiral Atlantic; May '12 3rd B.S. 1st Fleet (nucleus crew); May '12 2nd Fleet 5th Squadron Nore (fitted for seaplane experiments). (Collision with S.S. *Don Benito* 11 May '12 off Hythe); '12 5th B.S.

War: 5th B.S. Channel August '14-March '15 then ordered to Mediterranean to make good losses in Dardanelles. '19 Reserve depot.

Sold 1920.

"VENERABLE"

Commissioned at Chatham for Mediterranean (Rear-Admiral flagship) 12 November '02 (touched bottom Algiers harbour with slight damage 26 June '05); flagship transferred to *Prince of Wales* August '07; (f.c. fitted Malta '06-'07); big refit Chatham February-October '09; October '09 Atlantic; (w.t. fitted '09); May '12 reduced to nucleus crew in 5th B.S.

War: August '14 5th B.S. (operations off Belgian Coast until October '14 when she could no longer be usefully employed) bombarded Westende batteries March '15; ordered to Dardanelles May '15; replaced *Queen Elizabeth*; operations off Suvla 14-21 August; transferred to Adriatic with three other *Formidables* in conformity with agreement that we should provide a squadron of battleships and cruisers to help contain the Austrian Fleet.

"PRINCE OF WALES"

Joined Fleet Reserve at Chatham March '04; Commissioned for Mediterranean 18 May '04-'06 (collision with S.S. *Enidween* off Oran 29 July '05; her anchor was pushed through main deck plating of *Prince of Wales*). May '06 commissioned in Reserve Portsmouth; refit June-November '06; September '06 Mediterranean flagship Rear-Admiral August '07; transferred to Atlantic as Flagship C.-in-C. November '08-December '10; refit Gibraltar February-May '11; May '12 transferred to 3rd B.S. 1st Fleet (Flagship Vice-Admiral 1-13 May); then Flagship Rear-Admiral 2nd Fleet Portsmouth (engine-room accident 16 April '06, 3 killed 4 injured) (stokehold explosion 2 July '09); (run into by submarine C.32 during exercises 2 June '13, slight damage). '12-'14 5th B.S.

War: 5th B.S. Channel. Transferred to Dardanelles March '15 (covered Anzac landing 25 April); ordered to Adriatic to help stiffen Italian Fleet 12 May.

Sold 1920.

"QUEEN"

Commissioned at Devonport for Mediterranean 7 April '04.

1904-December '08 Mediterranean (Flagship from February '07); (grounded off Isola Point Malta 28 August '05 with slight damage); December '08 transferred to Atlantic (1 February '10 fouled Greek S.S. *Dafui*, slight damage); '09-'10 refit Devonport; May '12 transferred to 3rd B.S. 1st Fleet; Flagship Vice-Admiral 2nd and 3rd Fleets from May '12; 13 January '13 run into by *Starling* at Sheerness, slight damage); '12-'14 5th B.S.

War: August '14 5th B.S. Channel operations; ordered to Dardanelles March '15 (covered Anzac landing 25 April); ordered to Adriatic with *Implacable*, *London* and *Prince of Wales* to stiffen the Italian fleet 12 May '15 and remained as base ship at Taranto until '18.

Sold 1920.

The *Queen* passed most of her service as a flagship, and was noteworthy for her large house on the after bridge. She is here seen with the high w.t. masts carried before the war. Torpedo nets and yards on the main mast were removed about '13.

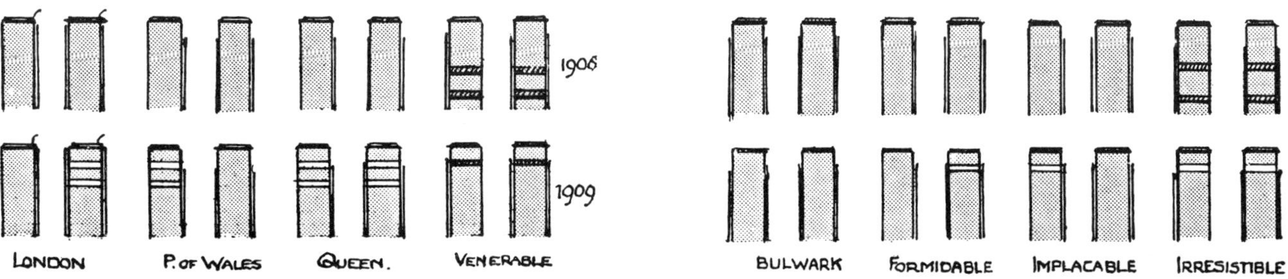

Chapter 70

CONTEMPORARY PROPOSALS FOR ANTI-TORPEDO PROTECTION

REFERENCE has already been made to Reed's *Enterprise* design incorporating an armoured double bottom (p. 82), which although turned down by the Admiralty may have germinated several schemes for under-water defence tried out in the French and Russian navies about this time. The increased accuracy of torpedoes under gyroscopic control plus greater efficiency in torpedo craft had made the risk of loss from torpedoes almost as great as from shell fire, and the question of how a hull should best be protected against torpedo attack began to exercise the ingenuity of constructors the world over.

The disparity in safeguarding against what might well be equally efficient methods of destruction cried out for adjustment. Armour protection against gun fire was absorbing from 25 to 30 per cent. of a battleship's displacement, while the weight allotted to torpedo defence was almost negligible.

But although under-water protection was indicated, there was little information as to what might be expected as the result of a torpedo hit upon a modern vessel. The only big ship lost by torpedo attack had been the Brazilian battleship *Aquidaban* during the Peizoto-Melloist operations in 1894, and she was well on the antiquated side. In her case a short-range hit by a Schwartskopf torpedo carrying 125 lb. of guncotton had struck close to a bulkhead near the port bow, blown a hole 20 ft. × 6½ ft. big, and torn the skin for 6 ft. at each end of it, flooding four compartments. The water shipped was estimated at 500 tons. There was also a hole 3 ft. in diameter on the opposite side, thought to have been made by the head of the torpedo being driven through the ship.

But as the French 17·7-in. torpedo carried 220 lb. of guncotton, the resulting concussion would be considerably more, and it was a question whether armour would stand up against it. The alternative was to increase and improve methods of subdivision with disposal of compartments, so that water, when admitted, should not remain on one side only and endanger stability. Longitudinal bulkheads promoted this risk, and these—without adequate compensating arrangements—were to prove a source of disaster to torpedoed ships in the 1914-18 war.

FRENCH "HENRI IV" SYSTEM

The first practical attempt to protect the lower hull by means of armour was adopted after experiments made at Lorient in 1894. In his design of the *Henri IV*—already referred to on p. 402—Bertin had included a novel system of semi-circular bulkheading in the monitor-like hull which it was hoped would make her torpedo-proof. The main armour deck at belt top level was separated from a lower splinter deck by a cellular layer, and this deck was curved round against the inner bottom to form a semi-elastic cushion bounded internally by a longitudinal bulkhead. The resemblance to Reed's arrangement will be noticed, except that he employed 4-in. armour and Bertin only 1½-in. While the ship was under construction a partial test of the system was made, the *Yachting Gazette* of Paris giving the following description:

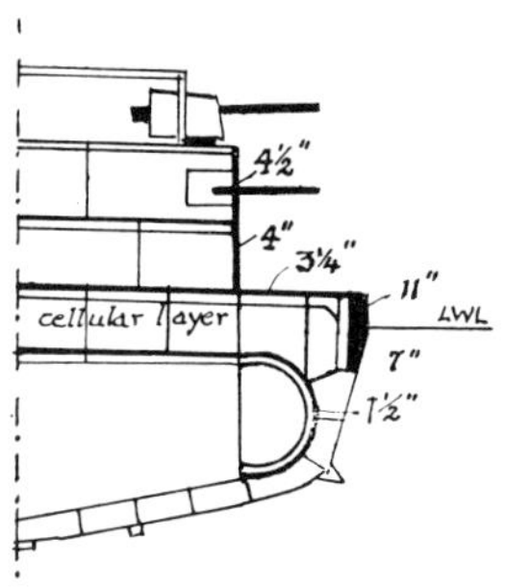

"This caisson (representing the ship's hull) carried the same armour, the same armoured deck, the same coal chutes, compartments, and bulkheads as the type ship. Its length was 40·6 ft., height 40 ft., draught 25 ft. and displacement 490 tons.

The torpedo, represented by a war head 17·7 in. in diameter, carrying a charge of 220 lb. of guncotton, was placed in contact with the caisson's side at a depth of from 10 to 11 ft. In the rear of the charge was placed a compressed-air reservoir, containing air at 100 lb. pressure—the remaining pressure of a torpedo at the end of a normal run. The charge was fired from a near-by boat by an electric fuse, and an enormous column of water was thrown up, the caisson sinking immediately. After great difficulty the caisson has been raised, and it was found that the torpedo had made a large hole, breaking through the double bottom."

BRITISH AND RUSSIAN SYSTEMS

For comparison with the bulkheading in the French-built *Tsarevitch* (1901) a short description of our own system—employed in all classes from the *Royal Sovereign* to the *King Edward VII*—may here be given. It provided the oldest defensive measure in hull construction with water-tight sub-division and coal bunkers between the outer skin and vitals, the inner skin being taken up as a longitudinal bulkhead. But all this was intended mainly as protection against gun fire as the result of the 1878 experiments at Portsmouth and Shoeburyness, when 2 ft. of coal was shown to have a resisting power equal to 1 in. iron, and was neither set on fire nor diplaced by shell explosion. The effectiveness of coal against torpedo explosion had not yet been determined.

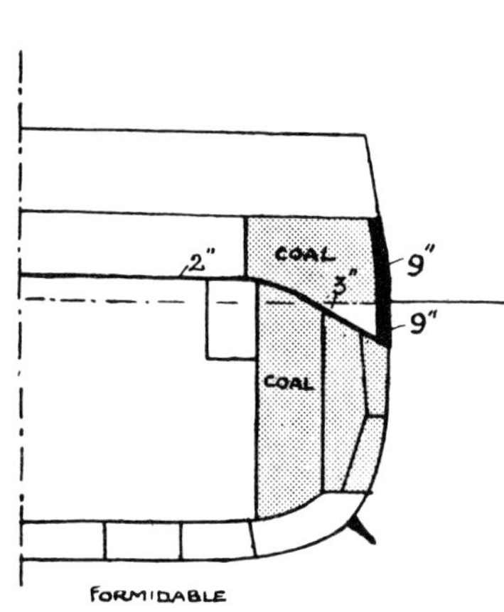

Typical British arrangement of thin bulkheads forming coal bunkers (*Formidable*)

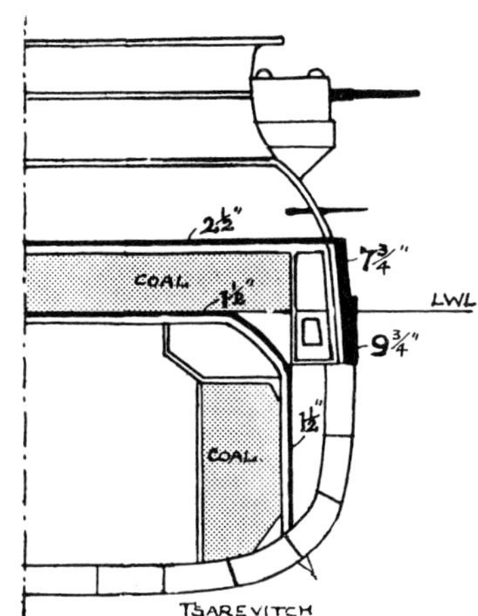

Tsarevitch showing armoured bulkhead formed by extension of protective deck.

As an alternative to ordinary bulkheads, which it was considered would be too weak to withstand torpedo explosion, *armoured bulkheads* were introduced in the French designed *Tsarevitch* (1901) formed by extensions of the lower protective deck and running 6½ ft. from the outer skin. In the Russian-designed *Borodino* class, intended as improvements on the *Tsarevitch* but generally very similar, extensive under-water armouring was proposed. Official plans are not available, but according to the description given in the 1902 edition of *Fighting Ships* the hull beneath the belt was to be covered with nickel steel of 4 in. nearly down to the double bottom with an internal vertical bulkhead of the same maximum thickness running the whole length of the ship's side. Above the armour deck proper—given as 4 in.—there was to be a 2-in. deck, the interspace being filled with coal. All this meant a tremendous weight of armour which could not possibly have been carried on a nominal displacement only 566 tons in excess of the *Tsarevitch*, but tests caused the scheme to be dropped and the class was completed with bulkheading along *Tsarevitch* lines.

To try out the value of such heavy plating, a barge was built and completely armoured with 4-in. steel below water and an internal lateral 4-in. bulkhead, and torpedoed. The result was the entire destruction of the barge, and the plating seems to have aggravated the explosion rather than mitigated it.

As it happened the *Tsarevitch* was torpedoed at Port Arthur at the outbreak of the Russo-Japanese war, but hit under the quarter where there was no special protection. The shell plating and frames were ruptured over an area of 30 ft. × 10 ft., the 2½-in. end of the belt pushed inwards, and supporting frames greatly deformed. Of the *Borodino* class the *Kniaz Suvouroff*, sunk at Tsushima, was driven out of the line by gun fire and forty minutes after the battle started had lost a mast and both funnels (3.10 p.m.); attacked by destroyers at 3.40 and again at 4.45, when one torpedo was known to have hit, which left her with a 10° list. As regards the final attack, accounts differ. One states:

> "There was a heavy sea running at the time of the attack on the *Kniaz Suvouroff* at the end of the first day of the Battle of the Sea of Japan; the ship was disabled apparently; she was attacked by six destroyers coming up from astern, three on each quarter, and torpedoed at a range of 800 metres (875 yards). She appeared to be only able to use one gun in her defence."

The other version, given by an officer in charge of one of the destroyers, says:

> "Four boats attacked at dusk and approached to within 200 to 300 yards. They were received by a hot fire, which seemed curious as the ship had been subjected to a very severe shell fire. Of the four torpedoes fired, three struck the ship, and in five minutes she sank."

Two torpedoes fired by the *Harusame* got home—one near the engines and the other aft, and she sank at 7.20. Driven from the line leaking and in flames, she had been kept afloat for over five hours, although twice torpedoed two hours before she went to the bottom. As the ship was loaded with coal above water but with empty bunkers and had no range of stability worth mentioning, her under-water protection must have served her well.

THE "BELLEISLE" TESTS

The effectiveness of coal against torpedo attack was not tested experimentally in this country until 1904, when the old *Belleisle* served as a target. A cofferdam 2 ft. deep filled with cellulose was built outside the hull, while between the skin and boiler rooms were six closely spaced longitudinal bulkheads forming bunkers filled with coal.

The explosion of an 18-in. torpedo very effectively demonstrated that protection as against gun fire did not apply to such under-water attack. A hole 8 ft. × 12 ft. was formed and a large portion of the cofferdam and its cellulose blown away, instead of the cellulose expanding and filling up the hole as had been anticipated. Inboard the damage extended to the inner bulkhead which remained intact, but the decks were blown up and the coal scattered all over the ship, so that not 1 ton remained in the bunkers. This test led to the provision of internal armoured screens covering the magazines in the *Dreadnought* (1905), which developed into the continuous armoured screens in the *Bellerophon* class.

Chapter 71

THE "DUNCAN" CLASS

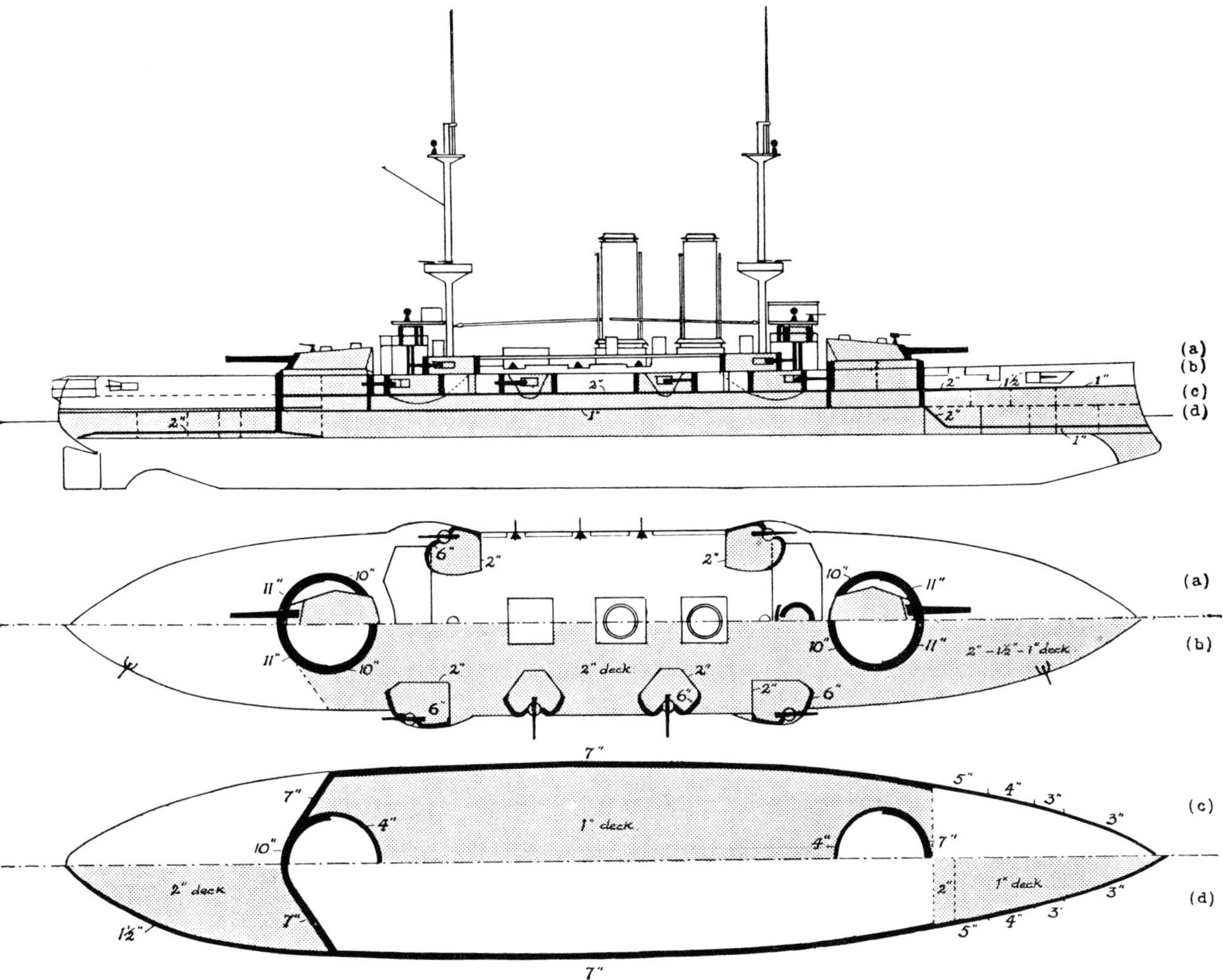

The *Canopus* protective deck arrangement is here reversed with 2-in. on the main and only 1-in. on the waterline and the "Duncans" were adversely criticized on that account.

Six "DUNCAN" Class (1898 (Supplementary) and 1899 Estimates)

	Built by	*Laid down*	*Launched*	*Completed*	*Cost*
"*Duncan*"	Thames I.W.	10 July '99	21 March '01	Oct. '03	
"*Cornwallis*"	Thames I.W.	19 July '99	13 July '01	'04	
"*Exmouth*"	Lairds	10 Aug. '99	31 Aug. '01	May '03	Average
"*Russell*"	Palmers	11 March '99	19 Feb. '01	'03	£1,093,000
"*Albemarle*"	Chatham	8 Jan. '00	5 March '01	Nov. '03	
"*Montagu*"	Devonport	23 Nov. '99	5 March '01	'03	

Dimensions 405′ (432′ o.a.) × 75½′ × 25·2′/26·3′ = 14,000 tons.

	Load draught	*Deep load (tons)*
"*Duncan*"	13,640	15,100
"*Cornwallis*"	13,745	15,200
"*Exmouth*"	13,500	15,120
"*Russell*"	13,270	14,900
"*Albemarle*"	13,440	14,930
"*Montagu*"	13,420	14,950

Armament	4 12-in. 40 cals. (80) 12 6-in. 45 cals. (200) 10 12-pdrs. (300) 2 12-pdrs. (boat) 6 3-pdrs. (500) 2 Maxims.	*Torpedo tubes:* 4 18-in. submerged. *Torpedoes carried:* 18 18-in. 6 14-in.

Protection Belt (KC and KNC) 7″-3″; bows 3″, stern 1½″.
Bulkhead (aft) 11″-7″.
Barbettes 11″-4″; shields 10″-8″.
Ammunition tubes 2″; conning towers 12″-3″.
Casemates 6″-2″.
Decks Lower 2″ and 1″; middle 1″; main 2″-1″.
Total 3,655 tons.

Machinery Engines by: Builders in first four. "*Albemarle*" Thames I.W. "*Montagu*" Lairds.
Two sets 4 cyl. inverted triple exp. H.P. 18,000=19 knots.
Boilers 24 Belleville with economizers; 300 lb. pressure.
Grate area=1,375 sq. ft.; heating surface=43,260 sq. ft.
Cyl. 2=33½″; 2=54½″; 4=63″.
Stroke 4′. Revs. 120.

Coal 900-2,240 tons.

Complement 720.

Points of interest:

(1) First battleships to steam at 19 knots.
(2) Were without ventilating cowls.
(3) Last battleships to be painted black, white and buff.

As already noted, the design of the *Duncan* class was drawn up in reply to the threat of a group of alleged fast Russian battleships of which the *Peresviet* and *Osliabia* were launched in 1898 and the *Pobieda* in 1900. Actually these ranked as second-class ships, carrying four 10-in. and eleven 6-in. guns with moderate protection and a continuous sea speed of 16 knots, so the six *Duncans* provided a generous marshalling of force with a liberal eye towards superiority on all counts—armament, protection and speed.

In order to obtain 19 knots on the eight hours trial the hull was made 5 ft. longer than in the *Formidable*, with 6 in. more beam and 3 in. less draught allowing for a displacement of 14,000 tons—or a saving of 1,000 tons. The same armament was provided, but considerable inroads had to be made on protection, which was cut down by about 675 tons; further improvements in armour and engineering were responsible for most of the balance, and it may be noted that this saving was not utilized in improving military qualities as in the *Formidable*, but just deducted from displacement. A 19-knot *Formidable* would have meant a considerable increase in tonnage, and as a rather weighty public element in criticism was in favour of smaller ships—or at least no further increase in size—the Board's decision on displacement was influenced accordingly.

HULL WEIGHTS

As designed the estimated hull worked out at 5,400 tons—250 tons less than the *Formidable*—and special attention was paid to keeping down weights during construction, with the result that all showed improvement upon the office figures and some very remarkable savings were achieved—which it is of interest to record as their details influenced future standard practice.

		Weight of hull	*Saving in tons*
Russell	Palmers	4,870	530
Albemarle	Chatham	5,020	380
Montagu	Devonport	5,030	370
Exmouth	Lairds	5,182	218
Duncan	Thames I.W.	5,271	129
Cornwallis	Thames I.W.	5,345	55

ARMAMENT

The four 12-in. guns were carried in barbettes of 36½ ft. diameter—1 ft. smaller than the *London's*. Above the side armour the walls were 11 in. with 10 in. rears—a reduction of 1 in.—but below there was only 7 in. with 4 in. rears in place of 12 in. and 6 in.

The same 6-in. casemate protection was retained for the 6-in. guns, and amidships the 12-pdrs. fired over a low breastwork as in the *Queens* instead of through ports like *Canopus* and *Formidable*.

With the object of reducing top weight and increasing stability the height of the after 12-in. guns was reduced by 15 in. to 21 ft. 9 in. above water, so that the class appeared to favour a trim by the stern.

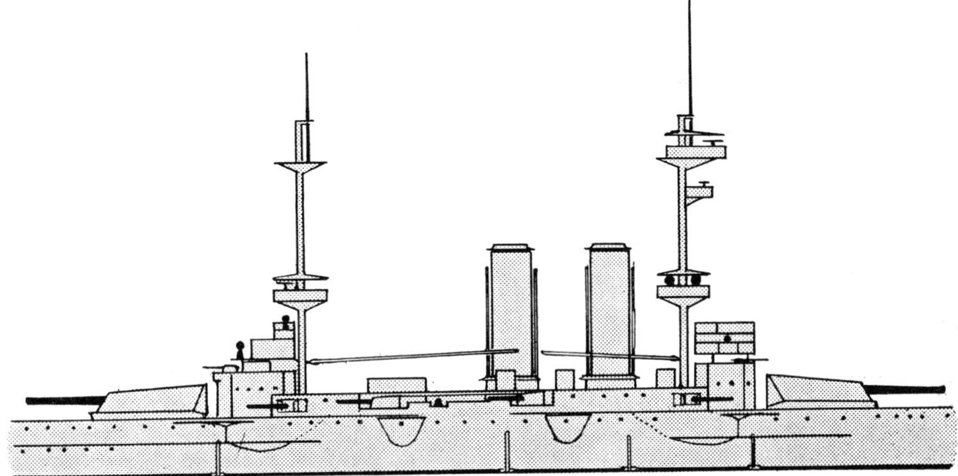

Albemarle with main deck battery suppressed and 6-in. guns on upper deck.

In 1917 *Albemarle* had her main deck battery suppressed and four 6-in. guns transferred to the upper deck amidships, where they had shield protection only. Despite experience in plenty and no lack of very candid criticism it had taken sixteen years for the defects of the main deck battery to be admitted, and the weakest point of White's designs to be corrected in these older ships.

PROTECTION

When the construction of the *Duncans* was postponed, the system of armour distribution decided upon for them was incorporated in the *Londons* and has already been described. But in the smaller ships with only 3,655 tons for disposal in place of 4,330 tons, very substantial reductions in armour had to be made averaging 1 in.-2 in. over the general distribution. Amidships for 238 ft. the belt became 7 in. to a depth of 15 ft. of which 4½ ft. was below water; this was continued to the bows as 5-in., 4-in. and 3-in. plating with a 1½-in. strake along the water-line aft. As in the *London*, this plating replaced the forward bulkhead, the after one sacrificing 2 in. Except that the stern protective deck lost ½ in., the horizontal plating was similar to that in the *London*.

It was in these ships that the competing claims of vertical and horizontal armour first led to adverse criticism of White's designs. It will be seen that while the main deck was 2 in., the water-line deck—which in the *Majestic* ran to 4 in.-3 in.—had been reduced to 1 in. only, both being of mild steel.

Now, the *Majestic's* 9-in. Harvey belt could be pierced by the contemporary French 9·4-in. gun at 3,000 yards,

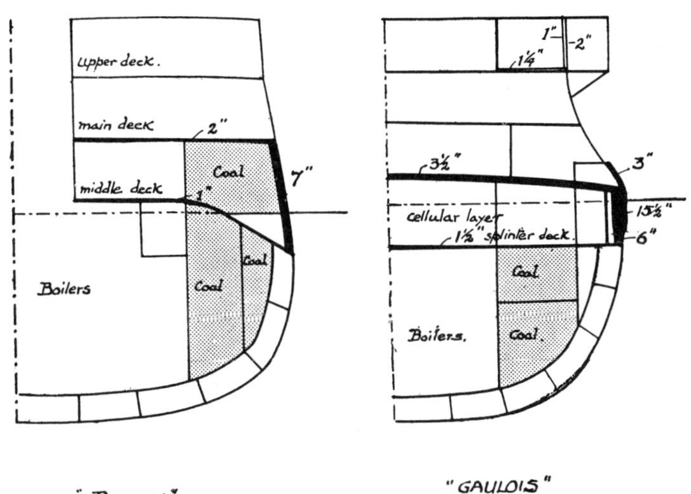

Cross-sections to show schemes of armour-belt and protective deck.

and relied upon reinforcement by armour deck and coal to preserve the integrity of the water-line. Although 7-in. Krupp was regarded as equal to 9-in. Harvey, the *Duncan's* 1-in. deck offered nothing like the same reinforcement to a belt only just proof against their 6·3-in., which meant that these ships were not worthy of first-class status. Their critics pointed out that as a 1-in. deck across a width of 75 ft. weighed as much as 5 in. of vertical armour—which would have afforded almost perfect security to engines, boilers, and water-line—it would have been better to have followed the *Majestic* system omitting the armoured main deck and making the ships battle-worthy. The French were still wedded to the complete *narrow* belt with a "cellular layer" and the contemporary *Gaulois* class of 11,105 tons carrying four 12-in. guns had 15¾ in. amidships with 10-in. ends of Harvey nickel steel for a depth of 6½ ft. only.

Now, although the howitzer armament in French ships—which had been responsible for the armoured main deck in the *Canopus*—had not materialized, the Board took rather an extreme view of the danger of deck hits in a rolling ship, even with the practically horizontal fire at the battle ranges which then obtained. As White pointed out in defence of the upper protective deck ("*Brassey*," 1904, p. 128) in the case of the *Duncan*, the total deck area would be 22,000 sq. ft. and a 10° roll from the vertical involved the exposure of a vertical (projected) height of target exceeding by 3½ ft. (nearly 40 per cent.) that of the side armour when the ship was upright. Very serious damage could be inflicted unless there was adequate deck strength, and large fragments of deck plating and supports could be blown down by the impact of heavy projectiles with powerful bursting charges. It was therefore necessary (1) to make the exposed protective deck at the top of the vertical armour of sufficient strength, and (2) to reinforce this deck by another protective deck, curved down at the edges to meet the lower edge of the armour, and made capable of stopping debris and fragments from the upper protective deck.

This splinter deck originated in France, but in many of their ships it had been placed too close to the upper protective deck, or else so rigidly connected to it that injury to the upper one would almost invariably have involved the splinter deck in serious damage. Considerably more than 25 per cent. of the total weight of protective material was now being worked into deck armour in our ships, although abroad proportionately much less was assigned to horizontal defence—a fundamental difference ignored by tabulated comparisons. We considered it to be of primary importance that the stronger of the two protective decks should be situated at the upper edge of the side armour. High-explosive common shells with large bursters must obviously burst on impact with the upper deck; the lower protective deck being placed so far below the main deck, there was little risk of serious injury to it from fragments of plating or projectiles. Also, with the abolition of the forward bulkhead, the upper protective deck became of greater importance to the defence of the barbette bases, engines, boilers and magazines—especially in a pursuit action, where the great longitudinal extent of the deck target and the slow change in the relative position of the ships tended to increase greatly the risks of deck injury by gun fire.

Critics of the *Duncan's* upper armour deck pointed out that it was by no means easy to see what the main deck was expected to safeguard. While it would certainly prevent pieces of shell which burst between the casemates from going down into the flats above the lower armour deck this was more or less immaterial, as these flats would be empty during action; also because of the armour such shells might blow up the upper deck and wreck the 12-pdr. battery, which would have been safer with the *Majestic* arrangement.

Having limited the legend displacement to 14,000 tons with a first-class armament, and an additional knot with an increased maximum coal supply, a compromise in the matter of armour was inevitable. But while the virtue of the system adopted was never put to the test of battle, the value of 7-in. armour forming the water-line belt in the *Duncan* may be judged from the experience of the Japanese flagship *Mikasa* at the battle of Round Island on 10 August 1904. Here the 7-in. armour below the fore barbette was blown in by a 12-in. projectile at about 13,000 yards, which having penetrated struck the inclined armour deck and was deflected upwards into the latter, where it danced about wreaking destruction. On the other hand, deck hits were few and did not cause much damage, except when the Russian ships were exposed to high-angle fire in Port Arthur harbour—then A.P. sometimes went clean through and pierced the hull bottom. It may be mentioned in passing that the *Osliabia* of the *Peresviet* class turned turtle and sank after three 12-in. hits up forward.

SPEED

For the designed continuous sea speed of 18 knots power was increased to 13,000 h.p. with 24 instead of 20 Bellevilles; for the full power 8 hours trial this was raised to 18,000 n.d. for 19 knots, the *Cornwallis* putting up the best figures with 19·56 knots. Both the Dockyard-built ships just failed to reach 19 knots.

When this class with the *Swiftsure* and *Triumph* composed the Channel Fleet, the two ex-Chileans usually established a good lead during a spurt, but were overhauled when it came to a long-distance trial. The *Albemarle* established a reputation for being the fastest steamer of the class. In service they proved quite good sea boats, able to make their speed in almost any weather, and reliable steamers.

GENERAL

Easily distinguished from both *Canopus* and *Formidable* by the funnels being of equal diameter and larger; also the 12-pdrs. being in an open battery, the ships looked lower amidships.

The *Albemarle* was the only one of the "Duncans" to have her main deck batteries suppressed and two 6-in. behind shields put in the open 12-pdr. battery a deck higher. She is here seen at Devonport in 1919.

Albemarle and *Montagu* had stockless anchors, otherwise all six were practically identical.

When range controls were fitted the *Cornwallis* and *Albemarle* had square fore-tops and the rest elongated oval ones.

They were the first battleships in which cowls were replaced by wind sails.

Four were built under the 1898 Supplementary Estimates, the *Albemarle* and *Montagu* being provided for the following year.

Construction was held up and completion delayed by strikes in the engineering trades and all were four years in hand—five in the case of the *Cornwallis*.

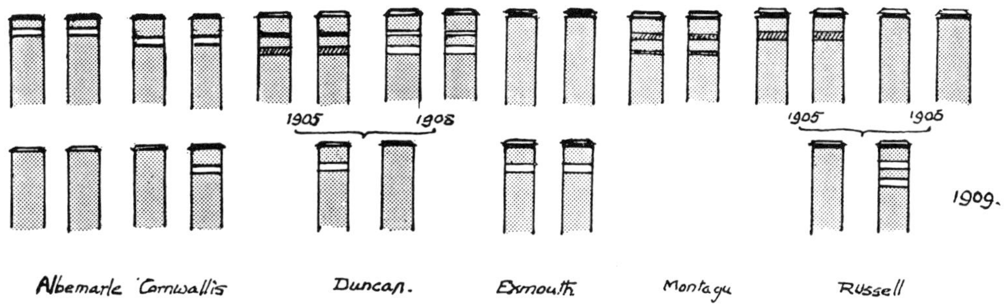

1905, red or white bands. 1909, white bands.
From starboard.

"ALBEMARLE"

Commissioned at Chatham November '03 for Mediterranean; served as 3rd Flagship until January '05 when she transferred to the Channel. In February '07 became Rear-Admiral flagship of Atlantic Fleet (collision with *Commonwealth* 11 February '07; slight damage only). Rear-Admiral Gibraltar January-May '09. In February '10 reduced to nucleus crew 3rd Division Home Fleet Nore, and then transferred to Portsmouth where she was Flagship Rear-Admiral from June-October '10. Long refit January-December '12 and then joined 4th B.S. Home Fleet. In May '13 went to Portsmouth as gunnery tender with a place in the 6th B.S.

War: Joined the Grand Fleet in August '14 and employed on Northern patrol. February '15 Channel Fleet 6th B.S. later 3rd B.S. both composed of "Duncan" class. On 11 November '15 when deeply laden with ammunition she met heavy weather in the Pentland Firth. One sea which passed just below the lower top on the fore mast smashed the charthouse and washed away the bridge. She rejoined at Scapa in December and was later employed at Archangel as an icebreaker and guardship. In '17 the main deck battery was suppressed and four 6-in. guns transferred to upper deck amidships with light shield protection. Remained in Reserve at Devonport.

Sold 1920.

"CORNWALLIS"

Commissioned at Chatham February '04 for Mediterranean (collision with Greek barque *Angelica* 17 September '04, no blame) until January '05, when she transferred to the Channel (primary fire control fitted '05-'06 and completed '07). Joined Atlantic Fleet February '07. Refit Gibraltar January-May '08 and transferred to Mediterranean Fleet in August '10 where she served until June '12 when she returned home to join the 4th B.S. Home Fleet.

War: Channel Fleet 6th B.S. Joined Mediterranean Fleet January '15 and fired the first shot in the preliminary bombardment of the Dardanelles forts on 18 February. Was actively engaged in all major operations until the final evacuation from Suvla Bay when she was the last ship to leave. Altogether she fired 500 rounds of 12-in. and 6,000 of 6-in. shell. Torpedoed and sunk 9 January '17 in the Mediterranean by U.32 but remained afloat after being hit by three torpedoes long enough for all hands to be taken off, except 15 killed by the explosions.

"DUNCAN"

Commissioned at Chatham 3 October '03 for Mediterranean where she served until January '05 and then transferred to the Channel Fleet (primary fire control fitted '05-'06; rammed *Albion* at Lerwick 26 September '05; repairs 22 days). Grounded on Lundy Island July '06 when trying to assist the stranded *Montagu*; repairs 72 days). Atlantic Fleet February '07; refit at Gibraltar November '07-February '08. Transferred to Mediterranean November '08; refit Malta '09; Rear-Admiral Flagship Mediterranean August '10-June '12. Returned home June '12 and joined 4th B.S. 1st Fleet until May '13 when she became gunnery tender at Portsmouth in 2nd Fleet.

War: August '14 6th B.S. 2nd Fleet on Northern patrol. In November joined the "King Edwards" in the 3rd B.S. and moved to Portland and later to Dover. Joined Mediterranean Fleet 1915 but took little part in the Dardanelles operations. Returned home in '17 and went into Reserve.

Sold 1920.

"EXMOUTH"

Commissioned at Chatham June '03 for Mediterranean. Returned home May '04 to become flagship of the Home (afterwards Channel) Fleet. Reduced to nucleus crew April '07 and re-commissioned as flagship Atlantic Fleet. Refit at Portsmouth '07-'08; became flagship Mediterranean Fleet November '08; refit Malta '08-'09. In July '12 transferred as Vice-Admiral flagship to 4th B.S. Home Fleet. Having served as a flagship for eight years she became a private ship in July '13 as gunnery training ship in the 2nd Fleet, Devonport.

War: Together with *Albemarle* and *Russell* formed part of 6th B.S. Grand Fleet. Employed on Northern Patrol in 3rd B.S. ("King Edwards" and "Duncans"); in November ordered to Portland, and together with the two "Lord Nelsons" and 7 "Formidables" formed the Channel Fleet. Bombardment of Zeebrugge 21 November. In May '15, together with *Venerable*, replaced *Queen Elizabeth* off Dardanelles having experience of Belgian coast firing. In action off Helles 4 June with *Swiftsure* and *Talbot* supporting assault which might have led to the capture of Achi Baba. Flagship of Admiral Nicholson at Cephalo where she lay with heavy nets down and colliers alongside after other battleships had been withdrawn from bombarding.

Returned home '17 and placed in Reserve.

Sold 1920.

"RUSSELL"

Commissioned at Chatham for Mediterranean February '03, returning to Home Fleet in April '04 which became Channel Fleet in April '06. Transferred to Atlantic Fleet February '07 (in collision with H.M.S. *Venus* off Quebec 16 July '08; slight damage only). July '09 to Mediterranean Fleet; refit Malta August-December '09 and again in June-September '11. August '12 returned home to 1st Fleet and in September '13 joined 2nd Fleet at the Nore.

War: Grand Fleet flagship 6th B.S. Employed on Northern Patrol in 3rd B.S. In November '14 joined Channel Fleet at Portland. Bombardment of Belgian Coast. Transferred to Mediterranean; in November '15, with *Hibernia*, was reinforcement ship at Mudros only taking part in action 7 January and covering evacuation. Mined off Malta 27 April '16 with a loss of 126 lives.

"MONTAGU"

Commissioned at Devonport in October '03 and served in Mediterranean until January '05 when she was transferred to the Channel Fleet. Wrecked on Lundy Island in a fog 30 May '06, where she was broken up.

The *Duncans* must be considered as the least satisfactory battleships of the White era. Conceived through faulty intelligence, the design suffered through a cut of 1,000 tons made to placate a vociferous group of economists, and the demands made upon protection by a quite unnecessary 19 knots. The claims of deck armour should have been investigated by experimental firing to determine what likely proportion of hits might find a deck target in a short-range action with gun platform and target ship rolling 10° each way. Certainly at that date such hits appeared to be as unlikely as subsequent war experience indicated.

Chapter 72

THE PRESSURE OF FOREIGN DESIGN AND ARMAMENT

In something over eight years twenty-nine battleships of the *Majestic* type had been built for the first line—an extraordinary tribute to White's genius. But when the *Queen* and *Prince of Wales* were provided for in the 1900 Programme it was realized that the time had come for a breakaway from what had become almost a standard model. So long as foreign designs showed no great improvement upon our own, traditional policy required that no changes should be introduced which could hasten developments militating against our numerical superiority. "To follow and overtake rather than to initiate" was the golden rule at Whitehall.

But for some time past British battleships had been criticized on the grounds of being under-gunned—and it was their designer who was held to blame rather than the Board. Secondary batteries had been augmented abroad by the introduction of guns of an intermediate calibre, and in both Italy and America the construction of ships carrying four or eight 8-in. guns in addition to a standard *Majestic* armament on about the same or even smaller displacement had lowered the prestige of our designs.

White circulated an Admiralty paper dealing with these comparisons, and referred especially to cruisers where his designs had come in for much uninformed criticism. Writing with some warmth, he said:

> "Comparisons of this kind have been made from time to time in the press, and in Brassey's Naval Annual or similar publications, always to the serious apparent disadvantage of our ships. The inference, of course, is that the designs prepared at the Admiralty are inferior to those prepared by private firms. In other words, that private firms 'do more on the dimensions and displacement.' No explanation is given why this should be so, or how the trick is done. It is thought sufficient to tabulate and compare dimensions, displacements, maximum (reputed or estimated) speeds, maximum thickness of protected decks or vertical armour, numbers, and calibres of guns, and bunker capacities (not coal actually carried at the displacement and speed). Such comparisons are incomplete and most misleading, but they serve their purpose with the public.
>
> As regards machinery, guns and gun-mountings, private designers draw upon the manufacturing engineering firms of the country, just as we do. In relation to the forms of ships, we possess enormously greater information, based on our experimental establishments and very numerous speed trials. Our structural arrangements are followed almost absolutely by private designers, although in scantlings (thicknesses of plates and bars) they sometimes go below what our experience shows to be necessary for durability as well as strength. Under these circumstances, there must obviously be some radical differences to account for the apparently superior results achieved by private enterprise. These differences are never mentioned in the tabulated comparisons, but they exist none the less and are well known.
>
> Admiralty speed trials are conducted by naval officers, entirely independent of the designer. All disturbing influences of tide and current are eliminated as far as possible. Runs are made over known distances. The reputed speed is the true speed. Speed trials for foreign cruisers built by private firms are not made under similar stringent conditions. In many cases the navies for which they are built have not officers of experience to conduct the trials. The runs are made under circumstances which often permit of tides and currents influencing the speed considerably, and sometimes the distances run are not beyond suspicion. In short, there is not the same independent guarantee of accuracy. As a rule the foreign cruisers are tried for maximum speed for much shorter periods than Admiralty cruisers; and the boilers are "forced" to a greater extent than we should accept. The loads (of coal, equipment, stores, etc.) carried on the speed trials are much less in proportion than would be carried on our cruisers. In many cases the speed trials are made at draughts and displacements corresponding to only *one-third* (or less) of the coal supply, and with *one-half* of the weights of equipment and consumable stores on board. This gives a fictitiously high speed and low displacement as compared with Admiralty practice. It is a significant fact that when firms who produce these very fast cruisers for foreign navies undertake "destroyers" for the Royal Navy, they do not achieve similar conspicuous successes.
>
> The armaments of foreign cruisers are much lighter (relatively to the numbers and calibres of guns carried) than those of British cruisers. . . . We carry much larger supplies of ammunition per gun. As an example, our practice gives 200 rounds for a 6-in. quick-firer. In foreign cruisers 100 rounds or less may be carried and included in the nominal displacement. Where we carry one such gun, the foreign cruiser might carry two guns (with reduced supply of ammunition) for the same weight, or might carry an 8-in. gun instead of a 6-in.
>
> It is the practice (as above mentioned) for foreign cruisers to be credited with their full bunker capacity, although this does not correspond with their reputed displacements. As an example, a recent case may be

mentioned. A cruiser nominally of 4,300 tons is said to have a coal supply of 1,000 tons. As a matter of fact, at the displacement named, she is to carry only 300 tons of coal. If she takes 1,000 tons on board, her displacement becomes 5,000 tons. We allow one-half the bunker capacity in our Navy List displacements (the ship referred to was the Japanese *Takasago*).

The weights of stores, provisions and equipment of all kinds carried are much less than in our cruisers. There is not nearly the same capacity for long and independent sea service. In our service, the provision made for comfort and accommodation goes far beyond what is found in foreign cruisers. Our ships are much more at sea. All these and many other items add considerably to the loads to be carried; and consequently produce increased displacements for a given speed, or tend to lower speeds. For speeds of 20 to 23 knots any addition to the load carried at a given draught of water and given speed will be trebled or quadrupled in the displacement.

In these tabulated comparisons we hear only of maximum thicknesses of armour on decks or sides, over guns, etc. Very often these maximum thicknesses extend over limited areas. Unless one knows what weights are assigned to protection, such statements are valueless for the purposes of comparison. Further, it is quite common to find no reference to important features of defence existing in our ships and costing a good deal to provide, but non-existent in foreign cruisers. For example: our first-class cruisers have armoured protection for their important quick-firing guns and heavier guns. Each casemate for a 6-in. gun involves weight enough to mount two 6-in. guns with shields as carried in most of these foreign cruisers. Not a word is said of this essential difference in design. Our system, introduced ten years ago and steadily adhered to, involves the protection, in battleships and large cruisers, of the more important guns, guns' crews, and transport of ammunition. The foreign cruisers of relatively small displacement are destitute of these features and necessarily so, just as our second-class cruisers have to be because space and weight cannot be found on the dimensions."

So far as the relative displacement value of our own and foreign battleships was concerned, White wrote in *Cassier's Magazine*:

"If the conditions of the problem were stated in identical terms to the leading warship designers of the world, the results obtained would not differ greatly as regards the sizes of ships proposed to fulfil the conditions. Differences in proportion and forms there would be, no doubt. But the differences that exist in dimensions of existing warships, in comparable classes, must be chiefly assigned to differences in the conditions laid down to govern the designs. . . . There is no monopoly of invention or technical skill. What has been accomplished in one country will speedily be rivalled, or perhaps temporarily excelled, elsewhere."

When details of the designs of the U.S. *New Jersey* and the Italian *Benedetto Brin* became known, Sir Arthur Wilson, the Controller, was anxious for our secondary armaments to be reinforced and asked for a series of alter-

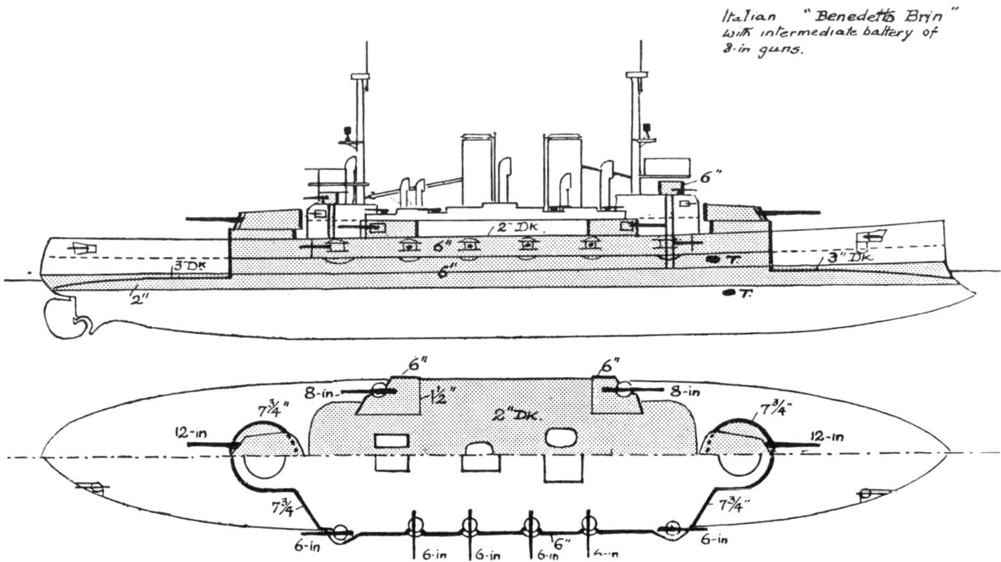

The Italian *Benedetto Brin* (1901) of 13,427 tons carried four 12-in., four 8-in., twelve 6-in., and twenty 12-pdrs. at 18-20 knots. Armour was of necessity on the moderate scale but covering a wide area, with a 3-in. protective deck. The 8-in. guns were later replaced by 6-in.

native designs to be prepared without, however, specifying any definite requirements. In the absence of the D.N.C. through ill-health Chief Constructor Henry Deadman became his deputy, with Constructor J. H. Narbeth in charge of battleship design. Mr. Deadman, groping for the mantle of Benedetto Brin, proposed a battleship which was to be a great advance on anything yet built—so great that no other Power would venture to compete with it. He would not, however, commit himself to any detail of this up-to-date edition of the *Duilio* or *Inflexible*, and response to the Controller's directions hung fire pending proper instructions to the staff. Finally, when the Controller had dismissed this fantastic conception, Constructor Narbeth drew up a series of designs based on the *Duncan* model with the addition of an intermediate armament of 9·2-in. or 7·5-in. guns, modifying the dimensions as length, speed, and stability were severally indicated. One which allowed for eight 7·5-in. guns on the upper deck in pairs, with a 6-in. main deck battery, was selected and approved *without the customary Board conference*.

This design was put in hand, but before the drawings were finished Sir William White returned to office. The Board directed him to consider and report on what had been done, and having gone carefully over the design approved of, the D.N.C. said to Mr. Narbeth: "The Board has asked me to report; I should like to say more than that I simply approve—can you mention anything that would be a big improvement?" He was then shown an alternative design with single 9·2-in. in place of the paired 7·5-in. guns and promptly minuted his opinion that this should be accepted inasmuch as twin 7·5-in. in hydraulically operated turrets were not worth mounting in a battleship, while 9·2-in. would give an adequate increase in offence on the displacement permitted. By such an alteration cost and general dimensions need not be affected and drawings and specifications could be completed without delay.

This modification having been approved by the Board, the drawings were completed although not actually issued when White resigned his post on the grounds of ill-health and left the Admiralty for the last time on 31 January 1902 "a broken-hearted, disappointed, and worn-out man." When his successor, Mr. Philip Watts, arrived from Elswick, he was instructed to examine the drawings, calculations and specifications and report to the Board.

(1) Did he concur in all details?
(2) Would he accept responsibility for the design as then completed?

The new D.N.C. expressed his high appreciation of the design, concurred, and accepted full responsibility by signing the plans for the *King Edward VII*. Officially, therefore, what is often regarded as White's Swan-Song and finest creation comes into the Watts era, although historically she ranks as the final development of the *Royal Sovereign* and the last battleship design produced in the White tradition.

STABILITY AND WEIGHTS

When first proposed in April 1901 the provisional statement was for a battleship limited to 16,000 tons with a length of 420 ft. amd 18 knots speed. In order to carry the additional guns on the upper deck while keeping down weight and assisting stability, the freeboard was to be reduced to 22 ft.—or 1 ft. less than the *London*—and the main deck also lowered 8 in. with the height between it and the upper deck increased by 3 in. to give better head room in the battery. An increase of 3 ft. in beam was necessary to secure the range of stability required.

For the accommodation of the 6-in. guns the *casemate* system was abandoned in favour of the *battery*. The Vickers-built Japanese battleship *Mikasa* largely inspired this change-over from established practice. When designed in 1899 with ten 6-in. guns along her main deck, space restrictions made it necessary to contain these in a continuous battery with armoured screens between the guns instead of in separate casemates as in the earlier battleships. The same considerations obtained in the case of the new British ship and the same solution was applied. The box battery had been also adopted in contemporary American, German, Japanese and Austrian ships, whereas the French, Russian and later Italian models favoured secondary turrets. The battery was regarded as being more economical in weight and cost of armour; on the other hand, it offered the maximum target compared with casemates or turrets and the thin screens between the guns did not afford the same isolation as casemates. Once a big projectile got inside, the outer wall would probably keep it in. It would have to go somewhere, and thin screens were not likely to check it from rebounding across, and across the battery.

ADMIRAL WILSON'S PROPOSALS

The Controller wished for a higher speed than 18 knots, as 19·5 and even 20 knots were being recorded in foreign battleships. But he was not prepared to recommend the increase in size it would have necessitated. He also wanted to carry side armour down for another 3 or 4 ft. and take the lower edge of the protective deck on to a longitudinal bulkhead running the length of the citadel about 6 ft. inboard, with the space between the bulkhead and the belt forming a coal bunker. But the anticipated difficulties arising from transporting coal without any doors in the bulkhead—which would weaken it—or by hoists up to the protective deck and then fore and aft to trunks running down to the stokeholds—too slow a process for rapid steaming—caused the scheme to be dropped. If oil fuel had then been in vogue it might well have been adopted, the outer coal bulkhead forming the boundary of an oil tank and thus anticipating the fore-and-aft protective bulkhead in the *Bellerophon*. Admiral Wilson proposed it as a protection from long-range heavy shell bursting in the water near the ship—in the *Bellerophon* it was introduced as an anti-torpedo measure.

HULL WEIGHTS

In view of the hull weight savings in the *Duncans*, the office estimate was reduced by 250 tons, and in 5,900 tons allowed for the hull, 2,560 tons were absorbed by gun supports and fittings for pumping, ventilating, lighting, magazines, etc., leaving 3,340 tons for the hull proper. During construction economy in weights and fittings resulted in the actual average displacement of the ships being from 15,585 to 15,885 tons, indicating a further saving of 400 tons besides the 500 tons of Board margin which was not drawn upon. This meant that although the legend displacement was 1350 tons more than the *Londons*, they actually only exceeded her by 588-885 tons!

Chapter 73

THE "KING EDWARD VII" CLASS

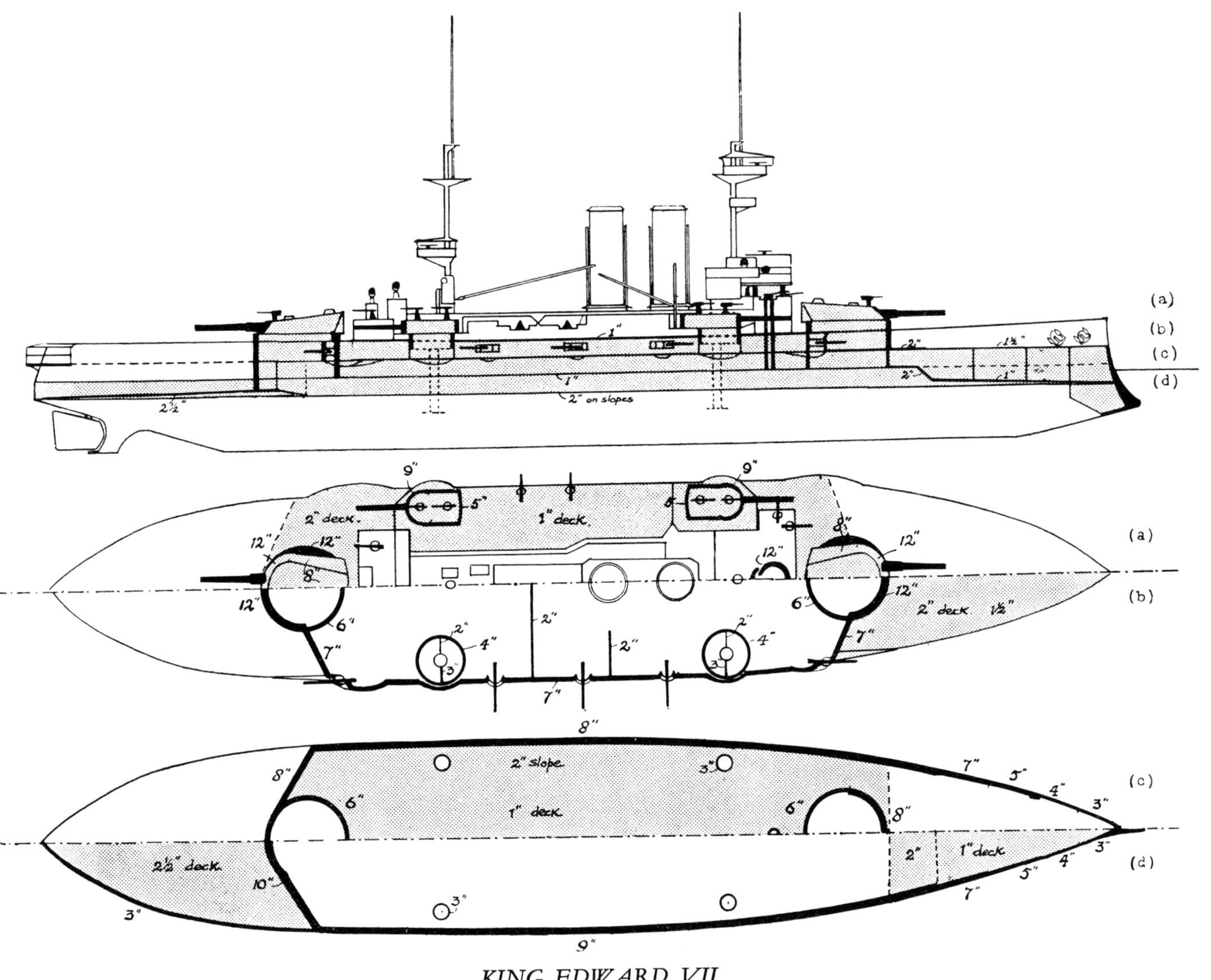

KING EDWARD VII

Eight "KING EDWARD VII" Class (1901-'02-'03 Estimates)

	Built at	*Laid down*	*Launched*	*Completed*	*Cost*
"*King Edward VII*"	Devonport	8 March '02	23 July '03	Feb. '05	£1,382,675
"*Dominion*"	Vickers	23 May '02	25 Aug. '03	July '05	£1,364,318
"*Commonwealth*"	Fairfield	17 June '02	13 May '03	March '05	£1,320,127
"*Hindustan*"	Clydebank	25 Oct. '02	19 Dec. '03	July '05	£1,361,762
"*New Zealand*" (Later "*Zealandia*")	Portsmouth	9 Feb. '03	4 Feb. '04	June '05	£1,335,975
				(Guns in above five £89,400)	
"*Africa*"	Chatham	27 Jan. '04	20 May '05	Nov. '06	£1,328,970
"*Britannia*"	Portsmouth	4 Feb. '04	10 Dec. '04	Sept. '06	£1,316,983
"*Hibernia*"	Devonport	6 Jan. '04	17 June '05	Jan. '07	£1,347,620
				(Guns in above three £91,070)	

Dimensions 425′ (453¾′ o.a.) × 78′ × 24½′/26¾′ = 16,350 tons.

	Deep load	Load draught
"*King Edward VII*"	17,009	15,630 tons
"*Dominion*"	17,020	15,645 „
"*Commonwealth*"	17,040	15,610 „
"*Hindustan*"	17,290	15,885 „
"*New Zealand*"	17,060	15,585 „
"*Africa*"	17,195	15,740 „
"*Britannia*"	17,270	15,810 „
"*Hibernia*"	17,100	15,795 „

Armament 4 12-in. 50-ton 40 cal. (80)
4 9·2-in. 45 cal. (150)
10 6-in. 50 cal. (200)
14 12-pdrs.
14 3-pdrs.
2 maxims.
Total (including turntables and gun shields) 2,575 tons.

Torpedo tubes: 4 18-in. submerged.

Protection Belt 9″-4″; bulkhead aft 12″-8″.
Side prot. plating bows and stern 2″ plus 1″ side plating.
Barbettes 12″-6″; shields 12″-8″.
9·2-in. barbettes 4″; shields 9″-5″.
Battery 7″ with 2″ screens.
Conning tower 12″; communication tube 6″.
Decks: lower 2½″, 2″-1″; middle 2″ and 1″; main 2″ and 1½″.
Total weight 4,175 tons.

Machinery Two sets 4 cyl. vert. triple exp. In contract ships by builders: "*King Edward*" and "*Hibernia*" by Harland and Wolff; "*Britannia*" and "*New Zealand*" by Humphreys and Tennant.
H.P. 18,000 = 18·5 knots. 120 revs.
Boilers: "*Dominion*" and "*Commonwealth*" Babcock and Wilcox. w.t. "*New Zealand*" 4/5 Niclausse, 1/5 cylindrical. Rest 4/5 Babcock and Wilcox, 1/5 cylindrical.
Pressure 210 lb.

Coal 950/2,200 tons.

Oil 380 tons except in "*New Zealand*"

Radius 3,150/17; 7,000/10.

Complement 777. *Constructor:* J. H. Narbeth.

Points of interest:

(1) The first British battleships to carry 9·2-in. guns as an intermediate calibre.
(2) The only White ships to have box batteries.
(3) The last to carry 6-in. guns primarily for action with other battleships.

The *King Edward VII* design having been endorsed by Mr. Watts, the three ships of the class built under the 1901 Estimates *King Edward VII*, *Dominion* and *Commonwealth* were put in hand, the *Hindustan* and *New Zealand* being provided for in the following year. But by 1903 the Board were considering drawings for a vastly superior ship carrying four 12-in. and twelve 9·2-in. guns, and had the preparation of this design reached a stage which would have allowed for the immediate commencement of the three ships of the 1903 Programme, we should have anticipated the *Lord Nelson* by a twelve-month and strengthened the Fleet accordingly. As it was, work had progressed so fast on the Dockyard ships that continuity of employment made it necessary to place the orders of these three battleships without delay. They were therefore allotted to the Yards instead of being given out to contract as first intended, and the *King Edward* design again repeated, bringing the class up to a homogeneous squadron of eight ships. But Sir Philip Watts in his I.N.A. paper of 9 April 1919 states:

> "After I became Director of Naval Construction in 1902, the design of battleships for the 1903-4 Programme came up for consideration. It was at length decided that they should have a powerful 'all big-gun' armament of two calibres, viz. four 12-in. guns and twelve 9·2-in. guns. The design was completed early in 1903 and approved; later on, however, it was decided to postpone building from this design till the following year, and to build three additional *King Edwards* for the 1903-4 Programme in order to complete a squadron of eight vessels of this type."

It need hardly be said that any Board which would choose to place in the line of battle three ships with battle range broadsides of 4,120 lb. in place of three able to discharge 5,560 lb. because of the value of squadron homogeneity would deserve to be pilloried.

Among the old rigged ironclads the *Achilles* was looked upon as being perfectly proportioned, and the same can be said of the *King Edwards*. The height of masts and funnels and their relative positions (rear of second funnel being midway between masts), together with the thickness of the funnels—which bore a generous relation to uptake requirements—were all calculated carefully to give an ensemble of balance and symmetry unique among the profiles of armoured ships. The original design had no fighting tops, the fire-control platforms being fitted during completion.

Forward the freeboard was 22 ft. with 18 ft. aft, the hull being without the 12-pdr. ports of the previous classes—in which they were sooner or later plated in and the guns transferred to the shelter decks. The Board having directed particular attention to the bridge and manœuvring qualities, the former was enlarged, the useless after bridge suppressed, and a large balanced rudder fitted. The deadwood aft was cut away as in previous ships and not to a greater extent, as in several cases vessels of the *Majestic* class had buckled their after keels where the ship first rested on the blocks when being docked.

KING EDWARD VII

ARMAMENT

The diversity of calibres in the armament came in for a good deal of adverse criticism in the Service when their details became known, the gist being that they did not carry enough guns for their size and that there were too many types. If the 9·2-in. was a desirable piece (and naval opinion was unanimous on this head), then the 6-in. was unnecessary, and the secondary armament could have been confined to the 9·2-in., which fired almost as quickly and was almost as easy to handle. By pairing these guns and disposing of them as in the Italian *Regina Elena*, six could have been carried on either broadside for very little more expenditure in weight, and the four 9·2-in. thus gained would have been infinitely preferable to two 9·2-in. and five 6-in. despite the disadvantage of pairs. It was also contended that, since the capped 9·2-in. was equal to the best armour, the heavy guns might just as well have been 9·2-in., and the ships could then have carried from eighteen to twenty of these pieces. Just how the extra turrets could have been worked in on the length was a debatable point, and the matter of stability with such a lot of extra weight up topsides was rather left in the air.

Other disliked features were the absence of any useful belt astern, and the relatively poor coal supply, so that —so far as "paper value" was concerned—the type was not regarded as standing well in comparison with many foreign battleships of less weight.

From the evolution of the design it will be appreciated that the hull of the *King Edward VII* was carrying as much weight as practicable and that a heavier 9·2-in. armament was out of the question. Had the gunnery officers been consulted in the first place it is quite on the cards that there would not have been this intermediate stage between the *Duncan* and *Lord Nelson*: but from the manner of selection between the 7·5-in. and 9·2-in. the choice of armament lay primarily with the Board, and the Navy—with no say in the matter—had to use the tools provided. Not until after the Great War were the positions reversed—when the Navy stated its requirements to the Admiralty, decided how the ships should be fought, and told the Controller's Department what it had to try to produce.

Although mounting 40 cal. 12-in., the mountings and shields were re-designed for 45 cal. guns and the outside diameter of the barbettes reduced from 37½ to 34 ft.—which meant a saving of about 300 tons on turn-tables, shields and barbettes. British gun positions at that time were far more spacious and vastly heavier than was customary abroad—from 45 to 80 per cent. for a given thickness of armour. Thus, viewed end-on, the *King Edward's* shield presented a target of 23 ft. and barbette 34 ft.; those of the *Gaulois* were about 25 ft. and 18 ft. respectively, the *Sevastopol* 25 ft. and 25 ft., and the *Rhode Island* 23 ft. and 27 ft., each housing two 12-in. guns. White was a great believer in plenty of room to give rapid handing of ammunition without interfering with the guns' crews. But less space meant heavier protection and a smaller target, so that any improvement in mountings which permitted this was all to the good, and the reduction of barbette diameter in these ships was the precursor to a still greater saving in the *Lord Nelson*.

The barbettes had 12-in. armour above the side plating, and 8 in.-6 in. behind it, the gun muzzles being 25 ft. above water forward and 22¾ ft. aft. Their turrets had 8-in. sides with 12-in. faces. Practically all warships suffered from blast effects when big guns were fired axially or nearly so, and the *King Edward's* short superstructures did little to shield the 12-in. turrets. So that when the after 9·2-in. trained astern the concussion in the 12-in. hoods was described as "very great," an officer in the nearest one being knocked senseless. When the after 12-in. fired 30° before the beam, blast in the 9·2-in. hood was unpleasant, although assessed as only "moderate."

For the 9·2-in. guns there were 9-in. turrets on 4-in. bases forming slight sponsons and covered by the 7-in. side armour, with light ammunition tubes taken down well below the belt. These shallow bases were criticized on the grounds that a shell below them would blow the whole thing into the air, but defended on the grounds that a whole shell room might well be expended without one bursting under the barbette. To succeed, direction would have had to be accurate to within 9½ ft.; elevation correct within 2 ft.; and the shell burst as much as 20 to 100 ft. from its point of entry (according to whether it was a broadside or a raking hit), which in itself was almost impossible. Even if a 12-in. shell did burst 2 ft. from the barbette floor, it was not considered likely that any great harm would result.

These 9·2-in. fired a 380-lb. shell capable of piercing a 14-in. steel plate at 3,000 yards four times a minute, and their inclusion gave the *King Edwards* considerable kudos for a year or so. But the times were unkind to them, as by 1906 when all eight were in service, long-range firing had discovered the drawbacks of a three-calibre armament—which looked better on paper than it proved to be in practice, fire control being greatly complicated by difficulty in distinguishing between 12-in. and 9·2-in. splashes and sighting confused by 6-in. gas discharge refraction. With the *King Edward's*, "smashing effect" of 9·2-in., and "smothering" of upper works and tertiary batteries, unprotected areas and control positions by 6-in. guns passed into the limbo of short-range action and ramming tactics.

The 6-in. guns were of 50 cals. and the first of this length to be mounted in a European ship—the Americans having jumped from 40 cals. in the *Alabama* (1898) to 50 cals. in the *Ohio* (1901). Although the full length of the main deck battery was about 210 ft., three guns aside had to be worked into a space of 90 ft. amidships between the 9·2-in. (whereas the *Duncan* allowed 160 ft. for four casemates) with the end guns in sponsons for axial fire. The three centre ports were in small sponsons which increased their arcs of fire, and all five could be sealed by hinged wings flush with the ship's side to prevent flooding. It was not a very satisfactory battery, as the gun muzzles were only 12 ft. 9 in. above water, wet and difficult to fight in a seaway, and dipping under at 14° roll. By 1917 this main deck battery had been replaced in the *Commonwealth*, *Zealandia*, *Britannia*, *Africa* and *Hibernia* by two guns aside behind shields on the upper deck amidships, where they served as defence against torpedo attack.

Fourteen 12-pdrs. and fourteen 3-pdrs. were distributed over the superstructures, in the amidships battery between the 9·2-in. and on the turret tops, their positions being altered to suit the caprices of the commanding officers. Thus when the *King Edward* was Lord Charles Beresford's flagship in 1907, she carried four on the roof of each of the big gun shields, where they had a good all-round bearing and were clear of surrounding structures—in which positions they set the fashion for many years to come.

Of the four under-water torpedo tubes, those forward fired at 10° before the beam and the after ones 35° abaft it; originally a stern tube was provided, but later on suppressed.

PROTECTION

Armour distribution was generally along *London* lines with a 3-in. belt extension aft instead of only 1½ in.; over the flanks there was a reduction to 8 in.; and a 7-in. battery wall and bulkheads along the main deck replaced casemates. Some redistribution of the horizontal armour became necessary, the upper protective deck having to be raised to crown the battery and for reasons of stability its thickness was reduced from 2 in. to 1 in.—which saving provided a good 5 in. towards the battery walls. Otherwise deck protection was similar to that in the *London*. The total armour was 4,175 tons, or 160 tons less than in *Formidable*.

But during their construction the *introduction of capped shell* and *increase in velocities* combined to give the gun ascendancy over armour, and theoretically the *King Edward's* protection suffered accordingly. For whereas when the *Formidable* passed into service her belt could resist 12-in. impact until ranges had closed to about 3,000 yards, in the *King Edward* it now became vulnerable at 5,000 yards to the old-type 12-in. and by a 9·2-in. at 3,000 to 4,000 yards. However, under average conditions of visibility the great increase in battle ranges would serve to neutralize this extra penetration to a large extent, although it was realised that three years' adherence to one design would have to mean drastic improvements in the ships to follow, if individual superiority over foreign ships was to be maintained.

MACHINERY

Four-cylinder triple-expansion engines were installed and the boiler plant suffered from the recommendations of the Boiler Committee in that only *Commonwealth* and *Dominion* had a full set of water-tube generators. With them the insensate "Battle of the Boilers" terminated.

"*King Edward*"	10 Babcock plus 6 cylindrical	18,138 h.p.	=19 knots.
"*Dominion*"	16 Babcock	18,438 „	=19·3 „
"*Commonwealth*"	16 Babcock	18,538 „	=19 „
"*Hindustan*"	12 Babcock plus 3 cylindrical	18,521 „	=19 „
"*New Zealand*"	12 Niclausse plus 3 „	18,440 „	=18·6 „
"*Africa*"	12 Babcock plus 3 „	18,698 „	=18·9 „
"*Britannia*"	12 Babcock plus 3 „	18,725 „	=18·7 „
"*Hibernia*"	12 Babcock plus 3 „	18,112 „	=18·1 „

Britannia was partially re-boilered in 1908 and *Dominion* in 1911.

SEA-GOING QUALITIES

Owing to reduced freeboard they were rather wet and felt the sea a good deal. Thus, the *Hibernia* had to abandon gun trials in weather which was not noticed aboard the *Dreadnought*. But they proved very handy, with a tactical diameter of about 340 yards at 15 knots.

The metacentric height was the greatest of any battleship in the White era, being 5·3 at load draught. This resulted in a 14 sec. period for the double roll and a 66·5° range of stability.

This increased stability helped to keep the *King Edward VII* and *Britannia* upright after receiving mortal injuries. When the former was mined she remained afloat for thirteen hours in rough weather with only a slight list. There were no casualties, and not until four hours after she had been abandoned did she capsize and sink. The *Britannia* received two torpedo hits but did not capsize for three and a half hours.

RIG

With these ships the fighting top was discarded. From the simple canvassed-in platform of the 'seventies it had grown into a distinctive and decorative adjunct of some value as a gun position as long as the 3-pdr. proved effective for torpedo defence. By 1902 this small gun had become discredited, although for some reason or other the *King Edwards* were given a dozen. But none of these went aloft and the masts had searchlight platforms only.

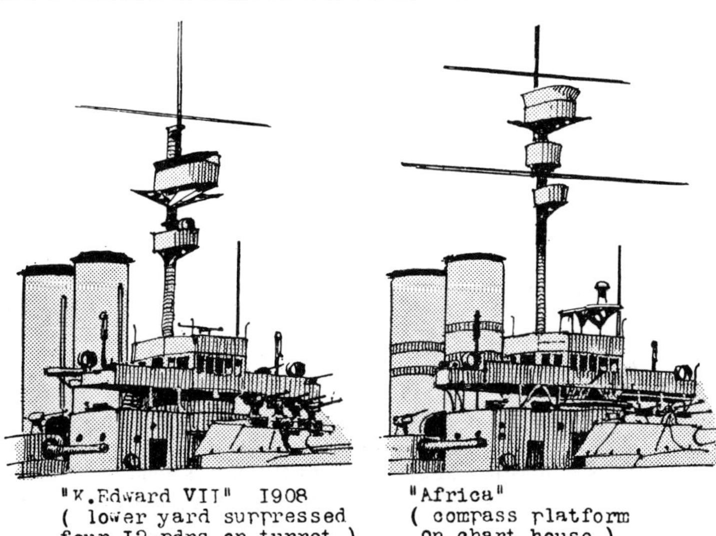

"K.Edward VII" 1908 (lower yard suppressed four 12-pdrs on turret.)

"Africa" (compass platform on chart house)

When the first rudimentary system of fire control was installed stations were placed on the foremast "starfish" and low down on the mainmast below smoke level; the last trio of the class were given three small tops right up on the foremast with the topmast abaft them—practically the only distinguishing feature.

When mast-head director towers became necessary, additional stiffening was afforded by tripod struts in *Commonwealth* and *Zealandia*. From 1914 in all the class the main topmast was unshipped and a light pole fitted.

REAPPEARANCE OF THE BALANCED RUDDER

The balanced rudder, introduced by Reed in the *Bellerophon* and fitted in all his subsequent designs, had been abandoned by Barnaby when the development of "rudder wobble" due to wear on the bearing surfaces, and

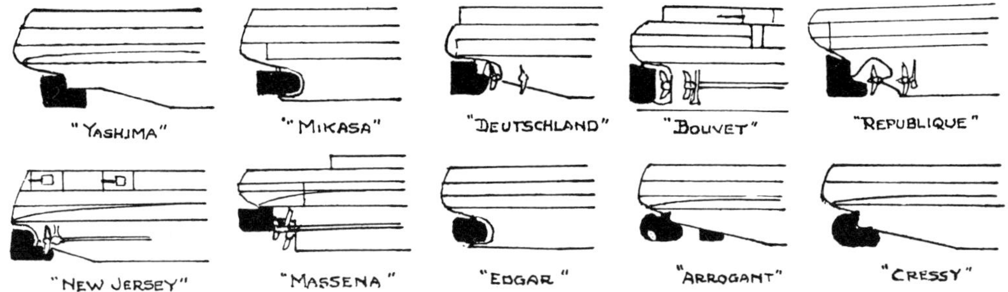

the drag—which was such a hindrance when under sail—led to its becoming thoroughly unpopular in the Service. Before the general adoption of steam steering it provided a great relief to the helmsmen; but when machinery replaced muscle this consideration lost weight and the pintle-hung rudder came back into favour for heavy capital ships. But several of White's cruisers were given partially balanced rudders with more area abaft than before the turning axis, while abroad this type in a variety of shapes had come into favour for the heaviest battleships, when seatings had been designed to withstand the tremendous strain thrown upon them during manœuvre at speed.

A few of the more interesting foreign patterns have been included in the sketches above for comparison with the British practice. It will be noticed that in the *King Edward VII* there was very little area forward of the axis but even this was too much for the seatings in the *Commonwealth* as she developed such a degree of rudder wobble during her first commission that there was nothing for it but to pay her off into dockyard hands for the seating to be modified and strengthened.

At the end of 1912, when our battleships were being concentrated in Home waters and the French moved the heavy units of their Northern Fleet into the Mediterranean to counter the entry into service of the new Austrian and Italian dreadnoughts, the retention up the Straits of a battle squadron composed of *Duncans* and *Swiftsures* was useless. These six vessels were therefore withdrawn and for the winter months 1912-13 their place was taken by six *King Edwards* which were fit to lie in the line until a fresh distribution placed the three *Indomitables*, *Indefatigable*, and four of the latest armoured cruisers in the Mediterranean.

Prior to April 1915, when the Grand Fleet battle squadrons became composed of *Dreadnoughts* only, the

COMMONWEALTH

Main deck battery removed, bulges and tripod mast.

presence of the 3rd Squadron made up of the *King Edward VII* class greatly complicated the rapid deployment of the Fleet for action, as their speed was three knots less than that of the rest of the Battle Fleet. In order to avoid reducing the fleet speed of the whole battle line to 14 knots during deployment, the cruising order adopted placed the squadron in rear of the *Dreadnoughts* squadrons, with orders to turn in the opposite direction to deployment, taking station in rear of the rest of the fleet, with consequent unavoidable delay in its coming into action.

While attached to the Grand Fleet of the 3rd Battle Squadron they were known as the "Wobbly Eight," and throughout hostilities bore the unfortunate distinction of never having been granted an opportunity of firing their guns at an enemy target, although on several occasions contact with the Germans was only missed by a narrow margin.

When altered for bombarding purposes in 1918, *Commonwealth* was given waterline "bulges" as torpedo protection, a tripod mast, and the main deck battery was suppressed in favour of two 6-in. aside behind shields on the upper deck as in *Albemarle*. *Zealandia* had her 6-in. armament similarly altered, and was given a tripod, but was not bulged.

"AFRICA"

Built at Chatham January '04-November '06, and commissioned for Atlantic Fleet. February '07 Channel Fleet (in collision with S.S. *Ormuz* off Portland March '07; repairs 21 days). April '09 2nd Division Home Fleet. Temporary Flagship Rear-Admiral. February '11 reduced to nucleus crew at Nore. April '11 Flagship Vice-Admiral of 3rd and 4th Divisions Home Fleet. Flag transferred to *King Edward VII* August '11. March '12 Home Fleet Nore, nucleus crew. May '12 Home Fleet 3rd B.S. (full crew). (In April was fitted with a temporary flight deck over forecastle for seaplane trials.) February '13 temporarily attached to 4th B.S. Mediterranean, rejoining 3rd B.S. in July.

War: August '14 3rd B.S. Grand Fleet. April '17-November '18 served with 9th C.S. Became an accommodation ship April '19.

Sold June 1920.

"BRITANNIA"

Built at Portsmouth February '04-September '06. October '06 commissioned for Atlantic Fleet. February '07 transferred to Channel Fleet. April '09 2nd Division Home Fleet Flagship Vice-Admiral February '10 (collision with barque *Loch Trool* 14 July '10, slight damage). May '12 2nd Division 1st Fleet. May '12 3rd B.S. temp. in Mediterranean (had received no large refit until '13).

War: August '14 3rd B.S. Grand Fleet. (January '15 stranded at Inchkeith and refloated in 2 days; badly damaged.)

Torpedoed 9 November '18 off Cape Trafalgar by U.B. 50; floated for 3½ hours, then sank with casualties.

"COMMONWEALTH"

Built at Fairfields June '02-March '05 and completed at Devonport. 9 April '05 commissioned for Atlantic Fleet. May '07 Channel Fleet temp. Flagship Rear-Admiral in '08 (collision with *Albemarle* 11 February '07 off Lagos; severe structural damage). Grounded at entrance to Lamlash 23 August '07. April '09 transferred to Home Fleet 2nd Division. June '11 Home Fleet 3rd Division Nore. May '13 3rd B.S. 1st Fleet. Temporarily in Mediterranean (had no refit until '12, although 8 times in dockyard hands).

War: August '14 3rd B.S. (refit December '14-February '15).

Big refit 1918 (6-in. batteries removed; bulges fitted. D.C. and tripod mast). Served as sea-going gunnery ship at Invergordon '19-'21.

Sold November '21. Broken up in Germany.

"DOMINION"

Built at Vickers May '02-July '05. Commissioned 5 August '05 for Atlantic Fleet (grounded in Chalon Bay, St. Lawrence August '16 and repaired at Bermuda September-January '07 and Chatham February-June '07). April '09 Home Fleet 2nd Division. May '12 2nd B.S. 1st Fleet. October '13 3rd B.S. Temp. in Mediterranean.

War: August '14 3rd B.S. Grand Fleet temp. Flagship Vice-Admiral August-September '15. Refit at Devonport. May '16 avoided 2 torpedoes from U-boat. 1917-18 Depôt at the Swin for Zeebrugge operations.

Sold May 1921.

"HIBERNIA"

Built at Devonport January '04-January '07. Commissioned 2 January for Atlantic Fleet. February '07 transferred to Channel Fleet Rear-Admiral; January '09 Channel Vice-Admiral. March '09 Home Fleet 2nd Division Flagship Vice-Admiral (14 July run into by *Loch Trool*, just in collision with *Britannia*). January '11 Flagship Rear-Admiral Home Fleet 2nd Division. January '12 Nore Division Home Fleet nucleus crew. May '12 3rd B.S. Flagship Rear-Admiral (fitted with temporary flight runway over forecastle from which Commander C. R. Samson made the first seaplane flight from a British warship. 4 May '12). Temporarily in Mediterranean.

War: August '14 3rd B.S. Grand Fleet. November '15 transferred to Dardanelles naval forces as Flagship Admiral Freemantle.

Nore Command accommodation ship 1919.

Sold 1921. Broken up in Germany.

"HINDUSTAN"

Built at Clydebank October '02-July '05. July '05 Reserve, Portsmouth. 22 August '05 commissioned for Atlantic Fleet. February '07 Channel Fleet. April '09 Home Fleet 2nd Division. April '12 Home Fleet Portsmouth sub-division. May '12 3rd B.S. 1st Fleet. February '13 4th B.S. (temp.). July '13 rejoined 3rd B.S. (no large repairs until '13 apart from annual refits).

War: August '14 3rd B.S. Grand Fleet. In May '16 after the Lowestoft raid the 3rd B.S. was based on the Thames.

Sold 1921.

"KING EDWARD VII"

Built at Devonport March '02-February '05. 7 February '05 commissioned for Atlantic Fleet Flagship. '06-'07 repairs and refit. March '07 Channel Fleet Flagship. March '09 Home Fleet 2nd Division Vice-Admiral Flagship transferred to *Hercules* June '11. Dec. '09-February '10. refit Portsmouth. August '11 Home Fleet Nore sub-division nucleus crew Vice-Admiral 3rd and 4th Division. May '12 3rd B.S. Vice-Admiral temporary in Mediterranean.

War: August '14 3rd B.S. Vice-Admiral Bradford. Flag. shifted to *Dominion* when *King Edward VII* left for Devonport to change cracked guns; rejoined 2 September. 6 January '16 at 7 a.m. mined in a very scattered field laid by the raider *Mowe* off C. Wrath—through which *Africa* had just proceeded safely. Both engine rooms filled and ship heeled to starboard in strong wind and rising sea. Attempted tow of collier *Melita* and leader *Kempenfelt* failed. Destroyers transferred all hands and she turned over and sank 8 p.m.

(When launched by King Edward VII, His Majesty stipulated that she should always be employed as a flagship. She was sunk on the only occasion when a private ship.)

"NEW ZEALAND" (*Zealandia*)

Built at Portsmouth February '03-June '05. 11 July '05 commissioned for Atlantic Fleet. October-December '06 refit at Gibraltar. June '07 Channel Fleet. March '09 Home Fleet 2nd Division Flagship Rear-Admiral temp. '09. August-November '08 refit Devonport. August '09 Home Fleet 2nd Division. August '11 Home Fleet Portsmouth sub-division Rear-Admiral (became *Zealandia* December '11). May '12 3rd B.S. 1st Fleet temp. in Mediterranean (received no thorough refit until '12).

War: August '14 3rd B.S. November '15 Transfer to Dardanelles naval force. '18 Big refit; 6-in. batteries removed; director tower and tripod. Accommodation ship at Portsmouth 1919.

Sold 1921. Broken up in Germany.

Distinguishing funnel bands in "*King Edward VII*" class.
From starboard.

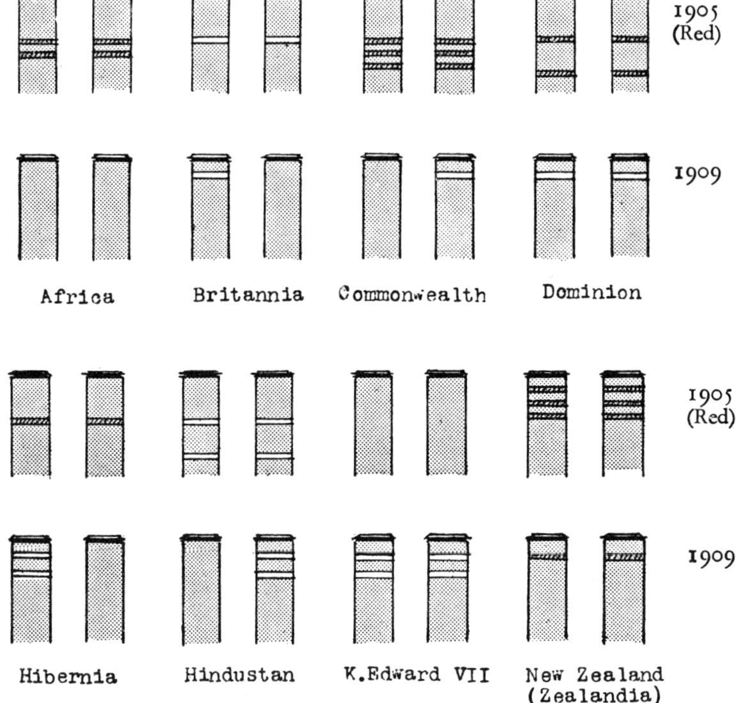

1906

CHANNEL	MEDITERRANEAN	ATLANTIC	RESERVE
Albemarle	*Bulwark*	*Commonwealth*	*Vengeance*
Cornwallis	*Formidable*	*Dominion*	*Ramillies*
Duncan	*Implacable*	*Hindustan*	*Repulse*
Exmouth	*Irresistible*	*King Edward VII*	*Resolution*
Montagu	*London*	*New Zealand*	*Royal Oak*
Russell	*Prince of Wales*	*Magnificent*	*Revenge*
Swiftsure	*Queen*	*Majestic*	*Empress of India*
Triumph	*Venerable*	*Victorious*	*Hood*
Albion			*Nile*
Canopus			*Trafalgar*
Glory			*Barfleur*
Goliath			*Centurion*
Ocean			
Cæsar			
Jupiter			
Prince George			

Chapter 74

THE RISE OF THE GERMAN NAVY

UNTIL 1898 the German Navy had been of secondary importance. Moltke had stated that Germany could never make claim to the command of the sea, and her miscellaneous assortment of ships bore no reasonable relationship to her growing trade and overseas interests. Obsessed by the success of her army in the war with France, and the small influence which sea power had exerted in that struggle, the ruling caste refused to shoulder the burden of any naval ambitions.

But the appointment of Admiral Tirpitz as Secretary of State for Naval affairs in January 1897 marked the beginning of a momentous change in the German outlook on sea power. By means of an elaborate Press Bureau for the education of the people, backed by the propaganda of the Navy League, he started to inculcate some realization of its meaning and importance, as well as the necessity for creating a ship-building industry sufficient to supply the demands of a large and efficient fleet, which at the same time might claim a share in the large profits appropriated by Great Britain as the world's shipbuilder. So successful were his efforts that in 1898 the Reichstag passed a Navy Act which incorporated the principle of fixed establishments and regular replacement of obsolete ships. The fleet considered necessary to fulfil the requirements of the empire was fixed at:

The Battle Fleet

19 battleships (2 as material reserve)
8 armoured coast-defence ships
6 large cruisers
16 smaller cruisers

with six large and fourteen small cruisers for the Foreign Service fleets. The period proposed for the attainment of this strength was seven years, which the Reichstag shortened by a year—*i.e.*, the end of 1903. Battleships and coast-defence ships were to be replaced at the end of twenty-five years, and the armoured ships built and building to be reckoned on this establishment were:

Battleships: 19 (5 *Wittelsbach*, 5 *Kaiser*, 4 *Worth*, 4 *Baden*, 1 *Oldenburg*)
Coast-Defence: 8 (6 *Siegfried*, 1 *Odin*, 1 *Aegir*.)

The "large cruisers" included the three old central battery ironclads *Konig Wilhelm*, *Kaiser*, and *Deutschland*.

Replacement of battleships was to be commenced in 1906 at the following rate: 1906-9 two yearly. 1910-16 one yearly. 1917 two.

The outbreak of the South African war, and such incidents as the seizure of the mail steamer *Bundesrat* and other German vessels on the African coast, roused hostility towards Great Britain to a white heat—and Tirpitz made prompt and full use of it. In the spring of 1900 the Act of 1898 was replaced by a new one setting up an establishment of almost twice its size, which, in its final form as published on 20 June 1900, provided for:

The Battle Fleet

2 fleet flagships
4 squadrons each of 8 battleships
8 large cruisers
24 small cruisers

Foreign Fleet

3 large cruisers
10 small cruisers

Reserve

4 battleships
3 large cruisers
4 small cruisers

Except in the case of total loss, battleships were to be replaced after twenty-five years and cruisers after twenty years. It was proposed to keep two battle squadrons fully manned on a war footing and two to form the Reserve Fleet, half the ships of which were to be kept in permanent commission.

But more remarkable than the actual terms of the Act was the character of the explanatory Memorandum in which occurred the following statement:

> "To protect Germany's sea trade and colonies, in the existing circumstances, there is only one means; Germany must have a battle fleet so strong that, even for the adversary with the greatest sea power, a war against it would involve such dangers as to imperil his position in the world.
>
> "For this purpose, it is not absolutely necessary that the German battle fleet should be as strong as that of the greatest naval Power, because a great naval Power will not, as a rule, be in a position to concentrate all its striking forces against us. But even if it should succeed in meeting us with considerable superiority of strength, the defeat of a strong German fleet would so substantially weaken the enemy that, in spite of a victory he might have obtained, his own position in the world would no longer be secured by an adequate fleet."

And further:

> "If the necessity for so strong a Fleet for Germany be recognized, it cannot be denied that the honour and welfare of the Fatherland authoritatively demand that the Home Fleet be brought up to the requisite strength as soon as possible."

This decision of the greatest military Power, to become at the same time something akin to the second naval Power, was an epoch-making event in world affairs. If carried into effect—and the principle of fixed establishments and regular replacements had by now become so recognized a feature of naval legislation that its opponents could only be found among the Socialists—it would create a situation of terrible significance to the British Empire.

Hitherto our Programme had been based upon a two-Power standard with adequate superiority over France and Russia. The addition of a third and even more formidable fleet meant that we could no longer afford to remain "in splendid isolation" from Continental affairs. Our foreign commitments would have to be adjusted to allow for a maximum concentration of naval force in Home and European waters, and to this end an Alliance was signed with Japan in 1901. Further, it would be necessary to improve our European relationships and put a stop to the recurring differences with France and Russia.

Meanwhile we preferred to regard Germany in the light of a traditional friend, and she was invited to join us in the Alliance with Japan and also to make a joint effort towards settling the Moroccan problem then disturbing the Chancelleries. It was a unique opportunity for Germany to attempt some reconciliation with Japan, although it is doubtful whether her behaviour in 1899 would have been forgiven. But if the breech had been closed, a neutral Japan would have made a lot of difference in the course of affairs in the Far East, fourteen years later.

However, Germany chose to decline both offers.

Chapter 75

"SWIFTSURE" AND "TRIUMPH"

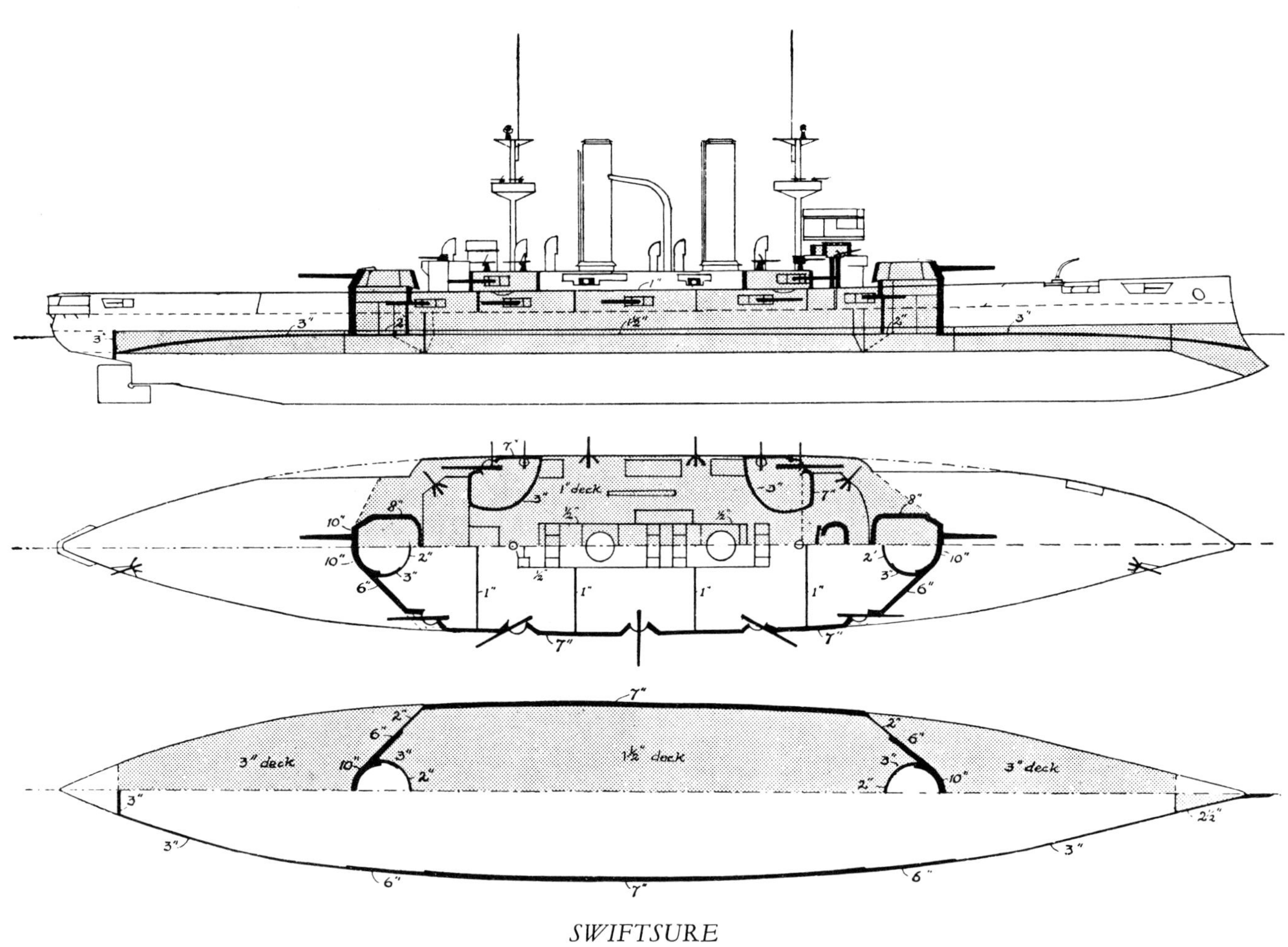

SWIFTSURE

"SWIFTSURE" and "TRIUMPH"

	Built at	*Laid down*	*Launched*	*Completed*	*Cost*
"Swiftsure"	Elswick	26 Feb. '02	12 Jan. '03	June '04	£846,596
"Triumph"	Barrow	26 Feb. '02	15 Jan. '03	June '04	£847,520
					(Guns in each £110,000)

Dimensions $(479\frac{3}{4}'$ o.a.$) \times 71' \times 25\frac{1}{3}' = 11{,}800$ tons.

	Deep load	*At load draught*
"Swiftsure"	13,840	12,175 tons
"Triumph"		

Armament

4 10-in. 45 cals.
14 7·5-in. 50 cals.
14 14-pdrs.
2 12-pdrs. (8 cwt.)
4 6-pdrs.
4 machine.

Torpedo tubes:
2 18-in. submerged.
carried 9 18-in.
4 14-in. for boats.

Protection Belt 7″-6″-3″; stern bulkhead 3″.
Lower deck side 7″ with 2″ bulkheads.
Battery 7″ with 6″ bulkheads.
Barbettes 10″-3″-2″; shields 10″-8″.
Casemates 7″ fronts; 3″ rears.
Screens in battery 1″.
Conning tower 11″.
Decks { reinforcing belt 3″ outside citadel. 1″ within citadel. above citadel 1″.
Total 3,075 tons.

Machinery Two sets vertical triple exp.
"*Swiftsure*" by Humphreys and Tennant.
"*Triumph*" by Vickers.
I.H.P. 12,500=19 knots.
Boilers 12 large tube Yarrow.
Coal 800/2,000 tons. Radius 3,360/17·6 or 6,250/10.
Complement 802.
Points of interest:
(1) The only British battleships to carry 7·5-in. guns.
(2) The fastest British battleships in 1904.
(3) The last British battleships to have bow scrolls.
(4) The last battleships designed by Sir E. J. Reed.

In December 1903 two light-weight battleships, *Constitution* and *Libertad*, were acquired from Chile, and renamed *Swiftsure* and *Triumph*. The purchase was arranged more to prevent their being taken over by another European Power than to make up for deficiencies in our own battleship force, which at this period was in a position of unassailable superiority.

Their construction had been decided upon at the end of 1901 as a counter measure to Argentina having ordered a couple of armoured cruisers (*Rividavia* and *Moreno*) in Italy at a time when relations between the two republics over the mutual boundary question had become strained almost to the point of hostilities. With those already in service the *Morenos* would have given Argentina a group of six fast ships carrying 10-in. and 8-in. guns, and as an offset Chile estimated her requirements as two battleships—either to be purchased or constructed as quickly as possible—which should displace about 11,000 tons, be able to steam at 19 knots and carry four 10-in. and ten or possibly twelve 7·5-in. guns of which four were to be on the upper deck. The design was dominated—so far as dimensions were concerned—by the consideration of the ships being able to enter the large double graving dock at Talcahuano, with sufficient clearance at all points to allow for the bottom to be cleaned and repaired.

Sir Edward Reed found himself in Chile when the ships were under consideration, and was entrusted with their design and construction by Admiral Moutt. He at once got into touch with Armstrongs, who became responsible for the drawings for one ship, while Vickers undertook the construction of the other.

Working to Chilean requirements, there was no question of their being "Reed ships" in which armament was secondary to protection. Actually they were the antithesis of his old-time models in every way. Great length was necessary because both beam and draught were limited by docking requirements, so that they were 30 ft. longer than the *Duncan* with 4½ ft. less beam and 2 ft. less draught for the nominal 11,800 tons. This figure was greatly in excess of the original estimate, but Reed showed that with a little more latitude the hull could be made to take five 7·5-in. aside on the main deck, which extra length would favour the high speed required. Freeboard was 21½ ft. forward—about 1 ft. less than the *Duncan's*, and they were more lightly constructed than our own ships.

To secure handiness for such a hull the deadwood aft was cut away, as in White's recent cruisers, and a balanced rudder fitted, the keel forward sloping up sharply to the ram.

As fighting ships they were by far and away the most interesting which had joined the Service for many years, but with an armament of 10-in. and 7·5-in. guns were very "odd volumes" in our establishment, although extremely powerful vessels for the displacement. Because of their speed they passed their pre-war service in company with the *Duncans* until sent out as flagships to the Eastern commands, and by virtue of special characteristics developed an individuality distinct from all other H.M. battleships and an intense rivalry between themselves.

ARMAMENT

Each ship was armed by her builders and there were certain small differences in equipment. The 10-in. guns weighed 31-32 tons and could fire a 500-lb. round through a 12-in. plate (Vickers) or 11½-in. (Elswick) at 3,000 yards. But Elswick listed three rounds a minute against the more modest Vickers claim of two; and four rounds a minute from each turret would be far in excess of any rival ship. Training, elevating and loading were all hydraulic, and loading was at anything between 5° elevation and 3° depression; in the Vickers mounting the breech screws were hand worked.

It will be seen that the barbettes thinned off to 2 in.-3 in. behind the bulkheads—an economy carefully avoided in descriptions of the ships—although the angled bulkheads made good the deficiency against horizontal hits. But the rear of the barbettes was exposed to an oblique deck hit over the end casemates, where the combined deck and barbette armour totalled 4½ in. to 5½ in. Apart from such a chance blow, the combined 10-in. to 8-in. plating was fairly adequate defence against the Argentine 10-in. and 8-in. guns. The gun houses were polygonal, but the port plates sloped at only 20° instead of the usual 30° to 35°, and so were not effective against capped projectiles.

The 7·5-in. was a new calibre in our Service, although the French were mounting it in the *Justice* class, and it was to become an accepted cruiser gun two years later. This 50 cal. model could fire a 200-lb. round through

8-in. steel at 3,000 yards and had a rate of fire of eight rounds a minute. A broadside of seven such guns constituted the heaviest secondary armament afloat, allowing the total weight of a minute's discharge (8,750 lb.), with the possible exception of the U.S. *New Jersey* which could bear six 8-in. and six 6-in., but with a rate of fire which was notoriously below the nominal figures.

Fourteen 14-pdrs. made up a far more formidable anti-torpedo armament than was carried in any British ship, and except for the forecastle guns, were well placed. Instead of only flat sloping face plates they had quite generous shields with side wings. The four hull guns were afterwards moved to the shelter decks.

Neither the 10-in. nor 7·5-in. were generally favoured in the Service, the one being regarded as too small and the other as too long for a main deck battery. Admiral John O. Hopkins, however, was of the opinion that the 10-in. was a perfectly adequate weapon for battleships, and maintained that the value of the *Swiftsures* should not be underestimated. They were certainly powerful enough to tackle the new German ships, and most of the Russian, while the French *Republiques* would offer a pretty target although their belts would be proof.

The *Swiftsure* in 1908 with r.c. platforms and the high W.T. gaff on the mainmast. She differed from standard British practice in having stocked bower anchors with a stockless sheet anchor on the *port* side.

Owing to chase length the 7·5-in. in the batteries were liable to dip their muzzles under a seaway, although Reed claimed that they would be no worse offenders than their squadron mates in this respect, the critical figures being:

	Height of main deck guns above water	*Heel bringing muzzles to water-line*
Swiftsure	13′ 2″	14°
King Edward	13′ 9″	14·15°
Duncan	13′ 2″	14·45°
Canopus	12′ 6″	14·3°

Although calculated for 11,800 tons, the normal displacement was actually 12,175 tons, which reduced freeboard by another 7 inches. When in sea-going trim at 13,840 tons their draught increased to 28½ ft. (submergence was 53·8 tons per inch), with the battery guns generally about 10 ft. above water in a calm and readily dipped in a seaway.

The ammunition supply of 86 rounds per 10-in. and 150 per 7·5-in. was generous and compared well with the 80 rounds per 12-in. and 200 per 6-in. in Admiralty designs.

PROTECTION

A comparison between the *Swiftsure* and *Duncan* in the matter of armour protection is apparently all to the advantage of the former, although actually 580 tons more protective material was carried in White's ships—as might be expected with their greater displacement. It will be seen that the whole amidships section to the upper deck was covered by 7 in. with shallow 3-in. extensions to bows and stern, the after end of the belt being closed by a 3-in. bulkhead over the rudder. There was only 1½ in. for a protective deck behind the citadel—although this was ½ in. better than the *Duncan's*—and the 3-in. at the ends was also superior; but the *Duncan* had a 238-ft. citadel side, while the *Swiftsure's* was reduced to 155 ft. and lacked the 5 in.-3 in. extension over the lower deck side, up forward. A great saving was made through the barbettes being only 22 ft. 8 in. in diameter with thinner plating, against *Duncan's* 36½ ft. in which there was a much greater arc of the maximum thickness.

On the upper deck the casemates had to be especially roomy to house the long guns, and with 7-in. sides and 3-in. rears afforded better protection than the standard 6 in. with 2-in. rears in White's designs.

Altogether, the armour distribution in Reed's ships was well arranged and afforded as good or better defence than in the *Duncan*. But they would have been very vulnerable to deck hits in the wake of the turrets, where the thin barbette armour could not have saved the magazine.

SPEED

Although there was a good deal of scepticism as to whether the two ships would make their designed speeds under strict service conditions—which were far more exacting than those observed during trials under foreign supervision—both came up to their builders' expectations in every way. *Triumph* designed for 19 knots with 12,500 h.p. reached this speed with 11,500 only and made steam for 14,000 h.p. on six runs over the measured mile at 20·1 knots. *Swiftsure* kept up 17·5 knots with 1-in. pressure for 30 hours with 8,700 h.p. only, reaching 20 knots on six runs during the 6 hours trials.

They were therefore the first battleships in H.M. Navy to record 20 knots, although three or four Italian ships had been credited with as much or just over when running light. There was a good deal of vibration at full power and at first they had some reputation as coal eaters, but in service proved fairly economical with 10 tons an hour at 10,000 h.p. for 18·4 knots. Their radius of action in descriptions published in 1904 was shown as 12,000/10 or 4,000/19, whereas the official figures were 6,250/10 or 3,360/17·6.

GENERAL

At one time *Swiftsure* exhibited a certain amount of structural weakness and Survey reports showed considerable trouble experienced through leaky compartments and buckling of plates and frames. Repairs and strengthening were carried out from time to time and by 1913 a survey pronounced the hull to be in good condition. *Triumph* was always staunch and there was no truth in the persistent story that they had to be shored up during the war.

The big goose-neck cranes handled boats far more expeditiously than the usual mast derricks, and gave an undue advantage in squadron exercises.

They were the last battleships to have bow ornamentation, the medallion being more prominent and conspicuous in *Swiftsure*. Another distinguishing feature—and the easiest to pick up—was the built-in dodger at each end of the *Triumph's* bridge; also *Swiftsure* had slightly higher cowls and lighter funnel caps.

Mixed anchors were fitted, with a single bed on each side and a stockless anchor in the second hawse on the *port* side, it being customary to reverse the British practice in South American ships. Owing to the retention of Spanish labels on the doors of the "offices" the ships were known as the "Occupado" and "Vacante" by their intimates.

"SWIFTSURE"

Built at Elswick February '02-June '04 for Chile. Purchased. Commissioned at Chatham June '04 for Home Fleet (collision with *Triumph* 3 June '05). July '06 Channel; Chatham for refit. Served in Channel Fleet until October '08 and then went to Mediterranean in March '09 where she remained until May '12 when she joined the 3rd Fleet at Portsmouth. Refit September '12 to March '13 when she went as flagship to East Indies.

War: August '14 Red Sea patrol and escort to Indian troopships as far as Aden; in November became flagship for the defence of Egypt in Suez Canal when she was in action against the Turks at Kantara. Joined the Dardanelles force in March '15, taking part in actions against the forts on 2 March '17-'18, and covering the landings on 25 April *et seq.*, when her firing was specially commended by the military. Covered the landing at Suvla. Attacked by submarine in September but not hit. After the evacuation returned U.K. and placed in Reserve at Chatham; later commissioned as overflow ship. In '19 was stripped for tests as target ship.

Sold 1920.

"TRIUMPH"

Built at Barrow February '02-June '04 for Chile. Purchased. Joined the Home Fleet June '04, which became the Channel Fleet in February '05. Ran into by Trinity House steamer *Siren* at Pembroke 17 September '04 with damage to side plating and main deck. Collided with *Swiftsure* 3 June '05 and bows damaged. Refit at Chatham October '08 and then rejoined Channel Fleet. Transferred to Mediterranean March '09 until May '12, when she joined the 3rd Fleet at the Nore. April '13 Devonport before proceeding to China, relieving *Tamar* at Hong Kong where she had her first thorough refit in '12.

War: Was in Reserve, and commissioned with crews from the River Gunboats for operations at Tsingtau with the Japanese warships. Joined the Dardanelles Fleet and took part in the attacks on the forts 18, 19, 25, 26 February, 3, 17, 18

March and 16 April for experimental firing at trenches. One of her boats destroyed the wrecked submarine E.15 which had run aground at Kephez. Covered the landing at Anzac. Sunk by submarine when firing off Gaba Tepe with nets down and watertight doors closed and one destroyer in attendance. *Chelmer* rescued a number of men before she capsized, floated bottom up for half an hour and then slowly sank. Three officers and 70 men were lost. She was sadly missed by the Australians who subscribed a month's pay all round towards salving her. Afterwards battleship support at the beaches had to be withdrawn, their place taken by destroyers.

1907

Channel	Mediterranean	Home	Reserve
King Edward VII	*Queen*	*Dreadnought*	*Barfleur*
Africa	*Formidable*	*Bulwark*	*Centurion*
Britannia	*Implacable*	*London*	*Renown*
Commonwealth	*Irresistible*	*Canopus*	*Hood*
Dominion	*Prince of Wales*	*Glory*	*Empress of India*
Hibernia	*Venerable*	*Goliath*	*Ramillies*
Hindustan		*Cæsar*	*Repulse*
New Zealand	Atlantic	*Hannibal*	*Resolution*
Ocean	*Exmouth*	*Magnificent*	*Royal Oak*
Vengeance	*Albemarle*	*Majestic*	*Royal Sovereign*
Swiftsure	*Cornwallis*	*Mars*	*Nile*
Triumph	*Duncan*	*Prince George*	
Illustrious	*Russell*	*Victorious*	
Jupiter	*Albion*		

THE WATTS ERA 1902 TO 1912

SIR PHILIP WATTS, K.C.B., LL.D., D.SC., F.R.S.

Philip Watts was born at Portsmouth in 1846, his father being one of the principal constructive officers in the Dockyard. In 1860 he was apprenticed as a shipwright in the Dockyard, and being of good physique and very diligent it was not long before he was able to turn out as good a day's work as a skilled man. Outstanding progress in the Dockyard school gained him selection as an Admiralty student in Naval Architecture, and led to an appointment in 1870 as Admiralty overseer on several ships building by contract, also to assist in making various calculations in connection with new designs, especially the proper size and strength of scantlings hitherto determined by custom or precedent.

On completion of this work he became assistant to William Froude in his tank experimental work on the behaviour of ships at sea, and was engaged upon the application of "Graphic Integration" to various problems.

As Assistant Constructor at Pembroke Dockyard he superintended work upon the *Shannon*, and became famous as an ingenious designer of mechanical details of all sorts. On returning to the Admiralty he organized a "Calculating section" supervising all detailed calculations of a scientific character including the design of the *Polyphemus* with all her special and unique features. In connection with the *Inflexible* he invented the "water chambers" to correct excessive rolling which although discarded in her case were again tried out in the *King George V* and *Von der Tann*. Until May 1885 he was Constructor at Chatham Dockyard when he retired from Admiralty service to succeed Sir William White as naval architect and general manager at Elswick at the age of 39.

There he became responsible for many famous warships including the Italian cruiser *Piemonte* of 2,600 tons which carried six 6-in. and six 4·7-in. guns at 23·5 knots, the second *Esmeralda*, *O'Higgins*, *Hatsuse*, *Asama* and *Iwate* which made fame for Armstrongs.

In 1902 he succeeded Sir William White as D.N.C. and his name is especially associated with the *Dreadnought* and *Invincible*—Fisher declaring that Philip Watts's name was enshrined in his heart. The designs of his era showed:

(1) More powerful armament upon a given displacement.
(2) Higher speed and greater manœuvring power than previously.
(3) Increased protection against guns and torpedoes, with better access, ventilation and drainage to watertight compartments.

The award of K.C.B. came in 1905. Twenty-nine battleships and battlecruisers and most of the cruisers and torpedo craft of the Grand Fleet at Jutland were built during his Directorship, and although he retired in 1912 his services were retained as consultant until 1916 when he rejoined Armstrongs as Director until his death in March 1926.

Elected to the Council of the I.N.A. in 1885 he became a Vice-President in 1901 and Vice-President of the N.E. Coast Institute of Engineers and Shipbuilders in 1915, and was Master of the Worshipful Company of Shipwrights 1915-16. Among other distinguished positions he was elected Vice-President of the Society for Nautical Research and Chairman of the Technical Committee for the restoration of the *Victory* to her Trafalgar condition. Elected F.R.S. in 1900 he was on the Council for two years and became Vice-President. He visited Japan in 1895 and 1913 and was awarded the Order of the Rising Sun for his services to the Japanese Navy.

Chapter 76

REVIVAL OF THE ARMOURED CRUISER

1899–1904

Our earliest armoured cruisers like the *Shannon* and *Nelson* were derated second-class battleships in which neither guns nor armour were heavy enough to justify inclusion in the line, while lack of speed—which was conveniently ignored—precluded their employment as cruisers. Consequently they were relegated to foreign service commands where their shortcomings were no embarrassment. The *Imperieuse* and *Warspite* (1886) came into the same category, and thereafter, except for the "belted cruisers" of the *Australia* class (1889), which were cruisers pure and simple but with a water-line belt of armour of no special virtue, a very definite distinction developed between capital ships carrying big guns and heavy armour, and cruisers relying upon speed and medium artillery.

Thus, the White Era was characterized by well-gunned first, second and third class cruisers designed for scouting duties and commerce protection, whose flotation and stability depended upon under-water armour decks, thick coal bunkers and subdivision.

But in France the extraordinary *Dupuy de Lôme* (1891) had introduced an entirely new aspect in cruiser design. Repeated with certain modifications in the *Bruix* (1894) and her derivatives, which later made way for the challenging but unsatisfactory *Jeanne D'Arc* (1899) and her successors, the type appeared well adapted for the commerce raiding and independent operations which, according to the "Jeune Ecole," were to bring England to her knees. Naval war was not to be waged by rival fleets with victory going to the superior forces, but by destruction of commerce, cutting off of food supplies, and the paralysis of trade. War against shipping was to relegate the Battle Line to the background, with numbers of fast and well-armed cruisers replacing the vulnerable and expensive battleships which could be looked after by swarms of torpedo craft.

As things turned out, successive Ministers of Marine did not accept Admiral Aube's theories as a definite policy, but continued to build battleships—and gave a marked preference to armoured cruisers, which were also appearing in considerable numbers in other navies. Until 1898 the Admiralty stuck to cruisers with protective decks only. Then, when the new Krupp process made possible the addition of side armour sufficiently tough to keep out steel 6-in. shell without any great increase in size and cost, they also adopted the armoured cruiser. Thus, the *Cresseys* (1899-01) were belted *Diadems* with a 9·2-in. fore and aft in place of 6-in. guns, followed by a procession of first-class *Drakes* (1902) and second-class *Kents* (1903) and *Devonshires* (1905) all designed to counter specific French armoured cruisers on the trade routes.

The end of the White Era coincided with a different outlook on armoured cruisers. Instead of being employed on cruiser duties only they were to be more heavily armed and protected, and serve as a fast wing to the Battle Fleet, with an eye on the German light battleships of the *Kaiser*, *Wittelsbach*, and *Braunschweig* types. Our traditional attitude to France and Russia was rapidly becoming less antagonistic in face of the rapidly growing German fleet, and although the new armoured cruisers might well be employed on commerce protection, it was realized that in squadron they would possess such battle value that no Commander-in-Chief would care to relinquish them from their duties with the Battle Fleet.

White ended his long tenure of office under a cloud. Increasingly hostile criticism to his designs both in and out of the Service ignored the fact that the D.N.C. was not a free agent, but had to work within specified limits in tonnage while incorporating the requirements of the Board as regards armament, protection, speed, fuel supply, stability, stores and accommodation, in conjunction with structural strength and sea-going qualities in conformity with British standards. In 1895 the *Majestics* had been the finest warships afloat; but by 1902 the *Queens* evoked no enthusiasm when compared with the paper virtues of their foreign contemporaries, while the *Diadems* and *Kents* added nothing to his reputation, which had suffered a grievous blow with the tragedy of the Royal yacht *Victoria and Albert* (p. 347). A breakaway from the long line of "four 12-in., twelve 6-in." ships in the *King Edward VII* was welcomed, but here again something better had been hoped for.

The new D.N.C., Mr. Philip Watts, came from Elswick with the reputation of putting in plenty of guns, and great things were expected from the designer of the *Esmeralda* and *O'Higgins*. He was known to be a great advocate of the 9·2-in. gun, which certainly was a very fine piece—fast firing with a good punch in its 380 lb. and capable of penetrating most armour at the then battle ranges. Naturally a cruiser carrying a broadside of such guns at the required speed of 23 knots or so could not be given battleship protection, but it was considered that the 6-in. scale would be adequate, and well up to foreign standards in view of the area which had to be covered.

So, as contemporaries of the second batch of *King Edwards*, two armoured cruisers of an entirely new type were ordered which, following the customary practice, had the same disposition of armament as the battleships.

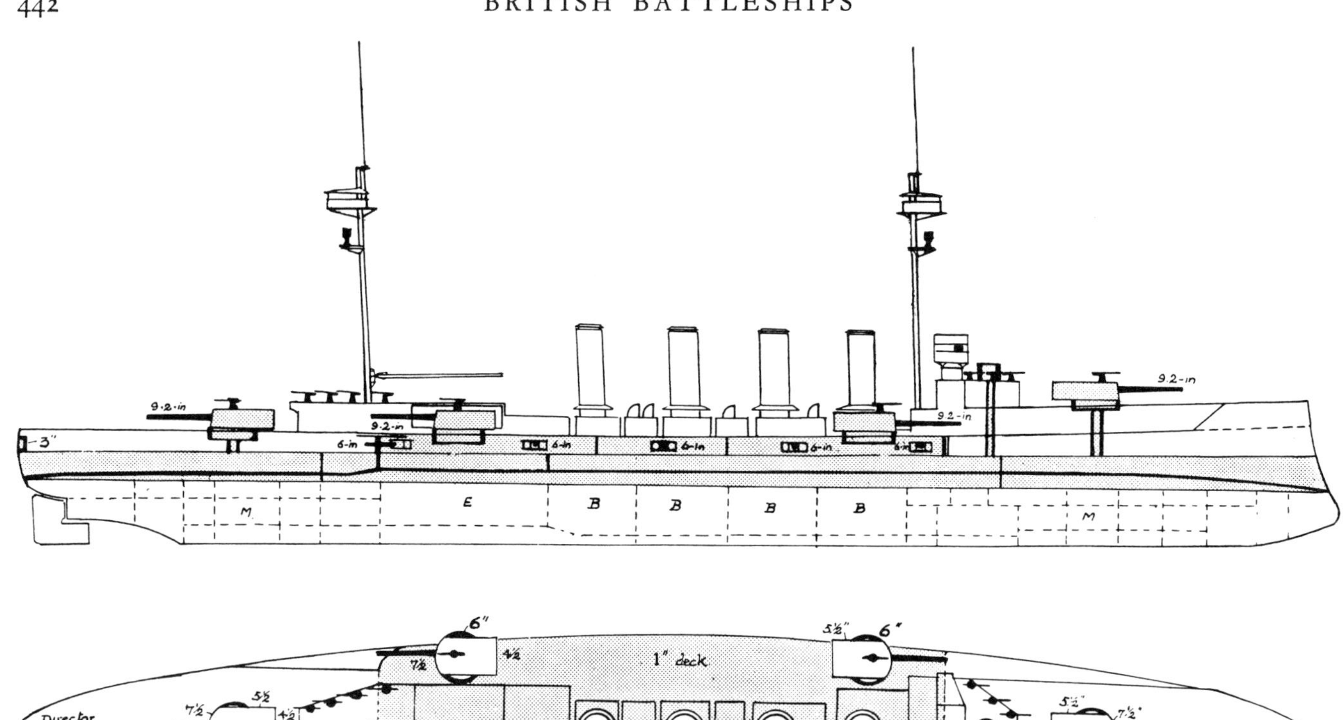

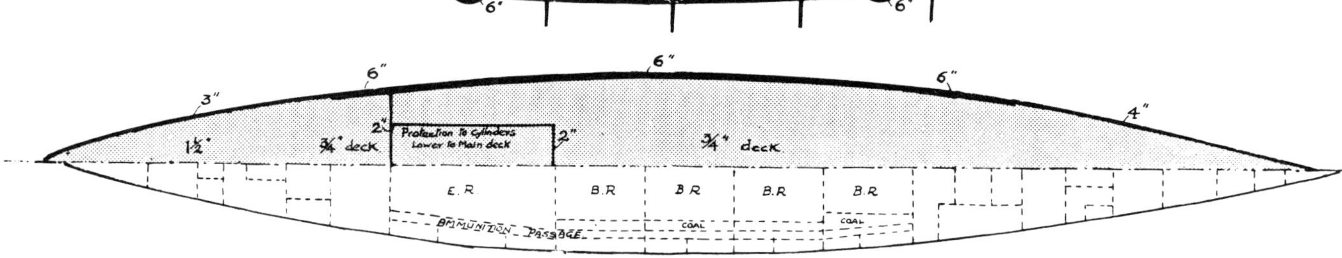

BLACK PRINCE

"DUKE OF EDINBURGH" Class (1902-'03 Estimates)

	Builders	*Laid down*	*Launched*	*Completed*	*Cost*
"*Black Prince*"	Thames I.W.	June '03	Nov. '04	Jan. '06	£1,201,687
"*Duke of Edinburgh*"	Pembroke	Feb. '03	14 June '04	March '06	£1,193,414 (including guns)

Dimensions 480′ (505½′) × 73½′ × 24′/27′ = 12,590 tons.
(Navy List displacement 13,550 tons. Deep load 13,965 tons.)

Armament 6 9·2-in./45. 10 6-in./50. 20 3-pdrs.
Torpedo tubes: 3 18-in. (submerged).

Protection Belt 6″ amidships, 4″ bows, 3″ stern.
Battery 6″; barbettes 6″-3″; shields 7½″-5½″-4½″.
Conning tower 10″.
Decks: Upper 1″; main 1″ and ¾″; lower 1½″-¾″.

Machinery Two sets 4-cyl. trip. exp. "*Duke of Edinburgh*" Hawthorn Leslie. "*Black Prince*" Thames I.W.
I.H.P. 23,000 = 22·84 knots ("*Duke of Edinburgh*").
f.d. 23,500 = 23·65 „ ("*Black Prince*").
Boilers 20 Babcock and Wilcox; 6 cyl.

Coal 1,000/2,150 tons. Oil 600 tons.

Radius 3,250 at 21 knots. 8,130 at 10 knots.

Complement 789.

Constructor: E. N. Mooney.

As cruiser editions of the *King Edward VII* these ships made a good show on paper, but were badly designed with 6-in. batteries placed too low to be fought in anything but calm weather. Thus, in a cruiser action on June 29 in the 1906 manœuvres the *Black Prince* with green seas sweeping her fore and aft was easily put out of action by the *Leviathan*. Looking back on that period it seems extraordinary that tradition kept such a hold on the Controller's Department as to retain this much abused feature of White's ships, in view of its very obvious shortcomings. When the *Drake* and *Good Hope*—Lord Goschen's "Mighty Cruisers" from which so much was expected—were first tried at sea, their inability to use their lower 6-in. guns caused much acid comment. The *Engineer* roundly proclaimed them as failures on that account. Nevertheless the longer guns in the *Duke of Edinburgh* were mounted at exactly the same height and proved even more unworkable in a seaway.

DUKE OF EDINBURGH

ARMAMENT

The 9·2-in. guns were on central pivot mountings with both hydraulic and hand gear, and arcs of fire of 285° for the end turrets. The beam guns were supposed to have axial fire, but blast effects limited their training to 30° of the fore and aft line. Rate of fire was about four rounds a minute.

The 6-in. guns had electric hoists and trained through about 120°, the aftermost guns firing through recessed ports to provide some fire astern.

With a tertiary armament of 3-pdrs. only, the anti-torpedo defence was futile against the 300-400 ton torpedo boats of their date. Disposition was in two groups on the shelter decks and on top of the gun houses—a novel arrangement which facilitated control and kept them clear of splinters.

In March 1916 both ships were ordered to be taken in hand for drastic alterations. All the gun ports on the main deck were closed and six 6-in. mounted on the upper deck; and in May 1917 two more 6 in. were added on the forecastle of the *Duke of Edinburgh*. Unfortunately the drawings and photographs of this period were destroyed during War II, but a rigging plan shows the fore tripod and an embrasure in the shelter deck, where presumably the forecastle guns were mounted as in the *Iron Duke* class.

With main deck batteries suppressed and 6-in. guns in shields along upper deck.
Tripod mast.

PROTECTION

The 6-in. armour providing belt and battery sides rose 14½ ft. above water and extended 4 ft. 10 in. below, the ends being closed by 6-in. bulkheads. Shallow screens separated the battery guns. Forward the belt was 4 in., aft 3 in., with the underwater protective deck reduced to ¾ in. except for a patch of 1½ in. over the steering.

The 7½ in.-4½ in. gun houses had 6 in.-3 in. shallow barbettes and hoists, similar to what had been provided from the *Cressy* onwards and about on a par with similar installations in French ships.

GENERAL

In accordance with instructions to keep funnel height to a minimum, they were completed with the caps level with the chart house screens, and it was not until some four years later that they were raised about 6 ft. to give a reasonable smoke clearance in a following wind.

Black Prince was one of the first cruisers in which oil fuel was sprayed into the coal-burning furnaces to increase combustion, and like the *Mars* and destroyers *Surly* and *Spiteful* her progress was then marked by a smoke cloud likened to that produced by the best Japanese steam coal.

It will be noticed that the legend tonnage was 1,000 tons less than the Navy List displacement, and although many vessels were able to show a saving on office calculations by some hundreds of tons, none was listed as having done better than the *Dukes*.

Duke of Edinburgh ran her trials in rough weather and strong wind and made 22·89 knots. *Black Prince* attained 23·65 knots in fine weather.

"BLACK PRINCE"

Commissioned January '06. Joined 2nd C.S. Atlantic Fleet until '08 when she was transferred to 1st C.S. Channel. In '09 when the big reorganization of the Fleet took place she joined 5th C.S. Atlantic serving until '12, when she went to the Mediterranean. Took part in the abortive operations against *Goeben* and *Breslau* in August '14, returning home to join the Grand Fleet 1st C.S. in December. Lost in the Jutland night action (857 killed).

"DUKE OF EDINBURGH"

Commissioned March '06 for 5th C.S. Home Fleet. In '08 went to 1st C.S. Channel. At the reorganization '09 formed one of the 5th C.S. Atlantic until '13 when she went to the Mediterranean. In August '14 engaged in the hunt for *Goeben* and *Breslau*, returning home to join the 1st C.S. Grand Fleet. (Jutland, no casualties.) When 1st C.S. was abolished in June '16 became one of the 2nd C.S. until September '17. Afterwards served on Atlantic convoys. Stricken 1919.

"WARRIOR" Class—4 Ships (1903-04 Estimates)

	Builders	*Laid down*	*Launched*	*Completed*	*Cost*
"*Achilles*"	Elswick	Feb. '04	17 June '05	March '07	£1,191,103
"*Cochrane*"	Fairfield	March '04	20 May '05	Feb. '07	£1,193,121
"*Natal*"	Vickers	Jan. '04	Sept. '05	'07	£1,218,244
"*Warrior*"	Pembroke	Nov. '03	Nov. '05	'07	£1,186,395
					(including guns)

Dimensions 480′ (505½′)×73½′×24¾′-25′=13,200-13,350 tons.
(Navy List displacement 13,550 tons. Deep load 14,500 tons.)

Armament 6 9·2-in./45
4 7·5-in./50.
24 3-pdrs.
1 3-in. A.A. (later).
5 Maxims.

Torpedo tubes:
3 submerged (1 stern).

Protection Belt 6″ amidships, 4″ bows, 3″ stern.
Upper deck 6″ amidships.
Turrets 7½″-5½″-4½″. Barbettes 6″ and 3″.
Decks: Upper 1″; main 1″ and ¾″; lower 2″-1½″-¾″.

Machinery 2 sets 4-cyl. trip. exp. "*Achilles*" Hawthorn Leslie. "*Cochrane*" Fairfields. "*Natal*" Vickers. "*Warrior*" Wallsend.
I.H.P. 23,000=23 knots.
Boilers 19 Yarrow (large tube) and 6 cyl.

Coal 1,000/2,050 tons. Oil 600 tons.

Radius 3,140/21; 7,960/10.

Complement 712.

Constructor: E. N. Mooney.

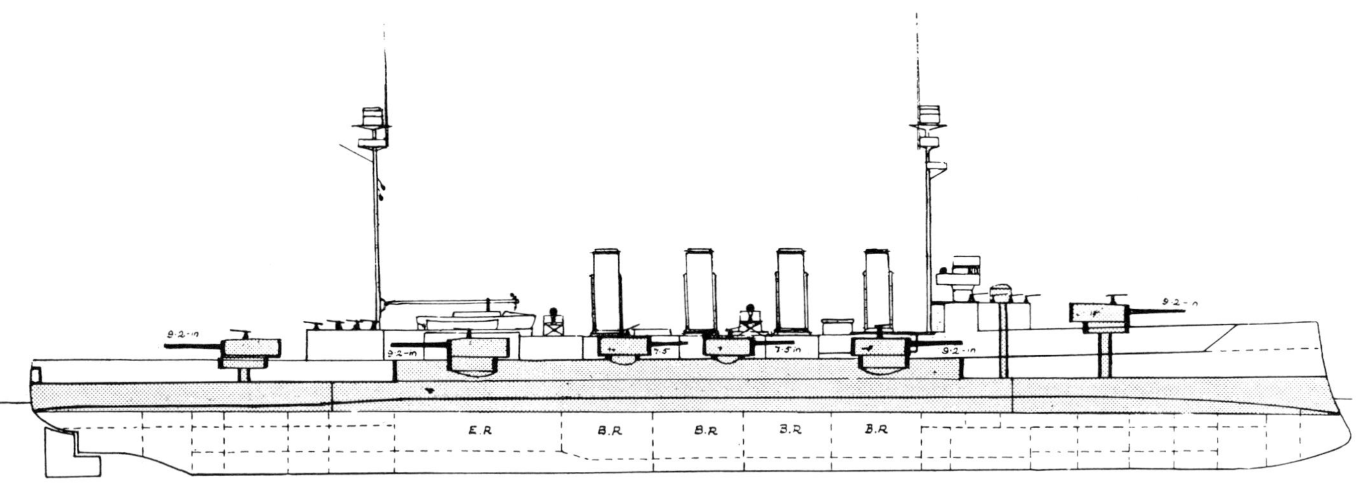

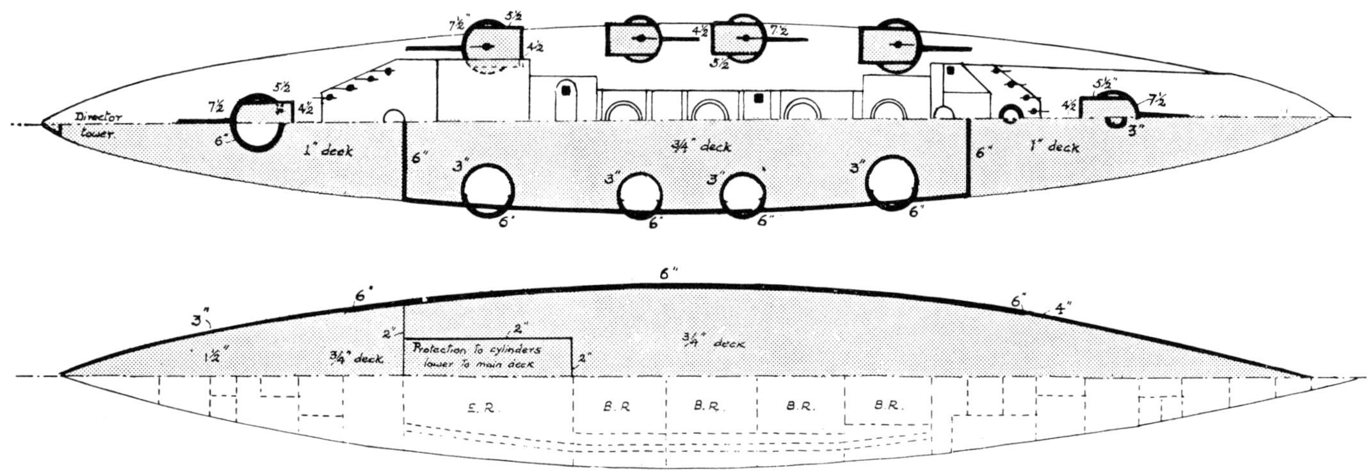

WARRIOR Class

These ships were to have been sisters to the *Dukes*, but at long last the disadvantages and faults of main deck batteries were realized, and at an early stage the design was altered and four 7·5-in. gun houses on the upper deck replaced the ten 6 in. The change was all to the good in every way. The full armament could now be fought in all weathers, and being very good sea boats they gained the reputation of being the best cruisers we ever built.

ARMAMENT

All guns manœuvred hydraulically and by hand. Arcs of fire: end guns 285°; beam 9·2 in. 120°; 7·5 in. about 110°.

PROTECTION

The 6-in. battery wall in the *Duke* was retained and served as a base for the amidships guns, distribution of armour being similar.

PROPULSION

Machinery was standardized and weighed 2,250 tons. Burned about 23½ tons an hour at full speed and 15 tons at 21 knots. At full power trials results were:

Achilles	23,977 I.H.P.	= 23·5 knots.	
Cochrane	23,654 ,,	= 23·29 ,,	
Natal	23,590 ,,	= 23·3 ,,	
Warrior	23,705 ,,	= 22·5 ,,	(22·9 by log).

Achilles. Black Prince Cochrane

Duke of Edinburgh Natal. Warrior

(From starboard.)

GENERAL

Were completed with short funnels which smoked out the bridge. *Warrior* later had fore funnel raised above the level of the chart house—the first large ship to have this unsightly arrangement—after which all four funnels were brought up to this height, and the rest of the class followed suit.

Completed with pole masts and small tops as in the *Britannia*, the *Cochrane* and *Warrior* having higher masts than the other two. After Jutland a director top was fitted and the foremast became a tripod.

Cochrane as completed with short funnels. *Natal* and *Achilles* were without the lower platform on the foremast, and *Cochrane* and *Warrior* had slightly higher masts.

Because of the additional weight on the upper deck and consequent reduction in metacentric height making them remarkably steady gun platforms, they usually showed up well in the gunnery returns. *Achilles* headed the list in 1907, *Natal* in 1909 (when she set up new records which included 13 rounds and 12 hits in 105 seconds with a 7·5-in. and 11 rounds and 10 hits with a 9·2-in.) and again first in 1910.

"ACHILLES"

Commissioned March '07. Home Fleet 5th C.S. Under reorganization became 2nd C.S. until '14 when it became 2nd C.S. Grand Fleet. 1914-September '17 (Jutland). Together with the Armed Boarding Steamer *Dundee* sank the raider *Leopard* 16 March '17 north of Shetlands. Refit February '18-December '18. Reserve Chatham as stokers' t.s.

Sold 1920.

"COCHRANE"

Commissioned February '07. Home Fleet 5th C.S. to '08. 2nd C.S. '09-'14. Grand Fleet 2nd C.S. '14-September '17; (Jutland) February '18-November '18. Wrecked in Mersey estuary 14 November '18.

"NATAL"

Commissioned '07 Home Fleet 5th C.S. 2nd C.S. '09-'14. Grand Fleet 2nd C.S. '14-'15. Blown up by internal explosion Cromarty Firth 30 December '15.

"WARRIOR"

Commissioned '07 Home Fleet 5th C.S. 2nd C.S. '09-'13; Mediterranean '14. Grand Fleet 1st C.S. '14-June '16. Foundered after being disabled by gunfire at Jutland 31 May '16.

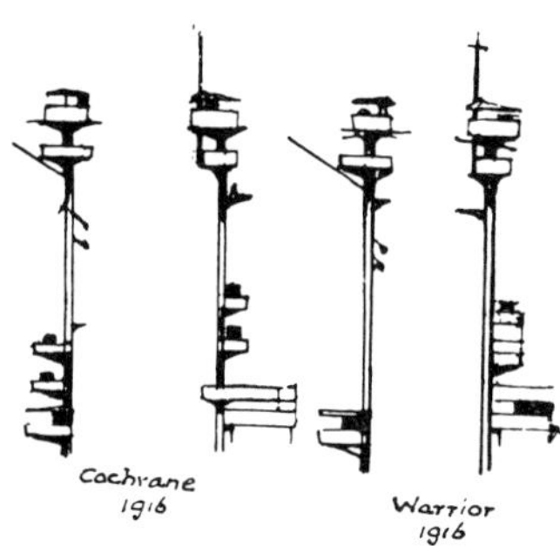

"MINOTAUR" Class 3 Ships (1904-'05 Estimates)

	Builders	*Laid down*	*Launched*	*Completed*	*Cost*
"*Defence*"	Pembroke	22 Feb. '05	27 April '07	April '08	£1,362,970
"*Minotaur*"	Devonport	2 Jan. '05	6 June '06	March '08	£1,410,356
"*Shannon*"	Chatham	2 Jan. '05	20 Sept. '06	March '08	£1,415,135

Dimensions "*Minotaur*" and "*Defence*" 490′ (519′)×74½′×26′=14,600 tons (16,100 full load).
"*Shannon*" 490′ (519′)×75½′×25′.

Armament 4 9·2-in./50. 10 7·5-in./50. 16 12-pdrs.
Torpedo tubes: 5 submerged.

Protection Belt 6″-4″ (bows)-3″ (stern).
Deck 2″-1½″.
Barbettes 7″; turrets 8″-7″, 8″-6″-4½″ (7·5″).
Conning tower 10″.

Machinery 2 sets 4-cyl. trip. exp. D.H.P. 27,000=23 knots.
Yarrow or Babcock boilers. 2 screws.

Coal 950 ("*Shannon*"), 1,000 ("*Minotaur*" and "*Defence*") 2,060 tons. Oil 750 tons.

Radius 2,920/20·5, 8,150/10.

Complement 755. *Constructor:* E. N. Mooney.

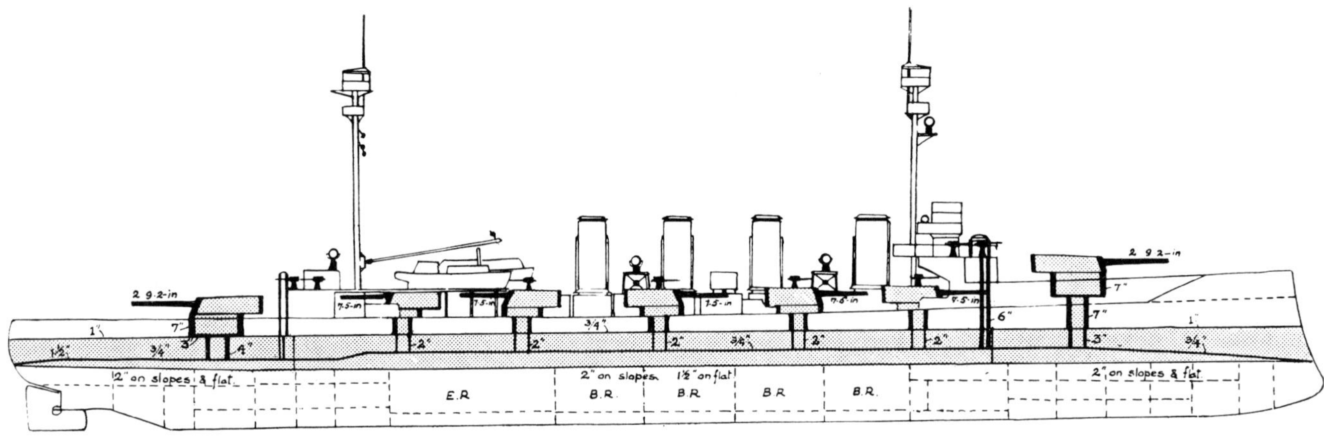

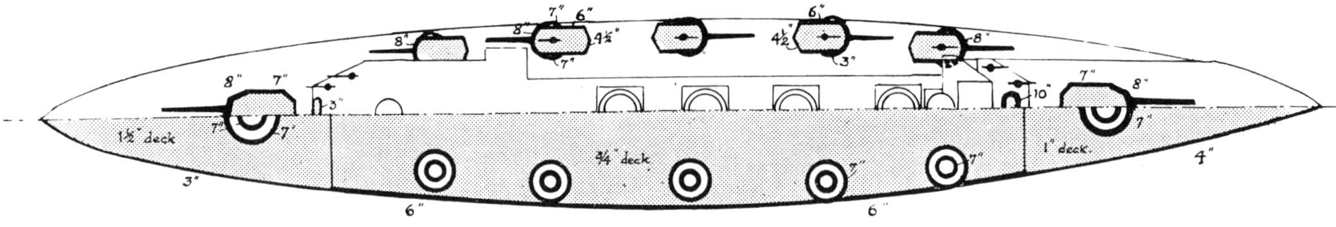

MINOTAUR

The 1904-05 Programme which provided for the commencement of the *Lord Nelsons* also included provision for three armoured cruisers—the last of the type carrying medium calibre guns to be built for the Royal Navy.

They were enlarged *Warriors*, 10 ft. longer with 1 ft. more beam and 1 ft. less draught, but with the same L/B proportions of 6·5 to 1. The *Shannons's* hull was a different shape with an extra 1 ft. in beam and 1 ft. less draught—which was no advantage and detracted from her speed.

ARMAMENT

They can be regarded as cruiser homologues of the *Lord Nelson*, although as a paired mounting for the 7·5-in. was not favoured the secondary guns were disposed singly. Compared with the *Warrior* there was a broadside advantage of three 7·5-in. just as the *Lord Nelson* brought five 9·2-in. to bear where the *King Edward VII* pointed only two.

The tertiary armament of sixteen 12-pdrs. marked a big improvement on the preceding class. The guns originally carried on the crown of the 9·2-in. gun houses were soon shifted to the shelter decks.

PROTECTION

Armour was disposed as in the *Warrior*, but without the main deck 6-in. strake, the barbettes having 7-in. hoists above the belt and 2-in. behind it down to the protective deck.

PROPULSION

The *Minotaur* had Babcock boilers, and the other two large tube Yarrow. By this time the opponents of the water-tube system had lost their influence and the expedient of mixed boilers could be discarded.

Defence	.. ..	27,570	I.H.P.	=22·9	knots.
Minotaur	.. ..	27,856	,,	=23·01	,,
Shannon	.. ..	28,553	,,	=22·49	,,

The different form of hull in the *Shannon* did not produce the additional speed expected and she failed to realize her designed figures by half a knot. The stumpy funnels originally fitted were raised 15 ft. in 1909, but the additional draught although increasing their power did not materially improve speed.

GENERAL

Solid bulkheads were first introduced in these ships for the engine rooms, which were without watertight doors.

In 1917 the foremast was made a tripod and a director tower fitted, with the searchlights from between the funnels grouped round the base of the main mast.

When on the China Station the *Minotaur* and *Defence* had as opposite numbers the *Scharnhorst* and *Gneisenau*, and as a gesture of friendly rivalry it was agreed that if they ever faced each other in action the *Minotaurs* would make a fair fight of it by withholding the fire from one 7·5 in.

MINOTAUR

All three were first completed with short funnels as directed by Admiral Fisher, and as in the preceding classes they had to be raised 15 ft.

"DEFENCE"

Commissioned 1908 for 5th C.S. Home Fleet; '09 1st C.S. '10-'12 China; Mediterranean '13-'14. Flagship 1st C.S. (*Black Prince*, *Duke of Edinburgh*, *Warrior*) in *Goeben-Breslau* search. Ordered to join Admiral Cradock but recalled; joined River Plate Squadron (Flagship Admiral Stoddart) in search for Von Spee; February '15 Cape Squadron, then ordered home after destruction of Von Spee's ships. Grand Fleet 1st C.S. January '15 (relieved by *Warrior* in May '16). Flagship Admiral Arbuthnot at Jutland; sunk by gunfire of German battle fleet (893 killed).

"MINOTAUR"

Commissioned March '08 for 5th C.S. Home Fleet, later 1st. C.S. Flagship China '10-'14. When the German Squadron left the station Admiral Jerram's ships searched the Dutch East Indies, covered the Australian convoys, and then joined the Cape Squadron (Flagship Admiral King-Hall). After Battle of Falklands returned home. Refit. Grand Fleet 2nd C.S. June '16-December '18 (Flagship, but for short intervals) Jutland (no casualties).

In Reserve until sold 1920.

Like her famous ancestor she served as a flagship throughout her active career.

"SHANNON"

Commissioned March '08 for 5th C.S. Home Fleet; 2nd C.S. '09-'11; 5th C.S. Atlantic Fleet '12 and again 2nd C.S. Home '13-'14 (Flagship). Grand Fleet 2nd C.S. January '15-December '18 (Jutland, no casualties). Flagship January '15-June '16 and May '18. Atlantic convoys '19. Reserve at Sheerness until sold 1920.

Shannon in 1917 with her funnels raised (1909), tripod foremast and searchlights grouped around base of mainmast.

Our construction of armoured cruisers carrying medium artillery ceased with the *Minotaurs*, as the design of the *Invincible* was already being worked out. The year 1905 also saw the commencement of the last American (*Washington*), French (*Waldeck Rousseau*), Italian (*San Marco*) and Russian (*Rurik* amd *Bayan*) ships of this type, and only the German *Blücher* and Japanese *Ibuki* were laid down in 1906. Thereafter for some years it appeared that scouting was to be relegated to big sea-going destroyers, and the protection of British commerce ensured by the Fisher conception of a perfect blockade of the North Sea rendered possible by wireless telegraphy and distant patrols. Only in Germany was the construction of light cruisers continued, and not until 1909, when the *Bristol* class were laid down, was our traditional policy resumed, with a proper realization of our needs for defence of the trade routes and the very serious deficiency in fast light cruisers.

On convoy duties the smaller armoured cruisers did good work, but as fast wing units of the Battle Fleet they proved to be death traps. Battle cruisers had put them out of court and gallant leadership merely proved their weakness.

Cochrane 1917 with tripod mast and searchlights regrouped.

Chapter 77

"LORD NELSON" CLASS

DURING the *King Edward VII* period there was a thorough reconsideration of battleship design when a large number of alternative types with many varieties in gun power, armour and speed were prepared and discussed. At the same time the new Controller, Sir William May, instituted an exhaustive enquiry into the relation between gun power and protection in different classes worked out by diagrams and graphs which, under the conditions assumed, showed:

(1) That very much better protection was required over a larger area of the ship than was customary.
(2) That in a ship action the value of the secondary armament was of little consequence, and that it would be swept away by big gun fire before coming into effective range.

The corollary being that only heavy armour-piercing guns and torpedo defence quick-firers should form the armament of future battleships.

Reference has already been made to the vastly improved design placed before the Board in 1903—which resolved into the *Lord Nelson* the following year—and it will be appreciated that this was drawn up solely to meet the requirements of the new conception—there was no question of foreign designs forcing our hand, as the other Powers were engaged on various adaptations of the *King Edward VII*, none of which were of any real competitive consequence. Watts therefore started work under entirely different conditions from those which had obtained during the White era. Now the Board supplied the initiative. Ships were no longer to be merely a little better than their rivals, but built to fight them on a basis of superiority due to a more practical conception of what fleet fighting really meant. The *Dreadnought* idea was in train. Before even the *Lord Nelson* design was finally approved, Constructor Narbeth submitted an alternative drawing carrying the above corollary to full conclusion and showing an armament of twelve 12-in. guns. But at that period the Board was not prepared to accept such a radical casting of the 9·2-in.

"LORD NELSON" Class (1904-'05 Estimates)

	Built at	*Laid down*	*Launched*	*Completed*	*Cost*
"*Lord Nelson*"	Palmers	18 May '05	4 Sept. '06	Oct. '08	£1,540,939
"*Agamemnon*"	Beardmores	15 May '05	23 June '06	June '08	£1,541,947
				(Guns in both	£110,400)

Dimensions 410′ (443½ o.a.) × 79½′ × 25¼′/27′ = 16,500 tons.

	Deep load	*Load draught*
"*Lord Nelson*"	17,820	16,090 tons
"*Agamemnon*"	17,683	15,925 „

Armament 4 12-in. 45 cal./80.
10 9·2-in. 50 cal./100.
24 12-pdrs./230.
2 3-pdrs.
8 Boat guns.

Torpedo tubes:
5 18-in. submerged.
(23 torpedoes carried)
plus 6 14-in. for boats).

Protection Belt 12″-4″ ends; bulkhead aft 8″.
Citadel 8″; bow plating 6″-4″.
Barbettes 12″-3″; turrets 12″.
9·2″ turrets 7″; glacis 6″; splinter protection 2″.
Conning tower 12″; communication tubes 6″; ford 3″ aft.
Decks: main 1½″; middle 4″-1″; lower 3″-1″.
Total weight 4,200 tons (excluding turrets).

Machinery Two sets vert. triple exp. by Palmers and Hawthorn Leslie.
H.P. 16,750=18 knots. Revs. 125. Pressure 275 lb.
Boilers 15 Yarrow ("*Agamemnon*") or Babcock.

Coal 900-2,171 plus 1,090 oil.

Radius 9,180/10 knots. cyl. 2=32¾″; 2=52¾″; 4=60″; 4′ stroke 235 lb.; piston speed 1,000′ p.m.

Complement 800-817.

Constructor J. H. Narbeth.

Points of interest:

(1) Last British battleship with mixed main armament.
(2) First to be without 6-in. guns since former *Agamemnon.*
(3) First British battleship to have solid bulkheads.
(4) Designed without any bridges.
(5) Last British battleship to have reciprocating engines.

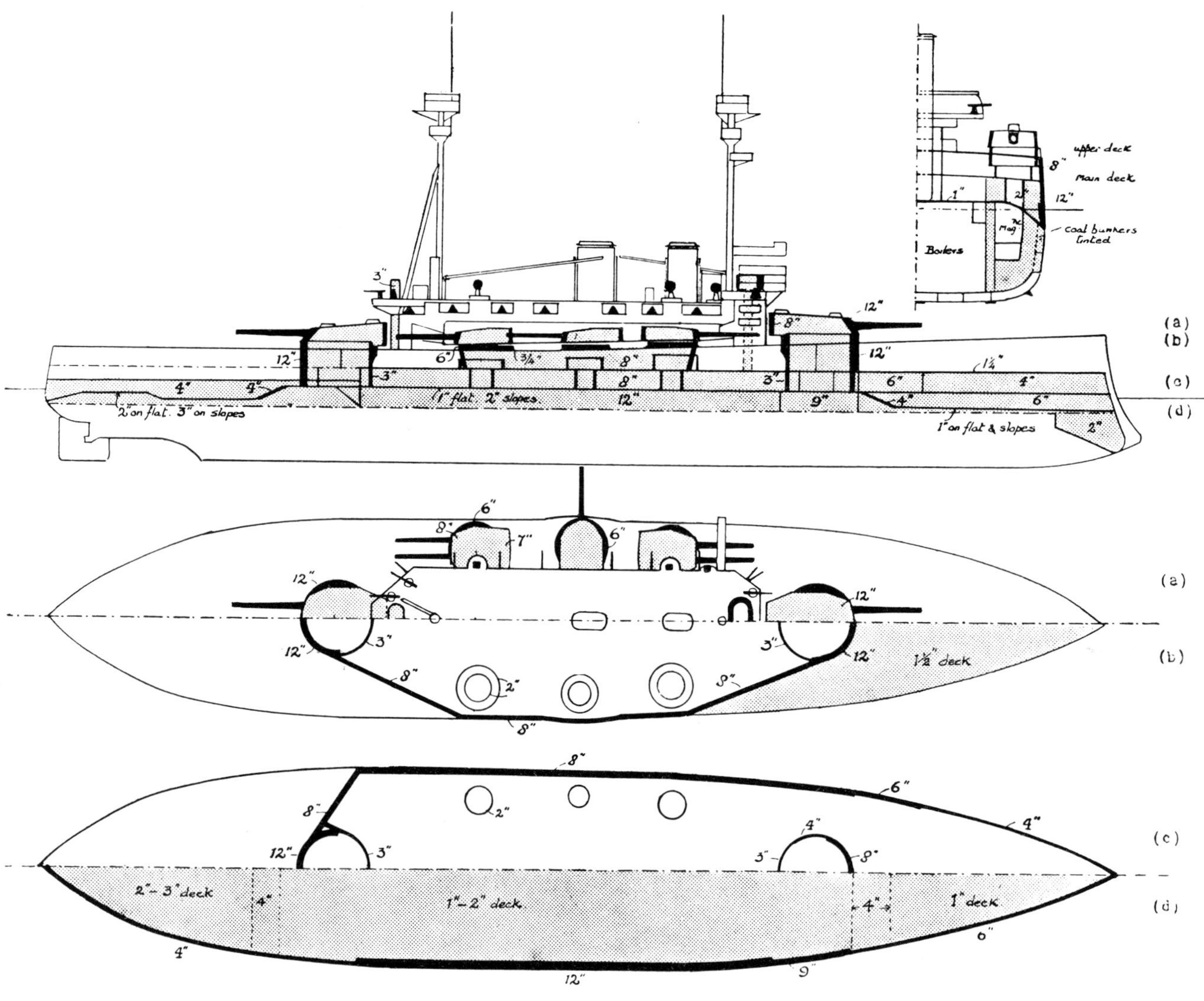

LORD NELSON

As a result of the purchase of the *Swiftsure* and *Triumph* Parliament was asked to approve of the commencement of only two battleships instead of three for the 1904 Programme.

Watts's earlier designs (*Duke of Edinburgh, Warrior* and *Minotaur* armoured cruisers) all carried a heavy 9·2-in. armament which at this period had a great reputation in the Service, and in the *Lord Nelson* he wanted to include twelve such guns in twin turrets amidships. Unfortunately the Controller laid down as a condition of the design that she should be able to dock in the then No. 9 at Chatham and No. 5 at Devonport—the former setting a limit to breadth and the latter to length. (I.N.A. paper 11.9.15.) This restriction was regarded as unfortunate and unnecessary—unfortunate because it meant lopping 11 ft. off the *King Edward* and restricting beam to 79½ ft., and unnecessary because by the time the ships were ready, new and ample docking accommodation was available at all the Dockyards. Because of this restricted beam the Board directed that the middle 9·2-in. turrets should be singles only; but Watts was very anxious to work in the full number of guns, and after some conversation with Sir William May gave orders for the design to be completed with twelve 9·2-in. Drawings were duly presented by the D.N.C. without his having taken preliminary steps officially on paper to secure Board approval for a variation from instructions, which led to an unfortunate position and a peremptory order for the complete design as directed.

Another result of restricted beam was that the magazines for the 9·2-in. could not be worked in along the centre of the ship, but had to be placed between coal bunkers along the sides. Here they would have been exposed to torpedo attack and to gun fire during a 10° roll—although as the ships proved remarkably steady the chances of such a hit were almost negligible. But it was a sore point with the Constructors for some time afterwards. Actually the *Lord Nelson* received a hit below the water-line during the attack on the Narrows (7 March 1915) which caused two bunkers to fill.

LINES

As the calculated displacement was 150 tons more than in the *King Edward* but with 15 ft. less length and 1½ ft. more beam, some difficulty was found in drafting the lines to give the necessary 18 knots. The Constructor in charge obtained his results by a bold experiment. He made the sides of the amidships section straight and parallel to the batter of the entrance to Chatham Docks, and the bottom of the ship quite flat so as to obtain as big a section and as much displacement as possible. From this the water-lines were drafted to make them as easy as possible forward and the same with the buttock lines aft, with the most satisfactory results, as the *Lord Nelsons* made their speed and proved exceptionally handy and steady.

LORD NELSON with funnels raised, 1918.

HULL WEIGHTS

Although carrying 360 tons in total load and armour *more* than the *King Edward*, the allowance for the hull of the *Lord Nelson* was only 5,720 tons—or 180 tons *less*. But by careful reduction of weights during construction she was finished with a displacement of only 16,090 tons in place of the 16,500 tons designed. This including the 100-ton Margin (not used) so showed a saving of 310 tons.

BULKHEADS

Following the Russian lead in the *Tsarevitch*, *Bayan* and *Pallada* the hull was divided into large sections by *solid* bulkheads, each section having separate drainage, pumping, ventilating systems and lifts. Such bulkheads made for safety but caused great inconvenience, especially in reaching the engine and boiler rooms—so much so that they were abandoned four years later in the *Neptune*.

For the first time magazine cooling arrangements were fitted during construction.

SUPERSTRUCTURE

To accommodate the numerous 12-pdr. battery and searchlights a very large flying deck was provided above which the boom boats were stowed. This involved considerable weight, and being of square section offered great resistance to rolling; as additional target it was of little consequence compared with the convenience and facilities it provided.

CONNING TOWER

Certain senior naval officers having strongly advocated a conning tower with clear, all-round vision and no obstructions, the usual bridge was omitted and all the navigating instruments placed inside the conning-tower. But as the commanding officers first appointed to both ships refused to be responsible for safe navigation without proper bridges after their first trials, a light flying bridge and wings were added to the *Agamemnon*, and *Lord Nelson* was given a chart house in addition to these.

ARMAMENT

Substantial increase in offence was also secured by later models of guns 5 cals. longer, the figures being:

		Cals.	*M.V.*	*Penetration of K.C. armour*	
King Edward	12-in.	40	2,612	12-in.	4,800 yards.
Lord Nelson		45	2,725		7,600 ,,
King Edward	9·2-in.	40	2,751	9·2-in.	4,550 yards.
Lord Nelson		45	2,875		5,200 ,,

the 12-in. guns having a command of 27 ft. forward and 22 ft. aft. With eight turrets on the upper deck, special steps were required to prevent interference and damage by gun blast and actual shell fire. As limiting stops were impracticable, a system of turret danger signals was devised by rubbing contacts on the revolving trunks and hoists which sounded a loud buzzer in the turret liable to do damage when the line of fire involved danger. When trained away from the fouling point the buzzer ceased. This arrangement proved most successful and was adopted in all later ships.

An anti-torpedo armament of twenty-four 12-pdrs. was by far the most powerful yet mounted, and was widely spaced in the superstructures and along the flying deck. It was reduced to eighteen guns during the war when 12-pdrs. were urgently required for other ships.

PROTECTION

Although exceeding the *King Edward's* total weight of armour by only 25 tons, the required increase in general protection was secured through restriction of armoured areas by most careful economy of space in armament disposition. A further reduction of 5 ft. in the barbette diameter made them only 29 ft. against 34 ft. in the *King Edward*, the total barbette armour being only 800 tons against 825 tons—and 1,210 tons in the *Majestic*! The citadel was also reduced by 35 ft. to only 190 ft., the 8-in. side armour being angled inboard beyond the secondary turrets to form an inclined bulkhead which wrapped round the 12-in. barbettes from main to upper deck. The belt showed a gain of 3 in. amidships and 1 in. on the deeper continuation aft, while the protective deck increased 1 in. on the slopes.

With her full load of oil fuel aboard she displaced 18,910 tons and drew 30 ft. 2½ in., which meant a sinkage of 3 ft. 10 in.—sufficient to place the 12-in. belt under water. Flotation would then depend upon 8-in. armour, but as Mr. Beardmore pointed out at her launch that this was equal to the 12-in. plate of four years previously, she was a good deal better off than figures suggested.

SEA-GOING QUALITIES

Having a metacentric height of only 3·4 as against 5·3 in the *King Edward* aided by the inertia due to eight heavy turrets and armour, plus resistance to rolling offered by flat sides and bottom with broad bilge keels, the *Lord Nelsons* proved good sea boats and steady gun platforms, with excellent manœuvring qualities. Their tactical diameter at 35° helm and 12 knots was only 395 yards compared with 460 yards of the *King Edwards*—so that in Service parlance "they were able to spin round on their sterns."

MACHINERY

These were the last British battleships to have twin screws and reciprocating machinery. The trial speeds were:

Lord Nelson	.. .. ..	17,445 h.p.=18·7 knots.
Agamemnon	.. .. ..	17,270 ,, =18·5 ,,

Agamemnon was the first British battleship to have forced lubrication for the main engines.

GENERAL

Owing to the narrow angle of support provided by the flying deck the tripod system in place of shrouds was revived for the main mast and derrick, and set a fashion which was to become general.

Fisher's predilection for short funnels and a small target resulted in the uptakes in the *Warrior*, *Minotaur* and *Lord Nelson* classes being cut down to bridge level. This uncomfortable state of things was remedied in the cruisers after a year or so, but the *Lord Nelsons* did not have their uptakes lengthened until 1917—and lost a good deal of their individuality thereby.

During the war searchlight platforms were fitted around the tripod base, and the projector previously beneath the fore control tops was lowered to funnel-cap level. *Lord Nelson* also had her chart house removed, so that the difference between the ships lay in the *Agamemnon* having two flying bridges.

In the post-war organization *Agamemnon*, devoid of turrets and general fittings, served as the first radio-controlled target ship. As such she was employed in working out new gunnery problems and as a mark for aircraft, whose practice in those days indicated that aerial bombing needed far more precision before it could imperil the existence of a steaming ship.

Main mast of "Lord Nelson" 1914. with S.L. removed from ends of flying deck.

"AGAMEMNON"

Built by Beardmore May '05 to June '08. Commissioned 25 June '08 for Nore Division Home Fleet. May '11 2nd Division Home Fleet (bottom and frames damaged through grazing an uncharted rock entering Ferrol 11 February '11). September '13 4th B.S. (temporary).

War: 5th B.S. Channel Fleet. February '15 transferred to Mediterranean for Dardanelles operations. Took part in preliminary bombardment of the forts on 19 and 25 February '15, and throughout the campaign during which time she was struck by over 50 projectiles including a 14-in. stone shot. On 5 May '16 she brought down Zeppelin L.85 at Salonika. When the battleships were withdrawn from coastal operations she was stationed at either Mudros or Salonika in readiness for any sortie by the *Goeben* from the Straits. The terms of the Turkish Armistice were signed on board. She returned to Chatham in February '19 where she remained until commissioned as a radio-controlled target ship in April '23 and served as such at Home and in the Mediterranean until paid off at Portsmouth 31 December '26, and sold for breaking up when relieved by the *Centurion*.

Agamemnon as a radio-controlled target ship.

"LORD NELSON"

Built by Palmers, Jarrow, May '05 to October '08. Commissioned December '08 for Nore Division Home Fleet with nucleus crew; full crew January '09; April '09 1st Division Home Fleet; January '11 2nd Division Home Fleet; May '12 2nd B.S.; September '13 4th B.S. (temporary).

War: Flagship of Channel Fleet. Covered the crossing to France of the B.E.F. and employed in defence of Southern ports. February '15 ordered to Dardanelles. Flagship of Vice-Admiral Wester Wemyss to 22 December '15 and then of Vice-Admiral John de Roebeck to 19 June '16; and later Flagship Eastern Mediterranean Ægean, and Black Sea until April '19.

Lord Kitchener had his Headquarters aboard at Mudros during November '15. Changed stations with the *Agamemnon* at Mudros or Salonika and was at Constantinople in January '19, returning home in May '19.

Was at Chatham or Sheerness until sold November '20.

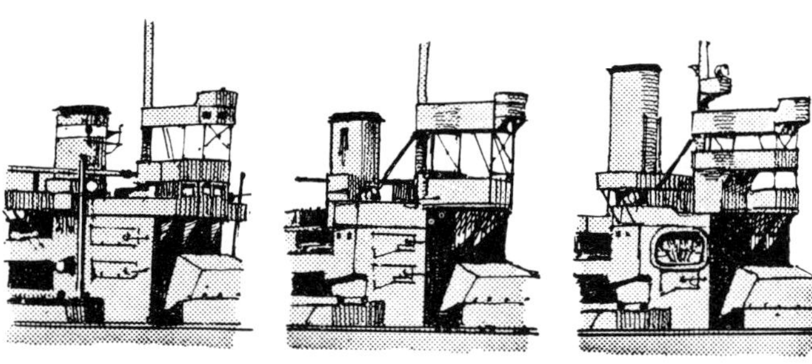

Lord Nelson showing charthouse, and *Agamemnon* as completed.

Agamemnon 1917 showing raised funnel and additional bridge.

Chapter 78

THE PROGRESS OF GUNNERY

Despite the great advances in design and armament which had so transformed our battle fleet during the past few years, the naval attitude towards the employment of the new weapons remained much as it always had been. The slow progress of an established order of things was accepted until 1899, when the extraordinary firing of the second-class cruiser *Scylla* (Captain Percy Scott) of the Mediterranean Fleet drew the attention of the Service and public to new possibilities in naval gunnery.

Scott had struck out on a line of his own. He had invented a loading trough to teach rapid loading and concerted handling of ammunition, and a "dotter" by which a hit or miss was shown on a miniature target, the men being trained to keep their sights on the target during the motions of rolling artificially produced. He taught his men to use extemporized telescopic sights in conjunction with a system of sub-calibre firing of his own devising against a target on which hits could be seen easily.

On 26 May 1899 the *Scylla* carried out her prize firing, to witness which three independent umpires were invited. Six 4·7-in. guns fired seventy rounds and made fifty-six hits (80 per cent.), which placed her at the top of the Fleet with a score so phenomenal as to be incredible when compared with the 20 to 40 per cent. usually attained.

Next year Scott was in command of the big cruiser *Terrible*, trained his men to use the 6-in. gun along *Scylla* lines, and placed her at the head of the Fleet with 77 per cent. of hits to rounds fired, against 28 per cent. for 6-in. Q.F. throughout the Service. In 1901 the *Terrible* scored 80 per cent. for the 6-in. with an average of 5·3 rounds and 4·2 hits per minute, while her 9·2-in. made 64 per cent. Ten men at her 6-in. guns hit with every round they fired, with Petty Officer Grounds[1] establishing a record of eight hits in eight rounds for the minute's firing.

With the 9·2-in., Petty Officers Taylor and Kewell scored nine hits out of twelve rounds, firing as quickly as did the average 6-in. in the Fleet.

Moreover, other ships on the China Station had copied Scott's methods and the *Barfleur* beat the *Scylla's* 4·7-in. record with 114 hits out of 159 rounds (71 per cent.), but at an average of 5·7 hits a minute, while the *Ocean* with her 12-in. scored fourteen hits out of twenty-six rounds—58 per cent. against the 33 per cent. Fleet average.

Scott and the *Terrible* became news. Grounds and Gunnery became news. A spirit of emulation and competition infused the Fleet, and in 1902 the Admiralty published the results of the annual prize firing with a return for general information, showing ships using the same calibre or type of gun grouped together to facilitate comparison.

The gulf separating the best shooting from the worst gave some indication of the leeway there was to make up, although allowances had to be made for weather conditions and equipment. The following selections give some idea of the great variations recorded:

13·5-in. gunned ships	*Hood*	88·35	*Empress of India*	13·25
12-in. „ „	*Ocean*	70·13	*Formidable*	4·12
9·2-in. „ „	*Crescent*	113·2	*Royal Arthur*	25·15

Sir John Fisher and Sir Edward Seymour instituted Station challenge shields for good shooting in the Mediterranean and China Stations, and the First Lord promised a decoration for good marksmanship in place of a money prize—the British bluejacket being more appreciative of a distinctive badge to prove his ability than an officer is of the C.B.

In 1903 Scott was selected to command the gunnery school at Whale Island and introduced a new system of training to replace book instruction. It was intended to bring ships and squadrons into direct competition in gunnery in the same way that they were in competition for everything else, but this plan did not commend itself to some of the senior officers afloat and was not put into execution until Captain Jellicoe came into office as Director of Naval Ordnance in February 1905. Instruction, however, was brought up-to-date and the teaching appliances used in China employed to bring about a high standard of shooting.

But although the Fleet was carrying out long-range firing it was not supplied with the necessary instruments or instructions, so that Commanders-in-Chief on various stations arranged things according to personal inclination —and some strange battle practices resulted.

Improvement in shooting so far applied only to the short-range gun-layers tests, when the men had to see whether they were hitting the target or not. Individual skill had increased, but ability to hit at 1,000 yards or so with separate guns in competition was not the sort of shooting required for long-range battle practice, which Scott was anxious to place on a sound and scientific basis.

---

[1] A tablet recording this feat was placed in St. Martin's Church, Birmingham.

The problem was how to record hits when the target cannot take fire, explode, or sink as in action, with the impossibility of seeing hits at four or five miles range. Some new method had to be devised which would indicate whether hits or misses were being obtained. Scott perceived that broadside firing would meet the case, as in a volley of say six guns the shots tend to open out, so that an observer spotting one shot short of the target could assume that others were hitting. To put theory into practice, he proposed that the armoured cruiser *Drake*, then commanded by Captain J. R. Jellicoe—a conspicuous gunnery officer—should be placed at his disposal for such "straddling" tests before a complete scheme for battle practice at what was then considered long range was put forward.

There was also the difficulty about our gun sights, which were proving very inaccurate. It was necessary to know into what space the broadside would fall, so that any guns shooting wide of the average could have their sights corrected (Scott called it "calibrating the guns"), and Admiralty attention had been directed frequently to faulty gun sights during the past three years but without much avail.

Unfortunately the Board would not sanction the proposed *Drake* experiments—which were not carried out until 1905—but instructed Rear-Admiral Sir Reginald Custance in the *Venerable* and Rear-Admiral Sir Hedworth Lambton in the *Victorious* to investigate the whole subject of long-range firing with a free hand to expend what ammunition they liked. A joint report was then to be sent in for a scheme of target practice, and against what sort of target; and whether the guns were to be controlled by a centralized system or by the gun-layers and battery officers.

Lord Chatfield has described the *Venerable's* three months' firing experiments at Prasa Island near Platea Bay in *The Navy and Defence*, and when they were over:

> "Hundreds of salvoes of ammunition had been fired and much coal and energy expended to prove what to many was a self-evident fact—*i.e.*, that you could not efficiently fire the powerful and long-ranged batteries of a modern man-of-war by the old plan of go as you please. Scientific centralized control alone could meet modern needs. To adopt it as the standard method in the fleets meant for the Admiralty and the gunnery schools new plans for the design and equipment of ships, new methods of training, new and better instruments, an accepted gunnery revolution. There was no time to lose. The Navy itself is the most rapidly moved weapon in the world; it can strike in its own way anywhere at a moment's notice, but it has one peculiarity; its material and men take long to produce."

The Committees in the two ships, however, came to very opposite conclusions on most points, so sent in two reports of which the Board decided that the *Venerable's* was the most promising and should be adopted in all ships, although "alternative systems might be used instead of it." But the suggestions put forward by the *Venerable* committee were so impossible that all ships took advantage of the escape paragraph, with the result that what was termed Battle Practice remained a "go as you please" operation with no Admiralty rules and no competition.

No steps were taken to remedy defective sights, which were more or less inefficient throughout the Fleet. The Admiralty knew it, but ignored every recommendation put forward from the *Excellent* until the *Centurion* scandal in 1904, which brought matters to a head. At her reconstruction, new sights had been supplied for her which, when tested by the Gunnery School, were found incorrect and not passed despite Admiralty pressure. So an official was sent down to Portsmouth who passed them, and the ship proceeded to China. There Admiral Sir Cyprian Bridge reported on them as follows:

> "It would not be possible to characterize with more than deserved severity the atrocious scandal of our inefficient gun sights; the sights of H.M.S. *Centurion's* guns were so defective that she was not fit to go into action."

In January 1904 Scott had written a stinging letter to their Lordships putting on record his frequent complaints of the inefficient sights throughout the Fleet which would lead to disaster in case of war, and now the state of things proved too much for the Board, who called a conference which discovered that *all the gun sights of the Fleet were inefficient, and that the guns of the whole Fleet would have to be re-sighted.* But though vitally important, very little was done towards re-sighting in 1904, although the First Lord (Lord Selborne) was telling the country that gunnery was of the first importance and wrote Scott that "the Lords of the Admiralty have for long devoted and are still devoting their whole heart and soul to improving the gunnery of the Fleet."

Fortunately Admiral Sir John A. Fisher became First Lord in October 1904 and gave Scott his backing. The appointment was received with national relief and *Punch* appeared with the famous "No more Gunnery Hash" cartoon showing John Bull in the Admiralty Grill Room with Fisher as chef.

In February 1905 Scott was promoted to flag rank and appointed Inspector of Target Practice. Incidentally, by the terms of the original Order in Council the appointment was described as "Director of Target Practice" (the title given to the post created for Captain W. Sims in the United States), but as the post carried no power of direction or Admiralty backing (Captain Sims was backed by the President and Navy Department), Scott had the title changed to "Inspector."

At the same time Sir John Jellicoe became Director of Naval Ordnance, and rescued the gun-layers test from the haphazard conditions which had obtained during the Selborne administration. In 1905 the tests were carried out in a more uniform manner, the improvement in shooting being maintained and for the first time hits exceeded misses with an excess of 1,017.

It was in that year that the Admiralty introduced a new test called "battle practice," already referred to in which every ship had to fire at a large towed target at from 5,000 to 7,000 yards range with all her guns simultaneously and altering course as she did so. The practice had a time limit of about five minutes. Points were awarded for the number of hits, rapidity of fire, early hitting, accuracy of the opening range, with penalties for rounds unexpended and other faults.

Scott records that the results were deplorable. No rules had been laid down, there were no efficient sights or necessary instruments for carrying out firing at any range except a short one, and each Fleet did as it liked with "independent," "salvoes," "control," "broadsides," "rapid," "slow," "group volleys" and a variety of other methods.

But for the first time the Director of Naval Ordnance, the Captain of the Gunnery School, and Inspector of Target Practice were all working in harmony to improve shooting.

The graph of the gun-layers tests between 1897 and 1907 shows how the percentage of hits rose from 32 to 79 in ten years, the improvement in battle practice keeping pace as efficient sights and proper instruments came into service.

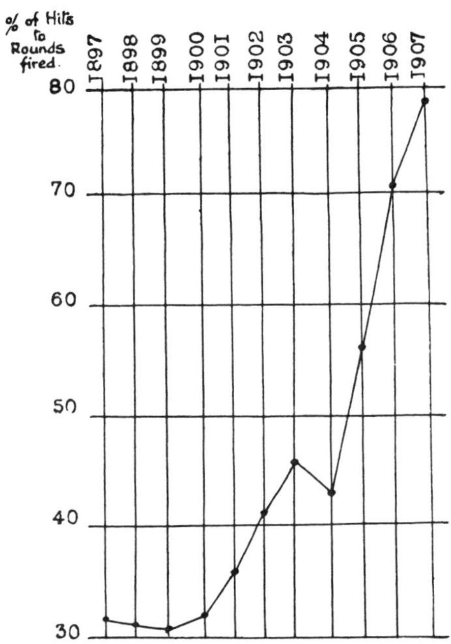

The drop in 1904 was due to increase in the range.

During 1905 Scott revived the old "Director" firing and, owing to the great advances made in electrical communications, was able to devise a satisfactory form of it. This was submitted to the Admiralty, who had it patented secretly, consigned it to themselves, and then pigeonholed it until 1911, when Jellicoe insisted on the *Neptune* being fitted with it.

It is interesting to recall the fire control system installed in the *Venerable* and other 12-in. and 6-in. gunned battleships of the era. The 12-in. turrets were fitted with a voice pipe to the conning tower; the 6-in. battery was divided into groups with three casemates in a group and a voice pipe to each group, the one casemate officer directing the other two guns. There was a small Barr and Stroud range-finder on top of the fore chart house with a voice pipe to the conning tower, and this instrument gave the range which was communicated to all guns. Realization that greater height was required to obtain a better approximation of whether splashes were over or under the target led to an observer and later a range-finder being installed on a platform at the foremast head, and in a lower position on the main mast below smoke level.

Range-finders then in use were generally of 3 ft. base and of the co-incidence type, in which vertical lines shown as "split" had to be focused until seen as unbroken, when the range was read off. The Zeiss system, in which double vision was adjusted until the image was seen as sharply stereoscopic for correct range, was not used in this country. As ranges increased and more accurate readings demanded, range-finders became longer and longer until in World War II the main armament was being controlled by instruments with a 36-ft. base.

GROWTH OF DESTROYERS

The tragic loss of one of our first two turbine-driven destroyers, the *Cobra*, through breaking her back in a North Sea gale on 18 September 1901, resulted in a complete change of policy as regards the construction of these vessels, and in the 1902 Programme provision was made for the 540-600-ton "River" class with a high forecastle in place of a turtle deck, and 25 knots reliable sea speed instead of a light draught trials 30 knots which could never be realized in service.

For the past few years German torpedo boats had been given raised forecastles—nothing like the height of the "Rivers," but certainly an improvement on the turtle deck.

With the "Rivers" destroyers entered upon a new phase in development, and within a few years the 870-ton "Tribal" type of ocean-going boats were entering service, with foreign designs following suit. The sea-going destroyer with a 4-in. armament able to make well over 30 knots at full load had arrived, and nothing under the 3-in. 12-pdr. gun was worth considering as battleship defence against them.

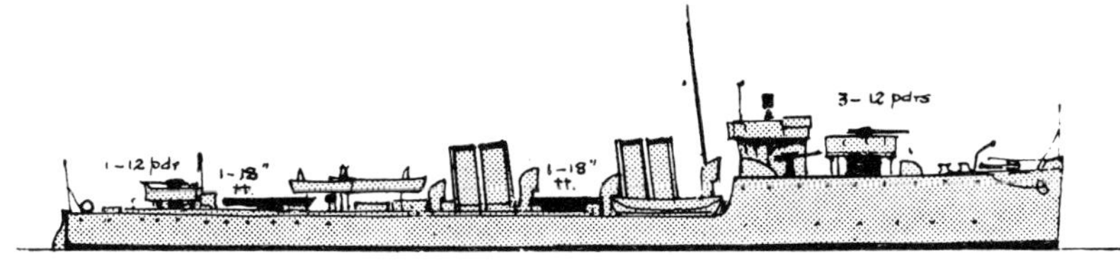

"River" type 1902. 540-600 tons. 25 knots.

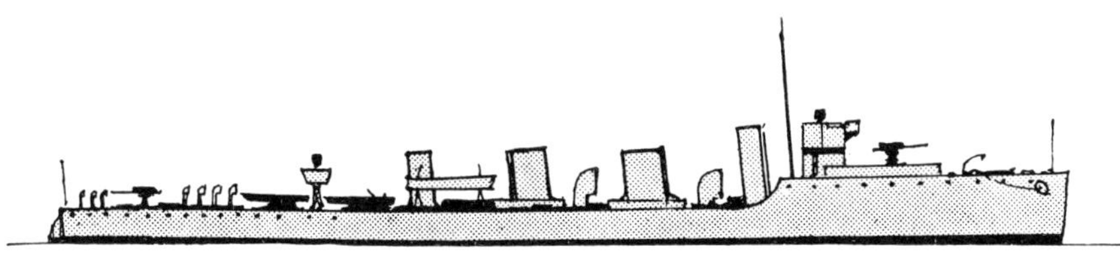

"Tribals" 1907-09. 855-1,045 tons. 33 knots.

Chapter 79

THE RUSSO-JAPANESE WAR 1904–05

So far as the design of capital ships and their equipment was concerned the "lessons of the late war"—to use the familiar cliché—were drawn mainly from the actions of 10 August off Port Arthur and the battle of Tsushima. From the first of these the outstanding facts were:

(1) The *Tzarevitch* and *Retvizan* opened fire at the extraordinary range of 18,000 metres and dropped shot 218 yards beyond the *Mikasa* and *Asahi*. The Japanese were outranged and the *Asahi* did not reply until the fleets had closed to 14,000 metres.

(2) Early in the action the *Mikasa* was hit at over 13,000 yards by a 12-in. projectile just above the heel of the second torpedo boom forward at the junction of the 5-in. and 7-in. armour of which a piece 3 ft. in diameter was knocked out making a hole extending to the wooden ledge. Had not the sea been smooth this wound might have been attended with serious consequences for the Japanese.

(3) The *Tzarevitch* was hit by a 12-in. shell between the upper and lower bridges which killed Admiral Witthoft, the fleet navigator, and severely wounded the chief of staff and the captain. These officers were outside the conning tower. Shortly after a second 12-in. struck the conning tower and exploded. Fragments were deflected by the roof, entered through the all-round slit 16-in. deep, killed or wounded everyone inside including the steersman who fell over the wheel and jammed it hard to starboard so that the ship sheered out of line and brought the fleet into confusion. These two shells decided the issue of the battle.

(4) The speed of the Japanese battle squadron was limited by that of its slowest unit, the *Fuji*, to 15 knots, which was only ½-1 knot more than that of the Russians. This prevented Togo from improving his tactical position and allowed the enemy to regain the shelter of Port Arthur when light failed.

Of these (1) and (2) demonstrated that opposing fleets may come into action at far greater distances than had ever been thought possible, and that at such ranges major injuries may be inflicted which could influence the result of the action. The inadequacy of conning towers in general at that time to house the personnel who required protection for the proper performance of their duties in control was fully recognized, and a radical change both in size and design was expected in post-war ships. The experience in the necessity for bigger and better conning towers, and the following note by a British observer, is of interest:

"The suitability of the conning towers in both fleets might be judged from the apparently universal avoidance of these structures by all who were supposed to use them. Apart from a sense of being able to command the ship from a place where everything 'looked so different,' it was felt that no properly constituted Captain could be expected to shelter himself behind armour so long as the upper and boat decks remained crowded with men stationed to repeat distances and pass orders. No suggestion for the improvement of the conning tower had been evolved, but in the Russian ships they were very large and roomy, but with no view aft. The look-out space above the armour was far too wide—especially in *Tzarevitch*, *Retvizan* and *Pobieda*.

"In both Fleets there was a general desire to con ships from the open, with the fore bridge as first choice.

"The *Asama* was conned from the fore top; aboard the *Mikasa* Togo and as many of his staff as could find standing room, were on the pilot house, the remainder being on the fore bridge; a shell, which had struck the semaphore, burst, and killed four of the Admiral's *entourage*. When the after bridge of the *Nisshin* was struck, also by a shell, Admiral Kataoka and his chief of staff had only just left in order to go forward. The remaining four staff officers, with the inspector of machinery at their head, were all killed. So far as is known, the captains and navigating officers throughout the Japanese fleet also occupied their usual navigational stations on the pilot-houses.

"In battle there are only two positions worth having—one is behind the thickest armour in the ship, and the next best is the most exposed that can be found, with perhaps just a screen of hammocks to keep off flying fragments, which are both plentiful and dangerous.

"When the conning tower is damaged, the people inside it killed, and the steering arrangements rendered useless, the next position is in the after director-tower, situated in the most inconvenient place, which at once alters the centre of command and the direction whence orders emanate, a proceeding needlessly baffling to organization. . . . To obviate all these drawbacks, the second directing position might be moved forward to within 20 feet of the principal one, where it could always supplement the other, and when necessary could replace it without loss of time or discontinuity of idea."

The dominating influence of the 12-in. gun both from a destructive and moral point of view was also stressed:

(1) "Although the 10-in. guns of the *Peresviet* and *Pobieda* were of 45 cals. and may also have been of greater range than the 12-in. 40 cal. guns in the Russian battleships, the fire effect of every gun is so much less than that of the next largest size, that when 12-in. guns are firing, shots from 10-in. pass unnoticed, while for all the respect they instil, 8-in. or 6-in. guns might just as well be pea-shooters, and the 12-pdr. simply does not count.

(2) The poor opinion expressed of the power of 6-in. and 8-in. guns prevented the addition of armoured cruisers to the Battle Fleet from being considered as any material accession to its strength. Only 12-in. and 10-in. guns were of decisive battle value and hits by smaller calibres were scarcely noticed. Increased ranges had quite put an end to any idea of smothering fire by secondary guns; they were not worth full-scale protection and were liable to be put out of action without

being able to make any effective contribution to offensive action; for use against torpedo craft they were regarded as being over-large.

(3) A prominent Japanese official stated 'If he were to order new ships of the *Nisshin* type, he would endeavour to insist on having a 12-in. 50-cal. gun.'

(4) Again 'The favourable opinion of Russian shooting was confined to that of the heavy guns. By the time the 6-in. came into play, the action was already going against Russia, but it is believed that an inspection of the ships would show that the fate of the day had been decided by heavy guns, *if not by the heaviest only.*'

RIG.—In the Japanese Fleet rig and masting came in for a general modification. Fighting tops were removed early in 1905, and the proximity of fore-mast and conning-tower was looked upon unfavourably as making a vital target. One mast amidships like in the cruisers *Nisshin* and *Kasuga* was considered the most satisfactory rig. Prior to the battle of Tsushima the armoured cruiser *Idzumo* hung hammocks around her foremast from the range-finder platform to the upper deck, giving it a curiously bloated appearance. The idea was to prevent splinters from hits on the funnels reaching the roof of the chart house where the Admiral and staff were likely to be. Very high top masts for wireless were fitted in most ships.

BULKHEADS.—The *Yakumo* appears to be the only ship in this fleet with intact water-tight bulkheads. Though tremendously abused at first, no inconvenience was felt as soon as it was understood the Japanese Admiralty would permit of no change to be made. Many ingenious minds have been at work in trying to improve the safety of the magazines by removing them from the influence of mine and torpedo explosions, or by protecting them against these, *as no ship has yet been sunk unless her magazines were affected* (September '04)."

Commenting on the fighting of 10 August, Captain W. C. Pakenham wrote early in May 1904:

> "Owing to long ranges, the battle was so prolonged that the Japanese may have forgotten that the crisis of such a fight lasts but a very few minutes after close action has once been engaged; and it may be found that, while the armoured cruiser division of Admiral Kamimura masked its fire while endeavouring to execute some ingenious manœuvre, the moment for snatching a victory has come and gone. If there is one thing more important than another in naval tactics, it is the early and simultaneous development of the whole gun effort of the fleet, and its maintenance in full development without intermission throughout the action. The crushing overthrow of the Russian gun effort on August 10th during the brief interval in which their fleet formation was duplicated (*i.e.*, when the *Tzarevitch* had turned out of line) is so recent it should not yet have been forgotten."

The battle of Tsushima was fought on 27 May 1905 in misty weather with a strong S.W. wind which threw showers of spray over the heavier ships and caused great inconvenience from water dashing through turret and casemate gun ports and from constant wetting of object glasses in sighting telescopes. The Japanese battle fleet included four battleships and eight armoured cruisers; the Russians had five modern and three older battleships, three small coast-defence ships, and four old armoured cruisers.

Nelson's advice, "out-manœuvre a Russian," proved to be unexpectedly easy to follow, while it is interesting to note that his statement that if he had to fight a Baltic fleet he would attack the head of the line and throw it into confusion was descriptive of what occurred after the battle had been in progress a short time. Rozhestvenski never attempted a tactical move of any description, allowed Togo to concentrate first on the leader of the port division, and afterwards on the head of his fleet, and tamely permitted his ships to be disabled in detail. Fresh from dockyard hands, the Japanese ships could steam at 15 knots; the Russians had crawled for seven and a half months through the tropics without docking; they carried all their boats and a large amount of inflammable fittings, being cluttered up with coal, much overloaded, and not good for more than 9 knots. This 6 knots speed advantage enabled Togo to select his range and assert a tactical superiority leading to decisive results.

The most recent Russian battleships had been modelled upon French practice with complete belts up to the main deck, bare or thinly armoured lower deck sides, and long towering superstructures; having a marked tumble-home, small initial stability, and inadequate protection for the high freeboard, they were inferior in stability to the Japanese ships, which followed our *Formidable* design. The five *Borodinos* had internal subdivision and lateral torpedo bulkheads like the *Tzarevitch* which apparently enabled them to resist torpedo attack, so that the *Suvarov* was only sunk after the fourth hit, when she lay on her beam ends for fifteen minutes. The *Alexander III* and *Borodino* were badly damaged by gun fire and fires aboard. The former capsized after her magazines blew up; the latter slowly heeled over and sank. When captured, *Orel* had her main armour intact although badly smashed up, and no torpedo hits had been received.

The *Osliabia* with her narrow belt, very high freeboard and great tumble-home had been designed for special steadiness with a period of oscillation of 10 seconds. But this had been secured at the expense of safety in action, and with her small beam and tumble-home she lacked stiffness and relied upon *high freeboard* for a proper range of stability. She presented a very vulnerable target and capsized as the result of wounds above the armour which led to flooding and a heel which put her 12-pounder gun ports under water. At normal draught these ships would have been rated as battleships, but at their condition of flotation at Tsushima this term was a misnomer. Had they all the full benefit of their waterline armour it seems fairly certain that the Japanese projectiles would have been *unable to impair their buoyancy or stability*, although just as efficacious against unarmoured parts. These would have been just as badly punished, and incendiary action no less severe; but less water would have come inboard and then would have drained away rapidly by the scuppers.

Apropos of the sinkings at Tsushima, the following comments by Commander W. Hovgaard, Royal Danish Navy, appeared in the 1906 *Fighting Ships*:

> "If we are to continue to build large battleships, it appears absolutely necessary that some radical change should be made in their design. A mere increase in size, if unaccompanied by a still greater increase in stability, is likely to lead to disappointment in time of war.
>
> Hence, battleships should be given a much greater initial stiffness than has hitherto generally been given to ships of this class. The stability at moderate angles of heel should be better protected by carrying the side armour, unimpaired by the presence of gun ports, up to the upper deck along the vitals. The tumble-home should be very small. The watertight subdivision should be designed with more particular regard to torpedo attack; lateral, eventually armoured, bulkheads should be carried along the vitals some 18 ft. from the sides, and the engine rooms should be reduced in size by the use of three or more propellers. Finally, compensating tanks, with a special and powerful flooding system, should be provided for righting the ship when it takes a heel.
>
> The advantages of a steady gun platform, so indispensable to a battleship, should be attained, not by sacrificing the safety in action, but by increasing the resistance to rolling.
>
> While in existing battleships of 14,000-16,000 tons we find a metacentric height of 3½-4 ft., future battleships of about 18,000 tons should not have less than 6-8 ft. metacentric height, even although this feature, *involving great beam*, as well as the fitting of *very large bilge keels* may be somewhat prejudicial to speed. With a proper system of subdivision and protection, the passive power of resistance of such battleships against attack on their stability would thus be more than twice that of existing battleships."

SHELLS

On 10 August the fuses of the Japanese shells filled with Shimose were too sensitive and exploded against almost anything they touched, so that the effect was outside instead of inside the plating. At Tsushima fuses were set to burst inside plating and consequently upper works were wrecked and greater internal damage resulted. Sensitive fuses caused several prematures, and a number of guns were disabled—three out of four 8-in. in the *Nisshin*, a 12-in. in the *Mikasa*, and one in the *Shikishima*.

INDIRECT FIRE ON THE PORT ARTHUR FLEET

Results from indirect fire by military 11-in. howitzers against the Russian ships in Port Arthur—by which the *Retvizan*, *Poltava* and *Peresviet* were put out of action during the first day's bombardment—were received with open incredulity by the Fleet. Without having any experience of the injuries indirect fire was capable of inflicting—even against ships protected by sand bags, then regarded as an adequate defence against dropping shell—the utmost expected had been a gradual destruction of their topsides.

In these ships the protective decks were thin—the *Peresviet's* had three ½-in. and one ¾-in., the *Poltava* totalled about 2¾ in. and the *Retvizan* about 2½ in. Several hits penetrated straight down to the magazines. These bombardments gave some indication of what might be expected from dropping shots at the very long ranges anticipated in advanced gunnery circles.

SPOTTING

During the battle of Tsushima it was considered that under the atmospheric conditions that prevailed and with the concentration of fire that took place, spotting was impracticable. The want of light prevented a projectile being seen during the latter part of its flight, and even if it had been possible to see it, spotting would have been accurate only when the shell fell considerably short. If it passed over the target, it was invariably lost sight of behind columns of water and spray thrown up by shell falling short, columns which rose to a great height and were at times so numerous as to hide the ship herself. If the shell fell a little short, the same thing would happen. To try and judge the accuracy of fire by the shell splashes was also misleading when concentration took place, as the only splashes invariably seen were those of the shell which fell shortest, these giving the impression that the sights should be raised—an impression which might never be received if the splashes beyond the target could have been seen. When the target was not under fire from any other ship, spotting was of use; but in a fleet action, and particularly when one fleet was drawing past the other, it was difficult to be certain that no other ship was sharing the target. During concentrated fire "one was apt to think that the bad shots were somebody else's, and that one's own ship was doing splendidly."

Next day it was possible to spot, as the fire was very deliberate and consisted practically of range-finding rounds only. The Japanese first rounds fell ahead of the Russians and short, but as soon as the range and deflection were accurately obtained firing ceased owing to the Russian surrender, and so no information was gained as to spotting under favourable conditions of light and weather and with a concentrated fire.

Although not germane to the material side, an official report describing the method of fire control employed by the Japanese at Round Island is of interest:

> "All ranges were taken from a large-size Barr and Stroud on the fore bridge. The Captain indicated the ship target and the officer having found the range passed target and range to an assistant, who repeated them by speaking trumpet, to the fore superstructure, whence they were forwarded, again by trumpet, to the after superstructure. From these two stations voice-tubes carried the orders to the batteries. When firing became more rapid, a man on the fore bridge replaced the first trumpet, and a nimble lad with a blackboard was substituted for the second one.
>
> Neither sextant, telescopic sights, nor mechanical telegraphs were used.
>
> The results were what might have been expected. As the firing increased in rapidity its accuracy improved, and when the noise had become sufficient to drown the cries of the repeaters, and no one had leisure to pay attention to the frenzied gyrations of the boy with the board, the system was at its best. It was at its best because it had gradually ascended through different degrees of diminishing harmfulness, until it had attained to total uselessness, which was the nearest approach to perfection such a system could know. Reduction of range had much to do with increased accuracy, but the coincidence of the improvement in shooting with the nullification of the method of fixing the range was significant."

TORPEDO WARFARE

The torpedo made its debut against battleships in this war—and achieved practically nothing. Only 2 per cent. of torpedoes fired against moving ships found their mark, and although the initial attack against the ships outside Port Arthur—anchored and practically unprepared for hostilities—inflicted some damage, it was soon repaired and the vessels returned to service.

The reasons for this poor showing of what might have proved a very potent weapon in Japanese hands were:

(1) Firing slow-running torpedoes at maximum distances.
(2) Enforced precaution against loss of ships.

As regards (1), torpedoes were set to run maximum ranges, said to be about 3,280 yards, for both the 14-in. and 18-in. Speeds were consequently reduced to about 14 to 15 knots and chances of hitting minimized, and to this adjustment must be attributed a large share of the responsibility for the unsuccessful attacks made by dashing and competent Japanese officers. (2) While the Russians could continue to build ships and reinforce their squadrons, Japan's naval strength throughout the term of hostilities was limited to the number of ships she possessed in August 1904. Warship building as a home industry was as yet quite undeveloped, and her fleet had all been purchased or acquired as prizes from the Chinese. For this reason her admirals and captains were instilled with the necessity for conserving their ships and risking nothing—a ship lost could not be replaced and there was no margin of superiority in material to justify forcing a decision in battle which might entail such a loss. The same caution was impressed upon the lesser commanding officers, and this caused them to avoid close action when employed upon their principal duty, however much their inclination prompted an opposite course.

Had the Japanese been able to make good their losses in destroyers, and their commanders free to carry out attacks at decisive ranges with fast-running torpedoes, results might have been very different. Other factors such as a shortage in trained torpedo ratings and failures from avoidable causes and climatic conditions could be assessed at their proper value, and those advocates of torpedo warfare who were in a position to judge results with a knowledge of the special circumstances which obtained both generally and on particular occasions saw the torpedo as a very real and growing menace to Sea Power of the Tradition.

But the official verdict, revealed in the war colleges and reflected in the schemes and rulings of our peace manœuvres, was that the torpedo would remain of very minor importance. Naval decisions were to be obtained, as in the past, by gun action between surface ships.

By this pernicious teaching torpedo and mine were belittled and no tests were carried out to determine the best methods of resistance against under-water explosions, nor were our ships properly designed to withstand them so far as bulkheading and the maintenance of proper trim when hit were concerned.

FACTORS WHICH CONFUSED TORPEDO ATTACKS

(1) Those with personal experience in attacking torpedo boats stated that it was quite impossible to see after the boat had once got within the beam of a searchlight. Searchlights used indiscriminately gave away a ship's position, as in the case of the *Kniaz Suvarov* at Tsushima. A Japanese captain said that he would have all upper

deck lights switched on immediately on sighting a destroyer, as it assisted in getting the guns into action, and further disguise was unnecessary. Searchlights would then be burnt, but never before. The *Kniaz Suvarov* burnt hers continually, and only drew the Japanese destroyers to her.

(2) Officers described the splashes made in the water by shot as being perfectly blinding and that under such circumstances they could see nothing but brilliantly irridescent fountains of spray.

(3) Those who attacked battleships at sea during the night explained failure to achieve hits by the conviction that the enemy altered course about four points and thus threw out the calculations for distance and deflection.

ANTI-TORPEDO GUNS

Torpedo attacks were made on the disabled Russians after they were more or less deprived of defensive gunfire. Although the largest destroyers on each side were from 300-400 tons only, the general opinion was that *nothing less than a 4·7-in. could be held as effective against them*; the 12-pdr. was of "little use in stopping an attack and should be the smallest calibre carried in torpedo craft."

Shields to 12-pdrs. were generally removed from the Japanese battleships in 1905.

POST-WAR DESIGNS

Early in 1905 the battleships *Aki* and *Satsuma* were laid down, but took over five years to build. On 19,800 tons they carried four 12-in. and twelve 10-in. with six 6-in. in *Aki* and twelve 4·7-in. in *Satsuma* and steamed at 19-20 knots. According to our reports, in 1908 the mixed armament was due to difficulties in supply of 12-in. guns. In the same year they also commenced the 12-in. gunned cruisers of the *Tsukuba* and *Kurama* classes, the latter with her 22 knot speed being classed as a battle cruiser.

But towards the end of the war our information showed that a *uniform armament of 12-in. guns* had been decided upon for future Japanese and Russian battleships, with a speed of 20 knots or over.

By virtue of the Alliance Captain Packenham had been accommodated aboard the *Asahi*, and although considerably hampered by linguistic difficulties had been able to furnish very full and accurate reports of the fighting, general equipment and damage sustained in the Japanese and captured Russian ships. But from a material viewpoint these and other reports from naval officers must have been largely of academic interest, as our designs had moved on far ahead of the ship types engaged, whose equipment had been largely outmoded. Thus, when Tsushima was fought on 28-29 May 1905 the *Dreadnought* Committee had completed their labours and four months' work had been done on the designs of the first single-calibre battleship.

On the other hand, reports and comments on a host of subjects—ranging from the uselessness of 12-pdrs. against destroyers to the remarkable freedom from fires caused by wooden decks and fittings—made by various British naval officers in touch with the Japanese Fleet were apparently completely ignored at Whitehall. A detailed record of how the Japanese prepared their ships for action at the later stages of the war could have been circulated to H.M. ships in 1914 with great advantage—and one minor benefit would have been the retention of wardroom furniture so hastily discarded in some ships.

NET DEFENCE

The Japanese in peace-time practised steaming with nets out, but did not do so during the war. They gained practically no experience in repelling torpedo attacks owing to the lack of Russian enterprise, but after their attacks on the Russian ships at Port Arthur the inadequacy of partial net defence was realized. Japanese battleships carried the same sort of protection as our own, and through about 60° of arc the nets gave no protection whatever; for another 100° or so they only slightly reduced the size of the target, and should the broadside be turned to an attack so as to get the benefit of the maximum length of net defence, the maximum of risk was invited by the offer of the unprotected ends.

In the flagship *Mikasa* an extension of the crinoline around the bows and stern was temporarily fixed, but discarded.

Some ships had large mesh nets, others small mesh. The Russians also used both sorts, and double nets around the *Sevastopol* stopped a number of torpedoes when she lay aground outside Port Arthur.

No reports of nets having fouled screws were received.

Japanese net cutters were of the scissors variety.

Chapter 80

GENESIS OF THE "DREADNOUGHT"

In the 1903 edition of *Fighting Ships* the celebrated Italian naval constructor Vittorio Cuniberti oulined "An Ideal Battleship for the British Navy" in which he described the design for a 17,000-ton ship carrying twelve 12-in. guns, protected by 12-in. armour, and steaming at 24 knots. This had been worked out as a feasible and attainable proposition, the argument for the numerous 12-in. guns being contained in the following extract:

> "If, however, the hit is an oblique one, and the distance is considerable, it appears necessary that we should adopt the calibre of 12-inch if we want to be absolutely certain of sinking the adversary, striking him only on the belt. But the loading of such guns is as yet very slow, although it has greatly improved of late. Besides, the number of hits that one can get in on the belt itself is small. From this it appears that in our ideal and intensely powerful ship we must increase the number of pieces of 12-inch so as to be able to get in at least one fatal shot on the enemy's belt at the water-line before she has a chance of getting a similar fortunate stroke at us from one of the four large pieces now usually carried as the main armament. . . . Without throwing away a single shot, without wasting ammunition, secure in her exuberant protection, with her twelve guns ready, she would swiftly descend upon her adversary and pour in a terrible converging fire at the belt."

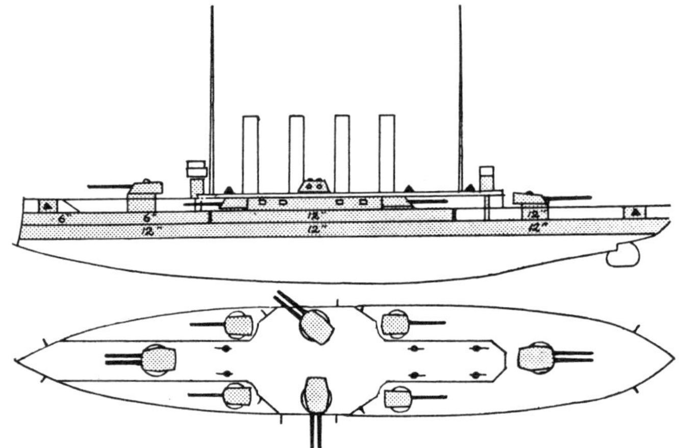

Cuniberti's proposed all big-gun battleship.

Cuniberti's high-speed ideal ship carried a big 12-in. armament heavily protected so as to bring an overwhelming volume of fire into action at *decisive range*. The *Dreadnought* was evolved for a totally different method of fighting, and in response to the demands of long-range gunnery.

In 1903 the fighting range of battleships was only about 3,000 yards, although both the French and Italians were carrying out experimental firing at much greater distances. Since 1899 shooting in the Mediterranean Fleet under Fisher had shown that 5,000-6,000 yards might become the battle ranges of the future, and that with proper fire control it would be possible to obtain a fair percentage of hits at 8,000 yards or more.

One fact that stood out prominently in these shoots was that accurate range control depended upon *salvo firing*, and that exact range could only be determined when of the strung-out bunch of splashes some fell short and some over the target. It was clearly impossible for guns of different calibres to be used, as owing to a variety of causes the range passed to 12-in. guns was not the range that would suit the 9·2-in. or 6-in. guns, although the same distance from the target; in addition there was possible confusion in differentiating between the splashes of 12-in. and 9·2-in. guns. Hence the difficulties in control of fire increased directly with the number of types of guns in the armament.

If the knowledge gained by such trials were to be properly utilized, it could only be done by a one-calibre armament eliminating splash and range confusion. Thus the main considerations which made the *Dreadnought* type inevitable were:

(1) Increasing battle range necessitated by the menace of long-range torpedo attack.
(2) Long-range hitting now being practicable, it might very well determine the result of an action.
(3) Salvo-firing was the only known method of control at long ranges.
(4) This necessitated a uniform heavy armament of eight or more guns.
(5) The heaviest guns made the most accurate firing with decisive results.

But for the threat of the torpedo and resultant increase in ranges, and the probability that the same conclusions about long-range hitting would be arrived at abroad, it would have been to our advantage *not* to have built the *Dreadnought*. As it was, the possibility that Germany might forestall us with ships able to fight at 10,000 yards built under the guise of conventional design made it impossible for the Admiralty deliberately to continue providing repeats of the *Lord Nelson*. Designed to carry as many armour-piercing guns as possible upon a limited displacement at a time when there were no formulated gunnery objections to heavy and semi-heavy calibres in the same hull, the *Lord Nelson* enjoyed a high appreciation at home and abroad as magnificently fulfilling the requirements of 1903. The absence of secondary guns certainly removed one of the complications experienced in the *King Edwards*, but was *per se* no qualifications for all-big-gun rank—indeed the Japanese retained the 6-in. and 4·7-in. in the battleships *Aki* and *Satsuma* (four 12-in., twelve 10-in.) laid down in May 1905, and in the course of a few years a 6-in. battery was again added to our *Iron Duke* class in keeping with the policy observed abroad when the all-big-gun became generally adopted.

It was the uniform armament of heavy guns in conjunction with high speed which placed the *Dreadnought* in a category by herself as the precursor of a new order in capital ships.

Lt.-Commander William S. Sims, U.S.N., responsible for improvements in gunnery in the American Fleet in the same way that Captain Percy Scott had revolutionized British shooting, had already come to the same conclusion as our own gunnery experts about the necessity for a one-calibre main armament, and his views undoubtedly had considerable influence with Fisher. Early in 1905 Congress had authorized the construction of two battleships, *Michigan* and *South Carolina*, of 16,000 tons carrying eight 12-in. and twenty-two 3-in. guns with 18·5 knots speed; indeed, the Navy Board had tried to get an increase to 19,000 tons and ten 12-in. This *Michigan* design had been worked out in the previous year—a fact quite overlooked by critics of the *Dreadnought* policy—but as the ships were not passed into service until September 1909 the British ship anticipated them by three years.

First proposals show the *Michigan* with twin turrets fore and aft and four singles on the beam, but at an early date the superfiring arrangement was adopted, blast effects being obviated by special screened sights projecting beyond the side walls of the turret in place of sighting hoods on the roof. In order to test the effects of blast conclusive experiments were carried out in which a 12-in. gun mounted in a battleship was fired over a monitor's turret in which observers were stationed. The lattice mast was also only adopted after a trial mast had been subjected to gun fire. (I.N.A. 1911 (2), p. 60.)

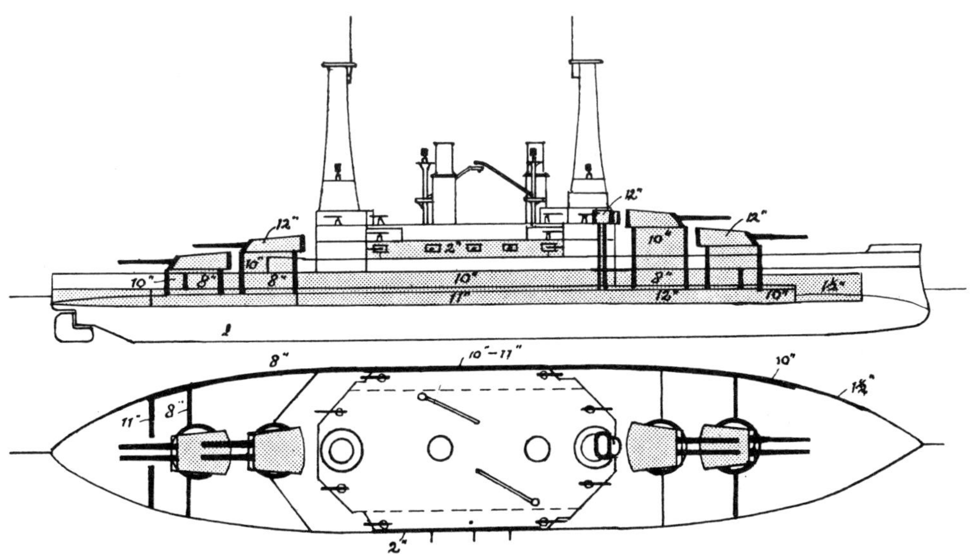

U.S.S. *Michigan*, the first warship to have an all big-gun armament along the centre line with superfiring guns.

The Americans had already experienced the effects of two-elevation firing in the *Oregon*—the double turrets of the *Georgia* and *Kentucky* presented other problems—and were therefore in a good position for testing the necessary remedies; but for a time the *Michigan* and *South Carolina* were classed with these unsatisfactory experimental designs and the significance of their gun disposition made little impression abroad. Any inadequacy of the 3-in. gun against torpedo attack was not accepted; it was still being mounted in destroyers, volume of fire being rated higher than the heavier shell of the 4-in. as in our own Service.

Had we delayed over the *Dreadnought*, the *Michigan* would have produced exactly the same effect upon battleship design when her details became known in 1905, by which time we should have started level with the Germans and without the experience gained through having our trial ship ready in 1906.

In his *Memories* Fisher states that the idea of the *Dreadnought* first came to him in 1900 when C.-in-C. Mediterranean Fleet and that it was developed in association with Mr. W. H. Gard, the Chief Constructor at Malta. When Fisher took over the Portsmouth Command, Gard was Manager of the Constructive Department there, and was kept busy working out various schemes for a battleship Fisher called the *Untakeable* and an armoured cruiser the *Unapproachable*. During the summer of 1902 he was very much influenced by Sir Andrew Noble's arguments in favour of the 10-in. as opposed to the 12-in. gun, mainly on the grounds that so many more could be carried on a given displacement. The *Swiftsure* and *Triumph* had caused considerable controversy, the 10-in. gun being greatly favoured as apparently fulfilling all the requirements for main armament while needing much less displacement to carry it. Sir Andrew submitted a number of designs from Elswick of which the most interesting was one of 17,000 tons carrying eight 10-in. and twenty 6-in. at 20 knots (October 1902), and later when Fisher's conceptions had eliminated the secondary battery a further set were sent in based upon a main armament of 10-in. and an anti-t.b. battery of 4-in. guns. From these was selected a design embodying sixteen 10-in. of a new type which were practically quick-firers, so disposed that ten could be fired ahead, astern, and on each beam. No sketch plan is available of this disposition, but presumably it would follow along Cuniberti lines with three twin turrets amidships.

An appreciation of this design was printed and given a very limited and secret circulation. Captains Madden, Jackson and Bacon all wrote in favour of the 12-in. gun and Fisher regarded Bacon's arguments as unanswerable. He asked Gard to prepare another design with eight 12-in. which he called Design "B," and incorporated Bacon's arguments in a further appreciation which apparently was placed before the Cabinet when he became First Sea Lord in October 1904.

Fisher's presentation of the two types of all-big-gun battleships contained so many novel proposals and demands that it is well worth quoting to some length, if only to preserve his forceful vision and cleverness in stressing as essentials, features which could well be relinquished after they had served as cockshies for the opposition. Much of what follows was lifted bodily from Captain Bacon's case for the 12-in. gunned ship, as "his arguments could not be bettered."

H.M.S. "UNTAKEABLE"

In designing this ship, the most powerful and powerfully arranged armament has been made the first consideration. Absolutely nothing has been allowed to stand in the way of the most nearly perfect power and scope of the guns. Alternative designs (A) and (B) have been prepared. In design (A) the new 10-in. gun has been chosen as, *par excellence*, the weapon to be carried; and barring the small 4-in. guns on the upperworks for use at night in repelling torpedo attacks, no other gun is admitted. By placing these guns in pairs in turrets, sixteen of them are mounted in such a disposition as to command the greatest possible arc of fire with any pair; and to give what is practically a uniform discharge of metal over the whole of the horizon with the large proportion of ten out of the sixteen guns. This is a very important feature of the design, and is regarded as indispensable for a truly effective and economical arrangement of guns, being the only method by means of which the very best results and offensive power can be obtained from a given weight of armament.

In design (B) on the other hand, we have eight 12-in. guns of a *new* type again a uniform armament, with the same distinctive features as to position and command of the guns in design (A); we will carefully review the comparative merits of the two designs.

Design (A)

The arguments for the 10-in. armament are that this gun is the biggest that can be carried in large numbers, that it is a much quicker firer than the 12-in. and therefore makes up in number of hits per minute for the heavier bursting charge of the 12-in. shell, apart from the greater number of guns that can be carried, and that the 10-in. gun is equal to the requirements in the matter of armour perforation and smashing of an enemy; that it is less expensive to mount, and involves the carrying of less and thinner armour; that is to say, we get a larger proportion of offence to defence on a given displacement.

Design (B)

The arguments in favour of the adoption of a uniform armament of 12-in. guns of the new type are as described hereunder; Of the eight guns six will fire in one direction at one time on any bearing from 60° before the beam to 60° abaft the beam, also right ahead and astern, and the following powerful arguments are advanced for the adoption of the six 12-in. guns versus ten 10-in. guns firing in one direction at one time, either of which is possible on the same displacement.

Being a battleship she will have to fight other battleships. Having speed, she can choose the range at which she will fight. This will naturally be a long range, so that gunnery skill can be used to the best advantage. Close ranges level individuality of marksmanship and therefore are to the advantage of the least trained crews.

Another reason which leads to long ranges is the dread of the torpedo, which limits the closeness of approach to 3,000 yards. But in large ships with good-sized turning circles, to ensure not approaching within 3,000 yards, the manœuvring distance will be at least 5,000, otherwise in an unappreciable time the two squadrons get within torpedo range.

Now the result of all long range shooting has gone to prove that if we wish to make good shooting at 6,000 yards and above, the guns must be fired slowly and deliberately, and the shots marked preferably one gun at a time. Hence the use of a larger number of guns disappears but the advantage of a few well-aimed guns with large bursting charge is overwhelming.

Hence speed and a few heavy guns go hand in hand when associated with scientific and practical shooting.

This argument is unanswerable.

The type of ship as previously considered for a uniform armament of sixteen 10-in. guns is in no way altered by this alteration in armament. H.M.S. *Untakeable* is H.M.S. *Untakeable* still, but is a more powerful hitting ship, whereas the other is the more rapid firing ship.

Referring to Sir Andrew Noble's paper, copy attached, and allowing him to be a master of ballistics, and giving all weight to his preference for the sixteen 10-in. guns, yet his knowledge of long range sea shooting is not that of personal experience and this is really the crux of the whole question. It is on the number of hits, not the number of shots fired, that the action depends.

The fast ship with the heavier guns and deliberate fire should absolutely knock out a vessel of equal speed with many lighter guns, the very number of which militates against accurate spotting and deliberate hitting.

The speed of firing at long range is no longer limited by the loading of the gun, but by the limitations imposed to obtain accuracy of fire.

Suppose a 12-in. gun to fire one aimed round each minute. Six guns would allow a deliberately aimed shell with a huge bursting charge every ten seconds.

Fifty per cent. of these should be hits at 6,000 yards.

Three 12-in. shells bursting on board every minute would be HELL!

The most advanced thinkers in the Navy and those having the greatest personal experience of the sea have come to the definite conviction that the battleship is really dead. No one need fight a battleship except with submarine boats or destroyers, and the sole function of battleships in future wars is to be sunk. They can defend nothing day or night with certainty.

But this new battleship now proposed will not only be a battleship but a first class cruiser superior to any but the very latest, hence for years to come she will be useful since whether battleships are or are not used in the future her speed will always make her of the greatest value.

The control of fire is also thought to be much more efficient in the (B) design with the smaller number of redoubts.

(Then follow notes on ammunition supply, hoists etc. The rate of fire of the 10-in. gun was to be 3 or 4 rounds p.m. and of the 12-in. gun nearly 2 rounds p.m.)

It will be seen that no guns are carried on the main deck. In this position they are practically useless. We know this from experience. Half the time they cannot see the object for want of view, and may hit a friend as readily as an enemy, and the other half they are flooded out by the sea. They are masked by the net defence unless this is carried close to the water, cause no end of trouble and expenditure of weight in the side arrangements, and necessitate side armour which might otherwise be dispensed with. In this ship the torpedo net defence will be carried at the height of the upper deck, out of the sea. With the nets at this height *Renown* got her defence out in 35 seconds, so that nothing is lost by the better placing of the net shelf as regards the management of the net defence. Main deck armaments are weighty and useless; highly placed guns which can see the enemy and fight in any weather are what is wanted. Where main deck guns are counted in the power of a design, they are better thrown overboard and the weight they involve turned to some useful purpose.

For ordinary work the midship guns in both designs would not, of course, be fired right ahead and astern, being fitted with stops which, for the time, would limit their use to angles at which they would not come into close proximity with the upper structure of the ship, but all this structure is so built and the conning tower so placed, that they can be used either right ahead or right astern without in any way interfering with other guns, or with other necessary operations or requirements, such as conning the ship, controlling fire, stowing the boats, etc.

(Next follows tables of comparison with foreign contemporaries.)

The quality to which attention has been next directed is *speed*. Apart from armament, this element of the design has been considered of vital importance, and the high rate of 21 knots has been here associated with the great power in guns already described. This speed cannot, of course, be obtained without length, and so we find this ship longer than any battleship hitherto contemplated. She is, however, of light draught and is high forward, so she will possess the most excellent sea keeping qualities. It may be noted her bows are 24½ ft. above water compared with 22 ft. in the *King Edward VII* and 24 ft. in the *Lord Nelson*, so the whole of her armament could be fought without let or hindrance in any weather. This is further secured by the great flare of the bows, and by her being comparatively of great length. . . . Too much attention cannot be directed to this feature of the design, as the arrangement of armament is what enables the speed to be properly utilized. The superiority in speed to be of value must be real. Thus a battleship which has a speed of 21 knots on trial is likely to be at least 3 or 4 knots faster in service than one which makes 18 knots on trial; and this 4 knots is just what is required to establish the supremacy of the fast ship as a fighting machine, the manœuvring powers being pretty nearly equal.

These two essential qualities of an eminently powerful armament and a high speed have been obtained without raising the displacement above that of recent ships; in fact, the total weight of the ship is less than theirs, the limit having been placed at 16,000 tons. This is a very important point, as indicating that the cost of the ship will fall within the bounds commonly recognized for expenditure, and that we are not paying an extravagant price for the purpose of securing unusual results.

Next comes a quality which is of paramount importance in view of the well known high power of the torpedo, and the vulnerability of the underwater portion of any ship to its deadly attack. This is *unsinkability*.

There has probably never been a question that every possible sacrifice should be made in every possible direction in order to prevent the loss of a valuable ship and more valuable lives by a single blow from a torpedo. It is a fact that so long as watertight doors exist in the bulkheads, so long will they be sources of danger and serious risk to the safety of the ship. It follows, therefore, that the only way to avoid this risk is to cut them out at whatever apparent expense to the usual facilities for working the ship. There can be no half-measures in this direction—and therefore no so-called water-tight doors are to be fitted in the transverse bulkheads of this ship. So far as possible, no holes of any kind, whether closed by water-tight covers or filled more or less by pipes, wires, cables, etc., can be allowed to affect this necessity. Facilities in advance of what are usually given will be necessary and can be provided. If the engine-room staff requires to be increased, it must be done. Communications, whether by lifts, telephones, or other improved and up-to-date appliances, can and must be fitted, but not holes in transverse bulkheads—this would be only courting disaster.

Each compartment is self-contained between two transverse bulkheads, with its own ventilation, pumping and drainage, etc. and vertical access. The only possible exception to this rule must be made in favour of the steam pipes, which extend only through the engine and boiler rooms. These cannot yet be dispensed with, but they are high up in the ship and can be shut off at each bulkhead as necessary by valves so that they may be well under control if damaged, but this is not a very probable contingency, so that they should not, if properly fitted, form a sensible menace to the safety of the ship. Arrangements are contemplated whereby each boiler room shall be supplied with feed water and oil fuel without the necessity of passing numerous pipes through the bulkheads.

In this way the ship will be made reasonably safe as possible against torpedo, the only weak point remaining being the magazines, which may conceivably be a source of vital risk if entered by a torpedo. It is contemplated, in order to reduce this risk to a minimum, to afford some protection by means of thick plating of special quality, so that if the torpedo were exploded on contact with the bottom of the ship, the effect would be limited and controlled by the thick inner wall of a magazine. . . . It will be noted that the magazines have been subdivided and placed as far away from the outer bottom as practicable.

Next in order of importance for design purposes comes protection. The system of mounting the guns here adopted originates the redoubts shown on the plans. In design (A) there are eight redoubts all covered with 10-in. armour, and in design (B) four redoubts covered with 12-in. armour—all extending down to the main deck. No armour is placed on the side of the ship above the main deck. It is thought better for many reasons to seat the redoubts in this deck which is 2 inches thick, of special steel, and to armour the side only up to this height. If it were not for the necessity of properly protecting the stability of the ship, it would be preferred to carry the redoubts down to the lower deck—*i.e.* to the height of the top of her belt armour, which in design (A) is 9-in. thick and in design (B) 12 in. But as it is clearly desirable to associate close subdivision with moderately thick armour and two protective decks above the vitals of the ship, the arrangement chosen is considered to be the best possible protection for the ship as a whole.

In design (A) the utmost protection has been given within the limits of the displacement, without diminishing the relative importance of speed and guns; moreover, the chosen position of this element of the design in the scale of value, would render more unnecessary, and it is both sound and serviceable protection. The amount of armour could be increased at the expense of speed and coal endurance, but if these qualities be whittled down, say, to enable thickness of armour on the side to be carried which may be theoretically not perforable by the heaviest guns afloat, the proper balance of the design would be lost, together with the distinctive feature of the ship as able to choose her own position in an action and her power of selection of the mode of attack; in fact, her value as a *fighting* machine would be gone.

In design (B) where the proportion of displacement absorbed by armament is about the same, we are able to provide a somewhat heavier and more extensive defence. In this ship a 12-in. belt has been possible, and this is considered by many to be inseparable from the 12-in. armament, and to represent more nearly a proper relation between offensive and defensive capacities of a design. But in both designs the general arrangement is the same. They are both protected on the same principle, but with different thicknesses of armour, the proportion of armour to weight of armament being not greater in the (B) design with 12-in. guns than in the (A) with 10-in. which may perhaps be considered to be just as it should be.

(Next follows a description of the coal supply and endurance.)

A very essential and substantial advantage that would accrue from the use of oil fuel would be the possibility of dispensing with watertight doors in the coal bunker bulkheads. These doors must always, in a coal-burning ship, be a source of great anxiety. They cannot be dispensed with, and they prevent the inner skin, the present coal bunker bulkheads, being made absolutely watertight, as they must always be open when burning coal. The greater the amount of oil carried, the smaller this risk by penetration of the outer skin becomes. Although it would take a sensible time to change from oil to coal, or *vice versa*, for feeding the fires, the necessity for this change in a ship carrying both kinds of fuel diminishes as the amount of oil carried is increased as compared with the amount of coal.

If we could use the coal only when making passages, and the oil when in the neighbourhood of an enemy, we should have done the best possible for the safety of the ship so long as we are bound to carry both fuels. And until a certain prospect of a constant oil supply for our fleets is provided, we shall never be able to make the inner skin absolutely watertight. We can use oil ships instead of colliers directly a constant source of oil is secured; and get rid of a lot of water-tight doors which we cannot dispense with so long as we burn coal, to say nothing of the weight saved by the reduction of complement due to cutting down of the stokehold party by two-thirds.

Conning Facilities

A conning tower of 12-in. steel is provided forward, and the arrangement is somewhat novel. Under the conning tower is the signal house and over it the forward fire control position. It is thus most conveniently situated with reference to the management of the guns in action, and is immediately over the main steering position below, pretty much as in the most recent battleships. This disposition enables the utmost simplicity to be obtained in the communications essential to the working of the ship from the conning tower, and no other conning tower is provided.

The lower part of the foremast forms the centre of the various stations, and enables them to be well supported and firmly knit together; and in addition is fitted with a ladder way for easy communication between them. The lower part of the foremast is 6-in. thick above the main deck and 2-in. thick below it. In this lower portion will be the latest improved arrangements of telephones and telegraph instruments with communications to the guns of each redoubt and to the fire-control stations.

A torpedo director tower will also be fitted on the after shelter. No conning position or tower, nor any navigation bridge or appliances are provided aft. They are quite superfluous and obsolete.

(Next follows Ventilation, of which there is to be a separate system for each main compartment. Drainage and pumping are similarly confined.)

Boats

The usual complement of boats is contemplated, but for the heavy boats cranes of a special type as fitted in the "Vulcan" and "Triumph" classes have been necessary, but lighter and less cumbersome.

It is undesirable to provide for such heavy boats as are at present carried in H.M. ships. For 10 or 12 tons we ought to get a good serviceable steamboat, and it is quite possible to do this if we give up the idea of its being a torpedo boat or carrying a comparatively heavy armament. The German and French navies carry much lighter boats than ours, and there is no known disadvantage in using such boats which are as handy, seaworthy and generally useful in all weathers as our heavier boats, and the lighter boat is of immense value in simplifying the lifting appliances to be fitted for handling them . . . two steam boats of 35 ft. in length and of light build will be carried in the designs presented.

The crane may not work in so well in the battleship design (B) with 12-in. guns, as it must be a single one placed in the middle line and of unusual dimensions and weight, but a preferable device may be found in a modified derrick system as indicated in the drawing.

Protection Generally

The armour at the belt at the water-line from redoubt to redoubt will be 9 in. thick in the (A) design and 12 in. thick in (B) design, tapering in both cases to 2 in. at the stem and stern,

The strake above this, rising to the main deck, will be 7 in. thick in the (A) design, this being also the thickness of the bulkheads. This 7 in. will be thickened up to 10 in. abreast the redoubts, which are also covered with 10-in. armour. In the (B) design the corresponding thicknesses will be 12 in. for the belt, and 9 in. on the upper strake and bulkheads, the redoubts being covered with 12-in. armour. Weight has been allowed for 2-in. special steel on the inner bottom in wake of the magazines to form protection against the explosion of a torpedo; but when the efficiency of this method of protection comes to be seriously considered and proper statistics become available, it may be necessary to modify this amount of protection, which is purely provisional.

Tha main deck in both designs will be of protective plating from the fore end to the after redoubt. Between redoubts it will be in two thicknesses each of 1-in. special steel. Before the forward redoubt it will be of two thicknesses each of ¾-in. plates. The lower protective deck from the fore end to the after redoubt will be in two thicknesses each ½-in. special steel, and abaft the after redoubt in two thicknesses each of 1 in. The conning tower is of 12-in. armour with a 6-in. communication tube.

(Description of armoured shutters, gratings and hatches.)

The ram has been given up. It was all very well when we were contemplating it as a valuable means of attack and ships were short, but it is not required in long, fast ships which under modern conditions will fight at long range. It is only extra length, which will make it more difficult to dock a ship, and more of a peril to friends in peace time than of any probable use in war. The stem of the projected ship is quite powerful enough to inflict damage if any occasion should arise for use of it on an enemy, and it is not advisable to carry about the useless weight of a weapon never likely to be wanted.

(Thirty Yarrow boilers working at 275 lb. pressure were to supply steam to triple expansion engines turning twin screws. The collective h.p. was to be 30,000 and revolutions 120 p.m.)

Unfortunately the sketch plans for these designs were not preserved, neither is there any record of the way in which the eight 12-in. gunned ship developed into the ten-gun and twelve-gun editions of the U.S. *Michigan* type with centre-line turrets. After becoming First Sea Lord (21 October 1904) Fisher had Constructor Gard transferred to Whitehall with the rank of Assistant Director of Naval Construction in order to supervise production of the finished drawings and calculations from his preliminary drafts.

The problem now was to get such radical departures from conventional design accepted by the Service with as little controversy as possible. Knowing full well that the fundamental reasons for the All-Big-Gun ship could not be divulged without giving away vital information, Fisher elected to make the change behind a barrier of secrecy and cloak his personal responsibility for the new types of warships he had decided to build by appointing a Committee on Designs composed of the most able naval officers and distinguished shipbuilders and scientists which would give an authority beyond reasonable cavil to any decisions arrived at. Their duties were to be of a deliberative and advisory nature only, but covered disposition of armament, fire control, protection, safety against under-water injury, torpedo nets, machinery, fuel, boat stowage, accommodation and communications.

The Board had already decided that new types of battleship, armoured cruiser, destroyer, torpedo boat and submarine were necessary and agreed as to their principal features. Thus, the Committee was not required to follow in the footsteps of the one appointed in 1870, but only to render assistance in consideration of details in design without in any way lessening the responsibility of the D.N.C. for fulfilling the Board's requirements.

Actually its labours more than justified Fisher's perspicacity, both as regards the design finally selected for the *Dreadnought* and the influence it exerted over national opinion when the new policy was assailed by a storm of criticism from those who believed that we had hazarded naval superiority by taking an unnecessary initiative in building her.

COMMITTEE ON DESIGNS, 1904

This Committee was appointed on 22 December 1904 and included:

Rear-Admiral Prince Louis of Battenberg	Director of Naval Intelligence.
Eng. Rear-Admiral Sir John Durston	Engineer-in-Chief of the Fleet.
Rear-Admiral A. L. Winslow	C.O. Torpedo and Submarine Flotillas.
Captain Henry B. Jackson	Controller.
Captain John R. Jellicoe	Director of Naval Ordnance.
Captain Charles E. Madden	Naval Assistant to Controller.
Captain R. H. S. Bacon	Naval Assistant to First Sea Lord.

Civilian Members

Philip Watts	Director of Naval Construction.
Lord Kelvin	
Professor J. H. Biles	Glasgow University.
Sir John Thornycroft	
Alexander Gracie	Fairfield Shipbuilding Co.
R. E. Froude	Superintendent Admiralty Experimental Works.
W. H. Gard	Chief Constructor Portsmouth Dockyard.
Commander Wilfred Henderson	Secretary to the Committee.
E. H. Mitchell (Assistant Constructor)	Assistant Secretary.

Constructor J. H. Narbeth acted as secretary to the D.N.C. and was responsible for working out details of the various designs considered.

The following instructions were to be observed in considering the features of the battleship and armoured cruiser designs.

(1) *Battleship*

Speed: 21 knots.
Armament: 12-in. guns and anti-torpedo-craft guns. Nothing between. 12-in. guns to be as numerous as possible. No guns on main deck, except a-t-c guns if necessary to place them there.
Armour to be adequate.
Must be capable of using docking accommodation at Portsmouth, Devonport, Malta and Gibraltar.

(2) *Armoured Cruiser*

Speed: 25 knots.
Armament: 12-in. guns and a-t-c guns. Nothing between. 12-in. guns to be as numerous only as is consistent with the above speed and reasonable proportions.
Armour: To be on similar scale to "Minotaur" class.
Docking facilities to be carefully observed.

Fisher was not a member of the Committee, but acted as chairman. The first meeting was on 3 January 1905 at the Admiralty, when the Fisher-Gard designs "E" and "F" came up for consideration. In the Report these are described as having been prepared chiefly in accordance with the strong recommendation of Admiral Sir Arthur Wilson, whose opinion had been asked for by the Board. Wilson had pointed out that the unfailing outcome of all fleet manœuvring in an action is that it becomes a *broadside* action; and that therfore the acme of battleship design would be one in which all guns fired on either broadside. Note that there was never any suggestion as to the real origin of "E" and "F," and this example of agile diplomacy representing Admiral Wilson as a strong advocate of all-centre-line turrets was typical of Fisher's methods in submerging his own personality and fathering his projects on to someone who had been persuaded into an expression of approval for them. Fisher evidently sponsored the superfiring gun designs with the idea that they would provide a maximum *axial* fire, being a strong advocate of this form of attack. In his *Memories* (p. 121) he states:

> "I am an apostle of 'End-on-Fire,' for to my mind broadside fire is peculiarly stupid. To be obliged to delay your pursuit by turning even one atom from your straight course on to a flying enemy is to me to be the acme of an ass."

He was therefore prepared to let "E" and "F" go forward as broadside designs, preferring to withhold his own opinion on their possibilities for concentrated axial fire.

Unfortunately the Committee fell foul of superfiring guns on the grounds of blast effects, and recorded the opinion that immunity from this could only be expected when training was within about 30° of the beam. Outside these beam limits it would only be possible to fight the end guns along the axis, so that right ahead and astern they would be no better off than the standard battleship.

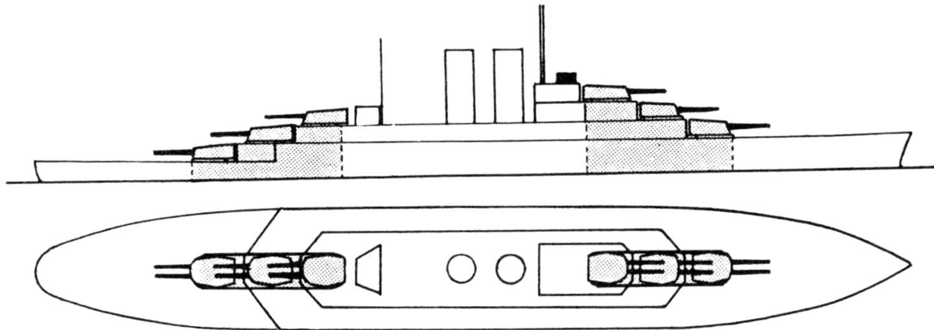

Fisher-Gard design 1. Battleship "E" reciprocating engines. $550 \times 85 \times 26\frac{3}{4}$ ft. = 21,000 tons. Twelve 12-in. 21 knots.

The design was considered unsatisfactory on these grounds, although it had been specifically drawn up to meet the requirements of *broadside* action. Incidentally, when referred to the Construction Department for check and examination it was found that the assistant officer had omitted certain weights in his calculations so that the displacement was insufficient to carry the weights proposed to the extent of 3,000 tons; also that the freeboard with only a proportion of coal aboard was but 18 ft. and quite inadequate for 21 knots.

The second design "F" was devised to reduce displacement and cost. But as the advantage of concentrating as much offensive power as possible in one unit had been insisted upon, the ten-gun design demanding 1,900 tons per gun was not so economical as the twelve-gun one requiring only 1,750 tons. Two turrets were carried forward and three aft—on a displacement of 19,000 tons.

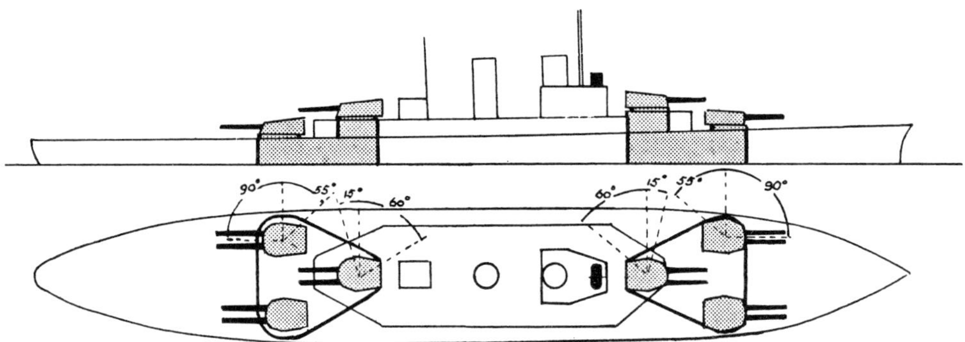

Battleship "D" reciprocating. $520 \times 84 \times 27\frac{1}{4}$ ft. = 19,000 tons. Twelve 12-in. 21 knots.

What was considered to be another serious disadvantage of both "E" and "F" was the large target presented by the turret groups at each end. Although at long range the turret and redoubt armour would be impenetrable, it was considered that with such good targets the chances of heavy shell bursting in close proximity to sighting hoods and gun ports would be so largely increased that damage to gun layers, sights, and even to the gun chases themselves would be invited rather than avoided by this disposition.

At the first two meetings Watts suggested the desirability of reverting to the *Lord Nelson* type with increased armament. He would have preferred four 12-in. and eighteen 9·2-in. guns, with three 9·2-in. placed in casemates beneath the muzzles of the fore and after 12-in. turrets and three pairs on each broadside; or, as an alternative, four 12-in. and sixteen 9·2-in. in four pairs abeam. But in the face of the Board instructions such alternatives found no support.

At subsequent meetings design "G" was turned down through objections to abreast turrets on the grounds of blast and sea-going qualities, although schematically providing good concentration axially and abeam. In all these three designs the group of turrets had a single redoubt in which there was no armoured subdivision between the barbette bases, so that one perforation might put all six guns out of action: and the impenetrability provided by maximum ranges was not always to be expected under average North Sea conditions.

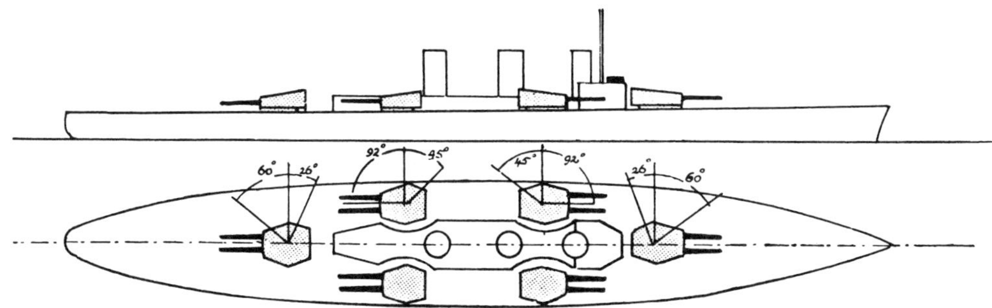

Battleship "G" reciprocating. 550×85×27 ft.=21,000 tons. Twelve 12-in. 21 knots.

Battleship design "D" carried the same armament as in those first considered but on 2,000 tons less displacement, and was generally acceptable apart from rather limited freeboard.

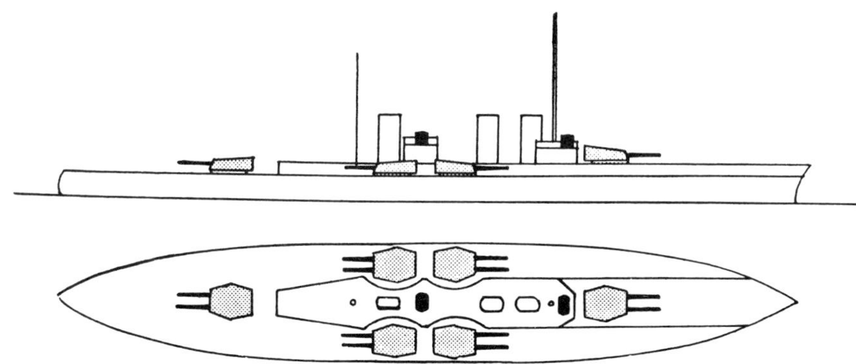

Battleship D.1 500×84×$27\frac{1}{4}$ ft.=18,500 tons. Twelve 12-in. 21 knots. Turbines.

As an alternative "D.1" showed a higher forecastle although having the beam turrets grouped closer amidships with magazines and shell-rooms adjoining. This arrangement allowed for some 500 tons being saved, but again blast considerations decided against it.

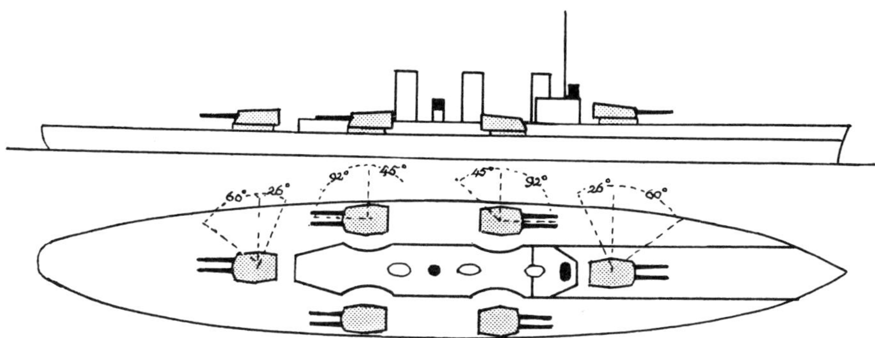

Battleship D.2. Similar to D.1 but with amidship turrets more widely spaced.

Attention was next directed to "D.2" with a forecastle and widely separated beam turrets, the arcs of training being as in "D" with the same armament. But the blast curves showed that the only arrangement giving better results—proposed by Prince Louis—was the substitution of a single turret amidships for the after beam turrets, broadside fire being then increased to a maximum. A further design "H" was therefore called for incorporating this change, which was accepted by the Committee on 13 January 1905 as a basis upon which the battleship should be worked out in detail.

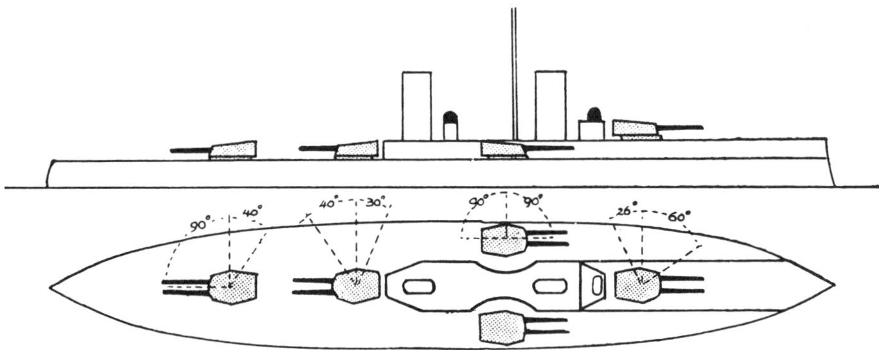

Battleship "H" with the accepted gun arrangement. 490 × 83 × 26½ ft. = 17,850 tons. Ten 12-in. 21 knots. Turbines.

The major features of the design were discussed in detail and the following decisions made:

MACHINERY

Owing to the inherent defects of reciprocating engines the effective speed of the Fleet was no more than 14 knots; and no fleet in the world could steam for eight hours at full power without ships breaking down. Fisher realized that only by a complete change-over to Parsons turbines could full steaming efficiency be assured, and their advantages were vividly described by Admiral Bacon in stressing the First Sea Lord's greatness in determination to get them installed in the *Dreadnought* (*Lord Fisher*, vol. 1. p. 263).

> "When steaming at full speed in a man-of-war fitted with reciprocating engines, the engine-room was always a glorified snipe-marsh; water lay on the floor plates and was splashed about everywhere; the officers often were clad in oilskins to avoid being wetted to the skin. The water was necessary to keep the bearings cool. Further, the noise was deafening; so much so that telephones were useless and even voice-pipes of doubtful value. In the *Dreadnought*, when steaming at full speed, it was only possible to tell that the engines were working, and not stopped, by looking at certain gauges. The whole engine-room was as clean and dry as if the ship was lying at anchor, and not the faintest hum could be heard."

Only two or three destroyers had so far been fitted experimentally with turbines, and the small cruiser *Amethyst* (14,000 h.p.) was still under construction when the Design Committee met. The naval members questioned the stopping and turning powers compared with reciprocating machinery, but Sir Charles Parsons was able to give assurances for a satisfactory power plant to meet all Service requirements. Four shafts were to be fitted, the inner ones being brought up close to the twin rudders so as to obtain plenty of work upon them. By thus adopting turbine engines there was a saving in weight of 1,000 tons and £100,000 in cost, and they were almost as much an epoch-making feature of the ship as were the big guns.

MAST

The control position was to be high up at the mast head above the fore funnel, and vibration reduced to a minimum. A mast of some light girder construction capable of standing without stays was considered, and nine alternative types with gallows or cranes for boat work submitted; of these the heavy tripod was accepted as being safe, rigid and strong.

BULKHEADS

Were to be solid without doors or perforations except for steam and hydraulic system pipes and electric leads.

ANTI-TORPEDO GUNS

Twenty of the new 18 cwt. 12-pdrs. were considered to be more effective than the equivalent fourteen 4-in. Q.F., and these were to be mounted on turret tops and superstructure.

SHELL-ROOM PROTECTION

As the shell rooms could not be placed more than 15 ft. from the ship's sides it was decided to allow weight for 2 in.-2½ in. protection to magazines and shell rooms by reducing elsewhere. (To this end the redoubts 12 in.-10 in. were made 11 in.-8 in.; turrets 12 in. reduced to 11 in.; fore c.t. 12 in. reduced to 11 in.) Also by omitting the thick slopes of the protective deck in the wake of the magazines, it was possible to fit a torpedo bulkhead as in the Russian *Tzarevitch* as under. (This ship had been struck many times by Japanese Whitehead torpedoes, but without serious results, and was brought into harbour and repaired.) The proposal to reduce the turret armour came from Captain Jellicoe, who pointed out that although 12-in. steel might be impenetrable at usual "action" ranges, no recent tests had been carried out to show whether the mechanism of the turret would stand the shock of a direct hit—which might put it temporarily out of action.

BOW SHAPE

It will be noticed that all the sketch plans considered had a clipper bow except "H," which showed the ordinary ram shape. Lord Fisher had wished a return to the long ram bow of the old paddler *Helicon* for the sake of appearances. As this "ram" was only incorporated in the *Helicon* to supply extra buoyancy forward and was both weak and wet, it could serve no useful purpose in the new ship. Instead a broad plough underwater snout was substituted as a placebo to the chairman and served as a model for many years.

POLICY

(1) To complete all ships building, as the *Lord Nelson* and *Agamemnon* were too advanced for 12-in. to be substituted for the 9·2-in.

(2) The *Dreadnought* to be laid down as soon as possible and completed in a year; trials were to be concluded without delay to afford experience for further ships.

(3) No new battleships to be ordered until these trials were completed.

Chapter 81

"DREADNOUGHT"

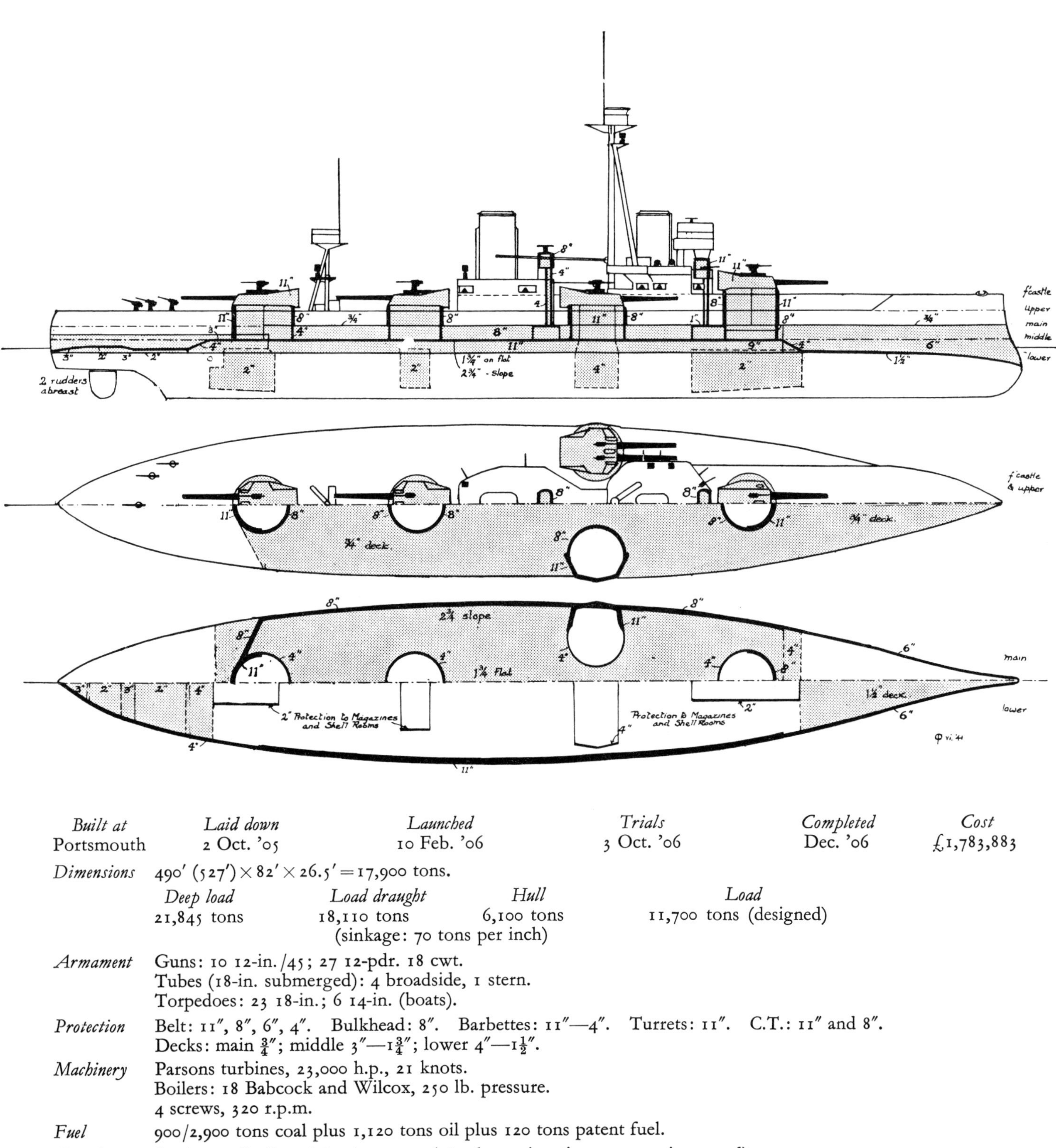

Built at	*Laid down*	*Launched*	*Trials*	*Completed*	*Cost*
Portsmouth	2 Oct. '05	10 Feb. '06	3 Oct. '06	Dec. '06	£1,783,883

Dimensions 490′ (527′) × 82′ × 26.5′ = 17,900 tons.

Deep load	*Load draught*	*Hull*	*Load*
21,845 tons	18,110 tons (sinkage: 70 tons per inch)	6,100 tons	11,700 tons (designed)

Armament Guns: 10 12-in./45; 27 12-pdr. 18 cwt.
Tubes (18-in. submerged): 4 broadside, 1 stern.
Torpedoes: 23 18-in.; 6 14-in. (boats).

Protection Belt: 11″, 8″, 6″, 4″. Bulkhead: 8″. Barbettes: 11″—4″. Turrets: 11″. C.T.: 11″ and 8″.
Decks: main $\frac{3}{4}$″; middle 3″—1$\frac{3}{4}$″; lower 4″—1$\frac{1}{2}$″.

Machinery Parsons turbines, 23,000 h.p., 21 knots.
Boilers: 18 Babcock and Wilcox, 250 lb. pressure.
4 screws, 320 r.p.m.

Fuel 900/2,900 tons coal plus 1,120 tons oil plus 120 tons patent fuel.

Complement 695/773. Radius; 6,620/10: 4,910/18.4 knots (continuous seagoing speed).

Constructor J. H. Narbeth.

POINTS OF INTEREST

(1) Introduced all-big-gun armament for long-range firing.
(2) First large warship to have turbines.
(3) First British battleship to steam at 21 knots.
(4) Officers berthed forward, men aft.
(5) Built in a year and a day.

In designing the *Dreadnought* extraordinary steps were taken to ensure that she should embody all requirements on the smallest dimensions and at the lowest cost, so that the anticipated opposition should not be founded on her excessive size and expense. In every way she proved an epoch-making warship. Brilliant in conception: the cynosure of naval interest during construction and of controversy afterwards: a magnificent success in every way structurally and mechanically: and the finest looking fighting ship of her day. Her detailed design was entrusted to Constructor J. H. Narbeth who drafted a set of lines specially calculated to carry the required displacement on the dimensions provisionally arrived at and requiring the smallest h.p. practicable for 21 knots. When the model was tried in the Haslar Tank it was found that 23,000 h.p. would suffice for this speed whereas Mr. R. E. Froude's best estimate made on previous forms of equal fullness required 28,000 h.p. Mr. Froude refused to accept this result and had the

The *Dreadnought* leaving Portsmouth in April 1907 as flagship of the Home Fleet after her course of sea and gunnery trials in the West Indies.

model destroyed as misleading. A second shared the same fate, and only when the seventh model was run and confirmed the earlier results did he feel safe in sending the usual E.H.P. curves to the Admiralty (*I.N.A. Trans.*, 1940, p. 148).

Although of extra strong construction to withstand the effects of salvo firing, the hull was actually of the same weight as that of the *Jupiter* (6,100 tons); the saving of 5,000 h.p. meant one row of boilers less and 25 ft. off the length. In order to get her built in record time considerable numbers of plates were ordered to standard sizes of the thicknesses required so as to avoid the usual labour and waste of time in cutting and sorting plates, and an ample supply of materials was maintained well in advance of the work in hand. In the Yard it was said that the ship was very largely built from the mould loft where Mr. J. R. Bond was responsible for the laying-off and preparation of detail drawings which contributed largely to her rapid, economical and efficient construction. It will be noticed that her load displacement was really 18,110 tons, or 210 tons in excess of the nominal Navy List figures.

HULL

A feature of the hull was the long forecastle giving a 28 ft. freeboard at the bow, 19 ft. amidships and 20½ ft. aft, the flare being continued as far aft as possible only reaching the upright amidships, where an almost rectangular section offered great resistance to rolling. Special attention was directed towards strengthening the forecastle deck and sides to withstand blast from the foremost and wing turret guns. The original order for a circular bulkhead beneath the arc traversed by the foremost gun muzzles was withdrawn, as it was considered that the deck would be beaten down on each side of it. Instead the deck was given a certain amount of elasticity with longitudinal girders well pillared at selected points, coupled with steel plating fitted on the upper side of the wood deck.

When it came to firing eight 12-in. on the broadside the most exacting moment of the trials had arrived, and one of the Constructors writes:

> "As to the result of this broadside, Sir Philip was a sceptic—that is, he was a little more than an agnostic. I well remember when we reached this point of the programme Sir Philip took me by the arm and led me along the upper deck forward on the port side and then below where we could look in and see the main deck. He selected a position on the port side of the forward barbette (the guns fired to starboard). He looked very grave and serious and I am quite sure that he fully expected the decks to come down wholesale. Presently there was a muffled roar and a bit of a kick on the ship. The eight guns had been fired and scores of men between decks had no idea what had happened."

Many great improvements were embodied in the hull especially as regards the water-tight subdivision. As the whole of the bottoms under the machinery spaces were to be used for oil fuel, the minute subdivision of the double bottom was dispensed with, thus saving considerable weight and cost in the matter of filling, pumping and ventilating arrangements and the means of access for cleansing the tanks. The structure of the ship was greatly simplified and water-tight doors generally abolished, the hull being built in large sections bounded by unperforated water-tight bulkheads with independent pumping, drainage and ventilating systems for each main compartment—which meant the abolition of the customary main drain running from end to end of the ship. Pumps were driven electrically instead of by steam, and allowed for the anchor cables being washed down as they came through the hawse pipes and so passed into the lockers in a clean condition instead of bringing a lot of filth aboard.

In place of w.t. doors electric passenger lifts were fitted in all the machinery compartments to facilitate communication.

The safety of the magazines was greatly enhanced by the gun disposition which allowed for their being placed in the middle line instead of along the sides as in the *Lord Nelson.*

ARMAMENT

In order to get the ship finished in twelve months the 12-in. guns for the *Lord Nelson* and *Agamemnon* with spares were appropriated, the armament weight including turrets and turn-tables being 3,100 tons—actually 10 tons less than in the *Lord Nelson.* A considerable saving in weight was effected by a new Admiralty design for the gun mountings worked out in detail by Vickers and followed by Armstrongs which allowed for the outside barbette diameter to be reduced from 34 ft. to 29 ft. This permitted of drastic reductions in weight for turn-tables and their supports, framing and plating of barbettes, and still more in the barbette armour. The system of construction of the circular bulkheads carrying the roller paths for the gun mountings was entirely novel and proved a complete success.

The turret disposition, allowing for eight guns on either broadside and four or possibly six to be fired ahead or astern, was never copied abroad, the German *Nassau* and Japanese *Kawachi* both showing the discarded "D" arrangement of twelve guns plus a main deck 6-in. battery—the retention of the after wing turrets marking a poor appreciation of economy in design. The gun heights above L.W.L. were 31½ ft. forward and 22½ ft. amidships and 23 ft. aft.

Of the twenty-seven 12-pdrs., twelve were in the superstructures two on each turret top, and five on the quarter deck; the original arrangement with four on the forecastle and one on the fore turret lasted only a short time. At a later date she carried four 12-pdr. A.A. and twenty of the 18-cwt guns. The forward and after guns were on disappearing mountings.

The general distribution was made as wide as possible to avoid one or two shells putting a whole battery out of action and on the principle that a gun in the open is safer than one firing behind thin plating.

PROTECTION

In the terms of reference to the design, armour was required to be "adequate"—which had to be interpreted in terms of what was possible after the claims of gun-power and high speed had been satisfied. It was the general feeling of the Committee that attention should be concentrated on obtaining the highest offensive power and that such reasonable thickness of armour should be accepted as would keep the general dimensions within moderate limits.

Although 5,000 tons of armour was carried—800 tons more than in the *Lord Nelson*—the 250 tons devoted to special magazine protection meant a general reduction of 1 in. on turrets and belt. Also the great length over the barbettes and of the protective decks "precluded a third strake along the upper deck side, which was not a vital target." Mr. Narbeth assures us that there was no question of protection being cut down to reduce displacement, and that the change from the more extensive distribution in the previous ships was accepted by the officers responsible without demur, in the same way that the massive plating of the *Trafalgar* was reduced in the *Royal Sovereign* without the general harmony of the design being affected (I.N.A. *Three Steps in Naval Construction*, 1922).

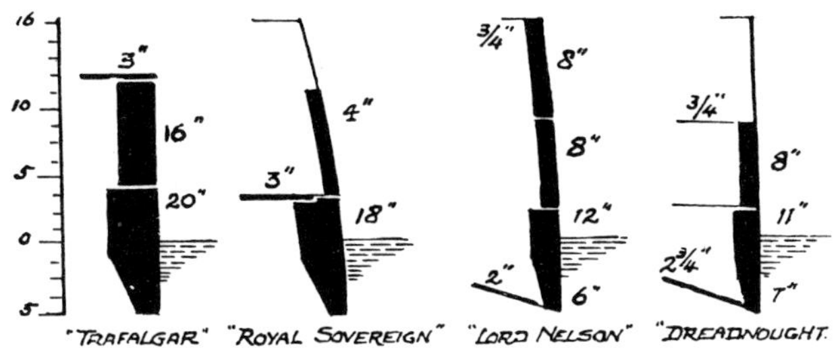

Under the gunnery conditions which obtained in 1905 the need for armour along the upper deck side was not so insistent as it became when longer ranges and dropping hits increased the risks of more vertical penetration; but as such additional protection could not have been worked in without a very considerable increase in displacement which would have militated against the *Dreadnought* being presented as a comparatively economical type of ship—its omission was accepted as a weak point in both her design and the succeeding classes until 1909 when upper deck side armour was again fitted.

In arranging distribution there was strong insistence on the great advantages of side armour being extended throughout the length with condemnation of "soft ends," so that the 8-in. and 11-in. strakes amidships were prolonged as 6 in. to the bows and 4 in. along the water-line aft. In the *Lord Nelson* with her fuller lines the 6-in. bow armour could be justified; with the *Dreadnought's* finer lines and reduced buoyancy up forward penetration would not have been so serious, and some of her critics contended that thinner plating should have sufficed, the weight being applied to better use elsewhere. It will be seen that in subsequent designs this bow armour was grea ly reduced.

The barbettes carried 11 in. on the outer faces with 8 in. on the less exposed perimeter, except the fourth position which was 8 in. only; all thinned to 4 in. below the main deck where side armour gave additional protection against direct hits.

As already noted the turrets were reduced to 11 in. with 3-in. to 4-in. roofs. Between the barbettes the upper armour deck was the usual $\frac{3}{4}$ in.; below, the water-line deck showed an extra $\frac{3}{4}$ in., being $1\frac{3}{4}$ in. on the flat and $2\frac{3}{4}$ in. on the slopes with 3 in. at the stern.

Special protection to the magazines was afforded by 2-in. side screens below water, increased to 4 in. for the wing positions.

For the past ten years or so the standard nominal coal supply in battleships had been about 900 tons and 1,900 to 2,200 tons with full bunkers, giving a sinkage in passing from load to deep load of about 2 feet. But in the *Dreadnought* although the legend supply remained at 900 tons a much greater bunker load had to be carried in order to sustain full speed for long stretches, so that at full capacity her fuel supply was 2,900 tons of coal, 1,120 oil and 120 tons patent fuel (used for protection). When full stores and water were added the deep load displacement rose to 21,845 tons changing the draught from $26\frac{1}{2}$ ft. to 31 ft. $1\frac{1}{2}$ in. (Sir William White stated that the ship could be seen drawing $31\frac{1}{2}$ ft.) As the side armour extended to a height of only 8 ft. 4 in. above water this meant that at deep load the 11-in. belt would be submerged with flotation dependent upon 8-in. plating only 4 ft. in height—or less. Above this the side was unarmoured and exposed to shell fire with grave risks of water accumulation above the $\frac{3}{4}$-in. deck if the hull was holed in a seaway, increasing consequent loss of buoyancy and stability with possibly disastrous results although the armoured side might remain intact.

This abnormal submergence of the belt at full load was a weak feature in all the subsequent 12-in. gunned battleships and battle cruisers as during the War they put to sea full of fuel. If an action had been fought soon after leaving harbour they would have been at grave disadvantage; but as it was usual for much fuel to be expended in high-speed steaming before action could be joined, their water-line protection consistently improved as bunkers were depleted.

UNDERWATER PROTECTION

In the *Dreadnought* and all subsequent battleships and battle cruisers special attention was paid to protection against underwater attack, the ships being designed to be safe against the explosion of two torpedoes in any position. The main bulkheads being unpierced by watertight doors to a height of 9 ft. above the water-line, sufficient stability was provided to ensure against capsizing from loss of stability due to flooding of compartments from below the armour deck. Such stability entailed a large metacentric height and a tendency to roll quickly

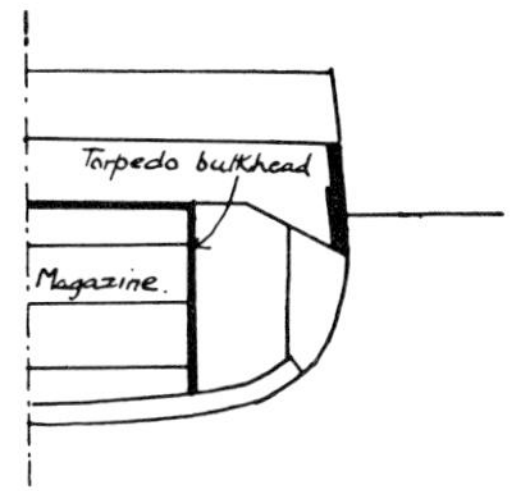

even with large bilge keels, but this had to be accepted as necessary for safety. The question of fitting anti-rolling tanks in the *Dreadnought* was considered, but the resulting increase in size could not be allowed—which was just as well in view of the unfavourable results in the *Inflexible* and *Colossus*.

LISTS OF WEIGHTS FOR TYPICAL SHIPS

	Majestic	*Formidable*	*King Edward VII*	*Lord Nelson*	*Dreadnought*
Water for 10 days	60	75	75	67	60
Provisions for 4 weeks	40	40	45	44	40
Officers' stores	55	55	55	45	42
Officers, men and effects	95	96	95	95	82
Masts, yards and tops	97	95	90	105	113
Cables and anchors	134	137	135	112	115
Boats	66	72	65	52	48
Warrant Officers' stores	90	90	80	90	90
Torpedo net defence	33	50	50	40	60
Total general equipment	670	710	690	650	650
ARMAMENT (including turn-tables and turrets)	1,580	1,730	2,575	3,110	3,100
PROPELLING AND AUXILIARY MACHINERY	1,320	1,415	1,800	1,660	1,990
Engineer's stores	45	60	60	60	60
COALS	900	900	950	900	900
Total	4,515	4,815	6,075	6,380	6,700
ARMOUR AND BACKING:					
Vertical, on sides and citadel	1,420	1,265	1,530	2,000	1,940
Plating on sides		175			
Protection to Magazines					250
Decks and gratings	1,200	1,240	1,060	1,170	1,350
Backing	140	85	85	120	100
Barbettes	1,210	1,035	825	800	1,260
Casemates	480	425	585	—	—
Conning-tower	85	110	90	110	100
Total armour	4,535	4,335	4,175	4,200	5,000
Total load	9,050	9,150	10,250	10,580	11,700
Hull	5,650	5,650	5,900	5,720	6,100
Total weight required	14,700	14,800	16,150	16,300	17,800
Board margin or displacement weight	200	200	200	200	100
Total displacement required	14,900	15,000	16,350	16,500	17,900

MACHINERY

Up to now the advantage of high speed for obtaining strategic advantage and also in enabling battle squadrons to choose the fighting range had not been recognized as a prime factor in capital ship design. In the *Dreadnought* Fisher's views found full expression and he had decided on turbine machinery to achieve it, confident that the results in liners and cross-channel steamers could be accepted as a basis for naval requirements. Parsons engines resulted in a saving in weight and reduction in the number of working parts with much reduced liability to breakdown; smooth working with ease in manipulation; saving in coal consumption at high speed and hence in boiler space and engine-room complement; and better protection through the machinery being placed lower in the hull. All these advantages laid most of the former bogies of engine-room equipment and working.

The one anticipated difficulty in providing sufficient power for stopping and quick manœuvre was met by placing astern turbines on all four shafts with one high and one low pressure astern turbine on each side. Thus all four shafts could be used economically when going astern with the proportionately greater power shown to be necessary in the trials of the cruiser *Amethyst* and destroyer *Eden*. Full power of 23,000 h.p. was developed at 320 revs., the trial figures being 26,350 h.p. with 21·6 knots at 328 revs., which was much faster than previous reciprocating machinery. Propellers for turbines have to be of comparatively small diameter to avoid excessive velocity at the tips.

Remarkable economy in weight resulted from the new system. Propelling and auxiliary machinery weighed only 1,990 tons—190 tons more than in the *King Edward* for an additional 5,000 nominal h.p. and 7,500 h.p. maximum. The reliability of turbines was demonstrated during the *Dreadnought's* return trip from the West Indies (7,000 miles) after a month's steaming and calibrating trials when she maintained an average of 17½ knots without any machinery defects. Compare this with the Second Cruiser Squadron's run from New York to Gibraltar in November 1905 when out of six ships only the *Drake*, *Berwick* and *Cumberland* got across at 18½ knots, finishing up with empty bunkers and requiring extensive repairs to their engines.

SEA-KEEPING QUALITIES

Although having a metacentric height of 5·07 compared with 3·42 in the *Lord Nelson*, her period for the double roll was only 13½ secs. compared with 15 secs., with a much diminished inclination due to the very square form of her section. On one occasion during her trials, when running across waves about 500 ft. long and 15 ft. high at 19 knots, the green seas came up a few feet above the stem head and when the crest had passed, exposed her forefoot for 20 or 30 ft. along the keel, but left the ship perfectly dry and steady.

At full load the metacentric height increased to 6·7 with an angle of maximum stability of 32°, vanishing at 72°. She was therefore considerably "stiffer" in this condition with a short period for the double roll and a quicker motion.

In view of the great length of the ship, the usual position of the Admiral's and Captain's quarters right aft was regarded as likely to be open to objection owing to delay in reaching the bridge and conning tower. By reversal of the time-honoured arrangement the officers were berthed forward and the men aft, so that the once sacred quarter deck became a promenade for the ship's company. Needless to say the men firmly believed that the change had been made because the vibration from the new machinery would be too much for the comfort of the officers, whereas the long-suffering British tar could be expected to stand anything. As it was, the officers had to put up with the inherent drawbacks of a forecastle at sea and the men reaped the benefit of a vibrationless stern (except at full speed) plus the amenities of the quarter-deck.

GENERAL

Captain Reginald Bacon was responsible for the system of torpedo net defence provided, the most complete ever fitted in a British ship. Leads taken from the brailing davits to the ends of the booms, down under the nets, and back to the heads of the booms served to roll up the nets on themselves and hoist them up to the edge of the upper deck right fore and aft in one continuous roll, the operation requiring only a few minutes. Letting out the nets took even a shorter time.

To judge the ship's condition, the heels of the booms were just awash at deep load draught.

STEERING

A novel departure was made in the steering arrangements in order that the extra length of the ship should not lead to a large turning circle. Two rudders were fitted, side by side and immediately abaft the inner pair of propellers—a position which helps in the steering directly the engines start turning and before the ship has gathered way. The rudders were balanced and completely underhung with their weight taken inside the ship.

Excellent manœuvring qualities resulted from this arrangement, the tactical diameter with 35° helm at 13 knots being 455 yards as against 395 yards in the *Lord Nelson*, 460 yards in *King Edward VII* and 493 yards in *Majestic*.

RIG

A Committee consisting of Captains Jellicoe, Madden and Jackson had been deputed to consider the arrangement of masts, fire control, boats and signals. The position of the big tripod just abaft the fore funnel came in for a good deal of criticism as under most conditions of wind furnace products affected the control top. When steaming against a head wind the mast near the top of the funnel became very hot, interfering with passage to and from the control. The mast would have served the main derrick equally well had it been stepped in front of the funnel with the struts running forward instead of aft as in the later *Erin*; the control top would then have been more happily placed and the bridge lifted from the top of the conning tower. The secondary control on the baby tripod was well below smoke level, but regarded as an unsightly erection and better suited as a searchlight platform to which it was converted in 1917.

In appearance the *Dreadnought* with her grim, awe inspiring sense of efficiency was something essentially British, outclassing anything else afloat, and unique in contrast to any other battleship. Her successors although bigger and better armed could never strike the same note of novelty and overwhelming power. The first sight of her completing in dock was an unforgettable experience, and as flagship of the Home Fleet she dwarfed her consorts to an extent that mere difference in tonnage would never suggest. Although accepted as a basis for future battleship development, in 1906 it was difficult to realize that we should one day possess her like in squadrons and that the mighty *Dreadnought* would in due course pass into obsolesence and the sale list.

"DREADNOUGHT"

Launched 2 February '06, only 130 days after keel had been laid; commissioned 1 September '06 in Reserve for trials. Left Portsmouth for preliminary trials 3 October '06; completed December '06. Attached to Home Fleet for "special service"; Flagship C.-in-C. from April '07 until May '12 when relieved by *Neptune* and went into 1st Division Home Fleet. Flagship 4th B.S. December '12 to '14.

War: Flagship 4th B.S. August '14 to May '16 (rammed and sank submarine U.29 on 18 March '15, thus avenging the sinking of the cruisers *Hogue*, *Aboukir* and *Cressy*). After the Lowestoft raid was transferred to the Thames estuary as Flagship 3rd B.S. In Reserve at Rosyth February '19 and placed on sale list in March '20.

Sold 1922 £44,000.

Chapter 82

EFFECTS OF THE "DREADNOUGHT" POLICY

UNTIL 1905 it had been the custom for the main features of new ships to be published openly in all countries, secrecy only being observed in specialized details. But the coming of the *Dreadnought* put a stop to this happy state of things. An official ban of secrecy was placed upon all details connected with her design, which were not made public until described in Parliamentary Paper Cd. 3048 of 1906. There was, however, no bar to the publication of unofficial details and in the 1905 edition of *Fighting Ships* she was shown as:

"DREADNOUGHT"

To be laid down at Portsmouth 1905

Guns	Ten 12-in. Eighteen 3·5-in.
Armour	12-in. belt.
Tubes	(submerged): 4 broadside. 1 astern.
Machinery	Turbines 23,000 h.p.=21 knots.

This silly farce unfortunately became an accepted Admiralty policy and reacted more and more to our disadvantage. In this country secrecy could never be enforced properly; in Germany it was. Consequently particulars of new British ships usually appeared in the German press when they were launched, while we knew but little of new German ships until they were almost complete. In May 1914 Mr. Churchill as First Lord wrote to the Prime Minister:

> "I wish to discuss the abandonment of secrecy in regard to the numbers and general characteristics (apart from special inventions) of the ships, built and building, in British and German dockyards. This policy of secrecy was instituted by the British Admiralty a few years ago with the worst results for us, for we have been much less successful in keeping our secrets than the Germans."

Germany was engaged upon the *Deutschland* class of 13,400 tons mounting four 11-in. and fourteen 6·7-in. with 18 knots speed, and the programme for 1905 included two battleships and a large cruiser. Limited in size by passage through the Kiel Canal these battleships were to have been of 16,000 tons and armed with eight 11-in. and twelve 7·6-in. guns with 19·5 knots speed. There would have been fore and aft and wing turrets, and a broadside of six 11-in. only would hardly have matched the *Lord Nelson*.

The *Dreadnought* brought confusion to this new programme. While the big cruiser (*Blücher*) could be proceeded with, there could be no question of carrying on with the battleships as designed. Germany had to choose between two alternatives. Either she must follow the fashion and build monster ships, or else abandon battleship ambitions, accept a *guerre de course* policy, and concentrate on improved armoured cruisers. Monster ships meant enlarging the Kiel Canal; greatly increasing big gun and mountings plant; larger docks; and considerable delay while new designs could be worked out and building facilities arranged.

But in a decision to follow the British lead, Germany saw she was going to benefit by unforeseen circumstances favouring her ambitions afloat. Within a few years, as *Dreadnoughts* took their place in the battle line, the earlier ships would have to be relegated to secondary duties long before their allotted span; by the time the alterations to the Canal were complete Britain's crushing preponderance in this type would be of little importance. Germany would thus be able to enter the lists on an equal footing and build up her battle fleet *pari passu* with our own.

The great Dreadnought Controversy which raged in 1906-07 is now almost forgotten history, and looking back it is interesting to recall the arguments put forward against the all-big-gun ship. Had the Admiralty thought fit to issue a statement explaining the real reasons for building the *Dreadnought* it is pretty certain that she would have been accepted by her opponents without question. But because the Germans had greatly increased the secondary battery in their new type, the Board evidently thought—or hoped—that they were ignorant about certain factors governing long range hitting, and so made our findings highly confidential.

As it was, Sir William White, Admiral Custance, Lord Brassey, Captain Mahon (U.S.N.), and many other well-known naval publicists wrote condemning the *Dreadnought* from every point of view. They argued that (1) there was no call for such a jump in displacement, speed and cost; (2) that her construction was premature and that we should have waited until the Germans showed their hand with the 1905 battleships; (3) that the "smothering effect" of 6-in. guns by demoralizing personnel was of more consequence than 12-in. fire; (4) that a greater number of smaller ships was preferable in battle; (5) with fewer large ships the loss or absence of one from the fighting line meant a serious reduction in strength, with the (6) premature obsolescence of the existing battleships as a general *liet motif*.

It was not until January 1907 that any comprehensive explanation of the Dreadnought policy was vouchsafed, and then in America where Lt.-Commander W. S. Sims was authorized by President Theodore Roosevelt to draw up an appreciation of the one-calibre ship, which was sufficiently convincing to dispose of any further criticism.

In addition to covering the range-control considerations already mentioned, Lt.-Commander Sims dealt with other arguments in favour of moderate dimensions and speed. Analysis of the battle charts of Tsushima showed that the Russian ships were damaged or sunk only when the "rate of change of range" was small, and that when this rate was large there was little or no evidence of damage being done by gun-fire. With his superior speed (actually 6-7 knots) and knowledge of the Russian fleet, whose gunnery training had for years been carried out with the object of bringing the enemy to close quarters, Admiral Togo must have gone into action with two definite objects in view:

(1) To fight at maximum range for effective hitting at 6,000 yards when the Russian fire would not be dangerous.
(2) So to manœuvre as to maintain the least practical rate of change of range as frequently as possible upon the head of the enemy's column.

His superior speed prevented the Russians from closing the range to 1,800 yards—the battle-range of their choice—when they would have made a large percentage of effective hits.

So far as numbers and cost were concerned, Commander Sims showed that for £56,000,000 twenty-eight "Dreadnoughts" or forty "Connecticuts" could be built, to form four squadrons of either seven or ten vessels. The former would be 1·4 miles long with a broadside of forty 12-in. guns per mile, and the latter 2·1 miles with twenty 12-in. and twenty 8-in. omitting smaller guns as not effective against *Dreadnought's* armour. The concentration of fire by the shorter line of heavier ships would mean successive annihilation of the smaller units.

As regards size, if 20,000 tons were required to obtain a broadside of ten 12-in. guns, no advantageous addition of turrets could be made on 21,000 or 22,000 tons, but it would mean going up to 25,000 or 26,000 tons to obtain the necessary space. Conversely if a 20,000 tonner were designed for 16 knots instead of 20 knots the weight saved could not be utilized by adding 12-in. turrets but only by a number of intermediate guns. This, of course, refers to twin turrets, as triple or quadruple mountings had not been considered.

Also, one of the great advantages of a big ship was that the hull could be designed to resist torpedo attack.

Finally, the same sum that would maintain a fleet of twenty small battleships would also provide for ten large ones greatly superior in tactical qualities, in effective hitting capacity, speed, protection, and inherent ability to concentrate its gun-fire, and still have a sufficient sum left over to build one 20,000-ton battleship each year, not to mention needing fewer officers and men to handle a more efficient fleet.

Chapter 83

GENESIS OF THE BATTLE CRUISER

EARLY in 1902, when the *Drake* was still regarded as our finest type of armoured cruiser, Fisher had started planning an entirely novel conception which he called H.M.S. *Unapproachable*. Chief Constructor W. H. Gard was responsible for working out the design, and as usual Fisher tapped a number of outside sources for advice about turbines, oil fuel, new gun types, etc. There was no question of an all-big-gun armament at this period, and the calibres selected at first were the 10-in. and 7·5-in. which had attracted so much attention in the *Swiftsure* and *Triumph*, the ship being intended to show the same superiority in gun-power and speed over foreign contemporary armoured cruisers as the *Untakeable* was to have over existing battleships.

The preliminary "Notes on the Imperative Necessity of possessing Powerful Fast Armoured Cruisers and their Qualifications" presented a general survey only and included the following special features:

(1) A superiority in speed over the fastest foreign armoured cruisers.
(2) A main armament of 10-in. guns fore and aft as the largest calibre which can be worked entirely by hand, with a secondary battery of 7·5-in. as the largest quick-firing gun.
3) Protection of all guns to be such as will resist 8-in. Melinite shell.
(4) Every gun to have its own fighting hood, range finder, and protection for the officer in charge.
(5) Disposition of armament to be such as will give the maximum fire ahead and astern and equal fire on all points of the horizon.
(6) No masts or fighting tops—only a pole for wireless. The necessity for masts and yards for signalling does not exist.
(7) Motor-operated gantries instead of hydraulic derricks, with light seamless steel boats. The largest practicable number of large Berthon boats to be stowed beneath the armour deck. No boats will float after an engagement.
(8) Telescopic funnels.
(9) Oil fuel indispensable.
(10) All bridges to be abolished except a light bridge as in the *Renown*.
(11) Turbine propulsion, strongly advocated.
(12) No wood anywhere.
(13) Stockless anchors.
(14) Magazines and shell rooms to be placed below all guns to get rid of ammunition passages and the number of men now employed passing ammunition to the guns.

The size of the ship will be determined by these requirements.

If it is feasible to place Boilers, Machinery and the whole propelling arrangements right aft there would be great practical advantages in mounting the armament to the best advantage, the after part being sunk below the rest of the upper deck, especially if, as is likely, the funnels can be got rid of. At all events telescopic funnels should be reverted to as formerly used. If practicable it would be desirable not to draw attention to the adoption of telescopic funnels so as to get a start over foreign navies, as they cannot suddenly be put into ships.

* * * * *

In a covering letter to Gard, Fisher stressed the advantage of cutting down funnels, masts, and superstructure in order to lessen detection on the horizon, and hoped that oil fuel would do away with funnels. Prince Louis of Battenberg was greatly in favour of gantries instead of derricks for handling boats, and evidently was responsible for section (7).

A later and undated paper on "The Design for a 25-knot armoured Cruiser" shows that an armament of four 9·2-in. guns in two turrets and twelve 7·5-in. in six turrets was as many as could be carried. The projected 10-in. gun was considered not to have sufficient advantage in ballistics over the 9·2-in. to be worth the extra weight involved in mounting it.

Displacement was to be about 14,000 tons with oil fuel and 15,000 tons if a coal burner. Length not less than 500 ft. with a 70 ft. beam as the minimum breadth which would admit of the desired arrangement of guns, although much would depend upon the length of the shield for the twin 7·5-in. mounting. A minimum of 35,000 h.p. would be required and from the allowance made for engine rooms and magazines the armoured portion would have to be at least 272 ft. At the designed draught of 26½ ft. (even keel) the forward tank would be full of oil, but with none in the double bottom where another 1,000 tons were to be stowed.

Armour protection was to be on the 6-in. scale with side plating 14½ ft. deep, the upper strake 5 in. and lower strake 6 in. tapering to 4 in. at the lower edge which was four feet under water. The big turrets were 6 in. and smaller ones 4 in., conning tower 10 in. and screen bulkheads 6 in., with an upper protective deck of 2 in. and a lower one 2½ in. forward, 1½ in. amidships, and 2½-3 in. aft.

No sketch plan of this design has been preserved, but it is noted that the disposition of armament does not allow for a forecastle or poop, and that it provided for a weight of metal to be discharged over a chasing arc of

10 degrees—such as had never been approached in a cruiser; while in addition the broadside fire was more powerful than in any other cruiser of the size. In this respect the following passage in a covering letter is of interest:

> "To meet the case of the midships 7·5-in. guns firing right ahead (which would presumably be taking place at long range) then to avoid the concussion which might be inconvenient in the conning tower the ship might be worked from conning positions over the top of either of the midships 7·5-in. guns, the two conning stations being connected by a light steel bridge running across the deck from one side to the other. It is not, however, considered that the effectual screening of the conning tower from the blast of these midships guns is unattainable."

Also a note by Prince Louis:

> "In most French ships and our latest battleships and cruisers the right ahead and right astern fire suffers the limitation that the line of fire is practically unable to cross the fore and aft line. The consequence is that, in chasing, even by keeping the chase absolutely right ahead, the slightest yaw will shut in either of the guns not on the middle line. The disposition of Mr. Gard's armament is most remarkable in this important particular, for the foremost and the after 7·5-in. turret on each side can cross its line of fire something like 25 degrees beyond the fore and aft line—that means that both in chasing and in retreating the entire theoretical end-on armament can be really used." (Ten out of sixteen guns.)

A disposition allowing for an all-round ten-gun concentration on the dimensions given in which the fore and after 7·5-in. guns can cross the axial line of fire by 25° is shown below.

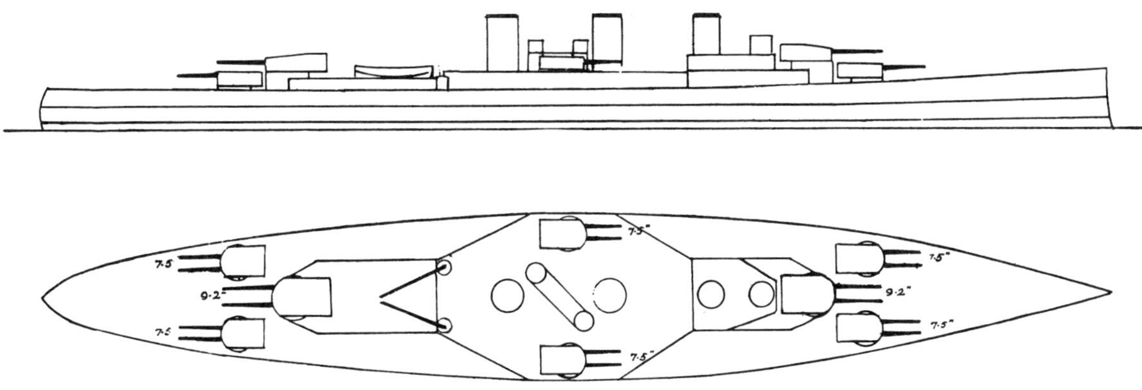

The "Shannon" class laid down in January 1905 with very much the same dimensions and carrying four paired 9·2-in. and ten 7·5-in. in single gun houses along the topsides amidships was the Board's response to Fisher's project. Single gun positions cost more weight and provided one gun less on the broadside and a theoretical two 7·5-in. axially, but the Service had no love for twin mounts after experience with the twin 6-in. in the "Counties," and doubling up the 9·2-in. was quite as far as very critical opinion was prepared to go.

White had been responsible for the *Cressy*, *Drake*, *County* and *Devonshire* types, and Watts came to Whitehall from Elswick with the reputation of "putting in plenty of guns." After his *Black Prince*—a cruiser edition of the *King Edward VII*—the 6-in. main deck battery was finally discarded and a row of 9·2-in. and 7·5-in. turrets along a low hull with a high forecastle characterized his *Warrior* (1904) and *Shannon* (1905) groups, which were to be the last of our armoured cruisers along conventional lines.

For towards the end of 1904 the Admiralty learned that the Japanese were laying down two armoured cruisers of a new type (*Tsukuba* and *Ikoma*) designed to carry four 12-in., twelve 6-in. and twelve 4·7-in. with 9 in.-7 in.-4 in. armour at 21 knots. Here was a new type of ship with exceptional potentialities—the merging of battleship and armoured cruiser which the constructional genius of Cuniberti had already anticipated in the Italian ships of the *Regina Elena* class laid down in 1901.

"IKOMA" and "TSUKUBA"

Dimensions	440′/475′×75′×26′=13,750/15,150 tons.
Armament	4 12-in.; 12 6-in.; 12 4·7-in.; 2 14-pdrs. 9 mg. 2 18-in. tubes (sub.). 1 (stern).
Protection	Belt 7″-4″; lower deck redoubt 5″; turrets and bases 7″; battery and casemates 5″; conning tower 8″ and 6″.
Machinery	D.H.P. 25,000=20·5 knots; coal 600/1,900 tons. Trials 21 knots.

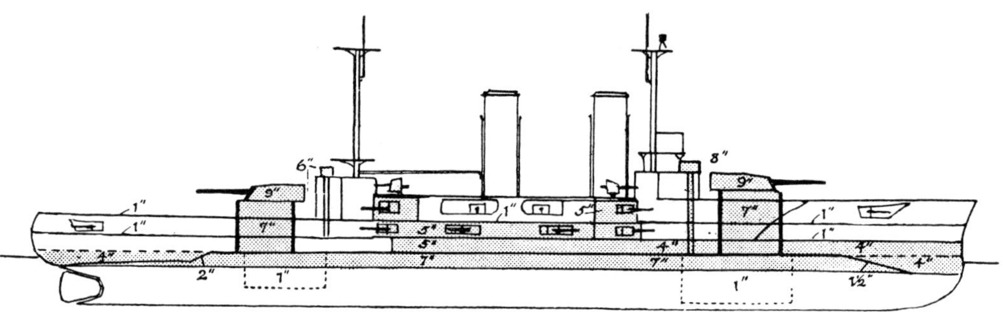

The curious Japanese hybrids with a battleship armament in a cruiser hull.

These *Tsukubas* of 14,000 tons were *Duncans* with 2 knots more speed and 2 in. less armour on the turrets but otherwise much the same standard in protection, and four 7-in. guns in place of the 12 pdrs. Both ships visited Portsmouth soon after completion and created a very good impression, but as by then we had the *Invincibles* in commission their novelty was overshadowed and they seemed already outdated.

Italy had four of her "Battle-cruisers" in hand—22 knotters carrying two 12-in. and twelve 8-in. with 9-in. 8-in. armour on Italian battleship scale. In their way these ships were a far more interesting and original conception than the *Tsukubas* especially as by skilful weight cutting their displacement had been kept down to 12,500 tons. They were still a year or so from entering service—the first, the *Regina Elena*, being launched in 1904 and the last the *Napoli* in 1907—but they played their part in bringing about the great change in design which was to characterize Fisher's new ships.

For in face of these unmistakable indications of future armoured cruiser development, our nextstep could

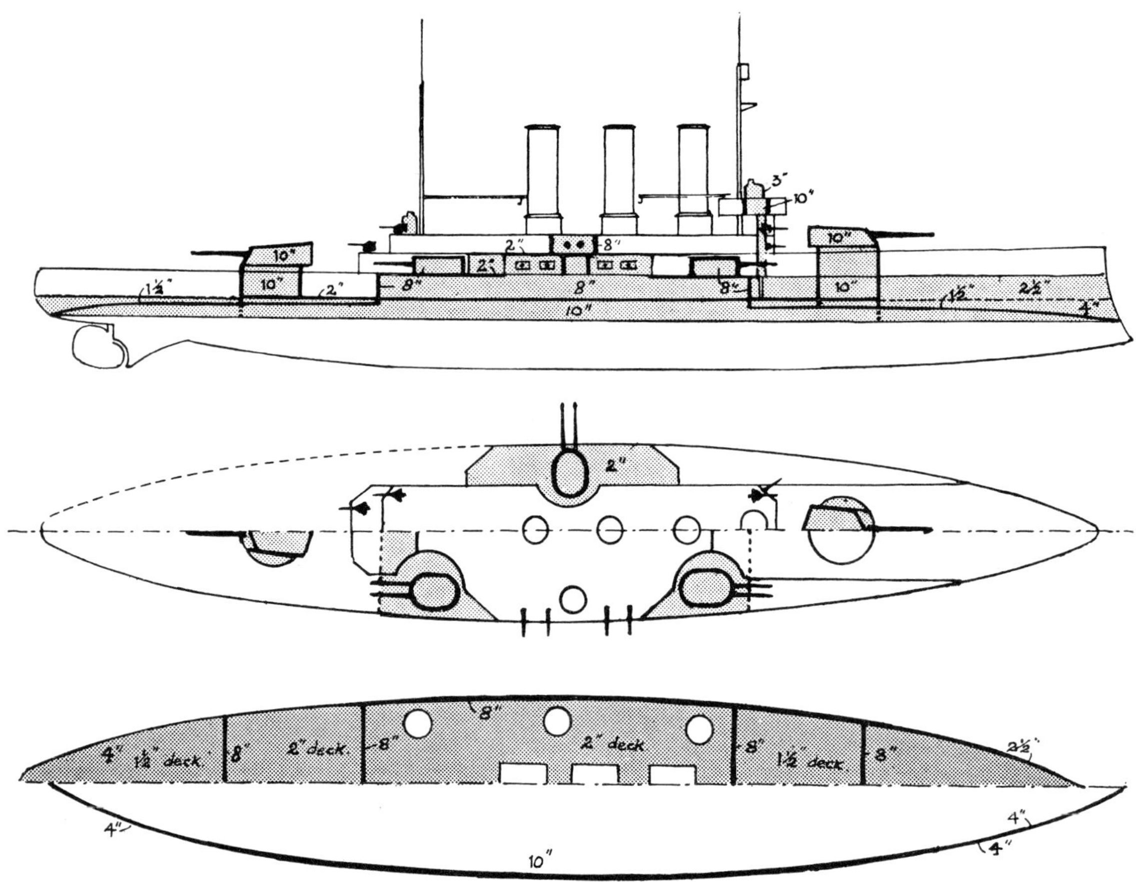

Cuniberti's *Regina Elena* with her powerful armament and high speed was another step towards the battle cruiser.

only be towards an artillery status with the capital ship. Already there was some difference of opinion as to the full employment of the *Warriors*, since theoretically the duties of large and heavily armed cruisers could include:

(1) Reconnaissance in force.
(2) Support and assistance of smaller scouting cruisers.
(3) Independent expeditions to round up enemy marauding cruisers.
(4) Pursuit of retreating enemy battle fleet and possibly bringing it to bay by concentrating on stragglers.
(5) Rapid concentration and enveloping movements during a fleet action.

which called for *far more powerful ships* than the *Warrior* or *Shannon*.

The official argument was that armoured cruisers could force their way up to within sight of a fleet and observe it, unless chased off by other armoured cruisers. But to do this they had to be given a certain amount of armour. The range of vision was constant—that of gun-fire had increased. Speed was necessary to ensure safety—armour to ensure vision.

The argument for the largest type of gun was the same for armoured cruisers as for the battleship, but the overruling qualification was speed; and as foreign armoured cruisers were to be 24 knotters, we must have 25 knots and—subject to docking limitations be content with the reduced armament and thinner armour such speed involved.

The fast armoured cruiser was to render all other cruisers useless. With 25 knots and 12-in. guns she should be able to overtake and annihilate everything afloat except the proposed battleship. No number or combination of unarmoured cruisers would be of the slightest avail against even one armoured cruiser.

Moreover, she had another mission to perform—to overtake and keep in touch with a fleeing battle fleet and possibly bring it to bay by concentrating her fire on stragglers at ranges up to seven miles (the *Mikasa* hit was stressed here).

The *Warrior* represented a hybrid type too weak for the battle line and yet too important to use as a scout, built to fight weaker cruisers and designed to have some superiority over contemporary armoured cruisers abroad. The new type of armoured cruiser was to be as much assured of supremacy beyond the battle line as the battleship was to have supremacy in it.

Fisher saw in speed the best form of protection. His new ships were to be able to command range and sink the enemy armoured cruisers without entering the target zone. Should they have to close the range on account of visibility, then the standard of armour protection of their hybrid contemporaries would suffice. There was no question of a mixed 12-in. and 9·2-in. armament—the same requirements of long range gunnery had to be observed although the broadside might be limited to six guns; with the sacrifice of a two-gun turret and 4 in. of armour along the belt and on gun positions it was hoped that a satisfactory design might be evolved without exceeding the *Dreadnought's* displacement, and allowing for 25 knots or more.

CHOICE OF THE "INVINCIBLE" DESIGN

The Committee on Designs considered five alternatives for the armoured cruiser gun disposition, all devised to secure the fire of not less than four guns ahead or astern and four to six abeam. As with the battleship sketches, a single redoubt was made to serve for pairs of turrets, and apart from this feature in protection no side or belt armour was included in the gun disposition. The Gard-Fisher design "A" (H.M.S. *Uncatchable*) showed eight guns, four firing ahead and astern, and six abeam, but as all the arguments against the disposition in the battleships "E" and "F" based on blast interference from super-firing guns were applicable to the after turrets (of which the aftermost was deemed to have insufficient command) the design could not be adopted. The following alternatives worked out by Mr. Narbeth were put forward by the Constructor's Department as embodying good all-round fire from four turrets, with 25 knots provided by reciprocating engines.

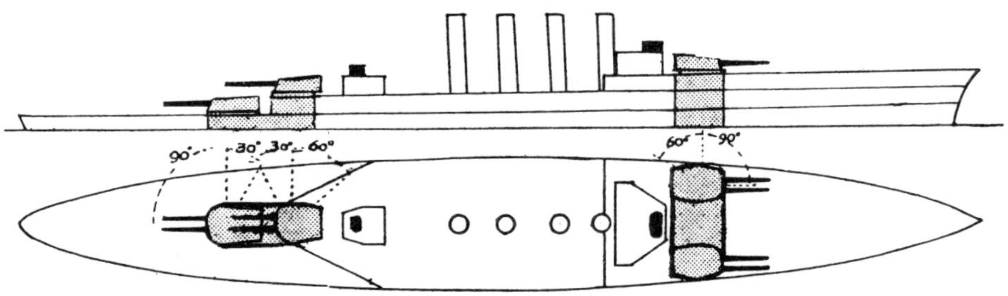

Armoured cruiser A. Reciprocating. 540×77×26½ ft.=17,000 tons. Eight 12-in. guns. 25 knots.

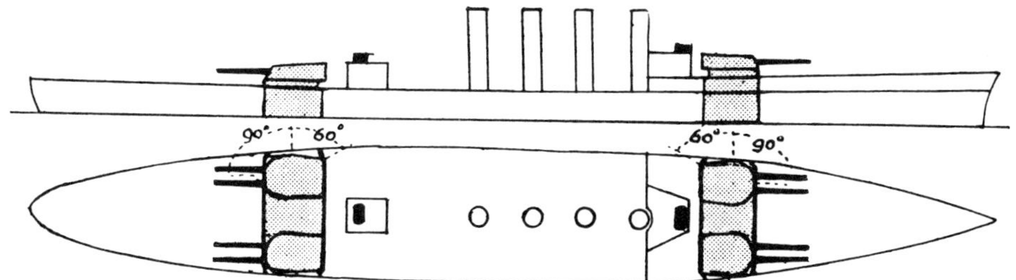

Design B. Reciprocating. $540 \times 77\frac{1}{2} \times 26\frac{1}{2}$ ft. = 17,200 tons. Eight 12-in. guns. 25 knots.

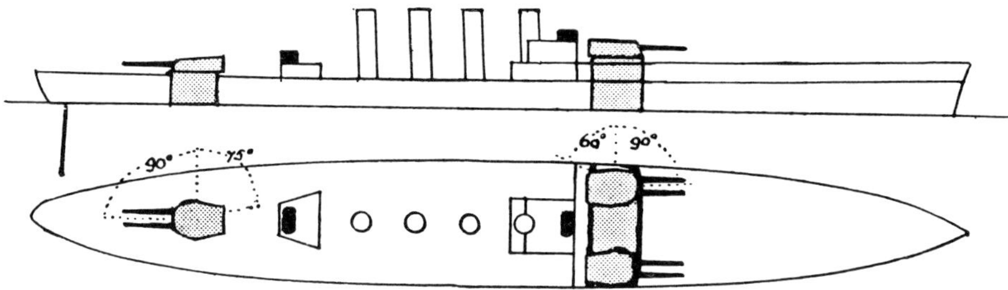

Design C. Reciprocating. $520 \times 76 \times 26$ ft. = 15,600 tons. Six 12-in. guns. 25 knots.

Both "B" and "C" suffered from the abreast turrets forward, which were regarded as objectionable in a sea-going ship, although in "C" they were brought well aft. In the past this arrangement had been seen in the French *Admiral Duperré* (1879), Austrian *Kronprinz Erzherzog Rudolph* (1886), Russian *Tchesma* (1886) and German *Siegfried* (1889) and dismissed as an expedient to be avoided.

An entirely different disposition "D" was then discussed and the Committee had no hesitation in deciding that as an ideal arrangement allowing both good concentration abeam and axially was impossible, strong broadside fire should have consideration over chase fire.

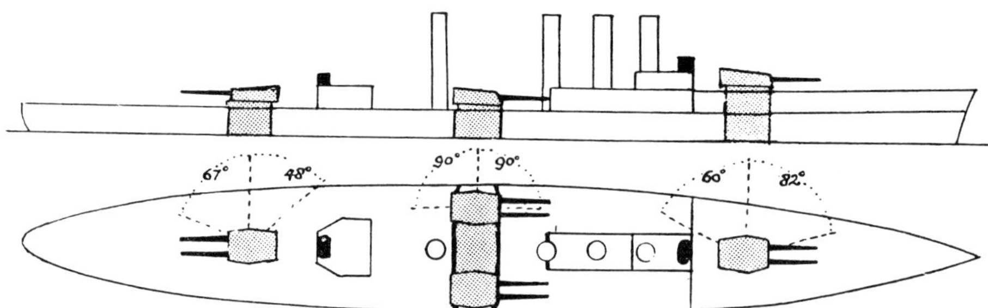

Design D. Reciprocating. $540 \times 77 \times 26\frac{1}{2}$ ft. = 16,950 tons. Eight 12-in. guns. 25 knots.

This arrangement gave six guns ahead and astern and on each side, but by placing the amidships turrets diagonally as in "E" each would be able to train on the opposite beam within an arc of about 30° if the *other were disabled.*

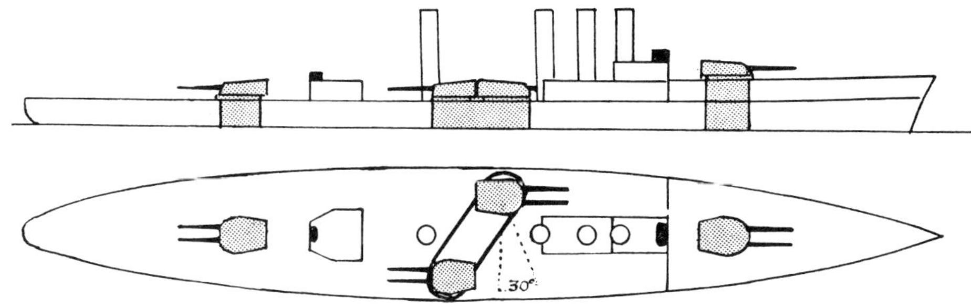

Design E. Reciprocating. $540 \times 77 \times 26\frac{1}{2}$ ft. = 16,950 tons. Eight 12-in. guns. 25 knots.

A more convenient broadside fire could have been obtained from a middle line turret, but this would have reduced chase fire to two guns only. An endeavour was made to get the diagonal turrets moved up forward, shifting the bow turret to a centre-line position amidships, but the fine lines made such a grouping forward impossible. The Committee therefore decided to adopt design "E" but with the addition of a long forecastle extending to the after turret to provide more seaworthiness and higher command for the amidships guns. There were to be two tripod masts, shelter decks for the secondary guns, etc., and a projecting bow as in the battleship. The single redoubt shown for the amidships turrets did not appear in the completed design as each turret was given a separate barbette.

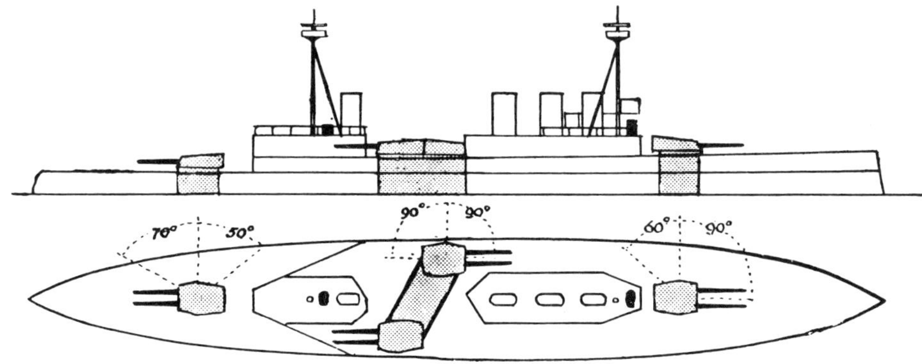

Chapter 84

THE "INVINCIBLE" CLASS (1905 PROGRAMME)

	Builder	*Laid down*	*Launched*	*Completed*	*Cost*
"*Indomitable*"	Fairfield	1 March '06	16 March '07	25 June '08	£1,662,337
"*Inflexible*"	Clydebank	5 Feb. '06	26 June '07	20 Oct. '08	£1,677,515
"*Invincible*"	Elswick	2 April '06	13 April '07	20 March '08	£1,635,739
					(armament £90,000)

Dimensions 530′ (567′)×78·5′×25·5′/26·8′=17,250 tons (Navy List).

	Deep load	*Load draught*
"*Indomitable*"	20,125	17,410 tons
"*Inflexible*"	19,975	17,290 „
"*Invincible*"	20,135	17,420 „

Armament 8 12-in./45; 16 4-in./45; 1 3-in.; 7 Maxims
Torpedo tubes: 5 18-in. submerged.
Torpedoes carried: 23 18-in.; 6 14-in.

Protection Belt 6″-4″; bulkhead 7″-6″; barbettes 7″-2″.
Turrets 7″; conning tower 10″ and 6″.
Decks: Main 1″-¾″; lower 2½″-2″-1½″.
Magazine screens 2½″.
Total

Machinery Parsons turbines 41,000 h.p.=25 knots. 4 screws.
"*Invincible*" by Humphreys and Tennant; others by builders.
Boilers: "*Indomitable*" Babcock, and others 31 Yarrow.

Fuel 1,000/3,084 tons Coal plus 725 tons oil ("*Inflexible*").
710 „ „ ("*Indomitable*").

Complement 784.

Constructor J. H. Narbeth, W. H. Whiting.

Points of Interest:

(1) The first Battle Cruisers.
(2) First large cruisers to steam at 25 knots.
(3) Had the highest h.p. yet installed afloat.
(4) Had the highest freeboard of any warship.

Of the four armoured ships of the 1905 Programme three were to be "armoured cruisers" ready for delivery in thirty months. No details were given in the First Lord's statement, nor was there any hint that the trio were to be anything more than the usual 9·2-in. gunned type. Not until the following year did any hint of the real armament leak out, and it was generally believed that the Germans designed the *Blücher* as a reply, giving her twelve 8·2-in. in the belief that the *Invincibles* would carry eight 9·2-in. guns.

When armour figures became known they did not get a very favourable press. To some critics the design appeared ill-balanced and "Brassey" summed them up in saying:

> "Vessels of this enormous size and cost are unsuitable for many of the duties of cruisers; but an even stronger objection to the repetition of the type is that an admiral having *Invincibles* in his fleet will be certain to put them in the line of battle, where their comparatively light protection would be a disadvantage and their high speed of no value."

Fisher had no use for small 6-in. gunned cruisers and expected to relegate their fleet duties to destroyers, while w.t. was to bridge the gaps in blockade and direct distant forces towards the enemy being shadowed. The *Swift* and *Tribal* destroyer classes intended to replace light cruisers were included in the five types outlined for consideration by the Committee on Designs. The folly of such a policy was not recognized for another three years, when the construction of the *Bristol* class was authorized and a start made towards remedying a culpable deficiency in the type of fighting ship especially needed in an Empire fleet. So far as the *Invincibles* were concerned, speed and gun-power proved their worth at the Falklands, but lack of armour led to tragedy at Jutland; while the criminal folly of using the battle cruisers to stop and search neutrals in the North Sea was not stopped until the end of 1914. The *Invincibles* certainly filled requirements (1) to (3) assigned to armoured cruisers, but were not

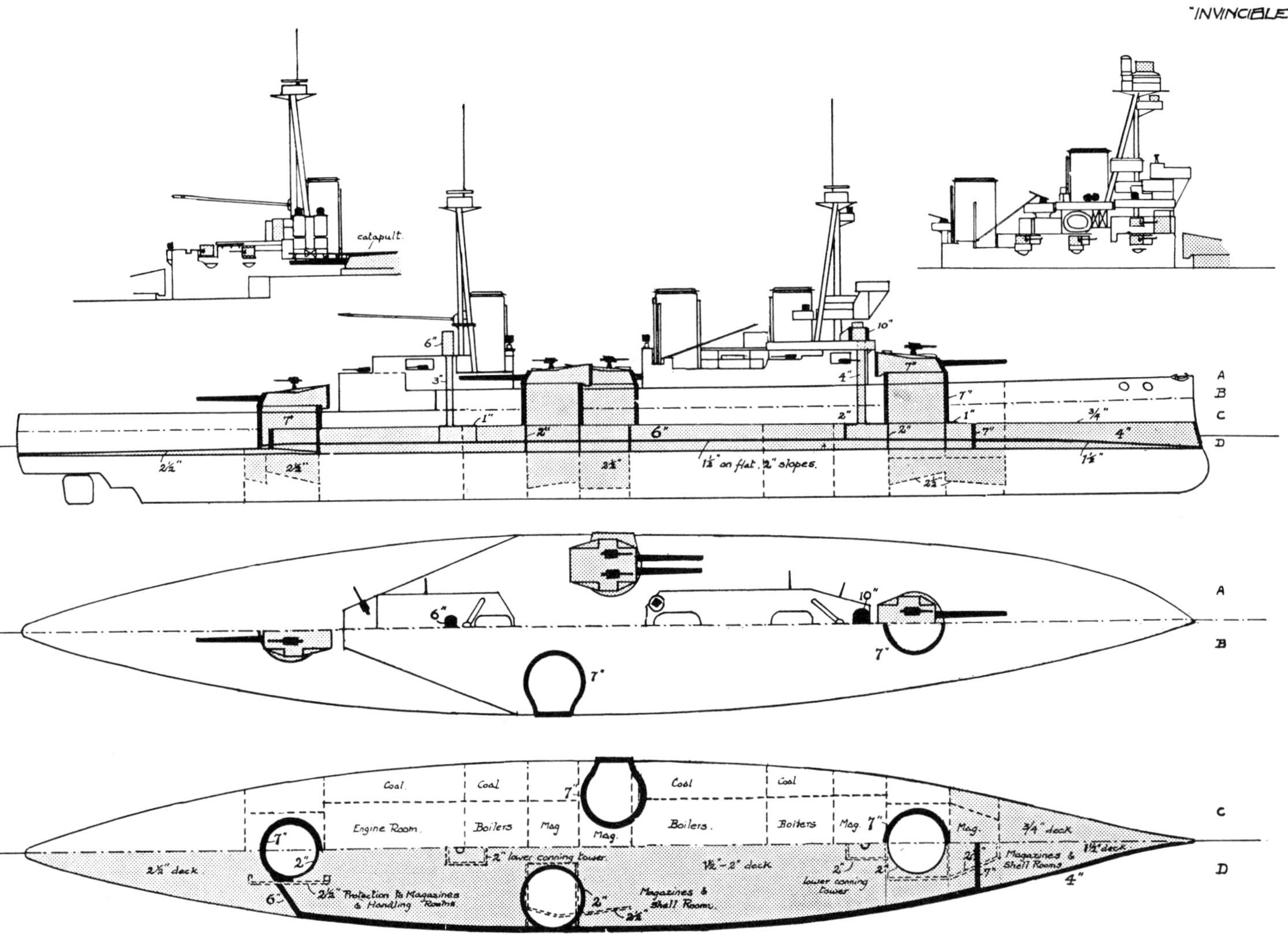

The Battle cruiser *Invincible*. Note the large expanse of unarmoured side and light deck protection. The insets show alterations to foremast, bridgework, 4-in. batteries, and searchlight positions carried out in 1917.

strong enough to carry out (4) and (5) which could be performed only by a fast battleship wing of ships of 60 per cent. greater displacement.

DESIGN

The design was entrusted to Constructor Narbeth and developed *pari passu* with that of the *Dreadnought*, until the detail stage was reached when speed pressure on the battleship required concentration for a time, and the work was handed over to Constructor Whiting for completion. But at an early stage it became obvious that the engine rooms would be so long as to be dangerous if flooded, and although this was pointed out to the engineers responsible they declined to accept a rearrangement with a large auxiliary engine-room cut out of the main engine-room. It may be said that the *Invincible* plan was developed more or less under protest on account of this and other internal arrangements.

The barbette disposition with the amidships turrets in close diagonal was the best which could be managed on the available length and beam, being dependent upon the internal capacity of the form with proper arrangement of magazines, shell-rooms, boilers and engine-rooms.

Fresh hull lines were worked out as for the *Dreadnought*, and proved even more successful, the designed speed being considerably exceeded at around the nominal h.p.

By combining the forward uptakes, two large flat-sided funnels replaced the three small ones in the original sketch, affording a most impressive sense of power and speed.

ARMAMENT

There was never any question of trying to obtain a broadside of eight guns by the diagonal placing of the amidships turrets, which at the best was only expected to enable those on the off-side to range over an angle of about 30° in the event of the other turret being disabled. Blast effects would have quite precluded any such practice with the near side turret in action.

The barbette diameter was 27 ft. as in the *Dreadnought*, with a thickness of 7 in. down to belt level, below which it was 2 in. only.

It had been intended to arm them with 12-pdrs., but thanks to a longer construction period there was time to substitute the new 4-in. firing a 31-lb. round twelve times a minute, and sixteen were mounted in the superstructures and on turret tops. In 1917 these were replaced by twelve 4-in. carried behind shields in the superstructures, with a 4-in. A.A. between the funnels and a 3-in. A.A. abaft the second one (*Inflexible* and *Indomitable*).

The *Invincible* was completed with electrical in place of hydraulic turret machinery, and Messrs. Vickers and Armstrongs supplied mountings of their own design—the former being responsible for the end and the latter

The *Invincible* at the Battle of the Falklands working up to full speed. The spiral around the fore topmast was to confuse its being used for a "cut" in range-finding. As the Germans used a stereoscopic range-finder it, and other such precautions were of no consequence.

for the wing positions. These installations were experimental in character and although satisfactory showed no superiority over the hydraulic system sufficient to warrant any change-over. The guns trials took place at the end of 1908 and in due course after various experiments and tests the electrical gear was replaced by hydraulic in 1914.

During her 1914 refit the 4-in. guns in *Invincible* were given shields and regrouped in the superstructures: stern torpedo tubes removed 1916.

PROTECTION

Although protection on the same scale as the *Minotaur* was considered adequate for the duties Fisher had visualized for the "armoured cruisers"—as they were called for the first year or so—it was insufficient for ships gunned on battleship scale which would inevitably be employed as fast battleships when necessity arose. With displacement limited to round about 17,000 tons, heavier armour could not be provided and this primary defect —unfortunately repeated in subsequent battle cruisers—was to have tragic consequences.

At Jutland Rear-Admiral Hood led the 3rd Battle Cruiser Squadron ahead of the *Lion* to engage the Germans, *Invincible* was struck by salvoes from the *König* and *Derfflinger* at 8,600 yards and destroyed in the same way as the *Queen Mary* (q.v.). Nothing but a heavily armoured ship could have withstood such an impact. Fisher's "Speed is the best protection" would have kept the ships at maximum range, but when occasion arose for gallant leadership in face of the enemy the dictates of design were brushed aside and the *Invincible* steamed at full speed into annihilation.

Although the naval annuals credited the *Invincibles* with 7-in. belts and up to 10-in. turrets in 1914, their real protection was only 6 in. amidships and 4 in. at the bows with no belt abaft the after turret. Gun positions had 7 in. above the belt and 2 in. below it, with a 2 in.-1½ in. waterline deck and 1 in.-¾ in. main deck. As in the *Dreadnought* the magazines were given 2½-in. side screens below water. Apropos of the *Invincible* scale of protection, Admiral Mark Kerr wrote:

> "When the *Invincible* was completing on the Tyne, Sir Philip Watts came to see me. Among other questions discussed I pointed out that the range at which I considered future actions would be fought, or anyhow commenced, would be at least 15,000 yards, and a shell descending from that range would go over the armoured barbette, penetrate the deck, and strike and burst against the armoured tube, going straight down to the magazine, which would result in an explosion that would destroy the ship. Sir Philip replied that he knew the danger, but his orders were to protect the vessel from a projectile fired at a range of 9,000 yards and he was not allowed sufficient weight to put on further armour." (*The Navy*, Admiral Mark Kerr, p. 47.)

Both conning towers had communication tubes to lower armoured positions behind the belt.

Inflexible during her last period of sea service in 1918. Note the aircraft and flight platform on the turret amidships and A.A. gun before and abaft second funnel. Searchlights are in towers around third funnel.

MACHINERY

The outer shafts were driven by L.P. ahead and astern and a cruising turbine, with H.P. ahead and astern turbines on the inner shafts above which were the condensers; and it will be seen that the engine-rooms presented an unusually large compartment, as the auxiliary machinery was not separately contained.

All three ships exceeded expectations on trial, their figures being:

Indomitable	43,780 h.p. = 25·3 knots.
Inflexible	43,390 „ = 25·5 „
Invincible	44,875 „ = 26·2 „

Better results were obtained in service when they had shaken down, and all reached 28 knots. On her return from the Quebec Celebrations with Prince George of Wales aboard in July 1908 the *Indomitable* maintained an average of 25·13 between Belleisle and the Fastnet. At continuous sea-going speed of 23·2 knots (22·3 knots at full load) coal consumption was 600 tons daily with 28,700 h.p., giving a radius of 2,340 knots or 3,090 if all the oil were also used.

SEA-GOING QUALITIES

Although reported as being good sea boats they were not particularly steady gun platforms.

GENERAL

Indomitable had her fore funnel lengthened in 1910 and *Inflexible* followed suit next year. *Invincible's* was not raised until after the Falkland Islands battle, when the necessity for smoke clearance caused the change to be made at Gibraltar on her way home (February 1915). In 1917 searchlights were re-grouped and mounted in towers around the third funnel, the forward superstructure was built up and shields fitted to the 4-in. guns; aeroplane runways were placed on the wing turrets and guns, and a director tower mounted on the fore control top. Stern torpedo tube removed 1916.

After Jutland: (*a*) additional armour to turret roofs and magazine crowns, ammunition hoists and decks around barbettes,
(*b*) special anti-flash protection to magazines and improved flooding arrangements. Shields to after superstructure 4-in. guns.

"INDOMITABLE"

Completed at Chatham by builders. Commissioned 25 June '08. Conveyed H.R.H. Prince George of Wales to Quebec for Tercentenary celebrations, when he joined the "black squad" as a stoker on the trip over. October '08 Nore Division Home Fleet. April '09 1st C.S.; July '09 Rear-Admiral Flagship until November '11 then p.o. for refit. February '12 2nd C.S. Flagship Rear-Admiral from March '12. December '12 attached temporarily to 1st C.S. as private ship. January '13 1st B.C.S. August '13 transferred to Mediterranean 2nd B.C.S.

War: 4-10 August shadowing and search for *Goeben* and *Breslau*; August-November Dardanelles blockade. 3 November long range bombardment of Sedd-el-Bahr. December returned home; refit; rejoined B.C.F. 24 January '15 Dogger Bank action; towed *Lion* home at 7 knots; 31 May '16 Jutland action (3rd B.C.S.) no damage or casualties. June '16 to January '19 2nd B.C.S.; February to July '19 Nore Reserve (Flagship). p.o. 31 March '20.

Sold December 1922.

"INFLEXIBLE"

Commissioned Chatham 20 October '08-January '09—damage due to gun trials being repaired. In Nore Division Home Fleet until April '09 and then transferred to 1st C.S. September-October '09 attended Hudson-Fulton celebrations at New York as flagship of Admiral of the Fleet Sir Edward Seymour (Senior Naval Officer present); 26 May '11 collision with *Bellerophon*, Portland. Damage to bows. November '12 Mediterranean (Flagship C.-in-C.).

War: August '14 2nd B.C.S. (Flagship). 4-10 August chase and escape of *Goeben* and *Breslau*; 19 August ordered home to Humber; 1-10 October Shetland patrol covering Canadian convoy; 4 November ordered to South America; repairs Devonport to 11 November; arrived Port William, Falkland Islands 7 December; 8 December 10 a.m. left harbour; 1.30 action against *Scharnhorst* and *Gneisenau*, both ships sunk by 6 p.m.; no damage to *Inflexible*; search for *Dresden*; 19 December ordered home; refit Gibraltar. 24 January '15 relieved *Indefatigable* as Flagship Admiral Carden; Dardanelles blockade; 18 March attack on the Narrows (bridge and fore control hit and set on fire, 9 casualties). Heavily hit and mined. Side at level of fore torpedo flat blown in. 29 killed. Retired from action with 2,000 tons of water in her, and much down by the bows. Repaired at Gibraltar. Rejoined Grand Fleet 19 June '15; 3rd B.C.S. (Jutland, no casualties). January '19. Nore Reserve until p.o. 31 March '20.

Sold December 1922.

"INVINCIBLE"

Completion delayed by electrical turret installations. Commissioned 20 March '09 Home Fleet 1st C.S. March-May '11 refit and alterations. May '11 1st C.S. January '13 1st B.C.S. (in collision with submarine C.34 in Stokes Bay 17 March no damage). August '13 transferred to Mediterranean until December '13.

War: Queenstown and Humber (Flagship). 28 August Heligoland Bight. Grand Fleet 2nd B.C.S. 4 November Flagship of Admiral Sturdee; left Cromarty for Devonport for stores and proceeded to South America 11 November. In action with Von Spee's squadron 8 December and with *Inflexible* sunk *Scharnhorst* and *Gneisenau*. Two hits below water but little damage. Leg on fore tripod shot away. 22 hits. 1 casualty. Rejoined Grand Fleet March '15 as Flagship 2nd B.C.S. May '15 Flagship 3rd B.C.S. (Rear-Admiral Hood) Jutland. At 6.34 p.m. after several hits, was struck in "Q" turret, when the magazine blew up and ship sunk in two halves. 1,026 killed. 2 officers and 3 men saved.

Chapter 85

THE "BELLEROPHON" CLASS

In the Memorandum issued by Lord Cawdor before leaving office at the end of 1905 the following passage occurred:

> "At the present time strategic requirements necessitate the building of four armoured ships only, and unless unforeseen contingencies arise, this number will not be exceeded. The period of building is to be two years, therefore four ships will be laid down each year, and there will be eight ships in course of construction in one year, either in the dockyards or by contract."

Thus the retiring First Lord not only anticipated the Programme to be determined by his successor in office, but laid down a rate of construction calculated to meet any contingency, Germany having announced her building period for battleships as three years. This "irreducible minimum" of four ships was fixed with full regard for this building period, and presumably in anticipation that there would be some delays over the large amount of work to be done in preparing designs for the proposed new German 16,000 tonners. Also, it would not be too much to suppose that Fisher would realize the effect that the *Dreadnought* might have on the design of the new German ships—that it would have to be re-cast in favour of something more competitive. This might very well have caused further delay, during which our strength in one-calibre ships could be built up. Thus the forecast for 1908, according to the Cawdor scheme, was that the Navy would possess five completed *Dreadnoughts*, three *Invincibles*, and the two *Lord Nelsons*—ten modern units—against which Germany would only muster two battleships of the 1906 Programme by the end of that year—if their construction were not postponed.

When Lord Tweedmouth took over the portfolio as First Lord under the new Liberal adminstration which followed the extraordinary Conservative landslide in January 1906 he retained the same Sea Lords as had been responsible for the Cawdor declaration of policy, but reserved the right of its further consideration.

On 27 July 1906 when the Shipbuilding Vote came before the House Mr. Robertson, Financial Secretary to the Admiralty, stated that the Naval Lords had "recommended us who are their colleagues to revise the new Programme." Further, he said: "The Sea Lords think that the balance of sea power will not be imperilled by the introduction of the changes we have recommended" in reducing the 1906-07 Programme to three battleships. This formal statement of the opinions and advice of the Sea Lords was unusual and only made "because so much had been said about dissensions and resignations" of Naval Members of the Board.

Such a *volte-face* on the part of the Sea Lords caused much surprise and indignation in the country, and came as a shock to public confidence in the naval advisers. Mr. Arthur Lee, Civil Lord under Lord Cawdor, wanted to know "What new facts had emerged since the Cawdor Memorandum was issued?" and Mr. Balfour wished that the House could have had "the advantage of cross-examining the Naval Lords."

Press comments were scathing, and journals which had strongly supported the protests against reduction which the Naval Lords were supposed to have made called loudly for explanation. Attempts were made to white-wash the Sea Lords in having to kow-tow before Liberal demands for retrenchment, but it seems that when asked to show cause for their "irreducible minimum" of November 1905 to the new Government, they found it impossible to do so and the demand for four new *Dreadnoughts* to be laid down in 1906-07 was judged to be unjustified.

The reasons given for dropping the one ship appeared adequate enough. Before the announcement of the *Dreadnought* policy it was expected that France, Germany and America would put in hand extensive programmes of new construction in 1906, whereas in fact no new battleships were laid down before the Admiralty decision was published. Then for a time foreign construction was held up as the Powers preferred to wait until the design of the *Dreadnought* became known before commencing new ships. Consequently, as our programmes were regulated by those of potential enemies and we could still build more rapidly than was possible abroad, the Board claimed justification in making the reduction. Such an outlook of course nullified the whole Cawdor conception, which was to take advantage of the delay and build a substantial nucleus of the new ships before competition set in again.

NAVY ACT 1906

Actually Germany's first replies to the *Dreadnought* were not laid down until August 1907. But in 1906 the Navy Act was amended by a single clause which increased the Foreign Fleet and Reserve by six armoured cruisers. With the passing of the 1900 Navy Act the 9·4-in. gun forming the main armament in the *Kaiser* and *Wittelsbach* classes was abandoned in favour of an 11-in. of 40 calibres, and the displacement of the new *Deutschland* class went up to 13,000 tons. The days of coast defence ships had passed and the High Seas Fleet was in the making. At about the same time German naval opinion made a complete *volte-face* in regard to the fighting value of the submarine. The entry into service of our first little boats of the Holland type (1901) had been hailed with something approaching derision, but by 1906 our 300-ton boats with a speed of 12/8 knots and a full speed radius of 3,000 miles on the surface could no longer be regarded as futile weapons. Germany began to treat the submarine with respect, and without any formality of announcement in the Reichstag or Press an experimental submarine was commenced at Kiel. Two years later legislative provision was made for the construction of "U" boats.

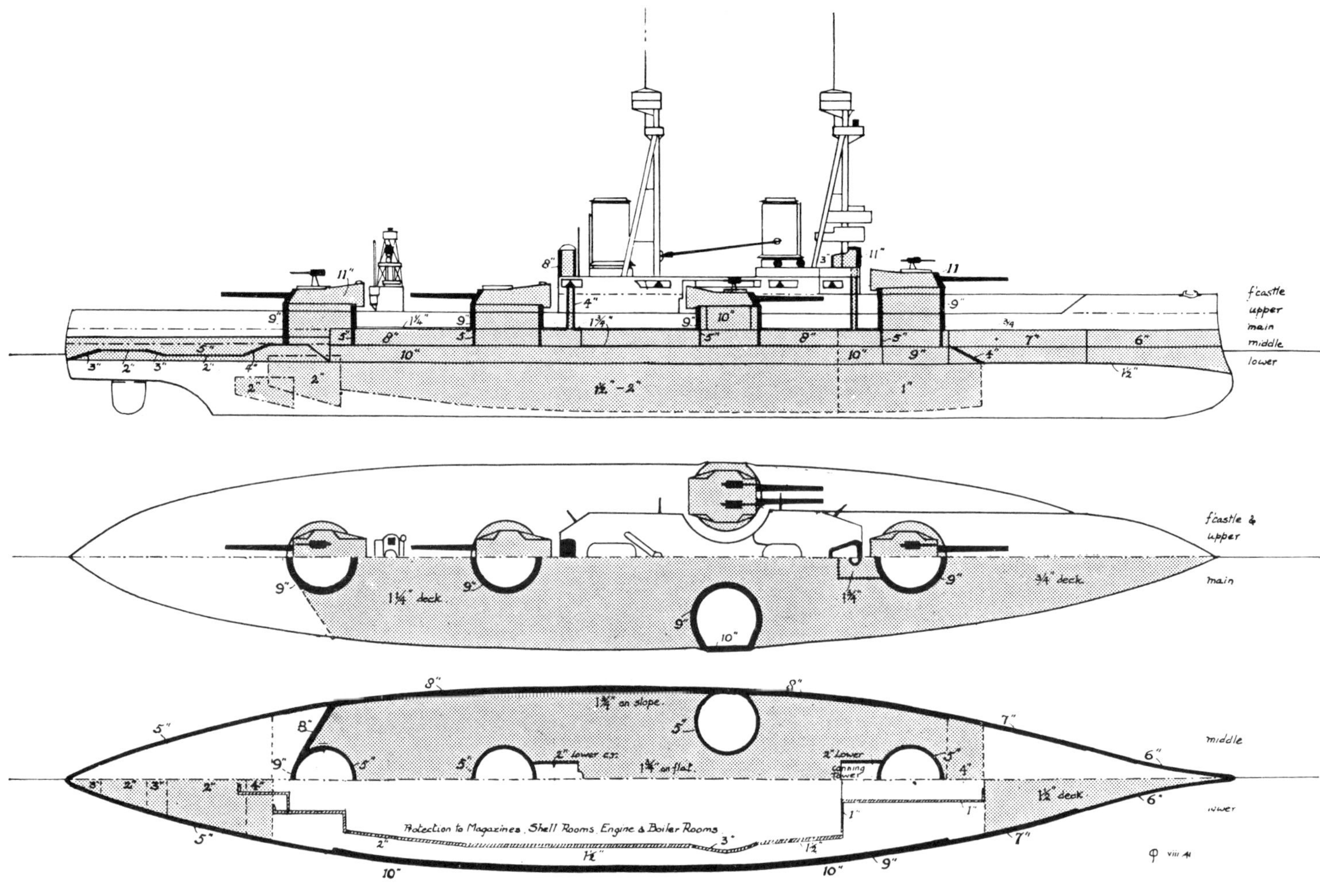

BELLEROPHON

3 "BELLEROPHON" Class (1906 Programme)

	Built at	*Laid down*	*Launched*	*Completed*	*Cost*[1]
"*Bellerophon*"	Portsmouth	3 Dec. '06	27 July '07	Feb. '09	£1,765,342
"*Superb*"	Elswick	6 Feb. '07	7 Nov. '07	May '09	£1,676,529
"*Temeraire*"	Devonport	1 Jan. '07	24 Aug. '07	May '09	£1,751,144

[1] including guns.

Dimensions 490′ (526′) × 82·5′ × 27·2′ (mean) = 18,600 tons.
Load displacement actually 18,800 tons. Full load 22,102 tons.

Armament

Guns	*Tubes*	*Torpedoes*
10 12-in./45	(18″ sub.)	14 18-in.
16 4-in./50	2 broadside	6 14-in. (9 boats)
4 3-pdrs.	1 stern	

Protection Belt 10″-9″-8″-7″-6″-5″; bulkheads 8″.
Barbettes 9″-5″; turrets 11″.
Conning tower 11″ and 8″.
Decks $\frac{3}{4}$″-$\frac{1}{2}$″ main; 3″-1$\frac{3}{4}$″ middle; 4″-1$\frac{1}{2}$″ lower.

Machinery	Parsons 23,000 h.p.=20·75 knots. "*Bellerophon*" Fairfield; "*Superb*" Wallsend; "*Temeraire*" Hawthorn Leslie. Boilers "*Bellerophon*" and "*Superb*" 18 Babcock; "*Temeraire*" 18 Yarrow.
Fuel	(tons) 900/2,648 coal plus 842 oil plus 170 patent fuel.
Radius	5,720/10; 4,250/18·3 knots (continuous sea-going speed).
Complement	733.
Constructor	J. H. Narbeth.
Point of interest:	
	First battleships to have anti-torpedo bulkheads.

Although reports from our observers with the Japanese fleet stressed that torpedo defence guns should not be smaller than 4·7 in. these seem to have been either overlooked or ignored by the Board when the *Dreadnought's* armament came to be fitted. However, as the Americans were mounting 14-pdrs. in the *Michigan* and the French

The *Superb* in 1910 with the original simple bridgework, searchlights abreast fore funnel, 4-in. guns on turret crowns, and torpedo nets fitted.

12-pdrs. in their *Danton* class of the 1906-07 programme she appeared to be in good company. On the other hand the Japanese—who had a better experience of war needs than anyone else—thought fit to retain 4·7-in. or 6-in. in their *Tsukuba* and *Aki* classes. Having substituted 4-in. for 12-pdrs in the *Invincibles*, the field was now open for further advance in calibre in the *Bellerophon*, and while the *Dreadnought* was building alternative armaments and variations in protection were proposed and investigated. Altogether twenty-five different sketch plans were considered, but after the *Dreadnought's* successful trials it was decided that the new ships should be of the same model with certain modifications.

Draught was therefore increased 6 in. providing 700 tons extra displacement to allow for a heavier torpedo defence battery, the fitting of anti-torpedo bulkheads, and an extra mast.

ARMAMENT

The sixteen 4-in. were disposed eight on turret tops and eight in the superstructures. During the 1916 refit those on the turrets were removed and double-decked in the superstructures with shield protection; in 1917 the secondary batteries in most of the earlier *Dreadnoughts* was reduced to thirteen guns to provide armament for small craft. By this time light A.A. guns were being served out to the Fleet and the *Bellerophons* received one 4-in. and one 3-in. both of which were mounted right aft. Stern torpedo tube removed during the war.

PROTECTION

A general re-adjustment of armour thicknesses reduced the belt to 10 in. amidships with an extra inch on the bow and stern continuations; barbettes were given a greater uniform thickness and the main deck armour increased from $\frac{3}{4}$ in. to $1\frac{1}{4}$ in. But the great feature was the replacing of the small magazine screens in the *Dreadnought* by a complete bulkhead running from the fore to the aftermost magazine and extending down to the double bottom, as protection against torpedo attack. Reports showed that during the Russo-Japanese war ships hit by torpedo or mine had only been lost if their magazines exploded, and this 1 in.-2 in. bulkhead—which absorbed the greater amount of additional displacement in the *Bellerophon*—was a first step towards the increasing allowance of weight devoted to defence against under-water attack which was to become a major feature in battleship design as the torpedo developed in power and accuracy.

RIG

Although to most observers the *Dreadnought* presented a profile of simple but awe-inspiring dignity, her rig provoked a good deal of adverse criticism in the Service. The small tripod was ridiculed and what was asked

The *Bellerophon* in 1914 when experiments in searchlight grouping were being carried out, keeping them amidships to confuse the course and length of the ship, and mounting them as high as possible.

for was a seemly two-masted rig with high control tops and w.t. masts. In *Bellerophon* the two tall, gaunt tripods gave a well-balanced and most majestic silhouette. During the 1914 refits developments in w.t. resulted in the reduction of topmasts to short poles.

SEARCHLIGHTS

The adoption of searchlight control considerably altered the silhouette when in 1914 the projectors were regrouped on platforms around the mast bases and funnels. In 1917 a new method of mounting was employed throughout the Fleet, the lights being housed in towers and raised when required; observation was through slots at a lower level and sheltered from glare. The *Bellerophons* had groups of three at different levels around the second funnel.

Additional bridgework and control positions helped to produce both a most impressive mass effect and an unusually imposing target.

FUEL

Machinery and boilers were as in the *Dreadnought*, but coal bunkerage was reduced by 252 tons to 2,648 tons, oil by 278 tons to 842, and patent fuel raised by 50 tons to 170 tons. The net result of this was a reduction of 760 miles in the steaming radius at 18 knots (4,230 miles) and 900 miles at 10 knots (5,720 miles). The coal consumption in 24 hours at 91·5 knots was 360 tons.

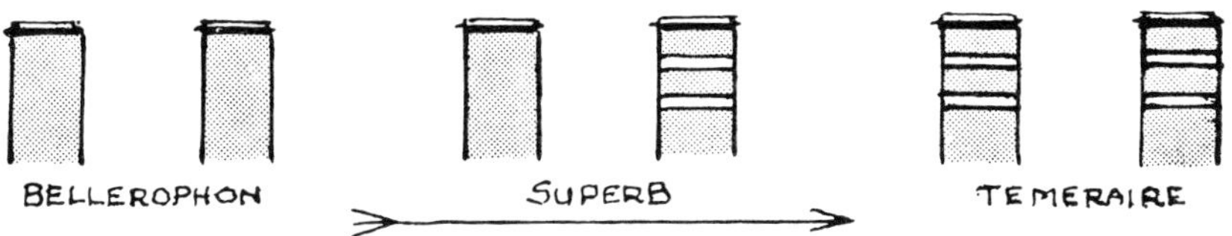

SPEED

The advantages of turbine machinery so far as designed horse power was concerned became manifest in these ships, which all put up good performances.

	Shaft h.p.	*Coal*	*Speed*
Bellerophon			21·8 (later 22·1)
Superb	25,400	1·38	21·64
Temeraire	24,600	1·74	22·07 (maximum)

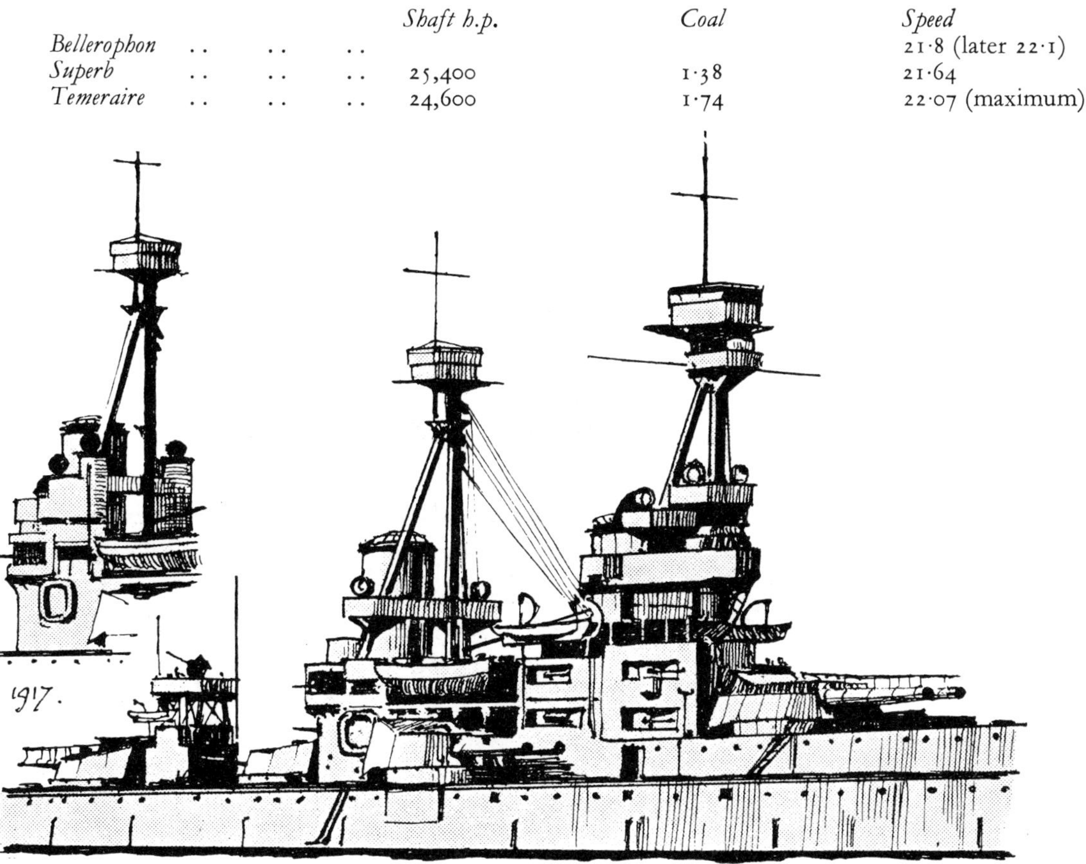

The *Bellerophon* in 1916 with the superstructures built up and the 4-in. guns removed from the turret crowns, aircraft runways on "A" and "Y" turrets, searchlight positions modified, and an A.A. gun on a platform aft. In 1917 searchlights were grouped in towers around the second funnel being raised when required, and controlled through slots lower down when the beam did not confuse the operator.

"BELLEROPHON"

Built at Portsmouth December '06-February '09. Commissioned February '09 for Home Fleet Nore. April '09 1st Division Home Fleet to May '12 (collision with *Inflexible* at Portland 26 May '11). May '12 1st B.S. Home Fleet (28 August '14 collision with S.S. *St. Clair*).

War: Grand Fleet 4th B.S. August '14 (Jutland. No casualties). 1919 Reserve. Sheerness. Turret drill ship. Scrapped under Washington Treaty.

Sold November 1921.

"SUPERB"

Built at Elswick February '07-May '09. Commissioned 29 May '09 for Home Fleet 1st Division. May '12 1st B.S. Home Fleet.

War: Grand Fleet 1st B.S. August '14. Jutland. 4th B.S. Flagship Rear-Admiral A. L. Duff. No casualties. '18 Mediterranean. Led the Allied Fleet through the Dardanelles (Flagship Vice-Admiral Gough-Calthorpe) after surrender of Turkey. '19 Reserve. Turret drill ship. Scrapped under Washington Treaty. Used as a target for shell attack.

Sold December 1922.

"TEMERAIRE"

Built at Devonport January '07-May '09. Commissioned for Home Fleet 1st Division. May '12 Home Fleet 1st B.S.

War: Grand Fleet 4th B.S. Jutland. No casualties. '18 Mediterranean. '19 Cadets sea-going training ship. Scrapped under the Washington Treaty.

Sold December 1922.

Chapter 86

THE "ST. VINCENT" CLASS

In presenting the Estimates for 1907-8 the First Lord (Lord Tweedmouth) stated that new construction for the year would include two or, unless an understanding between the naval powers was arrived at by the Hague Conference, three large armoured vessels of the *Dreadnought* type. But as no reduction in naval armaments was agreed to at the Conference, three battleships of the *St. Vincent* class were laid down in 1908.

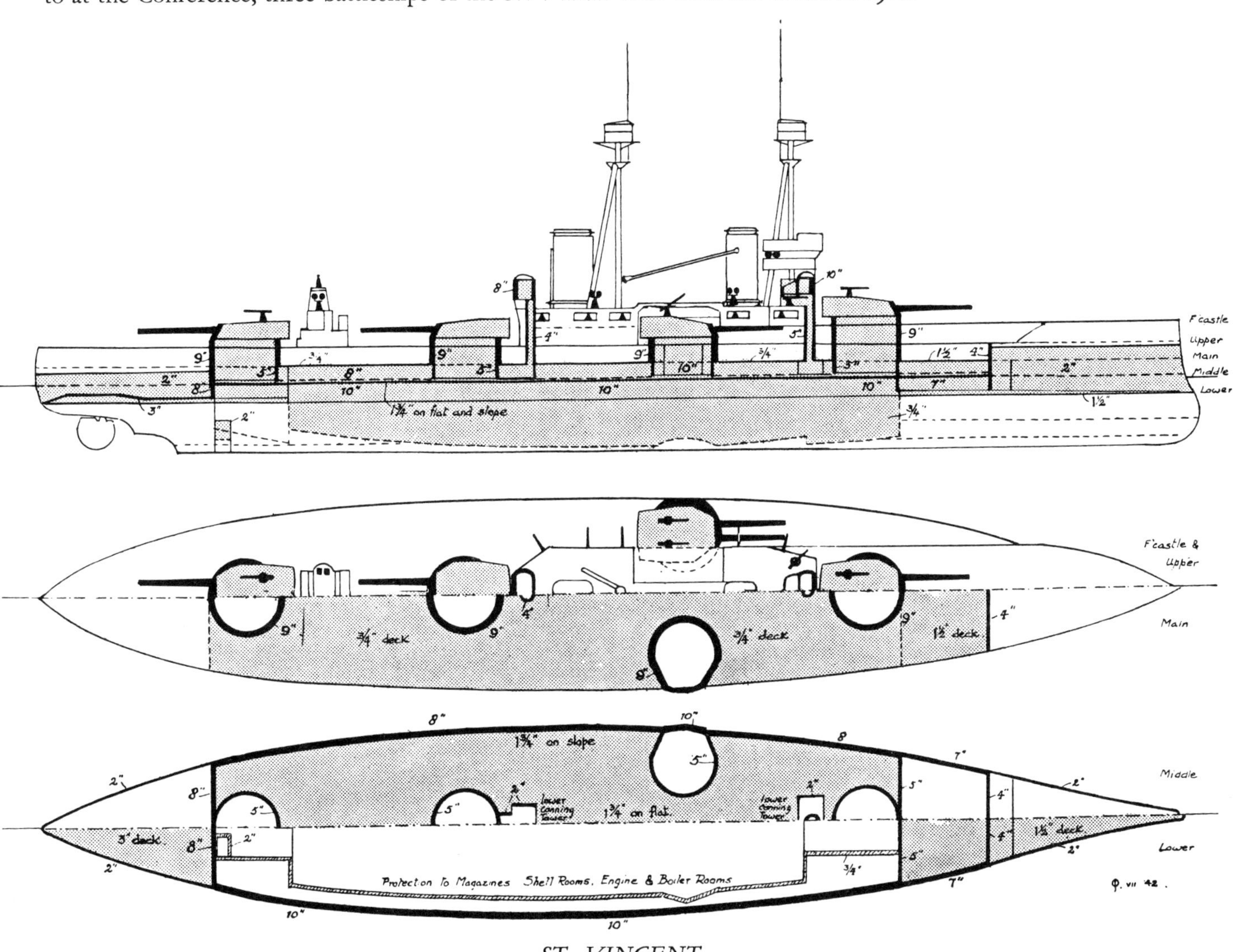

ST. VINCENT

"ST. VINCENT" Class (1907 Programme)

	Built by	*Laid down*	*Launched*	*Completed*	*Cost*
"*Collingwood*"	Devonport	3 Feb. '08	7 Nov. '08	April '10	£1,731,640
"*St. Vincent*"	Portsmouth	30 Dec. '07	10 Sept. '08	May '10	£1,754,615
"*Vanguard*"	Vickers	2 April '08	22 Feb. '09	Feb. '10	£1,607,780 (including guns)

Dimensions 500′ (536′) × 84′ × 25′ 3″/28′ 7″ = 19,250 tons.
Load displacement 19,560 tons; full load 23,030 tons.

Armament	Tubes (18″):	Torpedoes:
10 12-in./50.	2 abeam.	14 18-in.
20 4-in./50.	1 astern.	6 14-in.
4 3-pdrs.		

Protection	Belt 10″-8″-7″; bulkheads 8″-5″-4″. Barbettes 9″-5″; turrets 11″. Conning tower 11″-8″; signal tower 3″. Comm. tubes 5″-4″. Decks: $1\frac{1}{2}$″-$\frac{3}{4}$″ main; $1\frac{3}{4}$″ middle; 3″-$1\frac{1}{2}$″ lower.
Machinery	Parsons turbines 24,500 h.p. = 21 knots, 4 screws. "*Collingwood*" Hawthorn Leslie; "*St. Vincent*" Scotts; "*Vanguard*" Vickers. Boilers "*Collingwood*" Yarrow; "*St. Vincent*" and "*Vanguard*" Babcock.
Fuel	Coal 900/2,800; oil 940; Patent 190 tons.
Radius	6,900/10; 4,250/18·7 knots.
Complement	758.
Constructors	E. N. Mooney, A. M. Worthington.

Points of interest:

(1) Reversion to thin plating for waterline at bows and stern.
(2) First ships to carry 50-calibre 12-in. guns.

The *Vanguard* as completed, with a screen around the 4-in. guns on "A" turret roof. Searchlights were mounted in pairs—as can be seen on the structure between the after turrets—and she carries the high wireless topmasts in vogue until just before the war. Her funnel bands are red.

These ships were more or less repeats of the *Bellerophon* but armed with 50 cal. guns, which meant some increase in length and beam set off by reduction in draught, leading to a rise in displacement of 650 tons (nominal) and 760 tons on the actual load figures. However, the length : beam ratio tended towards easier speed, a full 21 knots being achieved with an increase of only 1,500 h.p.

In appearance they could be distinguished from the earlier trio by unequal funnel width and the stepping of the main topmast before instead of abaft the control top.

ARMAMENT

The increase from 45 to 50 cals. in the big guns was made to meet increasing battle ranges with combined armour piercing and shell effect, the longer weapons showing a rise from 47,875 to 53,400 ft. tons and 2,850 to 3,010 ft. secs. velocity, with the same weight of shell. The net gain was an increase in penetration of about $\frac{1}{2}$ in.

steel at 3,000 yards; the reverse was diminished accuracy as the higher velocity led to muzzle wobble. Thus, successive shells spread over two or three acres (*Lord Fisher*, 11, 83).

It will be seen that the first armament of twenty 4-in. was accommodated by placing additional guns in the superstructures. Those on the fore turret, although given a blast screen to protect them from nearby 4-in. were soon removed. In 1914 shields were fitted; in 1917 additional positions were built up at the base of the second funnel, and the forward superstructure heightened to contain four guns aside. Later when guns were required for a host of other vessels the armoured ships surrendered a portion of their secondary armament and the *St. Vincents* came down to thirteen 4-in. all in the superstructures. Single 4-in. and 3-in. A.A. were placed on the bakery between the after turrets or right aft.

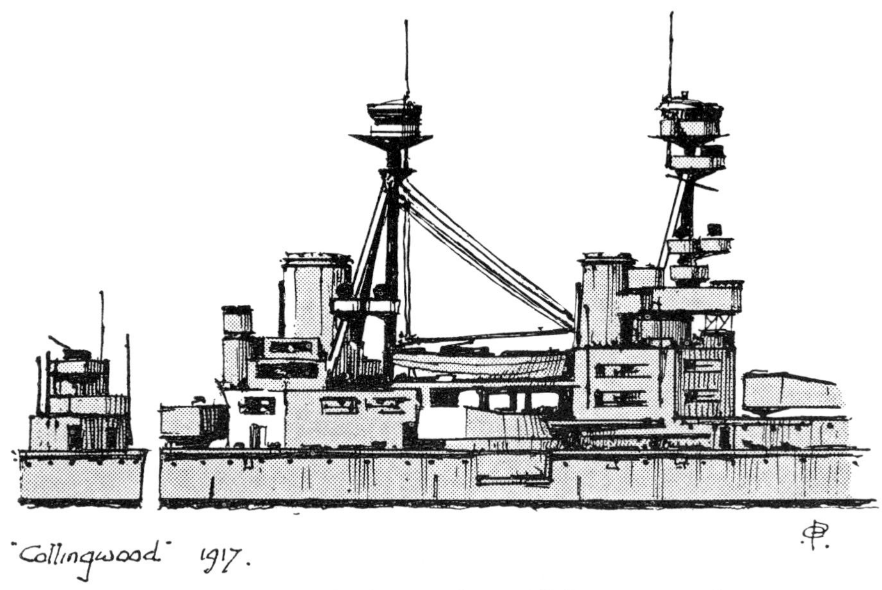

Superstructures built up and searchlights re-grouped.

PROTECTION

It will be recalled how protection at the bows and stern had been increased class by class from the *Majestic* to the *Bellerophon*; now we find the commencement of a reversion to soft ends with much the same changes as

The *St. Vincent* in 1919 with searchlight towers, the after control top removed, superstructure built up for the 4-in. gun re-grouping, and a clinker screen on the fore funnel to protect searchlights and mast platforms from funnel exhaust.

had marked the *Formidable-London* but in reverse. Forward the 7-in. strake was shortened and crossed by a 5-in. bulkhead, the former 6-in. being replaced by 2-in. extending to the upper deck; aft there was 2-in. in place of 5-in., the citadel being closed by an 8-in. bulkhead.

The weight saved by reductions in the belt was more or less absorbed by (1) armour having to cover 10 ft. extra space between the after turrets, (2) the increase in barbette diameter from 28 to 29 ft., and (3) the three cross bulkheads of 8 in., 5 in. and 4 in. In *Bellerophon* the magazines extended beyond the barbettes; in *St. Vincent* they flushed with the barbettes and were protected by the bulkheads instead of thick sloping decks.

SPEED

All three ships exceeded their designed speed, the figures for the 30 hrs. full power trial being:

	Shaft h.p.	*Coal.*	*Speed.*
"*Collingwood*"	26,319	1·8	21·5
"*St. Vincent*"	25,900	1·4	21·7
"*Vanguard*"	25,800	1·6	22·1

The *Vanguard* was completed in under the two years and as her contract was placed under considerable economical advantage she proved to be the cheapest battleship of her period, costing £53,000 less than *Superb*.

GENERAL

Similar changes in the search-light positions were made as in the *Bellerophon*, except that there was only one tower at each foot of the main mast instead of three. The original twin lights were later changed to larger singles.

Late in 1918 the control top was removed from the main mast in *Collingwood* and *St. Vincent*.

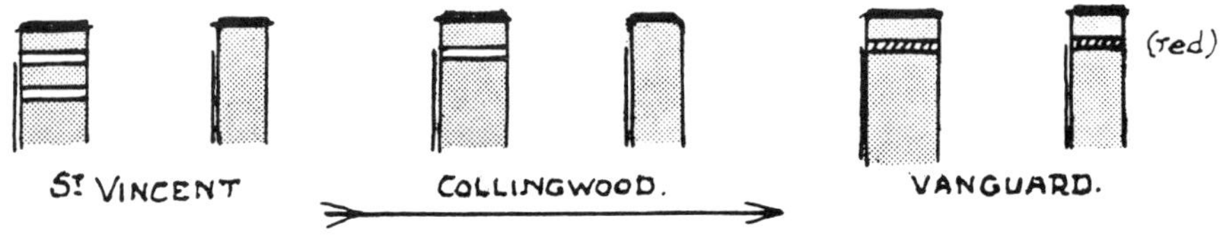

"COLLINGWOOD"

Built at Devonport February '07 to April '10. Commissioned 19 April for 1st Division Home Fleet (touched an uncharted rock at Ferrol February '11; bottom plating damaged). June '12 Vice-Admiral 1st B.S. (Bilge keels deepened 1913).

War: Grand Fleet 1st B.S. Jutland (no casualties. King George VI, then Duke of York, served aboard as a Lieutenant). 4th B.S. to '19. Devonport Reserve and gunnery ship until paid off. Discarded under Washington Treaty.

Sold December 1922.

"ST. VINCENT"

Built at Portsmouth December '07 to May '09. Commissioned 3 May '10 for 1st Division Home Fleet (Rear-Admiral Flagship from June). May '12 1st B.S. (Rear-Admiral Flagship).

War: Grand Fleet 1st B.S. (Flagship Rear-Admiral Sir Evan-Thomas until 1917). Jutland (no casualties). 4th B.S. until '19. Portsmouth Reserve and gunnery ship until paid off. Discarded under Washington Treaty.

Sold December 1922.

"VANGUARD"

Built at Vickers April '08 to February '10. Commissioned 1 March '10 for 1st Division Home Fleet. May '12 1st B.S.

War: Grand Fleet 1st B.S. Jutland (no casualties). Destroyed by internal explosion at Scapa 9 July '17. 804 killed.

THE ADVENT OF THE HARDCASTLE TORPEDO

In 1907 the propelling engines of the Whitehead torpedo underwent a more remarkable development than in any previous year since its appearance as an effective weapon. A device for heating the air used for driving the motor which, released from pressure is intensely cold, adds about 100 per cent. to the power available enabling either the range to be doubled or the speed to be increased about 10 knots at any range. Thus at 1,000 yards speed rose from 35 to 43 knots, at 4,000 yards 20 knots rose to 30, and in due course came the torpedo which ran with perfect accuracy for five or six miles carrying an explosive charge three or four times larger than anything previously known. A complete change in naval tactics and the defence of fleets would have to be the inevitable result, with torpedo craft possessed of a weapon which seriously challenged the hitherto proud superiority of the battleship.

Chapter 87

THE FIRST GERMAN DREADNOUGHTS

As the forecast for 1910 showed that we should have eight battleships and three battle cruisers completed against the German four and one respectively a further cut in the Cawdor programme was decided upon for the 1908 Programme, and in the face of such figures it was difficult for the Sea Lords to protest. Nevertheless they sent in a remonstrance to Lord Tweedmouth which showed their anxiety, not for the immediate future but for the years when German shipbuilding had really got into its stride. The memorandum dated 3 December 1907 ran:

> "We therefore consider it of the utmost importance that power be taken to lay down two more armoured ships in 1909-10 making eight in all, as unless there is an unexpected modification in Germany's anticipated shipbuilding programme, resulting in her not completing seventeen ships by the spring of 1912 it will be necessary to provide eight new British ships to be completed by this date, the last two being laid down at the end of March 1910."

The response to Liberals, anti-militarists, and pacifists came in the Estimates presented in March 1908 which provided for one battleship and one battle cruiser, six small cruisers and sixteen destroyers, a meagre programme put forward in the interests of economy and as a gesture for others to follow our lead. Unfortunately it only served to give the impression that our will towards Sea Power was waning.

Germany had commenced her first two Dreadnoughts the *Nassau* and *Westfalen* in 1906 and a second pair *Rheinland* and *Posen* in 1907. All details were kept secret and it is rather amusing to refer back to "Jane" for 1907 (14 11-in. guns), 1908 (10 or 12 11-in, but 14 or 16 11-in. alleged) and 1909 (10 11-in. for the two first disposed as in the Dreadnought, and 12 11-in. in the second pair, similar but turrets 4 and 5 *en echelon*) and recall the other ingenious designs in the press supposed to represent them. Curiously enough the secondary battery was usually estimated at about twenty 4·1-in. and presumed a two-calibre armament only. The writer photographed the ships completing in 1909 and these pictures gave the first true indication of their armament and appearance. They proved to be merely enlarged *Deutschlands* with six twin 11-in. turrets, twelve 5·9-in. along the main deck and sixteen 24-pdrs. Speed 20-21 knots. In dimensions they struck a new note having a beam of 88 ft. 3 in. to a length of 478 ft. (w.l.) the draught of 27 ft. 6 in. exceeding the design by a foot. They were cramped, overgunned, and had wretched accommodation but steamed well and made steady gun-platforms.

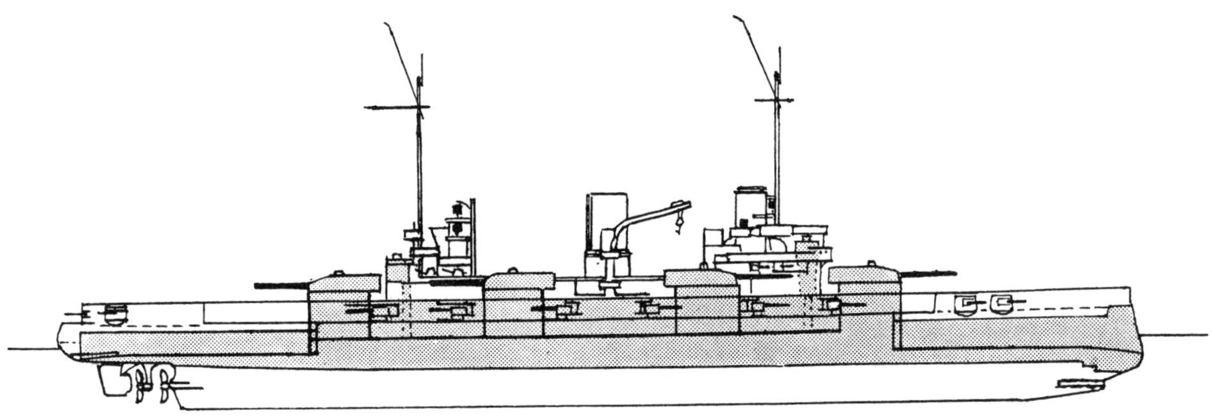

The *Nassau* had an almost complete waterline belt 11½-in. amidships, 6-in. forward and 4-in. aft with 7¾-in. bulkheads across the bases of the end turrets. Above this was the 6-in. battery. The barbettes and turrets were 11-in.

Our original intelligence reports credited their 11-in. with the 30° elevation allowed in earlier German battleships, and it was not until the *Nassau* had been in commission for some time that it was learned that the actual elevation was only 16°. The reason was that her 11-in. were of exceptionally high velocity designed for flat trajectory fire and consequently their range, even at moderate elevation, was far beyond that at which accurate aiming was considered feasible. It was therefore not thought necessary to give them more than 16° elevation—equivalent to 19,500 yards range—especially as high angle mountings were heavier, more complicated, and more expensive, besides needing a larger gun-port.

From 1907 Germany built twenty-six *Dreadnoughts* and battle cruisers and in every case the guns had a maximum elevation of 16°. Our 12-in. gunned *Dreadnoughts* had 15° elevation, which in those with 13·5-in. and 15-in.

guns was increased to 20°, so that while Germany lowered elevation, we increased it for reasons which will be given on a later page.

The third ship of the 1907 Programme was the *Von der Tann*, a battle cruiser, of 19,100 tons carrying eight 11-in., ten 5·9-in., and sixteen 24-pdrs. Although designed for 24 knots with 43,600 h.p. (Parsons) she made 27·75 with 79,800 on trials and touched 27·6 knots at the battle of Jutland. Comparison with the *Invincible* showed her general superiority and she was to prove an exceedingly tough antagonist in battle.

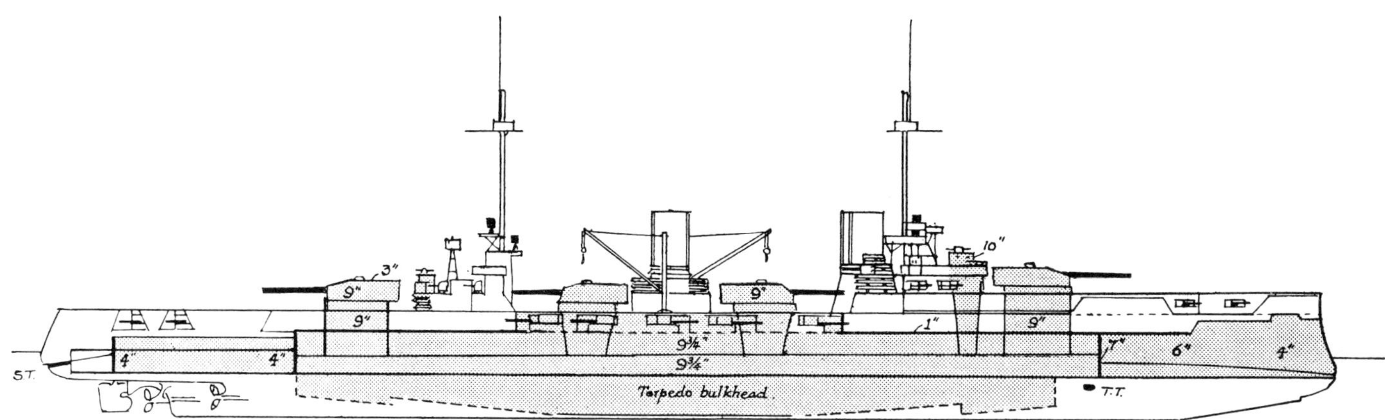

The *Von der Tann* was 562¾ ft. long against 530 ft. of the *Invincible*, and a beam of 87 ft. against 78 ft. which allowed wide arcs of bearing for the amidships guns. The secondary battery right amidships shared the barbette protection.

The Germans seem to have retained the 5·9-in. guns on general principles—for use against ships and also as torpedo defence in conjunction with the 24-pdrs. Incidentally during the war all but four of these latter were removed. Here again they showed a better appreciation of what would be required to ward off torpedo attack than did our people, and there was no question of employing 5·9-in. at long bowls with confusion of spotting. The *Von der Tann* showed a similar high proportion of beam to length—87 ft. 3 in. to 562 ft. 8 in. with 26 ft. 7 in. draught. Protection was considerably better than in our ships (9-in. gun positions; 9¾-in. belt and lower deck) and the target presented less portentous. Even in 1911 no authentic facts about her protection had been published, and to quote "Brassey": "The protection of the *Von der Tann*, as with British vessels of similar design, is less than that of the battleships, the belt according to foreign authorities being 6 in. at its thickest part, while the guns have 8-in. protection."

NAVY ACT 1908

By 1908 Britain had put in hand ten capital ships against the German five; in that year we provided for the *Neptune* and *Indefatigable* while Germany responded to our economy overture by voting three battleships and a battle cruiser. In addition, preparations for a new Navy Act were set in train with the object of constructing a larger number of armoured ships in the next few years than had been authorized by the Act of 1900. In order to make provision for these as simply and as unobstrusively as possible it was decided that the effective life of battleships should be reduced from twenty-five to twenty years, by which means a number of more or less obsolete ships which otherwise would have several years service still ahead of them could be scrapped and replaced by *Dreadnoughts*.

Accordingly a schedule was attached to the new Act of 1908 which set forth that four large armoured ships should be laid down annually between 1908 and 1911 both inclusive, and that from 1911 to 1917 two keels should be laid annually. The Marine Office also decided that each of the "large cruisers" specified in the 1900 Act should be of the *Invincible* type, so that instead of the 38 battleships and 20 armoured cruisers provided for by the Act of 1906, the new Act of 1908 increased the Fleet to 58 *Dreadnoughts* and *Invincibles*.

Thus, while the Government reduced the Cawdor "irreducible minimum" for the third time Germany provided for a vastly more powerful fleet and met our 1908 programme by laying down four keels to our two.

Chapter 88

"NEPTUNE"

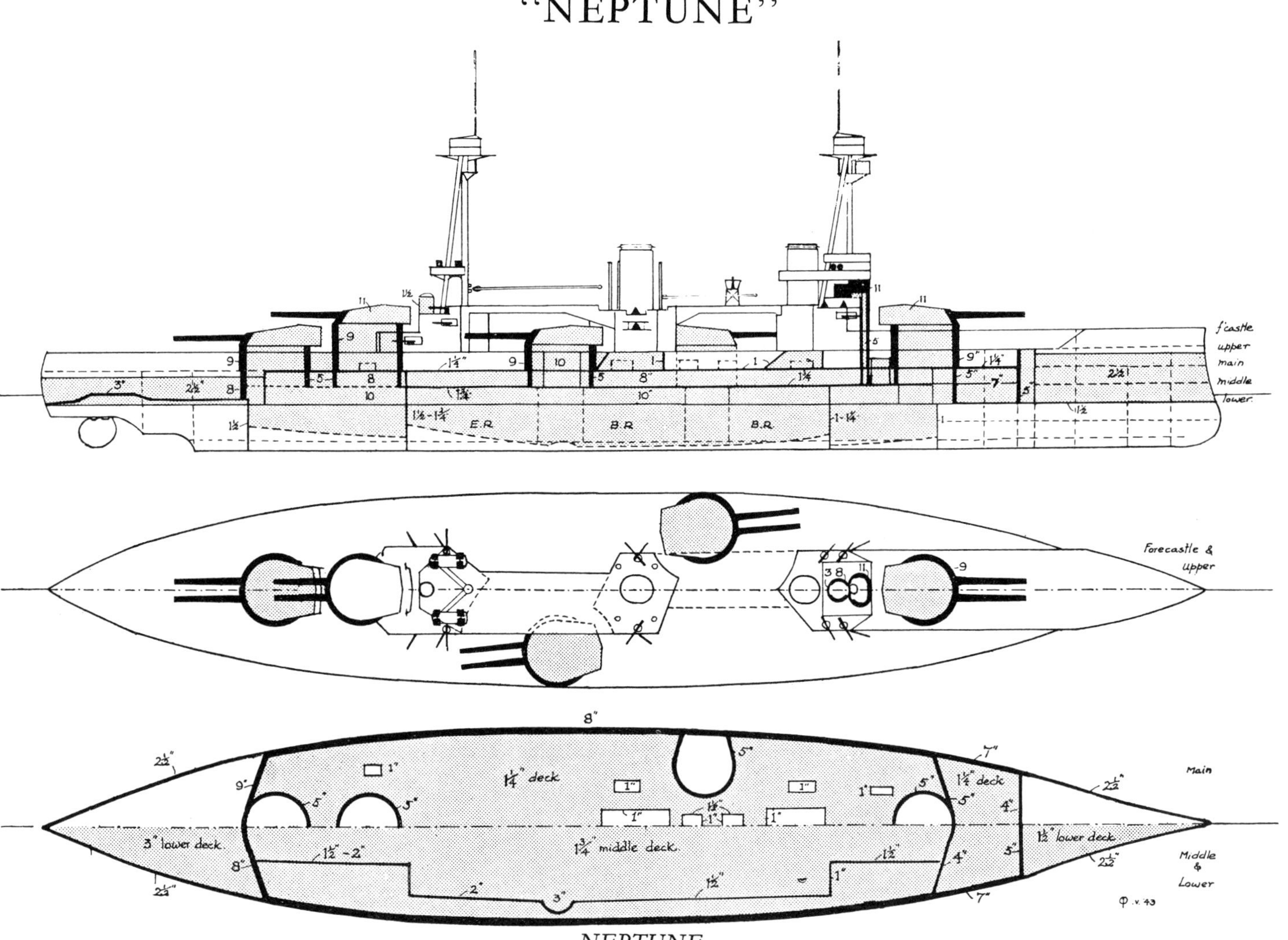

NEPTUNE

"NEPTUNE" (1908 Programme)

Built at	*Laid down*	*Launched*	*Completed*	*Cost*
Portsmouth	19 Jan. '09	30 Sept. '09	Jan. '11	£1,527,916 (guns £141,000)

Dimensions 510′ (546′) × 85′ × 24′/28′ 6″ = 19,900 tons.
Load displacement 19,680 tons; full load 22,720 tons.

Armament		
10 12-in./50.	Tubes (18″):	Torpedoes:
16 4-in./50.	2 beam	18 18-in.
4 3-pdrs.	1 stern.	6 14-in.

Protection Belt 10″-8″-7″-$2\frac{1}{2}$″; bulkheads 8″, 5″, 4″.
Barbettes 9″-5″; turrets 11″.
Conning tower 11″; signal tower 3″.
Communication tube 5″.
Decks: Main $1\frac{1}{2}$″-$\frac{3}{4}$″; middle $1\frac{3}{4}$″; power 3″-$1\frac{1}{2}$″.

Machinery Parsons (Harland and Wolff) 25,000 = 21 knots.
4 screws.
Boilers Yarrow.

Fuel Coal 900/2,710 tons; oil 790 tons.

Radius 6,330/10 knots; 3,820/18·5 knots.

Complement 759.
Constructors Mooney, Worthington.
Points of interest:

(1) First British ship to have a superimposed turret.
(2) First Dreadnought to train all big guns on either beam.
(3) Officers again berthed aft and men forward.

After the *St. Vincents* the original Dreadnought gun disposition ceased to provide an adequate broadside compared with what was possible on the all-centre-line model whereby the *Delaware* could concentrate ten guns aside, or the mixed superposed and *en echelon* design for the Argentine *Moreno* providing a broadside of twelve guns. It was obvious that in future the whole main armament would have to be available on either beam, and to meet this demand a number of plans were considered for the *Neptune*.

Advocates for the Fisher-Gard system were up against blast problems such as had influenced the Dreadnought Committee, but now considerations of length forced the issue. Only by raising a turret could excessive dimensions

The *Neptune* as she first appeared when flagship of the Home Fleet in 1911 before the fore funnel was raised. Note the length of the 12-in. guns compared with the turrets.

be avoided, and so a compromise was reached in which the *Dreadnought* wing turrets were staggered and given a considerable arc of cross-deck bearing while the extra space so employed was deducted from aft by raising the fourth turret, thereby saving about fifty feet of deck space.

There was no question of using the raised guns for firing astern—the sighting hoods in our turrets precluded this—and "stops" were fitted in the training arcs to prevent it happening. Axial fire from the wing guns was also ruled out, as blast effects on the bridge would have been intolerable, training being limited to 5° from the keel parallel ahead and astern, so that the disposition in practice worked out at two guns ahead, ten abeam, and two astern.

Secondary gun positions on the turret tops were abandoned the sixteen 4-in. being accommodated in the three superstructures. The flying bridges joining these carried the boats, but were so likely to become wrecked in action and foul the guns that the forward one was removed at the outbreak of the war. It will be noticed that the after flying bridge was disposed to starboard and that forward to port to get them as far from the muzzles of cross deck guns as possible.

DIMENSIONS

Compared with *St. Vincent*, length was increased by 10 ft. and beam by 1 ft. with a reduction of 8-in. in draught. Legend displacement was for the first time actually less than the true load displacement, the *Neptune* being 19,680 tons against the Navy List 19,900 tons.

The internal lay-out was complicated by the extra ammunition rooms required for amidships turrets and special cooling arrangements necessitated by their proximity to the boilers.

PROTECTION

This followed *St. Vincent* lines except that ½ in. was added to the bow and stern belting, and the funnel uptakes had 1-in. plating where they passed through the main deck. Hitherto uptakes had been exposed to shell splinters with the risk of decks being smoked out, and even thin plating was able to obviate this to a considerable extent. Solid bulkheads were abandoned in favour of water-tight doors.

Side armour extended 9 ft. 3 in. above water and 4 ft. 3 in. below at load draught; at full load the sinkage reached 3 ft. 3 in. when the *Neptune* relied upon 6 ft. of 8-in. armour for stability, which was some 2 ft. better than in the *Dreadnought*.

Cross-deck firing resulted in considerable strain to the deck, which had to be strengthened. But as in Barnaby's citadel ships, these arcs of training were reserved for battle and not covered as a practice procedure.

MACHINERY

The *Neptune* was the first battleship to have separate cruising turbines, which overcame the drawback of heavy fuel consumption when steaming at moderate and slow speeds. The proportion of power astern was also increased.

A mean of 27,721 h.p. on the eight hours trial gave 21·78 knots with 22·7 knots as a maximum—the highest yet recorded by a British battleship. Coal consumption worked out at 1·46 lb. per h.p. per hour.

"Neptune". July. 1914.

GENERAL

On completion she looked a well-balanced and beautiful ship, but was marred by a raised fore funnel in 1912. Next year six twin searchlights were grouped above the fore bridge on the grounds that such concentration would do much to prevent the size, angle, and course of the ship being recognized by the attacking torpedo craft. Two twin lights were left on the main mast as reserve. The twins were replaced by singles in 1916, and the

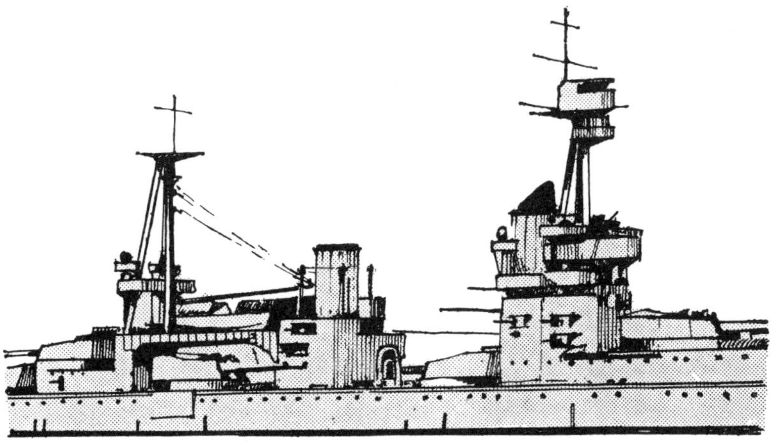

Neptune in 1916 with the forward part of the flying bridge removed and the forward shelter deck built up to house the 4-in. guns

following year came a re-distribution when only two were left above the bridge, three being placed in towers around the second funnel and those on the main mast raised to higher positions; in 1918 these latter were given tower accommodation.

As a wartime measure the forward flying boat-deck was removed, and the after control top suppressed as being more often than not put out of service by smoke and refraction.

She was the first ship to be fitted with a director tower for salvo firing, this being situated on the platform below the fore control.

"NEPTUNE"

Built at Portsmouth January '09-January '11 (cost only £86·8 per ton). Commissioned for temporary Special Service. Flagship C.-in-C. Home Fleet 11 May '11. May '12 1st B.S.

War: Grand Fleet 1st B.S. (collided with a neutral merchant ship in a fog 23 April '16). Jutland (no casualties). 4th B.S. '17-'18. Reserve. '19 Discarded under Washington Treaty.

Sold September 1922.

Chapter 89

THE "INDEFATIGABLE" CLASS

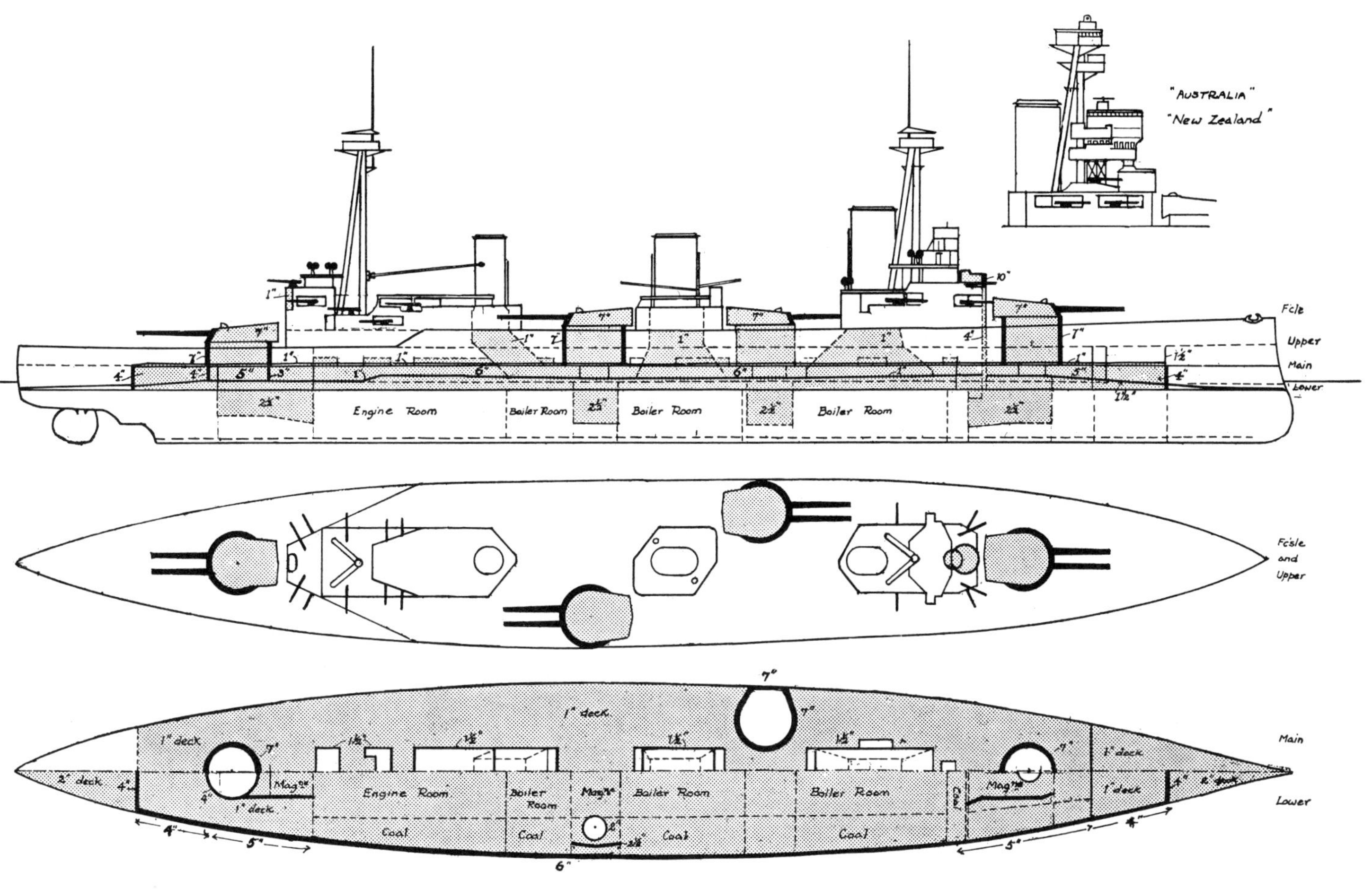

INDEFATIGABLE

"INDEFATIGABLE" Class

	Builders	*Laid down*	*Launched*	*Completed*	*Cost*
"*Indefatigable*"	Devonport	23 Feb. '09	28 Oct. '09	Feb. '11	£1,547,500
"*Australia*"	J. Brown & Co.	23 June '10	25 Oct. '11	June '13	
"*New Zealand*"	Fairfield	20 June '10	1 July '11	Nov. '12	£1,684,990 (guns £94,200)

Dimensions 555′ (590′) × 80′ × 24′ 9″/27′ = 18,800 tons (designed).
Load displacement 18,500 tons; full load 22,080 tons.

Armament 8 12-in./50. Tubes: 2 18″. Torpedoes: 12 18-in.
16 4-in./50. 6 14-in.
4 3-pdrs.

Protection Belt 6″-5″-4″ (11′ deep); bulkheads 4″.
Barbettes 7″-4″-3″; turrets 7″.
Conning tower 10″; communication tubes 4″-3″.
Spotting tower 6″-3″.
Magazine protection $2\frac{1}{2}$″.
Decks: main 1″; lower 1″; fore and aft $2\frac{1}{2}$″.
Funnel uptakes 1″-$1\frac{1}{2}$″.

Machinery Parsons ("*Indefatigable*" and "*Australia*" J. Brown; "*New Zealand*" Fairfield).
44,000 I.H.P. = 25 knots. 4 screws.
Boilers 31 Babcock and Wilcox.

Fuel	Coal 1,000/3,170 plus oil 840 tons.
Radius	6,330/10 knots; 3,140/22·8 knots; 2,290/23·5 knots.
Complement	800.
Constructor	W. T. Davis.

THE *Indefatigable*, second ship of the 1908 Programme, together with the *Australia* and *New Zealand* formed the second trio of battle cruisers. As a result of the violent controversy following the presentation of the 1908 Estimates the *Australia* and *New Zealand* were paid for by the two Dominions to help meet the deficiency in capital ships which the Government had neither the patriotism nor wisdom to provide. The former belonged to the Royal Australian Navy, the latter was presented to the British Navy. The worst results of secrecy were demonstrated in the case of the *Indefatigable*. From the start she was accorded distinction as a wonder ship—indeed, early rumours credited her as likely to be our first "motor driven" warship on the lines suggested by Mr. James McKechnie at the I.N.A. in 1907. She was to be a greatly improved *Invincible* with increased gunfire, higher speed, and stouter protection. Her real armament soon became known but unfounded optimism always placed her protection

The *Australia* in 1917 with aircraft ready to fly off the amidships turrets and searchlight towers around the second funnel, *New Zealand* was similar but had a small platform below the director tower on the foremast.

far above reality. *Jane* credited her with an 8-in. belt, 3-in. deck, and 10-in. turrets and every reference book listed some such figures. When she was reported to have steamed at 29-30 knots the tax-payer naturally regarded the ship as a fine investment and a splendid all-round fighting machine.

This of course may have suited the Admiralty book by "deceiving the enemy" but she certainly deceived the Nation, being nothing but an enlarged *Invincible* with the same weak protection and presenting a larger target. All that secrecy achieved was to hide the unpalatable fact that a ship regarded as equal or superior to the contemporary German design was unfit to get within range of her guns. If the *Indefatigable* and her protection could have been debated upon at the R.U.S.I. or I.N.A. it is safe to say that she would never have been built without drastic changes to make her battle-worthy. But unfortunately Fisher's dictum that "Speed is the best Protection" ruled design even when the original outline of employment for which these *Dreadnought* cruisers were intended became prejudiced by the announcement that in future German armoured cruisers would be of the *Invincible* type. Although the *Von der Tann* had been ordered in 1907 nothing was known about her—she might or might not carry heavier metal than our ships. But it was at once obvious that *Invincibles* acting as a fast battleship wing would have to contact their peers—when speed would offer no protection. Such engagements would mean exposure to heavy gun-fire when only adequate armour would ensure survival. There could be no question of relying upon superior gunnery to overwhelm enemy attack—the Germans were already building up a reputation for very remarkable long-range hitting, and the first salvoes could decide a ship's fate. Sir Eustace Tennyson D'Eyncourt put on record his own opinion of the design at the I.N.A. in March 1921 when he stated:

> "In reviewing the whole history of battle cruiser design, I cannot help thinking that it was unfortunate that it was decided virtually to repeat the 'Invincibles'—a design already becoming obsolescent—when the 'Indefatigable' class was ordered, instead of developing an improved design with protection which should have been at least equal to that of the 'Moltke' and 'Goeben' of about the same date."

At that period the battle cruiser edition of the contemporary battleship was allotted extra speed at the expense of guns and armour on about the same displacement. This compromise was accepted in explanation of the battle cruiser and generally regarded as reasonable, always presuming that such ships were capable of fulfilling a definite rôle in battle. But the *Indefatigable* could never be justified as such a compromise. She was over 1,000 tons lighter than the *Neptune* although requiring every ton of it, and more, to fit her for the battle line, and as planned with armour on the *Invincible* scale was simply a capital ship *pour rire* which showed a culpable want of vision on the part of the Board or, shall we say, the First Sea Lord. But what Fisher thought of her is best expressed when he wrote to Lord Esher in September 1908:

> "I've got Sir Philip Watts into a new *Indomitable* that will make your mouth water when you see it, and the Germans gnash their teeth."

Doubtless the question of expenditure had a lot to do with limiting displacement, although such an excuse would appear paltry. But having fixed on four turrets, spaced them to provide a full broadside, and drafted a hull to carry them at a legend 25 knots the question of protection would seem to have been almost of secondary consideration. Fisher did not believe in burdening his fast ships with armour—"handicapping the racehorses" as he used to put it—so would have been quite satisfied with 6 in. along the water-line and the high unarmoured freeboard, although this was most profligate in absorbing displacement.

Comparison with the *Von der Tann* shows to what extent high freeboard must have determined displacement considering dimensions and armour, although the German had somewhat finer lines.

	"INDEFATIGABLE"	"VON DER TANN"
Dimensions	555′ × 80′ × 25¾′.	562′ × 87′ × 26½′.
Displacement	18,500 tons (actual).	19,100 tons.
Armament	8 12-in.; 16 4-in. 2 21-in. tubes.	8 11-in.; 10 5·9-in. 16 3·4-in.; 4 20-in. tubes.
Protection	Belt 6″; turrets 7″. Decks 2″ (total).	Belt 9¾″-6″-4″; turrets 9″. Decks 3¾″ (total).
Designed h.p.	41,000=25 knots.	43,600=24 knots.
Fuel (maximum)	3,170 plus 840 oil.	2,760 plus 197 oil.
Complement (war)	800	1,300
Cost	£1,547,500	£1,833,000.

Allowing that the tonnage of the German ship is below what one might expect for the dimensions, she certainly shows a better bargain for the displacement. The main deck guns and battery would absorb over 1,000 tons, which is about what the British ship carried in excess fuel; both ships made over 1-2 knots more than the designed speed but the *Indefatigable* was somewhat the better sea boat.

No secret had been made of the *Von der Tann's* displacement being about 19,000 tons, and allowing that the Germans would save a lot on fuel and the lighter installations for their big guns, there was every indication that the ship would carry either a heavier armament or much sounder protection than in the *Invincible*, although in 1911 she was still believed to have a 6-in. belt only. (*Brassey*, 1911, p. 152.)

Given similar qualities a competitive British design must always show greater displacement than the Continental because of a necessary larger fuel supply and sea-going qualities, and there was no excuse for limiting the *Indefatigable* to 18,800 tons, indeed 20,000 tons might well have been allotted to her at an extra cost of about £100,000.

GENERAL DESIGN

As in the *Neptune* the internal lay-out was complicated by the wing turrets with separate central magazines placed between the boiler rooms, and needing special cooling arrangements. Space for the amidships guns was found by placing "A" and "B" turrets nearer the ends and adding 25 ft. to the length. On paper this arrangement gave eight guns aside and six ahead and astern, but actually the wing guns were limited to 5° of the keel parallel because of blast effects. Not that this was of any consequence, as pursuit actions would not be fought in the wake of an enemy and direct axial fire could but rarely be of any tactical value.

Because of the 50 calibre guns the barbettes were 28 ft. in diameter—1 ft. more than in *Invincible*—but "A" and "B" positions were placed where the beam was actually 6 ft. less than in the earlier ships.

In the two Dominion ships the after control top was suppressed owing to smoke and refraction difficulties.

ARMAMENT

The development of the echelon system was a mistake, but having accepted it for the *Invincible* it was only natural that a wider spacing of the amidships turrets to allow for a fuller broadside would be aimed at, when there was deck length to allow for it.

The echelon arrangement in Barnaby's ships was intended to provide end-on fire at a time when line abreast formations and ramming tactics held the field. It was discarded because in practice it failed to provide either a full broadside or axial concentration.

Unfortunately in 1905 the shortcomings of Barnaby's ships were either forgotten or ignored in face of the supposed necessity for end-on fire. When revived in Watts' *Inflexible* the slight stagger of the wing turrets served to give a very limited cross-deck bearing to a pair of guns which otherwise might never have come into action; but these amidships guns could not be fired directly ahead or astern without intolerable blast effects on bridge and control personnel. In the *Indefatigable* it would have been worse as the fore wing turret was placed so as to expose the bridge and controls to the maximum effect of blast from end-on fire.

Actually the provision of axial fire from the wing turrets would be of little consequence as the chances of encountering an enemy right ahead or astern were remote and in any case a very slight yaw could completely alter the situation. The gun concentration, therefore, may be taken as two guns ahead and astern and eight on the full beam but limited to six over certain arcs.

As in the *Invincible* and *Neptune* the port wing turret was the foremost so that only six guns could be trained towards an enemy on the port bow or starboard quarter, but all eight guns on the starboard bow or port quarter. In the *Von der Tann* there was the opposite arrangement, so that the British ship would have the German at a twenty-five per cent. disadvantage by keeping her on the starboard bow or port quarter while the German would have the same superiority with the British ship, on the port bow or starboard quarter.

The sixteen 4-in. guns were divided between the fore (6) and after superstructures (10), a distribution decided by available space rather than by the likelihood of torpedo attack from astern.

PROTECTION

Compared with the *Invincible* some fifty feet of 4-in. plating was removed from the bows and added to the belt aft, with 5 in. instead of 6 in. under "A" and "B" barbettes. The belt rose 8 ft. 1½ in. above water and extended for 2 ft. 10½ in. below at load draught, and with a sinkage of 75 tons per inch she drew 29 ft. 8½ in. at full load with only 4 ft. 3 in. of armour above water. This belt was closed by 4-in. bulkheads and covered by a deck of 1-in. only, below which the 7-in. barbettes were replaced by narrow 2-in. trunks to minimize magazine communication risks, except in the case of "X" which ran down to the lower protective 1-in. deck. Considerable weight was expended on 1-in. armour to the funnel uptakes from the lower protective deck to the forecastle deck as in the *Neptune*.

But however well these ships might be fought, such second-rate protection made their employment in the battle-line a hazardous risk.

MACHINERY

Although the higher powered *Von der Tann* managed with two boiler rooms by virtue of her small tube boilers, greater beam, and narrower bunkers, the *Indefatigable* required three whose different sizes were dictated by the position of the wing turrets and magazines. Over 100 tons more oil was carried than in the *Invincibles* and of the thirty-one boilers twenty-eight were fitted with three burners and three with two burners all at 300 lb. pressure.

No cruising turbines were fitted.

All three ships well exceeded designed speed on trials their figures being:

	Indefatigable	*Australia*	*New Zealand*
30 hours	31,717=24·6	25·1	31,794=24·7
8 "	47,135=26·7	26·9	45,894=26·3

GENERAL

These ships proved a lot cheaper to build than the *Invincibles*, the *Indefatigable* working out at £82 5s. per ton against £101 6s. of the earlier trio.

Searchlight towers were fitted to *Australia* and *New Zealand* in 1917.

"INDEFATIGABLE"

Commissioned at Devonport 24 February '11 for 1st C.S. which in January '13 became 1st B.C.S. December '13 transferred to Mediterranean 2nd B.C.S. Shared in search for *Goeben* and later blockade of Dardanelles. Bombardment of Cape Helles 3 November; Flagship of Admiral Carden until January '15 when relieved by *Inflexible*; refit Malta; joined Grand Fleet 2nd B.C.S. February '15. Sunk at Jutland (4.05 p.m.) on 31 May.

"At the other end of the line the duel between the *Indefatigable* and the *Von der Tann* had been growing in intensity till the British ship was suddenly hidden in a burst of flame and smoke. A salvo of three shots had fallen on her upper deck and must have penetrated to a magazine. She staggered out of line, sinking by the stern when another salvo struck her; a second terrible explosion rent her, she turned over and in a moment all trace of her was gone" (Naval Operations, 111, 336).

"AUSTRALIA"

Completed at Clydebank June '13 and proceeded to Australian waters.

War: Flagship of N.A. and W.I. station and flagship of an Australasian force in defensive operations against German squadron in Pacific. After Falklands battle joined in search of German armed merchantmen. Grand Fleet. Flagship 2nd B.C.S. (Rear-Admiral Pakenham). In collision with *New Zealand* 22 April '16 in a fog. Docked until 5 June; rejoined 2nd B.C.S. in which she was flagship for remainder of war. Returned to Australia as Flagship of Australian Navy 1919. When listed for disposal under Washington Treaty was sunk with honours off Sydney Harbour. 1924.

"NEW ZEALAND"

Completed at Fairfields November '12 at the charge of New Zealand Government and presented to the Royal Navy. Was visited by the King at Portsmouth and on 7 February '13 proceeded on a world cruise visiting the Dominions and several Colonies. Joined the B.C.F. December '13 for the visit to Russian Baltic ports.

War: Grand Fleet 1st B.C.S.; Rear-Admiral Flagship 2nd B.C.S. January-February '15. Dogger Bank 24 January '15 (Flagship Rear-Admiral Moore). In action with *Blücher* and succeeded to command when *Lion* was out of action. In collision with *Australia* 22 April '16 and in dock until May. Jutland battle. Received one hit on "X" turret; no casualties. June '16. 1st B.C.S. replaced by *Renown* in September and reverted to 2nd B.C.S. for remainder of war. '19 Conveyed Admiral Sir John Jellicoe for his tour of the Dominions, when he drew up a scheme of defence and future naval forces. Listed for disposal under Washington Treaty.

Sold December 1922.

Chapter 90

"WE WANT EIGHT" PROGRAMME

ON the death of Sir Henry Campbell-Bannerman early in 1908 Mr. Asquith succeeded to the Premiership with Mr. Lloyd George at the Exchequer. Mr. Churchill went to the Board of Trade with a seat in the Cabinet, and banded with the Chancellor and Mr. Lulu Harcourt to carry out social reforms and reduce armaments.

During 1908-9 for the first time the Navy became a subject for party controversy. The Liberals and their political henchmen persuaded themselves that the German Emperor's assurances regarding his fleet could be accepted at their face value, while the Conservatives claimed that there had been an acceleration of construction and that the German ships would be completed ahead of schedule. Feeling was considerably heightened by the incident of the Tweedmouth letter. An association called the Imperial Maritime League which had as its chief object the hounding of Lord Fisher from the Admiralty had canvassed Lord Esher for support and received a scathing letter which pointed out that Fisher was the most dreaded man in Germany from the Emperor downwards. A copy of this came into the Emperor's possession and his annoyance took the form of a letter to Lord Tweedmouth commenting on Lord Esher in a most uncomplimentary way. In March 1908 it became known that in his reply he had communicated to the Kaiser some information regarding the forthcoming Naval Estimates. Lord Tweedmouth was unjustly censored, he having framed his answer with the full knowledge and sanction of his colleagues. There was, in fact, no premature disclosure of the Naval Estimates to the German Emperor. The First Lord, a sick man, handled the matter badly. The Press made the most of what was presented as a correspondence between Lord Tweedmouth and the Kaiser and to appease an indignant public Mr. Reginald McKenna became First Lord.

Fisher, looking ahead, saw the relation between (1) the big German naval programme which would be completed in 1914, (2) the rebuilt Kiel Canal also to be finished that year, and (3) the end of the harvest—and fixed on September or October 1914 as the probable outbreak of war. He even went so far as to confide to the King his opinion that the German fleet should be "Copenhagened" before then—by which he meant sunk inside Kiel or led out of the harbour as prisoners. The King's comment was "Fisher, you're mad." (*Lord Fisher*, II, p. 75.)

However, a full-sized European crisis was to show Germany in her real light. On 5 October Austria, without warning or parley, proclaimed her annexation of Bosnia and Herzegovina. Britain and Russia demanded a conference but Austria, supported by Germany, refused. There was danger of Serbia's taking some violent action, and Sir Edward Grey while making it plain that we would not be drawn into a Balkan war, gave full diplomatic support to Russia's championship of Serbia. But Austria had decided that unless Serbia recognized the annexation she would declare war. Here Germany intervened, insisting that Russia should advize Serbia to give way—and do this without discussions with Britain or France, otherwise Austria would commence hostilities *with the full support of Germany*. Russia, unprepared for war with both Austria and Germany, gave way—and the Teuton triumph was complete.

In the autumn of 1908 the Admiralty became thoroughly alarmed. Evidence was forthcoming, from Mr. Mulliner of the Coventry Ordnance works and other sources, that Germany was going to take advantage of our reduced programmes to try and equal our Dreadnought fleet. From the figures submitted it looked as if by 1912 we should both have the same number of battleships and battle cruisers, twenty-one being the estimated number. Fisher presented the following memorandum to the First Lord viewing the situation as it then appeared:

> "We concur in the *statement* of the First Lord that there is a possibility that Germany by the spring of 1912 will have completed twenty-one Dreadnoughts; and there is a practical *certainty* that she will have seventeen by that date; whereas, presuming we lay down six during the coming year, we shall have only eighteen.... The question might be asked why warning was not given at an earlier date, but the information about the ante-dating of the laying-down and completion of the German ships of the 1909-10 programme, and the further evidence pointing to a continuous acceleration of shipbuilding in subsequent years, was not known until quite recently."

In the Cabinet battle which ensued Mr. McKenna stood practically alone. Mr. Churchill led the opposition and vehemently contested the Admiralty figures, claiming that the Germans had not commenced secret building and that our pre-Dreadnought margin added to the new programme of four ships proposed for 1909 would assure us an adequate superiority for 1912. Fisher was informed by Mr. McKenna that he was going to resign after Mr. Churchill and his adherents had apparently gained the day at the last Cabinet meeting. Then Sir Edward Grey stepped in. The First Lord's resignation raised the situation to one of first importance. The Admiralty statements were closely scrutinized and at Grey's request the Premier called a further Cabinet meeting. With certain provisos to cover the conduct of the Admiralty critics the Programme was accepted and the "We want Eight. and we wont wait" ships authorized.

Without the full eight we should have had sixteen Dreadnoughts to the German fourteen in August 1914; the loss of the *Audacious* would have reduced us to a level fifteen; in January 1915, by fleet casualties through collision, there would have been fifteen to meet sixteen Germans.

Fortunately the Admiralty figures were wrong. There was no acceleration in the building programmes and our margin was on the right side in 1912 when thirteen German capital ships were completed to our twenty-two. As Mr. Churchill puts it:

> "In the end a curious and characteristic solution was reached. The Admiralty had demanded six ships; the economists offered four; and we finally compromised on eight. . . . But although the Chancellor of the Exchequer and I were right in the narrow sense, we were absolutely wrong in relation to the deep tides of destiny. The greatest credit is due to the First Lord of the Admiralty, Mr. McKenna, for the resolute and courageous manner in which he fought his case and withstood his Party on this occasion. Little did I think, as this dispute proceeded, that when the next Cabinet crisis about the Navy arose our roles would be reversed; and little did he think that the ships for which he had contended so stoutly would eventually, when they arrived, be welcomed with open arms by me." (*The World Crisis*, 1, p. 37.)

The eight ships provided in 1909 belonged to three classes, of which *Colossus* and *Hercules* were half sisters to the *Neptune*; four battleships of the *Orion* class were of an entirely new type; with the *Lion* and *Princess Royal* as their battle cruiser editions. Thus the year saw the commencement of eight capital ships—the greatest accession to our armoured forces ever undertaken in a twelvemonth.

"COLOSSUS" and "HERCULES" (1909 Programme)

	Builders	*Laid down*	*Launched*	*Completed*	*Cost*
"*Colossus*"	Scotts	8 July '09	9 April '10	July '11	£1,540,402
"*Hercules*"	Palmers	30 July '09	10 May '10	Aug. '11	£1,529,540 (guns £131,700)

Dimensions 510′ (546′) × 85′ × 25′ 3″/28′ 9″ = 20,000 tons (designed).
Load displacement 20,225 tons; full load 23,050 tons.

Armament			
	10 12-in./50 cals.	Tubes (21″):	Torpedoes:
	16 4-in./50 „	2 beam.	18 21-in.
	4 3-pdrs.	1 stern.	6 14-in.

Protection Belt 11″-8″-7″.
Bulkheads 10″-8″-5″-4″.
Barbettes 11″-10″-9″-7″-6″-5″-4″.
Turrets 11″.
Conning tower 11″; signal tower 3″.
Communication tube 5″.
Decks: main $1\frac{1}{2}$″; middle $1\frac{3}{4}$″; lower 4″-3″-$2\frac{1}{2}$″-$1\frac{3}{4}$″.

Machinery Parsons (by builders) H.P. 25,000 = 21 knots.
4 screws.
Boilers 18 Yarrow ("*Hercules*"), Babcock ("*Colossus*").

Fuel Coal 900/2,900 tons; oil 800 tons.

Radius 6,680/10 knots; 4,050/18·5 knots.

Complement 755.

Constructors Mooney, Worthington.

Points of interest:

(1) First battleships to have 21-in. torpedo tubes.
(2) Secondary armament mainly concentrated forward.
(3) Reverted to magazine torpedo bulkheads only.
(4) Unarmoured ends.

Although nominally sisters to the *Neptune* these ships showed variations of considerable interest which served to place them in a class by themselves.

Two causes served to bring about the reversion to one mast abaft the funnel (1) the after control top was too often affected by smoke and gas fumes (2) w.t. aerials slung from a high topmast to short stumps aft had proved satisfactory. Suppression of the after tripod meant saving about 50 tons of topweight, and every ton meant a good deal in this design. Although displacing only 100 tons more than the *Neptune* according to the Navy List, the listed load figures showed an increase of 545 tons with an increase of 9-in. draught; but at 76·9 tons per inch

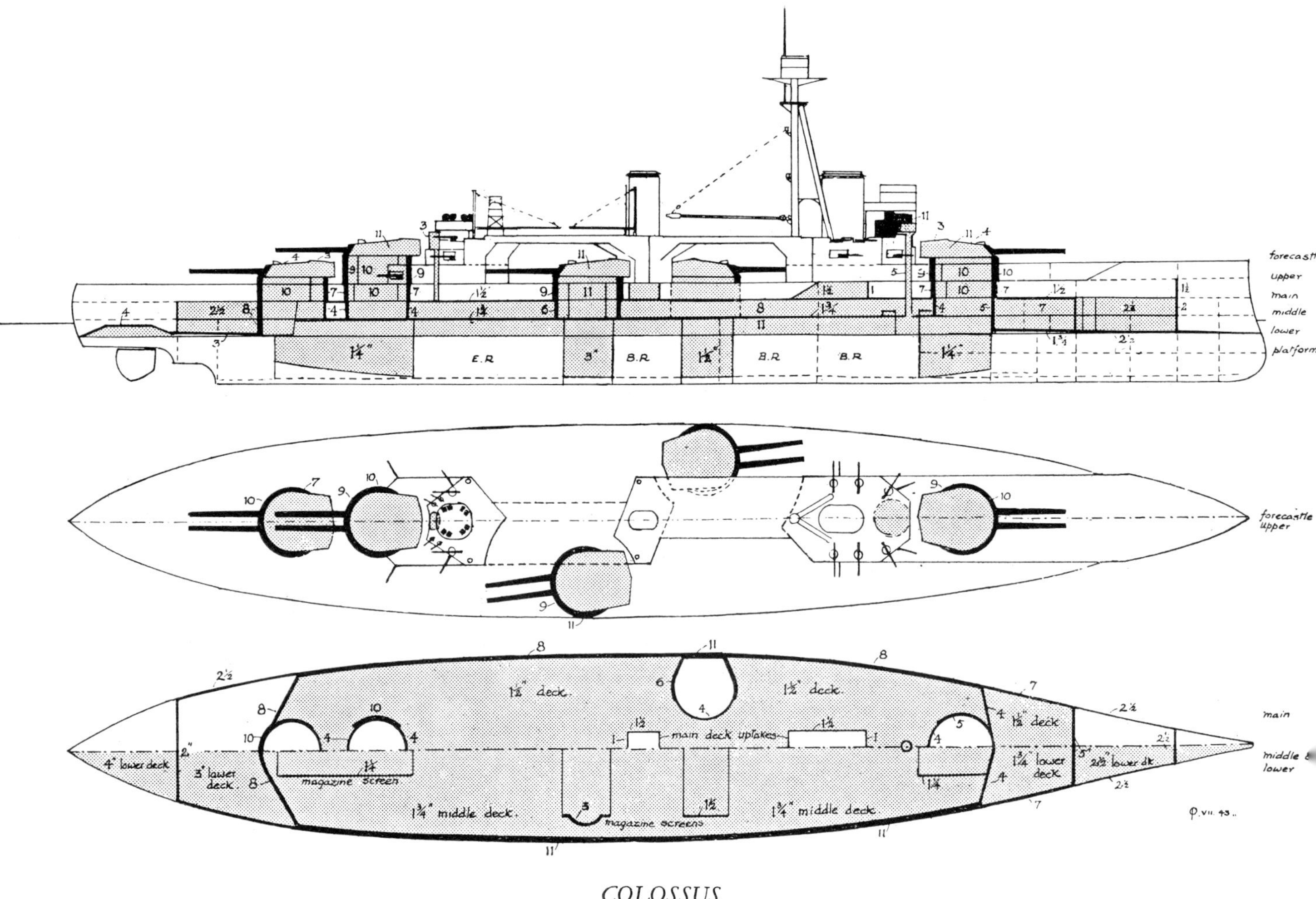

COLOSSUS

sinkage this meant 692 tons, which difference was probably nearer the mark. There were considerable changes in armour distribution, external protection being strengthened at the expense of internal.

ARMAMENT

In order to concentrate torpedo defence over the most likely quarters for attack the bulk of the 4-in. guns were mounted in the forward superstructure, lengthening it considerably. This entailed a considerable re-arrangement in turret positions, magazines and boiler rooms, as the middle superstructure deprived of 4-in. guns, became shorter and deck economy brought the wing turrets and their magazines closer together. This in turn reduced the size of the second boiler room and the generators had to be moved up to the forward one necessitating a wider funnel.

The arcs of fire of the wing turrets were from 5° of the fore and aft line as shown in the plan.

In 1917 the secondary armament was reduced to 13 guns, but a 4-in. A.A. and 3-in. A.A. were added.

The change from 18-in. to 21-in. torpedoes—which are considerably longer—required larger flats and torpedo rooms and so again added to the difficulties in restraining displacement. The Hardcastle-Elswick heater, by eliminating cold from the compressed air, increased speed to 45 knots over a range of 1,000 yards with an effective range of 7,000 yards.

PROTECTION

When the *Neptune* design was modified for the *Colossus* with the same length and beam it may be assumed that there was every intention of keeping to the same draught as any additional displacement would be a disability and merely serve to submerge the belt. But an essential feature of the modified design was to be better protection for gun positions and along the water-line. A halt had been called to the trend towards thinner plating observed

The *Colossus* in 1912 with her fore funnel raised. As a flagship *Hercules* had no funnel bands, while *Colossus* had one red on each before the alphabetical system with white bands was adopted.

in each class since the *Dreadnought*, which whittling away reached a stage in the *Neptune* when the 9-in. barbettes could be penetrated by 12-in. gunfire inside 11,000 yards and the 10-in. belt was not proof under 9,400 yards. An inch was therefore added to the lower belt and most exposed upper parts of the barbettes although elsewhere these were pared down by the same amount, and the seven thicknesses used in the different barbettes make interesting comparison.

As some compensation for the additional belt weight a return was made to the *Dreadnought's* local magazine

Colossus in 1918 with the after flying boat deck removed, director tower on control top, bridges built up, and searchlight towers around after funnel, her 4-in. guns fired through open ports without shields.

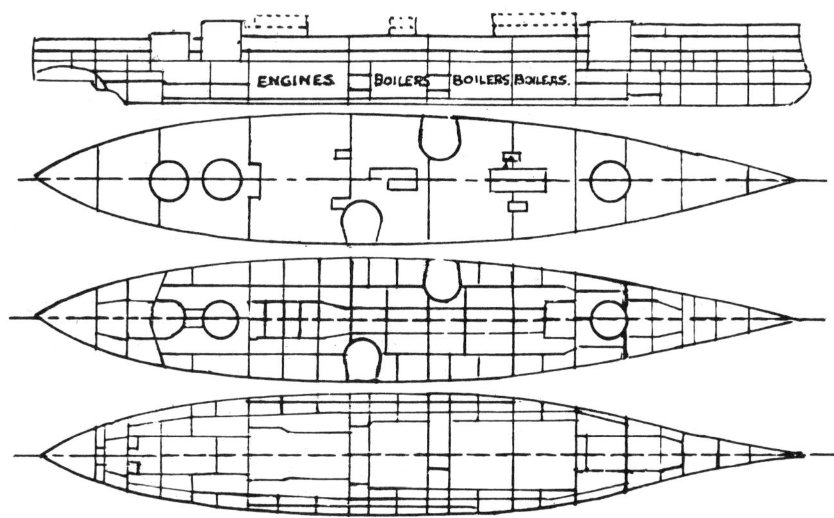

Watertight system of subdivision with *en echelon* turrets.

protection, the under-water screens being increased to 3 in.; also the bow and stern plating was suppressed and recourse made to a 4-in. deck over the steering.

MACHINERY

Was similar to that in *Neptune*. The trial figures were:

	30 *Hours*	8 *Hours*
Colossus	18,000=19·6	29,000=21·5 (maximum 22·6 knots).
Hercules	17,000=19·6	28,700=21·5 (maximum 21·9 knots). (bad weather).

Both ships were out on the measured mile in nineteen months and ready for the pennant in two years, despite labour troubles then delaying construction generally.

GENERAL

Boom boats were stowed on the forward flying deck, so that it was the after one which was removed at the outbreak of war. Changes during the next four years included extensions of the bridge-work and fitting of searchlight towers around the second funnel.

Hercules could be distinguished by having shields to her 4-in. while *Colossus* had open ports with dropping lids.

The short fore funnel proved troublesome to bridge duties and was raised in 1912.

After the war, when employed as a training ship at Devonport the *Colossus* was given the Victorian livery, the only *Dreadnought* to sport the black, white and buff.

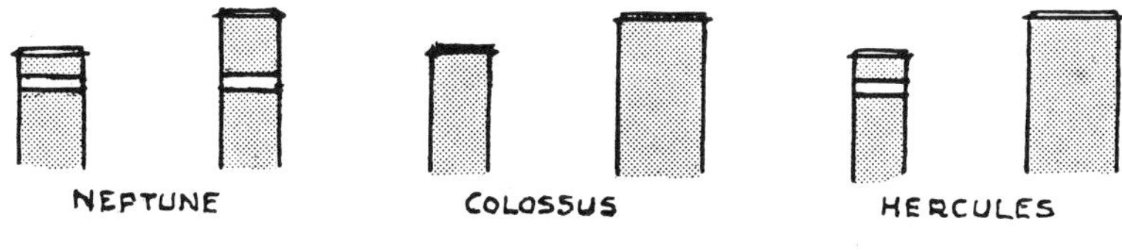

"COLOSSUS"

Built by Scott's July '09 to July '11. Commissioned 8 August '11 at Devonport for 2nd Division Home Fleet; May '12 2nd B.S.; December '12 1st B.S.

War: August '14 1st B.S. (Flagship Admiral Gaunt at Jutland. In action with enemy B.C. received 2 hits; 5 casualties; the only battleship in the main fleet to be hit); later 4th B.S. After the war became training ship for cadets at Devonport. Discarded under the Treaty and sold 1920.

"HERCULES"

Built by Palmers at Jarrow July '09 to August '11. Commissioned July '11 at Portsmouth as Flagship 2nd Division Home Fleet. May '12 became Flagship 2nd B.S. until Flagship was transferred to *King George V* in March '13 (22 March '13 collided with a steamer in Portland Roads; temporary repairs at Portsmouth) June '13 1st B.S.

War: August '14 1st B.S. Grand Fleet. At Jutland in the 6th Division with *Marlborough* (13·5-in.), *Revenge* (15-in.) and *Agincourt* (12-in.) as mixed a Division as was the 3rd. Later became Flagship of Admiral Sturdee 4th B.S. and carried the Naval Commission to Kiel after the Armistice. Discarded under the Treaty and sold 1920.

Chapter 91

REVERSION TO THE 13·5-IN. GUN

In the *Orion* and *Lion* classes a return was made to the 13·5-in. gun last mounted in the old *Royal Sovereign* class. The fact that the larger calibre was to be carried became a very open secret, and although officially referred to as the "12-in. A" during trials the real size of the gun was given full publicity in the Press very soon after the ships were laid down, there being no restrictions against publication of such information "unofficially." Officially, of course, the farce had to go on and the British Ordnance List in 1913 "Brassey" gave as the most recent mark the 12-in. 45 cal. with a note at the head of the list "Other guns are mounted, but details are withheld from publication." Thus were the Germans foiled from discovering the sacred secrets of what our guns could do! Twelve pages further on the latest Vickers and Armstrongs model were listed, and presumably it was to be supposed that by some kind of miracle the British Navy had evolved guns altogether superior to those produced by the knowledge of technical gun-factors the world over. Actually for all practical purposes any two guns of equal calibre and equal date are equal in power, and the real difference lies in the man behind; and no gun ballistics can give details about him.

The official answer to which was "Why give away something for nothing" and there the matter ended.

The reasons for adopting the larger calibre were:

(1) Better shooting.
(2) Greater hitting effect.

In the *Hercules* the 12-in. gun had been developed to the limits of its capacity in length, weight of shell, and muzzle velocity. Under the stress of constant practice firing erosion was considerable and accuracy soon suffered. Although quite capable of piercing the thickest armour at battle ranges, its shells could not carry the heavy bursting charge required after perforation. Guns of larger calibres were the obvious solution as the heavier shell could contain the required charge, while a lower muzzle velocity—causing less erosion—still provided ample striking energy. The life of the gun was thus lengthened, and more accurate shooting could be obtained. The shooting defects of the 12-in. 50 cal. have already been mentioned (p. 503) and to these difficulties a magnificent corrective was found in the 13·5-in.:

	12-in. 50 cal.	*13·5-in. 45 cal.*
Length in inches (total)	617	625·9
Weight in tons	65·6	75·4
Projectile in lb.	850	1,250/1,400 (heavy)
M.V. in foot-seconds	3,010	2,700
M.E. in foot-tons	53,400	63,190
Full charge in lb.	307	293/297

"ORION" Class (1909 Programme)

	Builders	*Laid down*	*Launched*	*Completed*	*Total cost*
"*Conqueror*"	Beardmore	5 April '10	1 May '11	Nov. '12	£1,860,648
"*Monarch*"	Armstrongs	1 April '10	30 March '11	March '12	£1,886,912
"*Orion*"	Portsmouth	29 Nov. '09	20 Aug. '10	Jan. '12	£1,918,773
"*Thunderer*"	Thames I.W.	13 April '10	1 Feb. '11	June '12	£1,885,145

Dimensions 545′ (581′)×88′ 6″×24′ 11″/28′ 9″=22,500 tons.
Load displacement 22,200 tons; deep load 25,870 tons.

Armament		
10 13·5-in./45	Tubes (21″):	Torpedoes:
16 4-in./50.	2 broadside.	20 21-in.
4 3-pdrs.	1 stern (later removed).	6 14-in.

Protection Belt 12″-9″-8″ (17′ 2″ above water, 3′ 4″ below).
Bulkheads 10″-8″-6″-3″.
Barbettes 10″-9″-7″-6″-3″.
Turrets 11″.
Conning tower 11″; spotting tower 6″; director 3″.
Decks: main 1½″; middle 1″; lower 4″-3″-2½″-1″.
Magazines 1¾″-1″.

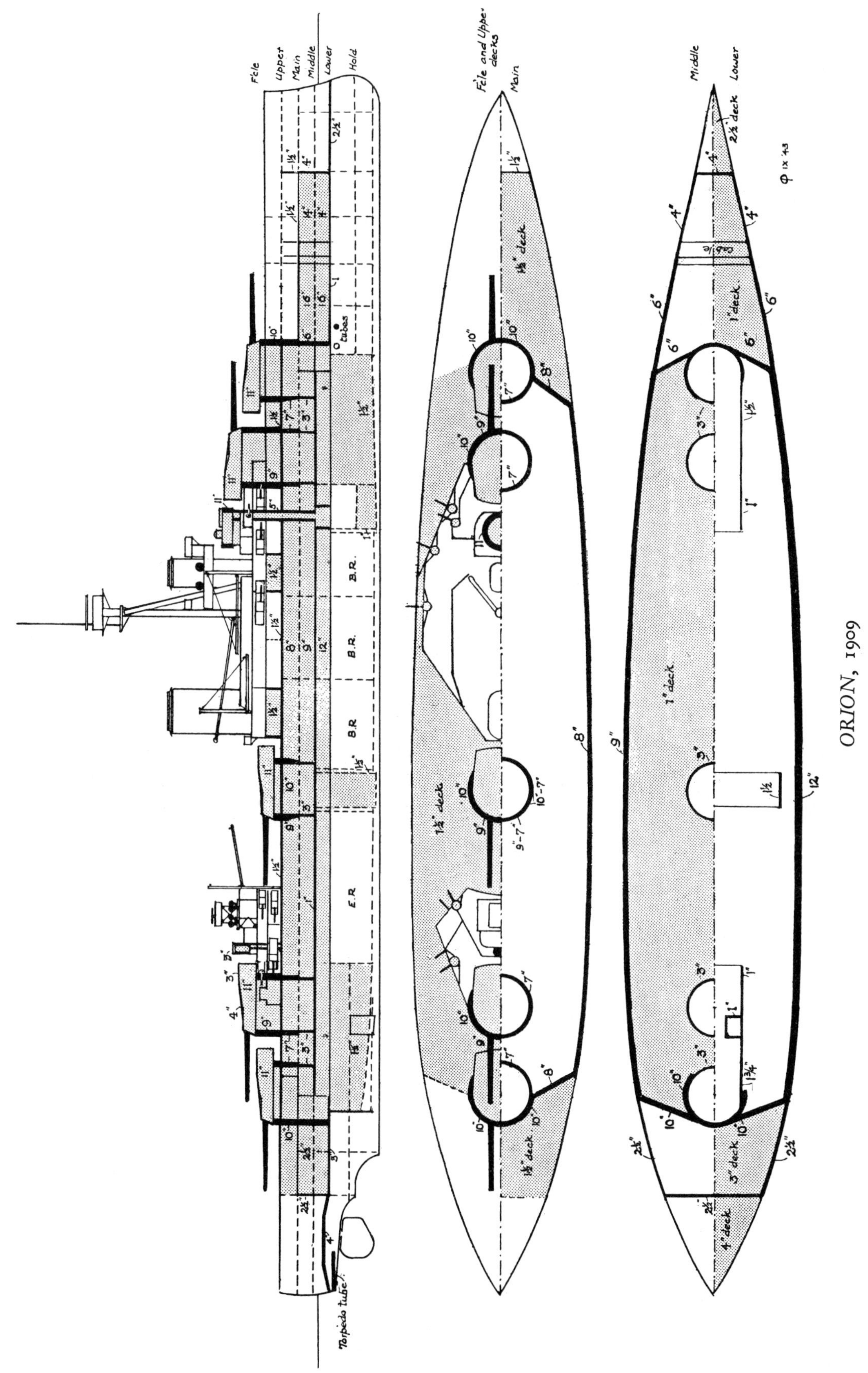
Fc'le
Upper
Main
Middle
Lower
Hold
Torpedo tube
tubes
B.R.
B.R.
B.R.
E.R.
Fc'le and Upper decks
Main
1½" deck
1½" deck
1½" deck
Middle
Lower
2½" deck
1" deck
1" deck
3" deck
4" deck

ORION, 1909

Machinery	Parsons. "*Conqueror*" and "*Thunderer*" by builders. "*Monarch*" Hawthorn Leslie. "*Orion*" Wallsend. 27,000 s.h.p.=21/20·5 knots; 4 screws. 18 Boilers: "*Conqueror,*" "*Thunderer,*" "*Orion,*" Babcock. "*Monarch,*" Yarrow.
Fuel	Coal 900/3,300; oil 800 tons. 3 sprayers at 300 lb. pressure.
Radius	6,730/10 knots; 4,110/19 knots.
Complement	752.
Constructors	E. N. Mooney, A. M. Worthington.

Special features:

(1) First all-centreline Dreadnoughts.
(2) Return to 13·5-in. guns.
(3) Return to main deck side armour.
(4) Splinter and blast screens to boats.

One outstanding feature of the capital ships of the 1909 Programme was the unprecedented rise in displacement of the *Orion* and *Lion* classes. Sir Philip Watts has recorded (I.N.A. 1911) that for once the Construction Department had almost a free hand without the restrictions imposed by financial considerations. There was a growing

Conqueror on completion November 1912 showing the restricted charthouse kept clear of the conning tower, and net defence.

sense of impending trouble in the not distant future which tended to ease the string round the money bags, and having decided upon a clean sweep in design and fighting equipment the ships were to be generously fashioned. Hence a rise of 2,500 tons in the *Orion's* nominal displacement—the biggest jump yet recorded in our tale of battleships.

In adopting the centre-line disposition of turrets we followed the American lead in the *Delaware* with modifications necessitated by our retention of 4-in. guns in two superstructures in place of medium-sized artillery along the main deck. In the past American designs had been often experimental and not particularly successful, but from the inception of the Dreadnought era they showed a better appreciation of fighting qualities than did our own. Their turret sighting arrangements allowed for super-firing without the observers being concussed; we persisted in the old form of sighting hoods in which they would have been, and so limited the raised guns to more or less broadside fire.

A belated but inevitable discarding of the wing turrets in favour of the centre-line facilitated internal arrangements and insured development upon a sound basis. Actually the change was less of a break-away then it appeared. So long as the after superstructure was retained five centre-line turrets could not have been accommodated in the *Hercules*, and the echelon arrangement was the only one providing a ten-gun broadside. But having adopted the superposed guns in the *Neptune* as a necessary expedient, it was but a short step to the *Orion* arrangement with the after wing turret moved to the centre-line and the forward one shifted to "B" position. As the new 45 cal. 13·5-in. guns were only some 8 in. longér than the 50 cal. 12-in., no increase in barbette diameter was necessary, but the re-arrangement added 35 ft. to the deck line—a turret's length and clearance.

The additional topweight of "B" turret plus a main deck strake of armour raised the centre of gravity considerably, so that an increase of beam was necessary to preserve the proper metacentric height and provide initial stiffness. Despite the additional length the beam increase was limited to 3½ ft. only, giving a length : beam ratio of 6·16 : 1—the highest since the old *Minotaur*. It will be seen that this ratio had steadily risen in each class of *Dreadnought*—so much so, that had the *Dreadnought's* proportions been retained the *Orion's* beam would have been 91 ft. instead of 88½ ft.

The advantages of a more generous beam in providing better anti-torpedo protection and stability were considered, but set aside in favour of an increase just sufficient to give the requisite initial stability and a metacentric height of 5 ft. On the other hand the German *Helgoland* class of the 1908-9 Programme were allowed an abnormally high proportionate beam which besides permitting their side turrets to be placed well inboard provided wide wing-passages with torpedo bulkheads—the first demonstration of a principle which characterized their capital ship designs from now onwards.

The question of docking facilities and the influence of dock width upon the design of the *Orion* and subsequent classes continued to be a limiting factor.

A comparison between the dimensions of the British and German ships is interesting, and had the *Orion* been allowed the same beam as the *Helgoland* her displacement would have risen to about 24,000 tons.

Orion	581′×88½′×27′=22,500. 27,000 h.p.=21 knots.
Helgoland	546′×93½′×27′=22,400. 25,000 h.p.=20·5 knots.

(Lengths are w.l.; draughts are mean.)

The h.p.—speed results were noteworthy considering the great difference in dimensions, and at full power the German ships made over 21 knots with from 31,000 to 35,000 h.p.

A fresh series of hull lines had been worked out for the *Orions* in which the full beam was carried further abaft than forward of amidships; also, in the absence of wing turrets the forecastle was carried at full width to practically amidships before being angled inboard to allow for "Q" turret's arc of fire.

Although the office calculations showed an increase of 2,500 tons over the *Hercules*, the actual load displacement was brought down to 22,200 tons—a saving of 300 tons.

The faulty mast-funnel positions persisted, but whereas in the *Hercules* the fore funnel served twelve boilers, in the *Orion* the boiler rooms were reversed so that the control top was not exposed to such an upblast.

For the first time the conning tower was kept clear of all bridge-work and quite unobstructed. In consequence the bridge became a very restricted structure with a tiny chart-house right up against the funnel, and proved so cramped that it had to be extended as soon as the ships entered service. Eventually it became a two-storey gallery around the funnel with the lower gallerv housing searchlights.

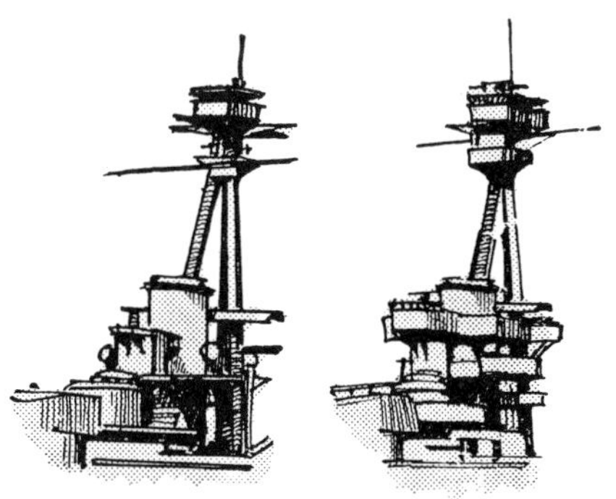

Orion in 1909 with range-finder in upper top, and minimum of bridge-work. Open 4-in. gun in shelter deck.

Orion in 1918 with armoured range-finder on upper top and director on platform below it. Increased bridge-work with 4-in. guns in shields and aeroplane runway on turret roof.

ARMAMENT

First impressions of the *Orion* were that the silhouette was just turrets and funnels and the very antithesis to the such monstrosities as the old French *Hoche* and *Magenta* types whose vast superstructures so held the eye. On the turret crowns were the usual sighting hoods, and although official plans show an arc of 300° for the raised guns, axial line firing was rarely carried out; on such occasions as it was, the blast was described as "unpleasant," which was a mild description of the effects.

In the old *Admiral* class the difference between the 12-in. guns in the *Collingwood* and the 13·5-in. in the later units was most marked; but because of her size the 45 cal. 13·5-in. in the *Orion* looked no bigger than the 12-in. in the *Dreadnought*.

Hitherto the elevation for turret guns had been 15°, but with the introduction of the 13·5-in. this was increased to 20° as against a maximum of 16° in all the latest German capital ships. This rise of 5° became necessary as the new piece had a lower muzzle velocity than the 12-in. and needed a higher elevation to maintain equality of range. As during this time target practice in both fleets was being carried out at a maximum range of 10,000 yards the difference between their gun elevation standards did not seem of much consequence. It was not until 1911 when the development of long range firing became extraordinarily rapid that the difference became of importance.

The sixteen 4-in. guns, divided equally between the fore and after superstructures, were arranged to give the maximum of end-on fire, the shelter decks being cleverly angled to secure this. As in the previous ships they were reduced to thirteen during the war and A.A. guns placed on the quarter deck and/or athwart the mast.

AEROPLANE FITTINGS

By 1917 the need for spotting aircraft to mark the shooting of each individual ship led to the fitting of flying-off platforms on the turret tops with runways fixed along the chases of the guns. Wheeled biplanes (Sopwith "Camel") were employed and these were flown either from turret top over guns, or in reverse with the guns elevated which gave a steep run, the turret being turned for flight into the wind.

Thunderer had runways to "B" and "X" turrets, the rest to "B" turret only (1917-18).

Thunderer during a sweep at full speed in 1917, showing extensions to the bridgework and searchlight towers around after funnel. Net defence removed. Boats between funnels hidden by screens.

PROTECTION

Although the 12-in. gun constituted the main armament in most foreign battleships, it was considered that a general rise in calibre would soon come along and in anticipation of this the *Orion* received a considerable increase in vertical protection. The main and lower belts were made 1 in. thicker with 6 in. and 4 in. up forward in place of 7 in. and 2½ in. For the first time in our *Dreadnoughts* an upper deck strake was fitted and this additional 8 in. meant that at full load armoured stability was superior to that in the *Lord Nelson*. Barbettes showed some variation in thickness and should be compared with those in *Hercules*.

Despite assurances to the contrary at the time of the *Dreadnought* design, the provision of an upper belt may be taken as implying that its absence in the previous classes of *Dreadnoughts* was countenanced not because it could be dispensed with as superfluous, but for reasons of financial considerations restricting displacement.

The main, middle, and lower protective decks were only partial, the main (uppermost) being laid above the 8-in. strake and then dropping to form the main deck over the 6-in. and 4-in. forward and 2½-in. aft; the middle one covered the 12-in. strake at the water-line dropping to the lower edge of the bow and stern plating to form the lower deck.

To preserve the boats during action they were stowed in a well amidships formed by the battery walls with an angled screen above this—a feature unique in warship design and never repeated.

SPEED

All did well on trials and easily exceeded the designed h.p. *Conqueror's* figures may be taken as typical. On the 30 hours trial six runs gave a mean of 19,200 s.h.p. and 19·36 knots. At full power she maintained a mean of 22·12 knots with 33,200 h.p., the coal consumption being 1·6 lb. *Thunderer* did not quite reach these figures.

SEA-GOING QUALITIES

The *Orion* as the first to be completed was sent out to the Bay of Biscay and was found to roll so heavily (21°) that she and the rest of the class had wider bilge keels fitted. In service they proved quite good sea boats.

GENERAL

Although built during a period of strikes and labour unrest the *Monarch* was ready in under two years, and but for the four months lock-out would have left the Tyne well under the twenty months.

Her launching weight was 11,500 tons which included boilers, funnels and uptakes, a large amount of auxiliary machinery and some 2,000 tons of armour and bulkheads—a unique condition for a battleship on the stocks. By installing the boilers, uptakes and barbettes the usual process of riveting-in the decks temporarily and later removing some hundreds of tons of plating to open out the boiler rooms was obviated; the decks and upper deck structures were completed and work in the boiler rooms well advanced when she went afloat.

Thunderer was the last warship of any size to be built on the London River, her contract being awarded with the hope that the Thames I.W. would survive their labour and rating difficulties. But these proved too much of a handicap for economical shipbuilding, and soon after her completion the old firm was wound up. Incidentally, the earlier *Thunderer* was being broken up a mile away from where the new vessel was building.

She was the second ship to have Scotts director system of firing fitted late in 1911, but it was not until November 1912 that the long anticipated trials against the *Orion* came off. The *Orion* had been nine months longer in commission with the reputation of being the best shooting ship in the Fleet. The range was 9,000 yards with the ships and targets making 12 knots. Immediately the "open fire" was made both ships commenced firing, the *Thunderer* making beautiful shooting. At the end of three minutes came the "cease fire" and the targets showed that *Thunderer* had scored six times as many hits as *Orion*.

"CONQUEROR"

Built by Beardmore April '10 to November '12. Commissioned 23 November '12 for service in 2nd B.S. (27 December '14 collided with *Monarch* and sustained serious damage to her bows). Jutland battle—no damage or casualties. Post-war service in B.S. until discarded under Washington Treaty 1922.

Sold 1922.

"MONARCH"

Built by Armstrongs April '10 to March '12. Commissioned 27 April '12 for 2nd Division Home Fleet and in May for 2nd B.S. (27 December '14 collision with *Conqueror* and sustained serious damage aft). Casemates fitted to 4-in. guns '13. Post-war service in B.S. until stricken under Washington Treaty. Used as a fleet target 20 January '25—'planes in the morning, cruisers in afternoon and battleships at night. Was still afloat when shoot was completed and had to be sunk by *Revenge* under searchlights by deliberate fire.

"ORION"

Built at Portsmouth November '09 to January '12. Commissioned 2 January '12 as Flagship Rear-Admiral 2nd B.S. Home Fleet (7 January '12 collision with *Revenge* when latter broke moorings and drifted across her bows). During the War was Flagship 2nd B.S. Grand Fleet and present at Jutland (Rear-Admiral A. C. Leveson). Service in post-war fleet. B.S. until discarded under Washington Treaty 1922.

Sold December 1922.

"THUNDERER"

Built by Thames Iron Works April '10 to June '12. Commissioned 15 June '12 for manœuvres and later joined 2nd B.S. Home Fleet. War service in 2nd B.S. Grand Fleet and present at Jutland. In post-war service was sea-going training ship for cadets.

Sold November 1926.

Chapter 92

GERMAN CAPITAL SHIPS OF THE 1908 AND 1909 PROGRAMME

IN reply to our 1908 Programme which included only the *Neptune* and *Indefatigable* the Germans laid down four big ships (three battleships and one battle cruiser).

Ostfriesland, *Helgoland*, *Thuringen*	22,400 tons.	12 12-in. 14 5·9-in.	25,000 h.p.=20·5 knots.
Moltke	22,640 tons.	10 11-in. 12 5·9-in.	52,000 h.p.=25 knots.

and against our eight capital ships in 1909 they commenced three battleships and one battle cruiser.

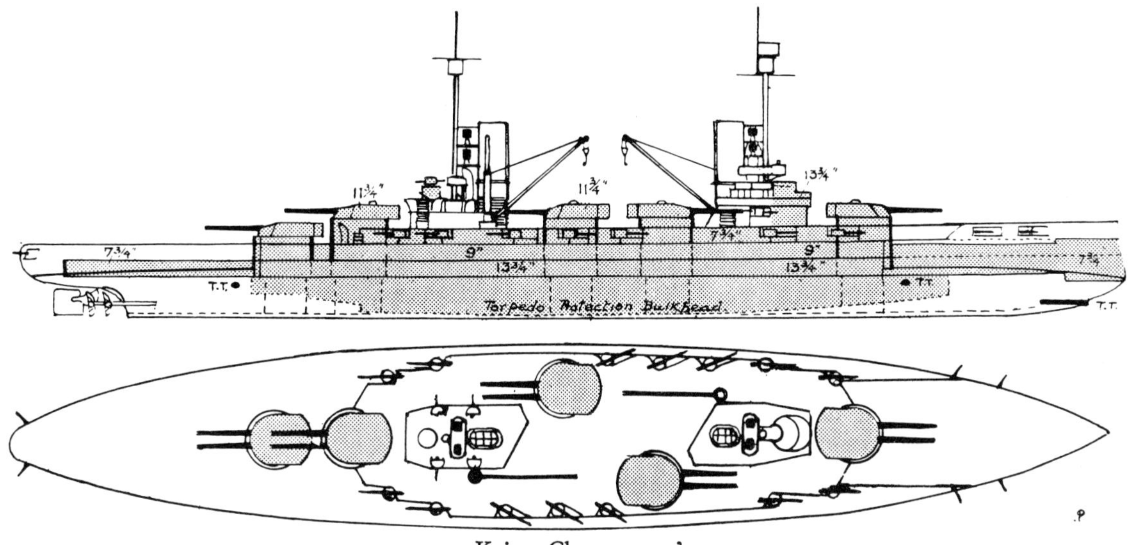

5 *Kaiser* Class, 1909-'12.

$564\frac{1}{2}' \times 95' \times 27\frac{1}{4}'$=24,380 tons. 10 12-in.; 14 5·9-in.; 12 4·1-in.; 5 torpedo tubes. Belt $13\frac{3}{4}''$-$7\frac{3}{4}''$; upper belt 9″; battery $7\frac{3}{4}''$; turrets $11\frac{3}{4}''$. I.H.P. 28,000=20·5 knots. 21·5 to 23 on trials.

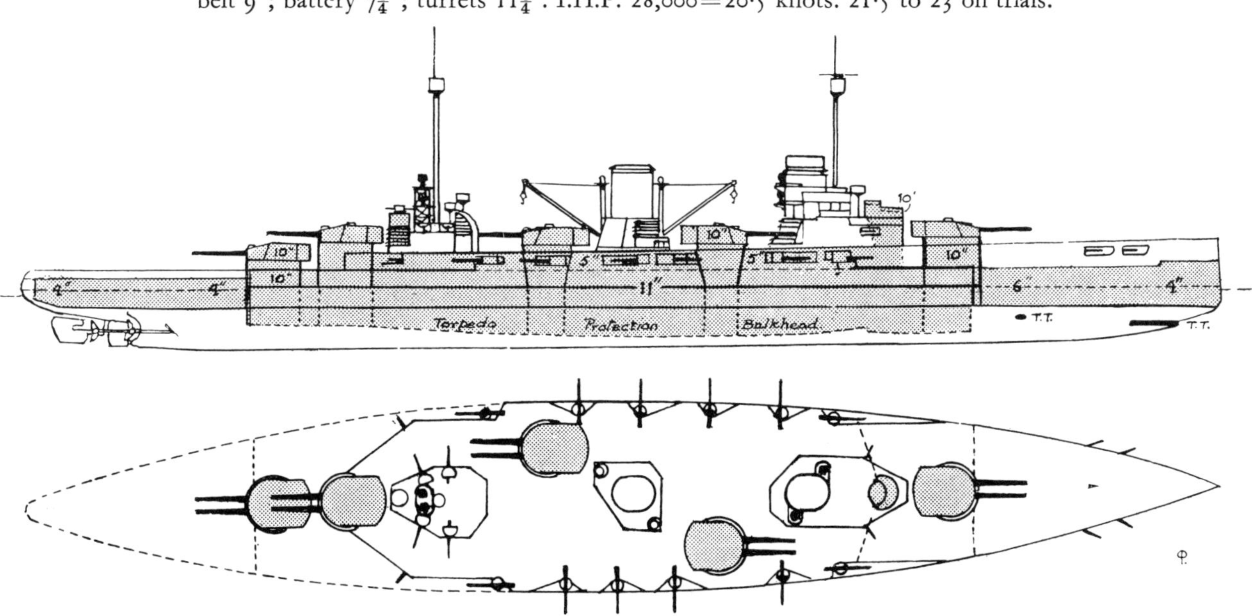

Moltke and *Goeben*. 1908-'12, 1909-'13.

$610\frac{1}{4}' \times 96\frac{3}{4}' \times 27'$=22,640 tons. 10 11-in.; 12 5·9-in.; 10 4·1-in.; 3 torpedo tubes. Belt 11″-6″-4″; upper belt 11″; battery 5″; turrets I.H.P. 52,000=25 knots. Trials 85,782=28·4 knots.

Oldenburg (sister to *Ostfriesland*)
Friedrich der Grosse } 24,400 tons. 10 12-in. } 28,000 h.p.=20·5 knots.
Kaiser } 14 5·9-in. }
Goeben (sister to *Moltke*).

The *Ostfrieslands* were enlarged *Nassaus* with a broadside of only eight 12-in. and seven 5·9-in ; the *Kaiser* was modelled upon our *Neptune* with echelon turrets amidships and a raised turret aft giving a broadside of ten 12-in. and seven 5·9-in. *Moltke* and *Goeben* were enlarged *Von der Tanns* with a raised turret aft[1] and a broadside of ten 11-in. and six 5·9-in., but had battleship protection with 11-in. belts and 10-in. barbettes and turrets. On the measured mile *Moltke* did 28·4 knots with 85,782 h.p. and 27·25 knots with 76,795 h.p. for 6 hours forced draught.

But such details were not forthcoming in 1909. We knew next to nothing about the *Moltke*, she being credited with twelve 11-in. or ten 11-in. disposed *Dreadnought* fashion with armour on the 7-in. scale. By and large it was generally accepted that she would be on a par with our ships as regards speed and protection with a more numerous but considerably lighter calibre main armament, and the *Lion* was designed as a reply. The penetration and smashing power of the 13·5-in. was regarded both from the offensive and defensive aspect—it would have the range of the German guns and prove effective before they could achieve decisive hitting.

---

[1] The writer's photographs of this ship under construction in 1911 showed this turret arrangement for the first time.

Chapter 93

"LION" CLASS (1909 AND 1910 PROGRAMMES)

	Builders	*Laid down*	*Launched*	*Completed*	*Cost (with guns)*
"*Lion*"	Devonport	29 Nov. '09	6 Aug. '10	May '12	£2,086,458
"*Princess Royal*"	Vickers	2 May '10	29 April '11	Nov. '12	£2,089,178
"*Queen Mary*"	Palmers	6 March '11	20 March '12	Sept. '13	£2,078,491

Dimensions 660′ (700′ c.a.) × 88′ 6″ × 26′ 5″/28′ 10″ = 26,350 tons.
Load displacement 26,270 tons; full load 29,680 tons.
"*Queen Mary*" 89′ beam and 27,000 tons (normal).

Armament		Tubes:	Torpedoes:
	8 13·5-in./45.	2 21″.	14 21-in.
	16 4-in./50.		6 14-in.
	4 3-pdrs.		

Protection Belt 9″-6″-5″-4″; bulkheads 4″.
Barbettes 9″-8″-4″-3″; turrets 9″.
Conning tower 10″; signal tower 6″; tubes 4″-3″.
Decks: upper 1″; lower 1″-1¼″ with 2½″ ends.
Magazines and shell rooms 2½″-1½″-1″.
Funnel uptakes 1½″-1″. "*Queen Mary*" ¾″.
Total 6,200 tons = 23 per cent. displacement.

Machinery Parsons. 4 screws. "*Lion*" and "*Princess Royal*" Vickers. "*Queen Mary*" Clydebank.
Boilers 42 Yarrow. S.H.P. 70,000 = 27/26 knots. Pressure 235 lb.

Fuel Coal 1,000/3,500; oil 1,135 tons ("*Lion*" and "*Princess Royal*").
„ 1,000/3,700; „ 1,130 „ ("*Queen Mary*").
5,610/10. 2,420 at continuous sea speed (23·9 knots).

Complement 997.

Constructors W. T. Davis and E. L. Attwood.

Special features:

(1) First battle cruisers with 13·5-in. guns, and centre-line turrets.
(2) Largest and fastest capital ships yet laid down.
(3) Entailed the biggest rise in displacement yet recorded.
(4) First ships to cost over £2,000,000.

UNTIL now the armoured cruisers—not yet accorded the dignity of battle cruisers—had been of less displacement than their battleship opposite numbers, but when the *Lion* came to be planned previous standards of tonnage restriction had to go by the board. Of all the factors which absorb displacement, none make a greater demand than high speed—and the new ship was to be a 27 knotter. In the *Orion* heavier guns and armour only required some 2,500 tons over the *Hercules'* figures, and on this displacement of 22,000 tons the *Indefatigable* could have been given 13·5-in. guns and a general rise in protection to the 9-in. scale. But to achieve the 27 knots required in the *Lion* to offset the 25 knots of the *Moltke*, length had to be increased by over 100 ft. with a consequent addition to displacement of some 8,000 tons.

Of the alternative sketch plans considered, the one finally drafted to cover the requirements of the Board can only be regarded as an unfortunate lapse from our high standards of design—at least, so far as the general lay-out was concerned. This battle cruiser edition of the *Orion* exhibited three errors in design which were inexplicable. (1) The suppression of "X" turret instead of "Q" in order to secure space for the additional boilers, thus limiting the arc of fire to 120° on each beam instead of securing one of 350° in the after position. (2) The retention of *Orion's* mast-funnel positions with the funnel close up against the bridge and mast when fourteen boilers were being served instead of only six. The only reason for placing the mast where the funnel ought to be in the *Dreadnought*, *Hercules*, *Orion* and *Lion* seems to have been that it should continue to perform its traditional duties as a support for the boat boom. In the *Lion* every indication pointed to its best position being forward of the funnel to obviate risk and nuisance from heat and smoke such as was encountered in the *Dreadnought*—and here to a much greater degree. (3) The bridge was placed on top of the conning tower—but for the last time in a British warship.

The results anticipated were confirmed during preliminary trials, as the control top became untenable and

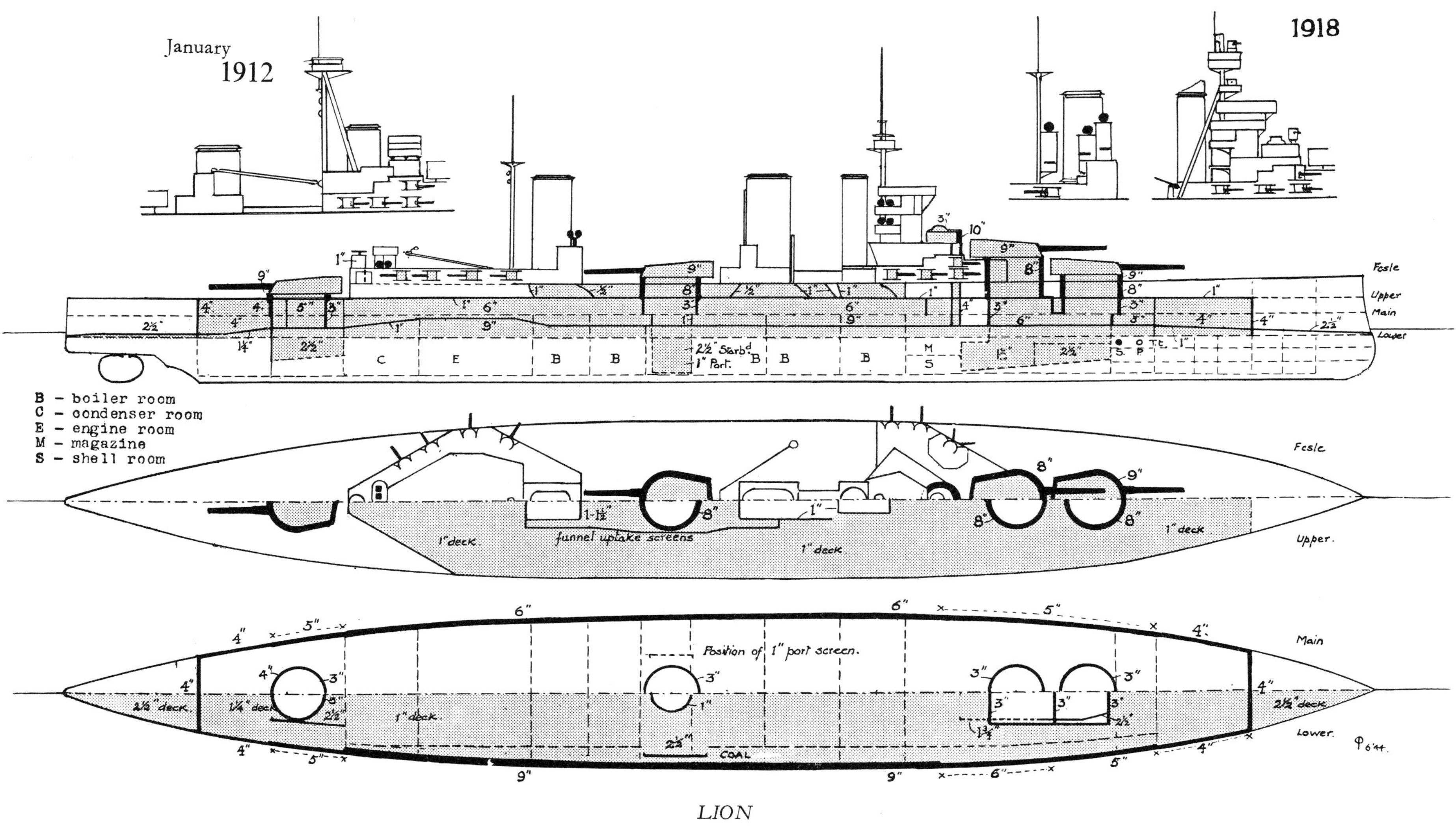
January
1912
1918
Fcsle
Upper
Main
Lower
B - boiler room
C - condenser room
E - engine room
M - magazine
S - shell room
2½" Starbd
1" Port.
funnel uptake screens
1" deck
Position of 1" port screen.
2½" deck
1¼" deck
COAL

LION

the mast legs got so hot that passage through them was impossible when the ship worked up to full speed; the bridge and fittings also suffered. On Mr. Churchill's instructions—and against the advice of the Board (*Scott*, p. 265)—*Lion* and *P. Royal* were taken in hand for alterations, at a cost of £60,000 each.

In the reconstruction the bridge was set back abaft the conning tower and considerably enlarged, the big tripod being replaced by a light mast for which the bridge was to afford stiffening in place of struts. All three funnels were raised, the uptakes to the foremost being sloped aft so that the stack could be placed abaft the mast. The new mast carried a light spotting-top only, as the Board was favouring Commander F. C. Dreyer's system of range control which obviated the heavy tripod. The main rangefinders were placed in "B" and "Y" turrets with another in an armoured tower on top of the conning tower. At first the control position was inside the conning tower, but later was again shifted to the mast head, with an additional range-finder, the mast being

Lion on trials in January 1912 with her bridge above the chart house and heavy tripod abaft the fore funnel. The erection abaft the after funnel is a water measuring tank.

stiffened by short struts. And so in about five years the big tripod found its substitute in a piecemeal-assembled makeshift.

ARMAMENT

The best explanation which can be put forward for the amidships position of "Q" turret was that it divided the boiler rooms and so made for safety where a transverse bulkhead between them might be struck by torpedo and lead to extensive flooding—an unnecessary precaution if it were ever seriously intended as such. Screens of 2-in. plating protected the funnel bases from blast.

The inclined 4-in. batteries allowed six guns to train ahead, four astern, and eight abeam—when the primary guns were not in action. In the *Queen Mary* the upper single guns were moved down to make a battery of four, where they had the barbette as rear protection.

The torpedo tubes were staggered just below the base of "A" barbette.

Queen Mary. *Lion* and *Princess Royal.*
Showing single and two-deck batteries.

PROTECTION

Although protection was heavier and more extensive than in the *Indefatigable* it was still very much on the second class scale and unworthy of 26,000-ton ships. But as gunpower ranked so much higher than armour, and speed demanded length which again meant a greater area to be covered by available weight of plating, the *Lions* were regarded as good value for their tonnage.

For the first time in battle cruisers the side-armour was taken up to the main deck, with a maximum of 9 in. on the lower belt and 6 in. on the upper, tapering to 4 in. at the ends and leaving the extremities unprotected. This of course was a great advance on the previous classes, but the sides of the forecastle which extended right aft to the main mast were still unarmoured except for some 1½-in. internal plating over the forward uptake, continued around "Q" barbette as ¾-in. and then doubling the ¾-in. after funnel uptakes. This exposed flank might be excused as it was in the *Dreadnought*, and would not have mattered so much against flat trajectory fire which apparently was the sort of attack the Board still had in mind judging by the ranges still laid down for battle practice in 1910. But against the plunging fire foreseen by the more advanced gunnery officers it meant serious exposure, especially as the armour deck was only 1-in., below which the barbettes ran to a meagre 3-in. It was this weakness which led to the loss of the *Queen Mary* at Jutland.

Above the belt, barbettes "A" and "Y" were 9-in. and "B" and "Q" 8-in., tapering to 3-in. as they passed behind armour; the turrets had 9-in. sides and faces with 4¼ in.-3½ in. crowns. Horizontal protection was meagre, with only 1-in. upper and lower decks and 2½ in. at the extremities. Below water the side screens covered magazines only, and it will be noted that under "Q" turret the port screen was 1-in. only and well inboard; elsewhere the plating ran to 1½ in.-2½ in. After Jutland in common with the other capital ships the magazines were given thicker bulkheads and decks to an average of 2 in.

Although press reports referred to the *Lion's* protection as being "on battleship scale" it was a good 2 in.-3 in. below that of the *St. Vincent* our least heavily armoured ship, and theoretically could be pierced by 11-in. gunfire at normal battle range.

SPEED

A designed speed of 26 knots at full load and 27 knots at normal draught required 70,000 h.p. The trials of the *Lion* took place in heavy weather and although the contract s.h.p. was attained she did not reach designed speed. The *Princess Royal* made 28·54 knots with 78,600 h.p. as her highest mean speed.

The most extravagant reports of the steaming trials of these ships appeared in the Press, crediting them with figures which were ludicrous. Thus, the *Princess Royal* was said to have made a mean of 33·5 knots with a maximum of 34·7 knots over the measured mile (*Navy League Annual*, 1912, p. 33) and the *Lion* was stated to have logged 31·78 knots. As 34·78 knots would have required upwards of 200,000 h.p. the impossibility of such speeds is obvious. An official announcement that the ships were able to attain their designed speed would have satisfied the requirements of secrecy, but the acceptance of these persistently repeated reports may have induced foreign Powers to aim at speeds which, even if possible, would involve very great expense. They certainly gave the British people a very exaggerated idea of the capabilities of the *Lions*. In service they were ordered to steam at 28 knots during the Dogger Bank action, although this was regarded as beyond their powers.

MACHINERY

The engine rooms contained two sets of turbines and four shafts. Each set comprised a H.P. ahead with a cruising stage at the forward end for L.P. only, also a L.P. ahead; for astern both H.P. and L.P. turbines. The H.P. ahead and astern turbines were separate and mounted on the wing shaft, with the L.P. ahead and astern on the inner shaft. All four shafts could work ahead or astern.

Four sets of propellers were tried in the *Princess Royal* while the *Lion* was being altered and the set which served her best enabled the *Lion* to improve on her designed speed.

	Trials	*8-hour full power*
Lion	73,800 S.H.P.	=27 knots.
Princess Royal	78,600 ,,	=28·5 knots.
Queen Mary	78,700 ,,	=28 knots.

SEA-GOING QUALITIES

With a metacentric height of $5\frac{1}{2}$ ft. the ships were regarded as good seaboats although liable to roll. One of her officers wrote:

> "The *Princess Royal* steamed most beautifully and easily. Running at full speed she scarcely vibrated, but she rolled, in a beam sea, as much as 25°, while I served in her, with just that 'hang' at the end of the roll which is somewhat unpleasant." (Jeans, *Reminiscences of a Naval Surgeon*, p. 217.)

GENERAL

The "Splendid Cats" enjoyed a great reputation both in and out of the Service, although the losses at Jutland caused misgivings about battle cruisers generally. As altered they were magnificent looking ships. The main mast proved an easy method of recognition as *Lion* had the starfish above funnel level, *Princess Royal* below it, and *Queen Mary* was without it. In addition the latter had round instead of oval forward funnels, and one-storey forward 4-in. batteries.

PRINCESS ROYAL

During 1917 searchlight towers were fitted around the after funnel, and when secondary guns were being surrendered for arming small craft the *Lion* lost her port aftermost 4-in. and the *Princess Royal* the corresponding starboard gun. They received one 4-in. and one 3-in. A.A. carried abreast of the fore funnel.

In 1918 aeroplane runways crowned "Q" and "X" turrets and *Lion* shipped a clinker screen to her fore funnel.

At normal load with 1,000 tons of fuel aboard the mean draught was 27 ft. 7 in., so that with a sinkage of 98 tons per inch this was increased by 3 ft. 1 in. when fully bunkered (4,635 tons).

Accommodation in the *Lion* and *Princess Royal* showed a partial return to the earlier Dreadnought system as the Admiral's and officers' quarters were forward in the vicinity of the bridge and fighting controls with the quarter deck amidships; the crew were berthed two decks down below armour without scuttles except in a few mess decks right forward and aft to which armour did not fully extend. This arrangement had obvious wartime advantages, but it was largely negatived by the great discomfort to the ship's company as well as the seaman's dislike for losing the traditional position of the quarter deck and all it stood for. In the *Queen Mary* there was a reversion to established practice with the officers aft and the crew forward.

"LION"

Commissioned 4 June '12 for 1st C.S.; Flagship (Rear-Admiral Bayly) from July '12 and from January '13 of 1st B.C.S. (Rear-Admiral Beatty).

War: Flagship B.C. Fleet ('15-'18) (from 28 November '16 Vice-Admiral Pakenham). Dogger Bank 24 January '15. Received several hits including two on the water-line which drove in several plates which were not strongly enough supported. One abreast engine room forced 15 ft. of 9-in. armour on to armour deck and crushed in bottom plating abreast engine room below water; salt water entered fresh water tanks. Only a 12-in. pipe of ¼-in. copper concertinaed saved flooding of the main engine room—a large compartment. Fisher would not admit that the ship was sufficiently damaged to need dockyard repair, so she spent four months at Elswick (director control installed). At Jutland she had 100 dead and 50 injured. One shell penetrated the juncture of roof and face of "Q" turret blowing half of it away and igniting the cordite in the loading cage killing everyone in the gunhouse and working chamber; smouldering charges in the lower cages ignited when the ship turned into the wind killing magazine and shell room crews. But for the order given by the Officer of the Turret (Major Harvey) to flood the magazine, the ship would have been blown up. '19-'23 Flagship of 1st B.C.S. Discarded under Washington Treaty 1922.

Sold January '24 and broken up at Jarrow.

"PRINCESS ROYAL"

Commissioned 14 November '12 for 1st C.S. January '13 1st B.C.S.

War: Flagship 1st B.C.S. '15-'18 Heligoland Bight 28 August '14. Dogger Bank 24 January '15, no casualties; Jutland main fire control destroyed by two hits forward ten minutes after action was opened on her. Shell in admiral's cabin caused casualties to port forward 4-in. crews, and several fires; "X" turret hit by 12-in. shell killed 4 men and put turret out of action; "B" turret hit but not damaged; shell pierced starboard side aft wrecking after engine-room casings and exploded on port side causing casualties to after 4-in. crews. Numerous fires were extinguished with difficulty owing to failure of all lighting systems and damage to fire mains. '19-'23 1st B.C.S. Discarded under Washington Treaty 1922.

Sold December 1926.

"QUEEN MARY"

Built at Palmers March '11 to September '13 (2½ years) constantly being delayed by industrial troubles. Commissioned '13 for 1st C.S. January '13. 1st B.C.S. January '15-May '16.

War: Heligoland Bight 28 August '15; refitting at the time of the Dogger Bank action; Jutland—sunk by gunfire from *Seydlitz* and *Derfflinger* 4.26 p.m. 31 May '16. The *Derfflinger*, mistaking the *Princess Royal* for the Flagship, began firing on the next astern, which the *Seydlitz* was also engaging. Thus the *Queen Mary* at from 15,800 to 14,500 yards, became the target of both these ships. For about five minutes she stood it splendidly. The Germans say salvoes were coming from her with fabulous rapidity. Twice already she had been straddled by the *Derfflinger*, when at 4.26 (Corbett III, p. 337) a plunging salvo crashed upon her deck forward. In a moment there was a dazzling flash of red flame where the salvo fell, and then a much heavier explosion rent her amidships. "The *Queen Mary* seemed to roll slowly to starboard, her masts and funnels gone, and with a huge hole in her side. She listed again, the hole disappeared beneath the water, which rushed into her and turned her completely over. A minute and a half, and all that could be seen of the *Queen Mary* was her keel with her propellers still slowly revolving high in the air. In another moment, as the *Tiger* and *New Zealand* were smothered in a shower of black debris, there was nothing of her left but a dark pillar of smoke rising stemlike till it spread hundreds of feet high (900-1,200 ft.) like a vast palm tree." The casualties were 67 officers and 1,209 men killed; 2 officers and 5 men wounded. One officer and 1 man were rescued subsequently by German destroyers.

* * * * *

Under the direction of Captain R. H. Hall (later Sir Reginald Hall, D.N.I.) the *Queen Mary* was fitted with a chapel, a book stall, a cinematograph, much improved washing facilities, and washing machines for petty officers and the older seamen. He rebuilt the petty officers' messes, abolished the ship's police, and introduced a wartime three-watch system which was generally adopted when war broke out.

Chapter 94

ADVENT OF THE TRIPLE TURRET

DURING 1909 both Italy and Russia laid down their first Dreadnoughts, and armed them with twelve 12-in. guns all mounted in triple turrets on the centre-line. Armstrongs designed the mountings of the *Dante Aligheri* and a group of British firms were responsible for the Russian ships, so that the credit for this breakaway from conventional practice must be credited to our own ordnance experts, although it was to be many years before the Admiralty discarded the twin mounting.

In both the new types there was no superfiring, their design being to secure a full broadside with axial fire restricted to the end turrets, to which extent they presented the direct antithesis to generally accepted practice during the past forty years.

Hitherto the experiment of grouping more than two guns into one fighting position had not been successful, the U.S. *Kearsarge* and *New Jersey* types with secondary turrets on top of the primary ones having developed a lot of trouble. Now discussion was started on the probable shortcomings of a triple mount and whether it was better to risk having a quarter of the armament put out of action with one hit. But the real argument in favour of the multiple mount was that a much heavier armament could be carried without excessive length, and if three guns could maintain a rate of fire in excess of two, there could be no gainsaying the advantages it offered. Austria and America were soon to follow with the *Viribus Unitis* (1910) and *Oklahoma* (1912) types and in 1913 France laid down the *Normandie* group which were to carry their twelve 13·4-in. guns in three quadruple turrets.

Chapter 95

"KING GEORGE V" CLASS (1910 PROGRAMME)

	Built by	*Laid down*	*Launched*	*Completed*	*Cost*
"*Ajax*"	Scotts	27 Feb. '11	21 March '12	Mar. '13	Average
"*Audacious*"	Lairds	Feb. '11	Sept. '12	Oct. '13	£1,960,000
"*Centurion*"	Devonport	16 Jan. '11	18 Nov. '11	May '13	including guns
"*King George V*"	Portsmouth	16 Jan. '11	9 Oct. '11	Nov. '12	

Dimensions 555′ (597′ 6″)×89′×26′ 7″/28′ 8″=23,000 tons.
Load draught 23,000; full load 25,700 tons (sinkage 86 tons per in.).

Armament 10 13·5-in./45. 16 4-in./50. 4 3-pdrs.
Tubes: 2 21-in. beam. 1 21-in. stern (later removed).

Protection Belt 12″-9″-8″; bulkheads 10″-6″-4″.
Barbettes 10″-3″; turrets 11″.
For'd battery 3″.
Conning tower 11″; director tower aft 6″.
Decks: above and below battery 1″; main 1½″; middle 1″; lower 4″-3″-2½″-1″.
(Belt rose 16′ 10½″ above and 3′ 7½″ below water).

Machinery Parsons. "*Ajax*" and "*Audacious*" by builders. "*Centurion*" by Hawthorn. "*King George V*" by Parsons.
Boilers: "*Ajax*" and "*King George V*" Babcock. "*Audacious*" and "*Centurion*" Yarrow.
31,000 h.p. (4 hours)=21·7 knots; 27,000 (8 hours)=21/20·6 knots.

Fuel Coal 2,870 ("*King George V*"), rest 3,150/900 tons. Oil 800 tons.

Radius 4,060/18·15 knots.

Complement 782/759.

Constructors E. N. Mooney and A. M. Worthington.

Special features:

(1) Large conning tower with well separated two-platform bridge.
(2) Derrick stump for boat boom.
(3) Torpedo defence guns concentrated forward.

This second batch of *Orions* slightly enlarged and modified, proved somewhat of a disappointment, as it was generally supposed that they would carry a 6-in. armament in place of the inadequate 4-in. Nothing smaller than 4·7-in. as a secondary gun was being mounted in the battleships of the Powers, and that the *King Georges* retained the smaller calibre was purely a matter of finance—as Mr. McKenna put it, the substitution of 6-in. guns would have increased displacement by 2,000 tons; and presumably the Government were not prepared to allow some £170,000 additional expense for these ships. But with Lord Fisher still at Whitehall when the design was drawn up it was hardly likely that any departure would be allowed from the two-calibre armament which he had so strenuously advocated.

For this reason the *King Georges* excited comparatively little interest when their details became known. It was felt that the Board had failed to provide against the growing size of German torpedo craft, and allowed the ships to suffer from a cheese-paring economy. While the 4-in. might serve for destroyers because of the difficulties in fighting a larger calibre gun aboard such small craft, the Americans were putting 5-in., the French 5·5-in., and the Germans, Japanese and Austrians 6-in. in their latest ships—and this general ignoring of the original Dreadnought policy as regards secondary armament could only be regarded as highly significant.

The increase of 16 ft. in over-all length with 6 in. extra beam and 3 in. in mean draught provided 500 tons of displacement which was expended in extra protection. According to official data this included an "upper protective deck 1¾ in.-1½ in."—an impressive reinforcement, except that the plans show it is to be confined to the forward 4-in. battery. The increased proportion of length allowed for 21 knots with the same natural draught h.p. as in the *Orion*.

As in the altered *Lion* the fire control system obviated the need for a heavy tripod mast, and so the *Centurion* and *King George V* were completed with only a small spotting top on the pole mast. But before the *Ajax* and *Audacious* passed into service there was a swing back to the director system, and these ships carried a large circular control top and director tower at the mast head; and as the bridge did not provide sufficient stiffening the mast was made into a half-height tripod. *Centurion* was altered to this rig, but in the *King George V*

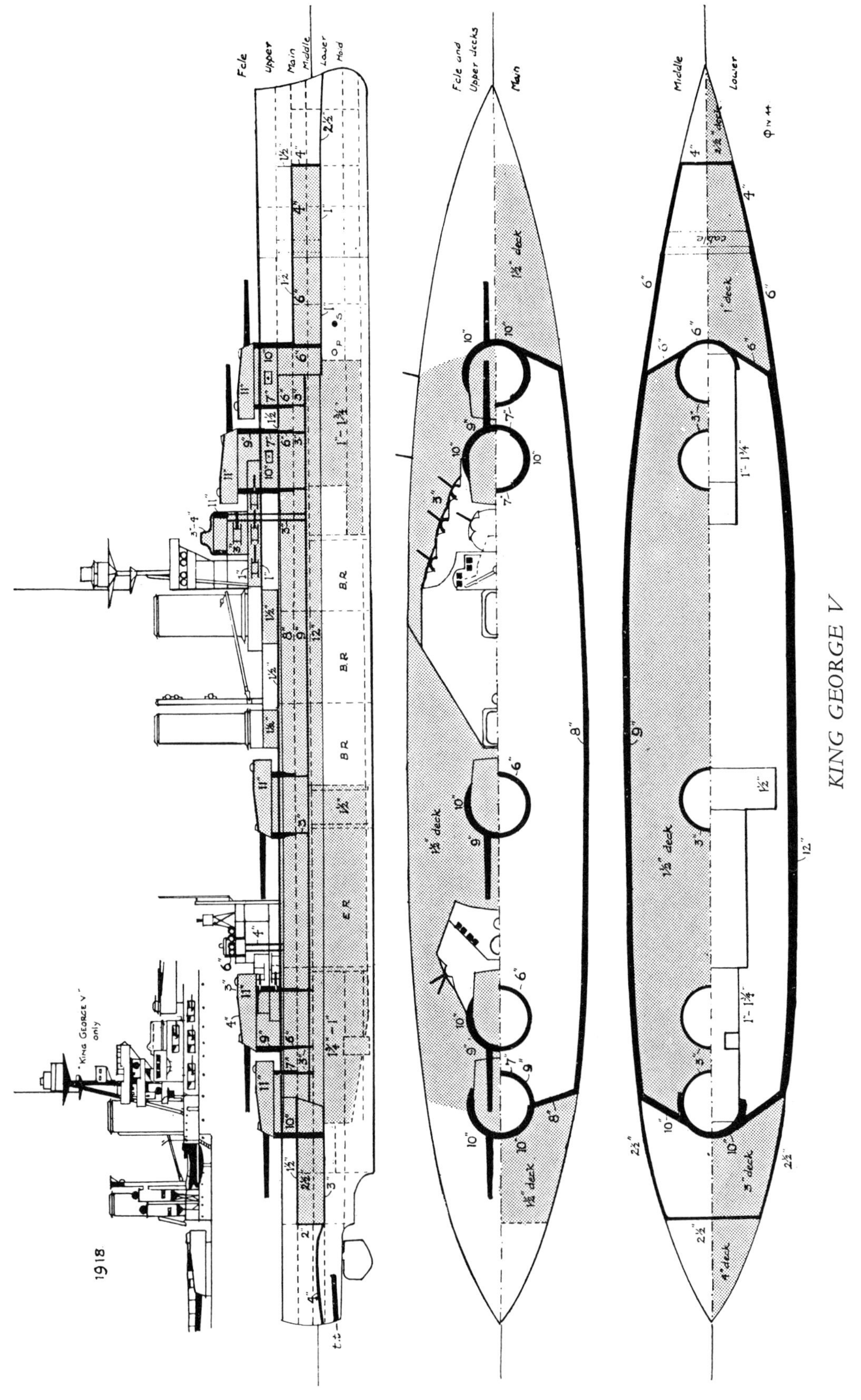
KING GEORGE V
1918
"King George V" only
Fcle
Upper
Main
Middle
Lower
Hold
Fcle and Upper decks
B.R
E.R
1½" deck
1" deck
4" deck
3" deck

the mast was stayed by wide flanges. This served until 1918 when she was given a larger control top and full height tripod.

Boats were again stowed in the open and a derrick stump carried the boom for the first time since the old *Imperieuse*.

ARMAMENT

The *Orion* distribution of turrets was followed, but with the forward superstructure cut away at a sharper angle allowing a wider training for "Q" turret guns.

Of the sixteen 4-in. guns, twelve had a bearing forward and four aft instead of being divided equally between the two superstructures. Practice torpedo attacks had shown that the forward guns had twice the work of those aft and had to draw on their ammunition. It will be seen that the forward guns were on three levels—single casemates below the conning tower, a group of three along the angle of the superstructure, and two in the forecastle abreast of "B" barbette; all had 3-in. protection. The four after guns had 3-in. shields, which replaced the original hanging port lids and unprotected mountings.

The forecastle ports were contra-indicated by the lessons of the Russo-Japanese war when particular attention had been drawn by our Naval Attaché to the inconvenience of ports opening into the forecastle when at sea. Certainly both the Americans and Germans were employing forecastle ports for light guns and often in sponsons in the bow flare; but the disadvantages from spray and flooding even so when placed far aft as in the *King George V* led to their being plated-in, those in the *King George V* being discarded in 1917.

The *King George V*, in 1918 with enlarged bridgework and a full tripod mast compared with the short struts supporting the mast in her sisters as shown in the elevation (p. 539).

At the same time two 3-in. or 4-in. A.A. were mounted on "Q" turret and the quarter deck.

At this time various methods of employing searchlights were being tried—especially as regards location, height above water, and grouping. In the *Neptune* (q.v.) they had been moved to the forebridge; in the *Centurion* they were alternatively grouped at a much lower level around the second funnel—an arrangement which proved more satisfactory so that when searchlight towers were introduced the after funnel position was retained for most of the lights. An experimental system of searchlight control was also installed in the *Centurion* and marked a first step towards subsequent practice.

The loss of the *Audacious* showed that the thin longitudinal bulkheading which covered the engine rooms was not sufficient to provide protection against mines. The port engine room was completely flooded and the central one partially so; the ship continued to sink slowly for twelve hours when an internal explosion occurred and she went down.

SPEED

On the eight hours trial the average for all four ships was about 28,200 s.h.p. with 330 revolutions. *King George V* registered 22·127 knots, *Centurion* 21·886 knots and *Ajax* 21·066 knots, but all four proved capable

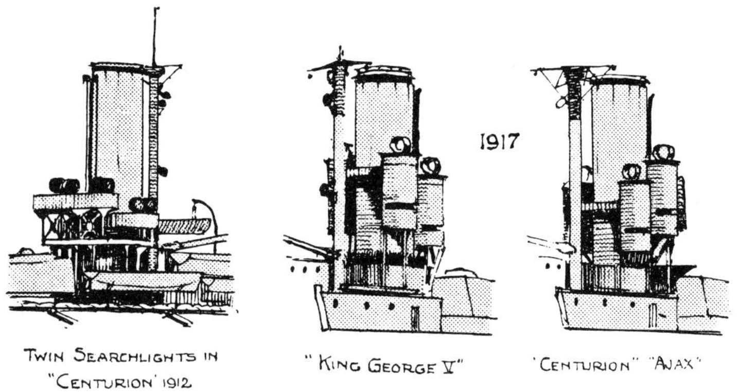

Location of searchlights.
In 1912 director control of searchlights was tried out for the first time in the *Centurion* when twin lights were sited around the after funnel. Later when mounted in towers out of which they could be raised and focussed by observers at the sighting slots they were carried at different levels as in *King George V*, *Centurion* and *Ajax*.

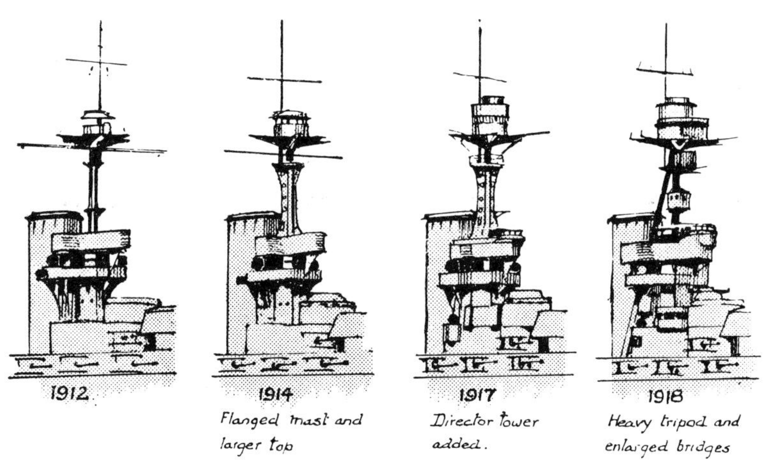

When the Dreyer system of fire control gave place to the director at the mast head, the light pole mast in the *King George V* was fitted with flanges to stiffen it against vibration. But as additional weights on the mast made these inadequate, full length struts became necessary.

of 22 knots. Each vessel had a different propeller varying in diameter, pitch and area. On the thirty hours trial at 290 revs. the s.h.p. averaged 19,800. *Ajax* was reported as having steamed at 22·47 knots on the measured mile, and her trials with a four-bladed experimental propeller showed that it was not so good as the three-bladed.

SEA-GOING QUALITIES

Owing to the low freeboard abaft of amidships they proved wet in a seaway, and a good deal of water used to come aboard. The anti-rolling tanks fitted in *King George V* did not act to any great advantage, their steadying effect being "not sufficiently marked to make it advisable to fit them in other ships." They were subsequently used as fuel tanks.

GENERAL

At the end of 1917 searchlights were shifted from the bridge and placed on towers around the second funnel.

Ajax, *Centurion* and *King George V* scrapped under the Washington Treaty, on completion of the *Nelson* and *Rodney*.

"AJAX"

Commissioned October '13 for the Home Fleet until '14. Grand Fleet 2nd B.S. '14-'19 (Jutland). Mediterranean, '19-'24 (Black Sea operations against the Bolsheviks). Nore Reserve '24-August '26.

Sold November 1926.

"CENTURION"

In collision with and sank S.S. *Derna* (Italian) during trials (9 December '12) and repairs took until March '13. Central searchlight controls fitted experimentally '13. Commissioned for Home Fleet March '13-August '14. Grand Fleet 2nd B.S. '14-'19 (Jutland). Mediterranean '19-'24 (Black Sea operations). Portsmouth Reserve '24-April '26; converted to radio con. target ship for gunfire up to 8-in. calibre. At Plymouth, in the Fleet Target Service until April 1941; converted into a creditable imitation of the new battleship *Anson* and set out on the 20,000 mile trip round the Cape to Bombay. Remained at Bombay (under her own name) until 1942, then sailed for Alexandria, arriving there in June 1942. Served as a floating anti-aircraft battery south of the Suez Canal until March 1944 and left Alexandria in April 1944 on return to the United Kingdom; was finally sunk as a blockship off the Normandy coast on 6 June 1944 to form a breakwater for landing craft.

Centurion as a radio-controlled target ship.

"KING GEORGE V"

Commissioned November '12 as Flagship Home Fleet (Vice-Admiral Sir George Warrender) July '14. Grand Fleet 2nd B.S. Flagship (Vice-Admiral Sir Thos. Jerram) (Jutland). Mediterranean '19-'23 Flagship. Devonport Reserve. '23-'26 gunnery ship.

Sold December 1926.

"AUDACIOUS"

Commissioned. '13 for Home Fleet. Grand Fleet 2nd B.S. '14. Mined and sunk by internal explosion while on gunnery exercises near Loch Swilly 27 October '14.

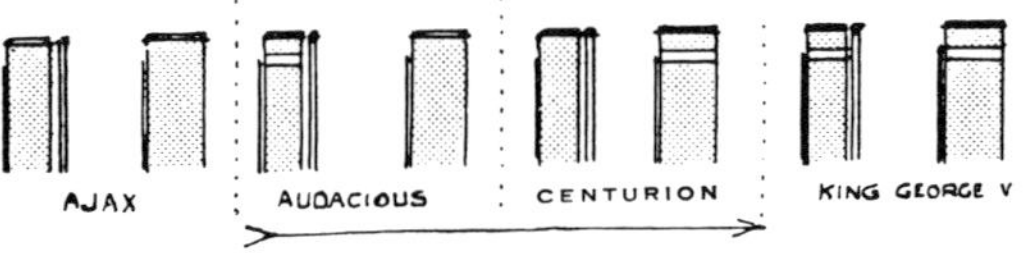

Chapter 96

COMPARATIVE BRITISH AND GERMAN PROGRAMMES 1909–1911

The British and German programmes for 1909, 1910 and 1911 included the following armoured ships:

British	1909	German
Colossus		*Oldenburg*
Hercules		*Friedrich der Grosse*
Orion		*Kaiser*
Conqueror		*Goeben* (b.c.)
Monarch		
Thunderer		
Lion (b.c.)		
Princess Royal (b.c.)		

British	1910	German
King George V		*Kaiserin*
Ajax		*Konig Albert*
Audacious		*Prinzregent Luitpold*
Centurion		*Seydlitz* (b.c.)
Queen Mary (b.c.)		
Australia (b.c.) } for Dominions		
New Zealand (b.c.) } for Dominions		

British	1911	German
Iron Duke		*Konig*
Marlborough		*Markgraf*
Benbow		*Grosser Kurfurst*
Emperor of India		*Derfflinger* (b.c.)
Tiger (b.c.)		

Of the 1909 programme the *Oldenburg* was a fourth of the *Helgoland* class with the *Kaiser* and *F. der Grosse* of a new type resembling our *Neptune* and *Goeben* a sister to *Moltke*. In 1910 there were three more *Kaisers* and an enlarged *Moltke* the *Seydlitz*. We were keeping a jump ahead in gun calibre and distribution of turrets, at the expense of protection; speed was about level with possibly a slight advantage on the German side.

In January 1910 Lord Fisher relinquished his post of First Sea Lord on reaching the age of 69. Although one year short of the retiring age for Admirals of the Fleet he was anxious for Sir Arthur Wilson (only two years his junior) to succeed him as soon as possible. "Tug" Wilson had a great reputation in the Service as an absolutely fearless, spartan, and unselfish martinet ("Old 'Ard 'Eart" was his other soubriquet); a great tactician, but wedded to a policy of absolute secrecy with regard to his own plans none of which could be worked out or discussed. An indefatigable worker, whom Fisher regarded as the only man fit to follow him.

Fisher will always be remembered as one of the greatest men of his time. For ten years or so he had been responsible for all the most important steps to enlarge, improve, and modernize the Navy—water-tube boilers, the all-big-gun ship, the introduction of the submarine ("Fisher's toys" as Lord Charles Beresford called them), nucleus crews for reserve ships (in place of care and maintenance parties), the development of the Home Fleet, minesweepers, and the adoption of the 13·5-in. gun. On the other hand he had created violent oppositions conducted with technicalities and personalities, and a deplorable schism so that officers became Fisher's men or Beresford's men. But "there is no doubt whatever that Fisher was right in nine-tenths of what he fought for. His great reforms sustained the power of the Royal Navy at the most critical period in its history. He gave the Navy the kind of shock which the British Army received in the South African war. It was Fisher who hoisted the storm-signal and beat all hands to quarters. He forced every department of the Service to review its position and question its own existence. He shook them and beat them and cajoled them out of slumber into intense activity. But the Navy was not pleasant while this was going on. . . . Fisher was maddened by the difficulties and obstructions which he encountered, and became violent in the process of fighting so hard at every step." (*Churchill* 1, p. 75.)

*   *   *   *   *

The Estimates for 1911 provided for the commencement of four battleships (*Iron Dukes*) and one battle cruiser (*Tiger*). The German additions for the year included three battleships of a new class (*Konigs*) and a battle cruiser (*Derfflinger*) all to be armed with 12-in./50 guns, which although listed as firing a 860 lb. shell actually fired one of 1,014 lb. In general design the *Konig* was a modified *Orion* with "Q" turret on the forecastle deck and a 6-in. battery along the upper deck. But her protection was on a far heavier scale than in our ships, while a beam of 96 ft. 9 in. allowed for better under-water protection.

"KONIG"

Dimensions	573′×96′ 9″×27′3″.
Displacement	25,390.
Guns	10 12-in.; 14 5·9-in.
Tubes	5 19·7″.
Lower belt	14″; upper 10″; 6″ fore and abaft citadel.
Barbettes	14″; turrets 14″ (fronts); battery 8″.
Decks	2·4″-2″.
S.H.P.	31,000=21 knots.
Fuel	Coal 3,543; oil 690.

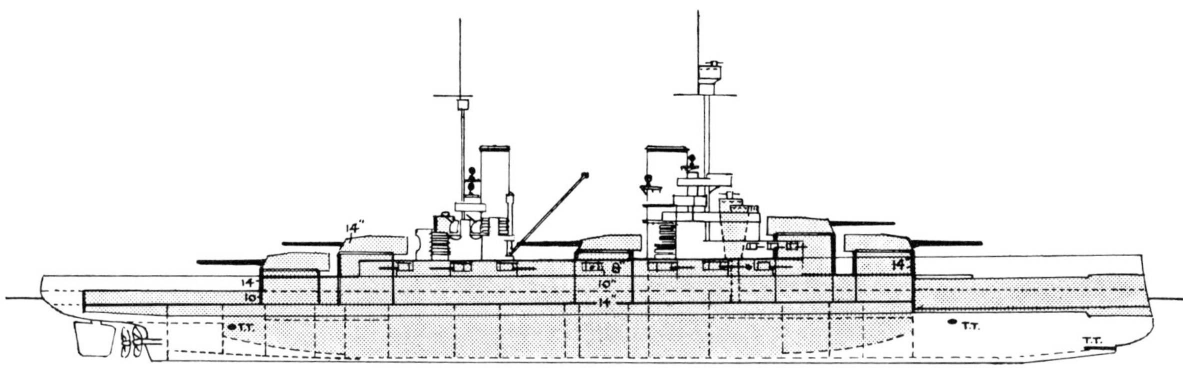

KONIG

The *Derfflinger* was a magnificent ship of which our people had the highest opinions. She differed radically from the *Seydlitz* in being flush decked with eight 12-in. along the centre-line and twelve 6-in. in the superstructure battery; plating was as heavy as in our battleships, with sound underwater protection. Designed speed figures were handsomely exceeded in service.

"DERFFLINGER"

Dimensions	689′×95′ 2″×27′ 3″=26,180 tons.
Freeboard	24 ft. forward.
Guns	8 12-in./50; 12 5·9-in.
Tubes	4 19·7″.
Belt	12″; upper 8″.
Barbettes	10″; turrets 11″; battery 7″.
Decks	1″-2″.
S.H.P.	63,000=26·5 knots.
Fuel	Coal 4,625; oil 984 tons.

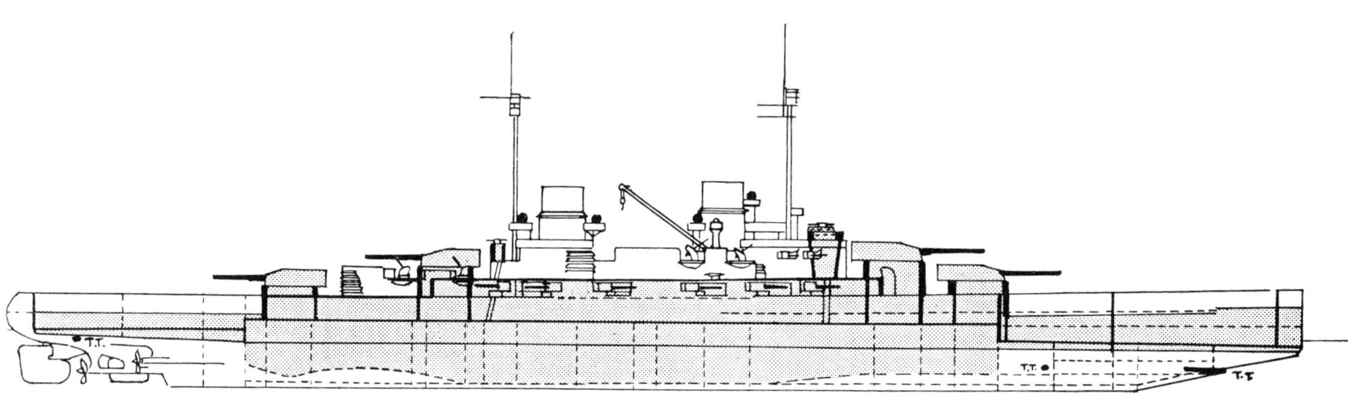

DERFFLINGER

Chapter 97

"IRON DUKE" CLASS (1911 PROGRAMME)

	Builders	*Laid down*	*Launched*	*Completed*	*Cost*
"*Iron Duke*"	Portsmouth	12 Jan. '12	12 Oct. '12	March '14	Average £1,891,122
"*Marlborough*"	Devonport	25 Jan. '12	24 Oct. '12	June '14	
"*Benbow*"	Beardmore	30 May '12	12 Nov. '13	Oct. '14	
"*Emperor of India*" (ex-"*Delhi*")	Vickers	31 May '12	27 Nov. '13	Nov. '14	

Dimensions 580′ (622′ 9″) × 90′ × 27′ 5″/29′ 6″ = 25,000 tons.
Load displacement (1917) 25,820 tons; full load 30,380 tons (sinkage 92 tons per in.).

Armament 10 13·5-in./45. 12 6-in./45. 2 3-in. A.A. (added). 4 3-pdrs.
4 21-in. tubes. (20 torpedoes).

Armour Belt 12″-9″-8″-6″-4″; bulkheads 8″-6″-4″-1½″.
Battery 6″-4″-2″ screens.
Barbettes 10″-3″; shield 11″; roofs 4″-3″.
Conning tower 11″; base 6″-3″; 4″ after tube.
Decks: forecastle over battery 1″; upper 2″-1½″; main (beyond turrets) 1½″; middle 1″; amidships, 2½″-1½″ aft; lower 2½″; over steering 1″.
Bulkheads to magazines and engines 1½″-1″.
Funnel uptakes 1½″.

Machinery Parsons, S.H.P. 29,000 = 21·25/20·7 knots. 4 screws.
("*Iron Duke*" Lairds; "*Marlborough*" Hawthorn; "*Benbow*" Beardmore; "*Emperor of India*" Yarrow.
Boilers 18 Babcock ("*Iron Duke*" and "*Benbow*"); 18 Yarrow ("*Marlborough*" and "*Emperor of India*"). Pressure 235 lb.

Fuel Coal 900/3,250 tons; oil 1,050 tons excluding 550 tons in emergency tanks.

Radius 4,840/19; 7,780/10.

Complement 942-925 (war 995-1,022).

Constructors E. N. Mooney and A. M. Worthington.

Special features:

(1) First British all-big-gun ships to carry 6-in. guns.
(2) Last coal-burning British battleships.

In describing the *Iron Duke* Admiral Mark Kerr relates the circumstances which led up to the adoption of the 6-in. battery (*The Navy in My Time*, p. 47) and throws an interesting light on gunnery tactics of the period:

> "In response to a request from Sir Philip Watts I wrote the following letter dated 27 June 1909, on the subject of the re-establishment of a secondary armament in capital ships."
>
> "You were kind enough to take an interest in my ideas about air-blast for clearing the conning tower of fumes on a shell bursting near, and also the pattern of cruiser conning tower with the movable chart-house above; so after some months in the North Sea I venture to send you a description of the effect the atmospheric environment I have lived in had on my ideas of the armament of the modern battleship.
>
> You remember that I am the father of the scheme of night defence that does away with the 4-in. guns etc. and substitutes shrapnel shell in the primary armament guns for the demoralisation of the enemy's flotillas, so you may rely on it that I have kept night and day actions both constantly in view while thinking this matter out in the daily surroundings where the final scene will one day be enacted.
>
> The officers of the Fleet are divided in opinion, but they are mostly in favour of retaining the 6-in. guns to "hail" on the enemy, if you find him close at hand on a misty day in the North Sea. They claim, and the Japanese applaud them, that the showers of water from the short shot will seriously disturb the laying of the enemy's guns, and perhaps put his telescope sights out of action, temporarily or permanently.
>
> I confess that these arguments cannot be ignored, and apparently they are borne in mind by most, if not all, of our possible adversaries.
>
> Again, there is one more danger that occurs to me, and for which a battery of 6-in. guns would be the best foil.

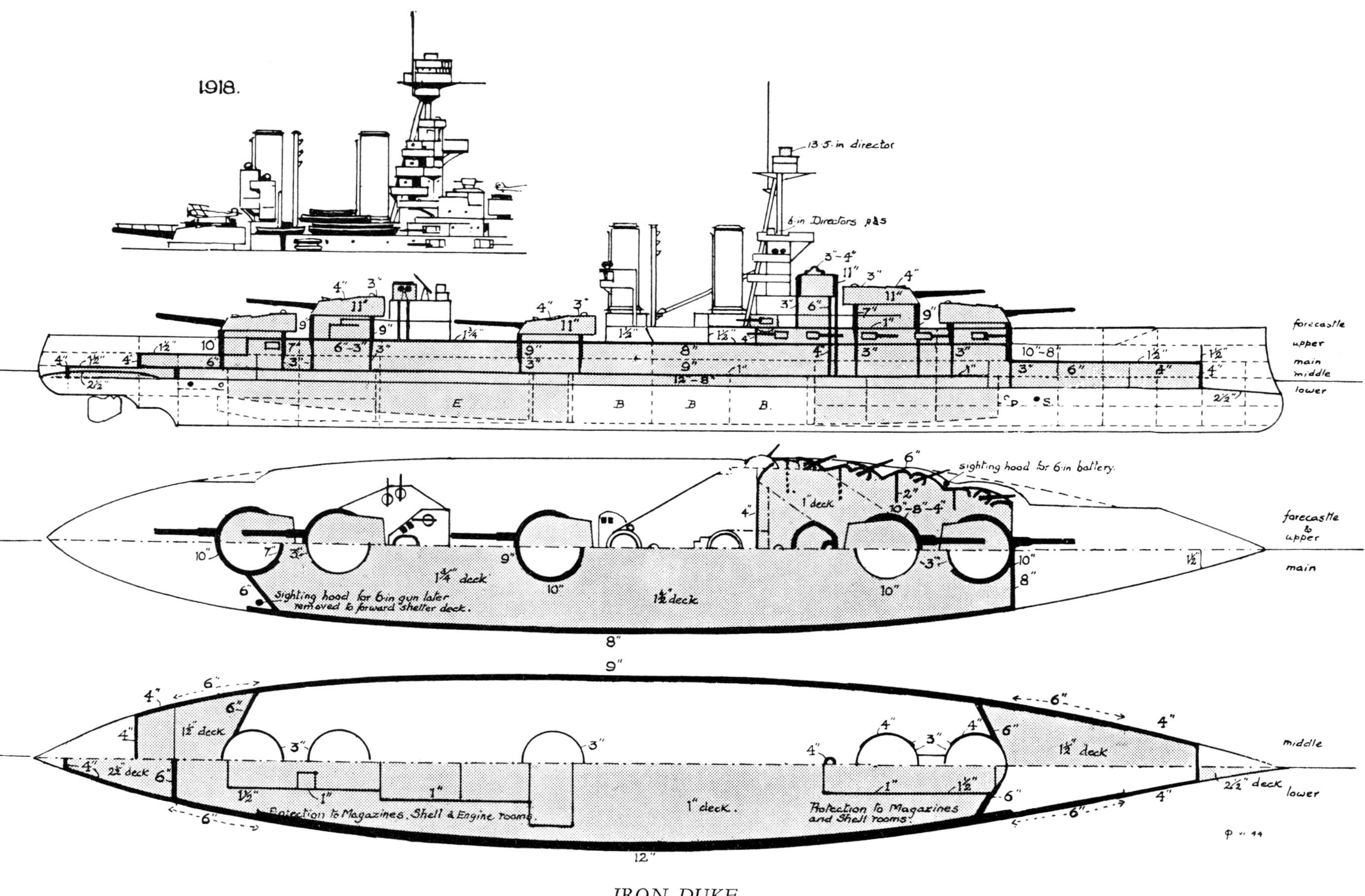

IRON DUKE

The 6th gun on each beam was originally carried in a casemate abreast "Y" turret, but was moved to the forward superstructure deck early in 1915.

Our neighbours use their flotillas in fleet actions, and in thick weather, it might be most unpleasant if they forced you to take your 12-in. guns off your opponent in order to fire at destroyers, remembering also that the 12-in. would not be loaded with shrapnel during a fleet action; and while it is a matter of some time to change the projectile in a 12-in. gun, it is only a matter of a few seconds to commence firing shrapnel with a 6-in. gun.

The all-big-gun enthusiasts claim simplicity of control and the enormous destructive power of one 12-in. as against a quantity of 6-in. projectiles; this is also the essence of truth and the difficulty is to find the compromise, which is the same old conundrum always being set to the Chief Constructor of the Navy, in slightly different forms.

The *Iron Duke* when paying off after serving in the Atlantic Fleet in 1929. Note the enlarged mast head control positions, searchlight towers, and W.T. mast aft.

After much observation, more discussion, and most thought, I have come to the conclusion:

(1) That it is advisable to have a 6-in. battery.
(2) That it is of necessity that it should take up but little room.
(3) That it should not interfere with the primary armaments when they have found the range and are hitting.
(4) That it should be of use for night attack, using shrapnel.
(5) That the weight economised by doing away with the 4-in. guns should assist to provide the 6-in. battery."

On receipt of this letter Watts made alternative plans for the next type of battleship with 6-in. batteries in one of them. The First Lord had also asked Admiral Kerr for some essays and letters he had written on the subject of armaments, tactics, and gunnery amongst which was the above quoted; after digesting them McKenna sent for Watts and asked if he could put 6-in. batteries into the next type of ship being designed, as he knew it was too late to make out new plans for those about to be built (*Iron Duke* class). Watts replied that he had already made alternative plans which allowed the *Iron Duke* class to carry such batteries, and the ships were ordered, forthwith.

Fisher having left the Admiralty early in 1910 design was no longer based upon his prejudices and opposition to a secondary armament. Economy may have had quite a lot to do with the absence of 6-in. guns in the *King George V*, but one cannot see the originator of the *Dreadnought* proposing or even acquiescing to the return of medium calibres.

The new ships were generally similar to the *King Georges* but 25 ft. longer with a foot more beam and draught. The additional length was divided between the forecastle and after part—forward to provide buoyancy against the weight of the battery and to get it back from the bows, and aft to accommodate the stern 6-in. guns. Industrial troubles hindered construction and delayed completion from two to six months.

In appearance they were easy to distinguish from the previous class by their narrower funnels, big tripod mast, and 6-in. battery. During the war mast-head control tops were augmented and searchlight towers fitted to the second funnel; in 1920 a small mast was stepped on the after superstructure.

ARMAMENT

The main armament remained unchanged, but in place of the 4-in. guns in the *King George V* batteries of twelve 6-in. re-appeared as a secondary armament, disposed five a side in the forecastle, and one abreast "Y" turret on the main deck, from which position it was thought the torpedo craft would be silhouetted against the horizon. This placing was far from happy as the guns were crowded, too far forward, and very low.

> "Early in the War it was found necessary to unship the ports altogether, as the sea washed them away constantly. Water then had free access to the inside of the ship through the opening between the revolving shield and the ship's side, and, except in fine weather, water entered freely. In bad weather the water, as deep as three to four inches, was constantly below through open hatches, to the great discomfort of the ship's company, who were continually wet, and to the detriment of efficiency. Arrangements were devised on board the *Iron Duke* to overcome this trouble. A partial bulkhead was fitted in rear of the guns to confine the water which entered the ship, and watertight india-rubber joints provided between the shields and the ship's side. The results were satisfactory and similar changes were made in the *Queen Elizabeth* class and *Tiger*. The two after 6-in. guns, which were on the main deck level, were removed altogether at the first opportunity and the ship's side and armour completed in the after embrasure in all these ships, as it was apparent that these guns could never be worked at sea, being only a few feet above the water-line. The guns themselves were mounted in new unarmoured casemates on the superstructure deck level." (*The Grand Fleet*, p. 174.)

The retention of "Q" turret at upper deck height precluded any other satisfactory disposition, but to have raised it a deck and spaced the 6-in. guns to greater advantage and with a drier command as in the *Erin* would have meant a longer strake of 6-in. armour and increased beam leading to a rise in displacement which would not have been sanctioned. Two 3-in. A.A. were placed on the after superstructure during the war.

Because of the unlikelihood of opportunity for using a stern torpedo tube as fitted in previous classes—and removed during the war—beam tubes were substituted in a submerged flat abaft "Y" barbette.

Director and spotting towers at the head of the foremast caused a return to the heavy tripod, the 6-in. gun directors being placed on the upper bridge with armoured sighting hoods for each battery at forecastle deck level forward and on the main deck aft. The 6-in. controls used to get badly smoked out at times, and gunfire was very inaccurate in a seaway.

Under fair conditions the main armament made very good shooting, although "Q" guns caused considerable superstructure strain when fired before or abaft the beam.

The two 3-pdr. A.A. guns mounted in the *Iron Duke* were thought to be the first to be sent afloat. In the absence of proper training they were quite useless, and this applies to A.A. armaments generally during War I except against comparatively slow moving targets like Zeppelins.

PROTECTION

Armour distribution was generally similar to that in the *King George V*. With the belt extended aft as 6 in.-4 in. instead of being only 2½ in. the bulkheads were modified accordingly, so that 4 in. and 6 in. replaced 2½ in. and 10 in. on both middle and lower decks. Extra protection by the battery armour led to thinning of the barbettes forward; the thicker belt aft reduced the after part of "Y" barbette, and led to the reduction of the deck over the steering from 4 in. to 2½ in.

The conning tower was quite a spacious structure of two storeys, the upper of 11 in. and the lower of 6 in. plating with a 4-in. communication tube leading to the middle deck.

After Jutland further protection was given to the magazines by means of bulkheads and thicker decks of 1 in.-2 in., with a rise in displacement of 820 tons.

Side screens of 1½ in.-1 in. covered the magazines and engine rooms, but two lines of coal bunkers up to 17 ft. wide at the waterline served to protect the boiler rooms. At Jutland the *Marlborough* received a torpedo hit amidships which made a hole 70 ft. in extreme length with a depth of 20 ft. at the point of explosion. She was able to keep station at 17 knots for a time and continued in action although with a list to starboard; twenty-four hours later she was drawing 39 ft. and making for the Humber at 10 knots. (When the *Tsarevitch* was torpedoed at Port Arthur the damage only spread over 30 ft. × 10 ft. and she again was not hit over a part covered by her internal anti-torpedo bulkhead. But the difference between the effects of torpedoes in 1904 and 1916 is instructive.) A comparison between the plans of the *Iron Duke* and *Kaiser* will show how the Germans preferred to run the anti-torpedo bulkhead along the full length of magazines, engine, and boiler rooms with coal bunkers acting as a buffer over as great an area as possible, while we massed our coal against "Q" magazine and the three boiler rooms. That the *Marlborough* shaped so bravely after being sorely wounded speaks well for solid coal pro-

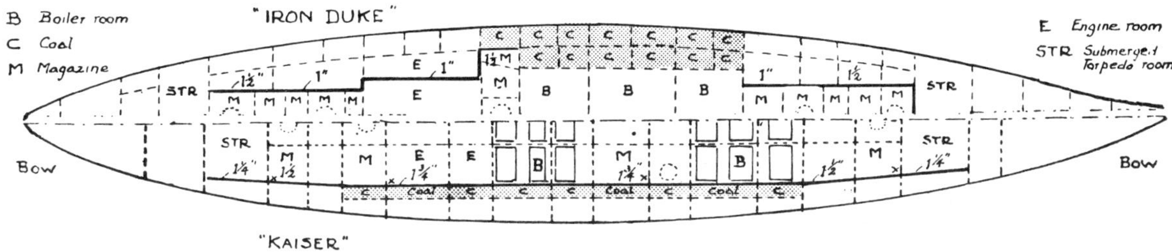

tection; that the several German capital ships we torpedoed also reached home is also a tribute to their system of defence although so far as we know they did not get hit amidships.

A comparison between the cross-sections of the *Iron Duke* and her contemporary the *Konig* shows the extent to which the British heavier guns necessitated armour protection on a lighter scale generally, especially along the water-line deck. On the other hand the German ships would have to face heavier projectiles, so that relatively they were not so well off as figures suggest.

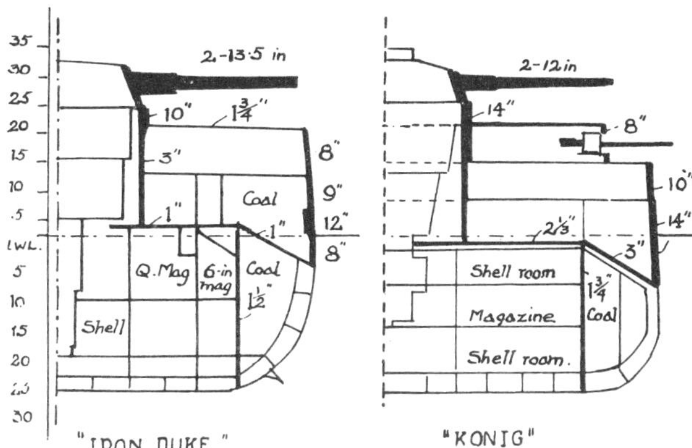

MACHINERY

The installation consisted of two sets of turbines working four shafts, all being available for ahead or astern. Each set had one H.P. ahead and one H.P. astern on the wing shaft and one L.P. ahead and one L.P. astern in the same casing on the inner shaft, working in series on the two shafts on the same side.

The 1,050 tons of oil stowed in the double bottom was burned by high pressure spraying on to coal, and used as an emergency fuel. With full bunkers trim was 18 in. by the head, so that the fore part of the thick belt lay a foot under water, and as draught measured 33 ft. even when 600 tons of oil had been expended, the belt was but rarely uncovered.

SPEED

As the addition of 25 ft. in length over the *King George V* was offset by only 1 ft. more beam the L/B ratio in these ships rose to 6·4 : 1, or 6·9 : 1 using the overall figures. But none of the class reached the trial figures of the *Conqueror* or *King George V*, although on full power trials they all made 21·5 to 21·6 knots with S.H.P. 29,000 to 32,500. During the war at full load they never did more than 20 knots and 17 knots as a squadron was quite enough.

SEA-GOING QUALITIES

Lacking the long clean run of forecastle in previous classes there was a lot of broken water up forward in a seaway, and a good deal used to come aboard owing to low freeboard abaft of amidships plus the slight tumble-home of the sides. But on the whole they were regarded as steadier gun platforms than the *King Georges*, although suffering more from wetness, and liable to plunge through heavy seas. As in other classes "Q" and "Y" turrets were difficult to man at times in rough weather without getting a soaking.

Manœuvrability was good and they were regarded as easy to handle.

GENERAL

As a class together they were very effective, and in many ways but little inferior to the *Royal Sovereigns*.

The *Emperor of India* was the only ship in which the Loyal Toast at dinner was "Gentleman, The King

Emperor." The crown on the ensign staff rested on a cushion as an Imperial Crown, and the Ship's Crest included a swastika right handed.

"BENBOW"

Built by Beardmore May '12-October '14. Joined the Grand Fleet on 10 December, and served in the 4th B.S. until '19. Flagship of Sir Douglas Gamble until February '15 and then of Sir Doveton Sturdee. Present at Jutland. No casualties. Served in the Mediterranean '19-'26. Black Sea operations. Atlantic Fleet until '29. Stricken under the terms of the Washington Treaty.

Sold January 1931.

"EMPEROR OF INDIA"

Built by Vickers May '12-November '14. Joined Grand Fleet December '14-'19. 4th B.S. (Jutland. No casualties.) For some time Flagship of Rear-Admiral A. L. Duff. 1st B.S. Flagship. Served in the Mediterranean '19-'26 (big refit '22). Atlantic Fleet '26-'29. Stricken under terms of the Washington Treaty. Used as a target for shell attack.

Sold December 1931.

"IRON DUKE"

Built at Portsmouth January '12-March '14. Home Fleet. Flagship '14 (Admiral Sir Geo. Callaghan). Grand Fleet Flagship of C.-in-C. (Admiral Sir John Jellicoe August '14-November '16). Present at Jutland. No casualties. 2nd B.S. '16-'19. Mediterranean '19-'26. Black Sea operations against Bolsheviks. Atlantic Fleet '26-'29. Reduced to gunnery and boys training ship under London Treaty '31-'32, when "B" and "Y" turrets, conning tower, belt armour and torpedo tubes were removed and boiler power reduced. Speed 18 knots. In 1939 removed to Scapa Flow and guns used for shore defence. As a depôt ship was injured by near misses from bombs 17 October '39 and bottomed, but continued in service.

Sold March 1946.

"MARLBOROUGH"

Built at Devonport January '12-June '14. Home Fleet 2nd Flagship. Grand Fleet 1st B.S. Flagship Sir Lewis Bayley to December '14 succeeded by Vice-Admiral Sir Cecil Burney '14-'19. Torpedoed at Jutland and repaired on the Tyne in three months. Mediterranean Fleet '19-'26. Black Sea operations. Big refit '20-'22. Atlantic Fleet '26-'29. Stricken under terms of the Washington Treaty.

Sold May 1932.

Chapter 98

TIGER (1911 PROGRAMME)

Builders	*Laid down*	*Launched*	*Completed*	*Cost*
J. Brown & Co.	20 June '12	15 Dec. '13	Oct. '14	£2,593,100 (including guns)

Dimensions 660′ (704′) × 90′ 6″ × 28′ 5″ = 28,500 tons.
Load displacement 28,430; full load 35,160 tons (sinkage 101 tons per inch).

Armament 8 13·5-in./45.
12 6-in./45.
4 3-pdrs.
2 3-in. A.A. (added).
Tubes:
4 21-in.
20 torpedoes.

Protection Belt 9″-6″-5″-4″-3″; bulkheads 4″-2″.
Barbettes 9″-8″-4″-3″-1″; shields 9″; roofs 4½″-3½″.
Batteries 6″; traverses 1″; bulkheads 5″-4″.
Conning tower 10″, 3″; torpedo control 6″.
Decks: forecastle 1½″-1″; upper 1½″-1″; main 1″; lower 3″ (bows) 1″.
After Jutland extra 1″ plating over magazines as in plan.
Screens to Magazines and shell rooms 2½″, 1½″, 1″.

Machinery Brown Curtis turbines, direct drive, 4 screws.
Boilers 39 Babcock and Wilcox, 235 lb. pressure.
S.H.P. 85,000 = 28 knots; 108,000 = 29 knots.

Fuel Coal 3,320/450 tons; oil 3,480/450 tons.

Complement 1,121.

Constructor E. L. Attwood.

Special features:

(1) The largest and fastest capital ship to date.
(2) Our only battle cruiser to mount 6-in. guns.
(3) Our last coal burning capital ship.

In January 1911 the Japanese Government caused general surprise by ordering a battle cruiser the *Kongo* from Vickers for delivery in two and a half years. Although for the past six years they had been building their own battleships, they wished to enjoy the advantage of the latest British practice in a class of four big ships and so had the prototype designed and constructed in this country. The *Kongo,* launched in May 1912 a month before the *Tiger* was laid down, may be described as a battle cruiser edition of the *Erin*—then building for Turkey as the *Reschadieh.* She displaced 27,500 tons, carried eight 14-in. and sixteen 6-in. guns with eight 21-in. tubes and was designed for 27·5 knots (64,000 s.h.p.). Protection was generally superior to the *Lions* and the nominal fuel supply of 1,200 tons had a maximum of 4,000 tons coal and 1,000 tons oil.

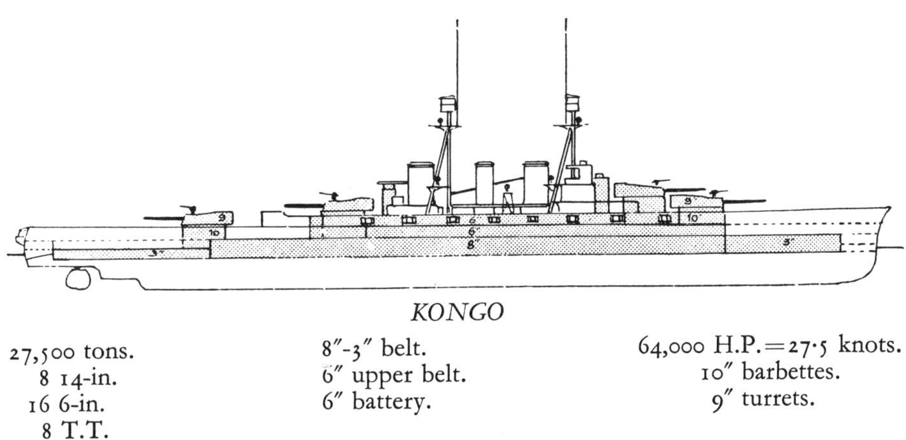

KONGO

27,500 tons.
8 14-in.
16 6-in.
8 T.T.

8″-3″ belt.
6″ upper belt.
6″ battery.

64,000 H.P. = 27·5 knots.
10″ barbettes.
9″ turrets.

As the first foreign capital ship of the Dreadnought Era to mount guns heavier than the 12-in. the design of the *Kongo* created considerable interest, especially in the arrangement of the four turrets and heavy secondary battery.

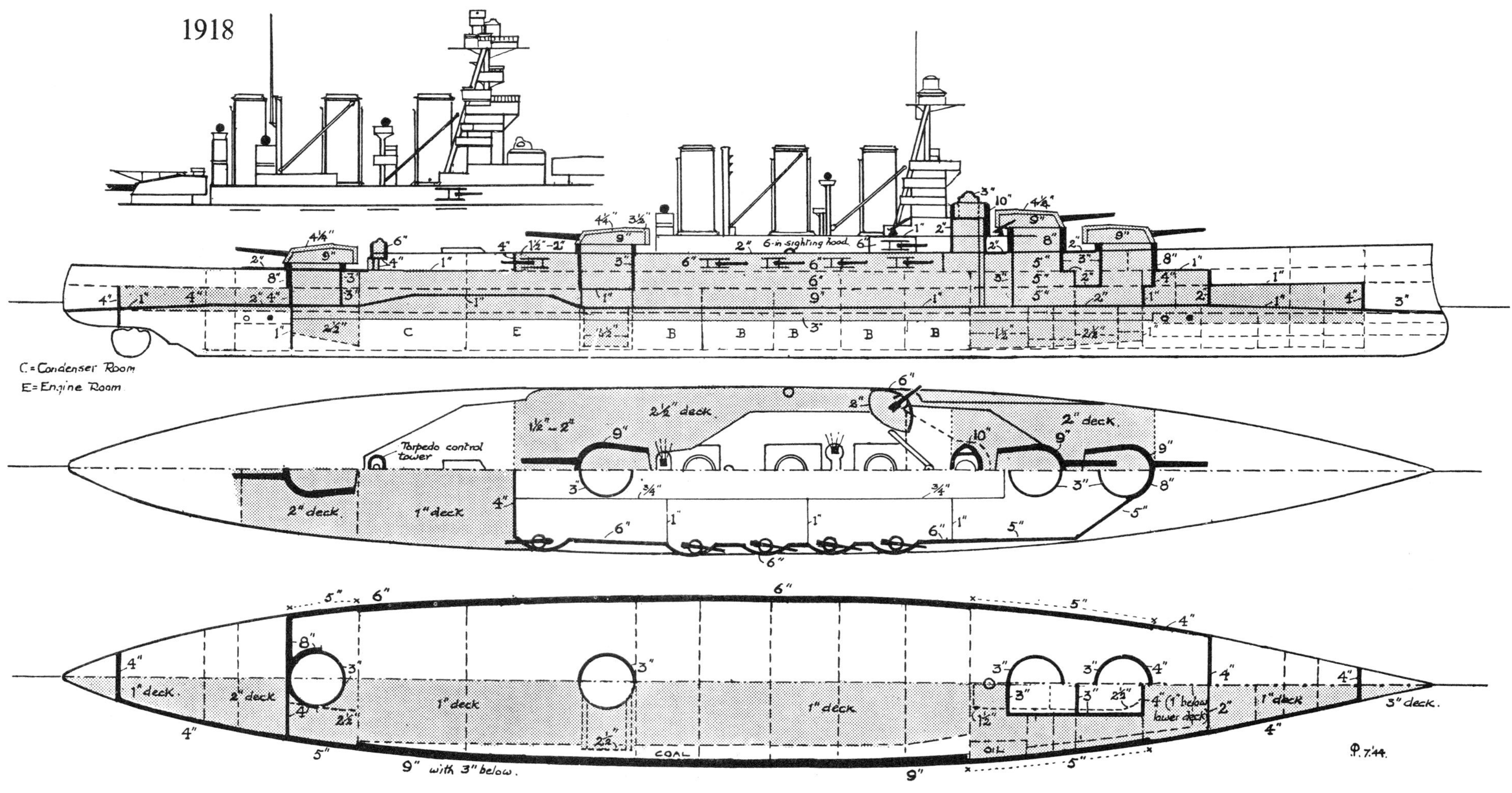
1918
C = Condenser Room
E = Engine Room
6-in sighting hood
2½" deck
1½"–2"
2" deck
1" deck
Torpedo control tower
4" (1" below lower deck)
3" deck.
COAL
OIL
9" with 3" below.

TIGER

Her superiority over the *Lion* was obvious and there could be no question of building a fourth ship of the class whan an all-round improvement was unmistakably indicated.

Hence although the *Tiger* was at first referred to as an enlarged *Queen Mary*, steps were taken to increase her power from the original 85,000 for 28 knots to 108,000 giving 29/30 knots and the influence of the *Kongo* can be seen in her general lay-out. The Board approved the selected sketch design in August 1911 and the final drawings in December. She was on the stocks for eighteen months, being rushed to completion in October 1914 and commissioned at Clydebank when day and night shifts were still working in her.

APPEARANCE

The majesty of a warship depends upon the mass of her hull bearing an aggressive array of guns being properly set off by impressive and well-placed masting and funnels. In the *Lion* and *King George V* the big flat-sided funnels

The *Tiger* in the Clyde when first completed for service.

produced a fine if somewhat asymmetrical mass effect which gained nothing from the rig. The *Iron Duke* was given a full-size tripod, and a reversion to equal sized round funnels made for symmetry with perhaps some loss in mass effect. But in the *Tiger* the *tout ensemble* had been as carefully planned as in the *King Edward VII*. "Speed and beauty were welded into every line of her. The highest ideals of grace and power had taken form at the bidding of the artist's brain of her designer. Wherever she went she satisfied the eye of the sailorman and I have known them to pull miles just that the sweetness of her lines might delight their eyes. She was the last warship built to satisfy the sailor's ideas of what a ship should be like, and nobly she fulfilled that ideal. Beside any others she made them look like floating factories. No man who ever served in her fails to recollect her beauty with pride and thankfulness." (*Years of Endurance*, Muir, p. 56.)

It is a thousand pities that a shifting of her topmast to the main derrick stump in 1918 was made necessary—it changed her in the same way that twisted eyebrows would spoil classic beauty.

Although retaining the *Lion's* length, beam was increased 2 ft. and draught 6 in. adding 2,150 tons to the legend displacement which reached 28,500 tons; at her official full load displacement of 35,160 tons draught touched 34 ft.! Freeboard at the bows was 34 ft. 4 in., amidships 31 ft. 3 in., and aft 19 ft. 9 in.

There was a three-decked bridge as in the *Iron Duke*, but this was later built up above funnel level when the mast controls were augmented and fresh tops added which displaced the topmast.

In addition to the main derrick-post shorter gallows-posts between the first and second funnels served derricks and carried searchlights at their heads—a feature unique to the *Tiger* and adapted from the American Dreadnoughts.

ARMAMENT

The change in position of "Q" turret increased its arc of bearing to 60° before the beam and 90° abaft it on either side, and by grouping all the boiler rooms amidships it was possible to provide a space of 75 ft. between its gun muzzles and "X" turret, which was considered sufficient to allow the guns to be fired dead astern when required (see Appendix IV. "Blast from Gunfire"). This space also served as a safety measure inasmuch as both turrets could not be knocked out at one blow—as occurred at Dogger Bank when the *Seydlitz* had her closely spaced after turrets put out of action by a hit which set fire to both magazines.

The height of the big guns above water at normal draught was A = 39 ft., B = 47 ft., Q = 39 ft., Y = 25 ft.

As the forecastle deck was carried aft beyond "Q" turret the 6-in. guns could be placed well amidships in a far better position for fighting than in the *Iron Duke* although the ports had to be treated in the same way to keep out water in a seaway. Direct fire astern was secured from the aftermost guns, but the two in shelter-deck casemates had broadside and ahead bearings only. The battery guns ranged from 80° ahead to 40° abaft the beam.

In 1918 the enlarged control top and addition of a long range finder made it necessary to shift the topmast to an after mast made from a heightened derrick stump which quite marred her profile.

The same protection as in the *Iron Duke* gave 6 in. over the battery with end bulkheads of 5 in. forward and 4 in. aft.

Port and starboard tubes were fitted before and abaft the end barbettes, the after tubes replacing the stern tube in the *Lion* which was removed during the war.

The wartime 4-in. A.A. can be seen near the base of the conning tower.

ARMOUR

Although the thickness of the main plating remained the same, protection was more extensive than in the *Lion*, the addition of 6-in. battery walls correcting a major deficiency in the earlier battle cruisers where the open forecastle deck made them so much more vulnerable to long range hits. Also the 4-in. belting was continued almost to the bow and stern along the water-line although shortened over the upper deck at the ends. After Jutland additional deck armour 1 in. thick was fitted over the magazines, and the plating on the forecastle and upper decks, magazines, and shell rooms was increased to 2½ in. with 3 in. on the lower deck.

A comparison between the system of amidships protection in the *Tiger* and her contemporary the *Derfflinger* shows how the extra beam and less space occupied by small-tube boilers allowed for additional bulkheading and coal protection below the water-line.

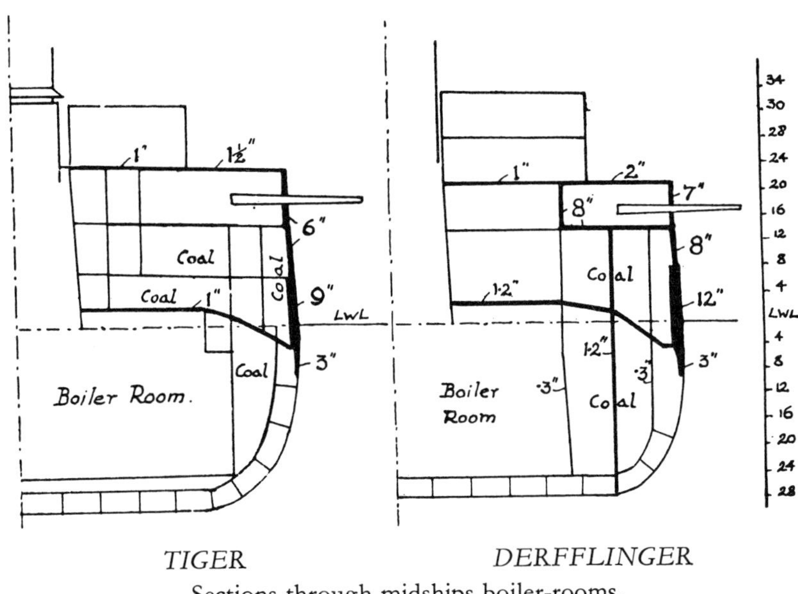

TIGER *DERFFLINGER*

Sections through midships boiler-rooms.

The percentage of displacement allotted to armour and protective plating was 26 per cent.

MACHINERY

The *Tiger* was the first British capital ship to have Brown Curtis turbines instead of Parsons, these being manufactured by the builders. Each of the four shafts was available for ahead and astern working, with the turbines in two sets each with H.P. ahead and H.P. astern on the wing shafts and one L.P. ahead and one L.P. astern in the same casing on the inner shaft. The D.N.C., Sir Eustace Tennyson D'Eyncourt was anxious to equip the *Tiger* with small-tube boilers and had urged the adoption of these for a number of years. But our engineers preferred the large tubes, which had certain advantages over the small tube type, but meant considerably more weight for their installation. He claimed that if geared turbines and small tube boilers had been available when the *Tiger* and *Queen Elizabeth* were designed, it would have been possible to give these ships speeds of 32 knots and 28½ knots respectively.

Admiral Jellicoe has recorded that when he was Controller in 1910 (while the *King George V* design was being

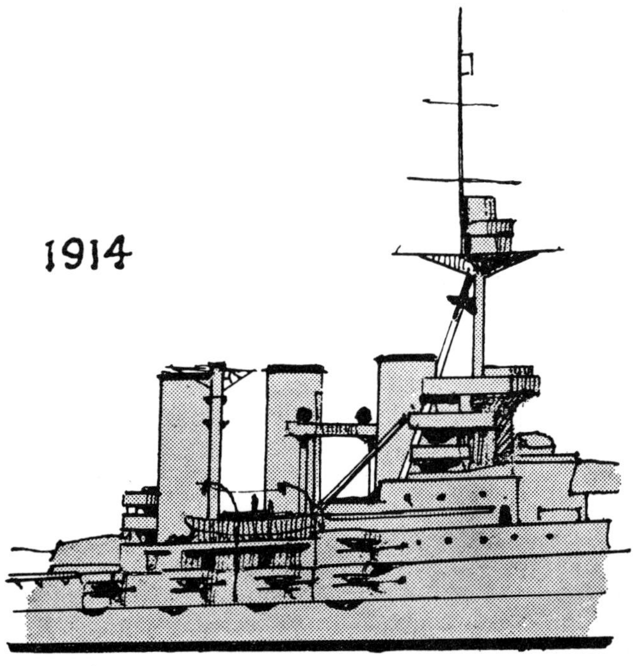

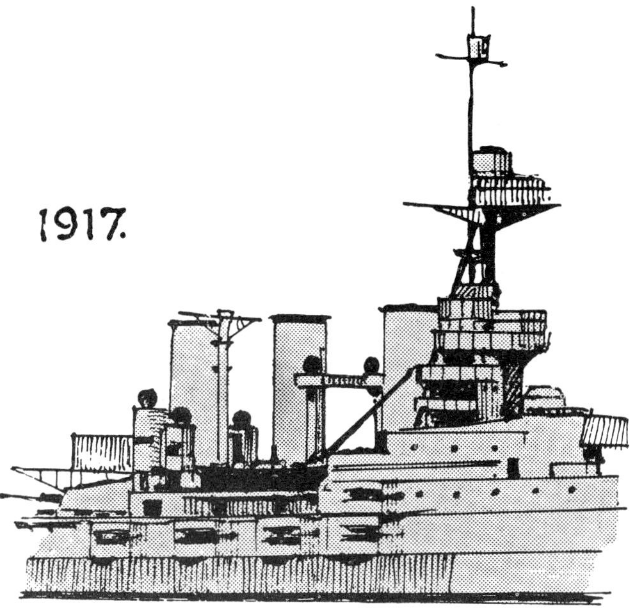

prepared) Sir Charles Parsons was strongly advocating the adoption of small-tube boilers in heavy ships. But when doing a round of the shipyards shortly afterwards "I mentioned this and asked the opinions of the various officers in charge—engineers, managers and so forth—but they one and all gave me no encouragement. I therefore had to drop it." (I.N.A., 24 March 1920.)

No exhaustive trials in deep water were carried out on commissioning, but runs made on the Polperro course showed that the designed horse power could be obtained easily although the highest recorded speed was 29 knots (d'Eyncourt, I.N.A., LXIII, p. 36). The enormous fuel capacity did not provide any exceptional radius of action as she burnt about 1,245 tons daily at 59,500 h.p. Figures showing radius of action were never included in official lists.

GENERAL

During 1917 searchlight towers were fitted around the third funnel, and the fore control enlarged. Later the addition of a mast-head range-finder caused the topmast to be fidded on the derrick stump, and 1918 saw aeroplane runways on "Q" and "B" turrets for flying-off a Sopwith biplane.

The percentages of load displacement were:

	%
General equipment	3
Armament	12·7
Armour and protecting plating	26·0
Hull	34·4
Machinery and engineers' stores	20·7
Fuel (at load draught)	3·2
	100·0

"TIGER"

Built at Clydebank June '12 to October '14, and joined the Grand Fleet at Scapa on 6 November after less than a month's shakedown. 1st B.S. At Dogger Bank: was hit on "B" turret and port gun disabled (2 killed and several wounded); a hit on the signal distributing station killed 8 and wounded 4. At Jutland she received 21 hits including a 12-in. on "A" barbette, an 11-in. on "Q" turret, an 11-in. on "X" turret (24 killed and 37 wounded). Repairs finished 2 July.

Post-war in B.C.S. Atlantic Fleet '19-'22. Sea-going gunnery ship '24-'29 and replaced *Hood* in B.C.S. '29-'31. On 30 March '31 took farewell cheers from the Atlantic Fleet, paid off at Devonport, and sold March '32 under life duration clause of Treaty.

Chapter 99

THE AGADIR CRISIS

DURING 1911 the Germans engineered what became known as the Agadir Crisis which kept Europe in tension for some months. France had occupied Fez in Morocco and as some sort of "lebensraum" counterblast the Germans claimed interest in Agadir and its hinterland although there was no German property there and no trade. To back up the claim the gunboat *Panther* was anchored off Agadir and when the British Government asked the reason why, it was left without a reply for many weeks. But Sir Edward Grey informed the German Ambassador that the Government could not disinterest themselves in Morocco and that until Germany's intentions were made known their attitude must be one of reserve.

The Press took a somewhat gloomy view of the situation. Was Germany angling for a pretext to attack France, or was it merely a test of the strength of the Entente, using uncertainty and diplomatic pressure in order to acquire some sort of colonial advantage? But with a certain schism in the Liberal cabinet between the Imperialist and Radical groups there was no certainty that we could speak with a decided voice if faced with a dangerous situation. Both Mr. Churchill and Mr. Lloyd George, then Chancellor of the Exchequer and a weighty influence in council, tended towards the Radical side of the Cabinet, but strangely enough it was the latter—then regarded as head of the Peace Party—who decided upon putting an end to the period of uncertainty. In July he took the occasion of an after dinner speech to the Bankers' Association to use these words:

> "If the situation were forced upon us in which peace could only be preserved by the surrender of the great and beneficient position Britain has won by centuries of heroism and achievement by allowing Britain to be treated, where her interests were vitally affected, as if she were of no account in the Cabinet of Nations, then I say emphatically that peace at that price would be a humiliation intolerable for a great country like ours to endure."

This pronouncement came like a thunderclap to the German Government and the national opinion of the Chancellor underwent a decided change. The Crisis ended with this diplomatic rebuff to Germany, and von Tirpitz wrote (p. 191) "It was a question of our keeping our nerve, continuing to arm on a grand scale, avoidign all provocation and waiting without anxiety until our sea power was established."

In October 1911 Mr. McKenna and Mr. Churchill exchanged portfolios and the latter commenced his association with the Admiralty which was to play such a vital part in the years to come.

Sir Arthur Wilson's tenure of office ended in January 1912 and the new Board included:

Sir Francis Bridgeman	First Sea Lord
Prince Louis of Battenberg	Second Sea Lord
Rear-Admiral Briggs	Controller and Third Sea Lord
Captain Pakenham	Fourth Sea Lord
Captain de Bartolemé	Naval Assistant
Sir Francis Hopwood	Additional Civil Lord

Sir George Callaghan became C.-in-C. Home Fleet with Sir John Jellicoe his second in command.

One of the first things Mr. Churchill set about was the creation of a Naval War Staff, which as he puts it "Takes a generation to form. At least fifteen years of consistent policy were required to give the Navy that widely extended outlook upon War problems and of war situations without which seamanship gunnery, instrumentalisms of every kind, devotion of the highest order, could not achieve their due reward." (*World Crisis*, p. 93.)

1912

The Agadir Crisis and steady strengthening of German policy towards increased naval power caused Mr. Lloyd George to adopt a more conciliatory attitude once the immediate danger of a flare-up was passed. If a formidable new Navy Law (in Germany) was to be forthcoming with increased antagonism in Britain, he thought it might be possible to avert the inevitable developments by friendly and intimate conversations aimed towards some mitigation of the dangerous naval rivalry. The Cabinet therefore invited Sir Ernest Cassel—who knew the Kaiser well—to go to Berlin and get into direct touch with him. The Memorandum he was to present was short and to the point: "Acceptance of English superiority at sea—no augmentation of the German programme—a reduction as far as possible in that programme—and on the part of England, no impediment to German expansions —discussion and promotion of German colonial ambitions—proposals for mutual declarations that the two Powers would not take part in aggressive plans or combinations against one another."

Cassel returned with a cordial letter from the Kaiser and a statement on the new Navy Law from von Bethmann-Hollweg, upon which the First Lord's comments were summarized as follows:

"The new Navy Law will be passed by the Reichstag and the naval increases are serious. Under the former Programme we should have built 4, 3, 4, 3, 4, 3 against their six years output of 2, 2, 2, 2, 2, 2. But if they are to build 3, 2, 3, 2, 3, 2 we cannot build less than 5, 4, 5, 4, 5, 4 to retain a 60 per cent. superiority in Dreadnought ships over Germany, with two keels to one on their additional ships."

"The creation of a third squadron in full commission is also a serious and formidable provision. At present in the six winter months the 1st and 2nd squadrons in the High Seas Fleet are congested with recruits, but the addition of a third squadron will impose a strain on us throughout the year. The maintenance in full commission of 25 battleships exposes us to constant danger but with some assurance against sudden attack in the fact that several Dreadnoughts are often the wrong side of the Kiel Canal which they cannot pass through and must therefore make a long detour. The deepening of the Canal will extinguish this danger signal. Since defenders are always liable to be attacked by an enemy at his maximum strength at his selected moment, it means that our margins will have to be very large. Against 25 battleships we could not keep less than 40 available within twenty-four hours."

"The only chance I see is roughly this. They will announce their new programme and we will make an effective and immediate reply. Then if they care to slow down the tempo so that the Fleet Law is accomplished in twelve and not six years, friendly relations would ensue, and we, though I should be reluctant to bargain about it, could slow down too. Let them make their quotas bienniel instead of annual; nothing would be deranged in their plan; twelve years of tranquility would be assured in naval policy. The attempt should be made."

The Cabinet decided that a Cabinet Minister should go to Berlin and Mr. Haldane was selected for that purpose, and with Sir Ernest Cassel left for Berlin on 6 February. He returned two days later and the Cabinet was summoned to receive an account of his mission. This may be given in Admiral Tirpitz's own words:

> "Haldane came out with a proposal of a certain delay in the building of the three ships; could we not distribute them over twelve years? . . . He only wanted a token of our readiness to meet England, more for the matter of form. . . . Haldane himself proposed that we should retard our rate of increase 'in order to lubricate the negotiations,' or that we should at least cancel the first of the three ships. He outlined in writing of his own accord the same principle which I had previously fixed upon in my own mind as a possible concession. *I therefore sacrificed the ship.*"

In return we "sacrificed" two hypothetical ships and our Programmes were declared at 4, 5, 4, 4, 4, 4, although the gift of the *Malaya* by the Federated Malay States raised the figure in the first year to five.

Chapter 100

REORGANIZATION AND THE COMING OF THE 15-IN. GUN

As a first step towards countering the augmented German battle fleet, a reorganization of our own squadrons was ordered at the instigation of the First Lord. Under this, the battleships available for home defence were divided into 1st, 2nd and 3rd Fleets comprising eight Battle Squadrons of eight ships each together with their attendant cruisers, destroyers, etc.

Hitherto the battleships comprising the Home Fleet had been organized in Divisions based upon Portsmouth, Devonport and the Nore. These "divisions" may have been tactical or administrative; the battle units were uneven in numbers, and the degree of readiness and efficiency of the different squadrons was not apparent from the classes in which they were grouped.

Under the new system came:

(1) The First Fleet comprising a Fleet flagship and four squadrons in full commission and always ready. This entailed basing the former Atlantic Fleet on Home ports instead of Gibraltar, and the battleships hitherto in the Mediterranean on Gibraltar instead of Malta.

(2) The Second Fleet consisting of two battle squadrons fully manned but having 40 per cent. of their ratings learning or qualifying in the gunnery or torpedo schools. It could fight at any minute, but for full efficiency would have to draw its balance from the schools.

(3) The Third Fleet of two squadrons made up of our oldest ships and manned by care and maintenance parties only. These could not be put into commission until after mobilization of the Reserves.

To facilitate mobilization of these squadrons and their attendant cruisers a special reserve was formed called the Immediate Reserve who received higher pay and periodical training, and were liable to be called up in advance of the general mobilization.

By adding a third squadron to their High Seas Fleet Germany was increasing her *always ready* strength from seventeen to twenty-five battleships. In reply the new organization raised our *always ready* Fleet from thirty-three to forty-nine with other forces in like proportion. On mobilization the German figures would rise to thirty-eight, and the British at first to fifty-seven and ultimately as the new organization was completed, to sixty-five. (*World Crisis*, 1, p. 117.)

The Mediterranean Fleet was to consist of the 2nd Battlecruiser Squadron of three *Indomitables* and *Indefatigable* with the 1st Armoured Cruiser Squadron in support.

THE COMING OF THE 15-INCH GUN

When Mr. Churchill was handed the portfolio of First Lord the Estimates and plans for the 1912 Programme were already far advanced. We were to lay down three battleships, one battle cruiser, three cruisers and twenty destroyers; the designs for the ships only awaited final approval before being passed by the Cabinet in February and presented to the House in detail in March. But a lot of uncertainty hung over these designs, especially those for the capital ships. We had built ten Dreadnoughts armed with 12-in. guns, before going one better in the 13·5-in.; already there were twelve battleships under construction mounting this larger calibre and although the *Kaiser* class were to have only 12-in. in their main armament, Krupp was listing 14-in. guns of 40, 45, and 50 cals. and there were reports that the *Konig* class were to be of 27,000 tons carrying 14-in. Both Japan and America were building 14-in. gunned ships. The time seemed ripe for another jump in calibre.

An increase of 1·5 in. from 12-in. to 13·5-in. had meant a jump from 850 lb. to 1,250/1,400 lb. in the weight of projectile; another 1·5 in. to 15-in. would result in a shell of over 1,900 lb. and an overwhelming broadside. But re-designing the 1912 ships to carry such guns meant a vast increase in size and cost. Moreover, there must be no delay over gun design, and the guns themselves would have to be ready as soon as the mountings.

The Ordnance Board rapidly produced a design which Armstrongs undertook to execute, but there could be no question of making a trial gun for thorough testing—it would mean the loss of a year and the new ships having to mount inferior weapons. Several responsible authorities considered it would be better to lose the year and avoid the risk of gun failure and the fiasco of marred and mutilated ships. As Mr. Churchill puts it:

> "I went back to Lord Fisher. He was steadfast and even violent in his advocacy. So I hardened my heart and took the plunge. The whole outfit of guns was ordered forthwith. We arranged that one gun should be hurried on four months in front of the others by exceptional efforts so as to be able to test it for range and accuracy and to get out the range tables and other complex devices which depended upon actual firing

results. From this moment we were irrevocably committed to the whole armament, and every detail in these vessels, extending to thousands of parts, was redesigned to fit them."

The first gun was known in the Elswick shops as the "hush and push gun" and invariably described officially as the "14-in. experimental." It proved a brilliant success, and hurled a 1,920 lb. shell 35,000 yards, and achieved remarkable accuracy at all ranges without shortening its existence by strain in any way.

The first conception was for a ship carrying ten such guns, at least 600 ft. long, with an unprecedented thickness of armour of 13 in., and steaming at 21 knots. But even eight 15-in. fired a broadside 2,800 lb. heavier than ten 13·5-in., and by accepting eight guns as the main armament the space occupied by the middle turret could be given over to additional boiler rooms for furnishing a much higher speed. Would it be possible to add another 4 or 5 knots and produce a real "fast division" capable of turning the enemy's van, destroying the head of his line, and throwing his fleet into confusion while our main squadrons came up with his rear and hammered away at a straggling tail?

The First Sea Lord, Sir Francis Bridgeman lately in command of the Home Fleet, and his principal officers were all in favour of such ships. They were the dream of their battle plans, and vastly more suitable for the job than the thinly armoured battle cruisers. Whatever might be the value of *Invincibles* and *Lions* against armoured cruisers it was going to be a very risky game pitting them against battleships. In the words of the First Lord:

> "If it is worth while to spend far more than the price of your best battleship upon a fast heavily-gunned vessel, it is better at the same time to give it the heaviest armour as well. You then have a ship which may indeed cost half as much again as a battleship, but which at any rate can do everything. To put the value of a first-class battleship into a vessel which cannot stand the pounding of a heavy action is false policy. It is far better to spend the extra money and have what you really want. The battle cruiser, in other words, should be superseded by the fast battleship, *i.e.*, fast strongest ship, in spite of her cost." (*World Crisis*, 1, p. 128.)

The War College decided that 25 knots would be necessary to contain the High Seas Fleet of 1914-15, and such a speed could only be attained by the use of oil fuel. Already we had some 56 destroyers dependent upon oil and most of the big ships used it as an auxiliary by spraying it on to coal. But to replace British coal by foreign oil in the battleships meant a change in the very foundation of our supplies and raised a whole series of vital problems embracing transport, storage, and financial outlay.

> "To commit the Navy irrevocably to oil was indeed to take arms against a sea of troubles. . . . If we overcame the difficulties and surmounted the risks, we should be able to raise the whole power and efficiency of the Navy to a definitely higher level; better ships, better crews, higher economies, more intense forms of war-power—in a word, mastery itself was the prize of the venture. A year gained over a rival might make all the difference."

The fateful plunge was taken when it was decided to create the fast division; the decision to drive the smaller ships by oil followed naturally upon this, and from that day no more coal burning battleships, cruisers or destroyers were ordered from Whitehall. The Government concluded an agreement with the Anglo-Persian Oil Co. when an initial investment of two millions (later increased to five millions) secured the Navy's future fuel, and led to the acquisition of a controlling share in oil properties and interests later valued at scores of millions, with very considerable economies in the purchase price of Admiralty oil.

Chapter 101

"QUEEN ELIZABETH" CLASS (1912 PROGRAMME)

	Builders	*Laid down*	*Launched*	*Completed*
"*Barham*"	J. Brown & Co.	24 Feb. '13	31 Oct. '14	Oct. '15
"*Malaya*"	Armstrongs	20 Oct. '13	18 March '15	Feb. '16
"*Queen Elizabeth*"	Portsmouth	21 Oct. '12	16 Oct. '13	Jan. '15
"*Valiant*"	Fairfield	31 Jan. '13	4 Nov. '14	Feb. '16
"*Warspite*"	Devonport	31 Oct. '12	26 Nov. '13	March '15

Dimensions 600′ (645′ 9″)×90′ 6″×29′ 7″/30′ 8″=27,500 tons.
(Load displacement (1917) 29,150 tons; full load 33,000 tons) sinkage 98 tons per inch.

Armament 8 15-in./42.
14 6-in./45 (16 in "*Queen Elizabeth*" as completed).
2 3-in. A.A.
4 3-pdrs.
Tubes: 4 21-in. 20 torpedoes carried.

Protection Belt 13″-6″; bulkheads 6″-4″.
Barbettes 10″-4″; turrets 13″-11″.
Conning tower 11″; director 6″; tubes 6″-4″.
Decks: Forecastle 1″; upper 1¾″-1¼″; main 1¼″ (forward and aft only); middle 1″ (amidships only); lower 3″-1″ (ends only).
Torpedo bulkheads 2″.
Uptakes 1½″.

Machinery "*Barham*" and "*Valiant*" Brown Curtis by builders; "*Malaya*" and "*Queen Elizabeth*" Parsons by Wallsend; "*Warspite*" Parsons by Hawthorn Leslie.
Boilers 24 Yarrow "*Barham*" and "*Warspite*. 24 Babcock and Wilcox in others.
Pressure 235 lb.
Designed h.p. 75,000=24 knots.
4 screws. 275 Revs.

Fuel Oil 650/3,400 tons; coal 100 tons.

Complement 925/951.

Constructor E. N. Mooney under W. H. Gard.

Points of interest:

(1) First battleships to mount 15-in. guns.
(2) First big ships to be oil-fired.
(3) First battleships to steam at 24 knots.
(4) Underwent more drastic reconstruction than any other British battleships.
(5) Had the greatest metacentric height of any British capital ship for forty years.

Looking back over the tale of our capital ships we can see at long intervals a few such as the *Achilles*, *Dreadnought*, *Majestic*, *Dreadnought* (1905) and *Tiger* which stand out by virtue of their fine appearance and exceptional military qualities. To them the *Queen Elizabeth* must be added and given pride of place as the most perfect example of the naval constructor's art as yet put afloat.

As a bigger-gunned battleship edition of the *Tiger* she presented an embodiment of power, speed, and majesty never surpassed until the coming of the *Hood*, and when Watts put his signature to this, the last of the eleven plans representing thirty-seven battleships for which he had been responsible as D.N.C. there may well have been some passing memory of the *King Edward VII* signed ten years previously to which, after many strange changes in silhouette, the *Queen Elizabeth* had a distinct, if glorified, resemblance.

With the advent of these "fast battleships" construction of battle cruisers fell into abeyance and a sixth unit of the *Queen Elizabeth* class, to be named *Agincourt*, was included in the 1914 Programme instead of a sister to the *Tiger*.

The original load displacement of 27,500 tons at 28 ft. 9 in. draught became 29,150 tons at 30 ft. 1½ in. after post-Jutland additions to protection. Compared with the *Iron Duke* length showed a 20 ft. increase with 6 in. extra on the beam and 9 in. more draught, giving a rise in displacement of 2,500 tons. In the absence of "Q" turret the forecastle deck could be carried to "X" barbette by an unarmoured extension which did not entail much top weight, and allowed the boats to be stowed abaft the funnels and worked by the mainmast boom.

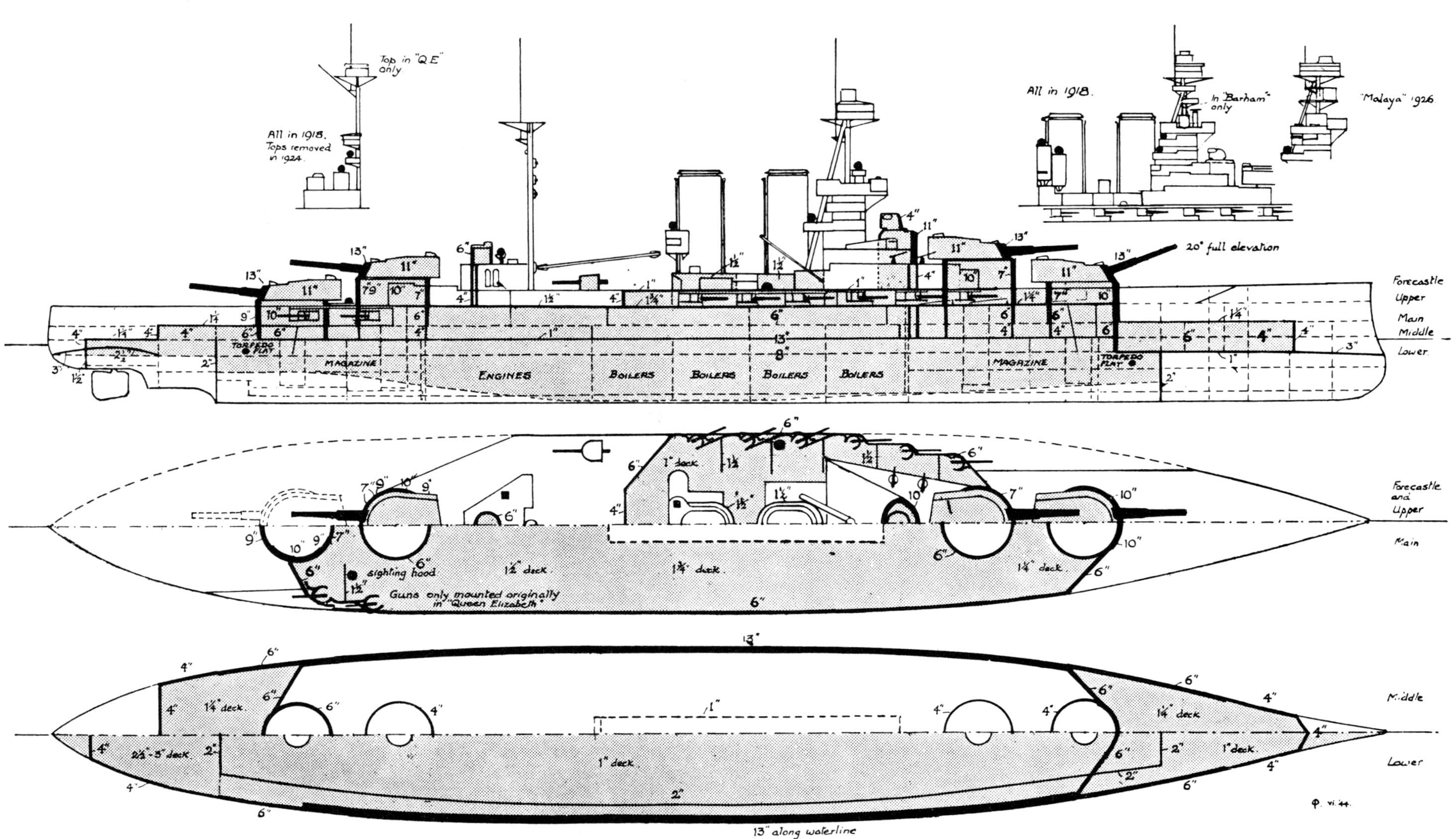

Queen Elizabeth class, showing a 6-in. gun on the upper deck amidships in place of two aside embrasured at the stern which the "Q.E." carried for a short time only.

ARMAMENT

The 15-in./42 cal. guns weighed 97·3 tons, fired a 1,920 lb. shell 23,400 yards with a m.v. of 2,450 ft. secs. using a full charge of 428 lb. cordite and maintaining a rate of fire of two rounds a minute. With barbettes measuring 34 ft. in diameter—2 ft. more than in the previous classes—the total weight of guns, mountings, barbettes and turrets was practically the same as for the five gun positions in the 13·5-in. gunned ships. As in the *Iron Duke* the barbette armour was steeply graded with the greatest thickness on the beam segment where it was likely to be hit, and thinning to the mid-line areas. Between decks, where there was side protection from the belts, thickness was reduced to 4 in.—or 1 in. more than in *Iron Duke*.

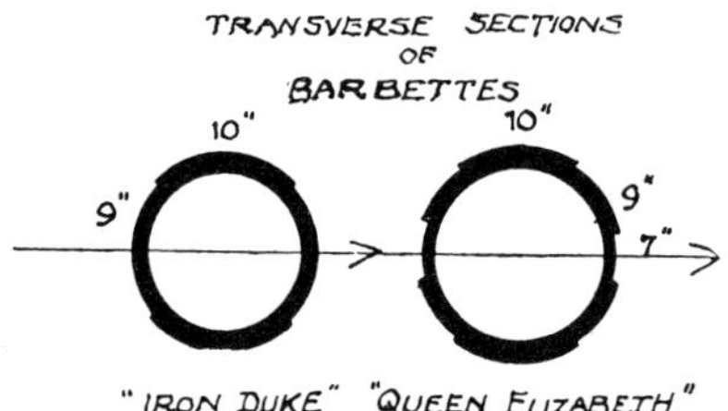

Queen Elizabeth as she appeared at the Surrender of the German Fleet 21 November 1918 with enlarged masthead control position, searchlight towers, and additional platforms on the main mast.

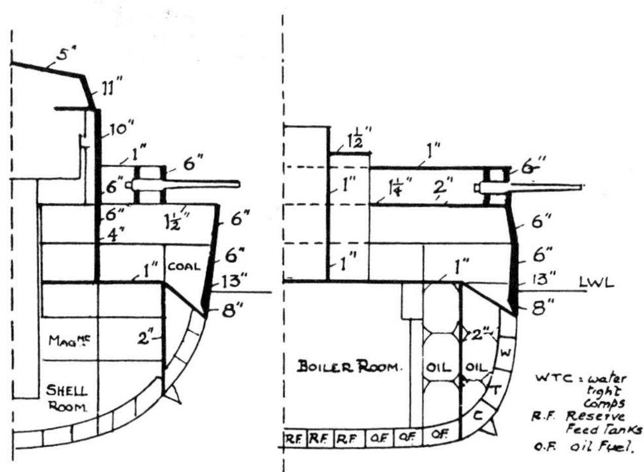

Cross sections of *Queen Elizabeth* through "B" turret and amidships to show deck protection and subdivision.

The turrets, of an enlarged *Iron Duke* pattern with 11-in. sides and 13-in. faces, had roof sighting hoods, so that the same blast conditions restricted overhead firing.

The position and spacing of the secondary battery was certainly a weak point in the design. For the *Iron Duke* the demand had been that the batteries should take up as little room as possible, which Watts had well and truly arranged. But in the *Queen Elizabeth* with her long forecastle deck, there was not the same necessity for crowding the guns up forward and the batteries could very well have been placed to run abaft of amidships. However, the *Iron Duke* was used as a model and the same restrictions observed, so that although grouped from below "B" instead of "A" barbette they suffered from the same defects and drawbacks. The forecastle sides being set well back to allow for the three foremost guns on each side (about 190 ft. from the bows) to bear ahead, there was troublesome wave resistance and considerable wetness in a seaway. The futility of the after 6-in. in the *Iron Duke*

After 6-in guns, starboard.

Port side 6-in gun. amidships.

not having been demonstrated when the *Queen Elizabeth* was nearing completion she went to sea with her full sixteen guns, but in the rest of the class these positions aft were plated in and replaced by a single gun on each side amidships with shield protection—which guns were often regarded as worth the whole battery a deck below. When space was needed for air defence these guns were replaced by 4-in. H.A.

The 6-in. battery guns were separated by screens of 1½-in. plating of full height between decks but extending only 15 ft. inboard. The gun bays were open to a passage on the inboard side and during the Battle of Jutland ready cordite charges were stowed in this passage. It was the flash caused by the explosion of these charges which caused the heavy casualties in the *Malaya*. In addition a coaming was fitted to the inboard side of the gun bays to deal with any water entering through the gun ports.

PROTECTION

Disposition of armour was along *Iron Duke* lines but generally slightly reduced in thickness. The waterline belt, increased from 12 in. to 13 in., also covered the middle deck in place of 9 in., with a reduction from 8 in. to 6 in. along the main deck. All bulkheads remained at 6 in., that under "A" barbette losing 2 in. Deck armour in places became ¼ in. thinner, but totalled 3¾ in. amidships instead of 3½ in., while the torpedo bulkheads—increased from 1 in.-1½ in. to a uniform 2 in.—covered the whole hull between the torpedo flats.

MACHINERY

The rise in horse-power to 75,000 providing 25 knots was phenominal for a battleship—a matter of 150 per cent. over the *Iron Duke's* 30,040 s.h.p. for 21·6 knots. The four-shaft installation gave two high-pressure turbines ahead and two high-pressure turbines astern directly coupled to the wing shafts, and two each low-pressure ahead and astern combined to the inner shafts. In addition cruising turbines were geared to the wing shafts. The revolutions at full power were 275 p.m.

Each of the funnels served twelve boilers in four rooms, with a working pressure of 235 lb. supplying steam at 175 lb. at the turbines.

Designed horse-power was exceeded on trials, but speeds are not on record.

Queen Elizabeth	75,130
Warspite	77,510
Barham	76,575
Valiant	71,112
Malaya	76,074

Although designed for 25 knots it is understood that 24 was about the best obtained. When reconstructed i.h.p. was over 80,000 for 24 knots. During fleet exercises the absence of smoke from these ships compared with the dense full-speed clouds from the coal burners was noteworthy.

SEA-GOING QUALITIES

With a metacentric height of 6·3 ft. in the deep and 4·6 ft. in the light condition, these ships had the greatest G.M. of any British warships since the *Glatton* (7 ft.) and old *Inflexible* (8·3 ft.). This while providing great stability and ability to stand considerable flooding of side compartments without incurring excessive list, made for quick rolling—which was largely controlled by the bilge keels.

GENERAL

War alterations included the fitting of searchlight towers to the second funnel, extra tops to the tripod and main masts, and some modifications to the bridgework. Both "B" and "X" turrets received flying-off platforms in 1918.

RECONSTRUCTION

The Washington Treaty of 1921 having restricted the construction of additional capital ships, the Powers had to be content with making the best they could out of the ships left to them, correcting deficiencies in design and equipment as far as possible by reconstruction of such vessels as were considered worth the heavy expenditure involved. In the *Queen Elizabeth* class this included (1) fitting of bulges (2) trunking the fore funnel into the second one to keep the bridge clear of smoke in a following wind (3) remodelling of bridgework (4) enlargement of control top (5) additional A.A. guns. The ships were put in hand at yearly intervals at a cost of about £1,000,000 apiece, the *Warspite* being the first completed (1924-26) and *Barham* the last (1930-33).

BULGES

Anti-torpedo bulges as fitted to the large monitors and *Edgar* class cruisers during the war were excrescences projecting up to 15 ft. from the ships' sides divided into air and water compartments, the latter being open to the sea. These acted as efficient cushions against torpedoes and served much the same way as the internal bulkheaded space in the *Bellerophon*, but were clumsy and detracted from speed, so had to be modified considerably when adapted for fast-steaming ships. In the *Ramillies* of the later *Revenge* class a much narrower form of bulge had been fitted, which projected only 7 ft. on each side; and this besides adding to her defence also served to increase stability without much reduction in speed. By 1924 docking restrictions had passed, so the same width could be used in the *Queen Elizabeths* although they measured 2 ft. more in the beam. The bulge stopped about 90 ft. short of the bows and stern.

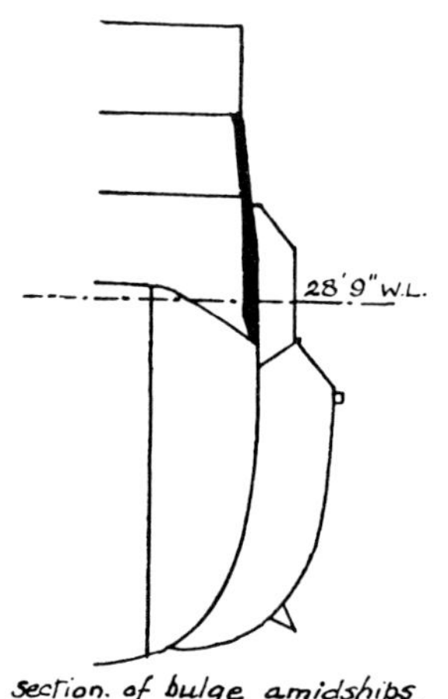

Section of bulge amidships.

The *Queen Elizabeth's* bulges differed from those in the *Ramillies* being in two sections, with a flat side and sloping top to the upper one, which extended well below the l.w.l. where it joined the much wider lower section with a marked jog. Forward the bulge was faired in to the run of the hull; aft it terminated in a cigar end at the level of the outer propellor shafts. The sloping top of the upper section showed a line of vent holes through which water driven upwards by a torpedo explosion could escape without resistance.

Bulges increased the G.M. from 6·3 ft. to 6·9 ft. in the deep condition and from 4·6 ft. to 6·1 ft. when light, but the "step" below water acted as a steadying influence and prevented excessive rolling.

With beam increased to 104 ft. load displacement reached 31,100 tons at 31 ft. 3 in. draught, with some reduction in speed, the best in service being about 24 knots.

TRUNKED FUNNEL

Funnel trunking designed to keep the bridge and control tops clear of heat, smoke, and refraction had been first introduced in the U.S. *Indiana* class of battleship abandoned under the Treaty of 1921, and later adopted by the Japanese in the cruiser *Yubari*.

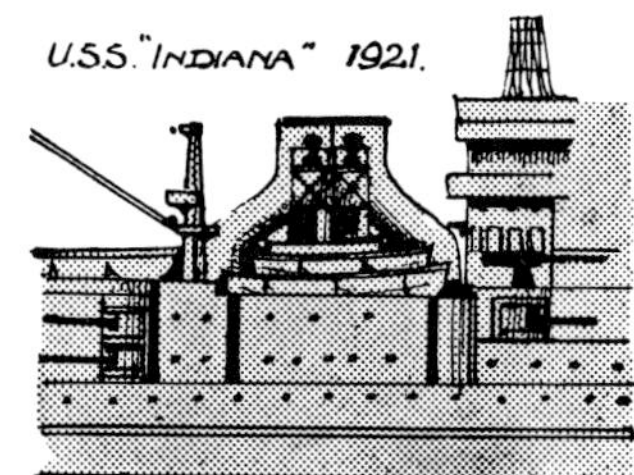

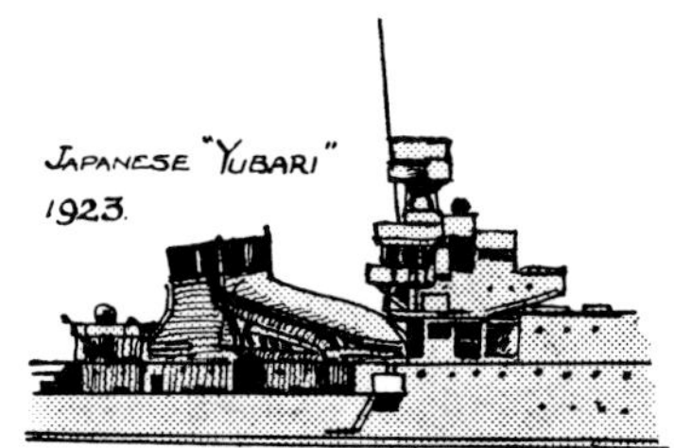

The origin of the trunked funnel as proposed for the U.S. battleships discarded under the Washington Treaty, and adapted by the Japanese to keep bridgework clear of funnel exhaust.

It was an efficacious but expensive expedient compared with the cowling and aft-discharging uptake now fitted when the funnel is close to the bridge, but unless sympathetically handled could be very unsightly. Happily in these ships the ugly trunk was largely masked by bridgework, so that the great flat-sided funnel became a most imposing structure, although at first sight rather an eyesore to the more æsthetic of ship-lovers.

Queen Elizabeth after her first reconstruction 1925-27 when she was fitted with bulges, additional control tops, A.A. guns amidships, and a trunked funnel.

ARMAMENT

As the Navy had to rely upon guns for air defence, the necessity for developing new and efficient designs which could deliver a rapid fire led to a series of trials in 1921, carried out under Rear-Admiral Usborne, which resulted in a form of multiple gun-mounting being decided upon as suitable for dealing with close-range bomb attack or torpedo dropping by aircraft—which the Fleet regarded as the greatest menace.

The task of producing this complicated mounting was entrusted to Elswick and Vickers, and after six years work Vickers succeeded in fulfilling all requirements with an 8-barrel 2-pdr. pom-pom. After a series of trials

Barham shows the 2-pdr. pom-pom at the base of the searchlight towers, and was given a tripod mainmast to support the torpedo control position. A McTaggart catapult is carried on the roof of "X" turret with a lattice work derrick for handling aircraft. The bridge structure is now merging into the mast.

at Portsmouth the gun was put into production, and four were to be mounted in each capital ship, at a cost of between three and four millions owing to the cost of ammunition. But the Treasury refused to allow such expenditure in the 1928 Estimates, although after much discussion it was agreed that a limited number of the guns should be put in hand, but with only a small allowance of ammunition. Serious delay resulted in equipping the Fleet and training the men to use an entirely novel weapon, but sufficient were afloat by 1939 to play a very substantial part in the air defence of the Fleet.

In the *Barham* the single 3-in. or 4-in. high angle guns were replaced by four 4-in. A.A. on the upper deck amidships with one of the multiple 2-pdr. pom-poms on a platform each side of the funnel. In place of the flying-off platforms on "B" and "X" turrets a McTaggart catapult was mounted on the roof of "X" turret where it was served by a special main-mast derrick.

MASTING AND BRIDGEWORK

A covered navigating bridge was added and the lower bridge wings extended, the whole structure now merging with the mastwork. The 15-in. gun director was below the upper control top with the 6-in. directors on each side of the lower platform. *Barham* alone had a tripod main-mast carrying a platform for the torpedo control tower.

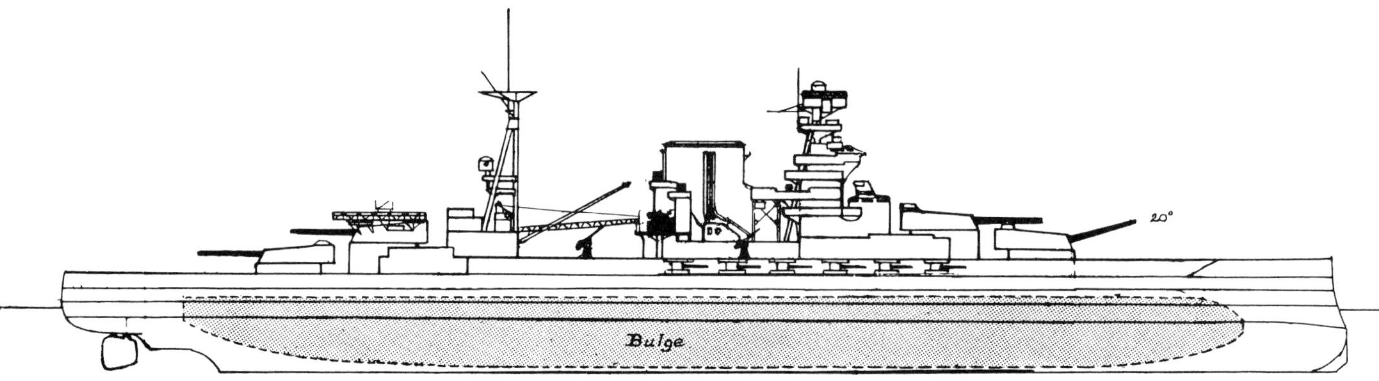

BARHAM. After refit 1930–33.

In 1934 *Malaya* and *Warspite* were taken in hand for further modernization, and upon their completion *Queen Elizabeth* and *Valiant* were withdrawn from service for similar treatment, the work being nearly finished in September 1939. *Barham* would have followed them, but the war cancelled her reconstruction and her career came to an end without further alterations.

BARHAM.

"BARHAM"

Built at Clydebank February '13-October '15. Grand Fleet. Flagship 5th B.S. '15-'19 (Jutland. In action with enemy battle cruisers and battleships. Six hits, with 26 killed and 37 wounded; worst hit near "B" barbette when 6-in. side was pierced and flash reached the battery deck and set fire to a quantity of cordite. Part of shell entered lower conning tower and put W.T. out of action. Repaired by July 4. Atlantic Fleet 1st B.S. (Flagship) '20-'24. Mediterranean Fleet '24-'27. Refitted '27-'28. Mediterranean '28-'29. Atlantic Fleet '29-'30. Big refit '30-'33. Home Fleet '33-'35. Mediterranean Fleet '35-'39.

War II. Bombardment and convoy duties. Torpedoed by U.30 north of Hebrides 28 December '39. Three months repair at Liverpool. Battle of Matapan 28 March '41 when she helped sink the cruiser *Zara*. In April was selected by the Board to serve as a block ship to close Tripoli harbour together with a "C" class cruiser; representations by Admiral Cunningham caused this sacrifice of a valuable ship with probably the loss of 1,000 lives to be dropped in favour of a bombardment in which she joined the *Warspite*, *Valiant* and *Gloucester*. In the Crete operations was hit by a bomb on "Y" turret, two bulges flooded by near misses, and a fire started which lasted two hours (27 May '41). Returned to Alexandria and later sailed for repairs at Durban. Rejoined the fleet in July.

When on patrol between Crete and Cyrenaica and expecting the appearance of enemy heavy ships with a convoy, was struck by three torpedoes from a German submarine which had passed through the destroyer screen. She rolled over on her beam ends, her main magazine blew up, and she disappeared with the loss of 56 officers and 806 men. 25 November '41.

MALAYA

MALAYA. LARGE REFIT 1934-36

By 1934 the menace of aerial attack and necessity for increased defence against it had become a very vital factor in modifying battleship design. Torpedo attack from the air was now as grave a danger as from surface craft or submarines, and deck protection against armour-piercing bombs quite as important as against long-range gun-fire.

The machinery and boilers remained unaltered.

The alterations carried out in the *Malaya* were not so drastic as in the other three ships, the cost being £976,900 against over £2,000,000. Above decks they included (1) the addition of hangars for four planes abaft the funnel with (2) a cross-deck catapult and large cranes for handling aircraft and boats, these latter being stowed around the funnel high on top of the hangars up out of the way of the A.A. guns. (3) Sponsons athwart the funnel for 8-barrel, 2-pdr. pom-poms, with twin 4-in. A.A. in place of the singles amidships.

She was the first battleship to have hangars fitted—a heavy and substantial addition to her profile—and all these extra topside weights were put into her without any substantial surrender of compensating material. There was naturally some loss in stability, which however, was accepted in view of the increase achieved when her

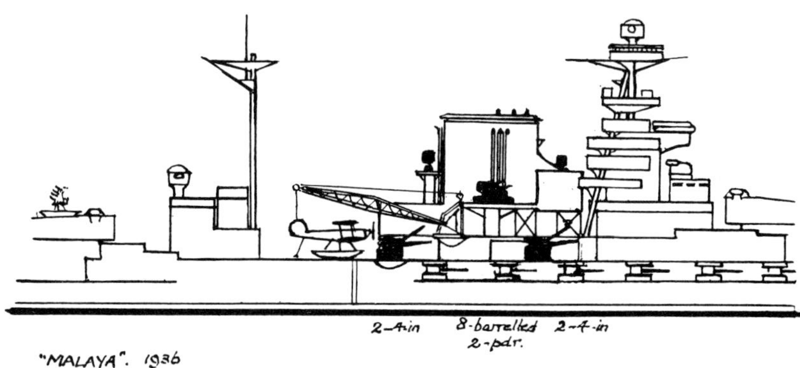

"MALAYA". 1936

bulges were added during the earlier refit. But her figures would not have been passed a few years later when more exacting standards of stability were required.

"MALAYA"

Built at Elswick October '13-February '15 as a gift of the Federated Malay States. Grand Fleet 5th B.S. '16-'19. At Jutland sustained 8 hits from large shells. 63 killed and 33 wounded. One shell pierced the f'cle deck and exploded in the starboard 6-in. battery, wrecking S.3 gun. Partial screens and cordite fires caused all her casualties. Two hits below the belt made a large hole, flooding inner and outer oil bunkers and wing compartments. Other hits caused local damage. Repairs completed by June. Visited Cherbourg for Peace Celebrations April '19. In '20 conveyed the Allied Naval Commission for its inspection of German naval ports during carrying out of Treaty obligations. In '21 made a courtesy visit to her donors in Malaya, taking H.R.H. the Duke of Connaught to India. Joined Atlantic Fleet on return from Far East, then ordered to Constantinople (Istanbul) during troubles in Turkey when the Sultan took refuge on board in November '22 and was taken to Malta. From '24-'27 Mediterranean 1st B.S. Refit '27-'29 (funnels trunked, bulged, etc.). Mediterranean '29-'30; Atlantic '30-'32 (thrice Royal guard ship at Cowes) Home '32-'34. Refit '34-'36 (£976,963). Mediterranean '37-'39. Her first War II service was escorting Canadian troops across the Atlantic, and in convoy protection. In March '40 the attitude of Italy led to her being sent to the Mediterranean. In July '40 she helped the *Warspite* to drive off a force of 2 battleships, 12 cruisers, and 20 destroyers. This was the first engagement with the Italian Fleet which turned away under smoke when the *Cesare* had been hit at 26,000 yards. Together with *Warspite*, *Ramillies*, and *Kent* she bombarded Bardia and Port Capuzzo and in October covered an important convoy from Port Said to the Dardanelles, and was largely engaged in escort work and attacks on enemy bases. Bombardment of works at Genoa February '41. Later as flagship of Admiral Somerville she joined Force H at Gibraltar for aircraft ferrying operations to Malta, supporting *Argus* and *Ark Royal*. Detached for Atlantic convoy service, and once sighted the *Scharnhorst* and *Gneisenau* which turned and escaped into the dusk. When after D-Day she bombarded the island of Cezembres off St. Malo her fourth salvo hit a large German battery and later two shells landed in the centre of a barracks at maximum range with aircraft spotting. After the War went into Reserve and later listed for disposal.

Sold April, 1948.

WARSPITE

The previous alterations to the "Old Lady"—as she was affectionately called during the 1939-45 War—could be regarded as a mere face-lifting compared with the complete gutting and reconstruction she underwent during 1934-37. Trials had shown that all the old capital ships were vulnerable to attack from the increasingly efficient shells, torpedoes, mines, and bombs, so that under-water and deck protection would have to be drastically strengthened. But in view of the great increase in battleship speed abroad and the certainty that this would continue to rise, it was essential that the 24 knots which the *Warspite* could still make at a pinch should not be reduced by any additional displacement entailed by this wholesale thickening of armour. To begin with the *Queen Elizabeths* were over-heavy with a designed hull weight of a lower percentage than usual, and the passing of twenty years had been marked by a continual rise in displacement, so that the major conversion decided upon was regarded by a good deal of misgiving in the Constructor's Department. The whole economy of the reconstruction turned upon

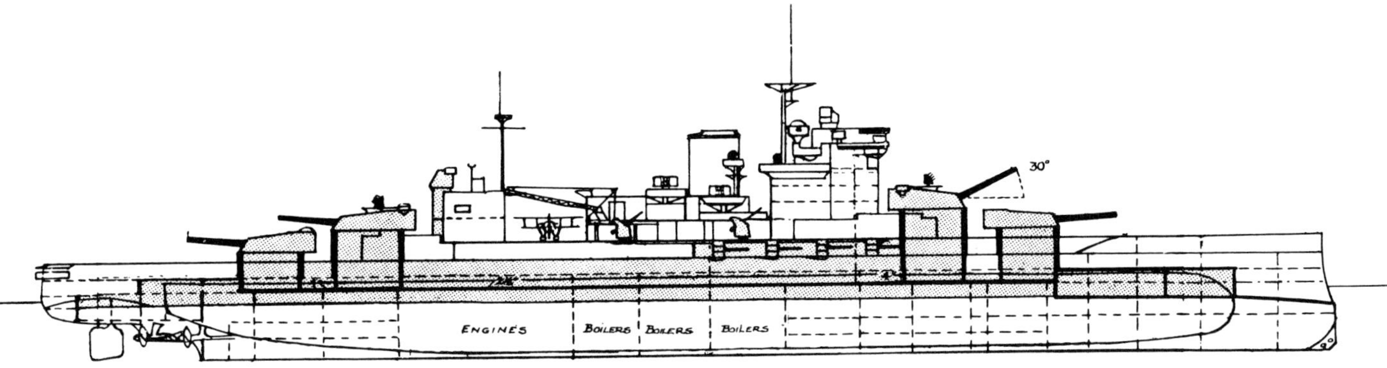

WARSPITE. Reconstructed 1934-37.

saving in weight made possible by modern high pressure boilers and the new geared turbines, plus such compensation as could result from the surrender of the heavy conning tower and four of the 6-in. guns and their side armour.

The removal of engines and boilers meant stripping the ship, opening up the decks, and gutting her amidships. The removal of the engine room bulkheads deprived the ship of much of her longitudinal strength and great care was required to preserve her form so that this, the first operation of its kind, meant a period of considerable anxiety to the Portsmouth Yard Officers. The heavy concentrated loads in way of the turrets coupled with the large areas opened up, gave rise to deformation difficult to correct.

Above decks the alterations included a tower superstructure carrying the control positions which replaced the former bridgework, with a pole mast in place of the heavy tripod. Amidships two hangars housing two Walrus planes served as a platform base for four multiple pom-poms, and became the new boat deck as a cross-deck catapult between the superstructures occupied the former stowage space for boats.

ARMAMENT

An increase of 10° bringing the elevation to 30° for the main armament marked the maximum[1] yet given to heavy guns, and necessitated strengthening the mountings and structure against recoil effects. The range was increased from 23,400 yards to 32,000 yards using an improved shell—an incredible shooting distance even against land targets.

A lingering belief in the necessity for retaining the 6-in. batteries for use against torpedo craft unfortunately still persisted, but the fore and aftermost guns were surrendered as a necessary compromise—and without any loss in efficiency, as *guns which could not be used against both sea and sky targets had no longer any place aboard ship.* Abroad the 5-in. "dual purpose" gun had come into favour in the U.S. Navy, where side batteries in battleships were to be plated in and the new pieces distributed along the topsides where they could have sky as well as sea command. On the Continent such side armament was only being retained in ships not worth the cost of reconstruction, and Italy was to embark on extensive modernization of her battle fleet with suppression of side batteries in favour of smaller "dual purpose" guns in deck turrets.

Four eight-barrelled pom-poms—an air defence weapon far superior to anything evolved abroad—sponsoned on each side of the funnel with twin 4-in. Mk. XVI A.A. below on the weather deck and multiple machine guns on the turret roofs constituted quite an adequate defence against bombers and torpedo planes according to the standards of the time. Additional Bofors and Oerlikons were mounted during the 1939-45 War.

All torpedo tubes were removed, their flats being used for the stowage of extra ammunition.

With the removal of the foremost 6-in. guns, the forecastle flare was extended further aft and the deck widened so that the embrasured sides flushed with what was formerly the second gun port. Aft the embrasures beneath "X" and "Y" turrets, which had persisted when the 6-in. guns were removed during her first commission, were also plated up and decked over.

PROTECTION

The armour from the battery over the surrendered guns was removed and the after bulkhead shifted forward, but that for the embrasures right aft was retained in position, forming an irregular shaped bulkhead between the barbette base and the hull side.

Additional armour was all put into horizontal protection over the magazines and machinery spaces, the original 1-in. H.T. plating on the middle deck being reinforced by 4-in. armour over the magazines and $2\frac{1}{2}$-in. armour over the machinery spaces. Forward, from under "A" barbette to the collision bulkhead across the end of the belt, the main deck was strengthened by $1\frac{7}{8}$-in. to protect the mess decks.

[1] Elevation of the 18-in. guns in the monitors *Lord Clive* and *General Wolfe* was 45°.

The original large conning tower was removed together with the lower navigating position, and in its place a new c.t. was constructed on No. 3 platform of the tower and fitted as the lower n.p. with an armoured communication tube from No. 2 platform. The armoured director tower for the 15-in. guns was removed from forward and replaced on the after island. Armoured gratings were fitted in the down- and uptakes.

Horizontal protection over the magazines totalled 6¼ in. (1¼ in. upper and 5 in. lower deck) and 5¾ in. over the engine and boiler rooms (1-in. f'le, 1¼-in. upper, 3½-in. middle deck).

MACHINERY

Here the greatest saving of weight resulted from the direct drive turbines being replaced by geared turbines, and twenty-four Babcock and Wilcox boilers by six Admiralty 3-drum small tube boilers. The former No. 1 engine room now served to store:

Hold: Diesel oil tanks; *Lower platform deck*: bomb room and spare gear; *Platform deck*: 2nd W.T. office, sub-calibre magazine, telephone exchange and H.A.C.P. with turbo generator rooms at sides; *Lower deck*: Central stores with S/L stabilizing room and engineer spare gear store at sides.

WARSPITE after reconstruction 1934-37.

TOWER SUPERSTRUCTURE

This imposing if target-making structure—which first appeared in the *Nelson* class in 1927—took the place of the tripod foremast and tiers of bridgework which only provided cramped and exposed accommodation for the increasingly numerous personnel now employed on fire control, signalling, and navigational duties. In the *Warspite* it comprised:

Shelter deck: General reading room and oilskin store.
No. 1 platform: C.P.O.'s reading room, Midshipmans study, officers sea cabins.
No. 2 platform: Admiral's, C. of Staff's and Captain's sea cabins. Two bathrooms. Cabins for Master of Fleet and navigation officers.
Conning tower and Signalling platform: Signal house, Signal Officer's cabin, Direction Finding office and cypher house with submarine look-out positions at sides and conning tower at forward end (3-in. armour).
Admirals bridge: Chart house, remote control office and plotting office, with Admirals shelter and chart house at forward end.
Wings: Searchlights.
On roof: 15-in. director tower, 6-in. directors on port and starboard.

GENERAL

After reconstruction the G.M. was reduced from 6·9 ft. to 6·4 ft. in the deep condition, and from 6·1 ft. to 5·1 ft. when light.

Acceptance for service was delayed owing to excessive vibration which developed aft when the helm was put over, which was traced to inter-action between the inner and outer propellors leading to very considerable axial and lateral vibration. Adjustment of the speed of the outer propellor when turning was adopted as a palliative to overcome the trouble, but the experience directed attention to the whole problem of shaft and propellor behaviour, when turning, and similar trouble did not develop in subsequent ships.

Although this skilful and expensive modernization enabled us to keep the *Warspite* in the first line of battle, the giant strides made in aerial attack during the war sadly discounted the value of the extra deck protection, so that the bomb hits at Salerno and off Crete both put her out of action. Again, at the time the reconstruction was planned it was considered necessary for both battleships and cruisers to carry their own reconnaissance aircraft but when war came the provision of fleet carriers led to these scouting planes being landed and the big hangars used for cinema performances.

On the debit side the reconstruction resulted in increased draught, reduced stability which made for greater vulnerability in the case of underwater damage, lower freeboard with wetness in bad weather coupled with impaired ventilation at sea. A considerable increase in war complement aggravated the loss in habitability with serious overcrowding in mess decks and washplaces, and strain on cooking facilities and arrangements for meals.

The old adage "Reconstruction never pays" would certainly have applied to the *Queen Elizabeth* class had we been free to build ships to replace them. But as the Treaty precluded such, there was nothing for it but to press new wine into old bottles and make the best we could of them, and the results cannot be dismissed as bad bargains, because ships which had reached their allotted span could not be armoured to withstand far heavier bombs than pre-war practice employed.

"WARSPITE"

Built at Devonport October '12-March '15. Grand Fleet 5th B.S. At Jutland hits by enemy shells jammed her steering gear and set her steaming in a wide circle towards the coast. All enemy guns were trained on her when she suddenly answered the helm again, and it is thought that another shell exploding righted the gear. In collision with *Barham* in '15 and with *Valiant* August '16 on both of which occasions she sustained severe damage. Atlantic Fleet 1st B.S. '19-'24; Refit '24-'26; Mediterranean '26-'30; Atlantic '30-'32; Home '32-'34; Reconstruction '34-'37 (£3,000,000); Mediterranean '37-'39. At Alexandria September '39. Went to Halifax N.S. to escort first contingent of Canadian troops to Britain. 13 April '40. Second Battle of Narvik. Flying the flag of Admiral Whitworth and attended by nine destroyers and dive bombers from *Furious* sunk eight torpedo craft which survived the First Battle. A week later engaged shore batteries there. May '40. Back in Mediterranean as Flagship of Admiral Cunningham. Bombarded Fort Capuzzo and Valona. Later attacked Capuzzo, Bardia and Tripoli. Battle of Matapan, 27-30 March '41. During the Battle of Crete over 400 bombs were aimed at her and all were dodged except the last which damaged her port side. Temporary repairs at Alexandria, then proceeded to Pearl Harbour via Singapore, and on to Bremerton N.Y., Seattle, for full repair to bomb damage. From there to Sydney and then joined Eastern Fleet at Colombo. From then on was at war with Japanese until recalled to Mediterranean for Salerno campaign after surrender of Italy. In Salerno bombardment 35 rounds out of 65 fired at long range fell exactly on the target and 8 were within 100 yards. On 16 September she was near-missed by one radio-controlled bomb and hit alongside the funnel by two others, which penetrated the boiler rooms and blew out her bottom. Except for one diesel engine there was no power aboard. All available salvage parties from U.S. ships went to her assistance and she was enabled to leave for Malta after dark in tow. Her three highly successful bombardments in support of the VI Army Corps earned a special message of appreciation for her splendid work with regrets for her casualties from Admiral H. Kent Hewitt, U.S.N. Temporary repairs were effected at Malta and Gibraltar before she returned home for permanent repairs. It was not possible to complete these before operation *Overlord*, and she had to be brought out for bombarding duties in her damaged condition. Again mined in June '44 and after quick repairs at Rosyth was again brought out for bombarding. In November supported the landings at Walcheren during the Scheldt operations, which were the last major operations of her outstanding career. In March '46 the Admiralty announced "Approved for H.M.S. *Warspite* to be scrapped after thirty years service through two wars." Went ashore at Prussia Cove, Cornwall, when under tow to the shipbreakers on 23 April '47 and was slowly broken up there.

QUEEN ELIZABETH. VALIANT. RECONSTRUCTION

The reconstruction of these two ships was carried out much along *Warspite* lines but with a completely new secondary battery and consequent modifications in protection. *Valiant* was taken in hand at Devonport, and the "Q.E." at Portsmouth. Work on both commenced in 1937, but many of the internal and armament fittings were still unfinished when war broke out. Every possible means were taken to expedite the completion of the "Q.E." even to the transference of equipment from ships of lesser importance. Thus, some of the 4·5-in. mountings were diverted from the carrier *Indomitable*, and HA directors were removed from the cruiser *Fiji* at Govan and sent down to Portsmouth.

During the heavy air raids in the latter half of 1940 the ruse was adopted of allowing the ship to be photographed by German reconnaissance planes on one side of Basin 3 during daylight, and then moving her to the opposite side at nightfall. This was successful for a long time, but in December she was moved up to Rosyth, and there completed on 31 January 1941.

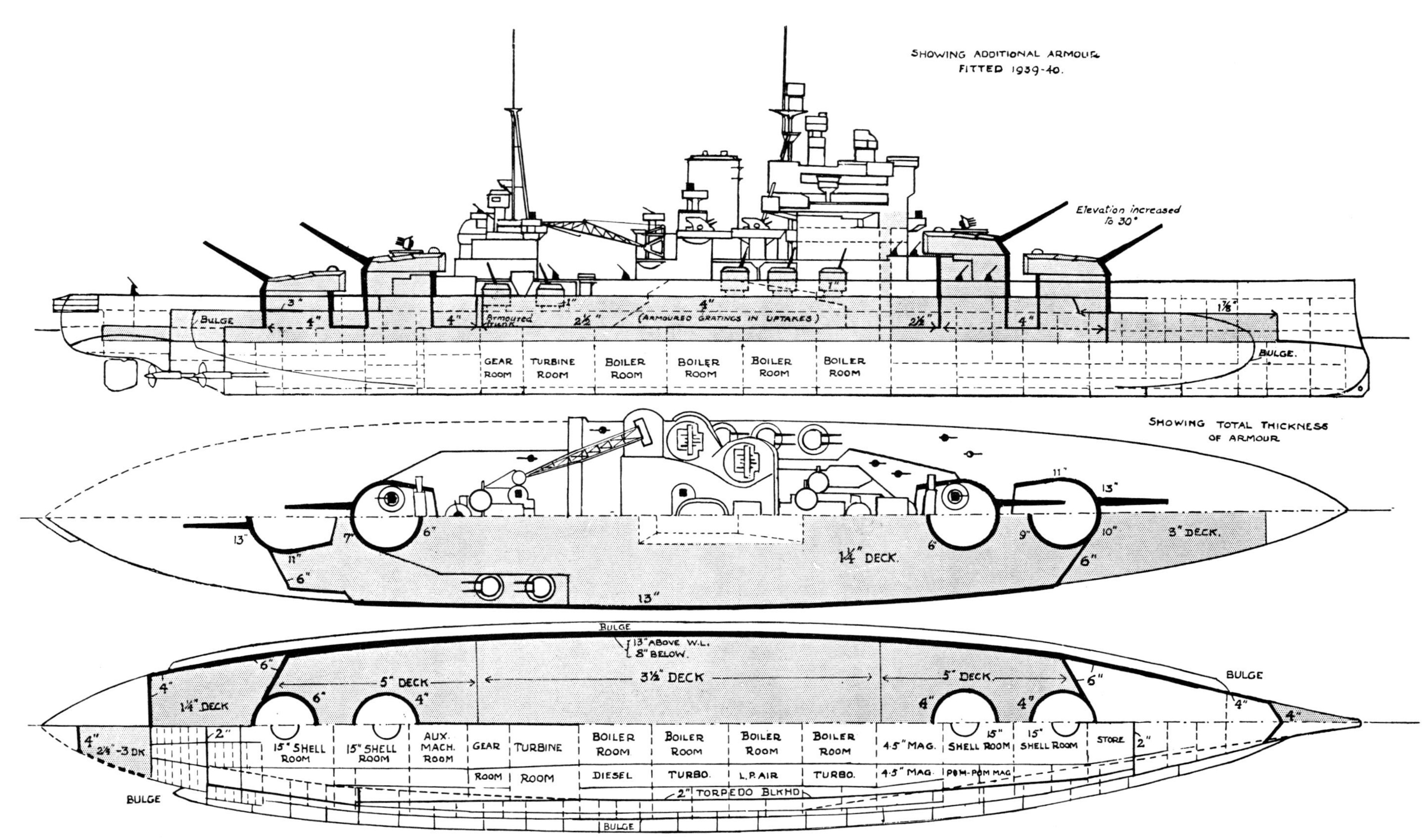

QUEEN ELIZABETH after reconstruction, 1941.

HULL

All the superstructure was removed together with the entire 6-in. batteries, the sides and upper deck being altered to conform with the general forecastle deck line, with a similar remoulding of the side and quarter deck line aft where the four embrasures were plated in. Abaft of amidships the forecastle deck was narrowed in order to accommodate four pairs of 4·5-in. guns below catapult level. Additional deck armour and bulges were fitted, and a completely new superstructure built up along *Warspite* lines. The internal arrangements of the hull were almost completely redesigned, and the system of subdivision considerably modified with more and smaller compartments. In the middle of 1940 internal demagnetization was introduced.

ARMAMENT

The 15-in. turrets were sent to Vickers Armstrongs and the mountings modified to give a maximum elevation of 30° and depression of 3°, elevation being obtained by altering the breach contacts. New guns were supplied, and projectiles became 5 ft. 7 in. long.

Whereas in the *Warspite* four 6-in. guns had been taken out as compensation for additional weights, in the *Queen Elizabeth* and *Valiant* the entire secondary armament was removed together with its covering armour, and twenty 4·5-in. guns in twin turrets—three aside abreast the forward superstructure and two aside abaft of amidships—were installed instead. The cupolas for these revolved on the weather deck with "between deck" mountings travelling on roller paths on the deck below, which permitted both flat trajectory or high angle fire.

The change to these dual purpose guns marked the beginning of a fresh cycle in secondary armament in which defence against air attack was to rank higher than that against surface torpedo craft. Medium calibre guns which could not be used in air protection were no longer worth their weight aboard, and although destroyers had reached cruiser standards in displacement and gun calibre (*vide* the French *Mogador* type, with the latest German, Russian and U.S. models running them close) it was felt that primary defence against such craft could be relegated to screening cruisers and destroyers. Against the smaller torpedo boats and motor boats now being produced in numbers by the European navies a smaller gun between 4-in. and 5-in. calibre would be quite efficacious. High ceiling defence against aircraft attack would also be well served by such guns and the 4·5-in. calibre was decided upon instead of the heavier 5·25-in. selected for the *King George V* class—laid down at the time the *Queen Elizabeth* and *Valiant* started their reconstruction—which guns could not have been carried in like number.

All except the left gun of S.2. mounting which was a Mark I were Mark III type, the mountings being Mark II twins. The maximum elevation was 80° and depression −5°. Special gear was fitted to the after guns in order to avoid the catapult when training forward. Ammunition was supplied by endless chain hoists and under good conditions their rate of fire was eighteen rounds per minute. Blast effects were described as bad. Control positions for these guns were placed on Y-shaped brackets abaft the heavy director tower above the bridge forward, (the starboard position being higher than the port one) and on the after superstructure.

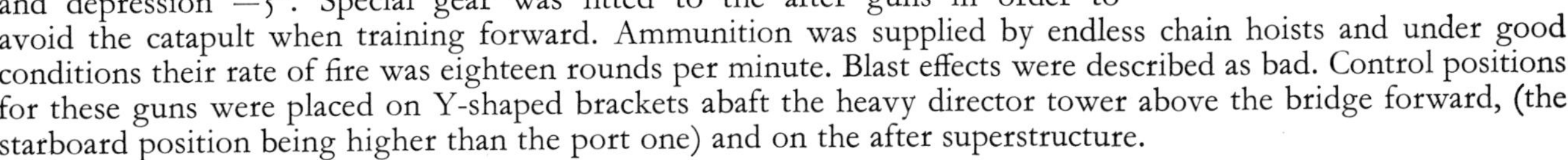

2-Pdr Pom.
Hangar roof
4·5" H.A.
Forecastle
LWL

Forward controls.

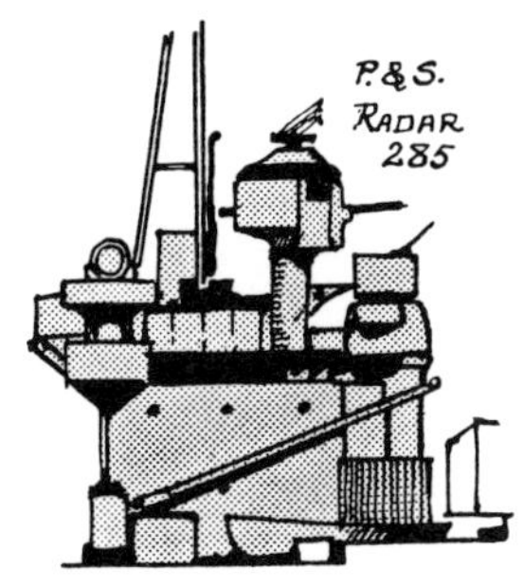

After controls.

For close-range A.A. defence four pom-poms were sponsoned on the amidships superstructure, with four Vickers Mark III quadruple ·5-in. machine guns in pairs on "B" and "X" turrets; all were controlled from the pom-pom directors. These latter were only 2 in. less in diameter than the 8 ft. platforms upon which they were mounted, so that clearance was very small and the fittings described as tricky.

Oerlikons were placed on deck and along the shelter decks so that towards the end of the war the *Queen Elizabeth* and *Valiant* carried one hundred guns in all.

AIRCRAFT

Hangars athwart the funnel housed four planes with a cross-deck catapult and handling cranes on each side. In 1944 when our growing fleet of carriers was able to provide accommodation for the Fleet Air Arm, capital ships were ordered to land their aircraft. In February 1945 no requirements for utilizing the catapult space apart from boat stowage had been formulated, but plans for a prefabricated deckhouse separate from the superstructure had been prepared.

The provision of aircraft in battleships was found to be a waste of effort and space, with the storage of petrol an added danger. The heavy hangars with boat stowage on top reduced stability, and provided a vulnerable target; they probably served best when used for cinema shows.

ARMOUR

All the 6-in. armour over the batteries was removed and 2-in. "D" plating fitted in way of the 4·5-in. casemates. ("D" steel with an ultimate tensile strength of 37 to 43 tons per square inch and a minimum elastic limit of 17 tons per square inch was first used in the *Nelson* and *Rodney* in place of the High Tensile quality.) The middle deck

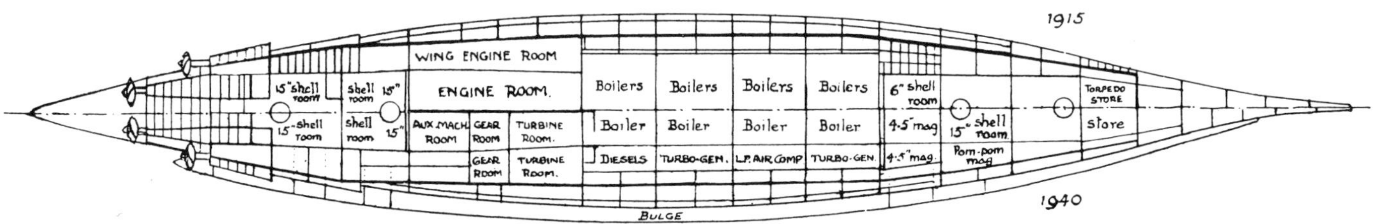

Platform deck sections to show the difference in the boiler and machinery spaces in 1915 (upper) and 1940.

was strengthened by 4-in. armour over the magazines and machinery compartments, with 3 in. in way of "Y" barbette and an extra 1½ in.-2 in. on the main deck between the two forward bulkheads, 3½ in. on the lower deck as far as bulkhead (a) and 2 in. on this bulkhead.

Splinter protection was fitted for exposed personnel around the close-range armament and bridges.

MACHINERY

Both ships had new geared turbines of 80,000 h.p. Parsons replacing Brown Curtis in the *Valiant*. But in order to provide more subdivision eight Admiralty 3-drum boilers were installed in four rooms instead of three as in the *Warspite*. It was in this new machinery that the greatest weight was saved, as may be seen from the following record:—

Item	*Weight when taken in hand*	*Calculated weight after reconstruction*	*Weight added or removed*
Equipment	1,256 tons	1,343 tons	+ 87 tons
Machinery	3,765 "	2,280 "	−1,485 "
Armament	5,108 "	5,704 "	+ 596 "
Armour, protection and hull	21,978 "	23,141 "	+1,163 "
Total	32,107 tons	32,468 tons	+ 361 tons

When completed the *Queen Elizabeth's* draught at light load in the dockyard was 32 ft.—a good 2 ft. more than in the original design, and indicating a displacement of 29,600 tons. Best speed in service about 22½-23 knots.

VALIANT

"QUEEN ELIZABETH"

Built at Portsmouth October '12-January '15. Commissioned 22 December '14 and joined Mediterranean Fleet in February '15 as Flagship of East Mediterranean Squadron. Employed in Dardanelles and supported Gallipoli landings. April '15 sank a Turkish transport in Nagara Liman by indirect fire, sinking her with third round. Grand Fleet May '15, and from '16-'19 was Fleet Flagship Admiral Sir David Beatty. Surrender of German Fleet was effected November '18 on board. Flagship Atlantic Fleet until July '24 when she was transferred to Mediterranean until '26 (refit '26-'27) Mediterranean '27-'29. Atlantic Fleet '29. Mediterranean '29-'37. Paid off August '37 for reconstruction at Portsmouth until December '40 when she was moved to Rosyth. Completed 31 January '41. Joined Home Fleet at Scapa, for working up. 2nd B.S. May '41 Mediterranean Fleet 1st B.S. Seriously damaged by limpet mines in Alexandria Harbour 19 December' 41. Heavily flooded and put out of action. Repaired in floating dock whilst a target for air raids. Sent to U.S.A. September '42 for reconditioning, sailing for U.K. June '43. In December left Scapa as part of 1st B.S. for Eastern Fleet arriving at Trincomalee 28 January '44 as Flagship of Admiral Sir James Somerville. Covering force for air attack on Sebang 19 April '44, also on Sourabaya 17 May, and again on Sebang 25 July '44, when for the first time the Eastern Fleet brought its guns into action against Japanese shore defences. Supported the landing at Ranree 21 January '45 (Flagship Vice-Admiral H. T. Walker). On 26 January '45 her Marines with detachment from cruisers were landed on the Cheduba Islands. Took part in covering operations for capture of Rangoon April-May when cruiser *Haguro* was sunk. Returned home July '45 and joined Reserve at Rosyth in August.

Sold June 1948.

"VALIANT"

Build by Fairfield January '13-February '16. Grand Fleet 5th B.S. (Jutland undamaged). Atlantic Fleet 1st B.S. '19-'24. Mediterranean '24-'29 (refit '29-'30). Atlantic '30-'32. Home Fleet '32-'35. Mediterranean '35-'37. Reconstructed '37-'39. In December '39 went to West Indies to work up. Formed part of convoy from Halifax to U.K. and joined Home Fleet February '40. Mediterranean August '40. In company with *Warspite* bombarded Valona December '40. On 3 January '41 bombarded coast N.W. of Bardia in support of Army in Western Desert, coming under fire from shore batteries. March '41 Matapan action in company with *Barham* and *Warspite*. May '41 operations off Crete, when she was bombed and hit aft twice, but without serious damage. 19 December '41 damaged by human torpedoes in Alexandria Harbour. Joined Eastern Fleet in April '42 coming home for refit in February '43. In June again in Mediterranean with Force H. Took part in Sicilian landings July '43 patrolling east coast to prevent attacks on Assault Forces. Bombarded between Reggio and Catona before landings on Italy. Took part in Salerno landings in September. Returned home in October for refit before joining Eastern Fleet in January '44. July '44 bombarded Sebang in company with 1st B.S. January '45 home for refit which lasted until the end of the war. Ended her career as one of four ships forming *Imperieuse* stoker mechanics' training establishment at Devonport.

Sold August 1948.

The announcement in February 1948 that the *Queen Elizabeth*, *Valiant*, *Renown*, *Nelson* and *Rodney* were to be discarded and scrapped came as a national shock. Never before had a group of warships been so close to the hearts of the people; each had for long years been a source of pride and confidence, a symbol of naval might, and to many tens of thousands of men a well-loved floating home of happy memories. That the time had come when they could no longer be employed was hard to realize, perhaps harder to accept. It was pleaded that they should be retained for training purposes or at least for subsidiary service of some sort. But although the First Lord admitted that he had signed the death warrant of five staunch old friends, the Board realized that on the grounds of lack of speed alone they would have to be ruled out of our future fleet organization; besides which there was the disconcerting fact that the battleship could no longer be regarded as the capital ship of today and tomorrow.

Of all the great flagships in our steam Navy—the *Minotaur*, *Agincourt*, *Alexandra*, *Majestic*, *Dreadnought*, *Iron Duke*, and *Lion*—the *Queen Elizabeth* with her thirty-three years service may be given pride of place, and long may her memory remain green as embodying the dignity and qualities of the battleship *par excellence*.

GENERAL

Valiant was given a pole mast aft like *Warspite* until 1945 when tripod legs were added to carry the heavy radar aerials as in *Queen Elizabeth*. Her fore topmast was also altered to that in the *King George V* doing away with the radar lantern etc.

The power boats carried included two 45 ft. picket boats, one 45 ft. launch, two 25 ft. boats, and a planing dinghy.

For secondary lighting self-contained battery-fed lanterns, coming into action automatically when normal lights failed, were adopted in place of the old oil lamps.

Chapter 102

THE U.S. "NEVADA" CLASS

REVERSION TO BARNABY PRINCIPLES

In the *South Carolina* and *Michigan* (1906) U.S. constructors had led the world in battleship design by employing an all-centre-line turret disposition; in 1912 they set a fresh fashion in protection for their *Oklahoma* and *Nevada*.

In these two remarkable vessels carrying ten 14-in. guns, a gun position was eliminated by the use of two triple and two twin turrets; and as the result of the firing tests against the old *San Marcos* which showed that light armour was useless in battleships, the fourteen 5-in. pieces were left unprotected. This conclusion, applied to the rest of the hull, left the main deck without the customary medium armour but gave 13½ in. along the middle and lower decks for 400 ft. out of the 575 ft. of waterline, and 8 in. for some 62 ft. aft to the rudder head. Big gun protection was on the same scale with 13½ in. on the barbettes and 18 in.-16 in.-10 in. over the turrets; 13½ in. also surrounded the funnel uptakes.

The *Nevada* was developed through the *Arizona-Idaho-California* to the *Maryland* of 1917 and it will be seen that her system of protection was more or less a reversion to Barnaby ideals on an extended scale. It is chronicled here because our *Rodney* and *Nelson* of 1922 were armoured along the same lines—what was known as the "All or Nothing" system—and in the American, Japanese, French and Italian battleships of the post-war period a similar scheme of protection was employed.

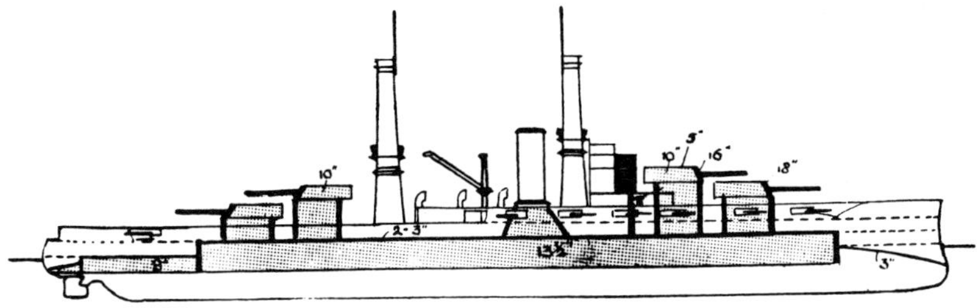

U.S.S. *OKLAHOMA*.

SIR EUSTACE H. TENNYSON D'EYNCOURT, BT., K.C.B., LL.D., D.SC., F.R.S.

DIRECTOR OF NAVAL CONSTRUCTION 1912-1924.

Eustace Tennyson D'Eyncourt was born at Hadley House in Hertfordshire on 1 April 1868 and educated at Charterhouse. On the advice of Sir Edward Reed he was first apprenticed to Armstrong Whitworth at Elswick and then after a two years' course at the Royal Naval College, Greenwich, returned to Elswick under Sir Philip Watts.

To gain experience in merchant shipbuilding he went to Fairfields at Govan as naval architect, and when Watts became D.N.C. in 1902 he returned to Armstrongs to replace Mr. J. R. Perrett, who had been responsible for the lines of the famous Elswick cruisers. Visits to Turkey, Brazil, Chile, Spain and the Argentine brought many important naval contracts to the Tyne and a record tonnage was under construction when he was called to Whitehall as D.N.C. in 1912.

During his term of office twenty-one capital ships, fifty-three cruisers, 133 submarines of eleven different classes and numerous other vessels were added to the Royal Navy. He introduced the bulge form of protection against torpedoes, and was entrusted with the design of rigid airships assisted by Mr. A. W. Johns (later D.N.C.) between 1915-17.

It was largely due to the progressive outlook of d'Eyncourt and Mr. J. H. Narbeth that British aircraft carriers led the world and evolved from the cross-Channel packet conversions through the *Campania* to the *Hermes* and *Eagle*, and converted *Furious*, *Glorious* and *Courageous*.

Outside the Navy he will be remembered for his work in connection with the first tanks, which was recognized by an award made by the Royal Commission on Awards to Inventors in 1919. He received his K.C.B. in 1917, and the American Distinguished Service Medal in 1918 when he was also made a Commander of the Legion of Honour.

In the post-war years Sir Eustace had to contend with the difficult problems consequent upon the Naval Treaty in 1922 which resulted in the *Nelson* and *Rodney* and the *Kent* class of cruisers.

In 1924 he resigned from the Admiralty to become a director of Armstrongs, and when the firm was closed in 1928 Sir Charles Parsons invited him to join the Board of Parsons Marine Turbine Co. with whom he remained until his retirement in 1948.

Sir Eustace was created a Baronet in 1930 and received the honorary degrees of LL.D. Cambridge and D.Sc. Durham and was elected Foreign Associate Member of the French Academie de Marine in 1937 in succession to Earl Jellicoe. A prominent and active member of many societies and institutions including Vice-Presidency of the Institute of Naval Architects, he remained for a long time an adviser to the Admiralty. He died on 1 February 1951.

The d'Eyncourt Era is associated with oil driven fine-looking ships, super-firing guns in light cruisers and destroyers, big submarines (although X.1 proved a failure), and all the strange wartime creations evolved by Fisher. The *Hood* stands out as the finest warship of her day, the *Nelson* as the ugliest; his destroyers served as a model in most foreign navies, and the various funnel and island arrangements in his carriers set a pattern to the world.

Chapter 103

THE "REVENGE" CLASS (1913 PROGRAMME)

	Builders	*Laid down*	*Launched*	*Completed*
"*Ramillies*"	Beardmore	12 Nov. '13	12 Sept. '16	Sept. '17
"*Resolution*"	Palmers	29 Dec. '13	14 Jan. '15	Dec. '16
"*Revenge*"	Vickers	22 Dec. '13	29 May '15	March '16
"*Royal Oak*"	Devonport	15 Jan. '14	17 Nov. '14	May '16
"*Royal Sovereign*"	Portsmouth	15 Jan. '14	29 April '15	May '16

Dimensions 580′ (624′ 3″) × 88′ 6″ × 28′ 7″/30′ = 27,500 tons.
(At load draught 28,000 tons; deep load 31,200 tons.)
Beam with bulges: "*Ramillies*" 102′ 6″.
Others 101′ 5″.
(Sinkage 91 tons-per-inch.)

Armament 8 15-in./42.
14 6-in./45.
2 3-in. A.A.
4 3-pdrs.
Tubes:
4 21-in. sub.
20 torpedoes.

Protection Belt 13″-6″-4″-1″; bulkheads 6″-4″.
Barbettes 10″-9″-7″-6″-4″; turrets 13″-11″-4½″.
Battery 6″; shields 3″.
Conning towers 11″ for'd; tube 6″-4″. 6″ aft, tube 4″.
Decks: F'castle 1″; upper 1¼″-1½″. Main 1″-1½″-2″. Lower for'd 2½″-1″; aft 2½″-4″-3″.
Torpedo bulkhead 1½″-1″.
Funnel casings 1½″-1″.
(Total 31·7 per cent. of displacement.)

Machinery Parsons S.H.P. 40,000 = 20·4/19·7 n.d.
22 /21·5 f.d.
("*Royal Sovereign*" Parsons; "*Revenge*" Vickers; "*Ramillies*" Beardmore; "*Royal Oak*" Hawthorn Leslie; "*Resolution*" Palmers.)
Boilers 18 Babcock and Wilcox or Yarrow.

Fuel Oil 3,400/900 tons; coal 140 tons.

Complement 908-936-997 (war).

Special features:

(1) First battleships to have bulge protection.
(2) Last to have main deck batteries.
(3) Protective deck at main deck level.
(4) Steadiest seaboats of all the Dreadnoughts with the lowest G.M.

In formulating the design of the *Revenge* the Board had in mind a 15-in. gunned edition of the *Iron Duke* with greater steadiness than had been provided in previous *Dreadnoughts* which had a metacentric height (G.M.) of 5 to 5½ ft. To this end the G.M. was to be reduced to 3 ft. retaining the same length as the *Iron Duke* while restricting beam by 1½ ft. and increasing the mean draught by 2 ft. As compensation for the reduced stability thus produced by which the safety of the ship could be imperilled if extensive flooding followed water-line damage, the protected freeboard was increased by raising the heavy armour deck to main deck level well above the deep-load line—which innovation of itself also served to lower the G.M. by raising the centre-of-gravity of the ship. The ship thus had greater steadiness but less stability, with special precautions to insure that that stability could be maintained in battle. But at one period the G.M. was down to less than 1 foot.

Additional anti-torpedo bulkheading was also installed and in the *Ramillies* the bold step was taken of fitting bulges, increasing her beam to 102½ ft. with a corresponding reduction in mean draught to 29 ft. 4 in. This again raised the metacentre, the G.M. being 2½ ft. or more than in the *Iron Duke.*

Uncertainty as to whether adequate supplies of oil fuel would be available in case of war led to a *reversion to coal*, the Board being satisfied with the standard 21 knots of the *Dreadnought* squadrons. Freeboard was to be the same as in the *Iron Duke*—the lowest of the *Dreadnoughts*—but to keep the 6-in. batteries as dry as possible they were shifted abaft of amidships well clear of the speed waves.

With only three boiler rooms to serve, it was possible to combine the uptakes into one large funnel, giving the class a most distinctive and impressive profile.

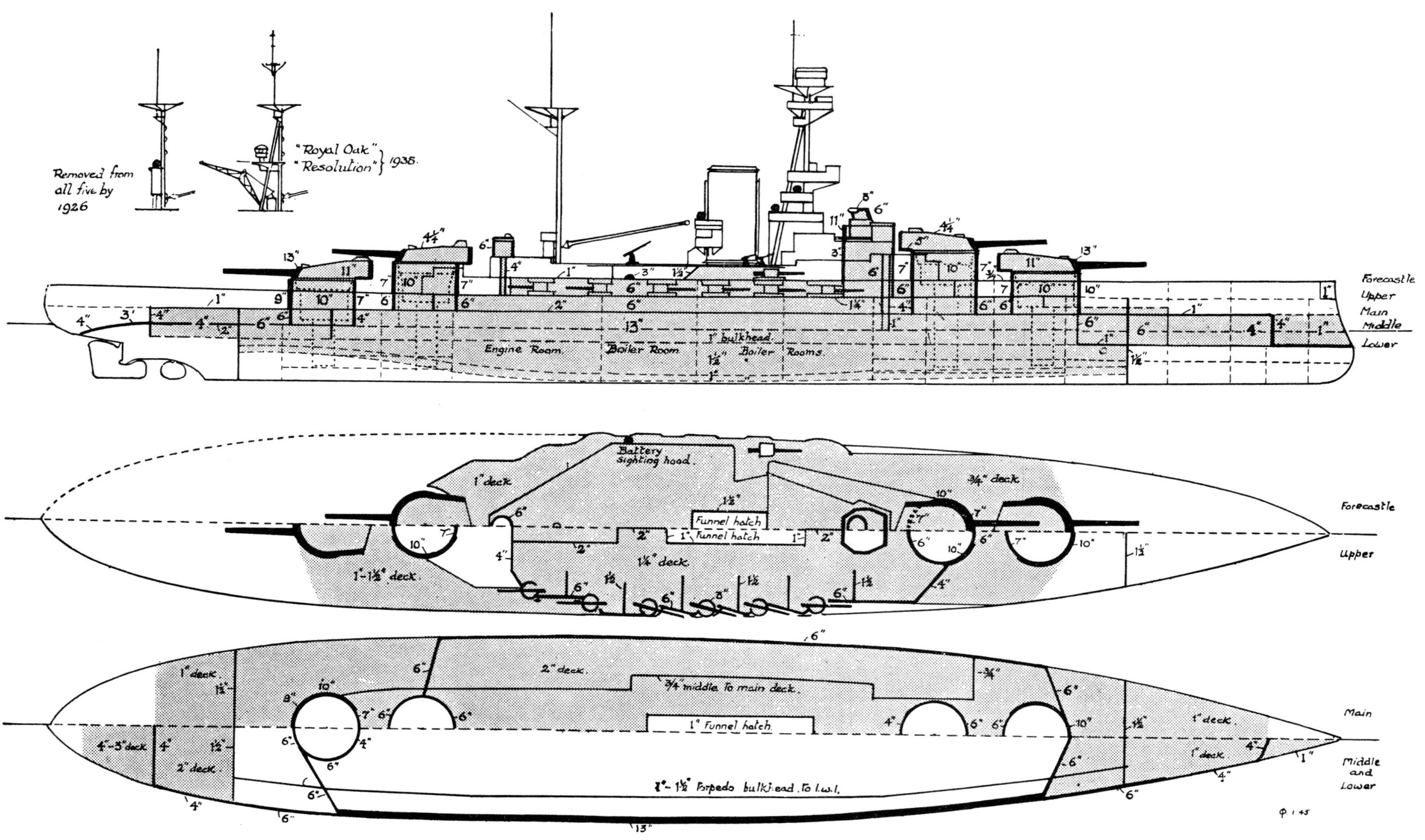

Revenge. Note that the main is the armoured deck instead of the middle as in *Queen Elizabeth*, with the 6-in. battery amidships.

But when Fisher was recalled to the Admiralty as the outbreak of war one of his first instructions was to have the design modified so that oil fuel could be bunkered instead of coal—a bold decision which allowed for a couple of knots more speed with all the amenities of oil fuelling, but giving hostages to fortune to an extent which at one time appeared likely to have serious consequences when oil supplies became short at the end of 1917.

ARMAMENT

Owing to lower freeboard the gun heights above l.w.l. were 31-40-31-22 ft., otherwise the main armament was similarly disposed to that in the *Queen Elizabeth*.

As already noted the 6-in. batteries were sited further aft with only the foremost guns (238 ft. from the bows) having ahead bearing. Although not sufficiently high above water for use in all weathers, the sea had a cleaner run forward and was not so troublesome as in the *Queen Elizabeth*. A single gun athwart the funnel on each side replaced the four stern guns in the *Queen Elizabeth*, their shields being afterwards enlarged to form a semi-casemate before the guns were removed in 1927-28. Unlike the previous class, only low 1½-in. screens separated the battery guns which served to assist water drainage. German ships of this period had complete bulkheads between the guns capable of saving life and limb from fire, gas, blast and splinters.

In 1924-25 the 3-in. A.A. were replaced by 4-in., and in November 1940 *Resolution* and *Revenge* had single

Revenge running her trials in 1916. The fitments on the funnel and around the main topmast are range-finding baffles.

4-in., replaced by four twin 4-in. mountings with two 2-pdr. 8-barrel guns and directors. Only twelve 6-in. were carried. The rest of the class received four twins during their big refits 1936-39. In the same period multiple 2 pdr. pom-poms were being supplied to capital ships as opportunity allowed, and the *Revenge* class had them mounted in large sponsons athwart the funnel. During 1939-45 Oerlikons, Bofors, and other close-range A.A. guns found mounting space on the quarter deck, turret tops, and wherever else was available.

TORPEDO TUBES

The torpedo tubes were removed during the late '20s (except in *Revenge* and *Resolution* which for a time retained two tubes) as it was considered they were not worth the space taken up or the men required to man them. *Royal Oak* during her last refit was given four above-water experimental tubes up forward, but these again were not considered worth having in such ships; all tubes were taken out by 1930.

SEARCHLIGHTS

As completed two 36-in. projectors were placed on the funnel platform and two on the after superstructure. During the war the former were replaced by towers each mounting two lights, with the after lights raised on single towers athwart the main mast. Only the *Ramillies* retained the original funnel platform and this served to identify her for a long time. During their large refits of 1936-39 a modified form of tower around the funnel allowed for a heavy multiple A.A. being sponsoned below.

AIRCRAFT

In 1917-19 "B" and "X" turrets received flying-off platforms and a fighter was sometimes carried; but was not of much use. At their last pre-war refits *Resolution* and *Royal Sovereign* had a McTaggart catapult fitted on the quarter deck, which worked well enough in calm weather. Later *Resolution*, *Royal Oak*, and *Ramillies* carried one on "X" turret served by a special crane. By 1939 *Revenge* and *Royal Sovereign* discarded their platforms and ceased to carry aircraft, all catapults being removed early in the war.

PROTECTION

Both external vertical and horizontal protection were on a par with that in the *Queen Elizabeth*, but the internal vertical protection was superior. Of the 20 ft. 9 in. depth of side armour in *Revenge* 7 ft. was submerged; in the *Queen Elizabeth* 5 ft. 4½ in. only was below water out of 20 ft. 6 in. The longer 6-in. battery abaft of amidships and absence of 6-in. guns aft meant more 6-in. armour along the upper deck and less over the main deck in way of the after barbettes, with additional 6-in. bulkheads. The quarter deck being about 20 ft. longer, the 4-in. strake stopped short of the fore instead of the after edge of the rudder, and right forward some 1-in. plating carried the belt up to the cutwater—a half-hearted return to *Bellerophon* ideas on bow protection.

But the principal feature of the protective system lay in the placing of a 2-in. deck on top of the 13-in. belt at main deck level instead of only a 1-in. deck along the waterline, thus providing additional armoured stability in case the belt were perforated. Comparison between the cross-sections of *Queen Elizabeth* and *Revenge* will show

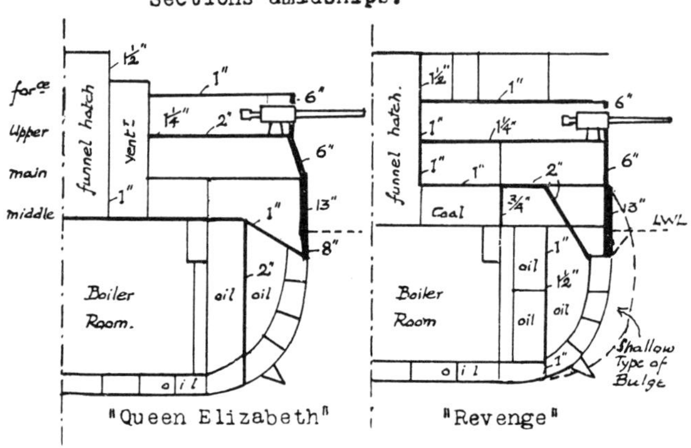

the different arrangements of the protective decks and also the additional middle-to-main-deck ¾-in. longitudinal bulkheading in *Revenge* which together with coal bunkers reinforced the armoured deck.

Ramillies was the first battleship to be completed for sea with shallow bulges, afterwards replaced by full-bellied things which rose to the main deck; *Royal Oak* was similarly flanked in her 1927 refit. In the rest of the class only the low type were fitted during their refits of 1926-30. The effect was to increase beam from 88 ft. 6 in. to

Ramillies in wartime mounting twin Bofors and Oerlikons on the turret crowns, quarter deck, and at after end of battery; radar lanterns at main top, and aerials on topmasts and elsewhere.

101 ft. 5 in. (low type) or 102 ft. 6 in., raised the G.M., and reduce speed by about ⅓ knot. That such protuberances should have so little effect on steaming was regarded as quite remarkable, the bulge being a pure addendum to the form which could not be faired at the ends to give the best results.

That the *Royal Oak* succumbed to submarine attack as she did was due to a cleverly contrived and well aimed salvo of torpedoes from dead ahead which exploded under the unprotected keel.

MACHINERY

As oil-driven ships it was estimated that they would be good for 23 knots at load draught (28 ft. 6 in.) with 40,000 h.p. but owing to their being passed into service during the war full trials were not carried out, and only deep load figures are available.

		Draught	*Displacement*	*S.H.P.*	*Revolutions*	*Knots*
Revenge	24.3.16	33′ 1½″	30,750	42,650	330	21·9
Ramillies (bulges) ..	30.9.17	32′ 1¼″	33,000	42,383	326	20·5

which represent the average speed for the two forms of hull. Commenting upon the steaming of the bulged ships in 1921 their designer says:

> "In spite of the extra displacement, amounting in all to over 1,500 tons, I have had frequent reports from the 'Royal Sovereign' class to the effect that when sailing in company at sea, the bulged ships keep pace with the unbulged at about the same revolutions and power of the engines. In fact, at sea the bulged form seems to do almost better than the actual experiments would lead one to suppose."

The turbine installation was disposed in a similar manner to that in the *Queen Elizabeth* with two H.P. ahead and astern coupled directly to the wing shafts and two L.P. ahead and astern combined to the inner shafts with cruising turbines geared to the wing shafts.

GENERAL

Compared with the other 15-in. gunned capital ships the *Revenge* class underwent very little in the way of alterations apart from being fitted with bulges. In their final refits the bridges and upperworks were modified for the extra A.A. armament, but there was no question of their being reconstructed like the *Queen Elizabeths* and *Renown* as by this time lack of speed had relegated them to the second line.

But in the inter-war period the ships showed individual changes to bridgework and funnels which served to identify them when funnel markings were no longer in fashion. The funnel bridge problem was met in the *Resolution*

All, in 1915.

Resolution, 1924.

Resolution, 1939.

Royal Sovereign, 1939.

Revenge, 1939.

by a clinker screen in 1922, disdained by the rest of the class until 1938-39 when the *Revenge* followed suit, as she had always been conspicuous by her piled-up bridgework which needed protection. They were then shipped by the rest as a wartime necessity.

Latterly *Ramillies*, *Resolution* and *Royal Oak* carried a tripod main mast, but *Resolution* reverted to a pole mast on her refit at Philadelphia Navy Yard in 1942.

The progressive additions to bridgework etc. are shown in the sketches, their final appearance being generally as in the photograph of *Ramillies*.

During the 1939-45 War Mr. Churchill wished to convert two or three of the class to inshore action ships, sacrificing one or two turrets and seven or eight knots for super bulges against torpedoes and strong armour decks. So protected and bristling with A.A. guns they would have served for North Sea and Baltic operations, and in the protection of Malta by bombarding Italian ports. However, their possible use on convoy work and other priorities in armour allotment precluded such transformation, and he tells us that "throughout the war the 'Royal Sovereigns' remained an expense and an anxiety. When the possibility of bringing them into action against the Japanese fleet which entered the Indian Ocean in April 1942 presented itself, the only thought of the Admiral on the spot, of Admiral Pound (First Sea Lord) and the Minister of Defence was to put as many thousands of miles as possible between them and the enemy in the shortest possible time." (*The Second World War.*)

SEA-GOING QUALITIES

Like the old *Revenge* class, these ships had a reputation for rolling as first completed, and the *Resolution* is described as having rolled 21° each way coming out of Arosa Bay in January 1920. Seemingly there was some improvement after they had been bulged, although they became difficult to handle at slow speeds.

The effect of the large rudder was intended to be supplimented by a small auxiliary one to produce good manoeuvring powers, but the latter was found to be ineffective and removed.

GENERAL

The gunnery control top was at times nearly untenable in a following wind, a condition of things improved by the clinker screen.

On forward bearing the after turrets shook up the ward room and gun room very badly when using full charges. Shooting with the 15-in. guns was very good, and with the 6-in. not too good in a seaway. The A.A. armament was too light to be effective. Elevation of "A" and "B" turrets in *Resolution* was to be increased to 30° in 1941.

"RAMILLIES"

Built by Beardmore at Dalmuir November '13-September '17. Injured rudder at launch and with great difficulty was towed to Liverpool and repaired by Cammell Laird. Completion much delayed. Commissioned May '17. Grand Fleet 1st B.S. '17-'19, and then in Mediterranean '20-'24 (was with *Revenge* at Ismid June '20 during operations in Turko-Greek War); 2nd B.S. Atlantic Fleet '24 (long refit)—'27 and 1st B.S. Mediterranean '27-'32 (refit '32-'33) and rejoined '33-'35. Reserve '36. Home Fleet 2nd B.S. '36-'39. September '39 covered passage of B.E.F. to France and then joined Force "J" at Aden. On 17 August '40 shared in bombardment of Bardia; in November on convoy duties to and from Malta; on 27 November joined in action with Italian Fleet off C. Spartivento when several enemy ships were damaged. In early '41 she was employed on convoy duty between Britain and the Middle East. During the *Bismarck* action when on convoy duty she was ordered to westward of the enemy to close the encirclement. Joined 3rd B.S. East Indies late in '41. Bombarded Diego Suarez on 7 May '42 when surrender followed. On the 30th she was torpedoed and damaged by a midget submarine off Diego Suarez, one compartment being flooded. After temporary repairs she left for Durban, arriving 9 June and returning to U.K. in September for repairs and refit. Sailed to join Eastern Fleet in September '43, returning to Home Waters in January '44. She covered the landings in Normandy and Southern France and took part in numerous bombardments in support of the Army. After the war became accommodation ship attached to *Vernon.*

Sold April 1948.

"RESOLUTION"

Built by Palmers at Jarrow November '13-December '16. Joined Grand Fleet 1st B.S. in August '16 to April '19 when she joined the Atlantic Fleet 2nd B.S. Was in the Mediterranean in '20 as Flagship 1st B.S. Long refit. Mediterranean January '24 to '30. Refit '30-'31; rejoined '31-'35. Reserve '36. Home Fleet '36-'39. In December '39 on North Atlantic convoy duty. During Narvik operations May '40 was bombed at Tjeldsundet, being hit by one bomb out of 50 dropped by four Heinkels. 2 killed, 27 injured. In August '40 joined Force "M" operating from Freetown. On 25 September '40 was torpedoed and damaged off Dakar. Returned to port, and after temporary repairs left for Portsmouth in March '41 being attacked by aircraft without damage. Proceeded to Philadelphia in April '41 for refit; returned to Plymouth September '41, and joined 3rd B.S. and in February '42 to Eastern Fleet as Flagship Vice-Admiral; operated in Indian Ocean throughout the year. In February '43 escort to a large convoy carrying Australian Division from Suez to Australia. Returned to U.K. in September '43 and in May '44 became part of *Imperieuse* stokers' training establishment, first in the Gairloch, then in '44 at Southampton, and then Devonport.

Sold May 1948.

"REVENGE"

Built by Vickers December '13-March '16. Grand Fleet 1st B.S. February '16-'19. (At Jutland Vice-Admiral Burney transferred to her when *Marlborough* had been torpedoed.) From November '16 Flagship of Admiral Madden, second in command of Grand Fleet. In June '20 was at Ismid for operations in Turko-Greek war. Was with 1st B.S. when Mudania was seized in July '20. Thereafter served with Atlantic and Mediterranean Fleets. Refits '28-'29 and '30-'31. 1st B.S. '31-'35 (refit '36). Home Fleet 2nd B.S. '37-'39. Convoy duties North Atlantic. Bombarded Cherbourg September '40 at 15,700 yards range. While on escort 2 September '41 in collision with *Orion.* Slight damage. Throughout '42 served with Eastern Fleet. In February '43 part escort to convoy of Australian Division from Suez to Australia. Returned to U.K. September '43 and in May '44 became part of *Imperieuse,* with *Resolution.*

Sold March 1949.

"ROYAL OAK"

Built at Devonport January '14-May '16. Grand Fleet 1st B.S. '16-'19 (Jutland). Atlantic Fleet 2nd B.S. '19-'22. Refit '22-'24. 2nd B.S. '24-'26. Mediterranean 1st B.S. '26-'34. Refit '34-'35. 2nd B.S. '35-'39. Torpedoed at Scapa Flow by U.47 (Lt. Prien) 14 October '39. Owing to the approaches not having been completely blocked with a passage left open between two sunken ships, the submarine was able to approach through the swirls of Holm Sound and Kirk Sound and fire a salvo at the anchored battleship, with one hit at the bows. After twenty minutes when the tubes had been reloaded four hits were scored with a second salvo, which ripped out the ship's bottom. She capsized and sank in ten minutes, so quickly that few below were able to escape. Casualties were 786 officers and men.

"ROYAL SOVEREIGN"

Built at Portsmouth January '14-May '16. Grand Fleet 1st B.S. '16-'19. Atlantic Fleet 1st B.S. '19-'26. Refit '27-'28. 1st B.S. '28-'35. Reserve '36. Training ship '36. Refit '37. Home Fleet 2nd B.S. '38-'39. Early in War II she took part in Atlantic convoy operations as Flagship of Rear-Admiral Bonham-Carter, Halifax Escort Force. Withdrawn in '41 to join 3rd B.S. of Eastern Fleet and her further war service was in eastern waters. Returned to U.K. and handed over '44 to the Soviet Union; operated in northern waters as *Archangelesk*, her transfer being kept a close secret. Handed back after much delay on 4 February '49.

Sold 1949.

Chapter 104

BUILDING AND DEVELOPMENTS IN THE PRE-WAR YEARS

THE lists of capital ships to be laid down year by year given on page 543 showed the totals up to 1911, after which the annual programmes included the following:

1912

British	German
Barham	*Kronprinz Wilhelm*
Queen Elizabeth	1 ship sacrificed
Valiant	*Lutzow* (b.c.
Warspite	
1 ship sacrificed	
Malaya (gift of Federated Malay States and additional to our programme)	

1913

British	German
Ramillies	*Baden*
Resolution	*Bayern*
Revenge	*Hindenburg* (b.c.)
Royal Oak	
Royal Sovereign	

1914

British	German
Renown	*Sachsen*
Repulse	
Resistance	
Agincourt	

making a total of fourteen British ships against six German.

The period was a bad one for building in the Reich. Some of the private yards were in an unenviable predicament as there was not enough Government work to go round. The effects of over-development and over-capitalization were now to be experienced, with expensive plant and skilled workmen threatened with idleness while British yards maintained full capacity with Admiralty and foreign contracts.

In the *Baden* and *Bayern* of 1913 a remarkable jump in gun calibre took place—from 12-in. to 15-in.—the ships being 21½ knot equivalents of the *Revenge*. And what at the time appeared almost as remarkable was the fact that the Marine Office announced details of their armament before even the keels were laid down.

This abandonment of the previous policy of exaggerated secrecy was a response to the wave of bitter criticism of capital ship design which rose in German technical circles. Hitherto warm supporters of the Navy Department agreed with their critics in condemning the *Konig* class as lacking in gun-power compared with foreign types, regretting that the adoption of more powerful ordnance had been so long delayed. The figures quoted—omitting smaller guns—show the broadside fire of ships of approximately equal date.

Laid down	*Ship*	*Broadside in lb.*	*Laid down*	*Ship*	*Broadside in lb.*	*British superiority*
February '07	*Superb*	6,800	August '07	*Nassau*	5,280	1,520 lb.
January '09	*Neptune*	8,500	January '09	*Oldenburg*	6,880	1,620 ,,
November '09	*Orion*	12,500	November '09	*Kaiser*	8,600	3,900 ,,
January '11	*King George V*	14,000	October '11	*Konig*	8,600	5,400 ,,
October '12	*Queen Elizabeth*	15,600	May '12	*Kronprinz Wilhelm*	8,600	7,000 ,,

The discovery that ships built with so much mystery were considerably inferior in gun-power to those they would have to face was not condusive to popular enthusiasm in the fleet. So, recognizing that a predeliction for concealment had been carried to excess, it was now largely discarded and the armaments for capital ships up to and including those of the 1914 Programme were divulged.

A favourite argument of some German writers was that the broadside method of calculating battle value was misleading since it left out of account the faster firing of 11-in. and 12-in. compared with 13·5-in. and 15-in. guns. The reply to this contention was that:

(1) The high level of efficiency which mounting and loading arrangements had now attained virtually synchronized the rate of fire from all guns above 9·2 in. in calibre.

and

(2) that under battle conditions it would be found impossible to keep up peace practice rates of firing, as smoke and refraction from broadsides made accurate aiming impossible until a certain interval had elapsed.

Director firing might obviate this difficulty to some extent, but authorities were fairly unanimous in agreeing that for guns above the 9·2-in. an actual rate of discharge under battle conditions would not exceed one round every ninety seconds.

Moreover, at long ranges heavier projectiles were more accurate than light ones fired with equal or higher initial velocity.

But the great value of the big calibre shell lay in its power to shatter a ship's structure. Germany might claim that her 12-in. was equal in penetration to our 13·5-in. but that did not imply all-round equality. As one authority pointed out:

"It is not so much a water-line penetration or several of them, that will cause the loss of a vessel, for the damage will be localized by the subdivision; it is the constant pounding, pulverising, and splitting of frames and armour backing, the straining and opening of seams, the shattering of bulkheads, and the destruction of the water-tightness of the whole which eventually sink the ship."

This condition was more likely to result from a pounding by 1,250 lb. projectiles with a heavier bursting charge and greater dislocating effect than from 12-in. shells variously given as of 776, 860, and 980 lb.—the second being that usually employed.

The maximum thickness of armour belt was also made public for the first time, and showed that the *Kaiser* class had 13½ in.—thicker than in any British ship afloat, and only to be equalled in the *Queen Elizabeth*. On a basis of proving ground results the *Kaiser* could not resist 12-in./50 cal. guns at 10,000 yards, but as such tests were made under the best possible conditions for the gun they were not regarded as affording a reliable indication of what might be expected against a floating target with armour at a constantly changing angle. But even 13-in. armour was not expected to stand up against the concussion effects of 13·5-in. and 15-in. shells.

In the case of the German battle cruisers, the official figures as to armour thickness came as rather a shock in this country—and there would have been some very candid criticism had the true details of our own ships been available. Thus, the *Von der Tann* had 9·8 in. against a credited 7 in. in the *Invincible* and 8 in. in the *Indefatigable*—when actually the belt was only 6 in. in both, while the *Moltke* with 11 in. put up a wonderful defence compared with the alleged 9¾ in. in the the *Lion* and 10¾ in. in the *Tiger*—whereas in reality both had only 9 in. It was evident that those responsible for German battle cruiser designs fully appreciated the axiom that "Armour is Vision" by equipping them with battleship protection in conjunction with guns which would enable them to act both as scouts and fast wing units in a fleet action.

By the decision made on 6 January 1912 to arm the *Baden* and *Bayern* with 15-in. guns the Navy Office did not follow in the wake of the *Queen Elizabeth* but almost anticipated her. In one stroke the ordnance gap between German and British practice was to be bridged and substantially overhauled—for Dr. Burkner writing in *Schiffbau* declared that when the calibre and arrangement of the *Baden's* guns were approved, no news as to the *Queen Elizabeth* had reached Germany beyond a rumour that a heavier gun than the 13·5-in. was contemplated. And with that decision all former German shibboleths as to the superior fire power from smaller but faster-firing weapons went by the board.

GERMAN BATTLESHIP "BADEN"

A short description of the *Baden* may be included here as she provides a good example of contemporary German practice in a ship similarly armed to our own. Hitherto a marked difference has been noted between British and German ships of the same year's Programmes, we having given preference to gunpower with weapons of higher calibre while the Germans provided greater protection in ships designed for the narrow seas with somewhat cramped accommodation for their crews. Where there was more or less equality in displacement and equal skill in designing, any difference between the ships must of necessity involve some feature in which each vessel is inferior to the other. Before Jutland the pros and cons of guns v. armour had to be decided by conjecture and reflection as distinct from hard-won battle experience. The Admiralty chose the offensive in design, the Germans the defensive and this difference was apparent until 1913 when in the *Revenge* and *Baden* we find ships of very similar displacement carrying the same armament at almost equal speeds and protected on much the same scale. As the *Baden* was thoroughly examined at Portsmouth in 1919 full data for a comparison is available.

	"Revenge"	*"Baden"*
Displacement (l.w.l.)	28,000	28,074
Dimensions	580′ × 88½′ × 28½′	560½′ × 98½′ × 27¾′
Armament	8 15-in. 14 6-in.	8 15-in. 16 5·9-in.

	"Revenge"	*"Baden"*
Armour	Belt 13″-6″	13¾″-6¾″ at bottom
		10″-6¾″
	Ends 6″-4″	8″-6″ for'd; 6¾″ aft.
	Turrets 13″	13¾″
	Torpedo bulkhead 1½″-1″	2″
	Decks: forecastle 1″	1½″
	upper 1¼″-1½″	middle 1¼″ amidships
	main 1″-1½″-2″	2¼″ for'd
	lower 1″-2½″	2¼″-4¾″ aft.
	for'd 1″-2½″	
	aft 4″-3″-2½″	
S.H.P. and speed	40,000=23 knots	52,815=22·3 knots
Maximum fuel	3,400 oil	3,650 coal, 600 oil

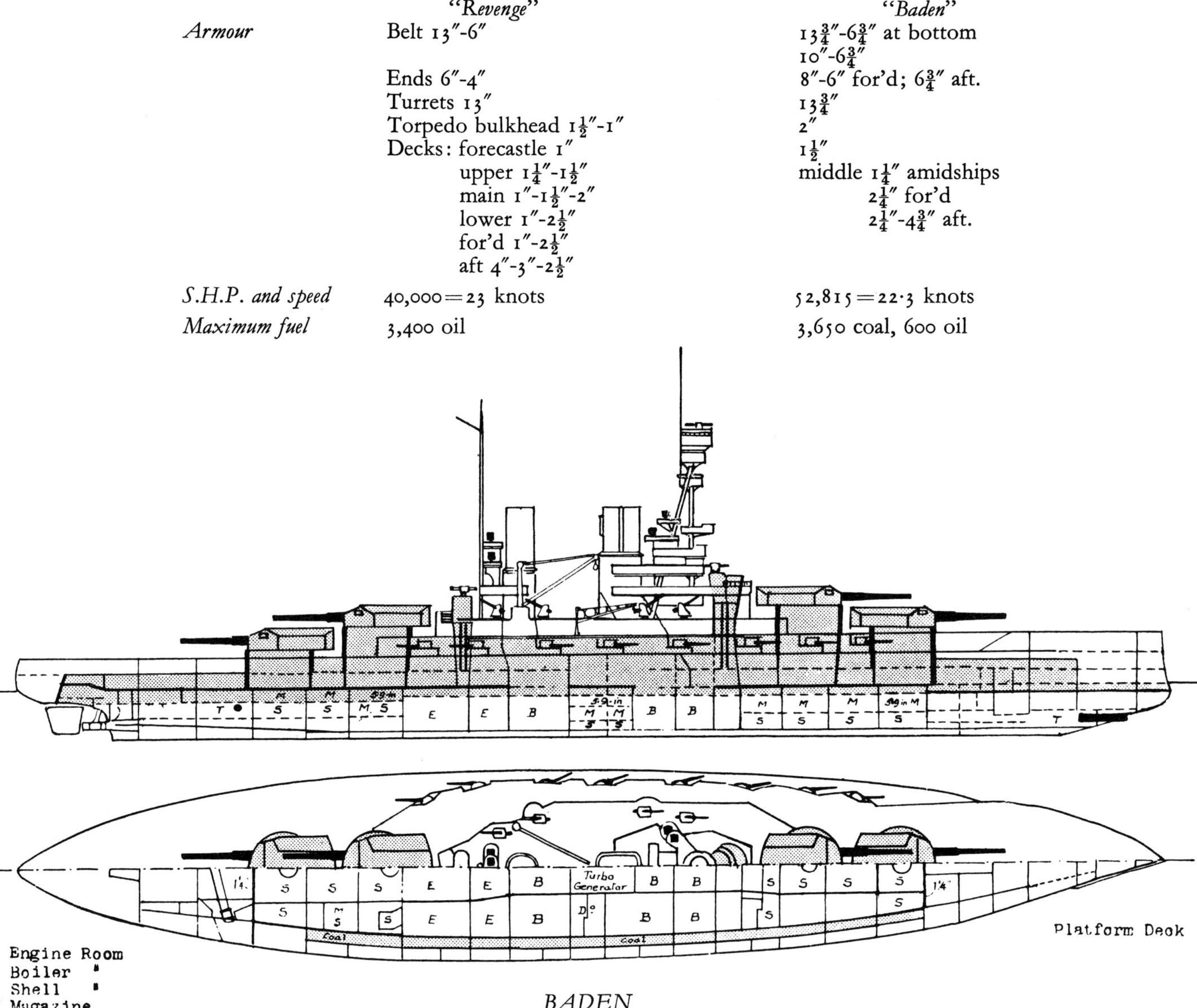

BADEN

In a paper on the *Baden* read before the I.N.A. in 1921 Constructor S. V. Goodall R.C.N.C.[1] presented the results of our investigations which with all due modesty corrected much of the fiction preached about the superiority of German designers. Special points about the *Baden* were:

(1) Her stability was worked out for North Sea operations with a metacentric height of 8·3 ft. (as advocated by Commander Hovgaard after the Russo-Japanese War, see p. 461) was greater than in any existing capital ship, providing great stiffness and enabling her to stand a large amount of damage and flooding of side compartments without incurring excessive list. Although suited for narrow seas where heavy rolling would be exceptional, it would result in a difficult gun platform in the Atlantic.

(2) Although four continuous longitudinal bulkheads allowed for very complete subdivision, nearly all the transverse bulkheads were fitted with doors pierced by voice pipes, sluice valves, suction pipes and ventilation trunks which reduced their efficiency as water-tight bulkheads.

(3) Weights allotted to protection as percentages of displacement were:

	Revenge	*Baden*
[2]Vertical armour	19·8	21·8
Horizontal	9·6	7·2
Under water	2·3	2·6
	31·7	31·6

[1] Afterwards Sir Stanley Goodall, K.C.B., D.N.C.

[2] Excluding turrets and conning tower.

(4) Armour plates were large, the 10″ plates of the upper belt being 7 ft. deep and over 25 ft. long.
(5) Five 21-in. sea valves on each side amidships permitted rapid flooding of certain side and end compartments made it possible to right the ship at the rate of 5° in 15 minutes. Two more aft and one forward sufficed for trimming purposes.
(6) Although the use of coal fuel was a necessity owing to the uncertainty of oil supplies, the 6 ft. wide side bunkers provided protection which enabled the torpedo bulkhead to be placed 13 ft. from the outer shell. These side bunkers were very difficult to empty and contained 1,740 tons.
(7) The foremost boilers burned oil fuel only; the remaining eleven burned coal and oil.
(8) Maximum elevation for the big guns was 16° only, giving a range of 22,200 yards. The shell weighed 1,653 lb. the time between rounds being 26 seconds or 50 seconds when shell and charge had to be transported from remote positions in shell rooms and magazines.

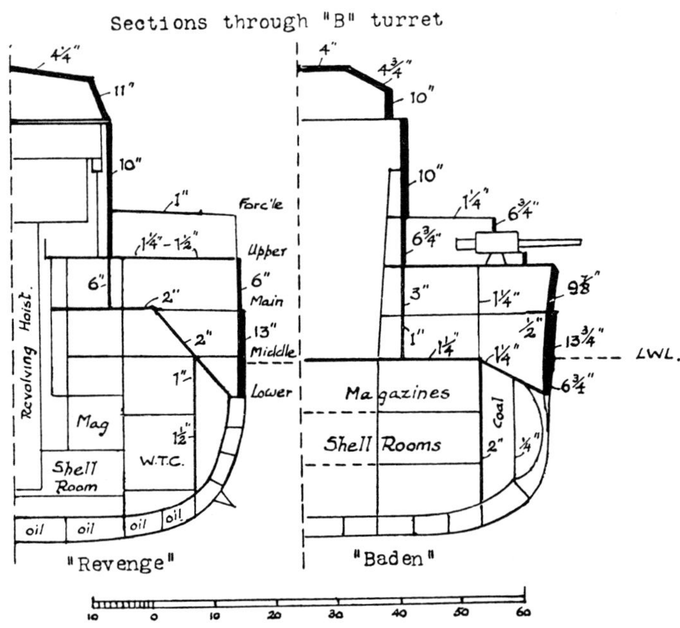

(9) Her armour did not stand the tests of actual firing which our own armour was called upon to stand in order to come up to specifications.
(10) Assuming the German legend condition included all ammunition, and average quantity of stores, and about 900 tons of coal it was estimated that the ship exceeded her legend draught by more than a foot.

As in other German ships construction was on a lighter scale than in our own, and taking bending moments on the same basis the Germans accepted stresses from 10 to 20 per cent. greater than were allowed in British ships. For local strength some of the plating was extraordinarily light, the *Baden's* outer bottom plating being only $\frac{5}{8}$ in. thick, whereas our corresponding plating was 1 in. It appeared that scantings were in many cases hardly sufficient to stand local stresses and ordinary wear and tear. (In the case of the *Seydlitz*, her officers reported that she leaked after being in action, this being due to damage caused by the shock of her own gunfire.)

Between 1907-14 there was a concentrated development in all types of warships which can only be compared with that seen in battleships between 1860-70. Capital ship displacement rose by over 50 per cent. and gun calibres by 25 per cent.; turbine machinery enabled long distance speed to be maintained without breakdown, and the later introduction of oil fuel heralded the passing of restricted radius and the delays and fatigues of coaling ships. Better armour and a fresh outlook on protection with improved subdivision, promised more adequate defence against heavier broadsides in conjunction with reduced penetration at longer ranges.

The battleship still reigned supreme, although not perhaps quite so unassailable as she had seemed say ten years previously. Comparative naval strength was estimated by the number of capital ships paraded by the powers with the British Navy comfortably first. Cruisers and smaller craft counted, but in a very secondary category, while docking facilities for larger and larger capital ships were more or less ignored—heavy expenditure on docks swelled the estimates without adding anything to our total of fighting strength.

Squadrons of from six to eight battleships were maintained in the Channel, Mediterranean, and Far East, and later in the Atlantic and Home Fleets when the *Canopus* class were withdrawn from China for the big concentration in home waters which marched with the evergrowing High Seas Fleet.

RANGE CONTROL

With the *Dreadnought* had come a new Gunnery Era.

Ever lengthening ranges so that the target might even be below horizon level when viewed from the turrets led to great difficulty in estimating the fall of shot and correcting the range, while alteration in course either by the ship firing or the target could change hits into misses. A high-up spotting position—and the higher the better—became essential, and led to the tall tripods in the earlier *Dreadnoughts* which combined rigidity with practical immunity from shell fire. Range-finders were becoming longer but were still inaccurate at long ranges, the longest in use before the war having a base of 9 ft. although in 1913 rangefinders of 25 ft. and 35 ft. were being supplied to foreign powers. During the war turrets received 9 ft., 12 ft., and 15 ft. instruments, and one with a 28 ft. base was lent on trial to the Navy in 1915, only to be returned the following year and then allocated to the War Office for coastal defence. The first 30 ft. instrument was supplied to the Navy in December 1919. Independent firing at ranges estimated from the spotting position aloft was generally favoured, and sporadic attempts to produce mechanical aids to range control were made by certain gunnery officers who realized how essential were rapid calculation and correction.

As the value of the battleship in action depended upon its ability to keep on hitting the target, it followed that the invention and development of such instruments of precision was a matter of the greatest national importance, comparable to Scott's revolution in the speed and accuracy of fire in the gun-layers' tests.

About 1908 two different systems of range-control came under discussion and test which ultimately brought about solutions to the complicated problems of long-range battle practice, Mr. Arthur H. Pollen, having discussed these difficulties with his brother aboard a cruiser in the Mediterranean, invented and had manufactured a set of control instruments. A gunnery officer Lieutenant F. C. Dreyer[1] had also worked out his solution, and in the so-called "Dreyer table" had produced a somewhat complicated machine which was sited in a "transmitting station" below the water-line. This combined the factors of (1) range of the enemy (2) course and speed of your own ship, and (3) estimated course and speed of the target, and produced a line or curve from which the rate of change of the target range could be measured. By a second instrument, invented by a torpedo officer, Lieutenant John S. Dumaresq,[2] this "rate" could be read off and set on the regulator of a special kind of clock which would then automatically grind out the *range* which was transmitted by instruments from the transmitting station to the director sites and guns.

Although the Admiralty decided to try out one system against the other the official attitude towards Pollen was indefendsibly churlish. Instead of welcoming him as an ally he was treated as a sort of intruder and Admiral Sir William James (who as a gunnery Lieutenant was working the "Dreyer system") writes:

> "One of my instructions was that if I met Pollen or Gipps (who worked the Pollen system) on shore I was not to speak to them!
>
> The verdict went in favour of the Dreyer system and so fierce internecine war broke out between those officers who were convinced that Pollen had had a raw deal and those who thought Dreyer was on the right lines. Pollen, undismayed by this blow to his hopes then invented a very clever mechanism which was fitted in my next ship, the *Natal*, and followed it with a still better design that was fitted in the *Queen Mary* when I was her Commander. So the man who I had been told to shun as a leper became a great friend.
>
> The irony was that the Admiralty design that eventually emerged after drastic alterations was hardly distinguishable from Pollen's design. Pollen claimed compensation and I think the adjudicators gave him a substantial sum, but the Admiralty fought the case inch by inch."

In the gunlayers' tests for 1909 the *Natal* set up new records for the 9·2-in. and 7·5-in. which have never been beaten—10 hits in 11 rounds by P.O. H. Fincken (9·2-in.) and 12 hits in 13 rounds by P.O. G. Eaton (7·5-in.). Her total score in points was 89·4 which she actually topped the following year with 90·4, and it was in the *Natal* that the first attempt at Director firing with a lash-up of instruments contrived in the ship made battle practice history.

Battle practice was carried out at 9,500 yards against a target about the size of a turret towed at some 10 knots, with the firing ship steaming at 14 knots. It was due to the insistence of Flag-Captain Chatfield of the *Lion* that the battle cruisers were allowed to carry out an experimental firing in April 1914 at two large targets towed at a range of 16,000 yards when steaming at 23 knots. The results showed the defects of our range-finders which could barely measure such a distance, and valuable lessons were learned when it came to ships firing together. Without such a practice the *Blücher* might not have been sunk eight months later.

Director control was first fitted in the *Neptune* in 1911, but not used in the battle practice for that year as the electrical connections were not satisfactory. *Thunderer* was the second ship to be fitted, and competitive shooting against the *Orion* in November 1912 showed that she had obtained six times as many hits. Only eight battleships had been equipped with directors by 1914, when it was by no means accepted generally as the best method of gunnery control.

---

[1] Admiral Sir Fredrick Dreyer, K.C.B.

[2] Vice-Admiral J. S. Dumaresq.

TORPEDO CRAFT

Until 1911 the last few years had seen but little change in torpedo craft. True with *River* class forecastles in place of turtle decks they had become sea-going vessels with some degree of habitability, but armament was still on the light side and torpedoes were still carried in single tubes without reloads. Our policy was "offence" as applied to battleships and very much "defence" in the matter of torpedo craft, so that while the Germans called their craft "torpedo boats" and gave them three or four 19-in. tubes and a couple of 24-pdrs., we dubbed ours "destroyers" and armed them with two 25-pdrs. and two 12-pdrs. for defending the fleet against torpedo attack and only a couple of 18-in. tubes for attacking the enemy.

Then in the "K" class (1911-12) came the tardy introduction of the twin tube, and we achieved what for some years became our standard destroyer armament of three 4-in. guns and four 21-in. tubes. The Germans followed suit with twin tubes in their V. 25-30 of the 1912 Programme.

German aspirations to sea power did not envisage big ship actions in which our superiority would be decisive —there was to be a gradual whittling away of our armoured strength by mine and torpedo. In the event of a fleet action, torpedo attack and smoke screens were to be employed to break contact and allow for safe retreat, and to this end their 150-odd torpedo craft were splendidly trained and fully efficient.

SUBMARINES

By 1907 underwater craft had passed from the experimental stage to one of definite efficiency, and their development into sea-going warships capable of dealing knock-out blows to battleships was to be expected in the near future.

No large scale realistic exercises were carried out to ascertain just what submarines were capable of, and they were generally regarded as fit for coastal work only although our 550/600 ton "D" class of 1910-11 and "E" class of 1912 were dependable seaboats well able to undertake extended trips and armed with 12-pdrs. and from three to five tubes. But no-one would have imagined that B.9 would have been able to make the passage to the Mediterranean under her own power, and penetrate the defences of the Dardanelles as she did in 1915.

From 1911 to 1912 German submarines developed along much the same lines as our own, and their 650/750 tonners from U.13 onwards were carrying out extended practices at sea before the war.

No practical measures were taken towards defence against submarines at sea, and both zigzagging and destroyer screens were not adopted until the war had been in progress for some time. Although Scapa Flow had been decided upon as a Fleet Base early in 1910, a committee of which Admiral Jellicoe was the most prominent member did not consider that boom defences there or at Cromarty and Rosyth could be provided on account of the limited expenditure available.

MINES

A few old cruisers of the *Apollo* class were fitted as minelayers, but we had no sea-mines worthy of the name and did not get them until 1917. Although the Germans were known to have highly efficient mines, our minesweeping service consisted of about a dozen torpedo-gunboats and half-a-dozen trawlers. All the German minefields were laid with the loss of only one minelayer.

AIRCRAFT

Trial seaplane flights had been made from runway platforms erected over the forecastles of the battleships *Africa*, *Hibernia*, and *London* in 1911-12 and then discontinued; various experiments with the light cruiser *Hermes* to find a suitable method of launching aircraft had not been satisfactory, and the least dangerous and most reliable method of getting seaplanes into the air was to lower them over the side in suitable weather and let them fly off the sea under their own power, reversing the procedure for regaining shipboard.

Reconnaissance held possibilities, but the clumsy aircraft of 1914 were unsuitable for offensive work with either gun, bomb or torpedo—although the great advantages of a torpedo-carrying plane had been advocated.

Attempts to construct dirigibles along the lines of the German Zeppelins had not been successful and the non-rigid airships, such as we had built, were no menace to warships. Hence the battleship appeared safe from aerial attack for many years to come, and the only A.A. guns mounted before the war were single 3-in. in the *Iron Duke* and *Marlborough*.

Chapter 105

WORLD WAR I

THE outbreak of hostilities against Germany in August 1914 found the battleship at almost the peak of her superiority among fighting ships—almost but not quite as unassailable as she had been say ten years previously when gunpower and armour reigned supreme. She could still overwhelm any other type of warship, but torpedo craft had grown to a seagoing size, and the 21-in. Hardcastle torpedo, effective at ever-increasing ranges, was a formidable weapon, to which the German 19·7-in. Schwartzkoff ran a good second. But for all that there was no longer the earlier fear of destroyer attack—the Russo-Japanese War had failed to substantiate many of the claims made for the "omnipotent torpedo," and post-war teaching had tended to minimize its bearing upon future warfare. True there were writers here and in Germany who prophesied great things from the German torpedo flotillas, and the massed assaults upon unsuspecting battle squadrons which were to herald the outbreak of war were supposed to destroy our margin of superiority and open the way to a British defeat at sea.

But nations still thought in *Dreadnoughts* and the Command of the Sea appeared safely vested in the Battle Fleet, with the battleship as the prime unit of naval force, omnipotent and unbeatable.

COMPOSITION OF THE GRAND FLEET

BATTLE FLEET

Fleet Flagship *Iron Duke.*

1ST BATTLE SQUADRON

Marlborough (Vice-Admiral), *St. Vincent* (Rear-Admiral), *Colossus, Hercules, Neptune, Vanguard, Collingwood, Superb.*

2ND BATTLE SQUADRON

King George V (Vice-Admiral), *Orion* (Rear-Admiral), *Ajax, Audacious, Centurion, Conqueror, Monarch, Thunderer.*

3RD BATTLE SQUADRON

King Edward VII (Vice-Admiral), *Hibernia* (Rear-Admiral), *Commonwealth, Africa, Zealandia, Dominion, Britannia, Hindustan.*

4TH BATTLE SQUADRON

Dreadnought (Vice-Admiral), *Temeraire, Bellerophon.*

6TH BATTLE SQUADRON

Russell (f), *Cornwallis, Albemarle, Duncan, Exmouth.*

1ST BATTLE CRUISER SQUADRON

Lion (Vice-Admiral), *Princess Royal, Queen Mary, New Zealand.*

2ND CRUISER SQUADRON

Shannon (Rear-Admiral), *Achilles, Cochrane, Natal.*

3RD CRUISER SQUADRON

(Smaller armoured cruisers)

Antrim, Argyll, Devonshire, Roxburgh.

1ST LIGHT CRUISER SQUADRON

Southampton (f), *Birmingham, Lowestoft, Nottingham, Falmouth, Liverpool.*

DESTROYERS 41

The Harwich Force of 2 light cruisers as flagships and 35 destroyers was intended to act with the Grand Fleet if ordered, but never did so.

The *Home Fleet* organization which was in force on 4 August lasted until the 7th, when the squadrons were reconstructed to form the Channel Fleet covering the passage of the Expeditionary Force to France.

CHANNEL FLEET

Fleet Flagship *Lord Nelson.*

5TH BATTLE SQUADRON

Agamemnon, *Prince of Wales* (Vice-Admiral), *Queen* (Rear-Admiral), *Venerable*, *Irresistible*, *Bulwark*, *Formidable*, *Implacable*, *London.*

7TH BATTLE SQUADRON[1]

Prince George (f), *Cæsar*, *Jupiter*, *Majestic.*

8TH BATTLE SQUADRON

Albion (f), *Goliath*, *Canopus*, *Glory*, *Ocean*, *Vengeance.*

9TH BATTLE SQUADRON[1]

Hannibal (f), *Victorious*, *Mars*, *Magnificent*, *Illustrious* paid off to provide a crew for the *Erin.*

MEDITERRANEAN FLEET

2ND BATTLE CRUISER SQUADRON

Inflexible (f), *Indefatigable*, *Indomitable.*

1ST CRUISER SQUADRON

Defence (f), *Warrior*, *Black Prince*, *Duke of Edinburgh.*

LIGHT CRUISERS

Chatham, *Dublin*, *Gloucester*, *Weymouth.*

Of the remaining armoured ships, *Swiftsure* was in the East Indies and *Triumph* in China with the *Minotaur.*

The pre-Dreadnoughts were withdrawn from the Grand Fleet and Channel early in 1915 when the decision was made to attack the Dardanelles, and the *Lord Nelsons*, *Duncans*, 6 *Londons*, 4 *Albions*, 2 *Swiftsures*, *Majestic* and *Prince George* were drafted to the Mediterranean. The remaining *Majestics* either surrendered their guns to the big monitors, or went to distant stations overseas for subsidiary service.

During the 1914-18 War battleships and battle cruisers were able to carry out their traditional duties in the line-of-battle, as convoy protection, and in the bombardment of enemy coastal defences, but not in the exercise of close blockade.

Until the middle of 1912 Admiral Wilson's scheme for close blockade along traditional lines was to be adopted but with the formation of a War Staff it was discarded as too precarious when faced with destroyer attacks, submarines and mine-fields. Instead, what was termed an observation blockade was substituted with a line stretching from the S.W. of Norway to the middle of the North Sea and then downwards to the Texel on the Dutch coast. This, however, meant watching some 300 miles with a very large number of cruisers and destroyers which the fleet could not spare. Such a watch could not be effective; the ships would be exposed to attack; and it would be far less likely to supply information than would the Close Blockade.

Mercifully such a plan was never adopted. It was abandoned in the summer of 1914 in favour of the Distant Blockade with a northerly line extending from Scapa Flow to Norway, and a southerly one across the Channel from Dover. This last-minute change meant shifting the Fleet from Rosyth to Scapa—which was undefended—and completely upset the German plan for defeating us by attrition afloat.

The German hopes of victory by "an equalization of strength" were based on our blockade plans for 1911 and 1912 when a blockade of the Bight would provide all the opportunities they wanted:

> "Before the war" says the official German historian "the whole training of our fleet and to some extent even our shipbuilding policy and even certain constructional details (for instance a small radius of action of a large number of our destroyers) was based on the assumption that the British would organize a blockade of the Helgoland Bight with their superior fleet."

---

[1] Withdrawn for Special Service.

We very nearly played in the German hands, and as late as May 1914 Vice-Admiral Scheer, the future Commander-in-Chief of the High Seas Fleet, wrote that in his opinion British prestige would not countenance the abandonment of the Bight Blockade. That we did so meant goodbye to the slow but sure attrition toasted in *Der Tag*, and the ultimate locking-up of their fleet in the Jade and the mutiny which led to the Great Surrender.

With the declaration of war, Germany's commerce came to a standstill. No more merchant ships put to sea, and those on passage came into our hands. Only the German cruisers on foreign stations remained at large, and with the exception of the *Goeben* and *Breslau* which, through mistakes in direction on our part and bold and well-judged decisions by the German Admiral, were able to reach Constantinople and implement the alliance with Turkey.

German minefields and encounters with submarines—of which twenty-four were sea-going—soon caused the fleet to confine its movements under ordinary conditions to the more northern part of the North Sea where it could cruise without attendant destroyers—which had fuel capacity for three days and nights only—and where distance from their bases and depth of water made minelaying without discovery improbable. During a southern sweep the shortage of fleet sweepers led to the older battleships of the 6th Squadron being stationed ahead of the Fleet to serve as "mine bumpers," such ships being referred to colloquially as the "Old Expendibles."

Being no longer able to carry out short-range attacks on close-blockading forces, the German Fleet was faced with the prospect of harbour service, relieved by occasional hit-and-run sorties when there was a good prospect of meeting an inferior force. Any deliberate engagement with the Grand Fleet was out of the question—losses which could turn the scale in favour of the Russian Fleet in the Baltic could not be risked. The employment of light forces on the Bight patrol was the only activity permitted, and then with the expectation of driving off British minelayers.

When Admiral Jellicoe took over command of the Grand Fleet at Scapa Flow it consisted of twenty *Dreadnoughts*, eight *King Edwards*, four battle cruisers, two squadrons of cruisers and one of light cruisers, with a few units still to join. Sir David Beatty was Vice-Admiral commanding the battle cruisers, armoured cruisers, and cruisers all of which formed "Cruiser Force A."

Chapter 106

"ERIN," "AGINCOURT" AND "CANADA"

In August 1914 we were fortunate in having a number of warships under completion to the order of foreign governments including three battleships, the *Reshadieh* and *Sultan Osman I* for Turkey and *Almirante Latorre* for Chile. The situation was therefore very much the same as during the Russian scare of 1878 with this difference: the *Neptune*, *Superb*, *Orion* and *Belleisle* then turned out to be of limited value, whereas the *Erin* (*Reshadieh*), *Agincourt* (*Rio de Janeiro*, *Osman I*) and *Canada* (*Almirante Latorre*) being all more or less in line with the main requirements of Admiralty design—proved themselves good bargains. Moreover in the case of the Turkish ships we now know that the Ottoman Alliance with Germany had already been concluded when war broke out, and had they been allowed to leave for the Golden Horn in August 1914 the odds against us in the Mediterranean would have required the employment of a squadron of *Dreadnoughts*. That the Turks strongly resented the transfer is hardly to be wondered at; but the contention that it was instrumental in bringing them in against us can now be dismissed. Seeing that they actually each counted two on a division the acquisition of these ships can be regarded as extremely fortunate, and on joining the Grand Fleet they proved very welcome additions at a time when our superiority over the High Seas Fleet was at its lowest.

All three needed certain modifications before entering our service, but these were of a "specialist" nature and did not unduly delay completion.

Two small Norwegian coast-defence ships the *Bjoervin* and *Nidaros* laid down at Elswick in January 1913 for completion the following year were also taken over and renamed *Gorgon* and *Glatton*, but must reluctantly be omitted from this review. Their namesakes in the 'seventies had been gunned and armoured on the heaviest scale and regarded as fighting machines of some consequence; but these two curious little craft were only suitable for coastwise operations and their category no longer bore any relationship to the huge sea-going ships of the line, either in size, guns, protection, or speed.

"ERIN" (ex-*Reshadieh*)

Builders	*Laid down*	*Launched*	*Completed*
Vickers	1 Aug. '11	3 Sept. '13	Aug. '14

Dimensions 525′ (559′ 6″)×91′ 7″×28′ 8″/28′ 2″=23,000 tons.
Load displacement 22,780 tons; full load 25,250 tons. Sinkage 82 tons per inch.

Armament 10 13·5-in./45.
16 6-in./50
6 6-pdrs.
2 3-in. A.A. (added).

Tubes:
4 21-in. beam.
10 torpedoes.

Protection (K.C.)
Belt 12″-9″-8″-6″-4″; bulkheads 8″-5″-4″.
Battery 5″.
Barbettes 10″-9″-5″-3″; turrets 11″-4″-3″.
Conning tower 12″-4″; torpedo control tower 4″.
Communication tubes: Forward 6″, aft 3″.
Decks: (H.T.) Forecastle over battery 1½″.
Upper outside battery 1½″.
Main 1½″.
Middle: amidships 1″, ends 3″.
Magazines and machinery 1½″.
Funnel uptakes 1″.
(Total weight 4,207 tons).

Machinery Parsons. Made by Vickers. S.H.P. 26,500=21 knots.
Boilers: 15 Babcock and Wilcox. 4 screws.

Fuel Coal 900/2,120 tons; oil 710 tons.

Radius 5,300/10.

Complement 1,070.

When Sir Douglas Gamble was in charge of a British naval commission in Turkey, he prepared a programme of new construction which was to include two capital ships, three cruisers and ten destroyers. Of these, orders for the two battleships *Reshad V* and *Reshad-i-Hamiss* were placed with Vickers and Armstrongs in 1911 to a design

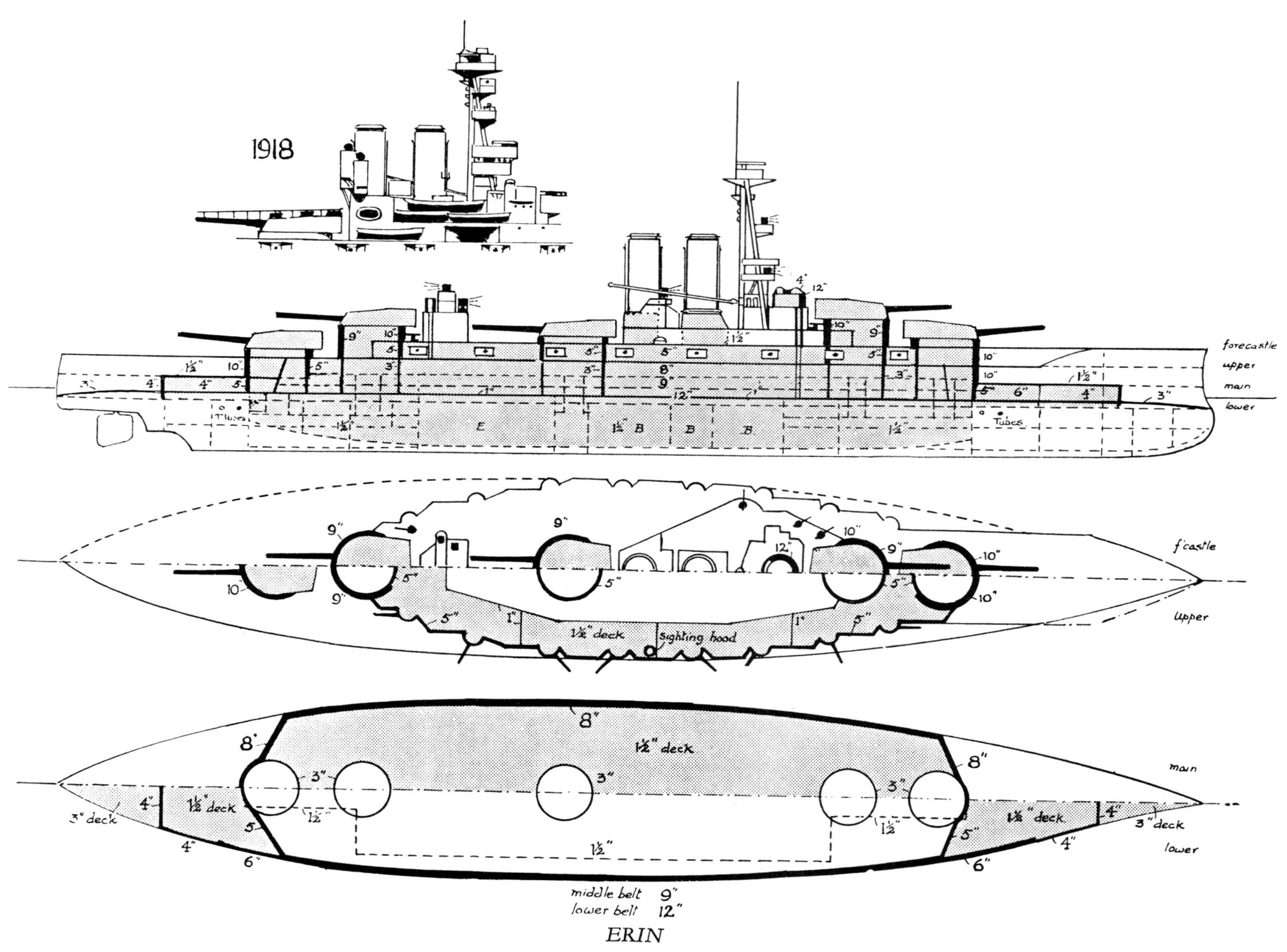
1918
forecastle
upper
main
lower
Tubes
f'castle
upper
sighting hood
1½" deck
3" deck
middle belt 9"
lower belt 12"

ERIN

prepared by Sir R. Thurston of Vickers. Work, however, was suspended in 1912 owing to the Balkan War and when resumed only the *Reshad V* (later *Reshadieh*) was proceeded with.

Intended to equal the most powerful battleships afloat in fighting power, her dimensions approximated to those of the *King George V* although for comparative purposes she was more like a compressed edition of the *Iron Duke*, giving away a couple of thousand tons on normal displacement while carrying a heavier secondary armament, very similar protection, and steaming only half a knot slower.

How the *Erin* came to be built on the same legend displacement as the *King George V* can be gathered from a study of their dimensions. The bugbear of British constructors at this period was the necessity for curtailing beam on account of docking facilities (see Appendix II); hence, when increased displacement was required it had to be found mainly by extra length so that the customary 28 ft. mean legend draught need not be exceeded. In the *Erin* such beam restrictions did not obtain, so that the necessary displacement could be effected by a very different set of dimensions. Length was reduced by 30 ft. while beam rose 2 ft. 9 in. to 91 ft. 7 in. (greater than that of the *Queen Elizabeth*) and mean draught by 1 ft. 5½ in. to 28 ft. 5 in.; also in section she was much squarer at the turn of the bilge amidships. The result was a hull with length : beam ratio of 5·7 as against 6·2 in the *King George V*. This excess of beam precluded her using any of the docks at Devonport, although they had a width

Erin as she appeared in 1918 with director platform on mast, searchlight towers, lights regrouped on after shelter deck with A.A. guns, and runways on "B" and "Q" turrets.

at entrance of 95 ft. A great floating dock for the new base to be created in the Gulf of Ismid, had been included in the scheme for Turkish naval reorganization.

Of the 30 ft. shortening, some of this was taken out of the forecastle and the rest from the amidships section where it had the greatest effect on displacement, although curtailing boiler rooms and coal supply. Freeboard was the same in both ships.

The additional beam and fullness below water provided the extra buoyancy necessitated by additional topside weight due to the long forecastle deck being continued aft to "X" turret with three more 6-in. guns aside in the battery, and a longer armour strake to cover them.

The plough bow made for dryness and gave a very distinctive finish to the profile.

First sketch plans as shown to the writer at the Turkish Embassy in 1911 had the mast placed abaft the funnel with a second tripod on the after superstructure. Later this latter was replaced by a pole, and mast moved forward of the funnel. During completion the pole was removed.

Limitations in space amidships and the fact that the mast legs were stepped forward to allow for the boats to be handled by one boom only, left no room for the bridgework on the *King George V* scale. Hence the chart house had to be built round the mast clear of the conning tower, and sea cabins were in the forward shelter deck. Accommodation was perhaps a little below our standard, cabins being on the small side, and a complement of 1070/1130 left none of the alleyways free from hammocks.

ARMAMENT

The ten 13·5-in. were disposed as in the British ships except that "Q" turret was a deck higher, their height above water at 28½ ft. draught being: forward 29½ ft. and 39 ft., amidships 29½ ft., aft 31½ ft. and 22 ft. The battery guns, 20 ft. above water, had wide arcs of fire, the first three bearing from 90° before the beam to 40° abaft it, the two amidships 65° each way, and the after three from 40° before to 90° abaft the beam. The three foremost tended to be wet in a seaway, but the rest had a reasonably dry command on a par with those in the *Tiger*. Screens of 1-in. steel separated them into pairs for localizing damage, with 5-in. armour along the battery walls. Behind the 5-in. strake the barbettes diminished to 5 in., and behind the 8-in. strake to 3 in. as against 6 in. in *King George V*.

The four torpedo tubes were Elswick side-loading pattern, in flats before and abaft the end barbettes. Originally *Erin* was listed with three tubes, but an after pair replaced a single tube in the stern.

In 1917 3-in. A.A. guns were placed above the searchlights on the after superstructure, the other projectors being moved to towers around the second funnel. Aeroplane runways crowned "B" and "Q" turrets in 1918.

PROTECTION

Distribution of armour was similar to that in the *King George V* but with the belts somewhat shallower. The different heights of the decks will be noticed and thus the 8-in. strake was deeper and the 9-in. shallower in the *Erin* while the 12-in. extended to 3 ft. 8 in. below water in the *Erin* and 3 ft. 7½ in. in the *King George V*. Fore and aft the 4-in. continuations were a little shallower in the *Erin* and her under-water 1½-in. internal screens were complete from "A" to "Y" barbettes, while in the *King George V* the boiler rooms were not so shielded. The total armour weight was 4,207 tons or 17·8 per cent. of the legend displacement.

MACHINERY

Although so much shorter and broader than the *King George V* the *Erin* was allowed 500 s.h.p. less for the same speed and made her 21 knots easily.

GENERAL

Behaviour at sea was good and she manœuvred easily with a small turning circle.

Her deficiency compared with Admiralty designs lay in fuel capacity, being 1,130 tons less than *King George V* and 1,280 less than *Orion*. But as she burnt 100 tons an hour less than these ships at $\frac{4}{5}$ power and 19·2 knots at deep load (360 as against 464 tons) her radius of action (never officially published) was ample for North Sea requirements.

In every way the *Erin* showed remarkable qualities for her tonnage, and needed but little alteration to bring her into line with British requirements.

"ERIN"

Built at Vickers August '11 to August '14 and joined the Grand Fleet the following month. Served in 2nd B.S. At Jutland was 4th ship in the line (no casualties). In 1919 went as Flagship (Admiral Sir H. Richmond) of Nore Reserve. Scrapped under Washington Treaty 1921.

"AGINCOURT" (War Emergency Purchase)

Builders	*Laid down*	*Launched*	*Completed*
Elswick	Sept. '11	22 Jan. '13	Aug. '14

Dimensions 632′ (671′ 6″) × 89′ × 27′ (mean) = 27,500 tons.
Load displacement 27,500 tons; full load 30,250 tons. 99 tons per inch submersion.

Armament 14 12-in./45. 20 6-in./50. 10 3-in. 2 3-in. A.A.
Tubes: 3 21-in. 10 torpedoes.

Protection Belt 9″-6″-4″; bulkheads 6″-3″.
Barbettes 9″-3″; ; turrets 12″-8″.
Battery 6″; conning tower 12″-4″.
Torpedo control tower 9″.
Decks: Forecastle over battery 1½″.
Upper deck outside battery 1½″.
Main 1″-1½″; middle 1″-1½″; lower 1″.
Forward 2½″ over rudder.
Torpedo bulkheads 1″-1½″ over magazines.

Machinery Parsons. 4 screws. Designed S.H.P. 34,000 = 22 knots.
Boilers: 22 Babcock and Wilcox.

Fuel 1,500/3,200 tons coal; 620 tons oil.

Complement 1,115 (1,267 in November '18).

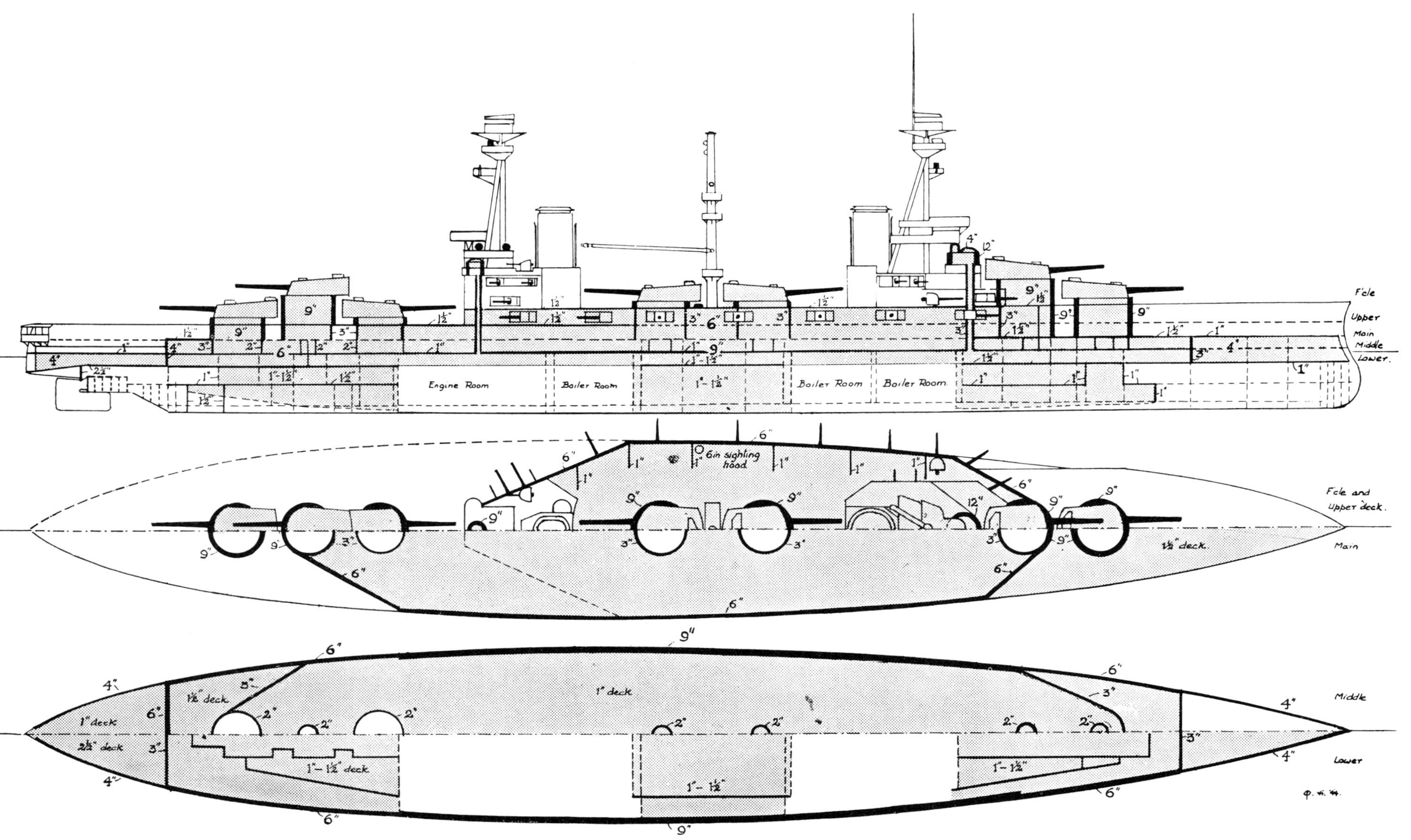

Agincourt with fore and aft flying bridge removed as she appeared when joining the Grand Fleet. Note the long angled bulkheads lapping the turret bases and extensive magazines.

Special features:

(1) Carried the largest number of heavy guns of any warship afloat.
(2) The last British 12-in. gunned ship.
(3) Had the highest length/beam ratio of any Capital ship except the *Tiger*.
(4) Carried the heaviest secondary battery afloat.

In reviewing those long vistas of ships stretching above and below the bridge in the days when the Grand Fleet turned the Forth into a sort of naval Venice, there was one ship which seemed to stand out in a splendid isolation from the sequence of *Queen Elizabeths*, *Iron Dukes*, *King Georges*, *Orions*, *Canada* and *Erin*—a solitary departure from the conventional profile which was more or less common to our later battleships—the *Agincourt*.

When first completed with the great "Marble Arch" boat deck spanning the amidships turrets no other ship afloat could equal her for aggressive magnificence. When stripped of this top hamper she seemed longer and there was something peculiarly attractive in the long lean hull bristling with guns and topped by a serried row of turrets, the quaint rig, and wide spaced funnels. She was one of those ships which appeared her best from every angle, and with all her guns trained on one beam there was no more ferocious looking fighter in the fleet.

The *Agincourt* had the curious distinction of being the property of three different Governments during twelve months. Her history evolves from that long-standing and insane spirit of rivalry existing between the South American Republics, which led to programmes of warship construction frankly in excess of their requirements and framed with but little regard to their geographical limitations. Brazil having opened the lists and thrown down the gauntlet of local Sea Supremacy by ordering the Dreadnoughts *Minas Geraes* and *Sao Paulo* in 1907 armed with twelve 12-in. guns, ten of which could be trained on either beam, Argentina and Chile began to look to their laurels. The former country after often and repeated traffickings with practically every firm in the world capable of producing a battleship was finally persuaded by the U.S. Government to place their orders for the twelve 12-in. gunned *Rividavia* and *Moreno* with the Fore River Co. early in 1910; and after much delay arising from divers importunities in the matter of speed, structural strength and what not, were able to add them to their fleet in 1915.

Not content to be out-bid by these very powerful vessels, Brazil tried to achieve an unassailable supremacy with a third ship the *Rio de Janeiro* which was to be the *ultima thule* in battleship design before Chile could come along with her contributions to this game of naval "beggar-my-neighbour."

The plans which were discussed and the design actually put in hand suggest an attack of warship megalomania only equalled in the history of naval construction by the Italian outbreak in the 'seventies. The extent of Brazilian ambition to be possessed of the biggest battleship afloat may be gauged from the following table:

	Rio de Janeiro	*Alexandrino*[1]	*Bacellar*[1]	*Perrett*[1]
Length (p.p.)	632′	650′	630′	650′
Beam	89′	92′	90′	90½′
Draught	29′	27′	28½′	29′
Displacement	27,500	31,600	30,500	31,250
Speed	22	22	23	23
Armament	14 12-in.	12 14-in.	8 16-in.	10 15-in.
	20 6- "	14 6- "	6 9·4-in.	14 6- "
	12 3- "	14 4- "	14 6- "	4 3- "
Torpedo tubes	3	3	4	3
Main belt	9″-6″-4″	12″-9″-6″	9″	9″
Upper belt	9″	8″	9″	9″
Battery	6″	6″		
Barbettes	9″	12″	12″-10″	12″

A contract for the *Alexandrino* design had been placed with Armstrongs, but a change of Government led to its being revised in favour of "a powerful unit which will not be built on exaggerated lines such as have not yet stood the test of experience." The new Minister had been to Germany, discussed the matter with the highest authorities, and been assured by the Kaiser that a 12-in. gun could pierce any existing armour. He was persuaded that it would be far better to have a ship able to use the same ammunition as the *Minas Geraes* and *Sao Paulo* and work in their company with a more numerous instead of heavier calibre weapons.

Exactly how the design for the *Rio de Janeiro* was accepted in face of foreign competition is a story of Mr. Eustace Tennyson D'Eyncourt (then working for Armstrongs) going out to Rio with a parcel of assorted plans drawn up by their Chief Constructor Mr. Perrett (who in the past had been responsible for working out the hull

[1] The originators of the designs.

lines of the famous Elswick cruisers); a discussion on competitive proposals; a strenuous all-night rush of draughtsmanship; and the production on the spot of striking drawings which captured the contract for Elswick.

Ten months after she had been launched there were reports that Brazil had repented of her bargain and wished to dispose of her; early in 1914 she was put on the market and acquired by the Turkish Government for £2,725,000 (raised by enthusiastic public subscription) and re-named *Sultan Osman I.* When the prospect of war became imminent the great ship was docking at Devonport. There her detention was arranged on sundry counts until the participation of this country in hostilities could no longer be in doubt, when she was taken over and re-named *Agincourt.*

As taken over from the Turks with flying boat deck.

Various modifications were effected to fit her for service under the White Ensign, the most noticeable being the removal of the big fore-and-aft boat bridge and torpedo nets, the boom boats necessarily being reduced to a pinnace and launch, carried on deck athwart the fourth turret. The main tripod was removed in 1916 and a short pole mast substituted, but later on this was dispensed with when the big derrick pole fitted with a topmast for W.T. again restored a well-balanced profile. In 1918 the bridge was enlarged and the searchlights were re-grouped in towers around the second funnel.

Like her namesake of the 'sixties the *Agincourt* could boast of being the longest battleship of her day with a length/beam ratio of 7·1 necessary to accommodate seven turrets. Had the Brazilians been willing to accept the triple turret a shorter ship would have carried fifteen big guns, but this was still only an experimental mounting yet to find general favour.

ARMAMENT

The seven turrets—named after the days of the week—had 12-in. faces and 8-in. rears with a big rear sighting hood placed towards the left side, and housed 45 cal. guns. Although this piece had not been mounted in our ships since the *Bellerophon* class the *Agincourts* thought the world of their vast broadside and were quite prepared to take on the *Queen Elizabeth* and smother her. At Jutland she was the last in the line and during the short time she came into action seized the opportunity to fire full fourteen-gun salvoes. "The sheet of flame was big enough to create the impression that a battle cruiser had blown up; it was awe inspiring."

Fourteen of the 6-in. guns were behind 6-in. armour and separated by 1-in. screens, the remainder on deck or in the superstructures having shields only.

The two side-loading submerged tubes just forward of the foremost barbette fired torpedoes differing from the standard pattern in having a smaller war-head due to the limited space athwartships in the flat. Incidentally it may be noted that during action the water admitted into the tube was immediately discharged into the flat preparatory to reloading and pumped out afterwards, so that the operators carried on sometimes in three feet of water when rapid firing was demanded.

PROTECTION

In view of the great length of the hull and number of turrets the weight available for armour precluded a maximum thickness of more than 9 in. along the water-line and on the barbettes, so that in this respect the *Agincourt* fell short of the Admiralty scale of protection. On the other hand, the 11-in. and 12-in. belts in our ships were so shallow that the upper 8-in. or 9-in. strake constituted the principal defence with the upper deck left open in all ships prior to the *Orion*, whereas the *Agincourt* had 6 in. along this and the forecastle deck. In our Service she was regarded as a floating magazine with a tremendous volume of gunfire as her best protection.

It will be noticed that only the end barbettes were 9 in. between decks, the rest being reduced to 3 in. when covered by 6 in. of side armour. The use of very long bulkheads afforded a saving of about 14 per cent. in armour weight under the second and sixth turrets.

Magazine protection was well carried out on our own scale with three to four 1½-in. decks providing good

AGINCOURT

cover, and in this respect she seems to have been somewhat superior to our ships. At the extremities two thin decks replaced the one thicker deck in Admiralty designs.

SPEED

The *Agincourt* was a good steamer and made 22·42 knots on trial with 40,279 s.h.p. She manœuvred well despite her great length, but had a larger turning circle than her consorts. In a seaway she was regarded as a good gun platform.

GENERAL

Having served in her for a time, the writer can support her reputation of being one of the most comfortable ships in the Navy and particularly well-appointed internally even after the special furnishing supplied for her first owners had been taken out. A knowledge of Portuguese was necessary to work many of the fittings—including those in the bath-rooms—and only the wardroom china retained Turkish inscriptions.

Being an odd-volume in our organization, the end of hostilities saw her placed in Reserve and then on the Disposal List with the hope that Brazil might wish to take her over.

Agincourt in 1918 with after tripod removed and searchlight towers around second funnel. A.A. guns on quarter deck.

"AGINCOURT"

Built at Elswick September '11-July '14 when she docked at Devonport. Taken over in August and joined Grand Fleet 4th B.S. at sea on 7 September. Having no sub-calibre guns there was difficulty in carrying out firing practices and delay in their supply retarded her battle efficiency for a time. At Jutland was in 1st B.S. 6th Division with *Marlborough*, *Revenge* and *Hercules*—as mixed a group as could be found. (No hits or casualties. Fired 144 rounds 12-in. and 111 rounds 6-in.) Transferred to 2nd B.S. On disposal list '19-'21 but re-commissioned at Rosyth '21 for experimental purposes.

Scrapped under Washington Treaty.

"CANADA" (ex-*Almirante Latorre*)

(War purchase)

Builders	*Laid down*	*Launched*	*Completed*
Elswick	Dec. '11	27 Nov. '13	Sept. '15

Dimensions 625′ (661′) × 92′ × 29′ (mean) = 28,000 tons.
Load draught 28,600 tons; full load 32,120 tons.
(Sinkage 101 tons per inch.)

Armament 10 14-in./45.
16 6-in./50.
2 3-in. A.A.
4 3-pdrs.
Torpedo tubes:
4 21-in.
20 torpedoes.

Protection Belt 9″-4″; bulkheads $4\frac{1}{2}$″-3″.
Barbettes 10″-4″; turrets 10″.
Battery 6″.
Conning tower 11″-6″; director tower 6″.
Decks: Shelter deck over casemates 1″.
Forecastle: over battery 1″.
Upper: outside battery $1\frac{1}{2}$″.
Main: aft $1\frac{1}{2}$″.
Middle 1″.
Lower: forward 2″; aft 4″.
Magazine screens 2″-$1\frac{1}{2}$″.

Machinery Brown-Curtis (H.P.) and Parsons (L.P.) turbines.
S.H.P. 37,000 = 22·75 knots. 4 screws.
Boilers 21 Yarrow (by J. Brown and Co.).

Fuel Coal 1,150/3,300 tons; oil 520 tons.

Radius 4,400/10

Complement 1,167.

Brazil having committed herself to the *Rio de Janeiro* it then became Chile's turn to decide her own venture and she placed a contract with Elswick for the construction of two monsters which were to outclass in gunpower anything yet ordered. As originally designed the *Almirante Latorre* and *Almirante Cochrane* were to have displaced 27,400 tons, and carry ten 14-in. and twenty-two 4·7-in. at 23 knots. But the increasing adoption of a larger calibre for the secondary guns by the powers caused the Chileans to follow suit and sixteen 6-in. were substituted with a corresponding rise to 28,000 tons, an increase in mean draught of $6\frac{1}{2}$ in. and reduction in guaranteed speed to $22\frac{3}{4}$ knots. The *Latorre* was commenced in December 1911 but the *Cochrane* could not be laid down until the *Rio* was launched in 1913.

In general design the *Latorre* was a lengthened *Iron Duke* with a slightly shorter forecastle, a much longer quarter deck, and extra space for boilers and engines. Freeboard was identical, but the Elswick ship looked much lower and appeared to trim by the bows, while the heavier funnels produced a more ponderous and majestic profile. As her sea-going displacement at load draught was 600 tons more than shown in the Navy List, at 29 ft. mean she was a good 6 in. lower in the water than as designed.

Although 100 ft. longer than the *Erin* her beam was only 7 in. more, the L/B ratio being 6·8 : 1.

Work ceased on both ships in August 1914, but the *Latorre* was purchased in September 1914 for completion, modified for British service and re-named *Canada*. The *Cochrane* remained on the stocks until taken over for conversion into an aircraft carrier and launched as H.M.S. *Eagle* in June 1918.

The principal structural changes included removal of the bridge and chart house and re-arrangement of the mast platforms for fire control: substitution of a single pole carrying a searchlight top for the twin stumps on the after superstructure; lowering of the funnels; replacing the two derrick posts athwart the fore funnel by a single larger stump abaft it; additions to the conning tower; and re-arrangement of the searchlights, etc.

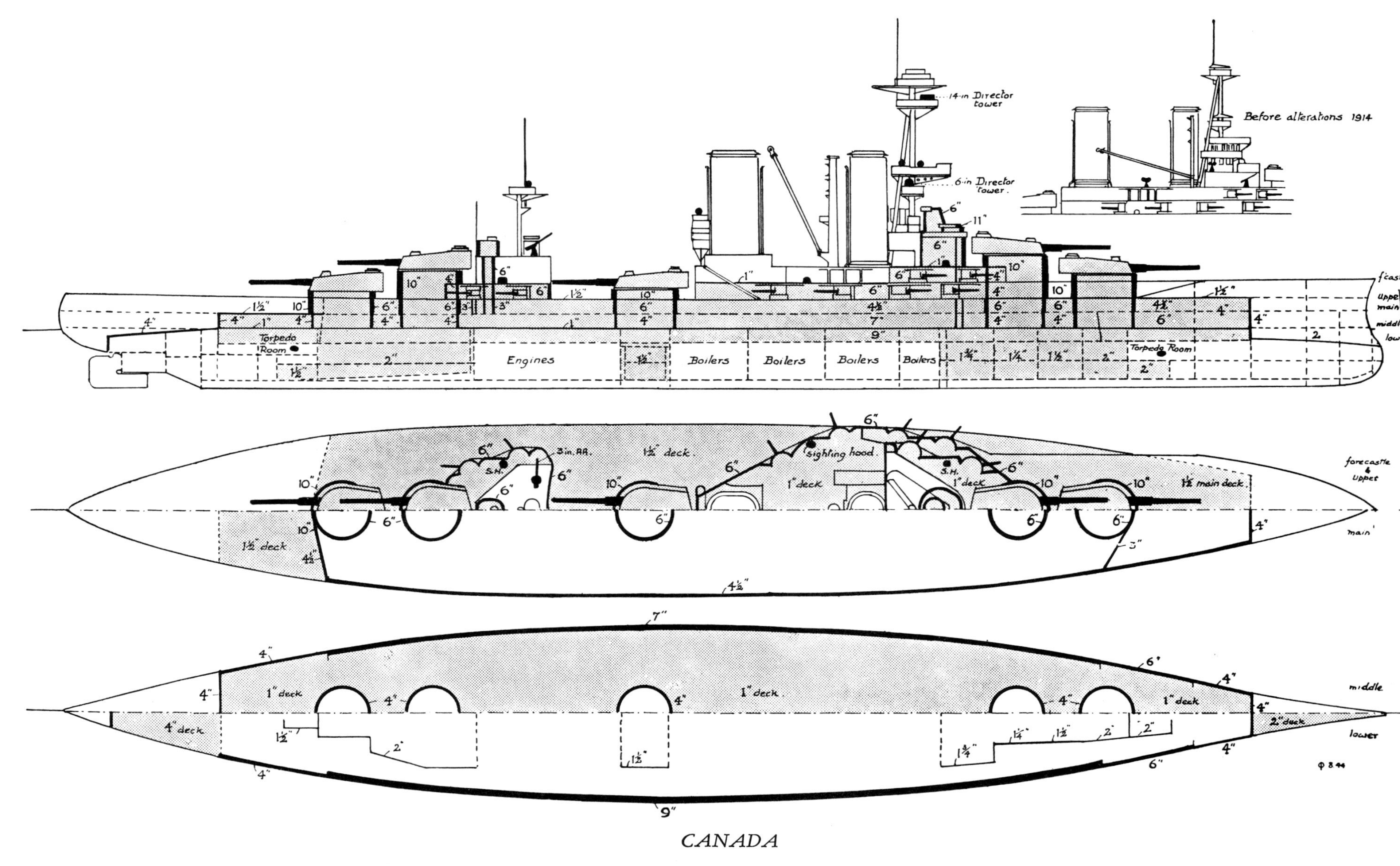

14-in Director tower
6-in Director tower
Before alterations 1914
Torpedo Room
Torpedo Room
Engines
Boilers
Boilers
Boilers
Boilers
f'castle
upper
main
middle
lower
sighting hood
3 in. AA.
S.H.
S.H.
1½" deck
1" deck
1" deck
1½" main deck
1½" deck
forecastle & upper
main
1" deck
1" deck
1" deck
4" deck
2" deck
middle
lower
φ 844

CANADA

ARMAMENT

The 14-in. gun weighed 85 tons and discharged a 1,400-lb. projectile with a m.v. of 2,700 f.s. penetrating 53·2 in. wrought iron at the muzzle. Normal rate of fire was two rounds a minute. There was little to choose between it and the 13·5-in. as mounted in the *King George V* which could discharge shells of the same weight and with a similar m.v.

It will be seen that the 6-in. battery was carried considerably further aft than in the *Iron Duke*, but the aftermost guns were removed and the ports plated-in during 1916 because of blast effects from "Q" turret. The shelter deck position was officially referred to as a casemate. A new type of Vickers gun-shield fitted in the *Canada* and *Erin* allowed for full elevation or depression at extreme angles of training, the wings of the side armour forming the gun recesses being semi-circular and provided with a port to take the gun at extreme angles.

PROTECTION

Of the belt armour, 16 ft. 6 in. was above and 4 in. below water at load draught, the 9-in. strake being submerged. Flotation thus depended upon 7-in. plating with only 4½ in. above it, so that the barbette bases were thicker than usual, the gradations in "B" and "X" being unique. Comparing the areas covered by side armour

Canada in 1917 with the aftermost 6-in. guns in the forward battery removed.

with the *Agincourt* plan will show the difference between the shorter belts and long angled bulkheads of that ship and the longer belts and short thin bulkheads in the *Canada*.

The magazine screens were thicker than in the *Agincourt* but without the series of 1-in. decks which were such a feature of that ship.

MACHINERY

An unusual combination of Brown-Curtis H.P. and Parsons L.P. turbines provided 37,000 s.h.p. for 22¾ knots—which was easily reached on trial. The *Canada's* fuel supply was the second heaviest in the fleet—1,150 instead of the usual 900 tons for battleships, but the maximum capacity of 3,820 coal and oil was 1,000 tons less than the *Iron Duke*. However, for North Sea operations this restriction in steaming radius was no great drawback.

GENERAL

Aeroplane runways fitted to "B" and "X" turrets in 1918.

"CANADA"

Built at Elswick December '11 to September '15 (launching weight 10,700 tons). Joined Grand Fleet October '15 and served in 4th B.S. at Jutland (no casualties). After the war was refitted at Devonport and transferred to the Chilean Navy as *Almirante Latorre*.

Chapter 107

"RENOWN" CLASS (EMERGENCY WAR PROGRAMME)

	Builders	*Laid down*	*Launched*	*Completed*
"*Renown*"	Fairfield Co.	25 Jan. '15	4 March '16	20 Sept. '16
"*Repulse*"	J. Brown and Co.	25 Jan. '15	8 Jan. '16	18 Aug. '16

Dimensions "*Renown*" 750′ (794′)×90′×25′ 8½″/27′ 6½″=26,500 tons.
"*Repulse*" 750′ (794′)×90′×25′ 4″/27′=26,500 tons.
"*Renown*" Load draught 27,947 tons; full load 32,727 tons.
"*Repulse*" Load draught 27,333 tons; full load 32,074 tons.
(Sinkage 103 tons per inch.)

Armament 6 15 in.
17 4-in. Mark IX B.L.
2 3-in. A.A.
4 3-pdrs.
Tubes:
2 21-in. (submerged).
10 torpedoes.

Protection Belt 6″-4″-3″-1½″; bulkheads 4″-3″.
Vertical plating 1½″ main and upper deck sides.
Barbettes 7″-5″-4″; turrets 11″-7″.
Conning tower 10″; tube 3″.
Decks: Forecastle 1½″-½″; upper ½″.
Main 3″-2″-1″; lower 2½″-2″-¾″; 3½″ over steering.

Machinery Brown-Curtis turbines by builders. 4 screws.
Boilers 42 Babcock and Wilcox.
S.H.P. 112,000 (n.d.)=30 knots.
120,000/126,000 (f.d.)=31·5/32·6 knots.

Fuel Oil 1,000/4,243 tons.

Complement 967.

Special features:

(1) Were a reversion to Fisher battle cruiser ideals.
(2) The fastest capital ships to date.
(3) Built in record time for their size.
(4) Mounted their 4-in. in triples.
(5) First to have bulges included in the hull structure proper.

Constructors Wm. Berry, E. L. Attwood.

At the outbreak of war in August 1914 work on the battleships of the 1914 Programme was held up in order to concentrate labour and material on such big ships as could be hastened to completion during hostilities—then anticipated at six months. But after the dramatic success of the two *Invincibles* at the Falkland Islands, Lord Fisher obtained Cabinet permission for the construction of two more ships of the type and gave orders for the *Renown* and *Repulse* to be re-designed as very fast battle cruisers.

It was Fisher's intention to employ them in the naval operations in connection with his Baltic Project, but what these were to entail he never divulged. So we can only regard the two ships as of "a special type for a special purpose" relying upon speed, power of manœuvre, and ability to get in the first blow.

Speed was to be of first importance and the design had to provide for 32 knots, an armament of 15-in. guns, and protection on the scale of the *Indefatigable*. They would thus represent the embodiment of Fisher's principles—able to catch and shoot down any enemy ship, while keeping out of range themselves. Von Spee's squadron had provided a target perfectly suited to his beloved *Invincibles*, and doubtless further opportunities of a like nature—or with even more formidable quarries—would be forthcoming to the ships he now visualized.

In the matter of guns, Fisher wanted 15-in. and as the D.N.C. put it "we had to cut our coat according to our cloth"—which was the number of guns and mountings available. Only six per ship could be managed—a number out of harmony with gunnery requirements of eight guns for salvo firing—and the design was drawn up accordingly.

As Palmers, who had contracted for one of the battleships, had no slip long enough for the new ships the construction of the *Repulse* was entrusted to Clydebank and the material collected at Palmers and Fairfields utilized as far as possible in the re-design. Instructions for this were given in December 1914, the general outline drawings being completed and approved of in ten days. Fisher insisted that the ships should be ready for sea in fifteen months—an abnormally short time for an entirely new type without any drawings prepared—so to obviate delay

RR

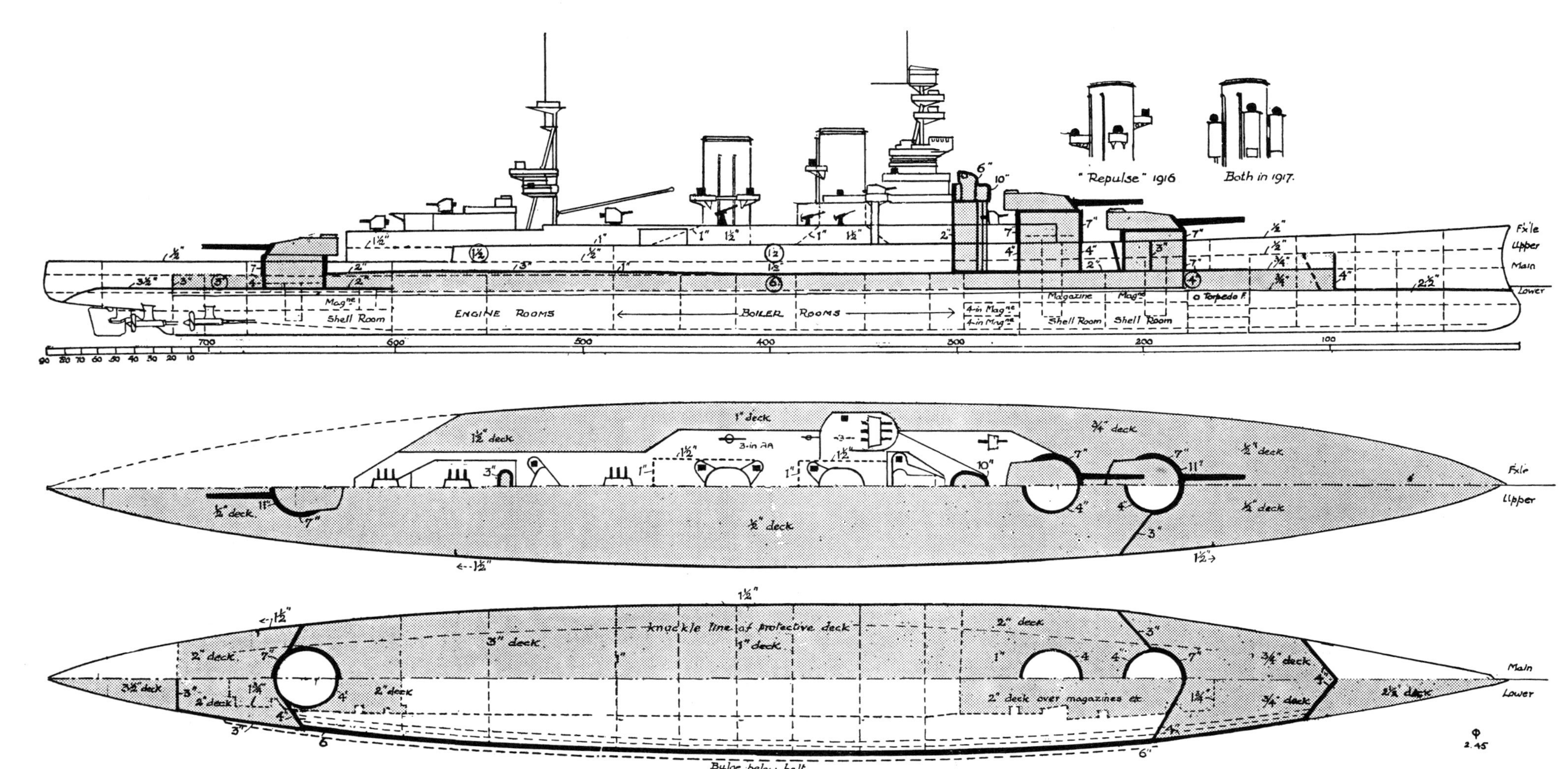

Renown as first commissioned with fore funnel raised. Insets show the arrangement of searchlights on the after funnel in *Repulse*, which was practically the only difference between them.

on the engineering side the *Tiger's* machinery was repeated with additional boilers. The *Tiger's* length had to be increased by 90 ft. to provide the necessary lines with a reduction of 6 in. in beam and 3 ft. in draught—the latter with an eye to their being able to operate in shallow waters. An extra margin of stability was provided to allow for subsequent modifications if required.

By 21 January 1915 the builders were supplied with sufficient information to allow them to get ahead with the structure, both keels being laid on 25 January (Fisher's birthday). Final drawings and specifications were approved in April. *Repulse* took the water in less than a year (15,156 tons) and ran her commissioning trials in August 1916: *Renown* lay three months longer on the slipway, but reached completion in September.

During their construction additional plating was worked in over the magazines (as shown in the plan) following the results of the Jutland action on 30 May.

That such ships could be built in a little over a year and a half from the first order to get out the design was a very remarkable achievement brought about by Fisher's driving power and the magnificent co-operation between the Constructor's Department and all the contractors concerned.

But upon joining the fleet at Scapa in September their reception was somewhat critical. Two long lines of scuttles proclaimed hulls devoid of armour, and armour in battle cruisers now not only meant "vision" but "survival" in a fleet action. Compared with the *Derfflinger* they were tin-cans, and although nothing could be done about side armour it was considered that their deck protection might be strengthened still further without much

Renown in 1917 when two rows of scuttles along her sides denoted absence of any armour.

difficulty. Proposals how this could be done were therefore made to the Admiralty, and approved; the work having been carried out at the fleet bases the two ships joined the B.C.F.—but very much as white elephants.

GENERAL DESIGN

Above decks they presented several novel features—the unusual bridgework and rig, searchlight platforms splayed out from the immense funnels (the fore funnel having been raised 10 ft. since first trials), and a well-considered disposition of the 4-in. guns to give a wide all-round concentration. There was majesty in the great hull, with a marked sheer forward and pronounced flare which moulded into the first plough bow since the old *Bellerophon*—an Elswick touch here—but any appreciation of fighting qualities was always tempered by the mute confession of those lines of scuttles.

The two ships could be distinguished by (1) the plating-in of the superstructure deck and (2) the searchlight gallery around the second funnel of *Renown*.

ARMAMENT

The forward pairs of guns ranged 35 ft. and 45 ft. above water, and the after pair 23 ft. in turrets with 7-in. sides, 11-in. fronts and 7-in. roofs. Elevation was 20°. Here the port plates (11-in.) were considerably thicker than in the *Invincible*, but the barbettes were almost the same 7-in., 5-in. (instead of 4-in.) and 3-in. Shell and ammunition stowage was 120 rounds per gun.

Lord Fisher and the D.N.O., Rear-Admiral Singer, were responsible for the return to 4-in. guns and their being mounted in triples. As such guns had not as yet been paired these triple mounts were years ahead of their time. On paper they provided quite a spectacular concentration of fire on all bearings but unfortunately the triple mounting was not a success. They made up a rather clumsy unit with separate breech mechanism instead of being in one sleeve, and required a crew of thirty-two men; the desired rate of fire was never achieved, and although retained in the *Repulse* right through her career, they were generally regarded as a mistake. Their centreline and wing disposition allowed for a concentration of thirteen abeam, eight ahead, and twelve astern.

The torpedo flat was forward of "A" barbette with single submerged tubes abeam. These were not a success. During her 1919 refit the *Repulse* received eight above-water tubes in twin mountings on the upper deck amidships.

AIRCRAFT

Flying-off platforms were fitted to "B" and "Y" turrets in 1917-18.

PROTECTION

As Lord Fisher wanted great speed as a complement to heavy armament at a time when his views on armour protection had not been confounded at Jutland, the *Indefatigable's* scale of plating was regarded as quite adequate.

It will be seen that the 4 in.-6 in.-3 in. belt only extended 2 ft. 2 in. below the water-line; above this the sides being of 1½-in. plating afforded strength with a certain amount of resistance of a negligible nature. The best that can be said for the defence in these ships was that the horizontal armour came up to standard after the decks had been twice strengthened over the magazines and shell rooms.

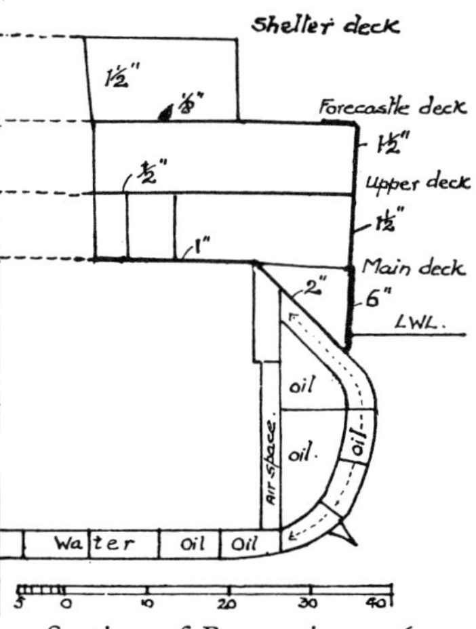

Section of *Renown* in 1916.

Forward of the 4-in. bulkhead a 2½-in. deck ran to the bows, with 3½ in. over the steering; the main curved protective deck was 1 in. on the flat and 2 in. on the slopes.

The outstanding feature of the defence was of course the "bulge," which unlike those fitted to the *Edgar* class and large monitors formed an integral part of the hull, replacing the anti-torpedo bulkhead in previous ships. The cross-section shows how it lay under the sloping part of the armour deck and consisted of an outer cellular skin covering a wide cushion of oil which was shut off from the hull compartments by a vertical cellular skin filled with air; the outer skin projected 3 feet beyond the belt, the hull side falling in so that a vertical from the edge of the forecastle deck cut the outer skin. The greatest width of the bulge was 14 feet.

The essential considerations in its design were to avoid much addition to the beam and to keep the protective structure external to the hull proper. Experiments showed what was later confirmed by war practice, that the gases resulting from a torpedo explosion were to a large extent vented in the air immediately above the bulge and did not penetrate to the interior of the ship. When bulges were hit by enemy torpedoes, some of the hits were near the top, some near the bottom, and some in the centre of the bulge, but in all cases adequate protection was given. These results applied to the *wide* bulges; to what extent the narrower *Repulse* type would have availed against 1914-18 marks of torpedoes was not ascertained as no ships thus bulged were hit.

MACHINERY

The four shaft turbines (Brown-Curtis) were in two sets, each with a H.P. ahead and astern on the wing shaft, and one L.P. ahead and astern in the same casing on the inner shaft.

Their forty-two Babcock and Wilcox large-tube boilers occupied five large rooms, with the uptakes protected by 1½-in. plating above the forecastle deck. They worked at 256 lb. pressure with 157,206 ft. of heating surface—the greatest installation to date. Had small-tube boilers been adopted the weight saved would nearly have allowed for a fourth 15-in. gun turret.

Fuel consumption at full speed worked out at about 1,400 tons a day.

SPEED

No full results of steaming trials are available, but at deep load *Repulse* reached 31·5 knots with s.h.p. 119,025 on the Skelmorlie mile; *Renown* at normal draught averaged 32·68 with s.h.p. 126,300.

Fantastic service speeds were claimed for both ships quite inconsistent with their official credit of 31·5 knots with s.h.p. 112,000, but they were good for 32 knots in service. At over 25 knots vibration became severe, and the quarter deck was flooded at full speed.

With a G.M. of only 3½ feet they were good seaboats and steady gun-platforms.

GENERAL

Renown's firing trials strained her hull considerably and after first commissioning constant recourse to dockyard hands earned her and her sister the nicknames of "Refit" and "Repair."

During the post-war period millions were spent in trying to make them battle-worthy by adding to their protection, and various drastic alterations were effected, the *Renown* being at last completely rebuilt. Their differences became so marked that from now on separate descriptions are necessary.

REPULSE

In the course of her 1919-20 refit (£860,684) deficiencies in the matter of vertical plating were as far as possible made good by the substitution of 9-in. armour in place of the 6-in. belt along the water-line with the addition of a strake of 6 in. along the main deck above this, together with the appropriate end bulkheads. The protuberance of the bulge limited armour depth below the LWL, and as the additional weight of some 1,600 tons increased the draught by 16 in. the underwater protection was about 2 ft. deep only.

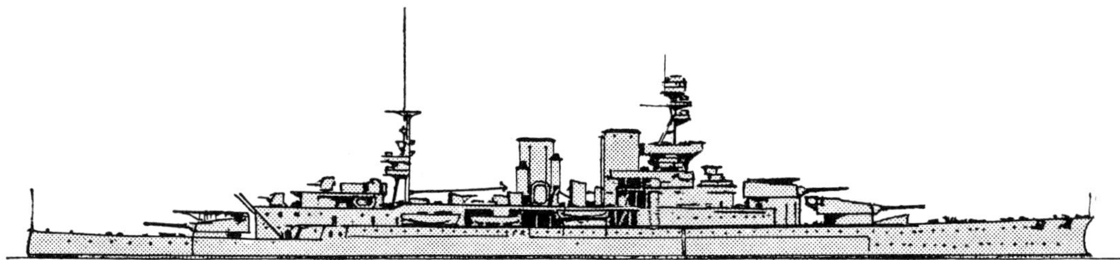

Repulse after her '19-'20 refit showing additional side armour and searchlight towers, and extensions to bridgework.

The two 4-in. B.L. singles were replaced by 3-in. H.A. guns making four in all, and eight 21-in. torpedo tubes added on the forecastle deck in pairs.

On the Skelmorlie mile after this refit the *Repulse* made just on 30 knots which was well in excess of capital ship speeds abroad.

BIG REFIT 1934-36

The life of our capital ships having been limited by the Washington Treaty to twenty-seven years—during which they were to undergo two large repair periods—the eighteen-year-old *Repulse* was docked at Portsmouth in 1934 for her second overhaul, with such modernization of equipment as could be contrived under the financial

Photo:—Richard Perkins, Esq.

Repulse in 1939 with additional A.A. gun sponsons, hangars and aircraft handling cranes, upper control top, etc. Note the twin torpedo tubes beneath the crane and after turret.

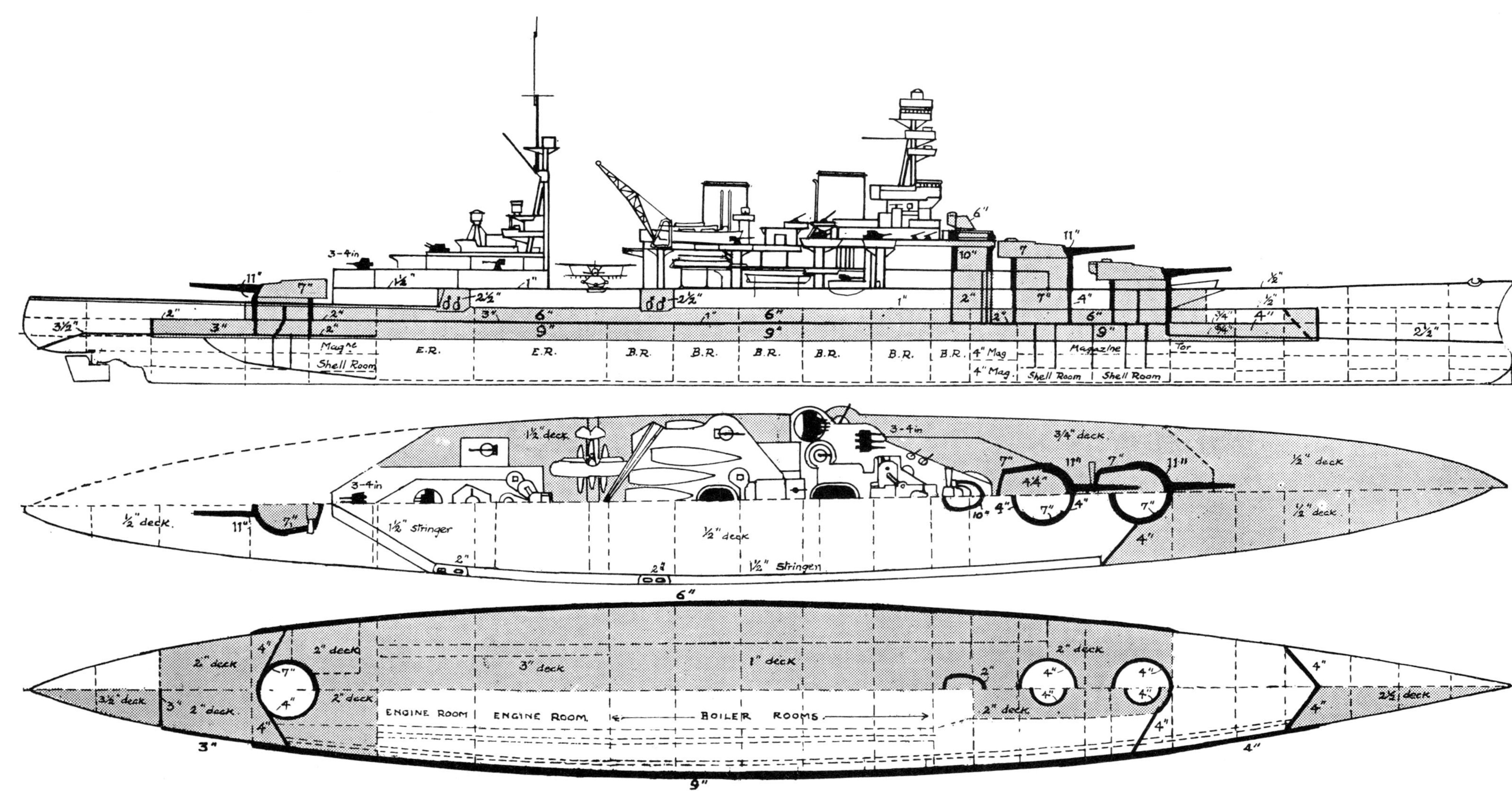

Repulse as refitted '34-'36, with hangars, aircraft, additional A.A. guns, and boats stowed around second funnel. An upper 6-in. belt has been added, and the water-line belt increased to 9 in.

stringency of the period. This included a hangar and an amidships cross-deck catapult in place of the flying-off platform on "X" turret; a considerable increase in the A.A. armament; and an imposing build-up of the superstructure to accommodate new gun sites and provide boat stowage.

Our meagre carrier force made it necessary for individual fighting ships to carry their own reconnaissance and spotting aircraft, and in the case of larger vessels, hangar stowage for four planes was being provided whenever possible, their wings being hinged and folded back to save space.

ARMAMENT

No alterations were made to the 15-in. gun installations, but the control arrangements were improved and an extra station fitted to the foremast head. Although four of the new eight-barrel pom-poms were to have been provided for each capital ship, only two could be allotted to the *Repulse* and these were sponsoned abreast the fore funnel. Here also, at a higher level, were placed a couple of the new 4-barrel 2-pdr. A.A. guns. The 4-in. H.A. were also sponsoned amidships and a couple added aft on the shelter deck—replaced in September 1936 by paired guns in small turrets.

As in the case of the *Malaya* all these additions and alterations were effected without any corresponding surrender of material as an offset, so that there was some loss of stability which had to be accepted as inevitable.

In December 1940 an inspection report stated that in a headwind suction of the funnel gases into the after part of the bridge where the torpedo, searchlight, and starshell control positions were situated was clearly noticeable, and that the question of fitting a cowl on the foremost funnel or lengthening it would have to be considered before any more extensions were made to the bridgework. A cowl to the funnel was approved in July 1941 but whether it was fitted or not cannot be determined.

She was also to be supplied with radar 282 (3 sets), 284 (1 set) and 285 (3 sets) of which 284 was fitted on the 15-in. Director forward; there is no record that she ever received the other sets, and this is significant as 282 and 285 sets much improved A.A. gunfire.

An armament refit in the U.S.A. was proposed in September 1941 to include substitution of fourteen 4-in./Mk. 16 on twin mountings for the triples.

"REPULSE"

Built at Clydebank January '15-August '16 (19 months). Joined Grand Fleet 1st B.C.S. until '19. In action November '17 with German light cruisers. Refit '19-'22. Atlantic Fleet B.C.S. '22-'32. In '22 visited Rio de Janeiro with *Hood* for the Centenary Celebrations in Brazil. Left Portsmouth in November '23 on a world cruise, visiting South Africa, Malaya, Australia, New Zealand, and then across the Pacific to Canada and the West Indies. Returned home in September '24. During '25 she took H.R.H. the Prince of Wales to visit South Africa and South America. From '26-'32 in Home waters. Big refit until '36. Mediterranean '36-'38 returning to U.K. in August. September '39 escorted Atlantic convoys against surface raiders. In December escorted the first Canadian troop convoy. During April '40 operating in Norwegian waters, and escorted the damaged *Suffolk* from Stavangar to Scapa. November '40 covered a raid on Jan Mayen Island, when a German scientific expedition was captured and the wireless transmission station destroyed. During December was covering minelayers laying a minefield off south-east coast of Iceland. Arrived Capetown October '41 and transferred to East Indies station to join Force "G" and proceeded to Colombo arriving 22 November. On 8 December left Singapore with *Prince of Wales* and four destroyers to attack an enemy force off Kota Bharu. Two days later off Kuantan they were attacked by 9 aircraft and *Repulse* was hit and a fire started. Thirty minutes later attacked by a wave of 9 torpedo planes and high level bombers. During a third attack was bombed amidships and steering gear jammed. Soon afterwards was torpedoed and began to list heavily, sinking six minutes later.

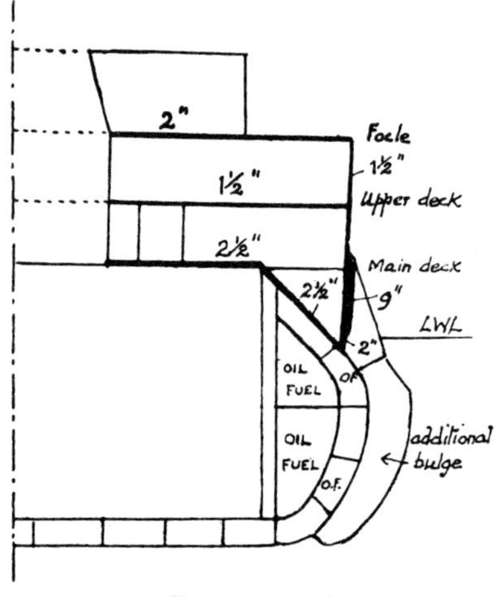

Renown 1926.

RENOWN

REFIT 1923-26 £979,927

Despite the increase in the vote for the *Renown's* refit compared with that of the *Repulse*, rising costs precluded any similar rearmouring and instead she was given extra protection against torpedoes instead of against shell fire, major alterations being confined to the fitting of additional bulges, and externally to winged sponsons for the multiple pom-poms and some extra bridgework with a big mast-head control top. A catapult was installed on the former boat deck amidships in 1933, with a single seaplane. This replaced a triple 4-in. mounting.

REFIT 1936-39 £3,088,008

As a battle cruiser the *Renown* had always been very much sub-standard in the matter of vertical protection, her preponderance having been on the side of gun-power and speed, and when reconstructed there could be no question of modifying this balance. The battle cruiser *per se* could no longer expect to carry out her classical duties, as from the nature of the fleets of England and Germany it was pretty obvious that the day of the line-of-battle had passed. In the hostilities which loomed more clearly each year the *Renown* as a heavy-weight commerce protector would have to rely upon speed, A.A. defence, and ability to withstand torpedo attack. Her outstanding requirements were therefore (*a*) a heavy dual-purpose battery to replace the obsolete triple 4-in. guns, (*b*) thicker deck armour over her magazines and machinery spaces, and (*c*) better protection against torpedoes.

When she steamed out of Portsmouth in June 1939 her "refit" represented only £30,000 less than her prime cost, but an out-of-date and very vulnerable ship had been given the teeth to defend herself from air attack, and by the then standards was well equipped to withstand it.

As with the *Queen Elizabeth* and *Valiant* the reconstruction hinged upon the weight saved by installing new machinery and high pressure small tube boilers, and amounted to a complete rebuilding from the bare hull.

Renown after her '23-'26 refit with additional bulge, mast head control top and bridgework, and catapult between funnel and mainmast.

Item	*Estimated legend as bulged* (1923-26)	*Light condition as reconstructed* (1936-39)	*Weight added or removed*
General equipment	800 tons	700 tons	— 100 tons
Machinery	5,890 ,,	3,200 ,,	—2,690 ,,
Armament	3,400 ,,	4,729 ,,	+1,329 ,,
Armour, protection and hull	21,430 ,,	21,396 ,,	— 34 ,,
Total	31,520 tons	30,025 tons	—1,495 tons

ARMAMENT

Elevation of the 15-in. guns was increased to 30° and the turret faces altered accordingly as in the *Queen Elizabeth*. Control was from two director towers with long base R/F, and later radar type 284 was added to the forward tower largely superseding the R/F for ranging and gunnery control.

A new secondary armament of twenty 4·5-in. were disposed in four groups ("four corner system") each controlled by a separate director with R/F height finder. Radar type 285 was added to all these in 1941. The mountings were similar to those in the *Queen Elizabeth*, the small turrets having gas-tight armoured crowns.

Three 8-barrel 2-pdrs. were fitted in 1939 and a 4-barrel 2-pdr. added in 1944 to the crown of "B" turret with twenty twin and twenty-four single Oerlikons. After 1942 a number of 20-mm. guns were mounted abeam lower bridge platforms and on hangars, and in 1945 40-mm. guns replaced some of the close-range armament.

Eight torpedo tubes in four pairs were placed along the upper deck. (Although 21-in. tubes were proposed in 1937, all records mention 18-in. Mk. XI torpedoes.)

PROTECTION

Additional 3-in. to 4-in. armour was fitted over the magazines, boiler, and turbine rooms, with 2½ in. over the steering gear. This was as much as could be worked in on the displacement and would have sufficed against bombing on the 1939 scale.

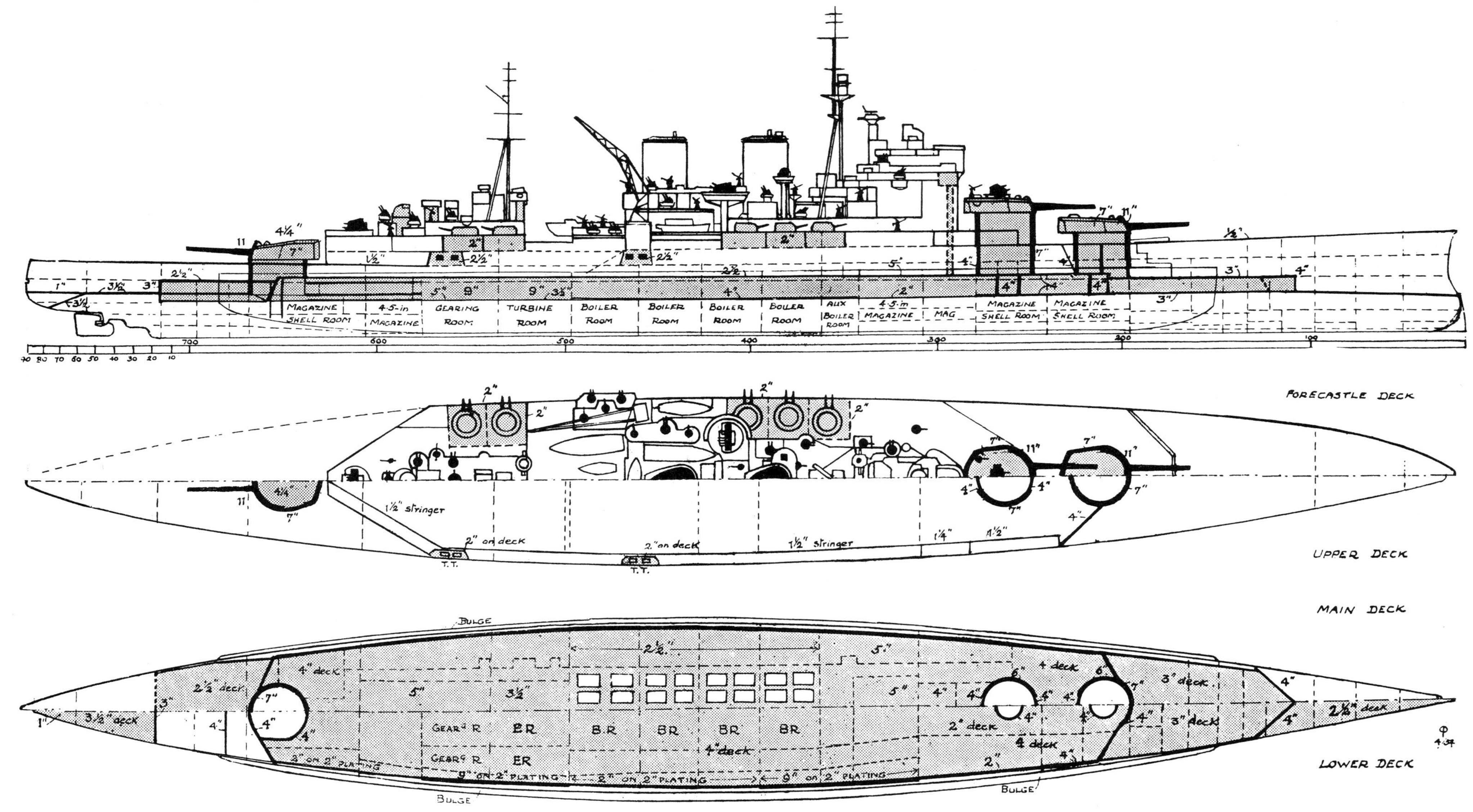

Renown after '36-'39 reconstruction with new bridgework, 4·5-in. gun turrets, hangars and aircraft handling cranes (the catapult was subsequently removed and the space utilized for boat stowage and additional A.A. guns), light tripod rig, etc. A pole mainmast as fitted was found to be too light for the radar and stiffened by struts. Additional lower deck and middle deck armour.

MACHINERY

Parsons geared turbines were supplied by Cammell Lairds, and eight Admiralty 3-drum boilers replaced the former forty-two Babcock and Wilcox. The machinery spaces were well separated from the hull sides, with the bulkheads over 26 ft. from the outer bulge casing, which should have rendered her reasonably torpedo proof. The saving in weight from new machinery and boilers was 2,690 tons, and her legend speed 29 knots with 130,000 S.H.P.

GENERAL

It will be seen that the fore and after shelter decks were built out flush to the ship's sides for siting the four groups of small turrets, with the usual provision of large hangars around the second funnel and a cross-deck

Photo:—Flight-Lt. P. A. Vicary

RENOWN

catapult. Modified tower bridgework was moved forward to just abaft "B" turret and well spaced from the stream-lined funnels so that there was none of the suction and smoke trouble experienced in *Repulse*. A light tripod forward was soon laden with radar lantern and aerials, and the pole mast aft was later given struts.

"RENOWN"

Built at Fairfields January '15-September '16 (20 months). Joined the Grand Fleet in September '16, and served in 1st B.C.S. until 1919. Conveyed H.R.H. the Prince of Wales in his tour to U.S.A. and Australasia '20-'21, and to India and Japan '21-'22. Underwent long refit '23-'26 prior to joining B.C.S. Atlantic Fleet. Conveyed H.R.H. the Duke of York to Australia '27. B.C.S. '28-'36. Refit '36-'39. Home Fleet '39. Vice-Admiral B.C.S. March-August '40. (8 April '40 in action with *Scharnhorst* and *Admiral Hipper* off Narvik at 18,000 yards steaming at 24 knots in very bad weather. Spray interfered with shooting, but hits observed. Enemy using after guns hit *Renown* twice, and drew out of range. August '40 Vice-Admiral, Force "H" Gibraltar. In November running action in company with 4 *Southampton* class for 90 minutes, defending convoy to Alexandria. February '41 Bombardment of Genoa. August '41 returned home as Vice-Admiral Home Fleet. April '42 Commodore-in-Command Force "W" when U.S.S. *Wasp* ferried aircraft to Malta. Returned to Home Fleet. October '42 joined Force "H" again to cover landings at Algiers. Based on Gibraltar until February '43. Refit five months at Rosyth. August '43 embarked Prime Minister and party at Halifax, Nova Scotia for passage to Scotland at 23½ knots through much fog. November '43 embarked Prime Minister, First Sea Lord, and party for passage to Alexandria. Returned to Rosyth. 27 December '43 Flagship Vice-Admiral Sir Arthur J. Power, Second-in-Command, Eastern Fleet, consisting of *Queen Elizabeth, Valiant, Illustrious, Unicorn*, frigates and destroyers. February-April working up at Singapore. May '44 4,000-mile voyage to Exmouth Bay, Australia for attack on Japanese base at Surabaya. Bombardment of Sebang with *Queen Elizabeth, Valiant* and *Richelieu*, cruisers and destroyers. August Bombardment of Car Nicobar. In November fleet divided and *Renown* and *Queen Elizabeth* remaining at Trincomalee with Eastern Indies Fleet. December sailed for refit at Durban returning to Trincomalee in March. Returned home with dispatch 30 March '45 to meet German capital ships, arriving at Scapa 14 April (7,642 miles in 306 steaming hours) and prepared to hoist the flag of C.-in-C., Home Fleet, but *Tirpitz* being out-of-action by R.A.F. bombing, *Renown* proceeded to Portsmouth and reduced to two-fifth complement. Finished up as part of the *Imperieuse* establishment at Devonport.

Sold: 1948.

Chapter 108

"COURAGEOUS," "GLORIOUS" AND "FURIOUS"

CONTEMPORANEOUSLY with the *Renown* and *Repulse* three extraordinary vessels were laid down as part of the huge fleet intended to carry through Lord Fisher's Baltic Project. As credits could not be obtained for any more large armoured ships Fisher described them as "large light cruisers"—a clever contradiction in terms successful in getting Treasury sanction, which would otherwise have been withheld had their true nature been divulged. But as additional light cruisers had already been approved, the *Courageous*, *Glorious* and *Furious* were put in hand and built under conditions of almost theatrical secrecy. The Board's—or rather, the First Sea Lord's—requirements were for very large cruisers mounting a few guns of the largest calibre, thin light cruiser protection, a speed of not less than 32 knots, and draught restricted to 22 feet—or 5 feet less than any capital ship—to enable them to operate in shallow Baltic waters non-navigable to other big-gunned ships. In Fisher's words "The *Furious* and all her breed were not built for salvoes. They were built for Berlin, and that's why they drew so little water and were built so fragile . . . their guns with their enormous shells were built to make it impossible for the Germans to prevent the Russians from landing on the Pomeranian Coast" and this was to be effected by these shells "bursting on reaching the ground far out of human sight, but yet with exact accuracy as to where they should fall, causing in their explosion craters somewhat like that of Vesuvius or Mount Etna; and consequently you can easily imagine the German Army fleeing for its life from Pomerania to Berlin."

For years Fisher had planned in the event of war to take an opening offensive against Germany by a landing on the Pomeranian shore 82 miles from Berlin, either by a British force or a Russian army, in conjunction with covering operations off the Frisian coast and extensive mining of the Sound and Felimern Belt, with flotillas of submarines working in the Baltic. To this end he placed contracts for 612 special vessels ranging from the *Furious*, large and small monitors, light cruisers, destroyers, minesweepers, and minelayers down to landing craft. The Germans feared such a landing and expected it to be attempted, and so grudged the transfer of battleships from the North Sea to Prince Henry's Baltic squadron; and that they expected such a landing may be taken as a measure of its being a practicable operation. Under Fisher's direction it might have succeeded; as a military operation planned on the Dardanelles level it would have failed. As it was, when Fisher left the Admiralty nothing more was heard of it.

But it was the Baltic armada, designed and built at a speed never before attempted, which provided all the special craft needed for the Dardanelles Campaign and initial reinforcements for the Grand Fleet. And if the *Furious* trio were looked on askance in the Grand Fleet it was because they were asked to fill a role for which they were not designed, in waters other than those in which they were specifically intended to operate. (That is how the ships themselves would have it.)

As "large light cruisers" they could have been omitted from this review; but in the official lists they were classed as "battle cruisers" and as such have a claim to recognition, although so deficient in the armour protection necessary for the efficient performance of battle cruiser duties. Among the ships of the Dreadnought era the trio stood unique. In the past they had their prototypes in the *Italia* and *Lepanto*, and to some extent in the Japanese *Matsushima* and *Hashidate* class (1890) whose single 12·6-in. Canet gun caused a certain moral effect in the Chinese and Russian wars, but no material damage to enemy ships. In close action the Japanese ships could have scored hits; at long range the four 15-in. could not and did not start hitting with the accuracy Fisher had imagined. As for the 18-in. pieces, the less said the better about their chances of securing a hit. Against land targets they would have been far better mounted in monitors, although when transferred to the *General Wolfe* and *Lord Clive* in 1918 there was no question of any "exact accuracy" when employed on long-range bombardment.

Exposing the largest tin-clad targets afloat, they presented a most vulnerable hull to 6-in. gunfire, and on the one occasion when they came into action with German light cruisers, received more damage than they inflicted.

Two "COURAGEOUS" Class (Emergency War Programme)

	Builders	*Laid down*	*Launched*	*Completed*
"*Courageous*"	Elswick	Mar. '15	5 Feb. '16	Jan. '17
"*Glorious*"	Harland and Wolff	May '15	20 April '16	Jan. '17

Dimensions 735′ (786′) × 81′ × 23·4′ = 18,600 tons.
Load draught 19,320 tons. Full load 22,690 tons.
(Sinkage 89 tons per inch.)

Armament
4 15-in.
18 4-in.
2 3-in. H.A.

Tubes:
2 21-in. singles.
(6 21-in. twins fitted later.)

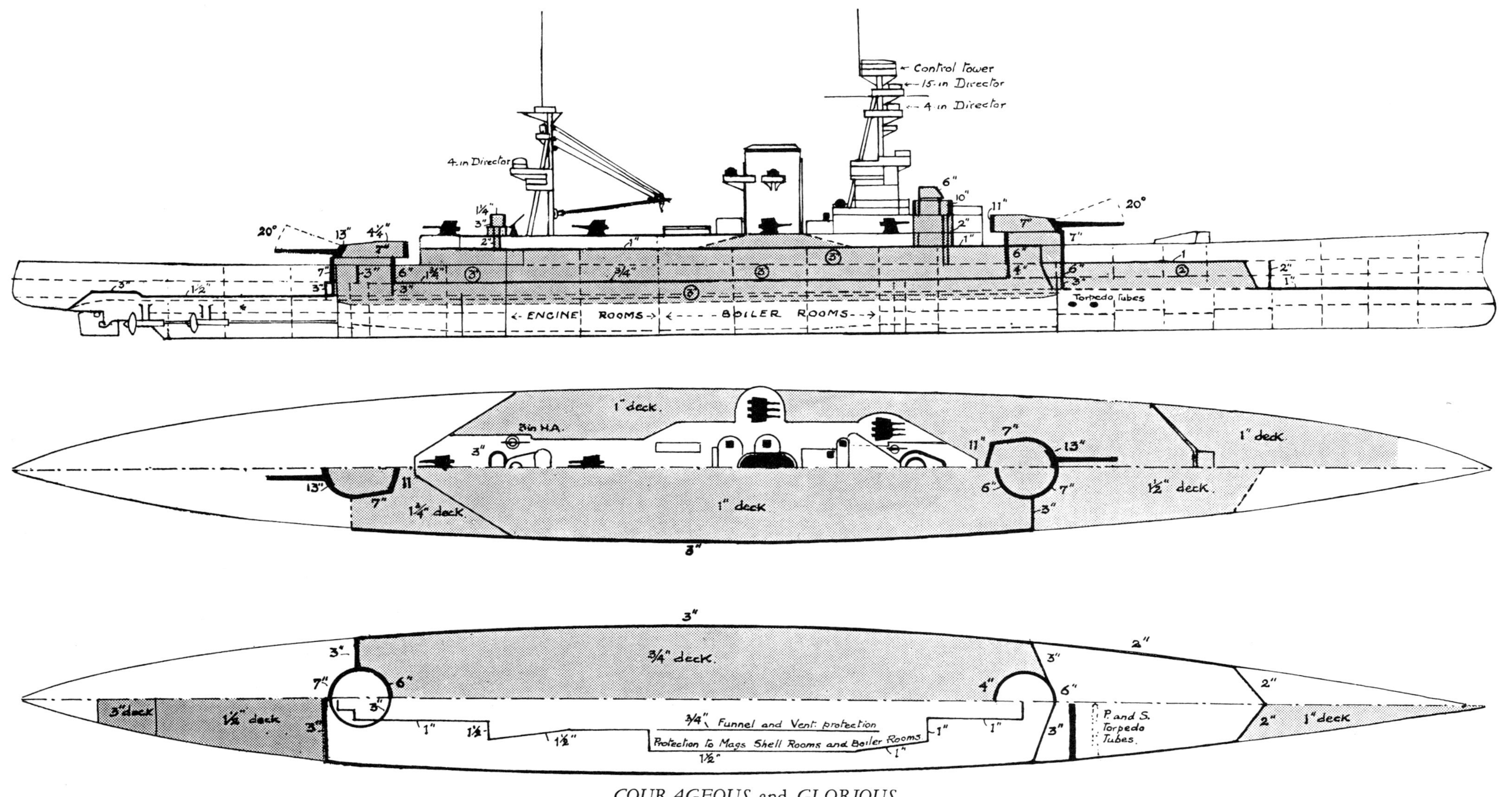

COURAGEOUS and *GLORIOUS*

Protection Belt 3″-2″; bulkheads 3″-2″.
Barbettes 7″-3″; turrets 13″-11″-7″-4½″.
Conning tower 10″.
Decks: Forecastle 1″; upper 1″; main 1¾″-¾″ (between barbettes).
Lower 1½″-3″ over steering.

Machinery Parsons all-geared-turbines. 4 screws.
S.H.P. 90,000=31-32 knots. 340 revs.
Boilers 18 Yarrow small tube.

Fuel Oil 750/3,160 tons.

Complement 829-842.

Constructor S. V. Goodall.

Special features:

(1) Carried the heaviest guns ever mounted in a light cruiser hull.
(2) Secondary guns in triple mounts.
(3) The fastest cruisers afloat in their day.
(4) First big ships with all-geared turbines.

It was intended that these ships should be finished in twelve months, but although commissioned in October 1916 they could not be accepted as completed until January 1917—which is their official date for completion. During her acceptance trials *Courageous* when running at full speed met very heavy weather and in a head sea showed signs of strain at the fore side of the forward turret where there is an inevitable discontinuity of longitudinal strength, which necessitated the addition of doubling plates. The *Glorious* after a year's service was similarly treated although showing no signs of weakness.

It will be noted that the load displacement was 720 tons in excess of the Navy List figures.

ARMAMENT

The barbettes and turrets were similar to those in the *Repulse*, the guns having 20° elevation and could be fired to 60° abaft the beam.

There was the same disposition of triple 4-in. guns but with additional sets abreast the funnel and no single guns. As already noted the mounting was not a success.

The original torpedo equipment consisted of single submerged tubes before the fore barbette bulkhead, but these could not be discharged at above 23 knots as the bars bent. In 1917 they received two pairs of above-water tubes on the upper deck abreast the main mast and four twin deck tubes around the after turret, making fourteen tubes in all. *Courageous* also served as a minelayer, her quarter deck being known as "Clapham Junction" from the four sets of rails which discharged over the quarters.

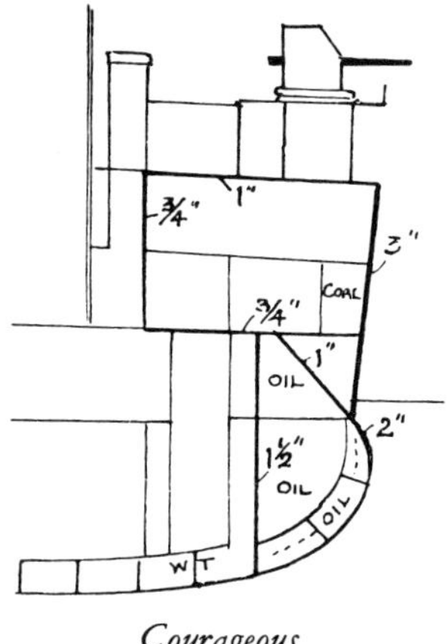

Courageous

PROTECTION

Being merely enlarged light cruisers there could be no question of anything beyond 2-in. plating over a 1-in. shell between the turrets, with 1½ in.-¾ in. on the decks except over the steering where it was 3 in. The little conning tower was 10 in. with a 6-in. hood, and 3 in. on the control position aft. Horizontal plating over the magazines was strengthened after Jutland.

The bulges were similar to those in *Renown* but shaped to allow for the reduced draught.

MACHINERY

Hitherto the installation of small tube boilers had been limited to light cruisers and destroyers, although the Constructor's Department had been pressing for their adoption in capital ships. Now came the opportunity of trying them out in a large hull as these large light cruisers were to be equipped along cruiser lines. To save time the machinery of the 3,750-ton *Champion* was duplicated, with four shafts instead of two for the double helical geared turbines and eighteen Yarrow boilers in place of eight, for 90,000 S.H.P. It may be noted that the *Renowns* needed forty-two large tube boilers for their nominal 110,000-120,000 S.H.P.

Both vessels exceeded 32 knots on service and it was claimed that they were 1½ knots faster at deep load than at legend draught.

GENERAL

When the *Renowns* joined the Grand Fleet their low standard of protection raised a nice problem as to how they could be profitably employed; in the case of the *Courageous* and *Glorious* it was simply a question of making the best use of a couple of white elephants. They formed the 1st Cruiser Squadron when the former cruiser squadrons had been so depleted at Jutland, and for a time *Courageous* was employed as a minelayer.

At first they could easily be distinguished by the position of the searchlights on the funnel which were on one level in *Courageous* and on two levels in *Glorious*. When these projectors were placed in towers the ships were identical.

In 1918 aeroplane runways were fitted to each turret. Both were converted into carriers in 1924.

"COURAGEOUS"

Built at Armstrong-Whitworth's Elswick yard May '15 to January '17. Served in 3rd L.C.S. and 1st C.S. Grand Fleet until '18 (in action with enemy light forces 27 November '17; sustained damage and casualties). Gunnery school at Portsmouth and later Flagship of Reserve. Conversion to aircraft carrier June '24-March '28. Cost £2,025,800. Sunk 17 September '39 by German submarine.

"GLORIOUS"

Built at Belfast March '15-January '17. Flagship 3rd L.C.S. and 1st C.S. Grand Fleet (in action with enemy light forces 27 November '17). Gunnery school ship Devonport '19 and later Flagship of Reserve. Conversion to aircraft carrier February '24 at Rosyth and towed to Devonport for completion January '30. Sunk off Narvik by *Scharnhorst* and *Gneisenau* 8 June '40.

Glorious on joining the Grand Fleet. Note the searchlight platforms on the funnel are at two different levels; in *Courageous* on same level.

"FURIOUS" (Emergency War Programme)

Builder	*Laid down*	*Launched*	*Completed*
Elswick	June '15	15 Aug. '16	July '17

Dimensions 750′ (786½′) × 88′ × 19¾′/24′ = 19,513 tons.
(N.L. tonnage 19,100. Deep load 22,890 tons.)

Armament 2 18-in. as designed; one as completed.
11 5·5-in.
2 3-in. H.A.
4 3-pdrs.

Torpedo tubes:
4 above water 21-in.
2 submerged 21-in.
(18 carried on completion.)

Protection Sides 2″-3″ armour over 1″ plating.
Bulkheads 2″-3″.
Barbettes 7″-4″. Turrets: 13″ faces; 11″ rears; 7″-4½″ sides.
Conning tower 10″; after 3″.
Decks: Forecastle 1″; upper 1″; main 1¾″-¾″ (between barbettes).
Lower 1½″; 3″ over steering.

Machinery Brown-Curtis geared turbines. 4 screws.
S.H.P. 94,000 = 31½ knots.
Boilers 18 Yarrow small tube.

Fuel Oil 750/3,160 tons.
Complement 880 (as a carrier).
Special features:

(1) Carried the heaviest guns in the world.
(2) The first warship to be converted into a carrier.

As originally designed she was to have been a sister to the *Courageous* and *Glorious*, but with a single 18-in. gun fore and aft and a slightly modified form of hull framing and structure; in fact, within certain restrictions, she was probably the ideal "Fisher" fighting ship, possessing guns of the maximum range and smashing power in conjunction with high speed, enabling her nominally to choose her own range and tactics. That she might not be fighting with maximum visibility, and that two-gun salvoes were not conducive to rapid ranging at sea, were considerations which could be disregarded. She was intended to bombard German shore forces, and there was no-one in a position to press the futility of employing such a ship for such service.

Fisher wanted her built in twelve months, but the spectacular construction of the *Dreadnought* with guns and mountings snatched from other ships and stocks of material accumulated before her keel was laid, could not be repeated, and it was two years before she was ready for commissioning. By that time the Baltic project for which she was built had passed into oblivion, and while completing the necessity for fast aeroplane carriers became obvious and it was decided that the *Furious* should be modified for this purpose. This entailed doing away with the fore turret and in its place a large hangar able to house ten machines was built along the forecastle deck with a flying-off platform 160 ft. long on its roof. In this hybrid state she joined the *Courageous* and *Glorious* in the 1st Cruiser Squadron, but for a short time only. The big gun was simply an encumbrance and in November 1917 she was back in the builders' hands to have the after turret removed and a hangar fitted in its place with a flight deck 300 ft. long extending from that forward to within some 75 ft. of the stern. In this guise she became a carrier pure and simple, subject to troublesome eddies caused by the funnel and bridgework which also curtailed landing space, so that in 1921 she was taken in hand for complete reconstruction and became a successful carrier performing invaluable service in World War Two.

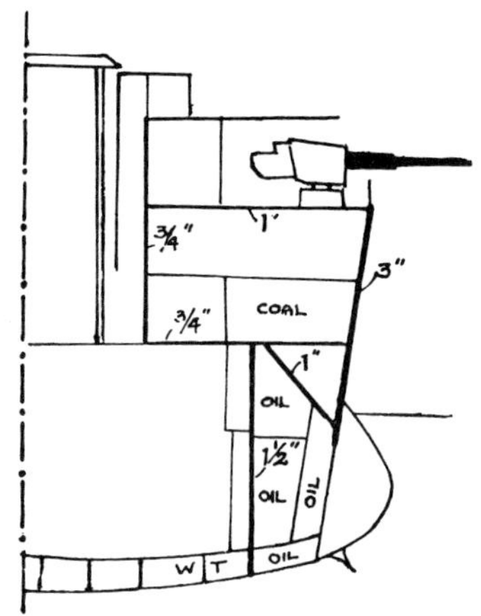

Cross section of *Furious* amidships showing variation in bulge and sub-division.

HULL

Was similar to that of the *Courageous*, but with a different form of midship section having a more pronounced bulge and a simpler form of main framing and structure.

ARMAMENT

The 18-in. gun weighed about 150 tons and fired a shell of 3,600 lb. In 1918 two spares were mounted aft in the monitors *Lord Clive* and *General Wolff* for bombarding the German bases inland from the Belgian coast, but hostilities ceased before they could be properly employed. Both guns were afterwards taken to Singapore. The design permitted for their replacement by twin 15-in. if required.

Single 5·5-in. replaced the triple 4-in. in the other two ships, the original eleven guns being spares provided for the cruisers *Birkenhead* and *Chester*. They weighed 6 tons 4 cwt. and fired an 82 lb. projectile with an m.v. 2,950 f.s. and m.e. 4,520 f.t.

The torpedo armament was heavy, with four sets of triple tubes on the upper deck aft and one pair each side on the upper deck forward.

PROTECTION AND MACHINERY

Was similar to that in the other two ships.

GENERAL

A trolley-and-rail method of launching seaplanes was employed, the seaplane resting on a trolley which ran down a slotted rail fixed to the deck. On reaching the end of the deck, the trolley was arrested by two arms fitted with shock absorbers. This method got over the difficulty of flight when it would not have been possible to get a seaplane off the water.

The first landing was made by Squadron Commander E. H. Dunning, D.S.C., in a Sopwith Pup in August 1917. With the ship steaming head to wind, the pilot flew past as close as possible, drifted round the bridge, and arrived over the forward flying deck. Here he throttled down and allowed his machine to sink to the deck where, as there was no sort of gear to hold her down it was grabbed by a party of officers and men while it was still in

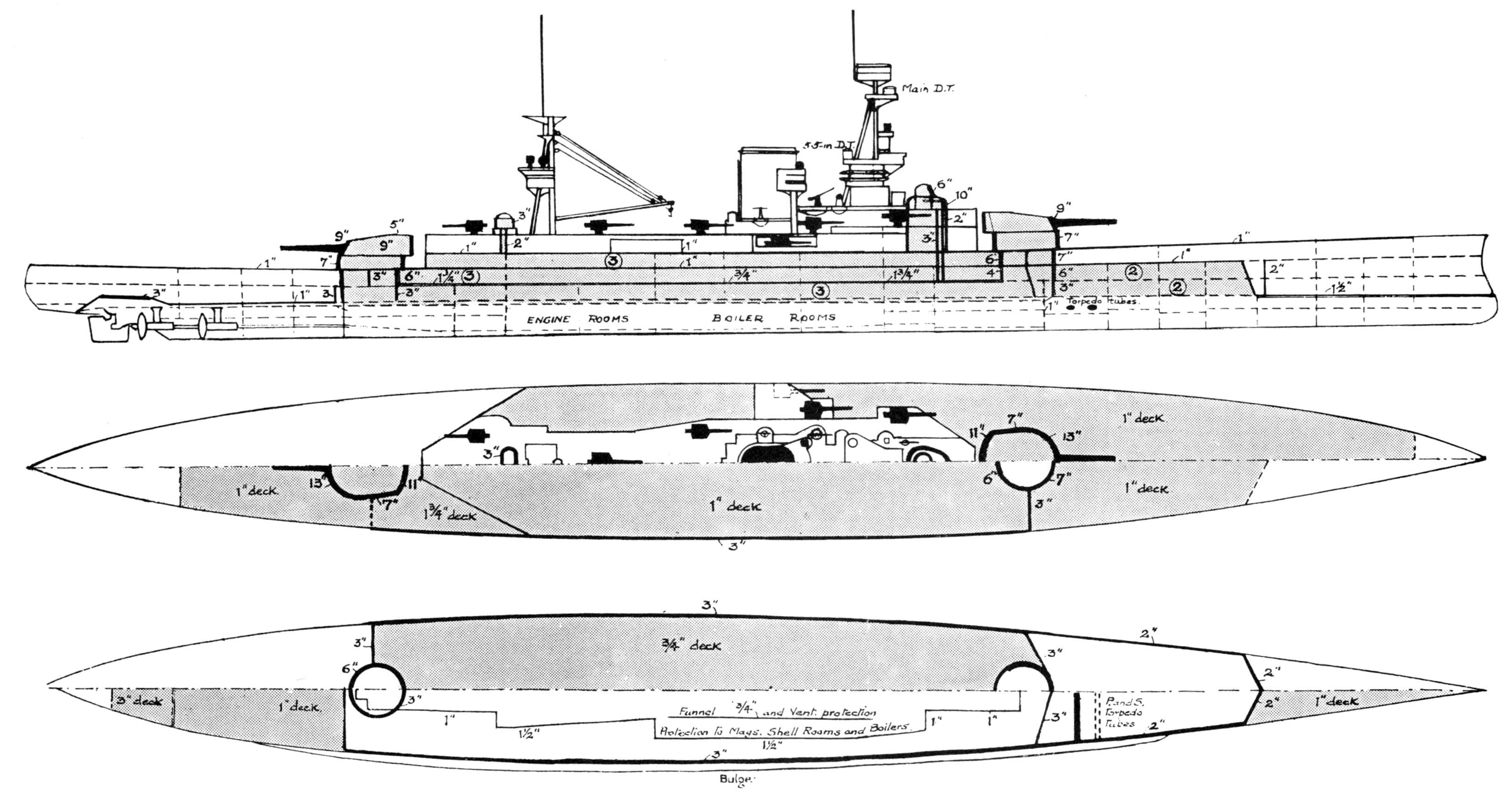

Furious as designed with the forward 18-in. gun turret which was replaced by a hangar and flight deck before her first commission. Single 5·5-in. replace the triple 3-in. guns in her half sisters and the searchlight arrangements are different.

the air. As this was not a practicable method, Dunning gave instructions that for his second attempt the plane was not to be touched until it was on the deck. So with the engine running he tried to land a second time, burst a tyre, and in the high relative wind the plane slewed over the side before it could be held and the pilot was drowned.

After her second alterations the *Furious* showed that lack of deck width was more dangerous than want of length, and that the funnel and bridge blanketed the natural wind and caused bumps so that a strong rope net was hung from a gallows at the forward end of the after flight deck which after determined attempts to break through stopped machines from hitting the funnel. Arresting wires attached to sandbags which were to be picked up by a hook on the undercarriage with the machine running between guiding wires did not come up to expectations.

A raid on the Tondern naval airship station—the most successful naval air operation of the war—was attended with so many aircraft casualties that it was decided no more landings should be made on the *Furious*. Actually only three successful attempts were recorded, and she was withdrawn from flight service and turned over to the captive balloon section which operated from a well in the after section of the flight deck.

Furious as first completed in 1917 with forward hangar and flight deck. Subsequently the after turret and mast were removed and another hangar and alighting deck added. But alighting was difficult and dangerous, so she was completely rebuilt 1921-'25 and her funnel replaced by smoke vents discharging at the rear of the after hangar, an unsatisfactory arrangement which contracted and overheated the hangar. Early in 1939 she too was given an island and a short mast to facilitate navigation.

Chapter 109

WORLD WAR I

OPERATIONS UP TO AND INCLUDING DOGGER BANK

As full descriptions of the battles and actions of the war can be found in the official "Naval Operations," only short accounts with some comments on the services and behaviour of the ships themselves need be included here. Of the major battles and actions:

(1) Heligoland Bight was a cruiser/destroyer action in which Beatty's battle cruisers arrived at a critical period in support.
(2) Dogger Bank was fought between the battle cruisers of both sides.
(3) Coronel being an armoured cruiser/cruiser engagement is outside the scope of this work.
(4) The Falklands was principally a battle cruiser/armoured cruiser action in which light cruisers were also engaged.
(5) Jutland commenced and developed as a battle cruiser engagement with the battle fleets mainly avoiding action.

Bombardments

(1) The Belgian Coast operations saw some old battleships firing at long range in support of troop movements or reducing enemy defences.
(2) The Dardanelles actions resulted from abortive attempts to force the Straits, in which mainly the older battleships were employed.

Convoy

Both the Scandinavian and Atlantic convoys were on occasion escorted by the older battleships and armoured cruisers.

HELIGOLAND BIGHT, 28 AUGUST 1914

A brilliant and timely action stultifying in its effects on German sea enterprise, which came as a welcome tonic to our people in the dark days of the Army's retreat in France.

A drive commencing at dawn by the Harwich destroyers under Commodore Tyrwhitt's destroyers and two light cruisers was to chase back the outcoming German patrol flotilla and if possible meet and destroy the incoming flotilla. Six of Commodore Keyes' submarines from Dover were to attack any heavy ships coming out in support, with the *Invincible* and *New Zealand* then stationed in the Humber as supports. Sir John Jellicoe offered to send down three battle cruisers and six light cruisers under Sir David Beatty as further support, although the German heavy ships in the Jade could not cross the outer bar until 1 p.m. and only light cruisers on patrol in the Elbe and Ems estuaries would be able to aid their flotillas.

The action did not turn out according to plan as the Admiralty message informing Keyes and Tyrwhitt of Beatty's presence did not reach them in time; nor did Beatty know whereabouts our submarines were working. There was a confused, dispersed and prolonged series of combats between our destroyers and light cruisers and the enemy light cruisers which came out in support, which lasted well into the afternoon, when Beatty suddenly appeared with his overwhelming force. In spite of the risk of mines and torpedoes and by that time the probability of meeting superior forces, he led his battle cruisers far into the Bight, sank the *Ariadne* and *Köln*, while the *Mainz* fell to the light cruisers and destroyers. The *Frauenlob*, *Strassburg* and *Stettin* managed to escape, but with heavy casualties. One destroyer was sunk.

No British ship was sunk, although the *Arethusa*, Tyrwhitt's flagship just commissioned, was severely damaged. Three destroyers also had serious damage when hit by salvoes from the *Mainz*.

More than a thousand of the enemy perished, including the Flotilla Admiral and Destroyer Commodore, and the effect on German morale was far-reaching. It was as if their ships had penetrated the Solent and sunk British ships on our own doorstep. Upon the Emperor the impression was decisive. As Admiral Tirpitz wrote "August 28th, a day fateful both in its after-effects and incidental results, for the work of our Navy. . . . The Emperor did not want losses of this sort. . . . Orders were issued by the Emperor after an audience with Pohl to restrict the initiative of the Commander-in-Chief of the North Sea Fleet: the loss of ships was to be avoided, fleet sallies and any greater undertakings must be approved by his Majesty in advance." In consequence only submarines and minelayers put to sea between August and November, while our own fleet was increased and harbour defences strengthened.

For the battle-cruisers it had been useful target practice, and an opportunity for showing their special qualities as a supporting force.

THE BATTLE OF THE FALKLANDS

8 December 1914

After the fateful action at Coronel on 1 November 1914 when Admiral Graf Spee's squadron sank Sir Christopher Cradock's flagship the *Good Hope* and the light armoured cruiser *Monmouth* the Germans disappeared into the wide Pacific. For over a month a net of four powerful squadrons made up of twenty-one armoured and eleven unarmoured ships were engaged in searching for them in the Atlantic with three more of mixed British and Japanese armoured ships in the Pacific.

Graf Spee knew that his doom was inevitable, that we should never rest until his force was destroyed. He was faced with the alternatives of scattering his ships and allowing each to act as a separate raider, living and fuelling on its captures—a course which would have presented us with an infinity of trouble in view of the exploits of the *Emden*, *Mowe*, and other corsairs—or by keeping them together as an individual command when their activities would be limited and their destruction facilitated. Coronel became fateful because it was followed by the sinking of all the German ships engaged, so that of the original forces only the *Glasgow* with her crew and a few captured Germans survived.

News of the loss of the *Good Hope* and *Monmouth* coincided with Prince Louis of Battenberg's resignation and Fisher's appointment as First Sea Lord in his place. The old man met the occasion with energy and drastic decision. He detached the *Invincible* and *Inflexible* from the Grand Fleet and directed them to Devonport in preparation for a flying passage to the South Atlantic. The Chief of Staff Admiral Sir Doveton Sturdee, whom Fisher blamed for the dispositions leading to Cradock's needless and useless sacrifice of 1,654 men (after he had been ordered to concentrate at the Falklands with the old battleship *Canopus* and armoured cruiser *Defence*), was ordered to make good his strategy as commander of an avenging squadron. No time was to be lost at Devonport, and if the two ships were not ready to proceed on 11 November, dockyard men would have to be sent with them.

Meanwhile Graf Spee had put into Valparaiso where he was entertained by the German colony, and then vanished into the blue. On 7 December Sturdee arrived at the Falklands without coming into sight of land and observing wireless silence, and forthwith proceeded to coal ship—bringing the Germans to book was likely to be a lengthy business.

Fate however willed otherwise. Next morning their ships appeared on the horizon off Stanley Harbour and *Gneisenau* and *Nürnberg* were detached for what was described as "a landing and action." Graf Spee had no intention of giving battle off the Falklands although the British forces judging by what could be seen of them, appeared inferior both in speed and force. He could, however, have closed the entrance and subjected each ship emerging to a concentrated fire—which was what our people expected would happen. Fortunately the two ships were recalled and the squadron steamed away.

When the British ships had left harbour it was seen by the Germans that two, larger and faster, had detached themselves from the rest and these were at first thought to be Japanese, on the assumption that none of our battle cruisers could possibly be out at the Falklands. A little later they were recognized, and recognition meant a fight to the death.

Retribution was to prove a lengthy and slow business. Sturdee had no intention of having his ships damaged, and with the whole day in front of him, excellent weather conditions, and perfect visibility he could afford to conduct the battle on his own terms. Fire was opened at 12.50 when the range was 16,000 yards, and seeing that escape was out of the question, the three light cruisers were ordered to scatter while the *Scharnhorst* and *Gneisenau* turned to cover their retreat. *Kent*, *Cornwall* and *Glasgow* went off after them, while the two battle cruisers and *Carnarvon* commenced a leisurely fire against the armoured cruisers.

The effective range for the 12-in. guns was 12,000-14,000 yards; the German 8·2-in. (turret) had an extreme range of 16,500 yards with 13,500 for the casemate guns, and 15,000 yards for the 6-in. But while the British armour was proof against the 8·2-in. at 14,000 yards, the Germans were everywhere vulnerable to the 12-in. Steaming at 25 knots the coal burners made an immense smoke and while the *Invincible* could count on a clear range, the *Inflexible* was generally blanketed by the flagship's smoke except for a brief period at 3.20 when alterations in course put her in the position of leader and she was able to fire without any sort of interference. By 3.30 *Scharnhorst* was listing badly with her funnels all awry, and on fire fore and aft and sinking. Spee signalled to the *Gneisenau* to escape if she could, then turned slowly towards the British, fired a last shot from her fore turret, and lay over on her beam ends, sinking at 4.4.

The *Gneisenau* was now subjected to leisurely target practice from all three ships and showed an extraordinary resistance as her upperworks were slowly wrecked, with great fires burning and only one gun left undamaged. She fired a torpedo at 5.25 and her last round at 5.45, and then turned over slowly with some 300 of her crew crowded on the wreck of the forecastle and quarter deck of which 200 were saved. She could have floated for another hour, but they opened her valves, discharged the lee torpedoes, and exploded charges in the engine-room bilges. The *Gneisenau* fired 200 8·2-in. at Coronel and did not use her 5·9-in.; the *Scharnhorst* fired 400 rounds and took over 100 from her sister so that each had 1,100 rounds of 8·2-in. and 1,200 of 5·9-in. for the Falklands.

The *Invincible* fired 630 rounds and *Inflexible* 560, but the latter's practice was badly affected by smoke—only for two intervals did she have a clear target. The action demonstrated that (1) against German ships heavy shell did not have the destructive effect anticipated, and that in long-range firing most damage is done by shell striking the upper deck and pieces penetrating the casemates; (2) their magazines did not explode, and ships could not be sunk by one or two salvoes. Even so single hits from heavy shell could have a big effect on armoured cruisers —one from *Invincible* struck the front plate of *Gneisenau's* turret and completely wrecked it. Another from *Inflexible* falling on the upper deck burst in an 8·2-in. casemate on the disengaged side and tumbled gun and ship's side-plating into the sea.

Two hits on the *Invincible* were below the water-line, but did little damage. One of the fore tripod legs was shot away, but the steadiness of the mast was unimpaired—a striking tribute to the efficacy of these heavy tripods. The front plate of the fore turret was hit, but the 7-in. armour was not penetrated. Two shells wrecked the ward-room, and a solid 8·2-in. projectile cut through the barrel of a 4-in. gun. The crew were kept behind armour, so there were no casualties from the twenty-two hits received.

The *Inflexible* was hit on the fore turret and main derrick. One man was killed.

It had been a hopeless fight against overwhelming odds, and satisfied (3) of the theoretical duties of large armoured cruisers for the rounding-up of enemy marauding cruisers, although Fisher was annoyed over the time taken and heavy expenditure of ammunition. Considering the reputation for good shooting enjoyed by both ships when on the China Station, Sturdee was perfectly right in keeping his distance; but had he placed the *Inflexible* on a bearing where she would have been clear of his smoke, and allowed her to keep out of it when changing course the battle could have been over in half the time.

Of the three light cruisers, the *Leipzig* was sunk by the *Glasgow* and *Cornwall*; *Nürnberg* fell to the *Kent*; and the *Dresden* was later run to earth at Mas-a-Tierra in Chilean waters and there sunk by the *Glasgow* and *Cornwall.*

BATTLE OF THE DOGGER BANK

24 January 1915

This was a full-speed pursuit action between Sir David Beatty's Battle Cruiser Force and the German First Scouting Group under Rear-Admiral Hipper. Here destroyers were first employed for purely defensive purposes in a fleet action, compelling their opponents to manœuvre thus upsetting control and accuracy of fire, and throwing pursuers back with increasing range. Smoke screens were also used for the first time.

The ships engaged were:

BRITISH

BATTLE CRUISER FORCE

Lion (Flagship), *Tiger*, *Princess Royal*, *New Zealand*, *Indomitable*. (*Queen Mary* en route for docking at Portsmouth; *Invincible* at Gibraltar; *Inflexible* in the Mediterranean.)

1ST CRUISER SQUADRON

Southampton (Commodore Goodenough), *Birmingham*, *Nottingham*, *Lowestoft*.

HARWICH FLOTILLA

Arethusa (Commodore Tyrwhitt), *Aurora*, *Undaunted*. 35 destroyers.

GERMAN

FIRST SCOUTING GROUP

Seydlitz (Flagship), *Derfflinger*, *Moltke*, *Blücher*.

LIGHT CRUISERS

Graudenz, *Rostock*, *Stralsund*, *Kolberg*. 19 destroyers.

The Commander-in-Chief, Admiral von Ingenohl's, order to Hipper to take his ships out to the Dogger Bank for a patrol, leaving by night and returning on the following night, was intercepted and decoded at the Admiralty. Beatty and Tyrwhitt were given a rendezvous off the Dogger to intercept them and the Grand Fleet ordered south in support, although chart and compass showed that Jellicoe could not reach the appointed spot until the following afternoon.

At 7.15 battle was joined when the *Aurora* sighted and engaged the *Kolberg* which retreated to the eastward, and sent the alarm to the German ships, which promptly headed for home at full speed. A stern chase ensued with the Germans leading by an estimated 28,000 yards, their speed limited by the *Blücher's* nominal 25 knots. The British ships worked up to 28 knots leaving the *New Zealand* and *Indomitable* astern, and at 8.52 the *Lion* opened on the *Blücher* at 22,000 yards but fell short. Both forces took up a line of bearing with Beatty on Hipper's starboard quarter and Goodenough to port with the destroyers between them. Visibility was good, but, cloaked by volumes of smoke from the battle cruisers and destroyers, sighting was difficult. It was now that Beatty reaped his reward for the long range "shoot" he had carried out in April 1914, and by 9.14 *Lion*, *Tiger* and *Princess Royal* were concentrating on the *Blücher* and the flagship was able to shift to the *Moltke*. The British ships were ordered to fire at their opposite numbers from left to right, while the Germans followed tradition by concentrating on the head of the line. But not realizing that the *Indomitable* was out of range, the *Tiger* fired at the *Seydlitz* leaving the *Moltke* undisturbed, and so able to make uninterrupted target practice on the *Lion*.

The flagship was hit twelve times. That at 10.0 put the fore turret temporarily out of action; at 10.18 she received a blow so severe that she was thought to have been torpedoed. As salvoes were arriving in pairs and groups of three and even five, it may have been combined hits from the *Derfflinger*, one of which below the water-line drove several plates through the timber backing and flooded the foremost port bunkers. Another pierced the armour on the water-line forward, burst in the torpedo flat, and in a few minutes all the adjacent compartments up to the main deck were flooded. The leading ships had got her range and their salvoes fell rapidly and accurately so that Beatty was forced to zig-zag. His squadron was ordered to take up a line of bearing N.N.W., proceed at the utmost speed, and press the advantage of our gunfire which was starting to punish the enemy severely. At 10.35 the *Lion* was again hit, and at 10.41 another shell caused a fire in "A" turret magazine. But the fire was put out, the magazine flooded, and she was still able to make 20 knots. Just before 11.0 a hit drove in the water-line armour abreast of one of the engine-rooms and so damaged the feed-tank and engine-room that the port engine had to be stopped. Both light and power failed, speed dropped to 15 knots, and a list to port increased to 10°.

Although full of fight, the *Lion* had to drop out just as a signal to turn to starboard to avoid an enemy submarine had been made. While the flagship fell far astern a misreading of Beatty's end-on final signals on the *Lion's* two remaining halyards turned his ships onto the dying but still defiant *Blücher*, while the three battle cruisers, half beaten, were allowed to escape. When Rear-Admiral Moore in the *New Zealand* decided to continue the chase they were a good 12 miles away and making their full 25 knots; it would take two hours to bring them into effective range again, by which time they would be close to Heligoland and the High Seas Fleet.

Meanwhile Beatty had boarded the destroyer *Attack* and raced after and boarded the *Princess Royal* which he found returning to the *Lion*. Bitterly disappointed he ordered the chase to be resumed, but realizing that further pursuit was useless he steered for the crippled flagship to make provision for her safe return to the Forth.

Incapable of steaming, the *Lion* was taken in tow by the *Indomitable*, escorted by destroyers, and at daylight on the 26th was brought safely to Rosyth.

Of the British ships *Lion* fired 243 rounds and received twelve hits. Casualties were twelve wounded. The driving in of her water-line armour has been attributed to deficient strength in hull construction, although it had been realized that the smashing force of heavy projectiles could be expected to displace plates without piercing them. With some 3,000 tons of water in her, mostly forward, she was 6 feet down by the bows, and only a 12-in. diameter ¼-in. thick copper pipe already concertinaed saved the huge main engine-room from being flooded.

Repair at Rosyth was impracticable and she should have gone to Plymouth for docking. But Fisher would not have it admitted that the ship was in need of dockyard facilities, and ordered her to be taken in hand by Armstrong's. In the Tyne she spent four months being heeled and repaired piece by piece by means of huge wooden coffer-dams—a needlessly difficult operation, made more so by the pouring of tons of cement into the leaky compartments by the Salvage Corps which had to be broken up by small charges of dynamite.

The *Tiger* received two hits with ten killed and eleven wounded, plus the foreman of the dockyard electricians still on board, who developed hysterical panic. When the *Lion* was disabled *Tiger* became leading ship and a target for the concentrated fire of three battle cruisers. A hit on "B" turret killed two men, wounded several, and put the port gun out of action; a second entered the signal distributing station and exploded killing eight men; a third hit the boat deck and set fire to the motor launch and petrol tank causing a huge blaze which made the Germans think the ship was disabled.

Newly commissioned and incomplete, denied a proper shake down period, and manned largely by an inexperienced crew she could not show to advantage and it is doubtful if she made any hits on the enemy. Had the very efficient *Queen Mary* been present the battle would have gone differently.

Of the other ships only the destroyer *Meteor* sustained any casualties. She was hit by a 8·2-in. shell from the *Blücher* and had four killed and one wounded.

Of the German ships, the *Seydlitz* had her two after turrets put out of action by the first hit from the *Lion*. This pierced the upper deck and 9-in. barbette armour of the rearmost turret where it exploded. The whole stern was wrecked, loading charges ignited in the loading chamber, and fire spread to the ammunition chamber and then through a door when men were escaping into the other rear turret via the ammunition chamber. Six tons of ammunition went up in a roar of flame half as high as the mast and 159 men perished. But the magazines were saved by the bravery of a chief petty officer who managed to turn the red hot wheels to the flooding valves with his bare hands.

The *Derfflinger* was hit once without casualties, although it was thought that she had been badly damaged. *Moltke* was not hit. No ship could have shown more courage and resistance than the *Blücher* which, hit by seven torpedoes and from seventy to one hundred shells until she was turned into a furnace, maintained a gallant resistance until her end. She had 792 killed, and 45 wounded and 189 unwounded were picked up by our people.

After the action attention was called to the weak turret roofs and defective magazine arrangements in our ships, but nothing was done to remedy these. On the other hand, the Germans installed improved rangefinders and made certain alterations to turrets and magazines which were thought to adequately prevent any repetition of the *Seydlitz* disaster, although at Jutland the *Derfflinger* was to undergo a similar ordeal.

As the *Indomitable* and *New Zealand* were left too far astern to do more than help finish off the stricken *Blücher*, and if the *Tiger's* shooting did not register any hits, it may be said that the action was fought between the *Lion* and *Princess Royal* and the four German ships. Our system of dispersed fire was baulked by smoke and fumes which made hitting extremely difficult, although it would have achieved its object had the *Tiger's* gunnery been worked up to the B.C.S. standard. By concentrating on the British flagship in the traditional manner, the Germans averted what could have been a costly defeat. All disabling hits are "unlucky" and the *Lion* had to leave the line when Beatty's leadership meant everything.

* * * * *

Sir David Beatty's official detailed despatch was so mutilated at the Admiralty before being issued to the public that no naval student could possibly understand the action in its true light. Both the original despatch and its official version are included in Filson Young's *With the Battle Cruisers* with this comment:

> "When the telegraphic report was published containing the entirely fictitious sentence 'The presence of the enemy's submarines necessitated the action being broken off' an American naval writer published an article analysing the action and saying that Admiral Beatty, on the evidence of his published report, ought to be shot. I showed this article to the Admiral at the time, and his only comment was 'I quite agree with him.'"

Chapter 110

COASTAL OPERATIONS AND THE DARDANELLES

ONE further engagement took place in which big ships took part—the indecisive action of 17 November 1917. The British had been laying intensive minefields in the Heligoland Bight further and further to seaward so that German sweepers had to come out some distance from their bases and within reach of Beatty's light forces. At intervals our light cruisers attacked the sweepers, whose losses made it necessary to give them battleship protection, and on this occasion a strong force was sent to the edge of the minefields where sweeping was in progress in the hope of surprising them. For the first time the *Courageous* and *Glorious* were to try to justify their existance in company with the First and Sixth Light Cruiser Squadrons, accompanied by destroyers and supported by the *Renown* and *Repulse* and the First Battle Squadron. Minesweepers were sighted midway between Horns Reef and Terschelling—about twenty small craft with ten destroyers and four light cruisers supported by the *Kaiserin* and *Kaiser*, later reinforced by the *Hindenburg* and *Moltke*. There was a running fight with hits on both sides, but mist and smoke screens made shooting very difficult, and neither force could deviate from the channel owing to surrounding mines. Rear-Admiral Napier in the *Courageous* stayed at the big ships while the cruisers pursued, until the two battleships started dropping salvoes but did not follow them.

The *Königsberg* (second of the name) was hit by a 15-in. shell which pierced all three funnels, went through the upper deck, and burst in a coal bunker causing a fire. Its pieces were picked up and calibre determined. One other 15-in. and three 6-in. hits caused twenty-one killed and forty wounded. Our casualties were one hundred killed and the *Courageous* suffered most; the *Calypso* had her conning tower hit and her Captain killed.

It was an unsatisfactory action in which the German light cruisers punished the *Courageous* and from German accounts caused her to sheer off, while they escaped lightly. But it did result in the Germans having to provide stronger support to their sweepers, so that our minefields gradually grew instead of being cleared up soon after being laid.

COASTAL OPERATIONS

THE BELGIAN COAST

In the early days of the operations off the Belgian coast old cruisers, destroyers, scouts, gunboats, flat-irons, and the three ex-Brazilian monitors of the *Severn* class were employed to help stop the enemy advance on the Channel ports. Not that they were specially suitable for the work, but were available and mounted guns of calibres for which there were reasonable reserves of ammunition. Later the *Venerable* was added to Admiral Hood's force for a short time, but it was found that the fire from the smaller ships was more efficacious against the numerous shore batteries. In August 1915 the old *Revenge* (with her big guns relined to 12-in., and fitted with temporary bulges), could be heeled to provide long range fire, and did good work in the bombardments of Zeebrugge and Ostend.

THE DARDANELLES

After the escape of the *Goeben* and *Breslau* from the Mediterranean to Constantinople, the Turkish attitude towards the Allies stiffened and she declared war on 1 November. Two days later a long range bombardment of the forts at the entrance to the Straits was carried out by the *Indefatigable* and *Indomitable* in company with the French battleships *Verité* and *Suffren*, seventy-six 12-in. rounds being fired. From the distance both Sedd-el-Bahr and Kum Kale forts appeared to have been reduced to rubble, the magazine of the former having blown up. Experience on the Belgian coast should have shown that this demonstration was of no military consequence, and it merely led to a strengthening of the defences.

Under German guidance Turkey then began preparing not only to invade Egypt, but to organize an enveloping movement in the Caucasus which caused grave anxiety to the Russian general in command. As no military relief could be spared from the Russian eastern front, the Grand Duke Nicholas asked for a diversion to be made against Turkey to relieve the tension in the Caucasus.

The evidence of history, however, ruled out any attempt to force the Straits by ships only. In 1906 the Committee of Imperial Defence had considered a combined attack and decided that the prospects of success were not worth the risks. Nevertheless in January 1915 the Government decided to prepare a naval expedition to bombard and take the Gallipoli peninsula with Constantinople as its objective. As Lord Kitchener was unable to allocate the necessary troops a combined operation was not possible, but it was considered that a naval demonstration, which could be called off at any time without loss of prestige, stood a good chance of getting through.

Old pre-Dreadnoughts could be employed without weakening the Grand Fleet although the Channel Fleet would suffer, and Fisher—who had returned to Whitehall as First Sea Lord—offered to add the *Queen Elizabeth*, hoping that high velocity/low trajectory guns could emulate the huge siege howitzers employed against Liége and Namur.

What a stupendous undertaking was being proposed can be gathered from the diagram. The outer defences at the entrance mounted nineteen guns of 11-in. to 6·8-in. in old-fashioned masonry forts; the intermediate defence mounted eighty-seven from 8·2-in. to 6-in. and at Nagara the most powerful works had six 14-in., six 11-in., seven 10·2-in., thirty-six 9·4-in., six 8·2-in. and fourteen 6-in. and numerous smaller guns with six 8·2-in. and seven 6-in. howitzers. At Kilid Bahr were three 18-in. torpedo tubes, but with only five torpedoes available. This arsenal of guns in forts difficult to destroy at long range made it impossible to sweep up the mines, and the mines made it impossible to close the forts.

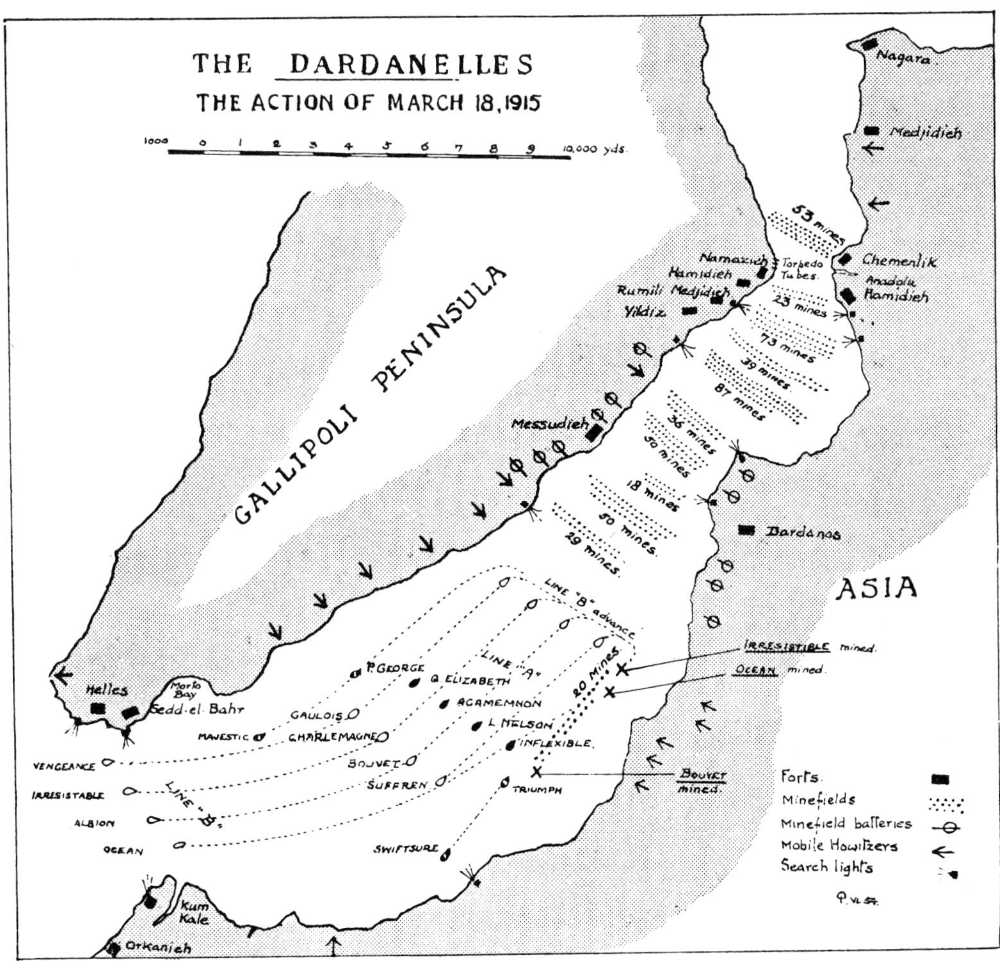

After the War Council Meeting of 28 January Fisher rejected the scheme, mainly on the grounds that it interfered with his own Baltic Project, but was talked into it by Lord Kitchener and the First Lord. "Naval opinion was unanimous," said Fisher afterwards, "Mr. Churchill had them all on his side. I was the only rebel."

If all went well the naval operations were to change the history of the world, cut the Turkish Empire in two, paralyse its capital, unite the Balkan States against our enemies, rescue Serbia, help the Grand Duke in the main operations of the war, and by shortening its duration save countless lives. (*World Crisis*, II, p. 167.)

We did not know until the Turkish General Staff admitted it after the war that on 19 March 1915 nearly all their ammunition at the Narrows had been shot away, and that a renewed attack on that day could have been decisive. That if our ships had appeared before Constantinople, the eight divisions there could not have defended it, and that the populace—convinced of the invincibility of the British Fleet—were demoralized.

* * * * *

Bombardment of the outer forts started on 19 February by the *Cornwallis*, *Triumph*, *Albion*, *Inflexible* and French *Bouvet* and *Suffren* under the command of Vice-Admiral S. H. Carden. The ships were kept under way at 8,000-11,000 yards, but firing was inaccurate and they later anchored out of enemy range when slow and observed fire was considered sufficiently effective for a closer attack to be made. There was no reply until 4.45 when the *Cornwallis* at 5,000 yards was shelled. The *Vengeance*, *Cornwallis*, *Agamemnon*, *Inflexible* and French *Gaulois* temporarily silenced the forts and the recall was made. Expenditure of 139 12-in. shells showed that (1) ships would have to anchor for accurate shooting (2) direct fire was the better, and (3) direct hits would have to be made on guns or mountings in order to silence them.

Bad weather prevented bombardment being resumed until 25 January when the *Agamemnon*, *Irresistible* and *Gaulois* with carefully checked firing obtained excellent results—direct hits knocked out guns in Fort Helles and Orkanieh, and later at close range all the outer forts were silenced. Sweeping the approaches and entrance to the Straits—where there was plenty of sea room and no mines—became possible on the 25th and 26th, and demolition parties were landed and destroyed all the guns in Sedd-el-Bahr and the two forts on the Asiatic side. By 2 March all the outer defences were accounted for, and the fleet was able to sweep and enter the Straits for 7 miles up to the Kephez minefield, but against considerable opposition from mobile defences.

The *Triumph*, *Albion*, and *Majestic* enlarged the intermediate works during the sweeping, and came up against some fifty large howitzers firing from hidden positions on the railways. More bad weather held up operations until 1 March when the same ships joined by the *Ocean* renewed the attack, but were hit repeatedly and their fire was ineffective against the mobile guns. Seaplanes from the *Ark Royal* (a converted tanker), spotting at low altitudes, reported that many new emplacements could be seen.

Next day was again stormy. The *Canopus*, *Swiftsure*, and *Prince George* aided by the French *Charlemagne* carried on the attack, but firing was delayed until the afternoon and little damage was done. That night the minesweepers were driven off by heavy and accurate fire. On 4 March landing parties were again put ashore to complete the demolition of the forts on both sides and sustained twenty killed and many wounded.

Late the next day the *Queen Elizabeth* opened the attack on the Hamedieh batteries of the inner defences by indirect fire over the western side of the peninsula at 14,000 yards range. Everything depended upon the spotting arrangements, but of the three seaplanes available the first crashed with a broken propeller; the pilot was wounded by rifle fire in the second; and the third only managed to report one correction. Admiralty instruction about the sparing use of ammunition, and the quite inadequate provision for aerial spotting led to indirect fire being prematurely discontinued and condemned.

Operations were continued from 7-12 March with fitful bombardments at long range, when the apparent silencing of any return fire was only due to conservation of ammunition. Against Fisher's wishes the precious *Queen Elizabeth* was taken up the Straits to attack Chanak, being uselessly exposed.

Although those on the spot were beginning to regard the passage of the Straits without land forces in support as impracticable, Carden was given instructions to use his maximum strength to force a passage, as the modest success achieved would justify the loss of ships and men. In preparation for the great attack the Bulair lines were bombarded as a diversion. Further attempts were made to sweep the minefields, but the terrific fire and loss from mines led to a withdrawal—the trawler Captains declared they could do no more. Volunteers from the fleet fared no better. Four trawlers were sunk, and the supporting cruiser *Amethyst* had her steering disabled and lost twenty-five killed and forty-five wounded. After this, thirty powerful trawlers were ordered from England, but arrived too late.

Carden's health broke down, and Vice-Admiral J. M. de Robeck took over the command. He decided to make the big attack ordered, but realized that even if he got through his fleet could not remain in the Marmora, nor could transports follow him.

March 18 was fixed for the great push, with twelve British and four French battleships in the Straits and three in reserve. The most powerful ships *Queen Elizabeth*, *Agamemnon*, *Lord Nelson* and *Inflexible* flanked by *Prince George* and *Triumph* in Line A were to steam towards Chanak and attack at 14,000 yards. When they had battered the forts, the second line B were to advance to close action, all keeping under way. (See diagram, p. 631.)

This time it was the smaller guns which proved so troublesome. Howitzers made twelve hits on the *Agamemnon* and the *Inflexible* had her tripod struck, the fore bridge set on fire, and her fore control top put out of action with three men killed and six officers and men wounded. Having dropped back to get the wounded down, she returned to the fight but was again heavily hit and badly mined. With 2,000 tons of water in her and down by the bows, she had to withdraw with twenty-nine men killed and reached Malta with extreme difficulty.

By midday the forts looked sufficiently knocked about for Line B to close up, and the four ships steamed in to press the attack when the Turkish fire suddenly blazed up. The *Gaulois* was repeatedly hit and badly damaged, being escorted by destroyers to Rabbit Island where she was beached. At 2 p.m. the *Bouvet*, hulled again and again by 14-in. shells was severely hit or probably struck a mine. A magazine blew up and she went under with 700 of her crew.

The Allies were unaware that they had run into a new minefield laid on 8 March in waters already swept and considered safe, through which the ships usually steamed when bombarding. In the same field the *Irresistible*, after having had both her turrets put out of action, struck a mine at 4.15. Her crew were removed with a loss of twenty and she was abandoned in a sinking condition. Later during the evening retirement the *Ocean*, badly damaged by gunfire, was also caught, and she too had to be abandoned. Both ships were sunk by Turkish fire as they drifted down the Straits. Other ships injured were the *Charlemagne* with a stokehold flooded; the *Agamemnon* with a 12-in. gun disabled; and the *Albion* with her fore turret out of action. Allied total losses were not published, but must have reached 800. The Turkish loss according to German reports was only twenty-four killed and seventy-nine wounded.

Thus the attack was a complete failure, and could hardly have been otherwise. Had it been properly planned and undertaken in settled April weather, with adequate air support and sweepers powerful enough to stem the current properly the ships *might* have got through. But as is known, the Germans and Turks were prepared to deal with anything which did get through to the Sea of Marmora, so no decisive result would have been forthcoming.

The First Lord was prepared to order a second attempt, but this was vetoed by Fisher and it was left to de Robeck's judgment. His estimation of the mine danger and the futility of employing high velocity guns against the forts led to the whole operation being abandoned on 23 March.

* * * * *

Subsequent naval operations in the Campaign were confined to covering the landings at Helles, Anzac, and Suvla and support of the troops during the trench warfare which followed. Further losses were the *Goliath* hit by three torpedoes from a Turkish destroyer when in Morto Bay, with 567 killed. After this the *Queen Elizabeth* was recalled, as on 25 May the *Triumph* was torpedoed by U-21 off Gaba Tepe, which heralded the appearance of German submarines in the Mediterranean. A destroyer screen was evaded, her nets pierced, and she sank in ten minutes with a loss of seventy-one. Two days later the same submarine sped a torpedo between protecting merchant ships and through the nets of the old *Majestic* off Cape Helles. She turned over in seven minutes with a loss of seventy-one. For some time her green hull showed above water as she rested on her masts, until these gave way and she disappeared.

As the monitors and bulged cruisers became available soon afterwards, battleship support to the land forces was then withdrawn and the ships lay at Mudros or Salonika awaiting the possible appearance of the *Goeben*.

* * * * *

In connection with the Dardanelles Campaign was the blockade of Smyrna, with a bombardment of the forts between 5 and 8 March by the *Triumph* and *Swiftsure* and the armoured cruiser *Euryalus*. Owing to minefields the batteries could not be approached closely and the minefields could not be swept because of the batteries, so the results were indifferent. On the 9th a passage was cleared to within 3,000 yards of the principal fort, and a truce concluded with the Governor.

* * * * *

AERIAL BOMBING

The only warship subjected to aerial bombing was the *Goeben* when she lay aground in the Bosphorus after being mined in 1917. Then only 25 lb. bombs were available, which were dropped by hand from as low a height as possible to obtain hits, in the face of rifle fire. Naturally she sustained only superficial damage, but the attacks were made to serve as evidence showing that either the ship possessed unusual resistance, or that aerial bombing was not a menace to big armoured ships—whichever way the argument was to be weighted.

Chapter III

THE BATTLE OF JUTLAND

31 MAY-1 JUNE 1916

In the Spring of 1916 it became necessary for the German fleet to undertake some operation which would justify its existence, and relieve the growing anxiety over the sacrifices at Verdun. Scheer therefore devised two plans. One, based on Hipper's bombardment of Sunderland with the H.S.F. in support and the employment of his submarines either off the G.F. bases or in defence of the Bight, involved the help of scouting Zeppelins and favourable weather conditions. The other was to stage a raid on our shipping off the Danish coasts by Hipper, again with the H.S.F. in support and the submarines in wait. Both were intended to entice Beatty into range of the H.S.F. and annihilate his forces, but the second did not entail the use of Zeppelins.

On 15 May the submarines left for their allotted stations, but adverse weather conditions grounded the airships until 30 May—by which time the U-boats would have to return. The more ambitious operation was therefore cried off, and Hipper was directed to proceed to the Skagerrak and show himself off the Norwegian coast to ensure that his presence would be reported to the Admiralty, while the battle fleet followed discreetly out of sight. This precaution was unnecessary as the reported movements of the submarines and signs of activity in the Jade roads showed that some important operation was afoot.

At 5.30 p.m. on 30 May Jellicoe and Beatty were therefore informed and ordered to concentrate as usual eastward off the "Long Forties," while Harwich and the Nore were warned for action. Our object was to be similar to Scheer's—for Beatty to engage Hipper with the battle fleet in support if necessary. But as Scheer had transferred his call sign to the shore establishment at Wilhelmshaven, and our directional wireless (then unknown to the Germans) had therefore placed him in the Jade roads at 11.10 a.m. on 31 May, neither Beatty nor Scheer imagined that the opposing battle fleets were at sea.

Beatty was to proceed to an area 70 miles southward of the rendezvous to ensure that the waters between the east coast and the line of advance should be widely swept before the concentration. The battle cruisers were not at this time regarded as an advanced squadron—when the distance would have been too great—but as a force whose primary function was to intercept raids on the east coast with the battle fleet sufficiently far back to prevent the enemy evading it to crush the 10th Cruiser Squadron (armed merchant ships) and raise the blockade.

The opposing forces were:

THE GRAND FLEET

1ST BATTLE SQUADRON

6th Div.:
Marlborough (Vice-Admiral Sir Cecil Burney)
Revenge
Hercules
Agincourt

5th Div.:
Colossus (Rear-Admiral Gaunt)
Collingwood
Neptune
St. Vincent

Light cruiser *Bellona*

2ND BATTLE SQUADRON

1st Div.:
King George V (Vice-Admiral Sir M. Jerran)
Ajax
Centurion
Erin

2nd Div.:
Orion (Rear-Admiral Leveson
Monarch
Conqueror
Thunderer

Light cruiser *Boadicea*

1ST CRUISER SQUADRON

Defence (Rear-Admiral Sir R. Arbuthnot)
Warrior
Duke of Edinburgh
Black Prince

4TH BATTLE SQUADRON

4th Div.:
Benbow (Vice-Admiral Sir D. Sturdee)
Bellerophon
Temeraire
Vanguard

3rd Div.:
Iron Duke (Admiral Sir J. R. Jellicoe)
Royal Oak
Superb
Canada

Light cruiser *Blanche*
Light cruiser *Active*
Minelayer *Abdiel*
Destroyer *Oak*

3RD BATTLE CRUISER SQUADRON

Invincible (Rear-Admiral Sir H. Hood)
Indomitable
Inflexible
Light cruiser *Chester*
Light cruiser *Canterbury*

2ND CRUISER SQUADRON

Minotaur (Rear-Admiral Heath)
Cochrane
Shannon
Hampshire (linking ship)

4TH LIGHT CRUISER SQUADRON

Calliope (Commodore Le Mesurier)
Constance
Comus
Caroline
Royalist

DESTROYER FLOTILLAS

Light cruiser *Castor* (Commodore Hawksley)

4th	11th	12th
nineteen	fifteen	sixteen

BATTLE CRUISER FORCE

1ST BATTLE CRUISER SQUADRON

Lion (Vice-Admiral Sir D. Beatty)
Princess Royal
Queen Mary
Tiger

2ND BATTLE CRUISER SQUADRON

New Zealand (Rear-Admiral Pakenham)
Indefatigable

5TH BATTLE SQUADRON

Barham (Rear-Admiral Evan-Thomas)
Valiant
Warspite
Malaya

1ST LIGHT CRUISER SQUADRON

Galatea (Commodore Alexander-Sinclair)
Phaeton
Inconstant
Cordelia

2ND LIGHT CRUISER SQUADRON

Southampton (Commodore Goodenough)
Birmingham
Nottingham
Dublin

3RD LIGHT CRUISER SQUADRON

Falmouth (Rear-Admiral Napier)
Yarmouth
Birkenhead
Gloucester

Aircraft Carrier *Engadine*

DESTROYER FLOTILLAS

1st	13th	9th and 10th
Fearless (light cruiser)	*Champion* (light cruiser)	
nine	ten	eight

Total 145

As the *Australia* was in dock and the three *Invincibles* had been detached from the B.C.F. at the end of May for routine gunnery practice at Scapa, Beatty had asked for the *Barhams* as a supporting force (the *Queen Elizabeth* was refitting) which although of two and a half knots less speed were far more powerful in every way than the early battle cruisers.

The composition of the 6th Div. 1st B.S. and 3rd Div. 4th B.S. are worth noting as indicative of how the claims of flagships and a diversity of ship types put homogeneity out of court—in the latter there were 15-in., 14-in., 13·5-in. and 12-in. guns.

HIGH SEAS FLEET

3RD SQUADRON

König (Rear-Admiral Behncke)
Grosser Kurfurst
Markgraf
Kronprinz
Kaiser (Rear-Admiral Nordmann)
Prinz. Luitpold
Kaiserin
Friedrich der Grosse (Vice-Admiral Scheer)

1ST SQUADRON

Ostfriesland (Vice-Admiral Schmidt)
Thuringen
Helgoland
Oldenburg
Posen (Rear-Admiral Engelhardt)
Rheinland
Nassau
Westfalen

2ND SQUADRON

(pre-Dreadnoughts)

Deutschland (Rear-Admiral Mauve)
Pommern
Schlesien
Schleswig Holstein
Hannover (Rear-Admiral Lichtenfels)
Hessen

2ND SCOUTING GROUP

Frankfurt (Rear-Admiral Boedicker)
Pillau
Elbing
Wiesbaden

1ST SCOUTING GROUP

Battle cruisers

Lutzow (Rear-Admiral Hipper)
Derfflinger
Seydlitz
Moltke
Von der Tann

3RD SCOUTING GROUP

Stettin
München
Frauenlob
Stüttgart
Hamburg

DESTROYER FLOTILLAS

Light cruiser *Rostock* (Commodore) Light cruiser *Regensburg* (2nd Commodore)

Sixty-one.

TOTAL 99

By 11.30 p.m. on 30 May all units of the Grand Fleet were clear of their bases. Two attacks by submarines were reported by *Galatea* and *Yarmouth* between 3.50 a.m. and 8 a.m. and a third boat sighted by the *Turbulent* soon afterwards, by which time the trap had failed. At 2 p.m. Beatty was within a few miles of his rendezvous and placed his squadrons ready for turning northward to meet Jellicoe. At this time Hipper was only about 50 miles to the eastward and his extreme left wing cruiser only 22 miles away, with Scheer some 50 miles astern of him.

"Enemy in sight" was reported by *Galatea* at 2.30 and forthwith Beatty made a general signal to alter course S.S.E., increase to full speed, and intercept the enemy. Jellicoe also took in the *Galatea's* signal when 65 miles to the northward, and ordered steam for full speed. Because of smoke Beatty's signal was not seen by the *Barham* or passed to her by the repeating ship *Tiger*, so Evan-Thomas held his course following instructions to keep a lookout to the north for Jellicoe. From being 5 miles ahead he was nearly 10 miles astern of the *Lion* before realizing the significance of Beatty's manœuvre, when he turned and followed at full speed.

The German battle cruisers were sighted at 3.30, converging N.N.W. at 25 knots. Hipper promptly turned away S.E. towards the H.S.F. and Beatty followed on a parallel course without waiting for the 5th B.S. to close—to have done so would have disclosed his ten ships and Hipper would certainly have declined battle. As it was, Beatty felt strong enough to tackle them before they could obtain support *if* the H.S.F. was out.

Visibility was good but patchy, with the British ships at a marked disadvantage being sharply silhouetted against a blue sky while the Germans were hull down 11 miles away and only dimly outlined. Rangefinding was difficult, and conditions gave readings far in excess of the actual range, so that Beatty held his fire longer than was necessary. Having thinner armour and heavier guns there was every advantage in fighting at maximum range, and the Germans had been expecting us to open fire for some minutes. By withholding his own fire as long as possible Hipper kept reducing the odds, but at 3.48 both sides saw the ripple of gun flashes followed by the splashes of shells which fell well over their target. We had fired at an estimated range of 18,000 yards when the actual distance was only 15,500 yards.

At 3.38 a seaplane from the *Engadine* had taken off from the water, but owing to the haze had only been able to signal the presence of German light cruisers when it had to come down because of a broken petrol pipe. The pilot Flight-Lieutenant F. S. Rutland, R.N. and Paymaster G. S. Trewen, R.N.—who were picked up—had the distinction of being the first airmen to take part in a naval battle.

For scouting we had to rely upon Goodenough with the 2nd L.C.S. who had refused to be drawn into the exchange with the German light cruisers in the movement to the N.W. with the 1st and 3rd L.C.S., but had placed himself where most needed—to watch the southern horizon.

The first phase of the battle now commenced—what is referred to as "The Run to the South" with the rival battle cruisers engaged on a parallel course and Hipper leading Beatty onto the H.S. Fleet. A signal by flags had been made from the *Lion* at 3.45 directing the distribution of fire—and Beatty was anxious to pay back something of what he had received at the Dogger. So with six ships against five the *Lion* and *Princess Royal* were to concentrate on Hipper in the *Lutzow*, the rest taking on the enemy in succession. But this signal is not recorded in the logs of the *Tiger* or *New Zealand* and was mistaken by the *Queen Mary* which engaged the *Seydlitz* leaving the *Derfflinger* undisturbed for ten minutes. Further down the line both the *Tiger* and *New Zealand*—which had correctly engaged the fourth ship—were both on the *Moltke* leaving the *Indefatigable* and *Von der Tann* to their fateful duel.

Conditions of light and blown smoke favoured the enemy, and within five minutes *Lion* and *Tiger* had both been hit. Our ships showed clear against the western sky and Beatty was closing the range by small turns to port,

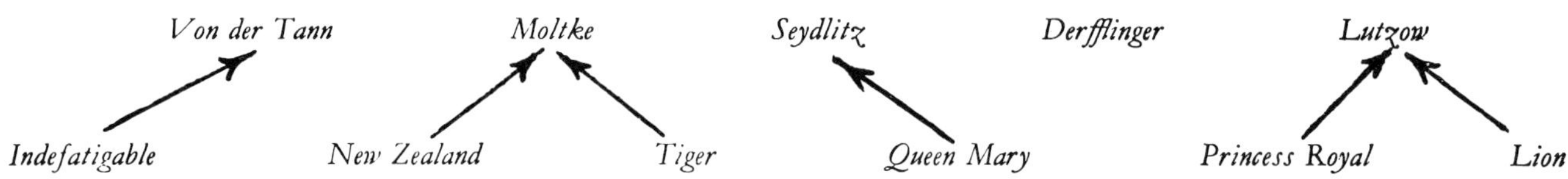

which quite soon enabled the enemy to bring their secondary guns into action, firing alternate salvoes with the main armament. Things were getting too hot to last, and Hipper turned sharply S.E. into line ahead, while Beatty bore two points to south, opening the range rapidly. Seven miles astern Evan-Thomas held to the eastward, clouds of smoke having masked these turns. As yet he had not seen the Germans.

During this period the enemy suffered no real damage, our ships being almost blinded by the smoke from a division of the 9th Flotilla (L class) determined to get into position for a torpedo attack but lacking the speed to do it.

At 3.58 we commenced rapid fire and the *Derfflinger* received her first hit of the hammering she was to undergo. By 4.0 the range had come down to 14,000 yards and *Lion's* "Q" turret was knocked out.

> "The shell penetrated the front armour plate at its joint with the roof plate, blowing half the roof of the turret into the air. It ignited the cordite in the loading cages, which were about to be entered into the guns. The explosion and fire caused had killed every man in the gunhouse and working chamber . . . but did not ignite other charges in the loading cages a little further down in the turret; but there must have been a good deal of smouldering material, which needed only a draught of air to burst into flame. This air current was provided when the battlecruisers altered course 180 degrees to the northward[1] bringing what wind there was ahead. It was at this moment that the other eight charges in the supply hoist caught fire, and a considerable explosion took place, a flame shooting up as high as the mast head. This explosion was greatly reduced in its effect by the vent given by the removal of the turret roof; and although the magazine bulkheads were bent inwards, they stood the strain and saved the ship. The turret's magazine and shell room crews, however —some seventy men—were all instantly killed." (*The Navy and Defence*, p. 142.)

At the time of the hit Major Harvey, R.M.L.I., officer in charge of "Q" turret, who had both his legs shot off, gave the order to close the magazine doors and flood the magazines, otherwise the ship would have gone up. For this selfless action he was awarded a posthumous V.C.

At 4.3 a salvo from the *Von der Tann* struck the stern of the *Indefatigable* causing an explosion. She hauled out of line but was again hit near the fore turret, with a second explosion. Under a colossal pall of grey smoke the ship slowly turned over and sank, both her after and forward magazines having been pierced or exposed to flash in quick succession.

A few minutes later Evan-Thomas got his first glimpse of Hipper's ships, and having conformed to the flagship's turn the *Barham* opened fire at 19,000 yards, straddled the *Von der Tann*, and soon the *Moltke*, *Seydlitz*, *Von der Tann* and *Lutzow* had all been badly hit. But at 4.26 we suffered a second catastrophe. Both *Derfflinger* and *Seydlitz* had been concentrating on the *Queen Mary* which was delivering her salvoes with "fabulous rapidity" (Von Hase) when at 4.20 "Q" turret was hit and the right gun put out of action. The left gun continued firing when four minutes later a salvo fell on her upper deck forward. There was a dazzling flash of flame and at the same time a terrific explosion amidships as "Q" turret magazine went up. Masts and funnels fell inwards, the bows plunged under, and with her screws slowly revolving the *Queen Mary* went down as the *Tiger* and *New Zealand* raced past her smothered in debris. A great pillar of black and yellow smoke shot with flame spread out like a palm tree hundreds of feet high to mark her passing.

Hipper was achieving results he could never have anticipated, but the 5th B.S. were now harassing his rear and the German shooting began to fall off. Ahead of them the 13th Flotilla was coming in for an attack, while Beatty turned 45 degrees towards the enemy to close the range which had opened to 18,500 yards.

The destroyer attack coincided with one launched from the German side, and developed into a spirited and courageous action with losses on both sides. Of the twenty torpedoes fired one discharged at a later stage from the *Petard* hit the *Seydlitz* forward under the belt and tore a hole 13 by 39 feet in her closely compartmented hull which reduced her speed. It was the first fleet torpedo action of its kind, and pushed through with courage and determination *forced the German battle cruisers to turn away.*

While the turn away was still in progress, the recall was made when Goodenough signalled having sighted the High Seas Fleet to the S.E., and forthwith Beatty turned to port direct for the reported position while the 5th B.S. continued to attack the German battle cruisers. Two minutes later the long line of Scheer's battle fleet could be seen from the *Lion* 12 miles away.

Goodenough's cruisers had prevented Beatty being taken by surprise, and if Scheer could be tempted to hold his course he would inevitably steam straight into the guns of the Grand Fleet, hastening down from the north.

---

[1] This turn was made at 4.40—about half an hour later.

It was Beatty's responsibility to see that this junction came about under conditions favouring Jellicoe, which meant that the German battle cruisers must be prevented from sighting the Grand Fleet and giving warning to Scheer of the trap into which he was steaming.

Hipper's turn away from our destroyers broke off the action at a most critical period, and gave Beatty the opportunity both to locate the High Seas Fleet and then to make a 16 point turn to the northward towards Jellicoe, during which his ships could otherwise have been badly punished.

In a brief fifteen minutes the whole aspect of the battle had changed to Beatty's advantage, although the 5th B.S. were to undergo a severe gruelling. By the time Evan-Thomas' turn north to follow Beatty had been completed he was under fire from Scheer's van as well as from Hipper. The *Barham* was badly hit with twenty-six killed and thirty-seven injured; *Valiant* and *Warspite* escaped the concentrated fire, but *Malaya* was amid salvoes falling every ten seconds and received two severe hits below the water-line and one in the starboard 6-in. battery which burst inside it. Along the passage at the rear of the screens between the guns, blast and an ensuing cordite fire killed sixty-three and badly burned thirty-three. Despite deepening obscurity on the eastern horizon where the Germans could only occasionally be seen, hits were made on their battleships *Grosser Kurfurst* and *Markgraf* and battle cruisers *Lutzow*, *Derfflinger*, *Seydlitz* and *Von der Tann* until about 5.30 when the 5th B.S. was out of range, and hastening to join Jellicoe with the enemy in full speed pursuit.

The second phase of the Battle—the run to the north of the Battle Cruiser Force—had now commenced.

From 3.55 the Grand Fleet had been pushing south at 20 knots, Admiral Hood with the three *Invincibles* and attached cruisers and destroyers having been ordered ahead to support Beatty. When some 20 miles ahead of the Grand Fleet the *Chester* on his starboard wing came into action with enemy light cruisers, and within five minutes only her after gun was in action and most of her guns' crews were casualties. Hearing gunfire, Hood swung round to starboard and a minute later the *Chester* and her pursuers came into view. While the battered cruiser ran across the *Invincible's* bows to safety, 12-in. salvoes reduced the *Wiesbaden* to a wreck with *Frankfurt* and *Pillau* badly hit. To save his squadron Boedicker resorted to torpedoes, from which Hood turned away and the cruisers were lost in the mist.

Meanwhile to the westward a dramatic situation was developing. By 5.26 Beatty decided that he had drawn far enough ahead of Hipper and that it was now time to head him away from reaching a point where he could sight the Grand Fleet. He therefore turned to starboard to shorten the range and cross Hipper's bows, and at 5.40 renewed action at 14,000 yards. Visibility was at last in our favour and Beatty's ships made full use of it. The *Lutzow* was again heavily hit and *Derfflinger* had some bow plating blown off and started to sink by the head; *Seydlitz* was on fire, and *Von der Tann* had all her heavy guns out of action. Determined that Hipper should be prevented from sighting the Grand Fleet, Beatty pushed across the enemy van and by 6.5 had forced him to retire under cover of Scheer's guns. To extricate himself Hipper ordered a destroyer attack, but here again Hood's battle cruisers showed up at an opportune moment. Their sudden appearance at 5.35 in the eastward haze frustrated the attack, and also prevented it from interfering with the deployment of the Grand Fleet.

For correct deployment of a battle fleet from its cruising formation of six columns of line abreast to a fighting formation of single column of line ahead depended upon a knowledge of the enemy position, his course, and speed —and Jellicoe wanted this information from visual touch and not through wireless which was regarded as unreliable. But high speed during the approach had prevented the old armoured cruisers from keeping more than six miles ahead of the battleships instead of the sixteen miles appointed, and miscalculations as to true geographical position in both the *Iron Duke* and *Lion* and the meagre information received precluded any reliable estimation as to the whereabouts of the German Fleet. Reports as plotted in the *Iron Duke* led Jellicoe to believe that Scheer would be sighted right ahead at about 6.30—that is, six miles further eastward and about nine miles further away than he was. When Beatty was at last sighted heading off an unseen enemy (Hipper) and without having sighted the High Seas Fleet for over an hour, the only information Jellicoe received to a signal "Where is the enemy battle fleet?" was that the German battle cruisers were bearing south-east. It now seemed that the enemy would be sighted on his starboard bow, and a turn south was ordered to gain ground in that direction. But as this would have brought his columns into an unfavourable formation for deployment to the eastward, course was altered again to S.E., bringing them again abreast.

Visibility was now about seven miles which was much less than gun range, and it was vitally important that the Grand Fleet should be in battle line with all its guns bearing when the enemy appeared through the fumes and smoke. But all Jellicoe could see was a blurred picture with Beatty's battle cruisers shrouded in smoke on his starboard bow crossing from west to east, more smoke from the *Defence*, *Warrior* and *Duke of Edinburgh* also passing across his lines, and beyond them murk from the blazing *Wiesbaden*. A first inclination to turn to starboard (west) where there were signs of battle would have placed his weakest ships in the van close under Scheer's guns. He therefore decided to deploy to port, keeping between the enemy and their coast, and this manœuvre was carried out between 6.15 and 6.26.

It has already been noted that Rear-Admiral Arbuthnot in the *Defence* followed by the *Warrior* were adding their smoke to the murk which was hiding the Germans. During the approach these two ships together with the *Duke of Edinburgh* and *Black Prince* had formed the starboard wing of the Battle Fleet whose appointed station after deployment was in rear of the battle line. Should the fleet deploy towards the wing on which he was stationed it would be necessary for him to move his squadron to the opposite flank, a distance of about five miles. This could be done by passing down the disengaged side of the fleet—which would be the proper course for comparatively slow and weak ships whose smoke would interfere with our gunnery at a critical period; by passing down the engaged side he would be exposing his ships unnecessarily and to no good purpose.[1] Unfortunately the gallant Admiral chose the more dramatic course, first steaming across the line until he was in the grain of the *Lion* and then turning S.S.W. so that he just crossed the bows of the battle cruisers, forcing Beatty to deviate from his course and to lose sight of the enemy. Having pumped some 9·2-in. and 7·5-in. into the helpless *Wiesbaden* both ships came under fire and four minutes later the *Defence* was hit by two salvoes in quick succession and disappeared in a volcano of flame with 903 officers and men. The *Warrior* with damaged engines was only saved from the same fate through being encircled by the wounded *Warspite* whose helm had jammed. For a time both were in a forest of water spouts until the fighting passed to the eastward and they were left in peace. She was, however, too badly holed to save herself and had to be abandoned next morning after being towed by the *Engadine*. Beatty, having placed Scheer in an impossible position by his outflanking movement aided by Hood having routed the Second Scouting Group, took up his allotted position at the head of the line where he was joined by Hood's squadron two miles ahead. At 6.25 the German battle cruisers appeared out of the mist at a range of 9,000 yards and Hood opened fire, the shooting of his squadron being described by both sides as magnificent. The *Derfflinger* was hit again and again so that she had to be steered out of line to clear the hail of fire. Suddenly silhouetted against clear sky the *Invincible* came under rapid salvoes from the *Derfflinger* and probably the *König*. One salvo amidships was followed by several explosions; flames shot up from the riven flagship, masts and funnels collapsed and beneath a huge column of smoke the mother of all battle cruisers split in two, her bow and stern standing up out of the water as she rested on the sea bed, like gravestones to her thousand and twenty-six dead. Only six were saved, including her gunnery officer Commander H. E. Dannreuther who attributed the disaster to a shell which pierced the roof of an amidships turret, bursting inside and causing both "X" and "Y" magazines to blow up. It is worth noting that it was a hit on "Q" (the amidships) turret which might have finished the *Lion*; a "Q" turret magazine explosion sunk the *Queen Mary*; and explosion of the "P" and "Q" amidships magazines which split the *Invincible*.

With the loss of the *Invincible* the third phase of the battle commenced—the period of close manœuvre with the battle fleets at grips for brief spells. Jellicoe had almost completed his deployment when Scheer was sighted, and promptly came under fire from some eight points of the compass, although smoke and mist saved him from its full weight. The head of the German line was being smashed in, with the *Lutzow* completely disabled, *Derfflinger* badly damaged with a large hole in her bows, *Seydlitz* flooded to the middle deck forward, and *Von der Tann* with all her turrets out of action. Only the *Moltke* was serviceable and to her Hipper shifted his flag.

Facing a great arc of gunfire Scheer's position was hopeless, and to get his neck out of the noose he ordered a manœuvre which we considered impracticable under fire—a 180° turn together. At 6.35 with his ships four to five cables apart he carried out an evolution to which there was no reply, and shielded by a smoke screen from his destroyers, disappeared into the murk and firing ceased.

To cut them off from their retreat to the Bight Jellicoe turned to the S.E. (6.44) and receiving no reports of the enemy being sighted by his cruisers swung round to the S (6.56) by which time Scheer was about 15 miles to the S.W. Five minutes later the *Lion* signalled "Enemy are to westward" and Jellicoe turned three points to starboard in order to close. Again Goodenough had added to his fine record by following the enemy until he was under fire, and was in a position to see that he had turned to the eastward in order to make the dash for home. Scheer thought our ships had continued on a S.E. course, but had divided in order to search for him; a glimpse of the isolated *Warspite* and Goodenough's cruisers to the N.E. reported as "Individual enemy heavy ships" suggested that a course to eastward would cut off this detached section and allow him to pass astern of the main body, rescue the crew of the *Wiesbaden*, and have his enemy at a gunnery disadvantage to the westward.

Scheer's return trip was sighted at 7.8 and the *Marlborough's* division opened fire and all observed hits. The 5th Division led by *Colossus* which were ahead of them saw Hipper's ships in the mist to starboard and poured in an overwhelming fire at 8,000 to 9,000 yards. The *Colossus* was hit by two shells with minor damage—the only ones sustained by the Battle Fleet in the whole action. At last the battleships' turn had come and soon all of them were in action at 9,000 to 12,000 yards against the battle cruisers and enemy van. Instead of having a clear path to eastward Scheer was in the worst possible situation with Jellicoe crossing his T.

There was nothing for it but another turn about, but this time under far more difficult conditions as his enemy was closer and his line bent. At 7.12 his destroyers were ordered to attack under a smoke screen, and the hard pressed battle cruisers told to "Charge the enemy. Ram. Ships denoted are to attack without regard to consequences." The *Derfflinger* under Captain Hartopp led what was called "The death ride of the battle cruisers" and in a couple of minutes had two turrets blown to pieces with decks a shambles, ablaze fore and aft, and her control gear out of action. Smoke from the burning *Lutzow* blinded her consorts and only a signal "Manœuvre off the enemy's

---

[1] *The Navy and Defence*, p. 146.

van" allowed this forlorn hope to break away as the second German turn was completed by 7.20 and a smother of haze and smoke from the destroyers again allowed Scheer to get away.

The destroyer attack was carried out at extreme range (7.23) and only eleven torpedoes were fired, but as Jellicoe turned away they were without effect. A second half flotilla attack two minutes later was broken up by the 4th L.C.S. and destroyers, the ten torpedoes being avoided by individual ships.

At 6.57 the *Marlborough* was struck by a torpedo thought to have been fired by the indomitable *Wiesbaden.* She was hit under the forebridge with extensive injuries; her diesel and hydraulic engine rooms were put out of action and two men killed. Listing 7° to starboard she could still steam at 17 knots and use her guns, maintaining her position in the line.

Only Beatty had not turned away, and he was in sight of the enemy battle fleet and reported its position at 7.45 when Jellicoe turned to the west. At 8.17 the German battle cruisers came into sight again and Beatty opened fire at 10,000 yards; before they could retire *Derfflinger's* last turret was put out of action and *Seydlitz* lost all her forebridge personnel. Hipper had decided to board the *Moltke* but had to postpone doing this for another hour, and she had 1,000 tons of water aboard when he transferred his flag. During this shoot *Princess Royal* had clear ranges free from *Lion's* smoke for the first time in four and a half hours.

For Scheer the situation had again become impossible, and he feared an attack in force in the dusk which would press him further to the westward—so turned again for the third time before our battle fleet lost sight of him, and by 8.35 he was once more lost in the mist. Jellicoe asked Beatty for a bearing, but there was a hitch in transmission and the reply did not get through until 9 when it was too dark to risk further fighting and the fleet turned in divisions to the south in close formation to prevent ships mistaking each other for enemy vessels. Jellicoe aimed to get between the enemy and their base and fight it out in the morning, but at 9.30 Scheer made a third thrust to break through the British fleet, and this time succeeded in passing astern of it and escaped home by way of the Horns Reef.

Cruisers and destroyers took part in some fierce and complicated fighting during the night, but apart from the *Black Prince* being caught and sunk while making her way home, our armoured ships had no active part in it. The pre-Dreadnought *Pommern* was sunk by torpedo, and the *Lutzow* with 8,300 tons of water aboard was finally torpedoed by G.38 at 3.45 when her survivors had been rescued.

British Losses		*German Losses*	
Queen Mary	*Ardent*	*Lutzow*	S.35
Indefatigable	*Fortune*		V.4
Invincible	*Nestor*	*Pommern*	V.27
	Nomad		V.29
Defence	*Shark*	*Elbing*	V.48
Warrior	*Sparrowhawk*	*Frauenlob*	
Black Prince	*Tipperary*	*Rostock*	
	Turbulent	*Wiesbaden*	

NOTES ON JUTLAND

Hits Received

Barham	6	*Grosser Kurfurst*	8
Malaya	7	*Kaiser*	2
Marlborough	(t)	*König*	10
Warspite	13	*Markgraf*	5
Lion	12	*Schlesien*	1
Princess Royal	6-9	*Schleswig Holstein*	1
Tiger	10-17		
		Derfflinger	20
		Lutzow	24
		Moltke	4
		Seydlitz	24
		Von der Tann	4

(Large projectiles only are included.)

THE CORDITE DANGER

The fact that our propellent cordite exploded when exposed to flash in the magazines explains the loss of the battle cruisers, although before the battle it was held that gelatinized smokeless powders themselves hardly ever explode unless very strongly confined, and the larger sizes, which are used for ordnance, will only burn however fierce the heat may be.

Our cordite charges were enclosed in silk covers, while the German ones were in two sections—the main charge in a heavy brass case and the second in a double silk case contained in an outer tin case from which it was only taken when actually loading. The half charges removed from their protective covering never exploded.

Their magazines were not flashtight in the later accepted sense of the term. When flames from the charges burning in the turret spread to the case chamber they only blazed and did not explode. In our ships four turrets were pierced and three ships blew up, the *Lion* being saved because her magazine doors were closed.

Of the German battle cruisers, turrets were pierced in the:

Lutzow	No. 2 penetrated with a cartridge fire.
Derfflinger	Two turrets completely burnt out.
Seydlitz	No. 2 penetrated and right gun put out of action.
	No. 3 penetrated twice. First burnt out the working chamber, and second caused a "Lion" fire.
	No. 4 hit twice and penetrated second time.
	No. 5 hit twice; the second caused a "Lion" fire.
Von der Tann	No. 1 penetrated with a small fire only.
	No. 2 penetration caused a big fire.

Thus, in nine penetrations there were eight fires but no ships were blown up.

ARMOUR

The claims that German ships survived because of our defective shells were based on German reports that our shells broke up on hitting at an oblique angle. But defective German shells were found in our ships, and there is German evidence that our shells did what theirs could not do. British armour was penetrated as follows:

Warspite	13″ once at 10,500 yards.
Lion	9″ once at 14,600 yards, the maximum range at which 9″ was pierced.
Princess Royal	9″ once.
Queen Mary	9″ say three times.
	German
Von der Tann	No. 1 barbette 9″ at 17,500 yards by 12-in. shell.
	No. 2 barbette and battery deck total 10″ at 17,500 yards by 12-in. shell.
Moltke	11″ belt armour at 17,500 yards by 12-in. shell. This exploded in a coal bunker and damaged battery deck.
Seydlitz	No. 2 turret 9¾″ front plate at 18,800 yards.
	No. 3 turret 8″ back plate at 18,800 yards.
Lutzow	No. 2 turret 9″ at 19,800 yards.

At shorter ranges apparently all German armour could be pierced. That the maximum range at which British 9-in. armour was pierced was about 14,600 yards, while our 12-in. shell were getting through 11-in. plates at 17,500 yards; 13·5-in. shell through 10-in. at about 19,000 yards and 9-in. at nearly 20,000 yards is some evidence of the superiority of our armour.

The claim that our fuses were defective on the grounds of German statements that shells had broken to pieces on turret armour—the hit on No. 1 of *Von der Tann*—led to a later issue of improved ammunition. But the above record shows that even at extreme ranges oblique hits got through thick armour. Tests with German plates and upon the battleship *Baden* showed that their resistance was not up to British standards.

SUBDIVISION

German designs showed greater subdivision than did the British, which made them almost unsinkable. Added to which their system of damage control kept ships on an even keel—the *Lutzow* with 8,000 tons of water in her was still upright when almost awash. It was usual for a sectional model showing compartmentation to be exhibited in large ships to facilitate instruction in counter flooding, drainage, and pumping.

The tragedy of Jutland was that the lateness of the hour and conditions of visibility prevented a beaten enemy from being defeated and destroyed. That our material losses were greater was beside the point. The British Fleet with an ample margin of strength was in full control of the North Sea, the Germans having escaped by brilliant evasive tactics from a trial by battle which they had no intention of facing. In the words of their chief naval critic Captain Perseus "Our Fleet's losses were very severe. On June 1st 1916 it was clear to any thinking person that this battle must, and would be, the last one."

On the afternoon of 1 June, unable to hide his disappointment at the result of the battle, Beatty repeated to his navigator "There is something wrong with our ships" and added "And something wrong with our system." There was, and when Beatty succeeded to the command of the Grand Fleet the rigid system of control, tactics, and training which had hitherto obtained was considerably modified, and Fisher shibboleths about speed and armour went by the board in favour of a balanced design for our capital ships.

* * * * *

No worthwhile comparison between the British and German battle cruisers can be made from their experiences at the Dogger. It required a willing enemy and plenty of time and sea-room to fight a conclusive action, and here the change in leadership deprived us of our chances of forcing a verdict. On the whole one can say that the larger British guns proved of more value than the thicker German side armour, but that at long range with dropping salvoes horizontal protection was worth more than vertical. As none of our ships underwent the experience of the *Seydlitz*, the need for thicker armour to protect magazines was not forced upon us.

At Jutland our battle cruisers were not lost through lack of vertical armour or better enemy shooting, but because cordite exploded when it should only have blazed. Exposure of the armoured cruisers to battleship gunfire could only have one ending, and Arbuthnot's squadron demonstrated it. That with the exception of the *Moltke*, Hipper's ships were rendered unserviceable was not all to the credit of Beatty's guns—they had also been under fire from 15-in. weapons, the like of which our ships had not to face, and no battle cruisers were then designed to withstand such guns. The *Derfflinger's* worst hits were from 15-in. shells one of which pierced "X" turret causing a bad ammunition fire and the death of seventy-three men, and the other penetrated "Y" roof causing a similar fire and killed eighty men. She was not repaired until the middle of October. The unlucky *Seydlitz* had hits on her second, third and fourth turrets causing bad fires and loss of life. A severe hit on the port side forward made a huge hole, and one on the bridge killed everyone up there and wounded several officers in the conning tower. She was also torpedoed. Damage and blood rendered her charts useless and illegible, and the reserve charts were in a flooded compartment. When the gyro compass broke down she ran ashore at Horns Reef, but got afloat again by her own screws. With a draught of 43 feet, leaking bulkheads and bucket gangs hard at work she went aground a second time near the reef but was got off five and a half hours later. Going astern to save her bulkheads and with the aid of two salvage pump steamers she reached the Jade on 2 June and was not repaired until the middle of September.

The experiences of our own ships may be summarized briefly:

Lion, 12 hits

The top of "Q" turret was blown off followed later by a bad fire which might have brought about her destruction. Two hits on the side armour did little damage.

Princess Royal, 9 hits

The main control top was put out of action for a short time by two hits forward in the first ten minutes. One shell exploded in the Admiral's cabin forward causing casualties among the 4-in. gun crews, started several fires, and filled the lower conning tower with fumes. "X" turret was struck and put out of action; a hit on "B" turret caused no injury. One shell pierced the starboard side aft, came through a bunker, and wrecked the after engine room casings; then exploded on the port side causing casualties among the 4-in. gun crews. Failure of all lighting systems and damage to the fire mains made fire fighting difficult.

Tiger, 17 hits

"Q" turret roof was struck on the central sighting hood, putting the left gun and loading gear out of action temporarily, later worked by hand loading—a difficult process with such large guns. "X" turret pierced and shell found between the guns with nose and fuse missing; loading gear damaged. A hit perforated the 9-in. side armour abaft "Q" turret and burst inboard penetrating the armour deck and just missing the main steam pipe in the port engine room. A bad cordite fire broke out near the 6-in. magazine which had to be flooded; heat and dense smoke filled the engine room. This hit caused many casualties.

Barham, 6 hits

One hit below the water-line did no damage. Another entered the glacis between No. 1 (S) 6-in. abreast after end of "B" turret wrecking the medical store rooms, fuelling pumps and auxiliary w.t. Many casualties. The flash passed up to the battery deck, igniting cartridges in S.2 casemate with loss of life. Some pieces of shell penetrated the middle deck and entered the lower conning tower (the only instance of shell splinters getting to magazine level in surviving ships). Others pierced the roof of the forward 6-in. magazine. Other hits were not serious.

Warspite, 13 hits (30 according to the account in *The Fighting at Jutland*, p. 148)

A hit below the water-line caused no damage. One through the side armour in the boys' mess deck caused a fire, controlled with difficulty; local damage only. There were several hits aft, one blowing in the side below the Admiral's cabin; others wrecked cabins and after flats and made a hole in the deck which admitted water. "X" turret redoubt hit, with casualties, water entering the hole in the side, flooding main deck and down central engine room trunk. One unexploded shell was found in the engineers' workshop. A shell entered the galley and wrecked it. A hit on the port side aft under the engineer's office blew off a piece of the main belt; a fresh water and oil fuel tank were destroyed and the deck bowed up. The hole could not be plugged and the entire compartment had to be filled with nearly 600 hammocks. Another hit aft by the 6-in. control hood did local damage. A shell burst in the starboard battery causing a bad fire in the superstructure from 6-in. cordite gases, with many casualties but the fire did not spread as in the *Malaya*. One shell through the after funnel hit the armoured grating over B boiler room and was deflected upwards smashing a cutter. Another went through the boys' mess deck from the embrasure overhead, the armour being holed. A 12-in. on the communication tube of the after director tower spun the tube right round—one killed and two wounded in the tower. A direct hit on "X" turret did no damage. All the boats were smashed, the quarter deck holed in several places, and searchlights looked like scrap iron The vessel was drawing 35 ft. aft when docked.

Malaya, 7 hits

Two hits forward, one indenting the upper armour plate, the other tearing the plating below the armour. Wing compartments flooded and ship shaken considerably. Another hit on plating above the water-line displaced it backwards. Two hits from a salvo amidships depressed the gun deck and galley, canteen, drying room and fittings wrecked by one passing through the forecastle deck and exploding in the 6-in. battery. A severe cordite fire destroyed the cables, and flame and debris passed down the air supply trunk to A boiler room damaging fittings and extended right back to the ammunition supply trunk and luckily stopped. The whole starboard battery was put out of action and most of the gun crews killed or burnt.

Two hits below the armour amidships caused a large hole and flooded the inner and outer oil bunkers and wing compartments with a 7° list for a time. A hit on the roof of "X" turret did not explode. Minor damage only.

Marlborough, torpedoed 6.55 p.m. 31 May

Struck by a torpedo in the diesel engine room amidships which flooded it and the hydraulic engine room, with water beginning to enter A boiler room. This caused a starboard list 7° and speed was reduced to 17 knots. Six minutes later three more torpedoes reported, two passing ahead and one astern. She remained in the line and did not have to haul out until 2 a.m. next day when the water started to gain. At 9.30 was attacked by two submarines and later a torpedo passed along her port side. She was escorted by destroyers and an oil track was laid to prevent seas breaking over the starboard upper deck, and reached Immingham at 10 a.m. 1 June.

* * * * *

When firing ceased with the oncoming darkness, and the enemy was lost to view in smoke and haze, the battle ended so far as the battle fleet was concerned. Neither Jellicoe nor Beatty wanted a night action and set course for a position which could cover the German retreat with the hope of renewed fighting next day. Both our cruisers and destroyers came into contact with the enemy during the night with severe fighting and ship losses, but the last engagement between battle ships had been fought and the German fleet never put to sea again with the intention of provoking a general action with the Grand Fleet.

Chapter 112

"HOOD"

As it was known that Germany was building several battle cruisers to be armed with 15-in. guns the D.N.C. was instructed in 1915 to prepare designs for ships of this type embodying the latest ideas as regards armament, speed and underwater protection. A considerable number were submitted to the Board, but as there were no large berths available, orders could not be placed before the spring of 1916. In March the approved design was worked out, and this formed the original basis for the *Hood*.

Dimensions	810′/860′ × 104′ × 25′ 6″ (normal) 29′ (deep)=36,300 tons.
Armament	8 15-in. guns. 16 5·5-in. guns. 2 21-in. torpedo tubes.
Armour	Equal to that of the *Tiger* with 8″ belt and 9″ barbettes.
Machinery	144,000 S.H.P.=32 knots. Small tube boilers.

Orders were placed for four ships in April 1916:

Anson ..	.. Armstrongs	*Howe*	.. Cammell Laird
Hood ..	.. John Brown	*Rodney*	.. Fairfields

In June came the reports on Jutland, when as a result of the damage done both to our own and the German battle cruisers it was decided that a radical increase in protection was indicated. Fisher's dictum that "Speed is the best Protection" went by the board, as did the former conception of the battle cruiser. There could be no longer any question of securing high speed by reducing armour weight in an elongated hull of approximately battleship displacement. Ships intended for the battle line would have to carry protection on battleship scale, and thus the original design for a battle cruiser with armour on the second class scale was scrapped in favour of an entirely new conception—the ultra fast battleship.

As redrafted a scheme of augmented protection was to be accommodated by increase in draught and a slight reduction in speed. The alterations included thickening of the belt from 8 in. to 12 in., barbettes from 9 in. to 12 in., and extra deck protection in region of the magazines. At the same time gun elevation was raised to 30° and modifications made in the torpedo equipment and anti-flash arrangements to the magazines. These changes involved an additional 5,000 tons raising displacement to 41,200 tons when carrying 1,200 tons of fuel at 28½ ft., and 45,200 tons at 31½ ft. with 4,000 tons in the tanks.

At this increased displacement stability conditions were satisfied with a metacentric height of 3·3 ft.

Consultations with the Commander-in-Chief delayed final approval for the design with all details of fire and torpedo control, arrangement of bridges, etc., until 1917, so that four years passed before the *Hood* was ready for service.

When it was learned that the Germans had ceased work on the *Graf Spee*, *Prinz Eitel Friedrich* and *Furst Bismarck* in 1917 the construction of the *Howe*, *Anson* and *Rodney* was stopped after some £860,000 had been spent on them; but the *Hood*, having been launched before the Armistice, was carried to completion.

"HOOD" (Emergency War Programme)

Builders	*Laid down*	*Launched*	*Completed*	*Cost*
Clydebank	1 Sept. '16	22 Aug. '18	5 March '20	£6,025,000

Dimensions	810′/860′ × 104′ × 28′ 6″=41,200 tons. Full load at 31′ 6″=45,200 tons.	
Armament	8 15-in./42 12 5·5-in./50. 4 4-in. A.A. 4 3-pdrs.	Torpedo tubes: 2 21-in. sub. 4 21-in. a.w.
Protection	Sides amidships 12″-7″-5″; bulkheads 5″-4″. „ forward 6″-5″. „ aft 6″. Barbettes 12″-6″-5″; turrets 15″-11″-5″ crowns. Conning tower 11″-9″; 6″ base; 5″ crown. Director tower 6″-3″; control towers 4″-3″. Funnel uptakes 1¼″.	

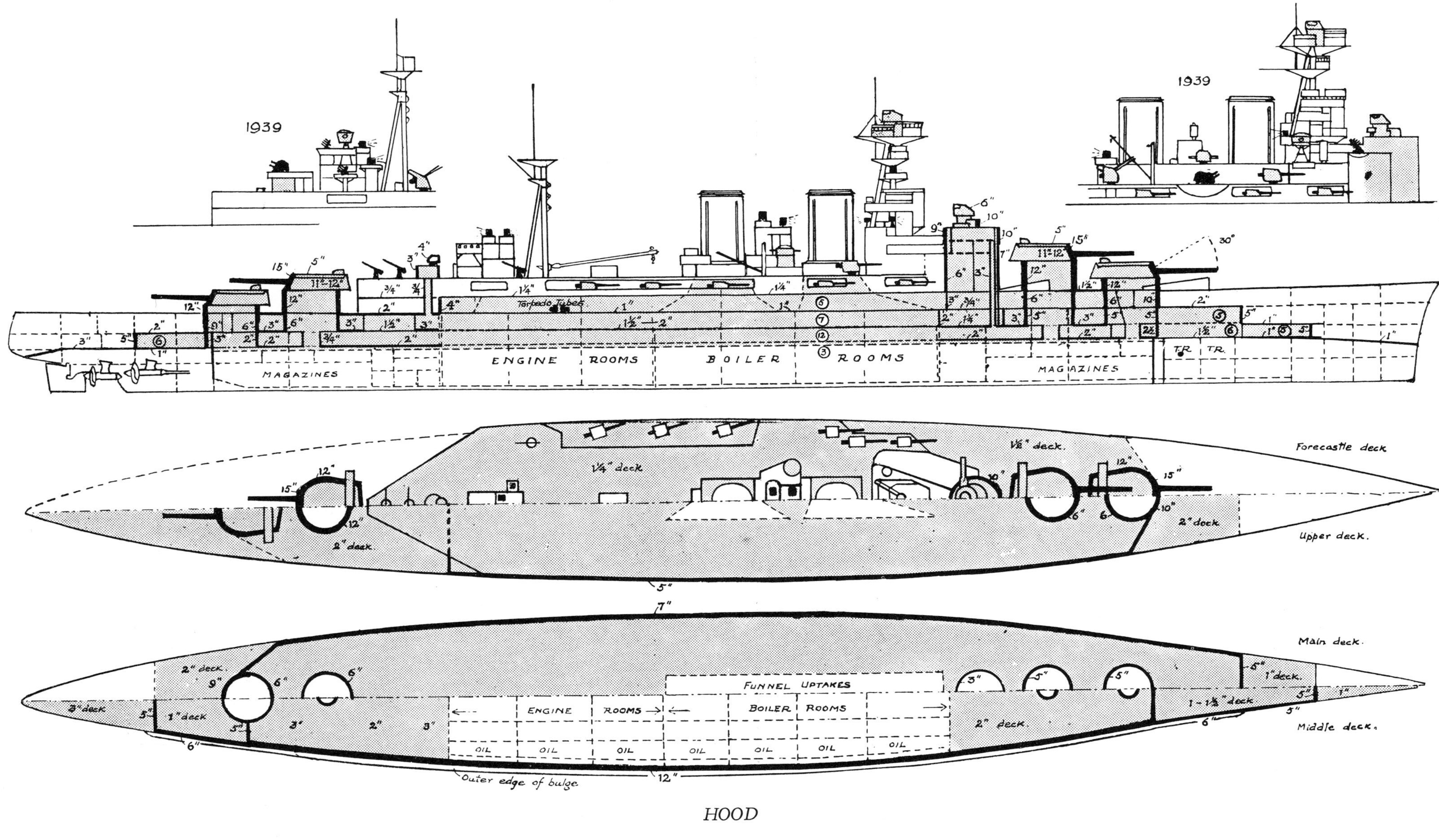
1939
1939
MAGAZINES
ENGINE ROOMS
BOILER ROOMS
MAGAZINES
Torpedo Tubes
TR TR
Forecastle deck
Upper deck.
1¼" deck
1½" deck
2" deck
2" deck
Main deck.
Middle deck.
FUNNEL UPTAKES
ENGINE ROOMS
BOILER ROOMS
OIL
2" deck
1" deck
3" deck
2" deck
1" deck
1-1½" deck
Outer edge of bulge

HOOD

	Decks: Forecastle 1½″.
	Upper (amidships) 1″.
	Main 1½″-2″; 3″ over magazines.
	Lower 1½″-1″ forward; 3″-1″ aft.
	Torpedo bulkhead 1½″-¾″.
	(Total weight of armour 13,800 tons.)
Machinery	Brown-Curtis geared turbines S.H.P. 144,000=31 knots. Boilers 24 Yarrow (small tube). 4 screws.
Fuel	Oil 1,200/4,000 tons.
Maintenance cost	(1934) £274,000 p.a.
Complement	1,477.
Constructors	E. L. Attwood. S. V. Goodall.

Weights expressed as percentages of normal displacement.

[1]Hull	36·0
Equipment	2·0
Armament	12·5
Machinery	13·0
Fuel	3·0
[1]Armour	33·5
	100·0

Special features:

(1) The largest, fastest, and finest-looking capital ship of her era.
(2) The last capital ship to have an open secondary battery.
(3) First British armoured ship to have small tube boilers.
(4) Last British capital ship to have mast-head control tops.

In designing the *Hood* Chief Constructor E. L. Attwood conceived as stately and gallant a fighting ship as ever hoisted an ensign. The Service knew her as "The Mighty 'Ood" and to the British Public she represented all that was finest in our Fleet. From first to last she retained her original profile without any disfiguring funnel

Hood on trials at deep load steaming at 32 knots.

[1] The plating of the decks and sides was of such thickness for strength that it contributed very materially to protection. Its weight, however, is included in "Hull".

alterations, and for full twenty years saw no rival to her proud position of Queen in the Fleets of the World in both beauty and strength.

HULL

Floating some 3 feet deeper than originally intended, the reduced freeboard was partially offset by a marked sheer at the bows and stern—but insufficient to keep the quarter deck from being flooded in a seaway.

Several fresh problems were presented when the additional armour was introduced, and the bending moment to be provided against—due to the great weight of the barbettes being so far apart—was very considerable; as in the *Renown* the riveting of the 1½-in. and 2-in. plating had to be very carefully arranged to get as large a proportion of it as possible effective for structural strength.

The marked flare of the hull side eliminated the chance of a hit at right angles when the cap held the shell point so that the belt could be pierced, and thus virtually increased the resistance of the armour while allowing for a much wider bulge than in the *Renown*, its width being determined by the weight of explosive charge in the torpedo of that day. It will be seen that the side plating was continued from lower deck to double bottom at a thickness of 1½ in. with an external bulge made up of an outer section of w.t. compartments separated by ½-in. plating from a buoyancy space also subdivided. The internal part of the anti-torpedo space, instead of forming part of the bulge as in the *Renown*, was a part of the hull proper composed of fuel compartments and separated from the working compartments by an air space. The bulge covered the water-line between the end turrets with the sides moulded to flush with it. There was no necessity for complete water-line protection because if some of the compartments forward of the magazines and the under-water torpedo-room had been blown in, the results would not have been serious. It was calculated that the ship could stand the explosion of several torpedoes and still remain in the line without serious loss of speed.

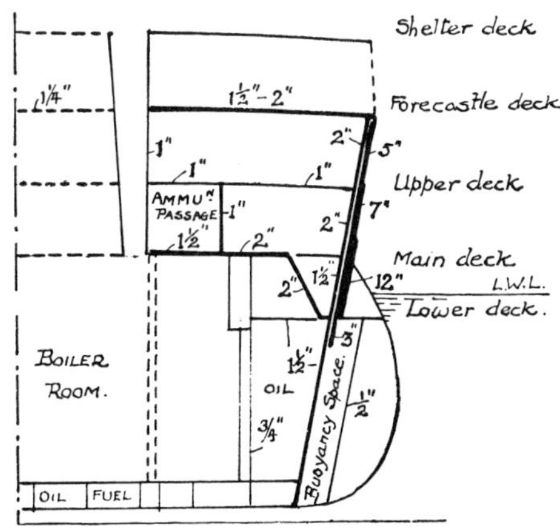

Section of *Hood* amidships to show inclined side armour, shallow belt and *Furious* type of bulge.

ARMAMENT

When the design was re-cast, the elevation of the 15-in. 100-ton guns was raised to 30°, their height above water being: Forward 32 ft. and 42 ft. with training 60° abaft the beam, and 31¾ ft. and 21¾ ft. aft with training 60° before the beam. The turrets had a flatter roof than formerly with 15-in. plating on the face, 11 in.-12 in. on the sides, and 5-in. roof—considerably thicker than in previous battleships. For the first time sighting hoods were abolished and a 30 ft. range-finder spanned each turret top, with small ports cut in the face plates. The turrets weighed 900 tons.

The 5·5-in. gun had been introduced into H.M. Service by two cruisers building for Greece at Armstrongs and re-named *Chester* and *Birkenhead* in 1915; it had also been mounted in the *Furious*. Its 82 lb. projectile was easier to handle than the 100 lb. 6-in. and little less effective against destroyers, being a mean between the 6-in. and 4·7-in. Their distribution in batteries also dates the design, as secondary guns were not as yet envisaged as for defence against aircraft, which were still almost a negligible factor against capital ships. The single pieces brought the axial concentration to six guns forward; none had a bearing aft, the four guns originally provided having been removed to save complement and the embrasured superstructure remoulded.

Four 4-in. on the after shelter deck and abreast the mainmast formed the original sky battery, but during her refit of 1929-31 multiple pom-poms replaced the boats slung between the second and third battery guns each side, and in 1939 a number of multiple machine guns were added abreast the conning tower and around the after control station, with twin 4-in. amidships in place of the single guns aft. During the World War close-range A.A. guns were installed wherever possible.

Torpedo armament being still in favour for capital ships twin 21-in. tubes were placed on the upper deck abreast the main mast and single tubes in the customary flat forward below water.

PROTECTION

Although completed after the Great War the *Hood* was not regarded as embodying any post-war ideas as regards protection, but only as an enlarged *Queen Elizabeth* with extra deck armour and thinner plating amidships. We had not yet accepted the "All-or-Nothing" scheme of protection, and thin armour was spread over the sides at the expense of decks and turret tops; only the unprotected 5·5-in. batteries showed a turning towards *Oklahoma* standards, although here any useful armour would have had a considerable effect on stability.

The 12-in. belt covered 562 ft. to a depth of 9½ ft. (of which 5½ ft. was above water) thinning off to 5 in.

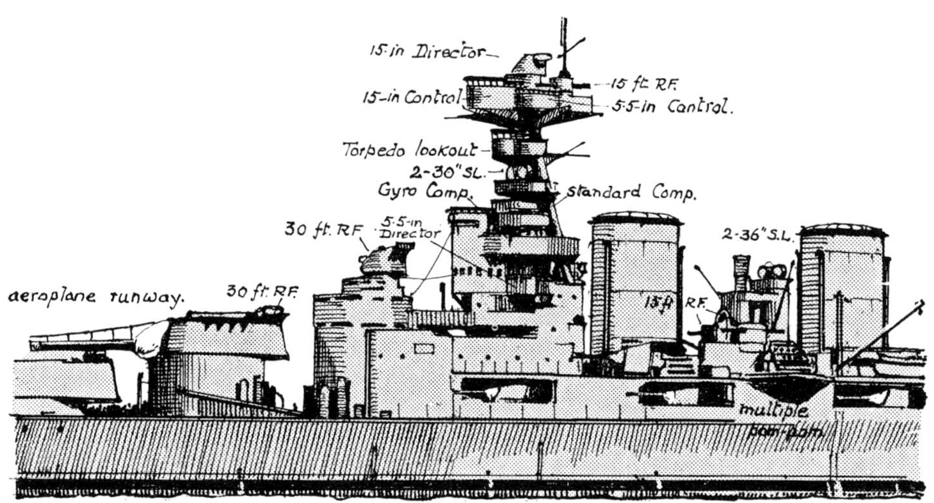

Some details of *Hood* after her 1929-31 refit.

towards the bows and 6 in. aft. Above this came a strake of 7 in. to the height of the upper deck and 5 in. between the upper and forecastle decks. But as all armour sloped outward from below, the virtual resistance was increased as shell could not hit with normal impact. Behind this armour came the side plating, mainly 2-in. with 1-in. fore and aft; this added to the side armour brought its thicknesses up to 13½-in., 9-in. and 7-in.

The additional armour allotted to horizontal protection in the revised design was largely distributed over the magazines. Forward this amounted to 1½ in. on the forecastle deck, 3 in. on the main, and 2 in. on the lower deck; aft the weather deck was 2 in., main 3 in. and lower deck 2 in.—by far the heaviest aggregate thickness yet fitted.

CONNING TOWER

This was by far the heaviest, most elaborate, and best devised position yet installed. It required over 600 tons of armour 11 in.-9 in. thick on the more exposed areas and carried a 30 ft. range finder in a revolving hood on its crown. The position at the after end of the shelter deck was a torpedo control tower.

MACHINERY

Geared turbines of 144,000 s.h.p.—the greatest power plant afloat—occupied three engine rooms, of which the forward one contained two independent sets for the outer shafts and the middle and after rooms one independent set each for the inner shafts. At full speed the propeller revolutions were only 210 p.m., which allowed for propellers of higher efficiency. On trial a mean speed of 32·07 knots was obtained with 151,280 s.h.p. at 42,200 tons, and 31·9 knots at deep load 44,000 tons—so that the actual speed with increased protection was equal to that intended in the lightly armoured original design.

The adoption of small-tube boilers—so long advocated by the Constructor's Department—markedly influenced the design by virtue of smaller space and reduced weight compared with the large-tube type. As the *Courageous*, *Glorious* and *Furious*—our first big ships to be equipped with small-tube boilers—were only regarded as large cruisers, the *Hood* ranks as the first capital ship to have them. The actual weight of the *Hood's* boilers and machinery generating 150,000 s.h.p. was almost exactly the same as that in the *Renown* and *Repulse* for 112,000-120,000 s.h.p., so that about 30 per cent. more power was obtained with the same weight. The pumps and ejectors could remove 20,000 tons of water per hour.

VENTILATION

Special attention was paid to the ventilating arrangements, supply and exhaust fans providing fresh air—warmed if necessary—at low velocity to all living spaces, with a full "natural" supply to the engine and boiler rooms; each of the main transverse compartments had a separate supply to avoid piercing any bulkheads. Accommodation was luxurious compared with that in ships ten or fifteen years old.

SEA-GOING QUALITIES

Although 3 ft. 6 in. lower in the water than had been arranged in the original design, the clipper bow and great flare forward kept her forecastle from being flooded at full speed; aft the lack of freeboard was felt considerably, the quarter-deck being awash in a seaway or at speed despite the appreciable sheer. But she made a steady gun platform, and was regarded as a good seaboat. But the effect of heavy seas may be judged from reports on patrol in Northern waters Christmas 1939 when huge waves swept the boat deck doing damage to the picket and motor boats.

GENERAL

The *Hood's* launching weight was 22,000 tons and she was sent afloat by Lady Hood, widow of Rear-Admiral Hood who was killed aboard the *Invincible* at Jutland. Her original cost was £6,025,000 (£145 per ton) with an annual upkeep of £400,000.

This ship was due for a major reconstruction following completion of the *Queen Elizabeths* if the political situation warranted the risk of putting our heaviest capital ship out of action for a couple of years or so. As it was, she had to accept all the wartime additions to equipment without being able to surrender any equivalent weight, so that the gallant old ship became overloaded and behaved more like a half-tide rock, as well as showing signs of strain.

As completed her displacement was 41,200 tons at legend draught and 45,200 tons at deep load. In 1940 these figures had risen to 42,462 tons with a G.M. of 3·25 ft. legend draught, and 48,360 tons with a G.M. of only 2·99 ft. deep load.

Her secondary armament was quite out-moded, and being ineffective against aircraft was regarded as so much dead weight.

The reconstruction of the *Hood* proposed early in 1939 was to include:

(*a*) Provision of new machinery.
(*b*) Modifications to underwater protection.
(*c*) Removal of the conning tower.
(*d*) Removal of the above-water torpedo tubes.
(*e*) Removal of the 5·5-in. and 4-in. guns and fitting eight twin 5·25-in. mountings.
(*f*) Fitting hangars etc.
(*g*) Increase of horizontal and vertical protection.

Items (*a*) to (*d*) would have resulted in the removal of about 4,000 tons and (*e*), (*f*) and (*g*) would have added about the same amount. Of this about 2,000 tons would have been available for improving the protection. War intervened before detailed investigations had reached a definite plan stage, and the whole project was dropped. But in general lines she would have resembled a modified *Renown*.

"HOOD"

Built at Clydebank September '16-March '20. Commissioned May '20 as Flagship B.C.S. (Acting Vice-Admiral Sir Roger Keyes) relieved by Rear-Admiral Sir Walter Cowan for Summer Cruise '21. '22 with *Repulse* represented the Royal Navy at Centenary Celebrations, Rio de Janeiro. Paid off May '23 and re-commissioned under flag of Rear-Admiral Sir Frederick Field. During a second visit to Scandinavian waters she flew the flag of King Haakon of Norway as hon. Admiral. '23 Flag-showing World Cruise with *Repulse* and 1st L.C.S. Sierra Leone—Cape Town—Durban—Zanzibar—Trincomalee—Malay States—Singapore—Fremantle W.A.—Adelaide—Melbourne—Hobart—Sydney—Wellington N.Z.—Auckland—Suva—Honolulu—Victoria B.C.—San Francisco—Kingston—Halifax—Quebec—Newfoundland. During ten months she had steamed 40,000 miles and been visited by nearly three-quarter million people. '24 January joined Atlantic Fleet for Spring Cruise and detached to Lisbon for Vasco da Gama celebrations. April Rear-Admiral Cyril Fuller. '26 Re-commissioned. Routine cruises Home and Mediterranean. '28 Re-commissioned. Admiral Sir Frederic Dreyer until April '29. Paid off at Portsmouth for refit June '29-May '31. '31 Re-commissioned in May, Atlantic Fleet. Flagship Rear-Admiral W. Tomkinson and Vice-Admiral Sir Wm. James ('32). '33 Re-commissioned Home Fleet. Vice-Admiral Sir Sidney Bailey (1934). '35 Collided with *Renown* 23 January '35; repaired at Portsmouth. '36 Re-commissioned in September Mediterranean Fleet. In November Vice-Admiral Sir Geoffrey Blake transferred flag from *Barham*. From April was patrolling North Spanish waters during Civil War. Autumn cruise in August visiting Mediterranean ports. '39 Refit at Portsmouth February-August. Joined Home Fleet as Flagship Vice-Admiral Sir W. J. Whitworth. October bombed in North Sea. No casualties. '40 Refit at Plymouth. 250 men joined Expeditionary Force to Norway. Convoyed New Zealand troops to England; procedeed to Gibraltar where Vice-Admiral Sir James Somerville joined the ship. Frequently bombed by Italian aircraft. Action against French ships at Oran in July. Returned Home in August (Vice-Admiral L. E. Holland). 19 May '41 sailed in search of *Bismarck*, with *Prince of Wales*; chase started 24 May and at 06.00 snowstorm abated and enemy sighted; enemy turned and closed at full speed. *Hood* opened fire—and shortly after was hit forward of "Y" turret. A great fire broke out, but *Hood* raced onwards, still firing. Then the magazines blew up and masts, funnels and structure hurled hundreds of feet into the air. Her bows tilted vertically and in four minutes only wreckage, smoke and flame remained. Three survivors were picked up. Her loss was broadcast at 9.0 p.m. 24 May and came as a staggering blow, ranking as a national disaster.

Chapter 113

THE POST-WAR YEARS

WITH the signing of the Armistice on 11 November 1918 the dispersal of the Grand Fleet started without delay. Day after day the gaps in the long lines grew bigger as battleships and battle cruisers flying their paying-off pennants steamed out of the Forth en route for Portsmouth, Devonport, or Chatham. Soon the Hamoaze, Medway, and upper reaches of Portsmouth Harbour were cluttered up with discarded warriors tied up in bunches—stripped, discarded, weatherbeaten, and forlorn. By the end of the war most of the pre-Dreadnoughts were being employed on subsidiary duties, and these were among the first to go, together with the once all mighty *Dreadnought*. In May 1921 a fleet of 113 warships were bought by Messrs. Ward of Sheffield for a flat rate of £2 10s. per ton of actual displacement—the largest sale of its sort ever recorded. Among them were the *Dreadnought*, *Hindustan*, *Dominion*, *Mars*, and *Magnificent*—the two last laid up and minus their guns after having served as troopers for the Suvla Bay campaign, but proud at having kept company with the once Queen of the Fleet as their lives drew to a close.

Later in the same year the remaining 12-in. gunned ships were placed on the Disposal List, and the *Colossus*, *Hercules*, *Neptune*, *St. Vincent*, *Collingwood*, *Temeraire*, *Bellerophon* and *Superb* went the way of their famous namesakes of the past. With the completion of the *Hood* the last of the big ships provided under the Emergency War Programmes passed into service, and according to a vociferous band of critics headed by Admiral Sir Percy Scott no more should have been built, as the battleship was doomed. *The Times* opened its columns to a long drawn out controversy on "Great Ships or . . . ?" when the chances of battleships surviving torpedo or bomb in a future war were argued from every point of view except, of course, that based upon a conception of future methods of attack and defence below and above water. For in the nineteen-twenties it was as much beyond man's range of vision to foretell the development of radar, magnetic and acoustic mines, pin-point bomb dropping with enormous armour-piercing bombs and other extraordinary means of attack and counter-attack as it would be for the nineteen-forties to hazard how war might be conducted in the nineteen-sixties.

In this country the "War to end Wars" was taken in a very literal sense. The German Fleet was at the bottom of Scapa Flow, and warnings by the Admiralty that the war-worn ships must be replaced and the Navy generally modernized were dismissed as merely being attempts to bolster up "bloated armaments." The public demand was for national economy, anti-waste, disarmament, and the abolition of the Capital ship; it was backed up in Parliament and by the Press. Naval Estimates were cut to the bone. Work ceased on all ships except those too far advanced to warrant scrapping, and the hulls of uncompleted carriers, cruisers, and a few destroyers were towed from the shipbuilders to the dockyards and there slowly finished off, with the result that year by year overhead charges swelled ultimate costs so that 6-in. gunned cruisers like the *Emerald* and *Enterprise* absorbed nearly one and three-quarter millions—a big sum for those days.

Unfortunately the effect of the Great War was little more than the temporary elimination of Germany as a naval power. It did nothing to end the struggle for sea supremacy, but merely substituted Japan for Germany, shifted the rivalry from the North Sea to the Pacific, and brought in the United States as a first-line competitor. Both America and Japan had drawn up programmes of new battleship construction during the War, but naturally these attracted no attention in this country. In any case they were not put into full production, and as both nations had fought with us as allies and the long standing alliance with Japan was still in active operation, any additions to their fleets could not be expected to cause apprehension. Our eyes had been centred on the North Sea for so many years, and the former Russian menace in the Far East had been banished by the Russo-Japanese war so that to the average man it looked as if we had no enemies capable of disturbing our future. Once the aftermaths of war had been cleaned up in Europe and the new national boundaries settled at the Peace Conference we might look forward to an indefinite period of peace. But the stage was already being set for the mightiest competition in naval armaments ever conceived. In order to preserve the "Freedom of the Seas" according to American interpretation a gigantic programme of armoured ships had been authorized by the U.S. Navy Department in 1916 although none had been laid down until 1919 when the six battleships of the *Indiana* class (43,200 tons, twelve 16-in.) and six *Constellation* battle cruisers (43,000 tons, eight 16-in.) had been commenced in full confidence that they would enjoy an unrivalled mastery of the seas. Japan had commissioned the 33,800 ton battleships *Nagato* and *Mutsu* carrying eight 16-in. by June 1921 while the *Kaga* and *Tosa* (39,900 tons, ten 16-in.) and battle cruisers *Amagi* and *Akagi* (43,000 tons, eight 16-in.) had been commenced in 1920, but about which nothing was known. Then early in 1921 U.S. Naval Intelligence was able to supply particulars of these ships and also of the 45,000 tonners with eight 18-in. to be laid down in the following years.

Faced with such a threat to her naval supremacy there was nothing for it but for Britain to follow suit, and the 1921 Estimates included four 48,000 ton battle cruisers to carry nine 16-in. which were to be followed by a group of 48,500 ton battleships with nine 18-in. At an average cost of £7 million apiece these three Powers were committed to an expenditure of £252 million on capital ships alone.

Confronted with the unpalatable fact that their mastodons, far from being unrivalled were already being equalled and threatened by heavier gunpower, the politicians responsible for the big American programme became only too eager to do something to stop the monstrous snowball they had set rolling. Domestic criticism was violently against the exorbitant cost of the new ships, and the Government was warned that a naval race in the Pacific would inevitably lead to war. By 1921 opposition had reached such a pitch that the completion of the Programme was no longer feasible. Mr. Hughes, Secretary of State, afterwards admitted that they could not have built all the battleships authorized. In addition funds had been voted for preliminary work in creating naval centres at Cavite and Guam which were to serve as advanced bases in a possible Pacific war.

There could be no question of scrapping the accepted designs and laying down more powerful units, owing to limitations in beam set by the locks in the Panama Canal. America did not want a Pacific war, and most certainly did not want an enormously expensive fleet of outclassed capital ships on her hands. The only solution lay in calling a Disarmament Conference without delay. In due course Great Britain, Japan, France and Italy were invited to such a Conference which was held at Washington in 1921-22.

THE 1921 BATTLE CRUISERS

Although work on these ships had only just commenced when the invitation to the Washington Conference caused them to be abandoned, they stand out as the most powerful British capital ships ever designed, incorporating a novel distribution of armament which had a good deal of influence on future design here and abroad, and deserve more than a casual reference.

It was generally understood that they would perpetuate the four "I" names of our first battle cruisers, but these were never officially given them, and they were just known by their numbers.

		Ordered	*Suspended*	*Cancelled*
No. 1	Swan Hunter	21 Oct. '21	18 Nov. '21	Feb. '22
2	Beardmore			
3	Fairfields			
4	Clydebank			

Dimensions 820′ p.p. (856′ o.a.) × 106′ × 32½′ (mean) = 48,000 tons.

Armament 9 16-in. in triple mounts.
16 6-in. 6 4·7-in. H.A.
32 2-pdr. pom-poms on four mounts.
2 24½-in. underwater tubes.
2 aircraft.

Protection Side amidships 14″ at 72° slope over magazines.
" " 12″ " 72° " " machinery and after magazines.
Bulkheads forward 12″-5″; aft 10″-4″.
Barbettes 14″ maximum.
Gunhouses 17″-13″-8″ roof.
Conning tower 12″-6″ roof.
Decks: Forecastle 1″; upper 8″, over magazines 7″ aft.
Lower 8″-7″ forward; 5″-3″ aft.

Propulsion Geared turbines 160,000 S.H.P. = 31-32 knots.

Fuel Oil 5,000 tons.

Complement 1,716.

Constructors E. L. Attwood and S. V. Goodall.

ARMAMENT

Although British firms had supplied triple 12-in. mountings for Italian and Russian ships since 1909 and the Americans had put them into various classes since 1912, the Admiralty had preferred the twin mount as being simpler, safer, and conducive to better shooting. The need for restricting length and concentrating armour however brought about the acceptance of the triple mount in these ships, which otherwise could only have carried six guns or eight in four turrets. Although deprived of direct fire astern, the superstructure around the funnel bases was so angled that the area of immunity aft was only 20° on each side—where it was considered unlikely that an enemy ship would be engaged.

The secondary guns were widely spaced to command large arcs of fire without interference, each group being separately controlled. For the first time 6-in. guns were mounted in turrets instead of in a battery, together with

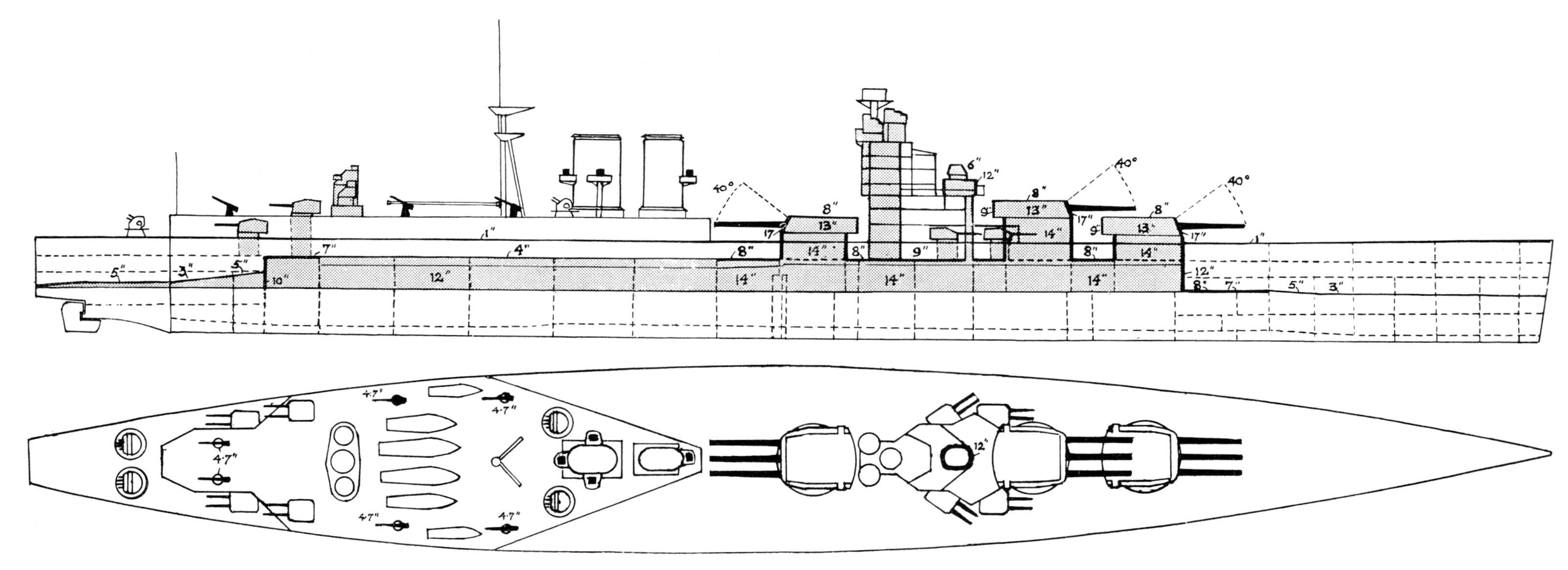

1921 Battle cruisers.

The third turret was placed amidships to provide wide arcs of fire abaft the beam. The three compartments abaft the 14-in. belt are boiler rooms with two engine rooms and 6-in. magazines beyond. Note the 8-in. and 9-in. deck over the forward magazines—the thickest ever intended for H.M. ships.

a heavy A.A. armament. During the World War II the after superstructure would have been lined with Bofors and Oerlikons, but in 1921 this was considered ample air defence.

PROTECTION

Hull armour was confined to the 12 in.-14 in. belt which thinned to 9 in. at its upper and 6 in. at its lower edge, and sloped inboard from the vertical as in the *Hood.* Water-line integrity was augmented by a bulge and underwater protection water jacket and tubes. Fore and abaft this citadel ran a protective deck only, 5 in over the steering. Horizontal protection over the magazines was the heaviest yet provided being 8 in.-9 in. thick amidships, over the machining spaces it was 4 in., and 7 in. aft over the 6-in. magazines.

The scale of armour protection followed that introduced in the U.S. *Nevada* and offered splendid defence against all forms of attack as then foreseen.

1921 Battle cruiser.

TOWER BRIDGE

In place of the customary bridgework and tripod mast a compact tower mast gave good protection and support to the range-finders and control stations and provided space for sea cabins, bridge, chart house, signal and plotting offices, look-out positions etc. It was exposed to blast effects when "X" turret fired forward of the beam or when the forward guns were trained abaft it, but was better adapted to withstand such stresses than the ordinary type of bridge.

It is perhaps difficult to realize that an interval of five years only came between this revolutionary design and the *Hood*, although the disparity does not compare with such earlier metamorphoses as the *Pallas* (1863)-*Devastation* (1869), or *Albemarle* (1900)-*Dreadnought* (1905).

The concentration forward of the main armament only appeared in the *Nelson* and the French *Dunkerque* and *Richelieu* classes; but the secondary turrets in place of a broadside battery were generally adopted, being a reversion to the medium gun disposition found in many pre-Dreadnought types (*Republique*, *Suffren*, *Rostislav*, *Poltava*, etc.). The tower mast-bridge in various forms was also widely copied after it appeared in the *Nelson* and became the outstanding feature of all battleships until their construction ceased.

The cancelling of these four contracts was as severe a blow as the Clyde shipbuilders had experienced, coming as it did at a time when naval construction was at its lowest ebb and the heavy armament industry almost threatened with extinction.

THE WASHINGTON CONFERENCE

There is no need to recount the misleading publicity and somewhat irregular circumstances which led to the final signatures of the contracting Powers. Suffice to say that agreement was reached on the following clauses affecting capital ships.

(1) The British and American battle fleets should be limited to 580,450 tons and 500,650 tons respectively, with Japan 301,320 (60 per cent.), France 221,170 and Italy 182,800 tons.
(2) Capital ships should be limited in displacement to 35,000 tons with 16-in. as the maximum gun calibre.
(3) Capital ships could be replaced by new construction twenty years after completion, and no fresh construction should be undertaken in the meantime.
(4) Reconstruction should be limited to defence against air and submarine attack to a limit of 3,000 tons. More latitude was allowed to France and Italy.
(5) The "Standard" displacement of a ship should be that when she was fully equipped for sea but without fuel and reserve feed water on board.

Britain was allowed to retain:

5 *Revenge* Class	1 *Hood*
5 *Queen Elizabeth* Class	2 *Renown*
4 *Iron Duke* Class	1 *Tiger*
3 *King George V* Class	
1 *Thunderer* (as training ship)	

but could build two 35,000 ton battleships in 1922 to offset Japan's retention of the *Mutsu*.

Britain scrapped 657 ships of a total displacement of 1,500,000 tons including twenty-two completed Dreadnoughts and four battle cruisers laid down in 1921. Dreadnought tonnage scrapped: 382,070 completed, 5,522 building.

America scrapped four completed Dreadnoughts and one partially completed together with the sixteen new ships varying from 4 per cent. to 38·5 per cent. completed. Total: 96,752 tons completed, 120,691 tons building.

The "building" tonnage represents weight of material actually worked in for each ship.

In addition to agreement on the reduction of naval armaments, America and Japan also agreed to abandon the great naval bases they had intended to create in the Pacific, and thus relinquished the only means of bringing their main battle fleets into action against each other. Without an adequate base overseas a fleet at that period was tied to its own coast, the fleet supply train being a creation of the then distant future.

The most difficult struggle our chief negotiator Rear-Admiral Chatfield had at the Conference was over the displacement of capital ships to be built in the future. A maximum limit of 32,500 tons had been proposed by the U.S.A. which was that of their *Maryland* class then under construction or completed. These carried eight 16-in. guns with a 16 in.-14 in. belt, 18 in.-9 in. on the four turrets at 21 knots, and they wished to retain 16-in. as the future limit. The Admiralty on the other hand thought that the 15-in. of the *Warspites* was sufficient when in conjunction with a higher speed than 21 knots, and did not consider a well-balanced design could be produced on 32,500 tons. If 16-in. guns were to be allowed, then displacement would have to rise to 35,000 tons, and designs were prepared showing "balanced" ships with the 15-in. and 16-in. guns.

But as the Japanese were building the two *Nagatos* with 16-in. which were too advanced to scrap, the U.S. delegates stood out for a 16-in. limit. It was finally agreed that a 35,000 displacement should be permitted and this without fuel oil and water—roughly 2,500 tons—and as British designs had to allow for a higher percentage of fuel and water than was customary abroad, the concession meant that this extra tonnage would not have to be taken out of protection. The U.S.A. were to retain three of their four 16-in. battleships scrapping the *Washington*, to match the two *Nagato's*, and our demand to build two new ships was agreed to after long debate.

"NELSON" Class (1922 Programme)

	Builders	*Laid down*	*Launched*	*Completed*	*Cost*
"*Nelson*"	Armstrongs	28 Dec. '22	3 Sept. '25	June '27	£7,504,055
"*Rodney*"	Cammell Laird	28 Dec. '22	17 Dec. '25	Aug. '27	£7,617,799

Dimensions 660′ (710′ o.a.) × 106′ × 30′ = 33,950 tons (38,000 full).

Armament
9 16-in.
12 6-in.
6 4·7-in. A.A.
8 2-pdr. pom-poms.
Tubes: 2 24½-in. submerged.

Final A.A. armament:
16 40 mm.
48 2-pdr. pom-poms.
61 20 mm.

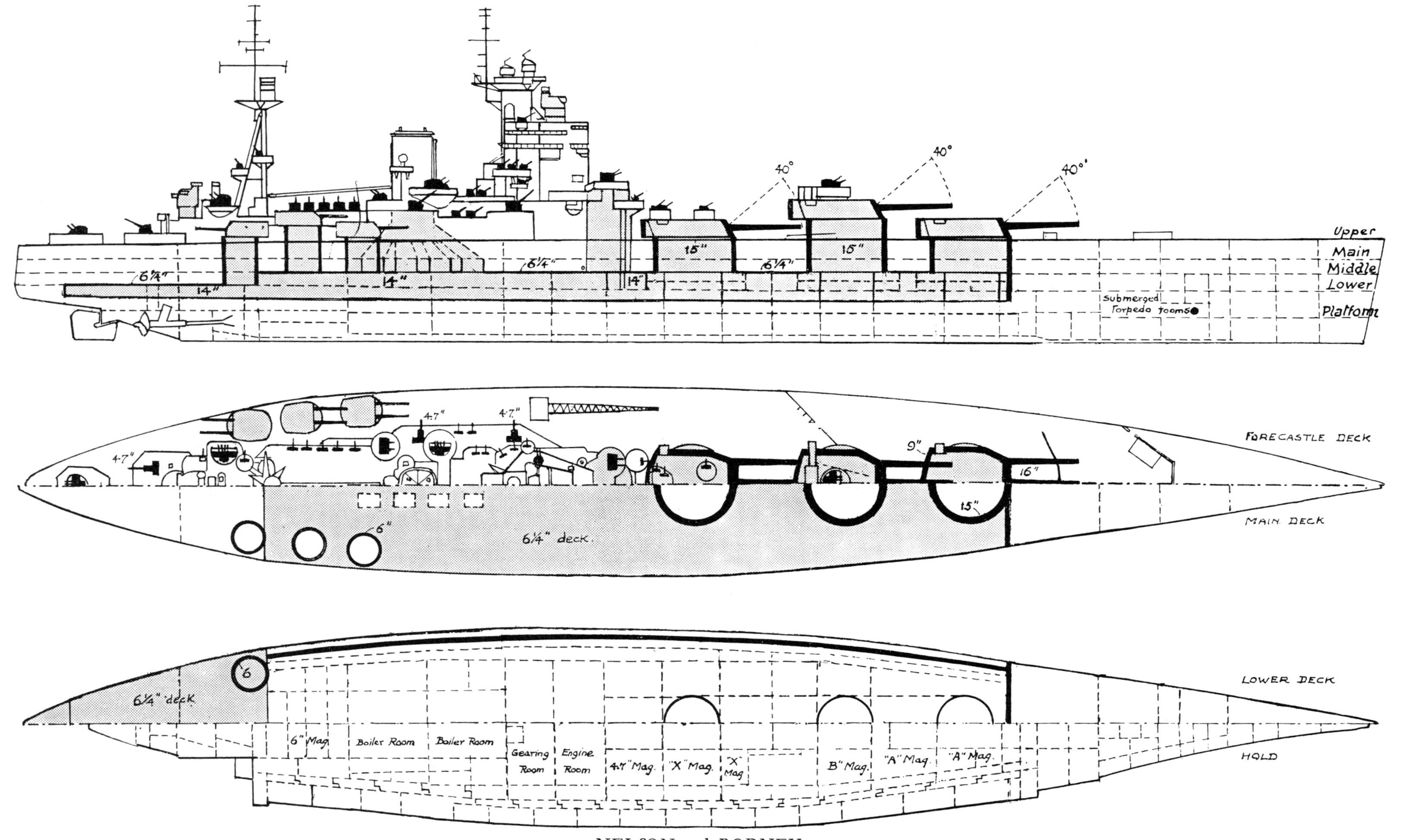

NELSON and RODNEY

Nelson is here shown with the A.A. armament she carried at the end of the War. As completed there were only the three 4·7-in. aside with a range finder in place of the multiple pom-poms abreast the funnel. The heavy structure on top of the tower replaced a light trunk carrying a control position, and there was an armoured director on the crown of the conning tower.

Protection	Belt 14″; bulkheads 14″. Turrets 16″-9″ backs. Barbettes 15″. Deck 6¼″ over magazines; 3″ over machinery.
Machinery	Brown-Curtis geared turbines. 2 shafts. Designed h.p. 45,000=23 knots. Boilers 8 3-drum with superheaters.
Fuel	Oil 4,000 tons. (Consumption: full speed 16 tons an hour; cruising speed 2·7 tons an hour.
Complement	As flagship 1,361; as private ship 1,314. Wartime 1,640.
Constructors	E. L. Attwood and S. V. Goodall.

Special features:

(1) Only British ships to mount 16-in. guns.
(2) First to have triple mountings.
(3) First warships to have a tower mast.
(4) First British battleships to have flush decks since the *Lord Nelson.*
(5) Main deck batteries replaced by small turrets.
(6) Engine rooms forward of boiler rooms.

As the terms of the Treaty permitted us to proceed at once with the construction of two 35,000 ton battleships—the last we should be able to build until 1931—alternative plans were considered during 1922 and the orders placed in December.

In the design accepted the general conception was for diminutives of the 1921 battle cruisers with the limitations

The *Nelson* with her main armament trained abeam as she appeared in 1944. The dazzle painting in blue, green and pink was supposed to baffle identity from the air.

imposed by a reduction in displacement of 13,000 tons. The same armament was to be carried with equally solid protection; high freeboard and good seakeeping qualities with a speed equal to or higher than foreign contemporaries were essential; and only thick armour on the all-or-nothing system for water-line and deck was to be fitted. The compromise presented much the same problem as confronted Barnaby in the case of the *Admirals*—side armour would have to be restricted to a water-line strake over the magazines and machinery spaces only, covered by a protective deck as thick as possible. This meant that forward of the turrets the whole hull would be as bare as the sides above the middle deck.

For the first time in the history of the Navy her constructors were prescribed by international limitations which were to be scrupulously observed. Weight estimation and economy became of first importance, and many standard Admiralty fittings were redesigned to save weight. Extensive use was made of "D" steel, aluminium in kit lockers, cupboards, mess racks etc. and the use of Douglas fir on deck in place of teak with plywood for dwarf and non-strength divisional bulkheads all contributed to such weight saving that the standard displacement was 1,000 tons below the Washington limit. All wood fittings were fireproofed.

The flush deck gave a freeboard forward of 29 ft., amidships 25½ ft., and 27 ft. aft, with more than half its length swept by the main armament. The bridge tower carried directors for the 16-in., 6-in. and A.A. guns, an Admiral's bridge, torpedo control, signalling and navigating platforms, various sea cabins and offices. "C" turret was placed exactly amidships, and in order to avoid smoke interference with the tower controls the engine rooms were immediately abaft the magazines and directly under the tower—the only instance of the usual sequence being reversed. But unfortunately 40 feet was not sufficient distance between the tower and funnel to prevent fumes permeating the bridge, especially when steaming head to wind when the tower caused excessive backdraught. A 15 ft. extension to the funnel or a cowl to its top was proposed and could have cured this troublesome defect.

They were the last ships to be built with a separate conning tower, which was surmounted by an armoured revolving director position.

ARMAMENT

In order to concentrate the magazine armour "Q" turret in the battle cruisers had to be placed forward of the tower so that its gun muzzles were close under the overhang of "B." This siting while enabling the nine guns to train forward of the beam without blast effects on the tower, made gunfire abaft the beam unbearable and the bridge almost untenable, especially with any elevation to "C" guns.[1] Consequently the after-training of the turrets was arbitrarily reduced, which was a disadvantage. Trials made in 1931 with the tower windows closed by special plate glass in small panes only, resulted in the windows being smashed and the bridge structure damaged. Special screens fitted in the *Rodney* did little to reduce the trouble, and it had to be accepted that gunfire abaft the beam was a contingency to be avoided. Between decks broadside fire before the beam was equally shattering, gunfire being only tolerable when the target was well abeam.

Armstrongs supplied the 16-in. mountings for both ships and 6-in. mountings for *Nelson*; Vickers supplied the *Rodney's* 6-in. mountings.

Comparison with the 15-in. gun was as follows:

	Length	*Weight*	*Shell*	*m.v.*	*Full charge*
16-in.	45 cals.	103½ tons	2,461 lb.	2,953 ft. secs.	640 lb.
15 „	42 „	97 „	1,920 „	2,450 „ „	428 „

Elevation was as much as 40° so that the guns could be used against distant aircraft; range was 35,000 yards; and the cost of a full salvo £700. Weight saving in the mountings led at first to frequent trouble, and it was a full five years before they could be relied upon to maintain salvo firing.

The 6-in. were the first to be power worked in the Service, the turrets being placed as far aft as possible to lessen blast effects from "C" guns trained aft. Elevation was 60° for A.A. defence. Six 4·7-in. A.A. in *Nelson* were later replaced in *Rodney* by eight 4-in. A.A. Two 8-2 pdr. pom-poms abreast the funnel were installed before the war, later increased to six. The final A.A. armament included 16-40 mm. and 61-20 mm.

Two 24·5-in. torpedo tubes were housed singly under the lower deck forward—the only examples of this calibre in the Service although carried by most major units in the Japanese Navy.

PROTECTION

In devising the system of protection the constructors were faced with considerable difficulties. The Board required the armour to be the thickest practicable—an All-or-Nothing application which severely restricted the area to be covered by the weight available after offence and propulsion had been satisfied, i.e. a thick but shallow belt over magazines and machinery spaces, in part covered by the stoutest horizontal armour since the cruisers *Powerful* and *Terrible* were given a 6-in. protective deck.

The D.N.C. would have liked to follow the *Hood's* inclined side armour and bulge system, but certain requirements made this impossible.

(1) The width of the bulge had to be increased considerably to counter torpedoes carrying a much greater charge, but if widened *pro rata* the ship would have been too beamy for existing docks.

(2) The armoured beam at the water-line had to be increased to ensure stability in the riddled condition.

Hence to proceed from *Hood* to *Nelson* the thick protective bulkhead had to be moved in and the armour belt moved out, so that they were no longer in line as an inner wall of a structure simple to design. Now displaced armour plates in the *Lion* at Dogger Bank and the *Derfflinger* at Jutland had demonstrated that plating and sections are relatively ineffective in supporting armour and that the best way is by armour itself. Hence in the *Nelson* if the armour belt were inside the curved hull the plates could be flat and keys driven straight down. Then at the top by recessing belt plates the thick deck would stop an armour plate being driven in; at its bottom the

[1] During the *Bismarck* action in 1941 blast from the *Rodney's* guns lifted the steel helmet from her Captain's head, which hit and knocked out a signalman standing some feet away.

protective bulkhead was run right up to the armoured deck which it helped to support, and used to back the belt armour. This made the top of the *Nelson's* citadel thus:

S-S¹ was a shelf of stout plating well supported; on it was an armour quality casting recessed to take the lower part of the armour plate. If the plate were struck it could not move at the top and would not move far at the bottom as this meant forcing the casting up hill and bringing into action the strength of the protective bulkhead. Hence this midship section:

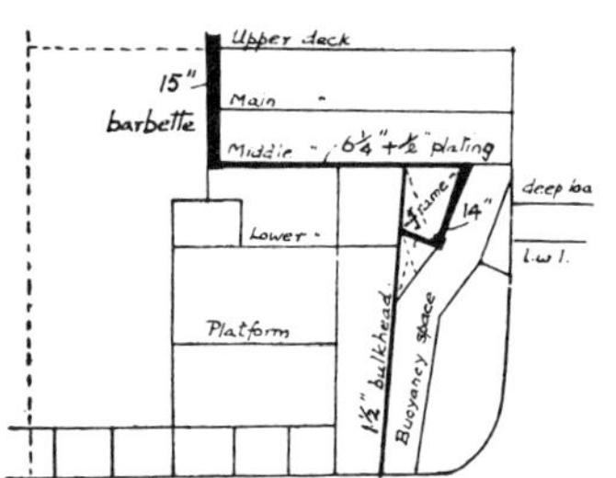

A full-sized target was tested and the shell exploded against the belt. All that happened was that splinters went down and struck the thick bulkhead. But although the ship might take damage outside without disaster, nobody liked the narrow belt, and there was always the fear that a shell might get below it owing to wave profile or the pitch and roll of the ship in action.

Published elevations of the *Nelson* show her side armour as a 14-in. belt extending from the middle deck down to the platform, which errs on the generous side by the height of a deck. The armoured deck was 6¼ in. on ½-in. plating over the magazines, reduced to 3 in. over machinery spaces—which was pierced when the *Rodney* was hit by a bomb aft, in 1940. When used as a target after the war, the *Nelson's* decks were pierced through and through, as by 1948 no warship afloat carried deck armour thick enough to withstand attack by heavy bombs.

PROPULSION

Steam at 250 lb. was supplied by six small-tube boilers of 5,600 h.p. each and two of 5,100 h.p. arranged two in each group of four boiler and engine rooms with central stokehold spaces. The groups of boiler and engine rooms were separated by a longitudinal bulkhead and the scheme of machinery subdivision was carried out to a degree never attained previously in large warships.

Nelson's machinery was by the Wallsend Slipway and Engineering Co., the *Rodney's* by her builders. Brown-Curtis turbines driving two shafts through single reduction gearing gave 23·5 to 23·8 knots for 46,000 h.p. at standard displacement. Oil consumption at full speed was 16 tons per hour and 2·7 tons when cruising. The turning circle at full speed was 670 yards or 2·7 times the ship's length, nevertheless the ships were described as exhibiting a majestic dilatoriness in answering the helm and propellers, with a tendency to hold the wind aft and turn into the wind owing to the large bridge structure. A Captain of the *Nelson* stated:

> "I am certain that every one of the commanding officers of the *Nelson* and *Rodney* would agree that the ships handled badly, especially in shallow water or in a wind. They were slow in starting to turn after helm was put over. Once they started to swing a very considerable amount of opposite helm had to be applied a long time before they reached the course on which it was desired to steady them. In a following sea they yawed badly, and steered badly when going astern and with sternway."

The effect of wind when at sea in these ships is shown by this report, "When proceeding at 12 kts. from Portland to Portsmouth with a wind of force 6 on the port beam, 12 degrees of starboard rudder was required to maintain course on the passage."

The *Nelson* had the very quick period of 11 seconds which was surprising in so large a ship, and made things uncomfortable in bad weather.

GENERAL

Accommodation for officers and men was on a generous scale with reading and recreation rooms, dressing rooms, wash places, drying rooms for wet clothing, and stowage spaces. Oil-fired galleys and electric bakery ovens were an innovation.

The full implications of "darken ship" under modern war conditions and its effect on ventilating arrangements had not been anticipated in peacetime. In these ships the exhaust to the crew's galley was mainly by means of the open skylight, which when closed for darken ship caused almost intolerable conditions for the cooking staff and distinctly bad elsewhere.

Although as ugly as the old *Sans Pareil* and *Victoria* they were our most impressive battleships evoking a truly British sense of solidity, especially when viewed from their best angle abaft the beam. When their ensigns were lowered for the last time it was felt that the day of the battleship was over with the remaining *King Georges* and *Vanguard* as just relics of a departed glory.

"NELSON"

Built by Vickers-Armstrongs at Newcastle-on-Tyne December '22 to June '27. Commissioned 15 August '27 as Flagship, Atlantic Fleet and for the next fourteen years wore the flag of seven successive Commanders-in-Chief in the Atlantic and

Home Fleets. She and the *Rodney* fell short of the record set up by the *Minotaur* and *Agincourt* by four years. She was at Scapa at the outbreak of war. Damaged by magnetic mine off Loch Ewe 4 December '39; repair and refit until August '40. Served with Home Fleet until August '42 (damaged by aerial torpedo during Malta convoy "Halberd" 27 September 1941). In August '42 as Flagship of Admiral Syfret transferred to Mediterranean with *Rodney*, 3 Carriers, 7 Cruisers and 32 destroyers, forming Force H. Took part in several Malta convoys including that of August '42, the African landings, and the invasion of Sicily and Italy. It was on board the *Nelson* at Malta that the Armistice with Italy was signed on 29 September '43 by General Eisenhower and Marshal Badoglio. In June '44 she was in the bombardment squadron for the Normandy landings. Mined and went to Philadelphia for a six months refit. On V.E. Day was at Malta *en route* for the East Indies where she became second Flagship of the East Indies Fleet. After operations against Japanese in Malaya she was at Trincomalee on V.J. Day and then proceeded to Penang for the surrender of that area which was signed on the same table as was that of Italy. At the end of '45 the *Nelson* returned to England, and after a further period as Flagship C.-in-C. Home Fleet joined the Training Battleship Squadron in August '46.

Sold February '48 and used as a bombing target before being broken up at Inverkeithing.

"RODNEY"

Built by Cammell Laird December '22 to August '27. Atlantic Fleet '28-'32. Home Fleet '32-'41. In April '40 when Flagship of Admiral Sir Charles Forbes was hit by a bomb during operations in the North Sea resulting from the invasion of Norway. Her armoured deck was pierced aft with 15 casualties. Escorting a convoy in May '41 she was ordered to leave it and join in hunt for *Bismarck*, when her engineers achieved speeds thought to be impossible, especially considering that she was long overdue for a refit, and had suffered both engine room and boiler breakdowns. Her third salvo was the first hit on the *Bismarck* and she finished the action with short range fire. In September '41 when Flagship of Sir James Somerville, Force H she led a Malta convoy, and during a similar mission in August '42 opened up at enemy aircraft with 16-in. guns at 9 miles. Refit December '41-May '42. Supported North African landings November '42, carrying out several bombardments, and engaged the Djebel Santon fort until it capitulated. Was at Spithead before operation "Neptune" and bombarded Caen and other strong points before the landing. Was attacked by human torpedoes, bombs, and shells but was undamaged. On August 12 her 16-in. fired over a hill to wipe out a German battery on Alderney Island. September '44 convoy to Murmansk. Steamed 156,000 miles on war service without a proper refit since '42 which she needed badly at the end of hostilities.

Sold February '48.

A Note on Radio-controlled Target Ships

In order to be able to carry out practice firing under more realistic conditions than could be afforded by the stationary battleship targets, the *Agamemnon* was stripped of her armament and equipped with radio-control to her steering gear which was activated from an attendant destroyer. She could then be manœuvred as required while being fired at by medium and small calibre guns, or used as a target for aerial bombing.

Some idea of the accuracy and estimated danger from air bombing in 1924 may be gathered from experiments carried out against the *Agamemnon* in July, which simulated war conditions as nearly as possible. A bomb dropped from 12,000 ft. requires 28 seconds to reach the deck of a ship. A 21-knot ship moves nearly 1,000 ft. on her course while the bomb is in flight, and if she zigzags the difficulties in estimating the trajectory with the means then available are tremendous. In these tests 114 bombs were dropped from a varying 5,000 to 12,000 ft., and not a single hit was made.

The *Centurion* became radio-controlled target ship in 1928 but no records of air attack upon her are available.

Chapter 114

THE TEN YEARS RULE

In 1930 a pernicious law came into operation in which it was to be assumed that there would be no great war for another ten years. Laid down for the guidance of Whitehall and the Services only, it went further than the Ten Years Battleship Holiday agreed to at Washington which assumed that the Services could be ready for war in 1932. As ships took a long time to build, and dockyards had to be restored to efficiency again, this provision permitted the Admiralty to resist drastic cuts in expenditure later on, as it could be argued that these could not be recovered from by 1933. So in order to give the Chancellor of the Exchequer a firm grip on the Economy Axe, the Cabinet decided that the Ten Year Rule should be renewed each year, thus ensuring each of the three Services and the next war would always be at ten years notice. In order that foreign governments should be in ignorance of this crippling procedure it was made secret, and Parliament was left unaware of it—and so, of course, were the People.

Consequently, for the next ten years the very roots of our naval existence—the Dockyards, private shipbuilding, the armament industries and skilled labour in vital factories upon which our existence as a great nation depended —were allowed to wither away. When the Rule was at length rescinded the power so unwisely wielded by the Exchequer had reduced the Empire's defences to a state that soon afterwards became a public scandal.

A second Naval Treaty in 1930 was called at the instigation of the United States who were concerned that our cruiser strength was greater than their own. They did not want to spend money upon cruisers or destroyers when they had neither a scattered Empire, long trade routes, nor a huge mercantile marine to protect. So as Prestige and Parity were seen as marching hand in hand, we were invited to keep down our cruiser expansion in order that by 1936 we could not have more than 50 ships, many of which would be over age. Admiral Chatfield, then First Lord, had a hard struggle with the Labour Prime Minister Mr. Ramsey MacDonald, but eventually won his claim for seventy cruisers even though it might cause a breach with the United States.

But in the matter of battleships there was a very different story. Mr. MacDonald had been considerably influenced by the theories of Admiral Sir Herbert Richmond who claimed that capital ships were unnecessary and that no warship need exceed 7,000 tons—that is, of sufficient force to defeat armed merchant ships. His writings in the British press had been eagerly accepted in political circles and by the Air protagonists, who were unable to weigh them correctly in relation to foreign navies. Unfortunately they led to the defeat of the Admiralty in the 1930 London Conference when we agreed with the U.S. and Japan to postpone building the battle-fleet replacement tonnage until January 1937 although France and Italy could lay down the new keels to which they were entitled. All we could do was to take advantage of the clause in the Washington Treaty permitting the displacement of existing ships to be increased by 3,000 tons in order to strengthen them against air and torpedo attack, which was then being carried out in the first rebuilding of the *Warspites*.

At the 1930 London Conference the Admiralty was defeated by the Foreign Office who wished to placate America, and the Treasury. Despite our totally different requirements, parity to the U.S. in cruisers and destroyers was accepted, placing our sea security in jeopardy, and in conjunction with the Ten Years Rule assuring the naval panic of 1936. New construction was to be limited to an allotted tonnage until January 1937 when both Treaties were due to expire. By that time we could have added a total of thirty-seven modern ships, by building 7,000-tonners like the *Leander* which had come into favour as off-setting the German *Köln* class.

* * * * *

During the next five years the campaign against the battleship as opposed to aircraft increased in intensity, and the Press in general encouraged it. Pictures showing battleships being blown to pieces by aircraft with the most lurid descriptions of the air wrath to come, were issued to educate the public and humiliate the Navy. That all the other maritime Powers were rebuilding their battle-fleets mattered nothing—the capital ship was doomed and so much bomb fodder. Their comparative cost was made much of, and unofficial estimates made out that for one ship a great number of aeroplanes could be built, sometimes covering only capital outlay, sometimes only maintenance and sometimes both. The number varied from 100 to 1,000, and to get at the truth the Admiralty and Air Ministry collaborated and worked out an agreed figure of forty-three twin-engine medium bombers as the nearest approximation to the equivalent in cost to one battleship, taking into account all those overhead, maintenance, and replacement and similar charges which should be included to make an effective comparison during the life of one capital ship.

The Admiralty view was simple. Advocates of the extreme air view wished the country to build no more capital ships although other powers continued to build them. If their theories turned out well-founded much money would have been wasted; if ill-founded, we would, in putting them to the test, have lost the Empire.

When a third Naval Conference was called in 1935 to discuss future building of capital ships, Mr. MacDonald firmly supported the Admiralty views on both battleships and cruisers. We were not in favour of monster vessels and put forward a design of about 25,000 tons with 12-in. guns costing about £5½m.—but the U.S. wanted big ships, while Japan wished to do away with them as being the only challenge to her supremacy in the East. Eventually a limit of 35,000 tons with 14-in. guns was agreed upon, with the proviso that if any of the parties to the Washington Treaty failed to enter into an agreement to conform to this provision not later than 1 April 1937, the maximum gun calibre should be 16-in. No limit was placed on the number of ships which could be built, economical rearmament being limited by eliminating the provocative factors of displacement and gun calibre.

In the event Japan did not conform to the agreement, and in due course produced the largest and most heavily gunned battleships ever to be built.

SIR STANLEY GOODALL K.C.B., D.N.C. 1936-1944

Stanley Vernon Goodall was born in 1883. Originally an Engineer Officer he transferred to Naval Construction Cadet in 1901, and after an exceptionally fine performance in the R.N. College, Greenwich examinations spent a few months as Assistant Constructor at Devonport prior to taking up appointment at the Experimental Works at Haslar in 1908. In 1911 he went to the Admiralty and served under Mr. W. H. Whiting and later under Sir William Berry on light cruiser design, his first assignment being the *Arethusa*, famous in War 1, which brought him the thanks of the Board.

In 1914 an appointment as resident lecturer at Greenwich was interrupted by the war, and he returned to the D.N.C. Department in February 1915 to serve under Mr. E. L. Attwood who was designing the *Renown* and *Repulse*. Later in the year promotion came to Acting Constructor with charge of the section dealing with design of the *Courageous*, *Glorious* and *Furious*. After Jutland he conducted the special investigation into the cause of our losses and later into the performance of projectiles and their improvement.

When with the Superintendant of Naval Construction Goodall had charge of the armour section and later was inspecting officer of submarines. Towards the end of 1917 he was specially appointed to the Embassy Staff at Washington and awarded the American Navy Cross for his "exceptionally meritorious services in assisting the U.S. Government in the prosecution of the War." He was also awarded the M.B.E.

Returning to the Admiralty in 1919 he took charge of the design of the *Hood*, surveyed the surrendered German battlefleet, and contributed a paper on the *Baden* to the I.N.A. in 1921. The design of the *Rodney* and *Nelson* was carried out in his section.

During the next few years he became responsible for work on graving docks, the supervision of underwater protection including special trials on the *Monarch*, the design of torpedo tubes, and was lecturer on warship design and construction to the Staff College and to the Senior Officers' Technical Courses.

From 1925-1927 Dockyard experience followed at Malta. Then promotion to Senior Constructor brought a return to Whitehall and charge of the designs for "A" and "B" class destroyers, with Committee work on anti-submarine weapons.

Promoted to Chief Constructor in 1930 he again supervised capital ships, this time the reconstruction of the *Warspite* and *Repulse* classes, and the gun, torpedo and bomb trials on old warships scrapped under the Treaty. Appointed Assistant Director in 1932 he was responsible for the design of many small craft and then took charge of submarine design.

After the *Nelson* and *Rodney* no battleships were laid down during the periods when Sir William Berry and Sir Arthur Johns held office as D.N.C., and the retirement of the latter in July 1936 brought Mr. Goodall the honour he had so well deserved. He was destined to lead the Royal Corps of Naval Constructors through perhaps the most difficult and certainly the most strenuous period in its history. The Navy had to be built up rapidly from its small interwar strength, during the searching war years when new types of ships had to be created and pace kept with war experience and scientific developments. To quote Their Lordships' letter of appreciation when he retired "During the period in which you have served as their principal technical adviser, the Navy has had to undertake, both during the period of rearmament and since the war began, the production of war vessels upon a scale unparalleled in British Naval history." All this had to be achieved with a very inadequate Corps which responded willingly to his inspiring leadership. He was created C.B. in 1937 and K.C.B. in 1938.

In October 1942 Sir Stanley was given the additional appointment of Assistant Controller for Warship Production and held both offices until January 1944 when he was succeeded as D.N.C. by Mr. (later Sir Charles) Lillicrap, and retired from the remaining appointment in October 1945. His name will always be associated with the designs of *Vanguard* and *King George V* class; *Illustrious*, *Colossus*, *Majestic*, *Implacable* and *Ark Royal* (1942) classes; *Fiji*, *Swiftsure*, *Tiger* and *Dido* classes and a very large number of smaller vessels including ships and craft of special character for Combined Operations. During his term of office the Cavitation Tunnel was installed at Haslar and the Naval Construction Research Establishment at Rosyth. The most recent recognition of his services has been his election as Renter Warden of the Worshipful Company of Shipwrights.

The particular problems confronting the D.N.C. were mainly due to limitations imposed by the Treaty. Thus, battleship displacement might not exceed 35,000 tons which meant pinching and scraping on the *King*

George V class; cruisers had to be reduced from 10,000 to 8,000 tons to provide more ships out of our allotted tonnage—and the resulting *Fiji* class in its time and as first completed were a class of which to be proud; and aircraft carriers of limited displacement had to have armoured flight decks to prevent small bombs bursting in the hangar and starting disastrous fires. Protection had to be devised against mines set to detonate against a ship's bottom, heavier torpedo charges, and modern shells and bombs. New types of ships such as landing ships, landing craft, midget submarines had to be devised, and a host of small craft provided.

But the outstanding difficulty of the whole period was that of personnel. Because of past Treasury niggardliness the Corps was woefully short handed, in particular of senior experienced men who could take over responsible posts entailed by expansion of the Fleet and other imposed activities. Drastic dilution brought a heavier burden upon the senior officers, and many jobs that demanded the attention of a constructor-officer had to be left to subordinates. That the Corps was able to respond as well as it did was something of a miracle.

Chapter 115

THE WASHINGTON TREATY TERMINATES

NEW CONSTRUCTION

WHEN the Washington Treaty terminated on 31 December 1936 the fifteen years of international limitations on our security came to an end and we are again able to proceed with battleship construction although on a qualitative basis. Japan had turned down the 1935 Agreement and Italy had not yet accepted it, so its observance lay principally with Britain, U.S.A. and France although the signatures of Russia, Scandinavia, and Turkey had also been obtained. A formidable shipbuilding programme was already in progress by 1937, two battleships having been laid down and three more approved for 1938—the largest practicable with our now limited ordnance output.

But a difficult problem had arisen over the calibre of the big guns to be mounted. The U.S.A. had agreed to wait until December 1936 when, if Japan had not ratified the Agreement to limit their calibre to 14-in., they would revert to 16-in. But the Admiralty could not wait until then. In France the *Dunkerque* and *Strasbourg* were completing; Germany had the *Scharnhorst* and *Gneisenau* well advanced; and the Italian *Littorio* and *Vittorio Veneto* had been two years on the stocks. A battleship's construction waits upon the delivery of her gun mountings and our 14-in. designs were already prepared. It was essential that guns and mountings should be ordered in June 1936 if the ships were not to be delayed—and yet we did not relish an armament of 14-in. when both the U.S. and Japan favoured the 16-in.

Ultimately the time factor decided things. The sense of tension with Germany was rising so fast that it seemed probable that by 1940—which was the earliest date the first two ships could be finished—we should be at war. A change to 16-in. would mean at least a year's delay; most of our skilled draughtsmen had gone, and it had not been possible with those available to turn out designs for both 14-in. and 16-in. mountings.

True we already had 15-in. designs, but on 35,000 tons a 14-in. armament allowed for a better balanced design. Pros and cons were thrashed out piecemeal by the Board, the Naval Staff, and Commanders at sea, and many were the alternative plans discussed. To get as many big guns as possible into the dimensions both triple and quadruple turrets were considered, and at length a design with three quadruple turrets was approved. Later when proof range firings with improved shells showed that further magazine protection would be required, it was decided to provide for the extra weight by altering "B" to a turret a twin, which again involved delay.

The secondary armament also led to much discussion as there were advocates for separate anti-destroyer and anti-aircraft batteries. This would have meant congested topsides with excessive blast interference, a multiplicity of fire control positions, difficult ammunition supply arrangements, and a greater complement. Eventually a HA/LA battery of 5·25 in. was accepted as firing a shell heavy enough to stop a destroyer and the heaviest which could be handled with sufficient rapidity to deal with attacking aircraft at long range.

"KING GEORGE V" Class (1936 Programme)

(Designed under Sir Arthur Johns, D.N.C.; built under Sir Stanley Goodall, D.N.C.)

	Builders	*Laid down*	*Launched*	*Completed*
"*Anson*"	Swan Hunter	July '37	24 Feb. '40	June '42
"*Duke of York*"	Clydebank	May '37	28 Feb. '40	Nov. '41
"*Howe*"	Fairfield	June '37	9 April '40	Aug. '42
"*King George V*"	Vickers-Armstrongs	Jan. '37	21 Feb. '39	Dec. '40
"*Prince of Wales*"	Cammell Laird	Jan. '37	3 May '39	March '41

Dimensions 700′ (p.p.), 745′(o.a.)×103′×35′ 6″=36,750 tons. As modified 38,000 tons, 44,460 tons full load.

Armament
10 14-in.
16 5·25-in.
64 2-pdrs. pom-poms.
10 40 mm. Bofors. } varied in each ship.
10 20 mm. Oerlikons. }
4 3-pdr. saluting.

Protection
Belt 15″ over magazines, 5½″ lower edge.
14″ over machinery, 4½″ lower edge.
Bulkheads 15″.
Turrets 16″ faces, 9″ roofs, 15″ sides.
Barbettes 16″.
Decks 6″ over magazines; ends 6″.
5″ over machinery.
Longitudinal torpedo bulkhead 2″.
Secondary turrets 6″.

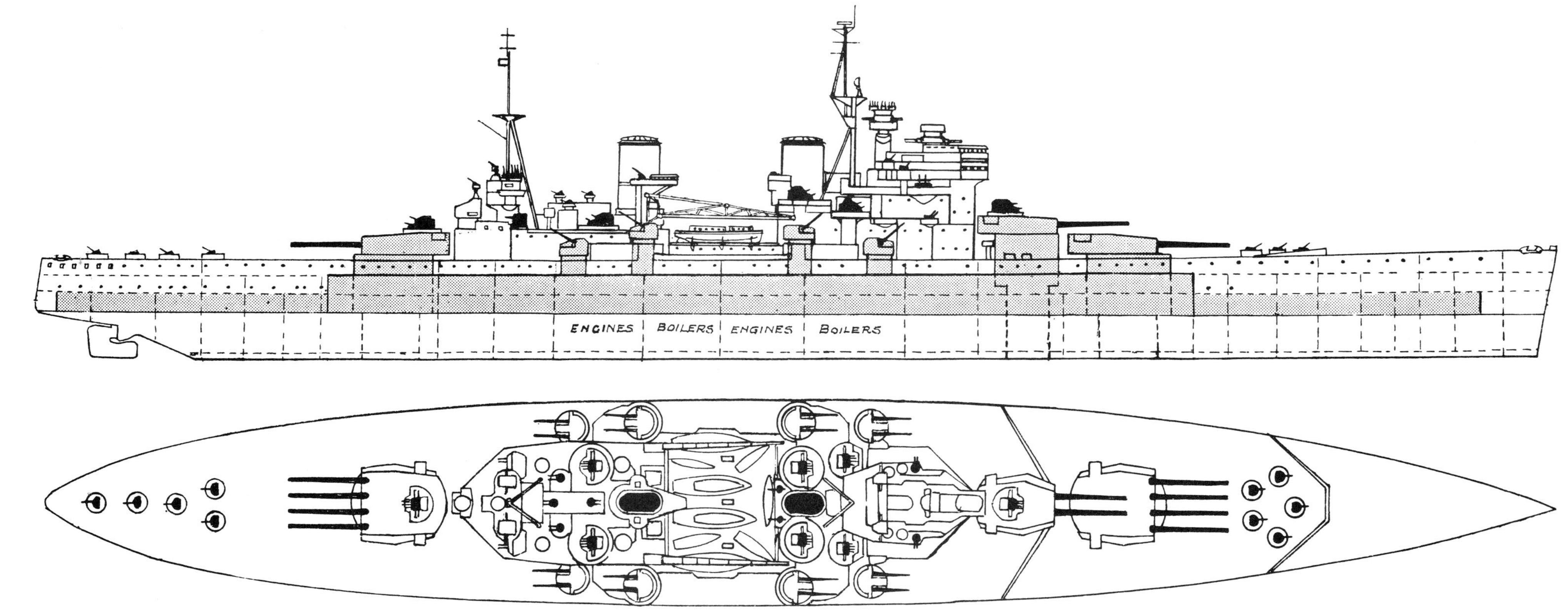

KING GEORGE V Class

As first completed there was a cross-deck catapult amidships, and boat stowage was between funnel and mainmast. When their aircraft were surrendered boats were stowed amidships and additional A.A. guns mounted in their former position. The Oerlikons on forecastle and quarterdeck were landed after the War. Fore and aft belt extensions are splinter-proof only.

Machinery	Single reduction geared turbines. 4 shafts. S.H.P. 110,000=27½ knots; 125,000=29¼ knots. Boilers 8 Admiralty 3-drum.
Fuel	Oil 3,842 tons.
Radius	15,000/10; 6,300/20; 3,200/27.
Complement	1,640.
Constructors	W. G. Sanders and H. S. Pengelly.

Special features:

(1) First British battleships to mount 14-in. guns since the *Canada*.
(2) First to have quadruple mountings.
(3) First to have a H.A./L.A. 5·25-in. battery.
(4) First battleships to be designed to carry aircraft.
(5) First to have main horizontal armour at upper deck level.

Until 1937 the heaviest programme of armoured ships we ever laid down in one year was that of 1910 when the "We want Eight" agitation produced the *Orion* (4), *Lion* (2) and *Colossus* (2) classes which, reduced to standard displacement represented roughly 175,300 tons. In 1937 the five ships of the *King George V* class had a total dis-

1940 *photo by favour of Messrs. Vickers-Armstrongs*

KING GEORGE V

placement of 175,000 tons, but as a concentrated force were far more powerful than the eight which served in War 1.

Originally the *Duke of York* was to have been called *Anson*, the *Anson*, *Jellicoe* and the *Howe*, *Beatty*, following the example of the Germans with their *Hipper*, *Graf Spee*, *Admiral Scheer*, and *Tirpitz*; but while still on the stocks these were altered to more traditional names.

As soon as war broke out the standard displacement limitations were disregarded, and further additions made to the protection of the machinery spaces and magazines. Later the *Bismarck* action showed the desirability of still more defence against shell splinters and also a greater endurance; and when our Carrier Force was sufficient to provide spotter and reconnaissance aircraft as required, their planes were landed and the hangars used as a cinema, with boat stowage in the catapult space. It is claimed by the *King George V* that her plane was the last to be flown from a capital ship. Altogether the principal changes made included additional A.A. armament and ammunition, more extensive radar equipment, more trunks for water-tight integrity, and increased fuel supply.

The effect on standard displacement was to increase this to about 38,000 tons, with a reduction in freeboard to 28 ft. forward and 24 ft. aft.

After their completion further additions to A.A. armament and ammunition, radar, and habitability aggregating about 1,500 tons added another 1½ ft. to their draught which then became 32 ft. instead of 27 ft. 8 in. as designed.

This reduction in freeboard would not have mattered so much had there been a good sheer forward; but unfortunately one of the requirements in the design was that "A" turret should have direct fire ahead without elevation. No satisfactory explanation for this unnecessary handicap has been forthcoming, but with the flat forecastle the ships are very wet forward at speed and easily buried in a seaway.

ARMAMENT

A *Nelson* disposition for the original three quadruple turrets was considered, but offered no advantage as the higher machinery power involved longer machinery spaces, the after ends of which would have been difficult to arrange satisfactorily in the fine stern section. The *Nelson* arrangement was also criticised on the grounds of blast effects when the guns were trained aft, and that the high superstructure made the ships difficult to handle under certain conditions of weather.

Weight of broadside was 15,900 lb., the rate of fire being two rounds per gun per minute. The maximum range was 36,000 yards, and penetrating power at 15,000 yards with full elevation was 13 in. of armour. The quadruple turret weighed 1,550 tons and the twin 900 tons.

The sixteen 5·25-in. were carried in eight 6-in. turrets weighing 80 tons each, and were fully automatic being capable of 18 rounds p.m. with a maximum range of 22,500 yards. But for the amidships catapult there would have been sufficient space for four more turrets as in the U.S. *California*. The close-range armament varied in each ship, and the single guns in pits fore and aft shown on the plan were afterwards landed. There were no torpedo tubes.

A decision to carry aircraft was the outcome of a long controversy. Opponents objected to equipment necessitating very inflammable accessories and stressed the poor qualities of the "Walrus" aircraft compared with carrier-borne aeroplanes, plus the risk to such a valuable ship when she slowed down to pick them up. Against this it was argued that without aircraft the area of vision would be strictly limited and fire control less effective, as carrier

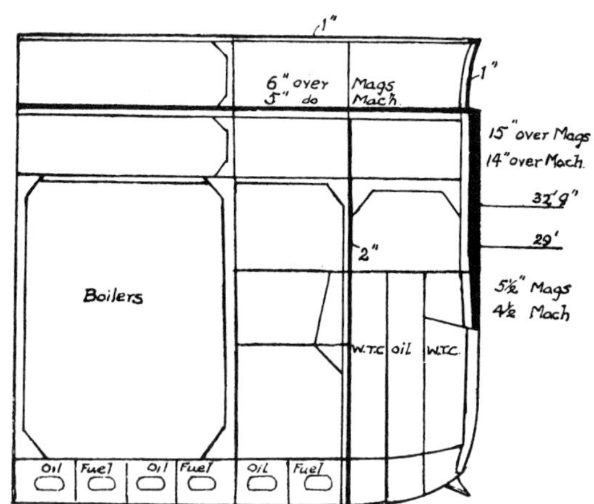

King George V. Full load displacement 44,550 tons. W.l. beam 103 ft.

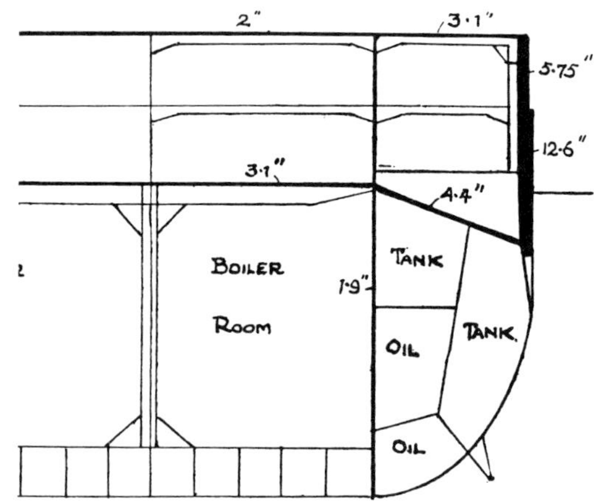

Tirpitz. Full load displacement 51,000 tons. W.l. beam 118 ft.

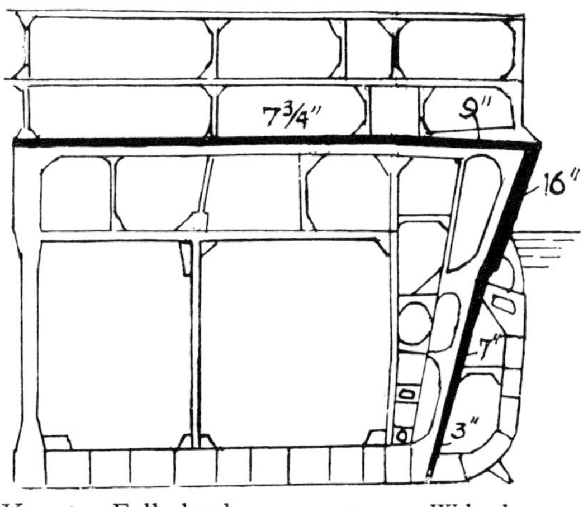

Yamato. Full load 72,000 tons. W.l. beam 121 ft.

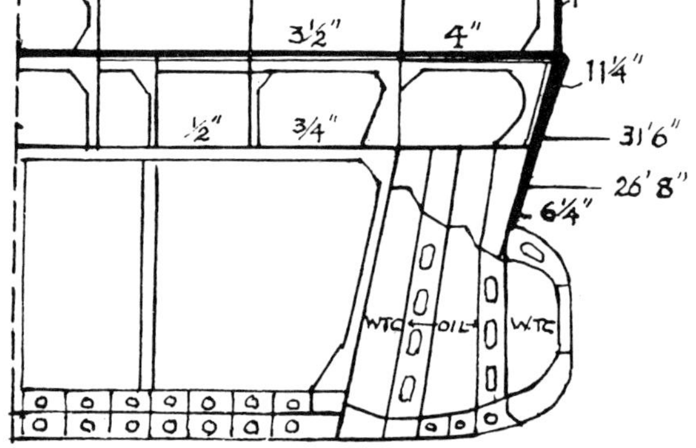

Washington. Full load displacement 42,000 tons. W.l. beam 108 ft.

attendance could not be available at all times. Four planes were housed in the hangars, and discharged from a fixed cross-deck catapult.

PROTECTION

Armour and protection absorbed one-third of the displacement—the proportion usually allotted in a well-balanced design. As the *Nelson* system of water-line protection did not commend itself to Sir Arthur Johns, a reversion was made to vertical armour on the ship's side with two watertight compartments and an oil space between it and the thick vertical bulkhead.

Portions of the belt over the magazines were 15-in., an inch thicker than in the *Nelson*, with 14 in. over the machinery spaces and the whole extending further below the water-line than in any previous battleship—a necessity demonstrated during shell attack on the *Baden* (ex-German), *Superb* and *Emperor of India*. Nevertheless a diving shell hit the *Prince of Wales* below the belt during the *Bismarck* action. At the extreme ends the sides were soft.

The horizontal armour was carried a deck higher than in *Nelson*, being 5 in. over the machinery spaces and 6 in. over the magazines with splinter protection at the magazine boundaries. Bombing of the *Marlborough* and "Job 74" mock-up demonstrated this thickness as sufficient to keep out bombs considered likely to be used in the war then foreseen. That was in 1936. But when the Japanese started on the designs for the huge *Yamato* and *Musashi* in 1934 they estimated that 9 in.-7 in. armour would have to go on the protective deck to ensure the unsinkable ships required.

In safeguarding against torpedo and mine attack the bulge was discarded and a novel form of bulkheading adopted, with increased pumping facilities. It was accepted that a mine detonated sufficiently close to the bottom would flood one or more main compartments, and structural and electrical arrangements were provided to minimize such effects. In the case of the *Prince of Wales*, it is understood that four torpedoes from aircraft (and Japanese aircraft dropped 24-in. weapons) struck her starboard side and the shock put out of action pumping and lighting arrangements and the port side lighting. Two more torpedoes on the port side laid her more or less on an even keel but made damage control impossible.

A new feature of the water-line protection was an arrangement by which the fuel tanks outside the protective bulkheads were automatically flooded as the oil was used, so these compartments, which were an important part of the protective system, were never empty. Subsequently it was found that voids could be just as efficacious as filled compartments in damping shock.

Comparison with the *Washington*, *Yamato* and *Tirpitz* as contemporaries shows that while the external bulge was adopted by the two former it was incorporated into the hull in the latter, while an armoured deck rising from the lower edge of the belt was retained, together with thick plating over the upper deck.

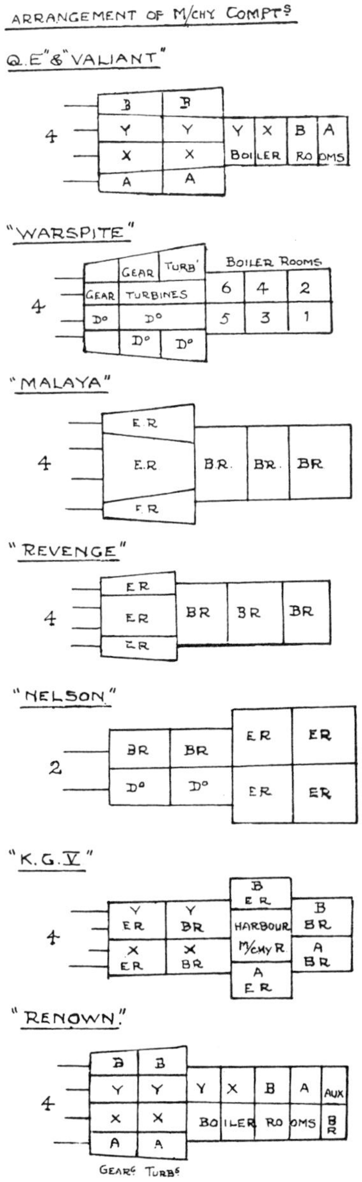

Diagrams to show the different arrangement of boiler and engine rooms in armoured ships of War II.

MACHINERY

There were eight boilers in four boiler rooms and four independent sets of geared turbines in four separate engine rooms, the boiler and engine rooms being staggered to reduce the chance of complete loss of motive power. Evaporators, dynamos and hydraulic engines were also in separate compartments. Improvements in boiler design are reported to have reduced boiler weights by about 15 per cent. as compared with *Nelson* and *Rodney*.

The designed S.H.P. 110,000 was for 27½ knots and 29¼ knots was actually logged with 125,000 S.H.P.

GENERAL

No conning tower was fitted, but as in the *Warspite* it was replaced by a splinter-proof position in the upper bridgework.

With her tight, almost square, bilge and great weight of side armour she made a good gun platform although with a G.M. of 6·1 ft. in the light and 8·1 ft. in the deep load condition—the highest figures of any of our armoured ships. But the low forecastle meant a lot of spray over the turrets in a seaway and affected speed. The *King George V* had a period of about 14 seconds, which meant easier behaviour in a seaway than was the case with the *Nelson* with an 11 second period.

The possibility of converting the four ships to carry guided missiles was considered, and rejected on grounds of expense.

"ANSON"

Built by Swan, Hunter and Wigham Richardson July '37-June '42. Flagship of 2nd B.S. Home Fleet (Vice-Admiral Sir Bruce Fraser until June '43, and of Vice-Admiral Sir Henry Moore until July '44). Mainly employed in shadowing forces in support of Russian convoys. Refit at Devonport. March '45 proceeded to the Pacific as Flagship 1st B.S. and entered the station in July, a short time before Japan surrendered. Her major work was the occupation of Hong Kong landing a force which included 200 Marines to police the area and the withdrawing of enemy troops, succour prisoners-of-war, and prevent looting. She was present for the surrender on 16 September '45. Became guardship at Tokio, returning to Australia in January '46. In February the Duke and Duchess of Gloucester and family took passage to Tasmania, and after a short visit to Sydney, she sailed for Japan and from there Home, arriving at Portsmouth in July. After a short refit became Training Ship for the new-entry of seamen under special service, and later "cocooned" and placed in Reserve.

Scrapped 1957.

"DUKE OF YORK"

Built at Clydebank May '37-November '41. Joined the Home Fleet and took part in many sweeps in northern waters covering Murmansk convoys. In December '43 as Flagship of Admiral Fraser intercepted the *Scharnhorst* which was being engaged by the cruisers *Belfast*, *Jamaica* and *Norfolk* and escorting destroyers. During a night action the *Scharnhorst* received at least four torpedo hits when under fire from the *Duke of York*, and was sunk. Sailed for Japan after the surrender of Germany and was Flagship of Admiral Fraser in Tokio Bay for the surrender of Japan. Returned U.K. in July '46 and after serving with the Home Fleet was placed in Reserve.

Scrapped 1957.

Official photo 1942

H.M.S. *DUKE OF YORK*

"HOWE"

Built by Fairfields June '37-June '42 when she was commissioned and completed in August. Joined the Home Fleet and in May was detached to the Mediterranean in support of the Sicily landings as Flagship of Vice-Admiral Power and took part in the bombardments and subsequent operations in Italian waters. Recommissioned July '44. Joined Eastern Fleet based on Trincomali and on formation of Pacific Fleet became Flagship of C.-in-C. Sir Bruce Fraser. Arrived at Sydney in January '45. Took part in several bombardments in support of U.S. forces before leaving in June to refit in South Africa. Arrived at Portsmouth in January '46 and became a Training Ship before being placed in Reserve.

Scrapped 1957.

"KING GEORGE V"

Built at Barrow January '37-August '40 and commissioned in October to join Home Fleet. In January took our Ambassador Lord Halifax to America and escorted a special convoy home. March '41 covered a landing force on Lofoten Islands and later in search for *Scharnhorst*. In April became Flagship of Home Fleet and took part in the search and sinking of the *Bismarck*. Attacked enemy shipping in Glom Fiord December '41. Search for *Admiral Scheer* February '42. Collided with and sank destroyer *Punjabi* whose d.c. damaged her. During '42 and '43 on convoy escort to and from Russia. July '43 covered Sicily landings, bombarding Favignaua and Trapani, and occupied Taranto September. Returned U.K. In December left Scapa for Mediterranean to bring home the Prime Minister. Refit '44 for Eastern service, and on passage bombarded Lakida Battery at Milos. Arrived in December and became second Flagship and during '45 covered air strikes on Japanese-held islands—the Ryukyus in March and Sakishima group in May. Together with U.S. force attacked Japanese mainland in July, shelling the Hitachi area of Honshu and Hamamatsu. Took part in naval occupation of Japan and surrender in September. January '45 conveyed the Duke and Duchess of Gloucester to Hobart, returning U.K. in March. Recommissioned as Flagship Home Fleet and later placed in Reserve.

Scrapped 1957.

"PRINCE OF WALES"

Built by Cammell Laird January '37-March '41. Took part in the *Bismarck* action in May before being properly worked up and received slight damage. Withdrew for a time when her gun mountings gave trouble. Scored two hits on *Bismarck*, one of which caused oil loss, reducing her speed and allowed contact to be regained and her subsequent sinking. In July conveyed the Prime Minister to Placenta Bay, Newfoundland to meet President Roosevelt in Atlantic Charter conference. Returned to Mediterranean for convoy duties, including a specially important one in September. In November was ordered to Singapore "to keep the Japanese quiet" together with *Repulse* as a first instalment of the Far Eastern Fleet. Pearl Harbour disaster on December 7 heralded Japan's entry into the war, and her operations against Britain commenced with an invasion of Malaya. Admiral Tom Phillips decided to proceed to Kota Bharu and check them landing there, but diverted to Kuantan further south and where another landing was reported. Attacked by waves of bombers and torpedo bombers and struck by several torpedoes close together. With port propellers out of control and unable to manœuvre properly she received further hits and bomb damage. Capsized and sunk, 1,285 being rescued by destroyers out of 1,612. Neither Admiral Phillips nor Captain Leach survived.

Chapter 116

THE NEW GERMAN NAVY AND BRITISH CONTEMPORARIES

UNDER the Versailles Treaty Germany was permitted an Establishment of six battleships with an age limit of twenty years, which were not to be replaced by ships of more than 10,000 tons standard displacement. In 1925 reconstruction of the navy was commenced when a cruiser *Emden* was laid down. Four years later the *Deutschland*, first of the heavy cruisers destined for commerce raiding, was laid down in February 1929. Admiral Raedar had planned an original and most provocative design providing for a ship of 26 knots, fast enough to escape from any battleship and armed with six 11-in. guns which could out-shoot any cruiser. The hull was welded to save weight and for the first time diesel engines were installed to allow for a radius of 10,000 miles at 20 knots. She was followed by the *Admiral Scheer* in June 1931 and the *Admiral Graf Spee* in 1932, both of the same type.

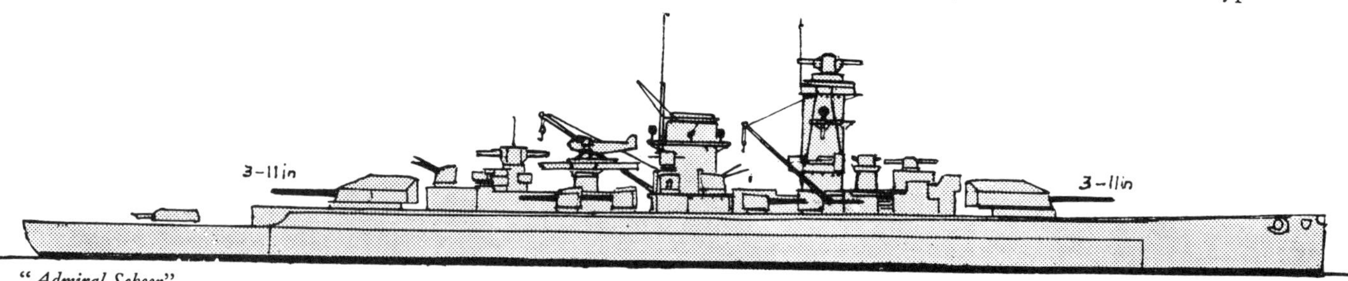

"Admiral Scheer"

"DEUTSCHLAND" (later "LUTZOW")

Dimensions 616′ 10″ (o.a.)×67′ 11″×19′=11,700 tons.
Armament 6 11-in.; 8 5·9-in.; 6 4·1-in.; 36 smaller. 8 torpedo tubes on quarter deck.
Protection Belt 3″; turrets 5½″-4″; deck 1¾″.
Machinery 3 sets diesels 56,800 S.H.P.=26/28 knots.
Fuel 3,280 tons.

"ADMIRAL GRAF SPEE." "ADMIRAL SCHEER"

Dimensions 616′ 10″ (o.a.)×71′ 9″×19′=12,100 tons.
Armament As above.
Protection Belt 4″-3″; turrets 5″-4″; deck 2¾″-1½″.
Machinery As above.
Fuel 2,800 tons.

(The permitted displacement was considerably exceeded allowing for increased protection.)

Now one of the clauses in the Versailles Treaty provided that the Allies should undertake a reduction in armaments when the disarmament of Germany had been carried out, and in 1934 Hitler announced that he would not remain bound by the naval restriction clauses unless disarmament were carried out by the Signatory Powers. That year the alleged 26,000-ton battleships *Gneisenau* and *Scharnhorst* were laid down, and it soon became known that Germany had started a rearmament programme which included twenty small submarines (built during 1935). On 16 March the Versailles Treaty was publicly renounced and in its place Hitler offered a permanent naval agreement which was accepted by the Government on Admiralty advice. Germany was to have a 35 per cent. ratio to British strength in each category of vessels with one exception—that of submarine tonnage. She was willing to abolish submarines or limit their size by international agreement, but in default of such agreement required a ration of 45 per cent. of our own tonnage. In addition, she claimed the right to increase her submarine strength to parity with the British—if circumstances warranted—by friendly negotiation.

As the opportunity for abolishing submarines had been thrown away at Washington in 1921-22 when France wished to retain them, and as we had planned a tonnage of 52,000, it was obvious that our best course was to come to an agreement which would delay German construction as long as possible.

The German naval staff intended to allocate the agreed tonnage of armoured ships to the three *Deutschlands*, two *Scharnhorsts*, and three larger ships with a legend displacement of 35,000 tons, on the assumption that war would break out in 1940. But when Hitler assured them that no war would take place until 1944 or 1945, they decided to embark on a long-term programme which would have provided a fleet of thirteen battleships, thirty-three cruisers, four carriers, about 250 submarines and a large number of destroyers—which would have constituted a threat capable of straining our resources to the utmost.

"GNEISENAU" and "SCHARNHORST"

Dimensions	771′ × 100′ × 32½′ = 31,300/38,100 tons.
Armament	9 11-in.; 12 5·9-in.; 14 4·1-in.; 36 smaller A.A.
	6 21-in. torpedo tubes.
	2 catapults. 4 aircraft.
Protection	Belt 13″-3¼″; turrets 13″; deck 3″; barbettes 10″.
Machinery	S.H.P. 160,000 = 32 knots. 31·5 full load.
	Fuel 6,300 tons. Radius 10,000/19.

(Data from "Flotten Taschenbuch" 1953.)

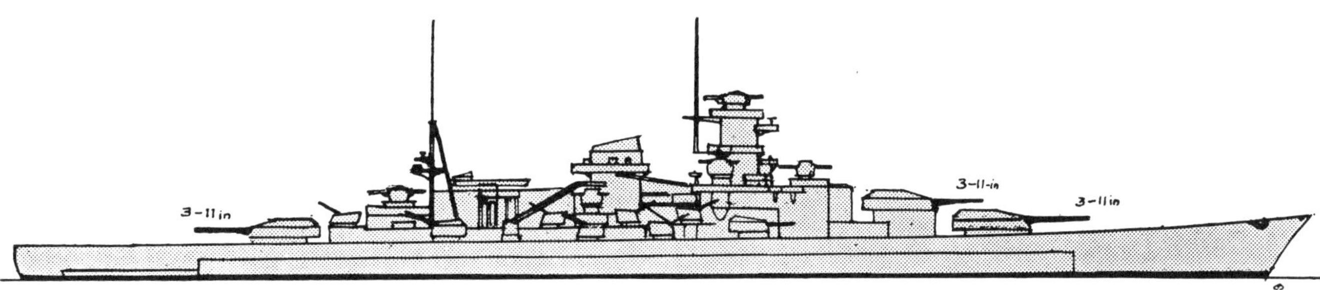

Originally these ships had a straight stem and a light pole mast against the after side of the funnel. But when the "Hipper" class of 8-in. cruisers were given a cutaway bow they followed suit, and also received an after tripod as shown. In silhouette the two classes were then so much alike that identification was difficult and confusion to be expected. Except for their having only three turrets instead of four they also closely resembled the *Tirpitz* in accordance with a policy to promote confusion in recognition.

Having signed the Agreement, two of the three larger battleships were laid down in 1936, the *Tirpitz* and *Bismarck* of 52,600 tons full load displacement. On 13 December 1938 Germany informed H.M. Government that she was taking advantage of the right to increase her submarine tonnage to that of our own. However, early in 1939 we denounced the Agreement as a protest against German aggression in Europe, so that it made little difference.

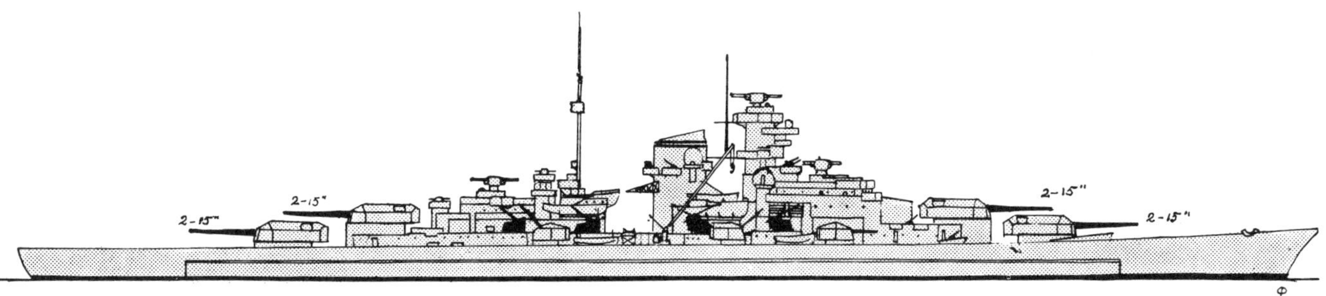

"BISMARCK" and "TIRPITZ"

Dimensions	823½′ × 118′ × 35·4′ = 41,700/52,600 tons.
Armament	8 15-in.; 12 5·9-in.; 16 4·1-in.; 56 smaller A.A.
	6 21-in. torpedo tubes ("*Tirpitz*" only).
	1 catapult. 4 aircraft.
Protection	Belt 12·6″; turrets 14″; deck 4½″-3½″ (lower).
	Upper deck side 5¾″; deck 3¼″-2″ (upper).
Machinery	S.H.P. 138,000 = 29/30·8 knots.
	Fuel 8,780 tons. Radius 8,100/19.

(Data from "Flotten Taschenbuch" 1953.)

In reply to these ships the Estimates for 1938 included two battleships the *Lion* and *Temeraire* with two more the *Conqueror* and *Thunderer* the following year. All four were cancelled subsequently when war was declared and our shipbuilding resources had to be devoted to ships which could be completed in two years.

THE GERMAN "PLAN Z"

Besides the various weapons with which Hitler hoped to achieve victory during the last stages of the war, there was also an orthodox weapon planned and provided for during the pre-war years, which would seem to have promised a very real chance of success in hostilities against Britain. This was a very powerful and well-balanced surface fleet, designed to destroy our commerce and extend the British Navy to the very limits of its protective capacity. It was known as "Plan Z" put forward by Admiral Raeder in March 1937.

It will be remembered that Hitler intended to delay hostilities against Britain until 1944 or 1945, by which time the greater portion of Europe would have become vassal states of the Reich, and he could have employed their shipbuilding resources. Seven or eight years would have been ample time to complete the work planned, which included the following vessels:

Six battleships (H, I, K, L, M, N) to be ready in 1944.
Three battle cruisers (O, P, Q) to be ready in 1943.
Four heavy cruisers to be ready in 1943-45.
Seventeen light cruisers to be ready in 1944-48.
Four carriers. Two to be ready in 1941.
221 submarines.
Destroyers, sweepers, etc.

this was not intended to be a battle fleet. Unlike the High Seas Fleet of 1914-18 there was no question of employing the ships against our Home Fleet in classical naval combat. They were to be used for commerce destruction only, just as the *Deutschlands*, *Scharnhorsts*, and *Bismarck* had orders to avoid action with enemy forces when possible, and apply themselves to the sinking of merchantmen. When we consider that in all some forty-eight surface ships were called upon to hunt down the *Bismarck*, the problem of dealing with such a force as is listed above when added to the navy of 1939 would have meant a very black outlook.

Chief interest centres in the battleships, which were to have been diesel-driven enlargements of the *Tirpitz* with a main armament of 16-in. instead of 15-in. guns. Two of the five, reported to have been named *Friedrich der Grosse* and *Gross Deutschland*, were laid down at Blohm and Voss' Yard, Hamburg, in May-June 1939, and their construction ceased after the Barents Sea engagement on 31 December 1942 when Captain Sherbrooke drove off superior enemy forces with his light escort group—a defeat which turned Hitler against large surface ships.

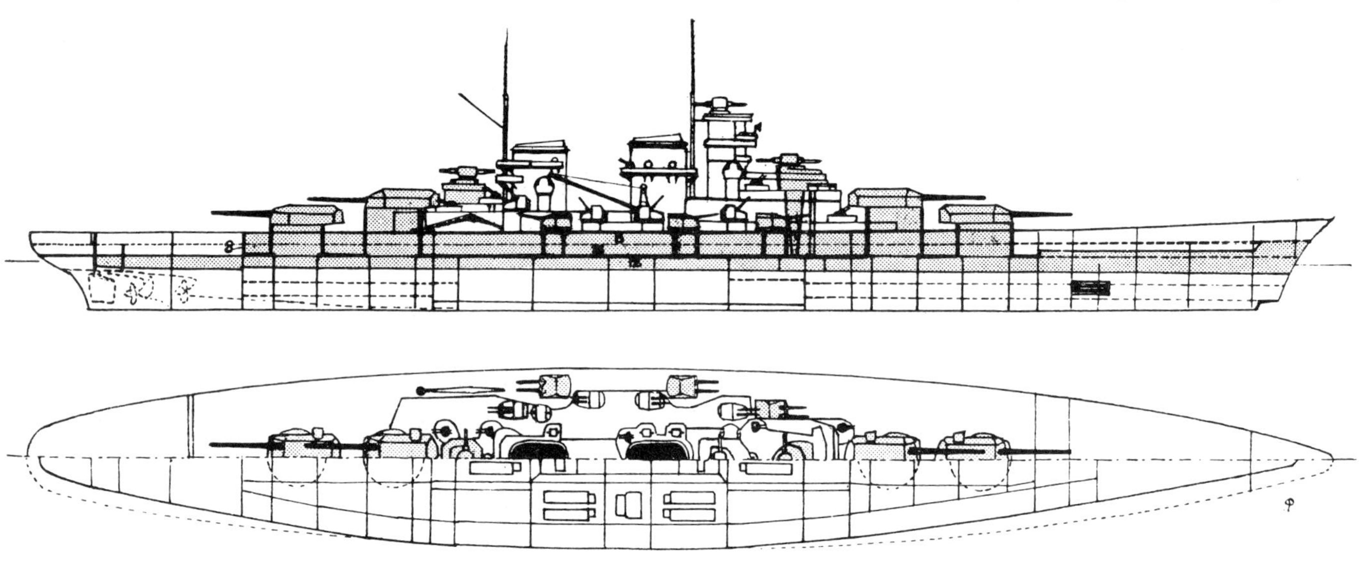

"H" (*Friedrich der Grosse*) "J" (*Gross Deutschland*) 50,000/64,000 tons.

Dimensions 820′ 3″ (o.a.) × 118′ 1″ × 35′ 5″ = 50,000/64,000 tons.
Armament 8 16-in.; 12 5·9-in.; 16 4·1-in.; 48 smaller. 6 torpedo tubes.
Protection Belt 11¾″; turrets 15″-4″; deck 4″-3¾″.
Machinery 165,000 S.H.P. = 30 knots.
Fuel 10,000 tons. Radius 16,000/19.

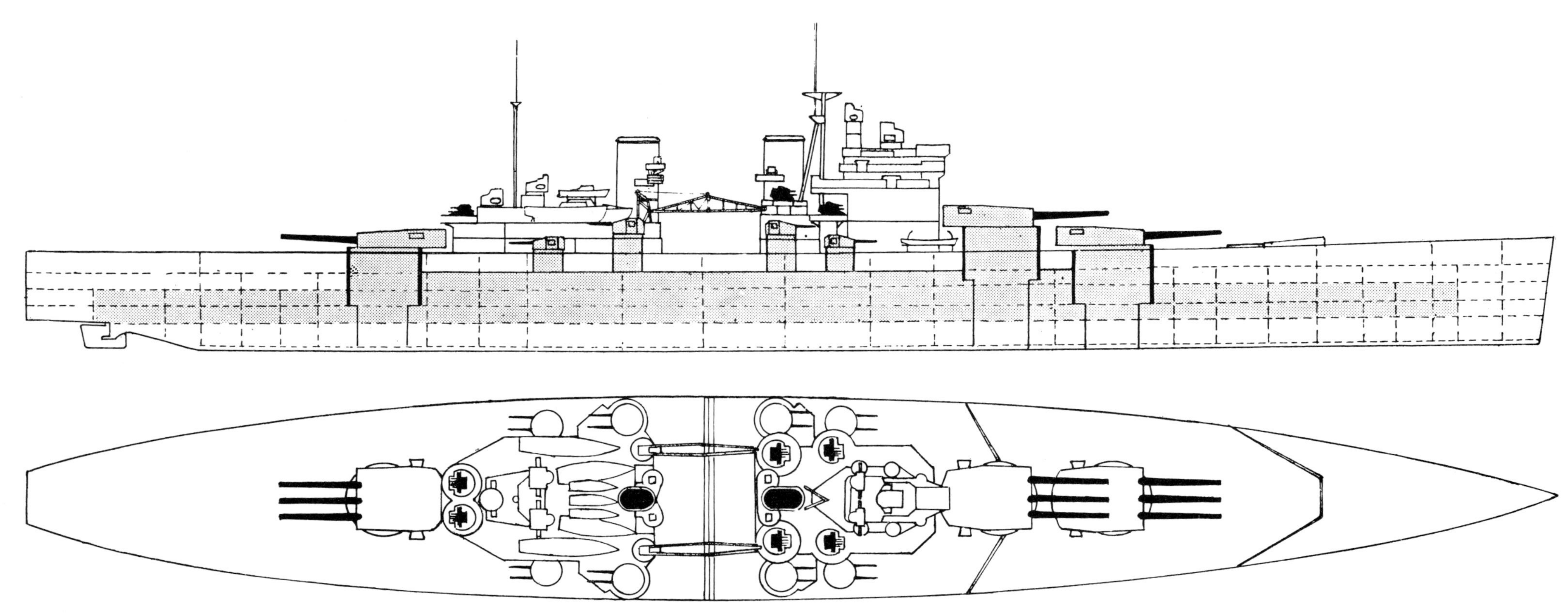

LION Class

An enlarged *King George V* design with triple turrets and a deeper belt. The close-range armament as shown would have been greatly augmented and the catapult space utilized with advantage.

"LION" Class (4 ships) 1938 and '39 Estimates

	Builders	*Ordered*	*Laid down*	
"*Lion*"	Vickers-Armstrongs	21 Feb. '39	4 July '39	Construction abandoned 1940
"*Temeraire*"	Cammell Laird	21 Feb. '39	1 June '39	
"*Conqueror*"	Clydebank	16 Aug. '39		
"*Thunderer*"	Fairfield	16 Aug. '39		

Dimensions 740′ (p.p.) 780′ (w.l.) 785′ (o.a.) × 105′ × 30′ (mean) = 40,000 tons.

Armament 9 16-in.
16 5·25-in.
6 8-barrel 2-pdr. pom-poms.

Protection Turrets 16″; barbettes 14″.
Belt 14″-15″.
Upper deck 6″.
Small turrets 6″.

Machinery Geared turbines. D.H.P. 130,000 = 30 knots.
4 screws. 8 3-drum boilers.

Fuel Oil 3,720 tons.

Constructors W. G. Sanders and H. S. Pengelly.

LION Class as projected.

With no international restriction on tonnage these ships were able to present a well-balanced design with the heaviest guns known to be carried afloat, the thickest armour required, and speed equal to that of any battleship building. As shown, they lack the wartime features added to the *King George V*, but would have received a tripod aft to support radar equipment, and additional A.A. guns.

A new and interesting feature in the design was the adoption of the square stern carried well down below the water-line. This saves deadweight, facilitates docking, and improves seakeeping and qualities of manœuvre. When the flat stern only extends down to the water-line as in several foreign designs, the run aft is affected when the ship dips her stern at speed and the flat surface becomes submerged.

Only the *Lion* and *Temeraire* had been commenced when the construction of all four was abandoned in 1940 as our shipbuilding resources had to be devoted to ships which could be built during the probable duration of hostilities.

Chapter 117

WORLD WAR II

FROM 1936 the years of disarmament and Collective Security through the League of Nations and the creation of a welfare state gave way to an all-too-short period of re-armament, when the Services paid a dreadful penalty for the political expediency which had brought about a near extinction of our sources for naval armaments and air strength. No longer did the heads of the great industries upon which our national survival depended have to come to the Controller at the Admiralty cap in hand, begging for contracts which would save skilled workers from being thrown out of employment on to the dole. Now, fifteen years of slow starvation made it impossible to spend the money voted. Crippled industries with the roots almost withered could not be revived overnight by an injection of political panic, nor could the men to man the ships be enlisted and trained when the naval and air schools had been forced to stagnate to merely nominal establishments.

As the power of the Nazis rose in Germany, so a vast system for re-armament over there became a national institution as an antidote to unemployment. A rigid secrecy allied to specious protestations for Peace and Non-aggression kept most of our pacifist leaders blinded to what was really happening in Germany. Churchill's warnings fell upon deaf ears.

Then came the Fascist revival in Italy with Mussolini's dream of Empire—and the attack upon Abyssinia, a member of the League of Nations. Here a united stand by Britain and France would have quashed the impulses of aggression. The Italians had always built better ships than they could fight, and our sadly reduced navy had no illusions about the quality of the new menace in the Mediterranean which war was to bring to light.

But instead we got the Hoare-Laval Pact, and half-hearted "sanctions" which would not ban the supply of oil, and only assured the dictators that they could go to any lengths they chose and encouraged America in her policy of isolation.

Hitler's ambitions led from the entry into Sudeten Germany to the subjugation of Austria and Czecho-Slovakia, and the threat to Poland. As a country we had to experience a national humiliation without precedent, as the expectations of those who had trusted in the League were allowed to go by default. A deluded electorate in this country saw the red light, but too late. The breathing space afforded by the Chamberlain-Hitler meetings at Munich and Berchtesgaden allowed a year of whole-time preparation for the inevitable war which the rape of Poland brought about.

War I was fostered by naval rivalry and the German invasion through Belgium. War II resulted from disarmament and a striving for peace through international pressure based on weakness and vacillation. The Navy and Merchant Navy entered it with the knowledge that they were still the foundations for our survival, as without food or oil neither the Army nor Air Force could exist. For over five long years the Battle of the Atlantic was fought without ceasing, and again it was the submarine which proved so dire an adversary. The battleship was no longer the prime unit of naval force, but the heavyweight member of a team and best fitted for leading a combined attack upon its opposite numbers.

There was no longer a question of matching ship against ship in line of battle. Instead of being designed for short range North Sea fighting German surface ships were intended for commerce raiding, with strict instructions to avoid contact with our warships, although with the guns and speed which could make for safety. A *Scharnhorst* in the Atlantic was a far greater menace than were Hipper's five battle-cruisers making hit-and-run raids in the North Sea, and to bring down the *Bismarck* meant marshalling every available battleship, battle-cruiser and carrier in order to close her bolt holes and bring her to action.

As the war progressed so the real potential of the battleship diminished. America rebuilt the ships disabled at Pearl Harbour and completed a group of the largest ever built in her yards, but they never came into action with Japan's battle fleet. For when fleet advanced to meet fleet it was the carrier planes on both sides which did the damage, and when the war ended the big armoured ships were the first to be put into Reserve.

GERMAN WAR DISPOSITIONS

Of the enemy ships the *Graf Spee* slipped away to her raiding station in the Atlantic on 31 August, to be followed by the *Deutschland* three days later together with their supply ships. Between the 19th and 29th August seventeen 500-700 ton U-boats were sent to the Atlantic, and twenty-two 250-ton coastal boats were ready in the North Sea out of a total of fifty-six completed. In October future construction was planned at thirty boats a month up to 850, but a definite programme was not settled until July 1940 when twenty-five a month became the target.

THE BLOCKADE

A blockade of Germany was declared on 3 September when war was declared, and the ships of the Home

Fleet under Admiral Forbes, the submarines and aircraft took up their patrols. By the middle of October the first of the twenty-five armed merchant cruisers was ready, and the contraband control base at Kirkwall was dealing with a steady toll of German ships attempting to run the blockade.

FLEET BASES

In the matter of fleet bases history was repeated. Scapa Flow had been stripped of its defences and until 1938 the three Services had agreed that the Home Fleet should be based on Rosyth as at the end of War I. But when the question was again examined in that year the Admiralty decided that Rosyth was too far south to prevent raiders breaking out into the Atlantic—now the main objective of the Home Fleet—and its long approaches were vulnerable to mining. On the other hand, Scapa was 150 miles nearer to the "Cutting-off position" between the Shetlands and southern Norway, while the turbulent Pentland Firth gave some protection against minelaying.

The Government however refused to take any steps towards defending Scapa as it would mean weakening the air defences of Edinburgh and Glasgow to provide protection for the north, with a call on equipment and labour of which there was a woeful shortage. In addition, there was a great objection to taking a step which "might alarm the populace" and antagonize Hitler, and so nothing was done until the outbreak of war when a few guns were mounted to protect the oil tanks and one squadron of naval fighters was stationed in the area. A single line of nets across the three main entrances and imperfectly blocked eastern entrances were the only anti-submarine defences, and unfortunately a further block ship was sunk on her way up and other arrived the day after the *Royal Oak* was torpedoed.

It was an ungrounded fear of heavy air attacks which led to its evacuation, while the fleet wandered between Loch Ewe, the Clyde and Rosyth. The loss of the *Royal Oak* proved the insecurity of Scapa: later the mining of the new cruiser *Belfast* confirmed the dangers attendant upon using Rosyth; and the unsuitability of Loch Ewe became patent when the *Nelson* was badly damaged in a minefield laid at its entrance. After a visit by the First Lord and Air Vice-Marshal Peirse to Admiral Forbes in the Clyde it was decided that Scapa should be thoroughly protected and that in the meantime the Clyde should serve despite its drawbacks as regards distance from the North Sea exit.

* * * * *

The part played by the Battle Fleet during the sixty-eight months of war was mainly in providing heavyweight convoy escort when one or more of the big German raiders were known to be out; or in hunting them down before they could close the convoy. All the armoured ships were constantly employed in the Battle of the Atlantic and the Mediterranean, and towards the end of the war went out East to join the U.S. forces against Japan.

THE SECOND BATTLE OF NARVIK, 13 APRIL 1940

During the invasion of Norway the enemy sent a force of ten destroyers to capture the port of Narvik at the head of the long and winding Vestfiord. Captain Warburton-Lee with the 2nd Destroyer flotilla was ordered to sink or take the transports lying there irrespective of what warships might be holding the port, and he led a spirited attack under shocking weather conditions to engage ten large 5-in.-gunned destroyers, sinking two and damaging five. We lost two with one damaged, and Captain Warburton-Lee was awarded a posthumous V.C. for his gallant leadership.

To complete the destruction of the remaining ships an attack was made by aircraft from the *Furious* without previous reconnaissance, in bad weather, when one squadron had to turn back and the other got through the low clouds but its bombs did no damage. Admiral Forbes therefore decided to send in the *Warspite* with nine destroyers under Admiral Whitworth.

Scouting ahead, the *Warspite's* aircraft bombed and sank U-64 and gave the enemy's strength and position. On information of our approach six German destroyers were ordered out and an hour's hot engagement took place in the narrow part of the fiord approach to Narvik. In all, eight destroyers and one U-boat were sunk at the cost of two *Tribals* damaged, and the risk of sending a battleship into such restricted waters was justified by the devastating effect of her big guns. It remains the only occasion on which a capital ship deliberately steamed in to attack destroyers.

ACTION OFF CAPE SPARTIVENTO, 27 NOVEMBER 1940

An Italian squadron consisting of the battleships *Vittorio Veneto* and *Guilio Cesare* with seven 8-in. cruisers and sixteen destroyers set out from Naples and Messina to attack a convoy of three merchant ships and the cruisers *Manchester* (Admiral Holland) and *Southampton* carrying 1,400 troops passing through from Gibraltar to Alexandria. They were being escorted by Force "H" under Admiral Somerville in the *Renown* with the *Ark Royal*, *Sheffield*, *Despatch* and nine destroyers which was to be met at the south of Sardinia by the *Ramillies*, *New-*

castle, *Berwick*, *Coventry* (A.A. ship) and five destroyers of the Mediterranean Fleet, for the passage of "The Narrows" between C. Bon and Sicily during darkness. Force "H" would then return to Gibraltar while the convoy and escort passed to the south of Malta to be met by the remainder of the Mediterranean Fleet next day.

At 6.30 a.m. a Sunderland flying boat from Malta reported the enemy off the C. Spartivento at the southern tip of Sardinia some 70 miles N.E. of Force "H" and the convoy. Although against vastly superior forces Admiral Somerville decided on a resolute offensive and at 11.30 a.m. spread Admiral Hollands cruisers in the van and turned towards the Italians at high speed. Soon afterwards the *Ramillies* and her consorts joined up, but the slow battleship was no great reinforcement. At 12.30 a short cruiser action in which the *Renown* joined led to the enemy retiring under smoke onto his battleships. Only the *Berwick* was hit. At 1 p.m. the enemy battleships were sighted ahead of our cruisers and opened fire on them, when the cruisers returned on *Renown*. However, when the enemy were seen to have turned away Admiral Holland at once followed and the *Ark Royal* launched eleven aircraft against the battleships. No hits were scored, and as we were approaching the Italian coast and the enemy had the heels of us, the action was broken off.

An indecisive action in which the Italians failed to molest the convoy or inflict damage upon our weaker forces, and turned to avoid possible action with the *Ark Royal's* aircraft. Lacking the degree of training and experience our aircrews did not slow up or damage the enemy so that our slower battleships could not bring them under fire.

BATTLE OF CAPE MATAPAN, 29 MARCH 1941

When news of impending Italian attacks on our convoys from Egypt to Greece reached Admiral Cunningham, (C-in-C Med.) our cruiser and destroyer forces, submarines, and torpedo bombers from shore stations were disposed so as to bring them to battle, with R.A.F. reconnaissance. When a flying boat reported three enemy cruisers (*Trento*, *Trieste*, *Bolzano*) and three destroyers off the south of Crete the flagship *Warspite* with the *Barham*, *Valiant*, and *Formidable* screened by nine destroyers sailed from Alexandria to meet them. They were sighted by the *Formidable's* air searchers south of Gadvo Island where Vice-Admiral Pridham-Whipple's lightforces were operating, and later a battleship (*Vittorio Veneto*) was seen 45 miles N.W. from the *Warspite* and another cruiser force (*Zara*, *Pola*, *Fiume*, *Garibaldi*, and *Abruzzi* reported as two *Cavour* class battleships and three heavy cruisers) with four destroyers to the north.

Attacked by aircraft from the carrier and our cruisers all three enemy divisions turned westwards, and to prevent their escape further air strikes were made, with a torpedo hit on the *V. Veneto* which reduced her speed to 8 knots, restored to 19 knots 3½ hours later. During the long chase she was steaming north-west with two destroyers ahead and astern and three heavy cruisers on each side flanked by columns of three or four destroyers, and a third striking force of eight torpedo bombers from the *Formidable* and two from Maleme aerodrome attacked at 7.30. A terrific barrage was put up confusing the targets and results of the attack, but the *Pola* was struck amidships and brought to a standstill. An hour later the *Zara* and *Fiume* were ordered back to assist her in the belief that our battleships were still far to the eastward—a fatal move which brought them under our guns.

With the *Pola* as the sole victim of the third attack Admiral Cunningham decided to force a night action before the enemy could reach air cover from Southern Italy and Sicily, and ordered his destroyers to attack. They reported passing a stopped unknown ship, so he turned to a westerly course at 20 knots. At 8.30 the *Valiant's* radar picked up this vessel about 8 miles away, and she was sighted at 10.30. The battleships formed into line ahead and opened fire at 3,000 yards, crippling the *Zara* and *Fiume* and leaving them to be finished off by the destroyers. The *Pola* had been the stopped ship, and she was found and put down by the *Jervis* and *Nubian*, while two of the accompanying destroyers fell to the *Stuart* and *Havoc*. No further contact was made with the *Vittorio Veneto* in the search which followed, and she reached Italy in safety.

We suffered no casualties, and this action gave us undisputed surface command in the Mediterranean.

THE "BISMARCK" CHASE, 24-27 MAY 1941

When the *Gneisenau* and *Scharnhorst* had become immobilized at Brest it was decided that both the *Bismarck* and *Tirpitz* would be required if our battleship escorts were to be defeated, and it was proposed to send the *Bismarck* into the Atlantic to tie these down while the heavy cruiser *Prinz Eugen* did the raiding.

After the *Prinz Eugen*—damaged by one of our magnetic mines—had been repaired, the two ships sailed from Gdynia on 18 May, their departure being duly reported in London. In the Denmark Strait between Greenland and Iceland where the *Norfolk* and *Suffolk* were on patrol they were sighted by both ships, the former coming under fire at 6½ miles and disengaging under smoke. Her report got through to Admiral Tovey in the *King George V* 600 miles away to the S.E., and Admiral Holland in the *Hood* with the *Prince of Wales* and four destroyers in company, closed at full speed.

Neither of these ships was in good fighting condition. The *Hood* had only completed her refit in March and gone on Atlantic patrol before gaining full efficiency. Designed twenty-five years previously before thick horizontal protection had become necessary, she was due for a major reconstruction when her armour would have been thickened to resist plunging fire. Thus she would become progressively more immune as ranges decreased to 12,000 yards and trajectories flattened. On the other hand the *Prince of Wales* was new and her armament not yet fully tested, but would be safe from heavy guns down to 13,000 yards. Such conditions would indicate closing the range with the *Prince of Wales* as the leading ship, in open order (1,000 yards) to give freedom of manœuvre.

As both ships were only good for about 28 knots while the *Bismarck* was rated at 30, a surprise attack was essential in bringing them to action, with reliance upon Admiral Wake-Walker's cruisers for guidance. Our ships prepared for action at 12.15 a.m. on 24 May expecting to contact the enemy after 1.40 a.m. in a night action. Unfortunately the cruisers lost touch with the German ships in a snowstorm, and thinking that this was because they had changed course to S.E. or by a turnabout Admiral Holland altered from a westerly intercepting course to due north and reduced speed to 25 knots. Visibility was too bad for the *Prince of Wales's* plane to undertake any reconnaissance work. If the enemy had not been sighted by 2.10 he intended to alter course to the south until the cruisers regained contact, while the destroyers searched to the north. The use of search radar in the *Prince of Wales* was forbidden in order to preserve secrecy.

At 2.47 the *Suffolk* regained contact and the enemy's position and speed could be plotted. Speed was increased to 28 knots and by 4.30 visibility was twelve miles, so the *Prince of Wales's* aircraft prepared to take off but found her fuel contaminated with sea water.

Admiral Holland intended to concentrate the fire of both his ships upon the *Bismarck* leaving the *Prinz Eugen* to the two cruisers, but when the enemy was sighted at 5.35 a.m. and action started eighteen minutes later their relative positions favoured the Germans. At a range of about 13 miles they were too fine on the starboard bow of the *Hood* for the after turrets to come into action, while to the *Bismarck* our ships were slightly before the beam and exposed to a full broadside. Thus, instead of bringing eight 15-in. and ten 14-in. to bear to the enemy's eight 15-in. and eight 8-in. the British squadron went in action with only four 15-in. and five 14-in. as one of the *Prince of Wales's* guns was defective.

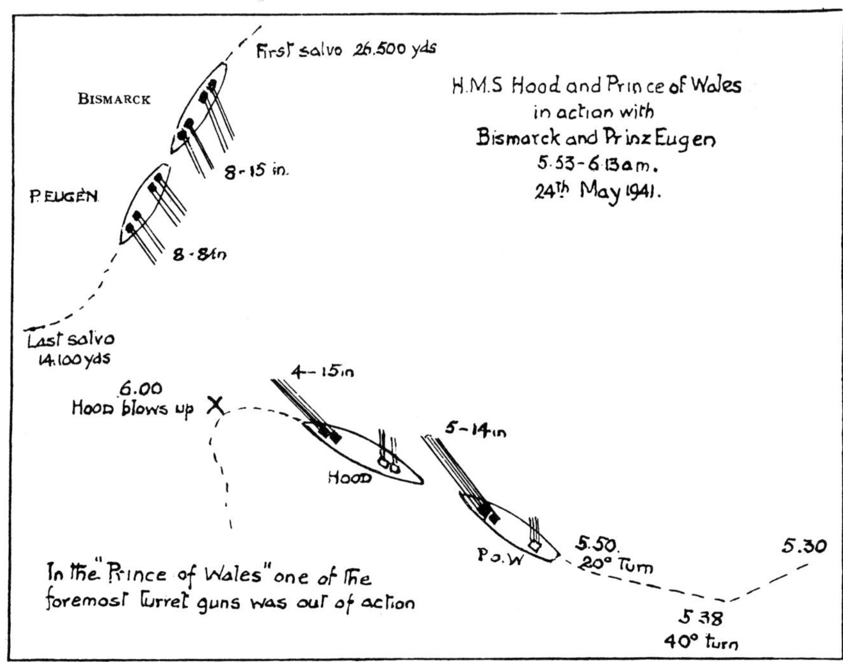

Fire was opened by all four ships at about 26,500 yards at 5.53 a.m., the Germans concentrating on the *Hood* which was leading. Admiral Holland had ordered his squadron to concentrate on the left-hand ship assuming that the *Bismarck* would be leading whereas it was the *Prinz Eugen*, and a shift to the *Bismarck* was not ordered until just before fire was opened. The gunnery officer of the *Prince of Wales*, having realized that the cruiser was in the lead, had already trained his armament on the right-hand ship. Certainly the *Prinz Eugen* was not troubled, and the control crew of the *Prince of Wales* saw only their own salvoes fall around the *Bismarck*—in which case the *Hood* bore the full weight of eight-gun broadsides. Only at the sixth salvo did the *Prince of Wales* straddle the *Bismarck* as neither of her radar sets was functioning, and owing to deficient freeboard forward spray had blanked both "A" and "B" turret rangefinders so that fire depended upon a 15 ft. instrument in the Director Control Tower aft which overestimated the range by about 1,000 yards.

To the distant cruisers *Norfolk* and *Suffolk* the *Hood's* fire apparently on the *Prinz Eugen* appeared excellent and her third salvo looked like a straddle; the *Prince of Wales* took longer to find her target and did not achieve a straddle until the sixth salvo. With both enemy ships concentrating on the flagship the *Prinz Eugen* with her more rapid fire scored a hit in less than a minute, causing a large fire by the *Hood's* mainmast which spread forward and blazed high above the upper deck. The cause of this was the additional magazines for her increased A.A. armament which were placed dangerously high up, plus about 9½ tons of useless A.A. rocket ammunition in light steel lockers in exposed positions.

At 5.55 the Vice-Admiral signalled for a 20° turn to port away from the enemy which would have brought the full broadships of both his ships to bear. But as they began to turn a salvo fell around the *Hood* and the cruisers saw an inferno of flame leap up hundreds of feet, and her place taken by an enormous column of smoke through which the bow and stern rose steeply as she broke amidships and disappeared.

The hit which exploded her after magazines situated below the turrets and shelter deck could either have entered beneath the shallow belt or pierced the horizontal armour around the turrets. This consisted of upper deck 2-in., main 3-in. and lower 2-in. which although thicker than contemporary protection was officially regarded as penetrable by high velocity shell at that range.

The fire of both German ships was now concentrated on the *Prince of Wales* and salvoes from 15-in., 8-in. and 5·9-in. guns began to fall every 15 seconds or so making it difficult to spot the fall of her own shell. One 15-in. hit on the compass platform killed or wounded every man there except Captain Leach; another landed under the fore 5·25-in. Directors and put them out of action; a third exploded on the aircraft crane just as the plane was preparing to take off, and the shattered machine with its load of petrol was hastily catapulted off. A fourth 15-in. pierced the side below the belt despite its depth, passed through several bulkheads and fetched up unexploded near the diesel dynamo rooms. Two 8-in. hit the water-line aft admitting 500 tons of water, and a third entered a 5·25-in. shell-handling room without exploding or hitting anyone.

To add to her troubles first one gun and then another kept on breaking down, and the builders' foremen who had been living on board completing the turrets' equipment did splendid work correcting these defects. But salvoes averaged only three instead of five guns, while the *Bismarck* appeared to be undamaged and was shooting with great accuracy, so Captain Leach wisely decided to break off the engagement until reinforcements arrived, and retired under a smoke screen. As she heeled on the turn the after turret jammed, leaving only four guns with two more rounds apiece until it could be cleared. These were fired under local control, making eighteen 14-in. salvoes which, according to German accounts, scored three hits, one of which passed through the *Bismarck's* bow below the bow wave and it was impossible to weld the holes without stopping the ship. The pipeline from the forward oil bunkers was cut, and the oil trickled out; the bows went down slightly and maximum speed was reduced to 27-28 knots. This reduced endurance sufficiently to cause the abandonment of the Atlantic raid and greatly improved the possibility of interception by Admiral Tovey.

This unfortunate action when the nominally superior force was defeated, was fought according to Admiralty fighting instructions with the ships in close order and manœuvred by signal from the flagship leaving no initiative to Captain Leach. As at the Falklands one ship was at a disadvantage—in this case not from smoke but by having to close to an unsuitable range at an angle when both ships were restricted to the use of their bow guns only. Had the closing been done alternatively, then one ship's full broadside could have covered her consort's advance with bow guns only. Had the *Prince of Wales* been allowed to fight at long range she would have been at an advantage when the time came for the Germans to change targets and alter the range.

The *Prince of Wales* now joined the *Norfolk* and *Suffolk* in shadowing the enemy as he steered S.W., attempting to shake them off. Some 300 miles away Admiral Tovey in the *King George V* with the *Repulse* and *Victorious*, four cruisers and nine destroyers was steaming at high speed to support them, and assuming the enemy could be kept in touch the earliest intercepting time would be about 7 a.m. next day (25th). But the prospects were not good unless his speed could be reduced. Then at 1.20 p.m. the *Suffolk* reported that the *Bismarck* had altered course to the south east and had reduced speed to about 24 knots.

At the Admiralty drastic steps were being taken to head off the German ships, and every available battleship, carrier and cruiser—nineteen in all—was ordered into the likely combat area. Force H (*Renown*, *Ark Royal* and *Sheffield*) under Admiral Somerville was called north from Gibraltar, the *Rodney* and four destroyers then about 550 miles S.E. of the enemy were ordered to close; the *Ramillies* with a Halifax convoy was ordered to place herself to the west, and the *Revenge* to leave Halifax and close towards the *Bismarck*; while the cruiser *Edinburgh* on Atlantic patrol was to join the shadowing force which was to be assisted by Coastal Command aircraft.

Not knowing whether the *Bismarck* had been damaged or was merely husbanding her fuel, aircraft from the *Victorious* were called upon to try and reduce her speed. The carrier together with the four cruisers therefore proceeded to a position within 100 miles of the enemy where her torpedo bombers could be launched. By 10 p.m. nine aircraft took off in very bad weather, manned by pilots on passage to Malta who had never flown off the deck of a ship, and at 11.27 radar contact was obtained. Attacks were pressed home under the worst conditions and one hit obtained amidships which did not do serious damage. All the Swordfish squadron regained the carrier and landed in the dark, but two of the shadowing Fulmers were lost.

Between 6 and 7 p.m. the *Bismarck* turned to engage her pursuers while allowing the *Prinz Eugen* to break away to the S.W. unobserved. No damage was done, and she resumed her southerly course. At 1 a.m. there was another brief skirmish which resulted in the *Suffolk* losing touch with her radar. Thinking the *Bismarck* had turned to the west she was searched for in that direction; actually she had altered course to the S.E. towards St. Nazaire. By this time the *King George V* was about 100 miles to the S.E. of the enemy and closing her rapidly; now with contact lost the *Bismarck* might adopt one of several courses, and all chances of an action within a few hours had to be given up.

The next period of 31½ hours was one of anxious searching, with Admiral Wake-Walker's squadron covering the W. and S.W. of the enemy's known position; the *Victorious* started air searches to the N.W. at dawn supported by the four cruisers; the *Rodney* had placed herself across the track to the Bay of Biscay, with the *Edinburgh* to the south. Approaching this area was the cruiser *Dorsetshire* with a convoy, and the *Ramillies* was patrolling to the south. In addition there was Force H still 1,300 miles away to the S.E. but approaching waters through which the *Bismarck* must pass if making for a French port.

Then came an unfortunate move due to an error in working out the enemy's position from a series of Admiralty reports which apparently showed that he had turned and was breaking back to the N.E. Admiral Tovey therefore reversed his course at 10.47 a.m., and the rest of the searchers were informed accordingly.

But Sir Fredrick Bowhill of Coastal Command—an old seaman—believed the *Bismarck* was bound for a French port and would make a safe landfall off Finisterre, and he persuaded the Admiralty to agree to a cross-over search covering that line. In support the Admiral of Submarines Sir Max Horton ordered six boats to take up a line covering first Brest and then St. Nazaire.

Not until evening was Admiral Tovey told to act on the assumption that the enemy was making for Brest, and throughout the 25th the Catalina aircraft of Coastal Command had been probing probable tracks towards the west of France, but only sighting our own ships. Next day a wider scheme took over the Biscay approaches and at 10.30 a.m. the enemy was sighted. The aircraft came under heavy and accurate fire, but managed to send a report that the *Bismarck* was 690 miles N.W. from Brest making a speed which would get him to the protection of U-boats and the Luftwaffe's heavy bombers in about 24 hours.

Meanwhile the ships were running short of fuel. The *Prince of Wales* and *Repulse* had to return to port, and supplies in both the *King George V* and *Rodney* were getting low. Of the searchers Force H was now admirably placed for the *Ark Royal's* Swordfish, who at last found the *Bismarck*. The *Sheffield* was sent off to the west to shadow her without the striking force having been warned, and was attacked with torpedoes when 20 miles north of the enemy. Later striking forces started attacks on the *Bismarck* at 8.47 p.m. in severe weather conditions against accurate A.A. fire, and two of the thirteen torpedoes made hits. One right aft wrecked the steering gear and jammed the rudders 15° to port, the propellers being undamaged. This hit sealed her fate, as she could not steer owing to the heavy gale and rudder jamming.

The aircraft were followed by five destroyers under Captain Vian which had been detached from a convoy. These carried out a series of night attacks between 1.20 and 7 a.m., which were repulsed by heavy radar-controlled gunfire. However, they kept in touch when air shadowing was impossible, and awaited the arrival of the battleships. It had been a close shave, for if the *Bismarck* had not been slowed down by midnight on the 26-27th the engagement would have had to be broken off. But the *Ark Royal's* Swordfish had enabled Admiral Tovey's ships to contact her by the narrow margin of three hours.

In the final gun action the *Rodney* was ordered to assume open order from the flagship and manœuvre as she liked. All three ships opened fire at 8.47 a.m. during an end-on approach starting at 16,000 yards. Gradually the range was reduced to what was described as "point blank target practice" against a flaming shambles. But the *Bismarck's* thick belt armour was not pierced and no shell or torpedo penetrated the engine rooms. Her machinery was intact when the turbine-engineer-officer was ordered to blow the explosive charges in the sea-valves of the engine room—a routine duty before abandoning ship.

Gunfire ceased at 10.15 and the *Dorsetshire* sent in two torpedoes to port and starboard which are claimed to have sunk her. She had fought to a finish with the greatest gallantry; only 110 survivors could be rescued by the *Dorsetshire* and *Maori* owing to the threat of enemy submarines.

All the primary warship types were closely concerned in the doom of the *Bismarck*. She was first spotted by cruisers and passed over to the battle cruiser squadron with disastrous results. Then when contact was lost it was an aircraft which found her and enabled the cruisers to carry on shadowing. Decisive blows were dealt by carrier aircraft, and destroyers harassed and held her through the night leading to the final battleship action.

Incidentally there is historical interest in the fact that radar was used for the first time to control gunfire in a night action.

ACTIONS WITH THE "GNEISENAU" AND "SCHARNHORST"

During War I two cruisers the *Gneisenau* and *Scharnhorst* caused us considerable if short-lived anxiety until sunk at the Battle of the Falklands. In War II the names were revived in two fast battleships which for four years remained a menace to Atlantic and North Sea convoys. They made several forays and were bombed or torpedoed, but weather conditions and their high speed enabled them to regain harbour; while under repair uncertainty as to when they were likely to emerge again locked up powerful forces which otherwise could have been used to build up our Eastern Fleet earlier.

During the Norwegian campaign the *Scharnhorst* caught the armed merchant cruiser *Rawalpindi* while on patrol and sunk her on 23 November 1939. Both battleships were encountered by the *Renown* in company with nine destroyers on 9 April 1940 when on their way to take up patrolling stations during the Norwegian campaign. Fire was opened at 4.5 a.m. at a range of nine miles in heavy seas and snow squalls, the *Renown's* gun sights clouded by spray and snow while the German ships could use their after guns without much interference. It was a short thirty minute action during which the *Gneisenau's* main armament control was put out of action by the first hit; a second crippled her forward turret and a third landed further aft without much injury. The *Renown* received two hits but was uninjured. A thick squall at 5 a.m. enabled the enemy to escape for the time being, and although the *Renown* worked up to 29 knots and got a further glimpse of them, both ships passed out of sight to the north. The weather was much too severe for the destroyers to keep up or take any part in the action.

The *Scharnhorst* was sunk in an engagement with a force under Admiral Sir Bruce Fraser, C.-in-C. Home Fleet on 26 December 1943, off the North Cape, when the battleship had come out to intercept convoys to and from Russia. It was a foray which the Admiral had anticipated and had prepared for accordingly. The outward bound convoy J.W.55B was escorted by fourteen destroyers, one frigate and two corvettes while the homeward bound R.A.55A had six destroyers and four corvettes in attendance. Two British forces were engaged:

Force 1. Cruisers *Belfast* (Vice-Admiral R. L. Burdett), *Norfolk*, *Sheffield*.
Force 2. *Duke of York* (C.-in-C.), cruiser *Jamaica*, four destroyers.

As it was unlikely that Force 2 could reach the operation area in time, the convoy J.W.55B was ordered to reverse course for three hours so that it should not be located by surface forces before dark. Pending the arrival of Force 2 it was the duty of Force 1 to shadow the *Scharnhorst* and keep her from attacking the convoy—a task made possible by the German directions that raiders should avoid contact with warships—and the 8-in. guns of the *Norfolk* could damage control positions in the same way that the *Exeter* treated the *Graf Spee*.

The enemy was picked up by *Belfast's* radar at 8.40 a.m., and at 9.24 she opened fire with star shell to be followed by the main armament of the *Norfolk* which claimed a hit with the second or third salvo on the port bridge director, causing several casualties. A second on the forecastle did little damage. The 6-in. cruisers did not open fire during this phase.

As the *Scharnhorst* was able to steam at 30 knots and Force 1's maximum against wind and sea was 24 knots the range continued to open and *Norfolk* ceased firing. The enemy's course was to the N.E., which would enable him to attack the convoy from another direction, and the cruisers therefore altered course to get between him and the convoy, thereby losing contact for about two hours. Rightly assuming that the attack would be renewed Force 1 held its course, and again *Belfast* made radar contact. A second action opened at 11,000 yards and again the enemy broke away after damaging *Norfolk*. His course was to the S.E. and any intention of attacking the convoy again had evidently been abandoned, so a shadowing pursuit was kept up on an advantageous course for interception by Force 1.

Contact with Force 2 at 40,000 yards was made at 4.40 p.m. and *Belfast* opened fire with star shell at 19,300 yards. Four minutes later Force 2 was engaging the enemy at 12,000 yards.

Evidently no reports from the enemy aircraft which had shadowed Force 2 had been passed to the *Scharnhorst*, which appeared quite unaware of the *Duke of York* and *Jamaica* with whom she had made no radar contact, and showed her turrets trained fore and aft. Her opening salvoes were erratic, and she altered course to the northward, when *Norfolk* again opened fire causing her to swing to the eastward to avoid Force 1.

Her tactics were to make a turn to southward and fire a broadside, then turn end-on away to the east until ready to fire the next, making *Duke of York's* gunnery a difficult problem. We adopted similar tactics while Force 2's screen *Savage*, *Saumarez*, *Scorpion* and *Stord* (Royal Norwegian Navy) crept in towards the enemy's quarters until they had closed to 10,000 yards.

Duke of York obtained hits with her first and third salvoes, one putting "A" turret out of action and another landing close to "C" turret; of three other hits one caused underwater damage and eventually reduced speed. *Jamaica* claimed one hit under difficulties. Fire ceased when the range had opened to 21,400 yards and it looked as if the *Scharnhorst* would escape—until the effects of the underwater damage became apparent.

When the destroyers closed to 10,000 yards they faced a heavy but ineffective fire which they returned at 7,000 yards. *Scorpion* fired eight torpedoes at 2,100 yards with one hit and *Stord* eight at 1,800 yards which were avoided, and the enemy then turned to a S.W. course when *Savage* and *Saumarez* attacked. *Savage* obtained three hits at 3,500 yards, and *Saumarez* one while being severely damaged with twenty-two casualties and reduced to 10 knots. One torpedo made a boiler room hit on the *Scharnhorst* and reduced her to 22 knots while another caused flooding aft. The Germans attributed the success of this gallant and relentless attack to the bad handling of the *Scharnhorst's* secondary and A.A. armament.

Meanwhile Force 2 had closed rapidly and re-engaged at 10,400 yards when the enemy was hit repeatedly, fires and flashes from exploding ammunition flaring up. She could only reply occasionally with part of her main armament and was compelled to shift her secondary guns from the destroyers to the *Duke of York*. Further attacks by the *Musketeer*, *Matchless*, *Opportune* and *Virago* claimed six hits making three cruisers and eight destroyers in the target area, a mêlée which the *Duke of York* avoided by turning to the northward. All that could be seen of the *Scharnhorst* was a dull glow through a dense cloud of smoke, which the searchlights and star shell could not penetrate. No ship saw her sink, but it seems certain that she went down after a heavy explosion about 7.45 p.m.

The *Duke of York* fought hard and well having drawn the enemy's fire for over 1½ hours. Although frequently straddled on all sides only her masts were shot through by 11-in. shells which failed to explode and by masterly handling aided by accurate advice from the plot, salvoes were avoided.

The engagement was marked by speedy radio communication and exceptional performance by radar personnel, which largely contributed to the success of a night action fought in heavy weather.

And so one of the two ships which had survived 112 air raids and some 4,000 tons of bombs while repairing in Brest, and had managed to return home through the Straits of Dover in the face of such air attack as could be mustered against them, was accounted for by heavy gun-fire.

BOMBARDMENTS AND COVERING OPERATIONS

During War I coastal attack by heavy warships suffered from inadequate or lack of aerial spotting when trying to reduce heavily fortified positions, which experience had shown could only be achieved by direct hits on guns or magazines. In War II they were employed against less formidable targets such as dockyards, coastal bases and the covering of amphibious operations when aerial defence was likely to be of greater effect than gunfire. Only two 15-in. monitors the *Abercrombie* and *Roberts* had been built to supplement the *Erebus* and *Terror* retained since War I, and of these the *Terror* had been lost off the Libyan Coast in February 1941; hence first-line ships had to be risked as at Salerno when there was a call for heavy calibre bombardment in extreme necessity.

BOMBARDMENT OF VALONA, 18 DECEMBER 1941

In order to assist the Greeks in their fight against the Italians in Albania, the main enemy supply base was bombarded by the *Warspite* and *Valiant* which fired 100 rounds of 15-in. shell into the town. In anticipation of bad weather the *Illustrious* had been detached, and without spotting indirect fire over intervening hills 2,000 ft. high probably did little damage.

BOMBARDMENT OF BARDIA, 3 JANUARY 1941

At the end of 1940 the Army of the Western Desert was temporarily held up before Bardia while supplies were being brought forward. The place was well fortified with a reported garrison of about 25,000. The assault was fixed for 3 January and the battle-fleet was asked to step-up the support from the sea hitherto given by the monitor *Terror* and river gunboats *Aphis* and *Ladybird*. The task was to prevent the large concentration of enemy troops and tanks in the northern part of the area from taking the Australians in the flank when they went in to attack.

A force consisting of the *Warspite*, *Barham*, *Valiant*, *Illustrious* with cruisers and destroyers went in to attack at 8 a.m. with fleet fighters overhead and Swordfish spotters. For forty-five minutes the three battleships drenched the area with their twenty-four 15-in. guns when all enemy movement had ceased. One coast defence battery replied without effect. The battleships retired that afternoon leaving the monitor and gunboats to continue the supporting fire. The Australian assault was successful and Bardia fell on 5 January with some 25,000 prisoners, its capture bringing the great relief of a proper water supply, and a port for running stores of every description for the Army.

GENOA, LEGHORN AND SPEZIA, 9 FEBRUARY 1941

What is described as "a cleverly disguised foray" was made into the Gulf of Genoa at dawn by the *Renown*, *Malaya*, *Ark Royal*, *Sheffield* and ten destroyers under Sir James Somerville and the shipbuilding yards and shore installations subjected to heavy sea and air bombardment when much damage was inflicted. At Genoa large fires were observed in the Ansaldo electric works, the main power station, dry docks, and round the inner harbour, and hits on oil tanks, the marshalling yard and merchant ships. More than 300 tons of shells were fired in this, one of the most successful bombardments of the war. Surprise was complete, and we suffered no casualties.

BOMBARDMENT OF TRIPOLI, 18 APRIL 1941

By April 1941 the situation in the North African campaign was such that the Admiralty decided on drastic measures to interrupt Axis communications for a considerable time. An attempt must be made to carry out a combined blocking and bombardment of Tripoli, the latter being carried out by the blocking ships at point blank range; and that the *Barham* and a "C" class cruiser should be expended to this purpose.

In answer to this extraordinary project Admiral Cunningham pointed out that we had mined some of the approach channels with magnetic mines from aircraft and that others were too shallow for a battleship; that the *Barham* drew 32 ft. and would be unhandy at slow speed with less than 2 ft. under her keel; and that she could not be expected to wedge herself in exactly the right position within point-blank range of enemy guns and dive bombers overhead. If successful it would mean the loss of a first-class fighting unit desperately needed in this and other theatres. He would rather attack with the whole battle-fleet, and should one of the battleships be seriously damaged than she could be used as a block-ship, her ship's company being removed by light craft subsequently.

After much argument the War Cabinet agreed to the Admiral's alternative of a combined bombing and shelling attack.

The attacking force *Warspite*, *Barham*, *Valiant*, carrier *Formidable* and cruisers *Phoebe* and *Calcutta* with screening destroyers sailed from Alexandria on the 18th ostensibly to escort a Malta convoy, then peeling off on the 20th at high speed to be off Tripoli before dawn next morning. R.A.F. Wellingtons and F.A.A. Swordfish were to make a preliminary attack while aircraft from the *Formidable* provided flare illumination besides spotting for our gunfire. Two days previously the submarine *Truant* was sent to fix herself accurately 4 miles off the harbour entrance, and show a seaward light as a navigation mark.

With perfect timing the three battleships supported by the cruiser *Gloucester* circled the *Truant*, passed along the line of the harbour and from 5 a.m. until 5.45 pumped 15-in. and 6-in. shell into the shipping and harbour works. Under clouds of dust from the previous bombing damage estimation was difficult, but the aircraft reported great damage and six ships sunk, with a big oil fire in the *Valiant's* area. Shore reply was very wild and scored no hits.

Had the *Barham* been sacrificed and our command of the Eastern Mediterranean jeopardized by her loss, it was by no means certain that Tripoli could have been closed as a supply base to Rommel or that the Tunisian ports might not have been able to afford the necessary supplies.

NORTH AFRICA LANDING ("OPERATION TORCH") 8 NOVEMBER 1942

Force H consisting of the *Duke of York* (flagship of Vice-Admiral Sir Neville Syfret), *Rodney*, *Renown*, the carriers *Victorious*, *Formidable* and *Furious*, three cruisers and seventeen destroyers were given the duty of covering both the British Task Forces and their follow-up convoys against attack from the sea by Italian or Vichy-French naval forces. In the event, no resistance from the sea was encountered.

THE INVASION OF SICILY, "OPERATION HUSKY," JULY 1943

We were taking no chances with the Italian fleet should they come out to defend their country, and our naval forces were brought up to a strength adequate for the task. Force H under Vice-Admiral Willis consisted of *Nelson*, *Rodney*, *Warspite*, *Valiant*, *Howe* and *King George V* with the 15th Cruiser Squadron *Newfoundland*, *Uganda*, *Orion* and *Mauritius* and the 12th C.S. *Aurora*, *Penelope*, *Cleopatra*, *Euryalus*, *Sirius* and *Dido*. Seven submarines acted as inshore beacons guiding the flights of landing-craft.

As the Italian fleet did not come out to protect their country only some support from the cruisers, destroyers and river gunboats *Aphis* and *Scarab* was required to cover the landing which was made in wild weather which the enemy decided would preclude any attack. Only at Gela, where a strong German counter-attack led to their tanks penetrating to the beach, were the Americans assisted by heavy gunfire from the monitor *Abercrombie*.

On 31 August the *Nelson* and *Rodney* entered the Straits of Messina and bombarded the Calabrian Coast—a striking instance of the employment of heavy guns in narrow waters.

After the capture of Messina a huge number of guns were sited to cover the crossing of the Straits (Operation "Baytown") made on 3 September and preceded by heavy bombardment of the Reggio and C. Pillaro coastal batteries by the *Nelson*, *Rodney*, *Warspite* and *Valiant*, *Mauritius*, *Orion* and monitors *Erebus*, *Roberts* and *Abercrombie*, six destroyers and two gunboats. But as the Italians were not fighting and the Germans had pulled out to the north, it was largely a waste of ammunition with a bloodless victory known as the "Messina Straits Regatta"—albeit a triumph of organization and landing technique, when the American "Ducks" appeared for the first time.

During the invasion the *King George V* and *Howe* forming Force Z bombarded Favignaua and Trapani and in September arrived at Taranto to occupy the naval base. Later they convoyed the surrendered Italian warships from Malta to Alexandria.

THE LANDING AT SALERNO, "OPERATION AVALANCHE," SEPTEMBER 1943

Five days after the landing when German resistance and counter attacks had forced the Americans to give ground and the military situation had become critical Vice-Admiral H. K. Hewitt U.S.N., the overall Naval Commander, asked for heavy air bombardment and naval bombardment by heavy guns over the enemy's rear. Admiral Cunningham called on the *Valiant* and *Warspite* with the *Nelson* and *Rodney* also available if required. Of sixty-two rounds of 15-in. shell thirty-five fell exactly on the target area and eight were within 100 yards of it, traffic concentrations being pounded and ammunition dumps blown up. After completing her third bombardment on the 16th at 21,800 yards the *Warspite* was hit by a radio-controlled bomb which after penetrating the mess decks exploded in No. 4 boiler room and went out through the double bottoms. Almost simultaneously a second bomb fell close alongside and blew another hole below the water-line. In five minutes the ship was without steam or power of any kind, in total darkness, and steadily flooding with water and oil fuel. Every deadlight was screwed down and below decks all was in stagnant darkness with fierce and tropical heat causing great thirst. In three days over 3,000 gallons of lime juice were consumed, and demand for solid food was negligible.

After an adventurous passage under tow sideways through the Straits of Messina she reached Malta on the 19th and later went on to Gibraltar where two enormous cofferdams were built onto her bottom. Although in need of extensive refit she was able to take part in bombarding during the Normandy landings in June 1944.

Admiral Hewitt's report on "Avalanche" stated "The margin of success in the landing was carried by the naval guns" and the Germans themselves attributed our final success to the devastating effect of naval gunfire, which held the ring when there was danger of the enemy breaking through to the beaches and when the overall position looked so gloomy.

THE NORMANDY LANDING, "OPERATION NEPTUNE," D-DAY, 6 JUNE 1944

This, the naval side of Operation "Overlord," covered the biggest amphibian operation in history. The actual landings on D-Day were preceded by a terrific bombardment of the enemy coastal defences, first from the air and then by combined British and U.S. naval forces. While "softening" from the air might knock out or damage some gun positions or batteries, block ammunition supplies and force dazed gunners to take shelter in deep dug-outs, they could not destroy the "West Wall" upon which four years of slave labour had been spent. It was during this temporary "heads down" period that naval units expected to close in and continue the process while the beach assault proceeded.

The first task was to silence the heavy batteries on each flank of the Assault Area. At Le Havre were four 16-in. and three 11-in. guns, and twenty-eight other guns of 6 in. and upwards, all within range of the eastern British Assault Area with its thousands of ships and landing craft packed with troops. On the western Cotentin Peninsula the batteries which could shell the U.S. Assault Area did not approximate to the same strength or calibre.

In the initial stages of the invasion the Eastern Bombarding Force was British and the Western one American, but it was not a hard and fast arrangement and when required there could be an exchange of forces. Admiral Sir Bertram Ramsey was Allied Naval C.-in-C. with Rear-Admiral Sir Philip Vian (*Scylla*) commanding the British Task Force. The Bombarding Squadron under Rear-Admiral W. R. Patterson with his flag in the cruiser *Mauritius* consisted of the *Warspite*, *Ramillies*, monitor *Roberts*, and cruisers *Arethusa*, *Danae*, *Dragon* and *Frobisher*. The *Warspite* was still in cofferdam repair after Salerno, and manned largely by personnel on passage from the Mediterranean.

Specially trained pilots from Lee-on-Solent spotted for each big ship working on pre-selected targets, and it was soon evident that the heavy Le Havre batteries were virtually immune to air or sea attack. Very thick reinforced concrete meant that nothing short of a direct hit or a shell through a casemate opening could knock a gun out. Also, a great many guns had been moved after the pre-D-day air bombardment of the coastal defences, so that the air attack before H-hour had only damaged the old positions. But it did drive the gunners to ground, and the new emplacements and defences were not complete when our assault was launched. However, nearly all the fixed batteries from the mouth of the Seine to Cape Barfleur were silenced temporarily before the landing ships came within range, and such intermittent fire as came from Le Havre was engaged with such accuracy that they again lapsed into silence.

The only sea attack on the big ships came early on through a smoke screen we had laid before Le Havre, when three torpedo boats suddenly emerged, fired torpedoes, and then beat a hasty retreat into the smoke. One torpedo sunk the Norwegian destroyer *Svenner*.

With the more formidable defences neutralized the bombarding cruisers came into action closer inshore against the pill-boxes, redoubts, anti-tank defences and machine-gun posts, with direct observation from the ships. This second phase again "kept the enemy's heads down" and allowed the landing craft to approach the beaches with far less opposition than had been anticipated. Then the third phase of the "fire plan" came into operation as the beaches and approaches from landward were "drenched" by the guns of seventy destroyers, L.C.G.'s (Landing

Craft, Guns) and mattresses of rockets from L.C.R.'s (Landing Craft, Rockets) which had a devastating effect against any defences not built of thick concrete.

All these, ranging up and down the sea front, laid a curtain of fire only lifted when the first assault wave touched the beaches. Timing was excellent and the lack of opposition to the degree expected was very largely due to the efficacy and timing of the naval "fire-plan."

After the advance inland supporting fire was accurately maintained at ranges between 20,000 and 24,000 yards. Enemy formations assembled for a counter attack were suddenly shattered by heavy shells coming from nowhere, and among the ships specially congratulated by the Army were the *Nelson*, *Warspite* and *Roberts*. Special mention must be made of the wonderful practice registered by the cruiser *Ajax* of River Plate fame, which will long be quoted as an outstanding example of naval gunfire against shore positions. The battery at Longues included four 6-in. in reinforced concrete casemates, and had been very troublesome from a position where they could do a lot of harm. *Ajax* fired 114 rounds at an average range of 12,000 yards, and when it was captured her shooting was found to have hit and damaged No. 2 casemate, hit and put out of action No. 3 gun, and destroyed No. 4 gun by more than one shell which had entered through the gun slot, and burst inside the casemate.

Accurate firing at such ranges depends upon the gun setting and allowances for wind, gun wear, temperature, and even the amount of the earth's revolution during the time of flight plus accuracy of navigation when firing at map references. At one period when the bombarding ships had been firing at 17,000 yards it was found that the average distance from the target of the first ranging shot was only 146 yards, which error was promptly corrected by the Forward Officer, Bombardment, or by aircraft.

The *Rodney* bombarded Caen and other strong points on the French coast. Although attacked by human torpedoes, bombs and shells she was undamaged. The *Nelson* also played her part, and was mined in June 1944.

After D-day the *Malaya* bombarded the German-held island of Cezembres off St. Malo whose two large batteries were to prevent the Allies using the port. She got onto her target at maximum range, and her last two shells destroyed the barracks.

THE WAR AGAINST JAPAN

In the Far East the theatres of operations were divided by the long spine of the Malay Peninsula and land formations stretching south-east through the E. Indian islands to Australia, and to the east of this division the war was predominantly American. The war in the Indian Ocean was a British responsibility, which was planned to take an ever-increasing part in the over-all campaign although limited by the enemy surrender before it could be developed.

In the Indian Ocean a naval force based on Port T, the name given to the Addu Atoll ring of coral islands surrounding a deep lagoon at the southern end of the Maldive Islands as big as Scapa Flow, was being built up. It included the *Queen Elizabeth* (flagship of Admiral Somerville), *Warspite*, *Valiant*, *Ramillies*, *Royal Sovereign*, *Revenge* and *Resolution* forming the 3rd Battle Squadron. Of these, the four "R"s with their sub-standard deck protection were regarded as a liability and brought home before the end of 1942, and *Warspite* was recalled to the Mediterranean in time for the invasion of Sicily. Three carriers, including the *Hermes*, seven cruisers including the Dutch *Heemskerck*, and sixteen destroyers completed the force.

ATTACK ON SABANG, 25 JULY 1944

An air strike was made against this Japanese naval base at the north-west end of Sumatra on 19 April when the *Queen Elizabeth* was one of the covering force, and again three months later when the 1st Battle Squadron had its first opportunity of offensive action against enemy shore defences. This and the bases in the Nicobars and Andamans controlled the approaches to the narrow neck of the Malay Peninsula and south-to-north sea route from Singapore to Rangoon along which Japanese supplies reached Burma.

* * * * *

Battleship reinforcements included the *Howe*, which became the flagship of Admiral Sir Bruce Fraser on the formation of the British Pacific Fleet in January 1945, and the *King George V* in December 1944 as 2nd flagship.

ATTACKS ON SUMATRA OIL REFINERIES, DECEMBER 1944-JANUARY 1945

To cut off Japanese supplies of oil a series of attacks were made upon the refineries in Sumatra by Carriers of the Fleet Air Arm under Rear-Admiral Sir Philip Vian at the request of Admiral Nimitz, Supreme Allied C.-in-C. Pacific. Covered by a strong force including the *King George V*, cruisers *Argonaut*, *Black Prince*, *Euryalus* and four destroyers, aircraft from the *Illustrious*, *Victorious*, *Indomitable* and *Indefatigable* attacked the installations at Medam in N. Sumatra on 20 December 1944 and 4 January 1945 with satisfactory results. In south-east Sumatra the refineries at Palembang, which were among the largest in the world and heavily defended by aircraft, A.A. guns and balloon barrages, were attacked on 24 January and made useless for a long time to come. As a result the enemy were deprived of sources of 75 per cent. of all aviation spirit at a time when fighting fronts were far nearer to Sumatra than Japan and the tanker fleet had been seriously diminished.

CAPTURE OF RANGOON, 2 MAY 1945

The seaborne assault and recapture of this great port marked the virtual end of the Burma campaign with a short term to any organized Japanese resistance. Naval and air operations were carried out over a wide area to prevent enemy interference with our landings and their consolidation. A long series of bombardments and strikes by carrier aircraft were made under a covering force under Admiral H. T. C. Walker, C.B. which included the *Queen Elizabeth* and French battleship *Richelieu*, cruisers *Suffolk*, *Ceylon* and Netherlands *Tromp* and destroyers *Rotherham*, *Paladin* and *Penn*.

BOMBARDMENT OF TRUK, 15 JUNE 1945

This great naval base in the Carolines called "The Gibraltar of Japan" with a garrison of 40,000 was heavily damaged when bombed and shelled for 48 hours by aircraft and cruisers. No battleships were engaged.

FINAL ASSAULTS ON JAPAN

On 17 July 1945 Admiral Halsay's Third Fleet joined up with a strong Task Force of the British Pacific Fleet under Vice-Admiral Sir Bernard Rawlings, and from that date until the final surrender in Tokyo Bay on 15 August the British and American Fleets did not separate.

In the bombardment of Tokyo and other parts of Honshu, the main island of Japan, the British force consisted of the *King George V*, cruisers *Black Prince* and *Newfoundland* and destroyers *Quickmatch*, *Barfleur*, *Grenville*, *Troubridge* and *Undine*.

This was the last occasion on which a British battleship fired her guns in action against enemy targets.

Chapter 118

"VANGUARD" (1940 EMERGENCY WAR PROGRAMME)

In December 1939 the D.N.C. Sir Stanley Goodall suggested that the 15-in. guns with their mountings and turrets which had been landed from the *Courageous* and *Glorious* on their conversion to carriers, could be used to arm a battleship which might be rushed to completion before the *Lion* class. As the time taken to design and produce her gun mountings usually determines the construction rate of a battleship, this proposal was welcomed by the First Lord as an expedient for increasing our strength in armoured ships during the probable duration of hostilities.

A sketch plan and costs having been submitted and approved by the Board, the design was drawn up and the ship ordered in March 1941 under the 1940 War Programme after work on the *Lion* class had been abandoned. As the *Hood* was not sunk until May 1941 it was not a question of replacing her, but of getting a fast battleship ready to meet an emergency in the West, or to join the Singapore fleet which we expected to form when Japan thought fit to come in against us.

"VANGUARD" (Emergency War Programme 1940)

Builders	*Laid down*	*Launched*	*Completed*	*Cost*
Clydebank	Oct. '41	30 Nov. '44	April '46	£9,000,000 (exclusive of armament)

Dimensions 760′ (p.p.) 814′ 4″ (o.a.) × 108′ × 36′ maximum = 51,420 tons full load; 44,500 standard.

Armament 8 15-in.; 16 5·25-in.; 11 twin 40 mm.; 4 3-pdrs saluting.

Protection Turrets 13″ faces, 11″ sides, 7″ backs, 4″ crowns.
Belt 14″ over magazines, 5½″ lower edge.
13″ „ machinery, 4½″ lower edge.
Barbettes 16″; small turrets 6″.
End bulkheads 15″; longitudinal torpedo bulkheads 2″.
Decks: 6″ over magazines; 5″ over machinery.

Machinery Parsons single reduction geared turbines. 4 shafts.
S.H.P. 130,000 = 30 knots.
Boilers 8 3-drum.

Fuel 3,800 tons.

Complement 1,600 (2,000 war).

Constructor W. G. Sanders (original design without sheer).

In general the design followed that of the *King George V* and *Lion* with extra length to accommodate four smaller turrets, their comparative dimensions as designed being:

King George V	745′ × 103′ × 27¾′ = 35,000 tons standard.
Lion	785′ × 105′ × 30′ = 40,000 „ „
Vanguard	814½′ × 108½′ × 28′ = 42,300 „ „

It had been intended to give her a straight bow and level forecastle, but experience with the *King George's* at sea demonstrated the need for extra freeboard forward and a cutaway bow with more flare, which again added to the over-all length. When the need for aircraft accommodation had passed her boats were stowed amidships with A.A. guns abaft the main mast which was placed close behind the after funnel. The stern was cut square in order to save weight and to facilitate docking.

ARMAMENT

In order to allow for extra elevation the turret faces were heightened and the ports enlarged, with range-finders laid across the roofs. Nine of the twin 40 mm. Bofors were mounted on the superstructure, one on "B" turret, and one at the stern with its own control position.

PROTECTION

This was similar to that in *King George V* the extra displacement being largely due to the longer belt. Subdivision is much along the same lines, with solid bulkheads between the main compartments so that access had to be down vertical shafts.

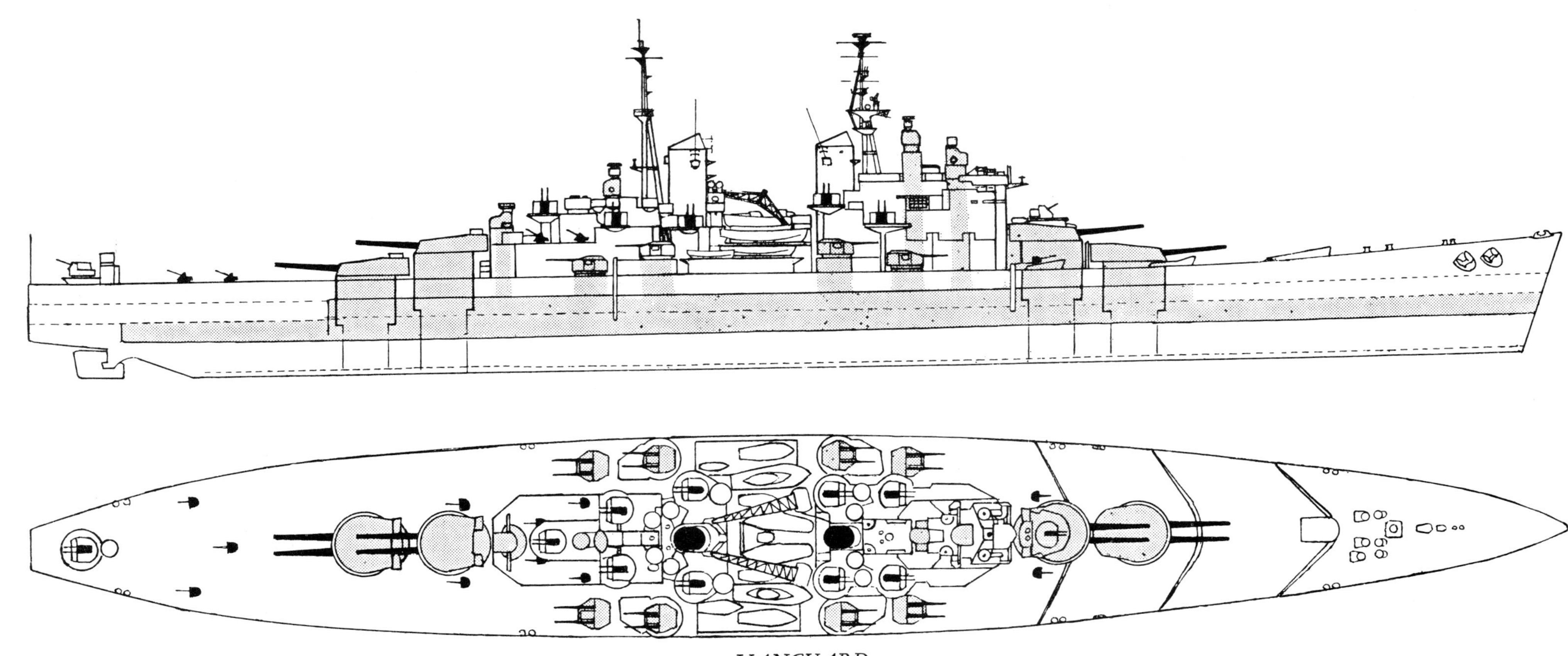

VANGUARD

MACHINERY

As in the *King George V* the engine rooms and boiler rooms were arranged in four separate units with four shafts. The designed h.p. was 130,000 for 30 knots at a legend displacement of 42,500 tons, but at her later increased load it was doubtful if she could have achieved this.

The system of humidity control in the engine and boiler rooms could keep an even temperature under Arctic or tropical conditions.

VANGUARD

SEA-GOING QUALITIES

She was proved a magnificent seaboat, dry and steady under severe weather conditions. During combined exercises with U.S. forces in September 1953 when the green seas taken in over the forecastle were checked by her breakwaters, the battleship *Iowa* shipped heavy water all over her decks which swept away everything in its path, and registered 26° roll each way while the *Vanguard* was making only 15°.

"VANGUARD"

Built at Clydebank October '41 to April '46, and accepted in August. Royal Tour to South Africa February-May '47. Refit at Devonport '47-'48; operational in Mediterranean January-July '49, followed by special trials. In November '49 became Training Ship at Portland, but temporary Flagship of C.-in-C. Home Fleet during cruises, and exercises. Refit at Devonport October '54. Was flagship of the Reserve Fleet at disposal of N.A.T.O. Scrapped 1960.

* * * * *

With the *Vanguard* the long tale of the gun-carrying battleship closed, and now that the line-of-battle is no more the *King Georges* have been discarded. To those of us who remember the rigged ironclads in Reserve, and have followed battleship development from the old *Royal Sovereign*, there is something infinitely pathetic in the passing of man's most wonderful creation afloat.

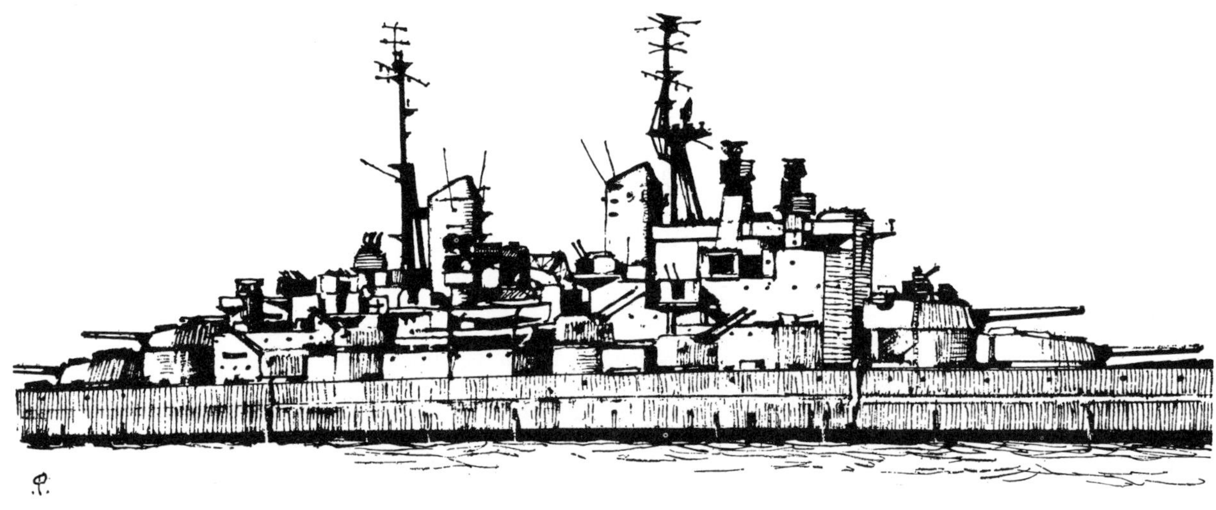

Appendix I

THE SAILING OF THE IRONCLADS

THE indifferent performance of the ironclads generally when under canvas was somewhat of a problem to their Captains. Men skilled in the art of getting the best out of sailing ships could not understand why splendidly modelled hulls with a fine entry like the *Minotaurs* and carrying a good spread of sail did not respond as they thought they should.

Reed professed to regard their dullness as merely due to restrictions imposed by the Board—given a free hand he was quite prepared to design an ironclad which should sail as well as an unarmoured ship. Because of pressure brought upon the Board to clear up the problem, Barnaby was instructed to prepare a full explanation at about the time when the Committee on Designs was sitting. This he did, and his explanation effectively took the wind out of Reed's sails.

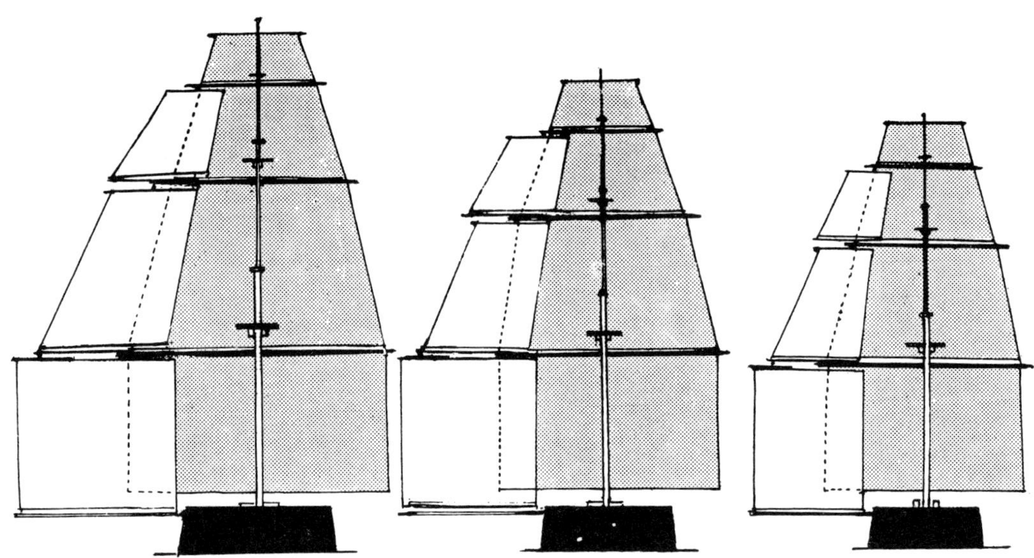

1ST SCALE	2ND SCALE	3RD SCALE
Warrior	*Defence*	*Favorite*
Black Prince	*Resistance*	*Pallas*
Achilles	*Hector*	*Penelope*
Monarch	*Valiant*	
Captain	*Royal Oak*	
Hercules	*Ocean*	
Sultan	*Caledonia*	
	Prince Consort	
	Minotaur	
	Agincourt	
	Northumberland	
	Royal Alfred	
	Zealous	
	Repulse	
	Lord Warden	
	Lord Clyde	
	Zealous	

Diagram to scale showing the three scales of masting and spars carried by the armoured ships of the mid-Victorian navy. Main mast only, with stunsails set on one side.

	Deck to truck	*Main yard*	*Topsail*	*Topgallant*	*Royal*
1st scale	175	105	74	46	$32\frac{1}{2}$ ft.
2nd scale	153	91	68	42	$30\frac{1}{2}$ ft.
3rd scale	140	$78\frac{1}{2}$	59	40	$29\frac{1}{2}$ ft.

He showed that the area of sail to a ton of displacement in sailing ships was from 6·15 to 13·9 sq. ft.; in the ironclads it was only 3·25 sq. ft. and would therefore need to be doubled to obtain the same results. The area of canvas in proportion to amidships section was 27·7 to 40, while in the *Hercules* it was 21·62. The *Hercules* should therefore hoist 49,740 sq. ft. instead of only 28,882 sq. ft. of plain sail, and to carry the necessary masting would require three times her stability—*i.e.*, with the same displacement, length and draught her beam would have to be 66 ft. instead of 59 ft., and it was a question whether crews to work such a windtrap could be berthed. Also, she would be much too stable and a shocking gun platform.

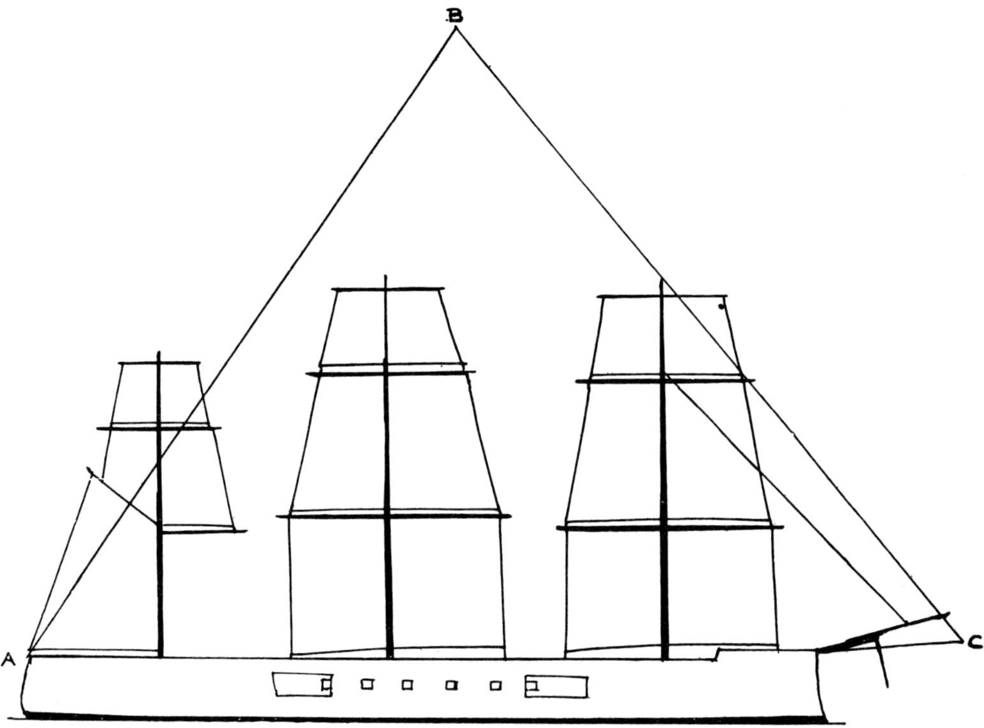

Above is the diagram Barnaby drew up to illustrate his calculations and argument, showing the *Hercules* under plain sail and ABC a triangle giving the necessary 49,740 sq. ft. of canvas.

Appendix II

DOCKS AND DIMENSIONS

THE rapid growth in battleship dimensions during the first Dreadnought decade was not accompanied, unfortunately, by the provision of docks of the necessary length and beam to take them. Even in 1914 the only Government docks on the east coast large enough to accommodate a Dreadnought or Invincible were the new dock at Chatham and the floating dock at Sheerness. The Chatham dock was more or less ruled out because of approach difficulties—the *Lord Nelson's* were the heaviest warships which ever entered the dockyard and then at light draught. Work on the new Rosyth yard was approaching completion and there would soon be three docks available with another at Invergordon, together with a floating dock. In the private yards there was only the big floating dock at Hebburn-on-Tyne, which pans out at two east coast floating docks to serve twenty-two battleships and eight battle cruisers in the event of a North Sea engagement, until Rosyth and Invergordon were ready.

Remote from the scene of action there were five docks and locks at Portsmouth, four at Devonport, one at Hawlbowline in Ireland, two at Southampton, one at Liverpool, one at Birkenhead, and several abroad.

From a constructional viewpoint it was not so much the shortage of docks as the limited width of those available. At a time when the Americans had been able to allow their 26,000-ton *Wyomings* a beam of 93·2 ft. and the *New Yorks* of 27,000 tons 95·2 ft., Sir Philip Watts was satisfied with 88·5 ft. in the *Orion*, although she was 22 ft. longer than the *Wyoming*. Germany's *Kaiser*, contemporary with the *Orion*, was 20 ft. shorter, but had nearly 7 ft. more beam. The British lines allowed for the required G.M. and about ½ knot higher speed with much the same h.p., but it was claimed that the extra beam permitted better water-line subdivision and protection against torpedoes outside the longitudinal protection bulkhead. Big German beam is also thought to have been partially determined by limitation in the water depth of the Kiel Canal. German ships at the period did not exceed 27 ft. draught.

The efficacy of this space between the hull side and the protective bulkhead depended upon the extent and nature of the subdivision; otherwise when the bulge or space was flooded and the bulkhead became the new water-plane edge, the ship would have been the better without the extra beam.

A space of about a foot between the hull and dock side was considered ample clearance.

Appendix III

DISTRIBUTION OF ARMOURED SHIPS AT TYPICAL PERIODS TO SHOW CHANGES IN SQUADRON STRENGTH

1863

CHANNEL
Black Prince
Warrior
Defence
Resistance
Revenge, 73

MEDITERRANEAN
Edgar, 89
London, 86
Marlborough, 121
Mars, 80
Meeanee, 60
Queen, 74
St. George, 84
Trafalgar, 70

CHINA
Sans Pareil, 70

NORTH AMERICA AND WEST INDIES
Nile, 78

1867

CHANNEL
Achilles
Bellerophon
Caledonia
Hector
Lord Clyde

MEDITERRANEAN
Enterprise
Ocean
Prince Consort
Royal Oak
Victoria, 102

PACIFIC
Zealous

CHINA
Princess Royal, 73

NORTH AMERICA AND WEST INDIES
Duncan, 81
Favorite

1871

CHANNEL
Agincourt
Minotaur
Northumberland
Hercules
Sultan
Monarch

MEDITERRANEAN
Defence
Caledonia
Lord Warden
Prince Consort
Royal Oak
Research

CHINA
Iron Duke
Ocean

PACIFIC
Zealous

NORTH AMERICA AND WEST INDIES
Royal Alfred

1876

CHANNEL
Black Prince
Defence
Resistance
Minotaur

MEDITERRANEAN
Devastation
Monarch
Hotspur
Rupert
Pallas
Hercules
Sultan
Swiftsure
Triumph
Research

CHINA
Audacious

PACIFIC
Repulse

NORTH AMERICA AND WEST INDIES
Bellerophon

1881

CHANNEL
Achilles
Agincourt
Minotaur
Northumberland

MEDITERRANEAN
Thunderer
Monarch
Temeraire
Alexandra
Invincible
Superb

PACIFIC
Triumph

CHINA
Iron Duke

1886

CHANNEL
Monarch
Agincourt
Minotaur
Iron Duke
Sultan

MEDITERRANEAN
Dreadnought
Thunderer
Agamemnon
Orion
Temeraire
Alexandra
Superb

NORTH AMERICA AND WEST INDIES
Bellerophon

PACIFIC
Triumph

CHINA
Audacious

1891

Channel	Mediterranean	North America and West Indies	Coast Guard and Reserve
Anson	*Benbow*	*Bellerophon*	*Ajax*
Camperdown	*Collingwood*		*Belleisle*
Howe	*Agamemnon*		*Hotspur*
Rodney	*Colossus*		*Northumberland*
	Edinburgh		*Neptune*
	Dreadnought		*Audacious*
	Trafalgar		*Invincible*
	Victoria		*Iron Duke*
	Inflexible		*Triumph*
	Temeraire		

1896

Channel	Mediterranean	China	Coast Guard and Port Guard
Magnificent	*Ramillies*	*Centurion*	*Benbow*
Majestic	*Revenge*		*Colossus*
Prince George	*Hood*		*Edinburgh*
Empress of India	*Barfleur*		*Dreadnought*
Repulse	*Anson*		*Sans Pareil*
Resolution	*Camperdown*		*Devastation*
Royal Sovereign	*Collingwood*		*Thunderer*
	Howe		*Inflexible*
	Rodney		*Alexandra*
	Nile		*Rupert*
	Trafalgar		

1901

Channel	Mediterranean	China	Coast Guard and Port Guard
Hannibal	*Canopus*	*Glory*	*Benbow*
Jupiter	*Ocean*	*Goliath*	*Camperdown*
Magnificent	*Cæsar*	*Barfleur*	*Howe*
Majestic	*Illustrious*	*Centurion*	*Rodney*
Mars	*Victorious*		*Collingwood*
Prince George	*Renown*		*Nile*
Repulse	*Empress of India*		*Trafalgar*
Resolution	*Ramillies*		*Hood*
	Royal Oak		*Sans Pareil*
	Royal Sovereign		*Colossus*
			Devastation
			Alexandra

1906

Channel	Mediterranean	Atlantic	Reserve
Albemarle	*Bulwark*	*Commonwealth*	*Vengeance*
Cornwallis	*Formidable*	*Dominion*	*Ramillies*
Duncan	*Implacable*	*Hindustan*	*Repulse*
Exmouth	*Irresistible*	*King Edward VII*	*Resolution*
Montagu	*London*	*New Zealand*	*Royal Oak*
Russell	*Prince of Wales*	*Magnificent*	*Revenge*
Swiftsure	*Queen*	*Majestic*	*Empress of India*
Triumph	*Venerable*	*Victorious*	*Hood*
Albion			*Nile*
Canopus			*Trafalgar*
Glory			*Barfleur*
Goliath			*Centurion*
Ocean			
Cæsar			
Jupiter			
Prince George			

1907

Channel
- *King Edward VII*
- *Africa*
- *Britannia*
- *Commonwealth*
- *Dominion*
- *Hibernia*
- *Hindustan*
- *New Zealand*
- *Ocean*
- *Vengeance*
- *Swiftsure*
- *Triumph*
- *Illustrious*
- *Jupiter*

Mediterranean
- *Queen*
- *Formidable*
- *Implacable*
- *Irresistible*
- *Prince of Wales*
- *Venerable*

Atlantic
- *Exmouth*
- *Albemarle*
- *Cornwallis*
- *Duncan*
- *Russell*
- *Albion*

Home
- *Dreadnought*
- *Bulwark*
- *London*
- *Canopus*
- *Glory*
- *Goliath*
- *Cæsar*
- *Hannibal*
- *Magnificent*
- *Majestic*
- *Mars*
- *Prince George*
- *Victorious*

Reserve
- *Barfleur*
- *Centurion*
- *Renown*
- *Hood*
- *Empress of India*
- *Ramillies*
- *Repulse*
- *Resolution*
- *Royal Oak*
- *Royal Sovereign*
- *Nile*

1910

Home Fleet

1st B.S.
- *Dreadnought*
- *Collingwood*
- *St. Vincent*
- *Vanguard*
- *Bellerophon*
- *Superb*
- *Temeraire*
- *Agamemnon*
- *Lord Nelson*

- *Indomitable*
- *Inflexible*
- *Invincible*
- *Defence*

2nd B.S.
- *Africa*
- *Britannia*
- *Commonwealth*
- *Dominion*
- *Hibernia*
- *Hindustan*
- *King Edward VII*
- *New Zealand*

- *Shannon*
- *Achilles*
- *Cochrane*
- *Natal*
- *Warrior*

Atlantic
- *Formidable*
- *Implacable*
- *London*
- *Prince of Wales*
- *Queen*
- *Venerable*

- *Black Prince*
- *Duke of Edinburgh*

Mediterranean
- *Cornwallis*
- *Duncan*
- *Exmouth*
- *Russell*
- *Swiftsure*
- *Triumph*

1913

Home Fleet
Fleet Flagship *Neptune*

1st B.S.
- *Colossus*
- *Hercules*
- *Collingwood*
- *St. Vincent*
- *Vanguard*
- *Bellerophon*
- *Superb*
- *Temeraire*

- *Lion*
- *Princess Royal*
- *Indefatigable*
- *Invincible*
- *Indomitable*

2nd B.S.
- *King George V*
- *Centurion*
- *Conqueror*
- *Monarch*
- *Orion*
- *Thunderer*
- *Agamemnon*
- *Lord Nelson*

- *Shannon*
- *Cochrane*
- *Achilles*
- *Natal*
- *Warrior*

4th B.S.
- *Dreadnought*
- *Africa*
- *Hindustan*
- *Albemarle*
- *Cornwallis*
- *Duncan*
- *Russell*

5th B.S.
- *Bulwark*
- *Formidable*
- *Implacable*
- *Irresistible*
- *London*
- *Prince of Wales*
- *Queen*
- *Venerable*

Mediterranean
- *Britannia*
- *Commonwealth*
- *Dominion*
- *Hibernia*
- *King Edward VII*
- *Zealandia*

- *Inflexible*
- *Black Prince*
- *Duke of Edinburgh*

6th B.S.
- *Vengeance*

1920

Atlantic Fleet
Fleet Flagship *Queen Elizabeth*

1st B S.
- *Revenge*
- *Ramillies*
- *Resolution*
- *Royal Oak*
- *Royal Sovereign*

2nd B.S.
- *Barham*
- *Malaya*
- *Valiant*
- *Warspite*

Battle Cruisers
- *Hood*
- *Repulse*
- *Renown*
- *Tiger*

Reserve Fleet (In Commission)

Erin
Orion
Monarch
Conqueror
Thunderer
Colossus
Collingwood

Hercules
Neptune
St. Vincent

Lion
Princess Royal
New Zealand

Mediterranean

Iron Duke
Emperor of India
Benbow
Ajax
Centurion
King George V

1925

Atlantic Fleet

Revenge
Ramillies
Royal Oak
Resolution
Royal Sovereign

Hood
Repulse

Mediterranean

Queen Elizabeth
Barham
Valiant
Malaya
Iron Duke
Benbow
Emperor of India
Marlborough

Reserve Fleet

Ajax
Centurion
King George V
Thunderer

1930

Atlantic

Nelson
Rodney
Barham
Malaya

Renown
Repulse
Tiger
Hood

Mediterranean

Warspite
Revenge
Ramillies
Royal Oak
Royal Sovereign
Resolution

3rd B.S.

Emperor of India
Marlborough

Paid Off

Valiant
Queen Elizabeth
Benbow

1935

Home Fleet

Nelson
Rodney
Royal Sovereign
Ramillies

Hood
Renown

Mediterranean

Queen Elizabeth
Resolution
Revenge
Valiant
Barham

Paid Off

Warspite
Repulse
Royal Oak
Malaya

SEPTEMBER 1939

Home Fleet

Nelson
Rodney
Royal Oak
Royal Sovereign
Ramillies

Hood
Repulse

Channel Force

Resolution
Revenge

Mediterranean

Warspite
Barham
Malaya

Refitting

Queen Elizabeth
Valiant
Renown

1957

Reserve Fleet

Vanguard (flag.)

Laid Up

King George V
Howe
Anson
Duke of York

Appendix IV

BLAST FROM GUNFIRE

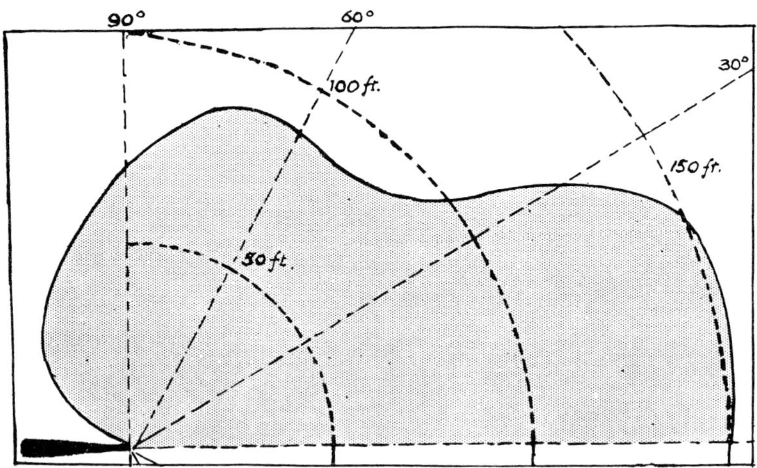

Curve showing pressure of 30 lb. per sq. ft. from the blast of a 12-in. gun. (Adapted from the Ordnance Committee Report, July 1895.)

DURING the discussions on the alternative designs for the Battleship and Armoured Cruiser by the 1905 Committee it became obvious that considerations of "blast" from 12-in. gunfire were of more importance in siting the turrets than concentration of armament over various arcs of training. In order to secure good practice from gunlayers, it was considered necessary that they should be guarded from the effects of "blast" to such an extent as to make it reasonably possible for them to take no notice of other guns firing. In the designs D.1 and D.2, using the model blast curves, it was found that immunity from blast could only be attained by separating the pairs of turrets to such an extent as to make the design impossible. The best results were found with a centre-line turret instead of the aftermost pair, and possible broadside training increased to a maximum, and guns could not fire into one another.

Captain Jellicoe was asked to collect information as to the effect on gunlayers in adjacent gun positions when 12-in. were fired without warning, with the following results:

Majestic — 12-in. fore turret 30°-45° before the beam.
Observer in sighting hood, fore casemate 63 ft. away at 118°.
Effect very considerable. Had to hold on with hands owing to *downward* blast.

Jupiter — 12-in. fore turret abeam.
Observer in sighting hood, fore casemate 58 ft. away at 88°.
Effect too great to allow him to control guns.

Magnificent — 12-in. fore turret on extreme training.
Observer in sighting hood of nearest casemate. Completely closed except for 9-in. slit with glass shutter inside. 34 ft., 52° to casemate port.
No blast through hood, but very considerable through port.

Exmouth — 12-in. up to 15° inside beam training.
Officer in sighting hood. Guns crew closed up at 6-in. gun. Gun on beam training. 32 ft. to casemate port, 44 ft. to sighting hood. 74°.
Effect not detrimental to men. Officer all right with *shutters closed.*

Exmouth — 12-in. beyond 15° training towards casemate.
Effect very considerable. Men could not stand a repetition of it. Officer all right with *shutters closed.*

King Edward VII — 9·2-in. right aft.
Observer in turret sighting hoods, 12-in. guns 32 ft. away at 41°.
Effect very great on the occupants of all three hoods. Officer in nearest hood rendered senseless.

King Edward VII — After 12-in. —30° before the beam.
Observers in sighting hood in 9·2-in. shield. Gun on same bearing. 35 ft. away at 46°.
Effect moderate.

The writer was informed that the 1895 blast graph was not produced when the *King Edward VII* was designed, otherwise the 9·2-in. guns would have been differently sited.

INDEX

[British Ships in Italics with date of Completion]